Philosophy of Religion: An Anthology

BLACKWELL PHILOSOPHY ANTHOLOGIES

Each volume in this outstanding series provides an authoritative and comprehensive collection of the essential primary readings from philosophy's main fields of study. Designed to complement the *Blackwell Companions to Philosophy* series, each volume represents an unparalleled resource in its own right, and will provide the ideal platform for course use.

Philosophy of Religion
An Anthology

Edited by

Charles Taliaferro and Paul J. Griffiths

Blackwell
Publishing

350 Main Street, Malden, MA 02148-5018, USA
108 Cowley Road, Oxford OX4 1JF, UK
550 Swanston Street, Carlton South, Melbourne, Victoria 3053, Australia
Kurfürstendamm 57, 10707 Berlin, Germany

First published 2003 by Blackwell Publishing Ltd

Library of Congress Cataloging-in-Publication Data

Philosophy of religion: an anthology / edited by Charles Taliaferro and Paul J. Griffiths.
    p.   cm. – (Blackwell philosophy anthologies; 20)
  Includes bibliographical references and index.
  ISBN 0-631-21470-4 (alk. paper) – ISBN 0-631-21471-2 (pbk.: alk. paper)
  1. Religion – Philosophy. I. Taliaferro, Charles. II. Griffiths, Paul J. III. Series.
BL51 .P532 2003
210 – dc21

                                  2002006824

A catalogue record for this title is available from the British Library.

Set in Ehrhardt 9/11pt
by Graphicraft Limited, Hong Kong
Printed and bound in the United Kingdom
by TJ International, Padstow, Cornwall

For further information on
Blackwell Publishing, visit our website:
http://www.blackwellpublishing.com

Contents

Contents

Contents

Acknowledgments

We thank Cleo Granneman for her wonderful assistance in helping to prepare this Anthology. We also thank Dan Arnold, Noah Holm, Kara Kandall, Z. Miller, Kurtis Parlin, Gretchen Ross, and Janelle Sagness. We are profoundly indebted to Beth Remmes and Sarah Dancy at Blackwell. Without their patience, attention to detail, and compassion for editorial inefficiencies (not to mention flaws of character), this book would never have reached production.

In addition, with the publisher, we gratefully acknowledge the permission granted to reproduce the copyright material in this book:

1   W. D. Hudson, "What Makes Religious Beliefs Religious?" reprinted by permission of Cambridge University Press from *Religious Studies* 13 (1977), pp. 221–42.

2   Stephen R. L. Clark, "World Religions and World Orders," reprinted by permission of Cambridge University Press from *Religious Studies* 26 (1990), pp. 43–57.

3   Paul J. Griffiths, "Religion," reprinted by permission of Oxford University Press from *Religious Reading* (New York: Oxford University Press, 1999), ch. 1.

4   Richard Swinburne, "God," reprinted by permission of Oxford University Press from *Is There a God?* (Oxford and New York: Oxford University Press, 1996), pp. 3–19.

5   Thomas V. Morris, "The Power of God" and "God's Knowledge," from *Our Idea of God: An Introduction to Philosophical Theology* (Vancouver: Regent College Publishing), pp. 65–81, 86–102.

6   Brian Leftow, "Eternity," from Philip L. Quinn and Charles Taliaferro (eds.), *A Companion to Philosophy of Religion* (Oxford: Blackwell Publishers, 1997), pp. 257–63.

7   Laura L. Garcia, "Divine Freedom and Creation," from *The Philosophical Quarterly* 42 (1992), pp. 191–213. Copyright © The Editors of *The Philosophical Quarterly*, published by Blackwell Publishers, Oxford.

8   Marjorie Hewitt Suchocki, "The Idea of God in Feminist Philosophy," reprinted by permission of the author and Indiana University Press from *Hypatia* 9 (Fall 1994), pp. 57–68.

9   Antony Flew, R. M. Hare, and Basil Mitchell, "Theology and Falsification: A Symposium," from Antony Flew and Alasdair MacIntyre (eds.), *New Essays in Philosophical Theology* (London: SCM Press; London and New York: Simon & Schuster Inc., 1955).

10   Adolf Grünbaum, "Psychoanalysis and Theism," reprinted with permission from *The Monist* 79 (1987), pp. 152–73. Copyright © 1987 *The Monist*, Peru, Illinois 61342.

11   William Alston, "Psychoanalytic Theory and Theistic Belief," from John Hick (ed.), *Faith and the Philosophers* (New York: St Martin's Press, 1964), pp. 63–102. Reprinted by permission of Macmillan Ltd.

12   William James, "The Varieties of Religious Experience," from *The Varieties of Religious Experience* (Longmans, Green and Co., 1902), pp. 485–501; 512–15. Not in copyright.

13   Rudolf Otto, "The Numinous," reprinted by permission of Oxford University Press from *The Idea of the Holy*, translated by J. W. Harvey (New York: Oxford University Press, 1936), chs. 2–6.

14   Caroline Franks Davis, "Religious Experience," reprinted by permission of Oxford University Press from *The Evidential Force of Religious Experience* (Oxford: Clarendon Press; New York: Oxford University Press, 1989), pp. 29–65. © Caroline Franks Davis, 1989.

15   Norman Malcolm, "The Groundlessness of Belief," reprinted by permission of the publisher, Cornell University Press, from Stuart Brown (ed.), *Reason and Religion* (Ithaca: Cornell University Press, 1977), pp. 143–57. Copyright © 1977 Royal Institute of Philosophy.

16   Søren Kierkegaard, "Thought-Project," reprinted by permission of Princeton University Press from *Philosophical Fragments* (Princeton: Princeton University Press, 1985), pp. 9–22. Copyright © 1985 Princeton University Press.

17   W. K. Clifford, "The Ethics of Belief," from *Lectures and Essays* (1874). Not in copyright.

18   Alvin Plantinga, "Religious Belief as 'Properly Basic'," from Alvin Plantinga and Nicholas Wolterstorff (eds.), *Faith and Rationality* (Notre Dame: University of Notre Dame Press, 1983). Copyright © 1983 University of Notre Dame Press.

19   Richard Swinburne, "The Cosmological Argument," reprinted by permission of Oxford University Press from *The Existence of God* (Oxford: Clarendon Press; New York: Oxford University Press, 1979), pp. 116–32.

20   J. L. Mackie, "Cosmological Arguments," reprinted by permission of Oxford University Press from *The Miracle of Theism: Arguments For and Against the Existence of God* (Oxford: Clarendon Press and New York: Oxford University Press, 1982), pp. 81–101. © John Mackie, 1982.

21   David Hume, "Teleological Argument," Part II from David Hume, *Dialogues Concerning Natural Religion*, edited by Henry D. Aitken (New York: Hafner Publishing Co., 1948).

22   Robert Hambourger, "The Argument from Design," from *Intentions and Intentionality: Essays in Honor of G. E. M. Anscombe* (Ithaca: Cornell University Press, 1979), pp. 109–31. Copyright © Blackwell Publishers, Oxford.

23   Norman Malcolm, "Anselm's Ontological Arguments," from *The Philosophical Review* 69 (1960), pp. 41–62. Copyright © 1960 Cornell University. Reprinted by permission of the publisher.

24   Michael Martin, "The Ontological Argument," reprinted by permission of Temple University Press from *Atheism: A Philosophical Justification* (Philadelphia: Temple University Press, 1990), pp. 79–95. Copyright © 1990 Temple University. All rights reserved.

25   Wilhelm Halbfass, "*Darśana, Ānvīkṣikī,* Philosophy," reprinted by permission from *India and Europe: An Essay in Understanding* (Albany: State University of New York Press, 1988), pp. 263–86.

26   Georges B. J. Dreyfus, "The Purview of the 'Real'," from *Recognizing Reality: Dharmakirti's Philosophy and its Tibetan Interpretations* (Albany: State University of New York Press, 1996), ch. 4. Copyright © 1988, State University of New York. All rights reserved.

27   Anne Carolyn Klein, "Finding a Self: Buddhist and Feminist Perspectives," from Clarissa W. Atkinson, Constance H. Buchanan, and Margaret R. Miles (eds.), *Shaping New Vision: Gender and Values in American Culture* (Ann Arbor: UMI Research Press, 1987), pp. 191–218.

28   David Loy, "How Many Nondualities Are There?" from *Nonduality: A Study in Comparative Philosophy* (New Haven: Yale University Press, 1988), pp. 17–37. Copyright © David Loy.

29   Mary Midgley, "The Problem of Natural Evil," from *Wickedness: A Philosophical Essay* (London and Boston: Routledge and Kegan Paul, 1984), pp. 1–16.

30   William L. Rowe, "The Problem of Evil and Some Varieties of Atheism," from *American Philosophical Quarterly* 16:4 (October 1979), pp. 335–41. Copyright © The Editors of *American Philosophical Quarterly*, published by Blackwell Publishers, Oxford.

31   Brian Davies, "The Problem of Evil," from *Philosophy of Religion: A Guide to the Subject* (London: Cassell, 1998). Used by permission of Continuum International Publishing Group.

32   Peter van Inwagen, "The Problem of Evil, the Problem of Air, and the Problem of Silence," reprinted from *Philosophical Perspectives* 5: *Philosophy of Religion* (1991), pp. 135–65.

33   Marilyn McCord Adams, "Horrendous Evils and the Goodness of God," reprinted by permission of Oxford University Press from Marilyn McCord Adams and Robert Merrihew Adams (eds.), *The Problem of Evil* (New York: Oxford University Press, 1990).

34   Mary Midgley, "Selves and Shadows," from *Wickedness: A Philosophical Essay* (London and Boston: Routledge and Kegan Paul, 1984), pp. 113–31.

35   Martin Southwold, "Buddhism and Evil," from David Parkin (ed.), *The Anthropology of Evil* (Oxford: Blackwell Publishers, 1985), pp. 128–41.

36   Nel Noddings, "Evil and Ethical Terror," from *Women and Evil* (Berkeley: University of California Press, 1989), pp. 5–34. Copyright © 1989 The Regents of the University of California, The University of California Press, Berkeley.

37   Edward Langerak, "Pluralism, Tolerance, and Disagreement," *Rhetoric Society Quarterly* 24 (1994), pp. 95–106.

38   Robert Merrihew Adams, "A Modified Divine Command Theory of Ethical Wrongness," from G. Outka and J. R. Reeder (eds.), *Religion and Morality* (Garden City: Anchor Press, 1975), pp. 318–47.

39   Baruch A. Brody, "Morality and Religion Reconsidered," reprinted by permission of Pearson Education, Inc., Upper Saddle River, NJ, from *Readings in the Philosophy of Religion*, 2nd edn (Englewood Cliffs: Prentice-Hall, 1974), pp. 592–603. Copyright © Baruch A. Brody.

40   George I. Mavrodes, "Religion and the Queerness of Morality," from R. Audi and W. J. Wainwright (eds.), *Rationality, Religious Belief and Moral Commitment* (Ithaca: Cornell University Press, 1986), pp. 213–26. Copyright © R. Audi and W. J. Wainwright.

41   Robert Merrihew Adams, "Pure Love," from *Journal of Religious Ethics* 8 (1980), pp. 88–99. Copyright © *Journal of Religious Ethics*, Inc., published by Blackwell Publishers, Oxford.

42   Richard Swinburne, "The Possibility of Incarnation," reprinted by permission of Oxford University Press from *The Christian God* (Oxford: Oxford University Press, 1994), pp. 192–215. Copyright © Richard Swinburne, 1994.

43   John Hick, "Religious Pluralism," from Philip L. Quinn and Charles Taliaferro (eds.), *A Companion to Philosophy of Religion* (Oxford: Blackwell Publishers, 1997), pp. 607–14.

44   Anthony O'Hear, "The real or the Real? Chardin or Rothko?" from Michael McGhee (ed.), *Philosophy, Religion and the Spiritual Life* (Cambridge and New York: Cambridge University Press, 1992), pp. 32–45. Copyright © The Royal Institute of Philosophy, 1992.

45   Holmes Rolston III, "Does Nature Need to be Redeemed?" from *Zygon* 29 (1994), pp. 205–29. Copyright © 1994 Advanced Study in Religion and Science, and Rollins College.

46   Blaise Pascal, "Pascal's Wager," from *Pensées and The Provincial Letters*, translated by W. F. Trotter and Thomas M'Crie (New York: Random House, 1941). Copyright © J. M. Dent & Sons Ltd.

47   Tim Chappell, "Why is Faith a Virtue?" reprinted by permission of Cambridge University Press from *Religious Studies* 32 (1996), pp. 27–36. Copyright © 1996 Cambridge University Press.

48   Roger Trigg, "The Metaphysical Self," reprinted by permission of Cambridge University Press from *Religious Studies* 24 (1988), pp. 277–89.

49   David Hume, "Of Miracles," reprinted by permission of Hackett Publishing Company Inc. from David Hume, *An Enquiry Concerning Human Understanding*, 2nd edn, edited by Eric Steinberg (Indianapolis: Hackett, 1977), pp. 72–90. All rights reserved.

50   Grace M. Jantzen, "Do We Need Immortality?" from *Modern Theology* 1:1 (1984), pp. 33–44. Copyright © Blackwell Publishers Ltd., Oxford.

51   Charles Taliaferro, "Why We Need Immortality," from *Modern Theology* 6:4 (1990), pp. 367–77. Copyright © Blackwell Publishers Ltd., Oxford.

52   A. Chakrabarti, "Is Liberation (*mokṣa*) Pleasant?" reprinted by permission of University of Hawaii Press from *Philosophy East and West* 33:2 (1983), pp. 167–82. Copyright © University of Hawaii Press. All rights reserved.

Every effort has been made to trace copyright holders and to obtain their permission for the use of copyright material. The publisher apologizes for any errors or omissions in the above list and would be grateful if notified of any corrections that should be incorporated in future reprints or editions of this book.

PART I

Religious Identity

Introduction

Paul J. Griffiths

Works in philosophy of religion, whether collections of readings such as this or writings devoted to a single topic such as the existence of God, tend to assume it to be obvious what makes a topic religious, and therefore also obvious what makes it belong to the philosophy of religion. But in fact none of these things is at all obvious, as the three readings in this section in various ways make clear.

Among the main reasons for the lack of clarity about what makes a topic or behavior or institution religious is the relatively short and complicated history of the idea that the term "religion" labels a phenomenon of importance. Matters are different with terms such as "law" or "politics": those terms have a much longer history than "religion" as terms of theoretical and practical importance, which is to say that they are more deeply rooted and intimately intertwined with the intellectual history of the West. It would, as a result, be less difficult to determine the topics that properly belong to the philosophy of law or the philosophy of politics than to decide those that properly belong to the philosophy of religion. "Religion" is, perhaps paradoxically, best understood as a recent, European invention, and one whose contours and boundaries are unclear and subject to dispute.

This probably reads oddly. Isn't religion, along with art, politics, and prostitution, among the oldest and most characteristically human activities? What then can it mean to say that it's a recent invention? The first point to note here is that the complex cultural formations that we now tend naturally to call "religions" – Buddhism, Hinduism,

Judaism, Christianity, and Islam, to name the usual big five – have only recently come to be called that, and are still not naturally thought of as such by most of their adherents. Christians, for instance, did not come to think of Christianity as a religion (much less as one religion among many) until after the Reformation; and Buddhism, to take another example, does not contain in its authoritative texts any term naturally or happily rendered by "religion." The same is true for the other traditions mentioned: each has its own vocabulary for self-identification and for identification of the alien other (Christians speak of pagans and heretics, for example, and Buddhists speak of *tirthikas*); but "religion" is not part of the discourse.

This is not surprising. "Religion" in its complex and confused modern sense was invented to deal with European political problems consequent upon the sixteenth-century fracturing of Christianity. In order to construct a political order that could accommodate Christians who found it difficult to resolve their differences about what constituted orthodox Christianity without violence, the idea that there are many religions and that the state must in some way acknowledge and accommodate this variety became of great importance. The British establishment of religion (the Anglican Church) and its limited toleration of others was one kind of solution; the passage of the First Amendment to the US Constitution in 1791 with its clauses about religion ("Congress shall make no law respecting an establishment of religion, nor prohibiting the free exercise thereof") was another. In all these cases, "religion" meant, essentially,

"Protestant Christianity and things like it"; and this, for the most part, is what it still means, which goes a long way toward explaining the tensions and difficulties that arise when Islam or neo-Confucianism is brought under the umbrella of "religion" – for these things are not very much like Protestant Christianity.

Among the essays in the first part of this volume, W. D. Hudson offers a particular interpretation of what constitutes or is essential to religious belief. It is, he says, the concept of God, and in so saying he both illustrates and sharpens the claim just made, which is that the concept "religion" tends to be arrived at by a process of abstraction from the concept "(Protestant) Christianity." But this is not the only virtue of Hudson's essay; it also shows with great clarity how someone who wants to think philosophically about the very idea of religion in conversation with the Austrian philosopher Ludwig Wittgenstein (1889–1951) is likely to do so.

Stephen Clark's "World Religions and World Orders," too, is alive to the difficulties of arriving at a philosophically useful understanding of religion, and to those involved in demarcating one religion from another. But he is especially interested in the future of religion (his essay was originally published in 1990) in an increasingly globalized and interconnected world. Is it possible, he asks (and he writes as a Christian), that the global religion (if there can be one) might be Abrahamic – that is, a proper offshoot of the tradition that stems from the call of Abraham described in Genesis 12?

Paul J. Griffiths offers a definition of religion quite self-consciously abstracted from Christianity (for he too writes as a Christian), but one nonetheless intended to be usable by those who are not Christians. If, he argues, you offer an account of things that seems to you comprehensive (to embrace all other accounts that you give), of central importance to your life, and not capable of being surpassed or subsumed by other accounts, then you offer a religious account of things. A Christian account of things has these features, he says, as does an Islamic or a Buddhist one: the particulars of such accounts of course differ, but in their formal features they are the same.

Further Reading

Introductions to the field:

Abraham, W., *An Introduction to the Philosophy of Religion* (Englewood Cliffs: Prentice-Hall, 1985). *A balanced, sympathetic approach.*

Clark, K. J., *Return to Reason* (Grand Rapids: William Eerdmans, 1990). *Lucidly written, Clark defends the reasonability of some religious convictions.*

Clarke, W. N., *Explorations in Metaphysics: Being–God–Person* (Notre Dame: Indiana and London, 1994). *A constructive account.*

Creel, R., *Religion and Doubt* (Englewood Cliffs: Prentice-Hall, 1991). *An engaging, constructive account.*

Davies, B. (ed.), *Philosophy of Religion: A Guide to the Subject* (Washington, DC: Georgetown University Press, 1999). *A fine collection that provides access to central themes in the field.*

Davies, B., *An Introduction to the Philosophy of Religion* (Oxford: Oxford University Press, 1993). *A popular, balanced text by a leading philosopher.*

Evans, S. C., *Philosophy of Religion* (Downers Grove: InterVarsity, 1985). *An introduction that is clearly written, commending theism.*

Gaskin, J. C. A., *The Quest for Eternity* (Harmondsworth: Penguin Books, 1984). *A critique of classical theism by a distinguished philosopher in the tradition of David Hume.*

Hick, J., *Philosophy of Religion*, 4th edn (Englewood Cliffs: Prentice-Hall, 1989). *A senior, distinguished philosopher writes on the central theme – with an emphasis on religious pluralism.*

Hudson, V., *The Philosophy of Religion* (London: Mayfield, 1991). *Covers most issues in the field.*

Le Poidevin, R., *Arguing for Atheism: An Introduction to the Philosophy of Religion* (London and New York: Routledge, 1996). *As the title suggests, this text has a definite orientation. The writing is clear and the arguments developed.*

Lewis, H. D., *Philosophy of Religion* (London: The English Universities Press, 1965). *A classic.*

Morris, T. V., *Our Idea of God* (Downers Grove: InterVarsity, 1991). *A non-technical, lucid investigation into theism.*

Nielsen, K., *An Introduction to the Philosophy of Religion* (New York: St Martin's Press, 1983). *A densely argued critique of classical theism.*

O'Hear, A., *Experience, Explanation, and Faith: An Introduction to the Philosophy of Religion* (London: Routledge and Kegan Paul, 1984). *A scholarly, refined work, critical of classical theism.*

Phillips, Stephen H., *Philosophy of Religion: A Global Approach* (Fort Worth, Texas: Harcourt Brace College Publishers, 1996). *One of the few clear surveys of all the major traditions in the philosophy of religion.*

Purtill, R., *Reason to Believe* (Grand Rapids: William Eerdmans, 1974). *A vigorous case for religious beliefs in the tradition of C. S. Lewis.*

Purtill, R., *Thinking About Religion* (Englewood Cliffs: Prentice-Hall, 1978). *A wonderful, engaging text.*

Ross, J., *Introduction to Philosophy of Religion* (New York: Macmillan, 1969). *Tough-minded, polemical, provocative.*

Rowe, W., *Philosophy of Religion*, 3rd edn (Belmont: Wadsworth, 2000). *A clear, systematic introduction by a prominent philosopher.*

Scharfstein, Ben-Ami, *A Comparative History of World Philosophy: From the Upanishads to Kant* (Albany, New York: State University of New York Press, 1998). *Covers more than the philosophy of religion, but a good part is devoted to those topics; especially good in indicating the independent development of similar arguments.*

Taliaferro, C., *Contemporary Philosophy of Religion* (Oxford: Blackwell, 1998). *Wide coverage of the field with an emphasis on philosophy of religion after the Second World War. Extensive suggested questions after each chapter.*

Tilghman, B. R., *An Introduction to Philosophy of Religion* (Oxford: Basil Blackwell, 1993). *Mostly focused on theism, Tilghman argues for a form of nonrealism.*

Wainwright, W., *Philosophy of Religion* (Belmont: Wadsworth, 1988). *Packed with provocative arguments.*

Yandell, K., *Christianity and Philosophy* (Grand Rapids: William Eerdmans, 1984). *An analytic text with meticulous arguments.*

Yandell, K., *Philosophy of Religion: A Contemporary Introduction* (London: Routledge, 1999). *A vigorous, analytic text with attention given to Eastern and Western philosophy of religion.*

From The Blackwell Companion to Philosophy of Religion, *see the following entries:*

Goodman, P. J., "Buddhism"
Hansen, C., "Chinese Confucianism and Daoism"
Nanji, A. A. and Esmail, A. A., "Islam"
Smart, N., "Hinduism"

Wainwright, W. J., "Christianity"
Westphal, M., "The Emergence of Modern Philosophy of Religion"
Wiredu, K., "African Religions From a Philosophical Point Of View"

And also:

Burrell, D., "The Islamic Contribution to Medieval Philosophical Theology"
Flannery, K. L., "Ancient Philosophical Theology"
MacDonald, S., "The Christian Contribution to Medieval Philosophical Theology"
Pereboom, D., "Early Modern Philosophical Theology"
Rudavsky, T., "The Jewish Contribution to Medieval Philosophical Theology"

Philosophy of religion is represented in virtually all the main philosophy journals, but it is the specific focus of *The International Journal for Philosophy of Religion, Religious Studies, Faith and Philosophy, Philosophy and Theology, Sophia, Philosophia Christi, Philo, American Catholic Philosophical Quarterly* (formerly *New Scholasticism*), *American Journal of Theology and Philosophy*, and *The Thomist.* Theology journals also carry considerable philosophy of religion, especially *The Journal of the American Academy of Religion, The Journal of Religion, Theological Studies, The Journal of Religious Ethics, Heythrop Journal, The Annual of the Society of Christian Ethics, Theology Today, New Blackfriars, Modern Theology, Harvard Theological Review,* the *Scottish Journal of Religious Studies,* and the *Scottish Journal of Theology.* Philosophy of religion can also be found in some cross-disciplinary journals, for example, *Law and Religion, The Journal of Law and Religion, Literature and Theology, The Journal of Humanism and Ethical Religions,* and *Christian Scholar's Review.* Blackwell has two anthologies in philosophy of religion which will be of interest: Eleonore Stump and Michael Murray (eds.), *Philosophy of Religion: The Big Questions,* and Mark Larrimore (ed.), *The Problem of Evil: A Reader.*

What Makes Religious Beliefs Religious?

W. D. Hudson

I want to put forward a certain view of the logical foundation of religious belief. It is, in a sentence, the view that religious belief is constituted by the concept of god. This view will be discussed under three headings. First, I shall explain as clearly as I can what I mean by it. Secondly, I shall indicate what seem to me to be interesting parallels, both with regard to universes of discourse in general and to religious belief in particular, between my idea of a constitutive concept and Wittgenstein's ideas of a fundamental proposition and a religious "picture". Thirdly, I shall try to substantiate the view I take of the logical foundation of religious belief by rebutting three conceivable objections to it: namely, that it rests on an illegitimate craving for generality, that it is at variance with common usage, and that it consigns religious belief to an intellectual ghetto.

I. The Logical Foundation of Religious Belief

In explaining the view that religious belief is constituted by the concept of god, I will say what I mean in general terms by a constitutive concept, then what I mean by the concept of god, and finally why I say that this concept is constitutive of religious belief.

W. D. Hudson, "What Makes Religious Beliefs Religious?" reprinted by permission of Cambridge University Press from *Religious Studies* 13 (1977), pp. 221–42.

A constitutive concept

I can best explain what I mean by a concept being constitutive if I take two examples, namely the concepts of a physical object and a moral obligation, and list the four things which I would mean by calling them constitutive of physical science and morality respectively.

First, everything which is said in physical science and morality respectively is said with reference to that to which these concepts respectively purport to apply. Physical science is about physical objects; morality about moral obligations. A physical object, however small its magnitude or brief its existence, is a particular which is identifiable by its spatial and temporal relationships with other such particulars in a system unified by these relationships. Whatever is said within physical science concerns the properties, operations and interactions of such spatio-temporally identifiable particulars. This is not to say, of course, that every statement within physical science must be an empirical description of a physical object (or objects). Other kinds of statement frequently come into it, e.g. mathematical deductions. But these other kinds of statement have their place in physical science only in so far as they make possible the more complete description of physical objects. A moral obligation on the other hand is a distinctive kind of constraint, logically different from constraints such as psychological compulsion or legal requirement. Its precise definition is a complicated matter about which moral philosophers are not agreed; but even so, if any utterance purports to be a moral one, it must (logically) concern the occurrence, grounds, or inter-relationships, of moral obligations. Once again, this does not mean that the only utterances which have a place in moral discourse are moral judgements. In support of the judgement, "Abortion is wrong" for example, it would, according to the view taken, be relevant to say that it causes unhappiness, contravenes the will of God, or whatever. These statements of natural or supernatural fact, however, have a place in moral discourse only in so far as they are premises from which moral judgements are deemed to follow. To say that the concepts of a physical object and a moral obligation constitute physical science and morality respectively is to say that, if any utterance does not purport to contribute to the description of physical objects in the one case, or the determination of moral obligations in the other, it has no place within these respective universes of discourse.

Secondly, the existence of that to which these concepts respectively apply cannot (logically) be doubted within their respective universes of discourse. It cannot be a fact of physical science that there are no physical objects nor of morality that there are no moral obligations. If anyone said that he doubted the existence of certain physical objects, say electrons, this could be regarded as a point of view, though an odd one, within physical science. But if he said that he doubted that there are any such things as physical objects and preferred to believe that they only appear to exist, what conceivable evidence within physical science could be adduced for or against this view? The proposition "There are physical objects" is not one hypothesis amongst others within physical science; it is the presupposition of all such hypotheses. Again, if anyone denied that abortion is wrong, there are two things which he could conceivably be doing. One is rejecting moral discourse altogether; the other is opposing one opinion about what we ought to do by another. What he could not be doing is both at the same time. From within moral discourse, that is to say, he could not be denying that there is such a thing as moral obligation. The proposition "There are moral obligations" is not one moral judgement amongst others. It is the presupposition of all such judgements. To say that the concepts of a physical object and of moral obligation constitute their respective universes is to say that there can be no doubt of the existence of that to which they purport to apply within those universes of discourse.

Thirdly, statements of the defining characteristics of these concepts in effect define what it is

logically possible or impossible to say in physical science and morality respectively. For example, from "Physical objects have magnitude and duration" it follows that it will always make sense to ask of a given physical object, "How big is it?" or "For how long does it exist?". Similarly, from "Moral obligations are constraints only upon human beings", for instance, it follows that, whilst it would make sense to say that John has obligations to his girl friend and perhaps to his dog Fido, it would make no sense to say that Fido has obligations to John or to the bitch next door. To say that the concepts of a physical object and of moral obligation constitute their respective universes of discourse is to say that definitions of them are what Wittgenstein called "grammatical propositions",[1] i.e. ones which in effect lay down what can, or cannot, be said.

Fourthly, the concepts of a physical object and of moral obligation are logically irreducible to concepts of any other kind. The futility of attempts so to reduce them may be illustrated from the following examples. Anyone wishing to show that statements about physical objects can be reduced without loss or change of meaning to statements about sense-perceptions will have to show that the latter can serve as the sufficient condition of the former: that if such-and-such statements about sense-perceptions are true, then such-and-such statements about physical objects are also true. But this cannot be shown because hallucination is always a logical possibility. Again, if anyone wishes to claim, as some Utilitarians like Bentham have,[2] that "ought to be done" can be defined as "conformable to the principle of utility", he will have to show that the one expression could be substituted for the other in any context. But as Moore pointed out,[3] the question "Ought what is conformable to the principle of utility to be done?" is an open, not a self-answering, question. Utilitarians of all people need so to regard it, otherwise their moral theory is reduced to the insignificant tautology that what is conformable to the principle of utility is conformable to the principle of utility. To say that the concepts of a physical object and a moral obligation respectively are constitutive of their universes of discourse is to say that whatever is said in terms of them cannot without loss or change of meaning be said in other terms.

These four points indicate what I regard as the necessary and sufficient conditions of a concept's being constitutive. I happen to think that my examples, the concepts of a physical object and of moral obligation, are in fact constitutive ones; but even if I am wrong about that, I have said enough to indicate what it would be for a concept to be constitutive in my view.

The concept of god

The concept of god constitutes religious belief in four ways similar to those I have been outlining. In a moment I will describe how I take it to do so, but first I want to explain what I mean by this concept of god.

To begin with, the concept of god is the concept of an object of belief. I must emphasize that I intend it to apply to objects of belief in all kinds of religions. This object of belief, as I conceive of it, may be singular or plural: "god" refers equally well to the one God of theism or to the many spirits of animism. Religious belief as such always has an object (or objects). This is so whether religious belief is conceived to be belief-in, belief-that, or some combination of the two. In so far as religious beliefs are beliefs-that, i.e. propositions to which the believer assents, they assert something to be the case concerning an object of belief. In so far as they are beliefs-in, i.e. affective or conative attitudes which the believer expresses or evinces, they are attitudes towards an object of belief. In order to conceive of religious belief at all one must conceive of an object of belief whose existence is logically distinct from that of the believer. The relationship between the believer and the object of his belief may be conceived in various ways, some of them very complicated. It may be held, for example, that the believer owes his existence to his god or that the goal of his existence is to attain oneness with his god; it may be said that his god abides in him and he in his god; and so on. But all such conceptions are conceptions of relationships between two logically distinct entities, the believer and his god. A man cannot logically be a religious believer unless there is something other than himself about which, or in which, he believes. And this something is what I mean by "god".

But now, does god have any characteristics common to all kinds of religious belief? I think we can find three such characteristics.

First, whatever is god is *aware* of the believer. Such awareness may be differently conceived in different religions. When, for example, the animist owner of a fetish beats it in order to secure the compliance of the spirit within, the awareness which he conceives the spirit to have is vastly different from that attributed by the author of Psalm 139 to the god who had searched him and known him. But for all such variation in the nature of the awareness, whatever is god is conceived to be in some manner and degree aware of the believer. Even in the most mystical of religions communion, rather than merely contemplation, is conceived ultimately to exist between the believer and the object of his belief; and communion is logically impossible without awareness of each other in all parties to it. Awareness, then, is a universal defining characteristic of god.

Secondly, whatever is god is conceived as *agency*. Here again there is much variation. The agency of god is differently conceived by, for example, the animist who goes in perpetual fear of evil spirits, the polytheist who has to cope with the fickleness of his gods, and a theist such as the author of Psalm 27 who was confident that when his father and mother forsook him the Lord would take him up. Divine activity may be conceived as a matter of intervention for good or ill in the events of this world; or of acceptance or rejection in some other world. But allowing for all such variations, what god does, or refrains from doing, is taken in all religions to make some difference to the believer. Agency is a universal defining characteristic of god.

The third characteristic common to god in all forms of religious belief I will call *transcendence*. There are two kinds of transcendence which I differentiate as the empirical and the logical. By "empirical transcendence" I mean that overplus of some property or properties which always seems to distinguish god from man. Whatever is god is always conceived to have some attribute (or attributes) in a degree which surpasses that in which man is conceived to have it (or them). Such attributes are often admirable ones, such as wisdom or goodness, but they may be morally neutral, like immortality, or morally obnoxious, like malice and cruelty. However, in some respect or other, there is always conceived to be more to god than there is to man. From the most primitive to the most sophisticated forms of religious belief, whatever god is, in that sense, believed to be empirically transcendent. By "logical transcendence" I refer to a constant feature of the language in which religious belief is expressed. This language always strains ordinary meanings in some respect or other. Consider, for example, those many religions in which whatever is god is conceived not to have any physical body and yet is spoken of as acting in the world. How is it logically possible for a being who has no body to act in the physical world? That is the kind of question to which religious language constantly gives rise. Philosophical difficulties about religion always have to do with how much strain ordinary language can bear before the point of unintelligibility is reached; and the philosophical defence of religion is always a matter of showing, in so far as this can be done, that what is said with reference to god is not completely unintelligible. However simple or abstruse the language in which religious belief is expressed, it is always in some respect and some degree logically odd. That is the sense in which I am saying that god is logically transcendent.

The concept of god, then, is the concept of an object of belief which is characterized by awareness, agency and both empirical and logical transcendence. I hope that I have said enough to show that, so defined, it is the object of belief in such differing cases as animism, polytheism, theism and mysticism.

How the concept of god constitutes religious belief

I must now give some account of how the concept of god constitutes religious belief in the four senses outlined above. I take them in turn.

First, everything said within religious belief is said with reference to god. It is true that much besides god is referred to in religious discourse: the beliefs-in or beliefs-that of which it consists may refer to things in the world, to one's fellow men or to oneself. A religious believer as such may believe *that* the world was made in a certain way, *that* his fellow men are of a certain nature, *that* his own duty is so-and-so; he may believe *in* this shrine, *in* that Church, *in* his own mission, etc. But all such beliefs are religious because in the last analysis they have some reference to god. They are beliefs *that* god is, or has done, something, e.g. created the world, made all men in his own image, given one a conscience, etc.; or they are beliefs *in god*, e.g. in this shrine as god's dwelling, in one's church as god's people, in one's mission as god's service, etc. When anything is part of the subject-matter of religious belief what makes it so in the eyes of the believer is the connexion which he conceives it to have with whatever is god for him. The first condition of a concept constituting a universe of discourse is therefore fulfilled in this case.

Secondly, the existence of god is something which cannot be doubted within religious belief. The distinction between "internal" and "external" questions, which Rudolph Carnap drew,[4] is relevant

here. He defined an "internal" question as one which has to do with the existence of entities within a framework and an "external" one as having to do with the existence of the framework itself. The question "Is there a white piece of paper on my desk?" would be an internal one where the framework is ordinary "thing-language", and "Does the world of things really exist?", an external one. Carnap observes that it is only philosophers, as distinct from scientists or men in the street, who raise "external" questions. I refer to this distinction because it may help to make clear what is meant by saying that god's existence cannot be denied within religious belief. There is, of course, much controversy in religion, but it is not about the existence of god; it is about who, or what, god is. It could no more be a religious – as distinct from a philosophical – belief that god does not exist than it could be a physically scientific one that physical objects do not exist or a moral one that there is no such thing as moral obligation. Since everything said in religious belief has reference to god, the existence of god is the logical presupposition of this whole universe of discourse. That is the sense in which the second condition of a concept constituting a universe of discourse is fulfilled in the case of the concept of god.

Thirdly, definitions of the concept of god are logically related to what can, or cannot, be said within religious belief. Above, I defined whatever is god as aware of believers, as agency and as empirically and logically transcendent. The correctness of this definition may be seen from what it makes, or does not make, sense to say in religion. Because god is aware of believers, the practice of prayer, or some form of communication with one's god, is always appropriate in religion. Because god is agency, the question "What is god doing?" is one which it always makes sense to ask in religion. The particular kind of empirical or logical transcendence ascribed to god in the case of any given religion is similarly related to what can, or cannot, be said within it. For example, certain things make sense on the empirical assumption that god is surpassingly merciful, others on the assumption that god is surpassingly malicious. In so far as a particular religion is based on the logical assumption that god is an agent without a body, it will not make sense in that religion to deny that god has done something because no one perceived, or could have perceived, god doing it; and in so far as it is assumed that god can be good even when appearances seem to be to the contrary, it will make sense to say things like, "all things work together for good to them that love God". The third condition of a concept's being constitutive is therefore fulfilled in the case of the concept of god.

Fourthly, the concept of god is logically irreducible. I think the "open-question" argument, used above to show that moral concepts cannot be reduced to non-moral ones, is *mutatis mutandis* applicable to "god". To illustrate this point let me take one particular example from Christianity (where God is god). Attempts have been made by some theologians, under the influence of the prevailing empiricism of our time, to say what the doctrine of Christ's Resurrection "really means" in empirical terms. They offer such accounts of its real meaning as: the Christian Church came into existence and flourished amazingly; Jesus' disciples experienced certain Christophanies; Jesus in his life and death evinced a freedom from anxiety which stimulated a similar insouciance in his disciples; meditation upon this freedom of Jesus can generate a like psychological condition in contemporary men and women; and so on. All such propositions could conceivably be tested for truth or falsity in the way that ordinary historical or psychological propositions can and that is their attraction. But there seem to me to be fatal logical objections to regarding any of them as what the doctrine of Christ's Resurrection really means for the following reason. This doctrine as ordinarily understood has always been to the effect that "God raised Jesus from the dead". It could conceivably be taken to mean that God had caused one of the above historical or psychological events to occur: that is to say, the predicate ". . . raised Jesus from the dead" could perhaps be taken as a figure of speech for ". . . caused Christophanies to occur", or ". . . inspired freedom from anxiety", etc. But even if some such meaning could be given to this predicate, the occurrence of any of these events would not be all that the doctrine of Christ's Resurrection affirms. They might be a necessary condition of its truth but they could not be a sufficient. What the doctrine affirms is that an act of god has occurred. The notion of an act of god cannot be equated with that of any historical or psychological event for the simple reason that when the occurrence of such an event has been stated, the question is always open: "Did god do it?" This is no more a self-answering question than "Ought what is conformable to the principle of utility to be done?" is one. As words are normally used, to say that an historical or psychological event is an act of god is to say more than

simply that it has occurred. On such grounds, then, I think the fourth condition of a concept's being constitutive is fulfilled in the case of the concept of god.

Such is the view I offer of the logical foundation of religious belief. I recognize that more penetrating work than I have done may need to be done on what precise conditions must be fulfilled when a concept constitutes a universe of discourse and on the exact and complete definition of the concept of god. I believe what I have said on these subjects to be correct as far as it goes but, of course, more may need to be said. Even so, I think the approach which I have taken to the question of what makes religious beliefs religious is the right one. The answer lies in the concept of that about which, and in which, such beliefs are held, a concept logically distinct from all others and constitutive of religious belief as a *sui generis* universe of discourse.

II. Parallels in Wittgenstein's Philosophy

My view of the logical foundations of religious belief took shape to some extent under the influence of Wittgenstein's philosophy and I will now try to give some indication of the connexions which I see between his views and mine at relevant points. There are parallels between what I have been saying about constitutive concepts in general and what Wittgenstein said about fundamental propositions in his latest work, *On Certainty* (written in 1950–1); and also between the account which I have given of religious belief in particular and some of the things which Wittgenstein had to say on this subject in his *Lectures on Religious Belief* (given in 1938).[5] I am not, of course, claiming anything more than that there are similarities; but in so far as these exist, it seems worthwhile to point them out both because they are interesting in themselves and because, having formed my view partly under the influence of Wittgenstein's later philosophy, I wish to show that I had good grounds for so doing.

Wittgenstein's *On Certainty* arose out of his reflections on G. E. Moore's claim[6] that there are some propositions which we all know for certain to be true. Wittgenstein thinks that Moore's claim to know them is open to the objection that it amounts to no more than feeling sure of them and is therefore uninteresting; but that the kind of propositions of which Moore did feel sure are of absorbing philosophical interest (*OC* 137). Among examples of such propositions which Wittgenstein considered are: that I have two hands; that physical objects exist; that the earth existed long before I was born; that nature is uniform; etc. Wittgenstein called such propositions fundamental and he was concerned in *On Certainty* to determine their logical role in language games. In his *Lectures on Religious Belief*, delivered more than a decade earlier, he had discussed how religious belief differs from unbelief, and, in attempting to answer that question, had said a good deal about the logical foundations of religious belief, though he said it in terms of "pictures" rather than of propositions. I find that the conditions on which Wittgenstein took a proposition to be fundamental, and those on which he took a "picture" to be a religious one, closely resemble the four conditions on which I have taken concepts to be constitutive of universes of discourse in general and the concept of god to be constitutive of religious belief in particular. I will now illustrate these comparisons.

The first condition of a concept's being constitutive which I gave was that everything said within its universe of discourse has reference to that to which it applies. Compare this with Wittgenstein's view in *On Certainty* that fundamental propositions are "anchored in all my *questions* and *answers*, so anchored that I cannot touch them" (*OC* 103). What he means is, for example, that the fundamental proposition, the earth existed long before I was born, is implicit in all historical questions and answers in the sense that if I denied that proposition, no one would know what I meant by a historical question or what I would regard as an answer to it. In other words, everything in history has some reference to the earth in times past and, if anything has no such reference, it cannot be part of history (cf. *OC* 231). I find a similar parallel to my first condition in what Wittgenstein had to say in his *Lectures on Religious Belief* about "pictures" such as those of divine judgement, life after death, the eye of God, etc. He took the content of religious belief to consist of such pictures, but the interest of his remarks is not, of course, in these particular pictures but in the logical role which Wittgenstein ascribed to all religious "pictures". He said that, for religious believers as such, they are "constantly in the foreground" (*LRB*, p. 56). He clearly meant that everything which the religious believer qua religious believer says has reference to them. To take the "picture" of divine judgement as an example, Wittgenstein said that when a believer is ill, he may ask "What have I done to deserve this?"

and answer "This is a punishment"; whereas the unbeliever when he is ill does not think in terms of divine judgement at all. Such, then, are the close parallels between what Wittgenstein said about fundamental propositions in general or religious "pictures" in particular and the first condition on which I said that the concept of god is constitutive.

The second of my conditions was that the existence of that to which a constitutive concept as such refers cannot be doubted within its universe of discourse. Again, Wittgenstein said the same of fundamental propositions and of religious "pictures". He excluded the possibility of doubt in their case by insisting repeatedly and emphatically that they are not hypotheses. Fundamental propositions, Wittgenstein says explicitly in *On Certainty*, "do not serve as foundations in the same way as hypotheses which, if they turn out to be false, are replaced by others" (*OC* 402). At times he seems to be saying that they cannot be doubted in any conceivable way, as for instance when he remarks that we can form no clear conception of what would count against, or even for, the fundamental proposition that things do not disappear when no one is perceiving them (*OC* 119). At other times, he seems to be making the more restricted claim that fundamental propositions cannot be doubted within their language-games. This latter seems to be his point when, for example, he imagines a schoolboy who, in the history class, keeps asking whether the earth existed before he was born, and in the science class whether nature is uniform, and in general whether things disappear when no one sees them; and comments that this boy's teacher would be justified in saying "Your doubts don't make sense" because, if the boy goes on like this, he will never learn the language-games, viz. history, etc., which the teacher wants to show him how to play (*OC* 310–17). However, be it in the wider or the more restricted way, Wittgenstein is consistently of the opinion that "there is no such thing as doubt" (*OC* 58) in the case of fundamental propositions. "Absence of doubt" about its fundamental proposition "belongs to the essence of the language-game" (*OC* 370). It is "presupposed in the language-game" in the sense that "one is not playing the game or playing it wrong" if one doubts the fundamental proposition (*OC* 446). Fundamental propositions are not presuppositions in the sense of hypotheses, but in that of logical presuppositions. In his *Lectures on Religious Belief*, Wittgenstein had been equally clear that religious "pictures" are not open to doubt in the way that hypotheses are. That, he said, is why we speak of them as "dogma" or "faith" rather than as "hypothesis" or "high probability" or "knowing" (*LRB*, p. 57). "Whatever believing in God may be, it can't be believing in something we can test, or find means of testing" (*LRB*, p. 60). Believers sometimes affirm that they have evidence for their beliefs, but it is not the kind of thing which would count as evidence for a scientific hypothesis (*LRB*, p. 61). Wittgenstein did not say this disparagingly. He was simply pointing out that to regard religious beliefs as hypotheses would be to misconceive of them (see e.g. *LRB*, p. 56). For a blunder that would be too big (*LRB*, p. 62). In religion, we do not speak of belief as we ordinarily do. Ordinarily, if we say that we believe – as distinct from know – something, we thereby imply that there are grounds for doubting it of which we cannot altogether dispose, even though we do not doubt it ourselves; but with regard to religion no one would ever say, "You only believe. Oh well . . ." (*LRB*, p. 60), as if there could be something in this case which was more assured than mere belief. But then again, according to Wittgenstein the word "believe", in the case of religion, "is not used as we generally use the word 'know'" (ibid.). Religious belief, that is to say, is not calculated acceptance but total commitment: "indubitability wouldn't be enough to make me change my whole life" (*LRB*, p. 57). One of Wittgenstein's ways of putting the difference between religious belief and ordinary belief was this: "Suppose someone were a believer and said: 'I believe in a Last Judgement,' and I said: 'Well, I'm not so sure. Possibly.' You would say that there is an enormous gulf between us. If he said 'There is a German aeroplane overhead' and I said 'Possibly. I'm not so sure,' you'd say we were fairly near" (*LRB*, p. 53). It is clear that Wittgenstein had thought of "pictures" when he gave his *Lectures* much as he thought of fundamental propositions in his latest work: both are conceived to be as far removed from the possibility of doubt within their appropriate contexts as my constitutive concepts.

My third condition of a concept's being constitutive was that definitions of it indicate what can, or cannot, be said within its relevant universe of discourse. Again, there are the closest parallels in Wittgenstein. He sees the role of fundamental propositions as regulative "like that of rules of a game" (*OC* 95). What was in his mind here can be illustrated, I think, from his remark that "it is part of the language-game with people's names that everyone knows his name with the greatest

certainty" (*OC* 579). He regards "Everyone knows his own name" as a fundamental proposition. The remark about it, which I have just quoted, can hardly have meant that, as a matter of empirical fact, no one ever forgets, or is misinformed about, his own name, for such things clearly happen from time to time. Even if they did not, there would be nothing self-contradictory in the thought of them doing so and therefore Wittgenstein can hardly have meant that the denial of his fundamental proposition is self-contradictory. What, then, does he mean when he says that the language-game with people's names "does presuppose that it is nonsensical to say that the majority of people are mistaken about their names" (*OC* 628)? Something like this seems to be the answer. Suppose I were selling someone my car and he asked me what the exact cubic capacity of the engine was and when I replied "1493" he said, "May I see the log book just to make sure?". That would not be an odd thing for him to say. But now suppose he asked me my name and, when I told him, he said "Shall we look at your birth certificate just to make sure?" I should think he was either joking or crazy. The proposition "Everyone knows his own name" regulates the language-game with people's names in the sense that it indicates what it makes sense to say within that game and what it does not. Think what irritation and delay would be caused by someone who wanted proof every time anyone gave him their name! We should all wonder what he was playing at. We find much the same idea in what Wittgenstein said earlier about religious belief. The "Eye of God" was one example of a religious "picture" which he used. He would have said that, in order to understand what is meant by it, you must see how it is used. There is a "technique of usage" to be learned where religious "pictures" are concerned: that is to say, there are some conclusions which believers draw from them and some they do not (*LRB*, p. 71). In the present instance, according to Wittgenstein, they would say that God's eye sees everything, but not that God has eyebrows (ibid.). For our purpose the point to take is this: there is a logical connexion between what is meant by the "picture" and what may or may not be said in expressing the belief which it sustains.

I said fourthly that if a concept is constitutive it is logically irreducible. I think it is fair to find a comparison to this in the logical ultimacy which Wittgenstein ascribed to fundamental propositions. He sees them as grounded in action: "It is our *acting*, which lies at the bottom of the language-game"

(*OC* 204). Such action is explicitly differentiated from assenting to a proposition (*OC* 204) or following a rule (*OC* 44). Fundamental propositions are, in the ordinary senses, neither propositions nor rules. Our certainty about them is "a form of life" (*OC* 358). It is difficult to be certain what Wittgenstein meant by "a form of life". He says that by so describing the certainty of fundamental propositions he wants "to conceive of it as something that lies beyond being justified or unjustified; as it were as something animal" (*OC* 359). Whatever he meant in the latter part of this quotation – and it has aroused considerable discussion[7] – there can be no doubt that in the former he was thinking of the logical ultimacy which attaches to fundamental propositions. Admittedly, to say that something lies at the bottom of the language-game, in the sense that there is nothing else by which it could logically be justified or unjustified, is not the same as saying that it lies there in the sense that there is nothing else to which it could logically be reduced; and I recognize that there is that difference between what Wittgenstein says about fundamental propositions and what I say about constitutive concepts. But, at least, there is this in common between his fundamental propositions and my constitutive concepts: that they are both seen as logical end-points. I hold that what is said in terms of this concept cannot be said in any other way; Wittgenstein, that what is said on the presupposition of this proposition can admit of no more ultimate presupposition. Does it not come to much the same thing? Are we not both contending that there is no saying this kind of thing except in these terms? Yet again, remarkably similar claims had been made earlier by Wittgenstein for his religious "pictures". He asked rhetorically, "Why shouldn't one form of life culminate in an utterance of belief in a Last Judgement?" (*LRB*, p. 58). The logical ultimacy of his religious "pictures" comes out very clearly, I think, in what Wittgenstein had to say about the logical impossibility of the believer and unbeliever contradicting one another. He remarked that you can say the unbeliever "believes the opposite" to the believer, if you like, but "it is entirely different from what we would normally call believing the opposite" (*LRB*, p. 55). Asked if he believed in a Judgement Day, it would seem to him, as an unbeliever, "utterly crazy" to say "No. I don't believe there will be such a thing" (ibid.). Why crazy? His answer is that, when he replies, "I don't believe in . . .", whatever description fills in the dots, "the religious person never believes in what I

describe". He concludes: "I can't contradict that person" (ibid.). His point is presumably that which I made above with regard to moral obligation, viz. that there is a difference between contradicting someone by denying what he says within the same universe of discourse and contradicting him by rejecting that universe of discourse altogether. It is the former which Wittgenstein thought he could not do because he and the believer simply did not speak the same language. But, of course, if what a believer says could be translated into the language which an unbeliever does speak, then Wittgenstein could contradict him. The fact that Wittgenstein thought he could not justifies us in supposing that he did not think any such translation possible. In other words, he thought religious discourse irreducible to any other kind of discourse.

Such, then, are the parallels which I find between what I mean by a concept being constitutive and what Wittgenstein meant by a proposition being fundamental; and again, between what I want to say about the concept of god and what Wittgenstein said about religious "pictures". It may be apposite to conclude by remarking that there is at least a hint in Wittgenstein's *On Certainty* that he would have been prepared to speak in terms of constitutive concepts. At *OC* 36, in a passage where he is discussing the fundamental proposition "There are physical objects", he remarks:

> "A is a physical object" is a piece of instruction which we give only to someone who doesn't yet understand either what "A" means or what "physical object" means. Thus it is instruction about the use of words *and "physical object" is a logical concept* (like colour, quantity, . . .). *And that is why no such* (sc. ordinary empirical) *proposition as: "There are physical objects" can be formulated.* (italics mine)

The points that "physical object" is a "logical concept" and that "There are physical objects" is a fundamental proposition seem here to be set alongside each other as amounting to the same thing.

III.   Defence of the View Taken

I drew out the above parallels between my account of the logical foundation of religious belief and certain ideas in Wittgenstein's later philosophy partly to rebut the criticism[8] that I am mistaken in supposing that my view owes anything to him. Now I wish to deal with three other, more general, objections which I have encountered to the view that religious belief is logically constituted by the concept of god.

The craving for generality

The first objection is that my attempt to define religious belief as constituted by the concept of god is an instance of that "craving for generality" (*BBB*, p. 17) which Wittgenstein so roundly condemned in his later philosophy. He said that we are inclined to think that there must be some property (or properties) common to every entity subsumed under a "concept-word" or "common noun" (*PG* 35) and that this common property (or properties) is our justification for applying the term in its various instances. What he had particularly in mind (*PI* 71) was Frege's insistence that definition must be complete, that a concept "must unambiguously determine, as regards any object, whether or not it falls under the concept".[9] Against this he said that if we "look and see" how general terms are actually used, we shall not discover common properties but only "family resemblances" (*BBB*, pp. 17–18, *PI* 66–7, *PG* 35). The general term "games" is one of his examples. Games form a family, e.g. board games, card games, ball games, writing games, ring games, etc.; and they have, so to say, family features, e.g. rules, scores, winnings and losings, teams, excitements, enjoyments, etc. These "family resemblances" "overlap and crisscross" each other (*PI* 67). Every member of the "family" bears some resemblance to at least one of the other members, but not necessarily to all the others. Like the links of a chain or the fibres of a thread, says Wittgenstein, the applications of a general term are bound together by intermediary connexions, so that some of them "belong to the same family without having anything in common" (*PG* 35). He is alive to the possible objection, as he puts it, that "a transition can be made from anything to anything, so that the concept isn't bounded" (ibid.). The point of this objection is that a link of some sort can always be discovered between any two things, whereas, so far as the applications of general terms are concerned, it is only certain links which bring things under certain concepts. As Wittgenstein himself recognizes, if we say that the applications of a general term form a "family", this "is not to say that we shall not mind what is incorporated into it" (*RFM* 26). What, then, is it to say? Wittgenstein's

forthright reply to the objection stated a moment ago is simply: "for the most part (the concept) isn't in fact bounded . . ." (*PG* 35). By which, no doubt, he meant that we cannot, as Frege proposed, invariably state the necessary and sufficient conditions for the application of a common noun or concept-word. We may take it from what Wittgenstein said about looking and seeing how general terms are actually used that he thought concepts are bounded simply by the conventions of ordinary use: it just is the case that the members of the family, links in the chain, fibres in the thread, are what they are. Nevertheless, it should be noted that in *Philosophical Grammar*, immediately after the words quoted a moment ago, Wittgenstein says that "in order to clear up philosophical paradoxes" we may sometimes find it convenient to set alongside the account of a general term's actual use a definition of it which is in many ways like the latter but draws the boundaries of the general term's application more clearly. I shall return to this concession in a moment.

The criticism which I am concerned to rebut is that my attempt to define religious belief is at variance with what Wittgenstein had to say about "family resemblances". He does not refer to religion in this connexion, but at least one of his expositors has offered it alongside games as an example of the force and validity of Wittgenstein's attack on our "craving for generality". Recalling that Wittgenstein read and admired William James' *Varieties of Religious Experience* (London, 1902), George Pitcher notes that in Lecture II James attacked essentialism with particular reference to religion. Said James: "let us rather admit freely at the outset that we may very likely find no one essence, but many characters which may be equally important in religion . . .". Pitcher elaborates the point thus:

> We call all sorts of things "religions", and it is plainly false that there are one or more characteristics to be found in each and every one of them. A philosopher can put forward a definition of the term "religion" which he thinks captures the "essence" of religion, but he can only think he has succeeded if he concentrates on a small group of religions and ignores all others. And more likely than not, his definition will merely express his own preference for what he thinks any proper religion ought to be. (*The Philosophy of Wittgenstein* (Englewood Cliffs, 1964), p. 218)

If this were so, then my definition of religious belief as constituted by the concept of god would be misguided. But I do not think it is.

In one of the passages to which I have referred above (viz. *BBB*, p. 17), Wittgenstein says that the quest for properties common to all applications of a general term – or as he puts it "the idea of a general concept being a common property of its particular instances" – is connected with ideas of the structure of language which are too "primitive" and "simple". What he clearly has in mind is the essentialism of, say, Plato or his own *Tractatus*. His strictures on "the craving for generality" are an attack on doctrinaire adherence to such essentialism on the part of those who ignore facts which make it implausible. Now, I have not the slightest inclination to defend essentialism; nor have I any quarrel with the following points which Wittgenstein makes. We do not learn the meaning of general terms by being told their defining characteristics but by being given instances of their use (*PI* 69). If this gives us a blurred concept, there is no good reason to say that it is not a concept: it makes perfectly good sense to say, for instance, "Stand roughly there" (*PI* 71). We must not suppose that, when we have given someone examples of the use of a general term, he has to see something common to them all, which we were unable to express by itself, before he can be said to understand the general term (ibid.). If the definition of a general term is thought of as a kind of mental picture, then we must be on guard against failure to recognize differences through being held captive by such pictures (*BBB*, p. 18, *PI* 115). We are entitled to ask people who want an exact definition of a general term what degree of exactness they require, for even the most exact definitions can be misunderstood (*PI* 71). There is no denying the open texture of general terms: they can mean different things to different people or in different situations and this in exact science no less than in ordinary speech (*PI* 79). All these points I accept; and for all these reasons Wittgenstein is doubtless justified in rejecting essentialism.

It does not follow, however, that any and every attempt to define the boundaries of a concept is necessarily mistaken. As we saw a moment ago, Wittgenstein allowed that it might be necessary to define a concept in order to clear up "philosophical paradoxes". All I wish to do is to extend that concession so that it will cover certain more general kinds of confusion. The sort of confusion which I have in mind may be illustrated as follows. Take

the concept-word "Christianity" for example. It applies to a "family" of things: viz. separate communions such as Roman Catholicism, Orthodoxy, Anglicanism, etc.; and, cutting across these denominational features, conservative evangelicalism, fundamentalism, modernism, Christian radicalism, etc. All these, in their present forms and in the somewhat different forms they have sometimes taken in the past, are comprehended by the term "Christianity". This term certainly has meant different things to different people. Most recently its meaning has been extended by some theologians to cover what would more normally be called humanism. Would Wittgenstein have considered that it evinces a reprehensible "craving for generality" when someone points out in criticism of such an extension of meaning, as Professor Bernard Williams did some little time ago,[10] that if the system of belief to which you are referring does not conceive God to exist whether human beings and their attitudes exist or not, it is a misnomer to call that system of belief Christianity? If "Christianity" is extended in ordinary use to cover what would normally be called "humanism", then the kind of thing which gets said is that everyone who acknowledges his own humanity really believes in God.[11] If that strikes us as a confusion – and how could it not? – then in order to clear up the confusion are we not entitled to draw clearer boundaries between what "Christianity" means and what it does not? I cannot think that Wittgenstein would have denied us that right. To exercise it, as Williams did, is to indicate a necessary condition of the application of the term "Christianity". Now, if it is possible to do that, in the case of "Christianity", it is at least conceivable that the same might be done in the case of "religious belief". And if necessary conditions may be indicated, why not sufficient ones? All I am claiming is that, where one believes confusion to exist, one is not prohibited by Wittgenstein's doctrine of "family resemblances" from attempting to resolve it by clearer definition of terms. That is the point of my attempt at a definition of religious belief above.

I must emphasize that, in making this attempt, I am simply trying to state the necessary and sufficient conditions for the application of "religious belief", as that expression is *most commonly* used in our society at the present time. I shall refer to this from now on as the common use.

When I claim that there is a concept, god, which constitutes religious belief, all I am saying is that, when the term "religious belief" is used as it commonly is, the conditions outlined above as those which make god the constitutive concept of religious belief must be fulfilled and, if fulfilled, suffice to make the use common. When "religious belief" is used without these conditions being fulfilled, that use is uncommon. If there is a difference of meaning between common and uncommon uses of "religious belief", it is important for clear thinking to recognize this. That is my point. I am not out to blanket differences by my attempt to define "religious belief"; on the contrary, I am bent upon exposing them. I see nothing alien to Wittgenstein's view of "family resemblances" in that.

Common use of "religious belief"

It may, however, be said that my definition of religious belief as constituted by the concept of god is *not* in accordance with the common use of the expression "religious belief", so I must next deal with that objection. It may take either of two forms. The criticism may be that, as "religious belief" is commonly used, being constituted by the concept of god is not a *necessary* condition of that to which the term applies; or alternatively, that it is not a *sufficient* condition. On the one hand, the objection is that religious belief can get on without the concept of god; on the other hand, that it cannot get on with that concept alone. I will consider these two forms of the objection in turn.

First, is the concept of god *necessary* to religious belief? Can such belief exist where there is no object of belief having the characteristics which I ascribe to god, namely, awareness, agency, empirical and logical transcendence? The counter-example usually adduced against my view is certain forms of Buddhism which have no concept of an object of belief, aware of believers and actively related to them. I do not deny that these forms of Buddhism exist; but my defence against this counter-example is as follows.

Let it be granted, for purposes of argument, that the characteristic, having the concept of god, is necessary to "religious belief", as that expression is commonly used; and also that this characteristic is neither a necessary nor a sufficient condition of "Buddhism", as that expression is commonly used. Let it also be granted, to recall Wittgenstein on "family resemblances", that, since adherents of some forms of Buddhism do believe in gods and goddesses, the characteristic, having the concept of god, can legitimately be listed among the family resemblances of Buddhism, even though some forms

of the latter do not possess it. From these premises two conclusions can be deduced validly. One is that it would be in accordance with common usage to call Buddhism as a whole an instance of religious belief – given that having the concept of god is a necessary condition of religious belief – because having that concept is among the family resemblances of Buddhism. The other conclusion is that it would be in accordance with common usage to call those forms of Buddhism which lack the concept of god instances of religious belief – even though having this concept is a necessary condition of religious belief – by virtue of the fact that they are already instances of Buddhism. On such grounds I would maintain that those forms of Buddhism which lack the concept of god will not serve as counter-examples to my view of the logical foundations of religious belief.

I turn to the second form of the criticism which I am considering, namely, that having the concept of god is not a *sufficient* condition of religious belief. Religious belief, it is said, is not simply a sort of conceptual thinking but a kind of emotional experience, such as Schleiermacher's "feeling of dependence", Otto's "sense of the numinous", or whatever. It provides us, not merely with explanations, but with experiences. All I have said of it as a universe of discourse, constituted by a concept, is alleged to leave out this element of feeling. To such criticism I would reply as follows.

First, I readily admit the affective and conative element in religious belief. It is apposite to recall the distinction between believing-that and believing-in, which H. H. Price and others have drawn.[12] Believing-*that* is simply assenting to some proposition that such-and-such is the case; believing-*in* is committing oneself affectively or conatively to the object of belief. I may believe that my bank manager knows a lot about stocks and shares; but to believe in him is not simply to be willing to assent to this proposition but to be prepared to invest my money in accordance with his advice. Without denying that belief-in presupposes belief-that, we can agree with those who say that a belief that God exists, if it were independent of any attitude towards him, would be of no interest, not even to God.[13] Religious belief is indisputably believing-in.

The important question, however, is, in whom or what? I may believe in all sorts of things or persons – British cars, the National Trust, my pupil Smith, my son Paul, etc. All these are affective and conative attitudes. What distinguishes religious belief from them? The answer can only be a certain distinctive object of belief. There is a logical connection between the concepts which constitute the universes of discourse in which we participate and the kind of experiences which we have. Wittgenstein was alive to this sort of connection in what he had to say about fundamental propositions. The latter are not simply "anchored in all our questions and answers" in the sense that they determine what counts as an explanation in their respective universes of discourse. Wittgenstein finds himself wanting to say "'That I regard this (sc. fundamental proposition) as certainly true also characterizes my interpretation of experience'" (OC 145). He does not think we can speak of certain experiences showing a fundamental proposition to be true, because this proposition, to which these experiences point, "itself belongs to a particular interpretation of them" (ibid.). The kind of thing he meant can, I think, be illustrated by the example that one could not have the experience of remorse unless one were already thinking in moral terms. Feeling remorse is not simply feeling sorry: it is feeling sorry that one has failed to do what one ought. The point is not, of course, that one must first say to oneself "There is moral obligation" and then and only then will one feel remorse. It is that some such fundamental proposition is implicit in moral experience in the sense that awareness of it *as* moral experience logically implies acceptance of this fundamental proposition. I would say in terms of the constitutive concept, god, what Wittgenstein said more generally to this effect in terms of fundamental propositions. So far from failing to account for religious feeling or experience, the view that religious belief is constituted by the concept of god offers the only plausible account of why religious feeling, or experience, has the distinctive character which it has. We feel "absolutely dependent", we sense "the numinous" – or however you choose to describe the distinctive emotional element in religious belief – because of the way in which we conceive of god. The fact that the ordinary meaning of "religious belief" includes some reference to affection or conation is not, therefore, incompatible with my account of the logical foundation of religious belief.

I would only add to my defence against the objection that my views are at variance with common usage the observation that, where some account other than mine of the logical foundations of religious belief is given, the concept of god has a way of creeping back unobserved. Otto, for instance, said that his "numinous" "completely eludes

apprehension in terms of concepts"; but in no time at all he is speaking of it as "objective and outside the self" and of its "energy", "majesty" and "mystery"; that is, of it as an active, empirically and logically transcendent, object of belief.[14] Tillichians substitute for god the concept of the Ground of our Being but in no time at all they are telling us that this Ground is gracious.[15] How could "Being" be gracious without being aware of other beings and actively related to them? Anders Nygren says that it is the concept of "the eternal" which is constitutive of religious belief; but in no time at all he is speaking of this concept thus: "The eternal means at once revelation, judgement, reconciliation and communion *with God*" (italics mine).[16] The concept of god is inescapable in religion.

Religious belief is no ghetto

The third objection which I shall consider is that my account of the logical foundation of religious belief reduces the latter to an intellectual ghetto. If it were correct that religious believers are definitively preoccupied with the concept of god, the criticism goes, this would shut them out *qua* believers from all the wonder of the works of nature and of man which science explores. I find this objection so totally misconceived that it is hard to imagine how anyone could suppose that they have grounds for it. However, it has been put[17] and a brief reply will enable me to make one or two things of some importance clearer about the way in which, on my view of it, religious belief is related to other universes of discourse. It is related in two ways at least.

First, it should be noted that to say that everything which is discussed within a given universe of discourse must be discussed in certain terms is not to say anything at all about *what* may or may not be discussed within that universe of discourse. In particular, to say that religious belief is constituted by the concept of god is not to say what may, or may not, form the subject-matter of such belief. Consider, for instance, morality, history and science as three distinct universes of discourse. Category confusion may certainly arise among them, but it is important to recognize what would constitute such confusion and what would not. I should be guilty of it, for example, if I asked how men ought to live and took this to be a historical or scientific question; or if I wanted to know why some historical event occurred and expected morality or science to tell me; or if I wished to discover the scientific explanation of some phenomenon and turned hopefully to morality or history. But I should be guilty of no category confusion at all, if, for example, I wrote a treatise on the morality of some historical personage's activities, or the history of some moral code, or the psychology of moral and historical thinking. There are, no doubt, some logical limits on what can be discussed within any particular universe of discourse; it is difficult to conceive, for instance, of what a treatise on the chemistry of moral judgements or the morality of chemical equations could be about. But there is certainly no logical frontier around religious belief, as I have defined it, which forbids the believer qua believer to think about history, morality or science. He can (logically) have religious beliefs in terms of god about the subject-matter of all such universes of discourse. Qua religious believer he could, for instance, spend some of his time thinking about the theology of history, sense his god's demand in facing his duty to his family, and approach his scientific work as a service to his god. The richness and depth of his religious life will depend upon how wide-ranging the subjects are for which he seeks religious explanations or with respect to which he has religious experiences. The matters on which religious beliefs may be held are as wide as the world.

But, in order to recognize that religion is not a ghetto cut off from the rest of man's intellectual life, it is also necessary to see that there are con-straints on what may be thought in terms of the concept of god which are imposed by what may be thought in more general terms. Discourse in terms of god is not logically isolated from other sorts of discourse. The language used to express and communicate religious belief is in large part the same language as that used in other kinds of discourse and is subject to the same constraints. Its meaning may be qualified by the religious context but only to a certain extent. To use language in a self-contradictory way, for example, is as futile in religion as elsewhere. To qualify words to such an extent that there ceases to be any reason why these, rather than other words, should be used is as inadmissible here as elsewhere. My account of the logical foundations of religious belief makes no demands which are incompatible with these requirements. Though I included logical trans-cendence in the defining characteristics of god, I made it clear that by this I did not mean that self-contradictory propositions are acceptable in religion or that language in religion can be qualified without limit. On my view of it, religious belief is rational, not in the sense that scientific, or any other kind of non-religious, reasons can be given for it, but in the sense that the meaning of lan-guage need not be so strained in religion that it becomes vacuous.

Nothing in my account of religious belief as constituted by the concept of god implies that religion is an intellectual ghetto.

Notes

1 See his *On Certainty*, 58.

2 J. Bentham, *Introduction to the Principles of Morals and Legislation*, I.X, in L. A. Selby-Bigge, *British Moralists* (Oxford, 1897).

3 G. E. Moore, *Principia Ethica* (Cambridge, 1903), chapter 1. What he says of "good" applies to "ought".

4 See his "Empiricism, Semantics and Ontology", in *Revue Internationale de Philosophie*, 1950.

5 References to L. Wittgenstein's works will be made in accordance with the following abbreviations: *OC*, *On Certainty*; *BBB*, *Blue and Brown Books*; *PI*, *Philosophical Investigations*; *PG*, *Philosophical Grammar*; *RFM*, *Remarks on the Foundations of Mathematics*; *LRB*, *Lectures on Religious Belief* in *Lectures and Conversations*. I deal further with fundamental propositions in my "Wittgenstein and Fundamental Propositions", *The South-western Journal of Philosophy* (USA), February 1977, and with religious "pictures" in chapter 5 of my *Wittgenstein and Religious Belief* (London, 1975).

6 See his papers "A Defence of Common Sense" (1925), "Proof of the External World" (1939), "Four Forms of Scepticism" (1959), "Certainty" (1959), all contained in his *Philosophical Papers* (London, 1959).

7 See e.g. G. F. M. Hunter, "'Forms of Life' in Wittgenstein's *Philosophical Investigations*", *American Philosophical Quarterly*, 1968.

8 See letter from D. A. Griffiths in the *Times Literary Supplement*, 21 February 1975, and the review of my *A Philosophical Approach to Religion* (London, 1974) by A. Ellis in *Philosophical Quarterly*, 1975. I would now concede that my use of *PI*, p. 173 was not the best way of making my point. I deal much more satisfactorily with the sense in which Wittgenstein thought that language-games have presuppositions in the paper referred to in note 7 above.

9 *Grundgesetze der Arithmetik*, 11.56.

10 B. Williams, "Has 'God' a Meaning?", *Question*, 1 (1968).

11   This seems to be the implication of P. Tillich's remark: "Genuine atheism is not humanly possible for God is nearer to a man than that man is to himself", *The Shaking of the Foundations* (Penguin, London, 1962), p. 131.

12   H. H. Price, "Belief 'In' and Belief 'That'", *Religious Studies* (1965), and *Belief* (London, 1969), 11,9; and e.g. N. Malcolm, "Is it a Religious Belief that God exists?" in *Faith and the Philosophers*, edited by J. H. Hick (London, 1964).

13   Malcolm, "Is it a Religious Belief that God exists?"

14   R. Otto, *The Idea of the Holy* (Oxford, 1923), chapters 1–3.

15   See, e.g., J. A. T. Robinson, *Honest to God* (London, 1963), chapter 3.

16   *Meaning and Method* (London, 1972), p. 344.

17   See M. Hesse's reference to my view in her review article on *Talk of God*, edited by G. A. N. Vesey (London, 1969) in *Philosophy* (1969), and P. Bertocci's review of my contribution to R. E. Davies, *We Believe in God* (London, 1968) in *Religious Studies* (1969).

2

World Religions and World Orders

Stephen R. L. Clark

Introduction

There are good reasons for being suspicious of the very concept of "a religion", let alone a "world religion". It may be useful for a hospital administrator to know a patient's "religion" – as Protestant or Church of England or Catholic or Buddhist – but such labels clearly do little more than identify the most suitable chaplain, and connote groupings in the vast and confusing region of "religious thought and practice" that are of very different ranks. By any rational, genealogical taxonomy[1] "Protestant", "Anglican", "Catholic" connote species, genera or families within Christianity, which is in turn a taxon within the multivariant tradition traced back to Abraham. "Buddhism" includes as many variants as would "Abrahamism". Most Abrahamists, traditionally, have been theists, but it is difficult not to suspect that Marxist socialism is an atypical (and probably non-viable) variant which has inherited a linear view of time, a contest between the chosen agents of justice and the doomed powers-that-be, and the prospect of a future in which "there shall be no more sea". Most Buddhists, correspondingly, have preferred to think of themselves as atheists (for even if the gods exist they cannot matter much); but there are Buddhist sects for whom the Buddha-nature does all the same work at least as Aristotle's God, even if not

Stephen R. L. Clark, "World Religions and World Orders," reprinted by permission of Cambridge University Press from *Religious Studies* 26 (1990), pp. 43–57.

Augustine's. Wilfrid Cantwell Smith has further reminded us all that stories, rites and doctrines cannot be contained within the artificial boundaries of any sect or great tradition. So stories that began as "Buddhist" flow into Christendom and back into yet another religious network, "Hinduism", and so return again to Christendom. One fascinating instance is the story of St Josaphat (which is to say, Gautama Buddha), transformed by Georgians from an Islamic source and exerting an influence on Tolstoy, and through him and Henry Salt on Gandhi.[2] Maybe in times past such links, associations and multiple reflections were the exception, and there were fairly readily distinguishable, isolated bodies of story, ritual and metaphysics. Maybe some traditions exist relatively unchanged for centuries, but most are in a constant flux of reinterpretation and expansion. Even now there are some Presbyterians who cannot imagine that they share anything significant with Papists, Christians who imagine that Hindus are all idolaters, Buddhists who suppose that Abrahamists are all simple-minded literalists (an error for which Christian missionaries who patronizingly and ignorantly tailored the faith to the capacities of a supposedly superstitious peasantry must bear a lot of the blame). But there is now no part of the world that can indefinitely be isolated: all humankind is now a single species even if there were millennia when normal biological criteria would have raised at least the probability that there were distinct sub-species. Equivalently, we are all at sea upon a single ocean of "religious faith and practice", and most of us are all too eager to borrow tips or tools or provender from any passing ship. Sooner or later, some have hoped, there will be one ship only, even if it is a construction quite unlike the slender vessels of our solitary past.

"There can only be one religion which is valid for all men and at all times. Thus the different confessions can scarcely be more than the vehicles of religion."[3] Kant, of course, had delusions – as most of us now think – of an ideal simplicity, the goal of all religious endeavours as the one true theory was the goal of science. Our problem is that, as good moderns, we cannot easily envisage such a closure, and rather expect that every supposed simplification will reveal deeper complexities and apparent contradictions. The single boat in which we shall one day sail will more likely be patched together from a thousand swarming vessels, with the bits that really don't fit being cannibalized or thrown away, but with no overarching blueprint that would tell us how to build the boat again.

So there are at least two futures for us that embody some ideal of unity: the rationally crafted Kantian vessel, and the baroque contrivance pieced together by a struggling crew. As far as our biological future goes, the latter has my vote: I had rather imagine humankind, lifekind, continue on its drunkard's walk through God's immensity than be "re-engineered" by certified experts. But not everyone will be at ease even with the tolerant, sprawling, unpredictable monster that emerges from the confluence of creeds. Need we, or should we, expect unity at all? Or if we do why should it take either the "essentialist" or the "inclusive" form? Perhaps at last there will be one boat only, since the others have all sunk, and all survivors will be packed inside that spruce, well-captained vessel as it comes into harbour. Perhaps the very attempts to throw away unnecessary trimmings, or to tack on the jetsam of another ship, will be what brings the failed ships down. If that be so, and we have reason to suspect it, no amount of flattery or abuse should make us fiddle with our seaworthy ship. Such an insistent conservatism would rather be neither elitist nor inhuman, but our one security.

It is implicit in the metaphor I have deployed that everything that matters to us is going on board the ships. The Sea, as it features here, is simple chaos, the barren and unharvested plains over which, perforce, we sail. I do not doubt that there are other allegorical uses for the sea. What I have already excluded is the thought that "religion", "our religion", is no more than a personal attitude, an individual's look away from other and less important matters, which are nonetheless secure

enough to provide a context for our life together. What we have gathered from the sea to make our boat, or the vessel in which we have been sailing from years uncounted (and none knows its origin), constitutes all the order that we have. Religion is not a video-game conducted in the vessel's saloon, having nothing to do with how the ship is built or where it's headed. Our religion determines our science, our politics, our psychology. This is no less true for those who think that they are atheists, agnostics, sceptics, humanists, even if (as is quite possible) what they have thrown out will one day turn out to have been the compass, tiller, pump or radio. It is true even for those who have wholly forgotten their position, and live for the night-life down below in the saloon.

> If we were all on board ship and there was trouble among the stewards I can just conceive their chief spokesmen looking with disfavour on anyone who stole away from the fierce debates in the saloon or pantry to take a breather on deck. For there he would taste the salt, he would see the vastness of the weather, he would remember that the ship had a whither and a whence. He would remember things like fogs, storms, and what had seemed in the hot lighted rooms down below to be merely the scene for a political crisis would appear once more as a thin eggshell moving rapidly through an immense darkness over an element in which men cannot live.[4]

But it is time to put the metaphor aside. The questions facing us are at least as follows: (i) are the multiple traditions of humankind, now brought, willy-nilly, face to face, genuinely different in their implications for our lives at sea? (ii) can we even detect a common, and important, core from which a smart new creed could be constructed? (iii) can we at least expect to patch something together which we can all endure to sail aboard? (iv) if not even this is possible, must we expect that only one ship, however enlarged or modified, will come to land, and the rest be lost? (v) what if all our ships go down? These questions, inevitably, must concern our personal lives and fate, but my intention is to concentrate on their significance for our lives together here, as would-be citizens of a single world. I would like to consider also what the implications of a radical enlargement of our horizons might be: what difference will inter-planetary or inter-stellar travel make to us? How shall we deal with alien sentience? But this one world, and the almost aliens on it, constitute a more immediate, and more manageable problem.

Essential, Secular, Inclusive Singularity

That there are in fact real differences between us is clear. It is not so obvious that these are unchanging or essential, nor that we always know quite what the differences are. As a reasonably well-informed philosopher, I grow weary of telling Christians that Buddhists do *not* seek to merge their identities in an Overmind, and Buddhists that Christians do *not* "heteronomously" obey an external law-giver. I am tired of hearing that Christianity/Judaism/Buddhism/Hinduism/Native American animism is at once the most materialistic and most spiritual of the great religions. I am tired of hearing Buddhists praised for their long tradition of psychological enquiry by people who have never troubled to discover the long tradition of Abrahamic psychological enquiry evidenced, say, in the *Philokalia*. I am as tired of hearing Christians praised for their compassion and "social outreach", as I am of hearing them denounced for their contributions to environmental catastrophe. Any differences I may allege may be as foolish, or as incompletely specified, as those. But I do not deny that there are differences.

Specifically, what differences in world order are dictated by the great religions? If, as Hocking declared many years ago, "precisely because we do not want a world state, we do require a world morale", which is to say a world religion,[5] it will obviously matter what that world religion is. If we are standing on the threshold of a new thing, civilization in the singular, spun by the religious community, what could it be like? Consider the Nazi attempt to create and sustain a new religion of blood and soil. Or the Marxist attempt to regulate the means of production by party dictatorship. Or Hindu Homo Hierarchicus, Islamic Shari'a, post-Christian humanism or romantic "naturism" (which last is a label for a form of thought and action that looks back to Native American, African or Celtic traditions for its inspiration). Consider other half-forgotten ways, and the possibility of their return: science fiction writers regularly conceive some version of Pharaonism as our future.

A religious order differs from a merely military or political one in that membership comes by self-identification, rather than being a function solely of birth or habitation, and obedience to its rules is a matter of loyalty rather than of enforced submission. A world state not animated by any corresponding religion could only be imperial. "For how can there be an international law or order or working league or federation of states until there is an accepted level of moral understanding among men to give vitality to its legal code?"[6] A global religion's qualification as a possible world order, a civilization transcending local loyalties, rests on its being available to citizens of any local state. In Arnold Toynbee's later analysis, such "religions" have a larger destiny than to carry the seeds of dying civilization into a new era: they are themselves the new creations which will one day transcend all merely local or coercive power.[7] Because they aim to be universal, and universal by inviting anyone's belief, they are seen to appeal to some essential human core of reason or will. What matters in them, it is then supposed, is what "just anyone" could see, no matter what her background, character or ritual preference. This Hellenist who extolled the Hebrews as "a nation of philosophers" made a radical distinction between ethical and contemplative principle and the merely ritual or superstitious elements of the Mosaic Law. Thus Vedantins who urge the "essential unity of all religions" downgrade the particular observances, and any doctrinal element that does not agree with their own favoured creed. Post-Christian humanists suppose that we would all agree (if only we were sensible) that every human being is a uniquely valuable individual to be accorded liberty and welfare-rights so as to co-operate in the progressive enterprise of deifying Humanity. All the great religions, we are regularly – and misleadingly – informed, speak of the Fatherhood of God and Brotherhood of Man – or else they can't be great religions. Oddly enough the "essential core" of all religions, and the core of such modern cults as have been contrived as candidates for global acceptability, always turn out to be cautiously expressed versions of the speaker's own personal or ancestral creed. Whatever cannot be made to fit in that is "obviously" superstition. If Hindus object to the maltreatment of cows, that is fanaticism; if humanists demand paid holidays for all (Article 24 of the United Nations Declaration) that is, at worst, a touching idealism.

One reply has been to agree that traditions, ideals, "religions" differ even in "essentials", in what believers mind most about, but to say that we can discover rules which all will accept, even if only so as to be free to get on with serious business. Such a would-be "secular" order would give all traditions such chances as could be equally agreed by all. But that hope is forlorn: either we are being asked to accept that "secular" order which reflects current power politics, or else one that embodies a particular vision. What could induce the powerful to bargain away their advantage, to give aboriginals a veto on the use of sacred sites? Even if a "secular" order did concede the "equal rights" of aboriginals, it would not give them more rights than ordinarily "secular" citizens, and would treat their attachment to the land as one more negotiable value, to be surrendered for the "common good". "Far from protecting cultural diversity, liberalism turns as by instinct to violence and war when cultural separateness shows signs of becoming serious, which is to say, political."[8] The powerful are at their most doctrinaire and moralistic when they think they are being impartial. To insist on "merely secular order" is to have decided that other people's sacred values do not seriously count.

So it is very doubtful that we can impartially identify either an essential core of "all religions" or even a minimal set of rules with which we'd all be satisfied. We might think it would be pleasant to arrange for "everyone" to treat, and be treated by, others according to the self-same rules. But we do not all agree on who is to count as "anyone". We do not all agree on the rules we would be prepared to live under. We do not all agree on what matters most to us. "Secularists", whether their ideology be post-Christian humanism or Marxism, are always very unimaginative in assessing what other folk might want to think. We don't all think that human beings matter most, nor that such beings last from birth to brain-death, nor that a relatively pain-free life is best for any individual, nor that a conciliatory expression always helps. In some societies vultures count far more than visiting anthropologists; in others the important individuals are families; in very many wisdom comes through pain. We help no one by pretending that the UN Declaration was anything but a piece of middle-class Western ideology adopted for want of anything better by people who openly interpret it in ways its authors disavowed. Such a Declaration could only be universally, and univocally, enforced by military action, not by the agreement of dissenting religions: it requires a world state just because there is no world religion to endorse it, but a state without religion (i.e. binding spirit) does not last for long.

So can we turn aside from the Kantian or quasi-Kantian dream of a rationally ordered vessel that could suit us all, and cobble a ship together from the rafts, boats, galleons, jetsam that the current

brings? This sort of world-religion would make no pretence to be coherent, minimal or rationally inventible. Instead we would all agree to give appropriate, differing, honours to "great religious leaders", allow inspiration from any number of "religious texts" and ceremonies, practice with more or less enthusiasm such techniques as will bring Krishna, Gabriel, Quetzalcoatl, Kuan Yin, Aphrodite, Jesus Christ before the imagination's eye. King Belshazzar gathered sacred vessels from the conquered nations, "drank wine and praised the gods of gold and silver, of bronze and iron, and of wood and stone"[9] (very much as moderns praise the artistry of medieval cathedrals, icons, ancient statuary). Any worshipper prepared to offer up a pinch of incense – a mere token of esteem – to the actual, over-arching laws of a global civilization, can travel where she pleases, and participate in any of the little, modest cults that crowd into our pantheon. To an outsider, the result will look a little like the Roman (or many another) Empire, and a little – though misleadingly – like Hinduism. No one need agree with anybody, and no one need suppose that imperial, global law is what we'd all desire, or accept if we had any choice. Perhaps we need not even have the emperor at hand: we could do without a political and legal centre, a single court of last appeal, if enough of us endorsed the world religion.

It would be a feature of that world religion that different classes thought quite differently about it. Most would never think to reason their way past their casual agreement that they were Catholics and their neighbours Mormons, and that there were some Buddhists or Vaishnavites or Celtic revivalists across the town. Some would agree that, had things been different or their family history changed, they would as readily have been Baptists, voodoo cultists, Parsees or Marxists. What matters, they say, is one's own national or family identity, one's roots. The Romans' objection to Christians, remember, was that they converted people away from those same stable roots. Some others insist upon a certain richness of imagination as the central theme of all religions ("Religion is really Art or Poetry"), or else talk of purity, ethical endeavour, psychological integrity. What does the particular story, mantra, guru, ritual matter? We all agree to disagree, because we have no disagreement worth mentioning: no one is ever wrong, or right.

I suspect that what I have described is already our world religion. Anyone who vehemently minds about a story, ritual, guru and wishes all alternatives away can already be typed as bad-mannered, if not fanatical. Missionary endeavour, sometimes with good reason, is condemned. In the face of this disapproval enthusiastic and committed Marxists, quite as much as enthusiastic Baptists, must support their enthusiasm by communal activity, mutual praise and occasional scape-goating. All enthusiasts can expect the patronizing tolerance of their peers – at least until their enthusiasm becomes a real offence, and the many-headed monster stoops to kill.

What I have described is a global religion, but I have done so in terms that should suggest a certain hesitation, and an apocalyptic image: the beast with ten horns and seven heads that John the Divine saw rising from the sea[10] "to mouth bombast and blasphemy" with the support of its marvel-working companion. I suspect that a very similar response would be made by those of other religious traditions: if the Christian can easily see a blasphemous parody and amalgam to divert us from true worship, a Buddhist can see a willed entanglement in the nets of death and illusion. Muslims will detect the familiar face of the *Dar al-Harb*, with which there can be no lasting truce. Even Hindus or Celtic revivalists, who are perhaps more used to seeing the divine in many shapes, must hesitate to endorse a creed that turns the gods into servants not of the "infinite and eternal of the human form" but of our shifting, self-congratulatory desires. Can the world-beast be religion after all? Does not all religion find us in the wrong before and in a real world that would have us better? Must it not be something more than a source of cheap thrills, marvels, gorgeous and self-serving fantasy?

Different Sorts of Global Religion

The Catholic Church, by derivation, is a church *kat'holou*, for the whole world. Mahayana Buddhism, by a similar derivation, is the Great Vehicle. The Anglican Communion has gloried in its diversity, and even such cults as have been considered local or merely tribal are often not too proud to accept converts. There is an aspiration to be available to all, and not just to spiritual athletes and enthusiasts. But of course the traditions, or communities that embody them, have not lacked positive doctrines. Being available for all need not, and usually does not, mean being amenable to all. Whereas the rationalist requires us to believe only what anyone could see or agree was true (if only she were rational enough), and the syncretist re-

quires us to believe (but not to believe *true*) whatever anyone at all believes, faith-holders of whatever persuasion demand particular beliefs out of many possible, and possibly rational, ones.

Faith-holders, rationalists and syncretists may not, in fact, be different people: any of us may acknowledge the attraction of any of these positions, and even if we finally endorse one thesis, we may still acknowledge elements of truth elsewhere. A faith-holder, in particular, may agree that holders of some other faiths, even if mistaken in her eyes, may, all unknowing, serve the real God. I have heard it said that such a belief is patronizing or offensive, but I do not see why it should be. If the *Logos* in fact is Christ, then anyone who serves and esteems the *Logos* does serve Christ, whether they know it or not. Their service may be incomplete, but whose is not? It must be part of any faith that the truth is not without its witnesses, that anyone may glimpse afar off what the chosen may see face-to-face. It may be irritating to be told that someone else knows more about what one is doing than one does oneself, but the irritations can be returned. Why is it worse for a Christian to tell a devout Jew that the Word and Wisdom that she seeks is actually embodied in a Jewish hasid, than for a Jew to tell a devout Christian that what she pictures to herself as Jesus can only at best be God's plan for humanity? Why is it offensive for evangelical Christians to preach the Gospel, but quite acceptable for Buddhist converts to recommend Buddhist thought and practice as a solution to ethical or scientific problems? Can it possibly have something to do with the charms of the unfamiliar, and the probable class of the preacher? We intellectuals are always very ready to rebuke the merely cultural and superstitious hang-ups of others, while ourselves displaying a quite crass cultural snobbery about TV evangelists! Fashionable forms of relativism usually stop well short of agreeing that Bible Belt fundamentalists, or creationists, might have a point, while simultaneously suggesting that it is racist to object to ritual slaughter of food animals, or to clitoridectomy. Everyone can be ethnic except rednecks. Everyone is right except those on the right. Everyone's religion can be taken seriously, unless it's Christianity.

But that is by the way. What I wish to consider here is the possible role for exclusivity in world religion, not in excluding anyone forever from the Kingdom, but in identifying particular conditions under which one may enter it. The Kantian Brotherhood of all Mankind reaches out to embrace all who will acknowledge themselves as equals of all other humans, ready to live under the same law. That brotherhood expressly excludes, and always, beings who do not rise to Kantian rationality, quite as much as the *Dar al-Islam* excludes, and must always be at war with, the *Dar al-Harb*. It also identifies the significant individuals in ways that not all humans have, ways that owe everything to a very specific religious and philosophical tradition. Kantianism and its offspring, post-Christian humanism, constitute particular religions that demand our allegiance. I doubt if either is attractive, or well-grounded, enough to secure it, or to give rational hope of a successful actualization of the Brotherhood.

Syncretism similarly demands allegiance, and its pretence of tolerance is easily exposed. Those who won't offer the pinch of incense, or carry the beast's number on their hand or head, can expect to be excluded from the benefits of the world-religion. To say anything is to deny something: to endorse one possible future is to flee from others. It follows that exclusions are inevitable, and that it is no final criticism of a candidate that it excludes.

So what sort of catholic, dogmatic religion might we look towards? My concern here, whatever that of other contributors to this conference, need not be with the metaphysical truth of the religion (though I am assuming, against the syncretist, that it is intended to be true). Instead, I want to consider what sorts of global religion are available, what different attitudes and methods could be brought to create "the coming world civilization".

There are three preliminary distinctions to be made, all implicit in what I have already said. Some projected world religions accept the division between spiritual authority and political power, and others do not. On the one side: Hinduism draws an absolute distinction between Brahmin and Kshatriya; Gautama chose to be a Buddha not a Cakravatin, to guide the world through the force for example and (perhaps) transmitted "merit" rather than by force of arms and delegated powers; Christians, Jews and Sunni Muslims all find their authorities elsewhere than in Princes; Kantians expressly distinguish sound republican governments as ones where the laws are proclaimed by those who can't themselves enforce them. On the other side, the half-forgotten but still deeply influential experiments of Egyptian Pharaonism, Constantinian theocracy, the Imamate, Tibetan Buddhism (under one interpretation) all postulate a God-King present in the flesh. My own prefer-

ence is for the former style, but Pharaonism et al. do have their attractions.

Secondly, some religions presuppose a diffused authority, others a more central one: for some any believer may speak with God's voice; for others only accredited officials may.

Another distinction lies between those who acknowledge themselves as faith-holders, and those who seek to fix their creeds as uniquely rational. Buddhists (and some Muslims) regularly comment unfavourably on a supposedly Christian appeal to "blind faith" and "dependence", and insist that we should rely upon ourselves, and on our reasoning powers. I have never myself been clear why such a project makes much sense if there is no self, and what our powers, images, thoughts are is irretrievably dependent on the manifold arisings of our aggregates. Believing in oneself, as Chesterton said, is a foolish superstition, like believing in Joanna Southcott: for a Buddhist it should be like believing in the accidentally accumulated "Prophecies of Merlin" (who does not exist). Christians, like the multiple authors of the *Philokalia*, proclaim their trust in the awakened intellect, but are strongly aware of the sluggish and beleaguered quality of how we actually now think. Most of us can rarely do much more than hang on desperately to the faint glimmer of watchfulness and clarity we have been blessed with. But temperaments do differ, and we place different emphases on what can be taught and what must be taken on trust. Some would-be global religions, accordingly, will think that they can spread by mere exposition of a doctrine (and conclude that unbelievers must be deliberately obtuse); others will also invoke ritual, art, poetry, and look to kindle the vision of enlightenment that no words can teach (pardoning those on whom no grace of vision falls). In brief, and obviously enough, the division between faith-oriented and reason-oriented creeds exists at the level of rhetoric, and neither thought nor practice. Suspect those preachers who appeal only to ungrounded commitment, and also those who appeal only to axiomatizable reason.

So let us consider other ways of distinguishing would-be world-religions. One option, and one of the most powerful, must be the kind of post-Christian humanism that is embodied in our scientific-industrial civilization. It is implicit in that system that there is no moral order in nature, that everything is readily at hand as tools or material for human purposes. Nothing is sacred, save the wills of accepted humans (which does not necessarily include infants, imbeciles or even "primitives") and – as I have already pointed out – the superstitions of primitive peoples cannot long be taken seriously. It is a little startling to find Northrop Frye seeking to defuse the implications of Spengler's vision of a declining West by referring to the global spread of such industrialism:[11] startling because Frye normally pays more respect to such possibilities as industrialism ignores, and because he offers this enchanting prospect immediately after rebuking Toynbee's wish-fulfilling expectation of a global Christendom that will transcend the dying West. Scientific industrialism – although its spokesmen regularly denounce old-fashioned dualisms of "matter" and "spirit" – actually embodies a powerful dualism of its own, between wild Nature and the technosphere. Sometimes its fantasies are of a space-travelling civilization that need never again adapt itself to a non-human environment (precisely by placing itself in that most alien and deadly space beyond the living Earth). Chardin's fantasies of the Overmind – which were a piece with much 1930s apocalypticism – are to be realized through computer networks, genetic engineering, bionic enhancement of sense and muscle. Those of us old-fashioned faith-holders who suspect that we shall not be allowed to "build a tower to heaven", nor yet to remake our bodies and the living earth, can expect to be denounced as backward-looking obscurantists, to be swept away (as Chardin hoped) in the tide of progress. It is worth adding that the self-congratulatory self-image embodied in dicta like "The Church fears criticism: we scientists welcome it"[12] is very far from my experience. Scientists emphatically do not welcome radical criticism, in ethics, metaphysics or methodology. Always suspect people who claim to be free of prejudice: they have just not noticed what their prejudices are!

But scientific industrialism does have other faces, maybe significant enough to be identified as yet another would-be global religion, or one that merges imperceptibly into this next one. While some believers seek to detach themselves from Earth, others seek the closest identification with our living world. Nature-worship is as powerful a form as Human-worship, and has many half-formed sects. Chardin himself may speak, or be heard, as a Naturist, though his heart is given to a nature fulfilled and transcended in the present human will. More typically, naturism involves an appeal to felt presences of stream and hill and forest, to the uncomplicated or supposedly uncomplicated) emotions of non-human animals, to supposedly "feminine" capacities of love or intuition rather than "masculine" and rule-governed intellect. Sometimes naturists, unconsciously, draw very close to that religion of blood and soil that almost established its leader as Viceroy of Hell a half-century ago: consider the rhetoric of pure nature, animal innocence, non-rational intuition; consider the use of ancient rituals to awaken gods from their long sleep; consider the abuse directed at the Jewish heritage of Western Europe; even the ancient stereotypes of what "women" are are now repeated, in praise of woman, where once they were recited with a hidden contempt. Obviously I do not mean to "refute" naturism by pointing out that some really despicable people have been naturists: plenty of despicable people have been anything you please, and plenty of naturists both were and are opposed to nearly everything the Nazis stood for. Plenty of very nice people, conversely, have held really despicable doctrines. But my point remains: naturism is a religious tradition as various as most others, but it does constitute, in its still formless and churchless state, a genuine possibility for global faith. Consider the widespread icon of the Earth as it is seen from space; consider our fascination with the world before us that was swept away, and the possibility that we might go down too, and yet Earth abide.

These opposing visions, of Gaia and the Technosphere, identify another real distinction amongst world-religions: some are humanist in their orientation, and others non-humanist or even anti-humanist. Is the divine to be discovered unambiguously within the human life, or does it loom outside or against us? Are we servants of Being, or its soon-to-be masters? Recent liberal theology in the West has been overwhelmingly humanist: the whole world is to be explained and justified by our presence in it; love of our (human) neighbour exhausts the meaning of the commandment to love God; the kingdom of Heaven, it almost seems, is to be a really friendly and unstructured party; human nature is no longer to be pruned, disciplined or crucified, but to be applauded as the real source of life. Even some Buddhists have caught the infection, and begun to explain away all tales of reembodiment in animals, all suggestion that the Buddha-nature counts as something more than human. Hinduism, on the other hand, could be contrasted with the syncretism it superficially resembles, exactly in that its multiple sects direct attention to the Absolute, not back to us. Naturists, in all their manifold sects, may have the bias toward an undisciplined human nature (for our errors, they say, are those of civilization, not the world), and may concede that humans occupy a special place in Nature, but find the images of the divine outside the merely human world.

So global religions, so far, may be parapolitical or political, centralized or decentralized, faith-holding or intellectual, humanist or non-humanist. Some are linear in their temporal outlook, others are, effectively, cyclical or "atemporal". Liberal theologians characteristically praise the former, though most of them have abandoned any expectation of that final ending which once defined linearity. "Worlds without end, Amen" is generally now heard in scientific-industrialist mode, as a promise that advancing humanity will always be able to cope, will leap from world to world and even remake the universe, or escape from it through infinitely extended hyperspatial tunnels. Such materiality and temporal involvement would once have been despised: both those who expected Judgement Day and those who "looked away" to eternity were emphasizing that "the things of this world" mattered, matter far less than we thought. The real distinction, I suspect, lies not between linear and cyclic images of time, but between those who expect a continually surpassed achievement here "in time" and those who "look away" to an infinite perfection present in eternity. For the former all limits exist to be transcended; for the latter limits are the mercy of God, the only way that eternity can mirror itself in the changeful.

Presumably a global religion, and civilization, that was "eternalist" would not expect unending change or progress. Presumably a "progressivist" religion must think our ancestors were foolish, long since obsolescent, creatures. "Process theology", with its curious conviction that God is always getting better and better, and will never be "corrupted by bad communications", can give no credit to past revelation when He knew no better. Like Aristotle I am not entirely convinced that a society founded on continuous revolution can expect to survive. All civilizations, and religions, must depend upon a pious respect for our predecessors, and for the creeds they taught us. Ritualized impiety and neophiliac enthusiasm, though popular options, strike me as obvious evolutionary failures.[13] If scientific-industrialism, post-Kantian humanism, Christian progressivism survive as the spirit of a global religion, they will have had to come to terms with tradition, and with real limits. The open future may still speak as myth, but not as "a realized eschaton".

A related set of distinctions that I shall not discuss just here. (1) Some traditions are Platonic, others anti-Platonic in that they do, or do not, acknowledge the presence of something over and above the sweep of particulars in which we seem, sometimes, to live. Naturism, most versions of Abrahamism, Hinduism are self-consciously "Platonic"; Buddhism, Marxism, humanism profess not to be. (2) Some traditions are deeply Platonic in another sense, and others anti-Platonic, in that some assert the rational incomprehensibility of the Divine, and consequently the strongly poetic character of credal utterances, while others think that things are well within human power. Abrahamists, Buddhists, Hindus on this account are all Platonic, while Marxists, Humanists and (some) Naturists are not. I repeat: contrary to the usual claims of comparative religionists, Abrahamists emphasize the apophatic character of orthodox theology, and their supposed susceptibility to the making of doctrinaire assertions about God is neither typical nor, above all, "typically Greek".

The Influence of Particulars

One last discrimination (though I don't doubt that there are others) and a credal statement: some religions are tied to precise historical associations and communities in ways that others are not. All "religions", to be religions, must be embodied in a continuing community with its particular customs and historical anecdotes. Even contrived religions quickly acquire such ornaments if they endure at all. Buddhism could doubtless survive the discovery that Gautama was a trickster, even that every named hero, arhat, lama, bodhisattva was fictional or a fraud, but actually being a Buddhist means more than the acceptance of the Four Truths. Inevitably the past and largely Asian history of the Buddhist community becomes one's own. Early British Buddhists made some attempt to interpret Druidism as a Buddhist missionary sect in order not to have to abandon their own national or ethnic past when they "entered the Stream". But the conversion does not really require one to shave one's head, learn Pali, take another name and feel oneself required to link hands with past Buddhists, or re-enact particular episodes of Gautama's life. There is certainly a case for saying that Buddhism is better suited to global authority than Abrahamic religions, which are crucially and indissolubly linked to the actual histories of Abraham, Israel,

Jesus, and Mohammed (though the Muslim branch might also claim a rational universality). Abrahamic scriptures are a closed canon; originative experience is normative. Those Christian missionaries who gave converts the impression that organ music, Gothic churches, trousers and the King James' Bible were central elements of Christianity (and correspondingly that Christians were overwhelmingly simple-minded, materialistic and subservient to imperial power) did enormous damage to existing pieties and to the reputation of Christendom. But they were not wholly absurd: they knew that what mattered in their faith was a close, material, historical association with the founding fathers, and with the Word himself. They knew that there was no single axiomatizable system to encapsulate necessary religious truth. They simply did not feel able to discriminate within their bundled traditions between what "really" went back to the beginnings and what did not, what "really" mattered and what was only disposable (or false) accretion. Perhaps if they had been better educated they would have done better, but it must be admitted that such discrimination is not easy. The Orthodox wing of Christendom can justly claim to have retained ritual, meditative practice and story more or less intact from the first beginnings – but no outsider doubts that Orthodox are also distinctively Greek or Russian, and sometimes preach to others what is only national custom. Muslim spokesmen have often claimed to preach only the age-old universal creed of creaturely obedience, but even if that claim is true they also carry their own historical baggage.

So must we accept that a Buddhist or Naturist religion is more likely to have a global, transcultural success than any religion resting on particular circumstance and grown up in and through particular histories? How can Papuan tribesmen possibly accept a creed that makes their personal, tribal history irrelevant? If they must become Westernized (i.e. given sugar, steel, knives, trousers, money) before they can grasp at Christianity, does that not amount to cultural genocide (maybe real genocide)? If they can "enter the stream", or reidentify the fourfold structure of the soul between earth and heaven, or even bow before the One who spoke through the prophets of every age and day (but perfectly through Mohammed), without ceasing to be Papuans is that not a gain?

But perhaps the problem is not quite so dire. The Koran is an Arabic document in a way that the Buddhist Scriptures are not fully or entirely Pali. To recite the Koran, as Cantwell Smith has

suggested, is a sacrament with the same function and power as to celebrate the Eucharist: the Word made Text and the Word made Flesh are both very particular things. But just because Koran and Eucharistic Christ express the *Logos* they are what makes us *logikos*. A full appreciation of either (if that is possible) must rest on fitting oneself into a particular tradition, learning one definite language, but their claim to be global religions rests on the fact that Papuans, Tupi-Guarani, Australians can find the features of that *Logos* in their own tradition. If they can't, they won't convert. If they do, it must be, after all, that their own tradition is not quite irrelevant, that Christ or the Koran fulfils both Hebrew or Semitic history and also Indian, Amerindian, Aboriginal or African. Quite how it does is for such converts to discover. As Hocking saw, we need both the general possibility that human beings be *logikoi*, and the particular fact that one such being absolutely is: but that is another story.[14]

So a global Abrahamic religion remains a real possibility: if it does win out, it will be obviously true that Israel is the source of the World's blessing. But something like that is already obvious: no one can understand global society and history without reference to Israel. Not only the obviously Abrahamic religions, but also scientific humanism and Marxism, are historically dependent on the Jews both for their theology and their particular progress. Naturism (or paganism) defines itself in opposition to those creeds, but has absorbed from a variety of sources a profoundly Jewish egalitarianism quite unlike the philosophers' Brotherhood of all the Wise.[15] Hinduism alone of the great creeds adopts an openly hierarchical mode of life, and must measure itself against Jewish (and Buddhist) condemnation of caste-structures before it should become global. I emphasize "should": it is all too likely that the world-beast will, as Spengler expected, be a hierarchical, caste-ridden civilization, and all the worst features of Hinduism be re-embodied there. Only Buddhism is any kind of independent rival to Abrahamism.

I said I would end with a credal statement. My own preference, as may already be obvious, is for a global religion that is parapolitical, decentralized, faith-holding, non-humanist, eternalist, Platonic and historically particular. My fear is that we shall instead live to see the rise and fall of Babylon, that tradition tells us must precede the Coming. My own commitment, over and above anything I can devise by way of rational argument, is to the body of Christ. The world and human kind are already unified eternally in that particular being, but we shall not be unified in time until there is a global acknowledgement of our single derivation and devotion. Even if that never happens, and the world-beast rules triumphant to the end, faith-holders may still "look away" to the eternal.

Much that pagan naturists, Hindus and Buddhists say is true, holy and of good report. In the absence of a particular incarnation and revelation in the flesh and speech of Israel they would together be the best that humankind could offer. Often enough they can justly rebuke Abrahamists (of whatever sect) for insincerity, stupidity and sin. But in the last resort there is one ship alone that comes in safe to harbour.

Notes

1 Modern biologists distinguish species (and higher taxa) not by any essential attributes but by common descent. The dodo, once extinct, will never reappear, even if birds indistinguishable from dodos someday evolve. And dogs are still dogs even though they are by now very unlike their wild ancestors. See E. Sober, "Evolution, population thinking and essentialism", *Philosophy of Science* XLVII (1980), 350–83.
2 W. Cantwell Smith, *Towards a World Theology* (London: 1981), pp. 8ff.
3 I. Kant, *Perpetual Peace*: H. Reiss, ed., *Kant's Political Writings* (Cambridge: 1970), p. 114.
4 C. S. Lewis, *Of Other Worlds*, ed. W. Hooper (London, Bles: 1986), pp. 59f.
5 W. E. Hocking, *Living Religions and a World Faith* (London: 1940), p. 264.

6 Ibid., p. 19.
7 A. Toynbee, *A Study of History*, vol. VII (Oxford: 1954), pp. 420–525.
8 B. Cooper, "A Imperio usque ad Imperium", *George Grant in Process*, ed. L. Schmidt (Toronto: 1978), pp. 22–39, 35. George Grant's thought is grievously neglected outside Canada.
9 *Daniel* 5.4.
10 *Revelation* 13.
11 N. Frye, *Spiritis Mundi* (Bloomington: 1976), p. 198.
12 See R. L. Slater, *World Religion and World Community* (New York: 1963), p. 241.
13 See my *Civil Peace and Sacred Order* (Oxford: 1989).
14 Hocking, *Living Religions*, p. 234.
15 See my "City of the Wise", *Apeiron* XX (1987), 63–80.

3

Religion

Paul J. Griffiths

Religion as an Account

Defining religion is a little like writing diet books or forecasting the performance of the stock market: there's a great deal of it about and none of it seems to do much good. This doesn't keep people from predicting share prices or prescribing eating habits, though it probably should. It won't keep me from offering a discursive definition of religion, either, though I may have a slightly better reason for it than does the usual diet-book author or stock-market prognosticator. Since I'm writing a book about religious reading, and since my understanding of what it is to be religious is different from that of many who call themselves religious, as well as from that of many academic professionals who think of themselves as studying religion, I can't avoid offering and defending my own understanding of religion.

I do this part of the work stipulatively. A religion is, for those who have it (or, better, are had by it), principally an account. To be religious is to give an account, where giving an account of something means to make it the object of some intentional activity – to tell a story about it, have some beliefs about it, direct some actions toward it, or the like. Mathematics, as an example of a human activity, gives an account whose chief objects are abstract entities and their relations, and whose main intentional activity is the construction, expression,

Paul J. Griffiths, "Religion," reprinted by permission of Oxford University Press from *Religious Reading* (New York: Oxford University Press, 1999), ch. 1.

justification, and ordering of beliefs about such objects and their relations. Being married, to take another example, is an account given by spouses (principally to one another, but also to others) of the history and current state of their relations, an account that involves the weaving of narratives, the regular performance of actions, the possession and nurturing of beliefs and affective responses, and much more.

Accounts that people offer may be distinguished one from another by their scope, their object, and the kinds of intentional activity they use. But there are no natural and inevitable distinctions among accounts. Decisions about the boundaries between mathematics and physics, or those between literary criticism and philosophy, are always indexed to the intellectual goals and interests of those making the distinctions. This is not to say that boundary decisions are completely arbitrary, that they have nothing to do with the accounts among which they draw boundaries. It is only to make the more modest claim that such decisions always and inevitably involve and are largely driven by the interests of those making them, and to suggest that other decisions are always both possible and defensible. Adjudicating rival boundary decisions must always involve reference to the interests implied by the decisions.

Nonetheless, paying attention to the scope, object, and kinds of intentional activity found in an account will typically give useful pointers as to how it might be demarcated from other accounts. Two accounts that differ significantly in even one of these matters are unlikely usefully to be classifiable as the same account, even though it will often be possible to imagine an account of which both are components. Consider, for instance, an account whose scope is whole numbers from one to 100, whose object is prime numbers within that range, and whose preferred intentional activity is squaring its objects. A giver of this account will, seriatim, find the square of each prime number within the chosen range. Imagine also an account identical in every respect, except that its object is even numbers within the same range. In spite of their deep similarities, these are likely, for most purposes, to be best thought of as different accounts, demarcated one from another principally by difference of object; though they might also for some purposes usefully be thought of as two components of a single account – perhaps the arithmetical account, or some such.

All human activities of cultural and conceptual interest are usefully capable of being understood as accounts in just this sense; and this means that religion must be capable of being so understood, since it is certainly of cultural and conceptual interest. If, then, to be religious is to give an account, what sort of account is it? I shall define it at a level of abstraction that makes the definition applicable to all particular religious accounts; and I shall define it by reference principally to how it appears to those who offer it. This is to say that I take the defining properties of a religious account to be both formal and phenomenal. They are formal because they are abstracted from the particularities of any particular religious account, and as a result address little if any of the substance of such an account. And they are phenomenal because they are not properties intrinsic to the account itself, but rather properties that explain how the account seems or might seem to those who offer it. These properties may also be non-phenomenal, just as the fastball that Frank Thomas of the Chicago White Sox hit out of the park last Friday may both have seemed to him to be traveling at 85 miles per hour (a phenomenal property) and have actually been doing so (a nonphenomenal property). But I shall not concern myself much with the interesting question of whether the phenomenal features of any particular account are also nonphenomenal features – for example, with the question of whether the Christian account, which indisputably possesses the property of seeming unsurpassably true to me, also possesses the nonphenomenal property of being unsurpassably true (of course, that I think it possesses the latter

property follows ineluctably from the fact that it possesses the former).

There are a number of advantages to describing religious accounts in terms of their formal and phenomenal properties. First (and most important for me), concentrating at the formal level on how accounts of this sort seem to those who offer them permits me to avoid controverted questions about the substantive and nonphenomenal properties of religious accounts. I do not need to decide, for instance, whether, in order to be called religious, a particular account must involve reference to a transcendent reality (God, nirvana, or the like). Neither do I need to decide whether religious accounts, in order properly to be called such, must engage certain kinds of questions – as to how we humans should most authentically live, for instance. Second, my interest in this book is principally in the modes of learning and teaching that most effectively foster the ability to come to give, to maintain, and to nurture a religious account. This is a formal question that can be answered largely without reference to the substance of what is read when one reads religiously, a question that is in most respects better answered without such reference; and so it too benefits from the approach taken here.

Consider an analogy. It is possible to say useful things about the modes of learning best designed to produce fluency in speaking some language without saying anything about the characteristics peculiar to any. Japanese and English are, in many important respects, different from one another. Fluency in speaking one obviously does not provide fluency in speaking the other. And yet there are clear and deep similarities between the formal and phenomenal properties of being a fluent speaker of Japanese, on the one hand, and those of being a fluent speaker of English, on the other. It's beyond my scope here to describe what it seems like to a fluent speaker of some language to be such a speaker, but it is surely obvious that it does seem like something. And this is the same as to say that being a fluent speaker of some language has phenomenal properties that can usefully be considered at the formal level, in abstraction from the particularities of any natural language. Considering them in this way is just what makes it possible for those who want to think and write about language learning in general to do so in ways that are of use (even if of limited use) to the teachers and learners of any particular language.

There is something of a difficulty at this point, a difficulty suggested by the language analogy. It is that the phenomenal properties of being a speaker of (say) English are rarely a matter for articulation on the part of those to whom they belong. I don't usually think about what it's like to be a speaker of English, and couldn't say all that much about it if pressed. This is to say that I can articulate only some of what it's like to be such a speaker; and what I can and cannot articulate may vary from time to time. But I want to extend the category "phenomenal property" to include properties of an account about which its offerers could say nothing, even if pressed. After all, as Thomas Nagel points out, it seems reasonable to think that it seems like something to a bat to be one, to think that a bat's experience has phenomenal properties.[1] And yet it is also true that the bat can say nothing about these, even to itself, while we nonbats might be able to say something.

In light of this, I use the phrase "phenomenal properties of accounts" to include (1) properties that givers of the account do or can articulate; and (2) properties they can't (or don't) articulate, but which it seems reasonable to observers and interpreters of their accounts to attribute to those accounts, even if their givers would not themselves articulate them (and even if they would deny them if they heard others articulating them). This means that an account's phenomenal properties may be articulable or nonarticulable, and this distinction is closely matched by one between their being occurrent (the account actually does seem at the moment to its offerers to be of such and such a kind, and they both can and would say so), and their being implicit (the account implies that it should seem to its offerers to be of such and such a kind, but in fact it does not explicitly seem to them like that or like anything just at the moment, and they might deny that it seems like that or like anything, if asked). So I shall understand "phenomenal properties" to embrace articulable, nonarticulable, occurrent, and implicit seemings, and this should be kept in mind as you read what follows, for I shall usually not signal all these distinctions. Bear in mind also that this way of talking about the accounts people offer is intended to explain only how they seem or might seem to those who offer them. The subjunctive mood in this second phrase ("might seem") covers the nonarticulable and implicit phenomenal properties of accounts.

Given all these qualifications, the phenomenal properties that religious accounts possess are three: comprehensiveness, unsurpassability, and centrality. The presence of these three will suffice to make

an account religious; the absence of any one will suffice to prevent it from being so. This means that to say of people that they are religious, or have a religion, is just to say that they give an account that seems to them to have these three properties – to be comprehensive, unsurpassable, and central. It is to say that one of the things religious people do, perhaps in the end the only thing they do, is to give a religious account, to be religious.

It might be objected that the construal of religion offered here is neither the only possible nor the obviously best one. It is certainly true that it rules out much that has often been called religious. Activities that are often taken to be paradigmatically such (belief in a god or gods, making offerings to the ancestors, using sacrifice to cure disease, and the like) can, according to this construal, only properly be called religious when a good deal is known about the account of which they form a part. It is true also that much not typically included under the rubric of religion may be so included under this construal. For instance, it might be that a thoroughgoing (if somewhat old-fashioned) Marxist would turn out to be religious; or that an unusually obsessive follower of the Chicago White Sox might. But disadvantages of this kind are shared by all construals of religion. And as to whether the construal offered here is the best possible of those in the field: since the desirability of any stipulative construal of this kind must be indexed to its effectiveness in helping or allowing certain intellectual or practical goals to be met, this question reduces to the more fundamental and also more modest question of whether a particular construal does effectively serve the ends it was constructed to serve. This book is principally concerned to describe and advocate a particular form of reading; and for this end (though certainly not for all) I judge the construal offered here to be both flexible and effective.

Comprehensiveness

What then is it for an account to seem to its offerers to be comprehensive? – for this is the first of the three properties that an account must possess in order to be religious. For an account to be comprehensive it must seem to those who offer it that it takes account of everything, that nothing is left unaccounted for by it. Most accounts are not comprehensive in this sense. For example, one account that I give of myself is as a parent, the father of two living children. But this is not a comprehensive account because, first, it does not comprehend (indeed, has little to say about) the accounts I give of myself as teacher, writer, spouse, citizen of the United States, and many other things. It stands alongside some of these other accounts, neither accounting for them nor being accounted for by them. But it is strictly subsumed by, accounted for by, some of the other accounts I offer, most especially the Christian account, according to which both the fact of my being a parent and the details of my acting as such are accounted for in terms of (as I see it) the fact that I am a Christian. So the parenting account is not for me (and I suspect this to be true for all who offer such an account) a comprehensive account, and as a result also not a religious account.

It is possible, indeed usual, for people to offer more than one comprehensive account at a time. I, for example, offer a Christian account that is comprehensive, and also the following (trivial) mathematical account: *everything is either a prime number or it is not*. This, like my Christian account, takes account of everything: of my being a parent (which is not a prime number), of my being a Christian (which is likewise not), of the number three (which is), and so forth to infinity.

These points may be put visually. Let a circle represent each account you offer. If you offer a comprehensive account, let that be represented by a circle within whose circumference all the other circles representing your noncomprehensive accounts are drawn. Some of these subsidiary circles (of which there will typically be a great many) may stand alone inside the great circle that represents the comprehensive account, neither subsuming nor overlapping nor being subsumed by any of the other subsidiary circles. But it will more frequently be the case that subsidiary circles will be related one to another by subsumption or overlapping. The full picture will typically be very complicated indeed. So the accounts that I offer of myself as parent, of the human activities of mathematics and music, of the physical states of affairs that partly constitute the cosmos, and of cultural facts like being an Englishman by birth who has become an American by choice are all (it seems to me) comprehended by the great circle of my Christian account. If you offer more than one comprehensive account, as I do, the line of your great circle's circumference will be increased in thickness for each comprehensive account you offer. Someone who offers a great many comprehensive accounts will have this fact represented by a great circle with a very thick line representing its circumference.

A couple of qualifications are necessary at this point. First, it is certainly not the case that everyone offers an explicit and articulable comprehensive account. That is, it may seem to you that no one of the accounts you offer comprehends all the others; if you're in this situation you're likely to deny offering such an account if a suggestion is made to you that you do. And this will mean that you are not, by my definition, religious, or are so only implicitly. Being explicitly religious is not, then, a necessary feature of human existence as such – and this conclusion is perfectly compatible with the truth of such claims as *all people were created by God*, and *all people have salvation made available to them through Jesus Christ*, and *God exists necessarily*. But it is rather less likely that anyone fails to offer an implicitly comprehensive account, and it is generally rather easy to persuade those who deny offering such an account that in fact they implicitly do. The easiest way to do this is to point at something (a book, say, or a table or a chair) and to ask whether it is what it is and not something else. The philosophically unschooled will rapidly agree that this is so, that everything must either be this thing or some other thing, and as soon as this is said a comprehensive account has been offered. The philosophically sophisticated may have more to say before they give their assent, or they may even withhold it altogether; but they, being sophisticated, will typically already have developed explicitly comprehensive accounts of their own. It seems a fair bet, then, that everyone offers a comprehensive account, though not that all do so explicitly.

The second qualification is that a comprehensive account, while it must provide rubrics under which the fact of all other accounts can be comprehended, need not determine just what the details of those other accounts are, and may often have nothing at all to say about those details. That is, it should not be supposed that offering a comprehensive account commits those who offer it to particular answers to all possible questions. Offering the Christian account does not, for example, commit me to any particular view as to whether Goldbach's Conjecture (that every even number greater than two is expressible as the sum of two primes) is true or not. But it does commit me to saying that the truth (or falsity) of this conjecture is one of the states of affairs eternally intended and known by God. Likewise, offering the comprehensive account *everything is either a prime number or it is not* commits me to no view about the relations between Father, Son, and Holy Spirit – except the view that such relations are not a prime number.

An account will be comprehensive, then, if and only if it seems to the person who offers it to take as its object strictly everything, and thereby to have universal scope. But some comprehensive accounts, like the prime-number account mentioned, are trivial even though their scope is universal. A trivial account is one that cannot organize a life. To find that an account is comprehensive is therefore not sufficient to make it religious; it must also appear to its offerer to be both unsurpassable and central, and as a result not to be trivial. I shall treat these two properties in order.

Unsurpassability

If I offer an account that seems to me unsurpassable, then I take it not to be capable of being replaced by or subsumed in a better account of what it accounts for.[2] So, for instance, one of the accounts I offer has my children as its objects. The chief elements of that account, its essential features, include beliefs such as that they are my children, bone of my bone and flesh of my flesh; that I love them; that I have nonnegotiable duties toward them and they toward me, duties produced directly by the fact of my parental relation to them – and so forth. It seems to me that this account is unsurpassable in its essential features, at least this side of death. This is not to say that the account will not change in its details; what I say and think about my children now, and how I act toward them, are obviously not the same in detail as what I will say, think, or do a dozen years from now. But the essential features of the account I offer will not, in my judgment, be changed, surpassed, or superseded. This is just what makes my account of my children unsurpassable for me. Unsurpassability, then, denotes an attitude toward what are taken to be the essential features of an account by the person who gives it.

When unsurpassability is coupled with comprehensiveness something close to a religious account is found. My account of my children, though unsurpassable, is of course not comprehensive, and as a result is not a religious account. My Christian account, by contrast, has both features. The importance of unsurpassability as a feature of religious accounts is that it highlights the fact that being religious, offering a religious account, is a commitment of a nonnegotiable kind. When coupled with comprehensiveness, such an account enters sufficiently deeply into the souls of those who offer it that the abandonment of its essential features is scarcely conceivable, and if conceivable, not desirable.

I take unsurpassability and nonnegotiability to be different ways of saying the same thing: if an account seems to you to be unsurpassable, this is just to say that you take what seem to you to be the account's essential features to be incapable of abandonment. This is to say neither that the formulation and expression of these essential features will not change, nor that they cannot be added to; the example of my account of my children shows this. But it is to say that any such changes or additions will not (or so it will seem to those who offer an unsurpassable account) involve or lead to the abandonment or alteration of these essential features. Christians, when considering the obvious fact that Christian doctrine appears to change over time, have often put this by saying that such apparent changes are to be understood as unfoldings, or unpackings, or flowerings (choose your metaphor) of what is already implied by Christian doctrine, and not as alterations or abandonments of it. Or, they have said that the content of the Christian account does not change, though its form may.[3] On such views (and they are typical of those found in religious accounts when their offerers become sufficiently reflective to pronounce on such matters), apparent change in the essential features of a religious account is always either developmental or cosmetic, and as a result is compatible with unsurpassability and nonnegotiability.

None of this is to say that religious accounts, once given, are never abandoned. You can cease to offer a religious account just as you can come to offer one. But it is to say that while a religious account is being offered, intrinsic to it is the feature that its offerer regards its essential elements as incapable of loss, supersession, or abandonment. This is a part of what Christians have meant by faith. But not even accounts that seem to their offerers both comprehensive and unsurpassable are necessarily religious. Some accounts of this sort may still be trivial, incapable of structuring the life of their offerer; or peripheral, not central to that life. This would be true, for example, of the prime-number account mentioned earlier. This account is, for me, both comprehensive and unsurpassable; but it is scarcely central to my life. Something more is needed, and it is centrality.

Centrality

For an account to seem central to you it must seem to be directly relevant to what you take to be the central questions of your life, the questions around which your life is oriented. Perhaps the account provides answers to these questions; or perhaps it prescribes guiding principles or intentional activities that contribute to answering, or provide ways of thinking about, these questions. Such questions may move in many areas. One is the general issue of how you should think about and relate to your fellow humans. Should you love them? Exploit them? Ignore them? Judge them to be perduring nonphysical individuals possessed of intrinsic worth? Treat them all the same, or some in one way and some in another? Another is the general issue of how you should think about and order your relations with the nonhuman order, both sentient and nonsentient. Should you treat sentient nonhumans significantly differently than you treat humans? Should you judge the nonsentient cosmos to be meaningful, or to be a collection of brutally irreducible states of affairs? Should you judge that what exists is limited to what you can perceive with your physical senses, and behave accordingly? And yet a third is the general issue of how you should think about yourself, and about what sorts of beliefs and actions you should foster in yourself, and what discourage. Should you make what seems to you to contribute to your own pleasure and happiness the central motivating factor in your decisions about what to do with your life? Should you judge that you are a perduring object of worth? Decisions about matters of these three kinds are life-orienting; they are also, when a decision already made about them is changed, life-changing. Not all may seem to everyone to be central questions, and the examples mentioned are only examples, not an exhaustive list. But they are ideal-typical representatives of questions central to the ordering of a life.

Most people do not explicitly ask themselves questions at this level of abstraction and generality. Doing so is characteristic of an uncommon level of reflection. But most people do explicitly ask and answer more concrete questions, and in so doing imply the asking and answering of abstract questions like these. For instance, a Hindu in Bihar might ask and answer a question such as this: Is my Muslim neighbor worthy of death just because he is a Muslim? A Muslim in Lyons might ask and answer the question: Should I wear the veil to school even though it is against French law to do so? A Jew in Hoboken might ask and answer the question: Should I marry a Gentile? A Christian in Leeds might ask and answer the question: Should I devote time and energy to becoming a concert pianist even though there are homeless and hungry people on the streets not a mile from my front door? Such concrete questions are likely to seem central to those who ask and answer them. And it is characteristic of religious accounts that they address such questions and that they do so in the context of offering a comprehensive and unsurpassable account.

That religious accounts must be central as well as unsurpassable and comprehensive is among the things that make it possible to be a person and yet not offer one. It's clear that not everyone explicitly offers an account that seems to them comprehensive, unsurpassable, and central; it's clear also that there are many who would deny offering such an account if asked. So some people, perhaps many, have no explicit and articulable religious account to offer. But perhaps they offer such an account implicitly, much as native speakers of English offer an implicit account of the grammar of the English language even when they can articulate little or nothing about that grammar. Perhaps, that is to say, offering religious accounts (being religious) is a necessary feature of human existence, a part of what it means to be human. Many have thought so, but it is not so. It is entirely possible to be human and to offer no religious account, even implicitly. I've already suggested that it is difficult, perhaps impossible, for anyone to avoid offering (at least implicitly) a comprehensive account. I suspect that similar things ought to be said about unsurpassable accounts: it turns out to be difficult not to offer at least one of these, even if it's of the pedestrian kind that denies (implicitly or explicitly) the possibility of offering an unsurpassable account – and in so doing, offers one. However, it is possible to fail to offer a central account with relative ease. Human beings can be (or can become) profoundly fragmented, their intentions and desires dispersed to such an extent that they do not, perhaps cannot, offer an account that seems to them directly relevant to what they take to be the questions around which their lives are oriented. For a deeply fragmented or dispersed soul, there may be no such questions: there may be only a series of disjointed, unconnected desires, chaotic in their proliferation and fragmentation. And in such a case, clearly, no central account can be offered, from which it follows that no religious account can be offered.

Being religious is therefore not an essential or intrinsic part of being human. It's important to note, though, that this is entirely compatible with the truth of claims such as *God created everyone* or *everyone's life comes from and is ordered to God*. These are metaphysical claims. Their truth (if they are true) does not require the truth of any claims about the phenomenal properties of the accounts that people offer – not even in the extended sense of phenomenal properties in play here. Returning to the analogy of language may help to show this. Suppose it's true that there is a deep structure common to all natural languages; it would then also be true that being a native speaker of English would imply (though distantly) the presence of that deep structure in every utterance. Analogously, if it's true that everyone's life issues from and is ordered to God, this fact will be implied by any account whatever (even one lacking in central questions). But in both cases the implication is a distant one and says nothing about the particulars of the account in question: it is applicable indifferently to all accounts. I am concerned here not with such distant implications, but only with those that have to do with the particulars of some account, the properties that differentiate it from other accounts, that make it the account it is and not some other. It follows that even if being a native speaker of English implies the presence and efficacy of a deep structure, and even if failing to offer a central account implies the existence of God, in neither case are these things among the phenomenal properties (implicit or explicit) specific to the accounts in question.

To reiterate: not everyone offers a religious account. But is it possible for anyone to have more than one religion (offer more than one religious account) at a time? The answer is no, and for strictly logical reasons. Bilingualism is possible, but bireligionism is not. It is, as I've said, possible simultaneously to offer more than one comprehensive and unsurpassable account. But the addition of centrality makes this no longer possible. For each person there is a finite (usually a small) number of questions that seem central, capable of organizing a life. Suppose you entertain two accounts, each of which seems to you comprehensive, unsurpassable, and central. Then either the two accounts will seem to you to be different in some of their essential features, or they will not. If the former, then it is both logically and

psychologically impossible for you not merely to entertain but actually to offer both accounts. This is because you cannot offer, simultaneously and with conviction, different answers to what seem to you life-orienting questions. Suppose you entertain different answers to the (possibly) life-orienting question: Should I kill and eat apparently sentient creatures? One answer might be: Never. Another might be: Only if they have two or more senses. A third might be: Whenever no other food is available. The first answer is incompatible with the second and third. You may entertain, but you cannot offer, an account that embraces all three. The second and third answers are different but not necessarily or obviously incompatible. You may entertain and come to offer an account that combines both. But then you are offering a single account that includes a complex answer to this particular question. In no case are you offering two different accounts at the same time.

The anthropologist Dan Sperber makes a formally identical point in his discussion of symbol systems:

> [T]here is no multi-symbolism analogous to multi-lingualism. An individual who learns a second language internalises a second grammar, and if some interference takes place, it is on a remarkably small scale. Conversely, symbolic data, no matter what their origin, integrate themselves into a single system within a given individual. If one could internalise several different symbolic devices, as one can learn several different languages, the task of the anthropologist would thereby become considerably simpler. But the anthropologist, who little by little penetrates the symbolism of his hosts, is never able to pass from one symbolism to another as easily as he passes from one language to another.[4]

Sperber's point is that for a user of symbolic systems there is only one active system at a time. You can act, or engage in other complex forms of pretense, when you deploy symbol systems; but this is never the same as genuine and authentic use. Transition from pretense to genuine use is possible, but it isn't possible to pretend and genuinely to use at the same time. Similarly for religious accounts. Many can be entertained at a time, but only one can be offered. This is not to say, of course, that a religious account need contain elements drawn from only one of those complexes of human thought and action called "Christianity" or "Islam" or the like. If you say that you are a Jewish Buddhist, for example, you typically mean that you offer a religious account some elements of which are historically Buddhist and some historically Jewish. You do not mean, because you cannot, that you simultaneously offer two religious accounts.

Skill and Information

Giving religious accounts is a practice, a human activity. It follows that every instance of giving a religious account, every token of the type, is learned, and learned in a particular social, linguistic, and institutional context. We are not born giving religious accounts any more than we are born using language, even though we may have deep and partly genetic tendencies to come to do both things, and even though there may be facts about the cosmos in which we live that strongly suggest to us the desirability of doing the former. Unless we are placed in a social and institutional context in which certain pedagogical practices are in place, we shall not, because we cannot, become religious: we shall not learn to offer a religious account. Analogously, unless we are placed in a community of language users, we shall not, because we cannot, become fluent users of any language. Rather few of us fail to become fluent users of some language or another, and we understand a good deal about the conditions necessary for becoming such. But very many of us fail to become religious, most often because the necessary social, institutional, and pedagogical practices are lacking. This has perhaps been especially true for inhabitants of Europe and the United States since the seventeenth century, but it is now becoming increasingly true for people in other parts of the world.

None of this is to say that there is a deterministic relation between the presence of the relevant practices and the offering of religious accounts. The practices, whatever they turn out to be, may in some cases be present and yet no religious account be offered. Necessary conditionality is not sufficient conditionality; human free will, divine grace, and various other imponderables have their proper part to play. Paying attention to the practices constitutive of religious learning is therefore not intended to suggest a reductionist view of any particular religious account, or of religious accounts in general. It is not intended to suggest that when the

learning practices have been analyzed there is no more to be said about religion. There is always the question of truth: is one, none, or several of the religious accounts offered true? But this is not my interest here.

Any kind of learning, including religious learning, results for us in one of two things: the acquisition and retention of information, on the one hand, or the possession of a skill, on the other. Each of these entails, in some measure, the presence of the other. Acquisition and retention of information is impossible without the possession and use of some skill that is not itself exhaustively accountable in terms of information. No human, for instance, can acquire and transmit information linguistically without being in possession of skills that go far beyond the information contained in dictionaries and manuals of syntax. The skills of reading or listening with understanding are complex and clearly not capable of analysis solely in terms of the possession of information. They involve dispositions and capacities that we do not fully understand, as is shown by the fact that we cannot program computers even to meet the test of producing a reasonable facsimile of reading or talking (one that could fool an averagely perceptive human observer), notwithstanding that the computer may have rapid access to a body of lexical and syntactical information many times larger than that possessed by any human. The same is true of other complex human skills. And even in the case of less complex skills, such as those of walking on two legs, riding a bicycle, making love, or playing the piano, skills in which the linguistic component is almost entirely (perhaps entirely) absent – even in the case of these it is at least arguable that the implicit possession of some information is among the necessary conditions for the exercise of the skill. You might need to know (even if you never need to formulate the knowledge) that pressing the pedal down will move the bicycle; that using the loud-pedal on the piano will make the noise continue; and that kissing the beloved will express your love and may be reciprocated.

There is, it should already be clear, a distinction between information presupposed by the possession of a skill and implied by its exercise, and information present to the minds of (or capable of being articulated by) possessors of that skill. Suppose you can speak a natural language; this is a skill that presupposes and implies all sorts of grammatical information, and yet you may be able to articulate little or none of it. Similarly for playing the piano or making love. This point can be clarified by speaking of three kinds of information. The first is occurrent: under this head comes all the information currently present to your mind. The second is dispositional: under this head comes information not at the moment present to your mind, but capable of becoming so when circumstance requires. And the third is implicit: under this head comes information implied in or presupposed by your skills, but not capable of articulation by you under any conditions.

Most of the information we possess is of the third kind, a good deal is of the second kind, and very little is of the first kind. This is as true of the information that belongs to religious accounts as of any other kind, and it is important to emphasize it, because only a tiny proportion of those who offer religious accounts have any but a vanishingly small proportion of the information implied by offering such an account either present to their minds or capable of articulation. Limiting the scope of this inquiry to information of the first kind would mean excluding the vast majority of people from learning to read religiously. I don't mean to do that, so when I speak of information in what follows I include all three kinds, though once again with the proviso that in the case of implicit information I am interested only in the kind specific to the account being studied.

Information and skill are never finally separable in practice. Nonetheless, it will be useful to have a fairly sharp distinction between them in mind when reading what follows, since I shall make some theoretical use of ideas about the difference between the two – between, as philosophers have tended to put it, following Gilbert Ryle and J. L. Austin, "knowing how" (possessing a skill) and "knowing that" (possessing some information).[5]

It should be pretty clear that offering a religious account will typically require much information and plenty of skill. Again, a good (though partial) analogy is with verbal fluency in some natural language. You need to know that a lot of things are the case (that, in Latin, nouns and adjectives agree, the subjunctive mood expresses possibility rather than actuality, and the like); and you need to know how to do a lot of things (how to construct a sentence with subordinate clauses, how to understand infinitives, and the like). So also with religious accounts. You need to know the grammatical and syntactical rules by which the account is structured, you need to know the semantic content of the claims made about human persons and the setting of their life, and you need to know what is

prohibited, what permitted, and what recommended in the sphere of human action. These are all examples of knowing that. But you also need to know how to offer the account: you need, to a greater or lesser extent, to possess the skills required to elucidate the account, to instantiate it in your life, to develop the capacities and proclivities that will make it possible for you to act in accord with what is prescribed or recommended by the account. Offering a religious account involves learning to play the piano as well as becoming a musicologist; and the virtuosos, the Barenboims and the Goulds, are the saints.

These points can be and should be put more strongly. Offering a religious account is, principally and paradigmatically, a skill. It consists essentially in knowing how to do certain sorts of things. Only secondarily, and quite inessentially, does it involve the possession of occurrent or dispositional information. Just as there are many more players of chess than theorists of the game, so there are many more faithful Christians than theologians, many more good Buddhists than analysts of dharma, and many more committed and ecstatic Śaivites than expositors of Śaivasiddhānta. Knowing how to offer a religious account is, as Ryle put it, "a disposition, but not a single-track disposition like a reflex or a habit" (Ryle was of course not speaking of religion, in which he had little interest).[6] This means that the complex disposition that is possessing the skill of offering a religious account does not issue in a single set of predictable actions. This is what makes it different from a habit. If I have the habit of drinking coffee or that of splitting infinitives, these facts will be evident principally in my repeated performance of such acts. But if I have a sarcastic disposition, this will be evident in many ways, including the bitter put-down, the abrasive parody, and the self-aggrandizing critique; there is no single set of actions in which this disposition issues, which is why it isn't a habit but instead a context-sensitive set of behaviors, each of which evidences my possession of the dispositional skill of being sarcastic (not a desirable disposition to be enslaved to, of course).

Being religious is more like being sarcastic than like being a coffee drinker or a splitter of infinitives. It may certainly contain and be partly constituted by habits (for example, repeating the Nicene Creed on Sundays, or praying the Paternoster daily), but it isn't limited to them or exhaustively describable in terms of sets of them. Like being sarcastic, it issues in context-specific behaviors such as acting charitably in response to a particular need, responding with forgiveness to an act of hostility, or meeting an act of injustice with denunciation. Since being religious is a skill in this sense, it's possible to get better at it (or worse). You're not, then, simply religious or not; you're more or less religious. To say that people are good (faithful, perceptive, discerning, vigorous, active) Christians is principally to say of them that they do certain things and do them in such a way that understanding of what they do is evident, and that deep commitment to it can be seen. Such people practice Christianity well, and the analogy with being a good chess player, lover, or philosopher is close and deep. In all these cases, the terms of approbation have to do with what is done rather than with what is known – even though doing always involves and implies knowing.

Ryle again:

> Learning how or improving in ability is not like learning that or acquiring information. Truths can be imparted, procedures can only be inculcated, and while inculcation is a gradual process, imparting is relatively sudden. It makes sense to ask at what moment someone became apprised of a truth, but not to ask at what moment someone acquired a skill. "Part-trained" is a significant phrase, "part-informed" is not. Training is the art of setting tasks which the pupils have not yet accomplished, but are not any longer quite incapable of accomplishing.[7]

If indeed being religious (offering a religious account) is a dispositional skill, then, as Ryle points out, it will have to be inculcated, which is to say that those who have (or come to have) the skill will have to be trained. Reading of a certain kind will be an important part of this training; and it is the central concern of this book to make clear just what kind.

The Christian Account

An example may be of use at this point, since almost everything said so far has been abstract. What are the lineaments of some religious account, and how are the possession of information and skill required of those who try to offer it? I shall take the Christian account as my example because it is the one I try to offer, and as a result the only one upon which I am qualified to pronounce as

a native.[8] It is for Muslims, Buddhists, Jews, and so forth, to say what the elements of their accounts might be. I shall have a good deal to say in later chapters about particular Buddhist artifacts that I take to illustrate some of the claims I shall be making about religious reading; but I shall be interested in those not for their substance but for their form, and I shall take pains to avoid normative pronouncements as to what should and what should not belong to a Buddhist account. Such restrictions do not constrain me when I write of Christianity, though of course any construal of that account I might offer is only one of many possible ones.

The sketch of the Christian account that follows is not meant to suggest that there is a single, unchanging account with just and only these features that has been offered by all Christians everywhere and always. *Semper, ubique, ab omnibus* (always, everywhere, by all) is a slogan with some uses and an important Christian lineage, but it should not be taken (and I do not take it) to indicate that the Christian account does not vary with time and place. That it does is obvious. But it is also obvious that there are features that have been and remain widespread among the accounts offered by those who call themselves Christians (though just what these are is matter for debate). It seems reasonable to think that when an account is offered from which some or all of these features are absent that account is no longer usefully thought of as a Christian account, much as the absence of any Latin-derived words in some idiolect probably indicates that the idiolect is no longer usefully thought of as English. It is features of this sort that the following sketch selects and calls essential.

The first and most fundamental essential feature of the Christian account as it appears to Christians is that the account itself is seen as a response to the actions of a divine agent who is other than those offering it. God, it seems to us Christians, has acted as creator, as guide of human history, and as redeemer of fallen and sinful humanity by becoming incarnate, dying, and rising from the dead. In order to learn how to offer our account, Christians must acquire both this basic item of information about it and the skills of responsive action that such a view of it implies. We Christians have been and continue to be acted upon, or so it seems to us; the account we offer is our response.

God's action requires a response from us. It is a response that we can give or refuse to give, wherein lies our freedom. And it is a response required of us not by compulsion, but by love: "For God so loved the world that he gave his only begotten Son, that whosoever believeth in him should not perish, but have everlasting life" (John 3:16). The response requires knowing that certain things are the case (what God has done, what God is like, what we are like, what we should do); it also requires knowing how to do certain things, the inculcation of skills that are difficult, learned slowly, learned hard, and never fully learned.

Principal among those skills is the ordering of the will and the appetites away from the self, away from self-centered gratification, and toward God first and other humans second. We come from God: the possibility of our existence and all its boundaries are from God and of God. This means that we are fundamentally restless and disordered until we come to see and acknowledge these facts, and to harmonize our wills with them. This restlessness and disorder is evident principally when we turn our wills and direct our appetites toward anything other than God. Things other than God are all of them necessarily and essentially good, since God made them. This means that they are proper objects of honor, affection, and use. But they are not, in themselves, proper objects of enjoyment, devotion, and reverence. Only God warrants those attitudes and responses, even though it's second nature to us to give them to things that are not God, which is to say that it's second nature to us to be idolaters. (Our first nature is given by God, and so is not idolatrous.) We must then, as Christians, inculcate the complex skill of directing our wills and appetites away from ourselves and our gratification, and toward God. Inculcating this skill and exhibiting it in our lives are proper and essential parts of the Christian account.

Closely associated with this necessity is the imperative to transform our attitudes toward humans other than ourselves. We have to learn to see each as an image of God, as created by God, and so as worthy of honor and affection. This involves learning the complex skill of discerning when to sacrifice our own interests (which are naturally dear to us, and which we naturally kill to defend and extend) for those of others, and when and how to witness to others in the hope that they might also become offerers of the Christian account, livers of the Christian life. Here, as so often, our paradigm is Jesus of Nazareth, who both gave his own life for others, and constantly taught and witnessed to them. But simple imitation is not possible, any more than simple imitation of Bobby Fischer's best games will make a good chess player, or simple imitation of Vladimir Nabokov's best novels will make a good novelist. The acquisition of a skill and the discernment to apply it well are what's needed.

The reordering of will and appetite away from self and toward God (first) and other humans (second) also has its application to the nonhuman parts of the created order, both sentient and otherwise. These also are God's creation, and are to be honored as such. They are not to be used solely for our gratification, not to be treated with casual violence or disrespect, and most emphatically not to become objects of idolatry, to be loved as if they were God. Seeing what all this means and applying it in the particular situations in which we find ourselves is, once again, a complex skill. It, too, is an essential part of the Christian account.

We Christians have often described and analyzed the inculcation of the skills mentioned in the immediately preceding paragraphs under the rubric of the training of conscience. All humans have a conscience, an internal witness and judge that instructs us in what we ought to do. But for most of us it is undeveloped, "weak" as St. Paul puts it (I Corinthians 8), clouded or obscured by sin and self-will. Inculcation of the skills I've mentioned (indeed, the whole process of religious learning for Christians) can usefully be understood as enlivening the lazy conscience.

Three kinds of practice are typically used by Christians as tools for the inculcation of these skills. The first is worship; the second, prayer; and the third, reading or hearing the Bible for nourishment. These are not finally separable one from another. All worship involves prayer, all prayer is a form of worship, and proper use of the Bible is both prayerful and worshipful. But it may nonetheless be useful to say a few words on each separately.

Worship, the first of these three, is a communal and individual returning of praise and love to the God who has acted in such a way as to make possible and to require the offering of the Christian account. Worship is, as we Christians have developed it, a complex and highly ordered collective activity. When, for instance, Catholic Christians offer the sacrifice of the mass, we perform actions that require a high level of understanding and skill. There are skills of bodily movement: knowing how and when to genuflect, to kneel, to stand, to make the sign of the cross, and so forth. There are skills of voice: knowing when and how to sing, to chant, and so forth. And there are skills of thought and attitude: knowing when and how to compose the mind, to direct the thoughts, to order the emotions and the will. All these skills presuppose and express a broad range of knowledge that: knowledge that God has acted in such and such a way; knowledge that such and such a response is appropriate; knowledge that the bread and wine on the altar have a peculiar significance – and so forth. The knowing how and knowing that evident in Christian worship are learned and inculcated by repetition; their inculcation produces a particular skill that is in turn part of the process by which the will and the appetites are ordered to God.

Prayer, the second practice used by Christians, has both communal and private aspects. Whether done with others or alone in your room behind closed doors (Matthew 6:6), it, too, is a returning of love, praise, and service to God. Its paradigm is the Paternoster, the prayer given by Jesus (Matthew 6:9–13; Luke 11:2–4), and its shortest and most pithy form is direct address to God in the form "Your will, not mine, be done." Like worship, it acknowledges and represents the facts about what God has done for us, and in so doing inculcates the skill of responding properly to those facts. It is part of the process by which our wills and appetites become aligned with God.

The third practice integral to the Christian account is the use of the Bible. We Christians possess what we take to be a peculiarly authoritative witness to God's actions and intentions. This authority is construed in various ways, but common to them all (or at least to all that warrant being described as Christian) are the ideas that the Bible has greater authority than any other work, that the reading of it should provide Christians with a set of tools and skills we can use to interpret the world, and that the world is to be interpreted in terms of the Bible, written into its margins, so to speak, rather than the other way around. Technically, this is to say that the Bible is a *norma normans non normata*, a norm that norms but is itself not normed. Here, too, many skills and much information are required: we Christians need to learn the skill of reading the Bible in a particular way, as well as a good deal of information about the Bible and about reading. George Herbert, in these lines from "The H. Scriptures I," puts the Christian's attitude to the Bible well:

Oh Book! infinite sweetnesse! let my heart
Suck ev'ry letter, and a hony gain

. . . .
. . . heav'n lies flat in thee,
Subject to ev'ry mounters bended knee.[9]

Sucking is another learned skill (as also was sucking at your mother's breast); learning it and practicing it contributes to the more fundamental and difficult skills of reorienting the will and the appetite.

The immediately preceding paragraphs have provided a very schematic outline of the Christian account. It has been meant only to illustrate the points made earlier about skills and information as integral parts of religious accounts. Similar schematic outlines could be given of Buddhist, Hindu, or Confucian religious accounts (though not by me). It should be clear even from this schematic version of the Christian account that it appears comprehensive, unsurpassable, and central to Christians. It also exhibits some other features likely to be found in religious accounts. It presents views about the setting of human life, and it presents them in such a way as to account in broad terms for every aspect of that life. All religious accounts are likely to do this. It presents views, also, about the nature of human persons, and about how we should conduct ourselves, and it does this in such a way as to embrace all dimensions of that life. This, too, is likely to be something that any comprehensive, unsurpassable, and central account will attempt. It also presents methods (worship, prayer, reading the Bible) intended to remind those who offer it of what they are doing, and to inculcate in them the skills needed for doing it well. It's unlikely that any religious account can get away without doing this, too. Enlivening the conscience, sharpening discernment, honing skill – whatever the preferred vocabulary, religious accounts must contain methods for doing this. That is, any religious account must contain a pedagogy. A final point about the Christian religious account that may also be applicable to others: central to its pedagogy is the teaching of a method of reading. What is read, for Christians, is primarily and paradigmatically the Bible, and this, of course, is specific to the Christian account. But it may be that the way in which its reading is taught is not specific in this way: perhaps all religious accounts recommend the kind of sucking at the nipple of the works important to them that George Herbert commends to Christians.

Notes

1   See Thomas Nagel, "What Is It Like to Be a Bat?" in his *Mortal Questions* (Cambridge, 1979), pp. 165–80.

2   On unsurpassability, see George Lindbeck, *The Nature of Doctrine* (Philadelphia, 1984), pp. 47–52.

3   J. H. Newman's *Essay on the Development of Christian Doctrine*, first published in 1845, is the classic example of an argument for the view that unsurpassability requires the essential doctrinal features of an unsurpassable account to change only in form or degree of explicitness, not in substance. Its thought underlies what I say in this section.

4   Dan Sperber, *Rethinking Symbolism* (Cambridge, 1975), pp. 87–8.

5   On "knowing how" and "knowing that," see Gilbert Ryle, *The Concept of Mind* (Harmondsworth, 1990; first published 1949); J. L. Austin, *Philosophical Papers* (Oxford, 1961), especially chapters 3 and 4.

6   Ryle, *Concept of Mind*, p. 46.

7   Ibid., p. 58.

8   The principal influences upon the version of the Christian account offered here are Augustine, Newman, John Donne, George Herbert, and Karl Barth.

9   C. A. Patrides, ed., *The English Poems of George Herbert* (London, 1974), pp. 76–7.

PART II

Theism and Divine Attributes

Introduction

Charles Taliaferro

The study of a religion is like the exploration of a world. In the course of learning about the faiths, which have Abrahamic roots, three worlds open up: the worlds of Judaism, Christianity, and Islam. In these three traditions as well as in some strands of Hinduism one finds a central role given to God as the creator and sustainer of the cosmos. To philosophically enter or, to be less metaphorical, to philosophically entertain these traditions requires reflection on the nature of God.

Some religious believers resist the philosophy of God on the grounds that God is beyond all conceivable human thought. To consider the scope and character of, say, God's power and knowledge may seem impious. But it is difficult to bypass a philosophy of divine attributes on religious grounds for at least three reasons. First, unless we can form *some* concept of the divine it is difficult to engage in many religious practices such as prayer and worship. How can one be in awe of some reality if one cannot form a concept of that reality? Second, even if human language and experience are too limited to fashion an exact portrait of the divine, can we not achieve at least *some* idea of God? Granted, you and I cannot imagine what it would be like to be omnipotent or omniscient. Even so, that does not mean we are entirely in the dark about the concepts of omnipotence and omniscience.

A third reason for the study of the concept of God is that this study can reveal what many of us value. Thinking of God in Judaism, Christianity, and Islam is to think of a reality, which believers take to be of great goodness and perfection. The power, knowledge, and goodness of God may be seen as the object of great human yearning and allegiance. To believe in God's essential goodness, for example, is to believe that the most fundamental reality is not evil or indifferent to the well-being of the cosmos. The exploration of divine attributes is therefore a study of values, and not merely some arcane academic undertaking.

In "God," Richard Swinburne provides an analytic understanding of God as the all-knowing, all-powerful, all-good, eternal, free Creator of the cosmos.

Thomas V. Morris provides a closer look at two divine attributes. The puzzle Morris faces over omnipotence involves the relationship between power and goodness. If God is essentially (or necessarily) good, are there some acts (such as doing evil for the sake of evil) that God cannot do? If there are some acts God cannot do, is God omnipotent? Morris proposes an engaging resolution to this quandary. On the topic of omniscience, Morris considers the scope of God's knowledge. If God knows of future free action (for example, if God knows that 10 minutes from now you will decide to go for a walk), can the action be truly free? Arguably, you freely do some act such as deciding to go for a walk when you take the walk and it was possible for you not to take the walk. But if God knows *now* that you will take a walk, it seems that your walk is fixed or guaranteed so that you are not free to remain seated. The problem is not: if God foreknows a future act, then God must have determined what you will do. You might foreknow who will win a race without fixing the outcome. The problem is, rather, that whoever and however the future is brought about, divine foreknowledge seems to threaten the possibility that the future is truly open so that you might act differently. Morris addresses this problem in light of the concept of God as perfect or unsurpassably excellent reality.

In "Eternity," Brian Leftow presents a series of reasons why some theists today think of God as a temporal reality. These theists believe God is without origin; no being created God and God will have no temporal end. Still, they believe there is a before, during, and after for God. On this framework, God has a future. Leftow believes instead that it makes sense to think of God as an atemporal or timeless reality.

In "Divine Freedom and Creation," Laura L. Garcia looks at a concern that goes beyond the topic of human freedom. To what extent is God, as traditionally conceived, free? In addressing this question, Garcia commends an analogy between human and divine creativity.

In the last entry of this section, Marjorie Hewitt Suchocki reminds us of the social, moral, and practical implications of the concept of God. To what extent do our concepts of the divine reflect or help shape our understanding of ourselves, including our gender? Suchocki examines two contemporary feminist theologians: Mary Daly and Rosemary Ruether.

Further Reading

From The Blackwell Companion to Philosophy of Religion, *see the following entries:*

Coakley, S., "Feminism"
Creel, R. E., "Immutability and impassibility"
Helm, P., "Goodness"
Hoffman, J. and Rosenkrantz, G., "Omnipotence"
Leftlow, B., "Eternity"
Mann, W. E., "Necessity"
Mavrodes, G. I., "Omniscience"
McCann, H. J., "Creation and conservation"
Sherry, P., "Beauty"
Stump, E., "Simplicity"
Taliaferro, C., "Incorporeality"
Tracy, T. F., "Divine action"
Wierenga, E. R., "Omnipresence"
Williams, C. F., "Being"
Zagzebski, L., "Foreknowledge and human freedom"

For some helpful texts that explore all the divine attributes see:

Davis, S. T., *Logic and the Nature of God* (Grand Rapids: Eerdmans, 1983). *A helpful treatment of central divine attributes.*
Flew, A., *God and Philosophy* (New York: Delta Books, 1966). *A highly critical text with bold arguments.*
Freddoso, A. J. (ed.), *The Existence and Nature of God* (Notre Dame: University of Notre Dame Press, 1983). *A fine collection on different divine attributes.*
Gale, R. M., *On the Nature and Existence of God* (Cambridge: Cambridge University Press, 1991). *Somewhat eccentric with off-beat humor, but important arguments for and against theism.*

Hughes, G. J., *The Nature of God* (London and New York: Routledge, 1995). *An analytic, constructive theistic philosophy.*
Kenny, A., *The God of the Philosophers* (Oxford and New York: Oxford University Press, 1979). *A prominent philosopher investigates key theistic attributes. Well informed by historical references.*
Kretzmann, N., *The Metaphysics of Theism* (Oxford: Clarendon, 1997). *Sophisticated essays on the coherence of theism drawing on medieval sources.*
Mann, W. E., "The Divine Attributes," *American Philosophical Quarterly* 12 (1975): 151–9.
Martin, M., *Atheism: A Philosophical Justification* (Philadelphia: Temple University Press, 1990). *The most sustained, systematic case for atheism in print; contains arguments on the incoherence of divine attributes.*
Meynell, H., *God and the World: The Coherence of Christian Theism* (London, SPCK Press, 1971). *A clear, accessible guide.*
Morris, T. V., *Anselmian Explorations: Essays in Philosophical Theology* (Notre Dame: University of Notre Dame Press, 1987). *Skillful, informative development of a theistic philosophy.*
Ross, J. F., *Philosophical Theology* (Indianapolis and New York: Bobbs-Merrill, 1969; 2nd edn, Indianapolis: Hackett, 1980). *A rich, aggressive defense of the coherence of theism, especially the divine attribute of necessity.*
Schlesinger, G. N., *New Perspectives on Old-Time Religion* (Oxford: Clarendon Press, 1988). *An odd title for papers of high quality on divine attributes.*
Swinburne, R., *The Coherence of Theism*, 2nd edn (Oxford: Clarendon Press, 1993). *A classic, refined text.*
Taliaferro, C., *Consciousness and the Mind of God* (Cambridge: Cambridge University Press, 1994). *Focuses on the coherence of believing God to be a nonphysical reality.*

Tracy, T. F. (ed.), *The God Who Acts* (University Park: Penn State, 1994). *Reflections on God as an agent.*

Wierenga, E., *The Nature of God: An Inquiry into Divine Attributes* (Ithaca and London: Cornell University Press, 1989). *A careful, intricate defense of divine attributes.*

For material on specific divine attributes, see:

Divine Simplicity

Davies, B., "Classical Theism and the Doctrine of Divine Simplicity," in Davis (ed.), *Language, Meaning and God* (London: Geoffrey Chapman, 1987). *An important articulation of this attribute.*

Hughes, C., *On a Complex Theory of a Simple God: An Investigation in Aquinas' Philosophical Theology* (Ithaca: Cornell University Press, 1989). *A systematic, vigorous text.*

Hughes, C., *The Nature of God* (London and New York: Routledge, 1995). *An illuminating, careful work.*

Kretzmann, N. and Stump, E., "Absolute Simplicity," *Faith and Philosophy* 2 (1985): 53–382. *An influential, challenging text.*

Mann, W. E., "Divine Simplicity," *Religious Studies* 18 (1982): 451–71. *An important defense of simplicity.*

Plantinga, A., *Does God have a Nature?* (Milwaukee: Marquette University Press, 1980). *A forceful critique of simplicity.*

Wolterstorff, N., "Divine Simplicity," in K. J. Clark (ed.), *Our Knowledge of God* (Dordrecht: Kluwer Academic Publishers, 1992). *A critical text.*

Divine Omnipotence

Frankfurt, H. G., "The Logic of Omnipotence," *The Philosophical Review* 73 (1964): 262–3. *This paper, along with those by Mavrodes and Savage listed here, are seminal, analytic treatments of omnipotence.*

Freddoso, A. J. and Flint, T. P., "Maximal Power," in Freddoso (ed.), *The Existence and Nature of God* (Notre Dame: University of Notre Dame Press, 1983). *A sophisticated analysis.*

Geach, P. T., "Omnipotence," *Philosophy* 48 (1973): 7–20. *An influential dismissal of formal treatments of omnipotence.*

Mavrodes, G. I., "Some Puzzles Concerning Omnipotence," *The Philosophical Review* 72 (1963): 221–3.

Savage, C. W., "The Paradox of the Stone," *The Philosophical Review* 76 (1967): 74–9.

Urban, L. and Walton, D. N., "Freedom within Omnipotence," in Urban and Walton (eds.), *The Power of God* (New York: Oxford University Press, 1978).

Divine Omniscience

Alston, W. P., "Does God Have Beliefs?" *Religious Studies* 22 (1986): 287–306. *Interesting look at divine awareness of the cosmos.*

Craig, W. L., *The Problem of Divine Foreknowledge and Future Contingents from Aristotle to Suarez* (Leiden: B. J. Brill, 1988). *Sweeping, bold defense of freedom and foreknowledge.*

Creel, R. E., "Can God Know that He Is God?" *Religious Studies* 16 (1980): 195–201. *A succinct, clever puzzle.*

Creel, R., *Divine Impassibility, An Essay in Philosophical Theology* (Cambridge: Cambridge University Press, 1986). *Can God know of the world if God does not suffer? Creel thinks so, and argues that theism does not require that God undergo pain or suffering.*

Flint, T. P., *Divine Providence: The Molinist Account* (Ithaca and London: Cornell University Press, 1998). *Essential reading for the debate over the compatibility of omniscience and freedom.*

Kretzmann, N. and Stump, E., "God's Knowledge and Its Causal Efficacy," in T. D. Senor (ed.), *The Rationality of Belief and the Plurality of Faith* (Ithaca and London: Cornell University Press, 1995). *A provocative, speculative proposal.*

Kretzmann, N., "Omniscience and Immutability," *The Journal of Philosophy* 63 (1966): 409–21. *Argument over the coherence of omniscience.*

Kvanvig, J. L., *The Possibility of an All-Knowing God* (New York: St Martin's Press, 1986). *A thorough, analytic analysis.*

Linville, M. D., "Divine Foreknowledge and the Libertarian Conception of Human Freedom," *International Journal of Philosophy* 33 (1993): 165–83. *Defense of freedom and foreknowledge.*

Prior, A. N., "The Formalities of Omniscience," *Philosophy* 37 (1962): 114–29. *Classic paper.*

Rudavsky, T., *Divine Omniscience and Omnipotence in Medieval Philosophy: Islamic, Jewish and Christian Perspectives* (Dordrecht, Boston, and Lancaster: D. Reidel Publishing Co., 1985). *Masterful essays on important historical sources.*

Taliaferro, C., "Divine Cognitive Power," *International Journal for Philosophy of Religion* 18 (1985): 133–40. *An argument that analyses of omniscience need to include not just a delineation of the scope of omniscience but an account of how God knows states of affairs.*

Eternity

Braine, D., *The Reality of Time and the Existence of God: The Project of Proving God's Existence* (Oxford: Clarendon Press, 1988). *A complex but substantial text.*

Craig, W. L., "God and Real Time," *Religious Studies* 26 (1990): 335–47.

Hasker, W., *God, Time, and Knowledge* (Ithaca: Cornell University Press, 1989). *A substantial text arguing for God in time.*

Helm, P., *Eternal God: A Study of God without Time* (Oxford: Clarendon Press, 1988). *A defense of divine eternity.*

Kretzmann, N. and Stump, E., "Eternity," *The Journal of Philosophy* 84 (1987): 214–19. *A classic defense of divine eternity.*

Leftlow, B., *Time and Eternity*, Cornell Studies in the Philosophy of Religion (Ithaca: Cornell University Press, 1991). *A host of arguments for God's eternity.*

Lewis, D., "Eternity Again: A Reply to Stump and Kretzmann," *International Journal for Philosophy of Religion* 15 (1984): 73–9.

Lucas, J. R., "The Temporality of God," in R. J. Russell, N. Murphy, and C. J. Isham (eds.), *Quantum Cosmology and the Laws of Nature* (Vatican City State: Vatican Observatory; Berkeley, CA: Center for Theology and the Natural Sciences, 1996).

Padgett, A. G., *God, Eternity, and the Nature of Time* (London: Macmillan; New York: St Martin's Press, 1992). *A clear, astute text.*

Pike, N., *God and Timelessness*. Studies in Ethics and the Philosophy of Religion (London: Routledge and Kegan Paul; New York: Schocken Books, 1970). *A gold mine of interesting arguments.*

Sorabji, P., *Time, Creation and the Continuum* (London: Duckworth, 1983). *A masterful look at theories of eternity, time, and God in antiquity and the Middle Ages.*

Wolterstorff, N., "God Everlasting," in C. Orlebe and L. Smedes (eds.), *God and the Good: Essay in Honor of Henry Stob* (Grand Rapids: Eerdmans, 1975). *Significant case for God as a temporal reality.*

Feminism and God

Anderson, Pamela Sue, *A Feminist Philosophy of Religion* (Oxford: Blackwell, 1998). *An important feminist examination of key religious narratives.*

Byrne, Peter, "Omnipotence, Feminism and God," *International Journal for Philosophy of Religion* 37:3 (June 1995): 145–65. *An appreciative note on the feminist critique of the philosophy of God, but also challenging whether feminism "can guide deep reflections in this area very far."*

Coakley, S., "Feminism," in P. Quinn and C. Taliaferro (eds.), *A Companion to Philosophy of Religion* (Oxford: Blackwell, 1997). *A brilliant example of feminist philosophy of religion.*

Jantzen, G. M., "Feminists, Philosophers, and Mystics," *Hypatia* 9:4 (1994). *Argues that feminist treatments of religious experience differ from prevailing, current views.*

Jantzen, G. M., *Becoming Divine* (Manchester: Indiana University Press, 1999). *A proposed radical shift in current philosophy of religion.*

Jantzen, G. M., *God's World, God's Body* (Philadelphia: Westminster Press, 1984). *A defense of the view that the cosmos is God's body.*

Divine Goodness

Garcia, L. L., "The Essential Moral Perfection of God," *Religious Studies* 23 (1987): 37–144. *Defense of God's perfection.*

Geach, P. T., "Could God Fail to Keep Promises?" *Philosophy* 52 (1977): 93–5. *A light, provocative essay in which Geach argues that God cannot fail to keep promises.*

Hasker, W., "Must God Do His Best?" *International Journal for Philosophy of Religion* 16 (1984): 213–23. *Important look at the divine attribute of goodness and its bearing on the problem of evil.*

Kretzmann, N. and Stump, E., "Being and Goodness," in T. V. Morris (ed.), *Divine and Human Action* (Ithaca: Cornell University Press, 1988). *A classical paper.*

Leftlow, B., "Necessary Moral Perfection," *Pacific Philosophical Quarterly* 70 (1989): 240–60. *An Anselmian understanding of God.*

Linville, M. D., "On Goodness: Human and Divine," *American Philosophical Quarterly* 27 (1990): 143–52. *Good analyses of key issues.*

Macdonald, S. (ed.), *Being and Goodness: The Concept of the Good in Metaphysics and Philosophical Theology* (Ithaca: Cornell University Press, 1990). *Solid collection, mostly arguing for a theistic metaphysic and theory of values.*

Plantinga, A., "The Perfect Goodness of God," *Australasian Journal of Philosophy* 40 (1962): 70–5.

Reichenbach, B. R., *Evil and a Good God* (New York: Fordham University Press, 1982). *Clear and systematic examination of the implications of divine goodness.*

Rowe, W. L., "The Problem of Divine Perfection and Freedom," in E. Stump (ed.), *Reasoned Faith* (Ithaca: Cornell University Press, 1993). *A sophisticated text.*

Zagzebski, L. T., *The Dilemma of Freedom and Foreknowledge* (New York: Oxford University Press, 1991). *Rigorously argued.*

4

God

Richard Swinburne

My topic is the claim that there is a God, under-stood in the way that Western religion (Christian-ity, Judaism, and Islam) has generally understood that claim. I call that claim theism. In this chapter I shall spell out what the claim amounts to. [. . .] I emphasize that, in this chapter, when I write that God does this or is like that, I am not assuming that there is a God, but merely spelling out what the claim that there is a God amounts to. I am not directly concerned to assess the claim that there is a God, where "God" is being understood in some quite different sense, as the name of a quite differ-ent sort of being from the one worshipped in West-ern religion. But, in arguing at various points that theism explains the observed data well, I shall occasionally point out that other hypotheses, in-cluding ones which invoke a "God" in some other sense, explain the data less well. Even within the mainstream of the Western tradition, there have been some differences about what God is like, and I shall draw attention to some of these differences in this chapter and suggest that some views about what God is like are to be preferred to others.

Theism claims that God is a personal being – that is, in some sense *a person*. By a person I mean an individual with basic powers (to act intentionally), purposes, and beliefs.

Richard Swinburne, "God," reprinted by permission of Oxford University Press from *Is There a God?* (Oxford and New York: Oxford University Press, 1996), pp. 3–19.

An *intentional action* is one which a person does and means to do – as when I walk downstairs or say something which I mean to say. A *basic action* is one which a person does intentionally just like that and not by doing any other intentional action. My going from Oxford to London is a *non-basic action*, because I do it by doing various other actions – going to the station, getting on the train, etc. But squeezing my hand or moving my leg and even saying "this" are basic actions. I just do them, not by doing any other intentional act. (True, certain events have to happen in my body – my nerves have to transmit impulses – if I am to perform the basic action. But these are not events which I bring about intentionally. They just happen – I may not even know about them.) By a *basic power* I mean a power to perform a basic action. We humans have similar basic powers to each other. They are norm-ally confined to powers of thought and powers over the small chunk of matter which each of us calls his or her body. I can only produce effects in the world outside my body by doing something intentional with my body. I can open a door by grasping the handle with my hand and pulling it towards me; or I can get you to know something by using my mouth to tell you something. When I produce some effect intentionally (e.g. the door being open) by doing some other action (e.g. pull-ing it towards me), doing the former is performing a non-basic action. When I go to London, or write a book, or even put a screw into a wall, these are non-basic actions which I do by doing some basic actions. When I perform any intentional action, I seek thereby to achieve some *purpose* – normally one beyond the mere performance of the action itself (I open a door in order to be able to leave the room), but sometimes simply the performance of the action itself (as when I sing for its own sake).

Beliefs are views, often true but sometimes false, about how the world is. When beliefs are true and well justified, they constitute knowledge. Our human knowledge of the world beyond our bodies is formed by stimuli – of light, sound, smell, and such like – coming from the world beyond our bodies and landing on our bodies. It is because light particles land on our eyes and sound waves (including those produced by speech) land on our ears that we acquire our information about the world. God is supposed to be like us, in having basic powers, beliefs, and purposes – but ones very different from ours. Human persons are either male or female. But the theist, of course, claims that God is neither male nor female. The English language alas does not have a pronoun for referring to persons without carrying any implication of their sex. So I shall follow custom in referring to God as "he", but I emphasize – without the implication of maleness.

God's basic powers are supposed to be infinite: he can bring about as a basic action any event he chooses, and he does not need bones or muscles to operate in certain ways in order to do so. He can bring objects, including material objects, into existence and keep them in existence from moment to moment. We can imagine finding ourselves having a basic power not merely to move objects, but to create them instantaneously – for example the power to make a pen or a rabbit come into existence; and to keep them in existence and then let them no longer exist. There is no contradiction in this supposition, but of course in fact no human has such a power. What the theist claims about God is that he does have a power to create, conserve, or annihilate anything, big or small. And he can also make objects move or do anything else. He can make them attract or repel each other, in the way that scientists have discovered that they do, and make them cause other objects to do or suffer various things: he can make the planets move in the way that Kepler discovered that they move, or make gunpowder explode when we set a match to it; or he can make planets move in quite different ways, and chemical substances explode or not explode under quite different conditions from those which now govern their behaviour. God is not limited by the laws of nature; he makes them and he can change or suspend them – if he chooses.

To use the technical term, God is *omnipotent*: he can do anything.

Human beliefs are limited in their scope, and some of them are true and some of them are false. God is supposed to be *omniscient* – that is, he knows everything. In other words, whatever is true, God knows that it is true. If it snowed on 1 January 10 million BC on the site of present-day New York, God knows that it snowed there and then. If there is a proof of Goldbach's conjecture (something mathematicians have been trying to discover for the past 300 years), God knows what it is; if there is no proof, God knows that there is no proof. All God's beliefs are true, and God believes everything that is true.

Human persons are influenced in forming their purposes by their desires, their in-built inclinations to make this choice and not that one. Our desires include those produced by our bodily physiology – such as desires for food, drink, sleep, and sex – and those formed in part by our culture – such as desires for fame and fortune. We are, it seems to us (I believe, correctly), free to some extent to fight against our desires and do some action other than one which we are naturally inclined to do, but it requires effort. Human beings have limited free will. But God is supposed to be not thus limited. He is *perfectly free*, in that desires never exert causal influence on him at all. Not merely, being omnipotent, can he do whatever he chooses, but he is perfectly free in making his choices.

God then, theism claims, is a person, omnipotent, omniscient, and perfectly free. But now we must be careful how we understand these claims. An omnipotent being can do anything. But does that mean that he can make the universe exist and not exist at the same time, make $2 + 2$ to equal 5, make a shape square and round at the same time, or change the past? The majority religious tradition has claimed that God cannot do these things; not because God is weak, but because the words – for example, "make a shape square and round at the same time" – do not describe anything which makes sense. There is nothing which would constitute a shape being both square and round. Part of what saying that something is square involves is saying that that thing is not round. So, in technical words, God cannot do what is logically impossible (what involves a self-contradiction). God can make the universe exist and God can make the universe not exist, but God cannot make the universe exist and not exist at the same time. The reason why theists ought to say what I have just said was first grasped clearly by the great Christian philosophical theologian, St Thomas Aquinas, in the thirteenth century.

It seems to me that the same considerations require that we understand God being omniscient in a similarly careful way. Just as God cannot be required to do what is logically impossible to do, so God cannot be required to know what is logically impossible to know. It seems to me that it is logically impossible to know (without the possibility of mistake) what someone will do freely tomorrow. If I am really free to choose tomorrow whether I will go to London or stay at home, then if anyone today has some belief about what I will do (e.g. that I will go to London), I have it in my power tomorrow to make that belief false (e.g. by staying at home). So no one (not even God) can know today (without the possibility of mistake) what I will choose to do tomorrow. So I suggest that we understand God being omniscient as God knowing at any time all that is logically possible to know at that time. That will not include knowledge, before they have done it, of what human persons will do freely. Since God is omnipotent, it will only be because God allows there to be free persons that there will be any free persons. So this limit to divine omniscience arises from the consequences (which God could foresee) of his own choice to create free agents. I must, however, warn the reader that this view of mine that God does not know (without the possibility of mistake) what free agents will do until they do it is not the normal Christian (or Jewish or Islamic) view. My view is, however, implied, I believe, by certain biblical passages; it seems, for example, the natural interpretation of the book of Jonah that, when God told Jonah to preach to Nineveh that it would be destroyed, he believed that probably he would need to destroy it, but that fortunately, since the people of Nineveh repented, God saw no need to carry out his prophecy. In advocating this refinement of our understanding of omniscience, I am simply carrying further the process of internal clarification of the basic Christian understanding of God which other Christian philosophers such as Aquinas pursued in earlier days.

All this does of course assume that human beings have some limited free will, in the sense that no causes (whether brain states or God) determine fully how they will choose. That is the way it often seems to us that we have such a power. Even the inanimate world, scientists now realize, is not a fully deterministic world – and the world of thought and choice is even less obviously a predictable world. [. . .]

God – the omnipotent, omniscient, and perfectly free person – is, according to theism, *eternal*. But there are two different ways of understanding "eternal". We can understand it, as clearly the biblical writers did, as everlasting: God is eternal in the sense that he has existed at each moment of past time, exists now, and will exist at each moment of future time. Alternatively, we can understand "eternal" as "timeless": God is eternal in the sense that he exists outside time. This latter is how all the great philosophical theologians from the fourth to the fourteenth century AD (Augustine, Boethius, and St Thomas Aquinas, for example) understood God's eternity. God does not, on this view, strictly speaking, exist today or yesterday or tomorrow – he just exists. In his one timeless "moment", he "simultaneously" causes the events of AD 1995 and of 587 BC. In this one timeless moment also he knows simultaneously (as they happen) what is happening in AD 1995 and in 587 BC. For myself I cannot make much sense of this suggestion – for many reasons. For example, I cannot see that anything can be meant by saying that God knows (as they happen) the events of AD 1995 unless it means that he exists in 1995 and knows in 1995 what is happening then. And then he cannot know in the same act of knowledge (as they happen) the events of 587 BC – for these are different years. Hence I prefer the understanding of God being eternal as his being everlasting rather than as his being timeless. He exists at each moment of unending time.

All the other essential properties which theism attributes to God at each moment of time follow from the three properties of omnipotence, omniscience, and perfect freedom. Thus God is supposed to be *bodiless*. For a person to have a body is for there to be a chunk of matter through which alone he or she can make a difference to the physical world and acquire true beliefs about it. But, being omnipotent, God can make differences to the world and learn about it without being thus dependent. So he will have no body; he does not depend on matter to affect and learn about the world. He moves the stars, as we move our arms, just like that – as a basic action. It follows too from his omnipotence that God is *omnipresent* (i.e. present everywhere), in the sense that he can make a difference to things everywhere and know what is happening everywhere just like that, without needing arms or sense organs or the normal operation of light rays in order to do so. But, although he is everywhere present, he is not spatially extended; he does not take up a volume of space – for he has no body. Nor, therefore, does he have any spatial parts: all of him is present everywhere, in the sense in which he is present at a place. It is not that part of him is in England, and another part in the United States.

God being omnipotent could have prevented the universe from existing, if he had so chosen. So it exists only because he allows it to exist. Hence either he causes the existence of the universe, or he causes or allows some other agent to do so. In this sense, therefore, he is the *creator of the universe*, and, being – by the same argument – equally responsible for its continued existence, he is the sustainer of the universe. He is responsible for the existence of the universe (and every object within it) for as long as it exists. That may be a finite time – the universe may have begun to exist a certain number of years ago; current scientific evidence suggests that the universe began to exist with the "Big Bang" some 15,000 million years ago. Or the universe may have existed forever. The theist as such is not committed to one or other of these positions. But the theist claims that, even if the universe has existed forever, its existence at each moment of time is due to the conserving action of God at that moment.

God is supposed to be responsible, not merely for the existence of all other objects, but for their having the powers and liabilities they do. Inanimate things have certain powers – for example, to move in certain ways, attract or repel each other. These are not "basic powers" in the sense in which I was using the term earlier; a basic power is a power to do something intentionally, by choice. The powers of inanimate things are powers to produce effects, but not through choice or for a purpose. In general inanimate things have to act as they do, have to exert their powers under certain circumstances – the gunpowder has to explode when you light it at the right temperature and pressure. That is what I mean by saying that it has a liability to exert its powers under certain circumstances. (On the very small scale, the world is not fully deterministic – atoms and smaller particles have only a probability, a propensity to do this rather than that. Their liability to exert their powers is only a propensity. But this randomness is not a matter of choice, and so their actions are not intentional.) God, theism claims, causes inanimate things to have the powers and liabilities they do, at each moment when they have them. God continually

causes the gunpowder to have the power to explode, and the liability to exercise the power when it is ignited at the right temperature and pressure. And likewise, theism claims, God causes plants and animals (and human bodies, in so far as they act non-intentionally – for example, when the blood is pumped round our arteries and veins) to have the powers and liabilities they do. And God is also responsible for the existence of humans. He could cause us to act of physical necessity. But, given that we have limited free will, God does not cause us to form the purposes we do. That is up to us. But God does conserve in us from moment to moment our basic powers to act, and thus ensures that the purposes we form make a difference to the world. God allows us to choose whether to form the purpose of moving a hand or not; and God ensures that (normally), when we form that purpose, it is efficacious – if we try to move our hand, it moves.

When God acts to produce some effect by conserving objects in existence, and conserving their powers and liabilities to act, he produces the effect in a non-basic way. When God makes the gunpowder explode by conserving its explosive power, and its liability to exercise the power when ignited, he produces the explosion in a non-basic way – just as when I cause the door to be open by pulling it towards me. God normally brings about ordinary historical events by these non-basic routes – that is, by making other objects bring about those events. But he could bring about any event by a basic action; and just sometimes, the theist normally claims, he does produce effects in a basic way. He occasionally intervenes in the natural world to produce effects directly – for example, curing someone of cancer, when they would not get better by normal processes. [. . .]

God is supposed to be *perfectly good*. His being perfectly good follows from his being perfectly free and omniscient. A perfectly free person will inevitably do what he believes to be (overall) the best action and never do what he believes to be an (overall) bad action. In any situation to form a purpose to achieve some goal, to try to achieve some goal involves regarding the goal as in some way a good thing. To try to go to London, I must regard my being in London as in some way a good thing – either because I would enjoy being there, or because thereby I can avoid some unpleasant occasion, or because it is my duty to be in London. To regard some aspect of being in London as good is to have a reason for going to London. If I had no reason at all for going to London, my going there would not be an intentional action (would not be something I meant to do). A person's intentional actions must, therefore, in part be rational; in them he must be guided in part by rational considerations. Yet, as noted earlier, we humans are not fully rational, being subject to desires. (In calling desires non-rational, I do *not* wish to imply that there is something wrong with them, and that we ought not to yield to them. I mean only that they are inclinations with which we find ourselves, not ones solely under the control of reasons.) But a person free from desires who formed his purposes solely on the basis of rational considerations would inevitably do the action which he believed (overall) the best one to do, or (if there is not, the person believes, a best action, but a number of equal best actions) one of the equal best actions.

Now, if there are moral truths – truths about what is morally good and bad – an omniscient person will know what they are. If, for example, lying is always morally wrong, God will know that. On the other hand, if lying is wrong only in certain circumstances, then God will know that. Despite the doubts of the occasional hardened sceptic, we do almost all of us think almost all the time that there are some acts which are morally good (and among them some which are morally obligatory), and some which are morally bad (and among them some which are morally wrong). It is morally good to give (at least some money sometimes) to the starving, and obligatory to feed our own children when they are starving; and it is wrong to torture children for fun. Who can seriously deny these things? The morally good is the overall good. To say that it is morally good to feed the starving is not to say that it is good in all respects; in depriving us of money, it may deprive us of some future enjoyment, and so giving will not be good in all respects. But it is good in the more important respect that it saves the lives of human beings and so gives them the opportunity for much future well-being. In consequence, it is overall a good act – or so someone claims who claims that it is a morally good act. God, being omniscient, will have true beliefs about what is morally good, and, being perfectly free, he will do what he believes is (overall) the best. So he will always do what is overall the best, and never do what is overall bad. Hence God will be perfectly good.

Some moral truths are clearly moral truths, whether or not there is a God: it is surely wrong to torture children for fun whether or not there is a

God. On the other hand, if theism is true, we owe our existence from moment to moment to the conserving action of God; and he gives us this wonderful world to enjoy. [. . .] God is a generous benefactor. One of the most fundamental human obligations (i.e. duties) is (within limits) to please our major benefactors – to do in return for them some small favour which they request in return for the great things they have given us. If theism is true, God is by far our greatest benefactor, for all our other benefactors depend for their ability to benefit us on God's sustaining power. We owe God a lot. Hence (within limits), if God tells us to do certain things, it becomes our duty to do them. Just as (within narrow limits) it becomes our duty to do certain things if our parents (when we are children) tell us to do them, or the state tells us to do them, so (within wider limits) it becomes our duty to do things if God tells us to do them. For example, it would not be a duty to worship God especially on Sundays if God did not tell us to do so; but, if God tells us to worship him then, it becomes our duty. (And if his command refers to Saturdays or Fridays instead, then our duty is to worship him then.) And, if God tells us to do something which is our duty anyway for other reasons (e.g. to ensure that our own children are fed and educated), it becomes even more our duty to do that thing. God is thus a source of moral obligation – his commands create moral obligations. But God clearly cannot make things which are our duty no longer our duty: he cannot make it right to torture children for fun. That being so, it follows from his perfect goodness that he will not command us to do so – for it is wrong to command what is wrong.

It may surprise some modern readers to suppose that a theist can allow that some moral truths are moral truths quite independent of the will of God. This is, however, an issue on which the Christian philosophical tradition has been split right down the middle; and I side with two of its greatest representatives – St Thomas Aquinas and the fourteenth-century Scottish philosopher Duns Scotus – in holding that there are moral truths independent of the will of God. God can only enforce these, not alter them. But, if there are moral truths such as "it is wrong to torture children for fun" which hold independently of the will of God, they will be like "no shape can be both round and square at the same time"; they must hold whatever the world is like, and that is because there is no sense ultimately in supposing them not to hold.

Good actions are of two kinds. There are obligations (i.e. duties), and there are good actions beyond obligation – called supererogatory good actions. We are blameworthy if we fail to fulfil our obligations but normally not praiseworthy for fulfilling them. Conversely, no blame attaches to us if we fail to do some supererogatory good act, but we are praiseworthy if we do it. Just where the line is to be drawn is not always obvious. But it is clear that there is a line. If I borrow money, I have an obligation to repay. If I fail to repay borrowed money, I am blameworthy; but I do not normally deserve any praise for repaying the money. Conversely, I have no obligation to throw myself on a grenade which is about to explode in order to save the life of a friend who is standing close. But if I do the action, I deserve the highest praise. Obligations mostly arise from benefits voluntarily accepted or undertakings voluntarily entered into. I have no obligation to marry and have children; but, if I do have children, I have an obligation to feed and educate them. This suggests that God before he creates any other persons has no obligations, though it is a supererogatory good act for him to create many other persons including humans. If he does create them, he will then incur certain obligations towards them. Exactly what those are may be disputed, but the Christian tradition has normally maintained, for example, that, if God makes promises to us, he is obliged to keep them.

To fail to fulfil your obligations is always an overall bad act, but obligations are limited. God can easily, and in virtue of his perfect goodness will easily, fulfil all his obligations. But there is no limit to the possible acts of supererogatory goodness which a person can do except any limit arising from his or her powers. We humans have limited powers; and can do only a few limited supererogatory good acts. I can give my savings to one charity, but then I will be unable to give anything to another charity. If I devote my life to caring for one group of children in England, I shall be unable to care for another group of children in a distant land. God's powers, however, are unlimited. But even God, we have seen, cannot do the logically impossible. And it is logically impossible to do every possible supererogatory good act. It is good that God should create persons, including human persons. But, however many he creates, it would be even better if he created more (perhaps well spaced out in an infinitely large universe). Given that human life is in general a good thing, the more of it the better. God cannot create the best of all possible worlds, for there can be no such world – any world can be improved by adding more persons to it, and no doubt in plenty of other ways as well. So what does God's perfect goodness amount to? Not that he does all possible good acts – that is not logically possible. Presumably that he fulfils his obligations, does no bad acts, and performs very many good acts.

So God's perfect goodness places very little restriction on which actions he will do. The restriction that he must perform no bad acts, and so fulfil all his obligations, may limit somewhat what he can do with creatures while he keeps them in being. But it does not, I suggest, oblige him to keep them in being forever (good though it is in some cases that he should), let alone create them in the first place. But there is open to God an infinite range of good acts: infinitely many different universes which he could create, and infinitely many different things he could do with them – all possible expressions of creative overflowing love. Yet, although there are infinitely many different universes he could create, there are perhaps only a small number of *kinds* of universe he could create. He could create universes containing some persons of limited powers such as humans, or universes without such persons. And the obvious goodness of at least one universe of the former kind makes it quite likely that he will create one. But there is no limit to the possibilities of how many persons it could contain, and indeed which persons they are. God must choose which to do of the infinitely many good actions, each of which he has a reason to do. So, like ourselves in a situation where we have a choice between actions each of which we have equal reason to do, God must perform a "mental toss-up" – decide, that is, on which reason to act in a way which is not determined by his nature or anything else. We can understand such an operation of non-determined rational choice, for we seem sometimes to experience it in ourselves.

So it follows from God being everlastingly omnipotent, omniscient, and perfectly free that he is everlastingly bodiless, omnipresent, creator and sustainer of the universe, perfectly good, and a source of moral obligation. But theism does not claim merely that the person who is God has these properties of being everlastingly omnipotent, omniscient, and perfectly free. It claims that God has these properties necessarily – these are *essential properties* of God. Let me explain what this means. Every object has some essential properties and some accidental (i.e. non-essential) properties. The essential properties of an object are those which it cannot lose without ceasing to exist. One of the essential properties of my desk, for example, is that it occupies space. It could not cease to occupy space (become disembodied) and yet continue to exist. By contrast, one of its accidental properties is being brown. It could still exist if I painted it red so that it was no longer brown. Persons are essentially objects with the potential to have (intentional) powers, purposes, and beliefs. I may be temporarily paralysed and unconscious and so have temporarily lost the power to think or move my limbs. But, if I lose the potential to have these powers (if I lose them beyond the power of medical or other help to restore them), then I cease to exist. On the other hand, my powers can grow or diminish, and my beliefs can change (I can forget things I once knew, and acquire new areas of knowledge), while the same I continues to exist through all the change.

By contrast, theism maintains that the personal being who is God cannot lose any of his powers or knowledge or become subject to influence by desire. If God lost any of his powers, he would cease to exist, just as my desk would cease to exist if it ceased to occupy space. And eternity (that is, everlastingness) also being an essential property of God, no individual who had begun to exist or could cease to exist would be God.

If, as theism maintains, there is a God who is essentially eternally omnipotent, omniscient, and perfectly free, then he will be the ultimate brute fact which explains everything else. God is responsible for the existence of everything else besides himself and for it being as it is and having the powers and liabilities it does; by his continual action at each moment of time, God's own existence is the only thing whose existence God's action does not explain. For that there is no explanation. In that sense God is a necessary being, something which exists under its own steam, not dependent on anything else.

So that is the God whom theists (Christian, Jewish, and Islamic among others) claim to exist. Why should we believe them? To answer that question we must look at the criteria which scientists, historians and others use when they put forward their theories about the causes of what they observe.

5

Omnipotence and Omniscience

T. V. Morris

The Power of God

[...]

The magnitude of divine power

Picking up on many passages in the Bible, Christians throughout the centuries have characterized God as "almighty" and "all-powerful." Philosophers and theologians have sought to register the magnitude of divine power by saying that God is *omnipotent*. They have also put a great deal of effort into trying to explain precisely what this means. What exactly is it to be perfectly powerful?

Philosophers have explored two ways of explicating the concept of omnipotence. There is first of all, and most commonly, the attempt to specify the magnitude of omnipotence by indicating the range of things an omnipotent being can do – the range of acts he can perform, tasks he can accomplish, or states of affairs he can bring about. This sort of analysis usually begins with the simple, commonplace religious assertion that:

(1)   God can do everything,

and proceeds to test its initially unrestricted universality ("everything") against various logical,

Thomas V. Morris, "The Power of God" and "God's Knowledge," from *Our Idea of God: An Introduction to Philosophical Theology* (Vancouver: Regent College Publishing), pp. 65–81, 86–102.

metaphysical, and theological intuitions which seem to call for more cautious qualification. For example, it is often pointed out that if "everything" is meant to encompass the logically impossible as well as the logically possible, then (1) entails that God can create spherical cubes, and married bachelors, as well as bring about states of affairs in which he both does and does not exist at one and the same time. But to say that God is so powerful that he can do the logically impossible is not pious or reverential; it is just confused. For logically impossible tasks are not just particularly esoteric and unusually difficult tasks – when you have attempted to describe an act or task and end up with the expression of a logical impossibility, you end up with nothing that can even be a candidate for power ascriptions. To put it vividly, in many such descriptions we can say that one half of the description just cancels the other half out, and vice versa. For instance, if we ask God to create a "married bachelor," each of the two terms cancels the other out. It is as if we were to write something down and then immediately erase it – the net result being nothing at all, no task specified. Now, not all impossibility can be thought of in even roughly this way. But the general point is that if we insist that God can do the logically impossible, we find that if we were to attempt to describe the results of his so doing, we violate the conditions under which, and under which alone, we are able to engage in coherent discourse capable of describing reality. So, most philosophers suggest that (1) be qualified accordingly, resulting in something like:

(2) God can do everything logically possible,

which is still quite an extraordinary claim. For the rest of us, there is a tremendous disparity between what is logically possible and what we can do. For God, (2) tells us, there is no such gap.

But even (2) seems insufficiently cautious, many philosophers have urged. For, assuming that each of us has free will, it is logically possible for us to do something not done by God. But we do not want to say that God can do something not done by God. That is to say, we do not want to commit ourselves to holding, because of what (2) stipulates, that God could possibly do something which would be such that, once done, it would properly bear the description "Not done by God." This, again, is just confused. So perhaps we need to be a little more careful still and express the range of God's power by saying that:

(3) Anything which it is logically possible for God to do, he can do.

And this is a phrasing which does not commit us to holding that God can do things "not done by God," or make things not made by God. It is impossible that God make a table thereafter properly described as "Not made by God," and so (3) does not locate such a task within the range of divine omnipotence. But (3) still expresses an extraordinary conception of divine power. It is logically possible for me to bench-press eight hundred pounds, but I can't do it. There is a tremendous disparity between what is logically possible *for me* and what is in my power. And (3) assures us that there is no such disparity faced by God.

But certain features of (3) can still be seen as problematic. The content of (3) leaves open the possibility that God could be by nature weak in numerous ways, that he could be such that many basic tasks are impossible for him, and yet by the conditions expressed in (3) still qualify as omnipotent. Any weakness that was essential to God, such that overcoming it would be logically impossible for him, would be compatible with calling him omnipotent. But do we want to allow this? Surely, some further rephrasing is called for. Perhaps:

(4) Anything that it is logically possible for a perfect being to do, God can do

would solve our problems. For any weakness is surely an imperfection. And an essential weakness would be an even greater imperfection. (4), accordingly, does not allow what (3) would seem to allow, namely, the compatibility between essential weaknesses and omnipotence.

The informativeness of (4), however, depends on our having some prior sense of what it is logically possible for a perfect being to do. And if part of perfection is omnipotence, we seem to confront here a sort of circularity that should at least give us pause. [. . .] There is an alternative, however. We can seek to explore the notion of omnipotence not in terms of the range of *things God can do*, but a bit more abstractly, and at the same time, at least potentially, more simply, in terms of *powers God possesses*.

The idea of a power is a very basic, fundamental idea. It is such a basic idea that it is very difficult to analyze or explain, since analysis and explanation typically break up the complex into the simple, or illuminate the unfamiliar by reference to the familiar. We normally give an account of one idea by explaining it in terms of more basic ideas. But the idea of a power is so basic in our conceptualization of the world that it is hard to find much to say in elucidation of it. But we can say a few things that are helpful for getting our bearings.

Our first acquaintance with power is, presumably, our experience of the power of personal agency. Other people act upon us, and we act upon them, as well as upon the world around us. When a small child wants a toy, he reaches for it and moves it closer to where he sits. He has exercised his power upon the world around him to get what he wants, to effect the satisfaction of his desires. He finds that he does not just have desires caused in him by things in the world; he finds that he himself can form intentions and cause changes in the world in response to those desires. He experiences, in his own small way, power – causal power.

This is arguably the most fundamental, or at least is closely related to the most fundamental, kind of power. The most fundamental sort of power, in the sense of ultimacy, would be the power to create *ex nihilo* ("from nothing"), the sheer power to bring into existence things which are not brought into being merely by the arrangement of previously existing things. Some philosophers categorize this as a kind of causal power – the power to cause being. Others divide the conceptual terrain a bit differently, and think of causal power as power which can only be exercised upon previously existing things, in accordance with causal laws which are already in place. Regardless of whether creative and causal power are distinguished as basically different kinds of power, or whether the former is treated as just the ultimate instance of the latter, both are metaphysical forms of power and are thus relevant to our understanding of the power of God.

In this regard, creative and causal power are to be distinguished from what we refer to as "political power" and "legal power." When we talk of political power we often mean to refer to no more than the entrenchment or institutionalization of personal influence or group influence with respect to matters of political governance. In legal matters, the power of attorney is just an authority, duly conferred upon one, to act for another person in business dealings or kindred actions. Political and legal power are powers defined in terms of, and dependent upon, previously existing rules or practices forming human social activity. If I am not a participant rightly placed in the appropriate practices or institutions, I cannot be said to have various powers of this sort. As God is not a creature participating in such creaturely institutions, he is not said to have power in these senses, but rather always in the more fundamental metaphysical sense.

Some further distinctions can be drawn to help us better understand the role of causal power in our conceptualization of the world. In our thought and talk about the world, we often attribute power, or the lack of certain powers, to objects and people. We often say what someone "can" or "cannot" do, and we sometimes assume that such talk always can be translated into talk about powers. But if I say of some task x that Jones cannot do x, I do not necessarily ascribe to Jones any lack of power at all. The little word "can" can serve many different functions; the word "cannot" cannot always be assumed to mean the same thing. Can-locutions sometimes attribute power. Often they do not. Likewise, cannot-locutions sometimes attribute lack of power. But often they do not. When I say "Jones cannot do x," I may mean that Jones lacks the *power* necessary for doing x. Or I may think he has the power, but lacks the *skill* requisite for using that power to do x. Or, again, I may grant him the power and the skill, but believe that he lacks the *opportunity* for drawing on that power, by means of that skill, in the circumstances in which he finds himself. But even with all the requisite power, skill, and opportunity, poor Jones may lack the *practical knowledge* of his situation – of his power, skill, and opportunity, as well as of how they could come together for the performance of x – necessary for the doing of x. And it may be *this* lack I mean to

convey, or which I have in mind, when I say "Jones cannot do x."

One other distinction can be drawn here, one relating to questions of moral character. Suppose that a young boy with a precociously obnoxious personality and a proclivity to mischief lives down the street from old Jones. He bothers Jones daily in extremely irritating ways. A neighbor who witnesses this regular harassment comments to a mutual friend, "If I were Jones, I'd throttle the kid. Why doesn't he just catch him, wrap his hands around that loud, whiny windpipe, and give it a good long squeeze?" The friend might reply, "Jones could not possibly do anything like that. He's not capable of such behavior." The friend need not be attributing to Jones any lack of physical power, skill, opportunity, or practical knowledge here. In fact, he's probably not. Often, when we say that a certain person is not "capable" of a morally dubious or improper line of action, what we mean to indicate is that doing such a thing would be contrary to a firmly entrenched character that person has, that the desire or inclination to perform the action is not within the range of his possible desires and inclinations, or that a serious intention to engage in the action is prohibited by a stable moral stance characteristic of that person. And this is a very different matter from anything having to do with power, skill, opportunity, or practical knowledge. We can somewhat stipulatively refer to this matter as a consideration of "moral capability," or just *capability*, to set it apart from the other factors we have identified as determinative with respect to what a person can or cannot do.

We can think of power, skill, opportunity and practical knowledge as comprising one cluster of factors concerning what an individual can or cannot do, and capability as defining the moral dimension relevant to this. But there is often one final factor potentially involved in action, and it is difficult to know whether to classify it with the larger cluster of factors which we can refer to as "the ability–cluster," or rather with the moral dimension of capability. What I have in mind is often called "will power," and is just the element of determination or persistence in pursuing a line of action which takes either time or effort to attain or complete. A person may have the requisite ability–cluster, as already identified, for x, and it may be that doing x is consistent with the person's settled values, but the individual cannot do x because of a lack of will power or determination. This can be viewed as something more akin to a

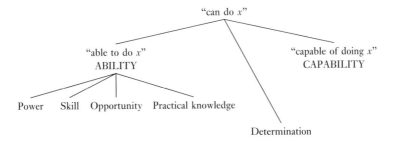

Figure 1

lack of power, or as something more like a moral weakness. Perhaps we can allot to it an intermediate status, as in figure 1.

Our informal, colloquial uses of "can" and "cannot" irregularly convey many different things. They do not always convey convictions about power. We can understand the conceptual terrain that our idea of power in the metaphysical sense is meant to cover only if we keep it distinct from these other many different ideas with which it is often confused when we talk simply of what an individual can or cannot do. This, in part, is what makes any explication of omnipotence in terms of what God can do such a complicated business. And it is this which, when kept in mind, will help us to understand and defend the simpler conception of omnipotence in terms of powers possessed.

[. . .] Along these lines, it can be said that when we describe God as omnipotent, we commit ourselves to his having every power which it is logically possible to possess. This is a very simple account of omnipotence, and seems clearly to present a view sufficiently exalted to accord with the perspective of perfect being theology. Indeed, it is a view which looks tailor-made for this perspective, for it is impossible to imagine coherently any greater account of perfect power.

Problems for divine power

Many critics of theism have alleged that calling God omnipotent, or perfect in power, lands the theist in a number of difficult philosophical problems. One particularly renowned problem is known as "the paradox of the stone." Somewhat akin to the form of argument known as the *reductio ad absurdum* ("reduction to absurdity"), the stone paradox arises in the asking and answering of a question. With this question-and-answer dynamic, the critic is trying to show that the ascription of

omnipotence to God is self-defeating, or that the notion itself of omnipotence is incoherent.

The question is this: If God is omnipotent, then can he create a stone which he cannot lift (cause to rise)? If the answer is "no," then, the critic reasons, there is something God cannot do, namely, create the sort of stone in question, and so he is not, after all, omnipotent. If the answer is "yes," he can create such a stone, then again there is a task he cannot perform, namely, lift the stone once created, and therefore again he is not omnipotent. Regardless of which answer is given to the question, the conclusion follows that God is not omnipotent. But we were assuming that he is. So the supposition that God is omnipotent must be ultimately self-defeating or incoherent. Therefore, there cannot be such a being. This is the critic's argument.

First, it should be noted that the critic is assuming throughout that if there is something specifiable that God cannot do, it follows that he lacks omnipotence. But if omnipotence is understood as perfect power, this is too quick an inference. For if it is true to say with respect to some particular act-description that God cannot perform the sort of act described, then it seems to follow only that God lacks either the power, the skill, the opportunity, the determination or the moral capability to exercise his power in that way. It does not directly follow that there is some power that God lacks. And if the act-description itself is incoherent, such as "create a married bachelor," it does not follow that God lacks anything at all, save perhaps the opportunity to exercise his perfect power in response to the act-description with which he is presented, since an incoherent act-description does not present even a possible candidate for action. [. . .]

The critic is asking whether God can create a certain kind of stone – a stone which is such that he, a being who by supposition is omnipotent, cannot lift it, or cause it to rise. What is the relevant act-description here? It seems to be "creating a stone that even a being with every logically possible power can't lift." But what would such a stone be like? What, for example, would it weigh? If God is omnipotent, then, presumably, he can create stones of any possible weight. But if he is omnipotent, then, presumably as well, for any possible weight n, he can lift stones of weight n. Realizing this has led some philosophers to one of the simplest solutions which has been offered to the stone paradox. They have just claimed that "creating a stone which even an omnipotent being can't lift," and all its analytical equivalents, is just an incoherent act-description. And since the phrase "the power to create a stone which even an omnipotent being can't lift" does not designate a logically possible power, it does not follow from the fact that God cannot create such a stone that God lacks any power required for omnipotence, or that he lacks in any other respect. This solution maintains that the proper answer to our original question is "no," but that does not cause any problems for the ascription of omnipotence to God.

Other philosophers remain unconvinced that we have here an incoherent act-description. They suggest that even if it is impossible to specify the weight or size of a stone that would render it unliftable by an omnipotent being, there still might be a possible form or source of immobility which can't be overcome even by God. One suggestion is that if God is supposed to be truly omnipotent, why couldn't he create a stone which was endowed with the property of being essentially unliftable, though not because of its weight, or size, or any such distinct feature? Why couldn't there just be a stone which directly, not because of or through other properties, has the property of being impossible to lift or move? And if such a stone is possible, then surely the creation of such a stone is possible as well. So if God cannot create it, then he lacks a power it is possible to have.

It may be difficult to imagine how something could be a physical object and have the property of being necessarily immobile or unliftable. What would account for such a property? How would it work? By means of what possible laws could it operate? But even if such a property is in the end inconceivable, such philosophers could suggest, couldn't God just create an ordinary stone and promise never to move it, thereby rendering it true that he subsequently cannot lift it? And, implausible as such a scenario might be, if it is possible, then the answer to our question is not "no" after

all but, rather, "yes": God can create a stone he cannot lift.

But any action from which God is debarred by having made a promise is not, in virtue of its inaccessibility to him, thereby indicative of a lack of *power*. This would clearly be a case in which God lacks not a certain *ability* but a *moral capability* of doing the evil of breaking his promise. So there is a potential threat to omnipotence only from the less likely, or more perplexing, possibility of a stone he brought into existence with the essential property of unliftability, or immobility.

Suppose for a moment that God could create and did create such a stone S. Should we then say that God lacks the power to lift S? Is there a discrete power properly individuated as "the power to lift S"? Well, if S is essentially unliftable, there can be no single exercise of a "power to lift S." Thus, lacking a power to lift S is not lacking a possible power, a power possible to have, and so no such lack would detract from God's being omnipotent.

I shall not argue for just one of these two possible solutions to the paradox of the stone. Either will suffice. If we choose to say that God *cannot* create a stone he can't lift, we can block the inference to his lacking omnipotence and explain the apparent divine inability by characterizing the act-description here as incoherent. If we choose to say that he *can* create such a stone which, once created, he cannot lift, we can block the inference to his lacking omnipotence by explaining that the subsequent inability to lift cannot be thought of as reflecting the lack of any power it is possible to have. But by either strategy the claim of omnipotence for God is defended.

[. . .]

In just the last few years another problem relating to omnipotence has emerged. A number of philosophers have suggested that necessary goodness is incompatible with omnipotence. The argument goes like this: If God is supposed to be omnipotent, he is supposed to have every power it is logically possible to possess. Now, surely, it is logically possible to possess the power to sin. This is a power all too common among human beings. So it is a power which should be ascribed to an omnipotent being, in accordance with the definition or explication of omnipotence we are using. But one cannot have the power to perform a certain type of action A unless it is possible for one to perform actions of this type. Possibility is required for power. But we have just argued in the previous chapter [not included here] that it is proper for the perfect being theologian to think of God as necessarily good, as being such that it is impossible for him to sin. On the perspective of perfect being theology, then, God must lack the power to sin. And so, on this way of thinking, he cannot be ascribed omnipotence after all.

There are two possible ways of responding to this objection. First, we could acknowledge that there is a special, discrete power to sin, a power humans have and God lacks. Along these lines, we would then have to revise our conception of the magnitude of divine power. We might still want to call God "omnipotent," but we would then have to qualify [the] account of what this means and offer something like the more restrictive gloss:

(P)   God has every power it is logically possible for a being perfect in every other respect to possess.

This strategy for reconciling ascriptions of perfect goodness and omnipotence to God might be judged effective as long as three important theistic beliefs about God's power were respected by any such restriction:

(1)   There can be no independent, externally determined constraints on God's power.

God is sovereign in the world. He is not hemmed in by any other competitive power. If moral principles are then thought of as constraints on God's power, morality cannot be thought of as independent of, or external to, God. [. . .]

(2)   The internally determined structure and scope of God's possibilities of action (the limits on divine action set by God's own nature and decisions) are not, and cannot be, such that he lacks any power which otherwise would be an ingredient in perfection.

Neither God's nature, in its other facets, nor his decisions can have a negative impact on the perfection of the power available to him. Perfection is not self-destructive or self-undermining. Finally,

(3)   God is the sole source of all the power there is or could be.

This assurance, along with a strong conception of divine goodness and wisdom, disallows the implication following from the restricted account of

divine power that there could even possibly be a being with all the power God does have *plus* a power to sin, a being independent of God who could possibly, through the having of this greater total array of power, ultimately thwart God's purposes and plans. With all this in mind, a restricted account of God's power could be a usable solution to the problem raised by the apparent existence of a power to sin.

But the best solution to this problem, I think, will involve denying that there is a discrete causal power to sin. If [. . .] we do hold that God is necessarily good, we do believe that it is impossible that God sin. This can be stated by saying that God cannot sin. But it may be sheer carelessness to think that this is the same as saying, or that it even implies, that God lacks some power, namely, what has been, so far, loosely referred to as "the power to sin."

How do we identify discrete powers? The idea of a power is a very fundamental notion. We typically identify powers with a certain standard locution, employing the infinitives of verbs along with verb phrases. We speak, for example, of "the power to lift one hundred pounds," "the power to communicate through an earthly language," "the power to create a stone." Now there are, no doubt, many sorts of power of which we have no conception and for which we have no ready-made power locutions of this type. But in another respect, our language is much richer than the underlying metaphysical realities having to do with power. For consider the two phrases (power locutions):

(A)   the power to lift a blue two-ounce pencil
(B)   the power to lift a yellow two-ounce pencil.

I have whatever power is designated by (A). I have whatever power is designated by (B). The power locutions (A) and (B) are two distinct locutions. It doesn't follow that they express two different powers, or that by being able to lift blue and yellow pencils I should be credited with two different powers. There is, presumably, only one basic power referred to differently by these two different power phrases.

So, distinct power locutions are no guarantee of correspondingly distinct powers. Nor is the mere existence of a power locution of the appropriate form any guarantee that there is a discrete power referred to by the phrase. Consider as an extreme instance: "the power to see to it that there never were any powers at all." There cannot be a discrete power referred to by this phrase. And whatever power is referred to by (A) and (B) has absolutely nothing intrinsically to do with anything regarding color. The surface grammar of power locutions can be misleading in numerous ways.

Following an example once presented by St. Anselm, we can see that to say of a certain man that "he cannot lose in battle" is not to attribute to him any lack of power. It attributes any real lack only to his enemies. Likewise, to say of God that he cannot sin should not be taken to imply on God's part any lack of power. It only indicates a necessarily firm directedness in the way in which God will *use* his unlimited power.

I would like to suggest that there is no discrete power referred to by the phrase "the power to sin." There are many powers necessary for sinning in various ways, but there is no single, distinct power to sin exercised in addition to all other powers exercised on any and every occasion of the intentional doing of evil. Suppose Jones wrongfully hits Smith in the face, intending to cause him pain. Jones must have and exercise the power to make a fist, the power to swing and aim his fist, and so forth, in order to commit the deed. Does he need an additional causal power once he has all those physical powers, a distinct power to sin? I do not think so. Drawing upon the chart presented earlier in this chapter (figure 1), we could say that Jones is capable of using his power in a way a more saintly person would not, and in a way a perfect person could not. The difference is not in the powers possessed, but in the moral capacity for employing those powers.

To account for why it is that a certain person cannot perform a certain kind of act, we need not, and should not, always suppose that a lack of power is what is involved. In the present case, to account for why God cannot do evil, we need not, and should not, attribute this divine guarantee to inability or lack of power. It is due, rather, entirely to God's perfection of character. There is no power to sin which God lacks. So there is here no exception to his being thought of as altogether omnipotent after all.

But the following problem could be raised. Even if it is granted that there is no incoherence about the ascription of omnipotence to God, and even if there is no glaring counterexample to the claim that God has every power it is logically possible to possess, how can the positive ascription of omnipotence ever be justified? To defend omnipotence against objections is not yet to provide any positive ground for thinking of God as omnipotent. And it can be thought that the provision of a positive ground would be impossible.

How do we justify power ascriptions? Typically, on the basis of observation. We see a person perform an action or range of actions and ascribe to him whatever kind or degree of power would be necessary for the performance we have witnessed. But under what conditions could any finite number of observations of divine conduct warrant or justify the ascription of omnipotence to God? Suppose God somehow were observed performing extraordinary miracles, in whatever mode of observation is appropriate. Would any number of such dramatic actions legitimate the claim that God has every power it is logically possible to possess? Suppose we know God to have created the entire existent universe. Would even *that* piece of astounding information call for the postulation of omnipotence, and nothing less? It is hard to see how any finite observations and data could ever demand, or even justify, so extreme an ascription of power as that ingredient in the attribution of omnipotence. And if this is so, one recent writer has suggested, not only could *we* never know or justifiably believe that God is omnipotent, he himself could not know or justifiably believe it. For, no matter how many tough tasks he proposed to himself and accomplished without the least effort, the literal ascription, or self-ascription, of omnipotence would go beyond the theoretical demands of explaining the observations made. Omnipotence is that extreme a notion.

The answer to this challenge is actually simple. First, God does not come to know himself inferentially, from making observations about his own conduct and extrapolating from those observations to their best theoretical explanations. God knows himself directly, as St. Thomas Aquinas taught us. Second, we do not have to rely upon observation and inference for all our ascriptions of properties to God. We hold that God is literally omnipotent because of the requirements of perfect being theology, as it encapsulates and extends the data of revelation. We derive the belief in strict omnipotence as a divine attribute not inductively from observation, but deductively from the conceptual and intuitive resources of perfect being theology. As a perfect being, God is perfect in power. We are justified in thinking of God as perfect in this respect, as in every other, unless there is well-attested revelation or credible human experience to the contrary. Observation is a constraint upon, but not the sole source of, our ideas about God.

God's Knowledge

[. . .]

God's knowledge and the future: the problem

The completeness of God's knowledge is often referred to as his *omniscience*. By claiming that God is omniscient, theists typically mean to say that

(1) God has all propositional knowledge

and

(2) God has perfect acquaintance with all things.

Propositional knowledge is, simply put, knowledge that can be expressed by indicative sentences or "that-clauses": God knows that football and philosophy are two active enterprises at Notre Dame; God knows that the earth is the third planet from the sun; God knows that $2 + 2 = 4$; God knows that equality is a transitive relation; and so forth. Following a number of their medieval predecessors (who wrote in Latin), philosophers often refer to this as knowledge *de dicto*. In ordinary language we sometimes distinguish between having knowledge *about* an object or person and more directly knowing that thing or person. I may have a great deal of knowledge about guitarist Eric Clapton without its being true that I know him. I may know about Paris from reading many descriptions and histories of that city. But ordinarily, I can't be said to know Paris unless I have been there to establish intimate firsthand acquaintance with its many delights. The firsthand intimacy of knowledge by acquaintance is often referred to by philosophers as knowledge *de re*. The extent of God's omniscience includes absolute completeness in both knowledge *de dicto* and knowledge *de re*.

God is also thought to be *infallible* as a knower. He cannot go wrong or possibly hold any false beliefs. Not only is God omniscient, he is *necessarily omniscient* – it is impossible that his omniscience collapse, fail, or even waver. He is, as philosophers nowadays often say, omniscient in *every possible world*. That is to say, he is actually omniscient, and there is no possible, complete, and coherent story about any way things could have gone (no "possible world") in which God lacks this degree of cognitive excellence.

In order to appreciate fully the status of divine knowledge, we need to make some further clarifications. The proposition that *God is omniscient* is a necessarily true proposition. There are no circumstances possible under which it is false. But the precise sense in which this is so needs to be clarified. For the proposition that *bachelors are unmarried men* is also a necessary truth, following, as it does, from the concept of bachelorhood. Yet we would never say of an individual bachelor, Ted, Fred, or Ned, that *he* is necessarily unmarried. However confirmed his bachelorhood may be, however apparently hopeless his nuptial prospects might be, it is always at least *possible* for him to marry. Even concerning someone who lives and dies a bachelor, it can be said that it was at least logically or metaphysically *possible* for him to have wed. Being unmarried is a logically necessary condition of bachelorhood, but being a bachelor is not a necessary life condition of anyone who happens to be single.

The case of God's omniscience contrasts with this in an interesting way. Consider the English sentence:

(B) Bachelors are unmarried men.

This sentence expresses a proposition (roughly, the content it conveys). It expresses a truth. It expresses a necessity. But it expresses a necessity only in the sense of conveying a necessary truth with respect to the conditions of bachelorhood. The concept of bachelorhood is such that it yields (B) as a necessary truth. That is to say, (B) expresses a necessity *de dicto*. It does not express a necessity *de re*, concerning some particular individual, some particular bachelor. It does not say of any particular bachelors that *they* are necessarily unmarried men.

Now consider the English sentence:

(G) God is omniscient.

This sentence expresses a proposition. It expresses a truth, and it expresses a necessity. In much the same way that (B) serves as a partial explication of bachelorhood, (G) can be seen as a partial explication of deity. On this reading, (G) presents a necessary condition for holding the exalted position, or having the maximal status, of *being God*. It expresses a necessity *de dicto*. But most theists influenced by the method of perfect being theology insist that it expresses a necessity *de re* as well. Not only is omniscience necessary for divinity, divinity is a necessary or essential property of any individual who has it. Unlike the property of being a bachelor, which is a contingent or accidental property, the property of being God is best thought of as a necessary or essential property. An individual who is God does not just happen to have that status. It is not a property he could have done without. Things at the top are more stable than this. In particular, omniscience is as firmly rooted in God, or God is as firmly rooted in omniscience, as it is possible to be. Omniscience is thus not only a necessary condition of deity, it is a necessary or essential property for any individual who is God. No literally divine person is even possibly vulnerable to ignorance.

This distinction in levels of necessity, so to speak, is customarily captured by different forms of expression such as:

(G1) Necessarily, God is omniscient,

which standardly expresses the necessity *de dicto*, and

(G2) God is necessarily omniscient,

which standardly expresses the necessity *de re*. In fact, the most exalted form of Anselmian theology will insist that (G2) expresses a necessity *de dicto* as well: Not only is omniscience a requirement for deity, necessary or essential omniscience is as well. A being who was even possibly vulnerable to ignorance would not be a greatest possible being. So perfection requires essential omniscience.

This is a very strong picture of the state of God's knowledge. In fact, many people have thought that it is far too strong. The problem is that if God's knowledge is absolutely complete and he cannot possibly hold a false belief about anything, an argument can be constructed which seems to show that there cannot be any genuine freedom, any authentically free will, in the world at all. The problem posed by this argument is widely known as the *problem of foreknowledge and free will*.

Initially, at least, it seems that in order for God's knowledge to be absolutely complete, he must know everything about the past, everything about the present, and everything about the future as well. But if he now knows, and always has known, how each and every one of us will act, in every detail, on every occasion in the future, how can we possibly be thought to be free in our actions, selecting among alternatives equally available to us? If God already knows exactly how we *shall* act, what else can we possibly do? We must act in that way. We cannot diverge from the path that he sees we shall take. We cannot prove God wrong. He is necessarily omniscient. Divine foreknowledge thus seems to preclude genuine alternatives, and thus genuine freedom in the world.

Notice that nothing has been said here about complete divine *predestination*, which is an exercise of God's *power* to determine the future in each and every detail. This argument has arisen solely from a consideration of the completeness of God's *knowledge*. In order to appreciate the distinctiveness of the problem posed by foreknowledge, let us first linger a bit over the distinct idea of total predestination.

Some theists endorse the idea that God has eternally predestined, or predetermined, the course of history in every detail. God is, remember, to be thought of as the omnipotent creator of all things. It is typically taken to be a corollary of this that God is sovereign over all things. He is, in the most ultimate way possible, in control of all things, however unlikely this may sometimes appear. So far, most theists are in agreement. Where total predestinarians diverge from other theists is in their interpretation of what such sovereign control requires. It is their contention that God could not be in complete control of the course of history unless he himself authored the story in all its details. Thus, they conclude, God predestines, or foreordains, or predetermines all things. But then, consider the following simple argument:

(1) God's power is irresistible.
Thus,
(2) For any event x, if God determines x, then no one is in a position to prevent x.
(3) For any event x, if no one is in a position to prevent x, then no one is free with respect to x.
(4) For every event x, God determines x.
Therefore,
(5) No one distinct from God is free with respect to any event.
And so,
(6) Human free will is a complete illusion.

In this argument, premise (1) follows from our understanding of the perfection of God's power. Line (2) is an immediate consequence of (1). Line (3) results from our ordinary conception of what it is to be free. Line (4) presents the thesis of total predestination. And finally, lines (5) and (6) draw the sad conclusions from these previous steps.

In so far as most theists believe that we are free, and thus morally responsible, for at least a great many of our actions, they reject (5) and (6), and so must reject one of the steps leading up to (5) and (6). The weak link in the argument is typically judged to be line (4), the thesis of total predestination, and so that view is rejected, in order to preserve the more deeply entrenched belief in human freedom. And, fortunately for those of us convinced of the reality of human freedom, whatever its limitations, it is possible to understand God's sovereignty as involving less than the predetermination of every detail of cosmic history. A teacher can be in control of a classroom without herself causing every move the students make. In order to endorse God's omnipotence, recognize his creation of all, and acknowledge his ultimate control of things, it is not necessary to embrace the doctrine of total predestination.

The challenge of foreknowledge has seemed to many people a little less easy to shake. It is a good deal more natural to suppose that the completeness of God's knowledge requires a full awareness of what the future holds than it is to suppose that the completeness of his control of creation requires that he causally predetermines everything that ever happens in the world. And the biblical documents seem to contain a great many instances of prophecy or prediction which appear to be based on a divine foreknowledge of the future. So the idea that God is a perfect knower of the future must be taken very seriously indeed.

But, as we have noted, this creates a problem. To appreciate the force of that problem, we should lay out a single straightforward argument, as we did for the idea of total predestination. Stating such an argument will help us to see the interrelation of ideas which generate the problem. To make everything as clear as possible, we'll start from a claim about God's *beliefs*, rather than stating the argument in terms of his knowledge. Whenever someone knows something, we can distinguish the object of knowledge, or the fact that is known, on the one hand, from the knower's mental state of belief, or awareness, by means of which he is connected with what is known, on the other hand. For God to have complete foreknowledge of the future is for him to have comprehensive belief states, or states of awareness, concerning the future, which constitute knowledge. With this in mind, and picking up on the claims about God's necessary omniscience, we have:

(1) God's beliefs are infallible.

Thus,

(2) For any event x, if God believes in advance that x will occur, then no one is in a position to prevent x.

(3) For any event x, if no one is in a position to prevent x, then no one is free with respect to x.

(4) For every event x that ever occurs, God believes in advance that it will occur.

Therefore,

(5) No one distinct from God is free with respect to any event.

And so,

(6) Human free will is a complete illusion.

What we have here is an argument perfectly parallel in form to the argument for the incompatibility of predestination and free will. Premise (1) expresses the conviction that God cannot possibly go wrong in his beliefs. This is an implication of his essential omniscience. Line (2) of the argument draws quickly the further implication that no one is free to act in such a way as to falsify one of God's beliefs. Step (3) unpacks part of our standard conception of what it is to be free with respect to something. Line (4) presents the thesis of complete divine foreknowledge. And lines (5) and (6) draw the inferences from what has preceded which seem so troubling.

Reactions to the problem

Thoughtful religious believers have reacted in many different ways to arguments like the one just presented. Some have felt compelled by this sort of reasoning to deny that we ever do have genuine freedom in what we do. And once freedom is given up, there is no longer any good reason to reject the total predestination interpretation of divine sovereignty. But few theists are willing to embrace so extreme a conclusion as the belief that we are never really free, never really faced with genuine options or alternatives of action, any one of which we are equally in a position to take. Most of us have such a deep and firm conviction that we are at least sometimes free in what we do, in precisely this sense, that we shall seek in any way possible to resist a philosophical argument which purports to show the contrary. Moreover, the Bible itself and other central theological doctrines seem to presuppose that we are free, and thus morally responsible for our sins as well as for whether or not we seek the proper relation with our creator. Thus, the outright denial of freedom is not a popular response to this argument and arguments of its type.

The harsh conclusions expressed by lines (5) and (6) of the argument can be avoided if we redefine "free will" in such a way that freedom doesn't require genuine options or alternatives for action. The view of freedom as compatible with a lack of options is, naturally enough, known as *compatibilism*. If compatibilism concerning free action is true, it can be argued that line (3) of the argument is false. The compatibilist suggestion is, roughly, that in order to be free with respect to an action, or with respect to the initiation of a train of events, I need not be in a position to refrain from performing the act or to prevent the sequence of events. I am free so long as my activity is in keeping with my intentions or desires in the matter, even if there are no genuine alternatives open to me. Thus, for the compatibilist, whether I have the power, or ability, or opportunity to deviate from the path God already believes I shall take is just irrelevant to the question of whether I am free in what I do. And if this is right, premise (3) of the argument we are examining is just false, and thus we are free to reject its conclusions.

Not many theists, however, have managed to content themselves with a compatibilist view of freedom. Most insist that in order to determine whether an action is free, we need to ask not only whether it occurs in harmony with the desires, choices, and intentions of its agent, but also whether those affective and volitional states – those desires, choices, and intentions – are themselves such that the agent could have refrained from, or prevented himself from, having them. In accordance with this, most theists hold that the ideal paradigm of free action does involve having real alternatives available. Of course, in the Christian world-view, God himself is viewed as the paradigmatically free agent. And he is held to be supremely free in precisely this sense. He is never without real alternatives. So, on a Christian scheme of things, freedom is most naturally viewed as involving alternatives.

The belief that genuine freedom, on any level, is *not* compatible with an utter lack of any real options is known, naturally enough, as *incompatibilism*. (This is the conception of freedom ingredient in the philosophical view known as *libertarianism*, the traditional view that we often are at liberty to originate our own lines of conduct.) An incompatibilist on the issue of how we should understand genuine freedom will insist on acknowledging the truth of premise (3) of our argument. So anyone who endorses this view of freedom, and is committed to the libertarian thesis that we are free, will have to find another point at which to resist this argument for the conclusion that we are never really free.

One possible strategy consists in the attempt to block the inference from premise (1), "God's beliefs are infallible," to line (2), "For any event x, if God believes in advance that x will occur, then no one is in a position to prevent x." In recent discussions of the problem of foreknowledge and free will, at least two versions of this strategy have been attempted. Some philosophers, who endorse a view known as *Ockhamism* (a view influenced by the great medieval thinker William of Ockham), have argued basically as follows: Suppose God has always believed that in exactly five minutes my right index finger will lightly scratch the tip of my nose. God is necessarily omniscient and so, as a believer, he is absolutely infallible. He cannot be wrong. Does it follow that no one is in a position to prevent it from being the case that, nearly five minutes hence, my finger will scratch my nose? Does it follow, in particular, that I am not free with respect to scratching? No, the Ockhamists insist, all that follows is that I *shall* scratch, not that I *must*, or that I lack the power to refrain from scratching. I can prevent the event in question. I can refrain from scratching. This option is open to me. I shall not take it, as a matter of fact, but the alternative is there. And, the Ockhamists add, if I did refrain from scratching, I would not prove God wrong. For if I were to exercise this option and leave the tip of my nose alone, God would have held a belief different from the one he in fact holds – he always would have believed that I would, at the appointed time, have done something else with my right index finger rather than scratching my nose. So the Ockhamists hold that for this event x, I am in a position to prevent x, but as a matter of fact will freely perform x instead. Generalizing, step (2) cannot legitimately be inferred from step (1) in our argument. But without this, the argument collapses and the problem with freedom is avoided.

The difficulty with the Ockhamist strategy is that, presumably, God has already held one particular determinate belief about what I shall do at the time in question. We have been supposing that he has always believed that I shall scratch. How then can I be said to have the option not to do this at the appointed time? I have a real option only if, in the circumstances, I can exercise it. But, by supposition, my circumstances include my already having been seen, or believed, to do one thing by

God, a being who cannot possibly be wrong. We cannot change what already has been. It is not plausible to think that I can act in such a way as to alter what God's belief has already been. Thus it seems that, given all my circumstances (including everything that is already true), I cannot refrain from scratching and so, despite what the Ockhamist says, I shall not be free with respect to that action. And, of course, given the completeness of God's knowledge, this consideration generalizes to all human actions at all times. If the Ockhamist insists that I can now act in such a way as to *change*, or otherwise determine, what God's beliefs in the remote past already were concerning what I shall do, then he swims upstream against some pretty strong intuitions most people have about the impossibility of changing or affecting the past in any substantive way whatsoever.

There is one other attempt to solve the problem of foreknowledge and free will which seeks to block the inference of step (2) from step (1) in the argument we are considering. It draws upon the work of another medieval thinker, Luis de Molina, and goes by the name of *Molinism*. The Molinist view is based on a distinctive conception of the makeup of God's knowledge. The range of divine knowledge is thought of as divided into three types: *natural knowledge* – knowledge God has prior to (conceptually prior to) any act of creation, concerning what all the possibilities of creation are; *free knowledge* – knowledge of everything that will actually happen in the world *given* God's free choice of which possibilities of creation to actualize; and *middle knowledge* – comprehensive knowledge of what contingently, as a matter of fact, *would* result from any creative decision he might make. In this threefold categorization, it is the category of middle knowledge which is most important. Middle knowledge is supposed to encompass an infinite array of propositions sometimes referred to by philosophers as subjunctive conditionals of freedom or, in a slightly less precise but more widely used terminology, *counterfactuals of freedom*. Simply put, a counterfactual of freedom is a proposition specifying how a free being would freely act if placed in a certain total set of circumstances. It is a proposition of the form: If placed in total circumstances C, person P would freely perform action A. The Molinist supposes that for every created person who could possibly exist, every total array of circumstances he could possibly exist in, and every action he could possibly perform, there is a truth of this form. For example, I suppose that there are

many total sets of circumstances in which, if I were offered one hundred dollars to refrain from eating lunch just once this week and go jogging for an hour instead, I would freely skip that meal with great pleasure. I would have the alternative of sticking to my ordinary schedule and not missing a meal. And it would be a genuine alternative. It's just true that I would not take that alternative. I would freely take the money and run. Now, the main way in which it seems that the typical Molinist proposes to reconcile foreknowledge and human freedom is by explaining *how* God foreknows the future free actions of his creatures in every detail. The story is basically very simple. Knowing how every individual he could possibly create would freely act in every complete set of circumstances he could possibly be placed in, God, by deciding who to create and what circumstances to create them in, completely provides himself with the knowledge of everything that will ever happen.

On the Molinist view, line (2) of our argument does not follow from line (1) and is not true because, to use our previous example, God's past belief that I shall scratch my nose is based on his knowing that if I were created and put in certain circumstances (involving, say, a sufficiently itchy nose) then I would *freely* scratch the tip of my nose with my right index finger, along with his deciding to create me in such a way that I would be in those circumstances at the right time. So, when the time comes, it cannot be said, as line (2) of our argument says, that "no one is in a position to prevent x." If I am truly free with respect to scratching, *I* am in a position to prevent its happening, by simply refraining from that action. God knows that I shall freely pass up that option, but it is an option I have. The counterfactual of freedom which provided for God's belief and thus his foreknowledge was precisely that – a counterfactual, or subjunctive conditional, *of freedom*. Molinism may provide the greatest hope for reconciling divine foreknowledge and human freedom. Unlike Ockhamism, it offers an interesting account of how God is able to know the future. And it carries no hint of an implication that, in order to be free, I must be able to act in such a way as to change or determine what God's beliefs about me have already been. It also goes a long way toward explicating a strong traditional view of God's providential governance of the world. And it puts questions about predestination in a new light. But it is a position which depends on many complex and controversial assumptions. How, for example, can the infinitely many counterfactuals of freedom which are supposed to be true attain that status prior to the creation of any people at all? What makes them true? There are serious questions which can be raised about any answer to this question that is attempted. The resources of Molinism may provide for the most exalted conception of God's knowledge and providential care imaginable, but their integrity, plausibility, and efficacy have not yet been established. And to some critics, the same problem plaguing Ockhamism will just seem to rear its ugly head once more: How can there possibly be truths and infallible divine beliefs about what I shall freely do far in advance of any deliberation and decision making on my part? If there are truths and infallible divine beliefs about what I shall do, it is hard to see how they can really be beliefs and truths about what I shall do *freely*. Unless I can refrain from scratching my nose, really refrain, regardless of my circumstances, I do not scratch freely. I do not have genuine options, and line (2) of our argument is after all, despite all that Molinists say to the contrary, true. This is a criticism it is not altogether easy to dismiss.

But there are at least two other strategies for responding to our argument which are well worth mentioning, however briefly. They both reject, in different ways, premise (4) of the argument, the claim that:

For every event *x* that ever occurs, God believes in advance that it will occur.

And they both attempt to do this in a way which does not detract from our being able to endorse the completeness of God's knowledge. In other respects, they are as different as can be imagined.

Many great philosophers and theologians of the past, including Augustine, Boethius, Anselm, and Aquinas, have believed that God exists outside the boundaries of time. He is not a temporal or time-bound being at all. Let us refer to this theological view as *atemporal eternalism*. According to atemporal eternalism, God does not believe anything *in advance* of the occurrence of anything, because to hold a belief, or to do anything, *prior to* or *in advance of* anything else is to be a temporal being subject to time. So when the time arrives for me, or for you, to make a decision or to choose one avenue of action over another, God has not *already* held a belief concerning exactly what will be done, and so it seems that there is nothing in our temporal circumstances to prevent our having a real array of options equally available to us. Another

way of putting this is to say that God's eternal knowledge of our actions is more like simultaneous knowledge than it is like advance knowledge. And just as your simultaneous knowledge that I am now scratching my nose does not detract in the least from the freedom of the act, so likewise, the atemporal eternalist assures us, God's eternal knowledge of my scratching does not inhibit at all its freedom.

The doctrine of atemporal divine eternity is itself a very difficult notion [. . .]. Here, it is important to point out only that it is difficult to see how its claim about God and time can alone reconcile the completeness of divine knowledge concerning our future with the reality of human freedom. Of course, if God is outside time, then premise (4) as it is stated is false, and so the precise argument we have been examining is blocked. But then a comparable argument for the same conclusions could be built around a slightly emended fourth premise:

(4') For every event *x* that ever occurs, God eternally believes that it will occur,

along with a correspondingly altered second line,

(2') For any event *x*, if God believes eternally that *x* occurs, then no one is in a position to prevent *x*.

And if (2') is true, the eternalist move alone will not suffice to reconcile the completeness of God's knowledge with our being genuinely free.

In order to evaluate the truth of (2'), we need to reflect for a moment on the following consideration. On the atemporal eternalist picture, God is related equally to all moments of time, in terms of his knowledge and power. But if that is so, then, presumably, he could have revealed to someone ten years ago his eternal knowledge that at a certain point in our future I shall scratch my nose. So suppose he has done this. Note that to be consistent with the atemporal eternalist view, we cannot say that ten years ago God made this revelation. He is not in time and does not act *at* times. But we can suppose that ten years ago someone received a revelation which God eternally willed to be received at that time [. . .], a revelation containing one piece of God's eternal cluster of beliefs, the information that at a certain time *t*, I shall scratch the tip of my nose in a certain way. When *t* arrives, will I be in a position to refrain from scratching and prove this revelation false? Surely not, for God is an infallible believer (the first premise of our argument) and God cannot lie (because of his necessary goodness). So it seems that even if God were atemporally eternal, outside of time, were such a revelation to be granted, I would be just as hemmed in as I would be if God had temporal foreknowledge of my actions.

What is important to note here is that whether God happens to reveal his eternal beliefs about our temporal actions or whether he keeps them to himself should not alone make any difference to whether we are free or not. It is not at all clear that, or how it could be the case that, it would be the act or fact of revelation itself that would act as a constraint. For, as critics of the eternalist strategy here have argued, whether God reveals it or not, on our assumptions it could have been truly said or believed by anyone ten years ago that God eternally knows that I shall scratch. And thus *it was true* ten years ago that God eternally sees this scratching at *t*. But this is enough to create the problem, to entail that at no time prior to *t* was anyone in a position to act in such a way that no scratching occurs at *t*. And this just means that we still have a problem concerning the completeness of God's knowledge, as it encompasses what is future to *us*, and our being free.

In fairness to this atemporal eternalist view, however, I should point out that not all philosophers are persuaded that, for any action *x* and time *t*, if I perform *x* at *t*, then at any time before *t* it was then true that I shall do *x* at *t*. Likewise, a philosopher can resist the inference from "God eternally believes that I do *x* at *t*" to "ten years before *t* it was true that God eternally believes that I do *x* at *t*." If this inference can be blocked, then perhaps some way can be devised for an eternalist to forge an argument for the compatibility of complete divine knowledge, encompassing our future and genuine free will. Perhaps this will involve the eternalist embracing the idea of middle knowledge and transposing it into an atemporal key, but to pursue this suggestion here would lead us into more complexities than our present purpose allows.

The eternalist tries to preserve the absolute completeness of God's knowledge and, by locating God and that knowledge outside time, to block the argument against free will. The suggestion is that God's knowledge of our future is not literally *fore*knowledge, and thus that premise (4) of the argument is strictly false. There is another response to the argument that consists in denying that there is complete divine foreknowledge of the future,

and thus in rejecting premise (4). But this strategy sees God as a temporal being who is everlasting – existing at each and every moment of time – and so it is a strategy which cannot seek to protect the completeness of God's knowledge by locating it in an atemporally eternal level of reality. It is a view which has been developed in recent years in interestingly different ways by a number of philosophers, including Peter Geach, J. R. Lucas, George Schlesinger and William Hasker. For the lack of any better-established name, we shall refer to it as *presentism*.

According to the Ockhamist, the Molinist, the atemporal eternalist, and the adherents of most other traditional views, the completeness of God's knowledge includes his having a comprehensive array of beliefs concerning everything in our future, in the most minute detail imaginable. The future is already, or eternally, known to God, and the passage of time is like the unrolling of a rug whose pattern has long been established. But this is not the view of presentism. According to the presentist, the future does not yet exist to be known. The forward edge of determinate reality is the present, and what comes next is no more than a realm of the possible and the probable. The passage of time is more like the weaving together of a rug afresh rather than the mere unrolling of one already there. And in a nondeterministic world, the results of this weaving cannot always be predicted. In particular, the free actions of human beings and other rational creatures cannot possibly be infallibly foreknown. Nor can they be eternally ascertained. As a perfect knower, God knows all possibilities for the developments in his creation. He knows what has occurred in every detail. And he is, in the words of Schlesinger, a perfect diagnostician of present tendencies. He knows present dispositions, proclivities, inclinations, intentions, and probabilities as well as they can be known. But in a world which is not deterministic, in a world peopled by free beings, this does not give him the whole future story of creation. In the very last sentence of a recent book treating this issue, J. R. Lucas says:

> If God created man in his own image, He must have created him capable of new initiatives and new insights which cannot be precisely or infallibly foreknown, but which give to the future a perpetual freshness as the inexhaustible variety of possible thoughts and actions, on the part of his children as well as himself, crystallizes into actuality.[1]

On this view, God's knowledge is as complete as it is possible for a state of knowledge to be, *given the sort of world which exists to be known*. The existence of freedom does preclude infallible foreknowledge, just as the latter prevents the former. But human freedom is no illusion. Thus, the perfect completeness of God's knowledge should not be understood to include comprehensive infallible beliefs concerning everything in the future. This is another way of rejecting premise (4) of our original argument, the premise which lays down the doctrine of complete foreknowledge.

As a response to the argument and as a view of God, presentism can be thought to have a couple of theological drawbacks. First, it offers a distinctively weaker conception of divine providence than what is provided by the more traditional view of Molinism. God does not have comprehensive access to our future, in all its details. Nor can he plan all in advance, if he leaves us truly free. Unanticipated innovations can occur in the created realm. Nothing, however, will utterly and fundamentally surprise God, on the presentist view. For he does know all possibilities. And nothing can ultimately thwart his plans, because of the perfect range of his power. So even though he cannot, on this view, foresee all future developments in his creation, we can nonetheless be assured that in the end his kingdom will prevail. It's just that, for presentism, the sort of meticulous providence allowed for by the Molinist is not a possibility. Of course, this may be judged by many theists not to be such a drawback after all. For it may make it a lot easier for us to deal with the problem of evil. On the Molinist view, God chooses all that will occur, including everything we judge to be evil. On the presentist view, it can be held that this aspect of creaturely history is just allowed, not planned, by God.

Second, it can be considered a weakness for presentism that this view has a greater difficulty accounting for the reliability of biblical prophecies, some of which seem to be about free actions and seem to capture both accurately and in advance quite specific details about what is to be (see for example Matt. 11: 27 and Mark 14: 27–30). Are the prophecies to be viewed as no more than the best divine extrapolations possible from present tendencies, which just happened, fortunately, to come true? Or do they all involve situations which were not, after all, situations involving genuine human freedom, but rather circumstances in which God himself acted in such a way as to see to it that what was predicted came to pass? Either supposition involves difficulties. But this is not to say that those difficulties cannot be overcome. There are ways in which the presentist can seek to offer a plausible account of biblical prophecies. Some prophecies are not so specific. Others seem somewhat conditional, rather than being outright, determinate predictions. It's just that more traditional views of the completeness of God's knowledge seem to have available more natural explanations for the accuracy of prophetic prediction in the Bible.

At the present time, there is no consensus among Christian or theistic philosophers, or among theologians, concerning which is the best response to the argument from foreknowledge (or divine forebelief) to the nonexistence of free will. It may be that something like a Molinist eternalism would be the most preferable sort of theological view *if* all its claims and implications can be sufficiently explained and defended. But there is serious doubt on the part of many philosophers concerning whether this can be done. And in that case, presentism may offer us the best conception of the completeness of God's knowledge. More than a thousand years of discussion have not managed to settle the issue. But in just the last few years, we have succeeded in attaining new levels of clarity concerning what exactly the problem is, what the alternative responses to it might be, and where both their strengths and weaknesses lie.

Note

1 J. R. Lucas, *The Future* (Oxford: Blackwell, 1989), p. 233.

6

Eternity

Brian Leftow

Western theists agree that God is eternal. They disagree over what "God is eternal" asserts. The Old Testament seems to take "God is eternal" to say that

(BE)   God exists without beginning or end,

through everlasting time. Influenced by Platonic philosophy, Christian thinkers came to treat "God is eternal" as saying that God is timeless, i.e. that

(GT)   God's existence does not endure through, and has no location in, time.

(GT) profoundly alters one's concept of God.

A timeless God does not remember, forget, regret, feel relief, or cease to do anything. For a timeless God has no past, and one can remember, forget, etc., only what is past. A timeless God does not wait, anticipate, hope, foreknow, predict, or deliberate. For a timeless God has no future, and one can anticipate, etc., only what is in one's future. A timeless God does not begin to do anything, if one can begin to do only what one then continues to do. If timeless, God does not change: what changes first has, then lacks, some property, and so must exist at at least two times. Thus a timeless God never learns or changes His attitudes or plans. All His knowledge and intentions are

Brian Leftow, "Eternity," from Philip L. Quinn and Charles Taliaferro (eds.), *A Companion to Philosophy of Religion* (Oxford: Blackwell Publishers, 1997), pp. 257–63.

occurrent, not dispositional. Further, if God is timeless, there is no temporal gap between His forming a plan and executing it, or executing it and seeing all its consequences.

If timeless, God's life lasts forever in the sense that at every time, it is true to say that, timelessly, God exists. Yet in itself, God's life is neither long nor short. We may say that a timeless God is forever unchanging. But from His own perspective, He knows and does what He does in the flash of a single now. A timeless God lives His whole life in a single present of unimaginable intensity.

(GT) and its concept of God reigned unchallenged from Augustine to Aquinas. Duns Scotus was the first to break ranks on (GT). His example was contagious, and (GT)'s foes now far outnumber its friends. Some who deny (GT) argue that while God is in time, His time is unlike ours. Some say that it is "metrically amorphous," i.e., that while events in God's life take time, there is no determinate amount of time they take. Some claim that God's time was amorphous until He created, at which point God entered ordinary time. Either proposal tries to save one benefit of (GT), that one need not say for how much of His life God waited before creating the universe.

Some argue that while God has a past, His "specious present" is unlike ours. To experience an extended event in one "specious present" is to presently experience a stretch of it, as when we seem to see motion. This seems to involve seeing a moving thing in a series of positions *in one present experience*, and so having a present perception which includes some of the moving thing's immediate past states. This "specious present" encompasses for us perhaps 0.05 seconds of the object's motion. God's (some say) encompasses His entire life. This proposal seeks to save an implication of (GT), that in some sense God never ceases to live any part of His life.

Debate over God's eternality has centered on whether to accept (GT). So I explore God's eternality by first examining two reasons to affirm (GT), then considering reasons to deny it.

Limits and Life

We begin and cease to live. Thus there are points in time beyond which we do not live: our life has limits. The writers of Scripture see God as unlimited, free from creaturely constraints. Thus (BE) was their way to say that God's life is boundless or limitless. Scriptural authors found it natural to gloss "without beginning or end" in terms of everlasting life in time.

Yet a life can have two kinds of limit. A life can have *outer* limits, a beginning or end. A life can also have *inner* limits, boundaries between parts, e.g. that between one's first and second year. If a life lasts forever in time, always one part of it is past and another is future. So any life in time contains at least one limit, an inner boundary dividing its past from its future. This inner limit is as real a constraint as outer limits are. For it walls us off from parts of our lives. We no longer live what is past, but can only recall it. We have not even memory's flawed access to our futures.

We are sometimes glad of this. Our pasts contain episodes it is good to be done with, and our futures contain events we might dread if we knew of them. But there are also past events we wish we could relive, and future days we are eager to see. Now God is perfect, and so lives a perfect being's life. What is a perfect being's life like? Plausibly, no part of such a life is on balance miserable: each part's balance of good and evil, or the qualities of its specific goods, are such that on balance, the perfect being is better off living that part of its life than not living it. If this is true, having a past and a future would be at best an only partly compensated loss for God. In not living part of His life, God would lose some good involved in living it. If God is on balance better off living than not living each part of His life, the loss of any evils that part of His life brings Him would not wholly compensate for the loss of that good. Thus having a

past and a future would limit the perfection of God's life.

Some suggest that this does not follow if God's "specious present" holds His whole past and God has perfect predictive knowledge or literal prevision of His future. But as time passes, we regret losing not just vivid experience of events but the events themselves – losing parts of our own lives. A continuing hallucination of the past would content nobody who knew that what seemed to be happening really was not. This holds a fortiori for a future one has yet to live at all. And what would it say about God if it made no difference to Him whether we lived with Him or ceased to exist, as long as His memory/prevision of us was intact?

Such thoughts have led many to hold that if God is a wholly perfect being, He has no past or future. If He does not, God is not in time. Note that if He is not in time, (BE) remains true. For only temporal lives begin or end. A life's beginning is earlier than its end, and any life with parts earlier than other parts is temporal.

The Creation of Time

Theists think that God is the source of whatever is not God. Time is not God. So theists want to see God as the creator not just of temporal things, but of time itself. This does not require theists to say that time is an independent thing, a container of events which exists whether or not filled. For God might create time *by* creating temporal things. If (say) for time to exist is for there to be events related as earlier and later, God may create time by causing such events to occur, or causing the existence of beings which do so. Whatever time's precise status, though, theists want to trace to God not just concrete things, but the most general conditions under which concrete things exist, time and space themselves.

Most theists think that God's creative activity is wholly free. As part of this, most think God is able to refrain from all creating. If He is, and time is a creature, it is possible that God exists even if no time exists: God is at least possibly timeless, and had He created nothing, He would have been timeless.

If this is so, the real question about God and time is whether God becomes temporal by creating time. This can seem true. If God exists and a minute goes by, it is natural to infer that God existed through that minute. All the same, we might want to resist this inference.

"God becomes temporal" suggests that God's life has first a timeless and then a temporal part. But God cannot first be timeless, then later be temporal. For then God's timeless phase is earlier than His temporal phase, and whatever is earlier than something else is in time. Nor can God be timeless during the time He is temporal. If t is a time at which God is timeless (as distinct from a time at which it is true to *say* that God is timeless), then God's timeless state, supposedly not earlier than anything, is earlier than every time after t. So the most "God becomes temporal" can mean is that God's life always consists of two temporally disconnected parts, one of which would not have existed had He not created time. But this is not what "God becomes temporal" tries to say. It tries to say that "before" there was time, God was timeless and not temporal, and once there was time, God was temporal and not timeless. What we have found is that there is no coherent thought here to express.

A second try at saying that making time makes God temporal goes this way: God is never anything but temporal, but He is only contingently so, and is so because He is always making time. This view also faces problems. If time is God's free creation and God is contingently temporal by making time, presumably God decided to be temporal. He could not have done so timelessly, for then He would have had to become temporal. But then when did He decide? If He did so at any time, it was then too late. As He was already *at* that time, He was already temporal.

But the temporalist has a reply here. It is that God's decision to become temporal would not have been temporal save for God's deciding to become temporal. Because God decided to make time, there came to be events or times later than this decision. So the decision came to *have been* temporal. Had God not decided to make time, nothing would have been later than this decision. This decision would then have been atemporal. So it is God's decision which accounts for His being in time.

This move works only at the price of denying (BE). Consider the instant of God's life which supposedly is temporal but could have been timeless. This instant either is or is not the first of God's temporal life. If it is not, then God was temporal before this instant. If so, a decision located at this instant can account for God's being temporal only by being effective *before* it occurs, i.e., by a backward causal relation which brings it about that God was temporal before He decided to be. This is

unacceptable. If the instant in question is the first instant of God's temporal life, God's life has a beginning, and so (BE) is false. Without (BE), God's life is not temporally unlimited. So this temporalist reply saves God's creation of time only by giving up temporalism's version of the claim that God is eternal.

It seems, then, that if God is eternally temporal, God cannot have decided to create time. But if not, and time is something God creates, then God cannot have decided to create *simpliciter*, i.e., to create anything rather than nothing. For at any time, He has already created something – time – without having decided to do so. But then God's creating *simpliciter* seems neither intentional nor free. Again, most Western theists think that God could have refrained from creating *simpliciter*. If God is eternally temporal and time is something God creates, it has always been too late for God to refrain from creating *simpliciter*. He may always have had the power to exist without a creation, but He has never had the opportunity to use it. However, when theists say that God was able to refrain from creating, they seem to mean that He had both power and opportunity.

Conjoined, then, (BE), the claim that God creates time, and the claim that God could have refrained from creating *simpliciter* seem to yield (GT). For it is not clear that God could become temporal by creating time.

Problems for Timelessness

Critics of (GT) argue that features of the Western theist concept of God require that God exist in time. Such arguments as these are current:

a   God is alive. But living involves changing. So God must change. Only beings in time can change. So God is in time.

b   God is alive. Lives are events. Events must occur in time. So God is in time.

c   God coexists with temporal things. So God's properties change: first He coexists with Abraham and not Moses, later with Moses and not Abraham. So God is in time.

d   God is omniscient. Thus God knows what time it is now. But only someone who exists now can know what time it is now. For whoever knows that it is now noon can say with truth, "it is now noon." But only at noon can someone say this with truth. So God is in time.

e If God is omniscient, He knows human actions which to us are future. If He is essentially omniscient, He cannot hold a false belief. If God is timeless, His knowledge cannot change, or depend on temporal events: what is eternal is as fixed as what is past. Were we to do other than God believes we will, either God would come to hold a false belief, or we would change God's timeless knowledge, or God's timeless knowledge would have been different because our temporal action was to be different, and so would have depended on our temporal action. Hence we cannot do other than God believes we will. So if God is timeless and essentially omniscient, we are not free. But we are free and God is essentially omniscient. So God is in time.

f If God is timeless, all He knows, He knows at once. So either His knowledge is all prior (in some non-temporal sense) to all temporal events or it is all (non-temporally) posterior to all temporal events. If the first, matters are as in (e). If the second, God knows what He does because temporal events turn out as they do. If so, His knowledge comes "too late" for Him to interfere providentially in time. God knows that Hitler kills Jews by seeing it happen. What one sees happen, one is too late to prevent. By contrast, if God is temporal, we are free, yet He can predict what we are likely to do and (if He chooses) act in time to save us or our victims.

g God acts. Actions are events. Again, events must occur in time.

h God is a cause. Either causal relations link only events, or they also link agents to events ("agent causality"). If the first, then as events occur only in time, God is in time. If the second, the agent's action is dated at the time of the effect. So if God has any temporal effects as an agent cause, He is again in time.

i God interacts with temporal things: we pray, He hears and responds. If God first hears, then responds, He hears before He responds. So He hears and responds in time.

j God became incarnate. So events in God's life have temporal dates. Whatever lives through temporally dated events exists in time.

k If God loves His creatures, He reacts appropriately to their present suffering: it pains Him. In the final state of things, "the Kingdom of Heaven," creatures no longer suffer, and so if God is perfectly rational, He feels less pain then than is appropriate while they suffer. So if

God always loves His creatures and is perfectly rational, God changes between now and then. If God timelessly beheld both present suffering and future happiness, His single, changeless overall state of feeling would be inappropriate to at least one of them.

Limits of space preclude my tackling all of these arguments. I choose to address the metaphysical worry behind (b), (g), and (h), that only occurrences in time can be events. I do so by exploring some arguments for this conclusion.

One might argue that:

(1) necessarily, any event which is a change in the things to which it happens occurs in time;

(2) necessarily, all events are such changes;

(3) so necessarily, all events occur in time.

But theists deny (2). Theists hold that God has created some things *ex nihilo* (from nothing). This cannot be a change in the things created, for they do not exist before being created.

Again one might reach (3) from

(4) necessarily, any event which occurs before or after another event occurs in time, and

(5) necessarily, any event occurs before or after another event.

But (5) is false. The mereological sum of all events is an event. So is the existing of all of space-time. No event occurs before or after either.

One might reach (3) from

(6) necessarily, any event with parts which follow one another occurs in time, and

(7) necessarily, all events have such parts.

But (7) is false. Consider a car continuously decelerating from 10 mph to zero. The car cannot do this without at some time having a speed of 5 mph. If the deceleration was continuous, though, the car was at 5 mph for only an instant. So the car's traveling at 5 mph was an instantaneous event, one without parts.

One might reach (3) from

(8) necessarily, any event which either follows or precedes another event or has parts which do so occurs in time, and

(9) necessarily, any event follows or precedes another or has parts which do so.

But (9) appears false. Many think it a live possibility that there be a topologically closed space-time, one structured like a circle, not a line. No event would occur before or after the existing of all of such a space-time, or the sum-event of its events. But neither event would have parts before other parts. The "before" relation is asymmetric (if A is before B, B is not before A) and irreflexive (A is never before A). Suppose, then, that space-time has a circular structure. If A and B are points in a circular space-time, then by proceeding around the circle in the direction time goes, we get from A to B *and* from B to A – time does both if it completes a circle from A back to A. Thus if in such a case A is before B, B is also before A and A is before itself. So in a circlelike space-time, nothing is before anything else.

Finally, one might reach (3) from

(10)   necessarily, every event has a date, and
(11)   necessarily, every date is the date of a temporal event.

Chisholm explicates the concept of an event without supposing that events have dates (Chisholm 1990). If his account is coherent, it is not clear why (10) should be true. Further, arguably (11) is false: eternity is itself a date.

A date is an answer to the question "when?" Asked when God knew that He would speak to Moses, a Hebrew Bible author might well have replied "eternally" or "from eternity." These answers give dates. Effectively, they say "at every earlier time." Later thinkers took (GT) as their account of God's eternality, but continued to see "eternally" as answering "when." Boethius' *De Trinitate* details the way statements about God fall into Aristotle's categories. When he turns to the category of "when," Boethius takes "God exists always" as his sample statement and explicates it in terms of God's timelessness (Boethius 1926, p. 20). The shift to a different doctrine of divine eternality did not change the question the doctrine answered. Thus if events require dates, "eternally" will serve.

If the arguments surveyed fail, it is not clear why one should deny that something atemporal could count as an event. Nor need the concept of a timeless happening cause pain. An event is something that happens at some present. An eternal event is just one which happens at a peculiar present, the eternal present. In a less liberal sense, an event is something *new* that happens. However, nothing is earlier than God's life if God is timeless. So for any f, if God is timelessly f, God is f, and nothing was f before God was. So arguably, God's eternally being f has the newness we associate with a happening. We do not think of it thus because we tend to think of whatever is eternal as infinitely old. What is old has a long past. But what is timeless cannot be old. There is no past in eternity.

Bibliography

Boethius: *The Theological Tractates*, tr. H. F. Stewart and E. K. Rand (New York: G. P. Putnam's Sons, 1926).

Chisholm, R.: "Events without times," *Nous*, 24 (1990), pp. 413–28.

Helm, P.: *Eternal God* (New York: Oxford University Press, 1988).

Leftow, B.: *Time and Eternity* (Ithaca: Cornell University Press, 1991).

Padgett, A.: *God, Eternity and the Nature of Time* (New York: St Martin's Press, 1992).

Pike, N.: *God and Timelessness* (New York: Schocken Books, 1970).

Stump, E., and Kretzmann, N.: "Eternity," *Journal* of *Philosophy*, 78 (1981), pp. 429–58.

Swinburne, R.: "God and time." In *Reasoned Faith*, ed. E. Stump (Ithaca: Cornell University Press, 1993), pp. 204–22.

Yates, J.: *The Timelessness of God* (Lanham, MD: University Press of America, 1990).

7

Divine Freedom and Creation

Laura L. Garcia

The claim that God acts freely in choosing to create us, or in choosing to create at all, holds a central place in theologies which accept an Anselmian understanding of God as the greatest conceivable being. Divine freedom assumes this importance for at least three reasons. First there is Thomas Aquinas' observation that freedom is a perfection. Just as humans are said to be more perfect than the lower animals in possessing the power of free choice, so God, who is the most perfect agent, must be said to have free choice in an even greater degree.[1] Aquinas makes it clear in his discussion of this topic that the perfection of freedom involves not only being master of one's own acts or willing for one's own sake, which might be construed in a deterministic way, but also a sort of election which is unnecessitated – the ability to choose freely among genuinely open alternatives.[2]

A second powerful impetus behind the doctrine of divine freedom is that it aids us in resolving the problem of evil. If ours is the only possible world God could have created, then the natural evils which occur in it cannot be seen as merely accepted by God on account of greater ends to be gained thereby. Rather, each earthquake, hurricane and illness that results from the ordinary workings of natural laws must be seen as necessary elements of the universe, as events God could not have done without. Further, theologians often appeal to human freedom as an explanation for the existence of moral evil, arguing that the value of creatures who respond to God and to one another *freely* outweighs the disvalue resulting from their wrong choices. But those who accept a necessitarian view of divine action often accept a similarly deterministic view of human action, and this raises the problem of moral evil to a deeper level. Necessitarians must see each instance of pain and suffering caused by human beings as absolutely inevitable, as an essential part of the world. Evil cannot be explained as a consequence of free human choices if there are no genuine choices open to humans; rather, God must be seen as the determining cause behind all the sins of mankind. The doctrine of divine freedom, on the other hand, allows that this world *could* have been other than it is, so that God *permits* evil (for purposes often obscure to us) and achieves his ends in part by means of it, but his ends in no way *require* that evil should exist, and God can create a world free from evil altogether if he so chooses.[3]

Finally, divine freedom seems important to a proper view of God's motives in creation, for God is traditionally viewed as creating out of a gracious love and kindness towards his creatures rather than out of necessity, whether of an internal or external kind. To deny divine freedom is to see the universe in all of its aspects as a necessary emanation from God's nature, so that God had no choice but to create us and our fellow creatures. On this scenario, gratitude towards God as creator seems inappropriate, but this runs counter to deeply ingrained theistic attitudes and beliefs. Consider the words of the Psalmist:

Laura L. Garcia, "Divine Freedom and Creation," from *The Philosophical Quarterly* 42 (1992), pp. 191–213. Copyright © The Editors of *The Philosophical Quarterly*, published by Blackwell Publishers, Oxford.

When I consider Thy heavens, the work of
  Thy fingers,
The moon and the stars, which Thou hast
  ordained;
What is man, that thou dost take thought of
  him?
And the son of man, that Thou dost care for
  him?
Yet Thou hast made him a little lower than
  God,
And dost crown him with glory and majesty!
                    (Psalm 8: 4–6)

Robert Adams observes that "Such utterances seem
quite incongruous with the idea that God created
us because if he had not he would have failed to
bring about the best possible state of affairs."[4]
Rather, it seems that the Psalmist is both amazed
and grateful that God has not only created but also
highly exalted such unworthy creatures as ourselves.

In spite of these substantial considerations in
favour of the doctrine of divine freedom, it has met
with opposition from many quarters over the years,
especially from rationalistic or idealistic metaphysical systems of the sort found in neo-Platonism,
Spinoza, Hegel and Whitehead. What I consider in
this paper, however, are two more recent attacks
on divine freedom from within the traditionalist
camp, where the Anselmian conception of God is
taken seriously and the transcendence of God is
emphatically asserted. Both thinkers behind these
attacks accept the claim that God exists necessarily
and is essentially omniscient, omnipotent, perfectly
good and outside space and time. Yet they either
reject outright or seriously compromise God's
freedom of will. I propose to consider here the
question of whether someone who agrees with the
conception of God shared by these thinkers must
accept a limitation or abandonment of the doctrine
of divine freedom.

Recently, Paul Helm has challenged the traditional understanding of divine freedom by reviv-
ing the Leibnizian view that a perfectly good and
rational agent must create the most optimific
possible world. Since, according to Helm, God
exists necessarily and has goodness and rationality
essentially, and since Helm holds that humans are
not free in the libertarian sense, it follows from his
view that the universe that does exist is the only
universe that could exist. One could qualify this if
one holds that God has created free creatures who
could choose differently than they do choose, but
even on such a view, the universe will be necessary

in every feature which is up to God, including the
number of free creatures (if any), the natural laws
under which they operate, his responses to their
choices, etc. On such a view, God would have less
freedom than creatures have. The second challenge
to God's freedom is found in some recent articles
by William Alston on divine action, where Alston
tries to fashion a functionalist account of human
agency into an appropriate model for divine agency.
Unlike Helm, Alston has no intention of compromising God's freedom within his account, but I
believe the model he proposes must ultimately have
that effect if it is to be at all useful to him in
illuminating God's activity. Following the discussion of these two challenges to divine freedom, I
will briefly sketch an alternative account of God's
creative act which I think avoids the difficulties of
Helm's and Alston's theories while still responding
to the concerns they express. The account I propose is based on Aquinas' analogy between God's
creative act and human creativity.

I. Helm's Denial of Divine Freedom

It is agreed by virtually every theologian that God's
freedom has *some* limitations, though most argue
that these restrictions should not be seen as
imposed upon God from outside his own nature.
Examples of such limitations are that God is not
free to do what is impossible in itself and that he
is not free to do evil, though perhaps the second
restriction can be construed as an instance of the
first. Theologians are also in general agreement with
respect to some of the things that divine freedom
includes. As Paul Helm puts it, "Because [God] is
a necessary being he is free from intellectual and
moral decay and weakness, and because he is the
omnipotent creator of all he cannot be dominated
or coerced by anything that he creates."[5] But disagreements arise over whether God has the freedom
to choose among various alternatives in creating
the universe, or whether he has the freedom to
choose between creating and not creating.

Helm suggests three distinct arguments for
the conclusion that the universe we inhabit is
the only possible world which God could have created. The first is based on God's immutability and
timelessness:

> The picture frequently sketched (for example
> by Leibniz), that among all possible worlds God
> has chosen to actualize one particular possible

world, supposes that God "stands back" from the array of possibilities to confer on one of them the dignity of actuality. And such a picture implies that while God chose A he might instead have chosen not-A. The "internal sources" of God's action incline but do not necessitate, but then this seems to suppose there could have been other reasons inclining other ways. But could there? Could there have been a situation in which God chooses neither A nor not-A, but is contemplating them both along with all other possibilities? Such a "situation" could only have been a time, and yet by supposition God is eternal and hence necessarily has no time in which to contemplate a range of possibilities before deciding which, if any, to actualize.[6]

Thus, if God first contemplates the different possibilities which he might create and then chooses one of these, his act of will must temporally succeed his act of knowledge, which entails that God is subject to change and hence to time. This conclusion is unacceptable to those who, like Helm and myself, believe that God exists timelessly.

Oddly enough, Helm seems to answer this objection himself in the very next sentence, so it is hard to believe that he places much store in it. Helm says at the end of the paragraph just quoted: "Consideration of possibilities is logically prior to actualizing one of them, but both contemplation and actualization are one eternal act of the divine nature, if God is timelessly eternal."[7] So Helm tentatively accepts the Leibnizian picture he sketches, as long as we understand the *knowledge* of God and the *willing* of God to be merely conceptually distinct and not temporally sequenced. This solution seems to me essentially correct, and various versions of it have enabled thinkers like Aquinas and John Duns Scotus to accept both divine freedom and divine immutability. We can distinguish various aspects of the divine intellect and will which bear logical connections to one another without turning these distinctions into a temporal sequence. Duns Scotus calls such distinct aspects within the life of God "instants of nature" to distinguish them from temporal instants.[8] The "instant" in which God *wills* the actual universe is posterior to, in the sense of dependent upon or informed by, the instant at which God *knows* all the possible worlds he could create, but these are merely relations of dependency within God's one eternal act. Thus it does not follow from the fact that God's choice of this universe depends upon

his knowledge of possible universes he might create, that his choice constitutes a change. Rather, God might have eternally willed that this universe exist, even though that choice was eternally informed by his knowledge of all the possible worlds he could actualize.

Helm next proposes an argument against divine freedom based on the claim that if God's choice of the world is an eternal act of a necessary being, then it must itself be logically necessary. His argument is this:

> For example, if we suppose with some (Anselm, for instance), that God's existence is itself logically necessary, and if this logically necessary being eternally wills that A, then it looks as if A is itself logically necessary since there is no possible world in which God does not exist, and no possible world in which God chooses some alternative to A.[9]

This argument requires an additional premise, namely, that whatever is eternally willed by God is necessarily willed by God, but this premise is far from an obvious truth. In fact, Aquinas argues for just the opposite claim in the course of his treatment of a related issue. In his discussion of whether or not creation constitutes a change in God in the *Summa Contra Gentiles* (Bk I, ch. 82), Aquinas considers the argument that the shift from contemplating different possibilities to electing one of them involves having a certain kind of *potency* and then undergoing a change when this potency is actualized. Such a result would compromise Aquinas' conception of God in a double way, since God for Aquinas is both fully actual and essentially immutable. He confronts the objection by means of an interesting distinction between two senses of the term "possible". In one sense, something is said to be possible with respect to a certain power or agent, as heating a hot dog is possible for a flame and knocking out Mike Tyson is possible for Buster Douglas. In this sense, "possible" bears the meaning of "potential"; what is potentially the case exists first in potency and then in act, though it may not come to be at all if the power involved is never actualized. Things are "possible" in this sense only relative to a power which is yet-to-be-actualized, where the actualization always involves a change from potency to act.

In Aquinas' second sense, "possible" means merely what is contingent, what is neither necessary nor impossible. In this sense, something can be "possible" relative to a power which is *always* in act, as long as that power is not *forced* to one alternative. It is this second sense in which Aquinas claims that different worlds are "possible" for God. He holds that God's will is never in potency but eternally in act, so that nothing can be "possible" for God in the first sense of the term; nothing is first potentially willed by God and then actually willed by him. But other worlds than ours are possible in the second sense, since God's will could have eternally been aimed at a different universe from ours, or at no created universe at all. Note that for Aquinas this is not merely a claim about God's power – that he is *able* to create these other worlds; it is a claim about his will – that he could have *chosen* other alternatives. Thus Aquinas argues that an act of will can be eternal without being necessary or determined, since even an eternal act of will might have had a different object. This means that Helm cannot move from the fact that God eternally wills *A* to the conclusion that *A* is logically necessary, so the second argument he proposes is unsound.

However, Helm's case against divine freedom rests less on the two arguments just discussed than on his claims about what is necessary to rational choice. Helm argues that a perfectly rational and good agent will choose what he takes to be the best option open to him, all things considered. To choose less than the best would be either irrational or wicked or both. Furthermore, unless there *is* a best option presented to an agent, the choice made must result from a kind of arbitrariness, a mere whim or fancy. So God chooses the best of all possible worlds in his act of creating, and it is impossible for him to choose otherwise, given that he is essentially both rational and perfectly good. Helm's argument here really involves two different premises:

(1) If God's willing a certain universe is rational, then that universe must be the optimific alternative.
(2) There is an optimific universe, a best of all possible worlds.

If one accepts that the divine will is essentially rational and that necessarily God wills *some* universe (even if that universe has no one in it but God), then (1) entails (2), since rational choosing will require choosing the optimific universe, which entails that there is an optimific universe. Helm seems to rely on this entailment, since all of his arguments aim at supporting (1), and he offers no independent

argument for (2). It should be noted, however, that a case against (2) would entail the falsehood of (1). I believe that both (1) and (2) are false, and will address them in order in what follows.

Constraints on rational choice

Helm's defence of (1), that rationality requires an optimific alternative, is somewhat obscure and scattered throughout the text, but I take the heart of it to be found in this passage:

> Certainly having a reason of a certain sort may, given a particular view of explanation, explain an action. But if having a reason for doing the action implies the possibility of having a reason for not doing it (in precisely similar circumstances), then the reason is what the action is due to, but that reason does not render it intelligible.[10]

Helm argues here that if a choice is to be fully explained, that is, intelligible, then the reason for that choice must be an overriding reason. Helm's suggestion that there cannot be even the *possibility* of having a reason for a different choice is far too strong, but this could be amended to the weaker claim that any reasons supporting other choices must be merely *prima facie* reasons that are overruled by the reasons for the choice actually made. Helm believes that if God must choose among *equally* optimific alternatives, his choice will be a product of "reasonless will",[11] "pure whimsy",[12] or "divine caprice".[13]

The underlying assumption here is that if one's *reasons* for an action are to make the action intelligible, or fully explain it, then the reasons must point to the act's being optimific. "Optimific" is left undefined by Helm, but presumably it has reference to the degree to which the act realizes one's goals or objectives, perhaps together with the total non-moral good or value produced by the act. Assuming that there exists such an optimific choice for God, then it may be that God as an essentially rational agent necessarily chooses it, though some philosophers would deny even this claim.[14] Of course, creaturely agents do not always choose the optimific alternative, but perhaps this merely shows that we are subject to ignorance, temptation and weakness of will. Richard Swinburne claims that a divine agent "will always do an action if he acknowledges overriding reasons for doing it rather than for refraining from doing it [where refraining includes the case of choosing some *other* action], if he judges that doing it would be overall better than refraining from doing it".[15] Thus if we were already convinced of the truth of (2), that there is a best possible world, then (1) would be fairly plausible, at least given the notion of "optimific action" Swinburne proposes – the action one has overriding reasons to choose. But Helm does not argue for (2) directly. Instead, he offers various reasons to accept (1), that rationality requires an optimific alternative, and these must be examined more closely.

Helm's acceptance of (1) seems to be based on a version of the principle of sufficient reason applied to acts of will. Leibniz phrases the principle this way in his correspondence with Samuel Clarke: "Nothing happens without a reason why it should be so, rather than otherwise".[16] In applying this principle to intentional actions, Helm seems to accept not only the relatively uncontroversial claim that every genuine action must be done for a reason, but also the much stronger claim that every action must be done for an overriding reason, at least if the action is to be fully explained or "intelligible". This would require that for every action, there are reasons why that very act was chosen in preference to any of the other alternatives open to the agent. Leibniz puts the strong version of his principle this way: "For a man never has a sufficient reason to act, when he has not also a sufficient reason to act in a particular manner."[17] But this principle seems empirically false. Even in cases where the options open to one are equally good, one might have good reasons not simply to *refrain* from acting. For example, suppose there are four exits from a room, equally accessible to you and equally convenient with respect to your present situation, and that a fire breaks out around the wiring just above your head. It is absurd to think that you have no sufficient reason to leave the room because you have no more reason to leave through *this* door than through *that* door. Your reason to leave is a compelling one, namely, that your life is in danger, and this can explain your departure perfectly well, even your particular action of racing through the door you did – you were fleeing the fire. It is true that the reasons offered do not fully determine or necessitate the specific act, and if full explanation requires such a deterministic account, there will be no full explanation of why you exited through the door you did. But this is not surprising, since some philosophers actually make the *absence* of a complete explanation the distinguishing feature separating free actions from other behaviour.[18]

Recent work on the concept of agent causation is in part the attempt to account for free choice in a way that allows for reasons which do not necessitate, and it seems that this is the sort of concept which fits best with divine agency.

In fact, it seems even more unlikely in the divine case that a complete explanation of God's actions could exist, since, unlike human beings, God is not moved by any forces or impulses external to his own reason and will. Thomas Aquinas holds that everything God wills is for the sake of his goodness. Clearly, some sorts of conceptually possible worlds will be such that God cannot will them, then, because they cannot be willed for the sake of his goodness.[19] But there is no reason to think that worlds different from our own in large and small ways could not reflect or embody God's goodness as well as ours does. Further, since God already possesses his goodness completely, no creature is *required* as a necessary means to the end which God wills, so there is no overriding reason for God to create at all, much less to create the particular creatures he does. Does this openness in the divine will entail that God's creative act is arbitrary? Not at all, since God does have a reason for creating, namely, his goodness, and this is a reason for creating the very universe which he creates, even though he may have had equally good reason to create another universe. Helm believes that in order for God's will to be moved to create a given universe, there must be a "further factor" in addition to his goodness which will steer his will in that particular direction.[20] But this is to assume the sort of determinism with respect to action which is the very point at issue. It is to assume with Leibniz that agents can only be moved to act and are never in any sense self-movers, an assumption we have already found reason to abandon.[21] Thus I reject Helm's claim that if God has equally good choices open to him, his free choice in creating must be "reasonless" or a matter of caprice. I would grant that it is in some sense "arbitrary", though in this instance I would prefer to use the term "gratuitous".

Is there a best possible world?

So far we have dealt only with Helm's premise (1), the claim that rational choices must be optimific ones, and we have found little reason for accepting it as a general principle. But what of premise (2), the claim that there is an optimific choice confronting God in his act of creating? If (2) is correct, then (1) would have far greater plausibility, as we have already seen. Various attempts have been made recently to determine whether or not the concept of a best possible world is even a coherent one, and the answer to this question depends upon having at least some understanding of what is meant by "best" when applied to possible worlds. Bruce Reichenbach has distinguished two different senses of "best" in this context. First, "best" might refer to the kinds of creatures found in the world, so that the best possible world is one containing either the best kinds of creatures or perhaps the richest variety of creatures. Along these lines, Leibniz argued against the possibility of a vacuum in space on the grounds that the best universe would contain as much matter as is possible and so God would have left no empty space in the universe.[22] But a moment's reflection shows that there is no upper limit to the perfections found in creatures, since for each level of finite knowledge or goodness they might have, there is always a higher level. Similarly, there is no upper limit to the amount of richness or variety present in a given world, as there is an infinite variety of possible life forms. So a "best" world in the first sense does not seem to be a coherent concept.

A second understanding of "best" would be in terms of the total value in the universe, where this might be understood as the total happiness, benefit or good in the world. But here again there does not seem to be any limit on how much happiness or good a world could contain. For any world with a total value of V, there will be a possible world with total value greater than V. Reichenbach concludes:

> It seems to be the case that when we speak of best as relating to the created world, we find that there is not a finite series such that there could be a best possible being or state of affairs. Rather, we are faced with an infinite series of characteristics, degrees of their actualization, or optimific states of affairs, in which for any given being or state of affairs there will always be a better. The entire series thus asymptotically approaches, but, as a finite, created world, cannot reach, the infinite perfection of God.[23]

Thus the notion of a "best of all possible worlds" seems incoherent on either interpretation. Reichenbach's argument here parallels a point made by Alvin Plantinga in the course of discussing Gaunilo's perfect-island objection to Anselm's ontological argument. Plantinga argues that "the idea of a greatest possible island is an inconsistent or incoherent idea; it's not possible that there be such a thing".

His reason is that "the qualities that make for greatness in islands – number of palm trees, amount and quantity of coconuts, for example – most of these qualities have no *intrinsic maximum*".[24] Plantinga's point here, I believe, can be generalized to the case of *any* finite object, including any created universe. Since the created universe by definition contains finite creatures with finite attributes, there cannot be a created universe which exhibits great-making qualities to the highest possible degree. Only God has such properties. So I believe Reichenbach's rejection of the notion of a "best possible world" in his two senses is well founded.

However, there are at least two further senses of the term "best" which Reichenbach does not consider in his essay. Philip Quinn suggests a definition of "best" in terms of the *moral* goodness found in a given universe. He introduces the notion of a "morally unsurpassable world", meaning a world which has at least as much moral value as any other possible world, however moral value is defined, and accepts the possibility that there is more than one world which falls in this category. Quinn then argues that a perfectly good moral agent would be obliged to create one of the morally unsurpassable worlds, since such an agent must be interested in maximizing the total moral value in the universe. Quinn says, "If he actualizes one than which there is a morally better, he does not do the best he can, morally speaking, and so it is possible that there is an agent morally better than he is, namely, an omnipotent moral agent who actualizes one of those morally better worlds."[25] Quinn restricts the field of possible worlds to those which are "actualizable" for God; that is, he is considering the amount of moral goodness in a given world, excluding God's own goodness, since God does not bring about his own goodness.

Quinn makes two assumptions here which seem problematic. First, he finds it very likely that there is such a thing as a morally unsurpassable possible world. But it is hard to see just what such a world would contain. If moral value is measured by the morally correct choices of free agents, then it seems that arguments similar to Reichenbach's and Plantinga's will show that there is no upper limit to the amount of moral value in a created universe – for any number of correct moral choices, there could always be a greater number. Similarly, if moral value is defined in terms of the number of creatures possessing certain virtues, then it is equally unlikely that there is an upper limit to the number of virtuous creatures or even to the degree of virtue in any given creature.

A second assumption Quinn makes is that a perfectly good being is obliged to create the world with the greatest amount of moral value, assuming for the moment that there is such a world. But it seems possible that even a perfectly good moral agent might have other purposes in creating besides maximizing moral value. Quinn suggests that in the case of a tie between morally unsurpassable worlds, considerations of beauty or simplicity might apply. It is not obvious that these other considerations could never outweigh the moral considerations that Quinn emphasizes, with the result that a perfectly good agent who is also perfectly wise, loving and holy might create a world less full of creaturely moral value than he could have. The main purpose of Quinn's article is to refute Robert Adams's suggestion that God might choose a world with less moral virtue in it than others he might have created, in order to bestow unmerited favour upon his creatures.[26] But it seems to me that Adams's suggestion makes perfect sense, and that God has no overriding reason to maximize creaturely moral value in preference to other values. We might well shrink from the prospect of a God who cared little for our happiness or contentment and only for turning us into moral heroes.

Let us consider one more attempt to define the term "best"; this time in the sense of the best relative to the ends or purposes one has in mind, so that the "best possible world" will be the one that is best for realizing God's purposes, whatever they may be. In this sense, even Adams might accept that if there is a world which is best for God's purposes, including his purpose in acting graciously towards his creatures, then this is the world that God must create. This notion of "best" is related to Swinburne's concept of having an overriding reason to act in a certain way. I believe it is also the notion that Helm has in mind, since he sees God's creative act to be determined by the purposes of God, which are largely unknown to us, not by some obvious features of the particular universe itself, such as its having the best creatures or the greatest amount of moral value. Helm says that in choosing to create a given world A, "God has a reason for willing A in preference to any alternative",[27] but "no further explanation of what takes place is possible than that it seemed good to the eternal God that these things should be so".[28] Helm believes that the existence of this particular universe is not entailed by anything about God's character; rather, it is simply the universe which God has the most reason to create. I believe that the notion of a best possible universe in this sense is at least a coherent one. And perhaps there is a universe which uniquely fits the purposes God has in mind, so that it is preferable from the divine point of view to any other, but this is far from obvious. The hesitation to affirm that there is such a world is in part due to the fact that we have so little to go on in determining what God's purposes are. Further, on Aquinas' picture of things, God's purposes cannot constrain him to create anything at all, much less to create any particular universe, since the only purposes he has necessarily are already fulfilled by his own existing. It is true that, according to Aquinas, God cannot will the absence of a good "which causes the nature of the good to be entirely lost. But there is no such good apart from God."[29] Finally, since God's goodness is infinite it can be participated in in an infinite number of ways, so God's purpose in ordering things to his goodness or creating things which participate in his goodness can be fulfilled by an infinite number of distinct possible worlds.

Even if Aquinas' picture of God's purposes is rejected, it still seems difficult, if not impossible, to show that those purposes must be so narrow as to restrict God's creative activity to one logically possible world. I believe this is the reason that Helm does not try to defend (2) itself, but spends his energies instead in the defence of principle (1). On this fourth understanding of best as "best for God's purposes", (2) is not very plausible unless we already know that (1) is true. If God's purposes must *fully* explain his creative act, then there must be one specific universe which fulfils those purposes. But so far we have seen no reason to accept Helm's requirement that every rational action must have such a complete explanation.

Before leaving Helm's treatment of divine freedom, we should note one unfortunate consequence of accepting (1) and (2). If these were correct, it would follow that the actual world (or, for libertarians, the part of the actual world strongly actualized by God) is the only possible world, since it is necessarily the only world which could have been created by the necessarily existing creator. If God's existence is necessary and his eternal act of will is also necessary, then for a soft determinist like Helm, there is only one possible world. This follows for Helm because he accepts divine determinism (and a version of compatibilism) with respect to human actions. But those who believe that humans have libertarian freedom and that God has neither foreknowledge of future contingent propositions nor middle knowledge of counterfactuals of freedom could accept here the existence of a restricted *set* of possible worlds, with only the divinely determined component fully fixed. God's response to each of our choices would be completely necessitated by his nature, but the universe would not be necessary in all of its details, since some of these would depend on our genuinely free choices. Obviously someone like Helm would find this view repugnant, since he cites the *Westminster Confession of Faith*, III.I, approvingly as follows: "God from all eternity did, by the most wise and holy council of his own will, freely and unchangeably ordain whatsoever comes to pass."[30] Helm tries to blunt this result by observing that worlds other than ours would still be epistemically possible (that is, they are possible for all we know) and conceptually possible (that is, we find no internal inconsistency in the description of them). But the fact remains that, as Helm puts it, "these possibilities are only abstract. They do not represent real possibilities and never did. The thought that they did was the product of our ignorance."[31] In the end, Helm must simply accept the counter-intuitive result that many things which appear to us to be eminently contingent, including on his view wicked human actions, are in fact metaphysically necessary. Further, even if humans and other creatures such as angels have libertarian freedom, the necessitarian view of divine action entails that God cannot *prevent* moral evil from occurring, since he cannot but create this universe, and in this universe some creatures do make evil choices. Helm does not seem to appreciate fully how deeply ingrained is our intuition that some things are not necessary, or how important this is for theology. He complains of one of Aquinas' arguments for divine freedom that it merely assumes that there is contingency in the universe.[32] But surely this assumption is about as unassuming as they come; one would need a very strong reason for rejecting it, and as far as I can see, Helm fails to provide such a reason.

II. Alston's Functionalist Account

The model of divine agency proposed by William Alston is not intended by him to compromise God's freedom in any way; in fact, Alston insists on the freedom of God in creating the universe. But it seems that if Alston's functionalist model of agency is to shed any light at all on divine action, it must incorporate elements that significantly undercut God's freedom of choice.[33] Alston is convinced that we need to find concepts within religious language that have a univocal sense when applied to creatures and to God, so he seeks to determine "how much of the *way we think of* human action can be carried over to our thought of divine action".[34] The way Alston proposes to understand human action is by means of the functionalist theory of mind, which attempts to predict (or explain) human behaviour by linking up the input into the human psyche (especially perceptual input) with the behavioural output (including linguistic behaviour). On most views of intentional action, whether functionalist or not, an action is done intentionally only if it results in the right way from the appropriate psychological states of the agent. These states are of two kinds: *goal-setting states*, or pro- and con-attitudes, and *cognitive guidance states*, or beliefs. Functionalism defines both types of psychological states according to the role they play in a system which connects the input and the output for a given agent. For humans, the input is their perceptual conditions and the output is their behaviour.

Functionalism provides an advantage over earlier behaviourist accounts in that it allows us to consider the possibility of beings very different from ourselves (for example, aliens or computers) with psychological states that play the same roles for them which our beliefs and attitudes play for us. This enables the functionalist to hold on to a token identity between mental events and brain states, where, for example, a given belief is identical with a certain brain state, without the embarrassing consequence that no one who is not in that very brain state can share that belief. This implication of functionalism leads Alston to suggest that even God's beliefs and attitudes might be understood on a functionalist model, thus providing the hoped-for univocal connection between divine action and human action. In the human case, a pro-attitude towards a certain goal G, together with the belief that some course of action A is the best way to obtain G, often results in doing A. But it might be that G is impossible to obtain or that doing A is incompatible with other goals we have, so that in the situation just described, A does not always occur. To account for this, Alston calls on the notion of a *tendency* to do A: "The rough idea is that a tendency to do A is a state that, in the absence of sufficient interference or blockage, will issue in doing A."[35] This definition allows for the possibility that a given tendency will be overridden by a stronger tendency or an incompatible tendency.

Of course, this model of action is still completely deterministic, since functionalism sees our beliefs and attitudes as completely necessitated by causes ultimately outside us, and then as combining to issue in actions in a causally deterministic way, with the strongest tendency prevailing. Given traditional claims about the perfect freedom of God, functionalism does not seem a very promising model for capturing divine activity.

Alston recognizes that the determinism implicit in functionalism poses an obstacle to applying that theory to God's actions. He asks, "Are we really prepared to think of God's behavior as issuing automatically from the interplay of motivational factors? Wouldn't that make God into a mechanism, a system the output of which is determined by the interplay of its parts, rather than a supremely free agent?"[36] But Alston tries to amend the functionalist account to avoid these problems by introducing the notion of agent causation. On Alston's view, an agent's free volition can intervene between her attitudes or motivational structure and behaviour, so that even her strongest tendency is not necessarily realized in action.[37] With the introduction of agent causality, one might think that Alston has moved completely away from functionalism, especially since he admits that "this is not a notion that can be given a functionalist interpretation".[38] But he believes that his revised functionalism can be applied to our understanding of God's agency. Alston summarizes revised functionalism in two conditionals:

(3) If S has a pro-attitude towards G, then S will have a tendency to do whatever S takes to be a way of attaining G.
(4) If S has a tendency to do A, then if this tendency is not successfully opposed by a stronger tendency or by an act of will, S will do A, if the external world co-operates in the right way.[39]

Objections to the functionalist account

Alston believes these conditionals can be applied to God's activity and to human activity alike, providing the univocal link he seeks between the two cases, but serious problems arise here. In the first place, God's actions do not have "input" in the sense in which human actions do; God does not learn or acquire knowledge and he is not in a perceptual situation when he acts. Further, as Alston points out, God has no biological urges, cravings or other external forces operating on him, and his knowledge and power are unlimited – he is not subject to natural laws as humans are. Thus, God's "situation" differs from ours dramatically.

Alston suggests that the input for the divine psyche might simply be conceived of as all the truths there are, but this will not do. It seems that the situation God is in "prior" to his decision to create, for example, is comprised of facts regarding God's own nature, other necessary truths and perhaps certain contingent counterfactual truths, statements about what agents would freely do in various circumstances in which they are placed.[40] Omitted from this original situation are all other contingent truths, since these depend causally upon the divine will and thus cannot serve as input into God's creative act. Alston holds, along with Aquinas and other theists in the classical tradition, that God is atemporal and that his willing should be understood as a single act. Thus, it cannot have as input the contingent truths which result from it. Furthermore, even if God exists temporally and acts at moments of time, not every contingent fact can be among those God considers as input to a given act, since some will be true only as a result of that act. Since the input for God's cognitive states "before" he creates does not include the contingent facts dependent on his creating, God has much more freedom with respect to his actions than do human beings, and divine actions differ significantly in this respect from paradigm cases of action in the functionalist model. For God, the input seems to leave the output radically under-determined, whereas in the human case, functionalists hope to find lawlike connections between the various inputs and resulting outputs.

One might reply that the original situation in which God exists "prior" (in some sense) to creating the universe includes God's *purposes and goals*, and that these can provide us with some predictive probabilities with regard to what God will create. But Alston accepts the traditional claim that in this original situation, God has no overriding reason to choose to create at all, much less to choose a particular universe. That is, even if God has some tendency to create *this* world, he can realize his goals equally well by creating another world or by creating no world at all. According to conditional (3) above, if God's purposes can be realized by the existence of an infinite number of different possible worlds, then God has some tendency to create an infinite number of different worlds and some tendency to create no world. And according to (4), these tendencies are such that they will issue in action unless blocked by stronger tendencies or by an act of will. But this presents us with a picture of a being who is pulled in an infinite number of directions at once, by tendencies which he does not create but simply finds himself subject to.

Much depends on the way in which these tendencies are to be understood. There seem to be three possible interpretations of the sort of tendency that is operative in cases of intentional action. First, a tendency might be understood as a causal force of some kind, an inclination or attraction which literally pulls one in a certain direction. Tendencies in this sense would be states which contributed causally (in a direct way) to the bringing about of an intentional action. A second interpretation of tendencies might be in terms of statistical laws, statements which describe how often a certain characteristic occurs within a particular group, for example, that women have a tendency to live longer than men. Finally, tendencies might be understood as expressing certain counterfactual truths, of the form: if S did not want G, S would do A.

I think it is clear that Alston must interpret tendencies in the first way, as causal forces, rather than in either of the latter ways. This is because conditionals (3) and (4) above describe tendencies as having different degrees of strength, as capable of being opposed by other tendencies, as succeeding, as being blocked or interfered with, and so on. Statistical tendencies, on the other hand, though they might be construed as having varying strengths in some sense, cannot really *oppose* one another or be blocked or interfered with. Similarly, counterfactual statements do not admit of degrees of strength, nor can they oppose one another or be blocked or interfered with, and thus they cannot figure in the functionalist theory as summarized in conditionals (3) and (4).[41] Although these counterfactuals might be true of God (for example, that if he had found ten righteous persons in Sodom he would not have destroyed it), by themselves they do not provide the link with functionalism that Alston desires. If God has such counterfactual "tendencies" to realize each of the various possible means to his goals, this is merely for him to have some reason to realize each of those means. Such reasons need not issue in action at all, even if they are not blocked by "stronger tendencies" (better reasons?) to do something else. This is clearest in cases where there are several incompatible means to one of God's goals.

If the tendencies do not causally move God to act in some way, but instead God acts only by a direct exercise of agent causality, then conditional (4) in Alston's description of functionalism does not apply to God after all. Conditional (4) will be false in the divine case because tendencies will not compete in strength and will not themselves produce or issue in an action (unless "blocked" by God's will). Rather, on this view, God's will produces the action, and the "tendencies" play no role in the action's production, but only come in to help provide a rational explanation of it. I am sympathetic to such a view, but it does not seem to correspond to functionalism as Alston describes it and as I understand it. Conditionals (3) and (4) contain the core of the functionalism that Alston wants to apply to both God and humans. If the tendencies in (3) are read in a counterfactual way and the claims of (4) are false in the divine case, then we seem to have lost any significant connection to functionalism.

Presumably, then, Alston must construe tendencies as some kind of causal force or impetus which points a person towards a certain action. Whenever an agent has a pro-attitude towards a goal, she automatically has a tendency towards whatever means she sees as a way of attaining that goal. There seem to be two ways in which pro-attitudes could generate tendencies of this sort. A first possibility is that the pro-attitude consists in *being attracted* by a certain good, being "pulled" in a particular direction. The will's being attracted in this way by the goal results in its also having a tendency towards (being attracted to) whatever the agent takes to be a means of realizing the goal. Of course, tendencies of this kind can be blocked by stronger tendencies or, in Alston's revised functionalism, by an act of will. But left unimpeded, they automatically produce an action. However, a serious objection to this model comes immediately to mind. On this account actions are really produced by the tendencies themselves and not by the agent, since the tendencies automatically issue in action if not blocked or impeded in some way. Whatever pro-attitudes the agent has prior to acting will automatically produce tendencies of varying degrees of strength, and normally the strongest tendency will produce the action. Even when the agent intervenes by a (self-caused) volition, the volition does not causally *produce* the action but only *prevents* some of the tendencies from producing the action, thus *allowing* other tendencies to win out and produce the action. This model is reminiscent of Leibniz's appeals to weights and physical forces which compete for supremacy. Further, Alston's introduction of agent causality fails to provide an active role for the agent in producing her actions; in fact, his theory makes her passive in the extreme, since even in "free" actions, where volitions play a role, her actions are produced not by her volition but by the strongest unblocked tendency. The role of the will here is analogous to the role of a bomb specialist, call her Prudence, who can block the bomb's exploding by defusing it, but cannot herself create the effect that the bomb does. If she blocks it, no explosion occurs, but if she fails to block it, the bomb is doing the exploding, and her failure to block it does not causally contribute to the explosion. (Prudence's refraining is part of the background conditions for the explosion, but it is not what helps *produce* the explosion.) Such a passive view of the will is extremely unattractive even for the theory of human behaviour, but it is doubly unattractive as a model for divine action. Surely God should not be viewed as subject to various tendencies which automatically result in actions unless blocked in some way by his will. Alston wishes to claim that "the things [God] directly brings about are the result of 'agent causality' rather than 'event causality', even where the events or states are states of His own psyche".[42] But the attraction model of revised functionalism *does* view God's actions as resulting from states of his psyche, namely tendencies, rather than from free volitions.

Given Alston's hesitation to adopt the implications of the attraction model of tendencies, we might consider a second way of understanding the link between pro-attitudes and tendencies, in which the agent is understood as *moving herself* towards the various means which would contribute to the realization of her goals. On this picture, the agent recognizes that something is good (has a pro-attitude towards it), and then seeks (or points herself towards) whatever she believes is a means to that goal. Since we have already seen that the tendencies here are to be understood as a type of causal force, this *seeking* must consist in a sort of *pushing* herself towards the means to her ends. While this does avoid the passivity inherent in the *attraction* view, it raises an equally vexing problem of its own. Since some tendencies will be directed towards actions which are incompatible with each other, this model must view the agent as striving to bring about incompatible actions and thus as operating irrationally. If David has some tendency (in this sense) towards digging a hole deeper and some tendency towards filling it in, he must be directing

himself towards both of these activities at the same time, which seems deeply irrational. One can be *attracted* towards mutually incompatible alternatives without being irrational, but one cannot actively *seek* what one knows are mutually incompatible alternatives if one is to remain rational. Therefore, agents viewed on Alston's functionalist model must be seen either as fundamentally passive or as irrational, both of which are repugnant to the traditional conception of God.

III. An Alternative Model

We have already seen that Aquinas' account of human action is much more cognitively oriented than is the functionalist account, and I believe it is an improvement over that view. Instead of beginning from pro-*attitudes*, seen as evaluative or affective states of the agent which generate tendencies, Aquinas begins from *reasons* to act, where these do not generate causal tendencies even when they involve viewing some states of affairs as good or desirable. For Aquinas, the end which God *necessarily* wills (namely, his own goodness) gives him no overriding reason to bring about any contingent means to that end, and produces no *tendencies* of Alston's sort towards realizing one of these means. God should not be viewed as having a tendency towards each of the actions that would realize his goals, and then as either allowing the strongest of these tendencies to win out or as blocking the strongest ones by an act of will so that the most forceful remaining tendency will produce an action. It is true that, within the set of things willed by God, some are willed as a means towards realizing others and some are willed as necessary conditions of others, but these cases do not translate easily into tendency-language. In the case of necessary conditions, God cannot but will what are necessary conditions to other things he wills, since he cannot will the ends without willing their essential conditions. Further, when God wills something as a *non-essential* means to a particular end, as in Alston's examples of sending Ezekiel to renew the faith of Israel or sending the Holy Spirit to guide the Church into the correct Trinitarian doctrine, it seems unlikely that there is such a thing as the *best* means to his ends. God has no need to minimize the amount of effort or expense and he is not subject to time constraints, natural laws, etc. It may be that a given means is optimal with respect to its cost to other goals or purposes of his, but even here it is not clear that he is required to realize that means. Finally, even if God *is* required to realize the best means to his ends in this sense, this does not seem to be a matter of a tendency towards *that* action winning out over tendencies towards less optimal actions. At most, God might be said to have a counterfactual tendency towards the other actions, since, given that he has a certain goal, perhaps he *would* choose those means were it not for other purposes of his. But given *all* of his goals and purposes and his omniscience, surely God would have no *actual* tendency or inclination towards the less optimal means. While Aquinas sees God's goals as rendering certain subsidiary actions "fitting" or "useful" or even "necessary", these considerations do not prevent God's willing of a particular order of things from being a free elective choice. I believe it is only a view like Aquinas', which takes agent causation seriously as the ultimate explanation of what God does, which will enable Alston to hold on to what he rightly

takes to be a central theistic doctrine: namely, that "God's activity is the activity of a free agent in the most unqualified sense".[43]

I believe Aquinas' understanding of God's creative act represents an equally significant advance over that of Helm. Whereas Helm has accused Aquinas of grounding the act of creation in God's "reasonless will", in the end it is Helm who cannot provide any reason for the creation of this universe other than that it seemed good to God to do so, while Aquinas suggests at least a partial explanation of what God does in terms of what is fitting, useful or conditionally necessary. In Aquinas' account, we find the metaphor of an artist, freely choosing the forms and materials that suitably realize his design. Surely this artistic metaphor, which has guided theological commentary on creation for centuries, is a far more congenial image of God's activity than either the Leibnizian metaphor of a divine calculator or the functionalist metaphor of a divine automaton.[44]

Notes

1 Thomas Aquinas, *Summa Contra Gentiles*, Bk I, ch. 88.
2 I understand "divine freedom" here in a libertarian sense, so that God's actions are free only if they are neither causally nor logically necessitated by any states of affairs.
3 In this paragraph I have assumed two things: (a) God knows in every detail how his creatures will act prior to creating them, and (b) there are no genuinely undetermined events in the world apart from those brought about by free agents (if any).
4 Robert Adams, "Must God Create the Best?", in Thomas V. Morris (ed.), *The Concept of God* (Oxford: Oxford University Press, 1987), p. 99.
5 Paul Helm, *Eternal God* (Oxford: Clarendon, 1988), pp. 171–2.
6 Ibid., pp. 178–9.
7 Ibid., p. 179.
8 See *Duns Scotus: Philosophical Writings*, ed. Allan Wolter (Edinburgh: Nelson, 1962), p. 66, where Duns Scotus distinguishes between the view that non-existence precedes existence by a "priority of duration" and his own view, that non-existence precedes existence merely by a "priority of nature". Duns Scotus attributes his view to Avicenna in *Metaphysics*, Bk VI.
9 *Eternal God*, p. 177.
10 Ibid., p. 174.
11 Ibid., p. 178.
12 Ibid., p. 180.
13 Ibid.

14 However, some have challenged this claim as well. See Michael Slote's discussion of so-called "satisficing consequentialism" (vs. "optimizing consequentialism") in his *Common-Sense Morality and Consequentialism* (London: Routledge, 1985), pp. 35–59.
15 *The Coherence of Theism* (Oxford: Clarendon, 1977), p. 148.
16 *The Leibniz–Clarke Correspondence*, ed. H. G. Alexander (Manchester: Manchester University Press, 1956), Leibniz's Second Paper, p. 16.
17 Ibid., Leibniz's Fifth Paper, p. 60.
18 For example, Richard Swinburne says in *The Coherence of Theism*: "An action, I suggest, is a free action if and only if the agent's choosing to do that action, that is having the intention to produce the result of that action, has no full explanation – of any kind, whether of the kind described by scientific explanation or of the kind described by personal explanation" (p. 143).
19 See my article "A Response to the Modal Problem of Evil", *Faith and Philosophy*, 1 (1984), pp. 378–88.
20 *Eternal God*, p. 176.
21 In the *Theodicy*, Leibniz actually compares the soul to a force which "acts on that part only where it finds the greatest ease or the least resistance. For example: air strongly compressed in a glass-receiver will break the glass to get out" (Clarke's Appendix, p. 131).
22 *Leibniz–Clarke Correspondence*, Leibniz's Second Paper, p. 16.
23 Bruce Reichenbach, "Must God Create the Best Possible World?", *International Philosophical Quarterly*, 19 (1979), p. 208.

24 *God, Freedom and Evil* (New York: Harper and Row, 1974), p. 91.

25 Philip L. Quinn, "God, Moral Perfection, and Possible Worlds", in Frederick Sontag and M. Darrol Bryant (eds), *God: The Contemporary Discussion* (Barrytown, NY: Rose of Sharon Press, 1982), p. 213.

26 In "Must God Create the Best?" Adams says, "The man who worships God does not normally praise him for his moral rectitude and good judgment in creating *us*. He thanks God for his existence as for an undeserved personal favour" (p. 98).

27 *Eternal God*, p. 178.

28 Ibid., p. 181.

29 *Summa Contra Gentiles*, Bk I, ch. 81.

30 *Eternal God*, p. 155.

31 Ibid., p. 189. Helm says that God's choice of this universe cannot be deduced from any set of logical truths, but of course many other necessary truths share this property – e.g., that red is a colour or that the number 7 is not purple.

32 Ibid., p. 177.

33 For a thorough discussion of Alston's theory, see his essays: "Divine and Human Action", in Thomas V. Morris (ed.), *Divine and Human Action* (Ithaca: Cornell University Press, 1988), pp. 257–80, and "Functionalism and Theological Language', *American Philosophical Quarterly*, 22 (1985), pp. 221–30.

34 "Divine and Human Action", pp. 259–60.

35 Ibid., p. 268.

36 Ibid.

37 As I understand it, Alston does not interpret volitions as pro-attitudes. Presumably, on his view, volitions are directly within the agent's control in a way that attitudes (most of the time) are not.

38 "Divine and Human Action", p. 272.

39 Ibid., p. 271. Alston points out that the last qualification in (4) becomes vacuous in the divine case.

40 This is my own view, in any case, though Alston does not commit himself on the question of whether or not there are true counterfactuals of freedom.

41 Some of these counterfactuals may be *true* because of the existence of tendencies of the first sort (causal forces), but they need not be based in tendencies of that kind.

42 "Divine and Human Action", p. 269.

43 Ibid.

44 I wish to thank Terry Christlieb, Wayne Davis, Jorge Garcia, Stephen Wykstra and the philosophy departments at the University of St Thomas and Georgetown University for invaluable comments and criticisms on this paper.

8

The Idea of God in Feminist Philosophy

Marjorie Hewitt Suchocki

The new wave of feminism desperately needs to be not only many-faceted but cosmic and ultimately religious in its vision. This means reaching outward and inward toward the God beyond and beneath the gods who have stolen our identity.

Mary Daly, Beyond God the Father

The notion of God has come under increasing critique in the recent past as scholars have dealt more seriously with the cultural roots of knowledge and with the question of the ability of language to express adequately any ontological reality beyond human experience. Although philosophers from a variety of perspectives have addressed these issues, feminists have arguably created the most devastating critique and the most constructive responses. Their sociological position on the boundary of a male-dominated tradition has given them a perspective that clearly shows the androcentric and cultural biases of traditional notions of God, even though feminists also encounter the common problem of critiquing categories they have to some extent internalized. Boundaries participate in the regions they define.

In this essay I explore feminist thought on the topic of God, giving major attention to Mary Daly and Rebecca Chopp. Both write from a strong background in the Christian tradition, with Daly vehemently rejecting this tradition in favor of totally new modes of talking about metabeing, and Chopp

Marjorie Hewitt Suchocki, "The Idea of God in Feminist Philosophy," reprinted by permission of the author and Indiana University Press from *Hypatia* 9 (Fall 1994), pp. 57–68.

staying more intentionally within her tradition. Ironically, however, Daly may reflect her rejected tradition more fully than she desires, so that both women together illustrate the possibilities for redeveloping the concept of God within the Western philosophical tradition.

The feminist critique of the concept of God is best characterized by Mary Daly's early comment, "If God is male, then the male is God" (1973: 19). Characteristics traditionally attributed to God, such as strength, wisdom, immutability, dependability, and righteousness, are similar to values stereotypically attributed to men, whereas the corollary values applied to humanity, such as weakness, ignorance, vacillation, and sinfulness, are stereotypically applied to women. Thus the concept of God as male serves to define men and male roles, and to reinforce the inferior definition and roles of women. How, then, is it a concept of *God* rather than androcentrism in faint disguise?

Responses to this question by feminist philosophers of religion include (1) rejection of the transcendence of God in favor of a totally immanent God, (2) replacement of God with Goddess, (3) reconsideration of the linguistic structure by which we name a reality beyond ourselves as God at all, and (4) reconceptualization of the presuppositions concerning the nature of reality as a whole, whether God or the world. Mary Daly offers an insightful illustration of all of these moves. Her works span – and arguably inaugurate – the past three decades of feminist reconsideration of God. Her own passionate journeying details successively the various ways of dealing with God and sexism.

Marjorie Hewitt Suchocki

In her earliest book, *The Church and the Second Sex* (1968), Daly offered a modest proposal. She exposed the patriarchal bias against women that pervades Christian history and reasonably suggested that such bias is against the Christian gospel. She recommended procedures by which the post-Vatican II church might more fittingly embody the grace of God in structures of equality for women, and she offered suggestions for changes in the concept of God that must parallel such changes. In a tentative way, she suggested that "vague identifications of God with the male sex" pervaded Christian theology, despite the paradox that "the masculine God" was held to be "above sex." She asked, "What can 'masculine' mean if predicated of a Being in which there is no sex?" (1968: 181), and went on to advocate reconsideration of notions such as the masculinity of God, omnipotence, immutability, and providence. These are suggestions only in this her first book; they would be developed later in her second book *Beyond God the Father* (1973). As for the reception of *The Church and the Second Sex*, Daly unfortunately did not account for the great depths to which patriarchy had molded the consciousness and the conscience of the church, nor the enormous threat to privilege and power that her proposals entailed: her book was not well received by the church hierarchy. However, it became the ground-breaking book in feminist philosophy of religion, launching an age of consciousness-raising among women.

Beyond God the Father was published five years later, and gave an answer to her own earlier suggestions relative to theology. With wonderful boldness she gave every theme within the Christian mythos a feminist reinterpretation. Echoing both process thought and Paul Tillich in much of the work, she assumed a position and perspective "on the boundary" of Christianity (patriarchal space) and asked "for whom" and "from whose perspective" theological judgments concerning the fall, sin, and redemption were fashioned. She exposed the hidden male authorship and agenda behind so-called universal pronouncements, considered the Christian concepts now nakedly exposed before her, and reclothed them in feminist dress. Her accomplishment is astounding, but the fundamental supposition operating throughout the work shows her boundary position to be more engrained within the tradition than she acknowledged. She never raised the question of the legitimacy of the fundamental Christian categories of thought; rather, she only questioned the male-oriented manner in which these categories were developed. Masculinist interpretation is countered with feminist interpretation, as if each essential concept were somehow ontologically deeper than its interpretation, pre-existing its linguistic and historical forms. This supposition is important, since it re-emerges in her fifth book, *Wickedary* (co-authored with Jane Caputi), as an assumption concerning the ontological status of language.

Each of Daly's reinterpretations of Christian categories invites dialogue, but for the purposes of this present investigation, I turn to her development of God as Verb (and I follow Daly's usage of capitalization and hyphenation). Daly translates Paul Tillich's "ground of Being" into Be-ing, and eventually, in echoes of Whiteheadian thought, to Becoming, or God the Verb. Her answer to the masculinization of God under patriarchy is the de-reification of God, positing God as dynamic energy, ever unfolding, drawing creation toward itself. God the Verb in this work is very much a transcendent God, but no longer in a way that suggests an "over and above" creation. Rather, God is in advance of creation, always transcending history by evoking new history, feminist history. The Unfolding Verb is the empowerment of women and the call to the Sisterhood of all humankind in new modes of community.

Many of the ideas of God Daly uses in this work are similar to those used in theology generally during the period: Wolfhart Pannenberg extensively developed the notion of "God as the Power of the Future"; process theologians such as John B. Cobb, Jr. had long worked with a notion of God as dynamic becoming; and Paul Tillich's own "on the boundary" position dealt with a God who was the Ground of Being and source of the "courage to be" in the face of existential anxiety. In Daly's integration of these positions, they became more than the sum of their parts. By integrating them within the framework of an angry "NO!" to sexism, Daly demonstrated that a new concept of God requires not only a new configuration of all thought patterns, but also a new configuration of society itself. Conversely, construction of a new society must proceed through a total revisioning of its theoretical grounding.

In the next few years Daly did indeed go beyond *Beyond God the Father*, but she never refuted this work as she did *The Church and the Second Sex*, even though *Beyond God the Father* contains an implicit endorsement of Christianity in its feminist interpretation of its key concepts. In *Gyn/Ecology* (1978), Daly redefined her boundary position as no longer attached to Christianity in any fashion. To the contrary, *Gyn/Ecology* is a violent rejection of Christianity and its notion of God on the basis of Christianity's own inherent violence toward women and toward the environment. In scathing rhetoric Daly satirizes the Christian God as trinity, naming its integral necrophiliac effects through such horrors as the atomic bomb, which was initially tested in 1945 at a site named "Trinity." The Christian God is irredeemable, being the epitome of maleness, which by now in this work is also to say the epitome of evil.

Gone is the relatively transcendent "God the Verb" of *Beyond God the Father*; transcendence is overshadowed by a deeper immanence. The book *Gyn/Ecology* itself is a primal form of immanence, described as a verb spun as a "gynocentric manifestation of the Intransitive Verb" (1978: 23). This Intransitive Verb is no longer a God above, nor even, in this book, the Unfolding Verb that calls us into a new future. Rather, the Intransitive Verb is the female Self. In place of the Word become Flesh, Daly sees the Verb become verbalized in radical metapatriarchal feminist writing, but the source of this Verb is the female Self of that psychic space beyond patriarchy called the Background. The language of unfolding first used in *Beyond God the Father* to describe God the Verb is now ascribed to the female Self, who is divine. The Verb becomes wholly immanent, incarnate in women's Background Selves and in the words spun from that space. The parallels with Christian theology are obvious: within the latter, the transcendent God becomes present within history through incarnation, creating a human/divine person. For Daly, the Verb becomes the female Self, and the Self is both divine and human.

Daly's language in *Gyn/Ecology* often includes references to Goddess, but the term does not seem to refer to that which is beyond the self, whether created through women's worship or pre-existing all humanity in association with earth (see, for example, such views in Carol Christ, *Laughter of Aphrodite* (1987), and the volume edited by Judith Plaskow and Christ, *Weaving the Visions* (1989)). For Daly, the Goddess seems to be solely the Goddess-within, or a name for woman's experience of her own activity as be-ing, know-ing, unfold-ing in metapatriarchal discovery of herSelf. God the Unfolding Verb of *Beyond God the Father* is the immanent female Self in *Gyn/Ecology*.

The total immanence of God or Goddess within women and/or within human communities of women and men marks the works of a number of feminists who explicitly name themselves Christian. Carter Heyward rejects the transcendence of God, redefining God as the power of love within community. For her, as for Daly, the self participates in divinity, but whereas Daly sees the divine Self inherently present in the depths of every woman (not men), Heyward does not identify divinity with the self, but with the power experienced by selves in communal togetherness. In her *The Redemption of God* (1982), God appears wholly immanent, to the point that God's own being is created in and through the human community. This immanence is mythologically contextualized in the collected essays of *Our Passion for Justice* (1984), where the ongoing creation of God through human community is itself generated by a God who is neither apart from creation nor reducible to creation, but forever with creation. In *Touching Our Strength*, God is "the empowering sparks of ourselves in relation" (1989: 3).

Rosemary Radford Ruether, while generally far removed from Daly's rhetoric and separatist feminist stance, nonetheless echoes in more muted language the spirit of Daly's transmutation of God first into Verb and then into the verb that expresses and is the female Self within each woman. In *Sexism and God-Talk* (1983), Ruether replaces the patriarchal word "God" with "God/ess" to name the reality to whom religion attempts to point. She is concerned to connect God/ess with the matrix of nature and with our own unfolding possibilities. She concludes her discussion of God/ess in consonance with Daly: "The liberating encounter with God/ess is always an encounter with our authentic selves resurrected from underneath the alienated self" (Ruether 1983: 71). Daly's parallel to this is woman's moving beyond her "foreground," which is alienation from herself in patriarchally defined space, to the Background, which is her inner, psychically authentic female space where she becomes Self, or Goddess. Ruether continues her text: "It [the liberating encounter] is not experienced against, but in and through relationships, healing our broken relations with our bodies, with other people, with nature" (ibid.: 71). For Ruether, as for Heyward and Daly in her *Gyn/Ecology* phase, the divine is deeply immanent. In *Gaia and God* (1992), Ruether's sense of the divine is a "personal center of the universal process, with which all the small centers of personal being dialogue in the conversation that continually creates and recreates the world" (1992: 253). The transcendence of the patriarchal God has given way to a radically immanent form of deity.

Daly's next book, *Pure Lust* (1984), spirals yet further into what she calls her metapatriarchal spinning away from Christianity. Again, as in her earlier works, her movement *away* from Christianity nonetheless continuously uses Christianity and its symbols as her touchstone. The biting satire of *Gyn/Ecology* gives way to a lighter laughter as she explores some of the constructive virtues of metapatriarchal space, where biophilia displaces necrophilia. Gone now is the use of the word Goddess introduced into *Gyn/Ecology*, replaced by metabeing: "The word *metabeing* is used here to Name Realms of active participation in the Powers of Be-ing. Be-ing, the Verb, cannot without gross falsification be reified into a noun, whether that noun be identified as 'Supreme Being,' or 'God,' or 'Goddess' (singular or plural). When I choose to use such words as Goddess it is to point Metaphorically to the Powers of Be-ing, the Active Verb in whose potency all biophilic reality participates" (1984: 26). Given the fact that for Daly the Self is no static term, but is itself a process of unfolding, the identification of Self with God (or Goddess or Supreme Being) is not reification. However, in this passage and *Pure Lust* as a whole Daly uses language that reintroduces the reality of the Verb as that in which the feminist community participates, but nonetheless as a reality that is not reducible to human community. Thus Verb is again both immanent *and* transcendent. In a sense, Daly has moved from transcendence and immanence in *Beyond God the Father* to immanence in *Gyn/Ecology* to immanence and transcendence in *Pure Lust*.

In *Wickedary* (1987, with Caputi) Daly completes the circle. There she reconstructs the Christian mythos, not through reinterpretation of basic concepts as in *Beyond God the Father*, but in a recasting of the Christian eschatological story, sans Christ (although one could argue that Daly herself takes that place as the female messiah she invoked in *Beyond God the Father*). She recasts this story through increasing her use of mythic language – a method that begins to appear in the conclusions of both *Gyn/Ecology* and *Pure Lust* but that intensifies in *Wickedary*. The content of this mythology still derives from that vision of reality presupposed beneath the masculinist and feminist theological interpretations in *Beyond God the Father*. The paradox, of course, is that she has explicitly rejected this vision of reality even while she continues to use it in transmuted form.

The very move to mythological narrative rather than rational reflection on the mythos is itself powerful, given the deep awareness in our own day that all religions live from a primal mythos concerning the nature of existence, the problematic aspects of existence, and some form of resolution. By working directly with the mythos, rather than interpreting it in rationalistic categories, Daly is attempting to refashion the fundamental sensitivity from which we live. She reconfigures the lines etched so deeply into our psyches. In this she shares the spirit of post-Christian or non-Christian feminists who work in the Wicce and/or Goddess movements (cf. Starhawk, Z. Budapest, Carol Christ). She differs, however, in the profoundly Christian structure of the mythos she develops (or redevelops).

Daly introduced this mythological method in her two earlier works, where she concluded each volume with construction of a dramatic scene of female biophilic fantasy as a coda to each work. In *Wickedary*, she places the fantasy between her introductory narrative and the Word-Web redefinitions of words that constitute more than half of this work. What we see in her myth is the "Peaceable Kingdom" of Christian lore, where the interconnectedness of all things (except men) is finally realized. Creatures of earth, sea, and sky join in the hilarity of women as they romp toward the eschatological banquet. There is also the resurrection of the just, so that great women of the past are alive again, joining in the throng. Full communion is established, as each one, whether of earth, sea, or sky, experiences the gift of speech for sharing with all others. Once again, the Verb has become verbs, even while remaining dynamically as Verb. Through its "verbing," the Verb sparks and spins in and through all in the creation of the beloved community. There are signs and wonders in the heavens, and, throughout, all are guided by a directing or controlling principle, the ever-unfolding Good as Verb.

Who, then, is "God" in Mary Daly's lexicon? "Be-ing the Verb, understood in multiple and diverse manifestations, e.g., Knowing, Creating, Loving, Unfolding – and through diverse Metaphors – e.g., the Fates, Changing Woman (Estsan Atlehi, Creatrix of the Navaho People), Shekhina (female divine Presence in Hebrew lore)" (1987: 88). This Verb is both immanent ("The ultimate Guide of each Weaver/Journeyer is her Final Cause, her indwelling, unfolding Purpose" (ibid.: 44)), and to some extent transcendent ("Goddess the Verb: Metaphor for Ultimate/Intimate Reality, the constantly Unfolding Verb of Verbs in which all be-ing participates; Metaphor of Metabeing" (1978: 76)). The Verb draws us toward realization of the reality of the interconnectedness of all existence, human and nonhuman, and toward the creation of life-loving communities. Daly's post-Christian God is very familiar to feminists who remain within the Christian tradition and in fact raises the question as to how thoroughly if at all Daly has succeeded in transcending rather than transforming her once-claimed tradition.

There are three pathways for the construction of the concept of God intimated in this final understanding of God in Daly's works: mythic, linguistic, and metaphysical. Mythically, as noted, Daly moves to the narrative of redemption that is pre-supposed by Christian concepts and recasts that narrative first in feminist adaptations and then in mythic terms. The systematic development of concepts falls away in order to make use of the more fundamental story. The power of the story is its ability to draw directly from the Christian mythic imagination. Thus *Wickedary*'s myth is not a contradiction of *Beyond God the Father*'s concepts; it is instead a different way of expressing the mythos that also gives rise to thought.

With regard to the linguistic move, Daly has been fascinated by the nature and role of language throughout her works. In *Beyond God the Father* Christian concepts have a strange status beyond their interpretation. In her following three works, language itself takes on a transcendent function. It is not simply that deity is named as the Verb; rather, it's as if verbs and all other words have ontological status apart from human usage, almost like Platonic forms of old, or the realism of medieval philosophy. These words reside within women: "Yet Wild words (e.g., words such as Amazon, Spinster, Virago, Angel) continue to live in Musing women's Metamemory. From these depths they howl and yell inside the women who have been made into their prisons and guards. Remembering women hear these howls as Calls of the Wild within and join the gagged Hag-words/Nag-words who Nag us into Naming" (1987: 34). But words are in some sense independent of women: there is a Race of Words (ibid.: 36), imprisoned in women much like the ancient gnostic myths of light imprisoned within finite being. Words are freed when spoken, and once spoken, they act as liberators in their turn. Words are "angels," messengers from the Verb come to empower us for our own participation in Be-ing. Even though Daly's spinning of such thoughts

often is couched in fantasy, the deep ontological sense goes beyond fantasy: in the Dalyan cosmos, the Verb sends off sparks that are verbs, empowering, releasing, and dancing with the community of freed Women. "God" is Word is Verb.

Finally, there is the reconfiguration of our basic conception of reality. By going beyond doctrine to the underlying story, Daly attempts to bypass the metaphysical suppositions of the doctrines. In both the reconceptualization of doctrine in *Beyond God the Father* and in the mythos of *Wickedary*, she implicitly replaces one metaphysical world with another. She throws off the metaphysics of substance presupposed by Christian concepts, and draws instead from a more fluid process/relational orientation. In a sense, one can read Daly as an illustration of what can happen to the Christian interpretation of existence when a relational metaphysics is substituted for a substantive metaphysics. Daly relies on the same mythic structure that undergirded Christian philosophies of substance, but like many another philosopher in the twentieth-century Christian tradition, she rejects substance philosophy without rejecting the underlying mythos. She spins it instead into the more fluid forms of relational philosophy.

Thus while Daly vehemently proclaims herself to be one who has radically rejected Christianity, one can read her work as Christianity in a revised form. Her latest work, *Outercourse* (1992), validates this interpretation, since the book is a "hagiography" that could only emerge from the Christian tradition. The book is a biographical account of her own journey as the paradigmatic journey of Everywoman; one could argue that she is the female Christ. She has left the Christian tradition only to embody its myths in new metaphysical forms.

In a sense, then, Daly illustrates a Christian feminist response to the notion of God in covert form. She provides an interesting contrast with Rebecca Chopp, a feminist Christian philosopher who shares Daly's feminist passion but with an explicit intent not to reject Christian faith but to transform it. For Chopp, as for Daly, the point of transformation is the concept of God. But whereas Daly uses myth, language, and metaphysics, Chopp is more directly involved in language as the primary instrument for overcoming the patriarchalization of God. She develops this most explicitly in her book, *The Power to Speak* (1989).

Quite unlike Daly, Chopp relies heavily and explicitly on Christian biblical texts for her revisioning of God. Like Daly, her metaphor for God refers to language itself: God is Word. Historically, the reference to God as Word had to do with God's logos as the ordering principle of creation, become incarnate in Jesus Christ; for Chopp, the reference is not so much the ancient connotation of logos as it is the contemporary connotations of semiotics. Chopp recognizes language as both definer and limit of our human existence. Word, as the metaphor for God, is liminal language drawn from the boundaries of our experience, pointing as a double referent toward ourselves, but also beyond ourselves toward that creative power that draws us toward our good. Like Daly's Verb, Chopp's Word empowers us toward community. Whereas Daly emphasizes the interconnectedness of the new community, Chopp emphasizes the justice of that community. This would be but a difference of emphasis save for the fact that by including men within the community of justice, Chopp envisions a more thoroughly interconnected community than does Daly.

Daly's Verb spins off angelic verbs that call women to recall old female wisdom; the verbs then become incarnate within women in their speaking. As speech, these verbs awaken other women toward recalling and remembering their strength, so that together, through the verbs, women's community of connectedness with themselves and all nature is established. Chopp's Word breathes in and around the many words contained within the biblical texts of Christian tradition. Through the words, the Word itself is communicated, empowering the hearers of the Word toward liberated communities beyond sexism, racism, classism, and anthropocentrism. For Chopp, as for Daly, there is an ontological power to the Word/Verb that includes but transcends the words of the text. Humans grasp the Word through words, but holding on to the Word, they find that the Word itself has already held onto them and, indeed, enabled their hearing of the words. The Word is a word of grace. The Word lives through humans, is communicated through textual words, but ultimately may transcend both texts and humanity. It is best heard not from the given order of society, but in one's approach to society from the margins, from that place of double vision where one sees things as they are publicly defined, but also as they are privately experienced from the different matrix of the margins. While Chopp's "Word" may be read as a metaphor for God, it is not as one alongside the more primal metaphor of God as Father. To the contrary: Chopp reads God as Father as inevitably and necessarily requiring a public/private dichotomy that makes the public

sphere of men dependent on the private and subordinate sphere of women. A supplemental metaphor is not sufficient to dislodge patriarchy and its necessarily entailed sexism. Rather, the Word is the "perfectly open sign" that cannot be relegated to any one order, since as "open" it necessarily generates a multiplicity of orders. God as "Word" is precisely *un*defined; "Word" generates "words" unendingly. The only qualifier of God as "Word" is drawn from biblical texts that indicate God's concern for the flourishing of existence. Unlike God as Father, with its exclusive blessing of patriarchy, God as "Word" conveys an inclusive blessing, and thus contradicts and *replaces* God as Father. Thus for Chopp, as well as for Daly, a feminist reconstruction of God takes us "beyond God the father."

No more than Daly does Chopp wish to reify deity, but Chopp, working more self-consciously within the limitations as well as the power of language, dares do no more than point to the open Sign that we experience in our liminality. It is sufficient that the Word calls us and empowers us in the various forms of just communities that we can achieve.

Daly's use of myth clearly implies a metaphysics of becoming, and her brilliant use of language illustrates rather than contradicts this metaphysics. Chopp's equally strong use of language moves in a different direction. For Chopp, language may well point beyond itself, but the power of language points most clearly to the sociological world of the humans who use it. Language implies a mystery and empowerment that is more than the human community, but the very naming of this mystery as "Word" underscores the origins of its naming not only in human community, but also within the very specific community of Christians.

Both Daly and Chopp argue that God is a guiding force toward organized complexity in more deeply relational forms of human community. Daly's Unfolding Verb, or the Metabeing that is the Power of Be-ing, guides or lures all creatures outside of patriarchy toward an idealized community. Chopp's Word as Perfectly Open Sign generates a multiplicity of orders all ordered toward a process of transformation into community and communities. Chopp's development is a Christian philosophy of religion, and Daly's is a proclaimed post-Christian philosophy of religion.

Precisely because she rejects Christianity, Daly provides the most interesting case of how feminist vision can transform Christianity. Her journey from reasonable reformist to "boundary" Christian to radical post-Christian, with the corollary transition from God the Verb to immanent Goddess to transcendent/immanent Goddess to the final Metapatriarchal Unfolding Verb, covers most of the feminist options within philosophy of religion for dealing with the issue of God. Daly highlights for us the ways by which God can be released from maleness, and the radical turn toward immanence that this release entails. The violence and necrophilia associated with the patriarchal God are countered with a vision of cosmic interconnectedness and biophilia, and the male-dominated society of the church is countered with a woman-and-nature free community for the celebration of life.

Through both Rebecca Chopp and Mary Daly one can see the depths of the problem of reconstructing the notion of God in an antisexist fashion within Western philosophy of religion. They illustrate the varieties of ways that feminists have sought to deal with the reality that the concept of God inherited in Western culture is so thoroughly enmeshed in the patriarchal oppression of women that the concept not only reflects this oppression but also fosters it. Both work from the supposition that only a radical reconfiguration of Western symbols and categories is sufficient to address the problem of reconstruction. Given the pervasiveness of the issues, to change only metaphors or only myths or only metaphysics is insufficient; all three must be part of the feminist reconstructive agenda.

Feminist reconstruction of the concept of God, using methods such as those of Daly and Chopp, insists finally that all concepts of God be tested heuristically by their effect on human community. For Daly, the litmus test is not only the well-being of women who finally become themselves, but it is also the total destruction of patriarchy. For Chopp, the test is not so much the destruction of patriarchy as the transformation of patriarchy into communities of emancipation into inclusive well-being.

The feminist reconstruction of the idea of God, then, uses the perspective from the margins of a male discipline to give a radical critique of traditional categories. Friedrich Nietzsche once posed the question concerning philosophy's sufficiency for self-criticism with the expression, "Can a tool measure itself?" With regard to the idea of God, a feminist response would simply be, "Yes, using the leverage of women's marginality in the culture and in the philosophical disciplines." From the margins, women reconfigure the center. In the process, they insist that the ultimate judge of any philosophical thinking is not simply coherence and consistency, but the pragmatic criterion of the philosophy's impact on communities of inclusive well-being. Their various modes of reconstructing the notion of God await the judgment of this test.

References

Budapest, Zsuzsanna. 1991. *Grandmother Moon: Lunar Magic in our Lives – Spells, Rituals, Goddesses, Legends and Emotions Under the Moon.* San Francisco: Harper.

Chopp, Rebecca. 1989. *The Power to Speak: Feminism, Language, God.* New York: The Crossroad Publishing Company.

Christ, Carol P. 1987. *Laughter of Aphrodite.* New York: Harper and Row.

Daly, Mary. 1968. *The Church and the Second Sex.* Boston: Beacon Press.

——1973. *Beyond God the Father.* Boston: Beacon Press.

——1978. *Gyn/Ecology: The Metaethics of Radical Feminism.* Boston: Beacon Press.

——1984. *Pure Lust: Elemental Feminist Philosophy.* Boston: Beacon Press.

——1985. *The Church and the Second Sex with the Feminist Postchristian Introduction and New Archaic Afterwords by the Author.* Boston: Beacon Press.

——1992. *Outercourse: The Be-dazzling Voyage.* San Francisco: Harper Collins.

Daly, Mary, and Caputi, Jane. 1987. *Websters' First New Intergalactic Wickedary of the English Language.* Boston: Beacon Press.

Heyward, Carter. 1982. *The Redemption of God: A Theology of Mutual Relation.* Lanham: University Press of America.

——1984. *Our Passion for Justice: Images of Power, Sexuality, and Liberation.* New York: Pilgrim Press.

——1989. *Touching Our Strength: The Erotic as Power and the Love of God.* San Francisco: Harper and Row.

Plaskow, Judith, and Christ, Carol P. 1989. *Weaving the Visions: New Patterns in Feminist Spirituality.* New York: Harper and Row.

Ruether, Rosemary Radford. 1983. *Sexism and God-Talk: Toward a Feminist Theology.* Boston: Beacon Press.

——1992. *Gaia and God: An Ecofeminist Theology of Earth Healing.* San Francisco: Harper Collins.

Starhawk. 1987. *Truth or Dare: Encounters with Power, Authority and Mystery.* San Francisco: Harper and Row.

PART III

Explanations of Religion

Introduction

Paul J. Griffiths

Explanation is a slippery and complicated idea. One might say that an occurrence has been explained when its causes have been discovered and described. Following this line, I might say that I've explained why you just shut the window by appeal to the fact that you were feeling cold. But why should explanation stop there? In order to explain why you shut the window shouldn't I also explain why you were feeling cold? There will be no end to such explanations. Ordinarily, then, explanation will seek not all the causes of what's to be explained, but only those importantly or relevantly related to the topic. Without having been born, for instance, you could not have closed the window. But it will surely sound odd to explain your action by appealing to your birth.

Explanation by appeal to causes, then, ordinarily proceeds by identifying the causes of special relevance or significance to the interests of the explainer. Sometimes, the one doing the explaining is interested mostly in explaining away, in showing that religion, say, is not what those who are religious think it is. An orthodox Jew, for example, may think that when he studies the words of the Torah, the law given to Moses contained in the first five books of what Christians call the Old Testament, what he does is best explained by the claim that God did in fact speak the words of the Torah. But a historian or a psychologist or an anthropologist may offer quite different explanations of what he is doing: they may say that his activity is exhaustively explicable in terms of human authorship of these texts; or that what he does can be explained as an instance of a widespread and well-understood human tendency to want to think that one's own culture possesses privileges and blessings not possessed by others; or that he's just ritualizing his reading activity. And so forth. An explanation that is also an explanation-away typically claims that what appears to be an *x* (a religious belief, an action responsive to God's initiative) is really a *y* (a common delusion, a side-effect of social or psychological needs, or what-have-you).

Philosophers and sociologists and anthropologists have engaged in a good deal of this. Antony Flew's contribution to the discussion with R. M. Hare and Basil Mitchell, for example, argues that what appear to be religious assertions – that God created the world, for example – are better understood as expressions of preference for a certain language, and this because there is, for those who like to speak about God as creator, no evidence that could possibly falsify the claim. An assertion is thus explained as something else.

Adolf Grünbaum and William Alston both address the relation between psychoanalytic theory and religious belief. It has often been claimed (and still is by some) that a complete explanation of why people come to have religious beliefs can be offered by psychoanalysts, whether of the Freudian or of some other persuasion, and that it is thereby easy to show that those who take such beliefs to be true are in the grip of an illusion. Grünbaum claims that Freud's thought on these matters was more complex than is often allowed, and although Grünbaum writes as an atheist, it seems, he does not take the truth of (some) psychoanalytic explanations of religion directly to entail the falsity of religious belief. Alston, too, explores the question of the relation between Freudian explanations of belief in God, and argues that even if Freudian explanations are substantially accurate, they are far from showing theism to be false.

The essays by William James, Rudolf Otto, and Caroline Franks Davis all in various ways treat the question of religious experience. This is relevant, clearly, to the topic of explaining religion because it is one of the things most commonly appealed to in constructing such explanations. People are religious, one might say, precisely because they have religious experiences – experiences, as James puts it, of "the fact that the conscious person is continuous with a wider self through which saving experiences come." Rudolf Otto offers an analysis of one important aspect of religious experience: that in which one is (or takes oneself to be) aware of the holy, something majestically and transcendentally above and beyond oneself. Caroline Franks Davis provides a more comprehensive analysis than Otto of the types of experience that might reasonably be called "religious," including data from a wide variety of particular religions. James, Otto, and Davis do not explicitly address the question of whether explaining religious belief by appeal to religious experience explains it away.

A particular claim or belief – "God exists," say, or "God is loving me now" – may also reasonably

be interrogated as to its grounds or basis. We may ask for the evidence or reasons a believer has for her belief, and if no answer is forthcoming, we may reject the belief in question as unreasonable or irrational, and we may do so just because it is (or appears) groundless. Norman Malcolm addresses this question and, under the influence of Wittgenstein, argues that it is normal for us to have beliefs for which we cannot provide grounds, and that it is therefore no objection to particular instances of religious belief that this is true of them. Søren Kierkegaard, in his "Thought-Project," offers a meditation on how it is that religious truths are learned – which is, according to him, in a way that altogether disposes of the question of grounds. In deep contrast to both Malcolm and Kierkegaard, W. K. Clifford propounds an ethic of belief according to which you should not believe anything without discovering the grounds of or evidence for the truth of what you believe. This principle, he thinks, applies as much to religious belief as to other kinds of belief. Alvin Plantinga, finally, offers a systematic analysis and rebuttal of what he calls the evidentialist objection to religious belief – the objection that religious belief is legitimately held only when sufficient evidence for it can be supplied by those who hold it.

Further Reading

From The Blackwell Companion to Philosophy of Religion, *see the following entries:*

Abraham, W. J., "Revelation and Scripture"
Mitchell, B., "Tradition"
Nielsen, K., "Naturalistic Explanations of Theistic Belief"

Other further reading:

Abraham, W. J. and Holzer, S. W. (eds.), *The Rationality of Religious Belief. Essays in Honor of Basil Mitchell* (Oxford: Clarendon Press, 1987).
Alston, W. P., *Perceiving God: The Epistemology of Religious Experience* (Ithaca: Cornell University Press, 1991). *Key, contemporary theistic reading of religious experience.*
Audi, R. and Wainwright, W. (ed.), *Rationality, Religious Belief, and Moral Commitment: New Essays in the Philosophy of Religion* (Ithaca: Cornell University Press, 1986).
Beaty, M. D. (ed.), *Christian Theism and the Problems of Philosophy* (Notre Dame: University of Notre Dame Press, 1990). *A look at a variety of religious concerns.*

Clark, K. J. (ed.), *Our Knowledge of God: Essays on Natural and Philosophical Theology* (Dordrecht, Boston, and London: Kluwer Academic Publishers, 1992).
Croft, J. and Hustwit, R. (eds.), *Without Proof or Evidence: Essays of O. K. Bouwsma* (Lincoln: University of Nebraska Press, 1984).
Evans, C. S. and Westphal, M. (eds.), *Christian Perspectives on Religious Knowledge* (Grand Rapids: Eerdmans, 1993). *Good quality essays.*
Evans, C. S., *Faith Beyond Reason* (Edinburgh: Edinburgh University Press, 1998). *Clearly written.*
Flew, A., *The Presumption of Atheism and Other Philosophical Essays on God, Freedom, and Immortality* (London: Pemberton Publishing Co.; New York: Barnes and Noble, 1976).
Gale, R. M., *On the Nature and Existence of God* (Cambridge, New York, Melbourne: Cambridge University Press, 1991). *A systematic criticism of theistic arguments, eccentric in places, but philosophically important.*
Garvey, Brian, "Adolf Grünbaum on Religious Delusions," *Religious Studies* 35:1 (March 1999): 19–36. *A reply to Grünbaum.*

Gaskin, J. C. A., *The Quest for Eternity: An Outline of the Philosophy of Religion* (Harmondsworth: Penguin, 1984).

Geivett, D. R. and Sweetman, B. (eds.), *Contemporary Perspectives on Religious Epistemology* (New York and Oxford: Oxford University Press, 1992).

Gutting, G. M., *Religious Belief and Religious Skepticism* (Notre Dame: University of Notre Dame Press, 1982).

Helm, P., *Faith and Understanding* (Edinburgh: Edinburgh University Press, 1997). *A good introduction.*

Helm, Paul, *Faith with Reason* (Oxford: Oxford University Press, 2000). *A clear, constructive account of faith and reason with a focus on Christian tradition.*

International Journal for Philosophy of Religion: The Special Volume on God, Reason and Religions 38: 1–3 (December 1995). *Eleven essays addressing the themes of this section.*

Jordan, J. (ed.), *Gambling on God: Essays on Pascal's Wager* (Lanham and London: Rowman and Littlefield, 1996). *Sophisticated recent contributions.*

Katz, S. T. (ed.), *Mysticism and Language* (New York and Oxford: Oxford University Press, 1992). *Critical, provocative essays.*

Katz, S. T. (ed.), *Mysticism and Philosophical Analysis* (New York: Oxford University Press, 1978).

Katz, S. T. (ed.), *Mysticism and Religious Traditions* (Oxford: Oxford University Press, 1983).

Kelly, K. J., *Return to Reason. A Critique of Enlightenment Evidentialism and a Defense of Reason and Belief in God* (Grand Rapids: Eerdmans, 1990). *Accessible, clear case for philosophy of religion not bound by evidentialism.*

Lewis, H. D., *Our Experience of God* (London: Allen and Unwin, 1959).

Martin, M., *Atheism: A Philosophical Justification* (Philadelphia: Temple University Press, 1990). *One of the best atheistic critiques.*

Matson, W. I., *The Existence of God* (Ithaca: Cornell University Press, 1965).

Mavrodes, G. I., *Belief in God: A Study of the Epistemology of Religion* (New York: Random House, 1970).

McCarthy, G. D. (ed.), *The Ethics of Belief Debate* (Atlanta: Scholars Press, 1986).

Mitchell, B., *Faith and Criticism* (Oxford: Clarendon Press, 1994). *Balanced, clear. A defense of the concord between faith and reason.*

Mitchell, B., *The Justification of Religious Belief* (New York: Oxford University Press, 1981).

Penelhum, T., *God and Skepticism* (Dordrecht: D. Reidel Publishing Co., 1987).

Phillips, D. Z., *Belief, Change and Forms of Life* (London: Macmillan, 1986).

Phillips, D. Z., *Faith after Foundationalism* (London: Routledge and Kegan Paul, 1988).

Phillips, D. Z., *Faith and Philosophical Inquiry* (London: Routledge and Kegan Paul, 1970; New York: Schocken Books, 1971).

Phillips, D. Z., *Reason without Explanation* (Oxford: Basil Blackwell, 1976).

Phillips, D. Z., *The Concept of Prayer* (London: Routledge and Kegan Paul, 1965).

Pike, N., *Mystical Union: An Essay in the Phenomenology of Mysticism* (Ithaca: Cornell University Press, 1992). *A constructive account of religious experience.*

Plantinga, A., *Warrant and Proper Function* (Oxford: Oxford University Press, 1993). *A trenchant, in-depth defense of a theistic epistemology.*

Schlesinger, G. N., *Religion and Scientific Method* (Dordrecht: D. Reidel Publishing Co., 1977).

Sessions, W. L., *The Concept of Faith: A Philosophical Investigation* (Ithaca and London: Cornell University Press, 1994). *The most thorough analysis of the concept of faith to date.*

Shalkowski, S. A., "Atheological Apologetics," in *American Philosophical Quarterly* 26 (1989): 1–19. *A brilliant reply to the presumption of atheism.*

Shepherd, J. J., *Experience, Inference and God* (London: Macmillan; New York: Harper and Row, 1975).

Trigg, R., *Rationality and Religion* (Oxford: Blackwell, 1998). *A vigorous defense of realism and reason in the assessment of religion. Exceptionally clear writing with a good overview of the literature.*

Trigg, R., *Reason and Commitment* (Cambridge: Cambridge University Press, 1973; University of Notre Dame Press, 1990). *A look at a variety of religious concerns.*

Wainwright, W. J., *Mysticism: A Study of Its Nature, Cognitive Value, and Moral Implications* (Madison: University of Wisconsin Press, 1981).

Wainwright, W. J., *Reason and the Heart: A Prolegomenon to a Critique of Passional Reason* (Ithaca and London: Cornell University Press, 1995). *A work that is both historical and constructive.*

Wittgenstein, L., *Lectures and Conversations on Aesthetics, Psychology and Religious Belief.* Compiled from notes by Y. Smythies, R. Rhess, and J. Taylor, ed. C. Barrett (Berkeley: University of California Press, 1967).

Zagzebski, L. (ed.), *Rational Faith. Catholic Responses to Reformed Epistemology* (Notre Dame: University of Notre Dame Press, 1993). *Essays that are critical of Plantinga's work.*

9

Theology and Falsification: A Symposium

Antony Flew, R. M. Hare, and Basil Mitchell

Antony Flew

Let us begin with a parable. It is a parable developed from a tale told by John Wisdom in his haunting and revelatory article "Gods".[1] Once upon a time two explorers came upon a clearing in the jungle. In the clearing were growing many flowers and many weeds. One explorer says, "Some gardener must tend this plot." The other disagrees, "There is no gardener." So they pitch their tents and set a watch. No gardener is ever seen. "But perhaps he is an invisible gardener." So they set up a barbed-wire fence. They electrify it. They patrol with bloodhounds. (For they remember how H. G. Wells's "Invisible Man" could be both smelt and touched though he could not be seen.) But no shrieks ever suggest that some intruder has received a shock. No movements of the wire ever betray an invisible climber. The bloodhounds never give cry. Yet still the Believer is not convinced. "But there is a gardener, invisible, intangible, insensible to electric shocks, a gardener who has no scent and makes no sound, a gardener who comes secretly to look after the garden which he loves." At last the Sceptic despairs, "But what remains of your original assertion? Just how does what you call an invisible, intangible, eternally elusive gardener differ from an imaginary gardener or even from no gardener at all?"

Antony Flew, R. M. Hare, and Basil Mitchell, "Theology and Falsification: A Symposium," from Antony Flew and Alasdair MacIntyre (eds.), *New Essays in Philosophical Theology* (London: SCM Press; London and New York: Simon & Schuster Inc, 1955).

In this parable we can see how what starts as an assertion, that something exists or that there is some analogy between certain complexes of phenomena, may be reduced step by step to an altogether different status, to an expression perhaps of a "picture preference".[2] The Sceptic says there is no gardener. The Believer says there is a gardener (but invisible, etc.). One man talks about sexual behaviour. Another man prefers to talk of Aphrodite (but knows that there is not really a superhuman person additional to, and somehow responsible for, all sexual phenomena).[3] The process of qualification may be checked at any point before the original assertion is completely withdrawn and something of that first assertion will remain (tautology). Mr. Wells's invisible man could not, admittedly, be seen, but in all other respects he was a man like the rest of us. But though the process of qualification may be, and of course usually is, checked in time, it is not always judiciously so halted. Someone may dissipate his assertion completely without noticing that he has done so. A fine brash hypothesis may thus be killed by inches, the death by a thousand qualifications.

And in this, it seems to me, lies the peculiar danger, the endemic evil of theological utterance. Take such utterances as "God has a plan", "God created the world", "God loves us as a father loves his children." They look at first sight very much like assertions, vast cosmological assertions. Of course, this is no sure sign that they either are, or are intended to be, assertions. But let us confine ourselves to the cases where those who utter such sentences intend them to express assertions. (Merely remarking parenthetically that those who intend or interpret such utterances as crypto–commands, expressions of wishes, disguised ejaculations, concealed ethics, or as anything else but assertions, are unlikely to succeed in making them either properly orthodox or practically effective.)

Now to assert that such and such is the case is necessarily equivalent to denying that such and such is not the case.[4] Suppose, then, that we are in doubt as to what someone who gives vent to an utterance is asserting, or suppose that, more radically, we are sceptical as to whether he is really asserting anything at all, one way of trying to understand (or perhaps it will be to expose) his utterance is to attempt to find what he would regard as counting against, or as being incompatible with, its truth. For if the utterance is indeed an assertion, it will necessarily be equivalent to a denial of the negation of that assertion. And anything which would count against the assertion, or which would induce the speaker to withdraw it and to admit that it had been mistaken, must be part of (or the whole of) the meaning of the negation of that assertion. And to know the meaning of the negation of an assertion is, as near as makes no matter, to know the meaning of that assertion.[5] And if there is nothing which a putative assertion denies then there is nothing which it asserts either: and so it is not really an assertion. When the Sceptic in the parable asked the Believer, "Just how does what you call an invisible, intangible, eternally elusive gardener differ from an imaginary gardener at all?" he was suggesting that the Believer's earlier statement had been so eroded by qualification that it was no longer an assertion at all.

Now it often seems to people who are not religious as if there was no conceivable event or series of events the occurrence of which would be admitted by sophisticated religious people to be a sufficient reason for conceding "There wasn't a God after all" or "God does not really love us then." Someone tells us that God loves us as a father loves his children. We are reassured. But then we see a child dying of inoperable cancer of the throat. His earthly father is driven frantic in his efforts to help, but his Heavenly Father reveals no obvious sign of concern. Some qualification is made – God's love is "not a merely human love" or it is "an inscrutable love", perhaps – and we realize that such sufferings are quite compatible with the truth of the assertion that "God loves us as a father (but, of course, . . .)." We are reassured again. But then perhaps we ask: what is this assurance of God's (appropriately qualified) love worth, what is this

apparent guarantee really a guarantee against? Just what would have to happen not merely (morally and wrongly) to tempt but also (logically and rightly) to entitle us to say "God does not love us" or even "God does not exist"? I therefore put to the succeeding symposiasts the simple central questions, "What would have to occur or to have occurred to constitute for you a disproof of the love of, or of the existence of, God?"

R. M. Hare

I wish to make it clear that I shall not try to defend Christianity in particular, but religion in general – not because I do not believe in Christianity, but because you cannot understand what Christianity is, until you have understood what religion is.

I must begin by confessing that, on the ground marked out by Flew, he seems to me to be completely victorious. I therefore shift my ground by relating another parable. A certain lunatic is convinced that all dons want to murder him. His friends introduce him to all the mildest and most respectable dons that they can find, and after each of them has retired, they say, "You see, he doesn't really want to murder you; he spoke to you in a most cordial manner; surely you are convinced now?" But the lunatic replies, "Yes, but that was only his diabolical cunning; he's really plotting against me the whole time, like the rest of them; I know it, I tell you." However many kindly dons are produced, the reaction is still the same.

Now we say that such a person is deluded. But what is he deluded about? About the truth or falsity of an assertion? Let us apply Flew's test to him. There is no behaviour of dons that can be enacted which he will accept as counting against his theory; and therefore his theory, on this test, asserts nothing. But it does not follow that there is no difference between what he thinks about dons and what most of us think about them – otherwise we should not call him a lunatic and ourselves sane, and dons would have no reason to feel uneasy about his presence in Oxford.

Let us call that in which we differ from this lunatic, our respective *bliks*. He has an insane *blik* about dons; we have a sane one. It is important to realize that we have a sane one, not no *blik* at all; for there must be two sides to any argument – if he has a wrong *blik*, then those who are right about dons must have a right one. Flew has shown that a *blik* does not consist in an assertion or system of them; but nevertheless it is very important to have the right *blik*.

Let us try to imagine what it would be like to have different *bliks* about other things than dons. When I am driving my car, it sometimes occurs to me to wonder whether my movements of the steering-wheel will always continue to be followed by corresponding alterations in the direction of the car. I have never had a steering failure, though I have had skids, which must be similar. Moreover, I know enough about how the steering of my car is made to know the sort of thing that would have to go wrong for the steering to fail – steel joints would have to part, or steel rods break, or something – but how do I know that this won't happen? The truth is, I don't know; I just have a *blik* about steel and its properties, so that normally I trust the steering of my car; but I find it not at all difficult to imagine what it would be like to lose this *blik* and acquire the opposite one. People would say I was silly about steel; but there would be no mistaking the reality of the difference between our respective *bliks* – for example, I should never go in a motor-car. Yet I should hesitate to say that the difference between us was the difference between contradictory assertions. No amount of safe arrivals or bench-tests will remove my *blik* and restore the normal one; for my *blik* is compatible with any finite number of such tests.

It was Hume who taught us that our whole commerce with the world depends upon our *blik* about the world; and that differences between *bilks* about the world cannot be settled by observation of what happens in the world. That was why, having performed the interesting experiment of doubting the ordinary man's *blik* about the world, and showing that no proof could be given to make us adopt one *blik* rather than another, he turned to backgammon to take his mind off the problem. It seems, indeed, to be impossible even to formulate as an assertion the normal *blik* about the world which makes me put my confidence in the future reliability of steel joints, in the continued ability of the road to support my car, and not gape beneath it revealing nothing below; in the general non-homicidal tendencies of dons; in my own continued well-being (in some sense of that word that I may not now fully understand) if I continue to do what is right according to my lights; in the general likelihood of people like Hitler coming to a bad end. But perhaps a formulation less inadequate than most is to be found in the Psalms: "The earth is weak and all the inhabiters thereof: I bear up the pillars of it."

The mistake of the position which Flew selects for attack is to regard this kind of talk as some sort of *explanation*, as scientists are accustomed to use the word. As such, it would obviously be ludicrous. We no longer believe in God as an Atlas – *nous n'avons pas besoin de cette hypothèse*. But it is nevertheless true to say that, as Hume saw, without a *blik* there can be no explanation; for it is by our *bliks* that we decide what is and what is not an explanation. Suppose we believed that everything that happened, happened by pure chance. This would not of course be an assertion; for it is compatible with anything happening or not happening, and so, incidentally, is its contradictory. But if we had this belief, we should not be able to explain or predict or plan anything. Thus, although we should not be *asserting* anything different from those of a more normal belief, there would be a great difference between us; and this is the sort of difference that there is between those who really believe in God and those who really disbelieve in him.

The word "really" is important, and may excite suspicion. I put it in, because when people have had a good Christian upbringing, as have most of those who now profess not to believe in any sort of religion, it is very hard to discover what they really believe. The reason why they find it so easy to think that they are not religious is that they have never got into the frame of mind of one who suffers from the doubts to which religion is the answer. Not for them the terrors of the primitive jungle. Having abandoned some of the more picturesque fringes of religion, they think that they have abandoned the whole thing – whereas in fact they still have got, and could not live without, a religion of a comfortably substantial, albeit highly sophisticated, kind, which differs from that of many "religious people" in little more than this, that "religious people" like to sing Psalms about theirs – a very natural and proper thing to do. But nevertheless there may be a big difference lying behind – the difference between two people who, though side by side, are walking in different directions. I do not know in what direction Flew is walking; perhaps he does not know either. But we have had some examples recently of various ways in which one can walk away from Christianity, and there are any number of possibilities. After all, man has not changed biologically since primitive times; it is his religion that has changed, and it can easily change again. And if you do not think that such changes make a difference, get acquainted with some Sikhs and some Mussulmans of the same Punjabi stock; you will find them quite different sorts of people.

There is an important difference between Flew's parable and my own which we have not yet noticed. The explorers do not *mind* about their garden; they discuss it with interest, but not with concern. But my lunatic, poor fellow, minds about dons; and I mind about the steering of my car; it often has people in it that I care for. It is because I mind very much about what goes on in the garden in which I find myself that I am unable to share the explorers' detachment.

Basil Mitchell

Flew's article is searching and perceptive, but there is, I think, something odd about his conduct of the theologian's case. The theologian surely would not deny that the fact of pain counts against the assertion that God loves men. This very incompatibility generates the most intractable of theological problems – the problem of evil. So the theologian *does* recognize the fact of pain as counting against Christian doctrine. But it is true that he will not allow it – or anything – to count decisively against it; for he is committed by his faith to trust in God. His attitude is not that of the detached observer, but of the believer.

Perhaps this can be brought out by yet another parable. In time of war in an occupied country, a member of the resistance meets one night a stranger who deeply impresses him. They spend that night together in conversation. The Stranger tells the partisan that he himself is on the side of the resistance – indeed that he is in command of it, and urges the partisan to have faith in him no matter what happens. The partisan is utterly convinced at that meeting of the Stranger's sincerity and constancy and undertakes to trust him.

They never meet in conditions of intimacy again. But sometimes the Stranger is seen helping members of the resistance, and the partisan is grateful and says to his friends, "He is on our side."

Sometimes he is seen in the uniform of the police handing over patriots to the occupying power. On these occasions his friends murmur against him; but the partisan still says, "He is on our side." He still believes that, in spite of appearances, the Stranger did not deceive him. Sometimes he asks the Stranger for help and receives it. He is then thankful. Sometimes he asks and does not receive it. Then he says, "The Stranger knows best." Some-

times his friends, in exasperation, say, "Well, what *would* he have to do for you to admit that you were wrong and that he is not on our side?" But the partisan refuses to answer. He will not consent to put the Stranger to the test. And sometimes his friends complain, "Well, if *that's* what you mean by his being on our side, the sooner he goes over to the other side the better."

The partisan of the parable does not allow anything to count decisively against the proposition "The Stranger is on our side." This is because he has committed himself to trust the Stranger. But he of course recognizes that the Stranger's ambiguous behaviour *does* count against what he believes about him. It is precisely this situation which constitutes the trial of his faith.

When the partisan asks for help and doesn't get it, what can he do? He can (*a*) conclude that the Stranger is not on our side; or (*b*) maintain that he is on our side, but that he has reasons for withholding help.

The first he will refuse to do. How long can he uphold the second position without its becoming just silly?

I don't think one can say in advance. It will depend on the nature of the impression created by the Stranger in the first place. It will depend, too, on the manner in which he takes the Stranger's behaviour. If he blandly dismisses it as of no consequence, as having no bearing upon his belief, it will be assumed that he is thoughtless or insane. And it quite obviously won't do for him to say easily, "Oh, when used of the Stranger the phrase 'is on our side' *means* ambiguous behaviour of this sort." In that case he would be like the religious man who says blandly of a terrible disaster, "It is God's will." No, he will only be regarded as sane and reasonable in his belief, if he experiences in himself the full force of the conflict.

It is here that my parable differs from Hare's. The partisan admits that many things may and do count against his belief: whereas Hare's lunatic who has a *blik* about dons doesn't admit that anything counts against his *blik*. Nothing *can* count against *bliks*. Also the partisan has a reason for having in the first instance committed himself, viz. the character of the Stranger; whereas the lunatic has no reason for his *blik* about dons – because, of course, you can't have reasons for *bliks*.

This means that I agree with Flew that theological utterances must be assertions. The partisan is making an assertion when he says, "The Stranger is on our side."

Do I want to say that the partisan's belief about the Stranger is, in any sense, an explanation? I think I do. It explains and makes sense of the Stranger's behaviour: it helps to explain also the resistance movement in the context of which he appears. In each case it differs from the interpretation which the others put up on the same facts.

"God loves men" resembles "the Stranger is on our side" (and many other significant statements, e.g. historical ones) in not being conclusively falsifiable. They can both be treated in at least three different ways: (1) as provisional hypotheses to be discarded if experience tells against them; (2) as significant articles of faith; (3) as vacuous formulae (expressing, perhaps, a desire for reassurance) to which experience makes no difference and which make no difference to life.

The Christian, once he has committed himself, is precluded by his faith from taking up the first attitude: "Thou shalt not tempt the Lord thy God." He is in constant danger, as Flew has observed, of slipping into the third. But he need not; and, if he does, it is a failure in faith as well as in logic.

Antony Flew

It has been a good discussion: and I am glad to have helped to provoke it. But now – at least in *University* – it must come to an end: and the Editors of *University* have asked me to make some concluding remarks. Since it is impossible to deal with all the issues raised or to comment separately upon each contribution, I will concentrate on Mitchell and Hare, as representative of two very different kinds of response to the challenge made in "Theology and Falsification".

The challenge, it will be remembered, ran like this. Some theological utterances seem to, and are intended to, provide explanations or express assertions. Now an assertion, to be an assertion at all, must claim that things stand thus and thus; *and not otherwise*. Similarly an explanation, to be an explanation at all, must explain why this particular thing occurs; *and not something else*. Those last clauses are crucial. And yet sophisticated religious people – or so it seemed to me – are apt to overlook this, and tend to refuse to allow, not merely that anything actually does occur, but that anything conceivably could occur, which would count against their theological assertions and explanations. But in so far as they do this, their supposed explanations are actually bogus, and their seeming assertions are really vacuous.

Mitchell's response to this challenge is admirably direct, straightforward, and understanding. He agrees "that theological utterances must be assertions". He agrees that if they are to be assertions, there must be something that would count against their truth. He agrees, too, that believers are in constant danger of transforming their would-be assertions into "vacuous formulae". But he takes me to task for an oddity in my "conduct of the theologian's case. The theologian surely would not deny that the fact of pain counts against the assertion that God loves men. This very incompatibility generates the most intractable of theological problems, the problem of evil." I think he is right. I should have made a distinction between two very different ways of dealing with what looks like evidence against the love of God: the way I stressed was the expedient of qualifying the original assertion; the way the theologian usually takes, at first, is to admit that it looks bad but to insist that there is – there must be – some explanation which will show that, in spite of appearances, there really is a God who loves us. His difficulty, it seems to me, is that he has given God attributes which rule out all possible saving explanations. In Mitchell's parable of the Stranger it is easy for the believer to find plausible excuses for ambiguous behaviour: for the Stranger is a man. But suppose the Stranger is God. We cannot say that he would like to help but cannot: God is omnipotent. We cannot say that he would help if he only knew: God is omniscient. We cannot say that he is not responsible for the wickedness of others: God creates those others. Indeed an omnipotent, omniscient God must be an accessory before (and during) the fact to every human misdeed! as well as being responsible for every non-moral defect in the universe. So, though I entirely concede that Mitchell was absolutely right to insist against me that the theologian's first move is to look for an *explanation*, I still think that in the end, if relentlessly pursued, he will have to resort to the avoiding action of *qualification*. And there lies the danger of that death by a thousand qualifications, which would, I agree, constitute "a failure in faith as well as in logic".

Hare's approach is fresh and bold. He confesses that "on the ground marked out by Flew, he seems to me to be completely victorious". He therefore introduces the concept of *blik*. But while I think that there is room for some such concept in philosophy, and that philosophers should be grateful to Hare for his invention, I nevertheless want to insist that any attempt to analyse Christian religious utterances as expressions or affirmations of a *blik* rather than as (at least would-be) assertions about the cosmos is fundamentally misguided. *First*, because thus interpreted, they would be entirely unorthodox. If Hare's religion really is a *blik*, involving no cosmological assertions about the nature and activities of a supposed personal creator, then surely he is not a Christian at all? *Second*, because thus interpreted, they could scarcely do the job they do. If they were not even intended as assertions then many religious activities would become fraudulent, or merely silly. If "You ought *because* it is God's will" asserts no more than "You ought", then the person who prefers the former phraseology is not really giving a reason, but a fraudulent substitution for one, a dialectical dud cheque. If "My soul must be immortal *because* God loves his children, etc." asserts no more than "My soul must be immortal", then the man who reassures himself with theological arguments for immortality is being as silly as the man who tries to clear his overdraft by writing his bank a cheque on the same amount. (Of course neither of these utterances would be distinctively Christian: but this discussion never pretended to be so confined.) Religious utterances may indeed express false or even bogus assertions: but I simply do not believe that they are not both intended and interpreted to be or at any rate to presuppose assertions, at least in the context of religious practice; whatever shifts may be demanded, in another context, by the exigencies of theological apologetic.

One final suggestion. The philosophers of religion might well draw upon George Orwell's last appalling nightmare *1984* for the concept of *doublethink*. "*Doublethink* means the power of holding two contradictory beliefs simultaneously, and accepting both of them. The party intellectual knows that he is playing tricks with reality, but by the exercise of *doublethink* he also satisfies himself that reality is not violated" (*1984*, p. 220). Perhaps religious intellectuals too are sometimes driven to doublethink in order to retain their faith in a loving God in face of the reality of a heartless and indifferent world. But of this more another time, perhaps.

Notes

1 *PAS*, 1944–5, reprinted as ch. X of *Logic and Language*, vol. 1 (Blackwell, 1951), and in his *Philosophy and Psychoanalysis* (Blackwell, 1953).
2 Cf. J. Wisdom, "Other Minds", *Mind*, 1940; reprinted in his *Other Minds* (Blackwell, 1952).
3 Cf. Lucretius, *De Rerum Natura*, II, 655–60:

> Hic siquis mare Neptunum Cereremque vocare
> Constituet fruges et Bacchi nomine abuti

> Mavolat quam laticis proprium proferre
>   vocamen
> Concedamus ut hic terrarum dictitet orbem
> Esse deum matrem dum vera re tamen ipse
> Religione animum turpi contingere
>   parcat.

4 For those who prefer symbolism: $p \equiv \sim\sim p$.
5 For by simply negating $\sim p$ we get $p: \sim\sim p \equiv p$.

10

Psychoanalysis and Theism

Adolf Grünbaum

Introduction

The topic of "Psychoanalysis and Theism" suggests two distinct questions. First, what is the import, if any, of psychoanalytic theory for the truth or falsity of theism? And furthermore, what was the attitude of Freud, the man, toward belief in God? It must be borne in mind that *psychological* explanations of any sort as to why people believe in God are subject to an important *caveat*. Even if they are true, such explanations are not entitled to beg the following *different* question: Is religious belief *justified* by pertinent evidence or argument, whatever its motivational inspiration? Freud's usage, as well as stylistic reasons of my own, prompt me to use the terms "religion" and "theism" more or less interchangeably, although in other contexts the notion of religion is, of course, more inclusive.

Freud declared himself to be an atheist. But I submit that when he offered his psychological account of religious allegiances, he did *not* succumb to the temptation of arguing for atheism by begging the question. He understood all too well that a purely psychological explanation – however unflattering – of why people embrace Judaism, Christianity or Islam does not itself suffice to discredit theism. Therefore, I claim, he did *not* fall prey to the well-known genetic fallacy, which is often called

Adolf Grünbaum, "Psychoanalysis and Theism," reprinted with permission from *The Monist* 79 (1987), pp. 152–73. Copyright © 1987 *The Monist*, Peru, Illinois 61342.

"the reductionism of nothing but." As he himself pointed out, those who commit this error overlook that the validity or invalidity of a doctrine as well as its truth or falsity are still left open by the psychological causes of its espousal. Thus, in a section on "The Philosophical Interest of Psychoanalysis," Freud wrote:

> [P]sycho-analysis can indicate the subjective and individual motives behind philosophical theories which have ostensibly sprung from impartial logical work. . . . It is not the business of psycho-analysis [itself], however, to undertake . . . criticism [of these theories] . . . for . . . the fact that [the acceptance of] a theory is psychologically determined does not in the least invalidate its scientific truth. (SE 1913, 13: 179)[1]

Like Nietzsche before him, Freud had become an atheist in his student days.[2] Then, in 1901, at the age of 45, he offered his first published psychiatric diagnosis of religion as an obsessional neurosis. He did so in order to illustrate his psychological account of superstition (SE 1901, 6: 258–9). As for the credibility of theism, he had reached a dismal verdict: "it is precisely the elements . . . which have the task of solving the riddles of the universe and of reconciling us to the sufferings of life – it is precisely those elements that are the least well authenticated of any" (SE 1927, 21: 27). But note how careful he was to stress the logical priority of his atheism vis-à-vis his psychology of theism:

Nothing that I have said here against the truth-value of religion needed the support of psycho-analysis; it had been said by others long before analysis came into existence. If the application of the psycho-analytic method makes it possible to find a new argument against the truths of religion, *tant pis* [so much the worse] for religion; but defenders of religion will by the same right make use of psycho-analysis in order to give full value to the affective significance of religious doctrines. (SE 1927, 21: 37)

In the same vein, he declared: "All I have done – and this is the only thing that is new in my exposition – is to add some psychological foundation to the [evidential] criticisms of my great predecessors" (SE 1927, 21: 35).

Apparently, Freud will be walking a tightrope. As we saw, he was very much aware that it is one thing to provide a *psychogenesis* of religious belief, and quite another to appraise that belief epistemologically, with a view to estimating its truth value. Yet, as he just told us, he also claimed that, after all, the *psychogenesis* of theism can have a *supplementary* philosophical bearing on the question of the truth or falsity of religion. And he sees his own contribution to the debate as being one of elucidating precisely that supplementary import. Hence, if we are to examine the philosophical case that Freud tries to make for atheism, we must first consider the evidential merit of the explanatory psychological hypotheses on which his psychogenetic portrait of religion relies.

My first task will be to develop the purely psychological content of Freud's theory of religion, but with a view to passing an epistemological judgment on its major psychological assumptions. These pivotal hypotheses are of three main sorts. Yet, only *two* of these sorts are *psychoanalytic* in the technical sense. Thus, only two-thirds of Freud's psychology of religion depends on the epistemic fortunes of his psychoanalytic enterprise. Later, I shall endeavor to articulate *and* appraise his sophisticated effort to harness his psychogenetic account of theism in the service of his irreligious philosophical agenda.

Freud's Psychogenesis of Religion

A short book entitled *The Future of an Illusion* is one of Freud's several major writings on religion

(SE 1927, 21: 3–56). Just what claims did he make about belief in God by characterizing it as an "illusion"? As he tells us "we call a belief an illusion when a wish-fulfilment is a prominent factor in its motivation, and in doing so we disregard its relation to reality, just as the illusion itself sets no store by verification" (SE 1927, 21: 31). Thus, this sense of the term "illusion" is both psychogenetic and epistemological. It requires that the wish-fulfilling character of the belief-content be an important motivating factor in its acceptance, whereas the availability of supporting evidence played no such psychogenetic role. In brief, Freud calls a belief an illusion, just when it is inspired by wishes *rather than* by awareness of some evidential warrant for it. Hence, as he uses the label, it is psychologically descriptive but epistemologically derogatory.

Yet clearly, it is then still an empirical question of actual fact whether any given illusion, thus defined, is true or false. Someone's wish-inspired belief to have bought a winning ticket to the Pennsylvania lottery may well be pathetically ill-founded, but just may turn out to be true after all. Christopher Columbus's conviction that he had discovered a new, shorter sea-route to the orient was at once wish-inspired and false. In the vast majority of cases, middle-class girls who have believed that a prince charming will come and marry them were concocting mere fantasies. Yet, in a few instances, this hope was not dashed. Hence Freud points out (SE 1927, 21: 30–1) that an illusion is not necessarily false. Nor is a false belief necessarily illusory. For example, the belief that the earth is flat may be induced mainly by inadequate observations, rather than by wishes. To qualify as an illusion, even a false belief needs to have been prompted mainly by a wish, rather than by known evidence.

There is an important subclass of false illusions whose generating wishes are complex enough to include unconscious desires. For example, according to Freud's theory of paranoia, the false notions of persecution entertained by a paranoiac are held to be inspired by repressed homosexual wishes, and by the operation of two unconscious defense mechanisms. Freud uses the term "delusion" to refer to such psychogenetically complex false illusions (SE 1927, 21: 31, 81; 1911, 12: 59–65; 1915, 14: 263–72; 1922, 18: 225–30). Thus, he also speaks of delusions of jealousy, delusions of grandeur, and the delusions associated with heterosexual erotomania.[3] In brief, every delusion is a false illusion, generated by requisitely complex wishes. Thus, a false illusion can fail to qualify as a delusion, if the desires that inspire it lack the stated psychogenetic complexity. But how do both illusions and delusions matter in Freud's philosophy of religion? They do, because the nub of his own philosophical argument for atheism will turn out to be the attempt to demonstrate the following: The theistic religions are delusions, rather than just illusions; in fact, they are mass delusions in important parts of the world.

It is to be borne in mind that these two technical notions differ importantly from the senses of "illusion" and "delusion" encountered in the *Psychiatric Dictionary*[4] published by the Oxford University Press. By contrast to Freud's wish-laden notion of "illusion," the Oxford *Psychiatric Dictionary* uses the same term to denote a false sense perception produced by a real external stimulus, as in the case of some mirages. Thus, when a straight pencil or glass tube is partially immersed in water, we have the so-called visual illusion that the submerged portion has bent and forms an angle with its free upper part, though it is actually still straight. In virtue of thus being induced by a real stimulus, an illusion in Oxford parlance differs from a *hallucinatory* sensation, which has no source in the subject's environment, but is produced endogenously.

Evidently, the Oxford sense of "illusion" requires that the perceptually induced belief be false, whereas Freud's wish-laden notion does not insist on a generic attribution of falsity. And instead of requiring a particular external physical object to be the eliciting cause, his concept calls for a psychological state. Later, when we address Freud's philosophical aim, we shall see just how the definition of "delusion" in the Oxford *Psychiatric Dictionary*[5] seriously diverges from his, no less than its notion of illusion does. In Oxford parlance, it is a matter of definition that there cannot be any mass delusions, but only idiosyncratic ones.

By saying that Freud's psychogenetic portrait of theism depicts it as a collection of "illusions," we have so far merely scratched its surface. That portrayal has at least two other major features.

1. The relevant illusions pertain to the fulfillment of those time-honored and widely shared human yearnings that the theologian Paul Tillich dubbed "ultimate concerns." Thus, in this context, Freud's accent was not on illusions – however strong – that are entertained only temporarily, or by only a relatively small number of people, let alone on more or less idiosyncratic ones. A purely wish-inspired belief that your favorite team will win

the Super Bowl does qualify as an illusion in the Freudian sense. But this illusion is both demographically and temporally parochial. By contrast, his theory of religion claims importance for evidentially ill-founded beliefs that envision actual "fulfilments of the oldest, strongest and most urgent wishes of mankind" (SE 1927, 21: 30). As he tells us, these beliefs, though still widespread today, were already held by "our wretched, ignorant, and downtrodden ancestors" (SE 1927, 21: 33). These forebears, we know, did not have the joys of American football. Therefore, we can refer to the sort of illusion already entertained by our ignorant, primitive ancestors as "archaic," if not as venerable.

2. A further, even more important psychological earmark of theism, in Freud's view, is that this doctrine is engendered by the cooperation or synergism of three significantly different sorts of powerful, relentless wishes. And for each of this trio of wishes, he offers a distinct scenario that specifies their content and mode of operation. Hence let us consider the relevant triad of hypotheses in turn.

As he points out (SE 1927, 21: 33), the first set of these psychogenetic assumptions features wish-motives that are largely conscious or "*manifest*," instead of being the repressed wishes postulated by psychoanalytic theory. Accordingly, this component of Freud's triadic psychology of religion does not rely on any of his technical psychoanalytic teachings. But what are the relevant archaic conscious wishes? He explains eloquently:

[T]he terrifying impression of helplessness in childhood aroused the need for protection – for protection through love – which was provided by the father; and the recognition that this helplessness lasts throughout life made it necessary to cling to the existence of a father, but this time a more powerful one. Thus the benevolent rule of a divine Providence allays our fear of the dangers of life; the establishment of a moral world-order ensures the fulfilment of the demands of justice, which have so often remained unfulfilled in human civilization; and the prolongation of earthly existence in a future life provides the local and temporal framework in which these wish-fulfilments shall take place. Answers to the riddles that tempt the curiosity of man, such as how the universe began or what the relation is between body and mind, are developed in conformity with the underlying assumptions of this system. (SE 1927, 21: 30)

Understandably, therefore, the protector, creator *and* law-giver are all rolled into one. No wonder, says Freud (SE 1933, 22: 163–4), that, in one and the same breath, Immanuel Kant coupled the starry heavens above, and the moral law within as both being awe-inspiring. After all, Freud asks rhetorically, "what have the heavenly bodies to do with the question of whether one human creature loves another or kills him?" And he answers: "the same father (or parental agency) which gave the child life and guarded him against its perils, taught him as well what he might do and what he must leave undone" (SE 1933, 22: 164).

Therefore, Freud deems it to be quite natural that man is receptive to the psychological subordination inherent in compliance with authority, especially authority that is claimed to derive from God. In this vein, Freud would presumably say that the Roman Catholic clergy astutely potentiates the religious fealty of its faithful by requiring them to call its priests "Father," to refer to the Pope as "the Holy Father," and to the Church itself as "Holy Mother Church." Again, Freud might adduce that when parents are asked by their children to give a reason for their commands, many an exasperated, if not authoritarian, mother or father will answer with finality: "Because!" No wonder, then, that religious systems too can secure the acquiescence of their believers, if they teach that the will of God is mysterious or inscrutable, and that some of their tenets transcend human understanding. In sum, it is one of Freud's recurrent psychological contentions that theism *infantilizes* adults by reinforcing the childish residues in their minds (SE 1927, 21: 49; 1930, 21: 85).

But even the liberal Catholic theologian Hans Küng goes so far as to say: "All religions have in common the periodical *childlike* surrender to a Provider or providers who dispense earthly fortune as well as spiritual health."[6]

The motivational account cited from Freud thus far is not predicated on psychoanalytic theory. Small wonder, therefore, that it was largely anticipated by earlier thinkers. At about age 18, Freud studied philosophy with Franz Brentano. Thereby he was exposed to the ideas of the early nineteenth-century German atheist-theologian Ludwig Feuerbach,[7] whose writings made a lasting impression on him. According to Feuerbach's psychological projection theory, it was man who created God in his own image, rather than conversely. Being dependent on external nature, and beset by the slings and arrows of outrageous fortune, man projects his cravings and fantasies outward onto the cosmos into a figment of his own imagination.

Feuerbach took it to be the task of his atheistic theology to *demystify* religious beliefs by showing in detail how God was an object "of the heart's necessity, not of the mind's freedom."[8] Freud (SE 1927, 21: 35, 37) used psychoanalysis to yield a further demystification by specifying additional, repressed feelings of human dependency on a father figure that would enhance the substance and credibility of Feuerbach's psychological reconstruction of religious history.

Likewise strongly influenced by Feuerbach, Karl Marx wrote: "Religion . . . is . . . the *protest* against real distress. Religion is the sigh of the oppressed creature, the heart of a heartless world, just as it is the spirit of an unspiritual situation. It is the *opium* of the people."[9] In Marx's time, opium was the most available painkiller and could be bought without any prescription. As he uses the name of this drug, its meaning is largely descriptive rather than pejorative. But Marx appreciated insufficiently that an impoverished nineteenth-century industrial proletariat and peasantry are not the only groups in society that crave supernatural consolation for the trials and tribulations of life. Freud took into account, much more than Marx did, that a good many of the rich and privileged in society also seek religious refuge from the blows of existence. At least to this extent, Freud was closer to Feuerbach's view than Marx was. Recently, Sidney Hook drew a germane comparison between Feuerbach and Marx, declaring Feuerbach to have been "more profound":

[W]hen Marx says, "Religion is the opium of the people," he is really echoing Feuerbach. In Feuerbach's day it wasn't a disgrace to take opium. It was a medicine, an anodyne. It was the only thing people had to relieve their pain. Feuerbach was really implying that under any system there will be tragedy, heartache, failure, and frustration. Religion, for him (he regarded humanism and even atheism as a religion), serves that function [of relieving distress] in every society. Marx ridiculed this view because he was more optimistic than Feuerbach. He believed that science would solve not only the problem of economic scarcity but all human problems that arise from it. He ignored other human problems. Feuerbach seems to me to be more realistic about most human beings.[10]

Insofar as Freud's psychogenetic portrayal of religion depicts it as the product of *conscious* wishes, his account draws, I submit, not only on Feuerbach, but also on common-sense psychology. After all, at least prima facie, it is rather a commonplace that people seek to avoid anxiety, and that they therefore tend to welcome the replacement of threatening beliefs by reassuring ones. Hence, for brevity, we can refer to this component of Freud's triadic psychology of religion as "the common-sense hypothesis," which is not to say, however, that it is obviously true. Each of the other two components of his trinity is a set of *psychoanalytic* claims, asserting the operation of repressed motives. And yet they differ from each other, because one of them relies on Freud's theory of the psychosexual development of the human individual, while the other consists of *ethno*psychological and psychohistorical averrals pertaining to the evolution of our species as a whole. Accordingly, we shall label the psychoanalytic assumptions relating to the individual as "ontogenetic," but will refer to the ethnopsychological ones as "phylogenetic."

As previously emphasized, the legitimacy of any psychogenetic portrait of religious creeds depends on the *evidential merit* of the explanatory psychological hypotheses adduced by it. Even the common-sense component of Freud's triad is subject to this *caveat*. Invoking the criticisms of his great predecessors, he took it for granted that there is no cogency in any of the arguments for the existence of God offered by believers. But he coupled this philosophical judgment with the daring motivational claim that the faithful who nonetheless adduce such proofs had not, in fact, themselves been decisively moved by them, when giving assent to theism. Instead, he maintained, psychologically this assent is emotional or affective in origin:

> Where questions of religion are concerned, people are guilty of every possible sort of dishonesty and intellectual misdemeanor. Philosophers stretch the meaning of words until they retain scarcely anything of their original sense. They give the name of "god" to some vague abstraction which they have created for themselves; having done so ... they can even boast that they have recognized a higher, purer concept of God, notwithstanding that their God is now nothing more than an insubstantial shadow and no longer the mighty personality of religious doctrines. (SE 1927, 21: 32)

In brief, he is telling us that, motivationally, the dialectical excogitations offered as existence proofs are post hoc rationalizations in which an elaborate intellectual façade takes the place of the deep-seated wishes that actually persuaded the theologians. Speaking epigrammatically in another context, Freud quotes Falstaff as saying that reasons are "as plenty as blackberries" (SE 1914, 14: 24). Hence, Freud could not have disagreed more with Edward Gibbon, who reversed the order of motivational priority as follows, though perhaps only tongue-in-cheek:

> Our curiosity is naturally prompted to inquire by what means the Christian faith obtained so remarkable a victory over the established religions of the earth. To this inquiry an obvious but satisfactory answer may be returned; that it was owing to the convincing evidence of the doctrine itself, and to the ruling providence of its great Author. But as truth and reason seldom find so favourable a reception in the world, and as the wisdom of Providence frequently condescends to use the passions of the human heart, and the general circumstances of mankind, as instruments to execute its purpose, we may still be permitted, though with becoming submission, to ask, not indeed what were the first, but what were the secondary causes of the rapid growth of the Christian church?[11]

It would seem to be basically a matter of empirical psychological fact whether the common-sense constituent of Freud's psychogenetic portrait of religion is sound. Yet, it is not clear how to design a cogent test even of this hypothesis. For note that the required design needs to have two epistemic capabilities as follows: (1) It needs to yield evidence bearing on the validity of the functional explanation of religious belief as being anxiety-reducing; presumably this explanation postulates some kind of stabilizing psychic servo-mechanism that reacts homeostatically to psychological threat. Furthermore, (2) the required test needs to be at least able to rank-order the intensity of the wish to escape from anxiety, as compared to the motivational persuasiveness of the theological existence proofs. Perhaps oscillating anxieties of believers who went through cycles of doubt and belief have already gone some way toward meeting the first condition by Mill's method of concomitant variations. In any case, it would seem that an explicitly *fideist* belief in the existence of God – which avowedly is *not* based on any arguments – calls for *psychological* explanation in terms of wish-motives. The second requirement, however, seems to be a tall order indeed, although it does not warrant putting a cap on the ingenuity of potential empirical investigators. It too must be met, because of Freud's bold claim that even the best of the arguments for the existence of God would not have convinced the great minds who advanced them, unless stronger tacit wishes had carried the day, or had prompted these intellects to prevaricate. But note that, so far, Freud's portrayal of the motives for religious belief has studiously refrained from claiming that this belief is false.

[...]

Let us turn to the two psychoanalytic ingredients of Freud's triad, consisting of his ontogeny and phylogeny of theism. In their case, we must ask, I claim, even whether there is good evidence for the existence of the repressed wishes postulated by them. Insofar as even the very existence of these hidden desires is questionable, one remains less than convinced, when told that they contributed significantly to the initial genesis and later persistence of religious creeds.

It is a major tenet of Freudian theory that psychopathology is rooted in the psychic conflict created by unsuccessfully repressed desires. Guided by this model of mental disorder, his ontogeny and phylogeny diagnose religion as a mixture of syndromes, featuring oedipal, paranoid, and obsessional elements. Yet he explicitly allowed that there are several interesting differences between, say, the illusions of a paranoiac and religious beliefs. For example, the specifics of the former are idiosyncratic, while the latter are usually shared, sometimes even widely (SE 1907, 9: 119–20; 1927, 21: 43–4). Let us now consider, in turn, some of the highlights of the ontogeny and the phylogeny.

In 1901, in his *Psychopathology of Everyday Life*, Freud traced superstitions to unconscious causes (SE 1901, 6: 258–60). The psychological mechanism operative here, we are told (SE 1913, 13: 92), is that of transmuting feelings and impulses into external agencies by *projection* or displacement.

[P]sycho-analysis can also say something new about the *quality* of the unconscious motives that find expression in superstition. It can be recognized most clearly in neurotics suffering from obsessional thinking or obsessional states – people who are often of high intelligence –

that superstition derives from suppressed hostile and cruel impulses [footnote omitted]. Superstition is in large part the expectation of trouble; and a person who has harboured frequent evil wishes against others, but has been brought up to be good and has therefore repressed such wishes into the unconscious, will be especially ready to expect punishment for his unconscious wickedness in the form of trouble threatening him from without. (SE 1901, 6: 260)

Obsessional neurosis features relentlessly intrusive, anxiety-producing thoughts, rumination, doubt and scruples, as well as *repetitive* impulses to perform such acts as ceremonials, counting, handwashing, checking, etc. One might include here perhaps the reported practice of a world-famous logician to cover his handwritten address on envelopes with transparent nail polish as prophylaxis against moisture. The hypothesized causes of a disorder X are said to be the "etiology" of X. Derivatively, the term "etiology" is also used to refer to the pertinent causal *hypothesis*, rather than to the presumed causes themselves.

[...]

Freud's psychopathological ontogeny of theism is not confined to obsessional neurosis. He thought that the Oedipus "complex constitutes the nucleus of all neuroses" (SE 1913, 13: 157, 129). Thus, we learn, the pathogens of obsessional neurosis are interwoven with those of the Oedipus complex. In its so-called "complete" form of ambivalence toward *each* parent, that complex is produced by the conflict between affectionate sexual feelings, on the one hand, and hostile aggressive feelings of rivalry, on the other, which are entertained toward both parents in the psyche of all children between the ages of three and six.[12] The special focus of these affects is the powerful, protective and yet threatening father, who has replaced the mother in her initial role of providing food and protection (SE 1927, 21: 24). Being too disturbing to be entertained consciously, these emotions are repressed.[13] It may be asked at once how the oedipal conflict can be deemed pathogenically relevant, if *all* people experience it in childhood, while only *some* become strikingly neurotic. The Freudian answer is that people do differ in regard to their success in *resolving* the infantile Oedipus complex (SE 1925, 20: 55–6). But some ambivalence toward the father figure lingers on into adulthood.

Hence the cosmic projection and exaltation of this authority figure as a Deity in publicly approved fashion has an enormous appeal. As Freud puts it: "it is an enormous relief to the individual psyche if the conflicts of its childhood arising from the father-complex – conflicts which it has never wholly overcome – are removed from it and brought to a solution which is universally accepted" (SE 1927, 21: 30). By the same token, a true child–father relationship is achieved, once polytheism yields to monotheism after man "creates for himself the gods whom he dreads, whom he seeks to propitiate, and whom he nevertheless entrusts with his own protection" (SE 1927, 21: 24).

Indeed, the psychoanalytically fathomed, unconscious wishes of the adult's residual Oedipus complex are held to combine *synergistically* with the urgent desire for relief from the *conscious* fears of enduring vulnerability, fears which are life-long intensifications of the child's dread of helplessness (SE 1927, 21: 23–4). The product is the belief in an omnipotent God, who is thought to love any of us, even if no one else does.

[. . .]

But what are the actual empirical credentials of Freud's sexual etiology of obsessional neurosis, and of his oedipal *ontogeny* of theism? In the context of the conjugal family, this oedipal plot calls for not only an erotic love–hate triangle prior to the age of six, but also a redemptive denouement of the guilt-laden parricidal wish by projective exaltation of the father into God. It is a clear moral of my recent book[14] that, far from having good empirical support, at best these obsessional and oedipal hypotheses have yet to be adequately tested, even prior to their use in a psychology of religion. A fortiori, the psychoanalytic ontogeny of theism still lacks evidential warrant, with the possible exception of the psychogenesis of the doctrine of the Virgin Birth of Jesus. Until and unless there is more warrant for the ontogeny, it is surely at least the better part of wisdom to place little explanatory reliance on it, brilliantly suggestive though it may be.

But Freud was not content to confine himself to explanatory reliance on the conscious quest for anxiety-reduction, and on his ontogeny of theism. Rather, he went on to develop a psychoanalytic *phlogeny* of theism (SE 1913, 13: Essay IV, 146ff). In his view, this historical ethnopsychology is a valid extension of psychoanalysis. He reasoned as follows:

The obscure sense of guilt to which mankind has been subject since prehistoric times, and which in some religions has been condensed into the doctrine of primal guilt, of original sin, is probably the outcome of a blood-guilt incurred by prehistoric man. In my book *Totem and Taboo* (1912–13) I have, following clues given by Robertson Smith, Atkinson and Charles Darwin, tried to guess the nature of this primal guilt, and I believe, too, that the Christian doctrine of to-day enables us to deduce it. If the Son of God was obliged to sacrifice his life to redeem mankind from original sin, then by the [Mosaic] law of talion, the requital of like by like, that sin must have been a killing, a murder. Nothing else could call for the sacrifice of a life for its expiation. And if the original sin was an offence against God the Father, the primal crime of mankind must have been a parricide, the killing of the primal father of the primitive human horde, whose mnemic image was later transfigured into a deity. (SE 1915, 14: 292–3; cf. also SE 1939, 23: 130–1)

Yet there is still the question of how Freud conjectured the *motive* for the inferred parricide. As he tells us: "Darwin deduced from the habits of the higher apes that men, too, originally lived in comparatively small groups or hordes [footnote omitted] within which the jealousy of the oldest and strongest male prevented sexual promiscuity" (SE 1913, 13: 125). In each of these hordes or families, the dominant male imposed such erotic restraint on his younger and subordinate male rivals by controlling their sexual access to the women of the clan. But this prohibition did not sit well with these rivals. Freud speculates that, driven by their ensuing hostility, and being cannibals, they banded together into a brother clan to *kill and eat* their own father (SE 1913, 13: 141–2). Yet they soon began to quarrel over the sexual spoils of his harem. Thus, they became highly ambivalent about their parricidal achievement. The memory of the homicide itself was repressed, and thereby generated guilt.

The resulting filial remorse, in turn, issued in two major developments: (1) the delayed enforcement of the father's original edict against incestuous sex within the clan made exogamy mandatory, thereby generating the incest taboo (SE 1913, 13: 5–6), and (2) the prohibition of parricide turned into the expiatory *deification* of the slain parent. As Freud put it: "the primal father, at once feared and hated, revered and envied, became the prototype of God himself" (SE 1925, 20: 68).

Freud assumed that over the millennia, our primitive ancestors re-enacted the parricidal scenario countless times (SE 1939, 23: 81). And, as a convinced Lamarckian, he believed that racial memories of it, cumulatively registered by our primitive ancestors – but subsequently repressed by them – were transmitted to us by the inheritance of acquired characteristics.[15] Thus, at least each male has supposedly stored this phylogenetic legacy in his unconscious, including the resulting sense of collective guilt over the primal crime (SE 1939, 23: 132). Hence, shortly before Freud's death, he confidently announced that "men have always known (in this special [Lamarckian] way) that they once possessed a primal father and killed him" (SE 1939, 23: 101). He explicitly credits the Scottish biblical scholar Robertson Smith and the anthropologist J. G. Frazer with the recognition that Christian Communion is a residue of the eating of the sacred totem animal, which in turn appeared to Freud to hark back to the eating of the slain primal father (SE 1925, 20: 68).

As he sees it, by combining ethnography with psychoanalysis, he has discerned a third set of strong wishes that unite synergistically with the other two classes of his triad, and make the psychogenesis of belief in God-the-Father the more imperative. Therefore he proclaimed: "We now observe that the store of religious ideas includes not only wish-fulfilments but important historical recollections. This concurrent influence of past and present must give religion a truly incomparable wealth of power" (SE 1927, 21: 42).

Moreover, the *ontogeny* of the Oedipus complex is, at least in its earlier stages, developmentally similar to its conjectured *phylogeny*. And this psychogenetic parallelism seemed all the more credible to Freud, because he saw it as the psychological counterpart of Ernst Haeckel's biogenetic law. According to Haeckel, the embryonic ontogeny of each animal, including man, *recapitulates* the morphological changes undergone by the successive ancestors of the species during its phylogeny. No wonder that Freud felt entitled to regard the early *ontogenetic* development of moral dispositions like remorse and guilt in each of us as both a replica and a phylogenetic residue of the primal father complex of early man (SE 1923, 19: 37).

At this point, standing at the portal of death in 1939, Freud is ready to deploy his repression-etiology of neurosis, together with his ethnopsychological retrodictions. And he joins them to explain the characteristic irrationality of traditional theism as follows:

A tradition that was based only on communication could not lead to the compulsive character that attaches to religious phenomena. It would be listened to, judged, and perhaps dismissed, like any other piece of information from outside; it would never attain the privilege of being liberated from the constraint of logical thought. It must have undergone the fate of being repressed, the condition of lingering in the unconscious, before it is able to display such powerful effects on its return, to bring the masses under its spell, as we have seen with astonishment and hitherto without comprehension in the case of religious tradition. (SE 1939, 23: 101)

As we learn on the same page, the "return" of the religious tradition refers to the *reawakening* of the repressed memory of ancestral totemistic parricide. And this reanimation was supposedly effected by two epoch-making episodes, each of which Freud claimed to be historically authentic: First, the murder of Moses by the ancient Hebrews, who rebelled against his tyrannical imposition of the intolerable prescriptions of monotheism; thereafter, "the supposed judicial murder of Christ" (SE 1939, 23: 101).

Daring and ingenious though it is, Freud's psychoanalytic phylogeny of theism is dubious, if only because it assumes a Lamarckian inheritance of repressed racial memories. Furthermore, contrary to the uniform evolution of religions required by his account, more recent historical scholarship seems to call for developmental pluriformity.[16] And if there are such differences of religious history, it becomes more difficult to sustain the historical authenticity of the common parricidal scenario postulated by Freud's phylogeny. Overall, Küng[17] emphasizes that hitherto no primordial religion has been found. Indeed, "the sources necessary for a historical explanation of the origin of religion are simply not available." Meissner devotes a chapter[18] to the scrutiny of Freud's psychoanalytic phylogeny of Mosaic monotheism. Writing from the standpoint of biblical archeology, exegesis, and anthropology, Meissner reaches the following verdict: "Subsequent years have subjected the whole area of biblical studies and criticism to a radical revision that makes it clear that the fundamental points of view on which Freud based his synthetic reconstruction were themselves faulty and misleading."[19]

Freud's Argument for Atheism

Having maintained that, psychogenetically, theistic beliefs are illusions, Freud deploys the following dialectical strategy on behalf of atheism: he aims to show that religious illusions, in particular, are very probably *false*. For that purpose, he deems it relevant – rather than *ad hominem* – to point out that religious illusions, though still widespread, were already commonly held by our ignorant, primitive ancestors. We shall designate *any* beliefs of such primitive vintage as "archaic," for brevity.

Freud makes only very cursory mention of the dread of the "evil eye" (SE 1919, 17: 240). But this belief is presumably archaic and still rampant. According to its adherents, the covetous glances of some persons have the malignant power to injure or kill people and animals, even involuntarily. Among the Greeks and Romans, as well as in the musical *Fiddler on the Roof*, spitting was used as a supposed antidote to the poison of the evil eye. Other gestures too – often intentionally obscene ones – were regarded as prophylactics on meeting the dreaded poisonous individual. By extension, praise for one's possessions or good fortune was thought to be an omen of bad luck. Thus, when I was a boy in Germany, even educated people who reported being in good health would *protectively* hasten to add the German word "unberufen," which literally means "uncalled for" or "unauthorized." Not to be outdone by Germans, Americans say "knock wood" with equal prophylactic efficacy. Presumably, no one has ever run a controlled study to determine whether envious glances have the pernicious effects envisaged in the evil eye doctrine. But it is safe to say that if there were any such dire effects, the wealthy and successful of this world, who have been known to dread evil eyes, would not fare nearly as well as they actually do. Hence we may conclude that the archaic belief in the evil eye doctrine is false.

How then does Freud invoke the *archaic* character of theism as a means of discrediting religious belief? He puts it as follows:

> To assess the truth-value of religious doctrines does not lie within the scope of the present enquiry. It is enough for us that we have recognized them as being, in their psychological

nature, illusions. But we do not have to conceal the fact that this discovery also strongly influences our attitude to the question [of truth-value] which must appear to many to be the most important of all. We know approximately at what periods and by what kind of men religious doctrines were created. If in addition we discover the motives which led to this, our attitude to the problem of [the truth of] religion will undergo a marked displacement. We shall tell ourselves that it would be very nice if there were a God who created the world and was a benevolent Providence, and if there were a moral order in the universe and an after-life; but it is a very striking fact that all this is exactly as we are bound to wish it to be. And it would be more remarkable still if our wretched, ignorant and downtrodden ancestors had succeeded in solving all these difficult riddles of the universe. (SE 1927, 21: 33)

In context, the opening disclaimer in this statement as to the scope of his inquiry is an ellipsis for his aforecited tribute to his atheistic predecessors. Presumably, by "religious doctrines," Freud means here beliefs, including totemism and polytheism, that *eventuated* in theism. And, in view of the phylogenetic history he postulated for theism, that religious belief qualifies as "archaic." Though the *word* "theism" was apparently coined in a book by Cudworth as recently as 1678, the belief itself antedates the birth of Christ by nearly a millennium, at least among the Jews. In its traditional form, it asserts the existence of an omnipotent, omniscient and omnibenevolent paternal creator – at once immanent and transcendent – who is accessible to personal communion with us. This divine being is to be respected, loved and feared. In fact, normally, compliance with His ethical demands holds out the promise of heaven, though there have been theists who disbelieved in personal immortality. On this construal, at least some forms of Buddhism and Taoism do not teach belief in the existence of God, as was noted by Supreme Court Justice Hugo L. Black in a decision he wrote in 1961.[20]

To reconstruct the logical framework of Freud's own case for atheism, we can encapsulate his argument in the following syllogism (SE 1933, 22: 168; 1927, 21: 33):

Premise 1:   All archaic, evidentially ill-supported illusions are very probably false.

Premise 2: Anyone's belief in theism is an archaic, evidentially ill-supported illusion.

Conclusion: Anyone's belief in theism is very probably false.

Note that since Freudian illusions are, by definition, evidentially unwarranted, the modifying adjective "evidentially ill-supported" in the two premises is redundant. But it is there for the sake of emphasis. Furthermore, observe that by talking about the belief-states of all theists, both the second premise and the conclusion are, in effect, making claims about *all known versions* of theism, except those that no one ever took seriously enough to believe them. Formally speaking, this syllogism is deductively valid, if we can regard probable falsity as a property of some beliefs. Hence the warrant for presuming its conclusion to be true depends, of course, on the epistemic merits of the two premises. In effect, the first premise says that the world being what it is, archaic illusions are, so to speak, too good to be true. The second premise, however, is a terse assertion of Freud's psychogenetic and epistemological thesis that religious beliefs are indeed archaic illusions; it states that these creeds were prompted not by cogent evidence, but by the need to fulfill a trio of "the oldest, strongest, and most urgent wishes of mankind" (SE 1927, 21: 30). Freud is making use of the fact that a belief-state can be characterized motivationally, while its content can be appraised as to the evidence for it, if any, and also as to its truth-value.

Consider the first premise. It would seem that he took it to be a legitimate induction from the discreditation of various archaic illusions by scientific advances. But prima facie, one might think that an example of his own from the history of alchemy furnishes evidence against the universal claim of Premise 1, which is that all archaic illusions are probably false. As he points out: "Examples of illusions which have proved true are not easy to find, but the illusion of the alchemists that all metals can be turned into gold might be one of them" (SE 1927, 21: 31). When Freud allowed in 1927 that the wish-inspired guess of the alchemists might perhaps be redeemed after all, he was presumably referring to the transmutation of elements known from the radioactive decay of metals of high atomic weight, such as uranium and thorium. Though relevant, let us ignore questions of practical and economic feasibility, and suppose that

all base metals can be turned into noble ones, as desired by the alchemists. Then this state of affairs would not refute Freud's first premise, which claims only that any archaic illusion is very likely to be false, rather than that it *is* categorically false. Besides, even the Greek and Egyptian alchemists of old probably towered in intellectual sophistication over the members of Darwin's primal hordes. Hence even these early alchemists presumably do not qualify as primitive and wretched ancestors by Freud's standards. And if not, then the belief in alchemy – though psychogenetically and evidentially an "illusion" for centuries – does not count as an "archaic" illusion.

Anyone who is still inclined to quarrel with Premise 1 will find it sobering to bear in mind how very difficult even science finds it to come up with true theories. Indeed, the history of science – both ancient and modern – is largely the history of discarded theories. Hence even for scientific theories that are now well-supported by evidence, it is a reasonable induction from the past that they, too, will be found wanting in due course. Moreover, success has eluded Karl Popper and others who have tried to develop a technical notion of relative proximity-to-the-truth or comparative verisimilitude, such that consecutive scientific theories would demonstrably get ever closer to being true. As we know, these bleak results have bedeviled the so-called "realist" philosophies of science. Thus, even the Australian aborigines of 12,000 years ago, if now alive, could be looking at Premise 1 undauntedly and say to Freud: "*Tu quoque.*" Therefore, the discreditation of archaic illusions by scientific advances, which presumably legitimates Premise 1, seems to pose a paradox: if the great scientific theories themselves eventually turn out to be false, by what right can Freud, or anyone, rely on *them* to scorn archaic illusory beliefs as sheer superstitions?

We have reason to think that Newtonian physics, and perhaps even general relativity theory, are partly wrong. But that does not prevent either from yielding otherwise unavailable, often stunningly accurate predictions of, say, the trajectory of the interplanetary Voyager 2, and of Halley's comet. Again, the current theories of neurotransmitters may well turn out to be wrong in some respects. Yet, the fact remains that dopamine and related medications – though of limited efficacy – control the symptoms of Parkinson's disease far more reliably than exorcistic rituals based on archaic illusions, such as shamanism, sorcery, occult art, thamaturgy, demonology, voodoo, hoodoo, incantation, mumbo-jumbo, hocus-pocus, and abracadabra. More often than not, the manifestly true *predictions* made by scientific theories – as distinct from their more speculative hypotheses – suffice to discredit archaic beliefs, such as that of the evil eye, which claims small amounts of visible light to be injurious, if not lethal. Thus, such discreditation does *not* stand or fall with the truth of the major scientific hypotheses themselves. Indeed, in striking contrast to the tenacity with which people cling to illusory beliefs, the methods of the scientific enterprise seem to have the following distinction: they are the only means of choosing theoretical beliefs that allow observational evidence to override, sooner or later, the appeal to wish-fulfillment.

It emerges after all that, though the history of science is the history of abandoned theories, scientific advances redound to the credibility of Premise 1, instead of leaving it devoid of support. Therefore, we can permit that premise to stand.

As for Premise 2, however, we need to recall our earlier hesitations and doubts. Let us grant Freud that theists have produced no proofs for the existence of God that are cogent, either severally or even collectively. Then there still remains the motivational question whether some of the faithful, when giving assent to theism, had not, in fact, been decisively moved by supposed proofs, rather than by deep-seated wishes. To be sure, the existence of a conscious wish for anxiety-reduction by reassuring beliefs is well attested. Yet it is not clear empirically that every case of religious belief can be attributed psychogenetically either to this wish or to the more speculative unconscious oedipal craving, let alone to the questionable repressed desire to expiate the parricidal guilt of Freud's Lamarckian phylogeny. Note that this *caveat* in regard to repressed oedipal wishes and parricidal guilt is not a matter of *generic* doubts as to the psychic operation of a mechanism of repression; instead, the doubts pertain to the existence of the *specific* sorts of repressed wishes invoked here by Freud, and to their explanatory role as the actual causes of the belief-phenomena he claims to explain. For his part, Freud thought that precisely by being so strong and urgent, his trio of wishes were psychologically theogenic. Anyway, the second premise seems to be the weak link in Freud's deductively valid syllogism.

Still, we can *allow* that all cases of belief in God may perhaps be inspired by conscious favoritism for consoling beliefs over ominous ones, combined with any repressed wishes that do turn out to have such psychogenetic credentials.

[. . .]

Notes

An earlier version of this paper constituted two of the author's 11 Gifford Lectures, delivered at the University of St Andrews, Scotland, in February and March 1985. The present, revised text was used in two lectures given in January and February 1986, as part of the 25th Anniversary Celebration Series of the Center for Philosophy of Science at the University of Pittsburgh. The author thanks Richard Gale for some helpful comments on an earlier draft.

1 All references to Freud's writings in English will be to the *Standard Edition of the Complete Psychological Works of Sigmund Freud*, translated by J. Strachey et al. (London: Hogarth Press, 1953–74), 24 volumes. Each reference will use the abbreviation "SE," followed by the year of first appearance, volume number, and page(s).

2 As a young student in Vienna, Freud took a course on the existence of God from Franz Brentano. For details, see W. J. McGrath, *Freud's Discovery of Psychoanalysis* (Ithaca, NY: Cornell University Press, 1986), pp. 101–20.

3 J. Laplanche and J. B. Pontalis, *The Language of Psychoanalysis* (New York: W. W. Norton, 1973), p. 296.

4 R. J. Campbell (ed.), *Psychiatric Dictionary*, 5th edition (New York: Oxford University Press, 1981), pp. 307–8.

5 Ibid., p. 157.

6 H. Küng, *Freud and the Problem of God* (New Haven, CT: Yale University Press, 1979), p. 120, italics added. For a critique of Hans Küng's theological views, see H. Albert, *Das Elend der Theologie* (Hamburg: Hoffmann & Campe, 1979).

7 Reported in P. E. Stepansky, "Feuerbach and Jung as Religious Critics – With a Note on Freud's Psychology of Religion" in P. E. Stepansky (ed.), *Freud, Appraisals and Reappraisals* (Hillsdale, NJ: The Analytic Press, 1986), pp. 231–2.

8 Quoted in Stepansky, "Feuerbach and Jung as Religious Critics," p. 223.

9 L. S. Feuer (ed.), Basic *Writings on Politics and Philosophy, Karl Marx and Friedrich Engels* (Garden City, NY: Anchor Books, Doubleday, 1959), p. 263.

10 S. Hook, "An Interview with Sidney Hook," *Free Inquiry* 5 (Summer 1985): 24–33.

11 E. Gibbon, *Decline and Fall of the Roman Empire* (New York: Peter Fenelon Collier, 1899), p. 523.

12 Laplanche and Pontalis, *The Language of Psycho-analysis*, pp. 282–6.

13 O. Fenichel, *The Psychoanalytic Theory of Neurosis* (New York: W. W. Norton, 1945), pp. 91–8; Laplanche and Pontalis, *The Language of Psycho-analysis*, pp. 282–6.

14 A. Grünbaum, *The Foundations of Psychoanalysis: A Philosophical Critique* (Berkeley, CA: University of California Press, 1984).

15 F. J. Sulloway, *Freud, Biologist of the Mind* (New York: Basic Books, 1977), pp. 274–5, 439–42.

16 Küng, *Freud and the Problem of God*, p. 67.

17 Ibid., pp. 70–1.

18 W. Meissner, *Psychoanalysis and Religious Experience* (New Haven, CT: Yale University Press), ch. 5.

19 Ibid., p. ix.

20 Cf. W. Safire, "Secs Appeal," *The New York Times Magazine* (January 26, 1986): 688.

11

Psychoanalytic Theory and Theistic Belief

William Alston

In this paper I am going to attempt to determine just what bearing, if any, the existence of an adequate explanation of theistic religious belief exclusively in terms of factors within the natural world would have on the acceptability of such beliefs; more particularly I shall examine the claims to the effect that such explanations render theistic belief unacceptable. It would be possible to proceed immediately to a consideration of this problem with no more specification of the sort of explanation in question than what I have just given. I believe, however, that the discussion will be more likely to be firmly anchored and that there will be a greater chance of focusing the discussion on real issues if the treatment of the philosophical issues is prefaced by a fairly detailed presentation of an actual example of the sort of explanation I have in mind. Indeed there may be those who, in the absence of such documentation, would suppose that the chance of success for such explanatory ventures is so remote as to render consideration of my problem useless. But I should not like to justify my prolegomenon in this way, for I fear that there is nothing in developments to date which could be relied upon to remove such a doubt.

If a man accepts a given belief that is widely accepted, he is not likely to feel a need to explain the fact that it is widely accepted. But if he does

William Alston, "Psychoanalytic Theory and Theistic Belief," from John Hick (ed.), *Faith and the Philosophers* (New York: St Martin's Press, 1964), pp. 63–102. Reprinted by permission of Macmillan Ltd.

not accept it, especially if it seems to him to be plainly false, he may well come to wonder why so many people do accept it. From ancient times there have been many attempts on the part of religious sceptics to answer this sort of question. To the question, "Why do people believe in the existence of supernatural personal beings?" some of the simpler answers which have been given are:

1   Man has a natural tendency to personify things in his environment.
2   Believing that the course of events is controlled by one or more personal beings which can, by suitable devices, be persuaded to direct it in a way favourable to man, serves to alleviate man's fear of the dangers in his environment.
3   These beliefs are a survival from the earliest human attempts to explain natural phenomena.

More elaborate attempts which have been made in the last 150 years include:

4   The Marxian theory that religion is one of the ideological reflections of the current state of economic interrelations in a society.
5   Durkheim's similar but more extensively developed theory that religious belief represents a projection into another realm of the actual structure of the society. This approach has recently been considerably elaborated by G. E. Swanson.[1]
6   The Freudian theory that belief in gods arises from projections which are designed to alleviate certain kinds of unconscious conflicts.

I have chosen the Freudian theory for detailed presentation for several reasons. First, it is the only theory which attempts to spell out in any detail the psychological mechanisms involved. Although Swanson, in supporting the Durkheimian theory, shows by statistical studies that there is a considerable correlation between certain features of the structure of a society and certain features of its theology, neither he nor any other protagonist of this point of view has, to my knowledge, done anything to indicate what psychological processes effect the transition between one's awareness of the structure of one's society and one's readiness to accept a certain theology. Second (though this point does not distinguish this theory from *all* the others), this theory is a live issue at present; there are men who are working to develop and extend it (though not, unfortunately, to test it) and so long as psychoanalytic theory continues to develop, this explanation of religious belief will have considerable growth-potential. Third, although it should be clear that no theory which proceeds in terms of one sort of factor can possibly be a complete explanation of religious belief, I am inclined to think, without really being able to support this, that Freudian theory is in possession of a larger segment of the complete explanation than any other.

I

A

To get the fundamentals of Freud's theory, we should look first at his great work, *Totem and Taboo*,[2] and I think it will be worth our while to retrace briefly the main stages of his investigation as he sets them out there. He began by considering the notion of taboo, which is very widely diffused in primitive societies. Certain things, persons, places, etc., are credited with a mysterious sort of sanctity or uncleanness (the two are not clearly distinguished) and from this character springs a strict prohibition against contact with them, except perhaps in very special circumstances. Freud noted some strong analogies between these taboos and certain compulsion neuroses, particularly those in which prohibitions are prominent. They are alike in the following striking features. (1) The prohibition has no rational explanation, or at least its violation will give rise to anxiety out of all proportion to the reasons against violating it. (2) The prohibition has to do chiefly with the act of touching and

secondarily with other sorts of contact. (3) The prohibitions are readily displaced from their primary objects to others associated with them in some way. For example, a person who has violated a taboo himself becomes a taboo, and a neurotic who finds it impossible to pronounce a certain name will also find it impossible to have any dealings with anything on a street which bears that name. (4) Violation can be expiated by carrying out certain stereotyped procedures such as repeated washings. Now the existence of these analogies gives us some hope of explaining taboos, for psychoanalysis, Freud thinks, has discovered the explanation for compulsion neuroses of these sorts. In early childhood the individual has a strong impulse to touch, look at, or otherwise come into contact with something, e.g., his mother or certain parts of her body. Some external authority (his father) prohibited him from doing so and backed the prohibition with strong sanctions. These threats plus the authority which the father's position gave him stopped the overt actions, but the desires were not destroyed – they were merely repressed, driven into the unconscious, from which they seek satisfaction in all sorts of disguised ways. The compulsion is a result of this psychic constellation of forces. The desire, blocked from its initial object, seeks substitute objects which are connected along various paths of association with the original object; but the prohibition, which has itself become unconscious as well, opposes each substitute in turn, the opposition now being manifested as a strange and inexplicable anxiety over the carrying out of the act. Thus both the tendency to touch the object and the fear of doing so are derived from sources which have been forgotten.

To give an analogous explanation of taboos we should have to show that at some earlier period of the race man had certain strong desires which were forcibly suppressed by external authority in such a way that both the desires and their suppression were forced into the unconscious, to emerge in the form of simultaneous desires for and fears of handling certain objects which are somehow associated with the original objects of desire. But where are we to find such phenomena? At this point totemism is brought into the picture. A totemic group is one which is bound together by a special regard for a certain species of animal or plant, the totem, which is regarded somehow as the original ancestor of the group and hence of one blood with it. If we make the assumption that totemism is the oldest form of religion and social organization, then we can take the fundamental totemic taboos as the basic ones, out of which all the others are derived by various associations. These are: not to kill the totem animal, and to avoid sexual intercourse with other members of one's totemic group. But even if we can somehow derive the other taboos from these, how does that help? These taboos themselves seem as inexplicable as can be. To what primordial trauma could they be related?

At this point two important clues present themselves. First the phenomenon of the totemic feast. In many totemic societies, the first taboo is cancelled on a solemn yearly occasion on which a member of the totemic species is killed and eaten in a rigorously prescribed way. The interesting thing is that this is both an occasion of mourning (for the slain totemic ancestory) and a joyful celebration. This clearly indicates that the ambivalence typical of the compulsion neurosis is present here; there are strong tendencies to both commit and abstain from committing (and hence regret committing) the tabooed act. The second clue comes once again from psychopathology, this time from the animal phobias of children. Freud's analysis of these, particularly his famous "Analysis of a Phobia in a Five-Year-Old Boy",[3] where the boy was afraid to even look at horses, convinced him that in each case the animal feared was a symbolic substitute for the father. If we can take the totem animal as a father substitute, then the desires against which the fundamental totemic taboos are in fact directed are those which Oedipus realized – to slay one's father and sexually possess one's mother – and we come within sight of the possibility of explaining totemism on the basis of the Oedipus complex, which, according to Freud, is at the root of all or most neuroses.

But we still need a racial analogue of the individual's infantile conflict with the father over his mother. At this crucial point in the argument I shall quote Freud's own summary of his position, in *Moses and Monotheism* and *Totem and Taboo*:

The argument started from some remarks by Charles Darwin and embraced a suggestion of Atkinson's. It says that in primaeval times men lived in small hordes, each under the domination of a strong male. . . . The story is told in a very condensed way, as if what in reality took centuries to achieve, and during that long time was repeated innumerably, had happened only once. The strong male was the master and father of the whole horde: unlimited in his power,

which he used brutally. All females were his property, the wives and daughters in his own horde as well as perhaps also those robbed from other hordes. The fate of the sons was a hard one; if they excited the father's jealousy they were killed or castrated or driven out. They were forced to live in small communities and to provide themselves with wives by robbing them from others. Then one or the other son might succeed in attaining a situation similar to that of the father in the original horde. . . . The next decisive step towards changing this first kind of "social" organization lies in the following suggestion. The brothers who had been driven out and lived together in a community clubbed together, overcame the father and – according to the custom of those times – all partook of his body . . . we attribute to those primaeval people the same feelings and emotions that we have elucidated in the primitives in our own times, our children, by psychoanalytic research. That is to say: they not merely hated and feared their father, but also honoured him as an example to follow; in fact, each son wanted to place himself in his father's position. The cannibalistic act thus becomes comprehensible as an attempt to assure one's identification with the father by incorporating a part of him.[4]

After they [the brothers] had got rid of him, had satisfied their hatred and had put into effect their wish to identify themselves with him, the affection which had all this time been pushed under was bound to make itself felt. It did so in the form of remorse. . . . The dead father became stronger than the living one had been – for events took the course we so often see them follow in human affairs to this day. What had up to then been prevented by his actual existence was thenceforward prohibited by the sons themselves, in accordance with the psychological procedure so familiar to us in psycho-analyses under the name of "deferred obedience". They revoked their deed by forbidding the killing of the totem, the substitute for their father; and they renounced its fruits by resigning their claim to the women who had now been set free. They thus created out of their filial sense of guilt the two fundamental taboos of totemism, which for that very reason inevitably corresponds to the two repressed wishes of the Oedipus complex.[5]

Thus the dictates of the father return in a disguised form in the totemic taboos, and their strength is based not only on the original power of the father, but on the enhancement of the power of his memory, as a result of the guilt felt for his murder.

However ingenious all this may be as an explanation of totemism, what does it have to do with religion as we know it today? Well, Freud tries to use these same principles to explain the development of religion up through Christianity. The basic point is that the memory of the primaeval murder(s), together with the ambivalent tender and hostile impulses toward the father associated therewith, have been repressed, and that like all repressed material, it is constantly seeking expression; but in order that the repression be maintained, this expression must be more or less disguised. The first step in the development is the replacement of the totem animal with a person deity; in transitional stages, he still bears the countenance of the animal, or the animal may be his inseparable companion; he may sometimes transform himself into the animal, or he may have attained his status, according to the myth, by vanquishing the animal. To represent the father as a personal deity is obviously closer to the truth of the matter, closer to an actual reinstatement of the father, and Freud suggests that this development was abetted by the fact that in the course of time the bitterness against the father abated and his image became a more ideal one, especially since, as none of the brothers could attain to his power and status, that status came to be an unattainable ideal for them. But the hostility had not disappeared. Just as the totem animal was ritually killed and eaten once a year, so the practice of sacrificing divine kings, gods in human form, grew up in many forms. This side of the picture was also reflected mythically in widespread stories of the divine son who committed incest with the mother in defiance of the divine father, only first to be killed by an animal and then resurrected amid joy and celebration.

The primaeval father is most fully restored in all his grandeur in monotheism, the worship of the one and only father-deity whose power is unlimited. In *Moses and Monotheism* Freud explains the fact that it was the Jews who most decisively attained this stage as a people by supposing, with some off-beat heterodox Old Testament scholars, that Moses was an Egyptian who tried to impose monotheism on the Jews and was murdered by them for his pains. The murder of this god-like figure formed such a close parallel with the primaeval murder that the Jews were, so to say, sensitized for a more complete return of the re-

pressed material, and so gradually came to accept the doctrines of their great leader. But this pure ethical monotheism is unstable; it tries to achieve a reconciliation with the father without taking into account the guilt of the sons, and as a result it cannot deal with the hostile tendencies and the guilt accruing therefrom; it offers them no expression. This deficiency is remedied in Christianity which takes as its starting-point man's original sin, and proclaims that the Son of God has suffered death to atone for that sin. (From Freud's standpoint, the attribution of innocence to the Son is part of the disguise.) But though the Son dies he rises again and henceforth occupies the centre of attention and worship so that the hostility to the father is triumphant after all.

Such is Freud's theory as we have it in his two major works on religion. There is no doubt that as historical explanation it is fantastic. There seems to be little basis for the assumption of the primaeval horde and its violent dissolution, other than its usefulness for a psychoanalytic explanation. And other features of the account have found as little acceptance among anthropologists and historians. For example, it is not generally thought nowadays that totemism is the earliest form of religion, or that every group passed through a stage of totemism. And practically no Old Testament scholars accept the thesis that Moses was murdered by the Israelites. An even more serious difficulty concerns the way Freud treats the race, or a society, like an individual man. By analogy with individual case-histories he supposes that cultural behaviour at a certain period of history can be viewed as a disguised manifestation of impulses and memories which had been repressed because of traumatic experiences in an early stage of the race or society. This presupposes that mental contents can persist in a repressed form over many generations, indeed over many millennia, and can from time to time profoundly influence people's behaviour. Being repressed, they cannot have been transmitted from one generation to another by oral teaching or anything of that sort. Despite Freud's disclaimer of Jung's concept of the collective unconscious, it seems that he is committed to something like that.

But really these objections do not strike at the root of the matter. We can look on this prehistoric "I was a Teen-Age Oedipus" story, and its unconscious sequels, as so much window-dressing to Freud's basic ideas. If we remember that, according to Freud, what the primaeval sons did is what every son wants to do but usually fails to carry out, and if we remember that, according to Freud, in the unconscious the wish is equivalent to the deed and gives rise to an equivalent guilt, we can see that the Oedipean conflict which each individual goes through in his childhood is for him an emotional equivalent of such a prehistoric deed persisting in the racial memory. Or to turn it around, we may look at Freud's narrative as a mythical exposition of the unconscious complex which every individual gets from his own early relations with his parents. By this revision we can consider Freud's theory in a form in which it can be taken more seriously as an account of the role played by individual development, rather than cultural evolution, in the formation of religious belief.

B

Unfortunately there is no canonical presentation of this more sober version of the Freudian theory. We shall have to rely on scattered and relatively undeveloped remarks in Freud, particularly in *The Future of an Illusion*,[6] supplemented with works by other psychoanalytic theorists, particularly T. Reik's *Dogma and Compulsion*[7] and *Ritual*,[8] J. C. Flugel's *Man, Morals, and Society*,[9] and M. Ostow's and B. Scharfstein's *The Need to Believe*.[10]

Translating Freud's pseudo-historical narrative into an account of those factors in the development of the individual which render him susceptible to belief in a theistic God, we get something like this. In his early life a boy's relations to his parents typically develop in such a way as to present grave problems to him. (To keep things within manageable length, we are restricting ourselves to the male believer. Perhaps the religious beliefs of females cannot be causally explained!) His parents, particularly his father, appear to him as almighty all-knowing beings, and as such they are regarded as mysterious and responded to with awe. The child is dependent on them in all sorts of ways and, of course, he normally develops a close attachment to them, feeling gratitude to them for their providential care and protection and vastly enjoying their company (a great deal of the time). But, of course, they also function as disciplinarians, restricting him in various ways and punishing him for transgressions, and so they are also regarded as stern judges and harsh taskmasters whose wrath is likely to be provoked at any moment, and this harshness naturally arouses resentment and hostility. (Of course there are wide variations between different sets of parents in these regards, but these differences may

loom larger to the adult observer than to the child.) Thus we have a striking surface similarity between the standard attributes of the theistic God – omnipotence, omniscience, inscrutability, providential concern and the small child's view of his parents and feelings toward them – and between the standard ways of relating oneself to the theistic God – utter dependence, awe, fear of divine punishment, gratitude for divine mercy and protection. Of course this similarity in itself is no evidence for a causal connection; at best it furnishes a clue.

So far, there is nothing to provide a decisive distinction between the parents in these regards, although it is generally assumed that the father is usually regarded as the chief source both of frustration and protection. Freud's main reason for regarding the father as the chief model for God (still restricting ourselves to the male child) comes from the Oedipean situation, and this is the chief point at which the theory of individual development parallels the "historical" account. As all the world knows, Freud supposes that the male child at around the age of four comes to desire the mother sexually and to regard the father as a rival. Depending more or less on actual indications, the child becomes so afraid of the father's hostility that he not only abandons his sexual aims but also represses the entire complex of desires, fears, etc. (Love for the father plays a role here too.) This complex remains, in greater or less intensity, in the unconscious, and it is because the theistic God provides an external figure on which to project this material that men have as much inclination as they do to believe in such a Being and to accept the attitudes and practices that go along with this belief.

This rough sketch of the theory leaves many questions unanswered. The most important of these is: just what does "projecting" this unconscious material do for the individual? To answer this question, we must first get a fuller idea of the nature of the material and the conditions of its existence in the unconscious.

Normally, the termination of the Oedipean situation leaves the individual with a number of conflicts, the exact nature of which are hidden from him because of the repression. There is the conflict between tendencies to rebel against the father and tendencies to submit to the father. And of course there is the conflict between the desires which his father opposed and the prohibitions against satisfying these desires; many of these prohibitions have now become internalized in the form of the "super-ego". Since these desires, fears, prohibitions, conceptions, etc., are excluded from consciousness, they are largely unavailable for further development and so retain their childlike form. But they also retain their strength; the desires press for some sort of satisfaction and the fears and prohibitions oppose this. And the lack of satisfaction and the continual vacillation manifest themselves in various kinds of conscious distress.

The projection of the childhood father-image onto a supernatural being serves to alleviate, or at least reduce, this distress in several ways. First, the mere fact of externalizing the problem is some relief in itself. Instead of mysterious discomfort with only vague intimations of its source, the individual has a clear-cut opposition between various desires of his own on the one hand and a forbidding external person on the other. At least he can understand the problem. Second, there is much less conflict because the balance has been tipped decisively in the direction of the prohibiting tendencies. (Perhaps the theory should hold that this decisive shift has to have already occurred in the unconscious before there is a very strong tendency to believe in the theistic God. See the detailed analysis from Freud below.) The external figure is so overpowering as to seriously weaken the rebellious tendencies, and on the other hand he is so idealized morally and credited with such perfect love as to render resentment and hostility much less appropriate. Third, as is suggested in our summary of Freud's historical account, the theology tends to be shaped in such a way as to give some vicarious satisfaction to the rebellious tendencies as well. Reik in *Dogma and Compulsion* carries out an elaborate analysis of the development of the Christian doctrine of the Trinity as a series of shifts in the balance of rebellious and submissive forces in the son–father conflict. And even if there are no female deities available there are feminine aspects of God, or perhaps the Virgin Mary, and in relation to these the individual may achieve some substitute satisfaction of the Oedipean desires.[11]

The Oedipean situation leaves a heavy deposit of guilt, as well as conflict, in the unconscious – guilt both for the continuing sexual desires for the mother and for the hostility against the father. Projection onto a supernatural deity can also serve to alleviate this guilt, for religion not only gets out into the open a figure, transgression against whom gave rise to the guilt and to whom reparations will have to be made, but also provides means for making the reparation and otherwise dissipating guilt – confession, penance, restrictions and renunciations of various kinds. Some Freudian writers, especially Ostow and Scharfstein, have placed the chief emphasis on this function of the religious projections in relieving guilt.

In *The Future of an Illusion*, a very chaotic work, the only clear suggestion made as to the psychological basis of theistic belief seems to be rather different from all the foregoing. There Freud speaks of the various dangers and frustrations of life, and says that the adult, in the face of these conditions, tends to regress to the infantile state in which he could rely on the love and protection of his almighty father. And since the adult can only carry this off by positing an invisible cosmic counterpart of the infantile image of the father he proceeds to do so.[12] Now in itself this suggestion differs from the old-age idea that belief in God is a wish-fulfilment only by invoking the well-attested mechanism of regression and calling attention to the fact that the infantile attitude toward the father provides an appropriate goal of regression. But it can also be viewed as a supplement to the Freudian theory as sketched above. In the concept of regression in the face of emotional difficulties it provides a possible way of answering questions as to the timing of conversion to or revivification of religious beliefs. The regression has three important features. First, it tends to reinstate various earlier modes of feeling toward, thinking about, and relating to, persons and things. This is the point made in the passage from *The Future of an Illusion* alluded to earlier in this paragraph. Second, it tends to strengthen the childhood desires, etc., already existing in the unconscious, thereby increasing the need for some sort of relief. Third, it lowers resistance to projection, since the further back we go in individual development the less sharp the distinction between oneself and the external world. All these factors are conducive to the sort of projection posited by the theory. We should also note that the difficulties which set off regression can themselves be intimately connected with the relevant unconscious material; for example, anxiety over intimate involvement with a woman unconsciously identified with the mother can play this role.

To sum up, Freudian theory can be construed as regarding an individual's tendency to accept belief in a supernatural personal deity (of the sort envisaged in the Judæo-Christian tradition) as partly due to a tendency to project a childhood father-image existing in the unconscious, this projection normally following on a regression set off by emotional difficulties of one sort or another and serving to alleviate, at least in part, unconscious conflicts and unconscious guilt. It would seem that *contra* many psychoanalytic writers the conflicts and guilt so alleviated need not be restricted to the Oedipean situation. It does seem that only conflicts between the superego and forbidden tendencies could be alleviated by this method, rather than conflicts between different morally neutral tendencies; but this still leaves a very wide field. And it would seem that unconscious guilt arising from any source could be interpreted by the individual as due to transgressions against divine commands. Hence I do not believe that this theory of religious belief is necessarily tied to the thesis that the Oepidean situation has the absolutely central importance attributed to it by Freud; although if we are to hold that projection of an unconscious father-image underlies theistic religious belief we have to suppose that relations to the father are extremely important in the life of the young child and that in the course of these relations difficulties arise which result in considerable repression.

What reason is there to suppose that this theory is correct? There is no scientifically respectable evidence for it. Such evidence might conceivably be gathered. If we could develop reliable measures of such factors as degree of unconscious conflict, degree of unconscious guilt, strength of tendency to regress under difficulties and strength of tendency to project, we could then determine the extent to which these correlate with degree of belief in a theistic God, provided we had some reliable way of measuring the latter. But we are a long way from this. Meanwhile the only backing for the theory consists of speculative extensions to religious belief of mechanisms like regression and projection, the existence and (to some extent) the conditions of which have been established elsewhere. These extensions are supported by analogies between cases of religious belief and cases of neurosis in which the operation of these mechanisms is fairly well established. The analogies are sometimes developed in great detail, as in Reik's analysis of the development of the doctrine of the Trinity, but no matter how elaborate, they remain suggestive rather than evidential. Nevertheless, the analogies and extrapolations seem to me impressive enough to make them worth taking seriously.

It may be in order to append to this rather abstract summary an actual example of an analysis by Freud of a particular case of coming to believe in God. Freud once received a letter from an American physician who had noted in a published interview with Freud a reference to the latter's lack of religious faith, and who communicated to Freud an account of his conversion experience. The account ran, in part, as follows:[13]

> One afternoon while I was passing through the dissecting-room my attention was attracted to a sweet-faced dear old woman who was being carried to a dissecting-table. This sweet-faced woman made such an impression on me that a thought flashed up in my mind, "There is no God: if there were a God he would not have allowed this dear old woman to be brought into the dissecting-room."
>
> When I got home that afternoon the feeling I had had at the sight in the dissecting-room had determined me to discontinue going to church. The doctrines of Christianity had before this been the subject of doubts in my mind.
>
> While I was meditating on this matter a voice spoke to my soul and said that "I should consider the step I was about to take". My spirit replied to this inner voice saying, "If I knew of a certainty that Christianity was truth and the Bible was the Word of God, then I would accept it".
>
> In the course of the next few days God made it clear to my soul that the Bible was his Word, that the teachings about Jesus Christ were true, and that Jesus was our only hope. After such a clear revelation I accepted the Bible as God's word and Jesus Christ as my personal Saviour. Since then God has revealed himself to me by many infallible proofs.
>
> I beg you as a brother physician to give thought to this most important matter, and I can assure you, if you look into this subject with an open mind, God will reveal the truth to your soul, the same as he did to me and to multitudes of others.

Freud proceeded to subject this account to psychoanalytic interpretation, with the following results:

> We may suppose, therefore, that this was the way in which things happened. The sight of a woman's dead body, naked or on the point of being stripped, reminded the young man of his mother. It roused in him a longing for his mother which sprang from his Oedipus complex, and this was immediately completed by a feeling of indignation against his father. His ideas of "father" and "God" had not yet become widely separated; so that his desire to destroy his father

could become conscious as doubt in the existence of God and could seek to justify itself in the eyes of reason as indignation about the ill-treatment of a mother-object. It is of course typical for a child to regard what his father does to his mother in sexual intercourse as ill-treatment. The new impulse, which was displaced into the sphere of religion, was only a repetition of the Oedipus situation and consequently soon met with a similar fate. It succumbed to a powerful opposing current. During the actual conflict the level of displacement was not maintained: there is no mention of arguments in justification of God, nor are we told what the infallible signs were by which God proved his existence to the doubter. The conflict seems to have been unfolded in the form of an hallucinatory psychosis: inner voices were heard which uttered warnings against resistance to God. But the outcome of the struggle was displayed once again in the sphere of religion and it was of a kind pre-determined by the fate of the Oedipus complex: complete submission to the will of God the Father. The young man became a believer and accepted everything he had been taught since his childhood about God and Jesus Christ. He had had a religious experience and had undergone a conversion.

C

I have been presenting the psychoanalytic explanation as an example of an explanation of theistic belief in terms of factors within the natural world. My central concern in this paper is to determine what bearing the adequacy of an explanation of this sort would have on the acceptability of theistic belief. But before settling down to this task, we must try to be clearer as to the defining features of the sort of theory in which we are interested and as to the extent to which the psychoanalytic explanation does or does not exemplify these features.

First, let me make more explicit what I mean by the adequacy of such an explanation. In saying of such an explanation ("causal" explanation, if you like, though I do not wish to import anything into "causal" other than what is specified here) that it is adequate, I simply mean that it specifies conditions which are such that whenever those conditions are satisfied theistic belief exists in some specified relation to the conditions. It might be argued that in order to explain the occurrence of a belief we need something further, e.g. some intelligible relationship between the antecedent conditions and the

belief. Thus it might be said that even if we found an absolutely unexceptionable correlation between theistic belief and level of blood sugar, so that on the basis of this we were convinced that wherever blood sugar is at a certain level theistic belief exists, that would not serve to *explain* such belief or to show that blood sugar *produces* such belief, for it is impossible to understand how there could be any connection between them. But if we did have a perfect correlation over a wide range of cases, then I would suppose that we should first look for intermediate factors which would bridge this conceptual gap, or, if persistent search should fail to uncover any, we should have to revise the basic principles in terms of which blood sugar level and theistic belief cannot be directly connected. This raises problems in the philosophy of science into which I cannot go.

One must recognize that Freudian theory, as it actually exists, is just not a theory of this sort. By this I do not mean that it has not been established as a theory of this sort, but that it is not put forward, and cannot plausibly be put forward, as a theory which specifies conditions sufficient to give rise to theistic belief. Remember that when I summed up the theory I presented it as claiming that an individual's *tendency* to accept belief in a supernatural deity is *partly* due to a tendency to project a childhood father-image. It can aspire to explain only a *tendency* to accept the belief, rather than simply the belief, because the theory in the form in which we are considering it is dealing with a situation in which the individual finds the belief ready-made in his culture, rather than dealing with the problem of the cultural origin of the belief. Therefore the cultural configuration with which the individual is faced and the learning processes by which he assimilates this will have to form part of the explanation of the fact that a given individual acquires theistic belief. Psychoanalysis can aspire only to explain the differential readiness of different people to accept what is thus proffered. And I have said "*partly* due" because even with this restriction there are obviously many other factors which play a part in determining the degree of this readiness. Both from everyday observation and from various systematic investigations, there is every reason to suppose that such things as intellectual capacity, temperamental factors such as a generalized enthusiasm or the reverse, the associations that he has formed with things religious, and the kinds of religious believers with whom he has been in personal contact, will affect an individual's readiness to accept certain beliefs with a given degree of assurance and a given sort of integration with other aspects of his personality. (Moreover, we should not lose sight of the possibility that theistic belief has very different psychological roots in different sorts of people and that psychoanalysis might give part of the explanation for some but not for all.) Given this obvious diversity in the determinants of theistic belief, if we try to inflate any of the current theoretical approaches into a theory which claims to provide a specification of sufficient conditions it becomes hopelessly implausible. And thus far no one has made any plausible suggestions as to how we might develop a theory which integrates all the relevant factors. Therefore, in the absence of any genuine actual example, I am going to take the psychoanalytic explanation as one which might, with suitable supplementation, be developed into the sort of theory in which I am interested, and in referring to it as an example I shall be pretending such supplementation has actually been carried out.

There are various other questions which might be raised concerning the boundaries of the kind of theory in which we are interested. Just what are we to count as theistic belief? For example, does the sort of religious belief which Paul Tillich says he has count? More generally, to just what extent does a Supreme Being have to be conceived as a person in order for the belief to be classified as theistic? And are we considering simply the bare belief that there exists an omnipotent perfectly good personal Being, or are we also including other typical components of a theistic theology, such as the doctrines of creation and predestination, and certain sorts of beliefs concerning human nature and destiny? Again, will the theory try to account for variations in the strength and/or persistence of such beliefs in terms of variations in the factors, or will it be simply an explanation of presence-or-absence, defined by some cut-off point? There are many such issues which would have to be settled by someone setting out to refine and develop such theories, but for our purpose we can leave these alternatives open. We shall simply suppose that a theory has been established which defines theistic belief in a way which makes it possible to reliably determine when we have it and when we don't, and in a way which does not significantly jar with the established use of the term; and that the theory relates the existence and/or degrees of such belief to certain factors in the natural world.

There is one further restriction on the theories in which we are interested which must be made

explicit. Let us suppose that there are one or more cogent arguments for the existence of God, and let us suppose that it can be shown that a grasp of one of these arguments, plus acceptance of the premises, is always sufficient to bring about theistic belief, unless certain specifiable and enumerable forms of irrationality are present. The fact that someone understands a certain argument and the fact that someone accepts certain propositions are surely facts within the natural world. Yet I suppose that no one would have the slightest inclination to say that the adequacy of this sort of explanation would have any tendency to show the belief to be unacceptable. I want to restrict my attention to possible explanations with respect to which there would be an inclination to say this. This restriction can be carried out by including a proviso that the theories specify conditions which do not include acquiring, considering or possessing good reasons for theistic belief. I shall put this by saying that these theories specify "reason-irrelevant" conditions. This will still leave us with a wide range of examples, including the psychoanalytic theory.

II

We can now turn to the central question of this paper: would the success of an explanation of religious belief in terms of natural factors have any tendency to show such belief to be unacceptable? We may as well begin by considering the most extreme claim which could be made on this matter, viz., that such explanations of religious beliefs as the Freudian show that these beliefs can no longer be considered serious candidates for acceptance. We can distinguish different versions of this view, depending on just what aspect of the explanation is supposed to give it this force. Presumably it will be either the general point that theistic belief is due to some reason-irrelevant natural causes[14] or others, or it will be the more specific point that it is due to the particular sort of natural causes specified in the psychoanalytic explanation. I shall consider each of these possibilities in turn.

A

Why should anyone suppose that the fact that there are causal factors within the world of nature which are responsible for theistic belief constitute any reason for rejecting the belief? One cannot appeal here to a general principle that any belief can be refuted by showing that it is due to natural causes. For if we accept causal determinism within the psychological sphere, and those whose positions are being considered presumably would, then such causal determinations could, in principle, be exhibited for any belief whatsoever. There would have to be something special about the belief in a theistic God which would render it specially liable to such refutation. Now there are undoubtedly some beliefs which could be refuted by showing them to be causally determined, e.g., the belief that no beliefs are causally determined (assuming that we can get around self-referential difficulties here). Similarly it might be supposed that theism has implications which are incompatible with a causal determination of theistic belief. For example, it might be claimed that it would not be in keeping with the character and/or purposes of a theistic God to allow belief or non-belief in his existence to be determined by any natural factors; that he would reserve such a sacred matter as this for his own direct jurisdiction.

I do not suppose that anyone would claim that such causal determination is *logically* incompatible with the existence of God. Surely there is nothing in the theistic notion of God which would make it impossible that God should set up the natural world in such a way that belief in his existence would be produced by certain natural mechanisms. The fact that such belief is especially important to him does nothing to establish any such conclusion. For there is no reason to doubt that he could so arrange things that the operation of such mechanisms would be such as to be in line with his purposes. Indeed there are many other things in the universe which are presumably very important to God's plans (indeed, what isn't?) which everyone admits to be causally determined, e.g. the revolution of the earth around the sun and the biological processes responsible for the functioning of plants. The most that could be claimed with any plausibility is that one would not *expect* a theistic God to arrange things so that theistic belief is so controlled. I will resist the temptation to oppose this on the grounds that no human being can have any grounds for expecting an omnipotent Creator to act in one way rather than another. For if that is the way the game is played we are also prevented from having any a posteriori grounds for deciding whether such a Being exists, and I would take that to be a severe blow to theistic belief. Moreover, in so far as our concept of God has any content we have some reason, on some level of generality, for expecting

one thing rather than another; and if the concept has no content then religion evaporates. However, in this particular case I would like to say that I do not see that the great importance or sanctity of this matter carries any strong presumption that God would not tie the belief to natural causes. I suppose I would admit to some mild surprise at finding a theistic God operating in this manner. But if anything is clear, it is that there are many features of the world which are not quite what one would initially expect from such a deity, and that if the belief can survive those that are repeatedly brought out in discussions of the problem of evil, it has nothing to fear from the present point.

There is one stronger reason for regarding such causal determination as discordant or even strictly incompatible with theism. This is the idea that it is part of God's plan to leave decision on belief or non-belief (in this matter) to the free choice of the individual. God has created man as a free moral agent and has left him to work out his own destiny. And among the most crucial choices which each individual has to make for himself is this one – whether to recognize the divine existence, with everything that this entails, or to blind oneself to it. (This line of thought requires the assumption that the divine existence is obvious to anyone who does not *avoid* it.) But if such belief is causally determined, then the individual does not have a free choice in this matter. *Ergo*: this line of argument, even if sound, does not show that causal determination of theistic belief is incompatible with certain views as to the divine purpose that are firmly entrenched in theistic thought.

This issue cannot be considered here because it raises all the fundamental problems about free will. The line of argument just sketched presupposes that if a certain belief is causally determined then one can't make a free choice as to whether to accept it or not. (I am leaving aside the further difficulty that it may be a mistake to use notions like choice and decision with respect to belief.) But whether this is so is perhaps the chief issue in discussions about free will, and there are powerful reasons for doubting that it is the case. In any event, if psychoanalytic theory comes into conflict with theism on this ground, it does so together with any view which regards human actions as causally determined. And so we are not faced here with a difficulty for theism which is in any way special to the causal determination of *theistic belief*.

But let us remember that we are dealing, not with explanations in terms of *any* natural factor, but specifically with those in terms of reason-irrelevant factors. And it might be thought that this restriction would put us in a better position to demonstrate an incompatibility. Can we suppose that a deity which is the source of rationality would structure things in such a way that theistic belief is produced by irrational factors; i.e., in such a way that those who have the belief are (or may be) without any real basis for the belief? Well, one can easily construe a concept of God which would rule out such causal determination, but it is not at all clear that the concept of God in, e.g., Christianity always or even usually is of this sort. References in Christian literature to God as the source of reason are far outnumbered by apostrophes to the inscrutability, mysteriousness or downright irrationality (by human standards) of the divine activity. God as a cosmic mathematician is a modern invention. And of course to a religious thinker like Kierkegaard rationality is the last thing in the world God is interested in promoting.

There seems, then, to be little reason to suppose that the fact, if it is a fact, that theistic belief is causally determined directly furnishes any *evidence* against theistic belief. And this is not surprising. For psychological investigations into the causation of beliefs, even this belief, is the wrong quarter in which to look for such evidence. One looks for evidence for and against the Darwinian theory of evolution not in the factors which make people accept it or the reverse, but in the results of palaeontology, comparative anatomy and the experimental production of mutations in fruit flies. And the fact that Kepler developed his heliocentric theory of the solar system under the influence of his quasi-religious sun-worship is not thought to be a relevant consideration if we are trying to determine whether his theory is correct. Of course in attempting to transfer these points to the theistic case we run into the fact that it is much more difficult here to say what would be relevant evidence. But in spite of all the problems that can be raised about the traditional arguments for the existence of God, I feel confident in saying that the order, or lack thereof, in the world, the existence of evil and the facts of human morality, are the right sort of thing to consider in a way that factors productive of theistic belief are not – if we are looking for positive or negative evidence.

I have still done nothing to rule out the possibility that a theory of the sort we are considering could do something in a more indirect way to weaken theistic belief, e.g., by showing that certain supposed reasons for acceptance are not sound ones, or by providing reasons for doubting that any adequate supporting reasons can be found. Something of the former sort is suggested by Freud in *The Future of an Illusion.*

Now, it is quite true that if anyone should argue that the existence of religious belief could only be explained by supposing that God himself had communicated it to men (that men could never have thought of all this by themselves, that the conceptions are too lofty to be initially formed by men, etc.), then showing another way in which such belief can be, and is, brought about disposes of this argument. It would nullify, e.g., the argument put forth by Descartes in his *Meditations* to the effect that the presence of the idea of God in the human mind can only be explained by supposing that God himself is ultimately responsible for putting it there. (Of course this does nothing to show that God has not in fact revealed truths to men; it only shows that we cannot hold that he has done so on *these* grounds. Note too that the sort of theory we are considering takes as one of the factors to be used in explaining the occurrence of theistic belief in the individual the existence of certain conceptions and certain beliefs in the culture to which that individual is exposed. This means that the ultimate origin of that cultural tradition is still unexplained, and as long as this is the case, a wedge is left for the revelationist.) But this is hardly a serious consequence; theism is not usually defended in this way.

There is one important way of supporting theistic belief which would certainly be adversely affected, perhaps fatally, by causal explanations. I am referring to the claim that one can be sure of the existence of God because one has directly experienced the presence of God.[15] Of course there are different sorts of experiences which have been so construed, and a complete discussion would have to take account of these differences, but for purposes of illustration we can once more revert to Freudian theory and consider a Freudian explanation of certain very pervasive features of mystical experience – (1) a breakdown of the usual boundaries of the self, a sense of a merging of oneself into the object, loss of separateness; (2) joy, which sometimes reaches rapturous intensity, combined with a profound sense of peace. If we look, as a Freudian would, for analogues of this in the development of the individual, we can find it in the experience of the infant. As reconstructed by psychoanalysis the infant's experience lacks the self–world distinction. He has to learn by hard experience what is part of him and what is outside him. Thus his consciousness is, in Freud's apt terminology, "oceanic". He feels an inseparable connection between himself and his environment; or rather he just feels, without referring contents to different sources. Moreover, if we consider the fed, satisfied baby on the edge of sleep, we may find the prototype of the profoundly peaceful rapture with which the mystic is suffused.

Then, by invoking the familiar concepts of fixation and of regression we can suppose that such experiences arise as follows. People differ in the extent to which they outgrow the desires, modes of thought, etc., of a given stage of development, and this certainly seems to be the case with respect to the early infantile stage; consider the well-established concept of the "oral personality". When an adult who still has strong but repressed desires to be in the infantile situation runs into severe difficulties and frustrations, a regression will ensue. One of the things this means is that the desires appropriate to that stage will be strengthened and press even more insistently for some sort of satisfaction. One form such satisfaction could take is an hallucinatory experience in which the individual feels himself to be in something like the infantile situation, suitably reinterpreted (as immediate union with God) so as to be acceptable to one's consciously held standards. Thus we find Ostow and Scharfstein quoting the following from Porphyry's *Life of Plotinus*: "Plotinus would tell his disciples how, at the age of eight, when he was already going to school, he still clung about his nurse and loved to bare her breasts and take suck: one day he was told he was a 'perverted imp' and so was shamed out of the trick." The authors then go on to say, "The tendency to retreat and demand the love and security granted an infant had already been established, and his later longing to join God in a union of love was a reappearance on a new level of the old desire."[16]

I do not want to suggest that there is any strong reason to believe that this is a correct explanation of such experiences. (There is, again, no direct evidence at all.) I simply present it as an example of the sort of explanation I wish to consider. Supposing that some such theory were established, what bearing, if any, would this have on claims that in such experiences one is directly apprehending God? There are those who maintain that the success of such explanations would constitute a refutation of the claim. So far as I can see the strongest way to support this position is to say that if we can show that there are natural factors which are sufficient to produce experiences of this sort, then one is unwarranted in claiming that divine activity or influence must be at least partly responsible for their occurrence, and hence that one has no basis for supposing that one is in contact with God when one has such an experience. To this it will, no doubt, be replied that causal origin is one thing and epistemological status another, and that answering questions about one does not suffice to answer questions about the other. More specifically, to say what one perceived on a given occasion is not to say what produced one's perception (or the sensations that were involved in the perception), and vice versa. Hence the fact that one's experience is produced by certain psychological factors, independently of any supernatural influence, leaves completely open the question whether one is perceiving God in that experience.

Clearly this raises fundamental questions concerning the concept of perception. There are those who affirm and those who deny that a necessary condition of perceiving x is that x be among the factors which produce the experience (sensation, awareness of sensa, etc.) involved in the supposed perception. (It is a further question whether the notion of perception can be completely analysed in such terms.) The parties to the above dispute will, of course, take opposite positions on this issue. I am unable to go into these matters here. I will only say that it seems to me plausible to say that the presence of x somewhere (not too far back) in the chain of causes giving rise to a certain experience is one necessary condition of that experience being involved in a perception of x. This principle seems to be supported by some of the procedures we use in determining whether or not someone has directly perceived something. If a thick brick wall was so placed as to prevent light waves from a house from reaching my eyes, then I could not have seen that house at that time.

It seems reasonable to take principles which are well established with respect to sense-perception, an area where we pretty much know what to say under a given set of conditions, and extend them to the discussion of purported direct experiences of God, an area where it is not at all clear what one should say. Thus I am inclined to agree that a successful explanation of certain mystical experiences in terms of purely natural factors would enable us to disallow claims that in these experiences one is directly apprehending God.

But even if there are certain ways of justifying theistic beliefs which could be discredited by psychological explanations – either of theistic belief in general or of the way in question – there would always remain the possibility that there were other modes of justification which would turn out to be valid. To do any real damage the Freudian theory would have to provide reason for supposing that no adequate justification could be given.

Construed in a certain way, Freudian theory will have this consequence. Up to now I have been interpreting a causal theory in such a way that it purports to specify *sufficient* conditions of religious belief. But suppose we understand our imaginary enriched Freudianism to put forward its factors as both sufficient and necessary for religious belief. Then it follows that no adequate reasons could be given. For if there were such reasons, the grasp of them by a rational man would itself be a sufficient condition of his accepting the belief.

I am sure that many will oppose this thesis on the grounds that reasons are one thing and causes quite another. Hence to say that someone has adequate reasons for a certain belief is to say nothing about the causes of his coming to have the belief, and to say that someone's belief is due to certain causes is to say nothing about the reasons that he might or might not have for it. But this seems to me to be mistaken. Of course a reason cannot be a cause, nor can a cause be a reason. They exist in logically different realms. But that does not mean that a statement about reasons cannot have implications concerning causes and vice versa. It seems quite clear to me that to say that A's reason for thinking that his lawn-mower is in his garage is that he saw it there in the morning, or that B's reason for thinking that the Republicans will show gains in the 1962 elections is that the party which does not have control of the presidency generally gains in off-year elections, is to imply something about the causes which have (or might have) given rise to his having this belief, or at least something about the causes which maintain his belief. It would be absurd to say "A has every reason to believe that *x*, but I can't imagine what led him to believe that". Conversely, to say that A's belief that there exists an omnipotent personal Being is *wholly* due to cultural conditioning in early childhood plus a projection of an unconscious father-image onto the Being envisaged in that cultural training is to deny that he has any reason for the belief. For if he had a reason, the psychological processes involved in becoming aware of the considerations involved in the reason, and in connecting them to the belief in question, would be at least part of what led him to have or retain the belief.

But this is a hollow triumph for the psychoanalytic critic of theistic religion. For the psychoanalytic factors could be established as necessary as well as sufficient conditions only if we could be sure that no one could acquire sufficient reasons for the belief; for if he could the belief could be produced in some other way.[17] Since the establishment of reason-irrelevant necessary and sufficient conditions presupposes that no sound reasons can be given, it can hardly be used to warrant that claim.

Now if we are dealing only with an established claim that there are reason–irrelevant causal factors which are sufficient to produce that belief (and furthermore are in general what is responsible for producing it), then what? Of course it follows that anyone whose belief is produced in this way lacks any sound basis for the belief. But what implication should I draw from it for *my* state of religious belief? Well, if I have adequate reasons for the belief myself it will do nothing to shake my confidence in those grounds. And justifiably. Why should I abandon what I can see to be sound reason for the belief just because it has been shown that many other people hold the belief without having any such grounds? It may be said that the demonstration that the belief is generally held as a result of unconscious projections might well make me suspicious of the cogency of my reasons. My belief might be caused by similar projections and I might be deceiving myself into thinking that I have good reasons in order to put a good face on the matter. And so I might. I would agree that the psychoanalytic results would properly make me suspicious and that in the light of this the reasonable thing for me to do would be to scrutinize my reasons very carefully. But if I have looked on them and have seen that they are good, what more is there for me to do?[18] And if I do not have adequate reasons for the belief, we have already seen that the existence of reason-irrelevant sufficient conditions does nothing to show that there could not be adequate reasons for the belief.

There still remains one way in which the success of a theory of the sort we are considering might have some relevance. If a man has no grounds of any magnitude for deciding the question of the existence of God one way or the other, he might be faced with the question of whether this is an issue which is worth considering further. After all, there are many important theses which at present we are unable to either prove or disprove, and we only have a limited amount of time and energy to devote to such matters. In this instance, he might take note of the fact that there are many people, including many intelligent and thoughtful people, who accept this belief, and this might lead him to conclude that it is a matter which should be looked into further. But now if it could be shown that, so far as we can tell, what leads these people to adopt this belief is something which is quite irrelevant to its truth or falsity, this would nullify the above reason for taking the issue seriously. Thus a causal explanation could, under these conditions, properly have the effect of counteracting a possible reason for regarding the question as one which is worth exploring further. Not much of a consequence, but something.

Thus I am forced to conclude that the fact, if it is a fact, that reason-irrelevant causal factors are sufficient to produce theistic belief has little or no tendency to show that the belief is false, unlikely to be true, or not worthy of serious consideration. And remember that we have arrived at this conclusion with respect to an imagined theory which would present at least sufficient conditions for the belief. As for theories of the sort we actually have, which can reasonably claim nothing more than a certain degree of correlation between theistic belief and certain factors, the case would be even worse. For such theories leave ample room for the operation of awareness of reasons in the production of the belief. And here there is even less reason to think that a theistic God would not set things up so that such partial correlations would not obtain.

B

Thus far we have simply been considering Freudian theory as an example of the general claim that theistic belief is in general due solely to reason-irrelevant causal factors. But the Freudian theory has some special features which distinguish it from some of the other theories of this class and some of these might be relevant to our problem. More specifically, the theory tends to assimilate religious belief to infantile modes of thought and to neurotic manifestations. Remember that, according to the theory, theistic belief, like many neuroses, is based on a regression to infantile modes of psychic organization and that it bears traces of this regression in the way it conceives God and in the ways it leads men to feel toward God. Moreover, as Reik points out in elaborate detail in his two books on the subject, religion exhibits many of the features of neurotic compulsions both in its ritual and in its doctrinal aspects. Michael Argyle summarizes the points of similarity as follows:

(a) . . . obsessions and compulsions simultaneously allow some substitute gratification both of the desire and of its prohibition. . . . Reik . . . similarly traces the development of ideas about the Trinity as a compromise between ideas of filial rebellion and veneration for the father.

(b) The neurotic's rituals have a compulsive character, in that he must carry them out conscientiously and experiences guilt if he fails to do so: this is to some extent true of religious rituals too.

(c) In religion there are taboos – of Sunday work, food before communion, and so forth: neurotics also have things which they must avoid touching or thinking about. . . . Reik . . . points out that the taboos surrounding religious dogma develop as a defence against scepticism: at the same time the dogma is developed in absurd detail, reflecting an underlying contempt for it.

(d) The real conflict in neurotics becomes displaced on to trivial details and verbal matters; this is also the case with religion, where the dogmas and rituals become elaborated in enormous detail, minute parts of which may become the basis for schisms and persecutions.[19]

On the basis of all this it is argued, or more often suggested, that beliefs which have this status, which are essentially infantile and/or neurotic in character, could not be taken seriously by rational, adult individuals. This sort of claim is clearly different from the one based on the mere existence of *some* sort of causal determination, and it must be examined separately.

But first note that it is not at all clear that *this* argument requires that we suppose the psychoanalytic theory inflated into a complete statement of causal conditions. It would seem plausible to suggest that the existence of substantial correlations between theistic belief and such factors as degree of unconscious conflict, tendency to regression, etc., would do as much, or almost as much, to show that theistic belief has an infantile and/or neurotic *character* as would the development of a complete theory integrating these factors with others. For presumably the other factors that would have to be included – degree of intelligence, cultural training, etc. – would not add anything to the force of the diagnosis. Hence in this section we can work with the theory as we actually have it.

In evaluating this claim we must first make some important distinctions which are generally overlooked. First, we must, as noted earlier, distinguish between the existence of similarities between the *forms* taken by theistic belief and the *forms* of infantile and neurotic behaviour, and the existence of causal factors for theistic belief of an infantile or neurotic kind. A great deal of the psychoanalytic discussion of religion consists simply of pointing out similarities, as with the similarities between obsessional neurosis and theistic belief listed above, and supposing that this shows that the two are fundamentally the same sort of thing. But such surface similarities are radically insufficient to bear the weight of such a conclusion. A man "obsessed" with a radically new idea, who is constantly preoccupied with thinking it through, seeing its implications, devising ways to test it, etc., exhibits striking similarities to obsessional neurotics, but it would be a great mistake to dismiss his theorizing on this basis. And in fact, despite the obvious similarities in patterns of overt behaviour, his "obsession" with the idea may be psychologically quite a different thing and may have very different psychological roots from the obsession of the neurotic. When I look at a snake in a zoo my experience may be phenomenally quite similar to that of a man suffering from hallucinations in delirium tremens, but it would be a great mistake to conclude from this that my experience is really an hallucination, or that this shows that there are really no such things as snakes. Surface similarities can be misleading.

But with respect to the charge that religion is a neurosis, the Freudian theory goes beyond these similarities and posits similar underlying mechanisms. But here, too, we must distinguish between two views which are not always distinguished. (1) Among the important causal factors producing theistic belief is always some neurosis of a commonly recognized sort. (2) Some of the important causal factors here are the same as some which play a crucial role in producing certain neuroses. There seems to be no evidence at all for (1), not even if we restrict our sample to neurotic believers. I shall confine my attention to (2).

If the Freudian theory as presented earlier is to be adequate, there are common causal conditions for neurosis and theistic belief – a substantial amount of unconscious conflict, a tendency to regression, etc. But the question remains as to whether this justifies Freud in terming religion "the universal obsessional neurosis of humanity".[20] Why should we not rather say that given these common causal conditions there are two ways in which the individual may respond – either by a neurosis or by religious faith? Of course we could say with Freud that this is just the

difference between an idiosyncratic neurosis and a socially approved neurosis. But we might also say, with Jung, that a religious orientation is an alternative to neurosis, or even constitutes a prophylaxis against, or cure for, a neurosis. How can we choose between these positions?

In considering this question, we are forced to get clearer about the term "neurosis", and more particularly about the sense of this term, if any, in which there would be any plausibility in saying that the fact that a belief arises out of a neurosis shows that we do not have to take it seriously. There are various ways of defining "neurosis" and more general terms like "psychological abnormality". If we define a neurosis in terms of underlying causal factors, as is often done, e.g., in terms of the amount of conflict which is unconscious and therefore not resoluble by rational deliberation, then in order to show that a belief can be dismissed from serious consideration on the grounds that it arises out of a neurosis we would need a supplementary argument to the effect that any belief so produced is unlikely to be correct. But we know too little about the effects of unconscious processes to have any confidence in any such principle. Moreover, if we widen the sphere to cover kinds of disguised resolutions of unconscious conflicts other than beliefs, we can think of many such cases which would not be classified as harmful or undesirable – e.g. (to take a couple of favourite textbook examples) the resolution of unconscious conflict over aggression by developing skill as a surgeon or resolution of unconscious conflict over love of one's mother by specializing in painting madonnas.

Therefore it seems that if we are to draw negatively evaluative implications from connection with a neurosis we shall have to build some negative evaluations into the concept of neurosis. And I believe that this is usually what is done. Included in the commonly used working criteria for calling a state a neurosis is the requirement that this state have the effect of hampering the individual in his "adjustments to the environment" or in his attempts to achieve his aims in life. If that is part of the definition of a neurosis, then there is some plausibility in holding that a belief which arises from a neurosis is, *ipso facto*, unlikely to be correct. For if a neurosis has the effect of hampering the individual's attempts to get along in his environment, then the hampering would presumably involve, among other things, producing false beliefs about the environment, or suppressing or warping true beliefs. And in fact this is one of the prominent features of neurosis. But now what happens is this. As people develop confidence in a theory of the causal basis of states which satisfy the initial criteria for neurosis, we get the familiar phenomenon of transition from synthetic to analytic connections; the underlying causal mechanisms come to be themselves used as criteria. It is then easy to assume unquestioningly, with respect to anything which satisfies these latter criteria, that it will have the unfortunate effects which were among the initial criteria. But, of course, the proposition that anything which results from certain sorts of unconscious processes will hamper the individual's pursuit of his goals is a generalization which must be tested separately for each new range of cases.

Hence the matter stands as follows. In order to argue that theistic belief, since neurotic, is unworthy of serious consideration, one must be holding the term "neurosis" subject to the evaluative criteria mentioned earlier. But so long as all we have shown is that this belief is due to certain unconscious processes, we have no right to call it neurotic in this sense. To gain this right we would have to show that a person who has a theistic belief is less able to function effectively than he would have been without it. And no one has ever begun to show this.

Moreover, there are some profound difficulties which intrude themselves when we consider the possibility of establishing such a conclusion. A psychoanalytically-minded writer who set out to do so would, presumably, proceed by determining whether religious believers were less able to establish satisfying personal relations, get ahead in their professions, etc., than non-religious believers who were identical in other respects. But even if this could be established the theist might complain we have been too restrictive in our survey of the "environment" and of what constitutes "success" or "effective functioning" therein. If we include the "supernatural environment" in our survey, it would seem plausible to suppose that theistic belief would be a powerful, or rather indispensable, aid to effective functioning with respect to *it*. And if we did not include it, our opponent might accuse us of stacking the cards against him. "You are", he would say, "using a criterion of effective functioning which already presupposes that my beliefs are false. For if they are not false, it would be quite reasonable to suppose that the conditions which were conducive to effective functioning and accurate apprehension with respect to two such different realms would be radically different." As James put it, "If there were

such a thing as inspiration from a higher realm, it might well be that the neurotic temperament would furnish the chief condition of the requisite receptivity."[21]

It is hard to know what to say about this issue. This may be one point at which there is, in the nature of the case, a complete *impasse* between the theist and his psychoanalytic critic.

To sum up, even if the psychoanalytic theory of the causal basis of theistic belief is correct, there seems to be no reason to say that therefore religion is a happy alternative to a neurosis; and therefore there is no reason for suggesting, on these grounds, that theistic belief is false, probably false, or unworthy of serious consideration.

The charge that theistic belief can be dismissed as infantile in character can be handled more briefly. This is based solely on the surface similarities between the theistic conception of God, and the believer's feelings and attitudes toward him, and the child's conception of, and feeling and attitude toward, his father. (The matter of regression to an infantile orientation has already been handled as part of the grounds for regarding religion as a neurosis.) Such similarities may be admitted. But the theist might well reply that whether such conceptions, attitudes, etc. are warranted is wholly a matter of whether his beliefs are true. It would be unworthy of an adult human being to take up such attitudes toward another human being. But if theism is correct, we do, as a matter of fact, stand in a relation to God very similar to that in which we stood to our fathers in early childhood, and therefore, if theism is correct, such attitudes and feelings are quite appropriate. In view of this fact one could hardly use such similarities as a basis for rejecting theistic claims. In general, a set of facts which are perfectly compatible with a theory can do nothing to weaken the plausibility of that theory.

We should note that here too it makes a difference whether the theory is asserting only sufficient, or necessary and sufficient, conditions. If it is the former (and we have seen that this is the only form of the theory which is not clearly unjustified), then in addition to the moves already considered it is open to the theist to hold that although many people may hold religious beliefs as the result of the unconscious mechanisms in question, the belief can be and sometimes is, held as a result of other factors. That is, it is open to him to distinguish between quasi-neurotic and non-quasi-neurotic ways of being religious. Of course he may not be able to show any sufficient conditions of the latter sort, but at least the theory in the weaker form does nothing to indicate that this would be impossible.

III

In this paper I have been considering the possible bearing of causal explanations of theistic belief on the question of whether there are, or might be, adequate reasons for or against such beliefs. What emerges from the foregoing discussion is the, by no means novel, conclusion that in religion as elsewhere there is no substitute for the detailed examination of evidence which has a direct bearing on the truth or falsity of a given belief, and that, in particular, investigation of the factors which generally produce the belief is no such substitute. As I say, this conclusion is nothing new; if the present discussion has added anything to previous discussions it is by way of considering more thoroughly and patiently some of the relevant distinctions.

But there is another way in which causal theories might be relevant to a decision on the acceptability of theistic belief. Consider the position of James in *The Will to Believe*, or the more extreme position of Kierkegaard, according to both of whom believing in God is somehow justifiable, even though no adequate reasons can be presented either for or against the proposition that God exists. (That is, even though we cannot discover adequate reasons in support of the proposition that God exists, we can discover adequate reasons for the proposition that it is justifiable to believe that God exists.) Such support may be of different sorts. In *The Will to Believe* James says that we are going to take some position on this problem without having adequate reasons for it in any event, so that we may as well recognize the inevitable and accept it with good grace. Kierkegaard supposes that if he presents the stance of faith and contrasting stances in sufficient concreteness, the reader will see that the former is the only possible stance for one who resolutely faces the facts of the human situation. One might wonder whether a psychoanalytic explanation of theistic belief, if established, would properly have any bearing on one's response to the position of these authors. That is, would an acceptance of the psychoanalytic explanation properly influence my decision as to whether or not it is justifiable to believe in God without adequate evidence for his existence?

This question presents very different problems from those already considered, problems that I cannot really discuss at the tail-end of a paper that is already too long. To settle the question we would have to decide what sorts of considerations properly influence a decision as to the justifiability of accepting a proposition under these conditions. I do not know how to lay down a criterion which will separate proper from improper considerations here, and perhaps no such separation can be made. Perhaps if we have abandoned the attempt to show that the proposition is true or false and are still trying to decide whether it is all right to believe it, then anything goes. But even if there still is a distinction between relevant and irrelevant considerations, it is hard to see how facts about the usual causal basis of the belief could be excluded. If one is to admit as relevant facts about the psychological consequences of accepting the belief, about the relative or absolute inevitability of taking some stand or other on a question, and about the way acceptance of the belief will have logical implications for the way various enquiries can and cannot be carried out (and facts of all these sorts have been adduced by philosophers who have discussed this sort of question), it is hard to see how facts about the causal basis of the belief can be excluded. Thus it might be quite pertinent, if not conclusive, in this sort of context to deny that theistic belief is justifiable, on the grounds that it involves acquiescing in a regression to an infantile mode of thought.

IV

There is one other sort of way in which causal explanations might be relevant to the status of theism, but, although I feel that this dimension of the problem is quite important, I am unable to formulate it clearly enough to even begin to determine just how much it does come to. It is often remarked that the general climate of thought in which supernaturalistic theology flourishes is very different from that in which intellectual endeavour is largely devoted to searching out empirically testable causal generalizations. Not that there is any logical incompatibility between a sophisticated theism and the search for such generalizations, or even between theism and a dogmatic determinism. It is just that the general cast of thought which naturally lead to taking the one or the other very seriously is quite different. So long as the search for natural causes shies away from human thought, experience and behaviour, it is relatively easy to distinguish the physical world, investigated by science, from the supernatural realm, which makes contact with man through religion. But when the search for natural causes extends to man, including religious thought, experience and behaviour, such compartmentalization is not so easy. It is still possible, as we have seen in the various moves made in the body of this paper, to distinguish causal expla-

nation of a belief from a disproof of that belief. But to carry it through introduces more and more strain. Therefore it seems that the thorough-going success of a theory like the Freudian would help to render the climate of thought even more antithetical to full-blooded theistic belief. But what implications, if any, this has on the justifiability of theistic belief, I do not know.

Notes

1 In *The Birth of the Gods* (Ann Arbor: University of Michigan Press, 1961).

2 In *The Basic Writings of Sigmund Freud*, tr. A. A. Brill (New York: The Modern Library, 1938).

3 Sigmund Freud, *Collected Papers*, ed. Ernest Jones, vol. III (London: Hogarth Press, 1956), pp. 149–242.

4 *Moses and Monotheism* (London: Hogarth Press, 1951), pp. 130–3.

5 *Totem and Taboo*, tr. James Strachey (London: Routledge and Kegan Paul, 1950), p. 143.

6 Tr. W. D. Robson-Scott (New York: Liveright, 1949; also London: Hogarth Press, 1928).

7 Tr. B. Miall (New York: International Universities Press, 1951; also London: Bailey Bros).

8 Tr. D. Bryan (New York: W. W. Norton, 1931).

9 New York: International Universities Press, 1947; also London: Duckworth, 1955.

10 New York: International Universities Press, 1954.

11 It is worth noting, however, that satisfaction of sexual desires in fantasy plays a very small role in Freud's account of religion, although, of course, it is primarily conflicts over sexual impulses that underlie the relationships to the father which he does take as crucial.

12 *The Future of an Illusion*, pp. 41–2.

13 Sigmund Freud, *Collected Papers*, "A Religious Experience", tr. J. Strachey (London: Hogarth Press, vol. 5, 1950), pp. 243–6.

14 Henceforth, when I use the phrase "natural cause", or even simply "cause", the appropriate qualifications are to be understood.

15 General explanations of theistic belief would not have any bearing on the force of this reason, except for the way in which a specification of necessary and sufficient reason-irrelevant conditions cuts off the possibility of any adequate reasons, as explained below.

16 Mortimer Ostow and Ben-Ami Scharfstein, *The Need to Believe* (New York: International Universities Press, 1954), p. 118.

17 It is significant that in *The Future of an Illusion* Freud prefaces his presentation of his explanation of theistic belief with a chapter in which he argues that there is no sound ground for the belief. Though if I am correct he should have gone further and argued that there *could be* no sound ground.

18 There is also the case in which I came to the belief via the Freudian route and then subsequently found really adequate reasons. In this case we should not say that in the later stages the belief is *really* due to the psychoanalytic factors alone. For now the situation has changed in such a way that even if the unconscious pressures should cease to operate I would still have a strong tendency to retain the belief.

19 Michael Argyle, *Religious Behaviour* (London: Routledge and Kegan Paul, 1958), p. 165.

20 Freud, *The Future of an Illusion*, tr. Robson-Scott, p. 76.

21 *The Varieties of Religious Experience* (London: Longmans, 1952; and New York: New American Library, 1958).

12

The Varieties of Religious Experience

William James

[...]

Summing up in the broadest possible way the characteristics of the religious life, as we have found them, it includes the following beliefs:

- that the visible world is part of a more spiritual universe from which it draws its chief significance;
- that union or harmonious relation with that higher universe is our true end;
- that prayer or inner communion with the spirit thereof – be that spirit "God" or "law" – is a process wherein work is really done, and spiritual energy flows in and produces effects, psychological or material, within the phenomenal world.

Religion includes also the following psychological characteristics:

- a new zest which adds itself like a gift to life, and takes the form either of lyrical enchantment or of appeal to earnestness and heroism;
- an assurance of safety and a temper of peace, and, in relation to others, a preponderance of loving affections.

In illustrating these characteristics by documents, we have been literally bathed in sentiment. In re-reading my manuscript, I am almost appalled at

William James, "The Varieties of Religious Experience," from *The Varieties of Religious Experience* (Longmans, Green and Co., 1902), pp. 485–501; 512–15. Not in copyright.

the amount of emotionality which I find in it. After so much of this, we can afford to be dryer and less sympathetic in the rest of the work that lies before us.

The sentimentality of many of my documents is a consequence of the fact that I sought them among the extravagances of the subject. If any of you are enemies of what our ancestors used to brand as enthusiasm, and are, nevertheless, still listening to me now, you have probably felt my selection to have been sometimes almost perverse, and have wished I might have stuck to soberer examples. I reply that I took these extremer examples as yielding the profounder information. To learn the secrets of any science, we go to expert specialists, even though they may be eccentric persons, and not to commonplace pupils. We combine what they tell us with the rest of our wisdom, and form our final judgment independently. Even so with religion. We who have pursued such radical expressions of it may now be sure that we know its secrets as authentically as any one can know them who learns them from another; and we have next to answer, each of us for himself, the practical question: what are the dangers in this element of life? and in what proportion may it need to be restrained by other elements, to give the proper balance?

But this question suggests another one which I will answer immediately and get it out of the way, for it has more than once already vexed us. Ought it to be assumed that in all men the mixture of religion with other elements should be identical? Ought it, indeed, to be assumed that the lives of all men should show identical religious elements? In other words, is the existence of so many religious types and sects and creeds regrettable?

To these questions I answer "No" emphatically. And my reason is that I do not see how it is possible that creatures in such different positions and with such different powers as human individuals are, should have exactly the same functions and the same duties. No two of us have identical difficulties, nor should we be expected to work out identical solutions. Each, from his peculiar angle of observation, takes in a certain sphere of fact and trouble, which each must deal with in a unique manner. One of us must soften himself, another must harden himself; one must yield a point, another must stand firm – in order the better to defend the position assigned him. If an Emerson were forced to be a Wesley, or a Moody forced to be a Whitman, the total human consciousness of the divine would suffer. The divine can mean no single quality, it must mean a group of qualities, by being champions of which in alternation, different men may all find worthy missions. Each attitude being a syllable in human nature's total message, it takes the whole of us to spell the meaning out completely. So a "god of battles" must be allowed to be the god for one kind of person, a god of peace and heaven and home, the god for another. We must frankly recognize the fact that we live in partial systems, and that parts are not interchangeable in the spiritual life. If we are peevish and jealous, destruction of the self must be an element of our religion; why need it be one if we are good and sympathetic from the outset? If we are sick souls, we require a religion of deliverance; but why think so much of deliverance, if we are healthy-minded? Unquestionably, some men have the completer experience and the higher vocation, here just as in the social world; but for each man to stay in his own experience, whate'er it be, and for others to tolerate him there, is surely best.

But, you may now ask, would not this one-sidedness be cured if we should all espouse the science of religions as our own religion? In answering this question I must open again the general relations of the theoretic to the active life.

Knowledge about a thing is not the thing itself. You remember what Al-Ghazzali told us in the Lecture on Mysticism – that to understand the causes of drunkenness, as a physician understands them, is not to be drunk. A science might come to understand everything about the causes and elements of religion, and might even decide which elements were qualified, by their general harmony with other branches of knowledge, to be considered true; and yet the best man at this science might be the man who found it hardest to be personally devout. *Tout savoir c'est tout pardonner.* The name of Renan would doubtless occur to many persons as an example of the way in which breadth of knowledge may make one only a dilettante in possibilities, and blunt the acuteness of one's living faith. If religion be a function by which either God's cause or man's cause is to be really advanced, then he who lives the life of it, however narrowly, is a better servant than he who merely knows about it, however much. Knowledge about life is one thing; effective occupation of a place in life, with its dynamic currents passing through your being, is another.

For this reason, the science of religions may not be an equivalent for living religion; and if we turn to the inner difficulties of such a science, we see that a point comes when she must drop the purely theoretic attitude, and either let her knots remain uncut, or have them cut by active faith. To see this, suppose that we have our science of religions constituted as a matter of fact. Suppose that she has assimilated all the necessary historical material and distilled out of it as its essence the same conclusions which I myself a few moments ago pronounced. Suppose that she agrees that religion, wherever it is an active thing, involves a belief in ideal presences, and a belief that in our prayerful communion with them, work is done, and something real comes to pass. She has now to exert her critical activity, and to decide how far, in the light of other sciences and in that of general philosophy, such beliefs can be considered *true.*

Dogmatically to decide this is an impossible task. Not only are the other sciences and the philosophy still far from being completed, but in their present state we find them full of conflicts. The sciences of nature know nothing of spiritual presences, and on the whole hold no practical commerce whatever with the idealistic conceptions towards which general philosophy inclines. The scientist, so-called, is, during his scientific hours at least, so materialistic that one may well say that on the whole the influence of science goes against the notion that religion should be recognized at all. And this antipathy to religion finds an echo within the very science of religions itself. The cultivator of this science has to become acquainted with so many groveling and horrible superstitions that a presumption easily arises in his mind that any belief that is religious probably is false. In the "prayerful communion" of savages with such mumbo-jumbos of deities as they acknowledge, it is hard for us to see what genuine spiritual work – even though it were work relative only to their dark savage obligations – can possibly be done.

The consequence is that the conclusions of the science of religions are as likely to be adverse as they are to be favorable to the claim that the essence of religion is true. There is a notion in the air about us that religion is probably only an anachronism, a case of "survival," an atavistic relapse into a mode of thought which humanity in its more enlightened examples has outgrown; and this notion our religious anthropologists at present do little to counteract.

This view is so widespread at the present day that I must consider it with some explicitness before I pass to my own conclusions. Let me call it the "Survival theory," for brevity's sake.

The pivot round which the religious life, as we have traced it, revolves, is the interest of the individual in his private personal destiny. Religion, in short, is a monumental chapter in the history of human egotism. The gods believed in – whether by crude savages or by men disciplined intellectually – agree with each other in recognizing personal calls. Religious thought is carried on in terms of personality, this being, in the world of religion, the one fundamental fact. Today, quite as much as at any previous age, the religious individual tells you that the divine meets him on the basis of his personal concerns.

Science, on the other hand, has ended by utterly repudiating the personal point of view. She catalogues her elements and records her laws indifferent as to what purpose may be shown forth by them, and constructs her theories quite careless of their bearing on human anxieties and fates. Though the scientist may individually nourish a religion, and be a theist in his irresponsible hours, the days are over when it could be said that for Science herself the heavens declare the glory of God and the firmament showeth his handiwork. Our solar system, with its harmonies, is seen now as but one passing case of a certain sort of moving equilibrium in the heavens, realized by a local accident in an appalling wilderness of worlds where no life can exist. In a span of time which as a cosmic interval will count but as an hour, it will have ceased to be. The Darwinian notion of chance production, and subsequent destruction, speedy or deferred, applies to the largest as well as to the smallest facts. It is impossible, in the present temper of the scientific imagination, to find in the driftings of the cosmic atoms, whether they work on the universal or on the particular scale, anything but a kind of aimless weather, doing and undoing, achieving no proper history, and leaving no result. Nature has no one distinguishable ultimate tendency with which it is possible to feel a sympathy. In the vast rhythm of her processes, as the scientific mind now follows them, she appears to cancel herself. The books of natural theology which satisfied the intellects of our grandfathers seem to us quite grotesque, representing, as they did, a God who conformed the largest things of nature to the paltriest of our private wants. The God whom science recognizes must be a God of universal laws exclusively, a God who does a wholesale, not a retail business. He cannot accommodate his processes to the convenience of individuals. The bubbles on the foam which coats a stormy sea are floating episodes, made and unmade by the forces of the wind and water. Our private selves are like those bubbles – epiphenomena, as Clifford, I believe, ingeniously called them; their destinies weigh nothing and determine nothing in the world's irremediable currents of events.

You see how natural it is, from this point of view, to treat religion as a mere survival, for religion does in fact perpetuate the traditions of the most primeval thought. To coerce the spiritual powers, or to square them and get them on our side, was, during enormous tracts of time, the one great object in our dealings with the natural world. For our ancestors, dreams, hallucinations, revelations, and cock-and-bull stories were inextricably mixed with facts. Up to a comparatively recent date such distinctions as those between what has been verified and what is only conjectured, between the impersonal and the personal aspects of existence, were hardly suspected or conceived. Whatever you imagined in a lively manner, whatever you thought fit to be true, you affirmed confidently; and whatever you affirmed, your comrades believed. Truth was what had not yet been contradicted, most things were taken into the mind from the point of view of their human suggestiveness, and the attention confined itself exclusively to the aesthetic and dramatic aspects of events.

How indeed could it be otherwise? The extraordinary value, for explanation and prevision of those mathematical and mechanical modes of conception which science uses, was a result that could not possibly have been expected in advance. Weight, movement, velocity, direction, position, what thin, pallid, uninteresting ideas! How could the richer animistic aspects of Nature, the peculiarities and oddities that make phenomena picturesquely striking or expressive, fail to have been first singled out and followed by philosophy as the more promising avenue to the knowledge of Nature's life? Well, it is still in these richer animistic and dramatic aspects that religion delights to dwell. It is the terror and beauty of phenomena, the "promise" of the dawn and of the rainbow, the "voice" of the thunder, the "gentleness" of the summer rain, the "sublimity" of the stars, and not the physical laws which these things follow, by which the religious mind still continues to be most impressed; and just as of yore, the devout man tells you that in the solitude of his room or of the fields he still feels the divine presence, that inflowings of help come in reply to his prayers, and that sacrifices to this unseen reality fill him with security and peace.

Pure anachronism! says the survival-theory – anachronism for which deanthropomorphization of the imagination is the remedy required. The less we mix the private with the cosmic, the more we dwell in universal and impersonal terms, the truer heirs of Science we become.

In spite of the appeal which this impersonality of the scientific attitude makes to a certain magnanimity of temper, I believe it to be shallow, and I can now state my reason in comparatively few words. That reason is that, so long as we deal with the cosmic and the general, we deal only with the symbols of reality, but *as soon as we deal with private and personal phenomena as such, we deal with realities in the completest sense of the term.* I think I can easily make clear what I mean by these words.

The world of our experience consists at all times of two parts, an objective and a subjective part, of which the former may be incalculably more extensive than the latter, and yet the latter can never be omitted or suppressed. The objective part is the sum total of whatsoever at any given time we may be thinking of, the subjective part is the inner "state" in which the thinking comes to pass. What we think of may be enormous, the cosmic times and spaces, for example – whereas the inner state may be the most fugitive and paltry activity of mind. Yet the cosmic objects, so far as the experience yields them, are but ideal pictures of something whose existence we do not inwardly possess but only point at outwardly, while the inner state is our very experience itself; its reality and that of our experience are one. A conscious field plus its object as felt or thought of plus an attitude towards the object plus the sense of a self to whom the attitude belongs – such a concrete bit of personal experience may be a small bit, but it is a solid bit as long as it lasts; not hollow, not a mere abstract element of experience, such as the "object" is when taken all alone. It is a full fact, even though it be an insignificant fact; it is of the kind to which all realities whatsoever must belong; the motor currents of the world run through the like of it; it is on the line connecting real events with real events. That unsharable feeling which each one of us has of the pinch of his individual destiny as he privately feels it rolling out on fortune's wheel may be disparaged for its egotism, may be sneered at as unscientific, but it is the one thing that fills up the measure of our concrete actuality, and any would-be existent that should lack such a feeling, or its analogue, would be a piece of reality only half made up.

If this be true, it is absurd for science to say that the egotistic elements of experience should be suppressed. The axis of reality runs solely through the egotistic places – they are strung upon it like so many beads. To describe the world with all the various feelings of the individual pinch of destiny, all the various spiritual attitudes, left out from the description – they being as describable as anything else – would be something like offering a printed bill of fare as the equivalent for a solid meal. Religion makes no such blunder. The individual's religion may be egotistic, and those private realities which it keeps in touch with may be narrow enough; but at any rate it always remains infinitely less hollow and abstract, as far as it goes, than a science which prides itself on taking no account of anything private at all.

A bill of fare with one real raisin on it instead of the word "raisin," with one real egg instead of the word "egg," might be an inadequate meal, but it would at least be a commencement of reality. The contention of the survival-theory that we ought to stick to non-personal elements exclusively seems like saying that we ought to be satisfied forever with reading the naked bill of fare. I think, therefore, that however particular questions connected with our individual destinies may be answered, it is only by acknowledging them as genuine questions, and living in the sphere of thought which they open up, that we become profound. But to live thus is to be religious; so I unhesitatingly repudiate the survival-theory of religion, as being founded on an egregious mistake. It does not follow, because our ancestors made so many errors of fact and mixed them with their religion, that we should therefore leave off being religious at all. By being religious we establish ourselves in possession of ultimate reality at the only points at which reality is given us to guard. Our responsible concern is with our private destiny, after all.

[. . .]

Let me then propose, as an hypothesis, that whatever it may be on its farther side, the "more" with which in religious experience we feel ourselves connected is on its hither side the subconscious continuation of our conscious life. Starting thus with a recognized psychological fact as our basis, we seem to preserve a contact with "science" which the ordinary theologian lacks. At the same time the theologian's contention that the religious man is moved by an external power is vindicated, for it is one of the peculiarities of invasions from the subconscious region to take on objective appearances, and to suggest to the Subject an external control. In the religious life the control is felt as "higher"; but since on our hypothesis it is primarily the higher faculties of our own hidden mind which are controlling, the sense of union with the power beyond us is a sense of something, not merely apparently, but literally true.

This doorway into the subject seems to me the best one for a science of religions, for it mediates between a number of different points of view. Yet it is only a doorway, and difficulties present themselves as soon as we step through it, and ask how far our transmarginal consciousness carries us if we follow it on its remoter side. Here the over-beliefs begin: here mysticism and the conversion-rapture and Vedantism and transcendental idealism bring in their monistic interpretations and tell us that the finite self rejoins the absolute self, for it was always one with God and identical with the soul of the world. Here the prophets of all the different religions come with their visions, voices, raptures, and other openings, supposed by each to authenticate his own peculiar faith.

Those of us who are not personally favored with such specific revelations must stand outside of them altogether and, for the present at least, decide that, since they corroborate incompatible theological doctrines, they neutralize one another and leave no fixed result. If we follow any one of them, or if we follow philosophical theory and embrace monistic pantheism on non-mystical grounds, we do so in the exercise of our individual freedom, and build out our religion in the way most congruous with our personal susceptibilities. Among these susceptibilities intellectual ones play a decisive part. Although the religious question is primarily a question of life, of living or not living in the higher union which opens itself to us as a gift, yet the spiritual excitement in which the gift appears a real one will often fail to be aroused in an individual until certain particular intellectual beliefs or ideas which, as we say, come home to him, are touched. These ideas will thus be essential to that individual's religion – which is as much as to say that over-beliefs in various directions are absolutely indispensable, and that we should treat them with tenderness and tolerance so long as they are not intolerant themselves. As I have elsewhere written, the most interesting and valuable things about a man are usually his overbeliefs.

Disregarding the over-beliefs, and confining ourselves to what is common and generic, we have in *the fact that the conscious person is continuous with a wider self through which saving experiences come*, a positive content of religious experience which, it seems to me, *is literally and objectively true as far as it goes*.

13

The Numinous

Rudolf Otto

"Numen" and the "Numinous"

"Holiness" – "the holy" – is a category of interpretation and valuation peculiar to the sphere of
religion. It is, indeed, applied by transference to
another sphere – that of ethics – but it is not itself
derived from this. While it is complex, it contains a
quite specific element or "moment," which sets it
apart from "the rational" . . . and which remains
inexpressible – an ἄρρητον or *ineffabile* – in the
sense that it completely eludes apprehension in
terms of concepts. The same thing is true (to take a
quite different region of experience) of the category
of the beautiful.

Now these statements would be untrue from the
outset if "the holy" were merely what is meant by
the word, not only in common parlance, but in
philosophical, and generally even in theological
usage. The fact is we have come to use the words
holy, sacred (*heilig*) in an entirely derivative sense,
quite different from that which they originally bore.
We generally take "holy" as meaning "completely
good"; it is the absolute moral attribute, denoting
the consummation of moral goodness. In this sense
Kant calls the will which remains unwaveringly
obedient to the moral law from the motive of duty
a "holy" will; here clearly we have simply the *perfectly moral* will. In the same way we may speak of
the holiness or sanctity of Duty or Law, meaning

Rudolf Otto, "The Numinous," reprinted by permission
of Oxford University Press from *The Idea of the Holy*,
translated by J. W. Harvey (New York: Oxford University Press, 1936), chs. 2–6.

merely that they are imperative upon conduct and
universally obligatory.

But this common usage of the term is inaccurate. It is true that all this moral significance is
contained in the word "holy," but it includes in
addition – as even we cannot but feel – a clear
overplus of meaning, and this it is now our task to
isolate. Nor is this merely a later or acquired meaning; rather, "holy," or at least the equivalent words
in Latin and Greek, in Semitic and other ancient
languages, denoted first and foremost *only* this
overplus: if the ethical element was present at all,
at any rate it was not original and never constituted
the whole meaning of the word. Anyone who uses
it today does undoubtedly always feel "the morally
good" to be implied in "holy"; and accordingly in
our inquiry into that element which is separate and
peculiar to the idea of the holy it will be useful, at
least for the temporary purpose of the investigation,
to invent a special term to stand for "the holy" *minus*
its moral factor or "moment," and as we can now
add, minus its "rational" aspect altogether.

It will be our endeavour to suggest this unnamed
Something to the reader as far as we may, so that
he may himself feel it. There is no religion in which
it does not live as the real innermost core, and
without it no religion would be worthy of the name.
It is pre-eminently a living force in the Semitic
religions, and of these again in none has it such
vigour as in that of the Bible. Here, too, it has a
name of its own, viz., the Hebrew *qādôsh*, to which
the Greek ἄγιος and the Latin *sanctus*, and, more
accurately still, *sacer*, are the corresponding terms.
It is not, of course, disputed that these terms in all

three languages connote, as part of their meaning, *good, absolute goodness*, when, that is, the notion has ripened and reached the highest stage in its development. And we then use the word "holy" to translate them. But this "holy" then represents the gradual shaping and filling in with ethical meaning, or what we shall call the "schematization," of what was a unique original feeling-response, which can be in itself ethically neutral and claims consideration in its own right. And when this moment or element first emerges and begins its long development, all those expressions (*qādôsh, ἅγιος, sacer,* etc.) mean beyond all question something quite other than "the good." This is universally agreed by contemporary criticism, which rightly explains the rendering of *qādôsh* by "good" as a mistranslation and unwarranted "rationalization" or "moralization" of the term.

Accordingly, it is worthwhile, as we have said, to find a word to stand for this element in isolation, this "extra" in the meaning of "holy" above and beyond the meaning of goodness. By means of a special term we shall the better be able, first, to keep the meaning clearly apart and distinct, and second, to apprehend and classify connectedly whatever subordinate forms or stages of development it may show. For this purpose I adopt a word coined from the Latin *numen*. *Omen* has given us *ominous*, and there is no reason why from *numen* we should not similarly form a word *numinous*. I shall speak then of a unique "numinous" category of value and of a definitely "numinous" state of mind, which is always found wherever the category is applied. This mental state is perfectly *sui generis* and irreducible to any other; and therefore, like every absolutely primary and elementary datum, while it admits of being discussed, it cannot be strictly defined. There is only one way to help another to an understanding of it. He must be guided and led on by consideration and discussion of the matter through the ways of his own mind, until he reach the point at which "the numinous" in him perforce begins to stir, to start into life and into consciousness. We can cooperate in this process by bringing before his notice all that can be found in other regions of the mind, already known and familiar, to resemble, or again to afford some special contrast to, the particular experience we wish to elucidate. Then we must add: "This *X* of ours is not precisely *this* experience, but akin to this one and the opposite of that other. Cannot you now realize for yourself what it is?" In other words our *X* cannot, strictly speaking, be taught, it can only be evoked, awakened in the

mind; as everything that comes "of the spirit" must be awakened.

The Elements in the "Numinous"

Creature-feeling

The reader is invited to direct his mind to a moment of deeply felt religious experience, as little as possible qualified by other forms of consciousness. Whoever cannot do this, whoever knows no such moments in his experience, is requested to read no further; for it is not easy to discuss questions of religious psychology with one who can recollect the emotions of his adolescence, the discomforts of indigestion, or, say, social feelings, but cannot recall any intrinsically religious feelings. We do not blame such a one, when he tries for himself to advance as far as he can with the help of such principles of explanation as he knows, interpreting "aesthetics" in terms of sensuous pleasure, and "religion" as a function of the gregarious instinct and social standards, or as something more primitive still. But the artist, who for his part has an intimate personal knowledge of the distinctive element in the aesthetic experience, will decline his theories with thanks, and the religious man will reject them even more uncompromisingly.

Next, in the probing and analysis of such states of the soul as that of solemn worship, it will be well if regard be paid to what is unique in them rather than to what they have in common with other similar states. To be *rapt* in worship is one thing; to be morally *uplifted* by the contemplation of a good deed is another; and it is not to their common features, but to those elements of emotional content peculiar to the first that we would have attention directed as precisely as possible. As Christians we undoubtedly here first meet with feelings familiar enough in a weaker form in other departments of experience, such as feelings of gratitude, trust, love, reliance, humble submission, and dedication. But this does not by any means exhaust the content of religious worship. Not in any of these have we got the special features of the quite unique and incomparable experience of solemn worship. In what does this consist?

Schleiermacher has the credit of isolating a very important element in such an experience. This is the "feeling of dependence." But this important discovery of Schleiermacher is open to criticism in more than one respect.

In the first place, the feeling or emotion which he really has in mind in this phrase is in its specific quality not a "feeling of dependence" in the "natural" sense of the word. As such, other domains of life and other regions of experience than the religious occasion the feeling, as a sense of personal insufficiency and impotence, a consciousness of being determined by circumstances and environment. The feeling of which Schleiermacher wrote has an undeniable analogy with these states of mind: they serve as an indication to it, and its nature may be elucidated by them, so that, by following the direction in which they point, the feeling itself may be spontaneously felt. But the feeling is at the same time also qualitatively different from such analogous states of mind. Schleiermacher himself, in a way, recognizes this by distinguishing the feeling of pious or religious dependence from all other feelings of dependence. His mistake is in making the distinction merely that between "absolute" and "relative" dependence, and therefore a difference of degree and not of intrinsic quality. What he overlooks is that, in giving the feeling the name "feeling of dependence" at all, we are really employing what is no more than a very close analogy. Anyone who compares and contrasts the two states of mind introspectively will find out, I think, what I mean. It cannot be expressed by means of anything else, just because it is so primary and elementary a datum in our psychical life, and therefore only definable through itself. It may perhaps help him if I cite a well-known example, in which the precise "moment" or element of religious feeling of which we are speaking is most actively present. When Abraham ventures to plead with God for the men of Sodom, he says (Genesis 18: 27): "Behold now, I have taken upon me to speak unto the Lord, which am but dust and ashes." There you have a self-confessed "feeling of dependence," which is yet at the same time far more than, and something other than, *merely* a feeling of dependence. Desiring to give it a name of its own, I propose to call it "creature-consciousness" or "creature-feeling." It is the emotion of a creature, abased and overwhelmed by its own nothingness in contrast to that which is supreme above all creatures.

It is easily seen that, once again, this phrase, whatever it is, is not a *conceptual* explanation of the matter. All that this new term, "creature-feeling," can express is the note of self-abasement into nothingness before an overpowering, absolute might of some kind; whereas everything turns upon the *character* of this overpowering might, a character which

cannot be expressed verbally, and can only be suggested indirectly through the tone and content of a man's feeling-response to it. And this response must be directly experienced in oneself to be understood.

We have now to note a second defect in the formulation of Schleiermacher's principle. The religious category discovered by him, by whose means he professes to determine the real content of the religious emotion, is merely a category of *self*-valuation, in the sense of self-depreciation. According to him the religious emotion would be directly and primarily a sort of *self*-consciousness, a feeling concerning one's self in a special, determined relation, viz., one's dependence. Thus, according to Schleiermacher, I can only come upon the very fact of God as the result of an inference, that is, by reasoning to a cause beyond myself to account for my "feeling of dependence." But this is entirely opposed to the psychological facts of the case. Rather, the "creature-feeling" is itself a first subjective concomitant and effect of another feeling-element, which casts it like a shadow, but which in itself indubitably has immediate and primary reference to an object outside the self.

Now this object is just what we have already spoken of as "the numinous." For the "creature-feeling" and the sense of dependence to arise in the mind the "numen" must be experienced as present, a *numen praesens*, as in the case of Abraham. There must be felt a something "numinous," something bearing the character of a "numen," to which the mind turns spontaneously; or (which is the same thing in other words) these feelings can only arise in the mind as accompanying emotions when the category of "the numinous" is called into play.

The numinous is thus felt as objective and outside the self. We have now to inquire more closely into its nature and the modes of its manifestation.

Mysterium Tremendum

The analysis of "tremendum"

We said above that the nature of the numinous can only be suggested by means of the special way in which it is reflected in the mind in terms of feeling. "Its nature is such that it grips or stirs the human mind with this and that determinate affective state." We have now to attempt to give a further indication of these determinate states. We must once again endeavour, by adducing feelings akin to them for the purpose of analogy or contrast, and by the use of metaphor and symbolic expressions, to make the states of mind we are investigating ring out, as it were, of themselves.

Let us consider the deepest and most fundamental element in all strong and sincerely felt religious emotion. Faith unto Salvation, Trust, Love – all these are there. But over and above these is an element which may also on occasion, quite apart from them, profoundly affect us and occupy the mind with a wellnigh bewildering strength. Let us follow it up with every effort of sympathy and imaginative intuition wherever it is to be found, in the lives of those around us, in sudden, strong ebullitions of personal piety and the frames of mind such ebullitions evince, in the fixed and ordered solemnities of rites and liturgies, and again in the atmosphere that clings to old religious monuments and buildings, to temples and to churches. If we do so we shall find we are dealing with something for which there is only one appropriate expression, "*mysterium tremendum*." (The feeling of it may at times come sweeping like a gentle tide, pervading the mind with a tranquil mood of deepest worship. It may pass over into a more set and lasting attitude of the soul, continuing, as it were, thrillingly vibrant and resonant, until at last it dies away and the soul resumes its "profane," non-religious mood of everyday experience. It may burst in sudden eruption up from the depths of the soul with spasms and convulsions, or lead to the strangest excitements, to intoxicated frenzy, to transport, and to ecstasy. It has its wild and demonic forms and can sink to an almost grisly horror and shuddering. It has its crude, barbaric antecedents and early manifestations, and again it may be developed into something beautiful and pure and glorious. It may become the hushed, trembling, and speechless humility of the creature in the presence of – whom or what? In the presence of that which is a *mystery* inexpressible and above all creatures.)

It is again evident at once that here too our attempted formulation by means of a concept is once more a merely negative one. Conceptually *mysterium* denotes merely that which is hidden and esoteric, that which is beyond conception or understanding, extraordinary and unfamiliar. The term does not define the object more positively in its qualitative character. But though what is enunciated in the word is negative, what is meant is something absolutely and intensely positive. This pure positive we can experience in feelings, feelings which our discussion can help to make clear to us, in so far as it arouses them actually in our hearts.

1. The element of awefulness To get light upon the positive "*quale*" of the object of these feelings, we must analyse more closely our phrase *mysterium tremendum*, and we will begin first with the adjective.

Tremor is in itself merely the perfectly familiar and "natural" emotion of *fear*. But here the term is taken, aptly enough but still only by analogy, to denote a quite specific kind of emotional response, wholly distinct from that of being afraid, though it so far resembles it that the analogy of fear may be used to throw light upon its nature. There are in some languages special expressions which denote, either exclusively or in the first instance, this "fear" that is more than fear proper. The Hebrew *hiqdīsh* (hallow) is an example. To "keep a thing holy in the heart" means to mark it off by a feeling of peculiar dread, not to be mistaken for any ordinary dread, that is, to appraise it by the category of the numinous. But the Old Testament throughout is rich in parallel expressions for this feeling. Specially noticeable is the *'ēmāh* of Yahweh ("fear of God"), which Yahweh can pour forth, dispatching almost like a daemon, and which seizes upon a man with paralysing effect. It is closely related to the δεῖμα πανικόν of the Greeks. Compare Exod. 23: 27: "I will send my fear before thee, and will destroy all the people to whom thou shalt come . . ."; also Job 9: 34; 13: 21 ("let not his fear terrify me"; "let not thy dread make me afraid"). Here we have a terror fraught with an inward shuddering such as not even the most menacing and overpowering created thing can instil. It has something spectral in it.

In the Greek language we have a corresponding term in σεβαστός. The early Christians could clearly feel that the title σεβαστός (*augustus*) was one that could not fittingly be given to any creature, not even to the emperor. They felt that to call a man σεβαστός was to give a human being a name proper only to the *numen*, to rank him by the category proper only to the *numen*, and that it therefore amounted to a kind of idolatry. Of modern languages English has the words "awe," "aweful," which in their deeper and most special sense approximate closely to our meaning. The phrase, "he stood aghast," is also suggestive in this connexion. On the other hand, German has no native-grown expression of its own for the higher and riper form of the emotion we are considering, unless it be in a word like *erschauern*, which does suggest it fairly well. It is far otherwise with its cruder and more debased phases, where such terms as *grausen* and *Schauer*, and the more popular and telling *gruseln*

Rudolf Otto

("grue"), *gräsen*, and *grässlich* ("grisly"), very clearly designate the numinous element. In my examination of Wundt's Animism I suggested the term *Scheu* (dread); but the special "numinous" quality (making it "awe" rather than "dread" in the ordinary sense) would then, of course, have to be denoted by inverted commas. "Religious dread" (or "awe") would perhaps be a better designation. Its antecedent stage is "daemonic dread" (cf. the horror of Pan) with its queer perversion, a sort of abortive offshoot, the "dread of ghosts." It first begins to stir in the feeling of "something uncanny," "eerie," or "weird." It is this feeling which, emerging in the mind of primeval man, forms the starting-point for the entire religious development in history. "Daemons" and "gods" alike spring from this root, and all the products of "mythological apperception" or "fantasy" are nothing but different modes in which it has been objectified. And all ostensible explanations of the origin of religion in terms of animism or magic or folk-psychology are doomed from the outset to wander astray and miss the real goal of their inquiry, unless they recognize this fact of our nature – primary, unique, underivable from anything else – to be the basic factor and the basic impulse underlying the entire process of religious evolution.

Not only is the saying of Luther, that the natural man cannot fear God perfectly, correct from the standpoint of psychology, but we ought to go farther and add that the natural man is quite unable even to "shudder" (*grauen*) or feel horror in the real sense of the word. For "shuddering" is something more than "natural," ordinary fear. It implies that the mysterious is already beginning to loom before the mind, to touch the feelings. It implies the first application of a category of valuation which has no place in the everyday natural world of ordinary experience, and is only possible to a being in whom has been awakened a mental predisposition, unique in kind and different in a definite way from any "natural" faculty. And this newly revealed capacity, even in the crude and violent manifestations which are all it at first evinces, bears witness to a completely new function of experience and standard of valuation, only belonging to the spirit of man.

Before going on to consider the elements which unfold as the "tremendum" develops, let us give a little further consideration to the first crude, primitive forms in which this "numinous dread" or *awe* shows itself. It is the mark which really characterizes the so-called "religion of primitive man," and there it appears as "daemonic dread." This crudely naïve and primordial emotional disturbance, and the fantastic images to which it gives rise, are later overborne and ousted by more highly developed forms of the numinous emotion, with all its mysteriously impelling power. But even when this has long attained its higher and purer mode of expression it is possible for the primitive types of excitation that were formerly a part of it to break out in the soul in all their original naiveté and so to be experienced afresh. That this is so is shown by the potent attraction again and again exercised by the element of horror and "shudder" in ghost stories, even among persons of high all-round education. It is a remarkable fact that the physical reaction to which this unique "dread" of the uncanny gives rise is also unique, and is not found in the case of any "natural" fear or terror. We say: "my blood ran icy cold," and "my flesh crept." The "cold blood" feeling may be a symptom of ordinary, natural fear, but there is something non-natural or supernatural about the symptom of "creeping flesh." And anyone who is capable of more precise introspection must recognize that the distinction between such a "dread" and natural fear is not simply one of degree and intensity. The awe or "dread" *may* indeed be so overwhelmingly great that it seems to penetrate to the very marrow, making the man's hair bristle and his limbs quake. But it may also steal upon him almost unobserved as the gentlest of agitations, a mere fleeting shadow passing across his mood. It has therefore nothing to do with intensity, and no natural fear passes over into it merely by being intensified. I may be beyond all measure afraid and terrified without there being even a trace of the feeling of uncanniness in my emotion.

We should see the facts more clearly if psychology in general would make a more decisive endeavour to examine and classify the feelings and emotions according to their qualitative differences. But the far too rough division of elementary feelings in general into pleasures and pains is still an obstacle to this. In point of fact "pleasures" no more than other feelings are differentiated merely by degrees of intensity; they show very definite and specific differences. It makes a specific difference to the condition of mind whether the soul is merely in a state of pleasure, or joy, or aesthetic rapture, or moral exaltation, or finally in the religious bliss that may come in worship. Such states certainly show resemblances one to another, and on that account can legitimately be brought under a common class-concept ("pleasure"), which serves to cut them off from other psychical functions, generically different. But this class-concept, so far from turning the various subordinate species into merely different degrees of the same thing, can do nothing at all to throw light upon the essence of each several state of mind which it includes.

Though the numinous emotion in its completest development shows a world of difference from the mere "daemonic dread," yet not even at the highest level does it belie its pedigree or kindred. Even when the worship of "demons" has long since reached the higher level of worship of "gods," these gods still retain as "numina" something of the "ghost" in the impress they make on the feelings of the worshipper, viz., the peculiar quality of the "uncanny" and "awful," which survives with the quality of exaltedness and sublimity or is symbolized by means of it. And this element, softened though it is, does not disappear even on the highest level of all, where the worship of God is at its purest. Its disappearance would be indeed an essential loss. The "shudder" reappears in a form ennobled beyond measure where the soul, held speechless, trembles inwardly to the furthest fibre of its being. It invades the mind mightily in Christian worship with the words: "Holy, holy, holy"; it breaks forth from the hymn of Tersteegen:

God Himself is present:
Heart, be stilled before Him:
Prostrate inwardly adore Him.

The "shudder" has here lost its crazy and bewildering note, but not the ineffable something that holds the mind. It has become a mystical awe, and sets free as its accompaniment, reflected in self-consciousness, that "creature-feeling" that has already been described as the feeling of personal nothingness and abasement before the awe-inspiring object directly experienced.

The referring of this feeling of numinous "tremor" to its object in the numen brings into relief a "property" of the latter which plays an important part in our Holy Scriptures, and which has been the occasion of many difficulties, both to commentators and to theologians, from its puzzling and baffling nature. This is the ὀργή (orgé), the Wrath of Yahweh, which recurs in the New Testament as ὀργή θεοῦ, and which is clearly analogous to the idea occurring in many religions of a mysterious *ira deorum*. To pass through the Indian pantheon of gods is to find deities who seem to be made up altogether out of such an ὀργή; and even

the higher Indian gods of grace and pardon have frequently, beside their merciful, their "wrath" form. But as regards the "Wrath of Yahweh," the strange features about it have for long been a matter for constant remark. In the first place, it is patent from many passages of the Old Testament that this "Wrath" has no concern whatever with moral qualities. There is something very baffling in the way in which it is "kindled" and manifested. It is, as has been well said, "like a hidden force of nature," like stored-up electricity, discharging itself upon anyone who comes too near. It is "incalculable" and "arbitrary." Anyone who is accustomed to think of deity only by its rational attributes must see in this "Wrath" mere caprice and wilful passion. But such a view would have been emphatically rejected by the religious men of the Old Covenant, for to them the Wrath of God, so far from being a diminution of His Godhead, appears as a natural expression of it, an element of "holiness" itself, and a quite indispensable one. And in this they are entirely right. This ὀργή is nothing but the "tremendum" itself, apprehended and expressed by the aid of a naïve analogy from the domain of natural experience, in this case from the ordinary passional life of men. But naïve as it may be, the analogy is most disconcertingly apt and striking; so much so that it will always retain its value, and for us no less than for the men of old be an inevitable way of expressing one element in the religious emotion. It cannot be doubted that, despite the protest of Schleiermacher and Ritschl, Christianity also has something to teach of the "Wrath of God."

It will be again at once apparent that in the use of this word we are not concerned with a genuine intellectual "concept," but only with a sort of illustrative substitute for a concept. "Wrath" here is the "ideogram" of a unique emotional moment in religious experience, a moment whose singularly *daunting* and awe-inspiring character must be gravely disturbing to those persons who will recognize nothing in the divine nature but goodness, gentleness, love, and a sort of confidential intimacy, in a word, only those aspects of God which turn towards the world of men.

This ὀργή is thus quite wrongly spoken of as "natural" wrath: rather it is an entirely non- or super-natural, i.e., numinous, quality. The rationalization process takes place when it begins to be filled in with elements derived from the moral reason – righteousness in requital, and punishment for moral transgression. But it should be noted that the idea of the Wrath of God in the Bible is always a synthesis, in which the original is combined with the later meaning that has come to fill it in. Something supra-rational throbs and gleams, palpable and visible, in the "Wrath of God," prompting to a sense of "terror" that no "natural" anger can arouse.

Beside the Wrath or Anger of Yahweh stands the related expression "Jealousy of Yahweh." The state of mind denoted by the phrase "being jealous *for* Yahweh" is also a numinous state of mind, in which features of the "tremendum" pass over into the man who has experience of it.

2. The element of "overpoweringness" (majestas)
We have been attempting to unfold the implications of that aspect of the "mysterium tremendum" indicated by the adjective, and the result so far may be summarized in two words, constituting, as before, what may be called an "ideogram," rather than a concept proper, viz., "absolute unapproachability."

It will be felt at once that there is yet a further element which must be added, that, namely, of "might," "power," "absolute overpoweringness." We will take to represent this the term *majestas*, majesty – the more readily because anyone with a feeling for language must detect a last faint trace of the numinous still clinging to the word. The "tremendum" may then be rendered more adequately *tremenda majestas*, or "aweful majesty." This second element of majesty may continue to be vividly preserved, where the first, that of unapproachability, recedes and dies away, as may be seen, for example, in mysticism. It is especially in relation to this element of majesty or absolute overpoweringness that the creature-consciousness, of which we have already spoken, comes upon the scene, as a sort of shadow or subjective reflection of it. Thus, in contrast to "the overpowering" of which we are conscious as an object over against the self, there is the feeling of one's own abasement, of being but "dust and ashes" and nothingness. And this forms the numinous raw material for the feeling of religious humility.

Here we must revert once again to Schleiermacher's expression for what we call "creature-feeling," viz., the "feeling of dependence." We found fault with this phrase before on the ground that Schleiermacher thereby takes as basis and point of departure what is merely a secondary effect; that he sets out to teach a consciousness of the religious *object* only by way of an inference from the shadow it casts upon *self*-consciousness. We have now a

further criticism to bring against it, and it is this. By "feeling of dependence" Schleiermacher means consciousness of *being conditioned* (as effect by cause), and so he develops the implications of this logically enough in his sections upon Creation and Preservation. On the side of the deity the correlate to "dependence" would thus be "causality," i.e., God's character as all-causing and all-conditioning. But a sense of this does not enter at all into that immediate and first-hand religious emotion which we have in the moment of worship, and which we can recover in a measure for analysis; it belongs on the contrary decidedly to the *rational* side of the idea of God; its implications admit of precise conceptual determination; and it springs from quite a distinct source. The difference between the "feeling of dependence" of Schleiermacher and that which finds typical utterance in the words of Abraham already cited might be expressed as that between the consciousness of *createdness* (*Geschaffenheit*) and the consciousness of *creature-hood* (*Geschöpflichkeit*). In the one case you have the creature as the work of the divine creative act; in the other, impotence and general nothingness as against overpowering might, dust and ashes as against "majesty." In the one case you have the fact of having been created; in the other, the status of the creature. And as soon as speculative thought has come to concern itself with this latter type of consciousness – as soon as it has come to analyze this "majesty" – we are introduced to a set of ideas quite different from those of creation or preservation. We come upon the ideas, first, of the annihilation of self, and then, as its complement, of the transcendent as the sole and entire reality. These are the characteristic notes of mysticism in all its forms, however otherwise various in content. For one of the chiefest and most general features of mysticism is just this *self-depreciation* (so plainly parallel to the case of Abraham), the estimation of the self, of the personal "I," as something not perfectly or essentially real, or even as mere nullity, a self-depreciation which comes to demand its own fulfilment in practice in rejecting the delusion of selfhood, and so makes for the annihilation of the self. And on the other hand mysticism leads to a valuation of the transcendent object of its reference as that which through plenitude of being stands supreme and absolute, so that the finite self contrasted with it becomes conscious even in its nullity that "I am nought, Thou art all." There is no thought in this of any causal relation between God, the creator, and the self, the creature.

The point from which speculation starts is not a "consciousness of absolute dependence" – of myself as result and effect of a divine cause – for that would in point of fact lead to insistence upon the reality of the self; it starts from a consciousness of the absolute superiority or supremacy of a power other than myself, and it is only as it falls back upon ontological terms to achieve its end – terms generally borrowed from natural science – that that element of the "tremendum," originally apprehended as "plenitude of power," becomes transmuted into "plenitude of being."

This leads again to the mention of mysticism. No mere inquiry into the genesis of a thing can throw any light upon its essential nature, and it is hence immaterial to us how mysticism historically arose. But essentially mysticism is the stressing to a very high degree, indeed the overstressing, of the non-rational or supra-rational elements in religion; and it is only intelligible when so understood. The various phases and factors of the non-rational may receive varying emphasis, and the type of mysticism will differ according as some or others fall into the background. What we have been analyzing, however, is a feature that recurs in all forms of mysticism everywhere, and it is nothing but the "creature-consciousness" stressed to the utmost and to excess, the expression meaning, if we may repeat the contrast already made, not "feeling of our createdness" but "feeling of our creaturehood," that is, the consciousness of the littleness of every creature in face of that which is above all creatures.

A characteristic common to all types of mysticism is the *Identification*, in different degrees of completeness, of the personal self with the transcendent Reality. This identification has a source of its own, with which we are not here concerned, and springs from "moments" of religious experience which would require separate treatment. "Identification" alone, however, is not enough for mysticism; it must be Identification with the Something that is at once absolutely supreme in power and reality and wholly non-rational. And it is among the mystics that we most encounter this element of religious consciousness. Récéjac has noticed this in his *Essai sur les fondements de la connaissance mystique*. He writes:

Le mysticisme commence par la crainte, par le sentiment d'une *domination* universelle, *invincible*, et devient plus tard un désir d'union avec ce qui domine ainsi. [Mysticism begins with fear, the sense of a universal and irresistible rule, and later becomes a desire for union with that which thus rules.]

And some very clear examples of this taken from the religious experience of the present day are to be found in W. James:

The perfect stillness of the night was thrilled by a more solemn silence. The darkness held a presence that was all the more felt because it was not seen. I could not any more have doubted that *He* was there than that I was. Indeed, I felt myself to be, if possible, the less real of the two.

This example is particularly instructive as to the relation of mysticism to the "feelings of Identification," for the experience here recounted was on the point of passing into it.

3. The element of "energy" or urgency   There is, finally, a third element comprised in those of "tremendum" and "majestas," awefulness and majesty, and this I venture to call the *urgency* or *energy* of the numinous object. It is particularly vividly perceptible in the ὀργή or "Wrath"; and it everywhere clothes itself in symbolical expressions – vitality, passion, emotional temper, will, force, movement, excitement, activity, impetus. These features are typical and recur again and again from the demonic level up to the idea of the "living" God. We have here the factor that has everywhere more than any other prompted the fiercest opposition to the "philosophic" God of mere rational speculation, who can be put into a definition. And for their part the philosophers have condemned these expressions of the energy of the numen, whenever they are brought on to the scene, as sheer anthropomorphism. Insofar as their opponents have for the most part themselves failed to recognize that the terms they have borrowed from the sphere of human conative and affective life have merely value as analogies, the philosophers are right to condemn them. But they are wrong, insofar as, this error notwithstanding, these terms stood for a genuine aspect of the divine nature – its non-rational aspect – a due consciousness of which served to protect religion itself from being "rationalized" away.

For wherever men have been contending for the "living" God and for voluntarism, there, we may be sure, have been non-rationalists fighting rationalists and rationalism. It was so with Luther in his controversy with Erasmus; and Luther's *omnipotentia*

Dei in his *De Servo Arbitrio* is nothing but the union of "majesty" – in the sense of absolute supremacy – with this "energy," in the sense of a force that knows not stint nor stay, which is urgent, active, compelling, and alive. In mysticism, too, this element of "energy" is a very living and vigorous factor, at any rate in the "voluntaristic" mysticism, the mysticism of love, where it is very forcibly seen in that "consuming fire" of love whose burning strength the mystic can hardly bear, but begs that the heat that has scorched him may be mitigated, lest he be himself destroyed by it. And in this urgency and pressure the mystic's "love" claims a perceptible kinship with the ὀργή itself, the scorching and consuming wrath of God; it is the same "energy," only differently directed. "Love," says one of the mystics, "is nothing else than quenched Wrath."

The element of "energy" reappears in Fichte's speculations on the Absolute as the gigantic, never-resting, active world-stress, and in Schopenhauer's daemonic "Will." At the same time both these writers are guilty of the same error that is already found in myth; they transfer "natural" attributes, which ought only to be used as "ideograms" for what is itself properly beyond utterance, to the non-rational as real qualifications of it, and they mistake symbolic expressions of feelings for adequate concepts upon which a "scientific" structure of knowledge may be based.

In Goethe the same element of energy is emphasized in a quite unique way in his strange descriptions of the experience he calls "daemonic."

The Analysis of "Mysterium"

Ein begriffener Gott ist kein Gott. [A God comprehended is no God.]

Tersteegen

We gave to the object to which the numinous consciousness is directed the name "mysterium tremendum," and we then set ourselves first to determine the meaning of the adjective "tremendum" – which we found to be itself only justified by analogy – because it is more easily analyzed than the substantive idea "mysterium." We have now to turn to this, and try, as best we may, by hint and suggestion, to get to a clearer apprehension of what it implies.

4. The "wholly other" It might be thought that the adjective itself gives an explanation of the substantive; but this is not so. It is not merely analytical; it is a synthetic attribute to it; i.e., "tremendum" adds something not necessarily inherent in "mysterium." It is true that the reactions in consciousness that correspond to the one readily and spontaneously overflow into those that correspond to the other; in fact, anyone sensitive to the use of words would commonly feel that the idea of "mystery" (*mysterium*) is so closely bound up with its synthetic qualifying attribute "aweful" (*tremendum*) that one can hardly say the former without catching an echo of the latter, "mystery" almost of itself becoming "aweful mystery" to us. But the passage from the one idea to the other need not by any means be always so easy. The elements of meaning implied in "awefulness" and "mysteriousness" are in themselves definitely different. The latter may so far preponderate in the religious consciousness, may stand out so vividly, that in comparison with it the former almost sinks out of sight; a case which again could be clearly exemplified from some forms of mysticism. Occasionally, on the other hand, the reverse happens, and the "tremendum" may in turn occupy the mind without the "mysterium."

This latter, then, needs special consideration on its own account. We need an expression for the mental reaction peculiar to it; and here, too, only one word seems appropriate, though, as it is strictly applicable only to a "natural" state of mind, it has here meaning only by analogy: it is the word "stupor." *Stupor* is plainly a different thing from *tremor*; it signifies blank wonder, an astonishment that strikes us dumb, amazement absolute. Taken, indeed, in its purely natural sense, "mysterium" would first mean merely a secret or a mystery in the sense of that which is alien to us, uncomprehended and unexplained; and so far "mysterium" is itself merely an ideogram, an analogical notion taken from the natural sphere, illustrating, but incapable of exhaustively rendering, our real meaning. Taken in the religious sense, that which is "mysterious" is – to give it perhaps the most striking expression – the "wholly other" (θάτερον, *anyad, alienum*), that which is quite beyond the sphere of the usual, the intelligible, and the familiar, which therefore falls quite outside the limits of the "canny," and is contrasted with it, filling the mind with blank wonder and astonishment.

This is already to be observed on the lowest and earliest level of the religion of primitive man, where the numinous consciousness is but an inchoate stirring of the feelings. What is really characteristic of this stage is *not* – as the theory of animism would have us believe – that men are here concerned with curious entities, called "souls" or "spirits," which happen to be invisible. Representations of spirits and similar conceptions are rather one and all early modes of "rationalizing" a precedent experience, to which they are subsidiary. They are attempts in some way or other, it little matters how, to guess the riddle it propounds, and their effect is at the same time always to weaken and deaden the experience itself. They are the source from which springs, not religion, but the rationalization of religion, which often ends by constructing such a massive structure of theory and such a plausible fabric of interpretation, that the "mystery" is frankly excluded. Both imaginative "myth," when developed into a system, and intellectualist Scholasticism, when worked out to its completion, are methods by which the fundamental fact of religious experience is, as it were, simply rolled out so thin and flat as to be finally eliminated altogether.

Even on the lowest level of religious development the essential characteristic is therefore to be sought elsewhere than in the appearance of "spirit" representations. It lies rather, we repeat, in a peculiar "moment" of consciousness, to wit, the *stupor* before something "wholly other," whether such an other be named "spirit" or "daemon" or "deva," or be left without any name. Nor does it make any difference in this respect whether, to interpret and preserve their apprehension of this "other," men coin original imagery of their own or adapt imaginations drawn from the world of legend, the fabrications of fancy apart from and prior to any stirrings of daemonic dread.

In accordance with laws of which we shall have to speak again later, this feeling or consciousness of the "wholly other" will attach itself to, or sometimes be indirectly aroused by means of, objects which are already puzzling upon the "natural" plane, or are of a surprising or astounding character; such as extraordinary phenomena or astonishing occurrences or things in inanimate nature, in the animal world, or among men. But here once more we are dealing with a case of association between things specifically different – the "numinous" and the "natural" moment of consciousness – and not merely with the gradual enhancement of one of them – the "natural" – till it becomes the other. As in the case of "natural fear" and "daemonic dread" already considered, so here the transition from natural to daemonic amazement is not a mere matter of degree. But it is only with the latter that the complementary expression "mysterium" perfectly harmonizes, as will be felt perhaps more clearly in the case of the adjectival form "mysterious." No one says, strictly and in earnest, of a piece of clockwork that is beyond his grasp, or of a science that he cannot understand: "That is 'mysterious' to me."

It might be objected that the mysterious is something which is and remains absolutely and invariably beyond our understanding, whereas that which merely eludes our understanding for a time but is perfectly intelligible in principle should be called, not a "mystery," but merely a "problem." But this is by no means an adequate account of the matter. The truly "mysterious" object is beyond our apprehension and comprehension, not only because our knowledge has certain irremovable limits, but because in it we come upon something inherently "wholly other," whose kind and character are incommensurable with our own, and before which we therefore recoil in a wonder that strikes us chill and numb.

This may be made still clearer by a consideration of that degraded offshoot and travesty of the genuine "numinous" dread or awe, the fear of ghosts. Let us try to analyze this experience. We have already specified the peculiar feeling-element of "dread" aroused by the ghost as that of "grue," grisly horror (*gruseln, gräsen*). Now this "grue" obviously contributes something to the attraction which ghost-stories exercise, insofar, namely, as the relaxation of tension ensuing upon our release from it relieves the mind in a pleasant and agreeable way. So far, however, it is not really the ghost itself that gives us pleasure, but the fact that we are rid of it. But obviously this is quite insufficient to explain the ensnaring attraction of the ghost-story. The ghost's real attraction rather consists in this, that of itself and in an uncommon degree it entices the imagination, awakening strong interest and curiosity; it is the weird thing itself that allures the fancy. But it does this, not because it is "something long and white" (as someone once defined a ghost), nor yet through any of the positive and conceptual attributes which fancies about ghosts have invented, but because it is a thing that "doesn't really exist at all," the "wholly other," something which has no place in our scheme of reality but belongs to an absolutely different one, and which at the same time arouses an irrepressible interest in the mind.

But that which is perceptibly true in the fear of ghosts, which is, after all, only a caricature of the genuine thing, is in a far stronger sense true of the "daemonic" experience itself, of which the fear of ghosts is a mere offshoot. And while, following this main line of development, this element in the numinous consciousness, the feeling of the "wholly other," is heightened and clarified, its higher modes of manifestation come into being, which set the numinous object in contrast not only to everything wonted and familiar (i.e., in the end, to nature in general), thereby turning it into the "supernatural," but finally to the world itself, and thereby exalt it to the "supramundane," that which is above the whole world-order.

In mysticism we have in the "Beyond" (ἐπέκεινα) again the strongest stressing and over-stressing of those non-rational elements which are already inherent in all religion. Mysticism continues to its extreme point this contrasting of the numinous object (the numen), as the "wholly other," with ordinary experience. Not content with contrasting it with all this is of nature or this world, mysticism concludes by contrasting it with Being itself and all that "is," and finally actually calls it "that which is nothing." By this "nothing" is meant not only that of which nothing can be predicated, but that which is absolutely and intrinsically other than and opposite of everything that is and can be thought. But while exaggerating to the point of paradox this *negation* and contrast – the only means open to conceptual thought to apprehend the "mysterium" – mysticism at the same time retains the *positive quality* of the "wholly other" as a very living factor in its over-brimming religious emotion.

But what is true of the strange "nothingness" of our mystics holds good equally of the *sūnyam* and the *sūnyatā*, the "void" and "emptiness" of the Buddhist mystics. This aspiration for the "void" and for becoming void, no less than the aspiration of our western mystics for "nothing" and for becoming nothing, must seem a kind of lunacy to anyone who has no inner sympathy for the esoteric language and ideograms of mysticism, and lacks the matrix from which these come necessarily to birth. To such a one Buddhism itself will be simply a morbid sort of pessimism. But in fact the "void" of the eastern, like the "nothing" of the western, mystic is a numinous ideogram of the "wholly other."

These terms, "supernatural" and "transcendent" (literally, supramundane: *überweltlich*), give the appearance of positive attributes, and, as applied to the mysterious, they appear to divest the "mysterium" of its originally negative meaning and to turn it into an affirmation. On the side of conceptual thought this is nothing more than appearance, for it is obvious that the two terms in question are merely negative and exclusive attributes with reference to "nature" and the "world" or cosmos respectively. But on the side of the feeling-content it is otherwise; that *is* in very truth positive in the highest degree, though here too, as before, it cannot be rendered explicit in conceptual terms. It is through this positive feeling-content that the concepts of the "transcendent" and "supernatural" become forthwith designations for a unique "wholly other" reality and quality, something of whose special character we can *feel*, without being able to give it clear conceptual expression.

The Analysis of "Mysterium," Continued

5. *The element of fascination* The qualitative *content* of the numinous experience, to which "the mysterious" stands as *form*, is in one of its aspects the element of daunting "awefulness" and "majesty," which has already been dealt with in detail; but it is clear that it has at the same time another aspect, in which it shows itself as something uniquely attractive and *fascinating*.

These two qualities, the daunting and the fascinating, now combine in a strange harmony of contrasts, and the resultant dual character of the numinous consciousness, to which the entire religious development bears witness, at any rate from the level of the "daemonic dread" onwards, is at once the strangest and most noteworthy phenomenon in the whole history of religion. The daemonic-divine object may appear to the mind an object of horror and dread, but at the same time it is no less something that allures with a potent charm, and the creature, who trembles before it, utterly cowed and cast down, has always at the same time the impulse to turn to it, nay even to make it somehow his own. The "mystery" is for him not merely something to be wondered at but something that entrances him; and beside that in it which bewilders and confounds, he feels a something that captivates and transports him with a strange ravishment, rising often enough to the pitch of dizzy intoxication; it is the Dionysiac element in the numen.

The ideas and concepts which are the parallels or "schemata" on the rational side of this non-rational element of "fascination" are Love, Mercy, Pity, Comfort; these are all "natural" elements of the common psychical life, only they are here thought as absolute and in completeness. But important as these are for the experience of religious bliss or felicity, they do not by any means exhaust it. It is just the same as with the opposite experience of religious infelicity – the experience of the ὀργή or Wrath of God – both alike contain fundamentally non-rational elements. Bliss or beatitude is more, far more, than the mere natural feeling of being comforted, of reliance, of the joy of love, however these may be heightened and enhanced. Just as "Wrath," taken in a purely rational or a purely ethical sense, does not exhaust that profound element of *awefulness* which is locked in the mystery of deity, so neither does "Graciousness" exhaust the profound element of *wonderfulness* and rapture which lies in the mysterious beatific experience of deity. The term "grace" may indeed be taken as its aptest designation, but then only in the sense in which it is really applied in the language of the mystics, and in which not only the "gracious intent" but "something more" is meant by the word. This "something more" has its antecedent phases very far back in the history of religions.

It may well be possible, it is even probable, that in the first stage of its development the religious consciousness started with only one of its poles – the "daunting" aspect of the numen – and so at first took shape only as "daemonic dread." But if this did not point to something beyond itself, if it were not but one "moment" of a completer experience, pressing up gradually into consciousness, then no transition would be possible to the feelings of positive self-surrender to the numen. The only type of worship that could result from this "dread" alone would be that of ἀπαιτεῖσθαι and ἀποτρέπειν, taking the form of expiation and propitiation, the averting or the appeasement of the "wrath" of the numen. It can never explain how it is that "the numinous" is the object of search and desire and yearning, and that too for its own sake and not only for the sake of the aid and backing that men expect from it in the natural sphere. It can never explain how this takes place, not only in the forms of "rational" religious worship, but in those queer "sacramental" observances and rituals and procedures of communion in which the human being seeks to get the numen into his possession.

Religious practice may manifest itself in those normal and easily intelligible forms which occupy so prominent a place in the history of religion, such forms as propitiation, petition, sacrifice, thanksgiving, etc. But besides these there is a series of strange proceedings which are constantly attracting greater and greater attention, and in which it is claimed that we may recognize, besides mere religion in general, the particular roots of mysticism. I refer to those numerous curious modes of behaviour and fantastic forms of mediation, by means of which the primitive religious man attempts to master "the mysterious," and to fill himself and even to identify himself with it. These modes of behaviour fall apart into two classes. On the one hand the "magical" identification of the self with the numen proceeds by means of various transactions, at once magical and devotional in character – by formula, ordination, adjuration, consecration, exorcism, etc.: on the other hand are the "shamanistic" ways of procedure, possession, indwelling, self-imbuement with the numen in exaltation and ecstasy. All these have, indeed, their starting-points simply in magic, and their intention at first was certainly simply to appropriate the prodigious force of the numen for the natural ends of man. But the process does not rest there. Possession of and by the numen becomes an end in itself; it begins to be sought for its own sake; and the wildest and most artificial methods of asceticism are put into practice to attain it. In a word, the *vita religiosa* begins; and to remain in these strange and bizarre states of numinous possession becomes a good in itself, even a way of salvation, wholly different from the profane goods pursued by means of magic. Here, too, commences the process of development by which the experience is matured and purified, till finally it reaches its consummation in the sublimest and purest states of the "life within the Spirit" and in the noblest mysticism. Widely various as these states are in themselves, yet they have this element in common, that in them the "mysterium" is experienced in its essential, positive, and specific character, as something that bestows upon man a beatitude beyond compare, but one whose real nature he can neither proclaim in speech nor conceive in thought, but may know only by a direct and living experience. It is a bliss which embraces all those blessings that are indicated or suggested in positive fashion by any "doctrine of Salvation," and it quickens all of them through and through; but these do not exhaust it. Rather by its all-pervading, penetrating glow it makes of these very blessings more than the intellect can conceive in them or affirm of them. It gives the Peace that passes understanding, and of which the tongue can only stammer brokenly. Only from afar, by metaphors and analogies, do we come to apprehend what it is in itself, and even so our notion is but inadequate and confused.

"Eye hath not seen, nor ear heard, neither have entered into the heart of man, the things which God hath prepared for them that love Him." Who does not feel the exalted sound of these words and the "Dionysiac" element of transport and fervour in them? It is instructive that in such phrases as these, in which consciousness would fain put its highest consummation into words, "all images fall away" and the mind turns from them to grasp expressions that are purely negative. And it is still more instructive that in reading and hearing such words their merely negative character simply is not noticed; that we can let whole chains of such negations enrapture, even intoxicate us, and that entire hymns – and deeply impressive hymns – have been composed, in which there is really nothing positive at all! All this teaches us the independence of the positive content of this experience from the implications of its overt conceptual expression, and how it can be firmly grasped, thoroughly understood, and profoundly appreciated, purely in, with, and from the feeling itself.

Mere love, mere trust, for all the glory and happiness they bring, do not explain to us that moment of rapture that breathes in our tenderest and most heart-felt hymns of salvation, as also in such eschatological hymns of longing as that rhyme of St Bernard in which the very verses seem to dance.

Urbs Sion unica, mansio mystica, condita caelo,
Nunc tibi gaudeo, nunc tibi lugeo, tristor, anhelo,
Te, quia corpore non queo, pectore saepe penetro;
Sed caro terrea, terraque carnea, mox cado retro.
Nemo retexere, nemoque promere sustinet ore,
Quo tua moenia, quo capitolia plena nitore.
Id queo dicere, quo modo tangere pollice coelum,
Ut mare currere, sicut in aere figere telum.
Opprimit omne cor ille tuus decor, O Sion, O Pax.
Urbs sine tempore, nulla potest fore laus tibi mendax.
O nova mansio, te pia concio, gens pia munit,
Provehit, excitat, auget, identitat, efficit, unit.[1]

This is where the living "something more" of the "fascinans," the element of fascination, is to be found. It lives no less in those tense extollings of the blessing of salvation, which recur in all religions of salvation, and stand in such remarkable contrast to the relatively meagre and frequently childish import of that which is revealed in them by concept or by image. Everywhere Salvation is something whose meaning is often very little apparent, is even wholly obscure, to the "natural" man; on the contrary, *so far as he understands it*, he tends to find it highly tedious and uninteresting, sometimes downright distasteful and repugnant to his nature, as he would, for instance, find the beatific vision of God in our own doctrine of Salvation, or the "Henosis" of "God all in all" among the mystics. "So far as he understands," be it noted; but then he does not understand it in the least. Because he lacks the inward teaching of the Spirit, he must needs confound what is offered him as an expression for the experience of salvation – a mere ideogram of what is felt, whose import it hints at by analogy – with "natural" concepts, as though it were itself just such a one. And so he "wanders ever further from the goal."

It is not only in the religious feeling of longing that the moment of fascination is a living factor. It is already alive and present in the moment of "solemnity," both in the gathered concentration and humble abasement of private devotion, when the mind is exalted to the holy, and in the common worship of the congregation, where this is practiced with earnestness and deep sincerity, as, it is to be feared, is with us a thing rather desired than realized. It is this and nothing else that in the solemn moment can fill the soul so full and keep it so inexpressibly tranquil. Schleiermacher's assertion [*The Christian Faith*, §5] is perhaps true of it, as of the numinous consciousness in general, viz., that it cannot really occur alone on its own account, or except combined and penetrated with rational elements. But, if this be admitted, it is upon other grounds than those adduced by Schleiermacher; while, on the other hand, it may occupy a more or less predominant place and lead to states of calm ($\dot{\eta}\sigma\upsilon\chi\acute{\iota}\alpha$) as well as of transport, in which it *almost* of itself wholly fills the soul. But in all the manifold forms in which it is aroused in us, whether in eschatological promise of the coming kingdom of God and the transcendent bliss of Paradise, or in the guise of an entry into that beatific Reality that is "above the world"; whether it come first in expectancy or preintimation or in a present experience ("When I but *have* Thee, I ask no question of heaven and earth"); in all these forms, outwardly diverse but inwardly akin, it appears as a strange and mighty propulsion toward an ideal good known only to religion and in its nature fundamentally non-rational, which the mind knows of in yearning and presentiment, recognizing it for what it is behind the obscure and inadequate symbols which are its only expression. And this shows that above and beyond our rational being lies hidden the ultimate and highest part of our nature, which can find no satisfaction in the mere allaying of the needs of our sensuous, psychical, or intellectual impulses and cravings. The mystics called it the basis or ground of the soul.

We saw that in the case of the element of the mysterious the "wholly other" led on to the supernatural and transcendent and that above these appeared the "beyond" (ἐπέχεινα) of mysticism, through the non-rational side of religion being raised to its highest power and stressed to excess. It is the same in the case of the element of "fascination"; here, too, is possible a transition into mysticism. At its highest point of stress the fascinating becomes the "overabounding," the mystical "moment" which exactly corresponds upon this line to the ἐπέχεινα upon the other line of approach, and which is to be understood accordingly. But while this feeling of the "overabounding" is specially characteristic of mysticism, a trace of it survives in all truly felt states of religious beatitude, however restrained and kept within measure by other factors. This is seen most clearly from the psychology of those great experiences – of grace, conversion, second birth – in which the religious experience appears in its pure intrinsic nature and in heightened activity, so as to be more clearly grasped than in the less typical form of piety instilled by education. The hard core of such experiences in their Christian form consists of the redemption from guilt and bondage to sin, and we shall have presently to see that this also does not occur without a participation of non-rational elements. But leaving this out of account, what we have here to point out is the unutterableness of what has been yet genuinely experienced, and how such an experience may pass into blissful excitement, rapture, and exaltation verging often on the bizarre and the abnormal. This is vouched for by the autobiographical testimony of the "converted" from St Paul onward. William James has collected a great number of these,

without, however, himself noticing the non-rational element that thrills in them.

Thus, one writes

> For the moment nothing but an ineffable joy and exaltation remained. It is impossible fully to describe the experience. It was like the effect of some great orchestra, when all the separate notes have melted into one swelling harmony, that leaves the listener conscious of nothing save that his soul is being wafted upwards and almost bursting with its own emotion. (*Varieties of Religious Experience*, p. 66.)

And another:

> The more I seek words to express this intimate intercourse, the more I feel the impossibility of describing the thing by any of our usual images. (*Ibid.*, p. 68.)

And almost with the precision of dogma, a third (Jonathan Edwards) indicates the qualitative difference of the experience of beatitude from other "rational" joy:

> The conceptions which the saints have of the loveliness of God and that kind of delight which they experience in it are quite peculiar and entirely different from anything which a natural man can possess or of which he can form any proper notion. (*Ibid.*, p. 229.)

Also this of Boehme:

> But I can neither write nor tell of what sort of Exaltation the triumphing in the Spirit is. It can be compared with nought, but that when in the midst of death life is born, and it is like the resurrection of the dead.

With the mystics these experiences pass up wholly into the "overabounding." "O that I could tell you what the heart feels, how it burns and is consumed inwardly! Only, I find no words to express it. I can but say: Might but one little drop of what I feel fall into Hell, Hell would be transformed into a Paradise." So says St Catherine of Genoa; and all the multitude of her spiritual kindred testify to the same effect.

What we Christians know as the experiences of grace and the second birth have their parallels also in the religions of high spiritual rank beyond the borders of Christianity. Such are the breaking out of the saving *Bodhi*, the opening of the "heavenly eye," the *Jñāna* by *Iśvaras prasāda*, which is victorious over the darkness of nescience and shines out in an experience with which no other can be measured. And in all these the entirely non-rational and specific element in the beatific experience is immediately noticeable. The qualitative character of it varies widely in all these cases, and is again in them all very different from its parallels in Christianity; still in all it is very similar in intensity, and in all it is a "salvation" and an absolute "fascination," which in contrast to all that admits of "natural" expression or comparison is deeply imbued with the "overabounding" nature of the numen.

And this is also entirely true of the rapture of Nirvana, which is only in appearance a cold and negative state. It is only conceptually that Nirvana is a negation; it is felt in consciousness as in the strongest degree positive; it exercises a "fascination" by which its votaries are as much carried away as are the Hindu or the Christian by the corresponding objects of their worship. I recall vividly a conversation I had with a Buddhist monk. He had been putting before me methodically and pertinaciously the arguments for the Buddhist "theology of negation," the doctrine of *Anātman* and "entire emptiness." When he had made an end, I asked him what then Nirvana itself is: and after a long pause came at last the single answer, low and restrained: "Bliss – unspeakable." And the hushed restraint of that answer, the solemnity of his voice, demeanour, and gesture, made more clear what was meant than the words themselves.

And so we maintain, on the one hand, following the *via eminentiae et causalitatis*, that the divine is indeed the highest, strongest, best, loveliest, and dearest that man can think of; but we assert on the other, following the *via negationis*, that God is not *merely* the ground and superlative of all that can be thought; He is in Himself a subject on His own account and in Himself.

In the adjective δεινός the Greek language possesses a word peculiarly difficult to translate, and standing for an idea peculiarly difficult to grasp in all its strange variations. And if we ask whence this difficulty arises, the answer is plain; it is because δεινός is simply the numinous (mostly of course at a lower level, in an arrested form, attenuated by rhetorical or poetic usage). Consequently δεινός is the equivalent of *dirus* and *tremendus*. It may mean evil or imposing, potent and strange, queer and marvellous, horrifying and fascinating, divine and daemonic, and a source of "energy." Sophocles means to awaken the feeling of "numinous awe" through the whole gamut of its phases at the contemplation of man, the creature of marvel, in the choric song of the *Antigone*: πολλὰ τὰ δεινά, χούδὲν ἀνθρώποθ δεινότερον πελει. This line defies translation, just because our language has no term that can isolate distinctly and gather into one word the total numinous impression a thing may make on the mind. The nearest that German can get to it is in the expression *das Ungeheuere* (monstrous), while in English "weird" is perhaps the closest rendering possible. The mood and attitude represented in the foregoing verse might then be fairly well rendered by such a translation as: "Much there is that is weird; but nought is weirder than man." The German *ungeheuer* is not by derivation simply "huge," in quantity or quality – this, its common meaning, is in fact a rationalizing interpretation of the real idea; it is that which is not *geheuer*, i.e., approximately, the *uncanny* – in a word, the numinous. And it is just this element of the uncanny in man that Sophocles has in mind. If this, its fundamental meaning, be really and thoroughly felt in consciousness, then the word could be taken as a fairly exact expression for the numinous in its aspects of mystery, awefulness, majesty, augustness, and "energy"; nay, even the aspect of fascination is dimly felt in it.

The variations of meaning in the German word *ungeheuer* can be well illustrated from Goethe. He, too, uses the word first to denote the huge in size – what is too vast for our faculty of space-perception, such as the immeasurable vault of the night sky. In other passages the word retains its original non-rational colour more markedly; it comes to mean the uncanny, the fearful, the dauntingly "other" and incomprehensible, that which arouses in us "stupor" and θάμβος; and finally, in the wonderful words of *Faust*, it becomes an almost exact synonym for our "numinous" under all its aspects.

Das Schaudern ist der Menschheit bestes Teil.
Wie auch die Welt ihm das Gefühl verteure,
Ergriffen fühlt er tief das Ungeheuere.[2]

Notes

1. "O Zion, thou city sole and single, mystic mansion hidden away in the heavens, now I rejoice in thee, now I moan for thee and mourn and yearn for thee; Thee often I pass through in the heart, as I cannot in the body, but being but earthly flesh and fleshly earth soon I fall back. None can disclose or utter in speech what plenary radiance fills thy walls and thy citadels. I can as little tell of it as I can touch the skies with my finger, or run upon the sea, or make a dart stand still in the air. This thy splendour overwhelms every heart, O Sion, O Peace! O timeless City, no praise can belie thee. O new dwelling-place, thee the concourse and people of the faithful erects and exalts, inspires and increases, joins to itself, and makes complete and one."

2. Awe is the best of man: howe'er the world's
   Misprizing of the feeling would prevent us,
   Deeply we feel, once gripped, the weird Portentous.
   (Goethe, *Faust*, Second Part, Act I, Sc. 5.)

14

Religious Experience

Caroline Franks Davis

1. What Counts as a 'Religious Experience'?

Proponents of arguments from religious experience often succumb to the demand to provide a brief, precise definition of 'religious experience'. Such definitions can do more harm than good, however. If one restricts the term to experiences in accordance with the doctrines of one tradition, then any argument from religious experiences to those doctrines begs the question.[1] On the other hand, to widen the definition to include all experiences referred to as 'religious' would be foolhardy, since people often use terms such as 'religious' and 'mystical' metaphorically, to refer to any experience which is overwhelming, extraordinary, thrilling, or sublime. A brief definition such as 'experiences of God', though plausible, excludes the many religious experiences of theists which are not 'of God' as such, as well as experiences from atheistic mystical traditions such as 'cosmic consciousness' and Buddhism. Definitions involving the term 'God' are difficult to work with in any case, since the term admits of such a variety of interpretations.

Because there are so many religious traditions and so many types of experience within those traditions, I look upon the quest for a neat, precise definition of 'religious experience' – even a definition 'for

Caroline Franks Davis, "Religious Experience," reprinted by permission of Oxford University Press from *The Evidential Force of Religious Experience* (Oxford: Clarendon Press; New York: Oxford University Press, 1989), pp. 29–65. © Caroline Franks Davis, 1989.

the purposes of this study' – as fruitless. Most people have a workable idea of what counts as a religious experience, based on the many uncontroversial examples available. What I shall do in this and the following sections is to sharpen up that idea with a few guidelines, comparisons with borderline experiences which I do not count as 'religious', and an extensive survey of different types of religious experience. Such a procedure should provide us with a much better understanding of religious experiences than a short definition ever could.

It is the auto-description to which one must normally turn to determine the religiousness of an experience. A believer may give a hetero-description such as 'that was the Holy Spirit working in you' of another's experience of new hope or peace, but such an experience would only be a 'religious experience' if the subject himself saw it in a religious light. Experiences such as ecstasy, being in love, deliverance from danger or despair, aesthetic experiences, and inspiration must all be given a religious incorporated or reflexive interpretation if they are to count as 'religious experiences'.

Some experiences are seen as religious by the subject because of their religious content or context – for instance, a vision or revelation with religious content, or a feeling of peace while praying or taking communion. However, not all experiences in a religious context are 'religious experiences' – an itch during communion is unlikely to be, for instance! Similarly, the perception of religious texts and works of art and the participation in religious rituals, though experiences with religious content, do not in themselves constitute 'religious experiences'. Thoughts with religious content will be religious if they seem to the subjects to have been the result of divine inspiration rather than produced by their own powers of reasoning. Again, though, not all 'flashes of insight' are religious experiences; suddenly seeing the solution to a mathematical problem, even if it seems to have 'come out of the blue', is usually not a religious experience, though it may be referred to metaphorically as such by an overjoyed mathematician.

The line dividing secular experiences from their religious counterparts is often difficult to draw, and rightly so. Sometimes, for instance, a subject may come to see things in religious terms over the course of a sustained experience which began non-religiously. In the aesthetic realm, works of art and the act of creating works of art can often trigger religious experiences, and aesthetic experiences sometimes merge into religious experiences with no clear moment of transition. Some artists, musicians and writers even see their activity as a religious exercise, though many may be using the word metaphorically.

Some religious experiences are what I call 'intrinsically religious'. Such experiences involve at least one of those 'other-worldly' factors which are missing in quasi-religions such as Marxism and humanism: the sense of the presence or activity of a non-physical holy being or power; apprehension of an 'ultimate reality' beyond the mundane world of physical bodies, physical processes, and narrow centres of consciousness; and the sense of achievement of (or being on the way to) man's *summum bonum*, an ultimate bliss, liberation, salvation, or 'true self' which is not attainable through the things of 'this world'. These are very general categories, and they include experiences as diverse as the sense of the presence of the risen Christ and the 'discovery' that the universe is guided by love. Unlike experiences of peace, joy, and so on, it is impossible for this type of experience not to be religious.

People occasionally describe an experience in religious terms such as 'holy presence' and 'ultimate reality', and yet refuse to apply the word 'religious' to it. This usually occurs where people restrict their application of the term 'religious' to things associated with institutional religion or to experiences which conform to a narrow set of doctrines. Since I am not restricting the scope of the term in this way, I count such experiences as religious, even though the word 'religious' could not

appear in the auto-description. (In fact, one rarely finds the *word* 'religious' in auto-descriptions, but it would normally be legitimate to use it.)

Generally, then, religious experiences are experiences which the subjects themselves describe in religious terms or which are intrinsically religious.

The characteristics outlined above do not presuppose any form of intervention on the part of a conscious deity, although they do exclude the extreme form of deism according to which 'the transcendent' is in *no* way 'immanent'. Some religious experiences are described in a way that suggests divine intervention; others suggest that God is working through natural causes or that the world and human nature are so constituted that with suitable effort, we can attain salvation on our own. At the moment, while I am still taking religious experiences at their face value, I am assuming neither interventionism nor non-interventionism. [. . .]

Before I go on to describe the different types of religious experience, a note on my sources would be in order. Mystics and ordinary believers from non-Christian religious traditions have generally been reluctant to give the world autobiographical accounts of their experiences, and as a result, pure, straightforward auto-descriptions are rare. They must be distilled from biographies (and hagiographies), manuals, treatises, hymns, poems, and other religious works – rather like learning of Hebrew religious experiences through the Psalms and the Prophets. This can be done, but much care must be taken: retrospective interpretation is probably included; the original experience may have been edited or embellished to fit doctrines more closely or to make an astonishing or edifying story; and much information about the subject's psychological make-up and the conditions under which he or she had the experience is lacking. With those caveats, I shall nevertheless cite texts such as passages from the *Bhagavad Gita* as examples of religious experiences.

In the West, autobiographical material is much more abundant, and many great mystics have provided us with detailed and sensitive accounts of themselves, their lives and experiences. Contemporary auto-descriptions of religious experiences are also readily available in the West; some of these are particularly useful because the subjects are not adherents of a religious tradition and so attempt to describe their experiences without using either the standard metaphors or the 'formulae' (e.g. 'I accepted Christ as my personal saviour') characteristic of the auto-descriptions of many people deeply immersed in one tradition. A useful collection of such contemporary experiences can be found in Alister Hardy's book *The Spiritual Nature of Man.* Unfortunately, Hardy provides little information about the subjects' background beliefs, psychological state, and so on, and so the evidential value of any individual experience is difficult to assess; however, the sheer number and variety of independent reports helps to overcome this problem.

There certainly is an abundance of material to be *considered* as the basis of an argument from religious experience. [. . .]

Let us turn now to the experiences themselves, to get an idea of the range and nature of 'the data'. I have divided the experiences into six categories: interpretive, quasi-sensory, revelatory, regenerative, numinous, and mystical. This is by no means the only possible classification of religious experiences. I have chosen it partly because many religious experiences seem 'naturally' to fall into certain categories, but its main function is to facilitate an orderly overview of the kinds of experiences we will consider as possible evidence for religious claims. The categories are not intended to be exclusive, since an experience may exhibit the characteristics of several categories at once. Indeed, they could be presented as six different aspects of religious experiences: how they are seen by the subject to fit into a larger religious pattern, the quasi-sensory element, the alleged knowledge gained in the experience, the 'affective' aspect and immediate 'fruits' of the experience, the 'holy' element, and the 'unitive' element. This approach might be misleading, however, since few religious experiences have all six of these features. Bearing these remarks in mind, then, let us proceed to the first type of religious experience.

2. Interpretive Experiences

Sometimes a subject sees an experience as religious not because of any unusual features of the experience itself, but because it is viewed in the light of a prior religious interpretive framework. Common examples of such experiences are seeing a misfortune as the result of sins in a previous life, going through an illness with joy because it is a chance to 'participate in Christ's suffering', experiencing love for all things of this world because of the belief that they are permeated by the divine, seeing an event

as 'God's will', and taking an event to be the answer to a prayer. Some people are such fervent believers that they see all they do and experience as in some way religiously significant, whether fortunes or misfortunes, great works or just daily chores. I am reminded of John Donne's 'Hymne to Christ, at the Authors Last Going Into Germany':

> In what torne ship soever I embarke,
> That ship shall be my embleme of thy Arke;
> What sea soever swallow mee, that flood
> Shall be to mee an embleme of thy blood.

Experiences which are seen as the answer to a prayer often make fragile evidence, since the subjects themselves are usually willing to admit that things could have turned out just as they did without any divine aid.[2] In particular, sceptics can have a field day with subjects who treat God as an invisible business partner or 'meat purveyor', ready to intervene in response to materialistic prayers. William James gives a good example of such 'primitive religious thought' in a footnote. An English sailor, prisoner on a French ship in 1689, is fighting his captors:

> and looking about again to see anything to strike them withal, but seeing nothing, I said, 'Lord! what shall I do now?' And then it pleased God to put me in mind of my knife in my pocket. And although two of the men had hold of my right arm, yet God Almighty strengthened me so that I put my right hand into my right pocket, drew out the knife and sheath . . . and then cut the man's throat.[3]

However, not all 'answers to prayers' use such a crude model of divine intervention. We will see in section 5 that many regenerative experiences such as renewed hope are seen as answers to prayers [. . .].

Paranormal experiences with no specifically religious content come into the 'interpretive' category when they are seen by the subject as due to some divine agency. I quote a clairvoyant experience from Hardy's collection at some length, to show how the religious interpretation seems to be 'tacked on' at the end:

> I was a young married woman with a 6-month-old baby daughter. My husband and I got an evening off to see a film at K——about 6 miles

away. One of the hotel staff had volunteered to baby sit. . . . We had not been long seated in the cinema when a terrible uneasiness overcame me. I could distinctly smell burning. . . . Eventually I told my husband I was leaving. He followed me reluctantly, muttering something derogatory about women.

. . . At last we were sprinting down the lane leading to the cottage. The smell of burning was now very definite to me though my husband could not smell a thing. We reached the door which I literally burst in. As I did so the dense smoke poured out and a chair by the fire burst into flames. I rushed through to the bedroom and got the baby out while my husband dragged out the unconscious girl. She had fallen asleep in the armchair and dropped her lighted cigarette into the chair which had smouldered for hours. Yes, God sent me home to save my baby. God was with me telling me to hurry home; of that I am convinced and also my husband.[4]

There is no evidence that the woman sensed a divine presence guiding her. Up to the last two sentences, the experience could have been described by an atheist.

These examples are extreme, but they still show typical features of interpretive religious experiences in which a remarkable or beneficial event with no specifically religious characteristics is attributed to a divine source by a person with prior religious beliefs. Such religious experiences have little evidential force on their own (as later arguments will show), since they are so clearly the product of a prior interpretive framework. That interpretive framework may well be the right one to use, but the experiences themselves cannot tell us that. This is not to say, however, that interpretive religious experiences have no value at all as evidence [. . .]. For instance, a preponderance of unexpected beneficial events might lead a person to suspect that there is a benevolent deity; but then it is no longer an argument from religious experience, rather an argument from providence or miracles. Ordinary events and feelings might be seen by a person to 'make sense' only when interpreted within some religious model; crises and difficult moral decisions might be dealt with better if interpreted religiously. Paranormal experiences which the subjects do not consider 'religious' may nevertheless lead them to religious beliefs: for instance, an out-of-body experience could convince someone that human beings have a soul which is distinct from and separable from the body; and even a paranormal experience as mundane as the clairvoyant experience of 'seeing' a hidden object could shake a person out of a materialistic world-view.

Perhaps many interpretive experiences should not strictly be called 'religious experiences'; however, they form such an important aspect of the lives of deeply religious people that they ought not to be ignored.

3. Quasi-Sensory Experiences

Religious experiences in which the primary element is a physical sensation or whose alleged percept is of a type normally apprehended by one of the five sense modalities are 'quasi-sensory' experiences. These include visions and dreams, voices and other sounds, smells, tastes, the feeling of being touched, heat, pain, and the sensation of rising up (levitation).

The most frequently discussed type of quasi-sensory religious experience is the apparent vision of a spiritual being who gives the subject advice. Unfortunately, this has led to the common view that quasi-sensory religious experiences are 'all-or-nothing' affairs: either a supernatural being really was present in some form, or these experiences are hallucinations and of no value at all. However, this is a false dichotomy; quasi-sensory experiences can be 'veridical' in several different ways.

(i)   In the type of quasi-sensory religious experience already mentioned, the quasi-sensory elements are taken to be representations of a spiritual entity which is actually present. The experience can then only be veridical if the alleged percept is actually present as it appears to the subject to be. This type of experience is not in fact the most common – even visions of saints are often placed by subjects in category (ii) (to be discussed below), and the conviction that a divine being is truly there often comes through a non-physical 'sense of a presence'[5] rather than through quasi-sensory features – but they certainly do occur. A good example of one such is the conversion experience of Sadhu Sundar Singh in 1904.[6] Sundar could find no satisfaction in his own religion (Sikhism) but was violently opposed to Christianity; he finally decided that if he got no answer from God about the right path, he would kill himself. He took his usual cold morning bath and then began to pray fervently.

At 4.30 AM I saw something of which I had no idea at all previously. In the room where I was praying I saw a great light. I thought the place was on fire. I looked round, but could find nothing. Then the thought came to me that this might be an answer that God had sent me. Then as I prayed and looked into the light, I saw the form of the Lord Jesus Christ. It had such an appearance of glory and love. If it had been some Hindu incarnation I would have prostrated myself before it. But it was the Lord Jesus Christ whom I had been insulting a few days before. I felt that a vision like this could not come out of my own imagination. I heard a voice saying in Hindustani, 'How long will you persecute me? I have come to save you; you were praying to know the right way. Why do you not take it?' The thought then came to me, 'Jesus Christ is not dead but living and it must be He Himself.' So I fell at His feet and got this wonderful Peace which I could not get anywhere else.

Sundar claimed after this experience 'that some new power from outside entered into his life from that moment, and that it was Christ Himself who appeared and spoke to him'.[7]

The disciples' post-resurrection experiences of Christ, if reliably recorded, would certainly come into this first category. They are particularly interesting, as they are less like hallucinations than are most experiences of apparitions.[8] Generally apparitions appear and disappear suddenly, do not leave physical traces, and do not interact with the subjects, although they may utter a message – as Sundar's Christ vision did. Whether this peculiarity supports the theory that Christ was actually present to the disciples or whether it provides further evidence for a demythologized view of their experiences, I cannot venture to say; such a question is beyond the scope of this book.

(ii)   More often, the quasi-sensory elements of a religious experience are considered by subjects to be like 'pictures', 'sent' by a divine being and requiring a certain amount of interpretation. As such, they are 'hallucinatory' – i.e. they are not veridical sensory perceptions – but they are nevertheless considered to be valid sources of religious insight. One does not say that the experience of looking at a film with the knowledge that it is a film is unveridical just because one's field of vision contains 'images' rather than real people or actually occurring events; and one can acquire true beliefs even from fiction. Where quasi-sensory elements in the form of a religious symbol, a divine being, or even a whole spiritual drama are thus seen (in the auto-description) as 'pictures' shown the subject by a divine being for the subject's edification, the experience will be veridical if the quasi-sensory elements were actually brought about by that divine being (perhaps through telepathy). The fact that the contents of the vision were not physically present would only make such experiences unveridical if one forced them into the mould of sense perception.

Examples of this attitude to visions can be found in the mystical works of all religious traditions. Julian of Norwich, for instance, describes in detail a vision she had of a lord and his servant when she wanted to understand how we could sin so much and yet never be blamed by God.[9] She says she did not fully understand this vision until twenty years had passed, when she analysed it as a detailed allegory. There is never any suggestion that the vision was veridical in the sense that she saw a really existing lord and servant; it was regarded as a divinely produced 'picture' from which she was able to derive valuable religious knowledge. Similarly, the author of *The Cloud of Unknowing* says that visions are generally sent to demonstrate religious truths to those who would have difficulty grasping them in any other way, so that St Stephen's vision in martyrdom of Christ standing in heaven was as if Christ had said to him, 'I am standing by you spiritually' – not to show the actual posture of the heavenly Christ.[10]

(iii)   In the third type of quasi-sensory experience, the quasi-sensory elements have no religious significance themselves and convey no religious insight. Light is by far the most common quasi-sensory element in this category, but one also finds reports of beautiful music, bells, sweet odours, and heat. Where these elements accompany a non-sensory or more complex religious experience, they are taken to be an indication that the experience was of special significance or originated from a spiritual realm – see, for instance, the 'flame-coloured cloud' of R. M. Bucke's experience, quoted in section 4 below, and the 'great light' of Sundar Singh's experience, both of which were so vivid that the subjects' first thoughts were of a real, immense fire. Where these quasi-sensory elements occur alone, they are only seen as religious because they occur during an exercise in meditation (when they are often accompanied by great joy), or because the subject has been taught to expect such experiences as 'favours' from God or as signs of progress. In other circumstances, an experience such as a sudden vision of flashing lights would be unlikely to make the subject think of God, rather more likely to send him off to the doctor.

Experiences where a non-religious quasi-sensory element predominates are regarded with somewhat more favour in the East than in the West, and Indian mystics have drawn up elaborate classifications of the types of sounds, colours, smells, and so on that meditators may experience, giving each of them a religious 'meaning'.[11] Nevertheless, the different traditions are remarkably unanimous regarding the ultimate value and role of this third type of quasi-sensory experience. Such experiences may be rewards for the beginner, but they are generally trivial and can even be obstacles to spiritual advancement. The general consensus is that they should be disregarded: they are particularly suspect, as 'diabolical' and pathological states can bring them on much more easily than they can the more intrinsically religious experiences; they can be coveted, or seen as a source of pride, which would undo much of the subject's training in renunciation and purification; and there is a danger that they may be mistaken for the end of the path, so that salvation is never attained. The same can be said of the psychic powers allegedly attained by many mystics, especially those of Indian traditions; subjects are specifically enjoined to pay them no heed and never to exercise them.

Quasi-sensory religious experiences, perhaps more than any other type, acquire their specific form largely from the subject's own store of religious ideas. People have visions of saints and deities as they are portrayed in the pictures and sculptures of their community – examples of this are legion. Even the *type* of quasi-sensory experience can be conditioned by background beliefs; David Brown points out that Protestants, Jews, and Muslims, who are very averse to any kind of 'graven image', tend to hear voices, while Roman Catholics and Hindus see visions.[12] Such conditioning need not imply that the experience was entirely determined by the subject's background, however.

4. Revelatory Experiences

Religious experiences of this category comprise what their subjects may call sudden convictions, inspiration, revelation, enlightenment, 'the mystical vision', and flashes of insight. They may seem to descend upon the subject out of the blue, unaccompanied by any other feature which would make the experience religious, in which case it is their religious content which makes them 'religious experiences'; or, more frequently, they are the 'revelatory' element in a more complex religious experience, very often a mystical experience. These experiences have distinctive features: (i) they are usually sudden and of short duration, though the after-effects may last a lifetime (especially in the case of conversion experiences); (ii) the alleged new knowledge seems to the subject to have been acquired immediately rather than through reasoning or sense perception; (iii) the alleged new knowledge usually seems to the subject to have been 'poured into' or 'showered upon' him (metaphors abound) by an external agency; (iv) the 'revelations' carry with them utter conviction, somehow even more than that which attaches to sense perception; and (v) the insights gained are often claimed to be impossible to put into words.

In Eastern religious traditions, though purity of soul is required, it is ignorance which is generally regarded as the greatest hindrance to liberation or salvation. 'Enlightenment experiences' are often seen as the goal of the mystical quest and the beginning of a new, 'true' life, particularly in atheistic traditions such as Buddhism. D. T. Suzuki describes the Zen Buddhist experience of satori thus:

> *Satori* is the sudden flashing into consciousness of a new truth hitherto undreamed of. It is a sort of mental catastrophe taking place all at once, after much piling up of matters intellectual and demonstrative. The piling has reached a limit of stability and the whole edifice has come tumbling to the ground, when, behold, a new heaven is open to full survey . . . Religiously, it is a new birth; intellectually, it is the acquiring of a new viewpoint.[13]

Not all revelatory experiences are as cataclysmic as these mystical 'enlightenment experiences', but they do share the characteristics of immediacy and certainty. Philo reports that

> Sometimes, when I have come to my work empty, I have suddenly become full; ideas being in an invisible manner showered upon me, and implanted in me from on high . . . for then I

Caroline Franks Davis

have been conscious of a richness of interpretation, an enjoyment of light, a most penetrating insight . . . having such effect on my mind as the clearest ocular demonstration would have on the eyes.[14]

St Teresa also asserts emphatically that these insights are from an external divine source, are immediate, and are even *more* certain than 'the clearest ocular demonstration':

The Lord is pleased that this knowledge should be so deeply engraven upon the understanding that one can no more doubt it than one can doubt the evidence of one's eyes – indeed, the latter is easier, for we sometimes suspect that we have imagined what we see, whereas here, though that suspicion may arise for a moment, there remains such complete certainty that the doubt has no force . . . The Lord introduces into the inmost part of the soul what he wishes that soul to understand . . . It is as if food has been introduced into the stomach without our having eaten it or knowing how it got there.[15]

It is '*knowing* in a quite different way from intellectual knowledge', says one of Hardy's respondents;[16] and the sentiment is echoed wherever there is religion. This sense of certainty is not restricted to revelatory experiences, of course; experiences of a holy presence, mystical experiences of 'oneness', and so on, are typically reported with the same sense of assurance, as we shall see in later sections.

Just what is claimed to be known in this utterly convincing manner varies. It may be a specific and easily articulable prophecy, revelation, or religious insight; it may be something so comprehensive and fundamental that the subject has extreme difficulty expressing it; it may be an obviously false claim to omniscience, as exhibited by one of Hardy's respondents who wrote, 'I knew that I was capable of answering any question or problem put to me, no matter how abstruse.'[17] Sometimes subjects may have the sense of 'having understood everything', and then devote much of their life to the struggle to spell out more specifically what they understood in that brief moment:

A great inward light seemed to illuminate my thoughts, I experienced a magnificent sensation of arrival. I was filled with joy as though I had just discovered the secret of world peace. I suddenly *knew*. The odd thing was that I did

not know what I knew. From then on I set out to define it.[18]

Others may never find the words to express their alleged knowledge – in which case there is no cognitive claim for which the experience could be used as evidence, and the experience is truly ineffable.

In most cases, however, the subject does make specific knowledge claims. In the simplest kind of case, the content of the 'insight' can be found in the sermon or religious text which suddenly struck the hearer as ineluctably true:

It was while listening to a sermon in St Mary's, that I became convinced of the reality of God. Emotion was at a minimum . . . this sense of being convinced was not basically intellectual either. It was just that I knew the preacher was speaking the truth.[19]

Usually, however, the alleged knowledge is held to be revealed in some more interior way. These claims are often of a personal nature, and sometimes very specific, as when St Teresa says she received instructions and prophecies from the Lord regarding the founding of St Joseph's convent.[20] More typical are experiences in which some fairly general but articulable religious truths are alleged to have been apprehended, even in cases where the subject claims ineffability. These range from the highly ramified Christian claims of St Teresa and Julian of Norwich regarding the Trinity[21] to the more broadly religious claims of R. M. Bucke (see below), which are found in innumerable cases. Often subjects draw a distinction between the intellectual belief previously held and the way they now 'see' or 'know' the doctrine to be true (Newman's distinction between 'notional' and 'real' beliefs[22]): 'Knowing with all my being what is meant by the concept God is Love';[23] 'what we hold by faith [i.e. the Trinity] the soul may be said here to grasp by sight'.[24]

Paradoxically, perhaps, these revelatory experiences, which inspire so much certainty, are also a type of experience spiritual authorities are very inclined to mistrust. Like secular 'intuitions', they are treated as unreliable sources of knowledge, guilty until proven innocent. There is a long tradition within the Roman Catholic church, for example, of subjecting alleged revelations to rigorous tests, many of which involve the same sort of criteria as we would apply to any perceptual claim. Innocence is confirmed by such factors as consistency with (though not necessarily prior inclusion in) the teachings of the Church and the integrity, health, education, and spirituality of the subject.[25] Even then, private matters revealed through visions and voices are not accorded a high degree of trust. Meister Eckhart writes, for instance, that 'private revelations' through angels or special illuminations can be deceptive, but there is a

> second knowledge, which is incomparably better and more profitable and happens often to all who are perfect in their love . . . when a man, through the love and the intimacy that exist between his God and him, trusts in him so fully and is so certain of him that he cannot doubt.[26]

St Teresa of Avila, practical as always, writes that even if alleged revelations fulfil the criteria of agreement with Scripture and of increasing the soul's tranquillity, confidence, and devotion to God, if they are important, require action, or involve another person, then a wise confessor should be consulted.[27] Other religious traditions have similar reservations about revelatory experiences. Within Buddhism, for instance, the monk Mettānando Bhikkhu cautions that the insights which meditators think they obtain are more often wrong than not; such 'intuitions' are only accepted if the subject has reached a very advanced stage of meditation, and the intuition is shared by other meditators of high rank, or if the subject has had a gift for 'intuition' from childhood and so is known to be reliable.[28] Generally, revelations obtained during mystical experiences and the revelations of 'recognized' prophets and saints are accepted as valid religious insights within most traditions, while revelations conveyed by other means and trivial or mundane revelations are more suspect.

Let me close by quoting an experience of R. M. Bucke, which is particularly rich in alleged insights, and to which we shall have cause to refer many times:

> All at once . . . I found myself wrapped in a flame-colored cloud. . . . Directly afterward there came upon me a sense of exultation, of immense joyousness accompanied or immediately followed by an intellectual illumination impossible to describe. Among other things, I did not merely come to believe, but I saw that the universe is not composed of dead matter, but is, on the contrary, a living Presence; I became conscious in myself of eternal life. It was not a conviction

that I would have eternal life, but a consciousness that I possessed eternal life then; I saw that all men are immortal; that the cosmic order is such that without any peradventure all things work together for the good of each and all; that the foundation principle of the world, of all the worlds, is what we call love, and that the happinesss of each and all is in the long run absolutely certain. The vision lasted a few seconds and was gone but the memory of it and the sense of the reality of what it taught have remained during the quarter of a century which has since elapsed. I knew that what the vision showed was true.[29]

5. Regenerative Experiences

Regenerative experiences are the most frequent type of religious experience among ordinary people – that is, people who are not mystics, ecstatics, prophets, or psychics. Most religious people find their faith sustained by such experiences; they are one of the features which make a 'living religion' more than the mere acceptance of a set of doctrines or the performance of certain rituals. Regenerative experiences, as their name suggests,[30] tend to renew the subject's faith and improve his spiritual, moral, physical, or psychological well-being; it is like, as a respondent in Michael Walker's study put it, having 'my "spiritual" batteries recharged'.[31]

This category includes a wide range of experiences: experiences of new hope, strength, comfort, peace, security, and joy, seen as 'religious' because they are obtained during a religious activity such as prayer, apparently brought about by a divine power, or accompanied by the sense of a divine presence; experiences of being guided, 'called', forgiven, and 'saved', usually by an external divine power; healing experiences; an apparently divinely aided increase in moral virtues and love for others; and the discovery of 'meaning' in life. These experiences may be mild or overwhelming, daily occurrences or extraordinary 'one-off' events, with or without other elements such as the quasi-sensory; they could be anything from a believer's vague feeling of peace during prayer to a combined vision, revelation, and 'sense of a holy presence' which converts and heals an alcoholic atheist.

It may be noticed that both the revelatory and regenerative categories have included 'conversion experiences'. Those who treat these as a distinct type of religious experience usually concentrate on the experience of being 'saved' at a revival meeting, but people can be converted by many different types of experience – e.g. visions (Sundar Singh), 'flashes of insight', and even nature mysticism. What makes these 'conversion experiences' is their effect on the subject. 'Senses of a presence' are likewise often put into a single category. I have chosen not to do so here, since one does not have just the sense of 'a presence', but the sense of some *kind* of presence (e.g. awesome, loving, guiding; individual, all-pervading) and of a certain relationship with the presence (e.g. devotion, union, feeling it at work within you); and these differences result in extremely diverse experiences. For some purposes, it can be useful to think of 'senses of a presence' as a separate category; later chapters will show that religious experiences which include a 'sense of presence' are of more value as evidence for the existence of a holy power than are experiences without it.

To return to regenerative experiences in general: one important type of regenerative experience, and a vital part of Christian tradition, is 'healing'. Although it is the physical effects which are considered most significant by the person looking for 'miracles' to convince unbelievers, those who have been healed and those who have done the healing very often stress other 'regenerative' effects, while still – importantly for this study – claiming that the experience was brought about by God. For instance, an elderly clergyman wrote of his healing ministry:

The one constant factor is a serenity of spirit that, as is commonly said, can almost be felt; it can be seen even in those whose physical ailment has not been healed. . . . Death is not always defeated – I mean even temporarily, for of course death will always come – but people with cancer die without pain or drugs and in such serenity of mind and spirit that their passing is a triumph. It seems to me that it is impossible for one human being to do this for another unaided. I have comforted, and have been comforted, by another, but always the comfort waned. This awareness of a power, beyond us humans, remains and grows and wholeness or, if you like, righteousness, increases. . . . [O]ne woman . . . was healed, in a week, of a vast varicose ulcer; on being told by some friends that she seemed remarkably casual about it, she said: 'I'm not casual or ungrateful, but the much more important fact than my healed ulcer and the

freedom from pain and discomfort is that whereas I was a worrier and built all my bridges before I came to them, now I pray and trust and have lost anxiety and fear.'[32]

A type of experience especially common in evangelical Protestant circles is the sense of being 'saved', especially through the forgiveness of sins. In John Wesley's Journal entry on 24 May 1738 we read:

In the evening I went very unwillingly to a society in Aldersgate-Street, where one was reading Luther's preface to the Epistle to the Romans. About a quarter before nine, while he was describing the change which God works in the heart through faith in Christ, I felt my heart strangely warmed. I felt I did trust in Christ, Christ alone, for salvation; and an assurance was given me, that He had taken away *my* sins, even *mine*, and saved *me* from the law of sin and death.[33]

The experience of being 'saved from the law of sin and death' is found in Eastern monistic religions as well, but there it usually takes the form of a mystical experience apparently liberating the subject from the round of rebirths and from the ignorant, sinful, precarious existence of the normal run of mankind.

Regenerative experiences often have dramatic results, lifting people out of depression, steering them through a crisis, starting them on a new, sounder path in life, even maintaining their will to live when all else has failed. Viktor Frankl, the psychiatrist who developed 'Logotherapy', described in *Man's Search for Meaning* how the assurance that there was meaning in life enabled him to survive a Nazi prison camp: 'I sensed my spirit piercing through the enveloping gloom. I felt it transcend that hopeless, meaningless world, and from somewhere I heard a victorious 'Yes' in answer to my question of the existence of an ultimate purpose.'[34]

The experience of being guided by a being or force beyond one's conscious self is also a common regenerative experience. Sometimes this may take the stronger form of being 'called'. Clergy, missionaries, and even social workers often express the opinion that they would not be doing what they are doing, had they not experienced an overwhelming conviction that this vocation was God's will for them and that he would give them the strength and the means to carry it out. 'I now *am* a missionary', writes one of Hardy's respondents; 'I know that nothing except a superhuman power could have got me out here, or having got me here could keep me here.'[35] This same person writes that she derives 'tremendous joy and satisfaction' from the work; like most people who have felt 'divine guidance', the action was one which she saw over time to be the best one for her. Occasionally, however, people have felt murders, purges, and other atrocities to be 'the will of God'. Such cases cannot be ignored [. . .].

Regenerative experiences are not always joyful affairs. They may be profoundly humbling, as when one becomes more aware of one's own failings when one sees oneself in the light of God's unconditional love.

Some regenerative experiences are so intense that they approach the mystical or the numinous. Experiences involving overwhelming love are particularly borderline, whether the love is one's own newly increased love directed towards other people or towards the deity, or the love of the 'presence' directed towards oneself. Leslie Weatherhead described an example of the former, when in a train in Vauxhall Station he suddenly 'felt caught up into some tremendous sense of being within a loving, triumphant and shining purpose':

> I loved everybody in that compartment. It sounds silly now, and indeed I blush to write it, but at that moment I think I would have died for any one of the people in that compartment.[36]

At a less intense level, the experience of a loving, comforting presence can be an almost daily occurrence. Such an experience is aptly described in one of William James's examples as 'the sense of a presence, strong, and at the same time soothing, which hovers over me. Sometimes it seems to enwrap me with sustaining arms.'[37]

That people the world over do find comfort and strength in experiences of a divine power is reflected in the abundance of references to God as our 'refuge', 'home', 'rest', 'strength', and so on. 'Even as the mighty winds rest in the vastness of the ethereal space, all beings have their rest in me. Know thou this truth', says the *Bhagavad Gita*;[38] and the Psalms declare, 'God is our refuge and strength, a very present help in trouble.'[39] The divine is experienced as that in which our souls can truly find rest, free from the uncertainties and petty cares of the world; it is always there, always the same, ready to sustain us; it is our 'true home'.

Experiences of yearning for this 'true home' and of seeming to arrive at it are explored in the next two sections.

6. Numinous Experiences

The previous section dealt in part with experiences of the divine in its loving, comforting, guiding aspects; in the experiences of this section, it is revealed in all its terrifying glory, its unapproachable 'holiness'. In *The Idea of the Holy*, Rudolf Otto describes 'the holy' as a combination of supreme moral goodness and something else, even more fundamental, which he calls 'the numinous'.[40] The 'feeling of the numinous' consists of 'creature-consciousness', that is, the feeling that mortal flesh is somehow despicable in the face of eternal majesty, and 'mysterium tremendum', which comprises (i) awe, dread, or terror before the numen, (ii) the sense of being completely overpowered in the presence of such majesty, (iii) an experience of intense, almost unbearable energy or urgency, (iv) the sense that the numen is 'wholly other', and (v) a fascination with or attraction to the numen, and rapture upon contact with it.

A 'numinous experience' may exhibit only one of these features, or any combination of them. Let us begin with 'creature–consciousness': When faced with infinite goodness, might, and majesty, it is natural for a person to realize how puny and insignificant he is, how fragile his existence, even how imperfect and 'unclean' he is in comparison. 'Woe is me!' he cries, 'For I am lost; for I am a man of unclean lips . . . for my eyes have seen the King, the Lord of hosts!'[41] Julian of Norwich writes, after being shown how all will ultimately 'be well':

> The bliss and the fulfilment will be so vast in its immensity that the whole creation, wondering and astonished, will have for God a dread so great and reverent and beyond anything known before, that the very pillars of heaven will tremble and quake! But there will be no pain in this trembling and dread; it is wholly right that the worth and majesty of God should thus be seen by his creatures, who tremble in dread and quake in humble joy, as they marvel at the greatness of God their Maker, and the insignificance of all that is made. The consideration of all this makes the creature wonderfully meek and mild![42]

There are surprisingly few examples of creature-consciousness in Hardy's book, although there are plenty of numinous experiences. Perhaps this is due to the current attitude towards submission and to the belief that human beings are themselves 'sacred'. Modern man is reluctant to say, 'We are not worthy to gather up the crumbs under Thy table'; though increased knowledge of the vastness of space has encouraged some to feel at least the degree of creature-consciousness expressed by Psalm 8: 'When I consider thy heavens, the work of thy fingers, the moon and the stars, which thou hast ordained, What is man, that thou art mindful of him?'[43] Creature-consciousness should not be seen as something negative, however; it is not, as Otto points out, 'impotent collapse and submission to a merely superior power', but rather a sign that one has recognized the 'mysterium tremendum' of the numinous presence.[44]

Certain things characteristically evoke this sense of 'mysterium tremendum'. It can be found, Otto writes, 'in the lives of those around us, in sudden, strong ebullitions of personal piety . . . in the fixed and ordered solemnities of rites and liturgies, and again in the atmosphere that clings to old religious monuments and buildings, to temples and to churches.' He continues:

> The feeling of it may at times come sweeping like a gentle tide, pervading the mind with a tranquil mood of deepest worship. It may pass over into a more set and lasting attitude of the soul, continuing, as it were, thrillingly vibrant and resonant, until at last it dies away and the soul resumes its 'profane', non-religious mood of everyday experience. It may burst in sudden eruption up from the depths of the soul with spasms and convulsions, or lead to the strangest excitements, to intoxicated frenzy, to transport, and to ecstasy. It has its wild and demonic forms and can sink to an almost grisly horror and shuddering. It has its crude, barbaric antecedents and early manifestations, and again it may be developed into something beautiful and pure and glorious. It may become the hushed, trembling, and speechless humility of the creature in the presence of – whom or what? In the presence of that which is a *mystery* inexpressible and above all creatures.[45]

The awe involved in numinous experiences is no ordinary fear. It is the dread before the uncanny which makes our hair stand on end, terror before such grandeur that we feel compelled to kneel, incomprehension before such mystery that we are struck dumb. 'Let all mortal flesh keep silence, and with fear and trembling stand', says the ancient Greek hymn; and the feeling is echoed in countless individual experiences.

> though the sight is the loveliest and the most delightful imaginable . . . because it so far exceeds all that our imagination and understanding can compass, its presence is of such exceeding majesty that it fills the soul with a great terror. It is unnecessary to ask here how, without being told, the soul knows Who it is, for He reveals Himself quite clearly as the Lord of Heaven and earth. This the kings of the earth never do: indeed, they would be thought very little of for what they are, but that they are acccompanied by their suites, or heralds proclaim them.[46]

If the 'Holy, holy, holy' visions of Isaiah and Revelation are paradigm numinous experiences for Judaic religions, theistic Hindus can look to the *Bhagavad Gita*'s magnificent revelation of Krishna to Arjuna on the battlefield (chapter 11):

> 12. If the light of a thousand suns suddenly arose in the sky, that splendour might be compared to the radiance of the Supreme Spirit.
> 14. Trembling with awe and wonder, Arjuna bowed his head, and joining his hands in adoration he thus spoke to his God.
> 17. I see the splendour of an infinite beauty which illumines the whole universe. It is thee! with thy crown and sceptre and circle. How difficult thou art to see! But I see thee: as fire, as the sun, blinding, incomprehensible.
> 20. Heaven and earth and all the infinite spaces are filled with thy Spirit; and before the wonder of thy fearful majesty the three worlds tremble.
> 24. When I see thy vast form, reaching the sky, burning with many colours, with wide open mouths, with vast flaming eyes, my heart shakes in terror: my power is gone and gone is my peace, O Vishnu!
> 25. Like the fire at the end of Time which burns all in the last day, I see thy vast mouths and thy terrible teeth. Where am I? Where is my shelter? Have mercy on me, God of gods, Refuge Supreme of the world![47]

Experiences of *evil* often involve a similar numinosity. In this example from Hardy's collection, the subject used a symbolic Christian act to dispel the evil and with it that paralysing terror peculiar to the numinous:

Suddenly I became aware of a sense of the uttermost evil, so much so that I became awake. I could feel this sense of evil enveloping me. I had the terrifying impression that this evil force or presence was bent upon taking possession of me. How does one describe evil? I only knew that I was enveloped by this revolting force, so vile and rotting I could almost taste the evil. I was in terror, so much so I could not call out or move. A part of my mind told me I must at all costs act or I would be lost. I recall that I managed by a great effort to stretch out my right hand and with my index finger I traced the shape of the Cross in the air. Immediately on my doing this the evil enveloping me fell away completely, and I felt a wonderful sense of peace and safety.[48]

The awe inspired by non-evil numina, unlike ordinary fear, does not drive the subject away. Subjects encountering the numen somehow realize that their ultimate bliss is to be found in the closest possible union with this awesome, mysterious power. This fascination or attraction is expressed in many ways, from St Augustine's longing to be with God ('Thou hast made us for thyself and our hearts are restless till they rest in thee')[49] to the more ardent rapture and almost physical agony of many mystics, their 'burning', and 'being wounded with the dart of love'[50] – or, as Ramakrishna rather less elegantly put it, feeling 'as if my heart were being squeezed like a wet towel'.[51] But this painful yearning is in itself a blissful experience, for it is centred on God. For Gregory of Nyssa, for instance, ecstasy is 'the intense experience of longing, desire, and love of which *epektasis* – following after God – is the fruit'.[52] True satisfaction is an unceasing quest for God, for to seek him unendingly is to find him.

Otto attributes this anguish to the 'energy' or 'urgency' of the numen, the same energy as 'the scorching and consuming wrath of God . . . only differently directed'. It can be seen in the mysticism of love, in that '"consuming fire" of love whose burning strength the mystic can hardly bear, but begs that the heat that has scorched him may be mitigated, lest he be himself destroyed by

it'.[53] Such intense devotion to and yearning for the holy 'other' often leads to visions, ecstasies, and mystical experiences of apparent union with the numen. In the latter, which will be described further in the next section, the mystic gladly allows himself to be annihilated by the overwhelming 'other'. In the 'Spiritual Marriage' symbolism, he is the bride awaiting the embrace of the bridegroom, when they will become forever one.

That the experience of the 'scorching fire' can be unspeakably joyful is demonstrated by Pascal's famous experience, recorded on a piece of paper found sewn inside his doublet after his death:

From about half past ten in the evening to about half an hour after midnight.
   Fire.
God of Abraham, God of Isaac, God of Jacob,
Not the God of philosophers and scholars.
Absolute Certainty: Beyond reason. Joy.
Peace.
Forgetfulness of the world and everything but God.
The world has not known thee, but I have known thee.
   Joy! joy! joy! tears of joy![54]

Not all numinous experiences are so overwhelming. One can apprehend the numen in a very mild manner, as a general sense of 'sacredness' in the world, a feeling of happy dependence upon or devotion to an 'other', or a gentle yearning for something, one knows not what – 'a sort of homesickness', one of Hardy's respondents called it.[55]

Numinous experiences are often claimed to be ineffable. The numen is so different from and so far surpasses all ordinary percepts that the subject has difficulty describing it, and the experience itself is often so overwhelming that the subject is 'struck dumb'. However, as the examples in this section show, subjects can describe their experiences, albeit in a way that does not do justice to the numen – for how can one do justice to 'ultimate reality'? For our purposes, the important thing to notice is that however inarticulate the subjects may be, they all claim to have perceived *something* which is holy and external.

It may have been noticed that most of these examples of numinous experiences have come from theistic sources. Numinous experiences are characteristically dualistic; the subject seems to become aware of an 'other'. [. . .] Not all numinous experiences are typical of a personal theism, however, as the following points will show: (i) The 'other' is not always described in personal terms – many of Hardy's respondents refer to it as 'It'; and a sense that the world is 'sacred' or 'imbued with a holy force' is consistent with deism. However, the former often occurs because personal terms seem anthropomorphic and crude, not because the numen is 'impersonal' in the sense of being inanimate, unconscious, or a mere 'principle'; and the latter types of experience are very mild and somewhat atypical examples of numinous experiences, perhaps more akin to the nature mysticism of the next section. (ii) Numinous experiences often incline subjects to kneel or to sing praises at the time of the experience, but they certainly do not always lead them to worship in any regular manner. (iii) Many numinous experiences approach and sometimes even slip into the 'oneness' of mystical experiences, either because the yearning and love is so completely and intensely centred on the divine, or because the combination of creature-consciousness and awe leads to the feeling that one's own self has been annihilated and the numen is the sole reality. To see such experiences in their truly mystical form, let us turn to the next section.

7. Mystical Experiences

Most discussions of mystical experience are full-fledged treatises on 'mysticism', but in this section I shall refer to doctrines, techniques, and so on only where necessary, and attempt to confine the discussion to mystical *experiences*. The term 'mystical' has been used to cover everything from the experiences of the great mystics of each religious tradition to mildly ecstatic, mysterious, or occult experiences. I shall restrict it – not rigorously, for the purpose of these categories is mainly to provide an orderly account of 'the data' – to experiences with the following characteristics: (i) the sense of having apprehended an ultimate reality; (ii) the sense of freedom from the limitations of time, space, and the individual ego; (iii) a sense of 'oneness'; and (iv) bliss or serenity. 'Ineffability' is often included in lists of characteristics of mystical experiences, but since it is a problem encountered in most categories of religious experience (i.e. it is not really a 'distinguishing mark' of *mystical* experience) [. . .] I shall not include it here. The most paradigmatic mystical experiences have all four characteristics – not surprisingly, since, as will be shown below, they are closely interrelated.

Stace makes a useful distinction between 'extrovertive' and 'introvertive' mystical experiences.[56] In an extrovertive experience, the multiplicity of external objects is seen as somehow unified and divine. 'Nature mysticism' is typically of this type, as we shall see later. Introvertive experiences, usually obtained through the practice of an 'introspective' meditative technique, are 'unitary' rather than 'unifying'; subjects shut out all external and internal diversity and dive deep within themselves to discover 'the One'. Both introvertive and extrovertive experiences can have the four 'mystical characteristics'.

(i) *The sense of 'ultimate reality'*. Mystical experiences are usually considered the pinnacle of the spiritual journey, the closest one may come in this life to seeing divine reality face to face. Even religions such as Judaism and Islam which stress the gulf between creator and creature have their mystics, their Sufis and their Kabbalah – though they often sit uneasily on the fringes of orthodoxy. When that yearning for union with the numen mentioned in the last section is consummated, the subject seems to apprehend something both more 'real' than and more 'ultimate' than the percepts of ordinary life. It seems to theistic mystics that the 'transcendent' reality of their numinous experiences has become 'immanent', to monistic mystics that they are now one with 'the Absolute', to nature mystics that they have glimpsed something fundamental underlying the apparently disparate things of this world. Normal objects of sense perception and all mundane matters are seen as in some way 'unreal' in comparison with the overwhelming reality of the divine, and are described as 'insignificant', 'a dream', 'a veil', 'a shadow', or 'illusion'. This is one foundation of the mystic's traditional ability to renounce the things of this world.

Insights gained during mystical experiences are similarly 'ultimate', never trivial matters: mystics feel they have penetrated to the very heart of things, that what has been revealed to them is eternally and universally true, that they now realize the true nature of human beings, the world, and their relationship to the divine. While the 'flashes of insight' described in section 4 are not always so fundamental, the remarks there on the sense of utter conviction and on the 'immediate' manner of acquisition of these insights apply just as well to this feature of mystical experience.

(ii) *The sense of freedom*. In this category I include the apparent transcendence of space and time, the sense that the boundaries of the individual ego have been dissolved, and the loss of concern for all worldly matters which so characterizes the mystic.

The transcendence of spatial limitations is usually explicitly mentioned only in accounts of extrovertive experiences, where subjects feel they are no longer limited by the physical boundaries of their bodies but are 'part of something Other/Bigger/Wider',[57] part of the unity underlying the whole external world. In introvertive experiences, space is not felt as a limitation to be transcended; it simply does not exist for the mystic at all.

Though mystical experiences are usually transient, sometimes lasting only a few seconds, their subjects often report a feeling of 'timelessness'. This sense of 'eternity' is more than the 'losing all sense of time' common during extreme concentration; combined with the loss of the everyday sense of identity and the sense that one has been suffused with some divine essence, it often takes the form of a conviction that one is immortal. Thus Bucke claims to have become 'conscious that he possessed eternal life' (see section 4), and Tennyson writes of his 'waking trances':

> This has come upon me through repeating my own name to myself silently, till all at once, as it were out of the intensity of the consciousness of individuality, individuality itself seemed to dissolve and fade away into boundless being, and this not a confused state but the clearest, the surest of the surest, utterly beyond words – where death was an almost laughable impossibility – the loss of personality (if so it were) seeming no extinction, but the only true life.[58]

Tennyson's last line is typical of descriptions of the sense that one has escaped the narrow prison of the individual ego. This 'boundless' state may be experienced in different ways, ranging from the isolation of the pure self or consciousness, through varying degrees of dissolution of the subject–object distinction, to the complete annihilation or absorption of the self. In Christian mysticism it is usually interpreted as a total surrender to God, a 'dying to oneself' so that God can take over. As Boehme writes:

> The soul here saith, *I have nothing*, for I am utterly stripped and naked; *I can do nothing*, for I have no manner of power, but am as water poured out; *I am nothing*, for all that I am is no more than an Image of Being, and only God is

to me I AM; and so, sitting down in my own Nothingness, I give glory to the Eternal Being, and *will nothing* of myself, that so God may *will all* in me, being unto me my God and All Things.[59]

From an agnostic tradition, Zen Buddhism, comes a different account of the dissolution of individuality:

> The individual shell in which my personality is so solidly encased explodes at the moment of satori. Not necessarily that I get unified with a being greater than myself or absorbed in it, but that my individuality, which I found rigidly held together and definitely kept separate from other individual existences . . . melts away into something indescribable, something which is of quite a different order from what I am accustomed to.[60]

Metaphors of 'melting', 'dissolving', 'sinking', and so on can be found in descriptions of this experience from all traditions. The Hindu *Brihadaranyaka Upanishad*, for instance, uses the following analogy to describe the merging of the self with the Absolute:

> as a lump of salt cast in water would dissolve right into the water . . . so, lo, verily, this great Being (*bhuta*), infinite, limitless, is just a mass of knowledge. Arising out of these elements (*bhuta*), into them also one vanishes away . . .
>
> For where there is a duality, as it were, there one sees another. . . . Where, verily, everything has become just one's own self . . . then whereby and whom would one see?[61]

Whether the loss of the sense of 'I' is seen as a merging into something 'wider' or merely as the transcendence of a human limitation, it is normally connected with renunciation – of worldly things, of all desires, of the very ideas of 'me' and 'mine'. 'Dying to oneself' is encouraged by all mystical traditions, whether it is seen as a prerequisite for the unitive experience or as a consequence of it. Hence the paradoxical passage in the Gospel of St John: 'He who loves his life loses it, and he who hates his life in this world will keep it for eternal life.'[62]

In Indian traditions this renunciation tends to take the extreme form of refraining from action and of indifference even to good and bad states of mind – 'attachment' to *anything* is supposed to be a hindrance to ultimate liberation. Indian mystics are thus often accused of indifference to the suffering of fellow humans and of feeling themselves to be beyond the distinctions of good and evil. Though this may be true of some cases, it is largely unjustified. It is clear from the biographies of Indian mystics that they see their prayer and purity as themselves working to help mankind, through 'spiritual vibrations', as it were;[63] and a major goal of Buddhist training is the cultivation of compassion and loving-kindness (*mettā*).[64] Nor is activity in the community shunned: the Ramakrishna Mission established schools, hospitals, and other charitable institutions, despite its strictly monistic mystical philosophy,[65] and even 'hermit' monks offer forms of assistance such as teaching and lending the prestige of their name to a worthy project in order to gain it backers.[66]

(iii)   *The sense of 'oneness'.* This may take four forms: (a) nature mysticism and other extrovertive mystical experiences; (b) integration or isolation; (c) introvertive monistic mysticism; and (d) introvertive theistic mysticism.

(a)   In the simplest kind of extrovertive experience of unity, all things are seen as intimately related, and the subject feels an extraordinary kinship with them: 'I heard a voice saying: 'All men are brothers! Every land is home,' And I felt quite stunned with joy.'[67]

The experiences known as 'nature mysticism' involve the transfiguration of external things, as if they have suddenly been imbued with deep meaning or with a living force; they also often involve the sense that everything is guided by Love or some inherently good power. R. M. Bucke's experience (section 4) is a good example of this, but a more paradigmatic example, since it deals with external objects, is this one from Hardy's collection:

One day I was sweeping the stairs down in the house in which I was working, when suddenly I was overcome, overwhelmed, saturated, no word is adequate, with a sense of most sublime and living LOVE. It not only affected me, but seemed to bring everything around me to LIFE. The brush in my hand, my dustpan, the stairs, seemed to come alive with love. I seemed no longer me, with my petty troubles and trials, but part of this infinite power of love, so utterly and overwhelmingly wonderful that one knew at once what the saints had grasped. It could

only have been a minute or two, yet for that brief particle of time it seemed eternity.[68]

William Blake's lines, 'To see a world in a grain of sand / And a heaven in a wild flower . . .' give concise expression to that mystical sense of the immanence of divinity in nature, so magnificently described in Wordsworth's *Tintern Abbey*:

. . . And I have felt
A presence that disturbs me with the joy
Of elevated thoughts; a sense sublime
Of something far more deeply interfused,
Whose dwelling is the light of setting suns,
And the round ocean and the living air,
And the blue sky, and in the mind of man:
A motion and a spirit, that impels
All thinking things, all objects of all thought,
And rolls through all things.

Scenes of natural beauty very often trigger these spontaneous extrovertive mystical experiences in Westerners out hiking:

[T]he setting sun blazed out turning the whole world crimson and gold, there was a gust of wind, and I felt as if I had been swept into the very heart of all that glory and colour, taken over by something outside myself of which I was yet a part.[69]

Michael Carrithers reports that there is little 'nature mysticism' in India because 'nature' is so much more dangerous than in the West, and tends to be avoided by villagers;[70] but nature mysticism is not a purely Western phenomenon. Oriental landscape paintings show a deep sense of harmony with nature, and Taoism glorified nature and the spirit within it.[71]

It is within Indian cultures that extrovertive mystical experiences of the most radical type are found – the alleged apprehension of a complete identity between external objects. This is the territory of the famous *tat tvam asi* (thou art that) of the Upanishads:

Whatever they are, whether tiger, lion, wolf, boar, worm, fly, gnat, or mosquito, they all become that (the ultimate reality). That which is the subtlest of the subtle, the whole world has it as its self. That is reality. That is the self, and that art thou.[72]

In its context in the Upanishads, this passage describes a doctrine rather than an experience; it is very probable, however, that Hindu mystics do have experiences of 'seeing' all things as Brahman, the supreme, hidden 'self' of the universe and all beings.

Nature mysticism and other extrovertive experiences are often associated with pantheism, but there is nothing to prevent other types of theists from having such experiences. The difference is that whereas pantheists feel that what they have seen in nature is the *whole* of the divine, monotheists (or pan-en-theists) believe that the divine has transcendent aspects as well as immanent ones.

(b) Introvertive mystical experiences are usually attained during the practice of a meditative technique which enables subjects to shut out all physical and mental distractions and to 'peel off' all the layers of the ego until they have – so mystics say – transcended the superficial, 'empirical' ego and arrived at a state in which there is no multiplicity, only pure 'unity'. In this state one loses all sense of 'oneself' as a separate being, as a subject observing objects from a distance. In its monistic form this is the experience of apparent identity with or complete absorption into the Absolute, the recognition that our 'true self' (as opposed to the empirical ego) is divine. In its theistic form it is the experience of apparent intimate union with but not identity with God, expressed by metaphors such as 'indwelling' and 'marriage'. In the experiences of this section, however, there is no union with anything, but simply an attainment of *internal* 'oneness'. This may take the form of 'personal integration', the realization of a 'self' in which all the elements are in such perfect harmony that it appears to be a unity. William James describes something of the sort in his account of his experiences with nitrous oxide:

> [T]hey all converge towards a kind of insight to which I cannot help ascribing some metaphysical significance. The keynote of it is invariably a reconciliation. It is as if the opposites of the world, whose contradictoriness and conflict make all our difficulties and troubles, were melted into unity.[73]

In the Theravada Buddhist mystical tradition (as opposed to many Mahayana Buddhist traditions, which are often close to theism), the subject claims to have arrived at a permanent, blissful state in which all external and internal multiplicity has been transcended. The sense of freedom from all attachments and limitations, as described in section (ii), is the primary thing; the subject sees it as the sign of release from the cycle of rebirth and suffering. By training themselves to regard everything, even their own states of mind, as inherently transient and imperfect, and by practising meditation, Theravada Buddhists strive to attain the supreme, enduring state of nirvana. Metaphysical questions about God, the form of 'existence' in nirvana, and so on are regarded in this agnostic tradition as distractions on the path to liberation, and subjects are therefore reluctant to 'ontologize the contents of their mystical experiences'.[74]

Somewhat similar to Buddhist experiences, but with the explicit assertion of the reality of the isolated, unified self, are experiences of the adherents of Yoga, whose doctrine Ninian Smart sums up as follows:

> That there is an infinite number of eternal selves, who through Yoga can attain isolation or liberation, a state in which the soul exists by itself, no longer implicated in nature and in the round of rebirth.[75]

(c) In the monistic mystical experience the subject feels himself (his 'Atman') to be identical with the One, the world-soul, or 'cosmic consciousness' ('Brahman'); in this state of pure unity he is 'a centre coincident with another centre' (Plotinus).[76] This is the experience sought by followers of Shankara's non-dualistic version of Hinduism, the Advaita Vedanta, whose doctrine Smart (once again) summarizes thus:

> That there is but one Self, which individuals can realize, and which is identical with Brahman as the ground of being (which at a lower level of truth manifests itself as a personal Lord and Creator) – such a realization bringing about a cessation of the otherwise continuously reborn individual.[77]

Even theists may have an experience of apparent identity with the 'ground of being', though they usually try to wriggle out of it somehow. Meister Eckhart tries to explain here how the soul can be absorbed and yet remain an individual soul separate from the Godhead:

> In this exalted state she [the soul] has lost her proper self and is flowing full-flood into the

unity of the divine nature. But what, you may ask, is the fate of this lost soul: does she find herself or not? . . . it seems to me that . . . though she sink all sinking in the oneness of divinity she never touches bottom. Wherefore God has left her one little point from which to get back to herself and find herself and know herself as creature.[78]

The 'God-intoxicated' Sufis of Islam are especially prone to express their experiences in terms of identity: 'In that Presence, says the Sufi mystic [Shabistari], "I" and "thou" have ceased to exist, they have become one: the Quest and the Way and the Seeker are one.'[79] Al-Ghazali tried to account for these 'blasphemous' Sufi utterances by dismissing them as 'the words of lovers when in a state of drunkenness'. In their sober moments, he claims, the mystics 'know that this was not actual identity, but that it resembled identity' – for they were 'drowned in pure solitude' and 'no longer had the capacity to recollect aught but God'.[80]

(d) Theistic mystics usually regard their type of mystical experience as the 'highest' type: other experiences may show that the subjects have attained, by their own efforts, absolute purity of soul and the kind of self-naughting required before union with God is possible, but to rest in them would be to miss out on the 'Beatific Vision', for which God's help (grace) is required. Many models have been used to describe this experience of near perfect union, just short of actual identity: 'Spiritual Marriage', which stresses intimacy, love, the indissolubility of the bond, the 'oneness' created by the act of consummating the marriage, and the sense of losing oneself completely in surrender to and rapt contemplation of the beloved; 'Indwelling' (sometimes called 'deification'), which implies that there is in human beings a 'divine spark' which the mystic has uncovered, or that the mystic has been transformed by a 'new birth', the birth of Christ or the spirit of God within him; and 'Absorption', which refers to the way the mystic feels entirely engulfed by the divine.

Mystics are not bound by one particular model. Even St Teresa, who generally uses the very personal imagery of marriage, sometimes describes her experience in the impersonal terms of absorption:

> [I]t is like rain falling from the heavens into a river or a spring; there is nothing but water there

and it is impossible to divide or separate the water belonging to the river from that which fell from the heavens.[81]

Descriptions of 'indwelling' are particularly frequent: 'it is no longer I who live, but Christ who lives in me' (Galatians 2: 20); 'I used unexpectedly to experience a consciousness of the presence of God, of such a kind that I could not possibly doubt that He was within me or that I was wholly engulfed in Him';[82] 'those who with devotion worship me abide in me, and I also in them';[83] and, from sources as diverse as Sadhu Sundar Singh and Jacob Boehme,[84] the analogy of red-hot iron:

> The iron is in the fire and the fire is in the iron, and yet the iron is not the fire and the fire is not the iron. In the same way we live in Christ and He lives in us and yet we do not become gods.[85]

(iv) The fourth characteristic of mystical experiences is what R. M. Gimello calls 'an extraordinarily strong affective tone':[86] exaltation, rapture, bliss, sublime serenity, the 'peace which passeth all understanding', and burning love. 'Might but one little drop of what I feel fall into Hell, Hell would be transformed into a Paradise', declared St Catherine of Genoa.[87] And Viktor Frankl, talking of his realization that 'the salvation of man is through love and in love', wrote, 'For the first time in my life I was able to understand the meaning of the words, "The angels are lost in perpetual contemplation of an infinite glory." '[88]

There are many indications that both the profound peace and the 'unspeakable rapture' are intimately bound up with the sense of freedom described in section (ii). They are not a peace or a joy for the faint-hearted or for those who find security in material things and familiar, narrow boundaries. Peace can come through such thoroughgoing renunciation that one thinks neither about one's reputation nor about one's next meal; and great joy can attend the sense of freedom from such intransigent human limitations as death and the boundaries of the individual ego. D. T. Suzuki suggests that the source of the bliss accompanying 'satori' is 'the breaking-up of the restriction imposed on one as an individual being . . . an infinite expansion of the individual'.[89] J. A. Symonds, quoted by William James, actually disliked his experience of the dissolution of his conscious self, and wrote of his 'return from the abyss', 'At last I felt myself once more a human being ... I was thankful for ... this deliverance from so awful an initiation into the mysteries of scepticism.'[90] This is the reverse of the Buddhist attitude, where the goal is precisely to plunge into that abyss! Just as some find skiing down a mountainside at top speed exhilarating, while others hate the sense of loss of control and prefer to stay at the bottom, so Symonds was like the majority of mankind, clinging to his everyday sense of identity rather than surrendering himself completely to receive a new and wider 'self'.

[...] It should be pointed out here, though, that there is a remarkable degree of agreement between vastly different traditions regarding method and stages of progress. Most have something approaching the triadic Dionysian scheme of 'purgation', 'illumination', and 'union', and agree that without adequate preparation the subject's mind may become so unstable and confused that the journey to enlightenment takes the terrifying route through madness. Guidance must be given by a confessor, yogi, or similar experienced person; the subject must be trained to transcend the cares and complexities of this world and his own self; and the final stage is regarded as not just one experience among others but as a continuing state of liberation or 'God-consciousness', and not just one end among others but a human being's *summum bonum*.

Notes

1   Such experiences would nevertheless have some small evidential force, since it could have been the case that no experiences ever occurred which were in accordance with that tradition's doctrines.

2   See Vincent Brümmer's study of prayer, *What Are We Doing When We Pray? A Philosophical Inquiry* (London: SCM, 1984).

3   William James, *The Varieties of Religious Experience: A Study in Human Nature* (Glasgow: Collins Fount, 1977), pp. 450–1, n.

4   In Alister Hardy, *The Spiritual Nature of Man: A Study of Contemporary Religious Experience* (Oxford: Clarendon Press, 1979), p. 46.

5   See the last chapter of Timothy Beardsworth, *A Sense of Presence* (Oxford: RERU, 1977).

6   Described in B. H. Streeter and A. J. Appasamy, *The Sadhu* (London: Macmillan, 1921), pp. 5–7. A more familiar example is St Paul's experience on the road to Damascus, which Sundar's vision echoes. [...]

7   Ibid., p. 8.

8   See the study by G. N. M. Tyrrell, *Apparitions* (London: Duckworth, 1953).

9   Julian of Norwich, *Revelations of Divine Love*, tr. Clifton Wolters (Harmondsworth: Penguin Books, 1966), ch. 51.

10 *The Cloud of Unknowing*, tr. Clifton Wolters (Harmondsworth: Penguin Books, 1961), ch. 58.

11 See Swami Sivananda, *Concentration and Meditation* (Rikhikesh: The Sivananda Publication League, 1945), ch. IX.

12 David Brown, *The Divine Trinity* (London: Duckworth, 1985), ch. I.

13 D. T. Suzuki, *An Introduction to Zen Buddhism* (London: Arrow Books, 1959), p. 95.

14 Quoted in James, *Varieties of Religious Experience*, p. 460.

15 St Teresa of Avila, *Life*, from *The Complete Works of Saint Teresa of Jesus*, tr. and ed. E. Allison Peers (London: Sheed & Ward, 1946), vol. 1, p. 172.

16 In Hardy. *The Spiritual Nature of Man*, p. 109.

17 Ibid., p. 56.

18 Ibid., p. 110.

19 Ibid., p. 100.

20 *Life*, ch. XXXIII.

21 St Teresa, *Interior Castle*, tr. and ed. E. Allison Peers (Garden City, NY: Image Books, 1961), 7. i; and Julian of Norwich, *Revelations of Divine Love*, ch. 58.

22 Made in *The Grammar of Assent*; see the discussion in H. D. Lewis, *Our Experience of God* (London: Allen & Unwin, 1959), p. 25.

23 In Hardy, *The Spiritual Nature of Man*, p. 109.

24 St Teresa, *Interior Castle*, 7. i.

25 See C. Wolters' introduction to Julian of Norwich, *Revelations of Divine Love*, pp. 11–13, for a good account of the church's attitude towards alleged revelations.

26 Meister Eckhart, *Counsels on Discernment* 15, tr. Edmund Colledge, from *Meister Eckhart: The Essential Sermons, Commentaries, Treatises, and Defense*, tr. and intro. Edmund Colledge and Bernard McGinn (London: SPCK, 1981), p. 264.

27 *Interior Castle*, p. 144.

28 Conversation with Mettānando Bhikkhu at Oriel College, Oxford, on 23 Feb. 1986.

29 In James, *Varieties of Religious Experience*, p. 385.

30 The term is from Peter Donovan, *Interpreting Religious Experience* (London: Sheldon Press, 1979), though what I include in the category differs slightly from what he includes.

31 Reported in Hardy, *The Spiritual Nature of Man*, p. 116.

32 In ibid., p. 48.

33 *The Journal of the Rev. John Wesley A.M.*, ed. Ernest Rhys, vol. 1 (London: J. M. Dent & Co.), p. 102.

34 Viktor Frankl, *Man's Search for Meaning*, tr. Ilse Lasch (New York: Washington Square Press, 1963), pp. 63–4.

35 In Hardy, *The Spiritual Nature of Man*, p. 71.

36 Ibid., p. 53.

37 In James, *Varieties of Religious Experience*, p. 86.

38 *Gita* 9: 6, tr. Juan Mascaró (Harmondsworth: Penguin Books, 1962). This is not the most reliable translation, but because of its eloquence I have used it where the translation is not inaccurate, as tested against the more reliable translations of R. C. Zaehner, Franklin Edgerton, and W. D. P. Hill. (The *Gita* 11: 18 says, 'Thou art the ultimate resting-place of this universe' (tr. Edgerton) and many other passages talk of 'abiding', 'rest', 'refuge', etc.)

39 Psalms 46: 1.

40 Rudolf Otto, *The Idea of the Holy*, tr. J. W. Harvey (London: OUP, 1936); [see also this vol., ch. 13].

41 Isaiah 6: 5.

42 *Revelations of Divine Love*, ch. 75.

43 See, for instance, the example in Hardy, *The Spiritual Nature of Man*, p. 82.

44 Otto, *The Idea of the Holy*, p. 78.

45 Ibid., pp. 12–13.

46 St Teresa, *Interior Castle*, p. 186.

47 Tr. Mascaró; see n. 38, above.

48 In Hardy, *The Spiritual Nature of Man*, p. 63. This book does not deal to any significant extent with the problem of alleged experiences of demonic or evil forces, but some of the remarks made in later chapters should prove relevant to the issue.

49 St Augustine, *Confessions*, tr. R. S. Pine-Coffin (Harmondsworth: Penguin Books, 1961), I, 1.

50 See, for example, Origen's *Commentary on the Song*, quoted in Andrew Louth, *The Origins of the Christian Mystical Tradition* (Oxford: Clarendon Press, 1981), p. 67; St Teresa, *Life*, ch. XXIX; Richard Rolle, *The Fire of Love*, tr. Clifton Wolters (Harmondsworth: Penguin Classics, 1971); and many passages from St Catherine of Genoa.

51 *Life of Sri Ramakrishna* (Mayavati: Advaita Ashrama, 1948), p. 71.

52 Louth, *Christian Mystical Tradition*, p. 97.

53 Otto, *The Idea of the Holy*, p. 24.

54 Quoted in F. C. Happold, *Mysticism* (Harmondsworth: Penguin Books, 1970), p. 39.

55 In Hardy, *The Spiritual Nature of Man*, p. 60. C. S. Lewis's childhood experience of 'Joy' seems to have been a somewhat more intense version of this type of experience; see his *Surprised by Joy* (London: Geoffrey Bles, 1955).

56 W. T. Stace, *Mysticism and Philosophy* (London: Macmillan, 1960), ch. 2.

57 In Hardy, *The Spiritual Nature of Man*, p. 89.

58 Quoted by James, *Varieties of Religious Experience*, p. 370 n.

59 Jacob Boehme (or Behmen), *Dialogues on the Supersensual Life*, tr. and ed. Bernard Holland (London: Methuen, 1901), p. 74.

60 D. T. Suzuki, *Essays in Zen Buddhism*, 2nd series (London: Luzac & Co., 1933), p. 18.

61 The *Brihadaranyaka Upanishad* 2.4.12 and 14, from Robert E. Hume, tr., *The Thirteen Principal Upanishads*, 2nd edn. (London: OUP, 1931).

62 12: 25.

63 See Winston L. King, *Buddhism and Christianity* (London: Allen & Unwin, 1962); this was also maintained by Mettānando Bhikkhu, in conversation.

64 See Happold, *Mysticism*, ch. 5 (anthology); and Michael Carrithers, *The Forest Monks of Sri Lanka* (Delhi: OUP, 1983), ch. 13.

65 See Geoffrey Parrinder, *Mysticism in the World's Religions* (London: Sheldon Press, 1976), p. 42.

66 See Carrithers, *The Forest Monks*, ch. 13.

67 In Hardy, *The Spiritual Nature of Man*, p. 113.

68 Ibid., p. 89.

69 Ibid., p. 72.

70 Carrithers, *The Forest Monks*, ch. 2.

71 See Parrinder, *Mysticism*, p. 71.

72 *Chandogya Upanishad* 6.10, tr. R. C. Zaehner, quoted in his *Mysticism Sacred and Profane* (Oxford: Clarendon Press, 1957), p. 139. The refrain, 'That which is the subtlest of the subtle . . . that art thou' is repeated frequently throughout this Upanishad. R. E. Hume has, 'That which is the finest essence – this whole world has that as its soul'; the remainder is the same.

73 James, *Varieties of Religious Experience*, p. 374.

74 R. M. Gimello, 'Mysticism and Meditation', in Steven Katz (ed.), *Mysticism and Philosophical Analysis* (London: Sheldon Press, 1978), p. 193.

75 'Interpretation and Mystical Experience', in ibid., p. 83.

76 Ennead VI.9 [9] 10, from *The Essential Plotinus*, tr. Elmer O'Brien (1964).

77 'Interpretation and Mystical Experience', p. 83.

78 Franz Pfeiffer, *Meister Eckhart* (Leipzig, 1857), tr. C. de B. Evans (London: Watkins, 1956), vol. i, Tractates II ('The Nobility of the Soul'), p. 282.

79 Margaret Smith, *The Way of the Mystics* (London: Sheldon Press, 1931, 1976), p. 9.

80 From al-Ghazali's *Mishkāt al-Anwār*, Zaehner tr., quoted in Zaehner, *Mysticism Sacred and Profane*, pp. 157–8.

81 *Interior Castle*, 7. 11.

82 St Teresa, *Life*, ch. x.

83 *Bhagavad Gita* 9: 29, tr. W. D. P. Hill (London: OUP, 1928).

84 Reported by Evelyn Underhill in her *Mysticism* (London: Methuen, 1911), ch. x.

85 Streeter and Appasamy, *The Sadhu*, pp. 66–7.

86 'Mysticism and Meditation'.

87 *Vita*, p. 94c (see Baron von Hügel, *The Mystical Element of Religion*, vol. 1, London: Dent, 1909, p. 159), quoted by Otto, *The Idea of the Holy*, p. 38.

88 Frankl, *Man's Search for Meaning*, p. 59.

89 *Essays*, p. 20.

90 In James, *Varieties of Religious Experience*, p. 372.

15

The Groundlessness of Belief

Norman Malcolm

I

In his final notebooks Wittgenstein wrote that it is difficult "to realize the groundlessness of our believing."[1] He was thinking of how much mere acceptance, on the basis of no evidence, forms our lives. This is obvious in the case of small children. They are told the names of things. They accept what they are told. They do not ask for grounds. A child does not demand a proof that the person who feeds him is called "Mama." Or are we to suppose that the child reasons to himself as follows: "The others present seem to know this person who is feeding me, and since they call her 'Mama' that probably is her name"? It is obvious on reflection that a child cannot consider evidence or even doubt anything until he has already learned much. As Wittgenstein puts it: "The child learns by believing the adult. Doubt comes *after* belief" (*OC*, 160).

What is more difficult to perceive is that the lives of educated, sophisticated adults are also formed by groundless beliefs. I do not mean eccentric beliefs that are out on the fringes of their lives, but fundamental beliefs. Take the belief that familiar material things (watches, shoes, chairs) do not cease to exist without some physical explanation. They don't "vanish in thin air." It is interesting

that we do use that very expression: "I *know* I put the keys right here on this table. They must have vanished in thin air!" But this exclamation is hyperbole; we are not speaking in literal seriousness. I do not know of any adult who would consider, in all gravity, that the keys might have inexplicably ceased to exist.

Yet it is possible to imagine a society in which it was accepted that sometimes material things do go out of existence without having been crushed, melted, eroded, broken into pieces, burned up, eaten, or destroyed in some other way. The difference between those people and ourselves would not consist in their *saying* something that we don't say ("It vanished in thin air"), since we say it too. I conceive of those people as acting and thinking differently from ourselves in such ways as the following: If one of them could not find his wallet he would give up the search sooner than you or I would; also he would be less inclined to suppose that it was stolen. In general, what we would regard as convincing circumstantial evidence of theft those people would find less convincing. They would take fewer precautions than we would to protect their possessions against loss or theft. They would have less inclination to save money, since it too can just disappear. They would not tend to form strong attachments to material things, animals, or other people. Generally, they would stand in a looser relation to the world than we do. The disappearance of a desired object, which would provoke us to a frantic search, they would be more inclined to accept with a shrug. Of course, their scientific theories would be different; but also their

Norman Malcolm, "The Groundlessness of Belief," reprinted by permission of the publisher, Cornell University Press, from Stuart Brown (ed.), *Reason and Religion* (Ithaca: Cornell University Press, 1977), pp. 143–57. Copyright © 1977 Royal Institute of Philosophy.

attitude toward experiment, and inference from experimental results, would be more tentative. If the repetition of a familiar chemical experiment did not yield the expected result this *could* be because one of the chemical substances had vanished.

The outlook I have sketched might be thought to be radically incoherent. I do not see that this is so. Although those people consider it to be possible that a wallet might have inexplicably ceased to exist, it is also true that they regard that as unlikely. For things that are lost usually do turn up later; or if not, their fate can often be accounted for. Those people use pretty much the same criteria of identity that we do; their reasoning would resemble ours quite a lot. Their thinking would not be incoherent. But it would be different, since they would leave room for some possibilities that we exclude.

If we compare their view that material things do sometimes go out of existence inexplicably, with our own rejection of that view, it does not appear to me that one position is supported by *better evidence* than is the other. Each position is compatible with ordinary experience. On the one hand it is true that familiar objects (watches, wallets, lawn chairs) occasionally disappear without any adequate explanation. On the other hand it happens, perhaps more frequently, that a satisfying explanation of the disappearance is discovered.

Our attitude in this matter is striking. We would not be willing to consider it as even improbable that a missing lawn chair had "just ceased to exist." We would not entertain such a suggestion. If anyone proposed it we would be sure he was joking. It is no exaggeration to say that this attitude is part of the foundations of our thinking. I do not want to say that this attitude is *un*reasonable; but rather that it is something that we do not *try* to support with grounds. It could be said to belong to "the framework" of our thinking about material things.

Wittgenstein asks: "Does anyone ever test whether this table remains in existence when no one is paying attention to it?" (*OC*, 163). The answer is: Of course not. Is this because we would not call it "a table" if that were to happen? But we do call it "a table" and none of us makes the test. Doesn't this show that we do not regard that occurrence as a possibility? People who did so regard it would seem ludicrous to us. One could imagine that they made ingenious experiments to decide the question; but this research would make us smile. Is this because experiments were conducted by our ancestors that settled the matter once and for all? I

don't believe it. The principle that material things do not cease to exist without physical cause is an unreflective part of the framework within which physical investigations are made and physical explanations arrived at.

Wittgenstein suggests that the same is true of what might be called "the principle of the continuity of nature":

> Think of chemical investigations. Lavoisier makes experiments with substances in his laboratory and now concludes that this and that takes place when there is burning. He does not say that it might happen otherwise another time. He has got hold of a world-picture – not of course one that he invented: he learned it as a child. I say world-picture and not hypothesis, because it is the matter-of-course (*selbstverständliche*) foundation for his research and as such also goes unmentioned. (*OC*, 167)

> But now, what part is played by the presupposition that a substance A always reacts to a substance B in the same way, given the same circumstances? Or is that part of the definition of a substance? (*OC*, 168)

Framework principles such as the continuity of nature or the assumption that material things do not cease to exist without physical cause belong to what Wittgenstein calls a "system." He makes the following observation, which seems to me to be true:

> All testing, all confirmation and disconfirmation of a hypothesis takes place already within a system. And this system is not a more or less arbitrary and doubtful point of departure for all our arguments: no, it belongs to the nature of what we call an argument. The system is not so much the point of departure, as the element in which arguments have their life. (*OC*, 105)

A "system" provides the boundaries within which we ask questions, carry out investigations, and make judgments. Hypotheses are put forth, and challenged, *within* a system. Verification, justification, the search for evidence, occur *within* a system. The framework propositions of the system are not put to the test, not backed up by evidence. This is what Wittgenstein means when he says: "Of course there is justification; but justification comes to an end" (*OC*, 192); and when he asks: "Doesn't testing come to an end?" (*OC*, 164); and when he remarks that "whenever we test anything we are already presupposing something that is not tested" (*OC*, 163).

That this is so is not to be attributed to human weakness. It is a conceptual requirement that our inquiries and proofs stay within boundaries. Think, for example, of the activity of calculating a number. Some steps in a calculation we will check for correctness, but others we won't: for example, that 4 + 4 = 8. More accurately, some beginners might check it, but grown-ups won't. Similarly, some grown-ups would want to determine by calculation whether 25 × 25 = 625, whereas others would regard that as laughable. Thus the boundaries of the system within which *you* calculate may not be exactly the same as *mine*. But we do calculate; and, as Wittgenstein remarks, "In certain circumstances . . . we regard a calculation as sufficiently checked. What gives us a right to do so? . . . Somewhere we must be finished with justification, and then there remains the proposition that *this* is how we calculate" (*OC*, 212). If someone did not accept any boundaries for calculating this would mean that he had not learned *that* language-game:

> If someone supposed that *all* our calculations were uncertain and that we could rely on none of them (justifying himself by saying that mistakes are always possible) perhaps we would say he was crazy. But can we say he is in error? Does he not just react differently? We rely on calculations, he doesn't; we are sure, he isn't. (*OC*, 217)

We are taught, or we absorb, the systems within which we raise doubts, make inquiries, draw conclusions. We grow into a framework. We don't question it. We accept it trustingly. But this acceptance is not a consequence of reflection. We do not decide to accept framework propositions. We do not decide that we live on the earth, any more than we decide to learn our native tongue. We do come to adhere to a framework proposition, in the sense that it forms the way we think. The framework propositions that we accept, grow into, are not idiosyncrasies but common ways of speaking and thinking that are pressed on us by our human community. For our acceptances to have been withheld would have meant that we had not learned how to count, to measure, to use names, to play games, or even *to talk*. Wittgenstein remarks that "a language-game is only possible if one trusts

something." Not *can*, but *does* trust something (*OC*, 509). I think he means by this trust or acceptance what he calls belief "in the sense of religious belief" (*OC*, 459). What does he mean by belief "in the sense of religious belief"? He explicitly distinguishes it from *conjecture* (*Vermutung*: ibid.). I think this means that there is nothing tentative about it; it is not adopted as a hypothesis that might later be withdrawn in the light of new evidence. This also makes explicit an important feature of Wittgenstein's understanding of belief, in the sense of "religious belief," namely, that it does not rise or fall on the basis of evidence or grounds: it is "groundless."

II

In our Western academic philosophy, religious belief is commonly regarded as unreasonable and is viewed with condescension or even contempt. It is said that religion is a refuge for those who, because of weakness of intellect or character, are unable to confront the stern realities of the world. The objective, mature, *strong* attitude is to hold beliefs solely on the basis of *evidence*.

It appears to me that philosophical thinking is greatly influenced by this veneration of evidence. We have an aversion to statements, reports, declarations, beliefs, that are not based on grounds. There are many illustrations of this philosophical bent.

For example, in regard to a person's report that he has an image of the Eiffel Tower we have an inclination to think that the image must *resemble* the Eiffel Tower. How else could the person declare so confidently what his image is *of*? *How could he know*?

Another example: A memory-report or memory-belief must be based, we think, on some mental *datum* that is equipped with various features to match the corresponding features of the memory-belief. This datum will include an image that provides the *content* of the belief, and a peculiar feeling that makes one refer the image to a *past* happening, and another feeling that makes one believe that the image is an *accurate* portrayal of the past happening, and still another feeling that informs one that it was *oneself* who witnessed the past happening. The presence of these various features makes memory-beliefs thoroughly reasonable.

Another illustration: If interrupted in speaking one can usually give a confident account, later on, of what one had been *about* to say. How is this possible? Must not one remember *a feeling of tendency to say just those words?* This is one's basis for knowing what one had been about to say. It justifies one's account.

Still another example: After dining at a friend's house you announce your intention to go home. How do you know your intention? One theory proposes that you are presently aware of a particular mental state or bodily feeling which, as you recall from your past experience, has been highly correlated with the behavior of going home; so you infer that *that* is what you are going to do now. A second theory holds that you must be aware of some definite mental state or event which reveals itself, not by experience but *intrinsically*, as the intention to go home. Your awareness of that mental item *informs* you of what action you will take.

Yet another illustration: This is the instructive case of the man who, since birth, has been immune to sensations of bodily pain. On his thirtieth birthday he is kicked in the shins and for the first time he responds by crying out, hopping around on one foot, holding his leg, and exclaiming, "The pain is terrible!" We have an overwhelming inclination to wonder, "How could he tell, *this first time*, that what he felt was *pain?*" Of course, the implication is that *after* the first time there would be *no* problem. Why not? Because his first experience of pain would provide him with a sample that would be preserved in memory; thereafter he would be equipped to determine whether any sensation he feels is or isn't pain; he would just compare it with the memory-sample to see whether the two match! Thus he will have a justification for believing that what he feels is pain. But the *first time* he will not have this justification. This is why the case is so puzzling. Could it be that this first time he *infers* that he is in pain from his own behavior?

A final illustration: Consider the fact that after a comparatively few examples and bits of instruction a person can go on to carry out a task, apply a word correctly in the future, continue a numerical series from an initial segment, distinguish grammatical from ungrammatical constructions, solve arithmetical problems, and so on. These correct performances will be dealing with new and different examples, situations, combinations. The performance output will be far more varied than the instruction input. How is this possible? What carries the person from the meager instruction to his rich performance? The explanation has to be that an effect of his training was that he abstracted the Idea, perceived the Common Nature, "internalized" the Rule, grasped the Structure. What else could bridge the gap between the poverty of instruction and the wealth of performance? Thus we postulate an intervening mental act or state which removes the inequality and restores the balance.

My illustrations belong to what could be called the *pathology* of philosophy. Wittgenstein speaks of a "general disease of thinking" which attempts to explain occurrences of discernment, recognition, or understanding, by postulating mental states or processes from which those occurrences flow "as from a reservoir" (*BB*, p. 143). These mental intermediaries are assumed to contribute to the causation of the various cognitive performances. More significantly for my present purpose, they are supposed to *justify* them; they provide our *grounds* for saying or doing this rather than that; they *explain how we know*. The Image, or Cognitive State, or Feeling, or Idea, or Sample, or Rule, or Structure, *tells* us. It is like a road map or a signpost. It guides our course.

What is "pathological" about these explanatory constructions and pseudoscientific inferences? Two things at least. First, the movement of thought that demands these intermediaries is circular and empty, unless it provides criteria for determining their presence and nature *other than* the occurrence of the phenomena they are postulated to explain – and, of course, no such criteria are forthcoming. Second, there is the great criticism by Wittgenstein of this movement of philosophical thought: namely, his point that no matter what kind of state, process, paradigm, sample, structure, or rule, is conceived as giving us the necessary guidance, *it* could be taken, or understood, as indicating a *different* direction from the one in which we actually did go. The assumed intermediary Idea, Structure, or Rule, does not and cannot reveal that because of it we went in the only direction it was reasonable to go. Thus the internalized intermediary we are tempted to invoke to bridge the gap between training and performance, as being that which shows us what we must do or say if we are to be rational, cannot do the job it was invented to do. It cannot fill the epistemological gap. It cannot provide the bridge of justification. It cannot put to rest the How-do-we-know? question. Why not? Because it cannot tell us how *it itself* is to be taken, understood, applied. Wittgenstein puts the point briefly and powerfully: "Don't always think that you read off your words from facts; that you portray these in words according to rules. For even so you would have to apply the rule in the particular case without guidance" (*PI*, 292). Without guidance! Like Wittgenstein's signpost arrow that cannot tell us whether to go in the direction of the arrow tip or in the opposite direction, so too the Images, Ideas, Cognitive Structures, or Rules, that we philosophers imagine as devices for guidance, cannot interpret themselves to us. The signpost does not tell the traveler how to read it. A second signpost might tell him how to read the first one; we can imagine such a case. But this can't go on. If the traveler is to continue his journey he will have to do something on his own, without guidance.

The parable of the traveler speaks for *all* of the language-games we learn and practice; even those in which there is the most disciplined instruction and the most rigorous standards of conformity. Suppose that a pupil has been given thorough training in some procedure, whether it is drawing patterns, building fences, or proving theorems. But then he has to carry on by himself in new situations. How does he know what to do? Wittgenstein presents the following dialogue: "'However you instruct him in the continuation of a pattern – how can he *know* how he is to continue by himself?' – Well, how do *I* know? – If that means 'Have I grounds?', the answer is: the grounds will soon give out. And then I shall act, without grounds" (*PI*, 211). Grounds come to an end. Answers to How-do-we-know? questions come to an end. Evidence comes to an end. We must speak, act, live, without evidence. This is so, not just on the fringes of life and language, but at the center of our most regularized activities. We do learn rules and learn to follow them. But our training was in the past! We had to leave it behind and proceed on our own.

It is an immensely important fact of nature that as people carry on an activity in which they have received a common training, they do largely *agree* with one another, accepting the same examples and analogies, taking the same steps. We agree in what to say, in how to apply language. We agree in our responses to particular cases.

As Wittgenstein says: "That is not agreement in opinions but in form of life" (*PI*, 241). We cannot explain this agreement by saying that we are just doing what the rules tell us – for our agreement in applying rules, formulae, and signposts is what gives them their *meaning*.

One of the primary pathologies of philosophy is the feeling that we must *justify* our language-games. We want to establish them as well-grounded. But we should consider here Wittgenstein's remark that a language-game "is not based on grounds. It is there – like our life" (*OC*, 559).

Within a language-game there is justification and lack of justification, evidence and proof, mistakes and groundless opinions, good and bad reasoning, correct measurements and incorrect ones. One cannot properly apply these terms to a language-game itself. It may, however, be said to be "groundless," not in the sense of a groundless opinion, but in the sense that we accept it, we live it. We can say, "This is what we do. This is how we are."

In this sense religion is groundless; and so is chemistry. Within each of these two systems of thought and action there is controversy and argument. Within each there are advances and recessions of insight into the secrets of nature or the spiritual condition of humankind and the demands of the Creator, Savior, Judge, Source. Within the framework of each system there is criticism, explanation, justification. But we should not expect that there might be some sort of rational justification of the framework itself.

A chemist will sometimes employ induction. Does he have evidence for a Law of Induction? Wittgenstein observes that it would strike him as nonsense to say, "I know that the Law of Induction is true." ("Imagine such a statement made in a law court.") It would be more correct to say, "I believe in the Law of Induction" (*OC*, 500). This way of putting it is better because it shows that the attitude toward induction is belief in the sense of "religious" belief – that is to say, an acceptance which is not conjecture or surmise and for which there is no reason – it is a groundless acceptance.

It is intellectually troubling for us to conceive that a whole system of thought might be groundless, might have no rational justification. We realize easily enough, however, that grounds soon give out – that we cannot go on giving reasons for our reasons. There arises from this realization the conception of a reason that is *self-justifying* – something whose credentials as a reason cannot be questioned.

This metaphysical conception makes its presence felt at many points – for example, as an explanation of how a person can tell what his mental image is *of*. We feel that the following remarks, imagined by Wittgenstein, are exactly right: "'The image must be more similar to its object than any picture. For however similar I make the picture to what it is supposed to represent, it can always be the picture of something else. But it is essential to the image that it is the image of *this* and of nothing else'" (*PI*, 389). A pen and ink drawing represents the Eiffel Tower; but it could represent a mine shaft or a new type of automobile jack. Nothing prevents this drawing from being taken as a representation of something other than the Eiffel Tower. But my mental image of the Eiffel Tower is *necessarily* an image of the Eiffel Tower. Therefore it must be a "remarkable" kind of picture. As Wittgenstein observes: "Thus one might come to regard the image as a super-picture" (ibid.). Yet we have no intelligible conception of how a super-picture would differ from an ordinary picture. It would seem that it has to be a *super-likeness* – but what does this mean?

There is a familiar linguistic practice in which one person *tells* another what his image is of (or what he intends to do, or what he was about to say) and no question is raised of how the first one *knows* that what he says is true. This question is imposed from outside, artificially, by the philosophical craving for justification. We can see here the significance of these remarks: "It isn't a question of explaining a language-game by means of our experiences, but of noting a language-game" (*PI*, 655). "Look on the language-game as the *primary* thing" (*PI*, 656). Within a system of thinking and acting there occurs, *up to a point*, investigation and criticism of the reasons and justifications that are employed in that system. This inquiry into whether a reason is good or adequate cannot, as said, go on endlessly. We stop it. We bring it to an end. We come upon something that *satisfies* us. It is as if we made a decision or issued an edict: "*This* is an adequate reason!" (or explanation, or justification). Thereby we fix a boundary of our language-game.

There is nothing wrong with this. How else could we have disciplines, systems, games? But our fear of groundlessness makes us conceive that we are under some logical compulsion to terminate at *those particular* stopping points. We imagine that we have confronted the self-evident reason, the self-justifying explanation, the picture or symbol whose meaning cannot be questioned. This obscures from us the *human* aspect of our concepts – the fact that what we call "a reason," "evidence," "explanation," "justification," is what appeals to and satisfies *us*.

III

The desire to provide a rational foundation for a form of life is especially prominent in the philosophy of religion, where there is an intense preoccupation with purported proofs of the existence of God. In American universities there must be hundreds of courses in which these proofs are the main topic. We can be sure that nearly always the critical verdict is that the proofs are invalid and consequently that, up to the present time at least, religious belief has received no rational justification.

Well, of course not! The obsessive concern with the proofs reveals the assumption that in order for religious belief to be intellectually respectable it *ought* to have a rational justification. *That* is the misunderstanding. It is like the idea that we are not justified in relying on memory until memory has been proved reliable.

Roger Trigg makes the following remark: "To say that someone acts in a certain way because of his belief in God does seem to be more than a redescription of his action. . . . It is to give a *reason* for it. The belief is distinct from the commitment which may follow it, and is the justification for it."[2] It is evident from other remarks that by "belief in God" Trigg means "belief in the existence of God" or "belief that God exists." Presumably by the *acts* and *commitments* of a religious person Trigg refers to such things as prayer, worship, confession, thanksgiving, partaking of sacraments, and participation in the life of a religious group.

For myself I have great difficulty with the notion of belief in *the existence* of God, whereas the idea of belief *in* God is to me intelligible. If a man did not ever pray for help or forgiveness, or have any inclination toward it; nor ever felt that it is "a good and joyful thing" to thank God for the blessings of this life; nor was ever concerned about his failure to comply with divine commandments – then, it seems clear to me, he could not be said to believe in God. Belief in God is not an all or none thing; it can be more or less; it can wax and wane. But belief in God in any degree does require, as I understand the words, some religious action, some commitment, or if not, at least a bad conscience.

According to Trigg, if I take him correctly, a man who was entirely devoid of any inclination toward religious action or conscience might believe in *the existence* of God. What would be the marks of this? Would it be that the man knows some theology, can recite the Creeds, is well-read in Scripture? Or is his belief in the existence of God something different from this? If so, what? What would be the difference between a man who knows some articles of faith, heresies, scriptural writings, and in addition believes in the existence of God, and one who knows these things but does not believe in the existence of God? I assume that both of them are indifferent to the acts and commitments of religious life.

I do not comprehend this notion of belief in *the existence* of God which is thought to be distinct from belief *in* God. It seems to me to be an artificial construction of philosophy, another illustration of the craving for justification.

Religion is a form of life; it is language embedded in action – what Wittgenstein calls a "language-game." Science is another. Neither stands in need of justification, the one no more than the other.

Present-day academic philosophers are far more prone to challenge the credentials of religion than of science, probably for a number of reasons. One may be the illusion that science can justify its own framework. Another is the fact that science is a vastly greater force in our culture. Still another may be the fact that by and large religion is to university people an alien form of life. They do not participate in it and do not understand what it is all about.

Their nonunderstanding is of an interesting nature. It derives, at least in part, from the inclination of academics to suppose that their employment as scholars demands of them the most severe objectivity and dispassionateness. For an academic philosopher to become a religious believer would be a stain on his professional competence! Here I will quote from Nietzsche, who was commenting on the relation of the German scholar of his day to religious belief; yet his remarks continue to have a nice appropriateness for the American and British scholars of our own day:

Pious or even merely church-going people seldom realize *how much* good will, one might even say wilfulness, it requires nowadays for a German scholar to take the problem of religion seriously; his whole trade . . . disposes him to a superior, almost good-natured merriment in regard to religion, sometimes mixed with a mild contempt directed at the "uncleanliness" of spirit which he presupposes wherever one still belongs to the church. It is only with the aid of history (thus *not* from his personal experience) that the scholar succeeds in summoning up a reverent seriousness and a certain shy respect towards religion; but if he intensifies his feelings towards it even to the point of feeling grateful to it, he has still in his own person not got so much as a single step closer to that which still exists as church or piety; perhaps the reverse. The practical indifference to religious things in which he was born and raised is as a rule sublimated in him into a caution and cleanliness which avoids contact with religious people and things; . . . Every age has its own divine kind of naïvety for the invention of which other ages may envy it – and how much naïvety, venerable, childlike and boundlessly stupid naïvety there is in the scholar's belief in his superiority, in the good conscience of his tolerance, in the simple unsuspecting certainty with which his instinct treats the religious man as an inferior and lower type which he himself has grown beyond and *above*.[3]

Notes

1 Ludwig Wittgenstein, *On Certainty*, ed. G. E. M. Anscombe and G. H. von Wright; English translation by D. Paul and G. E. M. Anscombe (Oxford, 1969), paragraph 166. Henceforth I include references to this work in the text, employing the abbreviation "*OC*" followed by paragraph number. References to Wittgenstein's *The Blue and Brown Books* (Oxford, 1958) are indicated in the text by "*BB*" followed by page number. References to his *Philosophical Investigations*, ed. G. E. M. Anscombe and R. Rhees; English translation by Anscombe (Oxford, 1967) are indicated by "*PI*" followed by paragraph number. In *OC* and *PI*, I have mainly used the translations of Paul and Anscombe but with some departures.

2 *Reason and Commitment* (Cambridge, 1973), p. 75.

3 Friedrich Nietzsche, *Beyond Good and Evil*, trans. R. J. Hollingdale, para. 58.

16

Thought-Project

Søren Kierkegaard

A

Can the truth be learned? With this question we shall begin. It was a Socratic question or became that by way of the Socratic question whether virtue can be taught – for virtue in turn was defined as insight (see *Protagoras, Gorgias, Meno, Euthydemus*). Insofar as the truth is to be learned, it of course must be assumed not to be – consequently, because it is to be learned, it is sought. Here we encounter the difficulty that Socrates calls attention to in the *Meno* (80, near the end) as a "pugnacious proposition": a person cannot possibly seek what he knows, and, just as impossibly, he cannot seek what he does not know, for what he knows he cannot seek, since he knows it, and what he does not know he cannot seek, because, after all, he does not even know what he is supposed to seek. Socrates thinks through the difficulty by means [of the principle] that all learning and seeking are but recollecting. Thus the ignorant person merely needs to be reminded in order, by himself, to call to mind what he knows. The truth is not introduced into him but was in him. Socrates elaborates on this idea, and in it the Greek pathos is in fact concentrated, since it becomes a demonstration for the immortality of the soul – retrogressively, please note – or a demonstration for the pre-existence of the soul.[1]

Søren Kierkegaard, "Thought-Project," reprinted by permission of Princeton University Press from *Philosophical Fragments* (Princeton: Princeton University Press, 1985), pp. 9–22. Copyright © 1985 Princeton University Press.

In view of this, it is manifest with what wonderful consistency Socrates remained true to himself and artistically exemplified what he had understood. He was and continued to be a midwife, not because he "did not have the positive,"[2] but because he perceived that this relation is the highest relation a human being can have to another. And in that he is indeed forever right, for even if a divine point of departure is ever given, this remains the true relation between one human being and another, if one reflects upon the absolute and does not dally with the accidental but with all one's heart renounces understanding the half-measures that seem to be the inclination of men and the secret of the system. Socrates, however, was a midwife examined by the god himself. The work he carried out was a divine commission (see Plato's *Apology*), even though he struck people as an eccentric (ἀτοπώτατος, *Theaetetus*, 149), and the divine intention, as Socrates also understood it, was that the god forbade him to give birth (μαιεύεσθαί με ὁ θεὸς ἀναγχάζει, γεννᾶν δὲ ἀπεχώλυσεν [the god constrains me to serve as a midwife, but has debarred me from giving birth], *Theaetetus*, 150c), because between one human being and another μαιεύεσθαι [to deliver] is the highest; giving birth indeed belongs to the god.

Viewed Socratically, any point of departure in time is *eo ipso* something accidental, a vanishing point, an occasion. Nor is the teacher anything more, and if he gives of himself and his erudition in any other way, he does not give but takes away. Then he is not even the other's friend, much less his teacher. This is the profundity of Socratic thinking, this his noble, thoroughgoing humanity, which does not exclusively and conceitedly cultivate the company of brilliant minds but feels just as kin to a tanner, and for that reason he soon "became convinced that the study of nature is not man's concern and therefore began to philosophize about the ethical in workshops and in the market-place" (Diogenes Laertius, II, V, 21) but philosophized just as absolutely with whomever he spoke. With half-thoughts, with higgling and haggling, with claiming and disclaiming, as if the individual to a certain degree owed something to another person but then again to a certain degree did not, with vague words that explain everything except what is meant by this "to a certain degree" – with all such things one does not go beyond Socrates or reach the concept of revelation, either, but simply remains in empty talk. In the Socratic view, every human being is himself the midpoint, and the whole world focuses only on him because his self-knowledge is God-knowledge. Moreover, this is how Socrates understood himself, and in his view this is how every human being must understand himself, and by virtue of that understanding he must understand his relation to the single individual, always with equal humility and with equal pride. For that purpose, Socrates had the courage and self-collectedness to be sufficient unto himself, but in his relations to others he also had the courage and self-collectedness to be merely an occasion even for the most stupid person. What rare magnanimity – rare in our day, when the pastor is little more than the deacon, when every second person is an authority, while all these distinctions and all this considerable authority are mediated in a common lunacy and in a *commune naufragium* [common shipwreck], because, since no human being has ever truly been an authority or has benefited anyone else by being that or has ever really managed successfully to carry his dependent along, there is better success in another way, for it never fails that one fool going his way takes several others along with him.

If this is the case with regard to learning the truth, then the fact that I have learned from Socrates or from Prodicus or from a maidservant can concern me only historically or – to the extent that I am a Plato in my enthusiasm – poetically. But this enthusiasm, even though it is beautiful, even though I wish for myself and for everyone else this εὐχαταφορία εἰς πάθος [disposition to passion], which only the Stoic could warn against, although I do not have the Socratic magnanimity and the Socratic self-denial to think its nothingness – this enthusiasm, Socrates would say, is still but an

illusion, indeed, a muddiness of mind in which earthly distinction ferments almost grossly. Neither can the fact that the teaching of Socrates or of Prodicus was this or that have anything but historical interest for me, because the truth in which I rest was in me and emerged from me. Not even Socrates would have been capable of giving it to me, no more than the coachman is capable of pulling the horse's load, even though he may help the horse do it by means of the whip.[3] My relation to Socrates and Prodicus cannot concern me with regard to my eternal happiness, for this is given retrogressively in the possession of the truth that I had from the beginning without knowing it. If I were to imagine myself meeting Socrates, Prodicus, or the maidservant in another life, there again none of them would be more than an occasion, as Socrates intrepidly expresses it by saying that even in the underworld he would only ask questions, for the ultimate idea in all questioning is that the person asked must himself possess the truth and acquire it by himself. The temporal point of departure is a nothing, because in the same moment I discover that I have known the truth from eternity without knowing it, in the same instant that moment is hidden in the eternal, assimilated into it in such a way that I, so to speak, still cannot find it even if I were to look for it, because there is no Here and no There, but only an *ubique et nusquam* [everywhere and nowhere].

B

If the situation is to be different, then the moment in time must have such decisive significance that for no moment will I be able to forget it, neither in time nor in eternity, because the eternal, previously nonexistent, came into existence [*blev til*] in that moment. With this presupposition, let us now examine the relations involved in the question: Can the truth be learned?

a. The preceding state

We begin with the Socratic difficulty: How is one able to seek the truth, since it is indeed equally impossible whether one has it or one does not. The Socratic line of thought in effect annulled the disjunction, since it appeared that basically every human being possesses the truth. That was his explanation. We have seen what resulted with regard to the moment. Now if the moment is to acquire decisive significance, then the seeker up until that moment must not have possessed the truth, not even in the form of ignorance, for in that case the moment becomes merely the moment of occasion; indeed, he must not even be a seeker. This is the way we have to state the difficulty if we do not want to explain it Socratically. Consequently, he has to be defined as being outside the truth (not coming toward it like a proselyte, but going away from it) or as untruth. He is, then, untruth. But how, then, is he to be reminded, or what would be the use of reminding him of what he has not known and consequently cannot call to mind?

b. The teacher

If the teacher is to be the occasion that reminds the learner, he cannot assist him to recollect that he actually does know the truth, for the learner is indeed untruth. That for which the teacher can become the occasion of his recollecting is that he is untruth. But by this calling to mind, the learner is definitely excluded from the truth, even more than when he was ignorant of being untruth. Consequently, in this way, precisely by reminding him, the teacher thrusts the learner away, except that by being turned in upon himself in this manner the learner does not discover that he previously knew the truth but discovers his untruth. To this act of consciousness, the Socratic principle applies: the teacher is only an occasion, whoever he may be, even if he is a god, because I can discover my own untruth only by myself, because only when *I* discover it is it discovered, not before, even though the whole world knew it. (Under the assumed presupposition about the moment, this becomes the one and only analogy to the Socratic.)

Now, if the learner is to obtain the truth, the teacher must bring it to him, but not only that. Along with it, he must provide him with the condition for understanding it, for if the learner were himself the condition for understanding the truth, then he merely needs to recollect, because the condition for understanding the truth is like being able to ask about it – the condition and the question contain the conditioned and the answer. (If this is not the case, then the moment is to be understood only Socratically.)

But the one who not only gives the learner the truth but provides the condition is not a teacher. Ultimately, all instruction depends upon the presence of the condition; if it is lacking, then a teacher is capable of nothing, because in the second case,

the teacher, before beginning to teach, must transform, not reform, the learner. But no human being is capable of doing this; if it is to take place, it must be done by the god himself.

Now, inasmuch as the learner exists [*er til*], he is indeed created, and, accordingly, God must have given him the condition for understanding the truth (for otherwise he previously would have been merely animal, and that teacher who gave him the condition along with the truth would make him a human being for the first time). But insofar as the moment is to have decisive significance (and if this is not assumed, then we do in fact remain with the Socratic), he must lack the condition, consequently be deprived of it. This cannot have been due to an act of the god (for this is a contradiction) or to an accident (for it is a contradiction that something inferior would be able to vanquish something superior); it must therefore have been due to himself. If he could have lost the condition in such a way that it was not due to himself, and if he could be in this state of loss without its being due to himself, then he would have possessed the condition only accidentally, which is a contradiction, since the condition for the truth is an essential condition. The untruth, then, is not merely outside the truth but is polemical against the truth, which is expressed by saying that he himself has forfeited and is forfeiting the condition.

The teacher, then, is the god himself, who, acting as the occasion, prompts the learner to be reminded that he is untruth and is that through his own fault. But this state – to be untruth and to be that through one's own fault – what can we call it? Let us call it *sin*.

The teacher, then, is the god, who gives the condition and gives the truth. Now, what should we call such a teacher, for we surely do agree that we have gone far beyond the definition of a teacher. Inasmuch as the learner is in untruth but is that by his own act (and, according to what has already been said, there is no other way he can be that), he might seem to be free, for to be on one's own certainly is freedom. And yet he is indeed unfree and bound and excluded, because to be free from the truth is indeed to be excluded, and to be excluded by oneself is indeed to be bound. But since he is bound by himself, can he not work himself loose or free himself, for that which binds me should also be able to set me free at will, and since that is himself, he should certainly be able to do it. But first of all he must will it. But just suppose that he was very profoundly reminded of that for which that teacher became the occasion (and this must never be forgotten) of his recollecting – just suppose that he willed it. In that case (if by willing it he could do it by himself), his having been bound would become a bygone state, one that in the moment of liberation would vanish without a trace – and the moment would not gain decisive significance. He would be unaware that he had bound himself and now set himself free.[4]

Considered in this way, the moment acquires no decisive significance, and yet this was what we wanted to assume as the hypothesis. According to the hypothesis, then, he will not be able to set himself free. (And this is truly just the way it is, for he uses the power of freedom in the service of unfreedom, since he is indeed freely in it, and in this way the combined power of unfreedom grows and makes him the slave of sin.)

What, then, should we call such a teacher who gives him the condition again and along with it the truth? Let us call him a *savior*, for he does indeed save the learner from unfreedom, saves him from himself. Let us call him a *deliverer*, for he does indeed deliver the person who had imprisoned himself, and no one is so dreadfully imprisoned, and no captivity is so impossible to break out of as that in which the individual holds himself captive! And yet, even this does not say enough, for by his unfreedom he had indeed become guilty of something, and if that teacher gives him the condition and the truth, then he is, of course, a *reconciler* who takes away the wrath that lay over the incurred guilt.

A teacher such as that, the learner will never be able to forget, because in that very moment he would sink down into himself again, just as the person did who once possessed the condition and then, by forgetting that God is, sank into unfreedom. If they were to meet in another life, that teacher would again be able to give the condition to the person who had not received it, but he would be quite different for the person who had once received it. After all, the condition was something entrusted, and therefore the receiver was always responsible for an accounting. But a teacher such as that – what should we call him? A teacher certainly can evaluate the learner with respect to whether or not he is making progress, but he cannot pass judgment on him, for he must be Socratic enough to perceive that he cannot give the learner what is essential. That teacher, then, is actually not a teacher but is a *judge*. Even when the learner has most fully put on the condition and then, by doing

so, has become immersed in the truth, he still can never forget that teacher or allow him to disappear Socratically, which still is far more profound than all unseasonable punctiliousness and deluded fanaticism – indeed, it is the highest if that other is not truth.

And, now, the moment. A moment such as this is unique. To be sure, it is short and temporal, as the moment is; it is passing, as the moment is, past, as the moment is in the next moment, and yet it is decisive, and yet it is filled with the eternal. A moment such as this must have a special name. Let us call it: *the fullness of time*.

c. The follower

When the learner is untruth (and otherwise we go back to the Socratic) but is nevertheless a human being, and he now receives the condition and the truth, he does not, of course, become a human being for the first time, for he already was that; but he becomes a different person, not in the jesting sense – as if he became someone else of the same quality as before – but he becomes a person of a different quality or, as we can also call it, a *new* person.

Inasmuch as he was untruth, he was continually in the process of departing from the truth; as a result of receiving the condition in the moment, his course took the opposite direction, or he was turned around. Let us call this change *conversion*, even though this is a word hitherto unused; but we choose it precisely in order to avoid confusion, for it seems to be created for the very change of which we speak.

Inasmuch as he was in untruth through his own fault, this conversion cannot take place without its being assimilated into his consciousness or without his becoming aware that it was through his own fault, and with this consciousness he takes leave of his former state. But how does one take leave without feeling sorrowful? Yet this sorrow is, of course, over his having been so long in the former state. Let us call such sorrow *repentance*, for what else is repentance, which does indeed look back, but nevertheless in such a way that precisely thereby it quickens its pace toward what lies ahead!

Inasmuch as he was in untruth and now along with the condition receives the truth, a change takes place in him like the change from "not to be" to "to be." But this transition from "not to be" to "to be" is indeed the transition of birth. But the person who already *is* cannot be born, and yet he is born.

Let us call this transition *rebirth*, by which he enters the world a second time just as at birth – an individual human being who as yet knows nothing about the world into which he is born, whether it is inhabited, whether there are other human beings in it, for presumably we can be baptized *en masse* but can never be reborn *en masse*. Just as the person who by Socratic midwifery gave birth to himself and in so doing forgot everything else in the world and in a more profound sense owed no human being anything, so also the one who is born again owes no human being anything, but owes that divine teacher everything. And just as the other one, because of himself, forgot the whole world, so he in turn, because of this teacher, must forget himself.

If, then, *the moment* is to have decisive significance – and if not, we speak only Socratically, no matter what we say, even though we use many and strange words, even though in our failure to understand ourselves we suppose we have gone beyond that simple wise man who uncompromisingly distinguished between the god, man, and himself, more uncompromisingly than Minos, Aeacus, and Rhadamanthus – then the break has occurred, and the person can no longer come back and will find no pleasure in recollecting what remembrance wants to bring him in recollection, and even less will he by his own power be capable of drawing the god over to his side again.

But is what has been elaborated here thinkable? We shall not be in a hurry with the answer, for someone who because of prolonged pondering never comes up with an answer is not the only one who fails to answer – so too the one who admittedly manifests a marvelous quickness in answering but not the desirable slowness in considering the difficulty before explaining it. Before we answer, we shall ask who ought to answer the question. This matter of being born – is it thinkable? Well, why not? But who is supposed to think it – one who is born or one who is not born? The latter, of course, is unreasonable and cannot occur to anyone, for this notion certainly cannot occur to one who is born. When one who is born thinks of himself as born, he of course is thinking of this transition from "not to be" to "to be." The situation must be the same with rebirth. Or is the matter made more difficult by this – that the non-being preceding the rebirth has more being than the non-being that precedes birth? But who, then, is supposed to think

this? It must, of course, be one who is reborn, for it would be unreasonable to think that one who is not reborn should do it, and would it not be ludicrous if this were to occur to one who is not reborn?

If a person originally possesses the condition to understand the truth, he thinks that, since he himself is, God is. If he is in untruth, then he must of course think this about himself, and recollection will be unable to help him to think anything but this. Whether or not he is to go any further, *the moment* must decide (although it already was active in making him perceive that he is untruth). If he does not understand this, then he is to be referred to Socrates, even though his opinion that he has gone much further will cause that wise man a great deal of trouble, as did those who became so exasperated with him when he took away some foolish notion from them (ἐπειδάν τινα λῆρον αὐτῶν ἀφαιρῶμαι) that they positively wanted to bite him (see *Theaetetus*, 151).

In *the moment*, a person becomes aware that he was born, for his previous state, to which he is not to appeal, was indeed one of "not to be." In *the moment*, he becomes aware of the rebirth, for his previous state was indeed one of "not to be." If his previous state had been one of "to be," then under no circumstances would the moment have acquired decisive significance for him, as explained above. Whereas the Greek pathos focuses on recollection, the pathos of our project focuses on the moment, and no wonder, for is it not an exceedingly pathos-filled matter to come into existence from the state of "not to be"?

This, as you see, is my project! But perhaps someone will say, "This is the most ludicrous of all projects, or, rather, you are the most ludicrous of all project-cranks, for even if someone comes up with a foolish scheme, there is always at least the truth that he is the one who came up with the scheme. But you, on the other hand, are behaving like a vagabond who charges a fee for showing an area that everyone can see. You are like the man who in the afternoon exhibited for a fee a ram that in the forenoon anyone could see free of charge, grazing in the open pasture." – "Maybe so. I hide my face in shame. But, supposing that I am that ludicrous, then let me put things right again with a new project. Admittedly, gunpowder was invented centuries ago; so it would be ludicrous of me to pretend that I had invented it. But would it also be ludicrous for me to assume that someone had invented it? Now I am going to be so courteous as to assume that you are the one who has invented my project – more courtesy you cannot expect. Or, if you deny this, will you then also deny that someone has invented it, that is, some human being? In that case, I am just as close to having invented it as any other person. Therefore you are not angry with me because I falsely attribute to myself something that belongs to another human being, but you are angry with me because I falsely attribute to myself something that belongs to no human being, and you are just as angry when I mendaciously want to attribute the invention to you. Is it not curious that something like this exists, about which everyone who knows it also knows that he has not invented it, and that this 'Go to the next house' does not halt and cannot be halted, even though one were to go to everybody? Yet this oddity enthralls me exceedingly, for it tests the correctness of the hypothesis and demonstrates it. It would indeed be unreasonable to require a person to find out all by himself that he does not exist. But this transition is precisely the transition of the rebirth from not existing [at være til] to existing. Whether he understands it later certainly makes no difference, for simply because someone knows how to use gunpowder, knows how to analyze it into its components, does not mean that he invented it. So go ahead and be angry with me and with any other human being who pretends to have invented it, but you do not for that reason need to be angry with the idea."

Notes

1 If the thought is thought absolutely – that is, so that the various states of pre-existence are not considered – this Greek idea is repeated in ancient and modern speculation: an eternal creating, an eternal emanating from the Father, an eternal becoming of the deity, an eternal self-sacrifice, a past resurrection, a judgment over and done with. All these ideas are that Greek idea of recollection, although this is not always noticed, because they have been arrived at by going further. If the idea is analyzed in a tallying of the various states of pre-existence, then the eternal "pre's" of that approximating thinking are similar to the eternal "post's" of the corresponding approximation. The contradiction of existence [Tilværelse] is explained by positing a "pre" as needed (by virtue of a prior state, the individual has arrived at his present, otherwise unexplainable state) or by positing a "post" as needed (on another planet the individual will be better situated, and in consideration of that, his present state is not unexplainable).

2 As it is said in our age, in which one has "the positive" more or less in the way a polytheist would make light of monotheism's negativity, because polytheism, of course, has many gods, the monotheist but one. The philosophers have many ideas – all valid up to a point. Socrates has but one, which is absolute.

3 I cite one passage in *Clitophon* merely as a remark by a third party, since this dialogue is considered to be spurious. Clitophon laments that, with respect to virtue, Socrates is only encouraging (προτ-ετραμμένος), so that from the moment he has adequately recommended virtue in general, he leaves everyone on his own. Clitophon believes that this conduct must have its basis either in Socrates' not knowing more or in his not wanting to communicate more. (See para. 410.)

4 We shall take our time – after all, there is no need to hurry. By going slowly, one sometimes does indeed fail to reach the goal, but by going too fast, one sometimes passes it. We shall discuss this somewhat in Greek fashion. If a child who has received the gift of a little money – enough to be able to buy either a good book, for example, or one toy, for both cost the same – buys the toy, can he use the same money to buy the book? By no means, for now the money has been spent. But he may go to the bookseller and ask him if he will exchange the book for the toy. Suppose the bookseller answers: My dear child, your toy is worthless; it is certainly true that when you still had the money you could have bought the book just as well as the toy, but the awkward thing about a toy is that once it is purchased it has lost all value. Would not the child think: This is very strange indeed. And so it was also once, when man could buy freedom and unfreedom for the same price, and this price was the free choice of the soul and the surrender of the choice. He chose unfreedom, but if he then were to approach the god and ask whether he could make an exchange, the answer presumably would be: Undeniably there was a time when you could have bought what you wanted, but the curious thing about unfreedom is that once it is purchased it has no value whatsoever, even though one pays the same price for it. I wonder if such a person would not say: This is very strange indeed. Or if two hostile armies faced each other, and there came a knight whom both sides invited to join; but he chose the one side, was defeated and taken prisoner. As prisoner he was brought before the conqueror and was foolish enough to offer him his services on the conditions originally offered. I wonder if the conqueror would not say to him: My dear fellow, you are my prisoner now; true enough, at one

time you could have chosen differently, but now everything is changed. Would this not be strange indeed! If it were otherwise, if the moment did not have decisive significance, then the child, after all, must indeed have bought the book and merely have been ignorant of it, mistakenly thinking that he had bought the toy; the prisoner, after all, must have fought on the other side, but had not been seen because of the fog, and had really sided with the one whose prisoner he now imagined himself to be. – "The depraved person and the virtuous person presumably do not have power over their moral condition, but in the beginning they did have the power to become the one or the other, just as the person who throws a stone has power over it before he throws it but not when he has thrown it" (Aristotle). Otherwise the throwing would become an illusion, and the person throwing, despite all his throwing, would keep the stone in his hand, since the stone, like the skeptics' "flying arrow," did not fly.

17

The Ethics of Belief

W. K. Clifford

I. The Duty of Inquiry

A shipowner was about to send to sea an emigrant ship. He knew that she was old, and not overwell built at the first; that she had seen many seas and climes, and often had needed repairs. Doubts had been suggested to him that possibly she was not seaworthy. These doubts preyed upon his mind, and made him unhappy; he thought that perhaps he ought to have her thoroughly overhauled and refitted, even though this should put him to great expense. Before the ship sailed, however, he succeeded in overcoming these melancholy reflections. He said to himself that she had gone safely through so many voyages and weathered so many storms, that it was idle to suppose that she would not come safely home from this trip also. He would put his trust in Providence, which could hardly fail to protect all these unhappy families that were leaving their fatherland to seek for better times elsewhere. He would dismiss from his mind all ungenerous suspicions about the honesty of builders and contractors. In such ways he acquired a sincere and comfortable conviction that his vessel was thoroughly safe and seaworthy; he watched her departure with a light heart, and benevolent wishes for the success of the exiles in their strange new home that was to be; and he got his insurance money when she went down in mid-ocean and told no tales.

What shall we say of him? Surely this, that he was verily guilty of the death of those men. It is admitted that he did sincerely believe in the soundness of his ship; but the sincerity of his conviction can in nowise help him, because *he had no right to believe on such evidence as was before him.* He had acquired his belief not by honestly earning it in patient investigation, but by stifling his doubts. And although in the end he may have felt so sure about it that he could not think otherwise, yet inasmuch as he had knowingly and willingly worked himself into that frame of mind, he must be held responsible for it.

Let us alter the case a little, and suppose that the ship was not unsound after all; that she made her voyage safely, and many others after it. Will that diminish the guilt of her owner? Not one jot. When an action is once done, it is right or wrong forever; no accidental failure of its good or evil fruits can possibly alter that. The man would not have been innocent; he would only have been not found out. The question of right or wrong has to do with the origin of his belief, not the matter of it; not what it was, but how he got it; not whether it turned out to be true or false, but whether he had a right to believe on such evidence as was before him.

There was once an island in which some of the inhabitants professed a religion teaching neither the doctrine of original sin nor that of eternal punishment. A suspicion got abroad that the professors of this religion had made use of unfair means to get their doctrines taught to children. They were accused of wresting the laws of their country in such a way as to remove children from the care of the natural and legal guardians; and even of stealing them away and keeping them concealed from their friends and relations. A certain number of men formed themselves into a society for the purpose of agitating the public about this matter. They published grave accusations against individual citizens of the highest position and character, and did all in their power to injure these citizens in the exercise of their professions. So great was the noise they made, that a Commission was appointed to investigate the facts; but after the Commission had carefully inquired into all the evidence that could be got, it appeared that the accused were innocent. Not only had they been accused on insufficient evidence, but the evidence of their innocence was such as the agitators might easily have obtained, if they had attempted a fair inquiry. After these disclosures the inhabitants of that country looked upon the members of the agitating society, not only as persons whose judgment was to be distrusted, but also as no longer to be counted honorable men. For although they had sincerely and "conscientiously" believed in the charges they had made, yet *they had no right to believe on such evidence as was before them.* Their sincere convictions, instead of being honestly earned by patient inquiring, were stolen by listening to the voice of prejudice and passion.

Let us vary this case also, and suppose, other things remaining as before, that a still more accurate investigation proved the accused to have been really guilty. Would this make any difference in the guilt of the accusers? Clearly not; the question is not whether their belief was true or false, but whether they entertained it on wrong grounds. They would no doubt say, "Now you see that we were right after all; next time perhaps you will believe us." And they might be believed, but they would not thereby become honorable men. They would not be innocent, they would only be not found out. Every one of them, if he chose to examine himself *in foro conscientiae,*[1] would know that he had acquired and nourished a belief, when he had no right to believe on such evidence as was before him; and therein he would know that he had done a wrong thing.

It may be said, however, that in both of these supposed cases it is not the belief which is judged to be wrong, but the action following upon it. The shipowner might say, "I am perfectly certain that my ship is sound, but still I feel it is my duty to have her examined, before trusting the lives of so many people to her." And it might be said to the agitator, "However convinced you were of the justice of your cause and the truth of your convictions, you ought not to have made a public attack upon any man's character until you had examined the evidence on both sides with the utmost patience and care."

In the first place, let us admit that, so far as it goes, this view of the case is right and necessary; right, because even when a man's belief is so fixed that he cannot think otherwise, he still has a choice in regard to the action suggested by it, and so cannot escape the duty of investigating on the ground of the strength of his convictions; and necessary, because those who are not yet capable of controlling their feelings and thoughts must have a plain rule dealing with overt acts.

But this being premised as necessary, it becomes clear that it is not sufficient, and that our previous judgment is required to supplement it. For it is not possible so to sever the faith from the action it suggests as to condemn the one without condemning the other. No man holding a strong belief on one side of a question, or even wishing to hold a belief on one side, can investigate it with such fairness and completeness as if he were really in doubt and unbiased; so that the existence of a belief, not founded on fair inquiry, unfits a man for the performance of this necessary duty.

Nor is that truly a belief at all which has not some influence upon the actions of him who holds it. He who truly believes that which prompts him to an action has looked upon the action to lust after it; he has committed it already in his heart. If a belief is not realized immediately in open deeds, it is stored up for the guidance of the future. It goes to make a part of that aggregate of beliefs which is the link between sensation and action at every moment of all our lives, and which is so organized and compacted together that no part of it can be isolated from the rest, but every new addition modifies the structure of the whole. No real belief, however trifling and fragmentary it may seem, is ever truly insignificant; it prepares us to receive more of its like, confirms those which resembled it before, and weakens others; and so gradually it lays a stealthy train in our inmost thoughts, which may some day explode into overt action, and leave its stamp upon our character forever.

And no one man's belief is in any case a private matter which concerns himself alone. Our lives are guided by that general conception of the course of things which has been created by society for social purposes. Our words, our phrases, our forms and processes and modes of thought, are common property, fashioned and perfected from age to age; an heirloom, which every succeeding generation inherits as a precious deposit and a sacred trust, to be handed on to the next one, not unchanged, but enlarged and purified, with some clear marks of its proper handiwork. Into this, for good or ill, is woven every belief of every man who has speech of his fellows. An awful privilege, and an awful responsibility, that we should help to create the world in which posterity will live.

In the two supposed cases which have been considered, it has been judged wrong to believe on insufficient evidence, or to nourish belief by suppressing doubts and avoiding investigation. The reason of this judgment is not far to seek; it is that in both these cases the belief held by one man was of great importance to other men. But forasmuch as no belief held by one man, however seemingly trivial the belief, and however obscure the believer, is ever actually insignificant or without its effect on the fate of mankind, we have no choice but to extend our judgment to all cases of belief whatever. Belief, that sacred faculty which prompts the decisions of our will, and knits into harmonious working all the compacted energies of our being, is ours not for ourselves but for humanity. It is rightly used on truths which have been established by long tradition and waiting toil, and which have stood in the fierce light of free and fearless questioning. Then it helps to bind men together, and to strengthen and direct their common action. It is desecrated when given to unproved and unquestioned statements, for the solace and private pleasure of the believer; to add a tinsel splendor to the plain, straight road of our life, and display a bright mirage beyond it; or even to drown the common sorrows of our kind by a self-deception which allows them not only to cast down, but also to degrade us. Whoso would deserve well of his fellows in this matter will guard the purity of his belief with a very fanaticism of jealous care, lest at any time it should rest on an unworthy object, and catch a stain which can never be wiped away.

It is not only the leader of men, statesman, philosopher, or poet, that owes this bounden duty to mankind. Every rustic who delivers in the village alehouse his slow infrequent sentences may help to kill or keep alive the fatal superstitions which clog his race. Every hard-worked wife of an artisan may transmit to her children beliefs which shall knit society together, or rend it in pieces. No simplicity of mind, no obscurity of station, can escape the universal duty of questioning all that we believe.

It is true that this duty is a hard one, and the doubt which comes out of it is often a very bitter thing. It leaves us bare and powerless where we thought that we were safe and strong. To know all about anything is to know how to deal with it under all circumstances. We feel much happier and more secure when we think we know precisely what we do, no matter what happens, than when we have lost our way and do not know where to turn. And if we have supposed ourselves to know all about anything, and to be capable of doing what is fit in regard to it, we naturally do not like to find that we are really ignorant and powerless, that we have to begin again at the beginning, and try to learn what the thing is and how it is to be dealt with – if indeed anything can be learned about it. It is the sense of power attached to a sense of knowledge that makes men desirous of believing, and afraid of doubting.

This sense of power is the highest and best of pleasures when the belief on which it is founded is a true belief, and has been fairly earned by investigation. For then we may justly feel that it is common property, and holds good for others as well as for ourselves. Then we may be glad, not that *I* have learned secrets by which I am safer and stronger, but that *we men* have got mastery over more of the world; and we shall be strong, not for ourselves, but in the name of Man and in his strength. But if the belief has been accepted on insufficient evidence, the pleasure is a stolen one. Not only does it deceive ourselves by giving us a sense of power which we do not really possess, but it is sinful, because it is stolen in defiance of our duty to mankind. That duty is, to guard ourselves from such beliefs as from a pestilence, which may shortly master our own body and then spread to the rest of the town. What would be thought of one who, for the sake of a sweet fruit, should deliberately run the risk of bringing a plague upon his family and his neighbors?

And, as in other such cases, it is not the risk only which has to be considered; for a bad action is always bad at the time when it is done, no matter what happens afterwards. Every time we let ourselves believe for unworthy reasons, we weaken our powers of self-control, of doubting, of judicially and fairly weighing evidence. We all suffer severely enough from the maintenance and support of false beliefs and the fatally wrong actions which they lead to, and the evil born when one such belief is entertained is great and wide. But a greater and wider evil arises when the credulous character is maintained and supported, when a habit of believing for unworthy reasons is fostered and made permanent. If I steal money from any person, there may be no harm done by the mere transfer of possession; he may not feel the loss, or it may prevent him from using the money badly. But I cannot help doing this great wrong towards Man, that I make myself dishonest. What hurts society is not that it should lose its property, but that it should become a den of thieves; for then it must cease to be society. This is why we ought not to do evil that good may come; for at any rate this great evil has come, that we have done evil and are made wicked thereby. In like manner, if I let myself believe anything on insufficient evidence, there may be no great harm done by the mere belief; it may be true after all, or I may never have occasion to exhibit it in outward acts. But I cannot help doing this great wrong towards Man, that I make myself credulous. The danger to society is not merely that it should believe wrong things, though that is great enough; but that it should become credulous, and lose the habit of testing things and inquiring into them; for then it must sink back into savagery.

The harm which is done by credulity in a man is not confined to the fostering of a credulous character in others, and consequent support of false beliefs. Habitual want of care about what I believe leads to habitual want of care in others about the truth of what is told to me. Men speak the truth to one another when each reveres the truth in his own mind and in the other's mind but how shall my friend revere the truth in my mind when I myself am careless about it, when I believe things because I want to believe them, and because they are comforting and pleasant? Will he not learn to cry, "Peace," to me, when there is no peace? By such a course I shall surround myself with a thick atmosphere of falsehood and fraud, and in that I must live. It may matter little to me, in my cloud-castle of sweet illusions and darling lies; but it matters much to Man that I have made my neighbors ready to deceive. The credulous man is father to the liar and the cheat; he lives in the bosom of this his family, and it is no marvel if he should become even as they are. So closely are our duties knit together, that whoso shall keep the whole law, and yet offend in one point, he is guilty of all.

To sum up: it is wrong always, everywhere, and for any one, to believe anything upon insufficient evidence.

If a man, holding a belief which he was taught in childhood or persuaded of afterwards, keeps down and pushes away any doubts which arise about it in his mind, purposely avoids the reading of books and the company of men that call in question or discuss it, and regards as impious those questions which cannot easily be asked without disturbing it; the life of that man is one long sin against mankind.

If this judgment seems harsh when applied to those simple souls who have never known better, who have been brought up from the cradle with a horror of doubt, and taught that their eternal welfare depends on *what* they believe; then it leads to the very serious question, *Who hath made Israel to sin?*

It may be permitted me to fortify this judgment with the sentence of Milton[2] – "A man may be a heretic in the truth; and if he believe things only because his pastor says so, or the assembly so determine, without knowing other reason, though his belief be true, yet the very truth he holds becomes his heresy."

And with the famous aphorism of Coleridge[3] – "He who begins by loving Christianity better than Truth, will proceed by loving his own sect or Church better than Christianity, and end in loving himself better than all."

Inquiry into the evidence of a doctrine is not to be made once for all, and then taken as finally settled. It is never lawful to stifle a doubt; for either it can be honestly answered by means of the inquiry already made, or else it proves that the inquiry was not complete.

"But," says one, "I am a busy man; I have no time for the long course of study which would be necessary to make me in any degree a competent judge of certain questions, or even able to understand the nature of the arguments." Then he should have no time to believe.

Notes

1 Before the tribunal of his conscience.
2 *Areopagitica*.
3 *Aids to Reflection*.

18

Religious Belief as "Properly Basic"

Alvin Plantinga

Belief in God is the heart and center of the Christian religion – as it is of Judaism and Islam. Of course Christians may disagree, at least in emphasis, as to how to think of God; for example, some may emphasize his hatred of sin; others, his love of his creatures. Furthermore, one may find, even among professedly Christian theologians, supersophisticates who proclaim the liberation of Christianity from belief in God, seeking to re-place it by trust in "Being itself" or the "Ground of Being" or some such thing. It remains true, however, that belief in God is the foundation of Christianity.

In this essay I want to discuss a connected con-stellation of questions: Does the believer-in-God accept the existence of God by *faith*? Is belief in God contrary to reason, unreasonable, irrational? Must one have *evidence* to be rational or reasonable in believing in God? Suppose belief in God is *not* rational; does that matter? And what about proofs of God's existence? Many Reformed or Calvinist thinkers and theologians have taken a jaundiced view of natural theology, thought of as the attempt to give proofs or arguments for the existence of God; are they right? What underlies this hostility to an undertaking that, on the surface, at least, looks perfectly harmless and possibly useful? These

are some of the questions I propose to discuss. They fall under the general rubric *faith and reason*, if a general rubric is required. I believe Reformed or Calvinist thinkers have had important things to say on these topics and that their fundamental insights here are correct. What they say, however, has been for the most part unclear, ill-focused, and unduly inexplicit. I shall try to remedy these ills; I shall try to state and clearly develop their insight; and I shall try to connect these insights with more general epistemological considerations.

Like the Missouri River, what I have to say is best seen as the confluence of three streams – streams of clear and limpid thought, I hasten to add, rather than turbid, muddy water. These three streams of thought are first, reflection on the evidentialist objection to theistic belief, according to which belief in God is unreasonable or irrational because there is insufficient evidence for it; second, reflection on the Thomistic conception of faith and reason; and third, reflection on the Reformed rejection to natural theology. In Part I, I shall explore the evidentialist objection, trying to see more clearly just what it involves and what it pre-supposes. In Part II, [. . .] I shall argue that the evidentialist objection [. . .] can be traced back to a common root in *classical foundationalism* – a per-vasive and widely accepted picture or total way of looking at faith, knowledge, belief, rationality, and allied topics. I shall try to characterize this pic-ture in a revealing way and then go on to argue that classical foundationalism is both false and self-referentially incoherent; it should therefore be summarily rejected. In Part III, I shall explore the Reformed rejection of natural theology; I will argue that it is best understood as an implicit rejection of classical foundationalism in favor of the view that belief in God is properly basic. What the Reformers meant to hold is that it is entirely right, rational, reasonable, and proper to believe in God without any evidence or argument at all; in this respect belief in God resembles belief in the past, in the existence of other persons, and in the existence of material objects. I shall try to state and clearly articulate this claim and in Part IV to defend it against objections.

Part I: The Evidentialist Objection to Belief in God

My first topic, then, is the evidentialist objection to theistic belief. Many philosophers – W. K. Clifford,[1] Brand Blanshard,[2] Bertrand Russell,[3] Michael Scriven,[4] and Antony Flew,[5] to name a few – have argued that belief in God is irrational or unreasonable or not rationally acceptable or intellectually irresponsible or somehow noetically below par because, as they say, there is *insufficient evidence* for it. Bertrand Russell was once asked what he would say if, after dying, he were brought into the presence of God and asked why he had not been a believer. Russell's reply: "I'd say 'Not enough evidence God! Not enough evidence!'"[6] We may have our doubts as to just how that sort of response would be received; but Russell, like many others, held that theistic belief is unreasonable because there is insufficient evidence for it.

But how shall we construe "theistic belief" here? I have been speaking of "belief in God"; but this is not entirely accurate. For the subject under discussion is not really the rational acceptability of belief *in* God, but the rationality of belief that God exists – that there *is* such a person as God. [. . .] The belief I mean to identify and discuss is not the belief that there exists some sort of imaginative construct or mental construction or anything of the sort. It is instead the belief, first, that there exists a *person* of a certain sort – a being who acts, holds beliefs, and has aims and purposes. This person, secondly, is immaterial, exists *a se*, is perfect in goodness, knowledge, and power, and is such that the world depends on him for its existence.

[. . .]

Now suppose we turn explicit attention to the evidentialist objection. Many philosophers have

endorsed the idea that the strength of one's belief ought always to be proportional to the strength of the evidence for that belief. Thus, according to John Locke a mark of the rational person is "the not entertaining any proposition with greater assurance than the proofs it is built upon will warrant." According to David Hume "A wise man . . . proportions his belief to the evidence." In the nineteenth century we have W. K. Clifford, that "delicious *enfant terrible*" as William James calls him, insisting that it is wicked, immoral, monstrous, and maybe even impolite to accept a belief for which you do not have sufficient evidence:

> Whoso would deserve well of his fellows in this matter will guard the purity of his belief with a very fanaticism of jealous care, lest at any time it should rest on an unworthy object, and catch a stain which can never be wiped away.[7]

He adds that if a

> belief has been accepted on insufficient evidence, the pleasure is a stolen one. Not only does it deceive ourselves by giving us a sense of power which we do not really possess, but it is sinful, because it is stolen in defiance of our duty to mankind. That duty is to guard ourselves from such beliefs as from a pestilence, which may shortly master our body and spread to the rest of the town. (p. 184)

And *finally*: "To sum up: it is wrong always, everywhere, and for anyone to believe anything upon insufficient evidence" (p. 186). (It is not hard to detect, in these quotations, the "tone of robustious pathos" with which James credits him.) Clifford, of course, held that one who accepts belief in God *does* accept that belief on insufficient evidence and has therefore defied his duty to mankind. More recently, Bertrand Russell has endorsed the same idea: "Give to any hypothesis which is worth your while to consider," he says, "just that degree of credence which the evidence warrants"; and in his view the evidence warrants no credence in the existence of God.

A. Flew: the presumption of atheism Still more recently Antony Flew has commended what he calls Clifford's "luminous and compulsive essay" (perhaps "compulsive" here is to be understood as "compelling"); and Flew goes on to claim that there is, in his words, a "presumption of atheism." What is a presumption of atheism, and why should we think there is one? Flew puts it as follows:

> What I want to examine is the contention that the debate about the existence of God should properly begin from the presumption of atheism, that the onus of proof must lie upon the theist.
>
> The word "atheism," however, has in this contention to be construed unusually. Whereas nowadays the usual meaning of "atheist" in English is "someone who asserts there is no such being as God," I want the word to be understood not positively but negatively. I want the original Greek preface "a" to be read in the same way in "atheist" as it is customarily read in such other Greco-English words as "amoral," "atypical," and "asymmetrical." In this interpretation an atheist becomes: not someone who positively asserts the non-existence of God; but someone who is simply not a theist.
>
> . . .
>
> What the protagonist of my presumption of atheism wants to show is that the debate about the existence of God ought to be conducted in a particular way, and that the issue should be seen in a certain perspective. His thesis about the onus of proof involves that it is up to the theist: first to introduce and to defend his proposed concept of God; and second, to provide sufficient reason for believing that this concept of his does in fact have an application.[8]

How shall we understand this? What does it mean, for example, to say that the debate "should properly begin from the presumption of atheism?" What sorts of things do debates begin from, and what is it for one to begin from such a thing? Perhaps Flew means something like this: to speak of where a debate should begin is to speak of the sorts of premises to which the affirmative and negative sides can properly appeal in arguing their cases. Suppose you and I are debating the question whether, say, the United States has a right to seize Mideast oil fields if the OPEC countries refuse to sell us oil at what we think is a fair price. I take the affirmative and produce for my conclusion an argument one of whose premises is the proposition that the United States has indeed a right to seize these oil fields under those

conditions. Doubtless that maneuver would earn me few points. Similarly, a debate about the existence of God cannot sensibly start from the assumption that God does indeed exist. That is to say, the affirmative cannot properly appeal, in its arguments, to such premises as that there is such a person as God; if she could, she would have much too easy a time of it. So in this sense of "start" Flew is quite right: the debate cannot start from the assumption that God exists.

Of course, it is also true that the debate cannot start from the assumption that God does *not* exist; using "atheism" in its ordinary sense, there is equally a presumption of aatheism. So it looks as if there is in Flew's sense a presumption of atheism, alright, but in that same sense an equal presumption of aatheism. If this is what Flew means, then what he says is entirely correct, if something of a truism.

In other passages, however, Flew seems to understand the presumption of atheism in quite a different fashion:

> It is by reference to this inescapable demand for grounds that the presumption of atheism is justified. If it is to be established that there is a God, then we have to have good grounds for believing that this is indeed so. Until or unless some such grounds are produced we have literally no reason at all for believing; and in that situation the only reasonable posture must be that of either the negative atheist or the agnostic. (p. 22)

Here we have a claim much more contentious than the mere suggestion that a debate about the existence of God ought not to start from the assumption that indeed there is such a person as God; here Flew is claiming that it is irrational or unreasonable to accept theistic belief in the absence of arguments or evidence for the existence of God. That is, Flew claims that if we know of no propositions that serve as evidence for God's existence, then we cannot rationally believe in God. And of course Flew, along with Russell, Clifford, and many others, holds that in fact there are not sufficient grounds or evidence for belief in God. Flew, therefore, seems to endorse the following two principles:

(1) It is irrational or unreasonable to accept theistic belief in the absence of sufficient evidence or reasons

and

(2) We have no evidence or at any rate not sufficient evidence for the proposition that God exists.

M. Scriven: atheism is obligatory in the absence of evidence According to Michael Scriven, if the arguments for God's existence fail, then the only rational posture is not merely not believing in God; it is atheism, the belief that there is no God. Speaking of the theistic proofs, he says, "It will now be shown that if they fail, there is no alternative to atheism."[9] He goes on to say: "we need not have a proof that God does not exist in order to justify atheism. Atheism is obligatory in the absence of any evidence for God's existence . . . The proper alternative, where there is no evidence, is not mere suspension of belief, e.g., about Santa Claus; it is *disbelief*" (p. 103). But Scriven's claim seems totally arbitrary. He holds that if the arguments *for* God's existence fail and the arguments *against* God's existence *also* fail, then atheism is rationally obligatory. If you have no evidence *for* the existence of God, then you are rationally obliged to believe there is no God – whether or not you have any evidence *against* the existence of God. The first thing to note, then, is that Scriven is not treating

(3) God exists

and

(4) God does not exist

in the same way. He claims that if there is no evidence for (3), then the only rational course is to believe its denial, namely (4). But of course he does not propose the same treatment for (4); he does not suggest that if there is no evidence for (4), then we are rationally obliged to believe *its* denial, namely (3). (If he *did* propose that (4) should be treated like (3), then he would be committed to supposing that if we had no evidence either way, the rational thing to do would be to believe the denial of (3), namely (4), and *also* the denial of (4), namely (3).) Why then does he propose this lack of parity between (3) and (4)? What is the justification for treating these propositions so differently? Could not the theist just as sensibly say, "If the arguments for *atheism* fail and there is no evidence for (4), then theism is rationally obligatory"? Scriven's claim,

initially at any rate, looks like a piece of merely arbitrary intellectual imperialism.

Scriven's extravagant claim, then, does not look at all promising. Let us therefore return to the more moderate evidentialist position encapsulated by

(1) It is irrational or unreasonable to accept theistic belief in the absence of sufficient evidence or reasons

and

(2) There is no evidence or at any rate not sufficient evidence for the proposition that God exists.

The evidentialist objection and intellectual obligation Now (2) is a strong claim. What about the various arguments that have been proposed for the existence of God – the traditional cosmological and teleological arguments for example? What about the versions of the *moral* argument as developed, for example, by A. E. Taylor and more recently by Robert Adams? What about the broadly inductive or probabilistic arguments developed by F. R. Tennant, C. S. Lewis, E. L. Mascall, Basil Mitchell, Richard Swinburne, and others? What about the ontological argument in its contemporary versions?[10] Do none of these provide evidence? Notice: the question is not whether these arguments, taken singly or in combinations, constitute *proofs* of God's existence; no doubt they do not. The question is only whether someone might be rationally justified in believing in the existence of God on the basis of the alleged evidence offered by them; and that is a radically different question.

At present, however, I am interested in the objector's other premise – the claim that it is irrational or unreasonable to accept theistic belief in the absence of evidence or reasons. Why suppose *that* is true? Why should we think a theist must have evidence, or reason to think there *is* evidence, if he is not to be irrational? Why not suppose, instead, that he is entirely within his epistemic rights in believing in God's existence even if he has no argument or evidence at all? This is what I want to investigate. Suppose we begin by asking what the objector means by describing a belief as *irrational*. What is the force of his claim that theistic belief is irrational, and how is it to be understood? The first thing to see is that this objection is rooted in a *normative* view. It lays down conditions that must be met by anyone whose system of beliefs is *rational*, and here "rational" is to be taken as a normative or evaluative term. According to the objector there is a right way and a wrong way with respect to belief. People have responsibilities, duties, and obligations with respect to their believings just as with respect to their actions, or if we think believings are a kind of action, their *other* actions. Professor Brand Blanshard puts this clearly:

> everywhere and always belief has an ethical aspect. There is such a thing as a general ethics of the intellect. The main principle of that ethic I hold to be the same inside and outside religion. This principle is simple and sweeping: Equate your assent to the evidence.[11]

and according to Michael Scriven:

> Now even belief in something for which there is no evidence, i.e., a belief which goes beyond the evidence, although a lesser sin than belief in something which is contrary to well-established laws, is plainly irrational in that it simply amounts to attaching belief where it is not justified. So the proper alternative, when there is no evidence, is not mere suspension of belief, e.g., about Santa Claus; it is disbelief. It most certainly is not faith.[12]

Perhaps this sort of obligation is really just a special case of a more general moral obligation; perhaps, on the other hand, it is unique and *sui generis*. In any event, says the objector, there are such obligations: to conform to them is to be rational and to go against them is to be irrational.

Now here what the objector says seems plausible; there do seem to be duties and obligations with respect to belief, or at any rate in the general *neighborhood* of belief. One's own welfare and that of others sometimes depends on what one believes. If we are descending the Grand Teton and I am setting the anchor for the 120-foot rappel into the Upper Saddle, I have an obligation to form such beliefs as *this anchor point is solid* only after careful scrutiny and testing. One commissioned to gather intelligence – the spies Joshua sent into Canaan, for example – has an obligation to get it right. I have an obligation with respect to the belief that Justin Martyr was a Greek apologist – an obligation arising from the fact that I teach medieval philosophy, must make a declaration on this issue, and am obliged not to mislead my students here. The

precise nature of these obligations may be hard to specify: What exactly *is* my obligation here? Am I obliged to believe that Justin Martyr was a Greek apologist if and only if Justin Martyr *was* a Greek apologist? Or to form a belief on this topic only after the appropriate amount of checking and investigating? Or maybe just to tell the students the truth about it, whatever I myself believe in the privacy of my own study? Or to tell them what is generally thought by those who should know? In the rappel case, do I have a duty to believe that the anchor point is solid if and only if it is? Or only only if it is? Or just to check carefully before forming the belief? Or perhaps there is no obligation to *believe* at all, but instead an obligation to *act on* a certain belief only after appropriate investigation. In any event, it seems plausible to hold that there are obligations and norms with respect to belief, and I do not intend to contest this assumption.

Now perhaps the evidentialist objector thinks there are intellectual obligations of the following sorts. With respect to certain kinds of propositions perhaps I have a duty not to believe them unless I have evidence for them. Perhaps I have a duty not to accept the denial of an apparently self-evident proposition unless I can see that it conflicts with other propositions that seem self-evident. Perhaps I have a duty to accept such a proposition as *I see a tree* under certain conditions that are hard to spell out in detail but include at least my entertaining that proposition and my having a certain characteristic sort of visual experience along with no reason to think my perceptual apparatus is malfunctioning.

Of course these obligations would be *prima facie* obligations; in special sorts of circumstances they could be overridden by other obligations. I have an obligation not to take bread from the grocery store without permission and another to tell the truth. Both sorts of obligation can be overridden, in specific circumstances, by other obligations – in the first case, perhaps, an obligation to feed my starving children and in the second (when the Nazis are pounding on the door) an obligation to protect a human life. So we must distinguish *prima facie* duties or obligations from *all-things-considered* or *on-balance* (*ultima facie*?) obligations. I have a *prima facie* obligation to tell the truth; in a given situation, however, that obligation may be overridden by others, so that my duty, all things considered, is to tell a lie. This is the grain of truth contained in situation ethics and the ill-named "new morality."

And *prima facie* intellectual obligations, like obligations of other sorts, can conflict. Perhaps I have a *prima facie* obligation to believe what seems to me self-evident, and what seems to me to follow self-evidently from what seems to me self-evident. But what if, as in the Russell paradoxes, something that seems self-evidently false apparently follows, self-evidently, from what seems self-evidently true? Here *prima facie* intellectual obligations conflict, and no matter what I do, I will violate a *prima facie* obligation. Another example: in reporting the Grand Teton rappel I neglected to mention the violent electrical storm coming in from the southwest; to escape it we must get off in a hurry, so that I have a *prima facie* obligation to inspect the anchor point carefully, but another to set up the rappel rapidly, which means I cannot spend a lot of time inspecting the anchor point.

Thus lightly armed, suppose we return to the evidentialist objector. Does he mean to hold that the theist without evidence is violating some intellectual obligation? If so, which one? Does he claim, for example, that the theist is violating his all-things-considered intellectual obligation in thus believing? Perhaps he thinks anyone who believes in God without evidence is violating his all-things-considered intellectual duty. This, however, seems unduly harsh. What about the 14-year-old theist brought up to believe in God in a community where everyone believes? This 14-year-old theist, we may suppose, does not believe in God on the basis of evidence. He has never heard of the cosmological, teleological, or ontological arguments; in fact no one has ever presented him with any evidence at all. And although he has often been told about God, he does not take that testimony as evidence; he does not reason thus: everyone around here says God loves us and cares for us; most of what everyone around here says is true; so probably *that is* true. Instead, he simply believes what he is taught. Is he violating an all-things-considered intellectual duty? Surely not. And what about the mature theist – Thomas Aquinas, let us say – who thinks he *does* have adequate evidence? Let us suppose he is wrong; let us suppose all of his arguments are failures. Nevertheless he has reflected long, hard, and conscientiously on the matter and thinks he *does* have adequate evidence. Shall we suppose he is violating an all-things-considered intellectual duty here? I should think not. So construed, the objector's contention is totally implausible.

Perhaps, then, the objector is to be understood as claiming that there is a *prima facie* intellectual duty not to believe in God without evidence. This duty can be overridden by circumstances, of course, but there is a *prima facie* obligation to believe propositions of this sort only on the basis of evidence. The theist without evidence, he adds, is flouting this obligation and is therefore not living up to his intellectual obligations. But here too there are problems. The suggestion is that I now have the *prima facie* duty to comply with the following command: either have evidence or do not believe. But this may be a command I cannot obey. I may not know of any way to acquire evidence for this proposition; and of course if the objector is right, there is no adequate evidence for it. But it is also not within my power to refrain from believing this proposition. My beliefs are not for the most part directly within my control. If you order me now, for example, to cease believing that the earth is very old, there is no way I can comply with your order. But in the same way it is not now within my power to cease believing in God now. So this alleged *prima facie* duty is one such that it is not within my power to comply with it. But how can I have a duty, *prima facie* or otherwise, to do what it is not within my power to do?

Can I have intellectual obligations if my beliefs are not within my control? This is a difficult and vexing question. The suggestion here is that I cannot now have a *prima facie* obligation to comply with a command which it is not now within my power to obey. Since what I believe is not normally within my power, I cannot have an obligation to believe a certain proposition or to refrain from believing it; but then, *contra* the objector, I do not have an obligation to refrain from believing in God if I have no evidence. This response to the objector is, I think, inadequate. In the first place the response is unbecoming from the theist, since many of those who believe in God follow St Paul (for example, Romans 1) in holding that under certain circumstances failure to believe in God is culpable. And there are cases where most of us – theist and nontheist alike – do in fact believe that a person is culpable or condemnable for holding a given belief, as well as cases where we hold a person responsible for *not* accepting certain beliefs. Consider the following. Suppose someone comes to believe that Jews are inferior, in some important way, to Gentiles. Suppose he goes on to conclude that Jews should not be permitted to share public facilities such as restaurants and hotels with the rest of us. Further reflection leads him to the view that they should not be provided with the protection of law and that the rest of us have a right to expropriate their property if that is convenient. Finally, he concludes that they ought to be eliminated in order to preserve the purity of the alleged Aryan race. After soul-searching inquiry he apparently believes in all honesty that it is his duty to do what he can to see that this view is put into practice. A convincing sort, he gets the rest of us to see things his way: we join him in his pogroms, and his policy succeeds.

Now many of us will agree that such a person is culpable and guilty. But wherein does his guilt consist? Not, presumably, in doing what he believes he ought to do, in trying to carry out his duty as he sees it. Suppose, to vary the example, he tries to encourage and institute these abhorrent policies at considerable cost to himself: he loses his job; his friends turn their backs on him; he is finally arrested and thrown into prison. Nonetheless he valiantly persists. Does he not deserve moral *credit* for doing what he sees as his duty? His guilt, surely, does not consist solely in his taking the *actions* he takes; at least part of the guilt lies in accepting those abhorrent views. If he *had not* acted on his beliefs – out of fear of the consequences, perhaps – would he not have been guilty nonetheless? He would not have caused as much trouble, but would he not have been guilty? I should think so. We do in fact sometimes think that a person is guilty – has violated norms or obligations – by virtue of the beliefs he holds.

The theist, accordingly, should not reply to the evidentialist objector by claiming that since our beliefs are not within our control, we cannot have a *prima facie* duty to refrain from believing certain propositions. But there is a second reason why this response to the evidentialist is inadequate. I have been using the terms "accept" and "believe" interchangeably, but in fact there is an important distinction they can nicely be used to mark. This distinction is extremely hard to make clear but nonetheless, I think, important. Perhaps we can make an initial stab at it as follows. Consider a Christian beset by doubts. He has a hard time believing certain crucial Christian claims – perhaps the teaching that God was in Christ, reconciling the world to himself. Upon calling that belief to mind, he finds it cold, lifeless, without warmth or attractiveness. Nonetheless he is committed to this belief; it is his position; if you ask him what he thinks about it, he will unhesitatingly endorse it. He has, so to speak, thrown in his lot with it. Let us say that he *accepts*

this proposition, even though when he is assailed by doubt, he may fail to *believe* it – at any rate explicitly – to any appreciable degree. His commitment to this proposition may be much stronger than his explicit and occurrent belief in it; so these two – that is, acceptance and belief – must be distinguished.

Take another example. A person may accept the proposition that alleged moral distinctions are unreal, and our tendency to make them is a confused and superstitious remnant of the infancy of our race – while nonetheless sometimes finding himself compelled to believe, for example, that gross injustice is wicked. Such a person adopts as his position the proposition that moral distinctions are unreal, and he accepts that proposition; but (at certain times and in certain conditions) he cannot help believing, *malgré lui*, that such distinctions are not unreal. In the same way, someone with solipsistic inclination – acquired, perhaps, by an incautious reading of Hume – could *accept* the proposition that, say, there really is no external world – no houses, horses, trucks, or trees – but find himself, under certain conditions, regularly believing that there are such things.

Now I am quite aware that I have not been able to make this distinction between acceptance and belief wholly clear. I think there is such a distinction in the neighborhood, however, and I believe it is important. It is furthermore one the objector may be able to make use of; for while it is plausible to hold that what I believe is not within my direct control, it is also plausible to suppose that what I *accept* is or can be at least in part a matter of deliberate decision, a matter of voluntarily taking up a certain position. But then the objector can perhaps restate his objection in terms of *acceptance*. Perhaps (because of an unfortunate upbringing, let us say) I cannot refrain from believing in God. Nevertheless it is within my power, says the evidentialist objector, to refuse to *accept* that proposition. And now his claim that there are duties with respect to our beliefs may be reconstrued as the claim that we have *prima facie* duties with respect to our acceptances, one of these duties being not to accept such a proposition as *there is such a person as God* in the absence of evidence.

Finally, while we may perhaps agree that what I believe is not *directly* within my control, some of my beliefs are indirectly within my control, at least in part. First, what I accept has a long-term influence upon what I believe. If I refuse to accept belief in God, and if I try to ignore or suppress my tendency to believe, then perhaps eventually I will no longer believe. And as Pascal pointed out, there are other ways to influence one's beliefs. Presumably, then, the evidentialist objector could hold that it is my *prima facie* duty not to accept belief in God without evidence, and to do what I can to bring it about that I no longer believe. Although it is not within my power now to cease believing now, there may be a series of actions, such that I can now take the first and, after taking the first, will be able to take the second, and so on; and after taking the whole series of actions I will no longer believe in God. Perhaps the objector thinks it is my *prima facie* duty to undertake whatever sort of regimen will at some time in the future result in my not believing without evidence. Perhaps I should attend a Universalist-Unitarian church, for example, and consort with members of the Rationalist Society of America. Perhaps I should read a lot of Voltaire and Bertrand Russell and Thomas Paine, eschewing St Augustine and C. S. Lewis and, of course, the Bible. Even if I cannot now stop believing without evidence, perhaps there are other actions I can take, such that if I were to take them, then at some time in the future I will not be in this deplorable condition.

So far, then, we have been construing the evidentialist objector as holding that the theist without sufficient evidence – evidence in the sense of other propositions that prove or make probable or support the existence of God – is violating a *prima facie* intellectual obligation of some sort. As we have seen, the fact that belief is not within direct control may give him pause; he is not, however, without plausible replies. But the fact is there is a quite different way of construing the evidentialist objection; the objector need not hold that the theist without evidence is violating or has violated some duty, *prima facie*, *ultima facie*, or otherwise. Consider someone who believes that Venus is smaller than Mercury, not because he has evidence, but because he read it in a comic book and always believes everything he reads – or consider someone who holds this belief on the basis of an outrageously bad argument. Perhaps there is no obligation he has failed to meet; nevertheless his intellectual condition is defective in some way; or perhaps alternatively there is a commonly achieved excellence he fails to display. Perhaps he is like someone who is easily gulled, or has a serious astigmatism, or is unduly clumsy. And perhaps the evidentialist objection is to be understood, not as the claim that the theist without evidence has failed

to meet some obligation, but that he suffers from a certain sort of intellectual deficiency. If this is the objector's view, then his proper attitude toward the theist would be one of sympathy rather than censure.

But of course the crucial question here is this: Why does the objector think these things? Why does he think there *is* a *prima facie* obligation to try not to believe in God without evidence? Or why does he think that to do so is to be in a deplorable condition? Why is it not permissible and quite satisfactory to believe in God without any evidence – proof or argument – at all? Presumably the objector does not mean to suggest that *no* propositions can be believed or accepted without evidence, for if you have evidence for *every* proposition you believe, then (granted certain plausible assumptions about the formal properties of the evidence relation) you will believe infinitely many propositions; and no one has time, these busy days, for that. So presumably *some* propositions can properly be believed and accepted without evidence. Well, why not belief in God? Why is it not entirely acceptable, desirable, right, proper, and rational to accept belief in God without any argument or evidence whatever?

Part II: Foundationalism

In this section I shall give what I take to be the evidentialist objector's answer to these questions; I shall argue that his answer is not in the least compelling and that the prospects for his project are not bright. [. . .]

The evidentialist objectors [hold] that belief in God is rationally acceptable only if there is evidence for it – only if, that is, it is probable with respect to some body of propositions that constitutes the evidence. And here we can get a better understanding of the evidentialist objectors if we see them as accepting some version of *classical foundationalism*. This is a *picture* or total way of looking at faith, knowledge, justified belief, rationality, and allied topics. This picture has been enormously popular in Western thought; and despite a substantial opposing groundswell, I think it remains the dominant way of thinking about these topics. According to the foundationalist some propositions are properly basic and some are not; those that are not are rationally accepted only on the basis of *evidence*, where the evidence must trace back, ultimately, to what *is* properly basic. The existence of God, furthermore, is not among the propositions that are properly basic; hence a person is rational in accepting theistic belief only if he has evidence for it. The vast majority of those in the Western world who have thought about our topic have accepted some form of classical foundationalism. The evidentialist objection to belief in God, furthermore, is obviously rooted in this way of looking at things. So suppose we try to achieve a deeper understanding of it.

Earlier I said the first thing to see about the evidentialist objection is that it is a *normative* contention or claim. The same thing must be said about foundationalism: this thesis is a normative thesis, a thesis about how a system of beliefs *ought* to be structured, a thesis about the properties of a correct, or acceptable, or rightly structured system of beliefs. According to the foundationalist there are norms, or duties, or obligations with respect to belief just as there are with respect to actions. To conform to these duties and obligations is to be rational; to fail to measure up to them is to be irrational. To be rational, then, is to exercise one's epistemic powers *properly* – to exercise them in such a way as to go contrary to none of the norms for such exercise.

I think we can understand foundationalism more fully if we introduce the idea of a *noetic structure*. A person's noetic structure is the set of propositions he believes, together with certain epistemic relations that hold among him and these propositions. As we have seen, some of my beliefs may be based upon others; it may be that there are a pair of propositions *A* and *B* such that I believe *B*, and believe *A on the basis of B*. An account of a person's noetic structure, then, would specify which of his beliefs are basic and which nonbasic. Of course it is abstractly possible that *none* of his beliefs is basic; perhaps he holds just three beliefs, *A*, *B*, and *C*, and believes each of them on the basis of the other two. We might think this improper or irrational, but that is not to say it could not be done. And it is also possible that *all* of his beliefs are basic; perhaps he believes a lot of propositions but does not believe any of them on the basis of any others. In the typical case, however, a noetic structure will include both basic and nonbasic beliefs. It may be useful to give some examples of beliefs that are often basic for a person. Suppose I seem to see a tree; I have that characteristic sort of experience that goes with perceiving a tree. I may then believe the proposition that I see a tree. It is *possible* that I believe that proposition *on the basis of* the proposition that

I seem to see a tree; in the typical case, however, I will not believe the former on the basis of the latter because in the typical case I will not believe the latter at all. I will not be paying any attention to my experience but will be concentrating on the tree. Of course I *can* turn my attention to my experience, notice how things look to me, and acquire the belief that I seem to see something that looks like *that*; and if you challenge my claim that I see a tree, perhaps I *will* thus turn my attention to my experience. But in the typical case I will not believe that I see a tree on the basis of a proposition about my experience; for I believe *A* on the basis of *B* only if I believe *B*, and in the typical case where I perceive a tree I do not believe (or entertain) any propositions about my experience. Typically I take such a proposition as basic. Similarly, I believe I had breakfast this morning; this too is basic for me. I do not believe this proposition on the basis of some proposition about my experience – for example, that I seem to remember having had breakfast. In the typical case I will not have even considered *that* question – the question whether I *seem* to remember having had breakfast; instead I simply believe that I had breakfast; I take it as basic.

Second, an account of a noetic structure will include what we might call an index of *degree* of belief. I hold some of my beliefs much more firmly than others. I believe both that $2 + 1 = 3$ and that London, England, is north of Saskatoon, Saskatchewan; but I believe the former more resolutely than the latter. Some beliefs I hold with maximum firmness; others I do in fact accept, but in a much more tentative way.

Third, a somewhat vaguer notion: an account of S's noetic structure would include something like an index of *depth of ingression*. Some of my beliefs are, we might say, on the periphery of my noetic structure. I accept them, and may even accept them firmly, but I could give them up without much change elsewhere in my noetic structure. I believe there are some large boulders on the top of the Grand Teton. If I come to give up this belief (say by climbing it and not finding any), that change need not have extensive reverberations throughout the rest of my noetic structure; it could be accommodated with minimal alteration elsewhere. So its depth of ingression into my noetic structure is not great. On the other hand, if I were to come to believe that there simply is no such thing as the Grand Teton, or no mountains at all, or no such thing as the state of Wyoming, that would have much greater reverberations. And suppose I were to come to think there had not been much of a past (that the world was created just five minutes ago, complete with all its apparent memories and traces of the past) or that there were not any other persons: these changes would have even greater reverberations; these beliefs of mine have great depth of ingression into my noetic structure.

Now foundationalism is best construed, I think, as a thesis about *rational* noetic structures. A noetic structure is rational if it could be the noetic structure of a person who was completely rational. To be completely rational, as I am here using the term, is not to believe only what is true, or to believe all the logical consequences of what one believes, or to believe all necessary truths with equal firmness, or to be uninfluenced by emotion in forming belief; it is, instead, to do the right thing with respect to one's believings. It is to violate no epistemic duties. From this point of view, a rational person is one whose believings meet the appropriate standards; to criticize a person as irrational is to criticize her for failing to fulfill these duties or responsibilities, for failing to conform to the relevant norms or standards. To draw the ethical analogy, the irrational is the impermissible; the rational is the permissible.

A rational noetic structure, then, is one that could be the noetic structure of a wholly rational person; and foundationalism, as I say, is a thesis about such noetic structures. We may think of the foundationalist as beginning with the observation that some of our beliefs are based upon others. According to the foundationalist a rational noetic structure will *have a foundation* – a set of beliefs not accepted on the basis of others; in a rational noetic structure some beliefs will be basic. Nonbasic beliefs, of course, will be accepted on the basis of other beliefs, which may be accepted on the basis of still other beliefs, and so on until the foundations are reached. In a rational noetic structure, therefore, every nonbasic belief is ultimately accepted on the basis of basic beliefs.

According to the foundationalist, therefore, every rational noetic structure has a foundation, and all nonbasic beliefs are ultimately accepted on the basis of beliefs in the foundations. But a belief cannot properly be accepted on the basis of just *any* other belief; in a rational noetic structure, A will be accepted on the basis of B only if B *supports* A or is a member of a set of beliefs that together support A. It is not clear just what this relation – call it the "supports" relation – is; and

different foundationalists propose different candidates. Presumably, however, it lies in the neighborhood of *evidence*; if A supports B, then A is evidence for B, or makes B evident; or perhaps B is likely or probable with respect to A. This relation admits of degrees. My belief that Feike can swim is supported by my knowledge that nine out of ten Frisians can swim and Feike is a Frisian; it is supported more strongly by my knowledge that the evening paper contains a picture of Feike triumphantly finishing first in the fifteen-hundred meter freestyle in the 1980 summer Olympics. And the foundationalist holds, sensibly enough, that in a rational noetic structure the strength of a nonbasic belief will depend upon the degree of support from foundational beliefs.

By way of summary, then, let us say that according to foundationalism: (1) in a rational noetic structure the believed-on-the-basis-of relation is asymmetric and irreflexive, (2) a rational noetic structure has a foundation, and (3) in a rational noetic structure nonbasic belief is proportional in strength to support from the foundations.

Conditions on proper basicality

Next we note a further and fundamental feature of classic varieties of foundationalism: they all lay down certain conditions of proper basicality. From the foundationalist point of view not just any kind of belief can be found in the foundations of a rational noetic structure; a belief to be properly basic (that is, basic in a rational noetic structure) must meet certain conditions. It must be capable of functioning foundationally, capable of bearing its share of the weight of the whole noetic structure. Thus Thomas Aquinas, [for example], holds that a proposition is properly basic for a person only if it is self-evident to him or "evident to the senses."

Suppose we take a brief look at self-evidence. Under what conditions does a proposition have it? What kinds of propositions are self-evident? Examples would include very simple arithmetical truths such as

(1) $2 + 1 = 3$;

simple truths of logic such as

(2) No man is both married and unmarried;

perhaps the generalizations of simple truths of logic, such as

(3) For any proposition p the conjunction of p with its denial is false;

and certain propositions expressing identity and diversity; for example,

(4) Redness is distinct from greenness,
(5) The property of being prime is distinct from the property of being composite,

and

(6) The proposition *all men are mortal* is distinct from the proposition *all mortals are men.*

There are others; Aquinas gives as examples:

(7) The whole is greater than the part,

where, presumably, he means by "part" what we mean by "proper part," and, more dubiously,

(8) Man is an animal.

Still other candidates – candidates which may be less than entirely uncontroversial – come from many other areas; for example,

(9) If p is necessarily true and p entails q, then q is necessarily true,
(10) If e^1 occurs before e^2 and e^2 occurs before e^3, then e^1 occurs before e^3,

and

(11) It is wrong to cause unnecessary (and unwanted) pain just for the fun of it.

What is it that characterizes these propositions? According to the tradition the outstanding characteristic of a self-evident proposition is that one simply sees it to be true upon grasping or understanding it. Understanding a self-evident proposition is sufficient for apprehending its truth. Of course this notion must be relativized to *persons*; what is self-evident to you might not be to me. Very simple arithmetical truths will be self-evident to nearly all of us, but a truth like $17 + 18 = 35$ may be self-evident only to some. And of course a proposition is self-evident to a person only if he does in fact grasp it, so a proposition will not be self-evident to those who do not apprehend the concepts it involves. As Aquinas says, some propositions are self-evident only to the learned; his example is the truth that immaterial substances do not occupy space. Among those propositions whose concepts not everyone grasps, some are such that anyone who *did* grasp them would see their truth; for example,

(12) A model of a first-order theory T assigns truth to the axioms of T.

Others – $17 + 13 = 30$, for example – may be such that some but not all of those who apprehend them also see that they are true.

But how shall we understand this "seeing that they are true"? Those who speak of self-evidence explicitly turn to this visual metaphor and expressly explain self-evidence by reference to vision. There are two important aspects to the metaphor and two corresponding components to the idea of self-evidence. First, there is the *epistemic* component: a proposition p is self-evident to a person S only if S has *immediate* knowledge of p – that is, knows p, and does not know p on the basis of his knowledge of other propositions. Consider a simple arithmetic truth such as $2 + 1 = 3$ and compare it with one like $24 \times 24 = 576$. I know each of these propositions, and I know the second but not the first on the basis of computation, which is a kind of inference. So I have immediate knowledge of the first but not the second.

But there is also a phenomenological component. Consider again our two propositions; the first but not the second has about it a kind of luminous aura or glow when you bring it to mind or consider it. Locke speaks, in this connection, of an "evident luster"; a self-evident proposition, he says, displays a kind of "clarity and brightness to the attentive mind." Descartes speaks instead of "clarity and distinctness"; each, I think, is referring to the same phenomenological feature. And this feature is connected with another: upon understanding a proposition of this sort one feels a strong inclination to accept it; this luminous obviousness seems to compel or at least impel assent. Aquinas and Locke, indeed, held that a person, or at any rate a normal, well-formed human being, finds it impossible to withhold assent when considering a self-evident proposition. The phenomenological component of the idea of self-evidence, then, seems to have a double aspect: there is the luminous aura that $2 + 1 = 3$ displays, and there is also an experienced tendency to accept or believe it. Perhaps, indeed, the luminous aura *just is* the experienced impulsion toward acceptance; perhaps these are the very same thing. In that case the phenomenological component would not have the double aspect I suggested it did have; in either case, however, we must recognize this phenomenological aspect of self-evidence.

Aquinas therefore holds that self-evident propositions are properly basic. I think he means to add that propositions "evident to the senses" are also properly basic. By this latter term I think he means to refer to *perceptual* propositions – propositions whose truth or falsehood we can determine by looking or employing some other sense. He has in mind, I think, such propositions as

(13)   There is a tree before me,
(14)   I am wearing shoes,

and

(15)   That tree's leaves are yellow.

So Aquinas holds that a proposition is properly basic if and only if it is either self-evident or evident to the senses. Other foundationalists have insisted that propositions basic in a rational noetic structure must be *certain* in some important sense. Thus it is plausible to see Descartes as holding that the foundations of a rational noetic structure include, not such propositions as (13)–(15), but more cautious claims – claims about one's own mental life; for example,

(16)   It seems to me that I see a tree,
(17)   I seem to see something green,

or, as Professor Chisholm puts it,

(18)   I am appeared greenly to.

Propositions of this latter sort seem to enjoy a kind of immunity from error not enjoyed by those of the former. I could be mistaken in thinking I see a pink rat; perhaps I am hallucinating or the victim of an illusion. But it is at the least very much harder to see that I could be mistaken in believing that I *seem* to see a pink rat, in believing that I am appeared pinkly (or pink ratly) to. Suppose we say that a proposition with respect to which I enjoy this sort of immunity from error is incorrigible for me; then perhaps Descartes means to hold that a proposition is properly basic for S only if it is either self-evident or incorrigible for S.

By way of explicit definition:

(19) p is incorrigible for S if and only if (a) it is not possible that S believe p and p be false, and (b) it is not possible that S believe $\sim p$ and p be true.

Here we have a further characteristic of foundationalism: the claim that not just any proposition is properly basic. Ancient and medieval foundationalists tended to hold that a proposition is properly basic for a person only if it is either self-evident or evident to the senses: modern foundationalists – Descartes, Locke, Leibniz, and the like – tended to hold that a proposition is properly basic for S only if either self-evident or incorrigible for S. Of course this is a historical generalization and is thus perilous; but perhaps it is worth the risk. And now let us say that a *classical foundationalist* is anyone who is either an ancient and medieval or a modern foundationalist.

The collapse of foundationalism

Now suppose we return to the main question: Why should not belief in God be among the foundations of my noetic structure? The answer, on the part of the classical foundationalist, was that even if this belief is *true* it does not have the characteristics a proposition must have to deserve a place in the foundations. There is no room in the foundations for a proposition that can be rationally accepted only on the basis of other propositions. The only properly basic propositions are those that are self-evident or incorrigible or evident to the senses. Since the proposition that God exists is none of the above, it is not properly basic for anyone; that is, no well-formed, rational noetic structure contains this proposition in its foundations. But now we must take a closer look at this fundamental principle of classical foundationalism:

(20)   A proposition p is properly basic for a person S if and only if p is either self-evident to S or incorrigible for S or evident to the senses for S.

(20) contains two claims: first, a proposition is properly basic *if* it is self-evident, incorrigible, or evident to the senses, and, second, a proposition is properly basic *only if* it meets this condition. The first seems true enough; suppose we concede it. But what is to be said for the second? Is there any reason to accept it? Why does the foundationalist accept it? Why does he think the theist ought to?

(211)

We should note first that if this thesis, and the correlative foundationalist thesis that a proposition is rationally acceptable only if it follows from or is probable with respect to what is properly basic – if these claims are true, then enormous quantities of what we all in fact believe are irrational. One crucial lesson to be learned from the development of modern philosophy – Descartes through Hume, roughly – is just this: relative to propositions that are self-evident and incorrigible, most of the beliefs that form the stock in trade of ordinary everyday life are not probable – at any rate there is no reason to think they are probable. Consider all those propositions that entail, say, that there are enduring physical objects, or that there are persons distinct from myself, or that the world has existed for more than five minutes: none of these propositions, I think, is more probable than not with respect to what is self-evident or incorrigible for me; at any rate no one has given good reason to think any of them is. And now suppose we add to the foundations propositions that are evident to the senses, thereby moving from modern to ancient and medieval foundationalism. Then propositions entailing the existence of material objects will of course be probable with respect to the foundations, because included therein. But the same cannot be said either for propositions about the past or for propositions entailing the existence of persons distinct from myself; as before, these will not be probable with respect to what is properly basic.

And does not this show that the thesis in question is false? The contention is that

(21) *A* is properly basic for me only if *A* is self-evident or incorrigible or evident to the senses for me.

But many propositions that do not meet these conditions *are* properly basic for me. I believe, for example, that I had lunch this noon. I do not believe this proposition on the basis of other propositions; I take it as basic; it is in the foundations of my noetic structure. Furthermore, I am entirely rational in so taking it, even though this proposition is neither self-evident nor evident to the senses nor incorrigible for me. Of course this may not convince the foundationalist; he may think that in fact I do *not* take that proposition as basic, or perhaps he will bite the bullet and maintain that if I really *do* take it as basic, then the fact is I *am*, so far forth, irrational.

Perhaps the following will be more convincing. According to the classical foundationalist (call him *F*) a person *S* is rational in accepting (21) only if either (21) is properly basic (self-evident or incorrigible or evident to the senses) for him, or he believes (21) on the basis of propositions that are properly basic for him and support (21). Now presumably if *F* knows of some support for (21) from propositions that are self-evident or evident to the senses or incorrigible, he will be able to provide a good argument – deductive, inductive, probabilistic or whatever – whose premises are self-evident or evident to the senses or incorrigible and whose conclusion is (21). So far as I know, no foundationalist has provided such an argument. It therefore appears that the foundationalist does not know of any support for (21) from propositions that are (on his account) properly basic. So if he is to be rational in accepting (21), he must (on his own account) accept it as basic. But according to (21) itself, (21) is properly basic for *F* only if (21) is self-evident or incorrigible or evident to the senses for him. Clearly (21) meets none of these conditions. Hence it is not properly basic for *F*. But then *F* is self-referentially inconsistent in accepting (21); he accepts (21) as basic, despite the fact that (21) does not meet the condition for proper basicality that (21) itself lays down.

Furthermore, (21) is either false or such that in accepting it the foundationalist is violating his epistemic responsibilities. For *F* does not know of any argument or evidence for (21). Hence if it is true, he will be violating his epistemic responsibilities in accepting it. So (21) is either false or such that *F* cannot rationally accept it. Still further, if the theist were to accept (21) at the foundationalist's urging but without argument, he would be adding to his noetic structure a proposition that is either false or such that in accepting it he violates his noetic responsibilities. But if there is such a thing as the ethics of belief, surely it will proscribe believing a proposition one knows to be either false or such that one ought not to believe it. Accordingly, I ought not to accept (21) in the absence of argument from premises that meet the condition it lays down. The same goes for the foundationalist: if he cannot find such an argument for (21), he ought to give it up. Furthermore, he ought not to urge and I ought not to accept any objection to theistic belief that crucially depends upon a proposition that is true only if I ought not to believe it.

Nearly everyone accepts as basic some propositions entailing the existence of other persons and some propositions about the past; not nearly everyone accepts the existence of God as basic. Struck by this fact, we might propose:

(22) p is properly basic for S if and only if p is self-evident or incorrigible or evident to the senses for S, or is accepted as basic by nearly everyone.

There are problems with (22). It is meant to legitimize my taking as basic such deliverances of memory as that I had lunch this noon; but not nearly everyone takes that proposition as basic. Most of you, I daresay, have not so much as given it a thought; you are much too busy thinking about your own lunch to think about mine. So (22) will not do the job as it stands. That is of no real consequence, however; for even if we had an appropriate statement of (22), it would suffer from the same sort of malady as does (21). Not nearly everyone takes (22) as basic; I do not, for example. Nor is it self-evident, incorrigible, or evident to the senses. So unless we can find an argument for it from propositions that meet the conditions it lays down, we shall, if we believe it, be believing a proposition that is probably either false or such that we ought not to believe it. Therefore we ought not to believe it, at least until someone produces such an argument for it.

Now we could continue to canvass other revisions of (21), and in Part III I shall look into the proper procedure for discovering and justifying such criteria for proper basicality. It is evident, however, that classical foundationalism is bankrupt, and insofar as the evidentialist objection is rooted in classical foundationalism, it is poorly rooted indeed.

Of course the evidentialist objection *need* not presuppose classical foundationalism; someone who accepted quite a different version of foundationalism could no doubt urge this objection. But in order to evaluate it, we should have to see what criterion of proper basicality was being invoked. In the absence of such specification the objection remains at best a promissory note. So far as the present discussion goes, then, the next move is up to the evidentialist objector. He must specify a criterion for proper basicality that is free from self-referential difficulties, rules out belief in God as properly basic, and is such that there is some reason to think it is true.

Part III: The reformed objection to natural theology

Suppose we think of natural theology as the attempt to prove or demonstrate the existence of God. This enterprise has a long and impressive history – a history stretching back to the dawn of Christendom and boasting among its adherents many of the truly great thinkers of the Western world. One thinks, for example, of Anselm, Aquinas, Scotus, and Ockham, of Descartes, Spinoza, and Leibniz. Recently – since the time of Kant, perhaps – the tradition of natural theology has not been as overwhelming as it once was; yet it continues to have able defenders both within and without officially Catholic philosophy.

Many Christians, however, have been less than totally impressed. In particular Reformed or Calvinist theologians have for the most part taken a dim view of this enterprise. A few Reformed thinkers – B. B. Warfield, for example – endorse the theistic proofs, but for the most part the Reformed attitude has ranged from tepid endorsement, through indifference, to suspicion, hostility, and outright accusations of blasphemy. And this stance is initially puzzling. It looks a little like the attitude some Christians adopt toward faith healing: it can't be done, but even if it could it shouldn't be. What exactly, or even approximately, do these sons and daughters of the Reformation have against proving the existence of God? What *could* they have against it? What could be less objectionable to any but the most obdurate atheist?

The objection initially stated

By way of answering this question, I want to consider three representative Reformed thinkers. Let us begin with the nineteenth-century Dutch theologian Herman Bavinck:

> A distinct natural theology, obtained apart from any revelation, merely through observation and study of the universe in which man lives, does not exist. . . .
>
> Scripture urges us to behold heaven and earth, birds and ants, flowers and lilies, in order that we may see and recognize God in them. "Lift up your eyes on high, and see who hath created these" (Is. 40: 26). Scripture does not reason in the abstract. It does not make God the conclusion of a syllogism, leaving it to us whether we

think the argument holds or not. But it speaks with authority. Both theologically and religiously it proceeds from God as the starting point.

We receive the impression that belief in the existence of God is based entirely upon these proofs. But indeed that would be "a wretched faith, which, before it invokes God, must first prove his existence." The contrary, however, is the truth. There is not a single object the existence of which we hesitate to accept until definite proofs are furnished. Of the existence of self, of the world round about us, of logical and moral laws, etc., we are so deeply convinced because of the indelible impressions which all these things make upon our consciousness that we need no arguments or demonstration. Spontaneously, altogether involuntarily: without any constraint or coercion, we accept that existence. Now the same is true in regard to the existence of God. The so-called proofs are by no means the final grounds of our most certain conviction that God exists. This certainty is established only by faith; that is, by the spontaneous testimony which forces itself upon us from every side.[13]

According to Bavinck, then, belief in the existence of God is not based upon proofs or arguments. By "argument" here I think he means arguments in the style of natural theology – the sort given by Aquinas and Scotus and later by Descartes, Leibniz, Clarke, and others. And what he means to say, I think, is that Christians do not *need* such arguments. Do not need them for what?

Here I think Bavinck means to hold two things. First, arguments or proofs are not, in general, the source of the believer's confidence in God. Typically the believer does not believe in God on the basis of arguments; nor does he believe such truths as that God has created the world on the basis of arguments. Second, argument is not needed for *rational justification*; the believer is entirely within his epistemic right in believing, for example, that God has created the world, even if he has no argument at all for that conclusion. The believer does not need natural theology in order to achieve rationality or epistemic propriety in believing; his belief in God can be perfectly rational even if he knows of no cogent argument, deductive or inductive, for the existence of God – indeed, even if there is no such argument.

Bavinck has three further points. First he means to add, I think, that we cannot come to knowledge of God on the basis of argument; the arguments of natural theology just do not work. (And he follows this passage with a more or less traditional attempt to refute the theistic proofs, including an endorsement of some of Kant's fashionable confusions about the ontological argument.) Second, Scripture "proceeds from God as the starting point," and so should the believer. There is nothing by way of proofs or arguments for God's existence in the Bible; that is simply presupposed. The same should be true of the Christian believer then; he should *start* from belief in God rather than from the premises of some argument whose conclusion is that God exists. What is it that makes those premises a better starting point anyway? And third, Bavinck points out that belief in God relevantly resembles belief in the existence of the self and of the external world – and, we might add, belief in other minds and the past. In none of these areas do we typically *have* proofs or arguments, or *need* proofs or arguments.

Suppose we turn next to John Calvin, who is as good a Calvinist as any. According to Calvin, God has implanted in us all an innate tendency, or nisus, or disposition to believe in him:

"There is within the human mind, and indeed by natural instinct, an awareness of divinity." This we take to be beyond controversy. To prevent anyone from taking refuge in the pretense of ignorance, God himself has implanted in all men a certain understanding of his divine majesty. Ever renewing its memory, he repeatedly sheds fresh drops. Since, therefore, men one and all perceive that there is a God and that he is their Maker, they are condemned by their own testimony because they have failed to honor him and to consecrate their lives to his will. If ignorance of God is to be looked for anywhere, surely one is most likely to find an example of it among the more backward folk and those more remote from civilization. Yet there is, as the eminent pagan says, no nation so barbarous, no people so savage, that they have not a deep-seated conviction that there is a God. So deeply does the common conception occupy the minds of all, so tenaciously does it inhere in the hearts of all! Therefore, since from the beginning of the world there has been no region, no city, in short, no household, that could do without religion, there lies in this a tacit confession of a sense of deity inscribed in the hearts of all.

Indeed, the perversity of the impious, who though they struggle furiously are unable to extricate themselves from the fear of God, is abundant testimony that this conviction, namely, that *there is some God*, is naturally inborn in all, and is fixed deep within, as it were in the very marrow. . . . From this we conclude *that it is not a doctrine that must first be learned in school* but one of which each of us is master from his mother's womb and which nature itself permits no one to forget.[14]

Calvin's claim, then, is that God has created us in such a way that we have a strong tendency or inclination toward belief in him. This tendency has been in part overlaid or suppressed by sin. Were it not for the existence of sin in the world, human beings would believe in God to the same degree and with the same natural spontaneity that we believe in the existence of other persons, an external world, or the past. This is the natural human condition; it is because of our presently unnatural sinful condition that many of us find belief in God difficult or absurd. The fact is, Calvin thinks, one who does not believe in God is in an epistemically substandard position – rather like a man who does not believe that his wife exists, or thinks she is like a cleverly constructed robot and has no thoughts, feelings, or consciousness.

Although this disposition to believe in God is partially suppressed, it is nonetheless universally present. And it is triggered or actuated by a widely realized condition:

Lest anyone, then, be excluded from access to happiness, he not only sowed in men's minds that seed of religion of which we have spoken, but revealed himself and daily discloses himself in the whole workmanship of the universe. As a consequence, men cannot open their eyes without being compelled to see him. (p. 1)

Like Kant, Calvin is especially impressed in this connection by the marvelous compages of the starry heavens above:

Even the common folk and the most untutored, who have been taught only by the aid of the eyes, cannot be unaware of the excellence of divine art, for it reveals itself in this innumerable and yet distinct and well-ordered variety of the heavenly host. (p. 50)

And Calvin's claim is that one who accedes to this tendency and in these circumstances accepts the belief that God has created the world – perhaps upon beholding the starry heavens, or the splendid majesty of the mountains, or the intricate, articulate beauty of a tiny flower – is entirely within his epistemic rights in so doing. It is not that such a person is justified or rational in so believing by virtue of having an implicit argument – some version of the teleological argument, say. No; he does not need any argument for justification or rationality. His belief need not be based on any other propositions at all; under these conditions he is perfectly rational in accepting belief in God in the utter absence of any argument, deductive or inductive. Indeed, a person in these conditions, says Calvin, *knows* that God exists.

Elsewhere Calvin speaks of "arguments from reason" or rational arguments:

The prophets and apostles do not boast either of their keenness or of anything that obtains credit for them as they speak; nor do they dwell upon rational proofs. Rather, they bring forward God's holy name, that by it the whole world may be brought into obedience to him. Now we ought to see how apparent it is not only by plausible opinion but by clear truth that they do not call upon God's name heedlessly or falsely. If we desire to provide in the best way for our consciences – that they may not be perpetually beset by the instability of doubt or vacillation, and that they may not also boggle at the smallest quibbles – we ought to seek our conviction in a higher place than human reasons, judgments, or conjectures, that is, in the secret testimony of the Spirit. (bk 1, ch. 7, p. 78)

Here the subject for discussion is not belief in the existence of God, but belief that God is the author of the Scriptures; I think it is clear, however, that Calvin would say the same thing about belief in God's existence. The Christian does not *need* natural theology, either as the source of his confidence or to justify his belief. Furthermore, the Christian *ought* not to believe on the basis of argument; if he does, his faith is likely to be "unstable and wavering," the "subject of perpetual doubt." If my belief in God is based on argument, then if I am to be properly rational, epistemically responsible, I shall have to keep checking the philosophical journals to see whether, say, Antony Flew has finally come up with a good objection to my favorite argument. This could be bothersome and time-consuming; and what do I do if someone does find a flaw in my argument? Stop going to church? From Calvin's point of view, believing in the existence of God on the basis of rational argument is like believing in the existence of your spouse on the basis of the analogical argument for other minds – whimsical at best and unlikely to delight the person concerned.

The Barthian dilemma

The twentieth-century theologian Karl Barth is particularly scathing in his disapproval of natural theology. *That* he disapproves is overwhelmingly clear. His *reasons* for thus disapproving, however, are much less clear; his utterances on this topic, as on others, are fascinating but Delphic in everything but length. Sometimes, indeed, he is outrageous, as when he suggests that the mere act of believing or accepting the Christian message is a manifestation of human pride, self-will, contumacy, and sin. Elsewhere, however, he is both more moderate and thoroughly intriguing:

> Now suppose the partner in the conversation [that is, natural theology] discovers that faith is trying to use the well-known artifice of dialectic in relation to him. We are not taking him seriously because we withhold from him what we really want to say and represent. It is only in appearance that we devote ourselves to him, and therefore what we say to him is only an apparent and unreal statement. What will happen then? Well, not without justice – although misconstruing the friendly intention which perhaps motivates us – he will see himself despised and deceived. He will shut himself up and harden himself against the faith which does not speak out frankly, which deserts its own standpoint for the standpoint of unbelief. What use to unbelief is a faith which obviously knows different? And how shocking for unbelief is faith which only pretends to take up with unbelief a common position. . . . This dilemma betrays the inner contradiction in every form of a "Christian" natural theology. It must really represent and affirm the standpoint of faith. Its true objective to which it really wants to lead unbelief is the knowability of the real God through Himself in his revelation. But as a "natural" theology, its initial aim is to disguise this and therefore to pretend to share in the life-endeavour of natural man. It therefore thinks

that it should appear to engage in the dialectic of unbelief in the expectation that here at least a preliminary decision in regard to faith can and must be reached. Therefore, as a natural theology it speaks and acts improperly. . . . We cannot experiment with unbelief, even if we think we know and possess all sorts of interesting and very promising possibilities and recipes for it. We must treat unbelief seriously. Only one thing can be treated more seriously than unbelief; and that is faith itself – or rather, the real God in whom faith believes. But faith itself – or rather, the real God in whom faith believes – must be taken so seriously that there is no place at all for even an apparent transposition to the standpoint of unbelief, for the pedagogic and playful self-lowering into the sphere of its possibilities.[15]

We must try to penetrate a bit deeper into these objections to natural theology, and suppose we start with Barth. Precisely what is the objection to which he is pointing? That somehow it is improper or un-Christian or dishonest or impious to try to prove God's existence; but *how* exactly? Barth speaks here of a *dilemma* that confronts the natural theologian. Dilemmas have horns; what are the horns of this one? The following, I think. In presenting a piece of natural theology, either the believer must adopt what Barth calls "the standpoint of unbelief" or he must pretend to his unbelieving interlocutor to do so. If he does the former, he deserts his Christian standpoint; but if he does the latter, he is dishonest, in bad faith, professing to believe what in fact he does not believe. But what *is* the standpoint of unbelief and what is it to adopt it? And how could one fall into this standpoint just by working at natural theology, just by making a serious attempt to prove the existence of God?

Perhaps Barth is thinking along the following lines. In *arguing* about the existence of God, in attempting to prove it, one implicitly adopts a certain stance. In adopting this stance one presupposes that it is not yet known whether there is a God; that remains to be seen; that is what is up for discussion. In adopting this stance, furthermore, the natural theologian implicitly concedes that what one ought to believe here depends on the result of the inquiry; if there are good arguments *for* the existence of God, then we – that is, we believers and unbelievers who together are engaged in this inquiry – ought to accept God's existence; if there are good arguments *against* the existence of God, we ought to accept its denial; and if the arguments on both sides are equally strong (and equally weak) then perhaps the right thing to do is to remain agnostic.

In adopting this stance one concedes that the rightness or propriety of belief and unbelief depends upon the outcome of a certain inquiry. Belief in God is right and proper only if there is on balance better reason to believe than not to believe – only if, that is, the arguments for the existence of God are stronger than those against it. But of course an inquiry has a starting point, and arguments have premises. In supposing the issue thus dependent upon the outcome of argument, one supposes the appropriate premises are available. What about these premises? In adopting this stance the natural theologian implicitly commits himself to the view that there is a certain set of propositions from which the premises of theistic and antitheistic arguments are to be drawn – a set of propositions such that belief in God is rational or proper only if it stands in the right relation to that set. He concurs with his unbelieving interlocutor that there is a set of propositions both can appeal to, a set of propositions accepted by all or nearly all rational persons; and the propriety or rightness of belief in God depends on its relation to these propositions.

What are these propositions and where do they come from? We shall have to enter that question more deeply later; for the moment let us call them "the deliverances of reason." Then to *prove* or *demonstrate* that God exists is to exhibit a deductive argument whose conclusion is that God exists, whose premises are drawn from the deliverances of reason, and each of whose steps is by way of an argument whose corresponding conditional is among the deliverances of reason. Aquinas' first three ways would be attempts to demonstrate the existence of God in just this sense. A demonstration that God does not exist, of course, would be structurally isomorphic; it would meet the second and third conditions just mentioned but have as conclusion the proposition that there is no such person as God. An alleged example would be the deductive argument from evil – the claim that the existence of evil is among the deliverances of reason and is inconsistent with the existence of God.

Of course it might be that the existence of God does not thus follow from the deliverances of reason but is nonetheless *probable* or *likely* with respect to them. One could then give a probabilistic or inductive argument for the existence of God, thus showing that theistic belief is rational, or

epistemically proper, in that it is more likely than not with respect to the deliverances of reason. Perhaps Aquinas' Fifth Way and Paley's argument from design can be seen as falling into this category, and perhaps the probabilistic argument from evil – the claim that it is unlikely that God exists, given all the evil there is – can then be seen as a structurally similar argument for the conclusion that unbelief is the proper attitude.

According to Barth, then, the natural theologian implicitly concedes that the propriety of belief in God is to be tested by its relationship to the deliverances of reason. Belief is right, or rational, or rationally acceptable only if it stands in the proper relationship to the deliverances of reason – only if, for example, it is more likely than not or at any rate not unlikely with respect to them.

Now to adopt the standpoint of unbelief is not, as Barth sees it, to reject belief in God. One who enthusiastically accepts and believes in the existence of God can nonetheless be in the standpoint of unbelief. To be in that standpoint it is sufficient to hold that belief in God is rationally permissible for a person *only if he or she has a good argument for it*. To be in the standpoint of unbelief is to hold that belief in God is rationally acceptable *only if it is more likely than not with respect to the deliverances of reason*. One who holds this belief, says Barth, is in the standpoint of unbelief; his ultimate commitment is to the deliverances of reason rather than to God. Such a person "makes reason a judge over Christ," or at any rate over the Christian faith. And to do so, says Barth, is utterly improper for a Christian.

The horns of the Barthian dilemma, then, are bad faith or dishonesty on the one hand and the standpoint of unbelief on the other. Either the natural theologian accepts the standpoint of unbelief or he does not. In the latter case he misleads and deceives his unbelieving interlocutor and thus falls into bad faith. In the former case he makes his ultimate commitment to the deliverances of reason, a posture that is for a Christian totally inappropriate, a manifestation of sinful human pride.

And this attempt to prove the existence of God certainly cannot end in any other way than with the affirmation that even apart from God's grace, already preceding God's grace, already anticipating it, he is ready for God, so that God is knowable to him otherwise than from and through himself. Not only does it end with this. In principle, it begins with it. For in what does it consist but in the arrogation, preservation and affirmation of the self-sufficiency of man and therefore his likeness with God? (p. 135)

Rejecting classical foundationalism

Now I think the natural theologian has a sound response to Barth's dilemma: she can execute the maneuver known to dialectician and matador alike as "escaping between the horns." As a natural theologian she offers or endorses theistic arguments, but why suppose that her own belief in God must be based upon such argument? And if it is not, why suppose she must pretend that it is? Perhaps her aim is to point out to the unbeliever that belief in God follows from other things he already believes, so that he can continue in unbelief (and continue to accept these other beliefs) only on pain of inconsistency. We may hope this knowledge will lead him to give up his unbelief, but in any event she can tell him quite frankly that her belief in God is not based on its relation to the deliverances of reason. Indeed, she can follow Calvin in claiming that belief in God *ought* not to be based on arguments from the deliverances of reason or anywhere else. So even if "the standpoint of unbelief" is as reprehensible as Barth says it is, his dilemma seems to evaporate.

What is most interesting here is not Barth's claim that the natural theologian faces this dilemma; here he is probably wrong, or at any rate not clearly right. More interesting is his view that belief in God need not be based on argument. Barth joins Calvin and Bavinck in holding that the believer in God is entirely within his rights in believing as he does even if he does not know of any good theistic argument (deductive or inductive), even if he does not believe there is any such argument, and even if in fact no such argument exists. Like Calvin, Kuyper, and Bavinck, Barth holds that belief in God is *properly basic* – that is, such that it is rational to accept it without accepting it on the basis of any other propositions or beliefs at all. In fact, they think the Christian ought not to accept belief in God on the basis of argument; to do so is to run the risk of a faith that is unstable and wavering, subject to all the wayward whim and fancy of the latest academic fashion. What the Reformers held was that a believer is entirely rational, entirely within his epistemic rights, in *starting with* belief in God, in accepting it as basic, and in taking it as premise for argument to other conclusions.

In rejecting natural theology, therefore, these Reformed thinkers mean to say first of all that the propriety or rightness of belief in God in no way depends upon the success or availability of the sort of theistic arguments that form the natural theologian's stock in trade. I think this is their central claim here, and their central insight. As these Reformed thinkers see things, one who takes belief in God as basic is not thereby violating any epistemic duties or revealing a defect in his noetic structure; quite the reverse. The correct or proper way to believe in God, they thought, was not on the basis of arguments from natural theology or anywhere else; the correct way is to take belief in God as basic.

I spoke earlier of classical foundationalism, a view that incorporates the following three theses:

(1) In every rational noetic structure there is a set of beliefs taken as basic – that is, not accepted on the basis of any other beliefs,

(2) In a rational noetic structure nonbasic belief is proportional to support from the foundations,

and

(3) In a rational noetic structure basic beliefs will be self-evident or incorrigible or evident to the senses.

Now I think these three Reformed thinkers should be understood as rejecting classical foundationalism. They may have been inclined to accept (1); they show no objection to (2); but they were utterly at odds with the idea that the foundations of a rational noetic structure can at most include propositions that are self-evident or evident to the senses or incorrigible. In particular, they were prepared to insist that a rational noetic structure can include belief in God as basic. As Bavinck put it, "Scripture . . . does not make God the conclusion of a syllogism, leaving it to us whether we think the argument holds or not. But it speaks with authority. Both theologically and religiously it proceeds from God as the starting point" (above, pp. 213–14). And of course Bavinck means to say that we must emulate Scripture here.

In the passages I quoted earlier, Calvin claims the believer does not need argument – does not need it, among other things, for epistemic respectability. We may understand him as holding, I think, that a rational noetic structure may very well contain belief in God among its foundations.

Indeed, he means to go further, and in two separate directions. In the first place he thinks a Christian *ought* not to believe in God on the basis of other propositions; a proper and well-formed Christian noetic structure will *in fact* have belief in God among its foundations. And in the second place Calvin claims that one who takes belief in God as basic can *know* that God exists. Calvin holds that one can *rationally accept* belief in God as basic; he also claims that one can *know* that God exists even if he has no argument, even if he does not believe on the basis of other propositions. A foundationalist is likely to hold that some properly basic beliefs are such that anyone who accepts them *knows* them. More exactly, he is likely to hold that among the beliefs properly basic for a person *S*, some are such that if *S* accepts them, *S* knows them. He could go on to say that *other* properly basic beliefs cannot be known if taken as basic, but only rationally believed; and he might think of the existence of God as a case in point. Calvin will have none of this; as he sees it, one needs no arguments to know that God exists.

Part IV: *Is* Belief in God Properly Basic?

According to the Reformed thinkers discussed in the last section the answer is "Yes indeed." I enthusiastically concur in this contention, and in this section I shall try to clarify and develop this view and defend against some objections. I shall argue first that one who holds that belief in God is properly basic is not thereby committed to the view that just about *anything* is; I shall argue secondly that even if belief in God is accepted as basic, it is not *groundless*; I shall argue thirdly that one who accepts belief in God as basic may nonetheless be open to arguments *against* that belief; and finally I shall argue that the view I am defending is not plausibly thought of as a species of *fideism*.

The Great Pumpkin objection

It is tempting to raise the following sort of question. If belief in God is properly basic, why cannot *just any* belief be properly basic? Could we not say the same for any bizarre aberration we can think of? What about voodoo or astrology? What about the belief that the Great Pumpkin returns every Halloween? Could I properly take *that* as basic? Suppose I believe that if I flap my arms with sufficient vigor, I can take off and fly about the room; could I defend myself against the charge of irrationality by claiming this belief is basic? If we say that belief in God is properly basic, will we not be committed to holding that just anything, or nearly anything, can properly be taken as basic, thus throwing wide the gates to irrationalism and superstition?

Certainly not. According to the Reformed epistemologist certain beliefs are properly basic in certain circumstances; those same beliefs may *not* be properly basic in other circumstances. Consider the belief that I see a tree: this belief is properly basic in circumstances that are hard to describe in detail, but include my being appeared to in a certain characteristic way; that same belief is not properly basic in circumstances including, say, my knowledge that I am sitting in the living room listening to music with my eyes closed. What the Reformed epistemologist holds is that there are widely realized circumstances in which belief in God is properly basic; but why should that be thought to commit him to the idea that just about *any* belief is properly basic in any circumstances, or even to the vastly weaker claim that for any belief there are circumstances in which it is properly basic? Is it just that he rejects the criteria for proper basicality purveyed by classical foundationalism? But why should *that* be thought to commit him to such tolerance of irrationality? Consider an analogy. In the palmy days of positivism the positivists went about confidently wielding their verifiability criterion and declaring meaningless much that was clearly meaningful. Now suppose someone rejected a formulation of that criterion – the one to be found in the second edition of A. J. Ayer's *Language, Truth and Logic*, for example. Would that mean she was committed to holding that

(1)   T'was brillig; and the slithy toves did gyre and gymble in the wabe,

contrary to appearances, makes good sense? Of course not. But then the same goes for the Reformed epistemologist: the fact that he rejects the criterion of proper basicality purveyed by classical foundationalism does not mean that he is committed to supposing just anything is properly basic.

But what then is the problem? Is it that the Reformed epistemologist not only rejects those criteria for proper basicality but seems in no hurry to produce what he takes to be a better substitute?

If he has no such criterion, how can he fairly reject belief in the Great Pumpkin as properly basic?

This objection betrays an important misconception. How *do* we rightly arrive at or develop criteria for meaningfulness, or justified belief, or proper basicality? Where do they come from? Must one have such a criterion before one can sensibly make any judgments – positive or negative – about proper basicality? Surely not. Suppose I do not know of a satisfactory substitute for the criteria proposed by classical foundationalism; I am nevertheless entirely within my epistemic rights in holding that certain propositions in certain conditions are not properly basic.

Some propositions seem self-evident when in fact they are not; that is the lesson of some of the Russell paradoxes. Nevertheless it would be irrational to take as basic the denial of a proposition that seems self-evident to you. Similarly, suppose it seems to you that you see a tree; you would then be irrational in taking as basic the proposition that you do not see a tree or that there are no trees. In the same way, even if I do not know of some illuminating criterion of meaning, I can quite properly declare (1) (above) meaningless.

And this raises an important question – one Roderick Chisholm has taught us to ask.[16] What is the status of criteria for knowledge, or proper basicality, or justified belief? Typically these are universal statements. The modern foundationalist's criterion for proper basicality, for example, is doubly universal:

(2)   For any proposition *A* and person *S*, *A* is properly basic for *S* if and only if *A* is incorrigible for *S* or self-evident to *S*.

But how could one know a thing like that? What are its credentials? Clearly enough, (2) is not self-evident or just obviously true. But if it is not, how does one arrive at it? What sorts of arguments would be appropriate? Of course a foundationalist might find (2) so appealing he simply takes it to be true, neither offering argument for it nor accepting it on the basis of other things he believes. If he does so, however, his noetic structure will be self-referentially incoherent. (2) itself is neither self-evident nor incorrigible; hence if he accepts (2) as basic, the modern foundationalist violates in accepting it the condition of proper basicality he himself lays down. On the other hand, perhaps the foundationalist will try to produce some argument for it from premises that are self-evident or

incorrigible: it is exceedingly hard to see, however, what such an argument might be like. And until he has produced such arguments, what shall the rest of us do – we who do not find (2) at all obvious or compelling? How could he use (2) to show us that belief in God, for example, is not properly basic? Why should we believe (2) or pay it any attention?

The fact is, I think, that neither (2) nor any other revealing necessary and sufficient condition for proper basicality follows from clearly self-evident premises by clearly acceptable arguments. And hence the proper way to arrive at such a criterion is, broadly speaking, *inductive*. We must assemble examples of beliefs and conditions such that the former are obviously properly basic in the latter, and examples of beliefs and conditions such that the former are obviously *not* properly basic in the latter. We must then frame hypotheses as to the necessary and sufficient conditions of proper basicality and test these hypotheses by reference to those examples. Under the right conditions, for example, it is clearly rational to believe that you see a human person before you: a being who has thoughts and feelings, who knows and believes things, who makes decisions and acts. It is clear, furthermore, that you are under no obligation to reason to this belief from others you hold; under those conditions that belief is properly basic for you. But then (2) must be mistaken; the belief in question, under those circumstances, is properly basic, though neither self-evident nor incorrigible for you. Similarly, you may seem to remember that you had breakfast this morning, and perhaps you know of no reason to suppose your memory is playing you tricks. If so, you are entirely justified in taking that belief as basic. Of course it is not properly basic on the criteria offered by classical foundationalists, but that fact counts not against you but against those criteria.

Accordingly, criteria for proper basicality must be reached from below rather than above; they should not be presented *ex cathedra* but argued to and tested by a relevant set of examples. But there is no reason to assume, in advance, that everyone will agree on the examples. The Christian will of course suppose that belief in God is entirely proper and rational; if he does not accept this belief on the basis of other propositions, he will conclude that it is basic for him and quite properly so. Followers of Bertrand Russell and Madelyn Murray O'Hare may disagree; but how is that relevant? Must my criteria, or those of the Christian community, conform to their examples? Surely not. The Christian community is responsible to *its* set of examples, not to theirs.

So, the Reformed epistemologist can properly hold that belief in the Great Pumpkin is not properly basic, even though he holds that belief in God is properly basic and even if he has no full-fledged criterion of proper basicality. Of course he is committed to supposing that there is a relevant *difference* between belief in God and belief in the Great Pumpkin if he holds that the former but not the latter is properly basic. But this should prove no great embarrassment; there are plenty of candidates. These candidates are to be found in the neighborhood of the conditions that justify and ground belief in God – conditions I shall discuss in the next section. Thus, for example, the Reformed epistemologist may concur with Calvin in holding that God has implanted in us a natural tendency to see his hand in the world around us; the same cannot be said for the Great Pumpkin, there being no Great Pumpkin and no natural tendency to accept beliefs about the Great Pumpkin.[17]

The ground *of belief in God*

My claim is that belief in God is properly basic; it does not follow, however, that it is *groundless*. Let me explain. Suppose we consider perceptual beliefs, memory beliefs, and beliefs ascribing mental states to other persons, such beliefs as:

(3)   I see a tree,
(4)   I had breakfast this morning,

and

(5)   That person is in pain.

Although beliefs of this sort are typically taken as basic, it would be a mistake to describe them as *groundless*. Upon having experience of a certain sort, I believe that I am perceiving a tree. In the typical case I do not hold this belief on the basis of other beliefs; it is nonetheless not groundless. My having that characteristic sort of experience – to use Professor Chisholm's language, my being appeared treely to – plays a crucial role in the formation of that belief. It also plays a crucial role in its *justification*. Let us say that a belief is *justified* for a person at a time if (a) he is violating no epistemic duties and is within his epistemic rights in accepting it then and (b) his noetic structure is not defective by virtue of his then accepting it.[18] Then

my being appeared to in this characteristic way (together with other circumstances) is what confers on me the right to hold the belief in question; this is what justifies me in accepting it. We could say, if we wish, that this experience is what justifies me in holding it; this is the *ground* of my justification, and, by extension, the ground of the belief itself.

If I see someone displaying typical pain behavior, I take it that he or she is in pain. Again, I do not take the displayed behavior as *evidence* for that belief; I do not infer that belief from others I hold; I do not accept it on the basis of other beliefs. Still, my perceiving the pain behavior plays a unique role in the formation and justification of that belief; as in the previous case it forms the ground of my justification for the belief in question. The same holds for memory beliefs. I seem to remember having breakfast this morning; that is, I have an inclination to believe the proposition that I had breakfast, along with a certain past-tinged experience that is familiar to all but hard to describe. Perhaps we should say that I am appeared to pastly; but perhaps that insufficiently distinguishes the experience in question from that accompanying beliefs about the past not grounded in my own memory. The phenomenology of memory is a rich and un-explored realm; here I have no time to explore it. In this case as in the others, however, there is a justifying circumstance present, a condition that forms the ground of my justification for accepting the memory belief in question.

In each of these cases a belief is taken as basic, and in each case *properly* taken as basic. In each case there is some circumstance or condition that confers justification; there is a circumstance that serves as the ground of justification. So in each case there will be some true proposition of the sort

(6)   In condition *C*, *S* is justified in taking *p* as basic.

Of course *C* will vary with *p*. For a perceptual judgment such as

(7)   I see a rose-colored wall before me

C will include my being appeared to in a certain fashion. No doubt *C* will include more. If I am appeared to in the familiar fashion but know that I am wearing rose-colored glasses, or that I am suffering from a disease that causes me to be thus appeared to, no matter what the color of the nearby objects, then I am not justified in taking (7) as basic. Similarly for memory. Suppose I know that my memory is unreliable; it often plays me tricks. In particular, when I seem to remember having breakfast, then, more often than not, I have not had breakfast. Under these conditions I am not justified in taking it as basic that I had breakfast, even though I seem to remember that I did.

So being appropriately appeared to, in the perceptual case, is not sufficient for justification; some further condition – a condition hard to state in detail – is clearly necessary. The central point here, however, is that a belief is properly basic only in certain conditions; these conditions are, we might say, the ground of its justification and, by extension, the ground of the belief itself. In this sense basic beliefs are not, or are not necessarily, *groundless* beliefs.

Now similar things may be said about belief in God. When the Reformers claim that this belief is properly basic, they do not mean to say, of course, that there are no justifying circumstances for it, or that it is in that sense groundless or gratuitous. Quite the contrary. Calvin holds that God "reveals and daily discloses himself in the whole workmanship of the universe," and the divine art "reveals itself in the innumerable and yet distinct and well ordered variety of the heavenly host." God has so created us that we have a tendency or disposition to see his hand in the world about us. More precisely, there is in us a disposition to believe propositions of the sort *this flower was created by God* or *this vast and intricate universe was created by God* when we contemplate the flower or behold the starry heavens or think about the vast reaches of the universe.

Calvin recognizes, at least implicitly, that other sorts of conditions may trigger this disposition. Upon reading the Bible, one may be impressed with a deep sense that God is speaking to him. Upon having done what I know is cheap, or wrong, or wicked, I may feel guilty in God's sight and form the belief *God disapproves of what I have done*. Upon confession and repentance I may feel forgiven, forming the belief *God forgives me for what I have done*. A person in grave danger may turn to God, asking for his protection and help; and of course he or she then has the belief that God is indeed able to hear and help if he sees fit. When life is sweet and satisfying, a spontaneous sense of gratitude may well up within the soul; someone in this condition may thank and praise the Lord for his goodness, and will of course have the accompanying belief that indeed the Lord is to be thanked and praised.

There are therefore many conditions and circumstances that call forth belief in God: guilt, gratitude, danger, a sense of God's presence, a sense that he speaks, perception of various parts of the universe. A complete job would explore the phenomenology of all these conditions and of more besides. This is a large and important topic, but here I can only point to the existence of these conditions.

Of course none of the beliefs I mentioned a moment ago is the simple belief that God exists. What we have instead are such beliefs as:

(8) God is speaking to me,
(9) God has created all this,
(10) God disapproves of what I have done,
(11) God forgives me,

and

(12) God is to be thanked and praised.

These propositions are properly basic in the right circumstances. But it is quite consistent with this to suppose that the proposition *there is such a person as God* is neither properly basic nor taken as basic by those who believe in God. Perhaps what they take as basic are such propositions as (8)–(12), believing in the existence of God on the basis of propositions such as those. From this point of view it is not wholly accurate to say that it is belief in God that is properly basic; more exactly, what are properly basic are such propositions as (8)–(12), each of which self-evidently entails that God exists. It is not the relatively high-level and general proposition *God exists* that is properly basic, but instead propositions detailing some of his attributes or actions.

Suppose we return to the analogy between belief in God and belief in the existence of perceptual objects, other persons, and the past. Here too it is relatively specific and concrete propositions rather than their more general and abstract colleagues that are properly basic. Perhaps such items as:

(13) There are trees,
(14) There are other persons,

and

(15) The world has existed for more than five minutes

are not in fact properly basic; it is instead such propositions as:

(16)   I see a tree,
(17)   That person is pleased,

and

(18)   I had breakfast more than an hour ago

that deserve that accolade. Of course propositions of the latter sort immediately and self-evidently entail propositions of the former sort, and perhaps there is thus no harm in speaking of the former as properly basic, even though so to speak is to speak a bit loosely.

The same must be said about belief in God. We may say, speaking loosely, that belief in God is properly basic; strictly speaking, however, it is probably not that proposition but such propositions as (8)–(12) that enjoy that status. But the main point, here, is this: belief in God, or (8)–(12), are properly basic; to say so, however, is not to deny that there are justifying conditions for these beliefs, or conditions that confer justification on one who accepts them as basic. They are therefore not groundless or gratuitous.

Is argument irrelevant to basic belief in God?

Suppose someone accepts belief in God as basic. Does it not follow that he will hold this belief in such a way that no argument could move him or cause him to give it up? Will he not hold it come what may, in the teeth of any evidence or argument with which he could be presented? Does he not thereby adopt a posture in which argument and other rational methods of settling disagreement are implicitly declared irrelevant? Surely not. Suppose someone accepts

(19)   There is such a person as God

as basic. It does not for a moment follow that he will regard argument irrelevant to this belief of his; nor is he committed in advance to rejecting every argument against it. It could be, for example, that he accepts (19) as basic but also accepts as basic some propositions from which, by arguments whose corresponding conditionals he accepts as basic, it follows that (19) is false. What happens if he is apprised of this fact, perhaps by being

presented with an argument from those propositions to the denial of (19)? Presumably some change is called for. If he accepts these propositions more strongly than (19), presumably he will give the latter up.

Similarly, suppose someone believes there is no God but also believes some propositions from which belief in God follows by argument forms he accepts. Presented with an argument from these propositions to the proposition that God exists, such a person may give up his atheism and accept belief in God. On the other hand, his atheistic belief may be stronger than his belief in some of the propositions in question, or his belief in their conjunction. It is possible, indeed, that he *knows* these propositions, but believes some of them less firmly than he believes that there is no God; in that case, if you present him with a valid argument from these propositions to the proposition that God exists, you may cause him to give up a proposition he knows to be true. It is thus possible to reduce the extent of someone's knowledge by giving him a sound argument from premises he knows to be true.

So a person can accept belief in God as basic without accepting it dogmatically – that is, in such a way that he will ignore any contrary evidence or argument. And now a second question: Suppose the fact is belief in God *is* properly basic. Does it follow that one who accepts it dogmatically is within his epistemic rights? Does it follow that someone who is within his rights in accepting it as basic *remains* justified in this belief, no matter what counterargument or counterevidence arises?

Again, surely not. The justification-conferring conditions mentioned above must be seen as conferring *prima facie* rather than *ultima facie*, or all-things-considered, justification. This justification can be overridden. My being appeared to treely gives me a *prima facie* right to take as basic the proposition *I see a tree*. But of course this right can be overridden; I might know, for example, that I suffer from the dreaded dendrological disorder, whose victims are appeared to treely only when there are no trees present. If I do know that, then I am not within my rights in taking as basic the proposition *I see a tree* when I am appeared to treely. The same goes for the conditions that confer justification on belief in God. Like the 14-year-old theist (above, p. 205), perhaps I have been brought up to believe in God and am initially within my rights in so doing. But conditions can arise in which perhaps I am no longer justified in this belief. Perhaps you propose to me an argument for conclusion that it is impossible that there be such a person as God. If this argument is convincing for me – if it starts from premises that seem self-evident to me and proceeds by argument forms that seem self-evidently valid – then perhaps I am no longer justified in accepting theistic belief. Following John Pollock, we may say that a condition that overrides my *prima facie* justification for *p* is *defeating condition* or *defeater* for *p* (for me). Defeaters, of course, are themselves *prima facie* defeaters, for the defeater can be defeated. Perhaps I spot a fallacy in the initially convincing argument; perhaps I discover a convincing argument for the denial of one of its premises; perhaps I learn on reliable authority that someone else has done one of those things. Then the defeater is defeated, and I am once again within my rights in accepting *p*. Of course a similar remark must be made about defeater-defeaters: they are subject to defeat by defeater-defeater-defeaters and so on.

Many believers in God have been brought up to believe, but then encountered potential defeaters. They have read books by skeptics, been apprised of the atheological argument from evil, heard it said that theistic belief is just a matter of wish fulfillment or only a means whereby one socioeconomic class keeps another in bondage. These circumstances constitute potential defeaters for justification in theistic belief. If the believer is to remain justified, something further is called for – something that *prima facie* defeats the defeaters. Various forms of theistic apologetics serve this function (among others). Thus the *free-will defense* is a defeater for the atheological argument from evil, which is a potential defeater for theistic belief. Suppose I am within my epistemic rights in accepting belief in God as basic; and suppose I am presented with a plausible argument – by Democritus, let us say – for the conclusion that the existence of God is logically incompatible with the existence of evil. (Let us add that I am strongly convinced that there *is* evil.) This is a potential defeater for my being rational in accepting theistic belief. What is required, if I am to continue to believe rationally, is a defeater for that defeater. Perhaps I discover a flaw in Democritus' argument, or perhaps I have it on reliable authority that Augustine, say, has discovered a flaw in the argument; then I am once more justified in my original belief.

[. . .]

By way of summary: I have argued that the evidentialist objection to theistic belief is rooted in classical foundationalism; the same can be said for the Thomistic conception of faith and reason. Classical foundationalism is attractive and seductive; in the final analysis, however, it turns out to be both false and self-referentially incoherent. Furthermore, the Reformed objection to natural theology, unformed and inchoate as it is, may best be seen as a rejection of classical foundationalism. As the Reformed thinker sees things, being self-evident, or incorrigible, or evident to the senses is not a necessary condition of proper basicality. He goes on to add that belief in God is properly basic. He is not thereby committed to the idea that just any or nearly any belief is properly basic, even if he lacks a criterion for proper basicality. Nor is he committed to the view that argument is irrelevant to belief in God if such belief is properly basic. Furthermore, belief in God, like other properly basic beliefs, is not groundless or arbitrary; it is grounded in justification-conferring conditions.

Notes

1 W. K. Clifford, "The Ethics of Belief," in *Lectures and Essays* (London: Macmillan, 1879), pp. 345f.

2 Brand Blanshard, *Reason and Belief* (London: Allen & Unwin, 1974), pp. 400f.

3 Bertrand Russell, "Why I am not a Christian," in *Why I Am Not a Christian* (New York: Simon & Schuster, 1957), p. 3ff.

4 Michael Scriven, *Primary Philosophy* (New York: McGraw-Hill, 1966), p. 87ff.

5 Antony Flew, *The Presumption of Atheism* (London: Pemberton, 1976), pp. 22ff.

6 Wesley Salmon, "Religion and Science: A New Look at Hume's Dialogues," *Philosophical Studies* 33 (1978): 176.

7 Clifford, "The Ethics of Belief," p. 183.

8 Flew, *The Presumption of Atheism*, pp. 13–15.

9 Scriven, *Primary Philosophy*, pp. 102–3.

10 See, for example, Plantinga, *The Nature of Necessity* (Oxford: Clarendon Press, 1974), ch. 10.

11 Blanshard, *Reason and Belief*, p. 401.

12 Scriven, *Primary Philosophy*, p. 103.

13 Herman Bavinck, *The Doctrine of God*, tr. William Hendricksen (Grand Rapids: Eerdmans, 1951),

pp. 78–9. *The Doctrine of God* is the translation of the second volume of Bavinck's *Gereformeede Dogmatiek*, published 1895–9.

14 John Calvin, *Institutes of the Christian Religion*, tr. Ford Lewis Battles (Philadelphia: Westminster Press, 1960), bk 1, ch. 3, pp. 43–4.

15 Karl Barth, *Church Dogmatics*, tr. G. T. Thompson and Harold Knight (Edinburgh: T & T Clark, 1956), vol. 1, part 1, pp. 93–5.

16 Roderick Chisholm, *The Problem of the Criterion* (Milwaukee: Marquette University Press, 1973), pp. 14ff.

17 For further comment on the Great Pumpkin objection, see Alvin Plantinga, "On Reformed Epistemology," *Reformed Journal*, April 1982.

18 I do not mean to suggest, of course, that if a person believes a true proposition and is justified (in this sense) in believing it, then it follows that he *knows* it; that is a different (and stronger) sense of the term.

PART IV

Theistic Arguments

Introduction

Charles Taliaferro

In Part III we considered a prominent area which some philosophers have construed as providing evidence of God's existence: religious experience. Arguments for the veracity of religious experience have their detractors (Grünbaum – see chapter 10 – but see also Matthew Bagger and Michael Martin in the suggested readings on pp. 231–2) but also their defenders (Alston, Davis, Gellman, Swinburne). In this section we consider three formal arguments for God's existence along with three entries which raise objections. While the theistic arguments are on a different footing from that of an appeal to religious experience, they need not be seen as taking on terrain which is completely foreign to religious experience. One may combine theistic arguments – for example joining an argument from religious experience with an argument from the apparent design of the cosmos – just as one may combine atheistic arguments – for example combining Grünbaum's explaining away of religious experience (see chapter 10) with Mackie's rejection of the cosmological argument which we will consider in chapter 20.

Standard philosophy introductions and anthologies in the 1960s through the 1980s set up traditional theistic arguments simply to knock them down with "decisive objections". The landscape has changed today in the philosophy of religion, where a host of theistic arguments are considered important challenges and also where a host of counter-arguments are fashioned and refashioned. In the journal *Philo*, which is dedicated to anti-theistic arguments, the editor (at the time of writing) Quentin Smith acknowledges this current change. Smith, an atheistic philosopher, paints this picture: "God is not 'dead' in academia; he returned to life in the late 1960s and is now alive and well in . . . philosophy departments. A hand waving dismissal of theism . . . has been like trying to halt a tidal wave with a hand-held sieve." Today there is ample opportunity for both believers and skeptics to undertake substantial philosophical work on theistic and anti-theistic arguments.

In the first entry of Part IV, Richard Swinburne argues that the existence of God offers a better account of the existence of this contingent cosmos than to suppose that the cosmos is uncaused and theism is false. J. L. Mackie seeks to undermine Swinburne's argument, as well as earlier versions of the cosmological argument advanced by William Craig, Aquinas, and Leibniz, which Mackie first explains and then critiques. Some of the argumentation between Swinburne and Mackie over the probability of God's existence is quite technical (though fortunately they also strive to put their points in straightforward, simple terms, e.g. Swinburne's conclusion in the last paragraph on p. 240). They use technical terms to distinguish degrees of probability. The existence of a contingent world may be a good "C-inductive argument" if it confirms the existence of God, whereas if an argument merely makes it more probable that God exists, it may be called a good "P-inductive argument." The point of distinguishing these is that a hypothesis may be made more probable by very modest evidence. The hypothesis that there has been intelligent life on

Mars is rendered more probable by the bare discovery that there was some kind of life on Mars. However, that discovery is so modest that the hypothesis "there has been intelligent life on Mars" is still far from secured. Swinburne and Mackie are the two leading figures in the late twentieth century who contributed to the probability of theism.

In the next exchange, we have an excerpt from David Hume's famous eighteenth-century *Dialogues Concerning Natural Religion*. Hume's dialogue includes three figures: Cleanthes argues that the apparent order and design of the cosmos is evidence of God; Philo objects to the argument on philosophical grounds; whereas the character Demea objects on religious grounds. The first speaker is Cleanthes. In "The Argument from Design," Robert Hambourger offers a contemporary version of the argument and an interesting defense.

The final exchange is over one of the most sophisticated theistic arguments. The "ontological argument" builds on a case for the coherence of theism. It has been argued that if it is reasonable to believe it is possible that God exists, then it is reasonable to believe that God actually exists. Most versions of the arguments are prompted by the view that God is not like contingent objects or states of affairs that are possible but do not obtain (the state of affairs of there being happy unicorns is possible but also not actual). If God exists, God exists necessarily. As such, God's existence seems to be either necessary or impossible. Consider this analogy: $3 + 7 = 10$ is not a contingent truth; it is either necessarily true (which it is) or impossible. If God's existence is possible, God's existence is not impossible – and, by analogy, if $3 + 7 = 10$ is possible, then $3 + 7 = 10$ is not impossible. A common version of the argument is that there are reasons to think it is possible God exists and thus good reasons to think God exists in reality. I will defer to the entries by Malcolm and Martin for a fuller development of the argument and a range of objections. The ontological argument probably stands out in the history of ideas as a supreme example of the philosophical fascination with the concept of God. The entries on the ontological argument in this volume will also stand as representations of two radically divergent attitudes: in the end Malcolm sees the argument as profoundly rooted in (and authenticated by) religious emotions, whereas Martin offers a disgruntled rejection of what he sees as simply a bad argument.

I end this Introduction by citing two contemporary philosophers who are not (at least not at this time) theists, but who highlight the philosophical significance and historical importance of the idea of God. Anthony Kenny, one of the leading contributors to the history of philosophy, puts the matter this way:

> If there is no God, then God is incalculably the greatest single creation of the human imagination. No other creation of the imagination has been so fertile of ideas, so great an inspiration to philosophy, to literature, to painting, sculpture, architecture, and drama. Set beside the idea of God, the most original inventions of mathematicians and the most unforgettable characters in drama are minor products of imagination: Hamlet and the square root of minus one pale into insignificance by comparison.[1]

Roger Scruton thinks that even if the religious belief in God were to disappear, investigation into the idea of God would remain vital.

> Our most pressing philosophical need, it seems to me, is to understand the nature and significance of the force which once held our world together, and which is now losing its grip – the force of religion. It could be that religious belief will soon be a thing of the past; it is more likely, however, that beliefs with the function, structure and animus of religion will flow into the vacuum left by God. In either case, we need to understand the why and wherefore of religion. It is from religious ideas that the human world, and the subject who inhabits it, were made.[2]

Speculation on the ontological and other arguments can be historically and philosophically illuminating even if, in the end, they do not establish theism. Of course, if some of the arguments are successful (as I believe they are), this area of philosophy of religion is of enormous importance.

Notes

1 Anthony Kenny, *Faith and Philosophy* (New York: Columbia University Press, 1983), p. 59.

2 Roger Scruton, *An Intelligent Person's Guide to Philosophy* (New York: Penguin Books, 1996), pp. 85–6.

Further Reading

Historical Sources:

The Cosmological Argument

Aquinas, Thomas: *Summa Theologica*, Part I, Question 2, Article 3
Aristotle: *Metaphysics*, Book XII
Descartes, René: *Meditations* III
Hume, David: *Dialogues Concerning Natural Religion*
Hume, David: *Enquiry Concerning Human Understanding*, Section XI
Kant, Immanuel: *Critique of Pure Reason*, Transcendental Dialectic, Book II, Chapters 2 and 3
Locke, John: *Essays Concerning Human Understanding*, Book IV, Chapter 10
Mill, John Stuart: "Theism," *Three Essays on Religion*
Plato: *Laws*, Book X

The Design Argument

Aquinas, Thomas: *Summa Theologica*, Part I, Question 2, Article 3
Hume, David: *Dialogues Concerning Natural Religion*
Kant, Immanuel: *Critique of Pure Reason*, Transcendental Dialectic, Book II, Chapter 3
Mill, John Stuart: "Theism," *Three Essays on Religion*
Paley, William: *Natural Theology: Or, Evidence and Attributes of the Deity, Collected From the Appearances of Nature*

The Ontological Argument

Anselm of Canterbury: *Proslogion*, Chapters 2–4
Anselm of Canterbury: *Reply to the Fool*
Gaunilo: *A Reply on Behalf of the Fool*
Hume, David: *Dialogues Concerning Natural Religion*

Descartes's Meditation V Argument

Descartes, René: *Meditations* III, V
Descartes, René: *Objections to the Meditations*, Part II, Objection II and Reply
Descartes, René: *Principles of Philosophy*, I, xviii
Kant, Immanuel: *Critique of Pure Reason*, "Transcendental Dialectic," Book II, Chapter 3
Leibniz, Gottfried Wilhelm: *New Essays Concerning Human Understanding*, Book IV, Chapter 10 and Appendix X
Liebniz, Gottfried Wilhelm: *Monadology*, Sections 44–5
Spinoza, Benedict: *Ethics*, Part I

From The Blackwell Companion to Philosophy of Religion, *see the following entries:*

Dore, C., "Ontological arguments"
Rowe, W. L., "Cosmological arguments"

Garcia, L. L., "Teleological and design arguments"
Evans, C. S., "Moral arguments"
Jordan, J., "Pragmatic arguments"
Schlesinger, G. N., "Miracles"
Yandell, K. E., "Religious experience"
Penelhum, T., "Fideism"
Plantinga, A., "Reformed epistemology"
Craig, W., "Theism and physical cosmology"
Hasker, W., "Theism and evolutionary biology"
Audi, R., "Theism and the scientific understanding of the mind"

Other further reading:

Adams, M. M., "Praying the Prosologion: Anselm's Theological Method," in T. D. Senor (ed.), *The Rationality of Belief and the Plurality of Faith* (Ithaca: Cornell University Press, 1995).
Bagger, Michael C., *Religious Experience, Justification and History* (Cambridge: Cambridge University Press, 1999).
Barnes, J., *The Ontological Argument* (New York: St Martin's Press, 1972). *Highly critical.*
Barrow, J. D. and Tipler, F. J., *The Anthropic Cosmological Principle* (Oxford: Oxford University Press, 1986).
Brain, D., *The Reality of Time and the Existence of God: The Project of Proving God's Existence* (Oxford: Clarendon Press, 1988).
Burrill, D. R., *The Cosmological Arguments* (Garden City, NY: Anchor Books, 1967). *Good anthology.*
Clarke, S., *A Demonstration of the Being and Attributes of God* (Oxford: Oxford University Press, 1969). *A classic.*
Craig, W. L. and Moreland, J. P. (eds.), *Naturalism: A Critical Analysis* (London and New York: Routledge, 2000). *A systematic case against naturalism.*
Craig, W. L. and Smith, Q., *Theism, Atheism, and Big Bang Cosmology* (Oxford: Clarendon Press, 1993). *Craig defends a theistic cosmological argument, while Smith defends naturalism.*
Craig, W. L., *The Cosmological Argument from Plato to Leibniz* (New York: Barnes and Noble, 1980). *Historic and contemporary cosmological arguments.*
Craig, W. L., *The Kalam Cosmological Argument* (New York: Barnes and Noble, 1979).
Creel, R. E., "A Realistic Argument for Belief in the Existence of God," *International Journal for Philosophy of Religion* 10 (1979): 233–53.
Davies, P., *God and the New Physics* (New York: Simon and Schuster, 1983).
Dawkins, R., *The Blind Watchmaker: Why the Evidence of Evolution Reveals a Universe Without Design* (New York: W. W. Norton and Co., 1986).
Dore, C., *Theism* (Dordrecht: D. Reidel Publishing Co., 1984). *Technical defense of theism.*
Edwards, P., "The Cosmological Argument," in D. R. Burrill (ed.), *The Cosmological Arguments* (Garden City, NY: Anchor Books, 1967). *Classical.*

Forrest, P., *God Without the Supernatural. A Defense of Scientific Theism* (Ithaca and London: Cornell University Press, 1996).

Grisez, G., *Beyond the New Theism: A Philosophy of Religion* (Notre Dame: University of Notre Dame Press, 1975).

Haldane, J. J. and Smart, J. J. C., *Atheism and Theism* (Oxford and Cambridge, MA: Blackwell Publishers, 1996). *An important debate. Haldane is the theist, Smart the atheist.*

Hartshorne, C., *Anselm's Discovery* (La Salle, IL: Open Court, 1965). *A take-no-prisoners defense of the ontological argument.*

Hartshorne, C., The *Logic of Perfection, and Other Essays in Neoclassical Metaphysics* (La Salle, IL: Open Court, 1962).

Leslie, J., "The Theory That the World Exists Because It Should," *American Philosophical Quarterly* 7 (1970): 286–98.

Leslie, J., *Universes* (London: Routledge, 1989). *The universe exists because it should.*

Lewis, C. S., *Mere Christianity* (New York: Macmillan, 1960). *Popular moral argument for theism.*

Mackie, J. L., "The Ontological Arguments," in *The Miracle of Theism: Arguments For and Against the Existence of God* (Oxford: Clarendon Press, 1982).

Mackie, J. L., *The Miracle of Theism: Arguments For and Against the Existence of God* (Oxford: Clarendon Press, 1982). *A critique of theistic arguments.*

Martin, M., *Atheism: A Philosophical Justification* (Philadelphia: Temple University Press, 1990).

Meynell, H., *The Intelligible Universe: A Cosmological Argument* (London: Macmillan, 1982). *A comprehensive defense of theism.*

Miller, B., *A Most Unlikely God: A Philosophical Inquiry into the Nature of God* (Notre Dame and London: University of Notre Dame Press, 1996). *Bears an ontological arguments.*

Miller, B., *From Existence to God: A Contemporary Philosophical Argument* (London and New York: Routledge, 1992).

Moreland, J. P. and Nielsen, K. (eds.), *Does God Exist? The Great Debate* (Nashville, Tennessee: Thomas Nelson, 1990).

Oppy, G., *Ontological Arguments and Belief in God* (Cambridge and New York: Cambridge University Press, 1995). *A critique of the ontological argument.*

Plantinga, A., "God and Necessity," in *The Nature of Necessity* (Oxford: Clarendon Press, 1974).

Reichenbach, B. R., *The Cosmological Argument: A Reassessment* (Springfield, IL: Charles C. Thomas, 1972).

Rowe, W. L., *The Cosmological Argument* (Princeton: Princeton University Press, 1975). *Nuanced, qualified defense.*

Swinburne, R., *Is There a God?* (Oxford and New York: Oxford University Press, 1996). *Swinburne answers "yes."*

Swinburne, R., *The Existence of God* (Oxford: Clarendon Press, 1981). *Constructive theistic stance.*

Taylor, R., *Metaphysics* (Englewood Cliffs: Prentice-Hall, 1963; 2nd edn, 1974; 3rd edn, 1983; 4th edn, 1992). *Defense of cosmological argument.*

19

The Cosmological Argument

Richard Swinburne

[. . .]

Two Forms of Cosmological Argument

Kant defined a cosmological argument as one which
starts from "experience which is purely indeterminate" or "experience of existence in general". Let
us say, more precisely, that it is one which starts
from the existence of a finite object, i.e. any object
other than God. However, other arguments called
cosmological have in effect started from something
rather more specific, the existence of a complex
physical universe; and I shall concentrate mainly
on these. I understand by a physical universe a
physical object consisting of physical objects spatially related to each other and to no other physical
object. (By "spatially related to each other" I understand "at some distance in some direction from
each other".) Our physical universe, *the* universe,
is the physical object which consists of all physical
objects including the earth, spatially related to each
other and to no other physical object. It consists of
the galaxies, stars, and planets, including the earth,
things on them, and gases between them. The universe is the only physical universe of which we
have knowledge, but I define it in such a way as not
to rule out the logical possibility of other physical
universes,[1] or of objects which are not part of any

Richard Swinburne, "The Cosmological Argument,"
reprinted by permission of Oxford University Press from
The Existence of God (Oxford: Clarendon Press; New
York: Oxford University Press, 1979), pp. 116–32.

physical universe (e.g. God or some finite spirit,
neither of which are physical objects). By a complex physical universe I understand one consisting
of many physical objects of diverse and of not
very natural volume, shape, mass, etc.; mostly
inert objects without powers of choice. Our universe
of material objects of galaxies, stars, planets, and
pebbles on the sea-shore is thus a complex physical
universe.

From time to time various writers[2] have told us
that we cannot reach any conclusions about the
origin or development of the universe, since it is
(whether by logic or just in fact) a unique object,
the only one of its kind, and rational inquiry can
only reach conclusions about objects which belong
to kinds, e.g. it can reach a conclusion about what
will happen to this bit of iron, because there are
other bits of iron, the behaviour of which can be
studied. This objection of course has the surprising, and to most of these writers unwelcome, consequence, that physical cosmology cannot reach
justified conclusions about such matters as the
size, age, rate of expansion, and density of the
universe as a whole (because it is a unique object);
and also that physical anthropology cannot reach
conclusions about the origin and development of
the human race (because, as far as our knowledge
goes, it is the only one of its kind). The implaus-
ibility of these consequences leads us to doubt the
original objection, which is indeed totally misguided.
One could perhaps circumvent it by regarding the
universe as consisting of two parts, divided by an
infinite plane, then reach conclusions about each of
these parts, and then conjoin them. But there is no

need for such subterfuge since the objection is totally misguided in ignoring the point that uniqueness is relative to description. Every object is unique under some description, if you allow descriptions which locate an object by its spatial position, i.e. by its distance and direction from other objects. Thus my desk is the one and only desk in Room 91 in Keele Hall of Keele University; and my house is the last house on the left along such-and-such a road. And even if you allow only descriptions in qualitative terms – e.g. the one and only desk of such-and-such a shape, such-and-such a weight, with such-and-such carvings on its legs, and scratches on its top – it is still plausible to suppose that most objects have a unique description.[3] In the first respect the universe is, like all physical objects, pickable out by a unique description – viz. the one which I gave above – "The physical object consisting of all physical objects including the earth spatially related to each other and to no other physical object". In the second respect too the universe is, very probably, describable by a unique description – e.g. "physical object consisting of physical objects, which are all spatially related to each other and to no other physical object". In all of this the universe is no more "unique" than the objects which it contains. Yet all objects within the universe are characterized by certain properties, which are common to more than one object. My desk has in common with various other objects that it is a desk, and with various different objects, that it weighs less than a ton, and so on. The same applies to the universe. It is, for example, like objects within it such as the solar system, a system of material bodies distributed in empty space. It is a physical object, and like other physical objects, has density and mass. The objection fails totally to make any crucial distinction between the universe and other objects; and so it fails in its attempt to prevent at the outset a rational inquiry into the issue of whether the universe has some origin outside itself.

So then, to return to the main thread, a cosmological argument is an argument to the existence of God from the existence of some finite object or, more specifically, a complex physical universe. There have been many versions of the cosmological argument given over the past two-and-a-half millennia; the most quoted are the second and third of Aquinas's five ways to show the existence of God.[4] However, Aquinas's "five ways", or rather the first four of his five ways, seem to me to be one of his least successful pieces of philosophy.[5] In my view the two most persuasive and interesting versions of the cosmological argument are that given by Leibniz in his paper, "On the Ultimate Origination of Things", and that given by his contemporary, Samuel Clarke, in his Boyle Lectures for 1704 and published under the title *A Demonstration of The Being and Attributes to God*.[6] The former seems to be the argument criticized by Kant in the *Critique of Pure Reason* and the latter the argument criticized by Hume in the *Dialogues*. In so far as I consider one detailed example of a cosmological argument, I shall consider Leibniz's version, but most of my remarks will apply to most versions of the argument.

The starting-points of cosmological arguments are evident facets of experience. There is no doubt about the truth of statements which report that they hold. It seems to me equally evident that no argument from any of such starting-points to the existence of God is deductively valid. For if an argument from, for example, the existence of a complex physical universe to the existence of God were deductively valid, then it would be incoherent to assert that a complex physical universe exists and that God does not. There would be a hidden contradiction buried in such co-assertions. Now, I believe,[7] the only way to prove a proposition to be incoherent is to deduce from it an *obviously* incoherent proposition (e.g. a self-contradictory proposition); and the only way to prove a proposition coherent is to show that it is deducible from an *obviously* coherent proposition, that is to spell out one obviously coherent way in which it could be true. Now notoriously, attempts to derive obviously incoherent propositions from such co-assertions have failed through the commission of some elementary logical error. Furthermore it seems easy enough to spell out in an obviously coherent way what it would be like for such co-assertions to be true. There would be a complex physical universe and no God, if there had always been matter rearranging itself in various combinations, and the only persons had been embodied persons; if there never was a person who knew everything, or could do everything, etc. Atheism does seem to be a supposition consistent with the existence of a complex physical universe, such as our universe. Of course things may not be as they seem, but in the absence of any worthwhile argument to the contrary known to me, I shall assume that the non-existence of God is logically compatible with the existence of the universe, and so that the cosmological argument is not a valid, and so not a good, deductive argument. Our primary concern is however to investigate whether it is a good C-inductive or P-inductive argument, and just how much force it has.

An argument from the universe to God may start from the existence of the universe today, or from its existence for as long as it has existed – whether a finite or an infinite time. Leibniz considers the argument in the latter form, and I shall follow him. So let us consider the series of states of the universe starting from the present and going backwards in time, S_1, S_2, S_3, and so on. (We can suppose each to last a small finite time.) Now clearly there are laws of nature L which bring about the evolution of S_3 from S_4, S_2 from S_3, and so on. (I shall assume for the purpose of simplicity of exposition that this process is a deterministic progress, viz. that L and S_5 together provide a full explanation of S_4, L and S_4 a full explanation of S_3, and so on; we can ignore any minor element of indeterminism – nothing will turn on it.) So we get the following picture:

$$\cdot > \cdots S_5 \xrightarrow{\;\;L\;\;} S_4 \xrightarrow{\;\;L\;\;} S_3 \xrightarrow{\;\;L\;\;} S_2 \xrightarrow{\;\;L\;\;} S_1$$

The series of states may be finite or infinite – which, we do not know. Now God might come into the picture in one of two ways, as responsible for L, and so as providing a complete explanation of the occurrence of each state S; or at the beginning of the series (if it has one) as starting the process off.

Before an argument of the second type can get off the ground, we would need to give reason to suppose that the universe had a beginning. I have argued elsewhere[8] that, although there is not much hope for any a priori arguments to show that the universe had a beginning, there is some possible future in a posteriori arguments to show it. These would be arguments of a scientific character, showing that the universe was now in a state S_1 and that the laws of nature were L, and that extrapolation backwards from S_1 via L eventually leads to a physically impossible state or a state with no matter, at a time t; whence we could conclude that the universe must have come into existence at a time after t, and not as a result of the operation of scientific laws. Thus science might discover that among the laws of nature was a law that conglomerations of matter (including the galaxies) necessarily over time recede linearly from each other. Then we might be able to retrodict from the present state of the universe that, if the universe existed say 14,000 million years ago, its matter must have been packed together with infinite density. But this, we may suppose, is

a physically impossible state. So there cannot have been conglomerations of matter subject to the law of expansion for as long as 14,000 million years. So the universe must have come into existence more recently. I do not think that a very strong inductive argument of this character could be constructed – because of the difficulty of getting any very strong confirmation for claims about what are the laws of nature in distant regions of space and time. Just how sure can we be, for example, that the laws of nature include laws of a continuous expansion of the universe, rather than laws of oscillation? Nevertheless, it is possible that the science of the future might provide us with such an argument of moderate strength for the conclusion that the universe had a beginning in time. (The science of the present, incidentally, in my view, is nowhere near providing us with a worthwhile argument either for the temporality or for the eternity of the universe.) In showing that the universe had a beginning in time, we would have shown that its first stage S_f had no scientific explanation in terms of a cause which was a prior state of the universe. There are then two alternatives – either S_f just happened (it had no cause) or S_f has a personal explanation. I shall not take this argument further here, because we are not likely to be able to show with very much force that the universe did have a first state; and because the other type of cosmological argument has much more force.

The Force of the First Form of the Argument

So let us revert to our series of states of the universe allowing for the possibility of an infinite regression. If the universe is infinitely old, then each state of the universe S_n will have a full explanation in terms of a prior state S_{n+1} and natural laws L. Clearly, since S_{n+1} consists of the state of the universe at the time in question, there can be no explanation of its occurrence in terms of any contemporaneous state. So if we take the most basic laws of nature L, then, keeping ourselves within the scientific scheme, L and S_{n+1} will provide a complete explanation of S_n [. . .]. Now L, being scientifically inexplicable, is either inexplicable totally, or it has an explanation of a non-scientific, viz. personal, kind. In the former case each state of the universe has a complete explanation, which is a scientific explanation, as the atheist believes. In the latter case there is a person, e.g. God, who brings about the operation of L at each moment of time, and a complete explanation of each state of the universe will involve reference to God who brings it about that L operates, viz. that S_{n+2} brings about S_{n+1}, S_{n+1} brings about S_n, and so on, and so keeps the universe in existence throughout infinite time.

It would be an error to suppose that if the universe is infinitely old, and each state of the universe at each instant of time has a complete explanation which is a scientific explanation in terms of a previous state of the universe and natural laws (and so God is not invoked), that the existence of the universe throughout infinite time has a complete explanation, or even a full explanation. It has not. It has neither. It is totally inexplicable. It has often been assumed and sometimes argued by philosophers, including Hume, that if we have a scientific explanation of each of a collection of states, then we have an explanation of the whole collection. Thus, Hume:

> In . . . a chain . . . or succession of objects, each part is caused by that part which preceded it, and causes that which succeeded it. Where then is the difficulty? But the *whole*, you say, wants a cause. I answer that the uniting of several parts into a whole, like the uniting of several distinct countries into a kingdom, or several distinct members into one body, is performed merely by an arbitrary act of the mind, and has no influence on the nature of things. Did I show you the particular causes of each individual in a collection of twenty particles of matter, I should think it very unreasonable, should you afterwards ask me what was the cause of the whole twenty. This is sufficiently explained in explaining the cause of the parts.[9]

To assess the worth of Hume's claim we need to develop general principles concerning the relation of causes of parts to causes of wholes.

One principle which might be proposed in this connection is that a cause of the occurrence of a collection of states is any collection of the causes of each. More particularly, a full cause of the occurrence of a collection of states is any collection of full causes of each. This principle clearly holds for any finite set of effects, where none of the causes of any member of the collection of effects is itself a member of the collection of effects. If a full cause of a is a', of b is b', of c is c', and of d is d', a, b, c, d, a', b', c', and d' being distinct states, then a full cause of $a + b + c + d$ is $a' + b' + c' + d'$. If a full

cause of one lamp's lighting up is its being connected to a battery, and a full cause of a second lamp's lighting up is its being connected to a different battery, then a full cause of the two lamps' lighting up is the connection of the two to batteries. This principle seems also to hold where the collection of effects is infinite, and none of the causes of any member of the collection of effects is itself a member of the collection of effects. If a full cause of the existence of every double-star system in the universe is the breaking-up of a single star, then a full cause of the existence of the double-star systems is still the breaking-up of single stars, even if the number of double-star systems is infinite.

However, the principle must be modified if it is to take account of cases where the cause of some member of a collection of effects is itself a member of that collection. For when b is the cause of a, and c is the cause of b, we say that the cause of $a + b$ is c, not $b + c$. If c is the lighting of a fuse, b is an explosion caused by c, and a an explosion caused by b, then the cause of $a + b$ is just c. To take account of this point, the previous principle must be expressed more generally as follows: a full cause of the occurrence of a collection of states is any collection of (full) causes of each, which are not members of the former collection. Hence if a full cause of a is b, of b is b', of c is d, and of d is d', then a full cause of $a + b + c + d$ is $b' + d'$. If a full cause of a is b, of b is c, of c is d, and of d is e, then a full cause of $a + b + c + d$ is e. In so far as some member of the collection does not have a cause, to that extent the collection of states does not have a cause. If a has no cause, but c is a full cause of b, then there is no full cause of $a + b$, but c is a partial cause. Hence in so far as a finite collection of states has a cause, it has its cause outside the set. Hence if the universe is of finite age, and the only causes of its past states are prior past states (i.e. scientific causality alone operates), the set of past states as a whole will have no cause and so no explanation.

The principle: "a (full) cause of the occurrence of a collection of states, is any collection of (full) causes of each, which are not members of the former collection" assumes, with the Hempelian account of scientific explanation, that causes are states, rather than objects, and it must be rephrased to allow object-causation (as in personal explanation, and in the powers-and-liabilities account of scientific explanation). The necessary rephrasing is as follows: "a (full) cause of the occurrence of a collection of states, is any collection of (full) causes of each, whose states as they cause are not members of the former collection." I shall in general use the original form, but shall also need to use the rephrased form shortly.

Now if the universe is of infinite age, a similar conclusion to that of the last paragraph but one applies. If the only causes of its past states are prior past states, the set of past states as a whole will have no cause and so no explanation. This will hold if each state has a complete scientific explanation in terms of a prior state, and so God is not involved. For although each state of the universe will have a complete explanation (unlike in the case where the universe is finite, where its first state will not have any explanation), the whole infinite series will have no explanation, for there will be no causes of members of the series, lying outside the series. In that case the existence of the universe over infinite time will be an inexplicable brute fact. There will be an explanation (in terms of L) of why, once existent, it continues to exist. But what will be inexplicable is the non-existence of a time before which there was no universe.

Further, the universe will have during its infinite history, certain constant features F_1 which are such that given that the universe has these features at a certain time and given L, the universe will always have them. But they are such that the universe could have had a different set of features F_2 equally compatible with L. What kind of features these are will depend on the character of L. But suppose for example that L includes a law of the conservation of matter, then given that there is a quantity M_1 of matter at some time, there will be M_1 at all times – and not merely that quantity of matter, but those particular bits of matter. Yet compatible with L will be the supposition that there was a different quantity M_2 made up of different bits. Then it will be totally inexplicable why the quantity of matter was M_1 rather than M_2. If L does not include laws of the conservation of matter, it is hard to see[10] how it could fail to include laws formulable as conservation laws of some kind (e.g. of energy, or momentum, or spin, or even the density of matter). And so a similar point would arise. Why does the world contain just that amount of energy, no more, no less? L would explain why whatever energy there is remains the same; but what L does not explain is why there is just this amount of energy.

I conclude that if each state of the universe at each instant of time has a complete explanation which is a scientific explanation, then the existence of the universe at each instant of time and its having

certain permanent features have no explanation at all. This is the point which Leibniz makes in his exposition of the argument:

Neither in any one single thing, nor in the whole aggregate and series of things, can there be found the sufficient reason of existence. Let us suppose the book of the elements of geometry to have been eternal, one copy always having been written down from an earlier one; it is evident that, even though a reason can be given for the present book out of a past one, nevertheless out of any number of books taken in order going backwards we shall never come upon a full reason; though we might well always wonder why there should have been such books from all time – why there were books at all, and why they were written in this manner. What is true of the books is true also of the different states of the world; for what follows is in some way copied from what precedes (even though there are certain laws of change). And so, however far you go back to earlier states, you will never find in those states a full reason why there should be any world rather than none, and why it should be such as it is. Indeed, even if you suppose the world eternal, as you will be supposing nothing but a succession of states and will not in any of them find a sufficient reason, nor however many states you assume will you advance one step forward giving a reason.[11]

Like Leibniz, I conclude that the existence of the universe over infinite time would be, if only scientific explanation is allowed, a brute inexplicable fact. Just the same would apply if the universe does have a first state. That state S_f would be a brute, inexplicable fact. The existence of the universe over time comes into my category of things too big for science to explain. If the existence of the universe is to be explained, personal explanation must be brought in, and an explanation given in terms of a person who is not part of the universe acting from without. This can be done if we suppose that such a person G brings it about at each instant of time, that L operates, and so brings it about for each S_{n+1} that S_{n+1} brings about S_n. We thus get the picture shown in figure 1.

It will clarify what is at stake here to rephrase our supposition, using the powers-and-liabilities account of scientific explanation. Our supposition that there is a full scientific explanation of the existence of each state of the universe in terms of the

Richard Swinburne

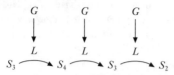

Figure 1

action of an immediately prior state then amounts to the following. The universe at any given time t_n is in a state S_n. At each such time it has power P to bring about its continued existence with whatever constant characteristics it has (e.g. same matter, or same quantity of energy), and a liability K necessarily to exercise P. Our supposition that a person G acts from without to conserve it in being is the supposition that G brings it about that it has the power P and the liability K. G makes it bring about its subsequent existence, and its subsequent possession of its permanent characteristics. At any time he could make the universe bring about different subsequent permanent characteristics or not give it the power to bring about its subsequent existence.

Now my earlier principle, in its rephrased form, runs as follows: "a (full) cause of the occurrence of a collection of states, is any collection of (full) causes of each whose states as they cause, are not members of the former collection". It follows under the conditions described in the last paragraph, whether the universe is of finite or infinite age, that G is a full cause of the existence of the universe throughout its history (with its permanent characteristics). For he is a full cause of each state of the universe, by his making it the case (through some intention of his) that the prior state brought it about, and yet his states are not states of the universe. G would be the cause of the existence of the universe (with its permanent characteristics) over all the time that it exists, by a series of intentions, or rather a continuing intention to keep it in being. If we are to postulate G we should postulate the simplest kind of G for the purpose, and that means a G of infinite power, knowledge, and freedom, i.e. God. A G of very great but finite power, much, but not all knowledge, etc. would raise the inevitable questions of why he has just that amount of power and knowledge, and what stops him having more, questions which do not arise with the postulation of God. The choice is between the universe as stopping-point and God as stopping-point.

Can we rest with the universe as a brute, inexplicable fact? Leibniz cannot, because the Principle of Sufficient Reason pushes him further. He writes:

The reasons of the world then lie in something extra-mundane, different from the chain of states, or series of things, whose aggregate constitutes the world. And so we must pass from physical or hypothetical necessity, which determines the subsequent things of the world by the earlier, to something which is of absolute or metaphysical necessity, for which itself no reason can be given. For the present world is necessary physically or hypothetically, but not absolutely or metaphysically. In other words, when once it is determined that it shall be such and such, it follows that such and such things will come into being. Since then the ultimate root must be in something which is of metaphysical necessity, and since there is no reason of any existent thing except in an existent thing, it follows that there must exist some one Being of metaphysical necessity, that is, from whose essence existence springs; and so there must exist something different from the plurality of beings, that is the world, which, as we have allowed and have shown, is not of metaphysical necessity.[12]

Leibniz has here deployed the principle of sufficient reason as a metaphysically necessary truth. The principle boils down to the claim that everything not metaphysically necessary has an explanation in something metaphysically necessary. A being has metaphysical necessity according to Leibniz, if from its "essence existence springs"; i.e. if it could not but exist. Whether this "could not" is a logical "could not" is, however, unclear. If the "could not" is a logical "could not", then the metaphysically necessary being with whom explanation is supposed to end is a logically necessary being. But against this claim that explanation ends with a logically necessary being I urge the point [that] the logically necessary cannot explain the logically contingent. Further, as I argued at the beginning of this chapter, it seems coherent to suppose that there exist a complex physical universe but no God, from which it follows that it is coherent to suppose that there exist no God, from which in turn it follows that God is not a logically necessary being. If there is a logically necessary being, it is not God.[13]

If, however, Leibniz's metaphysically necessary being is not a logically necessary being, but (speaking metaphorically) the supreme brute fact, then his principle boils down to the simple claim that there is a terminus to explanation, that everything which has a full explanation has an ultimate, or at least a complete explanation. [Elsewhere] we saw no general reason for accepting this claim. Whether it is rational to suppose that phenomena have complete explanations is a matter of whether we have potential explanations for them of great simplicity and explanatory power. Leibniz claims that the universe is not metaphysically necessary, and so that its existence needs explanation. He may be right, but I cannot see how you can argue for this claim except in terms of the relatively greater simplicity and explanatory power of a potential *explanans*. Leibniz does not provide such an argument. It is up to us to see the force of an argument along these lines for the existence of God.

Peter Geach has suggested[14] that four of Aquinas's five ways really have a somewhat similar form to the form which I have represented Leibniz's argument as having. He suggests, for example, that the first two ways should be understood as follows. The chain of objects *A*, *B*, *C*, etc. such that *A* brings about *B*, and *B* brings about *C* should be regarded as one big object, that is the universe which may have existed for infinite time. We look for the cause of this which is to be found outside the universe, in God. But if Aquinas's argument is to be represented in this form, the question arises as to why we should suppose that the universe has a cause. Aquinas might answer that we should suppose this because the universe is a complex whole of parts and is in the process of change.[15] But it is surely not a logically necessary truth that there is an explanation of the existence of any complex whole which is in the process of change. The argument can, surely, be only an a posteriori one from the simplicity and explanatory power of a postulated *explanans* in comparison with the complexity of the *explanandum*.

I commented [elsewhere] on the great simplicity of theism. What now of its explanatory power with respect to the universe? Let *h* be the hypothesis of theism, and *k* be mere tautological evidence. It is important at this stage to be clear about exactly what *e* is meant to be. We have seen that different versions of the cosmological argument interpret it somewhat differently. It can be taken, most generally, as the existence of a finite object. At the other extreme, it can be taken as the existence over time of a complex physical universe. I shall take it in the latter more specific form, and then comment on the effects of taking the premiss more generally. With this understanding of *e*, how does $P(e/h.k)$ compare with $P(e/k)$? *e* could not, as we have seen, have a scientific explanation. Either *e* occurs unexplained, or it is due to the action of a person, the most likely person being, as we have seen, God. For the sake of simplicity of

exposition we may, I suggest, ignore the alternative which we have shown to be a priori much less probable, that *e* was brought about by a person of very large but finite power, very considerable but limited knowledge, etc. Hence we may regard $P(e/ \sim h.k)$ as the probability that there be a physical universe without anything else having brought it about.

We saw in Chapter 6 [not included] that (for *h* as the hypothesis of theism) $P(e/h.k)$ may exceed $P(e/k)$ for one of two reasons. One is that $P(e/ \sim h.k)$ is very low, because *e* cannot be explained in any other way and has the kind of complexity which makes it a very unlikely stopping-point for explanation (at any rate in comparison with the simplicity of God). The other is that *e* is the kind of state which God can be expected to bring about (or allow others to bring about) more than other states. My appeal in connection with the cosmological argument is to the first reason only.

A complex physical universe (existing over endless time or beginning to exist at some finite time) is indeed a rather complex thing. We need to look at our universe and meditate about it, and the complexity should be apparent. There are lots and lots of separate chunks of it. The chunks each have a different finite and not very natural volume, shape, mass etc. – consider the vast diversity of the galaxies, stars, and planets, and pebbles on the seashore. Matter is inert and has no powers which it can choose to exert; it does what it *has* to do. There is just a certain finite amount, or at any rate finite density of it, manifested in the particular bits; and a certain finite amount, or at any rate finite density of energy, momentum, spin, etc. There is a complexity, particularity, and finitude about the universe which cries out for explanation, which God does not have. A priori the existence of anything at all logically contingent, even God, may seem vastly improbable, or at least not very probable. (Hence "the mystery of existence".) Yet whether this is so or not, the existence of the universe has a vast complexity, compared with the existence of God. [. . .] [T]he supposition that there is a God is an extremely simple supposition; the postulation of a God of infinite power, knowledge, and freedom is the postulation of the simplest kind of person which there could be. For this reason of the complexity of *e* $P(e/ \sim h.k)$ is low. If something has to occur unexplained, a complex physical universe is less to be expected than other things (e.g. God).

However I do not claim that $P(e/h.k)$ is especially high. $P(e/h.k)$ measures how likely it is if there is a God that there will be a physical universe. The choice before God among worlds to create includes a world where there is just God; a world where there are one or more finite non-physical objects (e.g. non-embodied spirits); a world consisting of a simple physical universe (e.g. just one round steel ball); and a world which is a complex physical universe. There are good reasons why God should make a complex physical universe. For such a physical universe can be beautiful, and that is good; and also it can be a theatre for finite agents to develop and make of it what they will. But I cannot see that God has overriding reason to make such a universe. (It is not obviously superior to any other sort of world; and he certainly has no moral obligation to make such a universe, for before he creates any rational agents, there are no rational agents to wrong.) Nor can I see that he has overriding reason to make or not to make any alternative world. Maybe God will leave things with God alone modifying his own states (and the succession of his own states would be a beautiful and so a good thing), and exercising his power in that way; or maybe he will create one or more finite beings, or just one physical object. That God is under no necessity to create a physical universe, or anything at all, is of course the traditional view of theism. So I conclude that $P(e/h.k)$ does not exceed $P(e/ \sim h.k)$ (and so $P(e/k)$) because God is especially likely to bring e about, although it does exceed it because e is very unlikely to come about but for God's agency. In view of the enormous number of different complex physical universes which there might be, neither $P(e/h.k)$ nor $P(e/k)$ will be very low. Since $P(e/h.k) > P(e/k)$, by the relevance criterion

$P(h/e.k) > P(h/k)$, and so the argument from the existence of a complex physical universe to God is a good C-inductive argument.

The same conclusion follows, I believe, if we take e, most generally, as the existence of a finite object. In that case both $P(e/ \sim h.k)$ and $P(e/h.k)$ are going to be greater, but I suggest that as before, $P(e/h.k)$ will exceed $P(e/ \sim h.k)$. $P(e/ \sim h.k)$ will be higher since it is more likely a priori that there should exist a finite object, than that there should exist a complex physical universe (a somewhat more specific hypothesis). Yet intuitively, any finite object would lack the simplicity of the God of Chapter 5 [not included here]. So, I suggest that $P(h/k)$ remains greater than $P(e/ \sim h.k)$ and both remain low. $P(e/h.k)$, however, will also be higher in virtue of the general principle [. . .] that the less specific is e, the higher is $P(e/h.k)$. For only if God refused throughout endless time to create any object other than himself could there fail, if there is a God, to be a finite object.

The argument of the last few pages can now be put in simple words as follows. There is quite a chance that if there is a God he will make something of the finitude and complexity of a universe. It is very unlikely that a universe would exist uncaused, but rather more likely that God would exist uncaused. The existence of the universe is strange and puzzling. It can be made comprehensible if we suppose that it is brought about by God. This supposition postulates a simpler beginning of explanation than does the supposition of the existence of an uncaused universe, and that is grounds for believing the former supposition to be true.

Notes

1 Another physical universe would be a physical object consisting of physical objects, spatially related to each other, but not to the objects of our universe such as the earth. For the logical possibility of other universes, see A. Quinton, "Spaces and Times", *Philosophy*, 1962, 37, 130–47, and the more extended discussion in my *Space and Time* (London, 1968), esp. ch. 2.

2 Including, for example, Hume. In Hume's *Dialogues Concerning Natural Religion* (first published 1779, H. D. Aiken (ed.), New York, 1948), p. 23, Philo objects to arguments to the cause of the universe as an object which is "single, individual, without parallel or specific resemblance". See also Hume's *Enquiry Concerning Human Understanding* (first published 1748, L. A. Selby-Bigge (ed.), Oxford, 1902), pp. 147f.

3 The claim that this is necessarily so for all objects is one version of the principle of the identity of indiscernibles. I do not rely on this principle, but only on the plausible empirical claim made in the text. For an introduction to the issues involved in discussion of the identity of indiscernibles see A. J. Ayer, "The identity of indiscernibles", in his *Philosophical Essays* (London, 1954).

4 See St Thomas Aquinas's *Summa Theologiae*, la.2.2. Aquinas's first way is sometimes said to be a version of the cosmological argument, but it does not count as one on my definition of a cosmological argument, since it argues not from the existence of physical objects, but from change in them. It claims in effect that, given that there are physical objects, change in them is so surprising that we need to invoke God

as its source. I cannot see that change as such is surprising at all. Given the existence of physical objects, it seems to me no more surprising that they should change than that they should remain changeless. Aquinas's supposition to the contrary arises from the Aristotelian physics which is so closely meshed with his philosophy. It is more plausible to suppose that the existence of *orderly* change is surprising, but the argument from orderly change is Aquinas's fifth way and is a teleological argument which I shall discuss in the next chapter [not included here].

5 For detailed criticism of Aquinas's five ways, see the full and careful discussion in A. Kenny, *The Five Ways* (London, 1969).

6 Clarke's argument, treated as a deductive argument, has received very full and interesting treatment in W. L. Rowe, *The Cosmological Argument* (Princeton and London, 1975). This is one reason why I concentrate on Leibniz's version.

7 I argue for this claim about how coherence and incoherence are to be proved in *The Coherence of Theism* (Oxford, 1977), ch. 3.

8 See my *Space and Time*, ch. 15.

9 David Hume, *Dialogues Concerning Natural Religion* (first published 1779, H. D. Aiken (ed.), New York, 1948), pp. 59f. The same argument is put forward, among modern writers, by Paul Edwards. He writes that "if we have explained the individual members" of a series "there is nothing additional left to be explained". ("The Cosmological Argument", in *The Rationalist Annual*, 1959, pp. 63–77. See p. 71.)

10 I write that this is "hard to see", for the reason that laws of nature tell us that a value of some quantity at some time is a function of some other value at an earlier time, e.g. $x = f(y)$. They can then be written as saying that something is conserved between the two times, e.g. that $x/f(y)$ or $x - f(y)$ remains constant.

11 G. W. Leibniz, *On the Ultimate Origination of Things*, trans. M. Morris, in *The Philosophical Writings of Leibniz*, Everyman Edn (London, 1934), pp. 31f.

12 Ibid., p. 33.

13 If this is correct, then of course the traditional ontological argument which attempts to prove that God exists of logical necessity, fails utterly. Kant accused the cosmological argument of being the ontological argument in disguise. His criticisms only have force if we suppose that the necessary being to which the cosmological argument purports to argue is a logically necessary being. See I. Kant, *Critique of Pure Reason*, Sect. 5: The Ideal of Pure Reason. For detailed discussion of Kant's treatment of the cosmological argument, see J. Bennett, *Kant's Dialectic* (London, 1974), ch. 11, and references contained there.

Kant holds that all necessity is either logical necessity or, more widely, necessity for human thought. Either way, for Kant, there is no necessity in things, only in our thought about them. ("The concept of necessity is only to be found in our reason, as a formal condition of thought; it does not allow of being hypostatised as a material condition of existence." *Critique of Pure Reason*, trans. N. Kemp-Smith, A620.) This is another of the general principles of Kant's philosophy which he brings to the philosophy of religion, and which spoils his treatment of it. Kant's principle is quite mistaken. Clearly there is a necessity in the conformity of material bodies to laws of nature which exists in things and not in our thought. For more extended discussion of kinds of necessity, see *The Coherence of Theism*, ch. 13.

14 G. E. M. Anscombe and P. T. Geach, *Three Philosophers* (Oxford, 1963), pp. 109–17.

15 Ibid., p. 113.

20

Cosmological Arguments

J. L. Mackie

The rejection of Berkeley's form of theism entails that if a god is to be introduced at all, it must be as a supplement to the material world, not as a substitute for it. The rejection of all forms of ontological argument then entails that the theist must argue from the world (or from some part or aspect of our experience) to a god. This brings us to the cosmological argument, which is *par excellence* the philosophers' argument for theism. It has been presented in many forms, but in one version or another it has been used by Greek, Arabic, Jewish, and Christian philosophers and theologians, including Plato, Aristotle, al Farabi, al Ghazali, ibn Rushd (Averroes), Maimonides, Aquinas, Spinoza, and Leibniz.[1] What is common to the many versions of this argument is that they start from the very fact that there is a world or from such general features of it as change or motion or causation – not, like the argument from consciousness or the argument for design, from specific details of what the world includes or how it is ordered – and argue to God as the uncaused cause of the world or of those general features, or as its creator, or as the reason for its existence. I cannot examine all the variants of this argument that have been advanced, but I shall discuss three intendedly demonstrative approaches and an inductive, probabilistic, approach. And although

J. L. Mackie, "Cosmological Arguments," reprinted by permission of Oxford University Press from *The Miracle of Theism: Arguments For and Against the Existence of God* (Oxford: Clarendon Press and New York: Oxford University Press, 1982), pp. 81–101. © John Mackie, 1982.

arguments to a first cause or a creator are more immediately attractive, and appeared earlier in history, than those which argue from the contingency of the world to a necessary being, the latter are in some respects simpler and perhaps more fundamental, so I shall begin with one of these.

(a) Contingency and Sufficient Reason

Leibniz gives what is essentially the same proof in slightly different forms in different works; we can sum up his line of thought as follows.[2] He assumes the *principle of sufficient reason*, that nothing occurs without a sufficient reason why it is so and not otherwise. There must, then, be a sufficient reason for the world as a whole, a reason why something exists rather than nothing. Each thing in the world is contingent, being causally determined by other things: it would not occur if other things were otherwise. The world as a whole, being a collection of such things, is therefore itself contingent. The series of things and events, with their causes, with causes of those causes, and so on, may stretch back infinitely in time; but, if so, then however far back we go, or if we consider the series as a whole, what we have is still contingent and therefore requires a sufficient reason outside this series. That is, there must be a sufficient reason *for* the world which is *other than* the world. This will have to be a necessary being, which contains its own sufficient reason for existence. Briefly, things must have a sufficient reason for their existence, and this must be found ultimately in a necessary being. There must be something free from the disease of contingency, a disease which affects everything in the world and the world as a whole, even if it is infinite in past time.

This argument, however, is open to criticisms of two sorts, summed up in the questions "How do we know that everything must have a sufficient reason?" and "How can there be a necessary being, one that contains its own sufficient reason?" These challenges are related: if the second question cannot be answered satisfactorily, it will follow that things as a whole cannot have a sufficient reason, not merely that we do not know that they must have one.

Kant's criticism of the Leibnizian argument turns upon this second objection; he claims that the cosmological proof depends upon the already criticized ontological proof.[3] The latter starts from the concept of an absolutely necessary being, an *ens realissimum*, something whose essence includes existence, and tries to derive from that concept itself alone the fact that there is such a being. The cosmological proof "retains the connection of absolute necessity with the highest reality, but instead of reasoning . . . from the highest reality to necessity of existence, it reasons from the previously given unconditioned necessity of some being to the unlimited reality of that being". However, Kant's claim that the cosmological proof "rests" or "depends" on the ontological one, that "the so-called cosmological proof really owes any cogency which it may have to the ontological proof from mere concepts", is at least misleading. The truth is rather this. The cosmological argument purports to show, from the contingency of the world, in conjunction with the principle of sufficient reason, that there must be something else which is not contingent, which exists necessarily, which is or contains its own sufficient reason. When we ask how there could be such a thing, we are offered the notion of an *ens realissimum* whose essence includes existence. This is the notion which served as the starting-point of (in particular) Descartes's ontological proof. But the notion is being used quite differently in the two cases. Does this connection imply that successful criticism of the ontological proof undermines the cosmological one also? That depends on the nature of the successful criticism. If its outcome is that the very concept of something's essence including existence is illegitimate – which would perhaps have been shown by Kant's thesis that existence is not a predicate, or by the quantifier analysis of existence in general, if either of these had been correct and uncontroversial – then

at least the final step in the cosmological proof is blocked, and Leibniz must either find some different explanation of how something might exist necessarily and contain its own sufficient reason, or else give up even the first step in his proof, abandoning the search for a sufficient reason of the world as a whole. But if the outcome of the successful criticism of the ontological proof were merely that we cannot validly start from a mere concept and thence derive actual existence – if we allowed that there was nothing illegitimate about the concept of a being whose essence includes existence, and insisted only that whatever a concept contains, it is always a further question whether there is something that instantiates it – then the cosmological proof would be unaffected by this criticism. For it does offer something that purports independently to answer this further question, namely the first step, the claim that the contingency of the world shows that a necessary being is required. Now our final criticisms, not only of Descartes's version of the ontological proof, but also of Anselm's and Plantinga's, were of this second sort. I said that the view that existence disappears wholly into the existential quantifier is controversial, and therefore did not press the first sort of criticism. Consequently the cosmological proof is not undermined by the so far established weakness of the ontological, though, since Kant thought he had carried through a criticism of the first sort, it would have been consistent for him to say that the cosmological proof was at least seriously threatened by it, that Leibniz would need to find some other account of how there could be a necessary being.

But perhaps we can still make something like Kant's point, even if we are relying only on a criticism of the second sort. Since it is always a further question whether a concept is instantiated or not, no matter how much it contains, the existence even of a being whose essence included existence would not be self-explanatory: there might have failed to be any such thing. This "might" expresses at least a conceptual possibility; if it is alleged that this being none the less exists by a metaphysical necessity, we are still waiting for an explanation of this kind of necessity. The existence of this being is not logically necessary; it does not exist in all logically possible worlds; in what way, then, does it necessarily exist in this world and satisfy the demand for a sufficient reason?

It might be replied that we understand what it is for something to exist contingently, in that it would not have existed if something else had been otherwise: to exist necessarily is to exist but not contingently in this sense. But then the premiss that the natural world as a whole is contingent is not available: though we have some ground for thinking that each part, or each finite temporal stretch, of the world is contingent in this sense upon something else, we have initially no ground for thinking that the world as a whole would not have existed if something else had been otherwise; inference from the contingency of every part to the contingency *in this sense* of the whole is invalid. Alternatively, we might say that something exists contingently if and only if it might not have existed, and by contrast that something exists necessarily if and only if it exists, but it is not the case that it might not have existed. In this sense we could infer the contingency of the whole from the contingency of every part. But once it is conceded, for reasons just given, that it is not logically impossible that the alleged necessary being might not have existed, we have no understanding of how it could be true of this being that it is not the case that it might not have existed. We have as yet no ground for believing that it is even possible that something should exist necessarily in the sense required.

This criticism is reinforced by the other objection, "How do we know that everything must have a sufficient reason?" I see no plausibility in the claim that the principle of sufficient reason is known a priori to be true. Leibniz thought that reliance on this principle is implicit in our reasoning both about physics and about human behaviour: for example, Archimedes argued that if, in a symmetrical balance, equal weights are placed on either side, neither will go down, because there is no reason why one side should go down rather than the other; and equally a rational being cannot act without a motive.[4] But what is being used by Archimedes is just the rule that like causes produce like effects. This, and in general the search for, and expectation of, causes and regularities and reasons, do indeed guide inquiry in many fields. But the principles used are not known a priori, and Samuel Clarke pointed out a difficulty in applying them even to human behaviour: someone who has a good reason for doing either A or B, but no reason for doing one of these rather than the other, will surely choose one arbitrarily rather than do neither.[5] Even if, as is possible, we have some innate tendency to look for and expect such symmetries and continuities and regularities, this does not give us an a priori guarantee that such can always be found. In so far as our reliance on such principles is epistemically

justified, it is so a posteriori, by the degree of success we have had in interpreting the world with their help. And in any case these principles of causation, symmetry, and so on refer to how the world works; we are extrapolating far beyond their so far fruitful use when we postulate a principle of sufficient reason and apply it to the world as a whole. Even if, within the world, everything seemed to have a sufficient reason, that is, a cause in accordance with some regularity, with like causes producing like effects, this would give us little ground for expecting the world as a whole, or its basic causal laws themselves, to have a sufficient reason of some different sort.

The principle of sufficient reason expresses a demand that things should be intelligible *through and through*. The simple reply to the argument which relies on it is that there is nothing that justifies this demand, and nothing that supports the belief that it is satisfiable even in principle. As we have seen in considering the other main objection to Leibniz's argument, it is difficult to see how there even could be anything that would satisfy it. If we reject this demand, we are not thereby committed to saying that things are utterly unintelligible. The sort of intelligibility that is achieved by successful causal inquiry and scientific explanation is not undermined by its inability to make things intelligible through and through. Any particular explanation starts with premises which state "brute facts", and although the brutally factual starting-points of one explanation may themselves be further explained by another, the latter in turn will have to start with something that it does not explain, *and so on however far we go*. But there is no need to see this as unsatisfactory.

A sufficient reason is also sometimes thought of as a final cause or purpose. Indeed, if we think of each event in the history of the world as having (in principle) been explained by its antecedent causes, but still want a further explanation of the whole sequence of events, we must turn to some other sort of explanation. The two candidates that then come to mind are two kinds of purposive or teleological explanation. Things are as they are, Plato suggested, because it is *better* that they should be so.[6] This can be construed either as implying that (objective) value is in itself creative [. . .] or as meaning that some intelligent being sees what would be better, chooses it, and brings it about. But why must we look for a sufficient reason of either of these sorts? The principle of sufficient reason, thus understood, expresses a demand for some kind of absolute purposiveness. But if we reject this demand, we are not thereby saying that "man and the universe are ultimately meaningless".[7] People will still have the purposes that they have, some of which they can fulfil, even if the question "What is the purpose of the world as a whole?" has no positive answer.

The principle of sufficient reason, then, is more far-reaching than the principle that every occurrence has a preceding sufficient cause: the latter, but not the former, would be satisfied by a series of things or events running back infinitely in time, each determined by earlier ones, but with no further explanation of the series as a whole. Such a series would give us only what Leibniz called "physical" or "hypothetical" necessity, whereas the demand for a sufficient reason for the whole body of contingent things and events and laws calls for something with "absolute" or "metaphysical" necessity. But even the weaker, deterministic, principle is not an a priori truth, and indeed it may not be a truth at all; much less can this be claimed for the principle of sufficient reason. Perhaps it just expresses an arbitrary demand; it may be intellectually satisfying to believe that there is, objectively, an explanation for everything together, even if we can only guess at what the explanation might be. But we have no right to assume that the universe will comply with our intellectual preferences. Alternatively, the supposed principle may be an unwarranted extension of the determinist one, which, in so far as it is supported, is supported only empirically, by our success in actually finding causes, and can at most be accepted provisionally, not as an a priori truth. The form of the cosmological argument which relies on the principle of sufficient reason therefore fails completely as a demonstrative proof.

(b)   The Regress of Causes

There is a popular line of thought, which we may call the first cause argument, and which runs as follows: things must be caused, and their causes will be other things that must have causes, and so on; but this series of causes cannot go back indefinitely; it must terminate in a first cause, and this first cause will be God. This argument envisages a regress of causes in time, but says (as Leibniz, for one, did not) that this regress must stop somewhere. Though it has some initial plausibility, it also has obvious difficulties. Why must the regress

terminate at all? Why, if it terminates, must it lead to a single termination, to one first cause, rather than to a number – perhaps an indefinitely large number – of distinct uncaused causes? And even if there is just one first cause, why should we identify this with God? I shall come back to this argument and to possible replies to these objections; but first I want to look at a more elaborate philosophical argument that has some, though not much, resemblance to it.

Of Aquinas's "five ways", the first three are recognizably variants of the cosmological proof, and all three involve some kind of terminated regress of causes.[8] But all of them are quite different from our first cause argument. The first way argues to a first mover, using the illustration of something's being moved by a stick only when the stick is moved by a hand; here the various movings are simultaneous, we do not have a regress of causes in time. Similarly the "efficient causes" in the second way are contemporary agents. Both these arguments, as Kenny has shown, depend too much on antiquated physical theory to be of much interest now. The third way is much more significant. This argument is in two stages, and can be freely translated, with some condensation, as follows:

First stage: If everything were able-not-to-be, then at some time there would have been nothing (because what is able-not-to-be, at some time is not); and then (since what does not exist cannot begin to be except through something which is) even now there would be nothing. It is plainly not true that there is nothing now; so it cannot be true that everything is able-not-to-be. That is, there must be at least one thing which is necessary.

Second stage: Everything that is necessary either has a cause of its necessity outside itself, or it does not. But it is not possible to go to infinity in a series of necessary things each of which has a cause of its necessity outside itself; this is like what has been proved about efficient causes. Therefore we must assume something which is necessary through itself, which does not have a cause of its necessity outside itself, but which is the cause of the necessity of the other things; and this men all call God.

This argument is quite different from our first cause argument and also from Leibniz's argument from contingency. Although it uses the contrast between things which are able-not-to-be (and therefore contingent) and those which are necessary, it is not satisfied with the conclusion that there is something necessary; it allows that there may be many necessary things, and reaches God only at the end of the second stage, as what has its necessity "through itself" (per se). Clearly "necessary" does not mean the same for Aquinas as for Leibniz. What it does mean will become clearer as we examine the reasoning.

In the first stage, the premiss "what is able-not-to-be, at some time is not" seems dubious: why should not something which is *able* not to be nevertheless just happen to exist always? But perhaps Aquinas means by "things that are able-not-to-be" (*possibilia non esse*) something like "impermanent things", so that this premiss is analytic. Even so, the statement that if everything were such, at some time there would have been nothing, does not follow: some impermanent things might have lasted through all past time, and be going to display their impermanence by perishing only at some time in the future. But we may be able to understand Aquinas's thought by seeing what is said more explicitly by Maimonides, by whom Aquinas appears to have been influenced here.[9] His corresponding proof seems to assume that past time has been finite – and reasonably so, for if past time has been finite there would seem to be an easier argument for a divine creator, such as we shall consider below. The suggestion is that it would not have been possible for impermanent things to have lasted throughout an infinite time, and hence they would have perished already.

However, another objection is that there might be a series of things, each of which was impermanent and perished after a finite period, but whose periods of existence overlapped so that there never was a time when there was nothing. It would be a clear logical fallacy (of which some commentators have accused Aquinas) to infer "at some time everything is not" from "each thing at some time is not". But we might defend Aquinas in either of two ways. First, if each thing were impermanent, it would be the most improbable good luck if the overlapping sequence kept up through infinite time. Secondly, even if this improbable luck holds, we might regard the series of overlapping things as itself a thing which had already lasted through infinite time, and so could not be impermanent. Indeed, if there were such a series which never failed, this might well indicate that there was some *permanent* stock of material of which the perishable

things were composed and into which they disintegrated, thereby contributing to the composition of other things.

A third objection concerns the premiss that "what does not exist cannot begin to be except through something that is". This is, of course, a form of the principle that nothing can come from nothing; the idea then is that if our series of impermanent things had broken off, it could never have started again after a gap. But is this an a priori truth? As Hume pointed out, we can certainly conceive an uncaused beginning-to-be of an object; if what we can thus conceive is nevertheless in some way impossible, this still requires to be shown.[10] Still, this principle has some plausibility, in that it is constantly confirmed in our experience (and also used, reasonably, in interpreting our experience).

Altogether, then, the first stage of Aquinas's argument falls short of watertight demonstration, but it gives some lower degree of support to the conclusion that there is at least one thing that is necessary in the sense, which has now become clear, that it is permanent, that *for some reason* it is not able-not-to-be.

The second stage takes this conclusion as its starting-point. One permanent thing, it allows, may be caused to be permanent, sustained always in existence, by another. But, it holds, there cannot be an infinite regress of such things. Why not? Aquinas refers us to his earlier proof about efficient causes, in the second way. This runs:

> It is not possible to go to infinity in a series of efficient causes. For in all ordered efficient causes the first item is the cause of the intermediate one and the intermediate is the cause of the last (whether there is only one intermediate or more than one); now if the cause is removed, so is the effect. Therefore if there has not been a first item among efficient causes there will not be a last or an intermediate. But if one goes to infinity in a series of efficient causes, there will not be a first efficient cause, and so there will not be a last effect or intermediate efficient causes . . .

Unfortunately this argument is unsound. Although in a *finite* ordered series of causes the intermediate (or the earliest intermediate) is caused by the first item, this would not be so if there were an infinite series. In an infinite series, every item is caused by an earlier item. The way in which the first item is "removed" if we go from a finite to an infinite series does not entail the removal of the later items. In fact, Aquinas (both here and in the first way) has simply begged the question against an infinite regress of causes. But is this a sheer mistake, or is there some coherent thought behind it? Some examples (some of which would not themselves have been available to Aquinas, though analogues of them would have been) may suggest that there is. If we were told that there was a watch without a mainspring, we would hardly be reassured by the further information that it had, however, an infinite train of gear-wheels. Nor would we expect a railway train consisting of an infinite number of carriages, the last pulled along by the second last, the second last by the third last, and so on, to get along without an engine. Again, we see a chain, consisting of a series of links, hanging from a hook; we should be surprised to learn that there was a similar but infinite chain, with no hook, but links supported by links above them for ever. The point is that in these examples, and in the series of efficient causes or of necessary things, it is assumed that there is a relation of *dependence* – or, equivalently, one in the reverse direction of *support* – and, if the series were infinite, there would in the end be nothing for the effects to depend on, nothing to support them. And the same would be true if the regress were not infinite but circular.

There is here an implicit appeal to the following general principle: Where items are ordered by a relation of dependence, the regress must end somewhere; it cannot be either infinite or circular. Perhaps this principle was intended by al Farabi in the dictum that is translated "But a series of contingent beings which would produce one another cannot proceed to infinity or move in a circle" (p. 83). As our examples show, this principle is at least highly plausible; the problem will be to decide when we have such a relation of dependence.

In the second stage of Aquinas's argument, therefore, the key notion is that any necessary – that is, permanent – thing either depends for its permanence on something else or is *per se necessarium* in a sense which can apply only to God. The actual text of the third way does not reveal Aquinas's thinking about this. But comparison of it with other passages in his writings and with Maimonides's proof suggests that the implicit assumption is that anything whose essence does not involve existence must, even if it is permanent, depend for its existence on something else.[11] This assumption would give the dependence which would call for an end to the regress and also ensure that nothing could end it but a being whose essence involved existence

– which would explain the assertion that what is *per se necessarium* is what men all call God.

But the final objection to the argument is that we have no reason for accepting this implicit assumption. Why, for example, might there not be a permanent stock of matter whose essence did not involve existence but which did not derive its existence from anything else?

It is obvious that, as I said earlier, Aquinas's third way is very different from Leibniz's cosmological proof. Yet there has been a tendency to assimilate the former to the latter.[12] This is understandable, in that Aquinas would need something like the principle of sufficient reason to support what I have called the implicit assumption against our final objection: for example, there being a permanent stock of matter would be just a brute fact that had no sufficient reason, whereas something whose essence involved existence would seem to have, in itself, per se, a sufficient reason for its permanence. But in view of our criticisms of Leibniz's argument, no borrowing from it can rescue that of Aquinas.

But what about the popular first cause argument? Can we not now answer our earlier queries? Why must the regress of causes in time terminate? Because things, states of affairs, and occurrences *depend* on their antecedent causes. Why must the regress lead to one first cause rather than to many uncaused causes, and why must that one cause be God? Because anything other than God would need something else causally to depend upon. Moreover, the assumption needed for this argument is more plausible than that needed for Leibniz's proof, or for Aquinas's. The notion that everything must have a sufficient reason is a metaphysician's demand, as is the notion that anything permanent must depend for its permanence on something else unless its essence involves existence. But the notion that an effect *depends* on a temporally earlier cause is part of our ordinary understanding of causation: we all have some grasp of this asymmetry between cause and effect, however hard it may be to give an exact analysis of it.[13]

Nevertheless, this argument is not demonstratively cogent. Though we understand that where something has a temporally antecedent cause, it depends somehow upon it, it does not follow that everything (other than God) *needs* something else to depend on in this way. Also, what we can call al Farabi's principle, that where items are ordered by a relation of dependence, the regress must terminate somewhere, and cannot be either infinite or circular, though plausible, may not be really sound. But the greatest weakness of this otherwise attractive argument is that some reason is required for making God the one exception to the supposed need for something else to depend on: why should God, rather than anything else, be taken as the only satisfactory termination of the regress? If we do not simply accept this as a sheer mystery (which would be to abandon rational theology and take refuge in faith), we shall have to defend it in something like the ways that the metaphysicians have suggested. But then this popular argument takes on board the burdens that have sunk its more elaborate philosophical counterparts.

(c) Finite Past Time and Creation

There is, as Craig explains, a distinctive kind of cosmological argument which, unlike those of Aquinas, Leibniz, and many others, assumes or argues that the past history of the world is finite.[14] This, which Craig calls, by its Arabic name, the *kalam* type of argument, was favoured by Islamic thinkers who were suspicious of the subtleties of the philosophers and relied more on revelation than on reason. Nevertheless, they did propound this as a rational proof of God's existence, and some of them used mathematical paradoxes that are descended from Zeno's, or that anticipate Cantor's, to show that there cannot be an actual infinite – in particular, an infinite past time. For example, if time past were infinite, an infinite stretch would have actually to have been traversed in order to reach the present, and this is thought to be impossible. Then there is an ingenious argument suggested by al Ghazali: the planet Jupiter revolves in its orbit once every twelve years, Saturn once every thirty years; so Jupiter must have completed more than twice as many revolutions as Saturn; yet if past time were infinite they would each have completed the same (infinite) number; which is a contradiction (pp. 101–2). The first of these (which Kant also uses in the thesis of his First Antinomy) just expresses a prejudice against an actual infinity. It assumes that, even if past time were infinite, there would still have been a starting-point of time, but one infinitely remote, so that an actual infinity would have had to be traversed to reach the present from there. But to take the hypothesis of infinity seriously would be to suppose that there was no starting-point, not even an infinitely remote one,

and that from any specific point in past time there is only a finite stretch that needs to be traversed to reach the present. Al Ghazali's argument uses an instance of one of Cantor's paradoxes, that in an infinite class a part can indeed be equal to the whole: for example, there are just as many even numbers (2, 4, 6, etc.) as there are whole numbers (1, 2, 3, etc.), since these classes can be matched one–one with each other. But is this not a contradiction? Is not the class of even numbers both equal to that of the integers (because of this one–one correlation) and smaller than it (because it is a proper part of it, the part that leaves out the odd numbers)? But what this brings out is that we ordinarily have and use a criterion for one group's being smaller than another – that it is, or can be correlated one–one with, a proper part of the other – and a criterion for two groups' being equal in number – that they can be correlated one–one with each other – which together ensure that *smaller than* and *equal to* exclude one another for all pairs of finite groups, but not for pairs of infinite groups. Once we understand the relation between the two criteria, we see that there is no real contradiction.

In short, it seems impossible to disprove, a priori, the possibility of an infinite past time. Nevertheless, many people have shared, and many still do share, these doubts about an actual infinite in the real world, even if they are willing to leave mathematicians free to play their Cantorian games – which, of course, not all mathematicians, or all philosophers of mathematics, want to play. Also the view that, whatever we say about *time*, the *universe* has a finite past history, has in recent years received strong empirical support from the cosmology that is a branch of astronomy. So let us consider what the prospects would be for a proof of the existence of a god if we were supplied, from whatever source, with the premiss that the world has only a finite past history, and therefore a beginning in time, whether or not this is also the beginning of time. Here the crucial assumption is stated by al Ghazali: "[We] know by rational necessity that nothing which originates in time originates by itself, and that, therefore, it needs a creator" (p. 102). But *do* we know this by rational necessity? Surely the assumption required here is just the same as that which is used differently in the first cause argument, that anything other than a god needs a cause or a creator to depend on. But there is a priori no good reason why a sheer origination of things, not determined by anything, should be unacceptable, whereas the existence of a god with the power to create something out of nothing is acceptable.

When we look hard at the latter notion we find problems within it. Does God's existence have a sheer origination in time? But then this would be as great a puzzle as the sheer origination of a material world. Or has God existed for ever through an infinite time? But this would raise again the problem of the actual infinite. To avoid both of these, we should have to postulate that God's own existence is not in time at all; but this would be a complete mystery.

Alternatively, someone might not share al Ghazali's worries about the actual infinite, and might rely on an empirical argument – such as the modern cosmological evidence for the "big bang" – to show that the material world had a beginning in time. For him, therefore, God's existence through an infinite time would be unproblematic. But he is still using the crucial assumptions that God's existence and creative power would be self-explanatory whereas the unexplained origination of a material world would be unintelligible and therefore unacceptable. But the first of these leads us back to the criticism stated in section (a), on pp. 243–4. The notion, embedded in the ontological argument, of a being whose existence is self-explanatory because it is not the case that it might not have existed, is *not* defensible; so we cannot borrow that notion to complete any form of the cosmological argument. The second assumption is equally questionable. We have no good ground for an a priori certainty that there could not have been a sheer unexplained beginning of things. But in so far as we find this improbable, it should cast doubt on the interpretation of the big bang as an absolute beginning of the material universe; rather, we should infer that it must have had *some* physical antecedents, even if the big bang has to be taken as a discontinuity so radical that we cannot explain it, because we can find no laws which we can extrapolate backwards through this discontinuity.

In short, the notion of creation seems more acceptable than any other way out of the cosmological maze only because we do not look hard either at it or at the human experiences of making things on which it is modelled. It is vaguely explanatory, apparently satisfying; but these appearances fade away when we try to formulate the suggestion precisely.

(d) Swinburne's Inductive Cosmological Argument

We might well have anticipated, from the beginning, the conclusion that our discussion in this chapter has thus laboriously reached. We have no general grounds for expecting to be able to demonstrate, by deductively valid arguments, using premises that are known with certainty, conclusions which go far beyond the empirical data on which they are based. And particularly since Hume and Kant philosophers have tended to be very sceptical about such a possibility. On the other hand we do have good general grounds for expecting to be able to confirm, provisionally but sometimes quite strongly, hypotheses that go far beyond the observational data that support them, and to confirm them in a sense that makes it reasonable for us to rely, for practical purposes, on their being either true or at any rate fairly close to the truth. The successful growth of the empirical sciences over the last 400 years justifies such a general expectation, no matter what problems there may still be in developing a satisfactory theory of the confirmation of hypotheses or of the justification of inductive reasoning. Though the theologians of the past wanted much more, many thinkers today would be content if theism were as well confirmed as one of the better-established scientific theories. So we might well consider whether there is a good inductive or hypothesis-confirming variant of the cosmological argument; and this is what Swinburne has tried to present.[15]

Swinburne prefixes to his whole discussion of the existence of a god an account of inductive reasoning in general. The statement that a hypothesis is "confirmed" by certain evidence is ambiguous: it may mean that the evidence has raised the probability of the hypothesis as compared with what it was, or would have been, apart from that evidence; or it may mean that the evidence makes the hypothesis more likely than not to be true. Swinburne speaks of a "good C-inductive argument", meaning one in which the premises or evidence confirm the conclusion or hypothesis in the former sense, and of a "good P-inductive argument" where they confirm it in the latter sense. As he says, it is harder to tell when we have a good P-inductive argument than when we have a good C-inductive argument. But in either case it is a question of an *argument*: we are concerned with relations of non-deductive support between certain evidence, in the light of some body of background knowledge or belief, and a hypothesis or conclusion. Any judgment that we reasonably make will be provisional, in that further evidence, or a change in the background knowledge or belief, may alter the degree of confirmation or the balance of probabilities, and one important kind of change in the background is the introduction of further, rival, possible explanatory hypotheses, or a change in the initial probability of such hypotheses.

There is an important principle which serves as a criterion for a good C-inductive argument. A hypothesis is confirmed by certain evidence if and only if (apart from or prior to that evidence's being observed) the addition of the hypothesis to the background knowledge or belief makes it more probable that that evidence would occur than it would be in relation to the background knowledge or belief alone. Symbolically, if "h" stands for the hypothesis, "e" for the evidence, "k" for the background knowledge or belief, and "$P(x/y)$" for the probability of x in relation to y, then h is confirmed – in the sense of having its probability raised – by e if and only if $P(e/h\&k) > P(e/k)$. Or, equivalently, a hypothesis is in this sense confirmed by evidence if and only if that evidence would have been more likely to occur if the hypothesis had been true than if it had been false: h is confirmed by e if and only if $P(e/h\&k) > P(e/{\sim}h\&k)$. In other words, the evidence raises the probability of the hypothesis if and only if the addition of the hypothesis raises the antecedent probability of the evidence. This holds provided that the initial probability of the hypothesis in relation to the background knowledge or belief is not zero.

This principle may be illustrated by a simple detective story example. The finding, in the dried mud of a path, of footmarks which closely match Fred's shoes in shape, size, and degree of wear, and the distances between which match the ordinary length of his stride, makes it more likely that Fred walked along that path when it was last wet than it would have been without this evidence. Why? Because the hypothesis that Fred walked there then raises the probability that there would now be just such footmarks as compared with what it would be without that hypothesis, or on the supposition that he did not walk there then. If our background information makes it quite likely that there would be such marks even if Fred had not walked there – for example, if Fred has a twin brother who frequently borrows Fred's shoes and

who uses that path – the addition of the hypothesis that Fred walked there does not raise the antecedent probability of the footmarks so much (since it was fairly high without that hypothesis, or even in relation to the denial of that hypothesis), and finding the marks is no longer so good a confirmation that Fred was there. Again (even if Fred has no twin brother) if our background knowledge makes it impossible that Fred should have walked on the path when it was last wet – for example, if Fred died before the last heavy rain – then although the addition of the hypothesis would raise the antecedent probability of that evidence, the evidence cannot confirm the hypothesis: its zero initial probability cannot be raised.

This principle concerns C-inductive arguments, the conditions for the raising of the probability of a hypothesis by evidence. When we come to P-inductive arguments, to the question whether the evidence makes the hypothesis on balance more likely than not, the initial probability of the hypothesis is very significant. Even if the evidence *raises* the probability of the hypothesis in comparison with what it was otherwise, it may fail to make it more likely than not, because the initial probability of the hypothesis was low. This was illustrated in our discussion of miracles [not included here]: because the initial probability of a miracle's occurring is so low, it would need very good evidence indeed to make it more likely than not that one had occurred. Even evidence which the miracle's occurrence would explain and make probable, but which would have been very unlikely to come about without the miracle, may be insufficient to overcome the antecedent improbability of the miracle so as to make it now more likely than not that it occurred.

These can be taken as agreed principles of inductive reasoning; the problem is to apply them to the cosmological argument. Swinburne's first point is an adaptation of one of Leibniz's. Even if the universe has an infinite history in which each event is causally explained by the conjunction of laws and earlier events, that history as a whole is still unexplained. It might have been radically different – either with different laws or with the same laws but different specific situations all the way along – or there might have been nothing at all; no explanation has been given to show why neither of these possibilities was fulfilled. But, secondly, Swinburne suggests, the hypothesis that there is a god would to some extent explain the existence and the actual history of the universe. He is claiming that there is a kind of explanation, quite different from causal explanation, which is used when we explain something as the intentional action of a rational being; he calls this "personal explanation". On the assumption that there is a god such as traditional theism proclaims, it follows that he could make a physical universe if he chose, and that he might have had some reason to do so. Swinburne does not, indeed, say that the hypothesis (h) that there is such a god makes it very probable that (e) there should be such a universe as this:

> However I do not claim that $P(e/h.k)$ is especially high. $P(e/h.k)$ measures how likely it is if there is a God that there will be a physical universe. The choice before God among worlds to create includes a world where there is just God; a world where there are one or more finite non-physical objects (e.g. non-embodied spirits); a world consisting of a simple physical universe (e.g. just one round steel ball); and a world which is a complex physical universe. There are good reasons why God should make a complex physical universe. For such a universe can be beautiful, and that is good; and also it can be a theatre for finite agents to develop and make of it what they will . . . But I cannot see that God has overriding reason to make such a universe . . . Nor can I see that he has overriding reason to make or not to make any alternative world. (pp. 130–1 [pp. 239–40, this volume])

Swinburne is not saying, then, that this is obviously the best of all possible worlds; so $P(e/h\&k)$ is not high. On the other hand, he thinks that $P(e/k)$ is still lower: a complex physical universe is "very unlikely to come about but for God's agency". Consequently we do have that $P(e/h\&k) > P(e/k)$, and therefore that there is a good C-inductive argument from the existence of a complex physical universe to the existence of the god of traditional theism.

As we have seen, this will hold only if $P(h/k)$, the initial probability of the existence of such a god, is not zero. Let us grant this. Still, all that is being said is that the existence of a complex physical universe *raises* the likelihood of a god, makes it more probable than it would have been otherwise, that is, if there had been no such universe. But it is hard to see how this helps us. How can we even think about the antecedent probability that there

should be a god, given that there was no such universe? Presumably we must think of an initial probability of there being a god, relative only to tautological information, and if we have rejected the ontological argument this will be pretty low. But there is very little analogy with Fred's case, where it was, perhaps, apart from the footmarks, not very likely that he had walked along that path, but the discovery of the footmarks makes it much more probable. The trouble is that if the evidence, e, is to be that there is a complex physical universe, then the background knowledge or belief k must exclude this, and so will be able to include only logical and mathematical truths. What likelihood could the god-hypothesis have had in relation to these?

We may be asking the wrong question, then, if we ask whether there is a good C-inductive argument from the sheer existence of a complex physical universe to the existence of a god. Swinburne's summary puts the issue differently:

> There is quite a chance that if there is a God he will make something of the finitude and complexity of a universe. It is very unlikely that a universe would exist uncaused, but rather more likely that God would exist uncaused. The existence of the universe is strange and puzzling. It can be made comprehensible if we suppose that it is brought about by God. This supposition postulates a simpler beginning of explanation than does the supposition of an uncaused universe, and that is grounds for believing the former supposition to be true. (pp. 131–2 [p. 240, this volume])

We are now comparing the two rival hypotheses, one that there is no further cause or explanation of the complex physical universe, the other that there is a god who created it. That there is this universe is common ground, shared by the two hypotheses. Swinburne is arguing that in relation to our background knowledge – which can now include everything that we ordinarily know about ourselves and the world, though it must exclude any specifically religious beliefs – it is more likely that there should be an uncaused god who created the world than simply an uncaused universe – that is, a universe with internal causal relationships, but no further cause for its basic laws being as they are or for its being there at all. The analogy would be with the reasoning in which we postulate a common ancestor for a group of similar manuscripts, on the ground that their otherwise unexplained and therefore improbable resemblances can be explained as being due to their having been copied, directly or indirectly, from this ancestor; the surviving-manuscripts-plus-common-ancestor hypothesis is more acceptable than a surviving-manuscripts-with-no-common-ancestor hypothesis.

But now the fact that the uncaused universe would, by definition, have no further explanation does not justify the claim that it is "strange and puzzling" or "very unlikely". The mere fact that it is a complex physical universe does not mean that it includes anything comparable to the resemblances between our manuscripts that would be surprising if not further explained. [. . .] On the other side, the hypothesis of divine creation *is* very unlikely. Although *if* there were a god with the traditional attributes and powers, he would be able and perhaps willing to create such a universe as this, we have to weigh in our scales the likelihood or unlikelihood *that* there is a god with these attributes and powers. And the key power, involved in Swinburne's use of "personal explanation", is that of fulfilling intentions *directly*, without any physical or causal mediation, without materials or instruments. There is nothing in our background knowledge that makes it comprehensible, let alone likely, that anything should have such a power. All our knowledge of intention-fulfilment is of *embodied* intentions being fulfilled *indirectly* by way of bodily changes and movements which are *causally* related to the intended result, and where the ability thus to fulfil intentions itself has a *causal history*, either of evolutionary development or of learning or of both. Only by ignoring such key features do we get an analogue of the supposed divine action. But even apart from this I see no plausibility in the statement that it is "rather more likely that God would exist uncaused". Swinburne's backing for this is that "the supposition that there is a God is an extremely simple supposition; the postulation of a God of infinite power, knowledge, and freedom is the postulation of the simplest kind of person which there could be", whereas "There is a complexity, particularity, and finitude about the universe which cries out for explanation" (p. 130 [p. 239, this volume]). (It is somewhat ironic that whereas God seemed to Anselm and others to be self-explanatory because he is something than which nothing greater can be conceived, he now seems to

Swinburne to be relatively self-explanatory because he is simple.) But, first, the "simplicity" achieved by taking everything to infinity is bought at the cost of asserting a whole series of real actual infinites, about which, as I mentioned, many thinkers, like al Ghazali above, have had doubts. Secondly, the particularity has not been removed, but only shelved: we should have to postulate particularities in God, to explain his choice of the particular universe he decided to create. And the very notion of a non-embodied spirit, let alone an infinite one, is intrinsically improbable in relation to our background knowledge, in that our experience reveals nothing of the sort.

Some of the themes we encountered in dealing with the older forms of cosmological argument recur here. Like Leibniz, Swinburne is looking for explanation and intelligibility. He does not, like Leibniz, demand a complete explanation, a sufficient reason for everything, or intelligibility through and through; but he is trying to minimize the unexplained part of our total picture. But without introducing the concept of something that contains its own sufficient reason, or whose essence includes existence – unsatisfactory though, in the end, these notions are – he has nothing to support the claim that by adding a god to the world we *reduce* the unexplained element. Although his starting-point is like Leibniz's, his conclusion is more like that of the *kalam* argument, in taking creation by a person as the one satisfactory beginning of things. But when we look hard at it, such "personal explanation" is not a satisfactory beginning at all, and certainly not one that is given any initial probability by the ordinary information that we have to take as our background knowledge.

The prospects for an inductive or probabilistic or hypothesis-confirming variant of the cosmological argument are, therefore, no better than those for a demonstrative one. However, our criticisms have been directed particularly against a *cosmological* argument in the sense explained at the beginning of this chapter, that is, one whose empirical datum is either the mere fact that there is a world at all or such very general facts about it as that there is change or motion or causation. These criticisms leave open the possibility that the hypothesis that there is a god may be confirmed by evidence of more detailed and specific kinds, for example by the existence of conscious beings, or the presence of what have been seen as "marks of design".

Notes

1 W. L. Craig, *The Cosmological Argument from Plato to Leibniz* (Macmillan, London, 1980). Quotations from al Farabi and al Ghazali are taken from this work.

2 The clearest account is in "On the Ultimate Origination of Things", printed, e.g., in G. W. Leibniz, *Philosophical Writings* (Dent, London, 1934), pp. 32–41.

3 *Critique of Pure Reason*, Transcendental Dialectic, Book II, Chapter III, Section 5.

4 *The Leibniz–Clarke Correspondence*, edited by H. G. Alexander (Manchester University Press, 1956 and 1976), Leibniz's Second Paper.

5 Ibid., Clarke's Third and Fifth Replies.

6 Plato, *Phaedo*, 97–9.

7 Craig, *The Cosmological Argument*, p. 287.

8 A. Kenny, *The Five Ways* (Routledge & Kegan Paul, London, 1969).

9 Craig, *The Cosmological Argument*, ch. 4.

10 *Treatise*, Book I, Part iii, Section 3; contrast Kenny, *The Five Ways*, p. 67.

11 Craig, *The Cosmological Argument*, pp. 142–3, 146–8.

12 Ibid., p. 283.

13 Cf. chapter 7 of my *The Cement of the Universe* (Clarendon Press, Oxford, 1980).

14 Craig, *The Cosmological Argument*, ch. 3.

15 In chapter 7 of *The Existence of God* (Oxford University Press, 1979). References in the text are to pages in this work. [See also ch. 19 in this volume.]

21

Teleological Argument

David Hume

Look round the world, contemplate the whole and every part of it: you will find it to be nothing but one great machine, subdivided into an infinite number of lesser machines, which again admit of subdivisions to a degree beyond what human senses and faculties can trace and explain. All these various machines, and even their most minute parts, are adjusted to each other with an accuracy which ravishes into admiration all men who have ever contemplated them. The curious adapting of means to ends, throughout all nature, resembles exactly, though it much exceeds, the productions of human contrivance – of human design, thought, wisdom, and intelligence. Since therefore the effects resemble each other, we are led to infer, by all the rules of analogy, that the causes also resemble, and that the Author of nature is somewhat similar to the mind of man, though possessed of much larger faculties, proportioned to the grandeur of the work which he has executed. By this argument *a posteriori*, and by this argument alone, do we prove at once the existence of a Deity and his similarity to human mind and intelligence.

I shall be so free, Cleanthes, said Demea, as to tell you that from the beginning I could not approve of your conclusion concerning the similarity of the Deity to men, still less can I approve of the mediums by which you endeavour to establish it. What! No demonstration of the Being of God! No

David Hume, "Teleological Argument," Part II from David Hume, *Dialogues Concerning Natural Religion*, edited by Henry D. Aitken (New York: Hafner Publishing Co., 1948).

abstract arguments! No proofs *a priori!* Are these which have hitherto been so much insisted on by philosophers all fallacy, all sophism? Can we reach no farther in this subject than experience and probability? I will not say that this is betraying the cause of a Deity; but surely, by this affected candour, you give advantages to atheists which they never could obtain by the mere dint of argument and reasoning.

What I chiefly scruple in this subject, said Philo, is not so much that all religious arguments are by Cleanthes reduced to experience, as that they appear not to be even the most certain and irrefragable of that inferior kind. That a stone will fall, that fire will burn, that the earth has solidity, we have observed a thousand and a thousand times; and when any new instance of this nature is presented, we draw without hesitation the accustomed inference. The exact similarity of the cases gives us a perfect assurance of a similar event, and a stronger evidence is never desired nor sought after. But wherever you depart, in the least, from the similarity of the cases, you diminish proportionably the evidence, and may at last bring it to a very weak *analogy*, which is confessedly liable to error and uncertainty. After having experienced the circulation of the blood in human creatures, we make no doubt that it takes place in Titius and Maevius; but from its circulation in frogs and fishes it is only a presumption, though a strong one, from analogy that it takes place in men and other animals. The analogical reasoning is much weaker when we infer the circulation of the sap in vegetables from our experience that the blood circulates in animals; and those who hastily followed that imperfect analogy are found, by more accurate experiments, to have been mistaken.

If we see a house, Cleanthes, we conclude, with the greatest certainty, that it had an architect or builder because this is precisely that species of effect which we have experienced to proceed from that species of cause. But surely you will not affirm that the universe bears such a resemblance to a house that we can with the same certainty infer a similar cause, or that the analogy is here entire and perfect. The dissimilitude is so striking that the utmost you can here pretend to is a guess, a conjecture, a presumption concerning a similar cause; and how that pretension will be received in the world, I leave you to consider.

It would surely be very ill received, replied Cleanthes; and I should be deservedly blamed and detested did I allow that the proofs of a Deity amounted to no more than a guess or conjecture. But is the whole adjustment of means to ends in a house and in the universe so slight a resemblance? the economy of final causes? the order, proportion, and arrangement of every part? Steps of a stair are plainly contrived that human legs may use them in mounting; and this inference is certain and infallible. Human legs are also contrived for walking and mounting; and this inference, I allow, is not altogether so certain because of the dissimilarity which you remark; but does it, therefore, deserve the name only of presumption or conjecture?

Good God! cried Demea, interrupting him, where are we? Zealous defenders of religion allow that the proofs of a Deity fall short of perfect evidence! And you, Philo, on whose assistance I depended in proving the adorable mysteriousness of the Divine Nature, do you assent to all these extravagant opinions of Cleanthes? For what other name can I give them? or, why spare my censure when such principles are advanced, supported by such an authority, before so young a man as Pamphilus?

You seem not to apprehend, replied Philo, that I argue with Cleanthes in his own way, and, by showing him the dangerous consequences of his tenets, hope at last to reduce him to our opinion. But what sticks most with you, I observe, is the representation which Cleanthes has made of the argument *a posteriori*; and, finding that that argument is likely to escape your hold and vanish into air, you think it so disguised that you can scarcely believe it to be set in its true light. Now, however much I may dissent, in other respects, from the dangerous

principle of Cleanthes, I must allow that he has fairly represented that argument, and I shall endeavour so to state the matter to you that you will entertain no further scruples with regard to it.

Were a man to abstract from everything which he knows or has seen, he would be altogether incapable, merely from his own ideas, to determine what kind of scene the universe must be, or to give the preference to one state or situation of things above another. For as nothing which he clearly conceives could be esteemed impossible or implying a contradiction, every chimera of his fancy would be upon an equal footing; nor could he assign any just reason why he adheres to one idea or system, and rejects the others which are equally possible.

Again, after he opens his eyes and contemplates the world as it really is, it would be impossible for him at first to assign the cause of any one event, much less of the whole of things, or of the universe. He might set his fancy a rambling, and she might bring him in an infinite variety of reports and representations. These would all be possible, but, being all equally possible, he would never of himself give a satisfactory account for his preferring one of them to the rest. Experience alone can point out to him the true cause of any phenomenon.

Now, according to this method of reasoning, Demea, it follows (and is, indeed, tacitly allowed by Cleanthes himself) that order, arrangement, or the adjustment of final causes, is not of itself any proof of design, but only so far as it has been experienced to proceed from that principle. For aught we can know *a priori*, matter may contain the source or spring of order originally within itself, as well as mind does; and there is no more difficulty in conceiving that the several elements, from an internal unknown cause, may fall into the most exquisite arrangement, than to conceive that their ideas, in the great universal mind, from a like internal unknown cause, fall into that arrangement. The equal possibility of both these suppositions is allowed. But, by experience, we find (according to Cleanthes) that there is a difference between them. Throw several pieces of steel together, without shape or form, they will never arrange themselves so as to compose a watch. Stone and mortar and wood, without an architect, never erect a house. But the ideas in a human mind, we see, by an unknown, inexplicable economy, arrange themselves so as to form the plan of a watch or house. Experience, therefore, proves that there is an original principle of order in mind, not in matter. From similar effects we infer similar causes. The adjustment of means to ends is alike in the universe, as in a machine of human contrivance. The causes, therefore, must be resembling.

I was from the beginning scandalized, I must own, with this resemblance which is asserted between the Deity and human creatures, and must conceive it to imply such a degradation of the Supreme Being as no sound theist could endure. With your assistance, therefore, Demea, I shall endeavour to defend what you justly call the adorable mysteriousness of the Divine Nature, and shall refute this reasoning of Cleanthes, provided he allows that I have made a fair representation of it.

When Cleanthes had assented, Philo, after a short pause, proceeded in the following manner.

That all inferences, Cleanthes, concerning fact are founded on experience, and that all experimental reasonings are founded on the supposition that similar causes prove similar effects, and similar effect similar causes, I shall not at present much dispute with you. But observe, I entreat you, with what extreme caution all just reasoners proceed in the transferring of experiments to similar cases. Unless the cases be exactly similar, they repose no perfect confidence in applying their past observation to any particular phenomenon. Every alteration of circumstances occasions a doubt concerning the event; and it requires new experiments to prove certainly that the new circumstances are of no moment or importance. A change in bulk, situation, arrangement, age, disposition of the air, or surrounding bodies – any of these particulars may be attended with the most unexpected consequences. And unless the objects be quite familiar to us, it is the highest temerity to expect with assurance, after any of these changes, an event similar to that which before fell under our observation. The slow and deliberate steps of philosophers here, if anywhere, are distinguished from the precipitate march of the vulgar, who, hurried on by the smallest similitude, are incapable of all discernment or consideration.

But can you think, Cleanthes, that your usual phlegm and philosophy have been preserved in so wide a step as you have taken when you compared to the universe houses, ships, furniture, machines, and, from their similarity in some circumstances, inferred a similarity in their causes? Thought, design, intelligence, such as we discover in men and other animals, is no more than one of the springs and principles of the universe, as well as heat or cold, attraction or repulsion, and a hundred others which fall under daily observation. It is an active

cause by which some particular parts of nature, we find, produce alterations on other parts. But can a conclusion, with any propriety, be transferred from parts to the whole? Does not the great disproportion bar all comparison and inference? From observing the growth of a hair, can we learn anything concerning the generation of a man? Would the manner of a leaf's blowing, even though perfectly known, afford us any instruction concerning the vegetation of a tree?

But allowing that we were to take the *operations* of one part of nature upon another for the foundation of our judgment concerning the *origin* of the whole (which never can be admitted), yet why select so minute, so weak, so bounded a principle as the reason and design of animals is found to be upon this planet? What peculiar privilege has this little agitation of the brain which we call *thought*, that we must thus make it the model of the whole universe? Our partiality in our own favour does indeed present it on all occasions, but sound philosophy ought carefully to guard against so natural an illusion.

So far from admitting, continued Philo, that the operations of a part can afford us any just conclusion concerning the origin of the whole, I will not allow any one part to form a rule for another part if the latter be very remote from the former. Is there any reasonable ground to conclude that the inhabitants of other planets possess thought, intelligence, reason, or anything similar to these faculties in men? When nature has so extremely diversified her manner of operation in this small globe, can we imagine that she incessantly copies herself throughout so immense a universe? And if thought, as we may well suppose, be confined merely to this narrow corner and has even there so limited a sphere of action, with what propriety can we assign it for the original cause of all things? The narrow views of a peasant who makes his domestic economy the rule for the government of kingdoms is in comparison a pardonable sophism.

But were we ever so much assured that a thought and reason resembling the human were to be found throughout the whole universe, and were its activity elsewhere vastly greater and more commanding than it appears in this globe, yet I cannot see why the operations of a world constituted, arranged, adjusted, can with any propriety be extended to a world which is in its embryo state, and is advancing towards that constitution and arrangement. By observation we know somewhat of the economy, action, and nourishment of a finished animal, but we must transfer with great caution that observation to the growth of a fœtus in the womb, and still more to the formation of an animalcule in the loins of its male parent. Nature, we find, even from our limited experience, possesses an infinite number of springs and principles which incessantly discover themselves on every change of her position and situation. And what new and unknown principles would actuate her in so new and unknown a situation as that of the formation of a universe, we cannot, without the utmost temerity, pretend to determine.

A very small part of this great system, during a very short time, is very imperfectly discovered to us; and do we thence pronounce decisively concerning the origin of the whole?

Admirable conclusion! Stone, wood, brick, iron, brass, have not, at this time, in this minute globe of earth, an order or arrangement without human art and contrivance; therefore, the universe could not originally attain its order and arrangement without something similar to human art. But is a part of nature a rule for another part very wide of the former? Is it a rule for the whole? Is a very small part a rule for the universe? Is nature in one situation a certain rule for nature in another situation vastly different from the former?

And can you blame me, Cleanthes, if I here imitate the prudent reserve of Simonides, who, according to the noted story, being asked by Hiero, *What God was?* desired a day to think of it, and then two days more; and after that manner continually prolonged the term, without ever bringing in his definition or description? Could you even blame me if I had answered, at first, *that I did not know*, and was sensible that this subject lay vastly beyond the reach of my faculties? You might cry out sceptic and rallier, as much as you pleased; but, having found in so many other subjects much more familiar the imperfections and even contradictions of human reason, I never should expect any success from its feeble conjectures in a subject so sublime and so remote from the sphere of our observation. When two *species* of objects have always been observed to be conjoined together, I can *infer*, by custom, the existence of one wherever I *see* the existence of the other; and this I call an argument from experience. But how this argument can have place where the objects, as in the present case, are single, individual, without parallel or specific resemblance, may be difficult to explain. And will any man tell me with a serious countenance that an orderly universe must arise from some thought and art like the human because we

have experience of it? To ascertain this reasoning it were requisite that we had experience of the origin of worlds; and it is not sufficient, surely, that we have seen ships and cities arise from human art and contrivance.

Philo was proceeding in this vehement manner, somewhat between jest and earnest, as it appeared to me, when he observed some signs of impatience in Cleanthes, and then immediately stopped short. What I had to suggest, said Cleanthes, is only that you would not abuse terms, or make use of popular expressions to subvert philosophical reasonings. You know that the vulgar often distinguish reason from experience, even where the question relates only to matter of fact and existence, though it is found, where that *reason* is properly analyzed, that it is nothing but a species of experience. To prove by experience the origin of the universe from mind is not more contrary to common speech than to prove the motion of the earth from the same principle. And a caviller might raise all the same objections to the Copernican system which you have urged against my reasonings. Have you other earths, might he say, which you have seen to move? Have . . .

Yes! cried Philo, interrupting him, we have other earths. Is not the moon another earth, which we see to turn round its centre? Is not Venus another earth, where we observe the same phenomenon? Are not the revolutions of the sun also a confirmation, from analogy, of the same theory? All the planets, are they not earths which revolve about the sun? Are not the satellites moons which move round Jupiter and Saturn, and along with these primary planets round the sun? These analogies and resemblances, with others which I have not mentioned, are the sole proofs of the Copernican system; and to you it belongs to consider whether you have any analogies of the same kind to support your theory.

In reality, Cleanthes, continued he, the modern system of astronomy is now so much received by all inquirers, and has become so essential a part even of our earliest education, that we are not commonly very scrupulous in examining the reasons upon which it is founded. It is now become a matter of mere curiosity to study the first writers on that subject who had the full force of prejudice to encounter, and were obliged to turn their arguments on every side in order to render them popular and convincing. But if we peruse Galileo's famous *Dialogues*[1] concerning the system of the world, we shall find that that great genius, one of the sublimest that ever existed, first bent all his endeavours to prove that there was no foundation for the distinction commonly made between elementary and celestial substances. The schools, proceeding from the illusions of sense, had carried this distinction very far; and had established the latter substances to be ingenerable, incorruptible, unalterable, impassible; and had assigned all the opposite qualities to the former. But Galileo, beginning with the moon, proved its similarity in every particular to the earth: its convex figure, its natural darkness when not illuminated, its density, its distinction into solid and liquid, the variations of its phases, the mutual illuminations of the earth and moon, their mutual eclipses, the inequalities of the lunar surface, etc. After many instances of this kind, with regard to all the planets, men plainly saw that these bodies became proper objects of experience, and that the similarity of their nature enabled us to extend the same arguments and phenomena from one to the other.

In this cautious proceeding of the astronomers you may read your own condemnation, Cleanthes, or rather may see that the subject in which you are engaged exceeds all human reason and inquiry. Can you pretend to show any such similarity between the fabric of a house and the generation of a universe? Have you ever seen nature in any such situation as resembles the first arrangement of the elements? Have worlds ever been formed under your eye, and have you had leisure to observe the whole progress of the phenomenon, from the first appearance of order to its final consummation? If you have, then cite your experience and deliver your theory.

Note

1 [*Dialogo dei due Massimi Sistemi del Mondo (1632)*.]

22

The Argument from Design

Robert Hambourger

The argument from design for God's existence is involved with important questions about the conditions under which it is reasonable to believe that a state of affairs was brought about intentionally. In this paper I shall offer a version of the argument and defend it, if not quite in the sense of trying to show conclusively that it succeeds, then, at least, in the sense of trying to show that it deserves to be taken seriously. In Part I, I shall present a number of objections to the argument that, for the most part, are quite well known and, I think, quite weighty. Most are descendants of objections to be found in the writings of David Hume.[1] Then, in Part II, I shall present the specific version of the argument I wish to offer here and, finally, in Part III, try to show that it does not succumb to the objections raised at the start.

Part I

At the beginning, I would like to distinguish two sorts of argument from design. Arguments of both sorts start with the fact that many natural phenomena look *as if* they might have been produced by design and try to show that such phenomena really *were* designed, and from this they hope that it will be concluded that the universe as a whole was produced

Robert Hambourger, "The Argument from Design," from *Intentions and Intentionality: Essays in Honor of G. E. M. Anscombe* (Ithaca: Cornell University Press, 1979), pp. 109–31. Copyright © Blackwell Publishers, Oxford.

by the intentional actions of a single being. But then, the arguments conclude, since the universe appears to be good, and since it would take an extraordinarily wise and powerful being to design and create it, the universe must have been created by a wise, powerful, and good being, and this is God.

Now I think it is clear that any argument of this type will face difficulties when it tries to conclude, from the claim that many natural phenomena were designed, that the universe as a whole was produced by the design of a single being. For it seems possible that the universe itself was not a product of design, even if many important parts of it were, and, further, even if we are willing to grant that the universe as a whole was designed, it still will not follow that it was created by the design of a single being.

This, however, does not seem to be the most serious objection facing the argument from design. For one thing, even if it is granted, the objection will not rob the argument entirely of its power. It would be a significant achievement to prove that certain natural phenomena were results of intentional action, even if one could not prove that the entire universe was created by a single being, and this achievement, by itself, would be enough to show that something was seriously wrong with the atheist's standard picture of the universe. Also, though, even if a demonstration that important portions of the universe were created by design would not actually entail the hypothesis that God exists, it would seem that, nonetheless, it would render that hypothesis more plausible than any competing one. In a contest with polytheism, monotheism is likely to prevail, and one who comes to hold that many natural phenomena were created intentionally probably will come to believe in God. This objection, then, does not seem to me to be a crucial one, and I shall not deal with it further in what follows. Instead, I shall be concerned with attempts by arguments from design to show that certain features of the natural world are products of design, and it is in the ways that they try to do this that the two sorts of argument I wish to distinguish here differ.

Arguments of the first of the sorts I want to discuss are true analogical arguments. One begins by pointing to ways in which certain natural phenomena resemble human artifacts. An animal's eye, for example, is much like a fine machine. And even where the likeness is not so direct, natural phenomena often share with artifacts what Cleanthes, in Hume's *Dialogues*, calls "[t]he curious adapting of means to ends".[2] That is, in the case of numerous natural phenomena, as in the case of human artifacts, states of affairs which plausibly could be desired as ends are brought about by phenomena that themselves might reasonably have been intended as means to those ends.

Once such resemblances are noted, arguments of the sort I have in mind proceed straightforwardly by induction. Certain natural phenomena have features in common with human artifacts. However, in many cases, namely, in cases of artifacts, phenomena with these features have been discovered to result from the intentional actions of intelligent beings. Further, in no cases have phenomena with the features been discovered not to result from such a cause; for we have not discovered that natural phenomena with the features are *not* ultimately the result of God's design, and human artifacts all are designed. But then, by induction, we can conclude that all phenomena with the relevant features are products of design and, so, that many natural phenomena are results of intentional action.

This argument, however, I think, must fail. One important principle of inductive reasoning is that, in making inductive inferences, one should not extrapolate from cases of one sort to others that differ too widely from them. For example, if one has studied a great many horses but no other mammals with respect to a certain anatomical feature and has found that all mammals studied have had the feature, one still cannot properly conclude that all mammals and, thus, all dogs have the feature. For the difference between horses and dogs is too great. The point here is not that one can never

make inductive inferences from one sort of case to another. If one has examined many animals of numerous mammalian species, though no dogs, with respect to a given feature, and if all mammals studied have had the feature, then it might well be proper to conclude that dogs have the feature, even though there are significant differences between a dog and any of the animals studied. For here the animals that have been studied vary as greatly among themselves as they do from dogs. But when all the cases one has examined for a property are alike in significant respects, and all differ in those respects from a new case that is being considered, then one can have little confidence that the new case will be like the others.

This, however, I think, is exactly the situation in which we find ourselves, if we attempt to infer – from the fact that human artifacts have been designed, and natural phenomena have not been proven not to result from design – that natural phenomena that resemble human artifacts have been designed. It is not that there are not clear analogies between artifacts and some natural phenomena. I think there are. But there are also important respects in which natural phenomena do not resemble artifacts. Consider, for example, the eye. One difference between an eye and a machine is the materials out of which the two are made. But I do not think this is the crucial difference. Suppose that a "mad scientist" some day should construct eyes exactly like natural ones out of flesh and blood. This, I think, would make us no more inclined than we would be otherwise to think that our own eyes were produced by design, nor would we conclude that the analogy between natural phenomena and artifacts was finally close enough for the argument from design to go through.

What seems to me a more important difference is this. Human artifacts, even in cases of automated production, result quite *directly* from intentional actions. Our eyes, on the other hand, while we were developing in the womb, originated from genetically controlled processes that themselves had natural causes, and so on, back as far as we can determine. These processes might have been the results of design, but, if so, the design seems, so to speak, to have been woven into the fabric of nature. And, it would seem, a similar disanalogy can be found in all cases between human artifacts and those natural phenomena that look as if they were produced by design.

This difference between natural phenomena and human artifacts, then, which involves the very features of natural phenomena to which a proponent of the argument from design would be most likely to point to justify his belief that such phenomena, if designed, must have been designed by a divine being, is, I suspect, a sufficiently great difference to block analogical versions of the argument from design. At any rate, I shall not pursue the attempt to work out such a version here. There is, however, another sort of argument from design which is not an analogical argument; and though it also faces serious difficulties, in the end, I think, much can be said for it. Indeed, the version of the argument I shall offer later might be classified as one of this sort.

Arguments of this second sort begin with the claim that, in numerous cases, desirable features of the universe have been brought about by complex states of affairs whose occurrences might seem totally fortuitous, if they were not produced by design. The fact that conditions on earth, for example, were suitable for the development of life probably depended on precise details of the planet's composition and the positioning of its orbit about the sun, and the earth might well have been lifeless, if these had been even slightly different as the planet developed.

Again, basic features of the physical world depend on the fact that bodies of the sort that exist will interact as they do, given the laws of nature that hold. If either the bodies or the laws had been sufficiently unlike what they are, the universe probably would have been quite different and, very possibly, less interesting than it is. Consider, as an example, the forces that bind particles together into bodies and physical systems, for example, the forces binding atoms to form molecules or the force of gravitational attraction. If these forces had been much weaker than they are, matter could not easily have been formed into stable configurations, and the universe might have been little more than a system of particles in flux. On the other hand, if the forces were significantly stronger than they are, it would seem that things would have been overly stable, and discrete, changeable bodies might be at a premium.[3]

It seems, then, not to be a matter of course that the universe is as impressive a place as it is. In many cases, desirable features of the universe would not have come about, unless seemingly unconnected states of affairs had come together in the right sort of way. But, also, one would think, it could not simply have been an accident that, in so many cases, things came together in ways that had such impressive results. Cases of this kind need explanation. However, someone who presents an argument of the sort I am describing would argue that such cases could not be explained unless they were results of design or, at any rate, that they could be better explained in this way than in any other. And if this is true, it would seem that we can conclude that in many noteworthy cases features of the universe were created by design.

Arguments of this second sort, notice, are not analogical arguments. They do not claim that the natural phenomena they hold to have resulted from design are very much like human artifacts. Instead, they hope to show on other grounds that the phenomena need explanation but can only be explained properly as results of design. Thus, these arguments seem to sidestep the problems that beset analogical versions of the argument from design. Nonetheless, arguments of this new sort are open to serious objections, and before presenting my own version of the argument from design I shall mention three that I think are the most serious:

(i) Arguments from design of the second sort depend on the view that certain natural phenomena have features that make it appropriate to explain them as results of intentional action, quite apart from any analogies that hold between them and phenomena that have previously been discovered to be products of design. But this would seem untrue. When we first come by the family of notions that are connected with intending, we are not, it seems, taught logical criteria that allow us to determine whether a state of affairs was brought about intentionally. Instead, we begin by learning to recognize cases of intentional *behaviour*, and, once we know what it is for a person to act intentionally, it would seem that we come to learn that states of affairs of certain sorts are brought about intentionally, only because we frequently find such states to result from actions we recognize as intentional. That is, it seems that there are no inherent features of a state of affairs that show it to have been produced by design. Rather, we can only know a state to have been brought about intentionally either by knowing directly that it was produced by intentional actions or by knowing it to be sufficiently like states that we have discovered to result from such actions. But if this is true, then the only sorts of argument from design that can succeed are analogical arguments, and we have already seen reasons to think that analogical arguments fail.

(ii) We can reach this same conclusion from more general considerations about causation. A justly celebrated feature of Hume's theory of causation is the thesis that there are no *a priori* connections between cause and effect.[4] One cannot by reason alone discover the cause of any state of affairs. One can only do this by having observed similar states to have been preceded by a given sort of occurrence in repeated instances. But then it will follow, again, that we can only know a state of affairs to have been caused by intentional actions if it is sufficiently like states we have already discovered to have had such causes, and if, as seems likely, the most general features of the universe are too dissimilar from those occurrences whose causes we have discovered for us to be able to reason by analogy from one to the other, then we will have to remain in ignorance about the ultimate causes in nature. These two objections, together with the objection against analogical arguments from design I presented earlier, seem to me to constitute the most serious challenge to the argument from design, and it should be noted that they challenge far more than just this single argument. Indeed, they call into question whether reason ever could provide adequate grounds for believing in the existence of God. For suppose one had adequate reason to believe in God. Then one would thereby have adequate reason to believe that the universe was caused by design. But if either objections (i) or (ii) succeed, one could not have such reason unless one had discovered states of affairs that both sufficiently closely resemble the universe as a whole and are known to have been produced by design. And, given the difficulties we saw with analogical arguments from design, it would seem that one could not do this.

(iii) Finally, non-analogical versions of the argument from design ask us to conclude that certain phenomena were produced by design, simply because no other adequate explanations seem to be available. However, even apart from the difficulties above, one should be suspicious of arguments of this form. It might, after all, be that alternative explanations are available but that we just have not been able to think of them. Indeed, it would seem that alternative explanations of many suggestive natural phenomena are available by using the sorts of devices employed by the theory of evolution in biology. For that theory seems to show a way in which purely natural processes can result in the most highly organized and impressive sorts of creatures.

Of course, the theory of evolution applies directly only to examples of seeming design in biological organisms. Nonetheless, the theory counts against the argument from design in two ways. First, it seems to rob the argument of many of its best examples. Using the theory, for example, one can explain why the various parts of the eye developed in just the way that would best promote good vision, without having to make reference to a designer. Second, even where evolutionary explanations cannot be employed directly, they seem to provide a model for explanations of phenomena that look as if they were designed. For it would seem that purely random processes could result in a universe filled with highly organized and, therefore, one would expect, impressive structures, as long as such structures came about on rare occasions and, once in existence, tended to remain in existence, while less highly organized structures tended to be less stable and more short lived.

I shall attempt to answer these three objections in Part III below. However, for now I shall set them aside and turn to the version of the argument from design I wish to offer.

Part II

The version of the argument from design I shall present here trades heavily on a distinction that is very similar to one worked out by Elizabeth Anscombe in a brief, unpublished paper, entitled "Cause, chance, and hap",[5] and to a great extent it grew from thoughts stimulated by Miss Anscombe's paper. In "Cause, chance, and hap" Miss Anscombe distinguishes what she calls "mere hap" from a sense of "chance" she defines as "the unplanned crossing of causes".[6] When an event occurs by mere hap, there is an element of randomness in its coming about; it might not have occurred, even if all of the conditions relevant to its production had been the same. To use Miss Anscombe's example, the wind might carry a sycamore seed to a certain spot and let it down, though, perhaps, it could have carried the seed just a bit further without anything relevant having been different. And if so, we can say that it merely happened that the seed dropped where it did and not a bit further on. Notice that in this case we will have a violation of the doctrine of determinism, and indeed determinism might be expressed simply as the thesis that nothing ever occurs by mere hap.

There are other sorts of cases, though, where we would say that something happened by chance, though there need be no violation of determinism. To use another example from "Cause, chance, and hap", a plane might jettison a bomb which hits a boulder as it rolls down a slope. And here Miss Anscombe will say that it was by chance that the bomb hit the boulder, if it was not intended that it should, even though it may be that no randomness was involved. Perhaps, given sufficient information about the path of the boulder and the manner in which the bomb was jettisoned, one could predict with certainty that the bomb was going to hit the boulder or, at least, that it would if nothing intervened.

The distinction on which the argument I shall present below depends is one between Miss Anscombe's sense of "mere hap" and a notion of chance quite similar to that of an unplanned or unintended crossing of causes. Consider as an example a typical case in which one would say that it was by chance that a friend and I met in a restaurant. One would not mean, in calling this a chance occurrence, that our meeting had no connexion with antecedent causal factors. It might well be that various occurrences brought it about that my friend was at the restaurant when he was and that others brought it about that I was there at the same time. If you wish, it might have been determined, perhaps it even always had been determined, that we would meet. None of this seems to be ruled out when one says that we met by chance. For if it were ruled out, it would be far easier than it is to refute determinism, or, rather, one would not be able to say that cases of this sort occurred by chance, unless one had refuted determinism.

What one does seem to mean in saying that it was by chance that my friend and I met, I think, is that there was no *common* cause of our meeting. I came for whatever reasons I did, and my friend for whatever reasons he did. There was nothing in common to the causal chains that got us there. Thus, if we met at the restaurant because we planned to meet, or if one of us went because he heard the other would be there, our meeting would not be a chance one. And, again, if we both went to the restaurant because a great chef was to give a one-night demonstration or because everyone in our circle of friends was there to celebrate a certain occasion, then, even if we had not intended to meet, one would not be inclined to say that we met by chance. These last two examples show, I think, that it need not be intended that two states of affairs occur together for their co-occurrence not to be by chance. It is enough if the causal chains by which the two come about contain a significant part in common.

In what follows I shall use the term "chance" in the sense I have described here. More precisely, I shall say that the co-occurrence of two states of affairs comes about by chance when neither is a significant part of the cause of the other, and no third state is a significant part of the cause of both; that is, when the two do not come about by causal chains that have a significant part in common. Also, corresponding to the distinction between mere hap and this sense of "chance", I shall find it useful to distinguish two ways in which one might explain conjunctions of states of affairs.

Suppose that I happen by chance to be standing up at the moment you read this sentence. Can one then hope to explain why I stand as you read? I think it would be natural to answer in the negative. There is no reason why I was standing as you read; things just happened to work out that way. However, someone who takes seriously the principle of sufficient reason, that every truth has an explanation, will not accept this reply as the last word. Rather, I think, he will want to say that all one has to do to explain the occurrence in question in the sense *he* has in mind is to conjoin explanations of why, at a certain time, I was standing and why, at the same time, you were reading the sentence you were. Corresponding to these two possible answers, let me say that a conjunction of two or more states of affairs, or the co-occurrence of the states of affairs, has a *basic explanation* when and only when each state in the conjunction has an explanation, and I shall say that a basic explanation of a conjunction is a conjunction of explanations of its conjuncts. Further, let me say that the states in a conjunction of two or more states of affairs have an *explanation in common* when and only when explanations of any two states in the conjunction contain a significant part in common. That is, the co-occurrence of a group of states of affairs will be guaranteed a basic explanation whenever no state in the group occurs by mere hap, and the states in the group will have an explanation in common if and only if no two occur together by chance.

Now there are two points I would like to make using these distinctions. First, there would seem to be no logical guarantee that two logically independent states of affairs will have an explanation in common. Things often happen by chance, and a supporter of the principle of sufficient reason can hope for no more than that every conjunction will have a basic explanation. Secondly, however, there are cases in which, as an epistemological matter of fact, we simply would not believe that certain states of affairs had occurred together by chance. And it is on this second point that the argument I shall present is based. For I believe there are natural phenomena which it would be extremely hard to believe occurred together by chance but which, it would seem, could only have an explanation in common if at least some of them were created by design. And thus, I think, by a two-step argument we might be able to prove that some natural phenomena are created intentionally.

I shall not offer an example of the sort of phenomena I have in mind until later. First, let me illustrate the reasoning I hope to use with a fictitious example which, if my memory has not deceived me, is adapted from one I was given a number of years ago by Miss Anscombe.

Suppose that one day a perfect picture, say, of a nativity scene were formed by the frost on someone's window.[7] I think we almost certainly would believe that this occurrence was brought about by design,[8] though not necessarily by the design of a divine being. And if we were asked why, I think we would probably respond that if this were not so, there would be no way to explain why ice formed on the window in the pattern it did. However, if by an explanation, we have in mind a basic explanation, this might well not be true.

Supposedly, in normal cases, various facts about weather conditions, the make-up of a pane of glass, the temperature and humidity in the room in which the pane is installed and the like, cause ice to form in the way it does on a window pane. And also, supposedly, there are possible conditions which, if they were to obtain, might cause ice to form a nativity scene on a given pane. Of course, these conditions might be very strange, but we do not know this. Suppose, in fact, that the nativity scene in our example arose by natural means from conditions that appeared quite normal, that those conditions themselves arose from normal-seeming conditions, etc. Then we can imagine that scientists could give a perfectly good basic explanation of why the pattern formed by the ice in our example was one that constituted a nativity scene.

First, one would explain why ice formed in the pattern it did on the relevant window in the way that one might hope to do so in normal cases, that is, by explaining why ice crystals of various sorts formed on various spots of the window. Then one would explain why the pattern that was formed made up a nativity scene, using facts about geometry,

about basic human perceptual mechanisms, perhaps, and the like. The result would be a basic explanation of why the pattern that formed was a nativity scene.

What I think is interesting here, though, is this. If we were given such an explanation of the nativity scene in our example, we would still, I think, be no less inclined than before to believe that it resulted from design. If anything, by showing that the scene arose from processes that were, so to speak, part of the course of nature, such an explanation would make us more inclined to believe that it was designed by a being deserving of our worship and not merely by someone who had made a technological breakthrough over ice.[9]

The question, then, I think, is: what reasoning do we use when we conclude that the nativity scene in our example was produced by design? And the answer, I believe, is the following. First, I think, we believe that ice could not form a nativity scene on a window merely by chance. That is, in our example, there must be an explanation in common of the fact that ice formed the pattern it did on a certain window and the fact that that pattern constitutes a nativity scene. Why we believe this is not completely clear. Ice very often forms beautiful patterns on window panes, and yet we are content to accept that it is by chance that the patterns that are formed are ones that strike us as beautiful. However, that we would not be content to hold similarly that a nativity scene resulted from chance I think is clear.

But if this is true, then the fact that the ice formed a certain pattern on the pane in our example and the fact that that pattern constitutes a nativity scene must share a significant part of their causes in common. And, therefore, either one of the facts is a significant part of the cause of the other, or a third state of affairs is a significant part of the cause of both. However, the fact that a certain pattern forms a nativity scene is a very general one. It results from facts about geometry, about what counts as a nativity scene, and, perhaps, about what patterns we see when we encounter various sorts of objects. And many of these facts are not caused at all, while the remainder, it would seem, as an empirical matter of fact, could be caused neither by the fact that ice formed in a certain pattern on a particular pane of glass nor by the sort of facts, for example, about local weather conditions and the make-up of a pane, that would cause ice to form in such a pattern. And, therefore, it seems that neither the fact that ice formed in a certain pattern nor causes of that fact could be significant parts of what caused the pattern to be a nativity scene.

However, in this case it must be that the fact that a certain pattern constitutes a nativity scene was an important part of what brought it about that the pattern appeared on the window in our example. And this, again as an empirical matter, seems to be something that could not happen unless the pattern was produced by design. For the fact that a pattern forms a nativity scene could give a designer reason to bring it about that it appeared on a window and, thus, play a significant role in an explanation of such a fact. However, if the pattern in our example was not brought about by design, then it seems out of the question to think that the fact that it constitutes a nativity scene might have been an important part of the cause of the very specific conditions holding in and around a particular piece of glass on a particular night that caused it to be formed in ice. And, thus, it seems that the nativity scene in our example must have been produced by design.

The case of the nativity scene, of course, is fictitious, but I believe that similar reasoning might well be able to show that in many actual cases natural phenomena have been produced by design. For in many cases complex states of affairs have come together in ways that have produced noteworthy features of the universe, and one might argue that it could not simply be by chance that they came together in ways that had such impressive results. That is, one might think that there must be an explanation in common of the facts that certain states of affairs have occurred and that, by having done so, they have produced the impressive results they have. However, the fact that various states of affairs would produce impressive results, if they occurred together, cannot, it would seem, be explained by the fact that the states actually did occur, nor by the sort of facts that would cause them to occur. And, therefore, the only alternative is that the fact that the states would produce impressive results helps to explain their occurrence. But, again, it would seem that this could not happen unless the states were caused to occur by a designer acting to produce their impressive results.

This, then, in brief, is the version of the argument from design I wish to put forward, and I want to claim that the reasoning employed in it gains plausibility from the fact that similar reasoning explains our intuitions in the case of the nativity scene. However, I think one might want to dispute this last claim. For, first, it might be thought that our intuitions about the example of the nativity scene are based, not on the complex argument I suggested, but on simple analogical reasoning. That is, one might think that, unlike the sorts of natural phenomena to which arguments from design appeal, the nativity scene in our example is sufficiently like works of art created by human beings for one to reason simply by analogy that it too must have been designed.[10]

And, secondly, one might want to argue that even if our intuitions about the nativity scene can be explained by the reasoning I proposed, that reasoning itself is only a disguised form of analogical reasoning. For it might seem that there is only one way in which one can discover that a group of phenomena have an explanation in common, assuming that one has not discovered this directly by first having discovered the causes of the various members of the group, and that is to find sufficient similarities between the group and others whose members are already known to have explanations in common. But in this case, it might be thought that the conjunctions of phenomena to which an argument from design points differ enough from those whose origins we have been able to discover to block an argument by analogy that their members have explanations in common.

I think, however, that these two objections fail. First of all, it is true that in many respects the nativity scene in our example closely resembles works of art we know to have been designed by human beings. Indeed, the image formed in the example can be supposed to look just like the sort of image artists put on canvas. Nonetheless, there are also ways in which the nativity scene differs from works of art. Most importantly, the process by which the scene came to be on its window differs greatly from that by which paint comes to be on a canvas, and this is just the sort of difference that earlier made us conclude that we could not claim that eyes were produced by design merely because they resemble machines.

That the similarities between our nativity scene and human works of art are not enough to permit a simple argument by analogy for the design of the scene can be shown, I think, by the following consideration. Frequently frost forms beautiful, symmetrical "snowflake" patterns on window panes, and these patterns often resemble man-made geometrical designs just as closely as the nativity scene in our example might be supposed to resemble works of art. Yet no one would conclude straight away that such frost patterns are produced by design. More than resemblance to works of art, then, is needed to show that the nativity scene in our example would have to have been created intentionally.

Secondly, it might be true that one can infer that phenomena whose causes are not known have an explanation in common, *only* if one does so by analogy from cases that already have been discovered to have such explanations, though shortly I shall suggest that this is not true. But even if it is true, it does not follow that one cannot infer that a group of phenomena have an explanation in common unless there are no significant disanalogies between that group and others that have been discovered to have explanations in common. For it must be remembered that we know phenomena of many different sorts to have explanations in common and, as a result, if a new group of phenomena has important features in common with those groups that have been discovered to have explanations in common, and if the differences between the new group and the other groups seem no more relevant than the differences between some of the other groups themselves, then one should be able to reason by analogy that the members of the new group have an explanation in common. That is, in this case our inference will be more like one which concludes that dogs have a certain feature from the fact that all mammals studied from a wide range of species do, than it will be like one which concludes that dogs have a feature because horses do and because no other mammals have been studied.

At any rate, the fact that the natural phenomena to which arguments from design point are not enough like human artifacts for one to argue by simple analogy that they came about by design is not sufficient to show that one cannot conclude that there must be an explanation in common of the facts that they took place as they did and that, by doing so, they brought about impressive states of affairs. Again, a case in point here is the eye. We cannot argue by simple analogy to machines that our eyes were designed, but it would be preposterous to maintain that the development of the various parts of the eye could be explained without bringing in the fact that they allow one to see. Indeed, one of the most attractive features of the theory of evolution is that it can provide explanations that meet this sort of requirement.

Earlier I suggested that when we infer that two states of affairs have an explanation in common, we might not be reasoning by analogy. In fact, I am

inclined to think that the judgement that certain states of affairs have an explanation in common is not dependent on but, rather, is presupposed by inductive reasoning, and I think it might well be the case that it is certain inherent features of states of affairs that make us judge them to have explanations in common, and, further, that we are justified in doing so, if we are justified in reasoning by induction.

Consider a case in which a coin is tossed 100 times and comes up heads each time. One would, no doubt, conclude from this both that the coin had been rigged and that it was almost certain to come up heads on future tosses. And what I think is important here is that these two judgements are connected. In particular, if one thought it was merely by chance that the coin came up the same way on each toss, then it would be as irrational to conclude, by induction, that future tosses would be like previous ones as it would be to conclude, by the gambler's fallacy, that a string of heads must be followed by one of tails. In each new toss the probability would still be one in two that the coin would land heads.

And this, I think, is true in general of inductive inferences. We can sensibly hold that unobserved cases will be like observed ones only when we believe the observed cases have had a significant part of their causes in common. Thus, if we do not believe observed emeralds have been green because of general features of the process by which they were formed, then it would not be reasonable to conclude that unobserved emeralds are green. But if this is true, then it seems that we must be able to make judgements that various phenomena have explanations in common before we can reason by induction and, therefore, it seems that such judgements are not based on induction.

Part III

Let me now turn to the three objections against the argument from design that I mentioned at the end of Part I. Objections (i) and (ii) from Part I tried to show that one could come to know that a state of affairs was brought about by design only directly or by straightforward analogical reasoning. However, if my remarks about our example of the nativity scene were correct, one could know that that scene was produced by design but could not do so in either of these ways. Further, even if I am mistaken, and one could infer by analogy that the scene in our example was designed, still, I think, one could also come to know that it was by the more complex reasoning I described, and such reasoning might let one know that a state of affairs was produced by design, even when this could not be shown by analogy.

Objections (i) and (ii), then, fail, and that they do, I think, should not come as too great a surprise. For the two objections hold, plausibly enough, that one cannot know *a priori* that any given state of affairs was brought about by intentional action. But it does not follow from this that one could know such a thing only directly or by analogy. The objections, then, do not show that there could not be a line of empirical reasoning that is not straightforwardly analogical but that, nonetheless, might allow one to infer that a state of affairs had been brought about by intention. They simply assume that there could be no such line. However, if I am correct, the reasoning I proposed to explain our intuitions about the nativity scene on the window is just such a bit of reasoning, and if the reasoning seems plausible, then objections (i) and (ii) should not stand in its way.

Let me move on, then, to objection (iii). I think many people today are taken by a certain picture of the origin of life in which the theory of evolution plays a large part. As things are represented by this picture, it was simply a matter of good fortune that the earth came to provide an environment suitable for living creatures, though the good fortune here was not particularly surprising. For in a universe as vast as ours there are many stars like the sun, and – often enough – such stars should have planets whose size, composition, and orbit are similar to those of the earth. Then, once the earth afforded the proper environment, the first primitive organisms came into existence as results of what, it is hoped, were not too improbable series of chemical reactions. Again, here, it was simply by chance that the chemical processes that occurred were ones that produced living creatures. Finally, once the first organisms were in existence, it is thought that the theory of evolution can account for the rest and that the mechanisms of chance mutation and natural selection embodied in the theory led to the development of more and more highly developed creatures until, finally, beings evolved that were capable of reason.

This picture of the origin of life seems to be widely held today. Indeed, I believe its popularity is an important feature of the intellectual history of the present age. Nonetheless, I think the picture is flawed. For one thing, we might believe that various chemical processes could produce very simple living creatures, even if the fact that they produced such creatures had nothing to do with the fact that the processes came about. But we would not accept that very complex creatures could come about in this way. However, as Geach has noted,[11] the process of natural selection itself seems to presuppose the existence of creatures with highly developed genetic mechanisms and, so, cannot be used to explain their origin. And, therefore, we must find another plausible account of the origin of these mechanisms.

Natural selection can only take place among creatures that bear offspring that closely resemble their parents without resembling them too closely. For if offspring are exactly like their parents, then natural selection can occur only among characteristics already in existence and, thus, will not lead to the development of new characteristics. On the other hand, if offspring do not closely resemble their parents, then even if certain parents have highly adaptive characteristics and bear many more children than others, their children will not be very likely to inherit the characteristics, and the process will stop.

Of course, in fact creatures do have genetic mechanisms that facilitate natural selection, but the mechanisms are very complicated, and though they might themselves have evolved to some extent by natural selection, it would seem that any mechanism that led to offspring that resembled their parents closely enough but not too closely would have to be very complicated. And so, one would have to ask how they could come about, if not by design. As Geach writes:

> There can be no origin of *species*, as opposed to an Empedoclean chaos of varied monstrosities, unless creatures reproduce pretty much after their kind; the elaborate and ostensibly teleological mechanism of this reproduction logically cannot be explained as a product of evolution by natural selection from among chance variations, for unless the mechanism is presupposed there cannot be any evolution.[12]

Thus, there is much that is noteworthy about the development of living beings that cannot be explained by the theory of evolution. But even if this problem can be surmounted without recourse to a designer, there is a second difficulty.

Simplified accounts of the theory of evolution might make it appear inevitable that creatures evolved with the sorts of impressive and obviously adaptive features that might otherwise be thought to have been designed. For over a sufficient period, one might think, a few individuals would develop such features by chance mutation, and once some creatures had them, the obvious desirability of the features would be enough to explain their proliferation. However, this impression of inevitability, I think, is quite misleading.

Evolutionary change generally proceeds very slowly. We can be confident, for example, that no ancestors of birds suddenly came by wings in a single step and, likewise, that no ancestor of man came to have a brain capable of reason because of one chance mutation. Instead, these sorts of noteworthy and obviously adaptive features come about only as results of long series of evolutionary changes, each of which has to be adaptive and has to become dominant among members of a species, and the noteworthy features themselves cannot come about unless all the others do. Further, these smaller evolutionary changes cannot be counted on to be obviously adaptive, nor always to be adaptive for the same reasons that the larger, more noteworthy changes are. And most importantly, as the term "adaptive" itself suggests, very often these small changes will be adaptive only because of fine details of, and changes in, the relationship between members of a species and their environment.

Consider the following passage from a recent biology textbook, for example:

> There is . . . good evidence that during the period in which *Australopithecus* lived there existed considerable expanses of lush savannah with scattered shrubs, trees, and grasses. There were berries and roots in abundance, and because such areas were suitable for grazing, these savannahs were well stocked with game. These areas provided new habitats, abundant in food, and so we surmise the australopithecines came down from the trees in which their own apelike ancestors lived in order to avail themselves of these new sources of food. . . . Although descent from the trees does not always result in evolution of upright posture in primates . . . through a lucky combination of anatomy and habits, these apemen became bipedal. Being bipedal meant that the hands were freed from locomotor function and could be employed in manipulative skills such as carrying and dragging objects, fashioning tools and weapons, and so on.[13]

This, in turn, led to improvements in the primitive tool-making ability that had preceded upright posture. And finally, "with the advent of toolmaking, hunting for big game became a possibility, and the brain and the hand were now subject to the molding force of natural selection".[14]

Now whether the precise details of the picture presented in this passage turn out to be true is not important here. What is important is that something of this sort almost certainly was true. Had not the grass in a certain area grown to the proper height, had not a certain food source become available or unavailable, had not various predators been present or absent, had not climatic conditions been what they were, etc. as ancestors of man developed, human beings would not have come into existence. And if they had not, there seems to be no reason to think other beings capable of reason would have evolved instead. After all, useful as intelligence is, no other species has come into existence with such a high level of it.

Furthermore, seemingly chance occurrences like these did not play a role only in the final stages of the evolution of human beings. It is likely that, at nearly every step in the evolutionary chain that led from the most primitive of creatures to people, similar sorts of occurrences played a role. In fact, without specific evidence one cannot assume even that it was inevitable that mammals, vertebrates, or even multi-celled creatures would evolve.

But then, one might ask, again, whether it could have been simply by chance that so many seemingly unconnected occurrences came together in just the way that would lead to the evolution of creatures capable of reason, and I think that one might well conclude that it could not have been.[15] At least, it would be very strange, if the myriad occurrences needed to produce human beings came about in just the right way simply by chance and equally strange if the occurrences had an explanation in common, but the fact that they would produce intelligent beings had nothing to do with the fact that they came about. However, one might wonder how so many different sorts of occurrences could have an explanation in common and, indeed, have an explanation in common with the fact that they would lead to the evolution of beings capable of reason, unless they were produced by design?

Of course, I must admit that I cannot prove that the occurrences that led to the development of beings capable of reason could not have taken place by chance. To do so in a fully satisfactory manner,

I think, would require a method for distinguishing those conjunctions of states of affairs which require explanations in common from those which do not, and this I do not know how to provide.[16] However, I find it hard to believe that so much could have happened simply by chance, and yet I think this is exactly what one must believe, if one believes that the universe was not created by design. I think, then, that it is safe to conclude that those who fear that the secular view of things, common today among so many intellectuals, robs the world of its mystery are quite mistaken.

Notes

1 See, in particular, the remarks of Philo in the *Dialogues Concerning Natural Religion* and those put into the mouth of Epicurus in Section XI of *An Inquiry Concerning Human Understanding*.

2 D. Hume, *Dialogues Concerning Natural Religion*, ed. Norman Kemp Smith (Bobbs-Merrill, Indianapolis, 1947), Part II, p. 143.

3 This example was adapted from one suggested to me by David Hills, and I am also indebted to Nancy Cartwright and Paul Humphreys for help in its construction.

4 For Hume's presentation of his thesis see, for example, Section IV of *An Inquiry Concerning Human Understanding*.

5 "Cause, chance, and hap" was written by the middle of 1968 and is four pages long in its handwritten manuscript. Much of the material in it, including the notion of "mere hap", appeared later in Miss Anscombe's "Causality and determination". I am relying on a photocopy of the manuscript.

6 This sense of chance and, therefore, the similar one I shall present below seem to be descendants of one discussed by Aristotle. See *Physics*, II, 4–6. I am indebted to Ian Hacking and Paul Humphreys for pointing this out to me and to Terry Penner for the reference.

7 While writing this paper I learned from Miss Anscombe of a similar example which she definitely has used in which a message is spelled out in perfect lettering in the ice on a window. Another, somewhat similar, example is given by Cleanthes in Part III of Hume's *Dialogues*: "Suppose . . . that an articulate voice were heard in the clouds . . . in the same instant over all nations, and spoke to each nation in its own language and dialect . . ." (D. Hume, *Dialogues*, p. 152). Either of these examples and, no doubt, many others besides could be used to make the points I wish to make below with the example of the nativity scene.

8 Anyone who believes a nativity scene could appear on a window without having been designed may substitute a more elaborate example for the one I am presenting. For example, it might be supposed that numerous perfect nativity scenes appear one Christmas morning on the windows of many practising Christians living in cold climates. Remarks similar to those I make below could then be made in connection with this example.

9 It should be noted that an analogous point could be made about the argument from design. Someone holding that certain natural phenomena were designed need not deny that the phenomena resulted from a chain of purely natural causes extending indefinitely far in the past. And, again, if a natural phenomenon one believes to have been produced by design turns out to have resulted from such a chain of causes, that fact may count as evidence for the eminence of its designer.

10 In his introductory material to Hume's *Dialogues*, Norman Kemp Smith makes a similar charge against Cleanthes' use of the example of the voice in the clouds, arguing that the example "chiefly serves to illustrate Cleanthes' entire failure to recognize the point and force of Philo's criticisms" (Hume, *Dialogues*, p. 101).

11 P. T. Geach, "An irrelevance of omnipotence", *Philosophy* vol. 48, No. 186 (1973), 327–33.

12 P. T. Geach, ibid., p. 330.

13 I. W. Sherman and V. G. Sherman, *Biology: A Human Approach* (OUP, New York, 1975), p. 456.

14 Ibid.

15 Of course, one might conclude that such occurrences could have come together by chance. In particular one might argue that, unlikely as it may be that all the conditions needed to produce beings capable of reason should have arisen on earth, still in a universe as vast as ours we can expect that it should have happened somewhere, and earth just happens to be a place where it did happen. However, I think this argument is little more than an appeal to scepticism. One could as well argue that we do not know that the speed of light is constant in a vacuum, because if the speed of light were random one still would expect it to appear constant in some region or other of a large enough universe. The point in both cases is the same. Random processes can be imagined and – in a large enough universe – expected to mimic controlled processes, but when phenomena of the right sort would be sufficiently improbable if they occurred by chance, we have a right to conclude that they did not occur by chance.

16 The problem here, I think, is closely connected with *one* of the problems of induction. If a coin is tossed 1,000 times, and the results form certain patterns of heads and tails (for example, if the coin lands heads on all and only the prime numbered tosses), then we will believe that the pattern that was formed did not occur by chance, and we will expect future tosses to result in a similar pattern. On the other hand, other patterns of heads and tails would strike us as "random", and one would not expect them to be repeated by future tosses. But how do we distinguish the random patterns from the others?

23

Anselm's Ontological Arguments

Norman Malcolm

I

I believe that in Anselm's *Proslogion* and *Responsio editoris* there are two different pieces of reasoning which he did not distinguish from one another, and that a good deal of light may be shed on the philosophical problem of "the ontological argument" if we do distinguish them. In Chapter 2 of the *Proslogion*[1] Anselm says that we believe that God is *something a greater than which cannot be conceived*. (The Latin is *aliquid quo nihil maius cogitari possit*. Anselm sometimes uses the alternative expressions *aliquid quo maius nihil cogitari potest, id quo maius cogitari nequit, aliquid quo maius cogitari non valet*.) Even the fool of the Psalm who says in his heart there is no God, when he hears this very thing that Anselm says, namely, "something a greater than which cannot be conceived," understands what he hears, and what he understands is in his understanding though he does not understand that it exists.

Apparently Anselm regards it as tautological to say that whatever is understood is in the understanding (*quidquid intelligitur in intellectu est*): he uses *intelligitur* and *in intellectu est* as interchangeable locutions. The same holds for another formula of his: whatever is thought is in thought (*quidquid cogitatur in cogitatione est*).[2]

Of course many things may exist in the understanding that do not exist in reality; for example,

elves. Now, says Anselm, something a greater than which cannot be conceived exists in the understanding. But it cannot exist *only* in the understanding, for to exist in reality is greater. Therefore that thing a greater than which cannot be conceived cannot exist only in the understanding, for then a greater thing could be conceived: namely, one that exists both in the understanding and in reality.[3]

Here I have a question. It is not clear to me whether Anselm means that (a) existence in reality by itself is greater than existence in the understanding, or that (b) existence in reality and existence in the understanding together are greater than existence in the understanding alone. Certainly he accepts (b). But he might also accept (a), as Descartes apparently does in *Meditation III* when he suggests that the mode of being by which a thing is "objectively in the understanding" is *imperfect*.[4] Of course Anselm might accept both (a) and (b). He might hold that in general something is greater if it has both of these "modes of existence" than if it has either one alone, but also that existence in reality is a more perfect mode of existence than existence in the understanding.

In any case, Anselm holds that something is greater if it exists both in the understanding and in reality than if it exists merely in the understanding. An equivalent way of putting this interesting proposition, in a more current terminology, is: something is greater if it is both conceived of and exists than if it is merely conceived of. Anselm's reasoning can be expressed as follows: *id quo maius cogitari nequit* cannot be merely conceived of and not exist, for then it would not be *id quo maius cogitari nequit.* The doctrine that something is greater if it exists in addition to being conceived of, than if it is only conceived of, could be called the doctrine that *existence is a perfection.* Descartes maintained, in so many words, that existence is a perfection,[5] and presumably he was holding Anselm's doctrine, although he does not, in *Meditation V* or elsewhere, argue in the way that Anselm does in *Proslogion* 2.

When Anselm says, "And certainly, that than which nothing greater can be conceived cannot exist merely in the understanding. For suppose it exists merely in the understanding, then it can be conceived to exist in reality, which is greater,"[6] he is claiming that if I conceived of a being of great excellence, that being would be *greater* (more excellent, more perfect) if it existed than if it did not exist. His supposition that "it exists merely in the understanding" is the supposition that it is conceived of but does not exist. Anselm repeated this claim in his reply to the criticism of the monk Gaunilo. Speaking of the being a greater than which cannot be conceived, he says:

> I have said that if it exists merely in the understanding it can be conceived to exist in reality, which is greater. Therefore, if it exists merely in the understanding obviously the very being a greater than which cannot be conceived, is one a greater than which can be conceived. What, I ask, can follow better than that? For if it exists merely in the understanding, can it not be conceived to exist in reality? And if it can be so conceived does not he who conceives of this conceive of a thing greater than it, if it does exist merely in the understanding? Can anything follow better than this: that if a being a greater than which cannot be conceived exists merely in the understanding, it is something a greater than which can be conceived? What could be plainer?[7]

He is implying, in the first sentence, that if I conceive of something which does not exist then it is possible for it to exist, and *it will be greater if it exists than if it does not exist.*

The doctrine that existence is a perfection is remarkably queer. It makes sense and is true to say that my future house will be a better one if it is insulated than if it is not insulated; but what could it mean to say that it will be a better house if it exists than if it does not? My future child will be a better man if he is honest than if he is not; but who would understand the saying that he will be a better man if he exists than if he does not? Or who understands the saying that if God exists He is more perfect than if He does not exist? One might say, with some intelligibility, that it would be better (for oneself or for mankind) if God exists than if He does not – but that is a different matter.

A king might desire that his next chancellor should have knowledge, wit, and resolution; but it is ludicrous to add that the king's desire is to have a chancellor who exists. Suppose that two royal councilors, A and B, were asked to draw up separately descriptions of the most perfect chancellor they could conceive, and that the descriptions they produced were identical except that A included existence in his list of attributes of a perfect chancellor and B did not. (I do not mean that B put nonexistence in his list.) One and the same person could satisfy both descriptions. More to the point, any person who satisfied A's description would *necessarily* satisfy B's description and vice versa! This is to say that A and B did not produce descriptions that differed in any way but rather one and the same description of necessary and desirable qualities in a chancellor. A only made a show of putting down a desirable quality that B had failed to include.

I believe I am merely restating an observation that Kant made in attacking the notion that "existence" or "being" is a "real predicate." He says:

> By whatever and by however many predicates we may think a thing – even if we completely determine it – we do not make the least addition to the thing when we further declare that this thing *is.* Otherwise, it would not be exactly the same thing that exists, but something more than we had thought in the concept; and we could not, therefore, say that the exact object of my concept exists.[8]

Anselm's ontological proof of *Proslogion* 2 is fallacious because it rests on the false doctrine that existence is a perfection (and therefore that "existence" is a "real predicate"). It would be desirable to have a rigorous refutation of the doctrine but I have not been able to provide one. I am compelled to leave the matter at the more or less intuitive level of Kant's observation. In any case, I believe that the doctrine does not belong to Anselm's other formulation of the ontological argument. It is worth noting that Gassendi anticipated Kant's criticism when he said, against Descartes:

Existence is a perfection neither in God nor in anything else; it is rather that in the absence of which there is no perfection. . . . Hence neither is existence held to exist in a thing in the way that perfections do, nor if the thing lacks existence is it said to be imperfect (or deprived of a perfection), so much as to be nothing.[9]

II

I take up now the consideration of the second ontological proof, which Anselm presents in the very next chapter of the *Proslogion*. (There is no evidence that he thought of himself as offering two different proofs.) Speaking of the being a greater than which cannot be conceived, he says:

> And it so truly exists that it cannot be conceived not to exist. For it is possible to conceive of a being which cannot be conceived not to exist; and this is greater than one which can be conceived not to exist. Hence, if that, than which nothing greater can be conceived, can be conceived not to exist, it is not that than which nothing greater can be conceived. But this is a contradiction. So truly, therefore, is there something than which nothing greater can be conceived, that it cannot even be conceived not to exist.
>
> And this being thou art, O Lord, our God.[10]

Anselm is saying two things: first, that a being whose nonexistence is logically impossible is "greater" than a being whose nonexistence is logically possible (and therefore that a being a greater than which cannot be conceived must be one whose nonexistence is logically impossible); second, that *God* is a being than which a greater cannot be conceived.

In regard to the second of these assertions, there certainly is *a* use of the word "God," and I think far the more common use, in accordance with which the statements "God is the greatest of all beings," "God is the most perfect being," "God is the supreme being," are *logically* necessary truths, in the same sense that the statement "A square has four sides" is a logically necessary truth. If there is a man named "Jones" who is the tallest man in the world, the statement "Jones is the tallest man in the world" is merely true and is not a logically necessary truth. It is a virtue of Anselm's unusual phrase, "a being a greater than which cannot be conceived,"[11] to make it explicit that the sentence "God is the greatest of all beings" expresses a logically necessary truth and not a mere matter of fact such as the one we imagined about Jones.

With regard to Anselm's first assertion (namely, that a being whose nonexistence is logically impossible is greater than a being whose nonexistence is logically possible) perhaps the most puzzling thing about it is the use of the word "greater." It appears to mean exactly the same as "superior," "more excellent," "more perfect." This equivalence by itself is of no help to us, however, since the latter expressions would be equally puzzling here. What is required is some explanation of their use.

We do think of *knowledge*, say, as an excellence, a good thing. If A has more knowledge of algebra than B we express this in common language by saying that A has a *better* knowledge of algebra than B, or that A's knowledge of algebra is *superior* to B's, whereas we should not say that B has a better or superior *ignorance* of algebra than A. We do say "greater ignorance," but here the word "greater" is used purely quantitatively.

Previously I rejected *existence* as a perfection. Anselm is maintaining in the remarks last quoted, not that existence is a perfection, but that *the logical impossibility of nonexistence is a perfection*. In other words, *necessary existence* is a perfection. His first ontological proof uses the principle that a thing is greater if it exists than if it does not exist. His second proof employs the different principle that a thing is greater if it necessarily exists than if it does not necessarily exist.

Some remarks about the notion of *dependence* may help to make this latter principle intelligible. Many things depend for their existence on other things and events. My house was built by a carpenter: its coming into existence was dependent on a certain creative activity. Its continued existence is dependent on many things: that a tree does not crush it, that it is not consumed by fire, and so on. If we reflect on the common meaning of the word "God" (no matter how vague and confused this is), we realize that it is incompatible with this meaning that God's existence should *depend* on anything. Whether we believe in Him or not we must admit that the "almighty and everlasting God" (as several ancient prayers begin), the "Maker of heaven and earth, and of all things visible and invisible" (as is said in the Nicene Creed), cannot be thought of as being brought into existence by anything or as depending for His continued existence on anything. To conceive of anything as dependent upon something else for its existence is to conceive of it as a lesser being than God.

If a housewife has a set of extremely fragile dishes, then as dishes they are *inferior* to those of another set like them in all respects except that they are *not* fragile. Those of the first set are *dependent* for their continued existence on gentle handling; those of the second set are not. There is a definite connection in common language between the notions of dependency and inferiority, and independence and superiority. To say that something which was dependent on nothing whatever was superior to ("greater than") anything that was dependent in any way upon anything is quite in keeping with the everyday use of the terms "superior" and "greater." Correlative with the notions of dependence and independence are the notions of *limited* and *unlimited*. An engine requires fuel and this is a limitation. It is the same thing to say that an engine's operation is *dependent* on as that it is *limited* by its fuel supply. An engine that could accomplish the same work in the same time and was in other respects satisfactory, but did not require fuel, would be a *superior* engine.

God is usually conceived of as an *unlimited* being. He is conceived of as a being who *could not* be limited, that is, as an absolutely unlimited being. This is no less than to conceive of Him as *something a greater than which cannot be conceived.* If God is conceived to be an absolutely unlimited being He must be conceived to be unlimited in regard to His existence as well as His operation. In this conception it will not make sense to say that He depends on anything for coming into or continuing in existence. Nor, as Spinoza observed, will it make sense to say that something could *prevent* Him from existing.[12] Lack of moisture can prevent trees from existing in a certain region of the earth. But it would be contrary to the concept of God as an unlimited being to suppose that anything other than God Himself could prevent Him from existing, and it would be self-contradictory to suppose that He Himself could do it.

Some may be inclined to object that although nothing could prevent God's existence, still it might just *happen* that He did not exist. And if He did exist that too would be by chance. I think, however, that from the supposition that it could happen that God did not exist it would follow that, if He existed, He would have mere duration and not eternity. It would make sense to ask, "How long has He existed?," "Will He still exist next week?," "He was in existence yesterday but how

about today?," and so on. It seems absurd to make God the subject of such questions. According to our ordinary conception of Him, He is an eternal being. And eternity does not mean endless duration, as Spinoza noted. To ascribe eternity to something is to exclude as senseless all sentences that imply that it has duration. If a thing has duration then it would be merely a *contingent* fact, if it was a fact, that its duration was endless. The moon could have endless duration but not eternity. If something has endless duration it will *make sense* (although it will be false) to say that it will cease to exist, and it will make sense (although it will be false) to say that something will *cause* it to cease to exist. A being with endless duration is not, therefore, an absolutely unlimited being. That God is conceived to be eternal follows from the fact that He is conceived to be an absolutely unlimited being.

I have been trying to expand the argument of *Proslogion* 3. In *Responsio* 1 Anselm adds the following acute point: if you can conceive of a certain thing and this thing does not exist then if it *were* to exist its nonexistence would be *possible*. It follows, I believe, that if the thing were to exist it would depend on other things both for coming into and continuing in existence, and also that it would have duration and not eternity. Therefore it would not be, either in reality or in conception, an unlimited being, *aliquid quo nihil maius cogitari possit.*

Anselm states his argument as follows:

> If it [the thing a greater than which cannot be conceived] can be conceived at all it must exist. For no one who denies or doubts the existence of a being a greater than which is inconceivable, denies or doubts that if it did exist its nonexistence, either in reality or in the understanding, would be impossible. For otherwise it would not be a being a greater than which cannot be conceived. But as to whatever can be conceived but does not exist: if it were to exist its nonexistence either in reality or in the understanding would be possible. Therefore, if a being a greater than which cannot be conceived, can even be conceived, it must exist.[13]

What Anselm has proved is that the notion of contingent existence or of contingent nonexistence cannot have any application to God. His existence must either be logically necessary or logically impossible. The only intelligible way of rejecting Anselm's claim that God's existence is necessary is to maintain that the concept of God, as a being a greater than which cannot be conceived, is self-contradictory or nonsensical.[14] Supposing that this is false, Anselm is right to deduce God's necessary existence from his characterization of Him as a being a greater than which cannot be conceived.

Let me summarize the proof. If God, a being greater than which cannot be conceived, does not exist then He cannot *come* into existence. For if He did He would either have been *caused* to come into existence or have *happened* to come into existence, and in either case He would be a limited being, which by our conception of Him He is not. Since He cannot come into existence, if He does not exist His existence is impossible. If He does exist He cannot have come into existence (for the reasons given), nor can He cease to exist, for nothing could cause Him to cease to exist nor could it just happen that He ceased to exist. So if God exists His existence is necessary. Thus God's existence is either impossible or necessary. It can be the former only if the concept of such a being is self-contradictory or in some way logically absurd. Assuming that this is not so, it follows that He necessarily exists.

It may be helpful to express ourselves in the following way: to say, not that *omnipotence* is a property of God, but rather that *necessary omnipotence* is; and to say, not that omniscience is a property of God, but rather that *necessary omniscience* is. We have criteria for determining that a man knows this and that and can do this and that, and for determining that one man has greater knowledge and abilities in a certain subject than another. We could think of various tests to give them. But there is nothing we should wish to describe, seriously and literally, as "testing" God's knowledge and powers. That God is omniscient and omnipotent has not been determined by the application of criteria: rather these are requirements of our conception of Him. They are internal properties of the concept, although they are also rightly said to be properties of God. *Necessary existence* is a property of God in the *same sense* that *necessary omnipotence* and *necessary omniscience* are His properties. And we are not to think that "God necessarily exists" means that it follows necessarily from something that God exists *contingently*. The a priori proposition "God necessarily exists" entails the proposition "God exists," if and only if the latter also is understood as an a priori proposition: in which case the two propositions are equivalent. In this sense Anselm's proof is a proof of God's existence.

Descartes was somewhat hazy on the question of whether existence is a property of things that exist, but at the same time he saw clearly enough that *necessary existence* is a property of God. Both points are illustrated in his reply to Gassendi's remark, which I quoted above:

I do not see to what class of reality you wish to assign existence, nor do I see why it may not be said to be a property as well as omnipotence, taking the word property as equivalent to any attribute or anything which can be predicated of a thing, as in the present case it should be by all means regarded. Nay, necessary existence in the case of God is also a true property in the strictest sense of the word, because it belongs to Him and forms part of His essence alone.[15]

Elsewhere he speaks of "the necessity of existence" as being "that crown of perfections without which we cannot comprehend God."[16] He is emphatic on the point that necessary existence applies solely to "an absolutely perfect Being."[17]

III

I wish to consider now a part of Kant's criticism of the ontological argument which I believe to be wrong. He says:

If, in an identical proposition, I reject the predicate while retaining the subject, contradiction results; and I therefore say that the former belongs necessarily to the latter. But if we reject subject and predicate alike, there is no contradiction; for nothing is then left that can be contradicted. To posit a triangle, and yet to reject its three angles, is self-contradictory; but there is no contradiction in rejecting the triangle together with its three angles. The same holds true of the concept of an absolutely necessary being. If its existence is rejected, we reject the thing itself with all its predicates; and no question of contradiction can then arise. There is nothing outside it that would then be contradicted, since the necessity of the thing is not supposed to be derived from anything external; nor is there anything internal that would be contradicted, since in rejecting the thing itself we have at the same time rejected all its internal properties. "God is omnipotent" is a necessary judgment. The omnipotence cannot be rejected if we posit a Deity, that is, an infinite being; for the two concepts are identical. But if we say, "There is no God," neither the omnipotence nor any other of its predicates is given; they are one and all rejected together with the subject, and there is therefore not the least contradiction in such a judgment.[18]

To these remarks the reply is that when the concept of God is correctly understood one sees that one cannot "reject the subject." "There is no God" is seen to be a necessarily false statement. Anselm's demonstration proves that the proposition "God exists" has the same a priori footing as the proposition "God is omnipotent."

Many present-day philosophers, in agreement with Kant, declare that existence is not a property and think that this overthrows the ontological argument. Although it is an error to regard existence as a property of things that have contingent existence, it does not follow that it is an error to regard necessary existence as a property of God. A recent writer says, against Anselm, that a proof of God's existence "based on the necessities of thought" is "universally regarded as fallacious: it is not thought possible to build bridges between mere abstractions and concrete existence."[19] But this way of putting the matter obscures the distinction we need to make. Does "concrete existence" mean contingent existence? Then to build bridges between concrete existence and mere abstractions would be like inferring the existence of an island from the concept of a perfect island, which both Anselm and Descartes regarded as absurd. What Anselm did was to give a demonstration that the proposition "God necessarily exists" is entailed by the proposition "God is a being a greater than which cannot be conceived" (which is equivalent to "God is an absolutely unlimited being"). Kant declares that when "I think a being as the supreme reality, without any defect, the question still remains whether it exists or not."[20] But once one has grasped Anselm's proof of the necessary existence of a being a greater than which cannot be conceived, no question remains as to whether it exists or not, just as Euclid's demonstration of the existence of an infinity of prime numbers leaves no question on that issue.

Kant says that "every reasonable person" must admit that "all existential propositions are synthetic."[21] Part of the perplexity one has about the ontological argument is in deciding whether or not the proposition "God necessarily exists" is or is not an "existential proposition." But let us look

around. Is the Euclidean theorem in number theory, "There exists an infinite number of prime numbers," an "existential proposition"? Do we not want to say that *in some sense* it asserts the existence of something? Cannot we say, with equal justification, that the proposition "God necessarily exists" asserts the existence of something, *in some sense?* What we need to understand, in each case, is the particular sense of the assertion. Neither proposition has the same sort of sense as do the propositions, "A low pressure area exists over the Great Lakes," "There still exists some possibility that he will survive," "The pain continues to exist in his abdomen." One good way of seeing the difference in sense of these various propositions is to see the variously different ways in which they are proved or supported. It is wrong to think that all assertions of existence have the same kind of meaning. There are as many kinds of existential propositions as there are kinds of subjects of discourse.

Closely related to Kant's view that all existential propositions are "synthetic" is the contemporary dogma that all existential propositions are contingent. Professor Gilbert Ryle tells us that "Any assertion of the existence of something, like any assertion of the occurrence of something, can be denied without logical absurdity."[22] "All existential statements are contingent," says Mr I. M. Crombie.[23] Professor J. J. C. Smart remarks that "Existence is not a property" and then goes on to assert that "There can never be any *logical contradiction* in denying that God exists."[24] He declares that "The concept of a logically necessary being is a self-contradictory concept, like the concept of a round square. . . . No existential proposition can be logically necessary," he maintains, for "the truth of a logically necessary proposition depends only on our symbolism, or to put the same thing in another way, on the relationship of concepts" (p. 38). Professor K. E. M. Baier says, "It is no longer seriously in dispute that the notion of a logically necessary being is self-contradictory. Whatever can be conceived of as existing can equally be conceived of as not existing."[25] This is a repetition of Hume's assertion, "Whatever we conceive as existent, we can also conceive as non-existent. There is no being, therefore, whose non-existence implies a contradiction."[26]

Professor J. N. Findlay ingeniously constructs an ontological *dis*proof of God's existence, based on a "modern" view of the nature of "necessity in propositions": the view, namely, that necessity in propositions "merely reflects our use of words, the arbitrary conventions of our language."[27] Findlay undertakes to characterize what he calls "religious attitude," and here there is a striking agreement between his observations and some of the things I have said in expounding Anselm's proof. Religious attitude, he says, presumes *superiority* in its object and superiority so great that the worshiper is in comparison as nothing. Religious attitude finds it "anomalous to worship anything *limited* in any thinkable manner. . . . And hence we are led on irresistibly to demand that our religious object should have an *unsurpassable* supremacy along all avenues, that it should tower *infinitely* above all other objects" (p. 51). We cannot help feeling that "the worthy object of our worship can never be a thing that merely *happens* to exist, nor one on which all other objects merely *happen* to depend. The true object of religious reverence must not be one, merely, to which no *actual* independent realities stand opposed: it must be one to which such opposition is totally *inconceivable*. . . . And not only must the existence of *other* things be unthinkable without him, but his own non-existence must be wholly unthinkable in any circumstances" (p. 52). And now, says Findlay, when we add up these various requirements, what they entail is "not only that there isn't a God, but that the Divine Existence is either senseless or impossible" (p. 54). For on the one hand, "if God is to satisfy religious claims and needs, He must be a being in every way inescapable, One whose existence and whose possession of certain excellences we cannot possibly conceive away." On the other hand, "modern views make it self-evidently absurd (if they don't make it ungrammatical) to speak of such a Being and attribute existence to Him. It was indeed an ill day for Anselm when he hit upon his famous proof. For on that day he not only laid bare something that is of the essence of an adequate religious object, but also something that entails its necessary non-existence" (p. 55).

Now I am inclined to hold the "modern" view that logically necessary truth "merely reflects our use of words" (although I do not believe that the conventions of language are always *arbitrary*). But I confess that I am unable to see how that view is supposed to lead to the conclusion that "the Divine existence is either senseless or impossible." Findlay does not explain how this result comes about. Surely he cannot mean that this view entails that nothing can have necessary properties: for this would imply that mathematics is "senseless or impossible," which no one wants to hold. Trying to fill in the argument that is missing from his article,

the most plausible conjecture I can make is the following: Findlay thinks that the view that logical necessity "reflects the use of words" implies, not that nothing has necessary properties, but that *existence* cannot be a necessary property of anything. That is to say, every proposition of the form "*x* exists," including the proposition "God exists," must be *contingent*.[28] At the same time, our concept of God requires that His existence be *necessary*, that is, that "God exists" be a necessary truth. Therefore, the modern view of necessity proves that what the concept of God requires *cannot* be fulfilled. It proves that God *cannot* exist.

The correct reply is that the view that logical necessity merely reflects the use of words cannot possibly have the implication that every existential proposition must be contingent. That view requires us to *look at* the use of words and not manufacture a priori theses about it. In the Ninetieth Psalm it is said: "Before the mountains were brought forth, or ever thou hadst formed the earth and the world, even from everlasting to everlasting, thou art God." Here is expressed the idea of the necessary existence and eternity of God, an idea that is essential to the Jewish and Christian religions. In those complex systems of thought, those "languages-games," God has the status of a necessary being. Who can doubt that? Here we must say with Wittgenstein, "This language-game is played!"[29] I believe we may rightly take the existence of those religious systems of thought in which God figures as a necessary being to be a disproof of the dogma, affirmed by Hume and others, that no existential proposition can be necessary.

Another way of criticizing the ontological argument is the following. "Granted that the concept of necessary existence follows from the concept of a being a greater than which cannot be conceived, this amounts to no more than granting the a priori truth of the *conditional* proposition, 'If such a being exists then it necessarily exists.' This proposition, however, does not entail the *existence* of *anything*, and one can deny its antecedent without contradiction." Kant, for example, compares the proposition (or "judgment," as he calls it) "A triangle has three angles" with the proposition "God is a necessary being." He allows that the former is "absolutely necessary" and goes on to say:

> The absolute necessity of the judgment is only a conditional necessity of the thing, or of the predicate in the judgment. The above proposition does not declare that three angles are

absolutely necessary, but that, under the condition that there is a triangle (that is, that a triangle is given), three angles will necessarily be found in it.[30]

He is saying, quite correctly, that the proposition about triangles is equivalent to the conditional proposition, "If a triangle exists, it has three angles." He then makes the comment that there is no contradiction "in rejecting the triangle together with its three angles." He proceeds to draw the alleged parallel: "The same holds true of the concept of an absolutely necessary being. If its existence is rejected, we reject the thing itself with all its predicates; and no question of contradiction can then arise."[31] The priest, Caterus, made the same objection to Descartes when he said:

> Though it be conceded that an entity of the highest perfection implies its existence by its very name, yet it does not follow that that very existence is anything actual in the real world, but merely that the concept of existence is inseparably united with the concept of highest being. Hence you cannot infer that the existence of God is anything actual, unless you assume that that highest being actually exists; for then it will actually contain all its perfections, together with this perfection of real existence.[32]

I think that Caterus, Kant, and numerous other philosophers have been mistaken in supposing that the proposition "God is a necessary being" (or "God necessarily exists") is equivalent to the conditional proposition "If God exists then He necessarily exists."[33] For how do they want the antecedent clause, "*If* God exists," to be understood? Clearly they want it to imply that it is *possible* that God does *not* exist.[34] The whole point of Kant's analysis is to try to show that it is possible to "reject the subject." Let us make this implication explicit in the conditional proposition, so that it reads: "If God exists (and it is possible that He does not) then He necessarily exists." But now it is apparent, I think, that these philosophers have arrived at a self-contradictory position. I do not mean that this conditional proposition, taken alone, is self-contradictory. Their position is self-contradictory in the following way. On the one hand, they agree that the proposition "God necessarily exists" is an a priori truth; Kant implies that it is "absolutely necessary," and Caterus says that God's existence is implied by His very name. On the other hand, they

think that it is correct to analyze this proposition in such a way that it will entail the proposition "It is possible that God does not exist." But so far from its being the case that the proposition "God necessarily exists" entails the proposition "It is possible that God does not exist," it is rather the case that they are *incompatible* with one another! Can anything be clearer than that the conjunction "God necessarily exists but it is possible that He does not exist" is self-contradictory? Is it not just as plainly self-contradictory as the conjunction "A square necessarily has four sides but it is possible for a square not to have four sides"? In short, this familiar criticism of the ontological argument is self-contradictory, because it accepts *both* of two incompatible propositions.[35]

One conclusion we may draw from our examination of this criticism is that (contrary to Kant) there is a lack of symmetry, in an important respect, between the propositions "A triangle has three angles" and "God has necessary existence," although both are a priori. The former can be expressed in the conditional assertion "If a triangle exists (and it is possible that none does) it has three angles." The latter cannot be expressed in the corresponding conditional assertion without contradiction.

IV

I turn to the question of whether the idea of a being a greater than which cannot be conceived is self-contradictory. Here Leibniz made a contribution to the discussion of the ontological argument. He remarked that the argument of Anselm and Descartes

> is not a paralogism, but it is an imperfect demonstration, which assumes something that must still be proved in order to render it mathematically evident; that is, it is tacitly assumed that this idea of the all-great or all-perfect being is possible, and implies no contradiction. And it is already something that by this remark it is proved that, assuming that God is possible, he exists, which is the privilege of divinity alone.[36]

Leibniz undertook to give a proof that God is possible. He defined a *perfection* as a simple, positive quality in the highest degree.[37] He argued that since perfections are *simple* qualities they must be compatible with one another. Therefore the concept of a being possessing all perfections is consistent.

I will not review his argument because I do not find his definition of a perfection intelligible. For one thing, it assumes that certain qualities or attributes are "positive" in their intrinsic nature, and others "negative" or "privative," and I have not been able clearly to understand that. For another thing, it assumes that some qualities are intrinsically simple. I believe that Wittgenstein has shown in the *Investigations* that nothing is *intrinsically simple*, but that whatever has the status of a simple, an indefinable, in one system of concepts, may have the status of a complex thing, a definable thing, in another system of concepts.

I do not know how to demonstrate that the concept of God – that is, of a being a greater than which cannot be conceived – is not self-contradictory. But I do not think that it is legitimate to demand such a demonstration. I also do not know how to demonstrate that either the concept of a material thing or the concept of *seeing* a material thing is not self-contradictory, and philosophers have argued that both of them are. With respect to any particular reasoning that is offered for holding that the concept of seeing a material thing, for example, is self-contradictory, one may try to show the invalidity of the reasoning and thus free the concept from the charge of being self-contradictory *on that ground*. But I do not understand what it would mean to demonstrate *in general*, and not in respect to any particular reasoning, that the concept is not self-contradictory. So it is with the concept of God. I should think there is no more of a presumption that it is self-contradictory than is the concept of seeing a material thing. Both concepts have a place in the thinking and the lives of human beings.

But even if one allows that Anselm's phrase may be free of self-contradiction, one wants to know how it can have any *meaning* for anyone. Why is it that human beings have even *formed* the concept of an infinite being, a being a greater than which cannot be conceived? This is a legitimate and important question. I am sure there cannot be a deep understanding of that concept without an understanding of the phenomena of human life that give rise to it. To give an account of the latter is beyond my ability. I wish, however, to make one suggestion (which should not be understood as autobiographical).

There is the phenomenon of feeling guilt for something that one has done or thought or felt or for a disposition that one has. One wants to be free of this guilt. But sometimes the guilt is felt to be so great that one is sure that nothing one could

do oneself, nor any forgiveness by another human being, would remove it. One feels a guilt that is beyond all measure, a guilt "a greater than which cannot be conceived." Paradoxically, it would seem, one nevertheless has an intense desire to have this incomparable guilt removed. One requires a forgiveness that is beyond all measure, a forgiveness "a greater than which cannot be conceived." Out of such a storm in the soul, I am suggesting, there arises the conception of a forgiving mercy that is limitless, beyond all measure. This is one important feature of the Jewish and Christian conception of God.

I wish to relate this thought to a remark made by Kierkegaard, who was speaking about belief in Christianity but whose remark may have a wider application. He says:

> There is only one proof of the truth of Christianity and that, quite rightly, is from the emotions, when the dread of sin and a heavy conscience torture a man into crossing the narrow line between despair bordering upon madness – and Christendom.[38]

One may think it absurd for a human being to feel a guilt of such magnitude, and even more absurd that, if he feels it, he should *desire* its removal. I have nothing to say about that. It may also be absurd for people to fall in love, but they do it. I wish only to say that there *is* that human phenomenon of an unbearably heavy conscience and that it is importantly connected with the genesis of the concept of God, that is, with the formation of the "grammar" of the word "God." I am sure that this concept is related to human experience in other ways. If one had the acuteness and depth to perceive these connections one could grasp the *sense* of the concept. When we encounter this concept as a problem in philosophy, we do not consider the human phenomena that lie behind it. It is not surprising that many philosophers believe that the idea of a necessary being is an arbitrary and absurd construction.

What is the relation of Anselm's ontological argument to religious belief? This is a difficult question. I can imagine an atheist going through the argument, becoming convinced of its validity, acutely defending it against objections, yet remaining an atheist. The only effect it could have on the fool of the Psalm would be that he stopped saying in his heart "There is no God," because he would now realize that this is something he cannot meaningfully say or think. It is hardly to be expected that a demonstrative argument should, in addition, produce in him a living faith. Surely there is a level at which one can view the argument as a piece of logic, following the deductive moves but not being touched religiously? I think so. But even at this level the argument may not be without religious value, for it may help to remove some philosophical scruples that stand in the way of faith. At a deeper level, I suspect that the argument can be thoroughly understood only by one who has a view

of that human "form of life" that gives rise to the idea of an infinitely great being, who views it from the *inside* not just from the outside and who has, therefore, at least some inclination to *partake* in that religious form of life. This inclination, in Kierkegaard's words, is "from the emotions." This inclination can hardly be an *effect* of Anselm's argument, but is rather presupposed in the fullest understanding of it. It would be unreasonable to require that the recognition of Anselm's demonstration as valid must produce a conversion.

Notes

1   I have consulted the Latin text of the *Proslogion*, of *Gaunilonis Pro Insipiente*, and of the *Responsio editoris*, in S. Anselmi, *Opera Omnia*, ed. F. C. Schmitt (Secovii, 1938), vol. I. With numerous modifications, I have used the English translation by S. N. Deane: *St. Anselm* (LaSalle, Illinois, 1948).

2   See *Proslogion* 1 and *Responsio* 2.

3   Anselm's actual words are: "Et certe id quo maius cogitari nequit, non potest esse in solo intellectu. Si enim vel in solo intellectu est, potest cogitari esse et in re, quod maius est. Si ergo id quo maius cogitari non potest, est in solo intellectu: id ipsum quo maius cogitari non potest, est quo maius cogitari potest. Sed certe hoc esse non potest." *Proslogion* 2.

4   Haldane and Ross, *The Philosophical Works of Descartes*, 2 vols. (Cambridge, 1931), I, 163.

5   Ibid., p. 182.

6   *Proslogion* 2; Deane, *St. Anselm*, p. 8.

7   *Responsio* 2; Deane, *St. Anselm*, pp. 157–8.

8   *The Critique of Pure Reason*, tr. Norman Kemp Smith (London, 1929), p. 505.

9   Haldane and Ross, *Philosophical Works of Descartes*, vol. II, 186.

10   *Proslogion* 3; Deane, *St. Anselm*, pp. 8–9.

11   Professor Robert Calhoun has pointed out to me that a similar locution had been used by Augustine. In *De moribus Manichaeorum* (Bk. II, ch. xi, sec. 24), he says that God is a being *quo esse aut cogitari melius nihil possit* (*Patrologiae Patrum Latinorum*, ed. J. P. Migne, Paris, 1841–1845, vol. 32: *Augustinus*, vol. 1).

12   *Ethics*, pt. I, prop. 11.

13   *Responsio* 1; Deane, *St. Anselm*, pp. 154–5.

14   Gaunilo attacked Anselm's argument on this very point. He would not concede that a being greater than which cannot be conceived existed in his understanding (*Gaunilonis Pro Insipiente*, secs. 4 and 5; Deane, *St. Anselm*, pp. 148–50). Anselm's reply is: "I call on your faith and conscience to attest that this is most false" (*Responsio* 1; Deane, *St. Anselm*, p. 154). Gaunilo's faith and conscience will attest that it is false that "God is not a being a greater than which is inconceivable," and false that "He is not understood

(*intelligitur*) or conceived (*cogitatur*)" (ibid.). Descartes also remarks that one would go to "strange extremes" who denied that we understand the words "*that thing which is the most perfect that we can conceive*; for that is what all men call God" (Haldane and Ross, *Philosophical Works of Descartes*, vol. II, 129).

15   Haldane and Ross, *Philosophical Works of Descartes*, vol. II, 228.

16   Ibid., vol. I, 445.

17   E.g., ibid., Principle 15, p. 225.

18   *The Critique of Pure Reason*, p. 502.

19   J. N. Findlay, "Can God's Existence Be Disproved?," in *New Essays in Philosophical Theology*, ed. A. N. Flew and A. MacIntyre (London, 1955), p. 47.

20   *The Critique of Pure Reason*, pp. 505–6.

21   Ibid., p. 504.

22   *The Nature of Metaphysics*, ed. D. F. Pears (New York, 1957), p. 150.

23   *New Essays in Philosophical Theology*, p. 114.

24   Ibid., p. 34.

25   *The Meaning of Life*, Inaugural Lecture, Canberra University College (Canberra, 1957), p. 8.

26   *Dialogues Concerning Natural Religion*, pt. IX.

27   Findlay, "Can God's Existence Be Disproved?," p. 154.

28   The other philosophers I have just cited may be led to this opinion by the same thinking. Smart, for example, says that "the truth of a logically necessary proposition depends only on our symbolism, or to put the same thing in another way, on the relationship of concepts" (*New Essays in Philosophical Theology*, p. 114). This is very similar to saying that it "reflects our use of words."

29   *Philosophical Investigations* (New York, 1953), sec. 654.

30   *The Critique of Pure Reason*, pp. 501–2.

31   Ibid., p. 502.

32   Haldane and Ross, *Philosophical Works of Descartes*, vol. II, 7.

33   I have heard it said by more than one person in discussion that Kant's view was that it is really a misuse of language to speak of a "necessary being," on the grounds that necessity is properly predicated

only of propositions (judgments) not of *things*. This is not a correct account of Kant. (See his discussion of "The Postulates of Empirical Thought in General," in *The Critique of Pure Reason*, pp. 239–56, esp. p. 239 and pp. 247–8.) But if he had held this, as perhaps the above philosophers think he should have, then presumably his view would not have been that the pseudo-proposition "God is a necessary being" is equivalent to the conditional "If God exists then He necessarily exists." Rather his view would have been that the genuine proposition "'God exists' is necessarily true" is equivalent to the conditional "If God exists then He exists" (*not* "If God exists then He *necessarily* exists," which would be an illegitimate formulation, on the view imaginatively attributed to Kant).

"If God exists then He exists" is a foolish tautology which says nothing different from the tautology "If a new earth satellite exists then it exists." If "If God exists then He exists" were a correct analysis of "'God exists' is necessarily true," then "If a new earth satellite exists then it exists" would be a correct analysis of "'A new earth satellite exists' is necessarily true." If the *analysans* is necessarily true then the *analysandum* must be necessarily true, pro-vided the analysis is correct. If this proposed Kantian analysis of "'God exists' is necessarily true" were correct, we should be presented with the consequence that not only is it necessarily true that God exists, but also it is necessarily true that a new earth satellite exists: which is absurd.

34   When summarizing Anselm's proof (in part II, above) I said: "If God exists He necessarily exists." But there I was merely stating an entailment. "If God exists" did not have the implication that it is possible He does not exist. And of course I was not regarding the conditional as *equivalent* to "God necessarily exists."

35   This fallacious criticism of Anselm is implied in the following remarks by Gilson: "To show that the affirmation of necessary existence is analytically implied in the idea of God, would be . . . to show that God is necessary if He exists, but would not prove that He does exist" (E. Gilson, *The Spirit of Medieval Philosophy*, New York, 1940, p. 62).

36   *New Essays Concerning the Human Understanding*, Bk. IV, ch. 10; ed. A. G. Langley (LaSalle, Illinois, 1949), p. 504.

37   See ibid., Appendix X, p. 714.

38   *The Journals*, tr. A. Dru (Oxford, 1938), sec. 926.

24

The Ontological Argument

Michael Martin

The ontological argument is an attempt to prove the existence of God by simply analyzing the concept of God. There is no appeal, as there is in the cosmological argument and the teleological argument, to premises about the world. The ontological argument is thus the paradigmatic a priori argument for the existence of God. Historically this argument has been used in various forms by St Anselm, its originator, as well as by Descartes, Spinoza, and Leibniz.[1] Until recently, Kant's critique of the argument was thought to be decisive by most philosophers. But the argument has been revived in contemporary philosophy by Charles Hartshorne, Norman Malcolm, Carl Kordig, and Alvin Plantinga. The argument seems to have a peculiar fascination for philosophers and refuses to die.

It is impossible to discuss all the variants of the argument here. But a refutation of the original version and four contemporary versions should provide good grounds for supposing that all versions are unsound.

Anselm's Ontological Argument

The most famous version of the ontological argument is that of St Anselm, the Archbishop of

Canterbury (1033–1109), in *Proslogion* 2. Anselm's argument takes the form of a commentary on the words of the Psalmist: "The fool hath said in his heart 'There is no God.'"

> And so, Lord, do thou, who dost give understanding to faith, give me, so far as thou knowest it to be profitable, to understand that thou art as we believe, and that thou art that which we believe. And, indeed, we believe that thou art a being than which nothing greater can be conceived. Or is there no such nature, since the fool hath said in his heart, there is no God? . . . But, at any rate, this very fool, when he hears of this being of which I speak – a being than which nothing greater can be conceived – understands what he hears, and what he understands is in his understanding, although he does not understand it to exist.
>
> For, it is one thing for any object to be in the understanding, and another to understand that the object exists. When a painter first conceives of what he will afterward perform, he has it in his understanding, but he does not yet understand it to be, because he has not yet performed it. But after he has made the painting, he both has it in his understanding, and he understands that it exists, because he has made it.
>
> Hence, even the fool is convinced that something exists in the understanding, at least, than which nothing greater can be conceived. For when he hears this, he understands it. And whatever is understood, exists in the understanding. And assuredly that, than which nothing greater

can be conceived, cannot exist in the understanding alone. For suppose it exists in the understanding alone: then it can be conceived to exist in reality; which is greater.

Therefore, if that, than which nothing greater can be conceived, exists in the understanding alone, the very being than which nothing greater can be conceived, is one, than which a greater can be conceived. But obviously this is impossible. Hence, there is no doubt that there exists a being, than which nothing greater can be conceived, and it exists both in the understanding and in reality.[2]

The argument proceeds as a *reductio ad absurdum* that purports to show that the fool has uttered a contradiction. It can be reformulated as follows: God is, by definition, a being such that no greater being can be conceived. Even the fool understands this is the meaning of "God." Consequently, such a being exists at least in the fool's understanding – that is, in the fool's mind. The fool, however, thinks that such a being exists only in his mind and in other minds, that it exists only as a mental object. But a greater being can be conceived that exists outside the fool's mind, in the real world. So the fool's thinking is incoherent; he thinks that he has conceived of a being such that no greater being can be conceived and that such a being exists only as a mental object. However, a being such that no greater being can be conceived must exist outside his mind, in the real world, thus contradicting his belief that God exists only as a mental object.

Clearly, one crucial assumption of this argument is that an entity is greater if it exists in reality than if it exists only as a mental object, merely something that someone is thinking about. This assumption can be and has been challenged. First, Kant questioned whether existence can be a property of an object.[3] If it cannot, then it can hardly be the case that, other things being equal, an existing object is greater than a nonexistent one. For it is plausible to suppose that a sufficient condition for entity A being greater than entity B is that A has all and only the properties that B has except that A has, in addition, a property P that makes A more valued or prized than B. On this account, a judgment that A is a greater entity than B, given that A is exactly the same as B, except that A exists and B does not, assumes that existence is a property of A. However, the assumption that existence is a property of objects is a very controversial one; and insofar as the ontological argument makes this assumption, it

is not a clearly sound argument. Kant's point still has force:

> By whatever and by however many predicates we may think a thing – even if we completely determine it – we do not make the least addition to the thing when we further declare that this thing *is*. Otherwise, it would not be exactly the same thing that exists, but something more than we had thought in the concept; and we could not, therefore, say that the exact object of my concept exists.[4]

Defenders of the argument at least have to show that existence is indeed a property. Although it may be possible to do this, Anselm did not attempt to show it.

Even if it is granted that existence is a property, the ontological argument further assumes that existence adds to the greatness of a being. After all, it may be the case that existence, although a property of an object, does not affect its greatness; indeed, it may be the case that existence even detracts from the object's greatness. God is supposed to be a perfect being. This means that He is all-good, all-knowing, and all-powerful. The assumption that God does not exist does not seem to take away from His perfection, as would, for example, the assumption that He is not all-knowing. Anselm seems to be using "a being, than which nothing greater can be conceived" as roughly synonymous with "a perfect being." So even if one allows that existence is a property of objects, the lack of existence would not detract from the greatness of a being who was all-good, all-knowing, and all-powerful. Furthermore, existence does not add to the greatness or value of other entities; hence it is difficult to see why it should with God. As Norman Malcolm points out:

> The doctrine that existence is a perfection is remarkably queer. It makes sense and is true to say that my future house will be a better one if it is insulated than if it is not insulated; but what could it mean to say that it will be a better house if it exists than if it does not? My future child will be a better man if he is honest than if he is not; who would understand the saying that he will be a better man if he exists than if he does not?[5]

On the other hand, it may be suggested that as far as religious believers are concerned, the existence of God is something that is valued and prized. Without the existence of God, life would be meaningless and without value. But this argument rests on a confusion. The existence of God adds not to the perfection or greatness of God per se, but to the value of something else, for example, human existence. This point suggests that we should amend the statement made above, which said that a sufficient condition for entity A being greater than entity B is that A has all and only the properties that B has except that A has, in addition, a property P that makes A more valued or prized than B. In order to be more accurate one should change the last phrase to read "in addition, a property P that makes A more valued or prized intrinsically than B."

Indeed, it may be argued that unless some such qualification is made, the value of the existence of God may be relativized to certain groups. Critics of religion may argue that the existence of God is not a desirable state of affairs. They may contend that a nonexistent God should be prized and valued as a beautiful and inspiring myth, while the actual existence of God would bring more problems than it is worth. If God existed, it may be argued, humans would lose a large part of their freedom and autonomy; they would be burdened with guilt and sin; they would have to accept repugnant ontology; they would be faced with the difficult problem of knowing what He commanded and forbade. So unless one restricts the value of God's existence to what is intrinsically valuable, whether the existence of God is valuable will be contextually determined. But so restricted it is not at all clear that existence adds to the greatness of God.

Moreover, supposing that existence is an essential part of the intrinsic value of God, why could not one argue that existence is an essential part of the intrinsic evilness of a completely evil being? Such a being, let us suppose, is all-powerful, all-knowing, and completely evil. Let us call it the absolute evil one. An ontological proof of the absolute evil one would proceed as follows.[6] By definition, the absolute evil one is a being such that no more evil being can be conceived. Even the fool understands that this is the meaning of "the absolute evil one." Consequently, such a being exists at least in the fool's understanding – that is, in the fool's mind. The fool, however, thinks that such a being exists only in his mind and in other minds, that it exists only as a mental object. But a more evil being can be conceived that exists outside the fool's mind, in the real world. So the fool's thinking

is incoherent; he thinks that he has conceived of a being such that no more evil being can be conceived and that such a being exists only as a mental object. However, a being such that no more evil being can be conceived must exist outside his mind, in the real world, thus contradicting his belief that the absolute evil one exists only as a mental object. Clearly something is wrong. One cannot prove the existence of both God and the absolute evil one, since they are mutually exclusive.

Along these same lines Gaunilo, a contemporary of Anselm, parodied the ontological argument by arguing that one could prove that a perfect island existed.[7] However, Anselm rejected Gaunilo's proof[8] as have contemporary proponents of the ontological argument. Unfortunately, Anselm's reply consists in little more than insisting that the reasoning used in the argument can only be applied to God. Charles Hartshorne, a contemporary philosopher, argues that Gaunilo's parody fails since it assumes that a necessarily existing island is a coherent notion.[9] But it is not, according to Hartshorne. By its very nature, says Hartshorne, an island is a contingent being, not a necessary being.

Plantinga also rejects the parody on the ground that it is not possible for such an island to exist. But Plantinga conceives of the island not as a necessarily existing island, but as one such that no greater island can be conceived of. He contends that the idea of a greatest island is similar to the idea of a largest number. This idea is incoherent since, no matter how large a number one picks, there could always be a larger one. In a similar way there could not be a greatest island since, no matter what island one conceives of, one could always conceive of a greater island.[10] For example, if one conceives of an island with 1,000 coconut trees, one could conceive of an island with twice as many. In Plantinga's terms, the qualities that make for greatness in islands have no *intrinsic maximum*. However, this is not true in the case of the greatest being that can be conceived of, since the greatness of a being is defined in terms of qualities that do have intrinsic maximums. For example, a being such that no greater being can be conceived of would be all-knowing. However, an all-knowing being is one that for any proposition p would know whether p was true or false.

Hartshorne's and Plantinga's critiques are not very telling.[11] We will consider later in this chapter whether Gaunilo's type of criticism can be applied to Hartshorne's own modal version of the ontological argument. For now it is only necessary to point out that not all forms of the ontological argument in all its forms presuppose the notion of necessary existence. Indeed, Anselm's argument in its most familiar form, the one introduced above, does not. Nor, as we shall see, does Plantinga's version.

Plantinga's critique fails because he assumes that the greatest conceivable island must have an unlimited number of entities such as coconut trees. But if one means by "the greatest conceivable island" a perfect island, it will not have an unlimited number of coconut trees but only the *right* number of coconut trees, whatever that may be. Too many coconut trees would spoil the perfection of the island. The same could be said of other properties, such as sunny days or pure water. Further, as we shall see when we come to Plantinga's version of the ontological argument, his own argument can be parodied without relying on the notion of greatness or an appeal to properties that have no intrinsic maximums. Plantinga's ontological argument can be used to show that it is rational to believe in the existence of a marvelous island (although not perhaps the greatest conceivable island) that has 360 sunny days per year, 10,000 coconut trees, a year-round temperature of 72 degrees, and a population that never grows old.

So by indicating that this mode of argument can lead to absurd results that proponents of the ontological argument can hardly accept, Gaunilo's parody can be used to undermine the ontological argument. The onus is then on the proponents of the ontological argument to show why the parody of the ontological argument should not be accepted while the ontological argument should be.

So far we have seen that the ontological argument of Anselm is based on two debatable assumptions: that existence is a property and that existence is an essential part of the intrinsic value of God. We have seen also that even if these assumptions are granted, one can give a parody of the ontological proof for the existence of God – namely, ontological proof for the existence of the absolute evil one. But the problem remains of where the argument goes wrong.

Mackie has suggested[12] that even if one grants that existence is a property and is part of the intrinsic greatness of God, the argument does not work. Anselm appears to suppose that the fool's concept is that of *a nonexisting being than which no greater being can be conceived*, where the entire italicized phrase represents the content of his concept. Given this concept and the assumption that existence is part of the intrinsic greatness of God, the fool does indeed contradict himself. However, the fool need not and should not conceptualize the situation in this way. The fool may simply have the concept of *a being such that no greater being can be conceived*. He does not include nonexistence within the concept, although he believes that the concept has no application in the real world. Viewed in this way, the fool does not contradict himself. But can the fool afford to admit that existence is part of the concept of a being such that no greater one can be conceived of? There is no reason why he cannot admit this, for he can still insist that such a concept has no application to reality.

To put this in a different way, the argument can be undermined by noting the following: Suppose the fool admits that existence is a property of an entity, that existence would add to the greatness of any being, and that God is a being such that no greater being can be conceived of. The fool could say definitionally that God exists in reality. Or to put it in still a different way, "God is nonexistent" would be a contradiction. But the fool would not be forced into admitting that God *in fact* exists in reality and not just in his understanding. He could insist that the following is not a contradiction: "It is not the case that God exists" or "There is no God."

To say something exists definitionally and not in fact means that by virtue of the way a certain concept is defined, existence is part of the concept. For example, one can define a Loch Ness monster as a large sea animal that inhabits Loch Ness and define a *real* Loch Ness monster as a Loch Ness monster that exists in reality. Such a creature would then exist definitionally, since existence would be part of the definition of a real Loch Ness monster. But whether a real Loch Ness monster *in fact* exists is another question. Further, it would be a contradiction to say that a real Loch Ness monster did not exist. But one would not be uttering a contradiction by saying: "It is not the case that a real Loch Ness monster exists" or "There is no real Loch Ness monster." Similarly, if the fool said that God exists definitionally but not in fact, he would in a way be acknowledging Anselm's point that God exists by definition while insisting that the concept that includes existence need not apply to the real world.[13]

Given the above diagnosis of the problem, I must conclude that Anselm's ontological argument as it is usually formulated is unsound and that it is difficult to see how it could be revived.

Malcolm's Ontological Argument

In a 1960 article in *The Philosophical Review* Norman Malcolm defended a version of the ontological argument that he attributes to Chapter 3 of St Anselm's *Proslogion*.[14] According to Malcolm, Anselm developed two versions of the ontological argument. He rejects the one that we have just expounded and criticized for the familiar reason that existence cannot be considered a perfection in that it does not add to the greatness of an entity. Malcolm argues, however, that although Anselm may not have realized it, he developed a different version of the argument to which this objection does not apply and, indeed, that this version is sound. In this second version, unlike the first, the modal notions of necessity and impossibility play a crucial role, and the conclusion of the argument is not merely that God exists but that God necessarily exists. Malcolm summarizes the argument in this way:

> If God, a being greater than which cannot be conceived, does not exist then He cannot *come* into existence. For if He did He would either have been *caused* to come into existence or have *happened* to come into existence, and in either case He would be a limited being, which by our conception of Him He is not. Since He cannot come into existence, if He does not exist His existence is impossible. If He does exist He cannot have come into existence (for the reason given), nor can He cease to exist, for nothing could cause Him to cease to exist nor could it just happen that he ceased to exist. So if God exists His existence is necessary. Thus, God's existence is either impossible or necessary. It can be the former only if the concept of such a being is self-contradictory or in some way logically absurd. Assuming this is not so, it follows that He necessarily exists.[15]

In order to understand this we must distinguish Malcolm's main argument from the ones supporting its premises. The main argument is this:

(1) If God does not exist, His existence is logically impossible.

(2) If God does exist, His existence is logically necessary.

(3) Hence, either God's existence is logically impossible or it is logically necessary.

(4) If God's existence is logically impossible, the concept of God is contradictory.

(5) The concept of God is not contradictory.

(6) Therefore God's existence is logically necessary.

Even before we evaluate the supporting arguments for the premises, serious problems are evident. Consider premise (5). Malcolm maintains that he knows of no general proof for the consistency of the concept of God[16] and that it is not in any case legitimate to demand such proof. He points out that there is no general proof that the concept of a material object is free from contradiction, yet it has "a place in the thinking and the lives of human beings."[17] The concept of God does as well, he says. But this answer is inadequate. Although there may be no general proof of the consistency of the concept of God, there have been many arguments purporting to show that the concept of God is incoherent. Malcolm makes no attempt to refute any of these, but if any of them are successful, premise (5) is then false, and instead of (6) one can derive the conclusion:

(6') Therefore, God's existence is logically impossible.

Further, Malcolm's second version of Anselm's argument can be parodied in the same way the first version was. Although islands are usually considered contingent entities, one could define a super island as a beautiful island paradise such that if it exists, it exists necessarily; and if it does not exist, its existence is impossible.[18] It would follow that the super island's existence is either logically impossible or logically necessary. It may be argued, moreover, that the concept of a super island is not contradictory, and hence a super island exists. Clearly this last step in the parody is the crucial one. For it would surely be argued by defenders of the ontological argument that a noncontingent island is incoherent, that an island is by its very nature dependent on other things for its existence, whereas a noncontingent being cannot be so dependent.

I will take up this problem when we evaluate Hartshorne's version of the ontological argument. For now it is sufficient to point out that by a perhaps less controversial parody of the argument one could also prove that a variant of the absolute evil one exists.[19] Let us define the super absolute evil one as a being having all the properties of the absolute evil one and in addition have the property that, if it exists, it exists necessarily; and if it does not exist, its existence is impossible. Since the concept of the super absolute evil one is not contradictory, the super absolute evil one necessarily exists. But since the super absolute evil one and God cannot both exist, one cannot accept both arguments. In this parody it cannot be objected that by its very nature the absolute evil one is dependent on other things and cannot therefore be noncontingent. As we have defined the absolute evil one, it has all the attributes of God except His moral ones.

When one examines the supporting arguments for some of the premises in Malcolm's main argument, further problems appear.[20] Let us assume initially that Malcolm means "logically necessary" and "logically impossible" to apply to propositions or statements. Thus when he says "God's existence is logically necessary" he intends that to be equivalent to "The proposition 'God exists' is logically necessary" or "N(God exists)." Given this interpretation, let us go back and look at Malcolm's argument.

Consider premise (1) where the phrase "logically impossible" refers to the following propositions:

(1′)   If God does not exist, N(God does not exist).

In the summary of the argument quoted above he seems to attempt to deduce premise (1′) from another statement:

(a)   N(God never has and never will come into existence).

But this inference is invalid. What follows is not (1′) but

(1″)   N(If there is a time at which God does not exist, then there is no subsequent time at which He does exist).

It should be noted that (1″) is compatible with the contingent existence of God – that is, with ~N(God exists) and ~N(God does not exist).

Malcolm purports to deduce premise (2) of the main argument, that is:

(2′)   If God exists, N(God exists)

from (a) and (b):

(b)   N(God never has ceased to exist and never will).

But this inference is incorrect as well. What follows is not (2′) but:

(2″)   N(If at any time God exists, then at every time God exists).

Elsewhere in his paper[21] Malcolm argues that the noncontingent nature of God follows from the necessary fact that God's existence is not dependent on anything and has neither beginning nor end. But again this inference is invalid. Neither (1′) nor (2′) follows from

(c)   N(If God exists, then His existence is not dependent on any other being and He has neither beginning nor end).

That Malcolm is assuming that "logically necessary" and "logically impossible" apply to propositions and statements is a natural interpretation to make, and it seems to be supported by the text. If it is not the correct one, however, then what Malcolm does mean is completely unclear.[22] In any case, we are certainly justified in concluding that Malcolm's version of the ontological argument fails.

Hartshorne's Ontological Argument

Charles Hartshorne, who maintains that he had shown long before Malcolm[23] that Anselm had two forms of the ontological argument, a modal form that was sound and a nonmodal form that was not, has perhaps written more on the ontological argument than any other contemporary philosopher. In *The Logic of Perfection* Hartshorne states the modal form of the argument in this way,[24] where q = There is a perfect being, N = It is necessary (logically true) that, ~ = It is not the case that, v = or, and p → q = p strictly implies q (see table 1).

Now, premise (1) is Anselm's assumption that perfection could not exist contingently. Premise (3) is a well-accepted postulate of modal logic that modal status is always necessary. Premise (5) can be derived from (1) using principles of modal logic. It says in effect that the necessary falsity of the consequence implies the antecedent; Hartshorne calls this a modal form of *modus tollens*. Premise (7) is the assumption that the existence of a perfect being is not impossible. Premise (8) is the modal axiom that if a proposition is necessarily true, it is true.

Table 1

(1) $q \rightarrow Nq$	Anselm's principle
(2) $Nq \lor \sim Nq$	excluded middle
(3) $\sim Nq \rightarrow N \sim Nq$	Becker's postulate
(4) $Nq \lor N \sim Nq$	from (2) and (3)
(5) $N \sim Nq \rightarrow N \sim q$	from (1)
(6) $Nq \lor N \sim q$	from (4) and (5)
(7) $\sim N \sim q$	intuitive postulate
(8) Nq	from (6) and (7)
(9) $Nq \rightarrow q$	modal axiom
(10) q	from (8) and (9)

There seems to be little doubt that the argument is valid. The crucial question is whether the premises are true. Clearly the most important ones for our purposes are premises (1) and (7). On Hartshorne's view, (7) is hardest to justify. He recommends using one or more of the theistic proofs that he claims demonstrate that perfection must be at least possible. But this seems to have things backward. The theistic proofs *presume* that the concept of God is coherent; they cannot demonstrate it. Furthermore, as we mentioned above, there have been many attempts to show that the concept of God is incoherent. Before one can claim that it is coherent, one at least needs to show that these attempts failed. Hartshorne has not done this, and consequently premise (7) is unjustified. Moreover, since [. . .] some of these attempts are successful, not only is premise (7) unjustified, but there is good reason to suppose that it is false.

Premise (1) is also problematic. Hartshorne seems to mean by "it is necessary that q" that it is *logically* necessary that q. However, there does not seem to be any reason to suppose that, if a perfect being exists, the existence is logically necessary. As R. L. Purtill has argued:

It seems to be contrary to our idea of logical necessity that whether or not a statement is logically necessary should be determined by the existence or nonexistence of something. If by "logically necessary statement" we mean "theorem of a logical system" or "tautology" or "analytic statement," it seems quite clear that the existence or nonexistence of something is irrelevant to the question of whether or not a statement is a theorem, or a tautology, or is analytic. Even if our idea of logical necessity is

claimed to be wider than any of these notions, it seems unlikely that any plausible account of logical necessity would allow it to be dependent on existence.[25]

Hartshorne believes that one cannot use the logic of perfection to prove the existence of a perfect island, but his attempt to meet a Gaunilo type of objection is not successful. He argues that it is incoherent to suppose that an island could be perfect, since in order to be perfect it would have to be a noncontingent being. However, he says, an island by its very nature is contingent. In response to Hartshorne, could one not introduce the concept of a super island that, if it existed at all, would exist necessarily? Hartshorne maintains that the concept of a necessarily existing island is "self-inconsistent."[26] What is his basis for this judgment? He maintains that a contingent being must have ten properties,[27] among which are being causally dependent for its existence on something else and being good for some legitimate purpose only. His argument seems to be that an island by its very nature must have these properties and consequently could not be noncontingent.

The trouble with this reply is that in the case of some of the ten properties listed, it is certainly not obvious that an island could not conceivably have them. For example, why does an island have to be causally dependent on other things? Islands are in fact so dependent, but it does not seem impossible to imagine an island that was not. To be sure, if such an island were to exist in our world it would be a miracle, since its existence would be in conflict with many laws of nature. But it would not, for that reason, be conceptually incoherent. In the case of some of the other properties listed by Hartshorne, although it is true that an island by its very nature must have them, it is unclear why he supposes that they are only properties of contingent beings. For example one may admit that even a perfect island is only good for some purposes. But why must a noncontingent being be good for *all* purposes?

It would also seem possible to "prove" the existence of the super absolute evil one by modal argument with a structure identical to Hartshorne's, the basic difference being in the interpretation of q. Statement q would now mean "A perfectly evil being exists." Since such a being would be all-knowing, all-powerful, uncreated, independent of everything else, and the cause of all contingent things, of the ten properties of a contingent being listed by Hartshorne it would lack only one: It would not be good for all legitimate purposes. But, as suggested above, it is unclear that this property has anything to do with noncontingency.

In an earlier work Hartshorne argued against an ontological proof of a perfect devil. Since the idea of a perfect devil has close similarities to our idea of the absolute evil one, it is important to consider his argument. He says:

> A perfect devil would have at the same time to be infinitely responsible for all that exists besides itself, and yet infinitely averse to all that exists. It would have to attend with unrivaled care and patience and fullness of the realization to the lives of all other beings (which must depend for existence upon this care), and yet must hate all these things with matchless bitterness. It must savagely torture a cosmos every item of which is integral with its own being, united to it with a vivid intimacy such as we can dimly imagine. In short, whether a perfect God is sense or nonsense, a perfect devil is unequivocally nonsense, and it is of no import whether the nonsensical does or does not exist, since in any case it necessarily does not exist, and its existence would be nothing, even though a necessary nothing.[28]

It is a mystery why Hartshorne attributes conflicting properties to the perfect devil, but in any case they are not the properties of the absolute evil one. As I conceive of the absolute evil one, although it is responsible for the existence of all contingent creatures in the sense that it is the ultimate cause of them, this is compatible with its inflicting great evil on these creatures. Thus the absolute evil one is not in one sense, at least, averse to all that exists since the torture of its creatures is its goal. It must create contingent sentient beings in order to cause them pain and suffering. It does not attend to their lives with care and patience in any sense that implies moral concern. It only attends to them in the way a torturer attends to his victims. The cosmos is not integral with its own being, for the absolute evil one transcends the cosmos and intervenes in it only for its own evil purposes. Thus Hartshorne has not shown that the super absolute evil one is a nonsensical notion, a "necessary nothing." Until this is shown, I must conclude that the ontological proof of the super absolute evil one is sound if the ontological proof of God is.

Kordig's Ontological Argument

Carl Kordig has recently presented a deontic version of the ontological argument that has two stages.[29] The first stage of the argument can be informally stated as follows: What is deontically perfect ought to exist. Since God is perfect He ought to exist. But Kordig argues that what ought to exist can exist. So it is possible that God exists. Stated more formally, with g standing for "God exists," and O the deontic operator, and $\lozenge$ the modal operator designating possibility, the first stage of the argument is this.

(1) Og
(2) Og → $\lozenge$g

(3) Hence $\lozenge$g

The first premise says that God ought to exist. The second premise says that if God ought to exist, it is possible that God exists. By *modus ponens* one concludes that it is possible that God exists.

Stated informally, the second stage of the argument is that since it was established in the first stage of the argument that the existence of God is possible, the existence of God is necessary. This is because God is not a contingent being. If it is possible that He exists, He must exist. It is formally stated, with $\square$ the modal operator designating necessity, as follows:

(4) $\lozenge$g
(5) $\lozenge$g → $\square$g

(6) Hence $\square$g

Premise (4), the conclusion of the first stage of the argument, says that the existence of God is possible. Premise (5) of the argument says that if the existence of God is possible, then the existence of God is necessary. Given these two premises, one concludes by *modus ponens* that it is necessary that God exists.

Even if there were no problems with the first stage of the argument, there would be serious problems with the second stage, problems identical to the one in Malcolm's and Hartshorne's versions of the ontological argument. For example, although islands are usually considered contingent entities, one can introduce the idea of a super island, an island paradise that not only has wondrous health benefits and the right number of coconut trees, days of sunshine, and so on but also has unusual modal properties. For example, if the super island exists at all, its existence is necessary. Since the concept of a super island is not logically impossible, by *modus ponens* one can conclude that the super island necessarily exists. Where s stands for "A super island exists" the argument is this.

(4') $\Diamond s$
(5') $\Diamond s \rightarrow \Box s$

(6') Hence $\Box s$

Now, it may be objected that the concept of a super island is incoherent and, consequently, that (4') is false. However, it is not at all obvious that there is anything any more incoherent about the concept of a super island than about the concept of God. As we argued above, such an island should not be considered analogous to the largest number, which clearly is an incoherent idea. Nor are the sort of considerations adduced by Hartshorne persuasive. In any case, at this point the first stage of Kordig's argument comes to our rescue. Even skeptics who doubt that a super island exists surely believe that it ought to exist. After all, as we have defined it, the blind and ill could be cured simply by being transported there. But if it ought to exist, then it is possible for it to exist. Stated more formally:

(1') Os
(2') $Os \rightarrow \Diamond s$

(3') Hence $\Diamond s$

As Patrick Grim has shown, all manner of bizarre deontically perfect beings can be demonstrated by this argument.[30] It is also possible to demonstrate the existence of the super absolute evil one. Let e stand for "The super absolute evil one exists." The argument then proceeds as follows:

(1a) $O{\sim}e$
(2a) $O{\sim}e \rightarrow \Diamond e$
(3a) Hence $\Diamond e$
(4a) $\Diamond e$
(5a) $\Diamond e \rightarrow \Box e$

(6a) Hence $\Box e$

Stated informally, this says that the super absolute evil one ought not to exist. So the super absolute evil one is possible. Since the super absolute evil one is by definition not a contingent being and it is possible that it exists, it must exist.

It seems clear that Kordig's deontic version of the ontological argument is no more acceptable than the other versions we have examined.

Plantinga's Ontological Argument

Plantinga has argued for the existence of God using a version of the ontological argument based on the logic of possible worlds.[31] He defines the property of maximal greatness as entailing maximal excellence in every possible world, and he defines maximal excellence as entailing omniscience, omnipotence, and moral perfection in every possible world. A simplified statement of his argument can be constructed as follows:

(1) There is a possible world where maximal greatness is exemplified.
(1a) There is some possible world in which there is a being that is maximally great. (From (1))
(2) Necessarily, a being that is maximally great is maximally excellent in every possible world. (By definition)
(3) Necessarily, a being that is maximally excellent in every possible world is omniscient, omnipotent, and morally perfect in every possible world. (By definition)
(4) Therefore, there is in our world and in every world a being that is omniscient, omnipotent, and morally perfect. (From (1a), (2), and (3))

Plantinga does not believe that this argument is a conclusive demonstration of the existence of God, since premise (1) is not rationally established; it could be denied by rational people. On the other hand, he maintains that (1) is not contrary to reason. Thus he concludes that the argument establishes not the truth of the thesis but "its rational acceptability."[32]

There are a number of problems with this argument. For one thing, technical questions can be raised about the use of possible world semantics and modal logic in his proof. In particular, it may be wondered if the system of modal logic used in Plantinga's proof is appropriate[33] and if Plantinga has provided adequate truth conditions for modal sentences.[34] We do not pursue these issues here, however, for there are more basic problems with the argument.

To begin with, Plantinga may well be mistaken that premise (1) is not contrary to reason. If, for example, omniscience, omnipotence, and moral perfection constitute an incoherent set of properties, as we shall soon see, then maximal greatness would be incoherent as well. Furthermore, one of Plantinga's arguments for supposing that the acceptance of premise (1) is not irrational is suspect. He compares (1) to Leibniz's Law:

(LL)   For any object x and y and property P, if x = y, then x has P if and only if y has P

and maintains that despite the fact that we have no proof of (LL) we are justified in accepting it. Similarly, Plantinga argues that despite the fact that we have no proof of (1) we are justified in accepting it.[35] However, it has been plausibly argued that the analogy between (LL) and (1) is weak. (LL) is a free English translation of a theorem of the first-order predicate calculus with identity, but (1) is not a translation of a theorem of any standard logic. Disputes about (LL) in the history of philosophy, unlike disputes about (1), seem to be metalinguistic and not over the truth value of (LL).[36]

In addition, Plantinga's argument can be parodied[37] by using an argument with the same form to show the rational acceptability of fairies, ghosts, unicorns, and all manner of strange creatures. One *reductio* of this mode of argument proceeds as follows: Let us define the property of being a special fairy so that it entails the property of being a fairy in every possible world. Let us define the property of being a fairy so that it entails the property of being a tiny woodland creature with magical powers in every possible world. Then:

(1′)   There is one possible world where the property of being a special fairy is exemplified.
(1a′)   There is one possible world where there is a special fairy. (From (1))
(2′)   Necessarily, a being that is a special fairy is a fairy in every possible world. (By definition)
(3′)   Necessarily, a being that is a fairy in every possible world is a tiny woodland creature

with magical powers in every possible world. (By definition)
(4′)   Therefore, there is a tiny woodland creature with magical powers in our world and in every world.

Since premise (1′) is no more contrary to reason than premise (1), one must assume that the conclusion (6′) is rationally acceptable. In a similar way one can show that there are gremlins, leprechauns, and unicorns. Using a similar mode of argument one can show the rational acceptability of a marvelous island of the kind specified above. One defines the property of a special marvelous island in such a way that it entails being a marvelous island in all possible worlds. One defines a marvelous island as an island where one never grows old, where there are 10,000 coconut trees, and so forth.[38] Then one has as the first premise of the argument:

(1″)   There is a possible world where the property of being a special marvelous island is exemplified.

Presumably, (1″) is not contrary to reason or, at least, no more contrary to reason than (1). The argument then proceeds in the way outlined above. One concludes that belief in a marvelous island is rationally acceptable. It can be shown as well that the absolute evil one exists in our world and every world. But, since the absolute evil one is omniscient, omnipotent, and completely evil, God and the absolute evil could not both exist.[39]

I must conclude that Plantinga's version of the ontological argument is no more successful than the others we have examined.[40]

Conclusion

Arthur Schopenhauer wrote, "Considered by daylight . . . and without prejudice, this famous Ontological Proof is really a charming joke."[41] One is tempted to agree. Yet, as we have seen, some well-known philosophers who have reputations as profound thinkers have taken it quite seriously. Given the problems with the argument outlined here, it is difficult to understand why they do.

Michael Martin

Notes

1 See Alvin Plantinga (ed.), *The Ontological Argument* (Garden City, NY: Doubleday, 1965), for relevant selections from St Anselm, Descartes, Leibniz, Kant, Spinoza, and Schopenhauer as well as contemporary philosophers.

2 St Anselm, *Proslogion*, ch. 2, in Plantinga, *Ontological Argument*, pp. 3–4.

3 For one influential contemporary critique see G. E. Moore, "Is Existence a Predicate?" reprinted in Plantinga, *Ontological Argument*, pp. 71–85.

4 Immanuel Kant, *The Critique of Pure Reason*, trans. Norman Kemp Smith (London: Macmillan, 1929), p. 505, reprinted in Plantinga, *Ontological Argument*, p. 62.

5 Norman Malcolm, "Anselm's Ontological Arguments," reprinted in Plantinga, *Ontological Argument*, p. 139. [See also ch. 23, this volume.]

6 Cf. David and Marjorie Haight, "An Ontological Argument for the Devil," *Monist*, 54, 1970, pp. 218–20. Richard Swinburne, *The Coherence of Theism* (Oxford: Clarendon Press, 1977), pp. 141–8, argues that the concept of an all-powerful, all-knowing, free, and completely evil being is incoherent. However, Swinburne is mistaken. See Michael Martin, "The Coherence of the Hypothesis of an Omnipotent, Omniscient, Free and Perfectly Evil Being," *International Journal for the Philosophy of Religion*, 17, 1985, pp. 185–91.

7 Gaunilo, "In Behalf of the Fool," reprinted in Plantinga, *Ontological Argument*, pp. 6–13.

8 St Anselm, "St. Anselm's Reply to Gaunilo," reprinted in Plantinga, *Ontological Argument*, pp. 13–27.

9 Charles Hartshorne, *The Logic of Perfection* (La Salle, Ill.: Open Court, 1962), p. 55.

10 Alvin Plantinga, *God, Freedom, and Evil* (Grand Rapids, Mich.: Eerdmans, 1983), pp. 90–1.

11 See Patrick Grim, "In Behalf of 'In Behalf of the Fool,'" *International Journal for the Philosophy of Religion*, 13, 1982, pp. 33–42.

12 See J. L. Mackie, *The Miracle of Theism* (Oxford: Clarendon Press, 1982), pp. 52–3.

13 A similar point is made in William Rowe, "The Ontological Argument," *Reason and Responsibility*, ed. Joel Feinberg (Belmont, Calif.: Wadsworth, 1985), pp. 14–22. Rowe argues that one can build existence into the definition of a concept. Modifying Rowe's example slightly, one can define a real magician as an existing magician. But it does not follow that there are any real magicians. The only thing that follows is that no nonexisting thing is a real magician. Similarly, if existence is part of the concept of God, the only thing that follows is that no nonexisting thing is God. But what if one supposes that God's existence is possible? Rowe shows that this indeed allows one to infer that God exists only because one has begged the question. In granting that God was possible, one is granting that God exists. In a similar way, if one granted that a real magician is possible, one would be granting that a magician exists.

14 Norman Malcolm, "Anselm's Ontological Arguments," reprinted in Plantinga, *Ontological Argument*, pp. 136–59.

15 Ibid., p. 146.

16 Malcolm rejects Leibniz's proof that since perfections are simple properties, they must be compatible with one another. See ibid., p. 157. Leibniz's argument is reprinted in Plantinga, *Ontological Argument*, p. 56.

17 Malcolm, "Anselm's Ontological Arguments," p. 157.

18 See Grim, "In Behalf of 'In Behalf of the Fool,'" p. 34.

19 Cf. Paul Henle, "Uses of the Ontological Argument," reprinted in Plantinga, *Ontological Argument*, pp. 172–80. Henle by parody of reasoning "proves" the existence of a whole family of necessary beings called Nec, NEc, and NEC.

20 See Alvin Plantinga, "A Valid Ontological Argument?" reprinted in Plantinga, *Ontological Argument*, pp. 160–71.

21 Malcolm, "Anselm's Ontological Arguments," pp. 143–7.

22 See Henle, "Uses of the Ontological Argument," p. 176. Although more than 25 years have passed, he has not clarified his meaning or indeed attempted in any way to answer his many critics. In addition to Plantinga, "Valid Ontological Argument?" and Henle, "Uses of the Ontological Argument," see R. E. Allen, "The Ontological Argument," *Philosophical Review*, 70, 1961, pp. 56–66; Raziel Abelson, "Not Necessarily," *Philosophical Review*, 70, 1961, pp. 67–84; Terrence Penelhum, "On the Second Ontological Argument," *Philosophical Review*, 70, 1961, pp. 85–92.

23 Hartshorne, *Logic of Perfection*, p. 25.

24 Ibid., p. 51.

25 R. L. Purtill, "Hartshorne's Modal Proof," *Journal of Philosophy*, 63, 1966, p. 408.

26 Hartshorne, *Logic of Perfection*, p. 55.

27 Ibid., pp. 74–5.

28 Charles Hartshorne, "The Necessarily Existent," reprinted in Plantinga, *Ontological Argument*, p. 127.

29 Carl R. Kordig, "A Deontic Argument for God's Existence," *Nous*, 15, 1981, pp. 207–8.

30 Patrick Grim, "Against a Deontic Argument for God's Existence," *Analysis*, 42, 1982, pp. 171–4.

31 Alvin Plantinga, *God, Freedom, and Evil* (Grand Rapids, Mich.: Eerdmans, 1983), pp. 108–12; *The Nature of Necessity* (Oxford: Clarendon Press, 1974), pp. 213–17.

32 Plantinga, *God, Freedom, and Evil*, p. 112.

33 See Mackie, *Miracle of Theism*, pp. 56–7.

34 See Michael Tooley, "Plantinga's Defense of the Ontological Argument," *Mind*, 90, 1981, pp. 426–7.

35 Plantinga, *Nature of Necessity*, pp. 220–1.

36 Peter van Inwagen, "Ontological Arguments," *Nous*, 11, 1977, pp. 388–9.

37 See Patrick Grim, "Plantinga's God and Other Monstrosities," *Religious Studies*, 15, 1979, pp. 91–7; Tooley, "Plantinga's Defense," pp. 422–7.

38 See Grim, "In Behalf of 'In Behalf of the Fool,'" p. 38.

39 Cf. Tooley, "Plantinga's Defense," p. 425.

40 For a milder criticism than the one given here, see William Rowe, "Modal Versions of the Ontological Argument," *Philosophy of Religion*, ed. Louis P. Pojam (Belmont, Calif.: Wadsworth, 1987), pp. 67–74. Rowe argues that the only thing Plantinga has established is that it *may* not be foolish to accept the argument, and he has not established that it is not foolish to accept. However, one would have thought that the various parodies of the argument suggest the folly of accepting the argument. Consequently, Plantinga has not even established this very weak conclusion.

41 Arthur Schopenhauer, *The Fourfold Root of the Principle of Sufficient Reason*, reprinted in Plantinga, *Ontological Argument*, p. 66.

PART V

Nontheistic Religions

Introduction

Paul J. Griffiths

Philosophy of religion as a Western (European and American) discipline has concerned itself very largely with questions about God. This is mostly because the discipline's idea of what religion is has been arrived at by a process of abstraction from Christianity (see the introductory remarks to Part I of this volume), and so has not been formed by any serious consideration of what religions very unlike Christianity might consider of philosophical importance. The topics discussed by Indian Buddhist scholastics, for instance, often have little or nothing to do with God and much to do with what Western philosophers are likely to think of as topics in metaphysics or psychology. What, for example, gives a material object or a human person the identity it has? Do such things endure through time, and if so, how? What is the origin of human suffering, and how (if at all) may it be removed? It seems not unreasonable to include readings on such topics since they have been of deep and continuing concern to many Buddhists, Hindus, Confucians, and so forth; and the extracts we provide here are intended to whet the appetite and to hasten the day when attention to these topics will be a standard part of the philosophy of religion.

Some have doubted that there is anything properly thought of as "philosophy" (and hence also anything properly called "philosophy of religion") outside Europe and those parts of the world whose culture is influenced by it. Wilhelm Halbfass's treatment of Indian (Sanskrit) terms for intellectual activities that might be thought of as philosophy is included here because it addresses this question in a detailed way. He shows, through a study of the uses of and definitions given to the Sanskrit terms *darśana* and *ānvīkṣikī* by Indian thinkers, that there was indeed in India an understanding of the use of reason in argument and systematic thought with significant parallels to what Europeans and Americans might think of as "philosophy" (itself, of course, a complicated matter). He also shows that most of this philosophical activity was related in one way or another to what are customarily thought of as the Indian religions. Halbfass's work is likely to be hard going for those without prior knowledge of Indian thought; but it repays the needed effort by showing that, and how, the topics and methods of philosophy and the philosophy of religion might be configured differently from how they have come to be in Europe and America.

The essay by Georges Dreyfus treats the thought of the seventh-century Indian Buddhist thinker Dharmakīrti on the question of what is real, which includes the question of how best to understand the nature of material objects. It may not seem immediately obvious why this is a topic in the philosophy of religion. An quick answer is that it is one much discussed by Buddhists, and therefore in that sense religious. But to this can be added the point that for Buddhists, as for many other religious people, coming to an accurate understanding of what is real is an essential part of making progress toward the abolition of suffering, which is (at the level of theory) what Buddhism is all about. The scholastic distinctions that Dharmakīrti's interpreters make are therefore a proper part of the religious enterprise of getting one's understanding of reality right.

Anne Carolyn Klein's essay brings together Buddhist and feminist perspectives on the nature of the self. Buddhists are typically concerned about the deep human tendency to paint a picture of the self that portrays it as enduring, changeless, and possessed of essential properties that it does not lose. Buddhist theorists have attempted to explain what it is to have a sense of self (and an understanding of what the self is) that paints a different picture: of the self as empty, imagined, and composed of events connected by causes but not consisting of an enduring substance. Klein proposes that there are ways in which a Buddhist view of the self as empty might be used to further one of the more important goals of feminism, which is the undercutting of a patriarchal social order. But she notes, too, that Buddhist theory has coexisted quite well with such social orders in Asia for more than two thousand years, and that the matter is therefore not straightforward.

The last piece in this section, David Loy's "How Many Nondualities Are There?," treats what he rightly calls a concept centrally important to Asian thought: that of the denial of duality. It is of course possible to deny duality in many ways, and to reject various different dualities. It is the burden of Loy's work to begin to make distinctions among the varieties of nondualism. Some nondualists, for example, reject the idea that the apparent multiplicity of objects in the world is real; others deny the distinction between subject (me) and object (the pen I hold as I write), and so forth. Again, it might be asked what the question of nonduality – the question, finally, of whether there is just one thing – has to do with the philosophy of religion. The answer this time is clearer: the question of nondualism is, at root, the question of the relation between what is taken to be maximally significant and what is not; and if ever there were a religious question, that is surely one.

Further Reading

From The Blackwell Companion to Philosophy of Religion, *see the entries on* Buddhism; Hinduism; Chinese Confucianism and Taoism

Collins, Steven, *Selfless Persons: Imagery and Thought in Theravada Buddhism* (Cambridge: Cambridge University Press, 1982). *The best single work on the Buddhist philosophical idea that there can be persons without selves – an idea of basic religious importance to the Buddhist tradition.*

Graham, A. C., *Disputers of the Tao: Philosophical Argument in Ancient China* (La Salle, Illinois: Open Court, 1989). *A counterpoint to Hansen: these are the two main views about the meaning of Taoist thought.*

Griffiths, Paul J., *On Being Mindless: Buddhist Meditation and the Mind–Body Problem* (La Salle, Illinois: Open Court, 1986). *A treatment of Buddhist analyses of the religious and philosophical significance of the idea that our mental life can come to a halt.*

Hansen, Chad, *A Daoist Theory of Chinese Thought* (New York: Oxford University Press, 1992). *A somewhat technical work, with special focus on philosophy of language and metaphysics.*

Mohanty, Jitendranath, *Classical Indian Philosophy* (Lanham, Maryland: Rowman and Littlefield, 2000). *A concise and elegant survey by a philosopher expert in both Western and Indian philosophy, much, but not all, devoted to philosophy of religion.*

Nagao, Gadjin, *The Foundational Standpoint of Madhyamika Philosophy* (Albany, New York: State University of New York Press, 1989). *An English translation of a key work by the most eminent Japanese interpreter of the Buddhist philosophy of emptiness.*

Perrett, Roy W. (ed.), *Indian Philosophy: A Collection of Readings* (New York: Garland, 2000). *A collection of important recent essays on the topic of its title.*

Phillips, Stephen H., *Classical Indian Metaphysics: Refutations of Realism and the Emergence of "New Logic"* (La Salle, Illinois: Open Court, 1996). *Translations and interpretations of important Indian philosophical works.*

Raju, P. T., *Structural Depths of Hindu Thought* (Albany, New York: State University of New York Press, 1985). *A long and difficult book, with many important insights.*

Schwartz, Benjamin, *The World of Thought in Ancient China* (Cambridge, MA: Harvard University Press, 1985). *A clear and thorough explanation of the development of Taoist and Confucian thought.*

Williams, Paul, *Buddhist Thought: A Complete Introduction to the Indian Tradition* (London and New York: Routledge, 2000). *The best single-volume introduction.*

25

Darśana, Ānvīkṣikī, Philosophy

Wilhelm Halbfass

1. While the European historians of philosophy in the nineteenth and early twentieth centuries still question whether the concept of philosophy can be applied beyond the tradition of European, fundamentally Greek thought, a process of globalization takes place in which non-European traditions not only adopt European philosophical concepts and teachings, but also reinterpret and reconceive their own ways of thinking *as* philosophy. India has played a conspicuous and significant part in this process. Indians have responded not only to specific philosophical ideas, but above all to the term and concept "philosophy" itself. For modern Hinduism, the concept of philosophy has become a vehicle of self-understanding, of assimilation and "Westernization," but also of self-affirmation against the West.

In modern Indian vernaculars as well as in modern Sanskrit, the word *darśana* is widely used as translation of "philosophy." *Darśana* is considered to be the traditional Indian word for "philosophy" – not merely in the sense of a lexicographic equivalent, but also as an answer which the Indian tradition has held in stock for its encounter with what is called "philosophy" in the European tradition. On the one hand, the word serves as a terminological device for the reception and assimilation of the European concept of philosophy, as an indigenous linguistic receptacle for foreign conceptual contents. On the other hand, specifically Indian apologetic

Wilhelm Halbfass, "Darśana, Ānvīkṣikī, Philosophy," from India and Europe: An Essay in Understanding (Albany: State University of New York Press, 1988), pp. 263–86.

claims are associated with the usage of this word. We often hear that *darśana* has to be understood in its etymological affiliation with *dṛś*, "to see," i.e. as "vision," "intuition," "realization," and that this meaning indicates something genuinely Indian, and characteristically different from the analytical, discursive, theoretically objectifying spirit of European philosophy.

2. Among Western historians of Indian philosophy, the terminological and conceptual correlation between "philosophy" and *darśana* is not normally accepted. Even those historians who are willing to concede that there is, or has been, philosophy in India, often maintain that there is no indigenous Indian word or concept corresponding to what we call "philosophy." It was only for a short period that, following H. Jacobi's suggestion, the word *ānvīkṣikī*, as used in Kauṭilya's *Arthaśāstra*, was taken seriously as a possible terminological equivalent. It is obvious that Jacobi was focusing on the critical and methodological implications of *ānvīkṣikī*, and he wanted to associate them with the ideas of critical, autonomous reasoning and "pure" theory which the European historians of philosophy tended to regard as criteria of "real" philosophy.

Jacobi's interpretation has been discussed in detail and rejected by P. Hacker.[1] Nevertheless, the issue is certainly not closed. The different approaches to the concepts of *ānvīkṣikī* and *darśana* reflect not only differences in the interpretation of classical Indian philosophy, but also in European self-understanding, and in the assessment of the encounter between India and Europe. Considering the great and symptomatic significance which *darśana* has gained for the Neo-Hindu self-understanding and self-definition, it seems surprising how little has been done to examine and clarify the traditional role and background of *darśana* and to trace and explain the hermeneutical processes of interpretation and reinterpretation which have led to the modern Indian adoption of *darśana* as a terminological equivalent or analogue of "philosophy."

3. An obvious basis for the semantic association between "philosophy" and *darśana* is given by the fact that *darśana* is a familiar and characteristic term in Indian doxographic literature, i.e. in that literature which summarizes and classifies the main schools or systems of what is commonly called "Indian philosophy." Most of the traditional Indian doxographies use the word *darśana* in their title, in particular those two which are the best known as well as the most interesting and significant ones: Haribhadra's *Ṣaḍdarśanasamuccaya* (eighth century) and Mādhava-Vidyāraṇya's *Sarvadarśanasaṃgraha* (fourteenth century). The short compendium by the Jaina Haribhadra is not only the older one of these two, but the oldest of all the Sanskrit doxographies which we have or about which we know.

The fact that Haribhadra chose the word *darśana* for the title of his doxographic treatise shows that by the time of the eighth century it had become a well-known designation for "philosophical" systems or doctrines. If we look, however, at earlier and contemporary and even at some later works, it is equally clear that it had by no means become *the* generally accepted standard term for the traditional systems of Indian philosophy. In fact, it plays no noticeable role in the self-characterization of the leading exponents of these systems. The philosophers themselves hardly ever use it when they refer to what they and their partners and opponents in debate, i.e. the representatives of other systems, are doing. It is generally absent in the older literature of the systems, i.e. in the *sūtras* and their immediate commentaries. [. . .]

Haribhadra's commentators, Maṇibhadra and Guṇaratna, often use *mata* [opinion] to paraphrase *darśana*. Haribhadra himself uses both terms interchangeably. On the other hand, Haribhadra distinguishes or even contrasts two meanings of *darśana* in the introductory verses of his work, when he first salutes the Jina Mahāvīra as one who is *ṣaḍdarśana*, i.e. has true and complete insight, and then proceeds to announce his program of describing the various philosophical "views" (*darśana*).

4. The terminology of Śaṅkara, who may have been a contemporary of Haribhadra, provides additional information. [. . .] In one significant passage he uses repeatedly the word *darśana*, even referring to the philosophical tradition advocated by himself as "our *darśana*" (*asmadīyaṃ darśanam*) or "the Upaniṣadic *darśana*" (*aupaniṣadaṃ darśanam*). However, this passage is a response to the statement of an opponent who had criticized the Vedāntic viewpoint as incoherent (*asamañjasam idam aupaniṣadaṃ darśanam*), and seems to adopt the opponent's own terminology. In another passage, Śaṅkara refers to the "systems (or 'views') like Sāṃkhya, etc., which are opposed to right insight" (*samyagdarśanapratipakṣabhūtāni sāṃkhyādidarśanāni*). It is evident that he is playing here on different connotations of *darśana*: As *samyagdarśana*, as the one true insight and realization, *darśana* appears appropriately in the singular, and it is to be distinguished from, and even contrasted with, that plurality of mere views which constitute the subject-matter of doxographic enumeration.

In the seventh century, and approximately one century earlier than Śaṅkara, the great Buddhist Madhyamaka commentator Candrakīrti referred to his own system, or rather method, as *madhyamaka-darśana* – a method which avoids the "false theories of the dichotomy of existence and non-existence" (*astitvanāstitvadvayadarśana*) and is thus different from the "mere views," i.e. "false theories" of the Vijñānavādins etc. (*vijñānavādidarśanādi*). Again a century earlier, the Vaiśeṣika teacher Praśastapāda referred to the false "views of the Buddhists, etc." (*śākyādidarśana*), which are "incompatible with the (true) Vedic insight" (*trayīdarśanaviparīta*).

The passages which we have quoted indicate that at the time of the composition of the *Brahmasūt-rabhāṣya* the word *darśana* had already assumed a certain doxographic connotation. [. . .]

At any rate, *darśana* in the doxographic sense, i.e. as "(mere) view," without qualifying epithets, such as *samyag-*, is clearly distinct from *darśana* in the sense of *samyagdarśana* or *tattvadarśana*, i.e., of right vision or realization. The doxographic meaning is a basically neutral, occasionally even pejorative meaning. The combination and merger of these two meanings, or the interpretation of the doxographic usage in the normative sense of "right vision," "realization," is a symptomatic innovation of Neo-Hinduism.

5. Our observations on the traditional usage of *darśana* may be supplemented by referring to its

close relative *dṛṣṭi* (Pali *diṭṭhi*), which is used most conspicuously, but by no means exclusively, in Buddhism. *Dṛṣṭi/diṭṭhi*, as used in chapter 27 of Nāgārjuna's *Madhyamakakārikā* or in the *Brahmajālasutta* of the *Dīghanikāya*, indicates something which is not only neutral or irrelevant, but soteriologically harmful – speculative views, mere theories which – by virtue of the fact that they are mere views and conceptualizations – constitute elements of bondage and obstacles on the way to liberation. With these "mere views," the Buddhists contrast the "right," i.e. soteriologically meaningful and helpful "view" or "orientation" (*samyagdṛṣṭi*, Pali *sammādiṭṭhi*), which is the first part of the "eightfold path" to final liberation (*nirvāṇa*). Although *dṛṣṭi* is much less conspicuous in Hindu philosophical literature, it occurs here, too, in the meaning "view" or "mere view." The same connotation of "speculation," "mere theory" may also occasionally be found in the usage of *darśana*.

The Jainas and Vedāntins who produced most of the doxographic literature do not normally use the word *darśana* in a pejorative sense. They tend to use it in a neutral, non-committal sense, and certainly without any normative or idealizing implications. As a matter of fact, the Jaina doxographers sometimes claim a complete and uncompromising neutrality, an attitude *sine ira et studio* [without anger and zeal], for their way of dealing with the various philosophical views. A verse from Haribhadra's *Lokatattvanirṇaya*, which both Guṇaratna and Maṇibhadra quote in their commentaries on the *Ṣaḍdarśanasamuccaya* and which is possibly based upon an older Buddhist verse, states that there is no partiality in favor of the Jina Mahāvīra nor any dislike or bias against teachers like Kapila. Such statements should certainly not be interpreted as programs for historical and critical research. Yet it is true that Jainism has developed a remarkable tradition of dealing with and relating to other schools and doctrines not just in order to criticize and refute them, but to put them into a systematic order and framework. And it is in this systematically coordinating, comprehensive and inclusive treatment of other doctrines that the Jainas find their own perspectivism, the *anekāntavāda*, fulfilled and confirmed.

6. [. . .]

The philosophical consummation of the Jaina approach is reached in the perspectivistic theory of world-views (*naya*) which we find most fully developed in the works of Siddhasena Divākara

and Mallavādin. Here, the enumeration of historically factual viewpoints merges with the construction of systematically possible standpoints in philosophy. Jainism is credited with a special and unique manner of coordinating, systematizing and completing the other world-views, of showing their attachment to partial truths and mere aspects, and of salvaging them from their self-imposed isolation and one-sidedness.

The conception of *naya*, and the procedures associated with it, are among the more distinctive contributions of Jainism to Indian philosophy, and their significance is not confined to the Jaina tradition. As for the word *naya* itself, it has also become quite familiar in non-Jaina doxographic and philosophical literature; it is frequently used as a virtual synonym of *darśana* and *mata*.

7. Quite obviously, the Jaina tradition provided a natural setting for the development of doxographic literature, as we find it represented by Haribhadra's *Ṣaḍdarśanasamuccaya*. Yet Haribhadra avoids the term *naya* with its systematic and "constructive" connotations, and uses *darśana* and *mata* instead. Haribhadra was a Brahmin by birth and education, and in his later career as one of the most learned and prolific Jaina authors he obviously tried to place Jainism in the broader framework of the Indian tradition, deemphasizing a terminology and phraseology which might have appeared as too technically and parochially Jainist. And it is not only the term *naya*, but also the systematic and constructivist claims of the *naya* theory which his doxography avoids. In choosing *darśana* as his doxographic title-word, Haribhadra did not simply continue or resume the old usage of *darśana*, but he also referred to a usage which had gained momentum outside of Jainism, and which had prepared the word *darśana* for its special doxographic role. The greatest representative of the Śabdādvaita [nonduality of speech] tradition, Bhartṛhari (who lived most probably during the second half of the fifth century), provides early and informative testimony for this usage.

Bhartṛhari was not a doxographer, and he did not use the word *darśana* in an explicitly doxographic sense. But his work shows us this doxographic usage *in statu nascendi* [coming to birth] and in preliminary stages of development, and in a peculiar affiliation with the philosophy of the absolute "word." In his *Vākyapadīya*, as well as in his commentary on Patañjali's *Mahābhāṣya*, Bhartṛhari uses *darśana* in the sense of "view" and "perspective,"

Wilhelm Halbfass

and then also of "way of thinking" and "doctrine." There are various "views," or "ways of seeing," with reference to one and the same "visible" object: *ekasmin api dṛśye 'rthe darśanaṃ bhidyate pṛthak*. The "seeing" and understanding of time varies: *bhinnaṃ kālasya darśanam*. We find different perspectives, different ways of seeing the same reality in many areas. There is the "perspective of unity" (*ekatvadarśana*) as well as the "perspective of aggregation" (*saṃsargadarśana*); in such and similar compounds, *darśana* is used in a way which recalls the Jaina concept of *naya*. In his commentary on the *Mahābhāṣya* Bhartṛhari also uses the more specifically doxographic expressions *vaiśeṣikadarśana* and *mīmāṃsakadarśana*. [Vaiśeṣika and Mīmāṃsaka are names for the adherents of particular schools of thought.] Towards the end of the second *kāṇḍa* of the *Vākyapadīya*, he refers to his *guru* as having studied other traditions as well as his "own system" (*svaṃ ca darśanam*), i.e. the tradition of grammatical philosophy; and he adds the general observation that insight gains distinctness from (the study of) different traditional views: *prajñā vivekaṃ labhate bhinnair āgamadarśanaiḥ*.

This statement sounds almost like a motto and a programmatic justification of the future doxographies, in particular if we consider the perspectivistic approach of the Jainas. It may be worth noticing in this connection that Bhartṛhari's commentator Helārāja uses *darśana* and *naya* as interchangeable terms.

8.   Indian as well as Western authors have emphasized that the philosophical "views" or "systems" which are the subject-matter of the Sanskrit doxographies should not be interpreted as systems of "pure theory" in the Greek-European sense. Indeed, the soteriological and practical perspective is as obvious in the basic texts of the systems (*darśana*) as in their doxographic recapitulations. Yet, in contrasting "pure theory" and "soteriological orientation," we have to be more cautious and discriminating than is often the case on both the Indian and the Western sides.

We do not have to repeat here the statements of those historians of philosophy who saw the "purely theoretical" attitude, the interest in "knowledge for the sake of knowledge," as a uniquely and exclusively European phenomenon. On the other hand, modern Hindu authors have invoked the traditional Indian disregard for "pure theory" as an element of Hindu self-affirmation. From their perspective, "knowledge for the sake of knowledge" and "value-free science" appear as idle curiosity, as compared to the soteriological commitment of Indian thought.

Indeed, declarations like those of Plato and Aristotle about "wonder" (θαυμαζειν) as the ground of philosophy, about the "desire to know" as a natural and inherently legitimate distinction of man, and about the ideal of the "theoretical life" (βιος θεωρητιχος) are absent in Indian literature. Instead, Indian philosophers usually take it for granted, or even postulate explicitly, that the desire to know has to be motivated and guided by a goal or purpose (*prayojana*). For the majority of philosophical systems (*darśana*), the ultimate purpose is final liberation (*mokṣa, mukti, apavarga*) from the cycle of rebirth and its inherent deficiency and distress (*duḥkha*).

9.   This soteriological motivation, which gained central importance in ancient Buddhism, is also generally present in the major works of classical Hindu philosophy, and it often appears as their starting-point and source of legitimacy. The *Sāṃkhyakārikā* by Īśvarakṛṣṇa provides one of the more conspicuous and memorable examples. It begins with the word *duḥkha* and presents suffering, and the desire to overcome it, as the basic incentive for the "pursuit of knowledge" (*jijñāsā*). A soteriological formula which seems to echo Buddhist ideas is among the opening statements of the *Nyāyasūtras*. Classical Vaiśeṣika tries to demonstrate its soteriological significance and to dispel doubts about its soteriological status which were raised in the *Nyāyabhāṣya* and other texts.

In contrast to the natural human urge to know which Aristotle proclaims in the first sentence of his *Metaphysics*, Indian philosophers tend to emphasize that the cognitive motivation is inseparable from the desire to obtain what is pleasant and to avoid what is unpleasant; just as human activities in general, intellectual, cognitive endeavors are said to be directed towards "fruits" or "results" (*phala*). On the other hand, the attainment of results and goals – and ultimately the goal of final liberation – depends upon right insight and cognition.

Indeed, the fact that traditional Indian self-understanding associates the "philosophical systems" (*darśana*) with practical, soteriological motivations, and even with the idea of a "science of final liberation" (*mokṣaśāstra*), cannot be disputed. Yet, this does not invalidate our earlier observation that the confrontation of "pure theory" and "soteriological orientation" requires caution and

302

discrimination. In order to avoid misleading simplifications, we have to be aware of the historical complexity and variability of both the Indian and the Western approaches, and of the deep problems and ambiguities associated with the concept of "theory," or "pure theory." The fact itself that the soteriological motivation has been postulated and proclaimed so explicitly in the Indian tradition, and that it has in turn become the object of *theoretical* inquiries, involves questions which are significant with regard to the historical development of Indian thought, as well as with regard to the conceptual relationship between "theory" and "practice."

10. The ideas of "pure theory" and "knowledge for its own sake" can hardly be considered as definitive and self-evident achievements of the European tradition; nor are they unquestionable standards for assessing or disqualifying non-European traditions. In the present context, we do not have to discuss the extent to which these ideas have been stylized by the historians of European and especially Greek thought. Nor do we have to investigate whether or how these historians have combined and contaminated fundamentally different phenomena and ideas – the Greek "theory" ($\theta\epsilon\omega\varrho\iota\alpha$), the Christian idea of contemplation, and finally the modern and secularized ideas of "science without presuppositions" and "value-free research." It will be sufficient to recall some exemplary questions which modern Western thinkers have raised with regard to the ideas of "pure theory" and "theoretical knowledge," and about the relationship between theory, practice, and human interests.

One of the most radical and challenging approaches to these questions is found in the work of M. Heidegger. Already in *Sein und Zeit* ("Being and Time"), he characterizes the theoretical contemplation of the object, the objectification which seems to be without any practical motivation, as a derivative mode of praxis. In Heidegger's later critique of the history of European metaphysics, the unfolding of theoretical objectification and of "re-presentational" thinking ("*Vor-Stellen*") appears as an increasing claim to power over the objects: Thus, "theory" cannot be separated from the technological drive towards mastery and domination. Descartes' attempt to establish man, through theory and metaphysics, as the "master and owner of nature" ("*maître et possesseur de la nature*") provides a conspicuous illustration. What is at the center in this case is not theory per se, but its

methodological, technical and anthropocentric "application." But such application is by no means a secondary phenomenon.

J. Habermas has distinguished some basic modes of interest which have determined the cognitive enterprise in the European philosophical and scientific tradition: the Greek "theoretical" interest in cosmic mimesis, i.e. in cognitive assimilation to the structure of the universe; the technical interest which dominates the natural sciences, i.e. "the cognitive interest in technical control over objectified processes"; the practical hermeneutical interest in the cultural sciences; the "emancipatory" interest, which modern philosophy shares with the critically oriented social and psychological sciences, which manifests itself in self-reflection, recognizes the illusory nature of "pure theory," and accepts the inseparability of knowledge and human interests.[2] M. Scheler has distinguished soteriological knowledge ("*Erlösungswissen*"), as the highest type of knowledge, from knowledge which aims at technical mastery ("*Leistungswissen*," "*Machtwissen*"), and knowledge which is committed to cultural ideas ("*Bildungswissen*").[3] Numerous other attempts have been made to define the relationship between theory and practice, knowledge and human interests, truth and relevance, and to clarify the ambiguities and complexities of this relationship. Regardless of the details – we cannot simply contrast the Indian "soteriological" commitment with the "purely theoretical" orientation of the West. There are various, often implicit forms of interaction and confrontation between theory and practice on both sides. We certainly can compare and contrast these, and the different historical directions which the relationship between theory and practice, or knowledge and its goals and uses, has taken in India and in Europe.

11. E. Frauwallner has tried to demonstrate that, prior to its domination by religious and soteriological interests, Indian thought went through a period of theoretical and "scientific" orientation.[4] In particular, he has tried to interpret the old Vaiśeṣika system as a fundamentally unsoteriological doctrine. Frauwallner's approach is obviously influenced by the ideals of "pure theory" and "objective science" as they were advocated by traditional European historians of philosophy, and it can hardly be justified in its entirety. Nevertheless, it raises important and legitimate questions.

It seems evident that the basic text of the Vaiśeṣika system, the *Vaiśeṣikasūtra*, contains numerous later additions and interpolations, and that attempts were made to strengthen and emphasize the religious and soteriological dimension of the system. The development of the Vaiśeṣika concept of *adṛṣṭa*, its increasing association with ethical and soteriological functions, and its identification with the principle of *karman* [action – and its results] illustrate this. In general, the theory of *karman* and rebirth becomes an unquestioned premise of Vaiśeṣika physics and cosmology. "Retributive" causality supersedes "natural" causality. The world becomes more and more a stage for karmic and soteriological processes. In the course of this development, the Vaiśeṣika also responds to the explicit doubts concerning its soteriological relevance which were raised in Vātsyāyana Pakṣilasvāmin's *Nyāyabhāṣya*. The Nyāya itself posits and emphasizes its soteriological commitment in a manner which appears somewhat forced. The Nyāya as well as other systems obviously tried to respond to and to neutralize the challenge of more genuinely and deeply soteriological movements, especially Buddhism.

More than other traditions, Buddhism has developed its critique of theory and speculation, and of merely factual knowledge. As Dharmakīrti states, "precise knowledge of the number of insects" (*kīṭasaṃkhyāparijñāna*) etc. is not part of the enlightenment which the Buddha teaches and exemplifies. Earlier in this chapter, we have referred to the role of *dṛṣṭi/diṭṭhi* in Buddhism. *Dṛṣṭi*, "speculation," "theorizing," "conceptualization," implies soteriological negligence and irresponsibility, and in general a waste of time. Beyond that, it also stands for the representational, reifying and possessive positing of objects and the relations between objects, the projection and reflection of that primeval "thirst" which attaches us to the world of passion and pain, the formation of a network of ideas in which the owner himself, the thinking and theorizing subject, gets caught.

12. Against all forms of theorizing and calculating attachment to the world, and regardless of all assurances that knowledge has to have a goal and purpose, and be a means to an end, the Indian tradition has developed conceptions of knowledge and ideals of contemplation which radically eliminate and transcend all goal-oriented interests, and the means–ends-relationship itself. This is not knowledge as "soteriological technique," but knowledge which tries to supersede all technique and instrumentality. Liberation cannot be attained through causal techniques, or the mastery of means–ends-relationships; but it means freedom from such relationships themselves, and from a world which functions and exists through them. It means pure, free, disinterested contemplation in which all causal and instrumental relations, and with them the world itself, become transparent and irrelevant. Accordingly, the soteriology of Sāṃkhya and Yoga postulates that the "spirit" (*puruṣa*) should withdraw from "being an actor" (*kartṛtva*) as well as from "being an enjoyer" (*bhoktṛtva*) and in general from all participation in the causal world. The same ideas are developed more radically in some schools of Buddhism and, within Hinduism, in Śaṅkara's Advaita Vedānta. Śaṅkara teaches that "knowledge" (*jñāna*) which coincides with liberation is something utterly incompatible with "works" (*karman*) which are accomplished in accordance with the means–ends-relationship (*sādhyasādhanabhāva*). Such "knowledge" can neither be a means for something else, nor can it be brought about by means or instruments. "Works" and "knowledge," *karman* and *jñāna* belong to fundamentally different contexts. Knowledge is not something to be done or performed; it is openness for absolute reality (*brahman*), i.e. a reality which is not a function and projection of "works" and desires.

Such "pure" knowledge abandons all claims to causal and conceptual mastery and explanation, and it transcends the world which is the realm of such apparent mastery and explanation, i.e. the world of "empirical transactions" (*vyavahāra*) and of *māyā*. Śaṅkara's predecessor Gauḍapāda, who is greatly indebted to the Buddhist Madhyamaka school, explicitly identifies "worldly existence" (*saṃsāra*) with "intentness upon," or even absorption by "causes and effects" (*hetuphalāveśa*). The soteriological orientation of Advaita Vedānta and Madhyamaka Buddhism is fundamentally different from a mere "technology of liberation." It implies an extraordinary level of "theoretical" awareness, and intense and uncompromising reflection upon the relationship between "knowledge" and "works," "theory" and "practice."

13. The doctrines and systems which the Indian doxographies present under the title *darśana*, provide clear and specific parallels to what is commonly called "philosophy" in the West: They are theoretically oriented, systematized "world-views," and they exclude more or less matters of religious practice. However, we are dealing here with "philosophy" as something given by tradition, i.e. as a certain spectrum of firmly established, fully developed doctrinal structures; we are not dealing

with "philosophy" as an open-ended process of asking questions and pursuing knowledge. *Darśana*, as used in the doxographies, is a fundamentally retrospective concept. It refers to what others have thought in the past, to views and systems which have been inherited from the past. There is no suggestion of progressive, future-oriented thought, and there are hardly any methodological implications in the doxographic usage of *darśana*.

On the other hand, there are obvious methodological implications in the concept of *ānvīkṣikī* – the concept which H. Jacobi tried to interpret as the proper Indian equivalent of "philosophy." Jacobi relied primarily on a passage in Kauṭilya's *Arthaśāstra*. Soon after the first publication (1909) of this work on government and politics, which had been considered lost for a long time, Jacobi referred to this passage,[5] translated *ānvīkṣikī* as "philosophy," and was obviously convinced that there was a precise conceptual correspondence. Several translations of the *Arthaśāstra* also render *ānvīkṣikī* as "philosophy."

The discussion was continued by M. Winternitz,[6] who dealt primarily with the relationship between the methodological notion of *ānvīkṣikī* and the soteriological idea of a "science of the self" (*ātmavidyā*). Winternitz rejects Jacobi's translation of *ānvīkṣikī*, and he warns against a superimposition of the European dichotomy of theology and philosophy. Even prior to the rediscovery of the *Arthaśāstra*, J. Dahlmann discussed the relationship between *ānvīkṣikī* and *ātmavidyā* on the basis of passages in the *Mahābhārata*.[7]

The most penetrating study of *ānvīkṣikī* which we have to this date was published by P. Hacker in 1958. Hacker's discussion, which provides a thorough critique of Jacobi's approach, not only supersedes most of the earlier work on the topic, but also various more recent contributions, such as the superficial observations by A. K. Warder.[8] Like Winternitz (of whose contribution he was apparently not aware), Hacker rejects Jacobi's correlation or identification of *ānvīkṣikī* and "philosophy." He emphasizes that *ānvīkṣikī*, as used by Kauṭilya, does not represent a generic concept, covering different "philosophical" systems, but "something that can be applied more or less,"[9] a method which is not restricted to any particular domain, and which has no specific affinity to the topics of philosophy. Concerning the role of *ānvīkṣikī* in the Nyāya system, Hacker argues that the Nyāya borrowed the term from the "science of politics" and adopted it for its own "self-definition."[10]

14. Hacker summarizes his argumentation against Jacobi as follows: "The origin of all false conclusions and improbable constructions in Jacobi's 'Frühgeschichte der indischen Philosophie' is his inadequate rendering of *ānvīkṣikī* as 'philosophy' – with which he then contrasts a 'theology' which he finds in *trayī*. His ingenious reflections tell much more about their author (i.e., that he was obviously so impressed with the Occidental emancipation of philosophy from theology that he projected this conflict into his own area of research, India) than about actual events in the history of Indian thought, which is still quite obscure as far as those centuries are concerned."[11] Hacker's challenging argumentation provides an appropriate starting-point for a renewed discussion of this highly significant and intriguing topic.

Kauṭilya introduces the word *ānvīkṣikī* while giving a list of "sciences" which he recognizes, and which includes his own "science of government and politics" (*daṇḍanīti*): *ānvīkṣikī trayī vārttā daṇḍanītiś ca-iti vidyāḥ*. While the explanation of *trayī* as "science of the three Vedas" and *vārttā* as "science of material welfare" (i.e., trade and agriculture) does not pose major problems, the definition of *ānvīkṣikī* turns out to be more difficult and elusive. Kauṭilya first presents an enumeration of three schools of thought, which are subsumed under, or at least associated with, the concept of *ānvīkṣikī*; *sāṃkhyaṃ yogo lokāyataṃ ca-ity ānvīkṣikī* [Sāṃkhya, Yoga, and Lokāyata are the three school names]. "Immediately thereafter, he describes, also in an etymologizing manner, what happens in *ānvīkṣikī*: 'The investigative science *investigates with reasons* what is right and wrong in the field of Vedic knowledge, what is advantageous and disadvantageous in the science of material acquisitions, and appropriate or inappropriate in the science of government, and moreover, the strengths and weaknesses of these (three sciences) . . .'" (*dharmādharmau trayyāṃ arthānarthau vārttāyāṃ nayānayau daṇḍanītyāṃ balābale caetāsāṃ hetubhir anvīkṣamāṇā*). Concluding this section, Kauṭilya cites a verse which is obviously taken from an older source: "The investigative science has always been considered as a source of light for all sciences, an instrument for all activities, a foundation for all religious and social duties" (*pradīpaḥ sarvavidyānām, upāyaḥ sarvakarmaṇām/ āśrayaḥ sarvadharmāṇāṃ śaśvad ānvīkṣikī matā*). This implies that *ānvīkṣikī* is not a special "science," side by side with other "sciences" and with an equally specific subject-matter, but a methodology which these other sciences themselves can and should utilize.

15. Already Jacobi has noticed that the verse quoted by Kauṭilya appears also, with a variant appropriate to the new context, in the *Nyāyabhāṣya* by Vātsyāyana Pakṣilasvāmin (ca. 400 AD); now it is the Nyāya itself which is presented as the fulfillment of that sense of *ānvīkṣikī* which the old verse describes. But there are also other ways in which the *Nyāyabhāṣya* supplements and modifies the information found in the *Arthaśāstra*. Vātsyāyana and his commentator Uddyotakara also define *ānvīkṣikī* as an "investigative," "reflective" science which reconsiders, re-examines what has been grasped through sense-perception and sacred tradition, and which applies valid criteria (*pratyakṣāgamābhyām īkṣitasya-arthasya-anvīkṣaṇam; pramāṇair arthaparīkṣaṇam*), and they assert that without its peculiar discipline of reasoning and argumentation the Nyāya would not be different from the Vedic-Upaniṣadic "science of the (supreme) self" (*ātmavidyā, adhyātmavidyā*).

Vātsyāyana emphasizes repeatedly that the Nyāya is indeed *ātmavidyā* and oriented toward the goal of final liberation (*apavarga*). The Nyāya, too, deals with the absolute self; as far as its goal and its subject-matter are concerned, it cannot and should not be distinguished from the Upaniṣads. Instead, its distinguishing feature is its methodology, to which it also owes its status as a general "auxiliary science," or even as a "meta-science." Hacker's statement that Vātsyāyana claimed a "special object" ("*besonderer Gegenstand*," i.e. subject-matter) for his system, on which he based its distinctive status, has thus to be taken with some caution. To be sure, the sixteen "themes" (*padārtha*) of the Nyāya system are indeed characterized as actual objects (*vidyamānārtha*), and they are presented as the special domain of the system. However, Vātsyāyana adds that liberation will result only from the adequate knowledge (*tattvajñāna*) of those twelve soteriologically relevant entities which are called *prameya*, "objects of knowledge," i.e. the self (*ātman*), body (*śarīra*), etc. The *prameya* are those entities which the Nyāya recognizes as objects in the full metaphysical and soteriological sense. The other – essentially logical or dialectical – "themes" of Nyāya are "objects" in a different sense and on a different level of reflection: They are thematized factors of knowledge, methods and perspectives of argumentation; the Nyāya has a special status insofar as it *objectifies* or thematizes them, insofar as it deals with them in an explicit and technical fashion. Uddyotakara defines the peculiar character of this "objectification" more clearly than Vātsyāyana;

what distinguishes Nyāya is not the occurrence of "means of knowledge" (*pramāṇa*), etc. per se (they are implicitly recognized by the other systems as well), but their explicit thematization and systematic refinement.

Vātsyāyana adds to the list of sixteen "themes" (*padārtha*) an enumeration of four "relevant matters" (*arthapada*), using a term which inverts the parts of the compound *padārtha*. This enumeration, just like a similar scheme in Vyāsa's *Yogabhāṣya*, clearly reflects the "four noble truths" of Buddhism (i.e., the truths of suffering, its origin, its cessation, and the way leading to this cessation). Several Nyāya authors have tried to coordinate all relevant "objects of knowledge" (*prameya*), or even all sixteen "themes" (*padārtha*), with the four *arthapada*, or to subsume them under these soteriologically "relevant matters," and thus to establish the pervasive soteriological significance of the Nyāya system in all its details. Bhāsarvajña (probably around 900 AD) discusses the issue in remarkable detail, and he refers explicitly to the "four noble truths" of the Buddhists.

16. Hacker maintains against Jacobi that Vātsyāyana's association of *ānvīkṣikī* and *ātmavidyā* should not be seen as an artificial and retroactive harmonization, or as an attempt to revoke a process of philosophical emancipation. He reminds us that this association fully agrees with a tradition which is documented by Kauṭilya himself: *Arthaśāstra* I,2 mentions that the school of the Mānava recognized only three sciences, and that it regarded *ānvīkṣikī* as a special kind of "Vedic science" (*trayī*). Kāmandaki explains *ānvīkṣikī* repeatedly as *ātmavidyā* or *ātmavijñāna*. In this sense, we may also understand Manu's phrase *ānvīkṣikīṃ ca-ātmavidyām* . . . There has also been a tradition which tried to coordinate the "investigative" *ānvīkṣikī* with the Vedic *trayī* in a manner analogous to the relationship between Pūrvamīmāṃsā and Uttaramīmāṃsā, or to associate it with *manana*, the "reflection" which, according to the Vedānta, should follow the "hearing" (*śravaṇa*) of the Vedic texts. Numerous other passages could be added to Hacker's references, especially from the Mahābhārata. Here, the term *ānvīkṣikī* is applied to questions of an Upaniṣadic type, and we hear about the "churning" of an Upaniṣad for the purpose of the "supreme ānvīkṣikī" (*ānvīkṣikī parā*). *Ānvīkṣikī* in these obscure passages seems to have a special connection with the *jñānakāṇḍa*, the Upaniṣadic "knowledge portion" of the Veda.

The Mahābhārata also contains Kauṭilya's list of "four sciences" (*trayī, vārttā, daṇḍanīti, ānvīkṣikī*), as well as the threefold list, which Kauṭilya ascribes to the Mānava and which does not recognize *ānvīkṣikī* as a separate "science." It is remarkable that the fourfold list emerges again in the *Vedāntacandrikā*, the anonymous pamphlet against Rammohan Roy which was published in 1817; in W. H. Macnaghten's attached English translation, *ānvīkṣikī* appears as "reasoning power," but also as "philosophy."

The concept of *ānvīkṣikī* which the classical Nyāya system adopts for its self-definition is certainly no emancipatory and anti-traditional concept: Any "investigation" or reasoning which is incompatible with sense-perception and with authoritative tradition (*pratyakṣāgamaviruddha*) can only be "petty," "trivial" reasoning (*kṣudratarka*), and it would be a "spurious Nyāya" (*nyāyābhāsa*). "Reasoning" and "investigation" have to accept and "follow" what is given by perception and tradition; this is an implication which the "orthodox" Naiyāyikas also find confirmed by the connotation of the prefix *anu-* within the word *ānvīkṣikī*.

17. Does all this mean that the question of the autonomy of methodical thinking and critical reasoning, and of its emancipation from the authority of religious and soteriological tradition, is a Eurocentric question which should not be applied to the Indian situation? Indeed, Jacobi's way of posing, or presupposing, this question reflects his European background and, more specifically, the actual historical conditions of his work as an Indologist. It reflects an obvious "prejudice" – but one which may still be useful, or even indispensable, as a heuristic device.

We have introduced our discussion of *ānvīkṣikī* by referring to its methodological implications. Most of our subsequent quotes postulate that such "methodological" and "investigative" reasoning should be compatible with the sacred tradition, should try to justify it, or at least be neutral. However, Kauṭilya himself is clearly less concerned about such compatibility than the Naiyāyikas and other "orthodox" groups; his *ānvīkṣikī* has a more independent status. Numerous references, accounts and allusions in ancient and classical Sanskrit literature, for instance in the great epics, document that this was by no means an isolated phenomenon. As a matter of fact, others had much more radical ideas about independent, critical reasoning than Kauṭilya, and in many instances, *ānvīkṣikī*, together with the

closely related notions of *hetuvidyā* [science of causality] and *tarkaśāstra* [teaching of logic], is clearly incompatible with, and opposed to, the Vedic tradition, or to the soteriologically relevant "science of the self" (*ātmavidyā*).

Kauṭilya's own presentation in the *Arthaśāstra* focuses on the "neutral" methodological aspect of the "investigative science," on the applicability and usefulness of *ānvīkṣikī* for other sciences which play a role in the education of the prince and in the successful conduct of government and administration. In this particular context, Kauṭilya is not interested in discussing the soteriological relevance of *ānvīkṣikī*, or its compatibility with the Vedic *ātmavidyā*. His primary concern with methodology is also illustrated by his list of schools of thought in which he finds *ānvīkṣikī* exemplified. The Sāṃkhya school, which he mentions first, has made important contributions to the formalization and systematization of the *pramāṇa* theory (i.e., the doctrine of the "valid means of knowledge"); it is, however, also a genuinely soteriological system. Such soteriological commitment is absent in the Lokāyata tradition, which Kauṭilya mentions last. The Lokāyata represents an openly secular attitude, which is critical towards the Veda and the traditions of *ātmavidyā*. What Kauṭilya means by *yoga*, the second item in his list, is not easy to determine. In a general sense, it is important to remember that the word *yoga* is by no means exclusively associated with the Yoga system of Patañjali, or with other doctrines and techniques of meditation and inner discipline. Its root *yuj-* also accounts for the word *yukti*, "reasoning"; and likewise, the word *yoga* itself is occasionally used to refer to disciplines of "reasoning" and "argumentation," such as Nyāya and Vaiśeṣika. This usage is documented in older as well as in more recent texts.

For instance, in his commentary on *Nyāyasūtra* 1,1,29, Vātsyāyana mentions "system-specific teachings" (*pratitantrasiddhānta*) of the "Yogas" which are obviously different from, and incompatible with, the teachings of Pātañjala Yoga. In the doxographic literature of the Jainas, the *Naiyāyikas* and *Vaiśeṣikas* are often referred to as "Yogins" or, more specifically, as *Śaiva* and *Pāśupata* Yogins; and their teachings are presented as doctrines of "Yoga."

18. For the "orthodox" groups, the methodological "neutrality" of Kauṭilya's *ānvīkṣikī*, i.e. its openness to different uses and interpretations, is in itself objectionable. On the one hand, reasoning can become an end in itself, and degenerate into

sheer intellectual vanity; on the other hand, it can serve anti-traditional, anti-Vedic purposes. There is ample evidence that such developments have, indeed, taken place in ancient India.

We do not have to discuss in detail the various forms which the critique of tradition and traditionalism, and the emancipation of reasoning and argumentation, have taken in India since the time of the Buddha and the Jina Mahāvīra, and how this relates to various movements of scepticism and materialism. Together with expressions like *tarkavidyā* ("science of reasoning"), the word *ānvīkṣikī* is directly associated with these tendencies. The "sophists" (*haituka*) who are addicted to "investigative reasoning" (*ānvīkṣikī tarkavidyā*) appear as "scorners of the Veda" and as persons who reject its authority (*vedanindaka, nāstika*). The "investigative intellect" (*buddhir ānvīkṣikī*) leads its "worldly," "secularizing" (*lokāyatika*) followers to a harmful anti-traditionalism. The Buddhists, too (whom the "orthodox" Hindus classify as "heterodox" addicts of reasoning), criticize and reject unrestricted critical reasoning and argumentation. [. . .]

In their usage by the critics of "autonomous," unrestricted reasoning, the terms *ānvīkṣikī, tarkavidyā, hetuśāstra*, etc., are closely related or even appear as synonyms. However, the pejorative connotation of *tarka* is more pronounced than that of *ānvīkṣikī* (or *yukti*). On the other hand, the Nyāya system, which adopts a positive and "orthodox" notion of *ānvīkṣikī* for its self-definition, also uses the term *tarka* with positive, "respectable" connotations, for instance in numerous titles of works.

19. Some of the most memorable invectives against all attempts to establish the fundamental metaphysical and soteriological truths without the guidance of the sacred texts, and against the vanity of "dry," "fruitless," "groundless" reasoning (*śuṣkatarka*, etc.) come from the great Śaṅkara. The sophist or dialectician (*tārkika*) who disregards the sacred tradition gets entangled in the fictions and constructions of his own intellect, and he falls into vanity, heresy and self-deception. Analytic reasoning alone, which is committed to the method of "positive and negative concomitance" (*anvayavyatireka*), cannot lead us to the truth about the absolute self. Only the Vedic-Upaniṣadic revelation provides access to this goal; and only that reasoning which understands itself as being grounded in this revelation, and applies the

anvayavyatireka method as an auxiliary device, is legitimate and fruitful.

"Reasoning" and "inference" are never final; they are never safe from future correction and refutation. It is in the very nature of human reasoning to constantly outdo and disprove itself, and to be unable to find a firm and permanent position. Several centuries before Śaṅkara, Bhartṛhari observed that anything established by skilled "logicians" (*anumātṛ*) was bound to be explained differently by other, even more ingenious ones; Bhartṛhari also used the expression *śuṣkatarka*, "dry," "fruitless" reasoning. Śaṅkara's statement in his commentary on *Brahmasūtra* II,11,11 that independent, unrestrained reasoning, i.e. human reasoning as such, is unstable and unfounded, is part of his response to an opponent who gave a positive interpretation to this phenomenon: In his view, the so-called instability of reason is in reality a distinction (*ayam eva tarkasya-alaṃkāro yad apratiṣṭhitatvaṃ nāma*), since it means openness for the correction of mistakes, i.e. for future progress. The fact that a predecessor was in error and confusion does not imply that we ourselves have to go astray (*na hi pūrvajo mūḍha āsīd ity ātmanā-api mūḍhena bhavitavyaṃ iti kiṃcid asti pramāṇam*). This statement of a defender of reasoning and "progress" may appear as a somewhat isolated curiosity; but even as such, it is worthy of notice.

Śaṅkara himself, as well as other leading advocates of Advaita Vedānta, also use *tarka* in their argumentation. But such usage is primarily a negative one, meant to refute or neutralize opposing doctrines. The rules of critical reasoning and argumentation are invoked against those systems which claim to be built upon reason; their own standards are used to demonstrate their deficiencies. In such contexts, reasoning and argumentation (which may also serve important exegetic, i.e. positive, functions) are used as devices of a *reductio ad absurdum*. After Śaṅkara, the great Vedāntic dialectician Śrīharṣa perfected this reductive use of reasoning (*vitaṇḍā*), this uncovering of undesirable consequences (*prasaṅga*) in accordance with the methods developed by Nāgārjuna and his Madhyamaka school. The Vedāntins seem convinced that by using *tarka* against their opponents they are only fulfilling and making explicit what those who rely on "groundless" reasoning are doing to themselves and to each other. Without any soteriological commitment, Jayarāśi, possibly Śaṅkara's contemporary, demonstrates a merely negative, reductive, dilemmatic use of reasoning in his *Tattvopaplavasiṃha*.

20.   The autonomy of human reasoning, the freedom from the forces of tradition, and the separation of philosophy and religion which the historians of philosophy in the nineteenth century saw as criteria of true philosophy, have not been proclaimed in the classical systems of Indian philosophy. Of course, religion and sacred tradition in India did not possess such uniformity and dogmatic compactness that they could have challenged and polarized critical reasoning in the same way as in Europe. There was less scope for conflict, less inducement for emancipation. And moreover, Indian mythology seems to be more susceptible to gradual transitions and reinterpretations than to confrontation with rationality, or to replacement by it. Nevertheless, the question of the autonomy of philosophical thinking and critical rationality which determined Jacobi's interpretation of *ānvīkṣikī* is not entirely inappropriate for the Indian situation. Although the tension between "free thinking" and the acceptance of tradition has never become as pronounced in India as in Europe, it has not been entirely absent. Of course, we have to view the relationship between "free thinking" and tradition, reason and revelation in a more cautious and balanced manner than many European historians of philosophy, whose treatment of the Pre-Socratic step "from myth to logos" and of the Cartesian freedom from prejudice has often been rather stereotyped and simplistic. In the meantime, the significance of "mythical" premises in the thought of the Pre-Socratics, or of "traditional" presuppositions in Cartesianism, has become increasingly evident. In general, there has been a new openness for the positive implications of "tradition," and a new readiness to acknowledge the constitutive role of "prejudice" in the pursuit of knowledge. On the other hand, the fact that there were no Cartesian "declarations of independence" of rationality in India does not mean that there was no critical search for the foundations of knowledge, for valid criteria, and no ability to reflect upon and question traditional sources and presuppositions.

21.   We must not limit our attention to explicit forms of anti-traditionalism and to programmatic declarations concerning the "independence" of critical thinking. Distance and alienation between reason and tradition can also be indicated by the deliberate effort to defend tradition and to restore its authority, and in general by its explicit thematization. A good deal of classical Hindu philosophy is, indeed, apologetics and restoration in this sense.

The extent to which tradition and revelation become thematic, and the focus of conceptual efforts of clarification and justification, testifies to the presence of a reflection which has by no means blindly surrendered to tradition. The commitment to tradition is not a mere habitual continuation of past ways of thinking. It is something actively asserted and pursued, something questioned, justified and rationalized. In a variety of ways, philosophers have tried to reconcile the acceptance of the Veda, or of other traditions and "revelations," with the spirit of critical argumentation which prevails in the classical systems and which is also reflected in the idea of *ānvīkṣikī*.

The Nyāya school takes an active part in these attempts. It tries to defend the Veda by using the means and standards of "rational" argumentation, and it tries to demonstrate that its teachings are fully compatible with the data of sense-perception and inference (*pratyakṣa; anumāna*). It also tries to anchor the truth and authority of the Veda in the idea of an omniscient and benevolent divine author (*īśvara*), who is by definition without error and deceit.

Likewise, the founders of particular schools of thought are often raised to the status of omniscient "seers" (*ṛṣi*). Yet this does not imply that their teachings are supposed to be inaccessible to rational scrutiny and justification. For instance, the Sāṃkhya tradition invokes the authoritative insights of its mythical founder Kapila, whom it regards as the "primeval sage" (*ādividvān*); but it continues to maintain that the Sāṃkhya teachings are based upon and justifiable by sense-perception and inference. On account of this claim, R. Garbe, the European pioneer of Sāṃkhya studies, has applied the somewhat misleading designation "Indian rationalism" to this system.

22.   Another, more radical attempt to justify and safeguard the Vedic tradition is represented by the Mīmāṃsā; this school of exegesis and apologetics tries to secure a domain for the Veda which is fundamentally inaccessible to the "worldly" means of knowledge (*pramāṇa*), and thus to reasoning and argumentation. However, reasoning and argumentation are indispensable in this process. They are needed to remove the contents of the Veda from the scope of sense-perception and inference, and of rational critique as well as rational justification. They are, in a sense, invoked against themselves. The authority of the Veda relates to the transempirical domain of the *dharma*, of what has to be done, i.e.,

primarily the ritual norms and duties. In this domain, there can be no conflict with the results and criteria of "worldly," i.e. empirical and rational cognition. The *dharma* is as inaccessible to "worldly" proof and justification, as it is to empirical and rational refutation. Moreover, the authority of the Veda does not imply that it is the work of an omniscient and absolutely reliable author. The Veda stands and speaks for itself as the timeless and uncreated testimony of *dharma*. It does not have an author; for this very reason, it has no room for error and deception. Outside of the domain of *dharma* and the exegesis of the Veda, the Mīmāṃsā has shown great openness for empirical criteria and for independent argumentation, and the school tradition has accommodated numerous innovations and variations.

In two different ways, the Nyāya and the Mīmāṃsā respond to the argumentation of the Buddhists and other "heterodox" groups, who criticized the Vedic tradition on the basis of sense-perception, inference, common sense, etc. Of course, the Buddhists themselves developed a wide spectrum of ideas concerning tradition and revelation, as well as attempts to clarify and resolve the relationship between reason and revelation. In the epistemological school of Dignāga and Dharmakīrti, we find the remarkable notion that the true doctrine of the "means of knowledge" (*pramāṇa*), and the proper use of sense-perception and inference, ultimately coincide with, and amount to, the revelation of the Buddha.

The tradition of Advaita Vedānta, which eventually took the lead among the "orthodox" systems of Hinduism, adopts the Mīmāṃsā theory of the "authorlessness" (*apauruṣeyatva*) of the Vedic texts.

23. The emphasis on the inseparability of *ānvīkṣikī* and *(adhy) ātmavidyā* which we found in the classical Nyāya texts is obviously part and symptom of a wider historical phenomenon, a process of returning to authoritative sources and traditions, and of restoring and defending a unity and harmony between revelation and reason, tradition and argumentation which had been challenged and threatened. In this process, the Vedic sources themselves whose authority is invoked and proclaimed undergo a far-reaching reinterpretation. They are associated with views and orientations for which they provide little recognizable evidence; and they are invoked to support a historical stability and continuity, and a deliberate traditionalism, which seems to have little in common with their own spirit.

As we have seen, the Nyāya establishes its identity and peculiarity against other types of "orthodox" thought by systematically developing the element of *ānvīkṣikī*, of "investigation" and argumentation. On the other hand, it constitutes itself as an "orthodox" system by postulating that its *ānvīkṣikī* is fully committed to the tradition, and nothing but a special kind of *ātmavidyā*. The suspicion to which *ānvīkṣikī* could easily be subject has to be eliminated. "Logic" and "reasoning" themselves, which so often appear to be allied with anti-Vedic movements, have to be "orthodox." They have to prove themselves against the "petty reasoning" (*kṣudratarka*) of the heterodox Cārvākas and against the "logical path" (*anumānamārga*) of the Buddhists. Logic and dialectic, if used properly, support the validity of the sacred texts. Argumentative and "questioning" thought, which seemed to be on the verge of a radical "emancipation," has once again committed itself to the tutelage of the tradition, and to religious goals and contents.

24. In his argumentation against Jacobi, Hacker emphasizes the central and symptomatic significance of the question how to relate the two terms *ānvīkṣikī* and *ātmavidyā* in Kāmandaki's statement *ānvīkṣiky ātmavidyā syād* . . . Against Jacobi's translation "Die Philosophie soll eine *ātmavidyā* sein" ("Philosophy should be an *ātmavidyā*"), Hacker insists that *ānvīkṣikī* is not the subject of this sentence, but its predicate nominative.[12] The implications of this alternative are clear: Does Kāmandaki demand that *ānvīkṣikī*, i.e. an independent, investigative, "philosophical" science, should commit itself to religious and soteriological goals? Or does he suggest that a fundamentally unbroken, soteriologically committed "science of the absolute self" should be "methodical" and "investigative"? Immediately following, Hacker refers to the phrase *ānvīkṣiky ātmavidyā* in Manu VII,43 and he claims that here, too, *ānvīkṣikī* is used "in its original function as the feminine form of an adjective."[13] It seems, however, evident that both Manu and Kāmandaki allude to Kauṭilya's fourfold list of sciences, that *ānvīkṣikī*, not *ātmavidyā* is the primary theme of their statements, and that *ātmavidyā* qualifies *ānvīkṣikī*, not vice versa. Accordingly, Manu's commentator Medhātithi explains that the *ānvīkṣiky ātmavidyā* is that *ānvīkṣikī* which is "good for the self" (*ātmane yā hitā*) and thus different from the *tarkavidyā* of the Buddhists and Cārvākas.

Ānvīkṣikī is legitimized as well as neutralized in this coordination with *ātmavidyā*. It is characteristic that later commentators no longer see the need for such neutralization. They often tend to explain *ānvīkṣikī* and *ātmavidyā* as two different sciences – an interpretation which already Medhātithi considered as a possibility. And even if they preserve the combination and coordination of the two terms – they are no longer aware of the historical situation in which *ānvīkṣikī*, together with *hetuvidyā*, *tarkaśāstra*, etc., was a living challenge and a threat to the stability and continuity of the tradition. By the end of the first millennium AD, *ānvīkṣikī* itself, together with other forms of critical, investigative and heterodox thinking, was more or less fossilized. It was itself part of the tradition, included in a timeless framework and inventory of legitimate "sciences" and possible views and orientations, superseded by the emerging "structure of Hindu traditionalism."

25. In spite of its critical and methodological potential, the concept of *ānvīkṣikī* did not come to represent an open-ended, future-oriented attitude of thought. The retrospective tendencies of the Hindu tradition prevailed in this case, too. In Kauṭilya's *Arthaśāstra*, *ānvīkṣikī* was a method not confined to one particular domain of objects, and to be used by various branches of learning. But in its adoption by the "orthodox" Nyāya school, it became the name of *one* traditional system, *one darśana*, *one śāstra*; in this sense, Jayanta speaks of the *śāstram ānvīkṣikam*. *Ānvīkṣikī* and *tarka* appear as titles of traditional "orthodox" branches of learning in the lists of fourteen or eighteen "sciences" (*vidyā*) which have become canonical in classical Hinduism, and they signify the Nyāya or the "expanded" Nyāya (*nyāyavistara*), which includes the Vaiśeṣika. *Ānvīkṣikī*, *tarka* and *nyāya* / *nyāyavistara*, as used in these lists, are basically synonymous.

Jayanta explains that the list of fourteen sciences is a list of soteriologically relevant branches of learning, in which Kauṭilya's merely secular and empirical sciences of government (*daṇḍanīti*) and material welfare (*vārttā*) would be out of place. Kāmandaki's *Nītisāra* subsumes the entire fourteenfold list under the science of the three Vedas (*trayī*). Unusual in its time, but much closer to Kauṭilya's own treatment of *ānvīkṣikī*, is the procedure of Rājaśekhara (tenth century?). He uses *ānvīkṣikī*, just like *tarka*, as a generic term for the "orthodox" systems of Sāṃkhya, Nyāya, and Vaiśeṣika, as well as the "heterodox" systems of Buddhism, Jainism and Lokāyata; that means, he uses it for all the argumentative disciplines of the Indian philosophical tradition, insofar as they are different from the exegetic disciplines of Mīmāṃsā and Vedānta.

Regardless of the role which the concept of *ānvīkṣikī* has played in certain periods of Indian history, and regardless of its undeniable association with tendencies of "autonomous" reasoning and critique of the tradition – its significance as an indicator of rational and methodological attitudes and programs has been ambiguous and temporary. As far as its overall historical role is concerned, it can hardly be considered as an equivalent to "philosophy."

26. Hacker concludes his article on *ānvīkṣikī* as follows: "It is a characteristic trait of the Hindu culture that it knew the concept of philosophy, but no word which expressed this concept fully and exclusively."[14] Earlier in his article, he notes in connection with a critical reference to Jacobi that philosophy in India was recognized as a "special science" ("besondere Wissenschaft"), but that the Indians did not have "a *word* which would have described this domain – *only* this domain, but in its entirety."[15]

Hacker's statements are intriguing as well as problematic, even if we disregard the philosophical implications and ramifications of the question whether or how there can be, in this particular context, a clearly identifiable concept without a corresponding word. What seems to be at stake in Hacker's statements is the claim that philosophy was present in India in the sense of a clearly identifiable and distinguishable cultural phenomenon, as a distinctive discipline, which, though without the proper linguistic label, was actually pursued and cultivated. How essential is a linguistically or conceptually explicit self-awareness and self-definition for the "reality" of philosophy? What would the reality of philosophy be like without explicit reflexivity? Whatever we may define as philosophy – a certain level of reflexivity and of explicit self-positing seems to be indispensable. In this loose sense, a "concept" of philosophy (which would not require a precise terminological label) would, indeed, be part of philosophy itself in a manner in which, for instance, a concept of painting is *not* part of the actual art of painting. Yet it would hardly be appropriate to say that philosophy cannot occur without a clearly corresponding, explicit term and concept. Even in the history of European philosophy, there has been much retrospective application and extrapolation of the term and concept of philosophy. Ways of thinking and intellectual orientations and pursuits which were not originally under the guidance of an "idea" of philosophy were interpreted, adapted and assimilated as philosophy. In an exemplary and highly significant sense, this has happened in the early period of Greek thought, when Plato and Aristotle adopted and appropriated Pre-Socratic thought *as* philosophy. The retrospective application and historical expansion of the concept of philosophy is also part of the reflexive self-positing of philosophy. Its self-definition is an ongoing historical process, and it is much more than a series of attempts to define an academic discipline or a specific conceptual domain. At important junctures in the history of European thought, the attempts to define and understand what philosophy is coincide with European self-proclamations and with attempts to comprehend the meaning and direction of the entire European tradition. Regardless of the conceptual correspondences between *darśana* or *ānvīkṣikī* and "philosophy," neither of these concepts has played a role in India which would be historically comparable to the role of "philosophy" in Europe.

Today, it is no longer necessary to argue that there was philosophy in India in a sense which is fully compatible with what European philosophers have actually been doing, and with what is documented in European philosophical literature. There has been practical wisdom and conceptual sophistication in India, constructive metaphysics as well as critical epistemology, ontology as well as linguistic analysis: and in general, there has been a level of reflexivity and conceptual articulation which is fully commensurable with what we find in Europe. This commensurability of actual philosophical thinking, and the peculiar and distinctive role which philosophy, as well as its name and concept, have played in Europe are equally fundamental premises for the comparative study of Indian and European thought, for any future cooperation of Indology and philosophy, and for the philosophical "dialogue" between India and the West.

Notes

1 Hermann Jacobi, "Zur frühgeschichte der indischen Philosophie," *Sitzungsberichte der Preussischen Akademie der Wissenschaften* (1911), pp. 732–43; Paul Hacker, "ānvīkṣikī," *Wiener Zeitschrift für die Künde Süd- und Östasiens* 2 (1958), pp. 54–83.

2 Jürgen Habermas, *Knowledge and Human Interests* (Boston: MIT Press, 1971), pp. 301–17, especially p. 309.

3 Max Scheler, *Werurteilsstreit*, ed. H. Albert and E. Topitsch (Darmstadt, 1971).

4 Erich Frauwallner, *History of Indian Philosophy* (Delhi: Banarsidass, 1973), vol. 1, introduction.

5 Jacobi, "Zur frühgeschichte der indischen Philosophie."

6 Moritz Winternitz, "Ānvīkṣikī und ātmavidyā," *Indologica Pragensia* 1 (1929), 1–8.

7 J. Dahlmann, *Das Mahābhārata als Epos und Rechtsbuch* (Berlin, 1895), pp. 251ff.

8 Hacker, "ānvīkṣikī."

9 Ibid., pp. 58, 60.

10 Ibid., p. 81.

11 Ibid., p. 74, note 18.

12 Ibid.

13 Ibid., p. 75.

14 Ibid., p. 81.

15 Ibid., p. 80.

26

The Purview of the "Real"

Georges B. J. Dreyfus

Atomic Theory

[Early Buddhist] criteria that separate the real from the conceptual [are] far from unambiguous concerning the status of macroscopic objects. Let us now further inquire into Dharmakīrti's ontology by asking questions such as, What is to be considered part of the fabric of reality and what is to be excluded from this category?[1] Are commonsense objects such as jars real? Or are they conceptual constructions? Rather than proposing a unified system, Dharmakīrti offers a variety of conflicting views which he sees as pragmatically compatible. These different strands have not been always recognized by both modern and traditional scholars, with the consequence that Dharmakīrti's system has been oversimplified. Following Śākya Chok-den's insight, I distinguish four strands in Dharmakīrti's ontology: three assume the existence of external objects while the fourth one rejects this presupposition. I show how these four standpoints are articulated within his overall system according to a scheme of ascending scales of analysis. This allows me to throw some light on the role of the fourth level in Dharmakīrti's thought, his Yogācāra view. I ask the readers to bear with this rather involved discussion, for it often plays on subtle differences that are nevertheless important, for they will lead us to a better understanding of Dharmakīrti's overall

Georges B. J. Dreyfus, "The Purview of the 'Real'," from *Recognizing Reality: Dharmakirti's Philosophy and its Tibetan Interpretations* (Albany: State University of New York Press, 1996), ch. 4.

philosophical strategy. The less specialized reader may choose to skip the more technical discussions, focusing on the first and last two sections of this chapter.

The ontological status of commonsense objects is a key topic of the debates that oppose Dharmakīrti's tradition to its Hindu opponents. There the Nyāya assert the notion of whole (*anavayin, yan lag can*), a notion the Buddhists reject. The Nyāya rejoin that Buddhist philosophers cannot account for the differences that we perceive between our experiences of aggregates (a bundle of threads) and those of unitary objects (a cloth). How can Buddhist thinkers account for such differences without accepting the reification of entities involved in the Nyāya view? To explain a possible Buddhist answer to this qualm, we have to explore how the tradition views the macroscopic objects that we experience as unities. How are they made from atoms (*paramāṇu, rdul phran*)?

In some respects, Dharmakīrti does not seem to have very original views on questions such as these. He accepts most of the standard Buddhist doctrines found in the Abhidharma texts and reinterpreted according to the Sautrāntika viewpoint. These include impermanence and dependent arising. He uses these as the basis of his logico-epistemological system. It seems quite likely that concerning the reality of atoms, Dharmakīrti would again follow the Sautrāntika reinterpretation of the Abhidharma view as explained by Vasubandhu in his commentary on his own *Abhidharma-kośa*.

The Abhidharma views material reality in two different ways: ontologically, material reality is made of the atoms of the four elements (*bhūta, 'byung ba*) of earth, water, fire, and wind. This schema does not, however, specify the status of material phenomena other than the elements. These macroscopic phenomena are just described as arising from elements (*bhautika, 'byung 'gyur*). They are included in another classification which describes these phenomena from a phenomenological point of view according to how they are perceived through the senses. These objects are the five types of sensible phenomena apprehended by the five sense organs: form, sound, odor, taste, and touch. Among these five, sound is considered apart; it is not required for a material object to exist. The other four are necessarily present in any material object including sound. Thus, in our ordinary world of desire, all material objects other than sound have eight components (four elements and four types of sensible phenomena). Sound has nine (the former eight plus sound).

The Vaibhāṣika system combines these two Abhidharmic typologies to create a list of building blocks for material reality, the dharmas. Consequently, this school holds that the five types of sensibilia are substances as real as the four elements. This grouping of two distinct typologies is a consequence of the Vaibhāṣika view of reality. The Vaibhāṣika school asserts that only phenomena that resist material destruction or analysis are ultimate (*paramārtha-satya, don dam bden pa*). The Vaibhāṣika school lists seventy-five phenomena that resist physical destruction or reduction to other elements. These are considered real. Included in this list are the four elements and five types of sensibilia apprehended by the five senses. Other phenomena are only conventionally or relatively real (*saṃvṛti-sat, kun rdzob bden pa*). A jar, for example, ceases to exist when broken. Other sorts of objects such as water cease to exist when analyzed into their atomic components. Such cessations signify that these synthetic things are not fully real. On the contrary, taste and smell retain their identity when reduced to their components. Hence, they are real.

Accepting objects such as color, smell and taste as building blocks of reality creates a tension in the Vaibhāṣika system. These objects are not just atomic components but empirically observable entities; that is, sensibilia. They are sense-objects and they are called *spheres* (*āyatana, skye mched*) in that they are elements of a given sense sphere. For the Vaibhāṣika, they are real, despite being composed of atomic elements. This is problematic, however, for if colors, shapes, and tastes are collections of atoms, how can

they be said to be real? Can they not be reduced to their atomic components? It would appear, then, that the Vaibhāṣika system is not coherent. It delineates reality according to contradictory criteria.

The Sautrāntika interpretation of Abhidharma presented by Vasubandhu seems to deal with this problem by reducing reality to simple elements. Vasubandhu refutes the Vaibhāṣika interpretation that large material objects are made up of eight substances. For him, this view is incorrect because it conflates two different senses of substance, ontological and phenomenological. Ontologically speaking, only the four elements are substances. From a phenomenological standpoint, by contrast, the four sense spheres can be called *substances*. This latter typology cannot, however, be assimilated to the former. Since we are here attempting to distinguish what really exists from what is merely conceptually added to reality, only the ontological meaning of substance must be taken into account. Vasubandhu thus eliminates the sensibilia (the spheres such as form) from the list of real phenomena. Among material objects, only the four elements are real. They are the building blocks out of which all macroscopic material objects are made. Consequently, they constitute these objects, which are not real in the full sense of the term. Our perceiving those objects is not due to their reality, but is the result of the causal efficiency of their constituent atoms. Hattori explains: "[Sautrāntikas] did not, like the Sarvāstivādins, consider as real what is seen by the organ of vision such as the blue color or the round shape; instead, by understanding as real that which has the efficacy to produce visual cognitions, they sought to resolve the difficulty inherent in the Sarvāstivādin atom theory."[2] According to this Sautrāntika explanation, only infinitesimal atoms and moments of consciousness are real. Everything else, such as a shape or a color, is real only inasmuch as it is taken as an object of conventional practice. This view is not unlike Wilfrid Sellars's claim that objects such as table, ice cubes, and colors do not really exist.[3] Our commonsense notions of such objects are false but cognitively useful. We will see that the parallel between Sellars and Dharmakīrti can be further extended to their theories of universals and perception.

This theory seems clear and unproblematic. And although Dharmakīrti never provides a detailed statement of his ontology, we could expect him to follow this Sautrāntika view. Several traditional and modern scholars have explained Dharmakīrti in this way, emphasizing that in his system reality is reducible to partless atoms interacting with moments of consciousness. This causal relation explains our perceptions of extended objects. In reality, there is no extension but just the causal interaction of infinitesimal atoms with partless moments of consciousness. I call this interpretation of Dharmakīrti's ontology *the standard interpretation*.

Despite its strength, I believe that the standard interpretation does not account for some of Dharmakīrti's ideas concerning ontology. I am suggesting that Dharmakīrti's account is not unified. Conflicting elements in his view contradict the Sautrāntika account that he adopts in some parts of his work. These elements suggest an alternative view according to which spatially extended objects are to be included within the purview of the real. According to this view, material reality is not reducible to its atomic components but also includes extended objects such as shapes and tangible objects. I am not arguing that this is Dharmakīrti's view, but, rather, that this view is present in his work. It represents a level of his analysis which is often not recognized by scholars who tend to present his view as being more unified than it is.

I believe that there is a tension within Dharmakīrti's ontology between an atomistic reductionism, which is in accordance with his overall ontological parsimony, and a less reductionistic delineation of reality, which allows for the reality of extended objects. This tension is due to the very close connection between ontology and epistemology in Dharmakīrti's system. On the one hand, Dharmakīrti's ontology emphasizes the particular over the general. Accordingly, spatial extension, which materially subsumes real individual elements, cannot but be seen as ontologically secondary, an artificial construct. Therefore, on purely ontological grounds, it seems quite reasonable to deny the reality of any kind of extension. On the other hand, however, Dharmakīrti also holds that perception offers an undistorted reflection of reality. Accordingly, what is perceived by perception must exist in reality. This creates a problem for Dharmakīrti's ontology, for we do seem to perceive extended objects. Since this perception is an undistorted reflection of reality, the extended object we perceive ought to exist.

Dharmakīrti seems to recognize this tension and handles the problem through what I described as a strategy of ascending scales of analysis. This explains one of the most puzzling elements in Dharmakīrti's system, the adoption of several contradictory ontologies. Through most of his works Dharmakīrti presents himself as a realist concerning the existence of the external world. He defends a so-called Sautrāntika position. Within this view, he also seems free to move between conflicting accounts. Sometimes he follows the view described previously, reducing reality to the interaction of partless particles and moments of awareness. At other times, however, he includes extended objects such as colors or taste or even commonsense objects. Finally, at other times he seems to leave behind this form of realism concerning the external world to move toward a more radical antirealism, a Yogācāra idealism. I believe that these moves are made by Dharmakīrti to solve the difficult problems raised by the ontological consequences of his epistemology.

The existence of such a diversity within Dharmakīrti's ontology explains the diversity of views on this subject entertained by his commentators, traditional and modern. Here I will examine some of the Tibetan contributions to this question, delineating the conflicting opinions existing in the Sa-gya tradition concerning the reality of extended objects before explaining Śākya Chok-den's way of reconciling them. These conflicting interpretations are not idiosyncratic accounts given by commentators but reflect conflicting ideas that are clearly present in Dharmakīrti. I first examine briefly two passages that suggest that extended phenomena such as sensibilia are to be included among real things.

To discuss the ontological status of extended objects, I would like to distinguish four sizes of material objects. First, there are substantial atoms (*dravyaparamāṇu, rdzas kyi rdul phran*). These are partless particles out of which all material phenomena are made. These atoms aggregate to form the second size, larger molecules (*saṃghātaparamāṇu, 'dus pa'i rdul phran*), which in turn form larger objects. When a sufficient number of molecules aggregate, they form the third type of material object, a collection (*samudāya, tshogs pa*). This collection is observable by perception. It is given to sense consciousness as sensibilia such as a patch of color, a shape, a taste, and the like. Such an object is markedly different from the fourth type of object, commonsense objects such as a jar. These objects, which are often described as coarse (*sthūla, rags pa*), are synthetic objects constructed through the aggregation of the different sensibilia (colors, shapes, tastes, etc.). Although both collections and coarse objects are extended, they differ. Whereas the former is a mere aggregation of atoms of a similar kind, the latter is a synthesis of different kinds of sensibilia.

An Alternative Interpretation

According to the standard interpretation of Dhar-makīrti's ontology, both collections and coarse objects are unreal. Some passages in Dharmakīrti, however, do not fit this interpretation. The first passage I examine is found in Dharmakīrti's explanation of sense perception (*indriya-pratyakṣa, dbang po'i mngon sum*). Here he examines the status of objects of sense perception in the context of refuting a Nyāya objection. The Nyāya adversary claims to have found a contradiction between the Buddhist textual tradition and its rejection of universals. This adversary argues that, according to the Abhidharma texts, what a sense consciousness takes as its object is an aggregate (*saṃcita, bsags pa* or *saṃghāta, 'dus pa*). Such a collection (*samudāya, tshogs pa*), he argues, is nothing but a whole. It is determined as such by differentiating it from its parts. Such differentiation necessarily involves some conceptual determination based on universals. Dharmakīrti states the objection: "[*Objection:*] An aggregate (*saṃcita, bsags pa*) is an assemblage (*samudāya, tshogs pa*), [and] this is a universal. And there is a sense cognition of this [universal]. Now cognition of a universal must doubtlessly involve conceptualization." For this Naiyāyika, Buddhists cannot maintain their assertion that perception is nonconceptual and ought to accept the existence of a determinate perception (*vikalpakapratyakṣa, mngon sum rtog pa can*) and its support in reality, real universals.

Dharmakīrti answers that sense perception does not take as its object a genuine synthetic entity but only an aggregate of atoms. Atoms in isolation are not noticeable, for they do not have the capacity to generate a perception in ordinary beings. To do so they must act in a group. The Abhidharma refers to just such a group when it describes the object of sense consciousness as a collection. Not being the product of a conceptual synthesis, a collection is not a bona fide universal. Nevertheless, it can be called such since it subsumes a multiplicity of elements. Dharmakīrti says: "When different atoms are produced in combination with other elements, they are said to be aggregates. [And] indeed those [aggregates] are the causes for the arrival of [sense] cognitions. In the absence of other atoms, atoms have no special [noticeable] characteristics. Since cognition is not restricted to a single [atom], it is said to have a universal as its sphere of operation." Since cognition cannot apprehend a single atom, it always perceives assembled atoms. This is why

the Abhidharma describes cognition as having a universal as its object, although this object is not a real universal. For the Buddhist, as described by Dharmakīrti, sense perception depends for its object upon an assemblage of parts that collectively generate the awareness of an external object. These passages seem to suggest that the collection of parts must be included among the objects of perception. Hence, material reality is not reducible to atomic components.

A second passage suggests a similar conclusion. This passage answers a Nyāya objector, who argues that without unitary wholes we cannot account for the sense of unitary objects that we derive from experience. Dharmakīrti responds that large objects do not have to be wholes to be perceived: "If several [elements] are not apprehended simultaneously despite their [belonging] to a single sphere [of activity of a sense], how is it that many sesame seeds can appear to be apprehended simultaneously?"

Dharmakīrti argues that a collection of atoms is the objective *relata* (the object condition, *ālambana-pratyaya, dmigs rkyen*) of sense perception. A heap of sesame seeds, for instance, can be apprehended by perception even though no synthetic entity pulls together the separate elements. Furthermore, since these elements are apprehended together, they must be real not just on an individual basis but also as a collection. So, Dharmakīrti accepts that extended objects such as a heap of sesame seeds are perceived. He also accepts that this perception corresponds to some element in reality. It is the cluster of atoms that corresponds to the extended objects we perceive. Commenting on a passage of Durveka Miśra's commentary on Dharmottara's *Commentary*, C. M. Keyt explains, "In conclusion, these last comments of Durveka Miśra leave no doubt that the sensory object is an aggregate of atoms (*paramāṇu*). The cognition of an aggregate is free from both error and *kalpanā* or the mental operation in perception and is hence a sensory cognition. The atoms remain many and do not, simply because they are immediately juxtaposed, converge into some single, solidly extended thing. The singular solidarity of the sensum recording them is not a misrepresentation of them because this is the correct way for atoms immediately juxtaposed to be represented."[4] According to Keyt's interpretation, Dharmakīrti considers clusters of atoms to be effective and, therefore, specifically characterized phenomena. This is so because perception of extended objects is an undistorted reflection of reality. Certain macroscopic objects are effective inasmuch as they produce the perceptions that apprehend and validate them.

This conclusion is further supported by Dharmottara's comments on Dharmakīrti's *Drop*. Dharmottara differentiates, as we have seen, between individual real fires and the concept of fire. His remarks indicate that the real fires to which he refers are not just atoms but extended objects that can be observed empirically. Thus Dharmottara appears to imply that reality is not limited to infinitesimal objects, but includes spatially extended objects as well. Reality consists of empirically available objects and, hence, is not reducible to atomic reality.

This conclusion is certainly surprising, for it goes against Dharmakīrti's tendency toward a maximal ontological sparsity. It also contradicts other passages, where Dharmakīrti seems to imply that material reality is reducible to atomic components. This latter view is Vasubandhu's account and seems more consistent. And yet, it is hard to ignore the existence of passages that clearly suggest a different account within Dharmakīrti's works. This apparent inconsistency is due, as I argued earlier, to a tension within Dharmakīrti's thought arising out of the double perspective that orients his thought: the ontological and the epistemological. Ontologically, Dharmakīrti tends toward an antirealist reduction of reality to simple elements. From this perspective, extension is reduced to infinitesimal particles. Epistemologically, however, such a reduction is harder to sustain. According to his fundamental thesis that perception accurately reflects reality, extension would seem to exist. Extension appears, after all, to perception. This seems to lead Dharmakīrti to accept at some level a minimal notion of extension.

This does not imply, however, that at this level of analysis commonsense objects such as a jar are real. These coarse, that is, commonsense, objects, which we usually take as being real individuals, are synthetic and thus unreal, since they are made by the aggregation of atoms that do not belong to the same sense sphere (*āyatana, skye mched*) such as color, taste, and so forth. Hence, the reasoning that demonstrates the reality of collections (through the capacity of the atoms to collectively produce a perception) does not apply to these coarse objects. At this level, Dharmakīrti's acceptance of the reality of extended objects applies exclusively to objects such as color patches, which are made of similar elements. It does not include commonsense objects.

These commonsense objects are presupposed, however, to be real at other times. For example, while discussing the way in which causal relations are understood, Dharmakīrti shows how we understand the relation between fire and smoke by observing how smoke follows the presence of fire. In this discussion, causal relations are described as involving commonsense objects such as smoke that are thus assumed at this level of analysis to be real. Hence, there seems to be a confusing diversity in Dharmakīrti's ontology. To gain some perspective, it will be useful to examine the opinions of Tibetan scholars. Our discussion focuses on the Sa-gya tradition, where revealing debates have taken place about whether extended objects are real in Dharmakīrti's system.

In the debates concerning the status of extended objects, all participants hold that partless particles and moments of consciousness are real. The disagreement concerns the reality, or lack thereof, of extended objects. The discussion has often been complex and arcane. For the sake of simplicity I will distinguish three positions: (1) Some Sa-gya scholars, such as Dak-tsang and in part Śākya Chok-den, hold the view that I have described as the standard interpretation. In it, only infinitesimal atoms or moments of consciousness are real. No extended object can ever be a specifically characterized phenomenon. (2) Other Sa-gya scholars such as Lo Ken-chen hold the view that I call the *collection view*. For them reality includes some extended objects (the sensibilia given to perception, such as the collections of particles belonging to the same kind of physical object). They exclude from the purview of reality, however, commonsense objects such as houses and trees. These they describe as coarse. (3) Finally, others such as Ngak-chö assert that reality includes even these commonsense objects. This view is defended by the Ge-luk traditions as well. In this chapter, I analyze these three views as they appear in the Sa-gya tradition as well as the way in which Śākya Chok-den reconciles them. [. . .] I conclude that all the three views are present within Dharmakīrti, but they do not function at the same level. They can be ordered according to an ascending scale of analysis.

No Extended Object Can Be Real[5]

Śākya Chok-den defines the specifically characterized as that phenomenon which is ultimately able to perform a function. He defines generally characterized phenomenon as that which cannot do so. Śākya Chok-den gives partless atoms and moments of consciousness as illustrations (*mtshan gzhi*) of the specifically characterized. Such specific existence also implies substantial existence (literally, substantial establishment, *rdzas grub*), and true existence (literally, true establishment, *bden par grub pa*).

In some parts of his works, Śākya Chok-den argues that no extended object can ever be real. Such an object always involves a synthesis of discrete elements. Dharmakīrti's arguments against the Nyāya wholes, which have been briefly examined earlier, accordingly apply to any kind of extended object, even the mere collection of atoms. For if such a putative extended object existed, it would have spatial parts. It would have to be either substantially identical (*rdzas gcig*) with those parts or different. It cannot be either, however. If an extended object were substantially identical with its parts, in reality (*don la gcig*) it would be one with those parts. In that case, either it would become manifold or its parts would become one. Since neither is possible, for such an extended object to really exist it would have to be substantially different from its parts. It would then exist apart from its parts like the Nyāya wholes. Therefore, Śākya Chok-den concludes:

> It is certainly not [possible] to accept that the special collection of the many substances that are its components and the continuum of moments grouped [together] are one substance [with their parts]. A description of them as existing substantially does not even exist in the texts of the author of the Seven Treatises [i.e., Dharmakīrti].

> *Question*: Can we accept in our system that everything that has parts must not be one substance?
> *Answer*: We should differentiate. We can accept that an object with substantial parts (*rdzas kyi cha*) must be so [not one substance], but we cannot accept this for objects with many distinguishers.

All objects extended in space and time, even special collections of atoms and continua, are not real. They are made of different substances put together and are, therefore, reducible to such. Real objects are not associated with more than one point in space and time. Hence, they do not have real parts. Still, we may apply conceptual distinctions to them, such as being impermanent and being produced.

For Śākya Chok-den, all material objects exist only atomically (*rdul phran du gnas*) although we conceive (*rlom pa*) them as extended in time and space. Material reality is made of the atoms of the four elements (earth, water, fire, and wind). All material phenomena other than these elements are constructed from these basic building blocks and, therefore, are not fully real. In particular, the phenomena arising from elements (*bhautika, 'byung 'gyur*) are not real. They are extended, so they are reducible to their ultimate components, the four kinds of atoms. They are not real substances but exist nominally (*btags yod*).

Up to this point Śākya Chok-den's position is similar to the standard interpretation of Dharmakīrti's ontology among modern Western scholars. The problem with this interpretation is that it makes it difficult to account for the status of extended objects. Once we grant that they are unreal, we have to admit that they are permanent and ineffective (since being a nonthing, permanent, a construct, and ineffective are equivalent almost by definition). While it is relatively easy to imagine a universal such as existence as permanent, it is more difficult to grant that colors and shapes are permanent as well! Most modern interpreters seem to have been unperturbed by this prospect, even though it seems to completely contradict our practical experience. They are ready to assert that for Dharmakīrti colors, tastes, and smells are not causally produced and perform no function. Rather they are conceptual overlays and as such they are changeless! Few Tibetan scholars find this prospect appealing. Strongly influenced by commonsense realism, they resist supporting a view that so directly contradicts our experiences of physical objects.

To solve this problem, Śākya Chok-den offers the following solution in some parts of his works, where he adopts Dak-tsang's view, breaking down the dyadic structure of Dharmakīrti's system through the creation of an intermediary category. In addition to real things (specifically characterized phenomena) and ineffective conceptual constructions, is a third category, conventional things (*kun rdzob pa'i dngos po*). This category includes sensibilia such as color, taste, and tangible objects as well as commonsense objects such as jars and trees. These objects are generally characterized phenomena but are impermanent. They perform a function but only conventionally. All phenomena that have extension in space and time belong to this intermediary category. They are not really effective, for the performance of their function boils down to the functions performed by their constituent atoms. Therefore, they are things but not specifically characterized phenomena. They are classified as nonassociated compositional factors.

Śākya Chok-den's view has drawn criticism from other Sa-gya commentators. They have not failed to use this opportunity to distance themselves from such a controversial figure. Go-ram-ba, for example, argues against his rival that the binary distinction between the real and the conceptual at both the ontological and epistemological levels constitutes the basic structure of Dharmakīrti's system. Introducing a triadic structure changes this system. To put it in modern terms, Go-ram-ba argues that Śākya Chok-den's interpretation contradicts the hermeneutical maxim that a genuine interpretation must attempt to retain the basic structure of the system while confronting any tension therein. The dichotomous nature of Dharmakīrti's system creates several problems (such as the status of macroscopic objects or the existence of nonassociated compositional factors), so the temptation is strong to establish an intermediary category. Nevertheless, a good interpreter, Go-ram-ba asserts, must resist the temptation to change the system even to solve its conceptual difficulties. Moreover, as Go-ram-ba gleefully observes, Śākya Chok-den's views conflict with Sa-paṇ's views, the highest authority in the Sa-gya tradition. The idea of conventionally effective things contradicts Sa-paṇ's emphasis on Dharmakīrti's dyadic system.

I think that Go-ram-ba is quite right in his criticism. I find it even puzzling that Śākya Chok-den would advance this view, which contradicts his global view of Dharmakīrti's system as consisting of a variety of views arranged according to an ascending scale. For, if the acceptance of commonsense objects as real is a lower standpoint, as we will see shortly, what is the need of introducing this triadic structure? It is as if Śākya Chok-den sometimes is carried away by his investigation of a topic and loses sight of his own overall system. Although this fearless spirit of investigation makes his works particularly attractive, it sometimes makes a rendering of his views difficult. In this case, it is hard to know what to do with his triadic analysis. Although it is introduced at this point, it does not reappear later. This view also seems to be quite different from Sa-paṇ's ideas, which express the middle position that only some extended objects are real. Let us examine this position.

Some Extended Objects Are Real

Sa-paṇ seems to support what I have called the *alternative interpretation* or *collection* view. While refuting the Nyāya presentation of six types of relation, Sa-paṇ depicts a collection as the result of a gathering of elements:

> from the gathering of the separate components of a collection, a lump which is a collection is produced. [This is a case of] causes affecting an effect, as, for example, a mountain [is produced] from the gathering of atoms and a heap from the gathering of seeds . . . [Dharmakīrti says] in [his] *Ascertainment*:

> Since the cause that establishes the collection
> Is a component of the collection . . .

Thus, Sa-paṇ seems to consider collections of atoms of the same kind (also referred to as *special collections, tshogs pa khyad par can*), as parts of causal reality. They are lumpy objects produced by the accumulation of parts. The parts act as the causes bringing objects into existence. Thus, for Sa-paṇ reality is not only made of partless entities. The reality of extended objects made by the aggregation of atoms is undeniable: "Atoms of objects and sense powers [form] collections whose every moment produces a consciousness which experiences [an object]. [Such] are the perceptions of ordinary beings." Extended objects are performing the function of producing consciousness. As such they meet the criteria for reality.

Sa-paṇ's teacher Śākya Śrībhadra had already stated a similar position on his first meeting with Sa-paṇ. When asked what he thought about the idea that there is such a thing as mere blue (*sngo tsam*), Śākya Śrībhadra said: "Sometimes I do not know very much, but blue exists in reality." He further adds that these comments contain the essence of the *apoha* theory. The meaning and implications of these cryptic comments will have to be explained gradually. For now, suffice it to say that Śākya Śrībhadra seems to be committed to the idea that colors are real. This seems to imply that reality must include some extended entities.

If this is so, the next question is this: Are then commonsense objects (such as a jar) also included among the real? That is to say, is Dharmakīrti (according to this interpretation) a realist concerning

Georges B. J. Dreyfus

commonsense objects? Lo Ken-chen gives an extremely lucid discussion of this question. Having criticized Śākya Chok-den's concept of conventional things, Lo Ken-chen discusses whether or not extended objects exist in reality. He distinguishes two types of extended objects: those renowned to the world (*'jig rten la grags pa*) and those renowned to [philosophical] treatises (*bstan bcos la grags pa*).

From the point of view of the world, substantial identity (*rdzas gcig*) concerns everyday objects such as jars and trees. They are substances. But when substances are analyzed from the point of view of their mode of apprehension, they are understood in terms of the spheres (*rdzas kyi skye mched*) apprehended by the senses as delineated by the Abhidharma texts. Then the sense spheres are referred to as "substance," not the commonsense objects reducible to those spheres. Thus extended objects such as patches of color or tangible objects belonging to sense spheres are real but commonsense objects are not. Lo Ken-chen said:

> When engaged [in practical activities], one applies terms such as substance, thing, etc., [to objects such as pot]. Nevertheless, when they are explained in the treatises by differentiating specific [and] general [characteristics], they are not established as things for the following reason: since the eight sense spheres belonging to a jar, etc., exist independently, nonconceptual perceptions are produced individually. Accordingly, there is no single perception corresponding to the term "jar." [Moreover] while explaining Dignāga and others' thesis in [his] *Commentary on the Four Hundred*, [Candrakīrti] says: "Here, the logicians state: [an object such as] jar definitively does not exist [as an object of] perception. The specific characteristic of [its] form and so forth is not showable. It is called [object of] perception because it is the object of a visual consciousness, etc. Since a jar is merely named by the mind, it does not exist as a specifically characterized phenomenon. With respect to something which does not exist as a specifically characterized object, not only is there no real perception possible but even metaphorically perception is not feasible in such a case."

We use convenient terms to designate objects we deal with in our daily life as if those objects were real and perceived as they are. These names are not given arbitrarily, but neither do they directly correspond to what exists. When we use the term *jar*, for example, we in fact refer to a component of the jar such as its shape or tangible aspect. We perceive such components, but not the jar itself which is a synthetic object constructed from eight components (four elements (wind, fire, water, and air) and four spheres of sensory objects (form, taste, smell, and tangible aspect)). Each of these exists on its own. Together they form what we commonly call *material objects*. These components are apprehended by different types of perception. For example, form (i.e., color and shape) is apprehended by visual consciousness, tangible objects by body consciousness, and so forth.

When we perceive the shape of a jar, we do not fully perceive that jar, which is constructed out of eight components. We perceive only some of these components, such as its form. This is because there is no overlap among the senses. The special capacities of the organs on which the senses rely are mutually distinct. Therefore, our vision of a jar is only the experience of color and shape and not that of the jar itself, conceptually constructed from the eight components. Similarly, when we touch the same jar, we experience only one aspect of that object, its tangible aspect. The label *jar* that we give to that object does not correspond to what we actually perceive. We refer to the jar as the sum total of its parts, but this totality is an abstraction unavailable to empirical experience. It is a label that we give for the sake of convenience.

Lo Ken-chen's exegesis explains how a jar as the sum total of its parts does not exist in reality, since it is not available in its entirety to any perception. Objects such as jars are conventional descriptions that we give to components such as color, taste, and the like, for the sake of coordinating our perceptions. This is a convincing account of what Vasubandhu means when he says: "In common usage, what is called 'earth' is the color and the shape." The word *earth* is given commonly on the basis of what is in reality earth's color. Similarly, what we call *jar* is in reality a shape. These are convenient ways of speaking but do not reflect reality.

Extension in Space and Time

We are moving toward the examination of the third group of commentators. They hold a more realist position than Lo Ken-chen concerning commonsense objects. Let us pause to examine a question raised by Lo Ken-chen's claim that the collection of atomic elements is real. Does this real status apply to objects extended in time; that is, to continua (*rgyun, santāna*), which are collections of temporal parts, as argued by Gyel-tsap and Kay-drup? Among all groups of Sa-gya scholars the answer is unambiguously negative. Go-ram-ba explains: "Continua are also not [real] for the following reason: each part among the many parts [of the object] produces a single individual cognition as its effect. It is impossible that all the parts put together produce a single cognition as their effect." According to Sa-gya thinkers, the temporal parts of an object cannot be treated in the same way as its spatial parts. Each type of part produces its effects in a different way. Spatial parts coexist and, therefore, are able to contribute to the production of a common effect. Since their effectivity is not reducible to that of their components, they have a reality as a collection. This is not the case with temporal parts. They do not exist at the same time and, therefore, cannot produce a common effect. The different moments that we string together to make a continuum have no effectivity as a collective body. Therefore, continua as such are necessarily unreal.

Moreover, as both Go-ram-ba and Śākya Chokden remark, the arguments directed by Dharmakīrti against the Sāṃkhya and used by Sa-paṇ against Tibetan realists also refute the reality of continua. If continua were real, they would have to be either one with their parts or different. In the first case, when the first moment disintegrates the continuum would disintegrate and hence would not be a continuum. Or it would remain for a second moment and, therefore, be permanent. Since neither is feasible and a continuum cannot be substantially different from its parts (for that would be a Nyāya whole), it must be unreal.

This argument is based on Dharmakīrti's refutation of a Sāṃkhya view. That view holds individuals to be one with their universal, Nature (*prakṛti, spyi gtso bo*, or *rang bzhin*), the all-inclusive substratum. Dharmakīrti argues that individuals and Nature cannot be one entity since individuals keep coming into and going out of existence but Nature does not: "If they are not distinct, they would be produced and disintegrate together." If Nature and individuals were one, that Nature would disappear when individuals do. However, this is not possible, for then it would not be the all-inclusive substratum imagined by the Sāṃkhya. If Nature remains when individuals disappear, it is of a different essence from those.

This argument, as well as Sa-paṇ's, relies on the explicitly stated premise that two phenomena cannot be substantially identical if they have different causes:

> It is contradictory for [two phenomena being] one substance to have different production and disintegration or different aspects. [Dharmakīrti says] in his *Ascertainment*: "It is not proper, when something is established, [for another thing which] is not established or [has] distinct causes to be [its] essence. The reality of things is to be distinct or [to have] different causes, [for] phenomena exclude [each other] or [have] distinct causes. If even that did not establish them as distinct, nothing would be distinct and everything would be one single block substance."

Two phenomena are one substance if they are produced by the same aggregate of causes. This is so because the substance, that is, the essence (*rang bzhin, svabhāva*), of things is determined by the causal aggregate that produces them (*rgyu tshogs pa, hetusāmagrī*). Therefore, their essential identity or difference is also determined by their causes. Since two phenomena that are substantially identical must be produced by the same direct causes (*dngos rgyu tshogs pa gcig*), they must abide and disappear at the same time. Therefore, a continuum cannot be one substance with its parts. Since it cannot be different either, it cannot be real.

Sa-paṇ reaches a similar conclusion by considering the temporal nature of continua, which are created by putting together past, present, and future moments. Only the present moment, however, is real. A continuum depending for its existence on unreal moments can be only unreal. It is like putting a jar between the two horns of a rabbit. Such a synthesis cannot produce anything real!

Sa-paṇ does not indicate a source for his analysis of how continua lack reality. A text of Dignāga extant only in Chinese, however, has a similar view: "If a continuant were identical with [each of its successive members], a person – who is an example of a continuant – would have lost his whole being and existence when he left his babyhood behind and, after gradual growth, achieved boyhood; [therefore], a continuant cannot be identical with [its successive members]." Dignāga expresses the same type of argument as Sa-paṇ against the view that continua are one substance with their parts. He also compares continua to wholes: Both are equally unreal since both are the products of synthesis.

Sa-paṇ's arguments rest on his refusal to accept a distinction made by Tibetan realists between oneness and substantial oneness. Sa-paṇ holds, for instance, that impermanence and thing are one in reality because they are substantially identical. Sa-paṇ does acknowledge four types of difference, but the realist distinction is not among them. They are (1) real things such as shapes and tangible objects are distinct (*tha dad*); (2) unreal phenomena such as nonthing and thing are merely not one (*gcig pa bkag pa*); (3) impermanence and thing are distinct distinguishers within the same entity (*ngo bo gcig la ldog pa tha dad*), that is, they are conceptually distinct but in reality one; (4) moon and the Cooling Light are equivalents whose names are synonymous (*don gcig la ming gi rnam grangs*).

Among these four, only the first distinction amounts to a real difference. Since the second distinction concerns quasi-entities, it is a quasi-distinction. Nonthing is no different from thing, it is just not one with it. Sa-paṇ furthermore rejects the idea of Tibetan realists that these two phenomena are distinct within the same entity (*ngo bo gcig la ldog pa tha dad*), because they are not entities at all. Consequently, Sa-paṇ also refuses the idea that the moments of a continuum are one entity with the continuum. If they were, these moments would all become one thing.

All Extended Objects Are Real

Finally, the third group of Sa-paṇ's followers holds that all spatially extended objects (i.e., both the special collections of atoms of similar kind and the commonsense objects, but not continua) are real. This view is not, as we noticed earlier, without support in Dharmakīrti's works. There, he often uses commonsense objects such as jars, fire and smoke as examples of real things. Moreover, this is supported by commonsense as well, for after all, we believe that we see objects such as jars, tables, and trees. Tibetan thinkers find it more difficult to resist this appeal to commonsense than their Indian predecessors. As we will see, this realism concerning commonsense objects is precisely the position of Ge-luk thinkers.

Within the Sa-gya tradition, Ngak-chö, for example, expresses a view of this sort: "Obviously, jar and so forth exist substantially since they are specifically characterized phenomena." For Ngak-chö, there seems to be little doubt that commonsense objects are real. Commenting on Go-ram-ba's passage, Ngak-chö states that a jar must exist substantially since it is a specifically characterized phenomenon. His position seems to be accepted by many contemporary scholars. They, like many other Tibetan thinkers, seem to feel the strong pull of commonsense. Even Go-ram-ba seems to feel this pull, although his position does not seem to be consistent. While commenting on Dharmakīrti's explanation on the identity conditions of real things, he takes jar as his illustration, thereby implying its reality. In other passages, however, Go-ram-ba seems to express a contradictory view. While refuting the reality of universals, he lists a number of unreal phenomena. He includes in this list commonsense objects such as jar, which we just saw him include among the real! I believe that this last view is closer to what Go-ram-ba has in mind. This would make his position an instance of the middle view, holding only some extended objects to be real. His reference to an object such as jar is probably a convenient description of the different sensibilia made from components of a similar kind (*rigs mthun, sajātīya*).

Whatever the interpretation of his position, its internal contradictions are significant. They point to a general tendency among Tibetan thinkers toward a realism concerning commonsense objects. This insistence on commonsense objects as real does not correspond to what is found in most Indian texts. Śākya Chok-den, who does not accept this dominant tendency in Tibetan epistemological thinking, remarks that no Indian proponent of either the Sautrāntika or Vaibhāṣika view has accepted the reality of such objects on the ontological level. Only at the most common level of analysis can such objects be accepted, as when examples are given or the objects of cognitions are described. These objects cannot be accepted, however, within any slightly systematic ontological analysis.

From an Indian point of view, the exclusion of commonsense objects from the domain of the real is not surprising. It is not unique to Dharmakīrti's school, but is a premise accepted by most Indian Buddhist philosophers, who hold onto the reality of external objects. This premise derives from the epistemological atomism of the Abhidharmic tradition, where material objects are described as formed by the aggregation of sensibilia. In this view, reality consists of partless components but is not reducible entirely to them. Extended objects such as shape and tangible objects (sensibilia) exist. They are apprehended by perceptions which offer a true picture of reality. We usually fail to pay attention to these experiences, instead remaining prisoners of conceptuality.

Stcherbatsky interprets this exclusion of commonsense objects from reality as indicating that Dharmakīrti views specifically characterized phenomena (svalakṣaṇa, rang mtshan) as some kind of transcendental a priori or unique instants. This is not the case. Rather, excluding commonsense objects from reality is the consequence of the epistemological atomism that runs through the Abhidharmic tradition. Lo Ken-chen quotes the Abhidharmic commentator Sthiramati as saying: "[Expressions] such as 'exist substantially, exists as [having its] own essence, exists ultimately' are equivalent. 'Persons' are [just] imputed, [they are] mere names [and] only exist conventionally. They do not exist substantially or as [having their] own essence." This epistemological atomism is basic to Buddhist liberative strategy. Buddhism teaches that human beings can liberate themselves from suffering through a correct understanding of reality. We usually understand reality through perception and form wrong views, such as the substantial existence of persons, on the basis of these experiences. So the first step in a Buddhist liberative strategy is to gain a clear understanding of experience. This is achieved by developing mindfulness toward the four kinds of objects: body, feeling, consciousness, and mental factors.

Analyzing experience into different elements is essential to developing this practice. It permits us to disengage from our tendency to reify diverse elements into unities. To cure us of our constant reification the Abhidharma differentiates objects into spheres (āyatana, skye mched) and elements (dhātu, khams). In applying this teaching to experience, commonsense objects are found to consist of an aggregation of elements. These elements come apart through the power of mindfulness. The objects in which we have such strong confidence are found under analysis to be reducible to their components. Being real only to the commonsense world, they exist only at a superficial level. They are to be displaced by the practice of the path.

Who Is Right?

Our analysis reveals a surprising diversity among Dharmakīrti's Sa-gya commentators. Some, such as Dak-tsang, hold that only infinitesimal parts exist. Others, such as Sa-paṇ, seem to argue that sensibilia are also real, although not commonsense objects. Finally, a third group argues that even these objects are real. Who is right?

This diversity, I would argue, is less due to mistaken interpretations than to a multiplicity of views within Dharmakīrti's own work. Hence, in a certain way all three interpretations are partly right, although they are wrong to claim to represent Dharmakīrti's exclusive view. This seems to be Śākya Chok-den's approach in some parts of his work. Such a view is quite helpful here. Contrary to other Sa-gya scholars and most modern commentators, he refuses to describe Dharmakīrti as opting exclusively for one or the other of the views we described here. Instead, he shows that Dharmakīrti's analysis of external objects is articulated around three levels of analysis: (1) At a commonsense level, objects such as jars and so on are said to exist. (2) At a deeper level, however, these preanalytical ideas cannot stand. When examined in relation to sense spheres (āyatana, skye mched), objects of commonsense disappear and the color of the fire is distinguished from the fire. This is the level of analysis corresponding to what I describe as the alternate interpretation. In the Buddhist tradition, this level is reflected in the Abhidharma, where commonsense objects are reduced to phenomenologically available entities. The ontological analysis, however, cannot stop there, for even entities such as color are not real. Therefore (3) at the deepest level, only their infinitesimal components are real. This third level corresponds to what I have described as the standard interpretation.

The important contribution to our inquiry is Śākya Chok-den's insight that Dharmakīrti does not choose between these different levels but uses them in dependence on the context of his inquiry. Thus, rather than following a logic of either/or concerning these views, Dharmakīrti pragmatically uses them according to his needs. This may sound at first surprising, to say the least, for these views contradict each other and Dharmakīrti knows it. How can a systematic thinker use views that undermine each other? Nevertheless, this is precisely what Dharmakīrti does. Throughout this work, we will encounter a similar strategy, which is basic to Dharmakīrti's way of doing philosophy. For example, Dharmakīrti discusses epistemological questions mostly on the ontological basis we are sketching here. This is the level described by Tibetan doxographers as the Sautrāntika view, which asserts that external objects exist. As we will see shortly, Dharmakīrti does not feel bound to always follow this view and sometimes introduces a conflicting Yogācāra view, which denies that external objects exist.

This mode of inquiry is not, as one may be tempted to think, an example of confusion or a deviant logic, for Dharmakīrti sees these positions as logically contradictory, but he also sees them as complementary or at least pragmatically compatible. The different levels (1), (2), and (3) function at different levels of analysis. When discussing epistemology, the first level is usually preferred for it is the closest to the way we conceive of things. At this level, we conceive of ourselves as perceiving objects such as jars. Such a description is not sustainable, however, for commonsense objects are not findable under analysis. Hence, we need to move to a higher level, at which our epistemic practices are redescribed as involving only phenomenologically available entities such as colors. But further analysis reveals that even these entities, which we usually think we perceive, are fictional. Hence, we need to move to a yet higher view, according to which only momentary particles are real (the standard interpretation) following a strategy of ascending scales. It is important to realize that Dharmakīrti does not believe that these levels are equally valid. Rather, for him, each level has its own limited validity within its own proper context of use. Ultimately, none of these three levels is valid, for they all assume the existence of external objects, a presupposition that Dharmakīrti ultimately rejects, as we will see shortly. However, Dharmakīrti does not refer to this ultimate but counterintuitive level very often. He prefers to move at a level more attuned to ordinary epistemic practices in accordance with his goal, the defense of the Buddhist logico–epistemological system first propounded by Dignāga.

Yogācāra in Dharmakīrti's System

So far this chapter has explored possible interpretations of Dharmakīrti's ontology. It has noticed a bewildering variety of views, suggesting that, on a certain level, Dharmakīrti's system might accommodate real extended objects. Accepting such objects would partly account for our spontaneous intuitions of perceiving unitary extended objects by showing that our notion of extension rests on some objective basis (the sensibilia). Nevertheless,

this would only partly respond to the Nyāya objection that we cannot account for such intuitions without positing substantial wholes, since the collections we perceive (the sensibilia) are not unitary objects but mere clusters. Where does our sense of unity come from?

For Dharmakīrti, ultimately, the answer to this question concerns reality itself less than our perception of it. Therefore, his answer moves toward an epistemological analysis of our subjective impressions of unitary objects. From this perspective, the relevant question is not about the objective support for our experiences of unitary objects. It is about the way in which these experiences arise. As we will see in our investigation of Dharmakīrti's theory of perception, we do not perceive objects directly but only through the intermediary of aspects (ākāra, rnam pa) that represent them. External objects provide the cause for such representations to arise in our minds. Thus, perception is really to be explained in causal terms.

Still, the question remains: what is the relation between our perception of objects as extended solid blocks of matter and their reality as aggregations of separate particles? How is the perception of extension generated? Does each atom contribute separately to the generation of such a perception or do they contribute collectively? Opinions among Indian Buddhist thinkers fall into two general categories. Some hold that atoms are merely parts of a collection (saṃghāta, 'dus pa) and that each atom contributes to a perception of unity without sharing in it. The other view holds that atoms form an aggregate (saṃcita, bsags pa) in which they acquire a dual aspect: on the one hand they keep their subtle aspect, while on the other hand, they collectively acquire a coarse aspect.

[. . .]

Although both views differ in their explanations of extension, they rest on a similar metaphysical realism: Objects exist according to the way we perceive them. We have the gut feeling that we perceive objects that exist outside of our awareness, as if they were facing us. Metaphysical realism attempts to systematize this intuition by providing an account of external objects and their perception. This account is problematic, however, for our intuition concerning the perception of external objects conflicts with other intuitions. We assume that our perception provides a true reflection of how external objects exist. We also assume, however, that external objects are made by aggregation. These two intuitions pull apart and lead to contradictions when systematized within a philosophical system. For if perceptions are unmistaken (*abhrānta, ma 'khrul ba*) reflections of reality, then the objects that they perceive should exist as they are perceived; that is, as unitary wholes. This unity is not confirmed, however, by an analysis of the way in which objects exist. When we analyze them, we discover that objects are not unitary but made of smaller particles. The collection view explains the nature of objects as being a mere collection of particles, whereas the aggregate view explains them as having a slightly greater degree of unity. Objects are aggregates of particles, which contribute together to the production of our impression of extension in a way that cannot be reduced to the contribution of individual particles. Both views attempt to explain how nonunitary objects made by collection or aggregation can give rise to perception of extension and unity. Both views face the same problem: If our perceptions are accurate reflections of the reality of external objects, how can these objects be made of atoms, which we do not perceive?

This tension is highlighted by Dignāga in his *Investigation of the Object*. There, he proposes the following argument against realism concerning external objects, both in its collection and aggregate versions: metaphysical realism is based on the intuition that our perception of external objects is accurate. External objects would exist then according to the way we perceive them; that is, as having extension and unity. This is not possible, however, since the individual particles, which compose the objects, cannot create individually the impression of extension. Since no individual atom has such an aspect, there is nothing in reality that corresponds to our impression of extension.

One might object that, although particles cannot produce individually perceptions of extended objects, they can collectively create the impression of extension. Against this, Dignāga proposes two possibilities: either atoms form a mere collection (*saṃghāta, 'dus pa*), like a forest or an army, or they are aggregates (*saṃcita, bsags pa*), possessing their own collective structure. The collection cannot be, however, the external support of perception since it is not real. Like a forest, which is a mere name given to a bunch of trees without overall unity, it is a mere conceptual overlay on the individual atoms and, as such, does not exist substantially (*dravya-sat, rdzas yod*). Since it is unreal, it cannot cause a consciousness to perceive extension. Similarly, the aggregate, the

second alternative, cannot be the external support, for it is attributable to the cognition, not to the object. No collective structure in the object itself exists over and above its individual parts. Otherwise, we would have Nyāya wholes existing over and above their parts. Therefore, concludes Dignāga, both collection and aggregate accounts fail to vindicate the intuition that we have concerning external objects. Such intuition does not hold to analysis, despite its attraction. It is inconsistent to assume that external objects exist and that we perceive them correctly.

Dharmakīrti's thinking concerning external objects follows the same line as Dignāga's. He does not seem to distinguish an aggregate from a collection. For him, atoms remain what they are whether they are aggregated or not. How then does Dharmakīrti account for our impression of extension in external objects? Like Dignāga, he does so by maintaining that this impression does not reflect the way things exist but the way we perceive them. A material object is perceived through the intermediary of its representation or aspect (*ākāra, rnam pa*). Each of its atoms causes a perception that has such representation to arise so that we see such an extended object. Thus, the impression of extension is a result of the aspected perception, not a reflection of the way atoms exist.

This answer does not close the debate. If extension does not exist in the object, how can the perception to which the object appears as extended be unmistaken and completely objective? To solve this problem, Dharmakīrti makes a radically new move, introducing a Yogācāra view that constitutes a fourth level in his ontology. Like Dignāga, he questions the assumption that external objects exist just the way we perceive them by denying the reality of the external world. In this way, he eliminates the source of the difficulty of knowing whether extended objects are real or not: "Therefore, the impression of coarseness (*sthūlabhāsa, rags snang*) does not exist in the cognition or in the object [because this coarse] essence is repudiated as existing in one [atom] and it does not exist either in many [atoms]." The reasoning proposed by Dharmakīrti hinges on a simple assumption: If extended objects exist externally, they must be either identical with each of their parts or different from them. Extended objects cannot be identical with their atomic parts, since they are extended (assuming they exist) and atoms are infinitesimally small. They cannot be different either, for in this case they would exist apart from these atoms. Since no such object has ever been observed, we have to accept that extended objects are not different from their atomic parts. Since they are not one either, we have to conclude that extended objects do not exist externally. Why, then, are we perceiving extended objects if they do not exist? Dharmakīrti answers: "The appearance of a cognition, which is not distinct [from its object], as being so is indeed a distortion." Our perception of extended objects is without support in the external world and therefore mistaken. Extended objects appear to exist separate from our consciousness, but in reality they do not exist externally. We perceive them as such, however, because our perceptions are distorted. This distortion does not concern just that we see extended objects but goes deeper to the root of the problem of distortion, the duality between subject and object. Dharmakīrti explains: "This [duality of objects existing independently of consciousness] is distorted [because] the dual [appearance] is also distorted. [The reason is conclusive because] the existence of objects different [from consciousness] depends on their appearance as distinct."

Here Dharmakīrti confronts the objection that the reasoning he stated earlier (*Commentary*, III:211) shows that external objects do not exist the way we perceive them but does not establish that they do not exist. His answer is that the view that external objects exist depends on the realist assumption that they exist as they appear to our mind. On this basis of objects appearing to our mind as existing independent from consciousness, we decide that there are objects external to consciousness. Once this basis is questioned, the view that there are external objects is deprived of main support. We then understand the plausibility of the Yogācāra view that consciousness does not need any external support to perceive objects, not even that of infinitesimal atoms. The impression of extended external objects is not produced from external conditions but arises from innate propensities (*vāsanā, bag chags*) we have had since beginningless time. Under the power of these internal conditions, we constantly but mistakenly project the false impression that there are external objects existing independent of consciousness.

This denial of the reality of external objects is where Dharmakīrti finds a solution to the dilemma created by an impression of a solid extended object produced by atoms, which do not have any extension by themselves. The problem is solved by rooting out its source, the assumption that

objects exist external to consciousness as a result of atomic aggregation. The Yogācāra view that objects exist only as reflections of consciousness is Dharmakīrti's answer to the problem created by extended objects.

Is Dharmakīrti Contradicting Himself?

This idealist solution differs from the so-called Sautrāntika view found throughout most of Dharmakīrti's works. There, Dharmakīrti assumes that external objects are real. He repeatedly articulates this position. All of our discussion has assumed this view. Nevertheless, at the crucial juncture of explaining the ontological status of spatial extension, Dharmakīrti appeals to a radically different view. Extension does not exist because there is no external world in which such phenomena could take place. Thus, it appears that Dharmakīrti holds two contradictory metaphysical views. Are they really contradictory or is it just we who see them as such? And if they are, how can Dharmakīrti maintain them in the same work?

It is tempting to believe these two views are not contradictory, for it is difficult to accept that an author takes two contradictory stances within a single work! This is precisely, however, what Dharmakīrti does repeatedly; for example, in *Commentary*, III:209–22, he states in short succession several conflicting views regarding the nature of aspects. Responding to the Nyāya charge that, in the absence of substantial wholes, experiences of unitary objects cannot be accounted for, Dharmakīrti answers that such experiences are due to the presence of aspects. The question of the status of these aspects is then raised: Are they real or not? That is, does this experience of extension have at least subjective validity or not? Dharmakīrti offers both answers without indicating a clear preference for either. Therefore, we have to accept that Dharmakīrti does introduce conflicting views within a single work.

This is supported by several Tibetan sources, which understand Dharmakīrti's texts to articulate two points of view: External objects are accepted provisionally (the so-called Sautrāntika view) and refuted at a deeper level (the Yogācāra stance). This interpretation corresponds to what I have described as a strategy of ascending scales. Lower positions are introduced according to needs, with the understanding that they will yield to higher standpoints when the analysis is pushed further. This is confirmed by Dharmakīrti when he says: "[Buddha's] enacting the shutting of the eyes of elephants [leaves] aside the meaning of the [ultimate] reality. [Acting] in a spirit of strict [agreement with] the world they display external activities." This stanza comes at the end of one of the few passages reflecting a Yogācāra view. It is important in that it indicates that Dharmakīrti does not take this Yogācāra philosophy as just a convenient element but holds it to be a deeper view of reality. Hence, the different standpoints in Dharmakīrti's philosophy reflect a definite hierarchy. More commonsensical views are subsumed by more critical but more counterintuitive views.

Still, a question remains: Why does Dharmakīrti rarely mention this deeper Yogācāra view, which he favors, preferring more commonsensical approaches? I believe that the scarcity of passages reflecting this view is not due to Dharmakīrti's belief in external objects but to a conscious strategic choice. For Dharmakīrti, this choice parallels Buddha's decision not to reveal the deeper meaning of reality in most of his teachings, instead focusing on simpler and pragmatically more appropriate teachings that do not provide an accurate vision of reality. Dharmakīrti's choice is dictated by the nature of his audience. Like Dignāga before him, Dharmakīrti is engaged in elaborating an epistemology based on Buddhist principles but addressed to the larger Indian philosophical community of his time. He is also responding to non-Buddhist thinkers who had severely criticized Dignāga's thought. Since he is engaged in a debate with a wide variety of philosophers, mostly non-Buddhists, he cannot refer to his typically Buddhist Yogācāra idealism, for such a view would be completely unacceptable to most of his audience.

As Dignāga did before him, Dharmakīrti provisionally adopts a view, which later doxographers will describe as Sautrāntika, according to which external objects exist, while maintaining the Yogācāra denial of external reality in final analysis. Although these two views contradict each other, they are pragmatically compatible. They contribute to Dharmakīrti's task, the articulation and defense of a systematic epistemology embodying Buddhist principles within a generally accepted philosophical vocabulary. For this, he relies on the lowest common denominator between competing Buddhist views and uses as much as possible terms that have broad acceptance outside of Buddhist circles. This presentation of a common system is accomplished on the basis of a provisional acceptance of external objects. This less radical and more realistic view is introduced to create a basis of discussion acceptable to both sides. The discussion, however, will not stop at this level and the audience will be led gradually to realize that a sound theory of perception is incompatible with a realist acceptance of external objects. Thus, the contradiction between this view and the Yogācāra view does not invalidate Dharmakīrti's system because they operate at different levels. Whereas the former Sautrāntika view offers a provisional basis for discussion, the latter Yogācāra view describes reality.

This seems to me the best explanation for Dharmakīrti's presentation of one view accepting the existence of external objects in most of his works and another view that clearly indicates the suspicion he ultimately bears toward such objects. This interpretation raises, however, another question: Given that Dharmakīrti is a Yogācārin, how important is this philosophy for him? Does Dharmakīrti develop a system that primarily aims at leading its auditors to realize the ultimate, the absence of duality between subject and object? Or does he offer a Yogācāra answer as a way to resolve certain epistemological problems? I will leave these questions aside for the time being, for they raise difficult problems such as the importance of Dharmakīrti's soteriological intentions.

Suffice to say that I take Dharmakīrti's essential preoccupation to be epistemology not metaphysics. His interest in defining the nature of reality is to ontologically ground his epistemology. Essential to this purpose is the distinction between real individuals and unreal universals, a distinction that parallels and supports the one between the two types of knowledge, perception and inference. The exact nature of real entities (whether, for example, they are ultimately mind dependent or not) is a lesser concern. Although Dharmakīrti has a definite view on this topic, the epistemological nature of his project confines the articulation of this view to a system in which ontological commitments are kept to a minimum.

The nature of Dharmakīrti's enterprise explains why he left so many questions unanswered. It also accounts for the fact that his commentators came up with widely diverging interpretations.

Notes

1 [Dharmakīrti was a seventh-century Indian Buddhist philosopher whose many works are largely concerned with the questions of what is real and how it may be known. Eds]

2 Masaaki Hattori, "Realism and the Philosophy of Consciousness-Only," *Eastern Buddhist* 21 (1988), 4.

3 Wilfrid Sellars, *Science, Perception, and Reality* (Atlantic Highlands, NJ: Humanities Press, 1963).

4 C. M. Keyt, "Dharmakirti's Concept of the Svalak-sana" (Ph.D. dissertation, University of Washington, 1980), p. 274.

5 [The texts quoted and discussed from this point until the end of the chapter are all by Indian or Tibetan Buddhist scholars, and are almost all translated by Dreyfus from previously untranslated sources. These sources are not easily available, and are not, in any case, of use to those who cannot read Tibetan and Sanskrit. Full details about the texts are given by Dreyfus in the book from which this chapter is taken. Eds]

27

Finding a Self: Buddhist and Feminist Perspectives

Anne Carolyn Klein

Overview of the Issues

To gain a sense of self that is genuinely one's own, and not a projection or product of patriarchy, is an important focus of concern for many women today. The background of this issue is complex and the feasibility of the project linked with our understanding that complexity. Western conceptions of an individual as the creative agent of his world, a construct much embellished in the last five hundred years, is today seriously challenged in the human sciences.[1] The theories of Freud, Marx, Foucault, or Kohut, for example, suggest that as individuals our responses and actions are largely, if not exclusively, shaped by external circumstances such as class, up-bringing, and social structure. Indeed,

> much of the intellectual history of the present century can be read in terms of a fundamental tension in the representation of an individual, a dismantling of the classical figure, and a simultaneous effort to reconceive it.[2]

That classical figure is of course male, and the privileged intellectual history also predominantly male. I note this familiar fact by way of introducing

Anne Carolyn Klein, "Finding a Self: Buddhist and Feminist Perspectives," from Clarissa W. Atkinson, Constance H. Buchanan, and Margaret R. Miles (eds.), *Shaping New Vision: Gender and Values in American Culture* (Ann Arbor: UMI Research Press, 1987), pp. 191–218.

the complexities and possibilities that ensue in developing a feminist theory of selfhood and identity using categories and paradigms from a traditional, embedded Buddhist culture that in many respects mirrors the one vanished from the West since medieval times.

Yet it is partly the traditional cultural context in which Buddhist theory raises questions about the nature of self that makes these theories relevant to women today. Women still must contend with the expectation that they will focus on or at least fulfill traditional roles as wives and mothers, and that they will function in society through the reflected identity gained from husbands and children. Although parallel expectations were once also incumbent on men, this has long since been questioned and repudiated by them; men are able to "reconceive" their status as individuals. "Individuation" has meant, by and large, the emergence of consciously chosen work and attitudes from the grey background of homogeneous roles and expectations. Men as a group have proceeded further in this direction than women, although their apparent freedom has brought its own limitations regarding what is acceptable for a man to be or do.[3] Feminists do not necessarily wish to follow the direction of male individuation, despite an insistence on freedom from women's roles as men have constructed them. Thus, when it comes to questions of how and what kinds of identity or selfhood are achieved and bestowed in our culture, the current unraveling of assumptions surrounding male individualism can open much fruitful discourse, but it should not lull us into thinking that men and women necessarily are struggling with the same issues, or that they share personal and social histories.

Among contemporary North American women, search for a strong and fresh identity is often motivated by the urgent need to avoid a patriarchal style of identity. This latter involves, by definition, a sense of self which is neither chosen by women nor in their best interest. From a feminist perspective, the oppositionality that characterizes patriarchal styles of selfhood is pernicious. An identity crucially maintained through opposition, whether this manifests itself as actual exclusion of others or as the projecting onto others of unwanted elements of oneself, is to be avoided.[4] Class, racial, national, and sexual chauvinism all rest on a style of identity which, regardless of content, is characterized fundamentally by its need to express unassailable differences between oneself and others. Indeed, to maintain such an identity *requires* an ideology that entails, in the words of Susan Griffin, "the creation of another, a not-I, an enemy."[5] Some other paradigm of selfhood is needed. But what? Is it possible or even desirable to avoid all oppositionality? Can we distinguish differences without setting in motion the dance of dualism and conflict? Is it possible, in short, to find or imagine a functioning and powerful selfhood that is not so predicted on an exclusionist ontology of identity that in creating strength it also creates a basis for rejecting those who do not share this "identity?" What is the significance of one's relationships to individuals, groups, or cultures in forming such a non-exclusive identity?[6] In exploring these issues we will have to contend with a possible tension between (1) the importance of relationships to a healthy sense of self, and (2) the crucial need to have an identity that is experienced as genuinely one's own and not the making of another. To put this another way, many women seek a style of identity that is powerful, yet favors the relational over the individual.

Indeed, feminist endeavor has a vision of empowered persons who, in the words of the French feminist Hélène Cixous, have "no commerce with a love that stultifies the strange."[7] Strength without stridency, an identity of embrace rather than distance, is a more subtle achievement than the physical or psychosocial brute force with which societies and individuals are accustomed to create themselves. The difficulty here is partly that both language and the reflective process operate by way of exclusion – that is, dualistically. Thus,

modern French feminists approach the dilemmas of identity by creating new ways of thinking and, especially, writing.[8]

Buddhist philosophy, with its radical questioning of common assumptions regarding identity, seems particularly relevant to the developing feminist agenda. Buddhism offers a critique of hyperindividualism as well as a positive view of an interdependently understood identity. Furthermore, Buddhism is important because it is not organized around one of the principal disjunctures in Western thought, the bifurcation of epistemology and ontology,[9] and the sub-split within epistemology between experience and knowing. Feminists in this country are just beginning to understand that these fissures in the intellectual landscape are inhospitable to women. At the very least, the separation of these areas contributes to the abstractness of modern philosophy, against which feminism seeks to develop theory anchored in and relevant to experience.

To this end, Buddhist literature offers much to explore in an attempt to further understand and change Western conceptual schemes that women find problematic. Buddhist writings are particularly valuable in opening two issues crucial to our discussion: categories of subjectivity and ontological questioning. For reasons I will suggest below, an expanded vocabulary of subjective states may be an important step in bridging epistemological and ontological areas of inquiry. In most Buddhist traditions, ontological and epistemological considerations are intimately and explicitly entwined. The attention given to ontological descriptions of persons or things is matched by detailed epistemological explanation[10] of what takes place in the mind or subject who knows this. Certainly, theories of what mind is and how it works are foundational to assumptions and questions regarding the nature of selfhood. Such theories of mind also figure strongly in current North American feminist exhortations to groundedness, clarity, and recognition of be-ing.

In developing the relevance of specific Buddhist material to feminist questions and criteria regarding selfhood, I will focus mainly on theories and practices in Indo-Tibetan Buddhism, especially the Gelukba order's discussion of the Middle-Way Consequentialist (Prasangika-Madhyamika) school of Mahayana thought. I will suggest that the way in which this material frames what it understands to be a profound search for identity uncovers a dynamic congruent with the one being developed by feminists.

Psychology and Ontology

The purpose of Buddhist theory and meditative technique in general is to develop particular subjective states, many of which belong to categories of personal growth and styles of identity that, as we will elaborate below, do not at present figure significantly in Western developmental models. Western psychology emphasizes the "vital importance of developing a sense of continuity, identity, and ongoingness in existence."[11] From the Buddhist perspective, this type of secure identity, though foundational to development, is intrinsically problematic, a source of chronic dissatisfaction. Western philosophy, in raising crucial questions about the ontology of identity, does not clearly elaborate how the philosophical insights it offers affect the epistemological state of the subject. Western psychology, in focusing on the subject, tends not to examine the assumed ontology of the self whose development it charts, and therefore does not envision a stage of development that depends on questioning this. Feminist critique in this country seems to imply a place for such development when it notes on the one hand the necessity for a strong sense of consciously chosen selfhood, and recognizes on the other the deeply relational nature of identity. Their critique turns on two central axes, questions regarding the content of women's identity as women would create it, and questions regarding the ontology that undergirds both particular content and the overarching experience of self. What I call "content" has to do with the emotional or psychological character of self, and "ontology" with the existential structure of that self.

Buddhist observations on the stages of personal development presuppose the presence of an appropriately functioning psychological self and address themselves primarily to an ontological critique of the self. Unlike the developmental levels of Western psychology, Buddhist theories seem to begin with an adult rather than a child. Their further premise is that erroneous ontological assumptions about both self and other govern virtually all other experiences of self. Spiritual growth – development beyond the state of merely viable identity – is charted in terms of the relinquishment of increasingly subtle errors regarding the ontology of self.[12] Similarly, the female quest for selfhood highlighted here involves ontological as well as psychological issues. In furthering discussion of the latter through Buddhist material, we will have to contend with the Buddhist claim that certain ontological truths are available only to particular subjective states. For example, direct insight of what Buddhism calls the empty nature of the self – a special quality of oneself – is only experienced by a mind conjoined with specifically defined styles of stability, clarity, intensity, and, ultimately, insight.[13] Such factors, largely outside the vocabulary of current psychological language, nonetheless presume much of what the West regards as psychological well-being. I emphasize this because it seems clear to me that the modern feminist engagement, like the Buddhist one, is with styles of personal development that expand the classical dimensions of psychological health. It is easy to see that the same psychological health associated with assured self-constancy can accommodate unfortunate and ultimately unhealthy tendencies such as self-inflation, denigration of others, or narrowness of vision.

The assumption that ultimate ontological truths are available to human subjectivity – to perception – has much to do with the unified unfolding of ontology and epistemology in Buddhist and other traditions that uphold the possibility of "sacred knowledge." Despite problems inherent in this claim, feminists also seek an understanding pertinent to both being and knowing.

Concern for the experiential content of this self, for such basic requisites of psychological health as self-esteem and internal cohesiveness, is therefore to be joined with an examination of the experienced ontological structure of that self. Buddhist analyses of these matters are in my opinion significantly consonant with important elements of feminist reflection. However, the relevant Buddhist discussions of self and selflessness – persons and the emptiness of persons – have never taken account of gender as a category governing analysis. Even though the wisdom of selflessness is frequently characterized as female,[14] to my knowledge no one within the 2,500-year-old tradition has analyzed Indo-Tibetan theories and practices connected with emptiness in the context of how they do or do not speak to women. I am not yet prepared to suggest how such an inquiry might proceed in Asian countries where Buddhism is practiced; I do think it possible to find relevance to questions significant for women in North America.

A small but influential group of modern feminist writers describes selfhood primarily in ontological terms. Mary Daly, though more than willing to encourage an identity antagonistic to males, characterizes woman ontologically as "rooted in the intuition that Powers are constantly unfolding and creating, communicating, Be-ing more."[15] Further, as Marilyn Massey points out, French feminists like Cixous and Irigaray, taking as their starting point woman's experience of her own unfettered body, also focus on the almost-paradoxical vision of an identity that is both self-contained and non-exclusive.[16] For Cixous, woman is to know herself as "a moving, limitlessly changing ensemble . . . an immense astral space not organized around any one sun that's any more of a star than the others."[17]

Emphasis on knowledge through the body is also important in the work of contemporary North American writers such as Carol Christ and Adrienne Rich. My purpose here is to suggest another way of thinking of a strong self whose power does not depend on its ability to oppose, project, or conceive itself as radically separate. The process entails both epistemological and ontological considerations.

In order to explore a subjective style relevant to feminist interest in a non-oppositional *modus operandi*, I will turn first to a Buddhist discussion of the mental state of awareness. Buddhists in general consider awareness salutary in its own right as well as an essential subjective component in accomplishing further growth, particularly insight into the actual ontological status of the self. The topic of awareness therefore leads to analysis of ontological principles pertinent to an identity that incorporates but moves beyond the "healthy ego" that Western patriarchal culture deems optimal. In this context we will also be able to contrast Buddhist discussions of emptiness with a form of nihilism that has been appropriated by recent feminist thought.

Accessing Experience

As a style or category of subjectivity, awareness is in several ways significant in enabling a non-oppositional or non-ideological sense of self. From a feminist perspective, awareness is a non-oppositional mental posture that is at the same time self-empowering. Let us try to analyze why.

First, simple awareness can watch internal processes without interfering with them.[18] It entails no oppression of oneself by an ideal – patriarchal or otherwise – against which one is measured. A number of Western feminists have written about the importance of such self-awareness. The "wandering" chronicled by Mary Daly, wherein a new naming presages an "entrance to the Arch Image,"[19] requires awareness and self-knowledge. Doris

Lessing, herself much influenced by another tradition of sacred knowledge, Sufism, makes awareness the starting point of Martha Quest's spiritual odyssey in *The Four Gated City*. Quest learns how to render herself "alive and light and aware";[20] she knows the advantages, walking in the London rain, of having "her head cool, watchful, alert."[21] She knows too the sense of "a quiet, empty space, behind which stood an observing presence."[22]

The "observing presence" is an important dimension of experience. It permits self-knowledge without the crippling weight of an ideal against which one inevitably falls short.[23] Engagement with ideals can become potentially debilitating self-negation which also distracts from self-understanding. Contrasting oneself to an ideal is debilitating if, despite an explicit message of striving and optimism, there is stronger implicit emphasis on one's present unsatisfactoriness. The daily bombardment of *Cosmo*-style advice for make-overs, and media injunctions to deodorize, paint, and polish, operate on the same principle. Fear of falling short of ideals is, especially for "religiously" oriented persons, a great obstacle to self-knowledge, particularly when, under the guise of offering hope for improvement, the present state is demeaned.

The paradigm of struggle against self is well known in religious and secular practice. Mary Daly, in *Pure Lust*, scathingly satirizes Christian ascetics, seen as emblematic of patriarchal religiosity, for glorying in denying who they were in order to be something else. She calls such self-denial "sado-ritual." Such oppositional striving against self may or may not be peculiar to patriarchy. Whatever its efficacy in some situations, it has built-in dangers for women. It makes self-knowledge difficult, especially for a woman in a patriarchal culture that is eager to tell her exactly who she is or should be (preferring, actually, to gloss over any possible difference between these). The less sense she has of her own integrity, the easier it is to drive the message home. This is one reason why the struggle toward ideals is, as Judith Plaskow says, a practice for those who already possess a certain kind of strength.[24] Socially constructed ideals are an excellent way of controlling those who can be persuaded they should live up to them. They require maintenance of an oppositional identity if one is to maintain self-integrity in the face of them. Buddhist literature makes the point that manipulation, like all oppression, depends on unconscious ontological assumptions regarding the self that oppresses and is oppressed.

Thus seen, the potential disadvantages of a quest for self, or any religious quest, that is dominated by ideals are fourfold: (1) hindering self-knowledge, (2) demeaning the self, (3) providing a means by which one may be manipulated and (4) continuing the oppositional style that many feminists explicitly seek to overcome.

In short, self-knowledge can be much hampered by the presence of demanding ideals. It can be stymied further by excessive admiration of the ideal in question. Yet, ideals are often intrinsically appealing, beckoning one to merge with them, so that a person without a strong sense of self is likely to be engulfed by them. The patriarchal solution seems to be to match the strength of an ideal with the strength of one's own individuality. In addition to the difficulty, in some contexts, of distinguishing these, this is unacceptable to most feminists. It simply perpetuates oppositionality. Admiration for an ideal needs to be balanced by an equal degree of self-knowledge. Otherwise, in addition to the perils just noted, one becomes impatient for personal change while at the same time remaining in a kind of personal vacuum, a vacuum thinly veiled off from awareness by unrealistic expectations. Self-abandonment, which must be distinguished from the Buddhist understanding of selflessness or emptiness,[25] is the result of allegiance to an idea. It is easy to acquire. A few years ago I overheard a conversation between two American practitioners of Buddhist meditation. One, speaking with a kind of rosy excitement, turned to another and asked, "How has meditation changed you?" She appeared to expect some kind of success story of triumph over unwanted personality traits. The object of this inquiry, not responding to her eager anticipation, said, "Change? I don't want to change. I just want to *be* there."

It is often hard to "be there." However, an observing awareness offers a religious endeavor or self-cultivation that does not operate via oppressive ideals. Awareness as a means for getting in touch with one's own experience is crucial here. It is uncritical, it simply sees and accepts. This non-judgmental awareness constitutes groundedness; it is the beginning of constructive personal power. Awareness can facilitate access to one's experience, but it will not resolve all the issues. It will not illuminate, for example, the extent to which experience is culturally conditioned; nor will it determine new directions of endeavor. It will not necessarily vitalize activity.[26] Yet, Buddhist traditions maintain that simply by its presence, uncritical

awareness is salutary. Being aware of an experienced weakness, defect, or confusion relieves the drain caused by trying to pretend that it does not exist. Psychologists might call it "owning one's feelings." Acknowledging feelings takes power from them and gives it to the conscious self. Mistaken ontological assumptions about that self are not altered, but the conditions for growth are provided. Growth can then take place, not without effort, but without the kind of fight that can divide the self from the source of its strength. Such awareness is not simply a self-consciousness in which one experiences oneself as an object, but, as we have seen, has specific subjective qualities of its own – among them clarity, energy, buoyancy.[27] Further qualities develop as simple awareness becomes associated with greater degrees of stability. In addition to accessing experience and offering a method of empowerment that is not demeaning, awareness is important to women because it is, in and of itself, grounding.

Valerie Saiving, the first feminist theologian to express how the failings of women *as women* are different from those of men, suggests that distractibility and diffuseness, the lack of an organizing center or focus, are among the chief female "sins."[28] Sustained awareness speaks directly to this need for focus. Again, it facilitates focus without depending on an external goal or threat to galvanize it. In this sense also it is non-oppositional. Moreover, the capacity for careful observation is often strong in women. Doris Lessing writes:

> Old people, servants, children, slaves, all of those who aren't in control of their own lives, watch faces for minute signs in eyes, gestures, lips, as weather-watchers examine the skies.[29]

To watch others in this manner, however necessary, is a defensive maneuver, not an empowering one. To draw on this same skill in observing oneself so that one can then observe others in the context of knowing the observer, is finally to become a true participant, capable of purposeful, aware engagement with others.

Thus, awareness may have specific significance for women. It enhances understanding of one's own experience, reduces distractedness, and grounds activity. It also presents a potential hazard: too much fascination with awareness can drain energies from other important areas of endeavor.[30] As with most things, balance is required.

Let us consider the value of non-oppositional awareness in a particular Buddhist understanding of selflessness or emptiness. On the basis of awareness, and in the context of having a healthy degree of self-constancy, one becomes familiar with one's own assumptions regarding not only the healthfully constant self, but the reified status of that self. Subsequent analysis will challenge the latter but not the former. One thereby opens the possibility of experientially separating the continuity essential to psychological health from mistaken reification of the self. Only when one can identify reification of the self in terms of one's own experience is one ready to reflect on whether or not such a self is a delusion. We will consider the Buddhist observation of and reflections about the reified self, and then consider the relevance of these to the feminist agenda of a non-oppositional, grounded self.

A Question of Self

Before meditation on emptiness or selflessness commences, one needs to become thoroughly familiar with the ordinary experience of self. One observes, uncritically and without correction, the existential status naturally attributed to it. For example, one might observe that when the strong sense of "I" is discerned, no matter what its psychological content, it seems to have a certain locus and a certain style or ontological ambience that appears to combine elements of mind and body but at the same time seems different from them. It is important to note that there is no one way the ontologically misconstrued self "should" appear, and there is no immediate critique of its contents. The point is to allow one's natural way of perceiving the self to unfold. Later it will be subjected to analysis, but only after the initial phase of identifying the ordinary sense of self has been navigated. Because this sense of self may initially be unclear, the classic Buddhist advice is to observe closely at times of strong emotion such as happiness, indignation, greed or sorrow.[31] It is precisely when strong feelings arise – for example, when one is defending against an unjust accusation, in a state of fright or exultation – that one can detect the self that one will defend, rescue, or to which one will give pleasure. These feelings do not define self, but they do enable one to identify the self that has these experiences. Weeks or months of observation are recommended to gain familiarity with one's own way of conceiving self. This is considered the most difficult phase of the process of coming to understand what Buddhists mean by selflessness. Indeed,

Tsong-ka-pa, a fourteenth-century Tibetan yogi and scholar, devotes to this topic nearly half of his discussion of the special insight (*lhag mthong*) into emptiness.[32]

Tsong-ka-pa begins his discussion of special insight with emphasis on awareness of one's present state. He describes the ordinary experience of selfhood in ontological terms:

> Just as, for example, in order to ascertain that a certain person is not here, you must know the person who is not here so in order to ascertain the meaning of "selflessness" or "non-inherent existence," you must identify well that self, or inherent existence, which does not exist. [Otherwise] . . . you will not unerringly ascertain the negative of it.[33]

The self observed by ordinary awareness and then denied in theories of selflessness is not a psychological self characterized by certain personality traits, dominant emotions and so forth. It refers rather to a *style* of selfhood, to the ontological or existential status of such a self. Specifically, it refers to the assumption of a greatly exaggerated existential status. In the language of Buddhist philosophy, this reified sense of self is known as true or inherent existence. This term signifies, in part, the sense of something as massively existent, unambiguously findable or concretely identifiable, as one can point to a rock and then pick it up. It is this self, but not self in general, that is to be negated. In the Buddhist perspective this concept of "true existence" easily becomes the basis for an overbearing sense of hierarchy and thus provides fuel for oppression. According to the Prasangika-Madhyamika system, the most subtle forms of a misapprehension are innately present, not learned or socially constructed.

The word "self" in the Buddhist term "selflessness," although a literal translation, can be quite misleading. The "self" negated in the theory of selflessness is synonymous, not with person, but with inherent existence; in this sense one can speak of the selflessness of stones, trees, and so forth. The unthinking attribution of status to others, and the appropriation of it for oneself, is considered by Buddhists to be the lived ontology that underpins all oppression. Or, to use Foucault's term, this misconception provides in Buddhist theory the "surface of inscription for power"; in the Buddhist context this signifies one's susceptibility to being overpowered by perceptions and feelings founded on that basic error.[34] Identifying one's experience of self is considered essential because it gives access to this error. Analyzing or denying such a self will have no significance unless one first identifies implicit conviction in it.

Many feminists, aware of how extensively men have controlled women's minds and bodies – the very constituents of self – distrust the idea of "finding" a true or natural female self.[35] They emphasize the need to recognize the patriarchally sustained one and then, implicitly at least, to move to a different, more genuinely rooted, experience of self. The dynamic of discovering the apparent, manipulated sense of self with the expectation of redefining self parallels the Buddhist use of awareness to identify, and subsequently correct, the ontologically mistaken sense of self.

But how can a different sense of self occur? There is tension between the feminist perception of a need to re-create self and the assumption that there is an as yet undiscovered presence of a true female way of being.[36] The Buddhist perspective emphasizes an inquiry that proceeds from awareness of experience, regardless of how culturally conditioned this may be, and leads to ontological insight. The self of untutored experience is, from different perspectives and at different points in the exploration, both undermined and valorized. However, not even the qualified valorization of the presently experienced self suggests that one will find one's deepest identity through awareness of it. Further, because contemporary understandings of "identity" pertain to matters of character and feeling rather than to ontology, there is no Western parallel to the contemporary concept of a "search for identity" in Buddhist terms. Rather, in the Gelukba approach, one comes to grips with a self or identity that is the basis on which one receives and is overpowered by the projection of others. In the long run, one can identify a viable self of a wholly different ontological order, and this identification will ultimately be accompanied by profound changes in one's character and relationship with others. Unlike many feminists, however, Buddhism does not concern itself with complex psychological analysis of the self. The focus remains ontological because the addiction to inherent existence is the basic characteristic of mind that predisposes one to oppressing and being oppressed, or to any other form of suffering. It is the assumed existential status of the oppressed and confused self as well as of the empowered and prideful self that is at issue. This status is not problematic for spiritual reasons

– as with Christian pride, for example – but because it provides a basis for unethical behavior and experience.

The method for bringing to light this ordinarily unnoticed sense of inherent existence is itself non-oppositional. It consists of a simple, uncritical awareness of one's own view of inherent existence – that is, of one's own sense of "I." Moreover, unless this term "inherently existent 'I'" is seen as descriptive of some aspect of experience, however subtle, it will be irrelevant for both Buddhists and feminists. This reified ontology can be experienced even when one's identity is unclear in terms of social role or psychological content. That is, one can feel "I don't know who I am" and still have a mistakenly reified sense of the "I" who does not know.

Thus one begins with awareness of one's own experience. This is not, as we have seen, because such perception is entirely correct, though such awareness may be more correct than other kinds of subjectivity – but because awareness, rather than any grand ideal, is regarded as the starting point of religious life and philosophical discourse. Moreover, as already indicated, all afflictions come about through dependence on an innate error, a particular reified self. Since this self is an important support of oppression, Buddhist emphasis on undermining this sense of self is of interest to persons who seek a non-oppositional, non-idealizing approach to issues of identity.

To this point we have discussed one style of subjectivity that Buddhists consider useful in accessing one's present experience of self. I will now turn to a description of the ontological qualities of the self that is denied in Indo-Tibetan Buddhism, and of the self that is affirmed; then I will distinguish both selflessness and the mind that understands selflessness from certain forms of Western nihilism.

The Ontological Self

The self of ordinary experience is described with varying degrees of subtlety in Gelukba texts. These descriptions pertain mainly to the ontology of the experienced self, rather than its content. Except in its discussion of compassion, seen as central to the project of Mahayana Buddhism, specific feelings or personal qualities are not emphasized. Attention centers on more widely applicable ontological patterns of the experienced self. Typical of the Gelukba position is this statement by one of the foremost contemporary scholars from that tradition, the present Dalai Lama:

> There are many different ways in which the person or I appears to our minds. In one way, the I appears to be permanent, unitary, and under its own power; in this mode of appearance the I seems to be a separate entity from mind and body with the person as the user or enjoyer and mind and body as what is used or enjoyed.[37]

Feminists have also expressed concern about such a depiction of self and have envisioned a different way of being. This would not mean that a woman is, in the words of Hélène Cixous, "an undifferentiated magma but that she doesn't lord it over her body or her desire."[38] "Lording it over" requires precisely the reified self, a self which is a fundamental component of the patriarchal self. Seeing self as distinct from a mind and a body in this manner opens the way to an oppositionality between self and mind or body, as well as between mind and body. For Tsong-ka-pa and the philosophical system of Prasangika in general, however, this exemplifies a relatively superficial mistaken sense of self. It is not the most deeply ingrained sense of self. Belief in it is easily dispelled by the reasoned reflection that will occupy the next phases of analysis. After all, it is argued, if the self were as independent of mind and body as it sometimes seems, it should be possible to experience this self, one's own or others', without any reference to mind or body. And this is patently not the case.[39] Yet, one could overcome oppositionality and still be mistaken regarding the nature of the self. The Dalai Lama, again referring to well known Gelukba categories, describes a more subtle, but still ontologically overbearing, sense of self:

> In another mode of appearance the I seems to have its own substantially existent or self-sufficient entity but to be of the same character as mind and body. There are both innate and artificial [or learned] forms of consciousness that conceive the I to exist in accordance with this appearance. . . . Another is the appearance of the I as if it exists inherently; our innate misconception of I is a consciousness which views the I in this last way as concretely existent in accordance with this appearance. This form of misconception exists in all beings, whether they have studied and been affected by a [religious or philosophical] system or not.[40]

The point is not that one *consciously* mistakes the self's ontology in this way, but that we all operate under the assumption that this is the case. It is this unintended assumption that must first be identified by non-oppositional awareness.

Subsequently, one subjects this sense of self to analysis. Without specifying how the analysis works,[41] I will describe its method. The mode of understanding is not textual but experiential. That is, having observed how the existential or ontological status of the self is ordinarily experienced, analysis is used to test whether a self like this could actually exist or not. Such reflection progresses in stages from the merely intellectual to an experiential integration of emptiness, the absence of reified selfhood. In early and middle stages of analysis, the intellect itself proceeds dialectically – that is, oppositionally. Because it is directed at undermining the ontological basis of its own oppositionality – the conception of inherent existence – it is able finally to undercut all inherently existent oppositionality, but not oppositionality in general. The possibility of hierarchical and other differences still exists, but not the ontological support that is the chief factor making differences problematic. For example, high and low are strictly relative designations, one cannot exist except in relation to the other; within nominally established differences, high and low have the common quality of being empty of reified or inherent status as high or low.

The conclusion that the self does not exist at all is not drawn, but rather that the self is utterly unreifiable, non-inherently existent. Understanding this emphasizes the contingent, dependent, interconnected, and non-autonomous nature of the self's existence. An active, effective self exists, but not in any sense independently. Again, the fact that persons do not exist in this way is, according to Prasangika, the most subtle emptiness qualifying the self. Only when this emptiness or selflessness is fully known can one discover the self affirmed in this Buddhist system, a fully functioning self which certainly exists, but its existence has no ontological fixedness. Although viable as an agent and object, the self affirmed in Buddhism is dependently constituted. It is created through association, rather than separation, and in relation, rather than from nothing.

Theories of emptiness and interdependence frame ontological dynamics crucial to current North American feminist reassessments of the inclusive and relational context of identity formation. In this view, other persons are not merely mirrors facilitating self-knowledge, but "the self is known in the experience of connection, defined not by reflection but by interaction, the responsiveness of human engagement."[42] The experience of emptiness discussed above is associated with the development of a compassionate sense of relatedness in which self and other are seen not as oppositional but as relative designations, like the far and near banks of a river.[43] The identity of each is utterly contingent on the other. This much is easy to understand. Mahayana texts suggest however that the real import of this perspective cannot be perceived so long as one maintains a reified sense of self or other. Emptiness theory is therefore crucial to the full development of relational understanding and compassionate involvement.

Broadly speaking, emptiness theory runs parallel to current feminist observations of the mutuality of self and other as constitutive of personal identity. For both Buddhists and feminists, however, the question remains: how does one live within this recognition, even if one takes it to be true? Is it something to be brought to consciousness at will? Is it only descriptive or is it also prescriptive? If the latter, what, precisely, does it prescribe? How might it influence individual behavior or social praxis? At the very least it calls attention to the foolishness of paying excessive homage to human autonomy. A case in point is our own culture's loyalty to an illusory independence. This glorification of independence may partially explain the low esteem in which the difficult and vital tasks of childbearing, child rearing, and primary education are held. Social, economic, and institutional failure to support parenting may stem in good measure from a deeply-rooted unwillingness to value the utter dependence all adults have had as children on the work of parents, and primary or secondary school teachers – most of whom are women. Moreover, in many colleges and universities, teaching, at its best a powerful expression of relationship, is not valued as much as "Lone Ranger" scholarship. There is an irrational but powerful clinging to the idea of "self-made" autonomous men.

According to psychologists such as Carol Gilligan and Nancy Chodorow, many women in our culture find it more accurate to think of themselves in terms of connectedness than separation. Because most models of powerful selfhood available to us in modern life feature autonomy and separateness, women who do not wish to claim power in this way often decline to claim it at all, partly because more appealing styles of power do not readily present themselves. A woman may react to the available model of power by behaving meekly, or she may experience herself only as helpmate to others, as incapable of further aspirations. The personal cost of such a stance is discussed widely. Scholars have emphasized the psychological and social context of this posture, but there is another sphere of influence operative regarding woman's sense of self, the ontological sphere.

Self-abandoning behavior is not merely a drain; it also fails to get at the ontological root of the issue. In the Buddhist view, it is not only the powerful, confident person who has an ontologically overwrought sense of self. A person with a fragile psychological self or low self-esteem is just as likely to have this, although the ontology of that self may be less accessible to awareness. To realize that one need not be attached either to a highly *or* lowly esteemed self is to open a fresh possibility of self-identity. This does not mean that ontological concerns necessarily take precedence over psychological ones. It would be foolhardy for anyone with an overly fragile sense of self to engage in a process which undermines her identity when what is needed on the psychological level is a stable, organized self.[44] Ontological inquiry may however strengthen the sense of self in a different way. To express this possibility in Western terms: the Buddhist analysis of self might help alleviate a person's tendency to become a reflecting pool for projections. Why? Because in the Buddhist view the ontologically inflated self is the fabric of the sail – the confidence or lack of it, for example – that catches the wind of such projections. Such a sail blows an erratic course. An ontologically false sense of self is distracting, leaving one at sea, ungrounded.

What potential do the principles associated with the Buddhist discussion of selflessness have to open non-oppositional reconstructions of individual identity? We can only evaluate this by considering once again, and from a different perspective, some subjective styles associated with this endeavor.

Mahayana Buddhist texts emphasize that the process of coming to understand non-inherent existence, or emptiness, involves a radical reorientation of the subject. Many subjective experiences are cultivated, such as simple awareness, an unshakable concentration known as calm abiding which is accompanied by physical and mental joy and agility, an increased benevolent concern for others, and a sense of no longer being entirely cut off from sense objects or from other persons. Awareness participates in a larger process of growth, not by

337

moving toward ideals but by making possible insights that alter the state – and thereby the content – of one's interiority. The insight into emptiness, facilitated by awareness, leads to an empowered compassion.[45] The relationship between such insight and concern for others is an important principle in Mahayana Buddhism. Insight, and its affective counterpart, compassion, are crucial for the Buddhist enterprise of ultimate liberation. To quote from Saraha, one of India's great Buddhist yogis:

> One who enters into emptiness without
>   compassion
> Will not find the most excellent path.
> Yet, should one cultivate only compassion
> One will not attain liberation, but remain in
>   cyclic existence.[46]

In Indo-Tibetan Mahayana Buddhism, neither compassion nor an understanding of selflessness comes to full flower without the other. Moreover, insight into the ontological principle of interrelatedness engenders understanding of interpersonal connectedness and hence in Mahayana is fundamentally conjoined with compassionate concern for persons who are no longer seen as other.[47] In other words, the subjectivity involved in experiencing emptiness is characterized by emotional richness. This is important to notice, because Buddhist emptiness has often mistakenly been associated with inner deadness and with certain forms of nihilism.

How then is emptiness distinguished from nihilism? What might distinguish it from, for example, Novak's "experience of nothingness," of which North American feminist theory has made considerable use? These terms must not be confused because of their semantic similarity. To do so would be to obscure the respective relevance for feminist issues of identity. In describing the distinction between Western "experience of nothingness" and "emptiness," I will refer to emptiness in two different ways: as a theoretical perspective and as a focus of experience. It is important to contrast descriptions of the experience of emptiness with descriptions of the experience of nothingness in order to take account of the ontological implications of each.

Emptiness and Feeling Negative

In *The Experience of Nothingness* Novak writes that "To choose against culture is not merely to disobey,

it is to die."[48] For Novak, "the source of the experience of nothingness lies in the deepest recesses of human consciousness, in its irrepressible tendency to ask questions."[49] Here nothingness signifies, in part, the bleakness and alienation that results from not seeing one's own reality mirrored in the larger one and the way this experience motivates many, many questions. Women have often described their own situation in these terms. Moreover, incessant questioning can be exhausting. Mary Daly, paraphrasing Simone de Beauvoir, observes that "women who have perceived the reality of sexual oppression usually have exhausted themselves in breaking through to discovery of their own humanity with little energy left for constructing their own interpretation of the universe."[50]

The angst associated with Novak's nothingness is something that "may lead either to madness or to wisdom."[51] In either case angst is a passageway, not an end point. Thus, as a focus of experience, its place in the developmental spectrum in which it is embedded is different from that of the realization of emptiness. Emptiness is not an experience that one passes through to something better, as in the mythic paradigm of a descent into hell. Rather emptiness is an awareness one continually cultivates so as to integrate it into more and more aspects of one's life, including one's relationship to others. Moreover, as understood in Buddhist Middle-Way (Madhyamika) systems, emptiness is not the void that Novak describes as "full of danger, insanity, destructiveness, rage."[52] Realization of emptiness is not a recognition, despairing or otherwise, of a lack of *telos* in life's trials, even though it undermines the ontological status of *telos*, as well as of the self that seems to require it. Nevertheless, both *telos*, construed in Buddhist terms, and self are valid constructs.

Whereas Novak's nihilism involves recognition of a lack of meaning, emptiness theory questions the ontological status of agents while preserving the meaning of their actions as valid.[53] Nihilism in general denies a posited totality of a whole – whether God or something else – on which one can depend and through which one incurs value. Madhyamika, agreeing that such a conception limits human possibilities, takes the discussion of emptiness and associated topics in epistemology to include a vast range of possibilities. Compassion, mental clarity, and energy are positive concomitants of understanding emptiness. These results do not depend on dismissing the world as illusion and offering a more stable realm; the world is said to be illusion-like, not "mere" illusion, and neither more nor less, ontologically, than emptiness itself. Insight into emptiness does not result from pushing aside one's experience of the world, but by observing it more closely. Unlike the experience of nothingness that Novak discusses, the emptiness discussed in Indo-Tibetan Madhyamika does not signify a state of alienation.

The new possibilities connected with realizing emptiness in this tradition are primarily developments in the person, not escape to another realm. In Buddhism the discussion of emptiness or selflessness aims at developing specific subjective insights and experiences. Emptiness does not become a focus for Buddhists simply because it is considered true. Emptiness is central to Buddhist theory and practice because realization of this is salutary in the short term and transformative in the long one. In order to have a direct experience of emptiness, as opposed to mediated, conceptual understanding, however vivid and psychologically affective, certain qualities of mind must be present. The factor of mindfulness discussed above must be developed and combined with other factors so that one achieves the pacification of mind known as calm abiding. This is the lowest form of concentration with which it is possible to cognize emptiness directly. Calm abiding is always associated with mental and physical joy. Meditators from many traditions, Buddhist and non-Buddhist, attest to the connection between mental concentration and pleasurable physical feelings. Therefore, in terms of its psychological aspect, the experience of emptiness is not one of emotional nothingness. Although some form of joyful release may follow Novak's "experience of nothingness," joy is not an integral part of the nihilistic perspective itself.

Emptiness as Inalienable

Having discussed the subjective features associated with emptiness, we can turn to ontological considerations. In addition to being the focus for specific experience, emptiness is an ontologically descriptive term. As such it is an ingredient in the dynamic agents as well as the inanimate objects of the world. It is, in short, an immanent quality of existing things, having no existence apart from them. This is another factor distinguishing Madhyamika emptiness from Novak's nothingness. The latter is part of alienation, the former of integration. For Buddhists, both the theory and experience of

"emptiness" undermine psychological or ontological self-sufficiency and confirm the existence of a self that is ontologically relational and whose primary emotional characteristic is compassion for others. Indeed, in Prasangika-Madhyamika interdependent existence is the necessary reciprocal meaning of emptiness; it is as all-encompassing a rubric as emptiness itself. Emptiness or selflessness is described as altogether compatible with functionality and existence. Both its religious significance and its potential import for feminist experientially-based theories of selfhood lie in this functionality.

Moreover, as an ontological theory, emptiness is descriptive of self as well as other, and contradicts the ontological oppositionality that feminists see as characterizing the patriarchal self, and which Buddhists see as characterizing an ontologically overwrought sense of self.

Emptiness is often credited with a generative quality that nothingness, used in the ontological sense of *ex nihilo*, does not possess. Unlike the nothingness or nihility which in Nishitani's pithy phrase "lies on the far side of phenomena,"[54] emptiness is part and parcel of all that it qualifies, and has no existence except as a quality of these things. Thus it is compatible with activity in ways that nihility is not. For all these reasons, emptiness "lies on the near side" of being, it is not "some point recessed behind the things that we see with our eyes and think of with our minds."[55] Rather, these are suffused with the quality of emptiness. Neither emptiness nor the sense-objects it qualifies can exist without the other. The *Twenty-Five Thousand Stanza Perfection of Wisdom Sutra* states:

> It is like this: a Bodhisattva [an altruistically motivated seeker of highest enlightenment] is empty of being an inherently existent Bodhisattva. A Bodhisattva's name is also empty of being a Bodhisattva's name. Why? It is their nature. It is like this: it is not that form is empty on account of emptiness; emptiness is not separate from a form. A form itself is [that which is] empty; just [that which is] empty is also the form.[56]

Emptiness is co-extensive and integrated with people and things, not set apart from them. To know emptiness therefore is not to be preoccupied with "the negation of everything that is."[57] Emptiness is not seen as opposed to being, but as an inseparable quality of all that exists. Thus, emptiness itself is empty – not a paradox, but a logical unfolding of the principle that nothing inherently exists. The theory of emptiness can help articulate the possibility of a strong identity not predicated on exclusion of unlike members. This is largely because the meaning of emptiness, which negates much of what is ordinarily conceived about the ontological nature of self, other, and the world, *simultaneously* underscores the interdependent, relational co-existence of self, other, and the world.

In these ways, the Prasangika-Madhyamika theory of emptiness parallels feminist critiques of patriarchy by questioning the ontological assumptions on which patriarchal power is premised. Moreover, and especially important for feminist thought, emptiness theory offers an option for a transformative perspective that need not, though it sometimes does, gain its leverage from a point outside the sphere of love, work, and relationship that is the domain of feminist endeavor.

Self-Concepts and Societies

In what ways, if any, might insights gleaned from Buddhist materials support, enrich, or shed light on the social issues women face today? On what basis do we even begin to assess this? Cultural disparities make it difficult to base judgment solely or even primarily on how women fared in traditional Buddhist societies. That they tended to have somewhat more respect and independence than their non-Buddhist Indian or Chinese counterparts does not clearly indicate how Buddhist theory might pertain to today's feminist concerns. In addition to the difficulty of taking the situation of pre-modern Asian women as a primary indicator here, there are other complexities.

Emptiness, understood as a quality of things and people, is equally compatible with terrorists, pacifists, misogynists, and feminists. As a quality of things therefore, emptiness is not a governing principle; it does not favor ontologically one type of quest over another. As a quality to be acknowledged or experienced however, emptiness does favor certain types of attitudes. We have also noted that the mind which understands or experiences emptiness is of necessity focused, clear, and inclined to be ethical, active, and compassionate. Any ethical or social implications of emptiness theory must derive primarily from the features and empathies of the mind engaged with it, and from the kind of society seen to foster the ontological and epistemological implications of this theory.

The further import of emptiness theory has to do with perceived integration of emptiness with, rather than its alienated distinctness from, those things and beings which are empty – that is to say, everything and everyone. This integration purveys an ontological model whose implications are at odds with much that is fundamental to patriarchy. The error of inherent existence that emptiness theory counters is a form of projection. According to the most prevalent system of Madhyamika such "projection" is automatic: it results from the erroneous way in which we make assumptions about what seems to inherently exist, and thus about the way things are by their very nature. By extension then, emptiness theory disputes the presumption that others, and in particular women, are by their nature persons to be molded by patriarchal projections in the name of family, culture, and tradition.

Emptiness theory undercuts patriarchal hierarchy in another way as well. It proposes the equal ontological *value* of all things and people, even though their functions may be assessed hierarchically. For example, in the "Advice to Singala Discourse,"[58] Buddha indicates the reciprocal, if not altogether equal, responsibilities between child and parents, student and teacher, master and servant and so forth. Although hierarchy is not questioned, each group is due specific forms of consideration and recognition from the other. This is similar to accepting equality before the law without at the same time asserting the equal talents of each individual. By contrast, patriarchy has often equated functional status with value. This results in the view that power inheres in the individuals and is not interdependently constituted. Emptiness theory can recognize existent hierarchies while maintaining the equal ontic value of each constituent.[59] Emptiness theory may not favor a particular social structure; yet, those who develop an understanding of emptiness presumably will also understand the interdependent nature of any social structure, and perhaps therefore may be freer from the constraints or rigidity of the patriarchal subject–object dyad. Whether this might bring about social change in North American culture as it has not in Buddhist cultures, and what sort of change that might be, cannot be predicted.[60]

Historically, emptiness theory has co-existed with intricately hierarchical societies in India, Tibet, China, and Japan. The Buddhist *sangha* or spiritual community itself, however, has not always reflected the hierarchical arrangement of the larger society. Indeed, since the inception of Buddhism, a distinction has been made between how the Buddhist spiritual community should operate and the politics of society at large. When the Buddhist community was initially formed in India during the fifth century BC, economic welfare and social stability were primary concerns. These were judged to be best maintained by supporting the monarchical institutions of the time.[61] Considerable emphasis was placed on the benevolent concern rulers should evince toward their subjects but the then-current tendency toward monarchy went unquestioned. The principle of benevolence was considered more important than egalitarianism. In other words, as is also true in Buddhist doctrines of karma and ethics, a king's or government's motivation and actual effect on persons was considered more crucial than social structure as such. Hierarchy itself was not repudiated. At the same time, the relational status of all constituents in the social hierarchy was emphasized.

In contrast to the larger social order, the Buddhist *sangha* operated by consensus.[62] "Every member of the *sangha* was regarded as having equality of rights in any deliberation concerning the life of the community."[63] This egalitarian trend deserves notice. Nevertheless, for a variety of reasons, the community of nuns was structurally subordinate to the community of monks, and younger monks subordinate to their elders. I. B. Horner has suggested that the former aspect of this structure was primarily a concession to Indian society. When Buddhism arose in the fifth century BC, the sanction of female clergy was itself a radical departure from centuries of tradition. At that period in Asia only the Jains had begun to offer similar opportunities to women. In any case, the legislated subordination of the community of nuns to that of monks does not seem to have been questioned. At the same time, there was open recognition of the equal spiritual possibilities for men and women, and in this important though not conclusive sense women and men – two groups in an institutionalized hierarchical relationship – were equal.[64]

Conclusion

Despite all the difficulties we face, many women have found and are finding ways to claim powerful identities that are not extensions of patriarchal value systems. Nevertheless, there are few theoretical models with which we can articulate and broaden such development. The Buddhist literature examined here offers an ontological model of selfhood that is non-oppositional and thus consonant with a feminist tendency to value connectedness over separation as a viable model for establishing identity.

An essential issue to date has been women's efforts to build a psychology of connectedness without addressing directly the assumed ontological status of the self that is so connected. The discrepancy between a psychology emphasizing connectedness and an ontology emphasizing reified isolation is counterproductive. Buddhist analyses of self as active and empty offers one approach to an articulation of selfhood that addresses the tension between social interrelatedness and psychological individuality.

Much of our discussion has focused on emptiness as an ontological theory. We have also considered the experiential dimension of emptiness, in particular the styles of subjectivity that occur in approaching and understanding it. Buddhist analysis here, uniting epistemological and ontological concerns, instances a closing of a major rift in Western thought, a rift currently critiqued by feminists. What we need is precisely to understand the subject – ourselves – *in relation to* the structures by which we organize meaning.

Having discussed the relevance of emptiness theory and the experience of emptiness for feminist questions regarding women's identity, and having distinguished briefly the import of emptiness and nihilism for feminist theory, we moved to its possible social import. This is ambiguous: on the one hand Buddhist traditions state that the effects of understanding emptiness are palpable. On the other hand, even in societies where significant portions of the population were either roughly familiar with or actively cultivating realization of emptiness, no one has yet claimed to discern a clear causal connection between that fact and specific social developments that affected women or men. Perhaps such effects will be hypothesized as our understanding of Buddhist cultures is refined. Still, it will be impossible to verify precisely how a particular given society has been tempered by its doctrines and practitioners of selflessness. Would any given culture have been more or less patriarchal, matriarchal, or hierarchical without exposure to these ideas? Nevertheless theoretical discussions of emptiness in Buddhist literature, including detailed descriptions of subjective styles associated with it, can help refine the categories of ontology and subjectivity on which feminist theory continues to build.[65]

Anne Carolyn Klein

Notes

1 Thomas C. Heller, Morton Sosna, and David E. Wellberry (eds.), *Reconstructing Individualism* (Stanford: Stanford University Press, 1986), p. 7.

2 Ibid., p. 10.

3 Ironically, although the main privilege patriarchy claims for its supposed beneficiaries is powerful autonomy, it sets in motion permutations of privilege that are in important ways confining. In commenting on an earlier version of this paper, Richard Niebuhr astutely observed that "one failure of patriarchy as it is commonly understood is that it does not take autonomy seriously enough; it substitutes a private or limited maxim for a true *nomos* or law."

4 See for example Marilyn Massey's discussion of Rich, Kristeva, and Irigaray in *Feminine Soul* (Boston: Beacon Press, 1985), pp. 184–8.

5 "The Way of All Ideology," *Signs* (Spring 1982), p. 643.

6 See Carol Gilligan, "Remapping the Moral Domain: New Images of Self in Relationship," in Heller et al. (eds.), *Reconstructing Individualism*, pp. 237–52.

7 Hélène Cixous, "The Laugh of the Medusa" in Elaine Marks and Isabelle de Courtivron (eds.), *New French Feminisms* (New York: Schocken Books, 1981), p. 264.

8 See Donna C. Stanton, "Language and Revolution: The Franco-American Disconnection," in Hester Eisenstein and Alice Jardine (eds.), *The Future of Difference* (Barnard College Women's Center) (Boston: G. K. Hall & Co., 1980), especially p. 76ff.

9 For excellent discussion of this, see Jane Flax, "Mother–Daughter Relationships: Psychodynamics," in Eisenstein and Jardine (eds.), *The Future of Difference*, p. 21ff.

10 Lee Yearley noted these categories to me in a different context, Stanford, January 9, 1987.

11 Jack Engler, "Therapeutic Aims in Psychotherapy and Meditation: Developmental Stages in the Representation of Self," in *Journal of Transpersonal Psychology* 16, no. 1 (1984), p. 25; this is a reworking of Engler's "Vicissitudes of the Self According to Psychoanalysis and Buddhism: A Spectrum Model of Object Relations Development," in *Psychoanalysis and Contemporary Thought* 6.1 (1983a), pp. 29–72.

12 For brief descriptions of these errors, see Jeffrey Hopkins, *Meditation on Emptiness* (London: Wisdom Publications, 1983), pp. 296–304.

13 Geshe Gedun Lodrö, "Calm abiding and Special Insight," unpublished MS, 1979, in discussion of Asanga's Levels of Hearers (*Śrāvakabhumi, Nyan sa*). There are four factors developed in the process of gaining calm abiding (*śamatha, gzhi gnas*). The factor of stability (*gnas cha*) signifies the ability to remain constantly with a chosen object; the factors of clarity refer to subjective clarity (*trang cha*), the clarity of both subject and object (*gsal cha*) and intensity (*ngar*).

14 For discussion of female symbolism associated with Buddhist wisdom see A. Klein, "Non-Dualism and the Great Bliss Queen," in *Journal of Feminist Studies in Religion*, vol. 1 (1985). Regarding the relationship between such female symbolism and the lives of actual women in Tibet, see "Primordial Purity and Everyday Life," in Clarissa Atkinson, Constance Buchanan, and Margaret Miles (eds.), *Immaculate and Powerful: The Female in Sacred Image and Social Reality* (Harvard Women's Studies in Religion Series) (Boston: Beacon Press, 1985), pp. 111–38.

15 *Pure Lust* (Boston: Beacon Press, 1984), p. 30.

16 *Feminine Soul*, p. 184.

17 "The Laugh of the Medusa," in Marks and de Courtivron (eds.), *New French Feminisms*, p. 259.

18 For a classic discussion of simple awareness, see the discourse on the "Foundations of Mindfulness" (*Mahā-satipatthāna sutta*), trans. in *Heart of Buddhist Meditation* (London: Rider and Co., 1969). For a concise discussion of the development of calm abiding, see Hopkins, *Meditation on Emptiness*, pp. 80–90. We can compare this developed awareness, for example, with Hegel's self-consciousness which, in revealed religion, is "aware of itself in pictorial objectification, not as yet *as* self-consciousness," *Hegel's Phenomenology of Spirit* VIII.788, trans. by Miller and Findlay (Oxford: Clarendon Press, 1977), p. 589. "Self-consciousness . . . necessarily involves consciousness of self as object . . . [it] is impossible apart from self-objectification" (Mark Taylor, *Journeys to Selfhood: Hegel and Kierkegaard* (Berkeley: University of California Press, 1980), p. 186). The object but not the *style* of such awareness is focal here. Further, if we accept Donna Stanton's statement that for Hegel "the knowing subject called 'consciousness of self' . . . emerges as a unity and passes through one transcendent act of cognition after another" (in Eisenstein and Jardine (eds.), *Future of Difference*, p. 74), this is patently not the case in Buddhism where awareness itself reveals the arising and ceasing of one moment of consciousness followed by another. See also Charles Taylor, *Human Agency and Language* (Cambridge: Cambridge University Press, 1985), pp. 80–8.

19 *Pure Lust*, pp. xii and 89.

20 *Four Gated City* (London: MacGibbon and Kee, 1969), p. 36.

21 Ibid., p. 37.

22 Ibid., p. 38.

23 In the literature on calm abiding, "simple awareness" is distinguished from the function of introspection (*samprajanya, shes bzhin*); this latter is the factor of mind that notices whether faults such as laxity or excitement are present. See Hopkins, *Meditation on Emptiness*, pp. 74–6. A classic distinction between

mindfulness and introspection is made in the Shantideva's *Engaging in the Bodhisattva Deeds* (*Bodhisattvacāryāvatāra, spyod 'jug*), 1979.

24 *Sex Sin and Grace: Women's Experience and the Theologies of Reinhold Niebuhr and Paul Tillich* (Washington DC: University Press of America, 1980).

25 Conversation with Constance Buchanan, Cambridge, Mass., July 1985.

26 Conversation with Hester Gelber and Rose Anne Christian, at Stanford University, April 1986, helped clarify this last point. The relationship between vitality or energy and clarity or awareness is an interesting one, especially if one takes account of tantric perspectives. I hope to do so elsewhere; space does not permit it here.

27 For a discussion of the characteristics of mind associated with *any* wholesome consciousness, including simple mindfulness, see Angarika Govinda, *The Psychological Attitude of Early Buddhist Philosophy* (London: Rider, 1969), pp. 120–1. The classic Theravada source for this is Buddhaghosa's *Visuddhimagga* (*Path of Purification*), Shambala, 1976 reprint.

28 Christ and Plaskow (eds.), *Womenspirit Rising* (New York: Harper & Row, 1979), p. 37.

29 *The Four Gated City*, p. 247.

30 Conversation with Courtney Thompson, Stanford University, November 1985.

31 Discussed in the chapter "Perfection of Wisdom" of the fifth Dalai Lama's "Sacred Word of Manjushri" translated by Jeffrey Hopkins as "Practice of Emptiness" (Dharamsala: Library of Tibetan Works and Archives, 1974), pp. 11–12.

32 Elizabeth Napper, "Dependent-Arising and Emptiness," unpublished Ph.D. dissertation, University of Virginia, 1985 [forthcoming from Wisdom Publications, London, 1987], p. 106. The text under discussion is "Great Exposition of Special Insight" from his *Great Exposition of the Stages of the Path* (*Lam rim chen mo*). Peking Tibetan Tripitaka, p. 6001, vol. 152.

33 Ibid., p. 269.

34 Michel Foucault, *Discipline and Punish: The Birth of the Prison*, trans. Alan Sheridan (New York: Vintage Books, 1979), p. 50; discussed in Massey, *Feminine Soul*, p. 40.

35 Conversation with Marilyn Massey, November 7, 1985, Stanford, Calif. For an exemplary discussion of the perils of such an idea, see Massey, *Feminine Soul*, passim, but especially pp. 26–9.

36 Buddhism also has both these models of discovery and development. As I hope to show elsewhere, this has been a major area of debate among numerous groups of Buddhist exponents.

37 Tenzin Gyatso, the Fourteenth Dalai Lama, *Kindness, Clarity, and Insight* (Ithaca: Snow Lion Publications, 1984), p. 162.

38 "The Laugh of the Medusa," p. 259.

39 For further discussion of this analysis, see Hopkins, *Meditation on Emptiness*, pp. 43–51, 677–97.

40 *Kindness, Clarity and Insight*, p. 262.

41 For discussion of this see Hopkins, *Meditation on Emptiness*, especially Part I, chapters 1–4, and Part II.

42 Gilligan, "Remapping the Moral Domain," pp. 240–1.

43 Kelsang Gyatso, *Meaningful to Behold* (London: Wisdom Publications, 1980), p. 236.

44 Harvey Aronson, "Altruism and Adversity: Perspectives from Psychoanalytic Object Relations Theory," unpublished paper delivered at the Tibetan Buddhist Learning Center, July 1985, pp. 12–16, and Aronson, "Guru Yoga – A Buddhist Meditative Visualization: Observations Based Upon Psychoanalytic Object Relations Theory and Self-Psychology," unpublished paper delivered at American Academy of Religion Meeting at Anaheim, Calif., November 1985, pp. 43–8.

45 For an exploration of how this is empowering and why all forms of compassion are not, see A. Klein, "Gain or Drain: Buddhist and Feminist Views on Compassion," *Spring Wind*, Ann Arbor, Mich., vol. 6, nos. 1, 2, and 3 (1986). For a discussion of early Buddhist views on the relationship between insight and compassion, see Harvey Aronson, *Love and Sympathy in Theravada Buddhism* (New Delhi: Motilal Banarsidas, 1980), pp. 93–4.

46 Quoted by Nga-wang-den-dzin-dorje in *Ra Dik*, 37.5; trans. Klein, unpublished ms., p. 14. Selections from this text appear in *Tibet Journal*, Spring/Summer 1987. Further reflections on the nature of the subjectivity involved in cognizing emptiness, as I hope to elaborate elsewhere, pertain to classic discussions of the "womb of the Buddha" (Tathāgathagarbha).

47 See chapter 13 of Shantideva's *Engaging in the Bodhisattva Deeds* (*Bodhisattvacāryāvatāra*) translated and commented upon by Kelsang Gyatso in *Meaningful to Behold* (London: Wisdom Publications, 1980), p. 237.

48 Michael Novak, *The Experience of Nothingness* (New York: Harper Torchbooks, 1978), p. 13.

49 Ibid., p. 14. See also Christ, *Diving Deep and Surfacing* (Boston: Beacon Press, 1980), pp. 14–15. She points out that Mary Daly was the first to notice the significance of Novak's categories for women, first in her review of Novak's book ("Critics' choices," *Commonweal*, vol. 93, no. 21 (February 26, 1971), p. 526, and later in *Beyond God the Father*.

50 *Beyond God the Father* (Boston: Beacon Press, 1973), p. 7.

51 *Experience of Nothingness*, p. 15.

52 Ibid., p. 65. The illuminating despair of which Novak speaks may roughly parallel how some in the Buddhist tradition initially relate to expositions of emptiness. This occurs because of misinterpreting their import nihilistically. Such misinterpretation is taken as a sign that instruction on emptiness is inappropriate for that person at that time. Tsong-ka-pa in the

Perfection of Wisdom section of his *Clarification of the Thought* (*dbU ma dgong ba rab gsal*) states that those who will construe the discussion of emptiness to mean that cause and effect are not operative, or that nothing really exists at all, are not suitable even to begin study of the topic of emptiness (Sarnath, 1983, 119.12.9ff). Their error results from overextending the significance of emptiness and therefore negating more than is intended. Tsong-ka-pa labels such an error an abandoning of emptiness. Because it denies the interdependent existence of agents, activities, and other phenomena, this view represents a failure of understanding, an abandonment of emptiness.

53 This emphasis is especially strong in Gelukba discussions of emptiness.

54 Keiji Nishitani, *Religion and Nothingness*, trans. Jan Van Bragt (Berkeley: University of California Press, 1982), p. 85 and p. 123ff.

55 Ibid., p. 123.

56 Quoted in *The Buddhism of Tibet* by H. H. Tenzin Gyatso, trans. Jeffrey Hopkins (London: Allen & Unwin, 1975), p. 73.

57 See Daly's critique of Tillich as unduly fascinated by non-being in *Pure Lust*, pp. 29–30.

58 From the *Dīghanikāya*, iii.180ff.; trans. in de Bary (ed.), *The Buddhist Tradition* (New York: The Modern Library, 1969), pp. 39–44.

59 This theoretical framework developed in conversation with Harvey Aronson, October 1986.

60 There is also the matter of what an individual's involvement with religious practices associated with emptiness might imply for the larger society. That such involvement, even in Buddhist countries, is not likely to be the province of large groups of a portion of the population, does not foreclose the possibility of their having some effect on society. Durkheim, focusing on how ascetics affect the social order, writes:

> It is necessary that an elite put the end too high if the crowd is not to put it too low. It is necessary that some exaggerate, if the average is to remain at a fitting level. [Quoted by Trevor Ling, *Elementary Forms of the Religious Life* (New York: Collier Books, 1961), p. 170.]

This assumes however that those who "exaggerate" – that is, who devote their lives to cultivating and living in accordance with the subjective styles associated with emptiness theory, are somehow significant cultural figures. Generations of women, for example, have lived their lives in ways antithetical to patriarchal perspectives ("unconcerned" with the hierarchies that obtain there) without this factor even being noticed, let alone seen as an example for the rest of society.

61 Quoted by Trevor Ling, *The Buddha* (New York: Collier Books, 1961), p. 3ff.

62 Ibid., pp. 172–4.

63 Ibid., p. 159.

64 See Nancy Falk, "The Case of the Vanishing Nuns," in Nancy Falk and Rita Gross (eds.), *Unspoken Worlds: Women's Religious Lives in Non-Western Cultures* (San Francisco: Harper & Row, 1982); see also I. B. Horner, *Women Under Primitive Buddhism* (London: Routledge and Kegan Paul, 1930; reprinted in Delhi: Motilal Banarsidas, 1975).

65 Thanks to P. J. Ivanhoe, of Stanford University, for a careful reading and good discussion of this article.

28

How Many Nondualities Are There?

David Loy

No concept is more important in Asian philosophical and religious thought than *nonduality* (Sanskrit *advaya* and *advaita*, Tibetan *gÑismed*, Chinese *pu-erh*, Japanese *fu-ni*), and none is more ambiguous. The term has been used in many different although related ways, and to my knowledge the distinctions between these meanings have never been fully clarified. These meanings are distinct, although they often overlap in particular instances. This chapter distinguishes these different meanings, explores the relationships among them, demonstrates their importance for what I call "the nondualist systems," and reflects on the significance of all the above.

The following types of nonduality are discussed here: the negation of dualistic thinking, the non-plurality of the world, and the nondifference of subject and object. In subsequent chapters [not included here], our attention focuses primarily on the last of these three, although there will be occasion to consider two other nondualities which are also closely related: first, what has been called the identity of phenomena and Absolute, or the Mahāyāna equation of *saṁsāra* and *nirvāṇa*, which can also be expressed as "the nonduality of duality and nonduality"; second, the possibility of a mystical unity between God and man. No doubt other nondualities can be distinguished, but most of them can be subsumed under one or more of the above categories. As the negative construction of the word

in all languages suggests, the meaning of each nonduality can be understood only by reference to the particular duality that is being denied. We shall quickly see that each of these negations has both an ontological and a soteriological function; the term is used to criticize our usual dualistic experience (or understanding of experience) as both delusive and unsatisfactory, and the corresponding nondual mode is recommended as both veridical and superior.

The Negation of Dualistic Thinking

> It is because there is "is" that there is "is not"; it is because there is "is not" that there is "is." This being the situation, the sages do not approach things on this level, but reflect the light of nature.
>
> ***Chuang Tzu***[1]

Our first nonduality is a critique of "dualistic thinking," that is, of thinking which differentiates that-which-is-thought-about into two opposed categories: being and nonbeing, success and failure, life and death, enlightenment and delusion, and so on. The problem with such thinking is that, although distinctions are usually made in order to choose one or the other, we cannot take one without the other since they are interdependent; in affirming one half of the duality we maintain the other as well.

> Without relation to "good" there is no "bad," in dependence on which we form the idea of "good." Therefore "good" is unintelligible.

There is no "good" unrelated to "bad"; yet we form our idea of "bad" in dependence on it. There is therefore no "bad." (Nāgārjuna)[2]

This abstract point becomes more relevant when, for example, we consider the problem of how to live a "pure" life. The implication of Nāgārjuna's argument is that attempting to live a pure life involves a preoccupation with impurity. In order to have only pure thoughts and actions, one must avoid impure ones, and this means determining to which of the two categories each thought and action belongs. It is generally claimed that this dichotomizing tendency of mind keeps us from experiencing situations as they really are in themselves, when no such dualistic categories as pure and impure, good and bad, and so on, are applicable. These warnings are especially common in Mahāyāna Buddhism:

> Dānapāramitā [literally, perfect or transcendental generosity] means relinquishment . . . of the dualism of opposites. It means total relinquishment of ideas as to the dual nature of good and bad, being and nonbeing, love and aversion, void and not void, concentration and distraction, pure and impure. By giving all of them up, we attain to a state in which all opposites are seen as void.

> Thinking in terms of being and non-being is called wrong thinking, while not thinking in those terms is called right thinking. Similarly, thinking in terms of good and evil is wrong; not to think so is right thinking. The same applies to all the other categories of opposites – sorrow and joy, beginning and end . . . all of which are called wrong thinking, while to abstain from thinking in those categories is called right thinking. (Hui Hai)[3]

The second passage contains a claim which negates itself, as Hui Hai must have realized: dualistic thinking is criticized as wrong thinking, but the distinction between right and wrong thinking is itself dualistic. So, in fact, is the very distinction between dualistic and nondualistic thinking, or between duality and nonduality generally. Carried to this extreme, "the perfection of wisdom (prajñāpāramitā) should not be viewed from duality nor from nonduality."[4] Therefore such teaching naturally tends toward self-negation and paradox, due to its apparent violation of logic, especially the law of identity:

Q: The Vimalakīrti Nirdeśa Sūtra says: "Whosoever desires to reach the Pure Land must first purify his mind." What is the meaning of this purifying of the mind?

A: It means purifying it to the point of ultimate purity.

Q: But what does that mean?

A: It is a state beyond purity and impurity. . . . Purity pertains to a mind which dwells upon nothing whatsoever. To attain this without so much as a thought of purity arising is called absence of purity; and to achieve that without giving that a thought is to be free from absence of purity also. (Hui Hai)[5]

In other words, "purity is not purity; that is why it is purity." This paradox – A is not A, therefore it is A – is found in its clearest form in the Prajñāpāramitā literature. The Diamond Sutra, for example, contains many instances:

> Subhūti, the so-called good virtues, the Tathāgata says, are not good, but are called good virtues.

> Subhūti, when [the Tathāgata] expounds the dharma, there is really no dharma to teach: but this is called teaching the dharma.[6]

This paradox finds its "purest" philosophical expression in Mādhyamika. Nāgārjuna insisted that the Buddha himself had no philosophical views, and his own approach was solely concerned to demonstrate that all philosophical positions are self-contradictory and untenable. In the process he had occasion to employ the term śūnyatā (emptiness), but woe to him who grasps this snake by the wrong end and takes śūnyatā as making some positive assertion about the nature of reality: "The spiritual conquerors have proclaimed śūnyatā to be the exhaustion of all theories and views; those for whom śūnyatā is itself a theory they declare to be incurable."[7] Insofar as the assertion of any philosophical position negates the opposite view, Mādhyamika may be said to have developed the critique of dualistic thinking to its most extreme philosophical conclusions. Ch'an (Zen) took this one step further and eliminated even Nāgārjuna's anti-philosophy:

> The fundamental dharma of the dharma is that there are no dharmas, yet that this dharma of no-dharma is in itself a dharma; and now that

the no-dharma dharma has been transmitted, how can the dharma of the dharma be a dharma? (Huang Po)[8]

The result of this was that no teaching whatsoever – not even anti-teaching – remained to be taught. Instead, Ch'an masters used various unconventional and illogical techniques to awaken a student, which in this context means to make the student let go of any dualities that he or she still clings to.

But isn't it the general nature of all reasoning to move between assertion and negation, between "it *is*" and "it is *not*"? The critique of dualistic thinking thus often expands to include all conceptual thinking or conceptualization.

> You can never come to enlightenment through inference, cognition, or conceptualization. Cease clinging to all thought-forms! I stress this, because it is the central point of all Zen practice. . . .
> . . . You must melt down your delusions. . . . The opinions you hold and your worldly knowledge are your delusions. Included also are philosophical and moral concepts, no matter how lofty, as well as religious beliefs and dogmas, not to mention innocent, commonplace thoughts. In short, all conceivable ideas are embraced within the term "delusions" and as such are a hindrance to the realization of your Essential-nature. (Yasutani)[9]

This expanded version of the critique seems to encompass all thinking whatsoever, obliterating Hui Hai's distinction between wrong thinking and right thinking. Now the problem with dualistic categories is that they are part of a conceptual grid which we normally but unconsciously superimpose upon our immediate experience and which deludes us by distorting that experience. Yasutani's admonition is so absolute that it seems to condemn all possible thought-processes, but such a radical "inflation" only strengthens the obvious objection to this type of critique: whether it is (more narrowly) dualistic thinking or (more generally) conceptual thinking that is problematic and to be rejected, what is the alternative? What kind of thinking remains? If all language seems to dualize, in distinguishing subject from predicate/attribute, how can there be such a thing as nondual, or nonconceptual, thinking? Can we get along without dualistic categories? And even if we can, is it desirable? The nature of any alternative – or is it no thinking whatsoever?

– needs to be explained, and its feasibility defended. But the issue cannot be resolved at this stage in our inquiry.

The Nonplurality of the World

> What is here, the same is there; and what is there, the same is here. He goes from death to death who sees any difference here.
> By the mind alone is Brahman to be realized; then one does not see in It any multiplicity whatsoever. He goes from death to death who sees any multiplicity in It.
> **Kaṭha Upaniṣad**[10]

It is due to the superimpositions of dualistic thinking that we experience the world itself dualistically in our second sense: as a collection of discrete objects (one of them being *me*) causally interacting in space and time. The negation of dualistic thinking leads to the negation of this way of experiencing the world. This brings us to the second sense of nonduality: that the world itself is nonplural, because all the things "in" the world are not really distinct from each other but together constitute some integral whole. The relation between these two senses of nonduality is shown by Huang Po at the very beginning of his Chun Chou record:

> All the Buddhas and all sentient beings are nothing but the One Mind, beside which nothing exists. This mind, which is without beginning, is unborn and undestructible. It is not green nor yellow, and has neither form nor appearance. It does not belong to the categories of things which exist or do not exist, nor can it be thought about in terms of new or old. It is neither long nor short, big nor small, for it transcends all limits, measures, names, traces and comparisons. It is that which you see before you – begin to reason about it and you at once fall into error.[11]

This asserts more than that everything is composed of some indefinable substance. The unity of everything "in" the world means that each thing is a manifestation of a "spiritual" whole because the One Mind incorporates all consciousness and all minds. This whole – indivisible, birthless, and deathless – has been designated by a variety of terms; as well as the One Mind, there are the Tao, Brahman, the Dharmakāya, and so on.

There is a beginning which contains everything.
Before heaven and earth it exists:
Calm! Formless!
It stands alone and does not change.
It pervades everywhere unhindered.
It might therefore be called the world's mother.
I do not know its name; but I call it the Tao.

(Tao Tê Ching)[12]

Now, all this [universe] was then undifferentiated. It became differentiated by name and form: it was known by such and such a name, and such and such a form. Thus to this day this [universe] is differentiated by name and form; [so it is said:] He has such a name and such a form. (Bṛhadāraṇyaka Upaniṣad)[13]

Changes in one's train of thought produce corresponding changes in one's conception of the external world. . . .
   As a thing is viewed, so it appears.
   To see things as a multiplicity, and so to cleave unto separateness, is to err. (Padmasambhava)[14]

The mechanism of differentiation identified in this passage from the Bṛhadāraṇyaka Upaniṣad – nāmarūpa (name and form), which is a common Vedāntic description of māyā – is also mentioned in the first chapter of the Tao Tê Ching, where it serves the same function in differentiating the Tao. Compare too the following quotation from Chuang Tzu:

The knowledge of the ancients was perfect. How perfect? At first, they did not know that there were things. This is the most perfect knowledge; nothing can be added. Next, they knew that there were things, but did not yet make distinctions between them. Next they made distinctions among them, but they did not yet pass judgements upon them. When judgements were passed, Tao was destroyed.[15]

Thus we have passages from four different traditions – the Upaniṣads, Tibetan Buddhism, Taoism, and Zen – which explicitly affirm the same relationship between these first two senses of nonduality: that dualistic conceptual thinking is what causes us to experience a pluralistic world.

If we compare the following two passages with the long quotation from Huang Po at the beginning

of this section, we have our first encounter with a controversy that develops into a major theme of this book:

This Self is that which has been described as not this, not this. It is imperceptible, for It is not perceived; undecaying, for It never decays; unattached, for It is never attached; unfettered, for It never feels pain and never suffers injury. (Bṛhadāraṇyaka Upaniṣad)[16]

Gaze at it; there is nothing to see.
It is called the formless.
Heed it; there is nothing to hear.
It is called the soundless.
Grasp it; there is nothing to hold onto.
It is called the immaterial . . .
   . . .
Invisible, it cannot be called by any name.
It returns again to nothingness.
Thus, we call it the form of the formless
The image of the imageless.

(Tao Tê Ching)[17]

These selections claim that the Ātman/Tao is not perceptible. Huang Po agrees that the One Mind is formless, colorless, and without appearance, yet he also says "it is that which you see before you." In the next chapter Śaṅkara is quoted to the same effect: "the universe is an unbroken series of perceptions of Brahman." This brings us to the inevitable question about the relationship between the nonplural Ātman/Tao/One Mind and the multiple sensible particulars of this world. Are phenomena merely delusive māyā (illusions) that obscure this attributeless Mind, or are they manifestations of It? Strictly speaking, perhaps the former view cannot be said to maintain nonplurality as the unity of phenomena, but rather postulates a monistic ground that "underlies" them. This seems to create another duality – between phenomena and Mind, between duality and nonduality – which becomes problematic, as we shall see. In contrast, the latter view does not necessarily imply monism at all, depending on how monism is defined. A weaker version of pluralism, that there are many things, may be compatible with a weaker version of monism, that there is only one type of thing (e.g., Mind), of which the many particulars are manifestations – a perspective which is important for understanding Mahāyāna metaphysics.

The Upaniṣads and the *Tao Tê Ching* also contain passages which imply another intermediate position between monism and pluralism: that the Ātman/Tao functions as a first cause which created the phenomenal world and then pervades it as a kind of spiritual essence. The first passage quoted above from the Bṛhadāraṇyaka Upaniṣad continues:

> This Self has entered into these bodies up to the very tips of the nails, as a razor lies [hidden] in its case, or as fire, which sustains the world, [lies hidden] in its source.[18]

There is the same claim in the Kaṭha Upaniṣad:

> As the same nondual fire, after it has entered the world, becomes different according to whatever it burns, so also the same nondual Ātman, dwelling in all beings, becomes different according to whatever It enters. And It exists also without.[19]

Such a view may be criticized as incomplete – as tending toward, but stopping short of, complete nonduality in the second sense; despite differences in their perspective, neither Huang Po nor Śaṅkara would accept such a distinction between pervader and pervaded. Perhaps the difference is due to the unrigorous nature of these early works, for both the *Tao Tê Ching* and the Upaniṣads are collections of mystical insights rather than systematic philosophical works.

It is noteworthy that, although there are many references to the Tao in Taoist texts and to Ātman/Brahman in Vedānta, there are fewer such references in Buddhism. There is not even any agreed-upon term; a variety of expressions are used: *dharmadhātu*, *dharmakāya*, *tathatā*, *vijñāptimātratā*, and so on. These are all Mahāyāna terms; there is no good equivalent in Pāli Buddhism because early Buddhism is more pluralistic in its preoccupation with the interrelations of dharmas. Generally, Buddhism, with the exception of Yogācāra, is hesitant to assert a nondual whole in this second sense, preferring to emphasize that everything is empty (*śūnya*) while offering admonitions against dualistic thinking. This inverse proportion is quite logical: dualistic thinking in the broad sense includes any conceptual labeling, hence one should not name even the nondual whole. After all, any Tao that can be Tao'd is not the real Tao.

The Nondifference of Subject and Object

> I came to realize clearly that mind is no other than mountains, rivers, and the great wide earth, the sun and the moon and the stars.
> **Dōgen**[20]

We have seen the connection between the first two dualities: it is because of our dualistic ways of thinking that we perceive the world pluralistically. The relationship between the corresponding nondualities is parallel: the world as a collection of discrete things (including *me*) in space and time is not something objectively given, which we merely observe passively; if our ways of thinking change, that world changes also for us. But there is still something lacking in this formulation. By itself it is incomplete, for it leaves unclarified the relation between the subject and the nondual world that the subject experiences. It was stated earlier that the nondual whole is "spiritual" because the One Mind includes my mind, but *how* consciousness could be incorporated has not been explained. The world is not really experienced as a whole if the subject that perceives it is still separate from it in its observation *of* it. In this way the second sense of nonduality, conceived objectively, is unstable and naturally tends to evolve into a third sense. This third sense, like the other two, must be understood as a negation. The dualism denied is our usual distinction between subject and object, an experiencing self that is distinct from what is experienced, be it sense-object, physical action, or mental event. The corresponding nonduality is experience in which there is no such distinction between subject and object. However extraordinary and counterintuitive such nonduality may be, it is an essential element of many Asian systems (and some Western ones, of course). Since the primary purpose of this work is to analyze this third sense of nonduality, it is necessary to establish in detail the prevalence and significance of this concept.

We begin with Vedānta. Several of the most important passages in the Upaniṣads assert this nonduality; for example, these famous ones from the Bṛhadāraṇyaka:

> Because when there is duality, as it were, then one smells something, one sees something, one hears something, one speaks something, one

David Loy

thinks something, one knows something. [But] when to the knower of Brahman everything has become the Self, then what should one smell and through what, what should one see and through what, [repeated for hearing, speaking, thinking and knowing]? Through what should one know That owing to which all this is known – through what, O Maitreyī, should one know the Knower?

And when [it appears that] in deep sleep it does not see, yet it is seeing though it does not see; for there is no cessation of the vision of the seer, because the seer is imperishable. There is then, however, no second thing separate from the seer that it could see. [To emphasize the point, this verse is repeated, in place of seeing substituting smelling, tasting, speaking, hearing, thinking, touching and knowing.][21]

The nonduality of subject and object also constitutes the heart of the short Īśā Upaniṣad: "To the seer, all things have verily become the Self: what delusion, what sorrow, can there be for him who beholds that oneness?"[22] The Taittirīya Upaniṣad concludes with it:

He [who knows Brahman] sits, singing the chant of the nonduality of Brahman: "Ah! Ah! Ah!"
"I am food, I am food, I am food! I am the eater of food, I am the eater of food, I am the eater of food! I am the uniter, I am the uniter, I am the uniter!
". . . He who eats food – I, as food, eat him."[23]

So many other passages could be cited that I can say, with no exaggeration, that asserting this third sense of nonduality constitutes the central claim of the Upaniṣads. It is most often expressed as the identity between Ātman (the Self) and Brahman, implied by the most famous mahāvākya (great saying) of all: tat tvam asi (that thou art).[24] Such an interpretation is of course crucial to Advaita (lit., nondual) Vedānta, and the great Advaitin philosopher Śaṅkara devoted an entire work to expounding it, the short Vākyavṛtti. A stanza from the Ātmabodha gives a clear and succinct expression of his view:

The distinction of the knower, knowledge, and the goal of knowledge does not endure in the all-transcendent Self. Being of the nature of Bliss that is Pure Consciousness, it shines of Itself.[25]

In his commentary on passages from the Bṛhadāraṇyaka quoted above, Śaṅkara insists that our usual sense of subject–object duality is delusive:

When, in the waking or dream state, there is something else besides the self, as it were, presented by ignorance, then one, thinking of oneself as different from that something – though there is nothing different from the self, nor is there any self different from it – can see something.[26]

The phrase "as it were" (Sanskrit, iva) emphasizes that the appearance to the subject of something objective is what constitutes avidyā, ignorance or delusion. This claim is by no means unique to Vedānta; it is found in virtually all the Asian philosophies that assert this third sense of nonduality: our experience not only can be but already is and always was nondual; any sense of a subject apart from that which is experienced is an illusion. According to this view, it is not correct to say that our usual experience is dualistic, for all experience is actually nondual. The spiritual path involves eliminating only the delusion of duality. However variously the different systems may otherwise characterize this nondual reality, the goal is simply to realize and live this nondual nature.

The foremost Advaitin of the twentieth century supports and restates the traditional Vedāntic position on nonduality:

The duality of subject and object, the trinity of seer, sight and seen can exist only if supported by the One. If one turns inward in search of that One Reality, they fall away.

The world is perceived as an apparent objective reality when the mind is externalized, thereby abandoning its identity with the Self. When the world is thus perceived the true nature of the Self is not revealed; conversely, when the Self is realized the world ceases to appear as an objective reality. (Ramana Maharshi)[27]

Advaita Vedānta clearly asserts nonduality in our third sense, to the extent of making it the central tenet. The case of Buddhism is more complicated. Ontologically, Pāli Buddhism, which bases itself on what are understood to be the original teachings of the Buddha, seems pluralistic. Reality is understood to consist of a multitude of discrete particulars (dharmas). The self is analyzed away into five "heaps" (*skandhas*) which the Abhidharma (the "higher dharma," a philosophical abstract of the Buddha's teachings) classifies and systematizes. So early Buddhism, while critical of dualistic thinking, is not nondual in the second, monistic, sense. Regarding the nondifference of subject and object, the issue is less clear. While the second sense of nonduality logically implies some version of the third, it is not true that a denial of the second sense implies a denial of the third. The world might be a composite of discrete experiences which are nondual in the third sense. I am not acquainted with any passage in the Pāli Canon that clearly asserts the nonduality of subject and object, as one finds in so many Mahāyāna texts. But I have also found no denial of such nonduality. One may view the *anātman* (no-self) doctrine of early Buddhism as another way of making the same point; instead of asserting that subject and object are one, the Buddha simply denies that there is a subject. These two formulations may well amount to the same thing, although the latter may be criticized as ontologically lopsided: since subject and object are interdependent, the subject cannot be eliminated without transforming the nature of the object (and vice-versa, as Advaita Vedānta was aware). [. . .]

Mahāyāna Buddhism abounds in assertions of subject–object nonduality, despite the fact that the most important Mahāyāna philosophy, Mādhyamika, cannot be said to assert nonduality at all, since it makes few (if any) positive claims but confines itself to refuting all philosophical positions. Mādhyamika is *advayavāda* (the theory of not-two, here meaning neither of two alternative views, our first sense of nonduality) rather than *advaitavāda* (the theory of nondifference between subject and object, our third sense).[28] *Prajñā* is understood to be nondual knowledge, but this again is *advaya*, knowledge devoid of views. Nāgārjuna neither asserts nor denies the experience of nonduality in the third sense, despite the fact that Mādhyamika dialectic criticizes the self-existence of both subject and object, since as relative to each other they must both be unreal.

Nāgārjuna holds that dependent origination is nothing else but the coming to rest of the manifold of named things (*prapañcopaśama*). When the everyday mind and its contents are no longer active, the subject and object of everyday transactions having faded out because the turmoil of origination, decay, and death has been left behind completely, that is final beatitude. (Candrakīrti)[29]

In comparison, Yogācāra literature contains many explicit passages asserting the identity of subject and object. These from Vasubandhu are perhaps the best known:

Through the attainment of the state of Pure Consciousness, there is the non-perception of the perceivable; and through the non-perception of the perceivable (i.e., the object) there is the non-acquisition of the mind (i.e., the subject).

Through the non-perception of these two, there arises the realization of the Essence of Reality (*dharmadhātu*).[30]

Where there is an object there is a subject, but not where there is no object. The absence of an object results in the absence also of a subject, and not merely in that of grasping. It is thus that there arises the cognition which is homogeneous, without object, indiscriminate and supermundane. The tendencies to treat object and subject as distinct and real entities are forsaken, and thought is established in just the true nature of one's thought. (Vasubandhu)[31]

The Yogācāra claim of *cittamātra* (mind-only), that only mind or consciousness exists, predictably gave rise to the misinterpretation (corrected in recent works) that Yogācāra is a form of subjective idealism. But subjectivism is not an aspect of any Buddhist school, nor, given the vital role of the anātman doctrine, could it be. As these two passages imply, for Yogācāra the apparently objective world is not a projection of my ego-consciousness. Rather, the delusive bifurcation between subject and object arises within nondual Mind. So in the *parinispanna-svabhāva* (absolutely accomplished nature), which is the highest state of existence, experience is without subject–object duality. In Yogācāra the claim that experience is nondual, in all three of our senses, attains full development and explicitness, and so it is fitting that with that claim Buddhist philosophy may be said to have reached its culmination. What followed were derivative elaborations and syntheses (popular in Chinese Buddhism, e.g., T'ien T'ai and Hua Yen) and the application of these philosophical perspectives to practice (especially Pure Land, Ch'an, and tantric Buddhism). What is most significant for us is that the third sense of nonduality, the nondifference between subject and object, was essential to all of them. (Hereafter, unless otherwise noted, the term *nonduality* will always refer to this third sense.)

The nonduality of subject and object is also the central concept of both Hindu and Buddhist tantra, according to S. B. Dasgupta:

The ultimate goal of both the schools is the perfect state of union – union between the two aspects of the reality and the realization of the nondual nature of the self and the not-self. The principle of Tantricism being fundamentally the same everywhere, the superficial differences, whatever these may be, supply only different tone and colour.

The synthesis or rather the unification of all duality in an absolute unity is the real principle of union, which has been termed *Yuganaddha* ... the real principle of *Yuganaddha* is the absence of the notion of duality as the perceivable (*grāhya*) and the perceiver (*grāhaka*) and their perfect synthesis in a unity.[32]

Evans-Wentz's translations of Tibetan Buddhist texts provide examples to support Dasgupta's view. From the "Yoga of Knowing the Mind," attributed to Padmasaṁbhava:

There being really no duality, pluralism is un-true.

Until duality is transcended and at-one-ment realized, enlightenment cannot be attained.

The whole *Sangsara* and *Nirvana*, as an inseparable unity, are one's mind. . . .

The unenlightened externally see the externally-transitory dually.[33]

We find this exemplified in the *Mahāmudrā* (Yoga of the Great Symbol), which provides a set of graded meditations. The final two practices are, first, "the Yoga of Transmuting all Phenomena and Mind, which are inseparable, into At-one-ment (or Unity)." This involves meditations on the nonduality between sleep and dreams, water and ice, water and waves. Finally, there is "the Yoga of Non-Meditation," which simply signifies the end of effort, since with the above transmutation into nonduality one has completed the Path: "one obtaineth the Supreme Boon of the Great Symbol, the Unabiding State of Nirvana."[34]

More recently, the Italian scholar Guiseppe Tucci has summarized the final objective of Tibetan Buddhist soteriology as follows:

Higher cognition is the penetrating to, and cognizing of, the true nature of these appearances, of these forms created by our discursive knowledge, these products of a false dichotomy between subject and object. . . . The final objective remains the awakening of that higher cognition, that *shes rab*, Sanskrit *prajñā*, in the adept's consciousness, which enables him to survey the ultimate nature of all things with the clarity of direct insight; in other words, the transcending of the subject–object dichotomy.[35]

In his voluminous writings on Zen, D. T. Suzuki repeatedly emphasized that the *satori* experience is the realization of nonduality. For example, in the first series of his *Essays on Zen Buddhism*, during a discussion of "original Mind," he states that "there is no separation between knower and known." Zen is "the unfolding of a new world hitherto unperceived in the confusion of the dualistically-trained mind."[36] There are many traditional Zen dialogues to support this:

MONK: If Self-nature is pure, and belongs to no categories of duality such as being and non-being, etc., where does this seeing take place?

CHIH OF YUN-CHU (8th Century): There is seeing, but nothing seen.

MONK: If there is nothing seen, how can we say there is any seeing at all?

CHIH: In fact there is no trace of seeing.

MONK: In such a seeing, whose seeing is it?

CHIH: There is no seer, either.

ANOTHER MONK ASKED WEI-KUAN: Where is Tao?

KUAN: Right before us.

MONK: Why don't I see it?

KUAN: Because of your egotism you cannot see it.

MONK: If I cannot see it because of my egotism, does your reverence see it?

KUAN: As long as there is "I and thou," this complicates the situation and there is no seeing Tao.

MONK: When there is neither "I" nor "thou" is it seen?

KUAN: When there is neither "I" nor "thou," who is here to see it?[37]

What is arguably the most famous of all Zen stories – purporting to describe how Hui Neng became the Sixth Patriarch – presents the Zen concept of "no mind" (Ch. *wu-hsin*, Jap. *mushin*), which asserts, in effect, the nonduality of subject and object. According to the autobiographical first part of the Platform Sutra, Shen Hsiu, head monk at the Fifth Patriarch's monastery, submitted a stanza comparing the mind to a mirror which must be constantly wiped free of all concept-dust. In response, Hui Neng composed a stanza denying that there is any such mind-mirror: "since all is empty from the beginning, where can the dust alight?" The Fifth Patriarch publicly praised Shen Hsiu's verse as showing the proper way to practice, but privately criticized it as revealing that Shen Hsiu had not yet become enlightened. His view was still dualistic, conceiving of the mind as a mirror which reflects an external world. Hui Neng's verse points out that there is no such mind apart from the world.

In his explanation of "no mind," D. T. Suzuki emphasizes the significance of this story for Zen.

> Hui Neng and his followers now came to use the new term *chien-hsing* instead of the old *k'an-ching* [to keep an eye on purity]. *chien-hsing* means "to look into the nature (of the Mind)." *K'an* and *chien* both relate to the sense of sight, but the character *k'an*, which consists of a hand and an eye, is to watch an object as independent of the spectator; the seen and the seeing are two separate entities. *Chien*, composed of an eye alone on two outstretched legs, signifies the pure act of seeing. . . . The seeing is not reflecting on an object as if the seer had nothing to do with it. The seeing, on the contrary, brings the seer and the object seen together, not in mere identification but the becoming conscious of itself, or rather of its working.[38]

The teachings of contemporary Zen masters also support the centrality of nonduality in Zen experience. Here are excerpts from Yasutani-rōshi's private interviews with Westerners during a meditation retreat:

> There is a line a famous Zen master wrote at the time he became enlightened which reads: "When I heard the temple bell ring, suddenly there was no bell and no I, just sound." In other words, he no longer was aware of a distinction between himself, the bell, the sound, and the universe. This is the state you have to reach.

> *Kenshō* [self-realization] is the direct awareness that you are more than this puny body or limited mind. Stated negatively, it is the realization that the universe is not external to you. Positively, it is experiencing the universe as yourself.[39]

Devotional Pure Land Buddhism, which emphasizes dependence upon Amitābha to help one be reborn in Sukhāvatī (the Western paradise of Mahāyāna), is not treated in detail in this work. But Shinran's development of Pure Land Buddhism into Shin Buddhism, a school that has been more popular in Japan than Zen, is relevant to my purpose. Shinran redefined Pure Land doctrine in the direction of nonduality. Rebirth in the Pure Land is not a stepping-stone to nirvana but is itself "complete unsurpassed enlightenment." Faith for Shinran was not merely belief in the power and benevolence of some external force; in the words of one commentator, "The awakening of faith in Shin Buddhism is an instant of pure egolessness."[40] This happens when we surrender to the infinite compassion of Amitābha, who is not an external God or Buddha but Reality itself, which is also our own true nature.

> The Compassion of all the Buddhas, though transcending all the categories of thought, including those of subject and object, appears to our ego-oriented perception as a force which acts upon us externally – as the Other Power [*tariki*]. This Shinran makes quite clear when he says "What is called external power is as much as to say that there is no discrimination of this or that." To surrender to the Other Power means to transcend the distinction between subject and object. As we identify ourselves with Amida, so Amida identifies himself with us. (Sangharakshita)[41]

Unfortunately, the emphasis upon *tariki* (Other Power) has too often led to minimizing the importance of any personal meditation practice, continuing the traditional division between Pure Land and Zen, which emphasizes *jiriki* (self-effort). This disagreement is due to a misunderstanding: nonduality seems to imply the negation of the opposition between tariki and jiriki in an effort which is not identified as either mine or another's. We might say that the effort Amida exerts to identify with me is at the same time my effort to identify with him.

None of the three classical Taoist texts – *Tao Tê Ching*, *Chuang Tzu*, and *Lieh Tzu* – is as definitive as Vedānta and Mahāyāna in denying subject–object duality. There are several passages in the *Tao Tê Ching* (e.g., in chapter 13) which may hint at such nonduality, but they are unclear. The *Chuang Tzu* is less ambiguous. "The perfect man

David Loy

has no self; the spiritual man has no achievement; the true sage has no name." "If there is no other, there will be no I. If there is no I, there will be none to make distinctions."[42] In chapter 6, "The Great Teacher," Nu Chü teaches the Tao to Pu Liang I:

> After three days, he [Pu Liang I] began to be able to disregard all worldly matters. After his having disregarded all worldly matters, seven days later he was able to disregard all external things; after nine days, his own existence. Having disregarded his own existence, he was enlightened . . . was able to gain vision of the One . . . able to transcend the distinction of past and present . . . able to enter into the realm where life and death are no more.[43]

This and other passages refer to the negation of duality while in meditative trance. We find the same in the *Lieh Tzu*, where Lieh Tzu learns to "ride on the wind" by meditating until "Internal and External were blended into Unity."[44] Such passages strongly imply, but do not explicitly state, that the goal, the resulting experience of Tao, is also nondual. Some other *Chuang Tzu* passages, however, are more explicit. The first quotation in this chapter is from the *Chuang Tzu*, criticizing dualistic thinking; it continues:

> Thereupon, the "self" is also the "other"; the "other" is the "self." . . . But really are there such distinctions as "self" and "other," or are there no such distinctions? When "self" and "other" lose their contrareity, there we have the very essence of the Tao.

Chuang Tzu repeatedly urges: "Identify yourself with the infinite"; "hide the universe in the universe."[45] But how are we to do this? "With the state of pure experience," explains Fung Yu-lan in the introduction to his translation of the *Chuang Tzu*:

> In the state of pure experience, what is known as the union of the individual with the whole is reached. In this state there is an unbroken flux of experience, but the experiencer does not know it. He does not know that there are things, to say nothing of making distinctions between them. There is no separation of things, to say nothing of the distinction between subject and object, between the "me" and the "non-me."

So in this state of experience, there is nothing but the one, the whole.[46]

Another contemporary commentator, Chang Chung-yuan, agrees: "the awareness of the identification and interpenetration of self and nonself is the key that unlocks the mystery of Tao."

> *Chih* [intuitive knowledge] is the key word to understanding Tao and unlocking all the secrets of nonbeing. In other words, intuitive knowledge is pure self-consciousness through immediate, direct, primitive penetration instead of by the methods that are derivative, inferential, or rational. In the sphere of intuitive knowledge there is no separation between the knower and the known; subject and object are identified.[47]

Having established the significance of subject–object nonduality for Taoism, the presentation of nondualities comes to an end. I have offered a number of passages from Vedāntic, Buddhist, and Taoist sources and have referred to the opinions of many respected scholars commenting on these traditions. The point of this exercise has been to establish, indubitably and in detail, the central importance of the concept of nonduality for these three traditions, which we now see can well be called "nondualist traditions." Various meanings of the term nonduality have been determined. The chapter began by distinguishing five such meanings and has analyzed three of them: the negation of dualistic (more generally, conceptual) thinking, the nonplurality of the world, and the nondifference of subject and object. Given the interrelations among these three meanings, it is significant that all three of them are important for all three of our nondualist traditions, although there are differences in emphasis. For example, Buddhist texts contain more admonitions against dualistic thinking and fewer claims about the nonplurality of the world, as we have seen. Generally, explicit assertions of subject–object nonduality are less common in China than in metaphysical India, reflecting their different philosophical interests, and as a consequence Indian sources are cited more often in the chapters that follow. My emphasis continues to be on the third sense of nonduality, but the relationships among all three also continue to be important. Many other passages could be quoted, and other traditions incorporated, both non-Western (e.g., Sufism) and Western (e.g., Plotinus and other examples of the *philosophia perennis*). These are not included partly for reason of space but primarily because our three nondual philosophies are the ones that have developed the concept of nonduality in the greatest detail, providing more than sufficient material on the topic.

When we put together the claims embodied in these three meanings of nonduality, what do we end up with? Due to our dualistic, conceptual ways of thinking, we experience the world as a collection of discrete objects interacting in space and time. One of these objects is *me*: I experience myself as a subject looking out at an external world and anxious about my relationship with it. Expressed in this way, the peculiarity of such an understanding becomes more obvious, for certainly I must be "in" my world in a different way than this pen I am writing with. The nondualist systems agree that

this way of experiencing is not the only possible way, and not the best way, because it involves delusion about the true nature both of the world and of ourselves, and that delusion causes suffering. If our thinking changes, if our dualistic ways of thinking are transformed in some as yet unspecified manner, we shall experience the world as nonplural and, most important of all, we shall overcome our alienation in realizing our nondual unity with it. This spiritual experience will reveal to us for the first time our true nature, which is also the true nature of the world: formless, indivisible, birthless and deathless, and beyond the comprehension of the intellect. But we have also noticed what may be a serious disagreement about the precise relationship between this imperceptible One and sensible phenomena.

Notes

1 "Selections from the Chuang-tzu," in *Sources of Chinese Tradition*, vol. I, ed. Theodore deBary (New York: Columbia University Press, 1964); as quoted by Francis H. Cook in *Hua-Yen Buddhism* (Pennsylvania State University Press, 1977), 27, with slight alterations by Cook. See also *Tao Tê Ching*, ch. 2.

2 Nāgārjuna, *Mūlamndhyamikakārikā* (hereafter *MMK*) XXIII, 10–11. Unless otherwise noted all *MMK* quotations are from Candrakīrti's *Lucid Exposition of the Middle Way*, tr. Mervyn Sprung (Boulder, Co.: Prajñā Press, 1979).

3 *The Zen Teaching of Hui Hai on Sudden Illumination*, tr. and ed. John Blofeld (London: Rider, 1969), 52, 49–50.

4 *Selected Sayings from the Perfection of Wisdom*, tr. and ed. Edward Conze (Boulder, Co.: Prajñā Press, 1978), 78.

5 Blofeld, *Zen Teaching of Hui Hai*, 81.

6 *The Vajracchedikā-Prajñā-Pāramilā Sūtra*, trans. from Chinese by Lu Ku'an-Yu (Hong Kong: Buddhist Book Distributor, 1976), 18–19.

7 Nāgārjuna, *MMK*, XIII 8.

8 *The Zen Teaching of Huang Po*, trans. and ed. John Blofeld (London: Buddhist Society, 1958), 64–5, with my alterations.

9 *The Three Pillars of Zen*, ed. Philip Kapleau (Tokyo: Weatherhill, 1966), 77, 79–80. Yasutani is not giving advice on how to lead everyday life; this admonition was presented during a *sesshin* (intensive meditation retreat) in which distractions are minimized and participants are expected to concentrate on their Zen practice full-time.

10 Katha Upaniṣad II.i.10–11, in *The Upanishads*, tr. and ed. Swami Nikhilananda (New York: Harper and Row, 1964), 78. Unless otherwise noted, all quotations from the Upaniṣads are from Nikhilananda.

11 Blofeld, *Zen Teaching of Huang Po*, 29.

12 My translation of ch. 25.

13 Bṛhadāraṇyaka Upaniṣad I.iv.7. The bracketed additions are Nikhilananda's.

14 "The Yoga of Knowing the Mind," attributed to Padma-Saṁbhava, in *The Tibetan Book of the Great Liberation*, tr. and ed. W. Y. Evans-Wentz (Oxford University Press, 1959), 231–2.

15 *Chuang-tzu*, with commentary by Kuo Hsiang, trans. Fung Yu-Ian (New York: Gordon Press, 1975), 53.

16 Bṛhadāraṇyaka Upaniṣad IV.iv.22.

17 Chang Chung-yuan, *Tao: A New Way of Thinking* (New York: Harper and Row, 1977), 38. From Chang's translation of ch. 14.

18 Bṛhadāraṇyaka Upaniṣad I.iv.7. Nikhilananda's bracketed additions.

19 Katha Upaniṣad II.ii.9.

20 Kapleau, *Three Pillars of Zen*, 205.

21 Bṛhadāraṇyaka Upaniṣad II.iv.14 and IV.iii.23. Nikhilananda's bracketed additions.

22 Īśā Upaniṣad 7.

23 Taittirīya Upaniṣad III.x.6; my bracketed additions. In a footnote to this passage Nikhilananda explains the exclamations: "An expression of extreme wonder. The cause of this wonder is that though the Seer is the non-dual Ātman, yet he himself is the food and the eater, that is to say, that he is both the object and the subject."

24 Chāndogya Upaniṣad VI.ix.4.

25 *Ātmobodha* 41, as quoted in Swāmī Satprakāshānanda, *Methods of Knowledge According to Advaita Vedānta* (London: Allen and Unwin, 1965), 276.

26 *The Bṛhadāraṇyaka Upaniṣad*, with commentary of Śaṅkarācārya, trans. Swāmī Madhavānanda (Calcutta: Advaita Ashrama, 1975), 474–5.

27 *The Teachings of Bhagavan Sri Ramana Maharshi in His Own Words*, ed. Arthur Osborne (Tiruvannamalai: Sri Ramanasramam, 1977), 251, 13–14.

28 T. R. V. Murti, *The Central Philosophy of Buddhism* (London: Allen and Unwin, 1960), 217.

29 Candrakīrti, *Lucid Exposition*, 35. Candrakīrti (6th C. AD?) was Nāgārjuna's main commentator within the *prāsaṅgika* tradition.

30 Vasubandhu, *Trisvobhāvanīrdeśa*, 36–7; quoted in Sangharakshita, *A Survey of Buddhism* (Boulder: Shambhala, 1980), 365. Sangharakshita's bracketed additions.

31 Vasubandhu, *Trimóikāvijñaptikārikā*; quoted in Edward Conze, ed., *Buddhist Texts Through the Ages* (New York: Harper and Row, 1964), 210.

32 S. B. Dasgupta, *An Introduction to Tantric Buddhism* (University of Calcutta, 1974), 4, 113.

33 Evans-Wentz, *Tibetan Book of the Great Liberation*, 206, 232.

34 *Tibetan Yoga and Secret Doctrines*, ed. and trans. W. Y. Evans-Wentz (Oxford University Press, 1958), 145–9.

35 Giuseppe Tucci, *The Religions of Tibet*, tr. Geoffrey Samuel (London: Routledge and Kegan Paul, 1980), 47–8.

36 D. T. Suzuki, *Essays in Zen Buddhism*, 1st ser. (London: Rider, 1927), 125, 230. Suzuki's description of prajñā is discussed in ch. 4.

37 In D. T. Suzuki, *Zen Buddhism* (New York: Doubleday Anchor, 1956), 207, 209.

38 Ibid., 160.

39 Kapleau, *Three Pillars of Zen*, 107, 137.

40 Philipp Karl Eidmann, quoted in Sangharakshita, *Survey of Buddhism*, 340.

41 Ibid., 341.

42 Fung, *Chuang-tzu*, 34, 46.

43 Ibid., 119–20.

44 *Taoist Teachings: From the Book of Lieh Tzu*, trans. Lionel Giles (New York: Dutton, 1912); quoted in Alan Watts, *Tao: The Watercourse Way* (Pelican, 1979), 92.

45 Fung, *Chuang-tzu*, 141, 116.

46 Ibid., 15, 16–17.

47 Chang Chung-yuan, *Creativity and Taoism* (New York: Julian Press, 1963), 20, 41. Nonduality remains an important element of some important contemporary Asian philosophical systems, including what has probably been the most influential Japanese philosophical work of this century, Nishida's *A Study of Good*: "What kind of thing is direct reality before we have as yet added the complexities of thought? That is, what kind of thing is an event of pure experience? At this time there is not as yet the opposition of subject and object, there is not the separation into intellect, emotion, and will, there is only independent, self-contained, pure activity." Nishida Kitaro, *A Study of Good*, trans. V. H. Viglielmo (Japanese Government Printing Bureau, 1960), 48–9. Many others (e.g. Krishnamurti) could also be cited.

PART VI

Evils and Goods

Introduction

Charles Taliaferro

If there is an all-powerful, all-knowing, all-good God, why is there evil? In brief, this is the standard "problem of evil" for theists. In this section we will consider extracts that explicitly wrestle with the problem of recognizing what we observe as evil or tragic events, while at the same time embracing theism. William Rowe argues that the existence of evil provides rational grounds for atheism. Van Inwagen is not convinced, and Marilyn McCord Adams goes on to offer a defense of theism in light of certain beliefs within religious tradition. Brian Davies makes the bold suggestion that Christian tradition is not committed to thinking of God as a moral agent. But while evil is a key element in the case for and against theism, we wish to cast the *problem* of evil as one that faces all of us, irrespective of our position on theism.

Mary Midgley opens this section with an entry on the concept of evil, its origin and allure. To what extent is evil natural or part of our innate constitution? You may find it useful to take some of Midgley's observations with you into the four readings on theism that follow.

It will be useful to note several aspects of theism and evil. In the current literature the term *theodicy* is used to refer to an extensive account of evil from a theistic point of view. A theodicy does not work with merely possible reasons why God allows evil, but points to features of the world that would actually make it permissible for an all-good, all-powerful God to sustain the world in existence. For example, it has been argued that evil is a necessary (or at least likely) result of great goods or a precondition for great goods. The existence of free, interdependent creatures may be such a great good. This state of affairs allows for the possibility of great harm, but it is also a condition for the goods of courage and all the virtues that come into play when persons justly provide for those who are vulnerable and in their care. Arguably, a world in which no ill were possible would not be one in which our actions have moral significance. Theists also sometimes appeal to what they see as greater all-encompassing goods such as the ecosystem as a whole which, in order to function, requires the merits and harms of, say, predator–prey relation.

Some theists today prefer what is often termed a *defense*, rather than a theodicy. A defense does not involve identifying goods that might justify (or warrant God's not destroying) evil. A defense takes the position that evil does not render theism unreasonable. A comparison of Rowe and Van Inwagen should prove to be of interest here. Both test the limits of what we may conclude, given the evident evils of the cosmos.

Marilyn McCord Adams's paper stretches the range of goods to be considered when thinking about evil. If she is right, then the problem of evil may (for a theist) require drawing on religious resources and insights and not simply addressing the problem restricted to secular values. Belief in the afterlife and the incarnation are certainly relevant to the problem of evil; papers on these may be found in Parts VII and VIII of this volume.

Midgley's essay "Selves and Shadows" returns us to the practical, psychological, and ethical implications of how we see good and evil. The problem of evil that she discusses is no mere academic undertaking but goes to the heart of our self-understanding.

In "Buddhism and Evil," Martin Southwold advances a philosophical analysis of evil in a cross-cultural context. This is a good example of how philosophical inquiry can be married to anthropological, social fieldwork. He locates a prevalent Western habit of categorizing some actions and events as radical evil as more at home in monotheism than in Buddhism. For further reflection on Southwold's observations on tolerance, you may wish to consider Edward Langerak's contribution, "Pluralism, Tolerance, and Disagreement," at the outset of Part VII.

In "Evil and Ethical Terror," Nel Noddings traces the moral, social, and personal implications of the concept of evil. This is a work in contemporary feminist philosophy that employs a variety of sources and methods: phenomenology (an analysis of experience) and mythology. Noddings highlights the danger of castigating others as evil. She offers a sustained critique of historical and contemporary theodicy, and opposes a traditional conception of God as pure goodness. Question: could a classical theist accept her critique, repudiate the ill effects of some theodicies, and argue that Jewish, Christian, and Islamic tradition should not in any way justify or ratify evil? In the Torah, the Christian Bible, and the Qu'ran, evil is often construed as something heinous; evil should not occur. And yet each tradition holds, in different ways, that while evil can never be redeemed or made good, nonetheless a person who does evil may reform, be forgiven, and be made whole and reconciled with the divine.

However you respond to the above suggestion, we believe that Noddings's analysis of evil and religious ideals demonstrates the importance of considering the inescapable moral implications of how the "problem of evil" is addressed. The concerns of this chapter are not easily cast as merely a matter of scholarship and speculation.

Further Reading

Historical Sources:

Plato: *Laws*, Book X
Hume, David: *Dialogues Concerning Natural Religion*
Hume, David: *Enquiry Concerning Human Understanding*, Section X
Mill, John Stuart: "Nature," *Three Essays on Religion*

From **The Blackwell Companion to the Philosophy of Religion**, *see the following entry: Peterson, M. L., "The problem of evil"*

Other further reading:

Adams, R., "Existence, Self-Interest, and the Problem of Evil," *Noûs* 13 (1979): 53–65.
Adams, M. M. and Adams, R. M. (eds.), *The Problem of Evil* (New York: Oxford University Press, 1990). *Superb anthology.*
Dupré, L., "Evil – A Religious Mystery: A Plea for a More Inclusive Model of Theodicy," *Faith and Philosophy* 7 (1990): 261–80.
Geivett, R. D., *Evil and the Evidence for God. The Challenge of John Hick's* (Philadelphia: Temple University Press, 1993). *Excellent on the problem of evil.*
Hasker, W., "On Regretting the Evils of This World," *The Southern Journal of Philosophy* 19 (1981): 425–37.

Hick, J. H., *Evil and the God of Love* (London: Macmillan; New York: Harper and Row, 1966; 2nd edn, 1978). *A classic modern text.*
Howard-Snyder, David (ed.), *The Evidentialist Argument from Evil* (Bloomington: Indiana University Press, 1996). *A collection of important papers.*
Martin, M., *Atheism: A Philosophical Justification* (Philadelphia: Temple University Press, 1990).
O'Connor, David, *God and Inscrutable Evil* (Lanham: Rowan and Littlefield, 1998). *A sophisticated, analytic treatment of the problem of evil, highlighting merits in both theistic and atheistic arguments.*
Schellenberg, J. L., *Divine Hiddenness and Human Reason*, Cornell Studies in the Philosophy of Religion (Ithaca: Cornell University Press, 1993).
Stewart, M. Y., *The Greater-Good Defense: An Essay on the Rationality of Faith* (Houndmills: Macmillan; New York: St Martin's Press, 1993). *Technical but very useful.*
Stump, E., "The Problem of Evil," *Faith and Philosophy* 2 (1985): 392–424.
Swinburne, R., "The Problem of Evil," in *The Existence of God* (Oxford: Clarendon Press, 1979).
Swinburne, R., *Providence and the Problem of Evil* (Oxford: Clarendon Press, 1998).
Swinburne, R., *Responsibility and Atonement* (Oxford: Clarendon Press, 1989).
Van Inwagen, P., *God, Knowledge, and Mystery: Essays in Philosophical Theology* (Ithaca and London: Cornell University Press, 1995).

29

The Problem of Natural Evil

Mary Midgley

What in the midst lay but the Tower itself?
  The round squat turret, blind as the fool's
    heart,
  Built of brown stone, without a counterpart
In the whole world. The tempest's mocking elf
Points to the shipman thus the unseen shelf
He strikes on, only when the timbers start.
      Robert Browning, "Childe Roland to
      the Dark Tower Came", stanza xxxi

Looking Towards the Darkness

This book [*Wickedness*] is about the problem of
evil, but not quite in the traditional sense, since I
see it as our problem, not God's. It is often treated
as the problem of why God allows evil. The enquiry then takes the form of a law-court, in which
Man, appearing both as judge and accuser, arraigns
God and convicts him of mismanaging his responsibilities. We then get a strange drama, in which
two robed and wigged figures apparently sit opposite each other exchanging accusations. But this
idea seems to me unhelpful. If God is not there,
the drama cannot arise. If he is there, he is surely
something bigger and more mysterious than a cor-
rupt or stupid official. Either way, we still need to
worry about a different and more pressing matter,
namely the *immediate* sources of evil – not physical

Mary Midgley, "The Problem of Natural Evil," from
Wickedness: A Philosophical Essay (London and Boston: Routledge and Kegan Paul, 1984), pp. 1–16.

evil, but moral evil or sin – in human affairs. To
blame God for making us capable of wrongdoing is
beside the point. Since we are capable of it, what
we need is to understand it. We ought not to be
put off from trying to do this by the fact that
Christian thinkers have sometimes been over-
obsessed by sin, and have given some confused
accounts of it. The phenomenon itself remains very
important in spite of all the mistakes that are made
about it. People often do treat each other abominably. They sometimes treat themselves abominably
too. They constantly cause avoidable suffering. Why
does this happen?

There is at present a strong tendency for decent
people, especially in the social sciences, to hold
that it has no internal causes in human nature –
that it is just the result of outside pressures which
could be removed. Now obviously there are
powerful outside causes. There are physical pains,
diseases, economic shortages and dangers – everything that counts as "natural evil". There are also
cultural factors – bad example, bad teaching, bad
organization. But these cultural causes do not solve
our problem because we must still ask, how did the
bad customs start, how do they spread, and how do
they resist counter-conditioning? Can people be
merely channels? If they are channels, out of what
tap do the bad customs originally flow? And if they
are not mere channels, if they contribute something, what is that contribution?

The idea that we must always choose between
social and individual causes for human behaviour,
and cannot use both, is confused and arbitrary. In
calling it arbitrary, I do not of course mean that no

reasons have been given for it, but that the reasons given are not, and could not possibly be, good enough to justify so crippling a policy. Causes of different kinds do not compete. They supplement each other. Nothing has one sole cause. And in this case, the inside and outside causes of human behaviour – its individual and social aspects – supplement each other so closely that they make no sense apart. Both must always be considered. It is understandable that embattled champions of the social aspect, such as Marx and Durkheim, were exasperated by earlier neglect of it, and in correcting that bias, slipped into producing its mirror image. Nothing is easier than to acquire the faults of one's opponents. But in the hands of their successors, this habit grew into a disastrous competitive tradition, a hallowed interdisciplinary vendetta. Social scientists today are beginning to see the disadvantages of this blinkered approach. Now that it has become dominant, these snags are very serious and call for sharp attention.

However great may be the force of the external pressures on people, we still need to understand the way in which those people respond to the pressures. Infection can bring on fever, but only in creatures with a suitable circulatory system. Like fever, spite, resentment, envy, avarice, cruelty, meanness, hatred and the rest are themselves complex states, and they produce complex activities. Outside events may indeed bring them on, but, like other malfunctions, they would not develop if we were not prone to them. Simpler, non-social creatures are not capable of these responses and do not show them. Neither do some defective humans. Emotionally, we are capable of these vices, because we are capable of states opposite to them, namely the virtues, and these virtues would be unreal if they did not have an opposite alternative. The vices are the defects of our qualities. Our nature provides for both. If it did not, we should not be free.

These problems about the psychology of evil cannot be dealt with simply by denying that aggression is innate. In the first place, evil and aggression are not the same thing. Evil is much wider. A great deal of evil is caused by quiet, respectable, unaggressive motives like sloth, fear, avarice and greed. And aggression itself is by no means always bad. [. . .] In the second place, and more seriously, to approach evil merely by noting its outside causes is to trivialize it. Unless we are willing to grasp imaginatively how it works in the human heart, and particularly in our own hearts, we cannot

understand it. [. . .] We have good reason to fear the understanding of evil, because understanding seems to involve some sort of identification. But what we do not understand at all we cannot detect or resist. We have somehow to understand, without accepting, what goes on in the hearts of the wicked. And since human hearts are not made in factories, but grow, this means taking seriously the natural emotional constitution which people are born with, as well as their social conditions. If we confine our attention to outside causes, we are led to think of wickedness as a set of peculiar behaviour-patterns belonging only to people with a distinctive history, people wearing, as it were, black hats like those which identify the villains in cowboy films. But this is fantasy.

In his book *The Anatomy of Human Destructiveness*, Erich Fromm explains his reasons for carefully analysing the motives of some prominent Nazis. Besides the interest of the wider human tendencies which they typify, he says:

> I had still another aim; that of pointing to the main fallacy which prevents people from recognizing potential Hitlers before they have shown their true faces. This fallacy lies in the belief that a thoroughly destructive and evil man must be a devil – and look his part; that he must be devoid of any positive quality; that he must bear the sign of Cain so visibly that everyone can recognize his destructiveness from afar. Such devils exist, but they are rare . . . Much more often the intensely destructive person will show a front of kindliness . . . he will speak of his ideals and good intentions. But not only this. There is hardly a man who is utterly devoid of any kindness, of any good intentions. If he were he would be on the verge of insanity, except congenital "moral idiots". *Hence, as long as one believes that the evil man wears horns, one will not discover an evil man.*[1]

In order to locate the trouble in time, we need to understand it. And to do this we have to grasp how its patterns are continuous – even though not identical – with ones which appear in our own lives and the lives of those around us. Otherwise our notion of wickedness is unreal.

The choice of examples in this book to avoid that difficulty is an awkward one. The objection to using the Nazis is that mention of them may give the impression that wicked people tend to be foreigners with funny accents, and moreover – since they are already defeated – are not very dangerous. Every other possible example seems, however, equally open either to this distortion or to arguments about whether what they did was really wrong. This last is less likely with the Nazis than with most other cases. I have therefore used them, but have balanced their case by others, many of them drawn from literature and therefore, I hope, more obviously universal. It is particularly necessary to put the Nazis in perspective because they are, in a way, too good an example. It is not often that an influential political movement is as meanly supplied with positive, constructive ideals as they were. We always like to think that our enemies are like this, but it cannot be guaranteed. To become too obsessed with the Nazis can therefore encourage wishful thinking. It can turn out to be yet one more way of missing their successors – who do not need to be spiritually bankrupt to this extent to be genuinely dangerous – and of inflating mere ordinary opponents to Nazi status. This indeed seems repeatedly to have happened since the Second World War when concepts like "appeasement" have been used to approximate other and quite different cases to the Nazi one – for instance by Anthony Eden in launching the Suez expedition. In general, politically wicked movements are mixed, standing also for some good, however ill-conceived, and those opposing them have to understand that good if their opposition is not to become distorted by a mindless destructive element.

What, then, about contemporary examples? These unfortunately are very hard to use here, because as soon as they are mentioned the pleasure of taking sides about them seems to exercise an almost irresistible fascination, and is bound to distract us from the central enquiry. We all find it much easier to denounce wickedness wholesale than to ask just what it is and how it works. This is, I think, only part of a remarkable general difficulty about facing this enquiry directly and keeping one's mind on it. This has something in common with the obstruction which Mary Douglas notices about dirt:

> We should now force ourselves to focus on dirt. Defined in this way, it appears as a residual category, rejected from our normal scheme of classifications. In trying to focus on it we run against our strongest mental habit.[2]

I have tried to resist this skiving tendency of the mind by many strategies, including another which may look even more startling and evasive, namely, not taking sides about religion. In my view it does not matter, for the purposes of analysing wickedness and its immediate sources, whether any religion is true or not. Neither embracing a religion nor anathematizing all of them will settle the range of questions we are dealing with here. I do not, of course, mean that the religious issue is not important in itself, or that it will make no difference to the way in which we view this matter. But it is not part of our present problem, nor a necessary preliminary for it. In particular, the idea that if once we got rid of religion, all problems of this kind would vanish, seems wild. Whatever may have been its plausibility in the eighteenth century, when it first took the centre of the stage, it is surely just a distraction today. It is, however, one often used by those who do not want to think seriously on this subject, and who prefer a ritual warfare about the existence of God to an atrociously difficult psychological enquiry. Since the useful observations which exist on this matter are scattered broadside across the works of many quite different kinds of writer, regardless of their views on religion and on many other divisive subjects, it seems likely that this warfare cannot help us, and that we had better keep clear of it.

Positive and Negative

To return, then, to our problem – how can we make our notion of wickedness more realistic? To do this we shall need, I believe, to think of wickedness not primarily as a positive, definite tendency like aggression, whose intrusion into human life needs a special explanation, but rather as negative, as a general kind of failure to live as we are capable of living. It will follow that, in order to understand it, we need primarily to understand our positive capacities. For that, we shall have to take seriously our original constitution, because only so can we understand the things which go wrong with it.

This means recognizing and investigating a whole range of wide natural motives, whose very existence recent liberal theorists have, in the name of decency, often denied – aggression, territoriality, possessiveness, competitiveness, dominance. All are wide, having good aspects as well as bad ones. All are (more or less) concerned with power. The importance of power in human motivation used to be considered a commonplace. Hobbes, Nietzsche,

Adler and others have treated it as central. This suggestion is of course wildly over-simple, but it is not just silly. All these power-related motives are important also in the lives of other social animals, and appear there in behaviour which is, on the face of it, sometimes strikingly like much human behaviour. If we accept that we evolved from very similar creatures, it is natural to take these parallels seriously – to conclude, as we certainly would in the case of any other creature we were studying, that, besides the obvious differences, there is a real underlying likeness. The physiology of our glands and nervous system, too, is close enough to that of other primates to lead to their being constantly used as experimental subjects for investigations of it. And common tradition has never hesitated to treat such dangerous motives as natural, and has often been content to call them "animal instincts". I shall suggest that the burden of argument lies today on those who reject this obvious and workable way of thinking, not on those who accept it.[3]

The rejectors bring two main charges against it. Both charges are moral rather than theoretical. Both are in themselves very serious; but they really are not relevant to this issue. They are the fear of fatalism and the fear of power-worship. Fatalism seems to loom because people feel that, if we accept these motives as natural at all, we shall be committed to accepting bad conduct as inevitable, and power-worship seems to follow because what seems inevitable may command approval. But this alarming way of thinking is not necessary. There is no need to conceive a wide and complex motive like aggression on the model of a simple drain-pipe, a channel down which energy flows ineluctably to a single outcome – murder. No motive has that simple form. Aggression and fear, sex and curiosity and ambition, are all extremely versatile, containing many possibilities and contributing to many activities. And the relation of motives to value is still more subtle. We do not need to approve of everything we are capable of desiring. It probably is true in a sense that whatever people actually want has *some* value for them, that all wanted things contain a good. But there are so many such goods, and so much possibility of varying arrangements among them, that this cannot commit us to accepting anything as an overall good just because it is in some way wanted. The relation of these many goods must correspond with the relation among the needs of conscious beings, and conflicts can only be resolved in the light of a priority system amongst

those needs. What we really want, if we are to understand them, is a full analysis of the complexities of human motivation.

This analysis, however, would be complicated. And many people still tend to feel that what we have here is an entirely simple issue. As they see it, the whole notion that a motive like aggression, which can produce bad conduct, might be natural is merely an unspeakable abomination, a hypothesis which must not even be considered. They often see this idea as identical with the theological doctrine of original sin, and consider that both, equally, just constitute the same bad excuse for fatalism and repression.

But this is to miss the large question. There is a real difficulty in understanding how people, including ourselves, can act as badly as they sometimes do. External causes alone do not fully explain it. And obviously external causes do not save us from fatalism. A social automaton, worked by conditioning, would be no more free than a physiological one worked by glands. What we need is not a different set of causes, but better understanding of the relation between all causes and free-will. Social and economic fatalism may look like a trouble-saver, because it may seem to make the problem of wickedness vanish, leaving only other people's inconvenient conduct, to be cured by conditioning. In this way, by attending only to outside causes, we try to cut out the idea of personal responsibility. If we blame society for every sin, we may hope that there will no longer be any sense in the question "Whodunnit?" and so no meaning for the concept of blame either. This policy has obvious attractions, especially when we look at the appalling things which have been done in the name of punishment. Certainly the psychology of blame is a problem on its own. Resentment and vindictiveness are fearful dangers here. But when we are not just dealing with blame and punishment, but attempting to understand human conduct generally, we find that this advantage is illusory. The problem hasn't really gone away; we have only turned our backs on it. The difference between deliberate wrongdoing and mere accidental damage is crucial for a hundred purposes. People who are knocked down no doubt suffer pain whether they are knocked down on purpose or not, but the whole meaning of their suffering and the importance it has in their lives are quite different if it was done intentionally. We mind enormously whodunnit and why they dunnit, and whether the action can eventually be justified.

Is Wickedness Mythical?

Ought we perhaps not to mind about this? Is our moral concern somehow superstitious and outdated? Have we perhaps even – oddly enough – a moral duty to overcome it? This thought hangs in the air today as a cloud which inhibits us from examining many important questions. It may be best to look at it for a start in a rather crude form. The *Observer* for Sunday, 28 February 1983 carried this report:

BRITISH STILL BELIEVE IN SIN, HELL AND THE DEVIL
Most Britons still believe in the concept of sin and nearly a third believe in hell and the devil, according to the biggest survey of public opinion ever carried out in the West. . . . Belief in sin is highest in Northern Ireland (91 per cent) and lowest in Denmark (29 per cent). . . . Even 15 per cent of atheists believe in sin and 4 per cent in the devil. . . . Most Europeans admit that they sometimes regret having done something wrong. The Italians and Danes suffer most from such regrets, the French and Belgians least. The rich regret more than the poor. . . . The rich are less likely to believe in sin than the poor.

What were these people supposed to be believing? "Belief in sin" is not a factual belief, as beliefs in God, hell or the devil certainly are, whatever else they may involve. "Sin" seems not to be defined in a restrictive way as an offence against God, or the minority of atheists could not have signed up for it. Belief in it can scarcely be identified with the sense of regret for having done wrong, since there might surely be people who thought that others sinned, though they did not think they did so themselves. Besides, the rich apparently do one but not the other. The word "still" suggests that this puzzling belief is no longer fashionable. But this makes it no easier to see what the belief is actually meant to be, unless it is the simple and obvious one that some actions are wrong. Is the reporter's idea really that up-to-date people – including most Danes and even more atheists – have now withdrawn their objections to all courses of action, including boiling our friends alive just for the hell of it? This is not very plausible. What the survey itself really means cannot of course be discovered from this report. But the journalist's wording is an interesting expression of a jumble of contemporary ideas which will give us a good deal of trouble. They range from the mere observation that the *word* sin is no longer fashionable, through a set of changes in what we count as sins, to some genuine and confusing reasons for doubt and rejection of certain moral views which earlier ages could more easily be confident about. At a popular level, all that is meant is often that sexual activity has been shown not to be sinful. This does not diminish the number of sins, because, where a sexual activity is considered justified, interference with it begins to be blamed. Recognized sins against liberty therefore multiply in exact proportion as recognized sins against chastity grow scarcer.

Original sin, however, is of course a different matter. On the face of it, this phrase is contradictory. Sin must, by definition, be deliberate. And our original constitution cannot be deliberate; we did not choose it. I cannot discuss here what theologians have made of this paradox. But many of them seem to give the phrase "original sin" a quite limited, sensible use, which has percolated into ordinary thought. They use it to indicate what might be called the raw materials of sin – natural impulses which are indeed not sinful in themselves, but which will lead to sin unless we are conscious and critical of them.[4] They are impulses which would not be present in a perfect creature – for instance, the sudden wish to attack an irritating person without delay. This kind of thing can also be described by the wider phrase of my chapter title: it is a "natural evil".

Now that phrase too may well seem paradoxical, particularly if we use it to describe human conduct. The phrase "natural evil" is often used to contrast unavoidable, non-human disasters, such as plagues and earthquakes, with "moral evil" or wickedness, which is deliberate. That is a useful distinction. But it leaves out an area between the two. *Moral evil too must surely have its "natural history"* – a set of given ways in which it tends to occur in a given species. Not every kind of bad conduct is tempting or even psychologically possible for a given kind of being. There might – for instance – be creatures much less partial than we are, creatures entirely without our strong tendency (which appears even in very small children) to prefer some people to others. Their sins and temptations would be quite different from ours. And within the set of vices which belongs to us, some are much more powerful and dangerous than others. If this is true, it seems to be something which we need to understand. We have to look into these trends, not only for the practical purpose of controlling them, but also for the sake of our self-knowledge, our wholeness, our integrity. As Jung has pointed out, every solid object has its shadow-side.[5] The shadowy parts of the mind are an essential part of its form. To deny one's shadow is to lose solidity, to become something of a phantom. Self-deception about it may increase our confidence, but it surely threatens our wholeness.

Mephistopheles Says "No"

The notion of these natural, psychological tendencies to evil will, I think, lose some of its strangeness if we are careful to avoid thinking of them primarily as positive tendencies with positive functions, and instead try thinking of them as failures, dysfunctions. Here we stumble over an old dispute about the negativity of evil, one which has suffered, like so many disputes, from being seen as a simple choice between exclusive alternatives, when there are parts of the truth on both sides. The choice is really one between models – patterns of thought which have distinct uses, do not really conflict, but have to be employed in their own proper fields. It has, however, been treated as a matter for fighting, and in the last couple of centuries has been caught up in the general warfare declared between romantic and classical ways of thought. The older notion of evil as negative – which is implicit in much Greek thought, and in the central tradition of Christianity – was marked as classical and shared the general discrediting of classical attitudes. This whole warfare should surely now be seen as a mistaken one, a feud between two essential and complementary sides of life. But its results have been specially disastrous about wrong-doing, because this is a peculiarly difficult subject to think clearly about in any case. Only a very thin set of concepts was left us for handling it, and we are deeply confused about it – which may well account for the blank denial of its existence implied by the reported "disbelief in sin" just mentioned. The first thing which seems needed here is to recover for use the older, recently neglected, idea of evil as negative – not because it contains the whole truth, but because it does hold an essential part of it.

Apart from its history – which we will consider in a moment – this idea is, on the face of it, natural enough. For instance, people have positive capacities for generosity and courage. They do not need extra capacities for meanness and cowardice as well. To be capable of these virtues is also to be capable of the corresponding vices, just as the possibility of physical strength carries with it that of physical weakness, and can only be understood if we think of that weakness as possible.[6] If we talk of evils natural to our species, we are of course not saying that it is as a whole just "naturally evil", which is an unintelligible remark. We are drawing attention to particular evils which beset it. And grasping these evils is an absolutely necessary part of grasping its special excellences. Indeed, the notion of the evils comes first. You could hardly have much idea of generosity if you did not grasp the dangers of meanness. A creature with a Paradisal constitution, immune to all temptation, would not have the vices. But it would not have or need the virtues either. Nor would it, in the ordinary sense, have free-will. Evil, in fact, is essentially the absence of good, and cannot be understood on its own. We constantly need the kind of analysis which Bishop Butler gave of selfishness – "The thing to be lamented is, not that men have so great regard to their own good or interest in the present world, for they have not enough; but that they have so little to the good of others."[7]

If we can use this idea, the existence of inborn tendencies to evil need not puzzle us too much. It only means that our good tendencies are not complete or infallible, that we are not faultless moral automata. But *is* evil negative? People resist this idea at once because they feel that it plays down the force of evil. Can a negative thing be so strong? Actually it can, and this is not a serious objection. Darkness and cold are negative, and they are strong enough. If we want to dramatize the idea, and see how a purely negative motive works out in action, we can consider the manifesto of Mephistopheles in Goethe's *Faust*. When Faust asks him who he is, he answers,

> The spirit I, that endlessly denies
> And rightly too; for all that comes to birth
> Is fit for overthrow, as nothing worth;
> Wherefore the world were better sterilized;
> Thus all that's here as Evil recognized
> Is gain to me, and downfall, ruin, sin,
> The very element I prosper in.[8]

This destruction is not a means to any positive aim. He is simply anti-life. Whatever is arising, he is against it. His element is mere refusal. Now whatever problems may arise about this diagnosis (and we will look at some of them in a moment) it scarcely shows evil as weak. All earthly good things are vulnerable and need a great deal of help. The power to destroy and to refuse help is not a trifling power.

Summary

The problem of evil is not just a problem about God, but an important and difficult problem about individual human psychology. We need to understand better the natural tendencies which make human wickedness possible. Various contemporary habits of mind make this hard:

(1) There is a notion that both method and morals require human behaviour in general, and particularly wrong-doing, to be explained only by external, social causes. But this is a false antithesis.
(i) As far as method goes, we need both social and individual causes. Neither makes sense alone.
(ii) Morally, what we need is to avoid fatalism, which is an independent error, no more tied to thought about individuals than about societies.

From this angle, however, the idea of natural sources of wrong-doing has been obscured because it was supposed that any such source would have to be a fairly specific positive tendency, such as aggression. But aggression certainly does not play this role, and it is hard to see what would. It is probably more helpful to use here the traditional notion of evil as *negative*, as a more general rejection and denial of positive capacities. The psychological task is then one of mapping those capacities, understanding what potential gaps and conflicts there are among them, spotting the areas of danger at which failure easily takes place and so grasping more fully the workings of rejection. (This does not have to involve identifying with it. The danger of identifying with a mental process just because we come to understand it exists, but it can be resisted.)

(2) Difficulty, however, still arises about this programme today from a suspicion that the whole problem is imaginary. Officially, people are sceptical now about the very existence of sin or wickedness. When examined, however, this position usually turns out to be an unreal one, resulting from exaggeration of reforming claims. It often means merely that different things are now disapproved of, e.g. repression rather than adultery.

The idea of evil as negative does not, of course, imply that it is weak or unreal, any more than darkness or cold. What it does imply is a distinct, original human nature with relatively specific capacities and incapacities, rather than total plasticity and indefiniteness. Unless evil is to be seen as a mere outside enemy, totally external to humanity, it seems necessary to locate some of its sources in the unevenness of this original equipment. But this negative conception has often struck enquirers as insufficiently dramatic.

Notes

1 *The Anatomy of Human Destructiveness* (Jonathan Cape, London, 1974), p. 432. Italics mine.

2 *Purity and Danger: An Analysis of the Concepts of Pollution and Taboo* (Routledge & Kegan Paul, London, 1966), p. 36.

3 I have argued this case at length in my book *Beast and Man* (Harvester Press, Sussex, 1979; Methuen, London, 1980) and shall try to avoid repeating much of it here.

4 Thus for instance C. B. Moss: "The Church, following St Paul's teaching, has always maintained that everybody is born with a tendency to sin, a weakness of the will which, if not checked, will result in sin. This weakness was called by the Latin Fathers 'original sin' (*originale peccatum*); it is not a good name, because, strictly speaking, original sin is not sin at all, but a weakness leading to sin, just as a weak chest is not consumption" (*The Christian Faith*, SPCK, London, 1943), pp. 149–50.

5 See for instance his *Modern Man in Search of a Soul* (Kegan Paul, Trench, Trubner, London, 1945, translated Dell and Baynes), pp. 46–8 and 234, and *Answer to Job* (Routledge & Kegan Paul, London, 1954, translated R. F. C. Hull), pp. 133–5 and 154.

6 Aristotle's notion that the vices are essentially just excesses or defects of the tendencies which, at a right level, produce the virtues is a typical expression of this approach. No doubt it is too schematic, but it can be very useful as a starting-point for bringing this problem in focus. See the *Nicomachean Ethics*, Book II.

7 Preface to the *Sermons*, section 40 (p. 24 of the edition of *Fifteen Sermons* published by G. Bell, London, 1969).

8 *Faust*, part 1, scene 2, translated by Philip Wayne (Penguin, Harmondsworth, 1949), p. 73.

30

The Problem of Evil and Some Varieties of Atheism

William L. Rowe

This paper is concerned with three interrelated questions. The first is: is there an argument for atheism based on the existence of evil that may rationally justify someone in being an atheist? To this first question I give an affirmative answer and try to support that answer by setting forth a strong argument for atheism based on the existence of evil.[1] The second question is: how can the theist best defend his position against the argument for atheism based on the existence of evil? In response to this question I try to describe what may be an adequate rational defense for theism against any argument for atheism based on the existence of evil. The final question is: what position should the informed atheist take concerning the rationality of theistic belief? Three different answers an atheist may give to this question serve to distinguish three varieties of atheism: unfriendly atheism, indifferent atheism, and friendly atheism. In the final part of the paper I discuss and defend the position of friendly atheism.

Before we consider the argument from evil, we need to distinguish a narrow and a broad sense of the terms "theist," "atheist," and "agnostic." By a "theist" in the narrow sense I mean someone who believes in the existence of an omnipotent, omniscient, eternal, supremely good being who created the world. By a "theist" in the broad sense I

mean someone who believes in the existence of some sort of divine being or divine reality. To be a theist in the narrow sense is also to be a theist in the broad sense, but one may be a theist in the broad sense – as was Paul Tillich – without believing that there is a supremely good, omnipotent, omniscient, eternal being who created the world. Similar distinctions must be made between a narrow and a broad sense of the terms "atheist" and "agnostic." To be an atheist in the broad sense is to deny the existence of any sort of divine being or divine reality. Tillich was not an atheist in the broad sense. But he was an atheist in the narrow sense, for he denied that there exists a divine being that is all-knowing, all-powerful and perfectly good. In this paper I will be using the terms "theism," "theist," "atheism," "atheist," "agnosticism," and "agnostic" in the narrow sense, not in the broad sense.

I

In developing the argument for atheism based on the existence of evil, it will be useful to focus on some particular evil that our world contains in considerable abundance. Intense human and animal suffering, for example, occurs daily and in great plenitude in our world. Such intense suffering is a clear case of evil. Of course, if the intense suffering leads to some greater good, a good we could not have obtained without undergoing the suffering in question, we might conclude that the suffering is justified, but it remains an evil nevertheless. For

William L. Rowe, "The Problem of Evil and Some Varieties of Atheism," from *American Philosophical Quarterly* 16:4 (October 1979), pp. 335–41. Copyright © The Editors of *American Philosophical Quarterly*, published by Blackwell Publishers, Oxford.

we must not confuse the intense suffering in and of itself with the good things to which it sometimes leads or of which it may be a necessary part. Intense human or animal suffering is in itself bad, an evil, even though it may sometimes be justified by virtue of being a part of, or leading to, some good which is unobtainable without it. What is evil in itself may sometimes be good as a means because it leads to something that is good in itself. In such a case, while remaining an evil in itself, the intense human or animal suffering is, nevertheless, an evil which someone might be morally justified in permitting.

Taking human and animal suffering as a clear instance of evil which occurs with great frequency in our world, the argument for atheism based on evil can be stated as follows:

(1) There exist instances of intense suffering which an omnipotent, omniscient being could have prevented without thereby losing some greater good or permitting some evil equally bad or worse.[2]

(2) An omniscient, wholly good being would prevent the occurrence of any intense suffering it could, unless it could not do so without thereby losing some greater good or permitting some evil equally bad or worse.

(3) There does not exist an omnipotent, omniscient, wholly good being.

What are we to say about this argument for atheism, an argument based on the profusion of one sort of evil in our world? The argument is valid; therefore, if we have rational grounds for accepting its premises, to that extent we have rational grounds for accepting atheism. Do we, however, have rational grounds for accepting the premises of this argument?

Let's begin with the second premise. Let s_1 be an instance of intense human or animal suffering which an omniscient, wholly good being could prevent. We will also suppose that things are such that s_1 will occur unless prevented by the omniscient, wholly good (OG) being. We might be interested in determining what would be a *sufficient* condition of OG failing to prevent s_1. But, for our purpose here, we need only try to state a *necessary* condition for OG failing to prevent s_1. That condition, so it seems to me, is this:

Either (i) there is some greater good, G, such that G is obtainable by OG only if OG permits s_1;[3]

or (ii) there is some greater good, G, such that G is obtainable by OG only if OG permits either s_1 or some evil equally bad or worse;

or (iii) s_1 is such that it is preventable by OG only if OG permits some evil equally bad or worse.

It is important to recognize that (iii) is not included in (i). For losing a good greater than s_1 is not the same as permitting an evil greater than s_1. And this because the *absence* of a good state of affairs need not itself be an evil state of affairs. It is also important to recognize that s_1 might be such that it is preventable by OG *without* losing G (so condition (i) is not satisfied) but also such that if OG did prevent it, G would be loss *unless OG* permitted some evil equal to or worse than s_1. If this were so, it does not seem correct to require that OG prevent s_1. Thus, condition (ii) takes into account an important possibility not encompassed in condition (i).

Is it true that if an omniscient, wholly good being permits the occurrence of some intense suffering it could have prevented, then either (i) or (ii) or (iii) obtains? It seems to me that it is true. But if it is true then so is premise (2) of the argument for atheism. For that premise merely states in more compact form what we have suggested must be true if an omniscient, wholly good being fails to prevent some intense suffering it could prevent. Premise (2) says that an omniscient, wholly good being would prevent the occurrence of any intense suffering it could, unless it could not do so without thereby losing some greater good or permitting some evil equally bad or worse. This premise (or something not too distant from it) is, I think, held in common by many atheists and nontheists. Of course, there may be disagreement about whether something is good, and whether, if it is good, one would be morally justified in permitting some intense suffering to occur in order to obtain it. Someone might hold, for example, that no good is great enough to justify permitting an innocent child to suffer terribly.[4] Again, someone might hold that the mere fact that a given good outweighs some suffering and would be loss if the suffering were prevented, is not a morally sufficient reason for permitting the suffering. But to hold either of these views is not to deny (2). For (2) claims only that *if* an omniscient, wholly good being permits intense suffering *then* either there is some greater good that would have been loss, or some equally bad or worse evil that would have occurred, had the intense suffering been

William L. Rowe

prevented. (2) does not purport to describe what might be a *sufficient* condition for an omniscient, wholly good being to permit intense suffering, only what is a *necessary* condition. So stated, (2) seems to express a belief that accords with our basic moral principles, principles shared by both theists and nontheists. If we are to fault the argument for atheism, therefore, it seems we must find some fault with its first premise.

Suppose in some distant forest lightning strikes a dead tree, resulting in a forest fire. In the fire a fawn is trapped, horribly burned, and lies in terrible agony for several days before death relieves its suffering. So far as we can see, the fawn's intense suffering is pointless. For there does not appear to be any greater good such that the prevention of the fawn's suffering would require either the loss of that good or the occurrence of an evil equally bad or worse. Nor does there seem to be any equally bad or worse evil so connected to the fawn's suffering that it would have had to occur had the fawn's suffering been prevented. Could an omnipotent, omniscient being have prevented the fawn's apparently pointless suffering? The answer is obvious, as even the theist will insist. An omnipotent, omniscient being could have easily prevented the fawn from being horribly burned, or, given the burning, could have spared the fawn the intense suffering by quickly ending its life, rather than allowing the fawn to lie in terrible agony for several days. Since the fawn's intense suffering was preventable and, so far as we can see, pointless, doesn't it appear that premise (1) of the argument is true, that there do exist instances of intense suffering which an omnipotent, omniscient being could have prevented without thereby losing some greater good or permitting some evil equally bad or worse?

It must be acknowledged that the case of the fawn's apparently pointless suffering does not *prove* that (1) is true. For even though we cannot see how the fawn's suffering is required to obtain some greater good (or to prevent some equally bad or worse evil), it hardly follows that it is not so required. After all, we are often surprised by how things we thought to be unconnected turn out to be intimately connected. Perhaps, for all we know, there is some familiar good outweighing the fawn's suffering to which that suffering is connected in a way we do not see. Furthermore, there may well be unfamiliar goods, goods we haven't dreamed of, to which the fawn's suffering is inextricably connected. Indeed, it would seem to require something like omniscience on our part before we could lay claim

to *knowing* that there is no greater good connected to the fawn's suffering in such a manner that an omnipotent, omniscient being could not have achieved that good without permitting that suffering or some evil equally bad or worse. So the case of the fawn's suffering surely does not enable us to *establish* the truth of (1).

The truth is that we are not in a position to prove that (1) is true. We cannot know with certainty that instances of suffering of the sort described in (1) do occur in our world. But it is one thing to *know* or *prove* that (1) is true and quite another thing to have *rational grounds* for believing (1) to be true. We are often in the position where in the light of our experience and knowledge it is rational to believe that a certain statement is true, even though we are not in a position to prove or to know with certainty that the statement is true. In the light of our past experience and knowledge it is, for example, very reasonable to believe that neither Goldwater nor McGovern will ever be elected President, but we are scarcely in the position of knowing with certainty that neither will ever be elected President. So, too, with (1), although we cannot know with certainty that it is true, it perhaps can be rationally supported, shown to be a rational belief.

Consider again the case of the fawn's suffering. Is it reasonable to believe that there is some greater good so intimately connected to that suffering that even an omnipotent, omniscient being could not have obtained that good without permitting that suffering or some evil at least as bad? It certainly does not appear reasonable to believe this. Nor does it seem reasonable to believe that there is some evil at least as bad as the fawn's suffering such that an omnipotent being simply could not have prevented it without permitting the fawn's suffering. But even if it should somehow be reasonable to believe either of these things of the fawn's suffering, we must then ask whether it is reasonable to believe either of these things of *all* the instances of seemingly pointless human and animal suffering that occur daily in our world. And surely the answer to this more general question must be no. It seems quite unlikely that *all* the instances of intense suffering occurring daily in our world are intimately related to the occurrence of greater goods or the prevention of evils at least as bad; and even more unlikely, should they somehow all be so related, that an omnipotent, omniscient being could not have achieved at least some of those goods (or prevented some of those evils) without permitting the instances of intense suffering that are supposedly related to them. In the light of our experience and knowledge of the variety and scale of human and animal suffering in our world, the idea that none of this suffering could have been prevented by an omnipotent being without thereby losing a greater good or permitting an evil at least as bad seems an extraordinary absurd idea, quite beyond our belief. It seems then that although we cannot *prove* that (1) is true, it is, nevertheless, altogether *reasonable* to believe that (1) is true, that (1) is a *rational* belief.[5]

Returning now to our argument for atheism, we've seen that the second premise expresses a basic belief common to many theists and nontheists. We've also seen that our experience and knowledge of the variety and profusion of suffering in our world provides *rational support* for the first premise. Seeing that the conclusion, "There does not exist an omnipotent, omniscient, wholly good being" follows from these two premises, it does seem that we have *rational support* for atheism, that it is reasonable for us to believe that the theistic God does not exist.

II

Can theism be rationally defended against the argument for atheism we have just examined? If it can, how might the theist best respond to that argument? Since the argument from (1) and (2) to (3) is valid, and since the theist, no less than the nontheist, is more than likely committed to (2), it's clear that the theist can reject this atheistic argument only by rejecting its first premise, the premise that states that there are instances of intense suffering which an omnipotent, omniscient being could have prevented without thereby losing some greater good or permitting some evil equally bad or worse. How, then, can the theist best respond to this premise and the considerations advanced in its support?

There are basically three responses a theist can make. First, he might argue not that (1) is false or probably false, but only that the reasoning given in support of it is in some way *defective*. He may do this either by arguing that the reasons given in support of (1) are *in themselves* insufficient to justify accepting (1), or by arguing that there are other things we know which, when taken in conjunction with these reasons, do not justify us in accepting (1). I suppose some theists would be content with

this rather modest response to the basic argument for atheism. But given the validity of the basic argument and the theist's likely acceptance of (2), he is thereby committed to the view that (1) is false, not just that we have no good reasons for accepting (1) as true. The second two responses are aimed at showing that it is reasonable to believe that (1) is false. Since the theist is committed to this view I shall focus the discussion on these two attempts, attempts which we can distinguish as "the direct attack" and "the indirect attack."

By a direct attack, I mean an attempt to reject (1) by pointing out goods, for example, to which suffering may well be connected, goods which an omnipotent, omniscient being could not achieve without permitting suffering. It is doubtful, however, that the direct attack can succeed. The theist may point out that some suffering leads to moral and spiritual development impossible without suffering. But it's reasonably clear that suffering often occurs in a degree far beyond what is required for character development. The theist may say that some suffering results from free choices of human beings and might be preventable only by preventing some measure of human freedom. But, again, it's clear that much intense suffering occurs not as a result of human free choices. The general difficulty with this direct attack on premise (1) is twofold. First, it cannot succeed, for the theist does not know what greater goods might be served, or evils prevented, by each instance of intense human or animal suffering. Second, the theist's own religious tradition usually maintains that in this life it is not given to us to know God's purpose in allowing particular instances of suffering. Hence, the direct attack against premise (1) cannot succeed and violates basic beliefs associated with theism.

The best procedure for the theist to follow in rejecting premise (1) is the indirect procedure. This procedure I shall call "the G. E. Moore shift," so-called in honor of the twentieth-century philosopher, G. E. Moore, who used it to great effect in dealing with the arguments of the skeptics. Skeptical philosophers such as David Hume have advanced ingenious arguments to prove that no one can know of the existence of any material object. The premises of their arguments employ plausible principles, principles which many philosophers have tried to reject directly, but only with questionable success. Moore's procedure was altogether different. Instead of arguing directly against the premises of the skeptic's arguments, he simply noted that the premises implied, for example, that he (Moore) did not know of the existence of a pencil. Moore then proceeded indirectly against the skeptic's premises by arguing:

(1) I do know that this pencil exists.
(2) If the skeptic's principles are correct I cannot know of the existence of this pencil.

(3) Therefore, the skeptic's principles (at least one) must be incorrect.

Moore then noted that his argument is just as valid as the skeptic's, that both of their arguments contain the premise "If the skeptic's principles are correct Moore cannot know of the existence of this pencil," and concluded that the only way to choose between the two arguments (Moore's and the skeptic's) is by deciding which of the first premises it is more rational to believe – Moore's premise "I do know that this pencil exists" or the skeptic's premise asserting that his skeptical principles are correct. Moore concluded that his own first premise was the more rational of the two.[6]

Before we see how the theist may apply the G. E. Moore shift to the basic argument for atheism, we should note the general strategy of the shift. We're given an argument: p, q, therefore, r. Instead of arguing directly against p, another argument is constructed – not-r, q, therefore, not-p – which begins with the denial of the conclusion of the first argument, keeps its second premise, and ends with the denial of the first premise as its conclusion. Compare, for example, these two:

I. p II.   not-r
     q q

     r not-p

It is a truth of logic that if I is valid II must be valid as well. Since the arguments are the same so far as the second premise is concerned, any choice between them must concern their respective first premises. To argue against the first premise (p) by constructing the counter argument II is to employ the G. E. Moore shift.

Applying the G. E. Moore shift against the first premise of the basic argument for atheism, the theist can argue as follows:

(not-3) There exists an omnipotent, omniscient, wholly good being.

(2) An omniscient, wholly good being would prevent the occurrence of any intense suffering it could, unless it could not do so without thereby losing some greater good or permitting some evil equally bad or worse.

Therefore:

(not-1) It is not the case that there exist instances of intense suffering which an omnipotent, omniscient being could have prevented without thereby losing some greater good or permitting some evil equally bad or worse.

We now have two arguments: the basic argument for atheism from (1) and (2) to (3), and the theist's best response, the argument from (not-3) and (2) to (not-1). What the theist then says about (1) is that he has rational grounds for believing in the existence of the theistic God (not-3), accepts (2) as true, and sees that (not-1) follows from (not-3) and (2). He concludes, therefore, that he has rational grounds for rejecting (1). Having rational grounds for rejecting (1), the theist concludes that the basic argument for atheism is mistaken.

III

We've had a look at a forceful argument for atheism and what seems to be the theist's best response to that argument. If one is persuaded by the argument for atheism, as I find myself to be, how might one best view the position of the theist? Of course, he will view the theist as having a false belief, just as the theist will view the atheist as having a false belief. But what position should the atheist take concerning the *rationality* of the theist's belief? There are three major positions an atheist might take, positions which we may think of as some varieties of atheism. First, the atheist may believe that no one is rationally justified in believing that the theistic God exists. Let us call this position "unfriendly atheism." Second, the atheist may hold no belief concerning whether any theist is or isn't rationally justified in believing that the theistic God exists. Let us call this view "indifferent atheism." Finally, the atheist may believe that some theists are rationally justified in believing that the theistic God exists. This view we shall call "friendly atheism." In this final part of the paper I propose to discuss and defend the position of friendly atheism.

If no one can be rationally justified in believing a false proposition then friendly atheism is a paradoxical, if not incoherent position. But surely the truth of a belief is not a necessary condition of someone's being rationally justified in having that belief. So in holding that someone is rationally justified in believing that the theistic God exists, the friendly atheist is not committed to thinking that the theist has a true belief. What he is committed to is that the theist has rational grounds for his belief, a belief the atheist rejects and is convinced he is rationally justified in rejecting. But is this possible? Can someone, like our friendly atheist, hold a belief, be convinced that he is rationally justified in holding that belief, and yet believe that someone else is equally justified in believing the opposite? Surely this is possible. Suppose your friends see you off on a flight to Hawaii. Hours after take-off they learn that your plane has gone down at sea. After a twenty-four hour search, no survivors have been found. Under these circumstances they are rationally justified in believing that you have perished. But it is hardly rational for you to believe this, as you bob up and down in your life vest, wondering why the search planes have failed to spot you. Indeed, to amuse yourself while awaiting your fate, you might very well reflect on the fact that your friends are rationally justified in believing that you are now dead, a proposition you disbelieve and are rationally justified in disbelieving. So, too, perhaps an atheist may be rationally justified in his atheistic belief and yet hold that some theists are rationally justified in believing just the opposite of what he believes.

What sort of grounds might a theist have for believing that God exists? Well, he might endeavor to justify his belief by appealing to one or more of the traditional arguments: Ontological, Cosmological, Teleological, Moral, etc. Second, he might appeal to certain aspects of religious experience, perhaps even his own religious experience. Third, he might try to justify theism as a plausible theory in terms of which we can account for a variety of phenomena. Although an atheist must hold that the theistic God does not exist, can he not also believe, and be justified in so believing, that some of these "justifications of theism" do actually rationally justify some theists in their belief that there exists a supremely good, omnipotent, omniscient being? It seems to me that he can.

If we think of the long history of theistic belief and the special situations in which people are sometimes placed, it is perhaps as absurd to think that no one was ever rationally justified in believing that the theistic God exists as it is to think that no one was ever justified in believing that human beings would never walk on the moon. But in suggesting that friendly atheism is preferable to unfriendly atheism, I don't mean to rest the case on what some human beings might reasonably have believed in the eleventh or thirteenth century. The more interesting question is whether some people in modern society, people who are aware of the usual grounds for belief and disbelief and are acquainted to some degree with modern science, are yet rationally justified in accepting theism. Friendly atheism is a significant position only if it answers this question in the affirmative.

It is not difficult for an atheist to be friendly when he has reason to believe that the theist could not reasonably be expected to be acquainted with the grounds for disbelief that he (the atheist) possesses. For then the atheist may take the view that some theists are rationally justified in holding to theism, but would not be so were they to be acquainted with the grounds for disbelief – those grounds being sufficient to tip the scale in favor of atheism when balanced against the reasons the theist has in support of his belief.

Friendly atheism becomes paradoxical, however, when the atheist contemplates believing that the theist has all the grounds for atheism that he, the atheist, has, and yet is rationally justified in maintaining his theistic belief. But even so excessively friendly a view as this perhaps can be held by the atheist if he also has some reason to think that the grounds for theism are not as telling as the theist is justified in taking them to be.[7]

In this paper I've presented what I take to be a strong argument for atheism, pointed out what I think is the theist's best response to that argument, distinguished three positions an atheist might take concerning the rationality of theistic belief, and made some remarks in defense of the position called "friendly atheism." I'm aware that the central points of the paper are not likely to be warmly received by many philosophers. Philosophers who are atheists tend to be tough minded – holding that there are no good reasons for supposing that theism is true. And theists tend either to reject the view that the existence of evil provides rational grounds for atheism or to hold that religious belief has nothing to do with reason and evidence at all. But such is the way of philosophy.[8]

Notes

1. Some philosophers have contended that the existence of evil is *logically inconsistent* with the existence of the theistic God. No one, I think, has succeeded in establishing such an extravagant claim. Indeed, granted incompatibilism, there is a fairly compelling argument for the view that the existence of evil is logically consistent with the existence of the theistic God. (For a lucid statement of this argument see Alvin Plantinga, *God, Freedom, and Evil* (New York, 1974), pp. 29–59.) There remains, however, what we may call the *evidential* form – as opposed to the *logical* form – of the problem of evil: the view that the variety and profusion of evil in our world, although perhaps not logically inconsistent with the existence of the theistic God, provides, nevertheless, *rational support* for atheism. In this paper I shall be concerned solely with the evidential form of the problem, the form of the problem which, I think, presents a rather severe difficulty for theism.

2. If there is some good, G, greater than any evil, (1) will be false for the trivial reason that no matter what evil, E, we pick the conjunctive good state of affairs consisting of G and E will outweigh E and be such that an omnipotent being could not obtain it without permitting E. (See Alvin Plantinga, *God and Other Minds* (Ithaca, 1967), p. 167.) To avoid this objection we may insert "unreplaceable" into our premises (1) and (2) between "some" and "greater." If E isn't required for G, and G is better than G plus E, then the good conjunctive state of affairs composed of G and E would be *replaceable* by the greater good of G alone. For the sake of simplicity, however, I will ignore this complication both in the formulation and discussion of premises (1) and (2).

3. Three clarifying points need to be made in connection with (i). First, by "good" I don't mean to exclude the fulfillment of certain moral principles. Perhaps preventing s_1 would preclude certain actions prescribed by the principles of justice. I shall allow that the satisfaction of certain principles of justice may be a good that outweighs the evil of s_1. Second, even though (i) may suggest it, I don't mean to limit the good in question to something that would *follow in time* the occurrence of s_1. And, finally, we should perhaps not fault OG if the good G, that would be loss were s_1 prevented, is not actually greater than s_1, but merely such that allowing s_1 and G, as opposed to preventing s_1 and thereby losing G, would not alter the balance between good and evil. For reasons of simplicity, I have left this point out in stating (i), with the result that (i) is perhaps a bit stronger than it should be.

4. See Ivan's speech in Book V, Chapter IV of *The Brothers Karamazov*.

5. One might object that the conclusion of this paragraph is stronger than the reasons given warrant. For it is one thing to argue that it is unreasonable to think that (1) is false and another thing to conclude that we are therefore justified in accepting (1) as true. There are propositions such that believing them is much more reasonable than disbelieving them, and yet are such that *withholding judgment* about them is more reasonable than believing them. To take an example of Chisholm's: it is more reasonable to believe that the Pope will be in Rome (on some arbitrarily picked future date) than to believe that he won't; but it is perhaps more reasonable to suspend judgment on the question of the Pope's whereabouts on that particular date, than to believe that he will be in Rome. Thus, it might be objected, that while we've shown that believing (1) is more reasonable than disbelieving (1), we haven't shown that believing (1) is more reasonable than withholding belief. My answer to this objection is that there are things we know which render (1) probable to the degree that it is more reasonable to believe (1) than to suspend judgment on (1). What are these things we know? First, I think, is the fact that there is an enormous variety and profusion of intense human and animal suffering in our world. Second, is the fact that much of this suffering seems quite unrelated to any greater goods (or the absence of equal or greater evils) that might justify it. And, finally, there is the fact that such suffering as is related to greater goods (or the absence of equal or greater evils) does not, in many cases, seem so intimately related as to require its permission by an omnipotent being bent on securing those goods (the absence of those evils). These facts, I am claiming, make it more reasonable to accept (1) than to withhold judgment on (1).

6. See, for example, the two chapters on Hume in G. E. Moore, *Some Main Problems of Philosophy* (London, 1953).

7. Suppose that I add a long sum of numbers three times and get result x. I inform you of this so that you have pretty much the same evidence I have for the claim that the sum of the numbers is x. You then use your calculator twice over and arrive at result y. You, then, are justified in believing that the sum of the numbers is *not* x. However, knowing that your calculator has been damaged and is therefore unreliable, and that you have no reason to think that it is damaged, I may reasonably believe not only that the sum of the numbers is x, but also that you are justified in believing that the sum is not x. Here is a case, then, where you have all of my evidence for p, and yet I can reasonably believe that you are justified in believing not-p – for I have reason to believe that your grounds for not-p are not as telling as you are justified in taking them to be.

8. I am indebted to my colleagues at Purdue University, particularly to Ted Ulrich and Lilly Russow, and to philosophers at The University of Nebraska, Indiana State University, and The University of Wisconsin at Milwaukee for helpful criticisms of earlier versions of this paper.

31

The Problem of Evil

Brian Davies

Does evil disprove God's existence or render it unlikely? I shall start by calling into question what seems to be a basic assumption of most contemporary treatments of the problem of evil. This is the assumption that the goodness of God is moral goodness (or, to put it another way, that God, if he exists, is a moral agent, or someone well behaved). Secondly, I shall say something about the Free Will Defence. Thirdly, I shall offer the reader comments on some questions which might be raised about what I argue concerning the goodness of God and the Free Will Defence. I shall then say something about evil and the mystery of God.

The Problem of Evil and the Goodness of God

The problem of evil, for many contemporary philosophical detractors of theism, is clearly a problem concerning God's moral integrity. J. L. Mackie and William Rowe [. . .] take it for granted that God's goodness is moral goodness. Mackie's talk about what "a good thing" will do makes no sense unless construed as talk about *a morally good thing* (presumably conceived of as something like a good human being). The same goes for Rowe's talk of justification for evils, and for his allusion to what accords with our basic moral principles. Rowe thinks

Brian Davies, "The Problem of Evil," from *Philosophy of Religion: A Guide to the Subject* (London: Cassell, 1998). Used by permission of Continuum International Publishing Group.

that God does not exist since, if he did, he would be morally culpable (and therefore does not exist).

What of contemporary philosophical defenders of theism? Taking their lead from arguments to be found in the work of people such as Mackie and Rowe, many of these are also clearly presuming that God's goodness is moral goodness. Alvin Plantinga, Richard Swinburne, William Alston and John Hick (like many other defenders of theism not mentioned above) are all evidently assuming that the proper theistic line on the topic of God and evil is one which defends God's moral integrity. Their positions on the topic of God and evil make no sense unless construed as starting from this assumption.

But should we begin by supposing that the goodness of God is moral goodness, or that God is a moral agent? I ask the question not in order to suggest that God is immoral or sub-moral, but in order to suggest that it is wholly inappropriate to think of God as something able to be either moral (well behaved) or immoral (badly behaved). I ask the question in order to suggest that both foes and friends of theism might do well to fight shy of statements like "God is a moral agent" or "God is morally good" (both of which I take to be equivalent to "God is well behaved").

To start with, note that goodness is not always moral goodness, and that "God is good" should not, therefore, automatically be deemed to be equivalent to "God is morally good". We speak, for example, of good doctors, good dinners, good singers, good houses, good exam results, good holidays . . . good *all sorts* of things. And we do so without suggesting that we are talking in moral terms (a good doctor or tenor, for instance, can be a morally bad person; a good house or a good holiday is neither morally good nor morally bad).[1] As P. T. Geach puts it, "good" is an "attributive" adjective, not a "predicative" one.

Let us say that "in a phrase 'an AB' ('A' being an adjective and 'B' being a noun) 'A' is a (logically) predicative adjective if the predication 'is an AB' splits up into a pair of predications 'is a B' and 'is A'". Let us also say that, if such is not the case, "A" is a (logically) attributive adjective.[2] On this account, "big" and "small" are attributive adjectives and "red" is predicative. As Geach says:

> "X is a big flea" does not split up into "X is a flea" and "X is big", nor "X is a small elephant" into "X is an elephant" and "X is small"; for if these analyses were legitimate, a simple argument would show that a big flea is a big animal and a small elephant a small animal. . . . On the other hand, in the phrase "a red book", "red" is a predicative adjective . . . for "is a red book" logically splits up into "is a book" and "is red".[3]

By the same token, "good" is logically attributive. It does not signify a common property shared by everything which has it. Its use on a given occasion cannot be understood unless one knows to what it is being applied. In this sense, goodness is relative: "good" works like "big" and "small", and differs from "red". To appreciate what is meant when told that something is good, one needs to know what is being talked about.

So what are we talking about when we talk about God? There is a long-standing Christian tradition (which exists in Islamic and Jewish thinking also) which says that we do not know what we are talking about since God is incomprehensible.[4] For present purposes, however, I take it that God is the creator.[5] And I take it that to call God "creator" is to say that he is the source of the being of everything, the reason why there is something rather than nothing, the cause of the existence of the universe (whether or not the universe had a beginning). I take "something" to be a word we use to allude to an individual of some kind, a member of the world, something we can distinguish from other things because of its own special characteristics (its own special way of being and acting), as a distinct thing recognizable as such because it exists in the context of a world in which there are many other such individuals and many other things with which

they may be contrasted as they exist alongside each other as possible objects of scientific enquiry. I take it that if you can single something out as an intelligible individual (something you can get your mind around, something there alongside you in the real world (no matter how far away and no matter how inaccessible to contemporary or future science), something with its own nature as part of a world), then it is being made *to be what* it is and *to be as it* is by God. And I take it that to call God "creator" is to say all this since the Bible (as I read it), and the mainstream Christian tradition (as I understand it), think along such lines.[6]

If that is so, however, theists (and their opponents) have very good reason for denying that God is or could be "well behaved" (a moral agent, morally good). It is people (limited, finite creatures) who can be well behaved as they live their creaturely lives in the order established by God.[7] It is people who are moral agents, or morally good or bad things. It is people who are well or badly behaved.

Theists (Jews, Muslims, Christians) will not, of course, find it amiss to speak of God as just. But they cannot (and, traditionally, do not) mean by this that God gives others what he owes them (commutative justice). For the notion of God being indebted to creatures makes no sense. If God is the source of everything creaturely, he cannot receive and gain by what is creaturely, and then return it to those to whom he is indebted. If we are entitled to call God just it can only be because he can be said to act in accordance with his own decrees (as revealed), or because he gives to his creatures what is good for them given their natures as made by him (this not implying that he gives the same to every creature). Such, in fact, is the view of God's justice found in the Old Testament. There, the justice (or righteousness) of God lies in him acting in accordance with his declared will for Israel (to whom he gives laws as one not bound by them). In Old Testament terms, the justice of God lies in his keeping of the law in accordance with the terms of the covenant as laid down by him. As one commentator puts it:

> The essence of the original biblical concept of God's righteousness lies neither in the ethical postulate of a moral world-order nor in an ideal of impartial retribution imposed by some inner necessity nor in the personification of the ethical by God. Instead it exalts over all abstract ethical ideas a *loyalty manifested in the concrete relationships of community.*[8]

It might be said that some creatures are such that God ought to give them certain things, e.g. that he ought to reward virtuous people with happiness.[9] At this point, however, we come to the issue of God's duties or obligations, and the point to make here is that we have good reason for resisting the suggestion that God can intelligibly be thought of as having duties or obligations.

Could he, for instance, have duties or obligations to himself? Should he, for example, strive to keep himself healthy? Should he try not to let his talents or abilities go to seed? Anyone seriously raising such questions would simply show a failure to grasp what the notion of God as creator amounts to.

One might say that God has obligations to creatures – that he is, for example, obliged to reward good people with happiness. But this suggestion also makes no sense. What can oblige God in relation to his creatures? Could it be that there is a law which says that God has obligations to them? But what law? And where does it come from? Is it something set up by someone independently of God? But how can anyone set up a law independently of God? Is God not the Maker of everything apart from himself?

Someone might say that there are duties and obligations binding on God, and that this just has to be accepted. But why should we believe that? What, indeed, are we to suppose ourselves to believe when believing that? Perhaps we should be thinking that there are moral laws (implying duties) with which God is presented just as he is presented with logical laws. And perhaps we should say that, just as God has to accept that there cannot be any square triangles (logical law), so he must accept that there are certain courses of action which he must either refrain from or adopt (moral law). But the cases cited here are not parallel. God must "accept" that there cannot be any square triangles. We can speak of him as "bound" by the truth that there cannot be any such things. But, since it cannot be known that there is any square triangle, that only means that God cannot know what cannot be known (that omniscience does not extend to knowing what is not an object of knowledge). It does not mean that God is bound by any command to do what can be done (e.g. by a human being). And it does not mean that he has a duty or obligation to do anything we care to mention. One has duties and obligations as part of a definite, describable context. A nurse, for example, has certain duties in the light of things such as hospitals, drugs, sickness, doctors, death and patients. The duties and obligations of nurses arise because of their role as nurses (something which makes no sense apart from the context in which nurses operate). A parent has obligations as someone living with families, children, money, schools, social services, and the like. The duties and obligations of parents arise because of their role as parents (something which makes no sense apart from the context in which parents operate). In that case, however, it seems fair to deny that God has duties and obligations. In the light of what context can he be said to have them? Given the notion of God as creator, there would seem to be no context at all (God is the cause of all contexts), and the notion of him having duties and obligations would therefore seem to be empty. If anything, it would seem better to say that God must be the source of all duties and obligations. For, if God is the creator, he must be the cause of there being situations in which people have duties and obligations.

Someone might reply that God does have obligations since he has obligations to his creatures as parents have obligations to their children. Before you produce a child, someone might argue, you have no obligations to it (because it is not there); but, having produced the child, you do have obligations. And, so the argument might continue, this is how it must be with God. Having fathered me, he is bound to act towards me in certain ways.

But this argument would simply miss the point I am now trying to make. Passing over the fact that God is not a human father living in the created world, let us suppose that God does have obligations towards his creatures. And let us ask how he is supposed to fulfil them. Being God, he can only do so by bringing it about that certain events come to pass. But he can only do that by bringing about the existence of things creatively (not by acting within a world over and against him, but by making the world to be). And how can he be obliged to do that? God, the creator, cannot be a labourer working on things existing over and against him before he sets to work on them. He makes the difference between things being there and things not being there. He is the creator *ex nihilo* (i.e. he makes the difference between there being something rather than nothing). God is also the sustainer *ex nihilo*, not in the sense that he sustains things which do not exist (a contradictory notion), but in the sense that what is sustained (made to continue to be) by him would not be there to be what it is over time (would be nothing, so to speak) if God were not making it to be what it is.

As Rowan Williams has recently put it (writing on the topic of God and evil): "God is never going to be an element, a square centimetre, in any picture, not because God's agency is incalculably greater but because it simply cannot be fitted into the same space."[10] Williams's point (to which he acknowledges a debt to Aquinas) is that to conceive of God as morally responsible is to commit a mistake of the kind which we would be making if we took "salt" or "beef" to be the names of things we might buy two of in a shop.[11] Rather, to use Aquinas's words, we should think of God as "existing outside the realm of existents, as a cause from which pours forth everything that exists in all its variant forms".[12] Aquinas certainly holds that God is good.[13] But it never seems to cross his mind that God's goodness consists in him doing his duty or being virtuous (being well behaved). For Aquinas, God is the source of the world in which people with duties exist (in this sense, Aquinas takes God to be the source of human moral obligations). And he would have thought it quite blasphemous to suggest that God displays virtues. For Aquinas (like Aristotle), virtues are what people need in order to be happy as human beings. But God, on his account, is not a human being and needs no human ways of being happy. To suggest the contrary, Aquinas thinks, would be to think of God in a deeply erroneous way: it would amount to confusing the creature with the creator. It would amount to idolatry. The same conclusion can, I think, be found (directly stated, or stated by implication) in the writings of the major patristic authors, including Augustine, and in the writings of major postpatristic Christian authors from the time of Augustine to the time of the Reformation and beyond. I also take it to be expressed (directly or by implication) in the Bible and in the teachings of the Church Councils up to and including Vatican II.

So, to be blunt, I suggest that many contemporary philosophers writing on the problem of evil (both theists and non-theists) have largely been wasting their time. It has been said that error in philosophy often consists in exploring the details of a road one should never have turned into in the first place. I am suggesting that philosophers who argue for or against God's existence by concentrating on God's supposed moral goodness are well down such a road. They are like people attacking or defending tennis players because they fail to run a mile in under four minutes. Tennis players are not in the business of running four-minute miles. Similarly, God is not something with respect to which moral evaluation (whether positive or negative) is appropriate.[14]

The Free Will Defence

Those who embrace the Free Will Defence take the topic of God and evil essentially to require an essay on God's morality. For the Defence suggests that God is allowing something (the evil committed by free agents) in order that there may come to pass a good (the existence of free agents) – and that God might therefore be defended as being morally good in spite of certain evils we encounter. But, forgetting about objections we may have to the project of defending God's moral integrity, there is another difficulty with the Free Will Defence which ought to be highlighted since it is commonly not alluded to by contemporary philosophers (not surprisingly, in my view, since contemporary philosophers frequently tend to conceive of God as if he were an item in the universe).

We can approach the difficulty in question by referring once again to something said by J. L. Mackie. As we have seen, he thinks it possible for God to have made a world in which people always freely act well. As we have also seen, however, Mackie's view has been contested (e.g. by Alvin Plantinga). But is it really obvious that Mackie is wrong?

Those (like Plantinga) who reject Mackie's view do so because they have in mind a certain picture of human freedom. On their account, there cannot be any such thing as a free human choice which is also caused by God. Why not? Because a choice caused by God would not be a choice at all. It would be something determined, or unfree. But why so?

Most philosophers (though there are some exceptions) would agree that if what I do is the result of something acting on me to make me behave as I do, then my freedom is infringed.[15] And this is a conclusion which seems right. If my arm hits the table because you are gripping my wrist and forcing my arm to the table, then I am not freely hitting the table. If I lunge to left and right because a drug is acting in me, then I do not freely move from left to right. But is it so obvious that if God causes me to do something I am also unfree in what I do?

If we think of God as something existing alongside us (as you are alongside me), and as something acting on us from outside to make us do as we do (like a drug), then it would seem that there cannot be any human freedom if what we do is caused by God. And that, I presume, is why authors such as Plantinga wish to reject Mackie's suggestion that God could have made a world in which people always act well. As we have seen, Plantinga holds that human actions can only be free if "no causal laws and antecedent conditions determine" that they occur or do not occur. I take "causal laws" to refer to codifiable ways in which unfree bits of the world behave of necessity. And I take "antecedent conditions" to mean "the state of the world prior to a human choice". And on that reading of Plantinga's words, I take him to be right.[16]

But Plantinga is wrong to speak as though divine causality is something subject to causal laws or as something exemplifying them somehow. And he is wrong to think of it as an antecedent condition of anything that happens. If we are thinking of God as the cause of the whole universe, if God is what makes things to be (whenever they are), then God (to use Rowan Williams's language) "cannot be fitted into the same space" as causal laws and antecedent conditions. He is not "an element" in "any picture" – including that of determining causes having their inevitable way with things with which they connect.

Here, once again, Aquinas proves illuminating. Just as he insists that God is good (though not morally good, like people), Aquinas also insists that we are able to choose freely. The view that all human action is determined is something he regards as "anarchic" and as undermining all sensible moral thinking. "Human beings", he says, "are masters of their own actions, able to act or not to act. But this can only be so if they can freely choose. So human beings can freely choose their actions."[17] Unlike fans of the Free Will Defence, however, Aquinas finds it unthinkable that any created event, including whatever we take to be there when human choosing occurs, should come to pass without God making it to be. Why? Because he takes seriously the claim that creatures really do owe their entire being to God. Or, in his words:

> God exists in everything; not indeed as part of their substance or as an accident, but as an agent is present to that in which its action is taking place. . . . Since it is God's nature to exist, he it must be who properly causes existence in creatures, just as it is fire itself that sets other things on fire. And God is causing this effect in things not just when they begin to exist, but all the time they are maintained in existence. . . . Now existence is more intimately and profoundly interior to things than anything else, for everything as we said is potential when compared to existence. So God must exist and exist intimately in everything.[18]

Does God's existence in things extend to his existence in human choices? Aquinas answers "Yes".

> Physical things are acted on in the sense that they are directed to an end by another; they do not act like self-determining agents who shape themselves to a purpose, in the manner of rational creatures who deliberate and choose by free judgement. . . . Yet because the very act of freewill goes back to God as its cause, we strictly infer that whatever people freely do on their own falls under God's Providence. . . . The divine power must needs be present to every acting thing. . . . God is the cause of everything's action inasmuch as he gives everything the power to act, and preserves it in being and applies it to action, and inasmuch as by his power every other power acts.[19]

With these points in mind, Aquinas argues that human freedom is not something to be thought of as threatened by God's causality. On the contrary. For Aquinas, I am free not *in spite of* God but *because of* God. My free choices are as much a part of creation as the rock of Mount Everest. And, so Aquinas reasons, if all that is real in Everest is made to be by God, the same is true of all that is real in me.

Aquinas has reason on his side in proposing this conclusion. Unless they are prepared to deny that the being of creatures is God's work, theists cannot view human free choices as not caused to be by God. In that case, however, the Free Will Defence is of no avail to them. It is useless as a way of defending God's moral integrity – even supposing that God has any moral integrity to defend. That is because it denies that humans acting freely are caused to act as they do by God. It conceives of human free actions as events which God must somehow stand back from and learn about as an observer. Effectively, it conceives of them as uncreated. But, as Herbert McCabe has nicely put it (assuming that God really is the cause of the entire being of creatures), "to be free means not to be under the influence of some other *creature*, it is to be independent of other *bits of the universe*; it is not and could not mean to be independent of God".[20]

The Goodness of God and the Freedom of People

I can imagine all sorts of objections being raised against what I have said about the goodness of God and about God's relation to human free choices. Since I cannot deal with all of them, I shall focus on what I would expect to be the first most likely to occur to the reader. They may be put in the form of two questions:

1 If God is not morally good, what can it mean to call God good?
2 How can one avoid holding that human choices are determined (or unfree) if one also takes them to be caused by God?

(1) If God is not morally good, what can it mean to call God good?

This question is forcefully pressed by the contemporary Christian philosopher Paul Helm. In *The Providence of God* Helm notes how some have resisted the suggestion that the goodness of God is moral goodness. But he finds their position puzzling. "What sort of goodness might God have that is not *moral* goodness?", he asks. "What is the concept of non-moral goodness?"[21] "The goodness of God", says Helm, "must bear some positive relation to the sorts of human actions we regard as good. Otherwise, why ascribe *goodness* to God?"[22] Helm's questions are perfectly fair ones. So let me try to answer them. I shall do so by suggesting (a) that God is good since God is perfect, and (b) that we have reason to call God good since we know him as the maker of all creaturely goodness, which must therefore reflect him somehow.

(a) God as perfect

I take it that to call something perfect is to imply that it is good (though not *vice versa*). If we have reason to call God "perfect", therefore, we have reason for calling him good. And it seems to me that we have reason to call God perfect. Furthermore, we have reason for calling God perfect in a way which does not imply moral excellence on his part.

I said above that we shall not understand "it's good" unless we know what "it" is. And the same is true when it comes to "it's perfect". What perfection amounts to in something of one kind (e.g. a

perfect wife) may be descriptively very different from what it amounts to in something of another kind (e.g. a perfect horse). But it does not follow from this that we are wholly at sea when trying to give some general account of what perfection is. For, though perfect things may not all share the same attributes or properties, they are all alike in one respect. For they are all succeeding in some respect. Or, rather, they are all as good as it is possible to be considering the sort of thing they are. A perfect X is an X which cannot be improved upon as an X. A perfect X is a wholly successful X which, as an X, cannot have anything added to it to make it better.

Now this notion of "not being improvable" is one we can employ when talking about God. For if God is the source of the being of everything, then God is no inhabitant of the world. And if God is no inhabitant of the world, then God is not something changing or changeable, for he is no inhabitant of space and time.[23] From this it follows that there can be no gap between what God is and what God might become, from which it follows, in turn, that the notion of God improving (or, for that matter, getting worse) can have no place in thinking about divinity. If God exists, then God is unchangeably all that it takes to be God. And from this I conclude that God can be said to be perfect and, therefore, good.

Here I agree with what Aquinas says when he turns to the topic of God's perfection. Aquinas thinks that perfection is the opposite of imperfection. He also thinks that imperfection is present when something which is potentially perfect (i.e. able to be perfect, though not actually perfect) is actually imperfect. For Aquinas, something imperfect fails because it is not what it could and needs (or ought) to be, because, in Aquinas's language, it lacks a certain sort of actuality.[24] And, since he takes God to be wholly actual, Aquinas therefore concludes that God can be thought of as perfect.

> The first origin of all activity will be the most actual, and therefore the most perfect, of all things. For things are called perfect when they have achieved actuality, the perfect thing being that in which nothing required by the thing's particular mode of perfection fails to exist. . . . Because things that are made are called perfect when the potentiality of them has been actualized, we extend the word to refer to anything that is not lacking in actuality, whether made or not.[25]

Aquinas is saying that God must be perfect since he is in no way potential – since there is nothing which he could be but is not. Since God, for Aquinas, has no potentiality, he cannot be modified and cannot, therefore, be either improved or made worse. There is with him no "could be thus and so but is not". For God to be, therefore, is for God to be as divine as it takes divinity to be. It is for God to be fully God and, therefore, perfectly God. Since I find Aquinas's reasoning sound at this point, I suggest that God is perfect and therefore good. The suggestion, please note, makes no claim to understand what the perfection of God amounts to. It belongs to what is sometimes called "negative theology" (theology which reminds us of what God cannot be). All the same, it is enough to give sense to the claim that God is good. And it does so without asserting that God is morally good like good, human, moral agents.

(b)   God as the maker of creaturely goodness

In suggesting that we have reason to call God good since we know him as the maker of all creaturely goodness, which must therefore reflect him somehow, I am again indebted to Aquinas. To be precise, I am in sympathy with what he says when he writes:

> Goodness should be associated above all with God. For goodness is consequent upon desirability. Now things desire their perfection; and an effect's perfection and form consists in resembling its cause, since what a thing does reflects what it is. So the cause itself is desirable and can be called "good", what is desired from it being a share in resembling it. Clearly, then, since God is the primary operative cause of everything, goodness and desirability fittingly belong to him. And so Dionysius (*The Divine Names*, 4, 4) ascribes goodness to God as to the primary operative cause, saying that God is called good as the source of all subsistence.[26]

This is a difficult passage, however, so let me try to unpack it a little.

In saying that "goodness is consequent upon desirability" Aquinas, echoing Aristotle, means that "good" can be thought of as equivalent to "attractive". In the *Nicomachean Ethics*, Aristotle says that goodness is "that at which all things aim".[27] According to Aristotle, goodness is what attracts or is desired. Aristotle, of course, is perfectly aware

that people might be drawn to what is bad for them and for others. So he does not assume that what I actually desire on a given occasion is actually good for me or for others. But, so he thinks, we can make nothing of the suggestion that something is good without introducing the notions of attractiveness or desirability. And that is what Aquinas thinks. He thinks, for example, that a *good* bicycle is one you would be *attracted* by if you wanted one for *cycling* (as distinct from, say, an object to photograph or help you over a wall). And, with this thought in mind, Aquinas wants to say that God is good since God is attractive.

But how is God attractive? In the above quotation from Aquinas, his answer lies in the words: "Now things desire their perfection; and an effect's perfection and form consists in resembling its cause, since what a thing does reflects what it is. So the cause itself is desirable and can be called 'good', what is desired from it being a share in resembling it. Clearly, then, since God is the primary operative cause of everything, goodness and desirability fittingly belong to him." Here Aquinas's idea seems to be (1) that all things seek their good (that which attracts), (2) that all things seeking their good are effects of God (things made to be by God), (3) that effects are somehow like their causes, and (4) that the goodness which creatures are drawn to is therefore like God, who can therefore be thought of as attractive (or good) like the goodness to which creatures are attracted. But, here again, we have some puzzling notions which need explanation. The most puzzling, perhaps, is the suggestion that effects are like their causes, which seems evidently false. A stew, for example, does not look at all like a human cook. A car crash does not look like the factors that brought it about.

In trying to understand Aquinas at this point, however, it is important to recognize that he is not asserting that effects always *look* like their causes (though he thinks that they sometimes do since, for example, children often look like their parents). Rather, his thesis is that causes (in the sense of agents in the world which bring about changes in the world) explain their effects and do so precisely because of what they are. For him, we have an explanation of some development in the world when we reach the point of saying "Oh, I see. Of course that explains it." And we have this, he thinks, when we see how a cause is expressing its nature in its effect.

Suppose that Fred is staggering around. We ask "How come?" Then we learn that he has drunk a lot of whisky, and we say "Oh, I see. Of course that explains it." But what do we "see"? One might be tempted to say something like "We see that it is not surprising that Fred should be staggering since people who drink whisky often do that". One might say that what "seeing" means here is that we note that what is now occurring has happened a large number of times before. But if one occurrence is puzzling (if, for example, Fred's staggering is puzzling), why should a thousand such occurrences be less puzzling? That drinking whisky is followed (or regularly followed) by staggering does not *explain* what has happened. It simply reports what we have become used to experiencing. Someone offering only such a report would be in the position of what Aristotle calls the man of "experience" as distinct from the "wise" men who do *see why* the drinking is connected with the staggering.[28]

Until quite recent times, nobody did see the connection. To see it you need a chemical account of alcohol and an account of the effect of this substance on the brain (molecular biology is relevant here), and of the effect of these events in the brain on the movements of the legs. Only when you have developed this kind of understanding to give an account of what is happening with the staggering drunk can you be said to *see why* he is staggering. And what you would at last see is why it has to be the case that the drunk is staggering. To see, in this sense, is to have what Aquinas would have called *scientia*. And when he says that causes are *like their effects* he simply means that seeing why the effects spring from their causes is seeing how the nature of the cause explains the effect and renders its effect necessary, and therefore unsurprising. He means that though, when drunk, I cannot be described as looking like alcohol, I am, when drunk, certainly showing forth what alcohol is. And in this sense, so he thinks, I resemble it. For him, the drunken man is, when properly understood, alcohol in action, alcohol expressing its nature in something – something which is, therefore, "like" alcohol.

Hence, so Aquinas argues, creatures which aim at their good can be thought of as expressing what God is in himself. We cannot, so he thinks, have a *scientia* which allows us to say something like "Now we can see why God has produced these particular effects". Aquinas does not suppose that God is something with respect to which we can develop a science which explains why God has the effects which he has. For him, any such thing would be a creature. But, trying to say something about the source of the being of all things, Aquinas finds it natural or appropriate (or, at least, not inappropriate) to suggest that since effects in nature show forth the nature of their causes, we can think of God as being shown forth in his effects. And since the goodness which creatures seek is something created by God, it can, thinks Aquinas, be thought of as being like what God is. Aquinas does not mean that God's goodness depends on his having created. Nor does he mean that we have any picture or image of God's goodness. But, so he thinks, we have grounds for calling God good since, whether or not God created, he would still be whatever he is as shown forth by the created world. And, since Aquinas thinks that the created world gives us grounds for calling God good as being "like" that to which all creatures are attracted (i.e. goodness), he thinks we have grounds for calling God "good".

And Aquinas, I think, is right. In the sense implied by him, effects do "resemble" their causes. If you pour exactly one mole of sulphuric acid on one mole of zinc metal, the zinc will always fizz, and disappear, and give off an inflammable gas, and the sulphuric acid will lose its corrosive power.[29] But why? Because:

$$Zn(s) + H_2SO_4(aq) \rightarrow ZnSO_4(aq) + H_2(g)$$

Here you see (in a literal sense) that what is on the right side of the $\rightarrow$ is the same as the elements on the left side. In this sense, the products of the reaction resemble the reactants. So you can now say "Yes, I see, of course". Effects really do reflect what their causes are. What Aquinas calls the likeness of an effect to its cause is precisely what we are seeking as we look for scientific explanations. And since all effects are ultimately God's effects, and since these include creatures who are attracted to what is good, God can be called "good" as the source of all that is attractive. He can be called this even on the (traditional Christian) assumption that the created world is in no way necessary to God (that there might never have been a world created by God). For, so we may say, in calling God good with an eye on his creation, we are alluding to what God is in himself, whether or not he creates – that the reality of the created order gives us a reason to say what God essentially is. Mary and John might decide never to have children. But the children they actually produce reflect what they are whether or not they choose to procreate. By the same token, so we may argue, the actual world reflects what God is apart from creation. You cannot give what you have not got, and God, so we may say, is what the goodness aimed at (and often achieved) by creatures is. He is attractive and, therefore, good (since "good" can be equated with "attractive" or "desired"). This is not, of course, to say that we have any understanding of what God's goodness amounts to. But it is to say, as I argued above with respect to "God is perfect", that we have a reason for calling God good – a reason which does not amount to the suggestion that God is a morally good individual, like a morally good human being. But, as should be obvious, it does not warrant the conclusion that God is good as a human moral agent is good. The argument I am now employing entails that human moral goodness reflects God and shows us something of what God is. So I have no problem in agreeing that human moral goodness reflects what God is. But that is not the same as saying that the goodness of God is moral goodness (a matter of being well behaved).

(2) How can one avoid holding that human choices are determined (or unfree) if one also takes them to be caused by God?

I have rejected the Free Will Defence since it rests on the assumption that human free choices are not caused by God. But how can my choices be caused by God without me being the puppet of God – something really lacking anything we can mean by "freedom"? Should we not equate "is caused" with "is determined" (the assumption being that if X is "determined" it cannot be "free")? And should we not therefore conclude that if human choices are caused by God they simply cannot be free?

I think that the answer to these questions is "No" since I see no reason to think of God as the sort of cause which can render what it causes unfree. Quite the contrary. For our knowledge of human free choices, and our knowledge of causes which determine their effects (i.e. render them necessary rather than free), depends on God as causing the existence of the world as a whole (including those things which act freely and those things which do not).

Consider, to begin with, what we mean when saying that a person chooses freely. The topic of human freedom has been hotly debated by philosophers over the centuries, but, when all the philosophical dust has settled, we surely have to say that human beings choose freely if nothing else alongside them acts on them from outside to make (force) them behave as they do.[30] By the same token,

someone behaves unfreely if the proper explanation of their behaviour lies in an understanding of the nature and action of something else, or of the purposes and action of someone else. Thus, my falling because of the poison I have taken is unfree and explicable in terms of the nature of the poison I have taken. So we say, for example: "He swallowed arsenic; that, of course, is why he fell to the ground." Or we say: "Jones hit him on the head; that, of course, was why he fell to the ground." But God, so I argue, is not something alongside human beings with a nature displayed by certain particular typical effects and not others (like arsenic or another human being). God accounts for there being a world in which some explanations of human behaviour rightly refer to the intentions of humans to act as they do (explanations in terms of free choices) and some explanations of human behaviour rightly refer to the action on us of other things with the power to make us behave in ways which cannot be thought of as chosen by us.

With these thoughts in mind, I again refer the reader to Aquinas, who seems to me to talk more sense than most on the topic of God and human freedom. We have seen him arguing that God exists "intimately in everything". Bearing in mind the question "How can we be free in a world made by God?", he argues that what we can understand as existing free and determined things must, as distinct or distinguishable existing things, all be caused to be by God, who must therefore be the condition of human freedom, not something which abolishes it.[31] Or, in Aquinas's words:

God's will is to be thought of as existing outside the realm of existents, as a cause from which pours forth everything that exists in all its variant forms. Now *what can be* and *what must be* are variants of being, so that it is from God's will itself that things derive whether they must be or may or may not be and the distinction of the two according to the nature of their immediate causes. For he prepares causes that must cause for those effects that he wills must be, and causes that might cause but might fail to cause for those effects that he wills might or might not be. And it is because of the nature of their causes that some effects are said to be effects that must be and others effects that need not be, although all depend on God's will as primary cause, a cause which transcends this distinction between *must* and *might not*. But the same cannot be said of human will or of any other cause, since every other cause exists within the realm of *must* and *might not*. So of every other cause it must be said either that it can fail to cause, or that its effect must be and cannot not be; God's will, however, cannot fail, and yet not all his effects must be, but some can be or not be.[32]

What Aquinas is driving at here has, I think, been nicely captured by James F. Ross. As he puts it:

The being of the cosmos is like *a song on the breath of a singer*. It has endless internal universal laws, and structures nested within structures, properties that are of *the song* and *not* of the singer or the voice or the singer's thought, though produced by them and attributively predicated of them. . . . The universe is continuously depending, like a song or a light show . . . ; its being is its own, yet it is from a cause, everywhere, and at no *including* time . . . God produces, for each individual being, the one that does such and such (whatever it does) throughout its whole time in being. . . . God does not make the person act; he makes the so acting person *be*. . . . The whole physical universe, all of it, is actively caused to be. Still, to say that freedom or human agency is thereby impeded is absurd. Nothing can be or come about unless caused to be by the creator. So the fact that God's causing is necessary for whatever happens cannot impede liberty; it is a condition for it. Similarly, in no way is our liberty impeded by the fact that God's causing is sufficient for the being of the very things that do the very things that we do. Nothing possible can be impeded by its necessary conditions. . . . God did not make Adam to be the first man to defy God; God made Adam, who was the first man to defy God, to be. God made Adam, who undertook to sin. . . . God makes all the free things that do *as* they do, instead of doing otherwise as is in their power, by their *own* undertaking. So God does not make Adam sin. But God makes the sinning Adam, the person who, *able* not to sin, does sin. It follows logically that if Adam had not sinned, God would have made a person who, though able to sin, did not. And, surely, God *might* have made a person who, though able to sin, did not. . . . It is the whole being, doing as it does, whether a free being or not, that is entirely produced and sustained for its time by God.[33]

What Aquinas and Ross have to say seems to me correct. So I therefore suggest that my grounds for rejecting the Free Will Defence allow me to believe in the reality of human freedom as well as in the reality of God, the source of the being of creatures.

Evil and the Mystery of God

I have now rejected the idea that God has some moral case to answer. And I have also denied that human choices should be thought of as uncaused by God. But I do not want to suggest that there is nothing more to be said on the topic of God and evil. On the contrary, I want to suggest that there is, indeed, a serious problem of evil. In my view, it is one which philosophy cannot solve. But I also think that it does nothing to suggest that God does not exist. Rather, it serves to highlight the mystery that God is to us as people trying to think about God in a philosophical way.

"Evil suffered" and "evil done"

To start with, we need to note that there are two kinds of evil. There is, as Herbert McCabe nicely puts it, "evil suffered" and "evil done".[34]

"Evil suffered" is anything which can be seriously thought of as diminishing or thwarting something. People who are ill are victims of evil suffered. So too are animals who are attacked (and maybe killed) by other animals (including us), or animals who endure pain for some other reason. Among victims of evil suffered we may even include plants, whose lives are ended by people who pluck them and eat them.

"Evil done" is what we have in mind when we say that someone acts badly (i.e. morally badly), for "evil done" is something which renders the badly acting agent bad in his or her self. We often think of moral evil chiefly with an eye on the victims of morally bad people. In thinking of people as morally bad we are often concentrating on, for example, the unhappiness they cause. And, if asked why they are bad, we may simply refer to this. But someone can act in a morally bad way without anything else suffering (the bomb I planted might not have gone off). And the same result as can be caused by a morally bad person can also come about simply in the course of nature (a human being murdered by someone using the branch of a tree might, to forensic experts, look just the same as someone struck by a branch falling from a tree in a storm). So we need to remember that people acting morally badly are *themselves* bad, regardless of their effects. Agents of "evil done" are first of all victims of themselves.

God and the badness of evil suffered and evil done

But what is the badness of evil suffered and evil done? With this question in mind, it seems to me that the *privatio boni* theory, noted above, is one which has to be taken very seriously. Evil is not an individual with a life or character of its own. Nor is it a positive quality, like being square or being plastic. Victims of evil suffered, and those who are morally bad, are all perfectly or entirely real. They are individuals there to be described. But what renders them bad is the gap between what they are and what they should be but are not. Human sickness would not worry us if it did not amount to there being people deprived of some thriving, prospering or flourishing. Acting people would not strike us as morally bad unless we recognized that, in acting as they do, they fail to do what they ought or need to do (or they fail to be what they ought or need to be). Such failure cannot, of course, occur without something positive being there. I cannot, for instance, murder someone if my body does not behave in certain ways. Evil done may exemplify skills and excellences which we might, without reference to context, desire and applaud. Successful practitioners of genocide tend to be people who exhibit unusual abilities in planning and organization (a good thing). They are normally rather intelligent or quick-witted (good again). And, given their goals, they employ their intellect to good effect (i.e. they succeed in their dreadful aims). But they are evil. And that is because of what they are not. While succeeding in what it takes to commit genocide, they are failing in some way. While perfectly real, they also lack something (e.g. justice, charity, proper concern for others).

With these thoughts in mind, an important point worth making with respect to God and evil is that evil cannot intelligibly be thought of as made to be by God (assuming that we take God to make the difference between something being and not being). So, at this point, I agree with what Aquinas says when he suggests (see above) that, though evil is no illusion, it cannot be thought of as a substance or quality the existence of which is caused by God.

There are holes in walls, but holes have no independent existence. There are holes in walls only because there are walls with something missing.

There are blind people. But blindness has no independent existence. There are blind people only because there are people who cannot see. In a similar way, evil has no independent existence. It "is there" only in the sense that something "is missing". But what is *not there* cannot be thought of as made to be by the source of the being of things. It cannot be thought to be made to be by God. Following Aristotle, Aquinas distinguishes between the use of "is" in sentences like "John is blind" and "John is" (i.e. exists). He takes the first use to signify that a predicate (i.e. "—— is blind") can be attached to the name "John" so as to result in a true statement. He takes the second use to signify that "John" is a genuine name (i.e. a word which labels something in the real world, something which has what Aquinas calls *esse*, or actual existence). In the light of these considerations, Aquinas maintains that, since God is the source of there being what has *esse*, God cannot be thought of as causing evil to be. For evil is not anything actual (whether a substance or a property). It is what we may talk of things as "being" only in the sense that we may speak of people as "being blind". It is the unreality we acknowledge when we call things bad, sick, maimed, defective, thwarted, and so on. And here, so I suggest, Aquinas is right. Evil cannot intelligibly be thought of as something which God has made to be.

On the other hand, however, there is evil suffered (e.g. there are ill human beings), and there is evil done (e.g. there are people who act unjustly). So what is going on when these come to pass?

Notice that, confronted by evil suffered, we naturally look for a natural explanation. If Mary is sick we try to discover what (in the world) accounts for her state. If we come across the corpse of a zebra, we assume that something (in the world) was responsible for the zebra's death. In other words, we never assume that evil suffered is *naturally inexplicable*. We assume, in fact, that there is something (even if we do not, as yet, know what exactly that is) which, by being *good in its way*, is causing something else to be *bad in its way*. We assume, in effect, that nothing ever suffers evil except at the hands of some other being which is gaining some good (even though, in the case of a free creature, it may be, in a deeper sense, damaging itself by practising evil done).[35]

What does this tell us about God and evil suffered? It tells us, I suggest, that evil suffered is a necessary concomitant of certain goods, and that God can only be said to have brought it about in the sense that he brought about those goods. As we have seen, it has been suggested that there is *too much* evil suffered in God's world (the implication being that God is either bad or non-existent). But, if evil means "evil suffered", there is no more evil than there need be. Any evil suffered that is *more than there need be* would be *lacking a natural cause*. It would be scientifically inexplicable. The evil suffered in the world is neither *more* nor *less* than what we can expect in a material world in which scientific explanations can be given for what happens. As we have seen, William Rowe thinks that there are multitudes of instances of "seemingly pointless human and animal suffering that occur daily in our world". But no human or animal suffering is pointless if "pointless" means "lacking a natural explanation" and if the suffering in question is what I am calling "evil suffered". For a natural explanation is exactly what we are looking for when seeking to account for evil suffered. One might, perhaps, say that evil suffered could always be prevented by a constant series of miracles and that it is, for this reason, pointless (sometimes or always). But a world governed by a constant series of miracles would not be a material world. It would not be an object of scientific enquiry. It could, perhaps, have been created by God, but the fact of the matter is that it has not been.[36] What God has created is a material world in which there is evil suffered. And in making this world to be, God is making what is good. Indeed, he is making nothing but what is good.

What about "evil done", however? Unlike evil suffered, this can hardly be thought of as *benefiting* something. People who wrong others harm their victims. And, in doing so, they are bad in themselves. With evil done, unlike evil suffered, there is no concomitant good. There is nothing but failure. Evil done often involves success, of course. To return to my previous example, the perpetrator of genocide may be succeeding in all sorts of ways – as a killer, a strategist, and so on. But agents of evil done are fundamentally failing to be good and nothing is benefiting from this (except accidentally). The evil in their actions is nothing but such failure.

In that case, however, it can hardly be thought to be made by God. The evil in a morally evil act is not something which God can make to be since it is not something existing. It is no kind of individual or positive quality. It can no more be made to be by God than can square circles. And, in that case, we have to say that evil done represents no action of God. Evil suffered does, and the same goes for the positive realities which are there in those who are morally wicked. But the evil in evil done is nothing but failure. Considered as such, it is not something produced by those who are morally evil. Nor can it be thought of as something produced by God.

What God might have produced and the problem of evil

If we think of God as the source of the being of things, then God can make to be whatever can be thought of as possibly existing. As Aquinas writes:

> Since every agent enacts its like, every active power has a possible objective corresponding to the nature of that activity which the active power is for. . . . The divine being, on which the notion of divine power is founded, is infinite existence, not limited to any kind of being, but holding within itself and anticipating the perfection of the whole of existence. Whatever can have the nature of being falls within the range of things that are absolutely possible, and it is with respect to these that God is called all-powerful.[37]

Aquinas means that created causes have a determinate range of effects depending on their natures, while God has no such range. And that seems to me to be true. There is no definite limited range of possibilities in what God can bring about. Things belonging to a distinct genus and species are limited in what they can bring about, for they can only produce effects which are characteristic of things in that genus and species. But God is not limited in this way. A man and a woman can bring it about that something is a human being. Two dogs can bring it about that something is a dog. But God can bring it about that something is, *period*. So if it *could be*, then God can bring it about, and his power is relative to the bringing about of what can be.

As far as I can see, it is this thought that gives us anything we might fairly call "the philosophical problem of evil". As I have suggested, the "problem" of God's moral integrity is a pseudo-problem. It is analogous to the problem expressed in the question "Why don't tennis players run a mile in under four minutes?" I have also suggested (a) that there can be no question of human free choices not being caused to be by God, and (b) that evil suffered could be abolished by a series of miracles. Since I take morally good behaviour to be something which can be, I take (a) to imply that God could have made a world in which there was no moral evil. And I take (b) to imply that, absolutely speaking, there might have been no evil suffered. So why has God not made a world in which there is no moral evil? And why has he not made a world in which there is no evil suffered?

Along with many thinkers, we might try to answer these questions by alluding to the good which often comes out of evil suffered and evil done. And it is true that good always comes out of evil in the case of evil suffered (in the sense that there is no evil suffered without concomitant good). It is also true that good sometimes (as a side-effect) comes out of evil done (in the sense that evil done is sometimes followed by consequences which can be thought of as good). But these truths do nothing to explain why there is any evil done or any evil suffered. Those who try to argue that God is well behaved think that they have such an explanation. It lies in God's morally good intentions. But if the notion that God is well behaved is suspect from the start, it can do nothing to explain why there is any evil done or any evil suffered. And if the Free Will Defence is brought in as a defence of God's moral integrity, it fails on two counts. It fails because its intention is to defend the morality of God. And it fails since it erroneously supposes that human free choices are not made to be by God. As far as I can see, God could have made a world in which people, angels, or any other creatures who might sensibly be thought of as moral agents (subject to duties, obligations and the like) always act well. So why has God not done so? And does his not having done so mean that he is bad?

To take the second question first, my suggestion is that we have no grounds for thinking of God as bad. I have been arguing that God is not good as a morally good human being is good. And I have given reasons for saying that God is good. One might suppose that God is bad since he has made the kind of world we inhabit (one which lacks various imaginable goods) even though he could have made a world with more good things in it (given that more good things than there are in the world are things able to be and, therefore, things which God can make or have made to be). But this supposition only makes sense on the assumption that God has a duty or obligation of some

kind to make a world which is different from the real one. And, so I have argued, such an assumption is misguided.

To take the first question second, I invite the reader to consider what people can mean by questions of the sort "Why has God . . . ?" Are they asking for an account of reasons which God has? Perhaps they are. If so, however, they are surely as off-beam as those who ask questions like "Why don't tennis players run a mile in under four minutes?" We know what it is to act with a reason since we know of human beings who, being language-users existing in time, sometimes act because they can conceive of something they want to come to pass in the future. But if God is the cause of the being of everything, he cannot be seriously thought of as a language-user existing in time acting because he wants something to come to pass in the future. The notion of God literally having "reasons for acting" seems highly dubious (if the literal sense of "reasons for acting" signifies what people have when they have reasons for acting). The notion of God literally having reasons for acting seems to imply that God is all too human. I am not denying that God has knowledge and will. Nor am I denying that what God has brought about can be talked of as intended. I am, however, suggesting that we cannot think of God as acting with reasons as human beings do. We can come to understand why Fred sold his house. We cannot, so it seems to me, come to any similar understanding of why God has made things to be the way they are and not otherwise.

And it is here, so it seems to me, that the real problem of evil lies. God could have created a world in which no evil suffered comes to pass (though I do not know what such a world would look like). And he could have created a world full of moral agents who always act well. But God has evidently not done that. Why not? I have no idea. And that is why I think that there is a problem of evil. But it is not a problem which casts doubt on what we say if we assert that divinity is not something fictional. It is not a problem which suggests that there is no God. Rather, it is something which invites us to reflect on the mystery of divinity, something which serves to remind us that God is nothing less than the beginning and end of all things, the source from which everything we can understand derives its existence.

Notes

1 For this reason, "good" can be taken to be the general word we use when approving or admiring things.

2 P. T. Geach, "Good and evil", reprinted in Philippa Foot (ed.), *Theories of Ethics* (Oxford, 1967), p. 64.

3 Ibid.

4 Cf. David Burrell, *Knowing the Unknowable God* (Notre Dame, 1986).

5 Christians traditionally deny that God has to create. So we may say that God is not essentially creator. But all discussions of God and evil start from the fact that God has created and that what should be said of God should be based on that. Note that, as countless theists have insisted, to say that God is Creator is not to deny that God is incomprehensible. For the most part, indeed, the claim that God is incomprehensible has sprung from reflection on the notion of God as Creator (coupled with reflection on the Old and New Testaments).

6 Throughout the Jewish and Christian Scriptures (the Old and New Testaments), God is the transcendent source of all things. He makes the world to begin, he keeps it in being, and he does with it what he wills. He is not a "god" – i.e. some material or spiritual individual conceived of (or conceivable as) as something alongside other things. He is the reality which lies beyond the world and makes it to be as it is.

7 We might include creatures such as angels, since the Christian tradition speaks of good and bad angels.

8 Walter Eichrodt, *Theology of the Old Testament*, vol. I (London, 1961), p. 249.

9 In the book of Job, a good man is afflicted by God. He is eventually recompensed to some extent, but it is never suggested that this is because God owes this to him.

10 Rowan Williams, "Reply: redeeming sorrows" in D. Z. Phillips (ed.), *Religion and Morality* (New York, 1996), p. 135. That is why the use of "he" (or "she") when talking about God is always a constant reminder of the limits of our language. Since theists want to say that God is real (not a fiction), they have to talk of God as if he were a thing in the world, for we naturally make assertions by singling out a subject (something nameable, something which might be a man or a woman or a material object) and by saying what properties it has. But God is not a nameable object in the world and our way of speaking of him as such needs to be understood accordingly.

11 You can buy two *boxes of* salt and two *portions of* beef. But you cannot buy two "salt" or two "beef".

12 Commentary on Aristotle's *De Interpretatione* or *Perihermeneias*, Book 1, chapter 9, 18b26–19a22: lectio 14.

13 Cf. *Summa Theologiae* I, 5.

14 I develop this point in "How is God love?" in Luke Gormally (ed.), *Moral Truth and Moral Tradition: Essays in Honour of Peter Geach and Elizabeth Anscombe*

(Dublin and Portland, OR, 1994). For an interesting development of the point see also D. Z. Phillips, *The Concept of Prayer* (London, 1965), ch. 5. See also Herbert McCabe, *God Matters* (London, 1987).

15 A good defence of this thesis can be found in Peter van Inwagen, *An Essay on Free Will* (Oxford, 1983).

16 Perhaps Plantinga would not accept this reading of his words. Perhaps he thinks that God's making-to-be of creatures is governed by causal laws and that God is something existing at times before particular human choices occur. If that is so, then all I can say is that Plantinga seems to think that God is a creature of some sort.

17 *Quaestio Disputata de malo* 6.

18 *Summa Theologiae* I, 8, 1.

19 *Summa Theologiae* I, 22, 2, *ad* 4; *De Potentia*, 3, 7.

20 *God Matters*, p. 14. Cf. Paul Helm, *The Providence of God* (Leicester, 1993). Helm refers to the notion that God does not cause, but somehow observes and waits upon, human free choices (which he may just have to put up with) as a denial of a "no risk" view of divine providence. As biblical texts supporting a "no risk" view of God, Helm (quite reasonably) cites 1 Thess 1: 5; Rom 1: 6; 9: 11; 1 Cor 1: 9; Eph 4: 4; 2 Tim 2: 25; and Eph 2: 8. Alluding to John 8: 36, Helm, rightly to my mind, observes that "The New Testament appears to find no incoherence in the idea of being made to be free" (p. 55).

21 Helm, *The Providence of God*, p. 167.

22 Ibid. Cf. also p. 201.

23 On these grounds I would reject the teaching of Moltmann and Sobrino noted above.

24 Cf. *Compendium of Theology*, ch. 20: "Imperfection occurs in a thing for the reason that matter is found in a state of privation. On the other hand, perfection comes exclusively from form."

25 *Summa Theologiae* I, 4, 1.

26 *Summa Theologiae* I, 6, 1.

27 I, 1, 1094a3.

28 Cf. Aristotle, *Metaphysics*, I, 1.

29 This is the language of Aristotle's man of "experience".

30 I know of no contemporary secular determinists who argue their case on theological grounds.

31 For an analysis of Aquinas on this topic, see Harm J. M. J. Goris, *Free Creatures of an Eternal God: Thomas Aquinas on God's Infallible Foreknowledge and Irresistible Will* (Leuven, 1996).

32 Commentary on Aristotle's *De Interpretatione* or *Perihermeneias*, Book 1, chapter 9, lectio 13.

33 James F. Ross, "Creation II" in Alfred J. Freddoso (ed.), *The Existence and Nature of God* (Notre Dame and London, 1983), pp. 128–34.

34 Cf. *God Matters*, ch. 3. Medieval authors distinguish between *malum poenae* (evil of penalty) and *malum culpae* (evil of fault) – a distinction presupposing

various theological beliefs about what results in what. Later writers distinguish between "natural evil" (or "metaphysical evil") and "moral evil" (a distinction presupposing various philosophical beliefs about what results in what). McCabe's distinction between "evil suffered" and "evil done" nicely avoids theological and philosophical theories about what results in what

while clearly drawing attention to the kinds of evil which we encounter.

35 Ibid., pp. 31–2.

36 Actually, I have no idea what I would be agreeing to if I agreed that God could have made a world continually governed by miracles.

37 *Summa Theologiae* I, 25, 3.

32

The Problem of Evil, the Problem of Air, and the Problem of Silence

Peter van Inwagen

It used to be widely held that evil – which for present purposes we may identify with undeserved pain and suffering – was incompatible with the existence of God: that no possible world contained both God and evil. So far as I am able to tell, this thesis is no longer defended. But arguments for the following weaker thesis continue to be very popular: Evil (or at least evil of the amounts and kinds we actually observe) constitutes evidence against the existence of God, evidence that seems decisively to outweigh the totality of available evidence *for* the existence of God.

In this essay, I wish to discuss what seems to me to be the most powerful version of the "evidential argument from evil." The argument takes the following form. There is a serious hypothesis h that is inconsistent with theism and on which the amounts and kinds of suffering that the world contains are far more easily explained than they are on the hypothesis of theism. This fact constitutes a prima facie case for preferring h to theism. Examination shows that there is no known way of answering this case, and there is good reason to think that no way of answering it will be forthcoming. Therefore, the hypothesis h is (relative to the epistemic situation of someone who has followed the argument this far) preferable to theism. But if p and q are inconsistent and p is (relative to one's epistemic situation) epistemically preferable to q, then it is not rational

Peter van Inwagen, "The Problem of Evil, the Problem of Air, and the Problem of Silence," reprinted from *Philosophical Perspectives* 5: *Philosophy of Religion* (1991), pp. 135–65.

for one to accept q. (Of course, it does not follow either that it is rational for one to accept p or that it is rational for one to reject q.) It is, therefore, not rational for one who has followed the argument up to this point to accept theism.[1]

In Section I, I shall present the version of the evidential argument from evil I wish to discuss. In Section II, I shall explain why I find the argument unconvincing. These two sections could stand on their own, and this essay might have consisted simply of the proposed refutation of the evidential argument from evil that they contain. But many philosophers will find the proposed refutation implausible, owing to the fact that it turns on controversial theses about the epistemology of metaphysical possibility and intrinsic value. And perhaps there will also be philosophers who find my reasoning unconvincing because of a deep conviction that, since evil just *obviously* creates an insoluble evidential problem for the theist, a reply to any version of the evidential argument can be nothing more than a desperate attempt to render the obvious obscure. Now if philosophers are unconvinced by one's diagnosis of the faults of a certain argument, one can attempt to make the diagnosis seem more plausible to them by the following method. One can try to find a "parallel" argument that is obviously faulty, and try to show that a parallel diagnosis of the faults of the parallel argument can be given, a diagnosis that seems plausible, and hope that some of the plausibility of the parallel diagnosis will rub off on the original. For example, if philosophers find one's diagnosis of the faults of the ontological argument unconvincing, one can construct an obviously faulty argument that "runs parallel to" the ontological argument – in the classical case, an argument for the existence of a perfect island. And one can then attempt to show that a diagnosis parallel to one's diagnosis of the faults of the ontological argument is a correct diagnosis of the faults (which, one hopes, will be so evident as to be uncontroversial) of the parallel argument. It is worth noting that even if an application of this procedure did not convince one's audience of the correctness of one's diagnosis of the faults of the original argument, the parallel argument might by itself be enough to convince them that there must be *something* wrong with the original argument.

This is the plan I shall follow. In fact, I shall consider *two* arguments that run parallel to the evidential argument from evil. In Section III, I shall present an evidential argument, which I feign is addressed to an ancient Greek atomist by one of his contemporaries, for the conclusion that the observed properties of air render a belief in atoms irrational. In Section IV, I shall present an evidential argument for the conclusion that the observed fact of "cosmic silence" renders a belief in "extraterrestrial intelligence" irrational. Neither of these parallel arguments – at least this seems clear to me – succeeds in establishing its conclusion. In each case, I shall offer a diagnosis of the faults of the parallel argument that parallels my diagnosis of the faults of the evidential argument from evil.

Finally, in Section V, I shall make some remarks in aid of a proposed distinction between facts that raise *difficulties* for a theory and facts that constitute *evidence* against a theory.

I

Let "S" stand for a proposition that describes in some detail the amount, kinds, and distribution of suffering – the suffering not only of human beings, but of all the sentient terrestrial creatures that there are or ever have been.[2] (We assume that the content of S is about what one would expect, given our own experience, the newspapers, history books, textbooks of natural history and paleontology, and so on. For example, we assume that the world was not created five minutes ago – or six thousand years ago – "complete with memories of an unreal past," and we assume that Descartes was wrong and the cats really do feel pain.)

Let "theism" be the proposition that the universe was created by an omniscient, omnipotent, and morally perfect being.[3]

The core of the evidential argument from evil is the contention that there is a serious hypothesis, inconsistent with theism, on which S is more probable than S is on theism. (The probabilities that figure in this discussion are epistemic. Without making a serious attempt to clarify this notion, we may say this much: p has a higher epistemic probability on h than q does, just in the case that, given h, q is more *surprising* than p. And here "surprising" must be understood as having an epistemic, rather than a merely psychological, sense. It is evident that the epistemic probability of a proposition is relative to the "epistemic background" or "epistemic situation" of an individual or a community: the epistemic probability of p on h need not be the same for two persons or for the same person at two times.)[4] That hypothesis is "the hypothesis of indifference" (HI):

> Neither the nature nor the condition of sentient beings on earth is the result of benevolent or malevolent actions performed by nonhuman persons.[5]

Here is a brief statement of the argument that is built round this core. We begin with an epistemic challenge to the theist, the presentation of a prima facie case against theism: The truth of S is not at all surprising, given HI, but the truth of S is very surprising, given theism. (For the following propositions, if they are not beyond all dispute, are at least highly plausible. Suffering is an intrinsic evil; a morally perfect being will see to it that, insofar as it is possible, intrinsic evils, if they are allowed to exist at all, are distributed according to desert; an omniscient and omnipotent being will be able so to arrange matters that the world contains sentient beings among whom suffering, if it exists at all, is apportioned according to desert; the pattern of suffering recorded in S is well explained – insofar as it can be explained: many instances of suffering are obviously due to chance – by the biological utility of pain, which is just what one would expect on HI, and has little if anything to do with desert.) We have, therefore, a good prima facie reason to prefer HI to theism.

How shall the theist respond to this challenge? The "evidentialist" (as I shall call the proponent of the evidential argument from evil) maintains that any response must be of one of the following three types:

The theist may argue that S is much more surprising, given HI, than one might suppose.

The theist may argue that S is much less surprising, given theism, than one might suppose.

The theist may argue that there are reasons for preferring theism to HI that outweigh the prima facie reason for preferring HI to theism that we have provided.

The first of these options (the evidentialist continues) is unlikely to appeal to anyone. The third is also unappealing, at least if "reasons" is taken to mean "arguments for the existence of God" in the traditional or philosophy-of-religion-text sense. Whatever the individual merits or defects of those arguments, none of them but the "moral argument" (and perhaps the ontological argument) purports to prove the existence of a morally perfect being. And neither the moral argument nor the ontological argument has many defenders these days. None of the "theistic" arguments that are currently regarded as at all promising is, therefore, really an argument for *theism*.[6] And, therefore, none of them can supply a reason for preferring theism to HI.

The second option is that taken by philosophers who construct *theodicies*. A theodicy, let us say, is the conjunction of theism with some "auxiliary hypothesis" h that purports to explain how S could be true, given theism. Let us think for a moment in terms of the probability calculus. It is clear that if a theodicy is to be at all interesting, the probability of S on the conjunction of theism and h (that is, on the theodicy) will have to be high – or at least not too low. But whether a theodicy is interesting depends not only on the probability of S on the conjunction of theism and h, but also on the probability of h on theism. Note that the higher $P(h/\text{theism})$, the more closely $P(S/\text{theism})$ will approximate $P(S/\text{theism \& } h)$. On the other hand, if $P(h/\text{theism})$ is low, $P(S/\text{theism})$ could be low even if $P(S/\text{theism \& } h)$ were high. (Consider, for example, the case in which h is S itself: even if $P(S/\text{theism})$ is low, $P(S/\text{theism \& S})$ will be I – as high as a probability gets.) The task of the theodicist, therefore, may be represented as follows: find a hypothesis h such that $P(S/\text{theism \& } h)$ is high, or at least not too low, and $P(h/\text{theism})$ is high. In other words, the theodicist is to reason as follows. "Although S might initially seem surprising on the assumption of theism, this initial appearance, like many initial appearances, is misleading. For consider the hypothesis h. The truth of this hypothesis is just what one would expect given theism, and S is just what one would expect [would not be all that surprising] given both theism and h. Therefore, S is just what one would expect [would not be at all surprising] given theism. And, therefore, we do not have a prima facie reason to prefer HI to theism, and the evidential argument from evil fails."[7]

But (the evidentialist concludes) the prospects of finding a theodicy that satisfies these conditions are not very promising. For any auxiliary hypothesis h that has actually been offered by the defenders of theism, it would seem that either no real case has been made for $P(h/\text{theism})$ being high, or else no real case has been made for $P(S/\text{theism \& } h)$ being high – or even not too low. Consider, for example, the celebrated Free Will Defense (FWD). Even if it is granted that $P(\text{FWD/theism})$ is high, there is every reason to think that $P(S/\text{theism \& FWD})$ is low, since of all cases of suffering (a phenomenon that has existed for hundreds of millions of years), only a minuscule proportion involve, even in the most indirect way, beings with free will. And no one has the faintest idea of how to find a proposition that is probable on theism *and*, in conjunction with theism, renders S probable. Therefore, given the present state of the available evidence, our original judgment stands: we have a good prima facie reason to prefer HI to theism. And, as we have seen, we have no reason to prefer theism to HI that outweighs this prima facie reason. It is, therefore, irrational to accept theism in the present state of our knowledge.

II

It will be noted that the evidential argument consists not only of an argument for the conclusion that there is a prima facie case for preferring HI to theism, but also of a list of options open to the theist who wishes to reply to that argument: the defender of theism must either refute the argument or else make a case for preferring theism to HI that outweighs the prima facie case for preferring HI to theism; if the defender chooses to refute the argument, he must do this by producing a theodicy in the sense explained in Section I.

This list of options seems to me to be incomplete. Suppose that one were successfully to argue that S was not surprising on theism – and not because S was "just what one should expect" if theism were true, but because no one is in a position to know whether S is what one should expect if theism were true. (Suppose I have never seen, or heard a description of, Egyptian hieroglyphs, although I am familiar with Chinese characters and Babylonian cuneiform and many other exotic scripts. I am shown a sheet of paper reproducing an ancient Egyptian inscription, having been told that it displays a script used in ancient Egypt. What I see cannot be described as "looking just the way one should expect a script used in ancient Egypt to look," but the fact that the script looks the way it does is not epistemically surprising on the hypothesis that it was a script used in ancient Egypt. I am simply not in a position to know whether *this* is the way one should expect a script that was used in ancient Egypt to look.)[8] If one could successfully argue that one simply could not know whether to expect patterns of suffering like those contained in the actual world in a world created by an omniscient, omnipotent, and morally perfect being, this would refute the evidentialist's case for the thesis that there is a prima facie reason for preferring HI to theism. If one is not in a position to assign any epistemic probability to S on theism – if one is not in a position even to assign a probability-range like "high" or "low" or "middling" to S on theism – then, obviously, one is not in a position to say that the epistemic probability of S on HI is higher than the probability of S on theism.[9]

The evidentialist's statement of the way in which the defender of theism must conduct his defense is therefore overly restrictive: it is false that the defender must either make a case for theism or devise a theodicy. At any rate, another option exists as a formal possibility. But how might the defender of theism avail himself of this other option? Are there reasons for thinking that the assumption of theism yields no prima facie grounds for expecting a pattern of suffering different from that recorded by S?

I would suggest that it is the function of what have come to be called "defenses" to provide just such reasons. The word "defense" was first employed as a technical term in discussions of the "logical" version of the argument from evil. In that context, a defense is a story according to which both God and suffering exist, and which is possible "in the broadly logical sense" – or which is such that there is no reason to believe that it is impossible in the broadly logical sense. Let us adapt the notion of a defense to the requirements of a discussion of the evidential argument: a defense is a story according to which God and suffering of the sort contained in the actual world both exist, and

which is such that (given the existence of God) there is no reason to think that it is false, a story that is not surprising on the hypothesis that God exists. A defense obviously need not be a theodicy in the evidentialist's sense, for the probability of a defense need not be high on theism.[10] (That is, a defense need not be such that its denial is surprising on theism.) In practice, of course, the probability of a defense will never be high on theism: if the defender of theism knew of a story which accounted for the sufferings of the actual world and which was highly probable on theism, he would employ it as a theodicy. We may therefore say that, in practice, a defense is a story which accounts for the sufferings of the actual world and which (given the existence of God) is true "for all anyone knows."

What does the defender of theism accomplish by constructing a defense? Well, it's like this. Suppose that Jane wishes to defend the character of Richard III, and that she must contend with evidence that has convinced many people that Richard murdered the two princes in the Tower. Suppose that she proceeds by telling a story – which she does not claim to be true, or even more probable than not – that accounts for the evidence that has come down to us, a story according to which Richard did not murder the princes. If my reaction to her story is, "For all I know, that's true. I shouldn't be at all surprised if that's how things happened," I shall be less willing to accept a negative evaluation of Richard's character than I might otherwise have been. (Note that Jane need not try to show that her story is highly probable on the hypothesis that Richard was of good character.) It would, moreover, strengthen Jane's case if she could produce not one story but many stories that "exonerated" Richard – stories which were not trivial variants on one another but which were different in important ways.

This analogy suggests that one course that is open to the defender of theism is to construct stories which are true for all anyone knows – given that there is a God – and which entail both S and the existence of God. If the defender can do that, this accomplishment will undermine the evidentialist's case for the proposition that the probability of S is lower on theism than on HI. Of course, these stories will (presumably) be *false* for all anyone knows, so they will not, or should not, create any tendency to believe that the probability of S on theism is *not* lower than it is on HI, that it is about the same or higher. Rather, the stories will, or should, lead a person in our epistemic situation to refuse to make any judgment about the relation between the probabilities of S on theism and on HI.

I shall presently offer such a story. But I propose to simplify my task in a way that I hope is legitimate. It seems to me that the theist should not assume that there is a single reason, or tightly interrelated set of reasons, for the sufferings of all sentient creatures. In particular, the theist should not assume that God's reasons for decreeing, or allowing, the sufferings of nonrational creatures have much in common with His reasons for decreeing or allowing the sufferings of human beings. The most satisfactory "defenses" that have so far been offered by theists purport to account only for the sufferings of human beings. In the sequel, I will offer a defense that is directed toward the sufferings of nonrational creatures – "beasts," I shall call them. If this defense were a success, it could be combined with defenses directed toward the sufferings of human beings (like the Free Will Defense) to produce a "total" defense. This "separation of cases" does not seem to me to be an arbitrary procedure. Human beings are radically different from all other animals, and a "total" defense that explained the sufferings of beasts in one way and the sufferings of human beings in a radically different way would not be implausible on that account. Although it is not strictly to our purpose, I will point out that this is consonant with the most usual Christian view of suffering. Typically, Christians have held that human suffering is not a part of God's plan for the world, but exists only because that plan has gone awry. On the other hand:

> Thou makest darkness that it may be night; wherein all the beasts of the forest do move.
> The lions, roaring after their prey, do seek their meat from God.
> The sun ariseth, and they get them away together, and lay them down in their dens.
>
> (Ps. 104: 20–2)

This and many other biblical texts seem to imply that the whole subrational natural world proceeds according to God's plan (except insofar as we human beings have corrupted nature). And this, as the Psalmist tells us in his great hymn of praise to the order that God has established in nature, includes the phenomenon of predation.

I will now tell a story, a story that is true for all I know, that accounts for the sufferings of beasts. The story consists of the following three propositions:

(1) Every possible world that contains higher-level sentient creatures either contains patterns of suffering morally equivalent to those recorded by S, or else is massively irregular.

(2) Some important intrinsic or extrinsic good depends on the existence of higher-level sentient creatures; this good is of sufficient magnitude that it outweighs the patterns of suffering recorded by S.

(3) Being massively irregular is a defect in a world, a defect at least as great as the defect of containing patterns of suffering morally equivalent to those recorded by S.

The four key terms contained in this story may be explained as follows.

Higher-level sentient creatures are animals that are *conscious* in the way in which (*pace* Descartes) the higher nonhuman mammals are conscious.

Two patterns of suffering are *morally equivalent* if there are no morally decisive reasons for preferring one to the other: if there are no morally decisive reasons for creating a world that embodies one pattern rather than the other. To say that *A* and *B* are in this sense morally equivalent is not to say that they are in any interesting sense comparable. Suppose, for example, that the Benthamite dream of a universal hedonic calculus is an illusion, and that there is no answer to the question whether the suffering caused by war is less than, the same as, or greater than the suffering caused by cancer. It does not follow that these two patterns of suffering are not morally equivalent. On the contrary: unless there is some "nonhedonic" morally relevant distinction to be made between a world that contains war and no cancer and a world that contains cancer and no war (i.e., a distinction that does not depend on comparing the amounts of suffering caused by war and cancer), it would seem to follow that the suffering caused by war and the suffering caused by cancer *are*, in the present technical sense, morally equivalent.

It is important to note that *A* and *B* may be morally equivalent even if they are comparable and one of them involves *less* suffering than the other. By way of analogy, consider the fact that there is no morally decisive reason to prefer a jail term of ten years as a penalty for armed assault to a term of ten years and a day, despite the indubitable facts that these two penalties would have the same deterrent effect and that one is lighter than the other. I have argued elsewhere that, for any amount of suffering that somehow serves God's purposes, it may be that some smaller amount of suffering would have served them as well.[11] It may be, therefore, that God has had to choose *some* amount of suffering as the amount contained in the actual world, and could, consistently with His purposes, have chosen any of a vast array of smaller or greater amounts, and that all of the members of this vast array of alternative amounts of suffering are morally equivalent. (Similarly, a legislature has to choose *some* penalty as the penalty for armed assault, and – think of penalties as jail terms measured in minutes – must choose among the members of a vast array of morally equivalent penalties.) Or it may be that God has decreed, with respect to this vast array of alternative, morally equivalent amounts of suffering, that *some* member of this array shall be the actual amount of suffering, but has left it up to chance which member that is.[12]

A *massively irregular world* is a world in which the laws of nature fail in some massive way. A world containing all of the miracles recorded in the New Testament would not, on that account, be massively irregular, for those miracles were too small (if size is measured in terms of the amounts of matter directly affected) and too few and far between. But a world would be massively irregular if it contained the following state of affairs:

God, by means of a continuous series of ubiquitous miracles, causes a planet inhabited by the same animal life as the actual earth to be a hedonic utopia. On this planet, fawns are (like Shadrach, Meshach, and Abednego) saved by angels when they are in danger of being burnt alive. Harmful parasites and microorganisms suffer immediate supernatural dissolution if they enter a higher animal's body. Lambs are miraculously hidden from lions, and the lions are compensated for the resulting restriction on their diets by physically impossible falls of high-protein manna. On this planet, either God created every species by a separate miracle, or else, although all living things evolved from a common ancestor, a hedonic utopia has existed at every stage of the evolutionary process. (The latter alternative implies that God has, by means of a vast and intricately coordinated sequence of supernatural adjustments to the machinery of nature, guided the evolutionary process in such a way as to compensate for the fact that a hedonic utopia exerts no selection pressure.)

It would also be possible for a world to be massively irregular in a more systematic or "wholesale" way. A world that came into existence five minutes ago, complete with memories of an unreal past, would be on that account alone massively irregular – if indeed such a world was metaphysically possible. A world in which beasts (beasts having the physical structure and exhibiting the pain-behavior of actual beasts) felt no pain would be on that account alone massively irregular – if indeed such a world was metaphysically possible.

A *defect in a world* is a feature of a world that (whatever its extrinsic value might be in various worlds) a world is intrinsically better for not having.

Our story comprises propositions (1), (2), and (3). I believe that we have no reason to assign any probability or range of probabilities to this story. (With the following possible exception: if we have a reason to regard the existence of God as improbable, then we shall have a reason to regard the story as improbable.)

We should have reason to reject this story if we had reason to believe that there were possible worlds – worlds that were not massively irregular – in which higher-level sentient creatures inhabited a hedonic utopia. Is there any reason to think that there are such worlds? I suppose that the only kind of reason one could have for believing that there was a possible world having a certain feature would be the reason provided by a plausible attempt to "design" a world having that feature. How does one go about designing a world?

One should start by describing in some detail the laws of nature that govern the world. (Physicists' actual formulations of quantum field theories and the general theory of relativity provide the standard of required "detail.") One should then go on to describe the boundary conditions under which those laws operate: the topology of the world's space-time, its relativistic mass, the number of particle families, and so on. Then one should tell in convincing detail the story of cosmic evolution in that world: the story of the development of large objects like galaxies and stars and of small objects like carbon atoms. Finally, one should tell the story of the evolution of life. These stories, of course, must be coherent, given one's specification of laws and boundary conditions. Unless one proceeds in this manner, one's statements about what is intrinsically or metaphysically possible – and thus one's statements about an omnipotent being's "options" in creating a world – will be entirely subjective, and therefore without value. But I have argued for this view of the epistemology of modal statements (that is, of modal statements concerning major departures from actuality) elsewhere, and the reader is referred to those arguments. In fact, the argument of those essays should be considered a part of the argument of the present essay.[13]

Our own universe provides the only model we have for the formidable task of designing a world. (For all we know, in every possible world that exhibits any degree of complexity, the laws of nature are the actual laws, or at least have the same structure as the actual laws. There are, in fact, philosophically minded physicists who believe that there is only one possible set of laws of nature, and it is epistemically possible that they are right.) Our universe apparently evolved out of an initial singularity in accordance with certain laws of nature.[14] This evolution is not without its mysteries: the very early stages of the unfolding of the universe (the incredibly brief instant during which the laws of nature operated under conditions of perfect symmetry), the formation of the galaxies, and the origin of life on the earth are, in the present state of natural knowledge, deep mysteries. Nevertheless, it seems reasonable to assume that all of these processes involved only the nonmiraculous operation of the laws of nature. One important thing that is known about the evolution of the universe into its present state is that it has been a very tightly structured process. A large number of physical parameters have apparently arbitrary values such that if those values had been only slightly different (very, very slightly different) the universe would contain no life, and a fortiori no intelligent life.[15] It may or may not be the "purpose" of the cosmos to constitute an arena in which the evolution of intelligent life takes place, but it is certainly true that this evolution did take place, and that if the universe had been different by an all unimaginably minute degree it wouldn't have. My purpose in citing this fact – it is reasonable to believe that it is a fact – is not to produce an up-to-date version of the design argument. It is, rather, to suggest that (at least, for all we know) only in a universe very much like ours could intelligent life, or even sentient life, develop by the nonmiraculous operation of the laws of nature. And the natural evolution of higher sentient life in a universe like ours essentially involves suffering, or there is every reason to believe it does. The mechanisms underlying biological evolution may be just what most biologists seem to suppose – the production of new genes by random mutation and the culling of gene

pools by environmental selection pressure – or they may be more subtle. But no one, I believe, would take seriously the idea that conscious animals, animals conscious as a dog is conscious, could evolve naturally without hundreds of millions of years of ancestral suffering. Pain is an indispensable component of the evolutionary process after organisms have reached a certain stage of complexity. And, for all we know, the amount of pain that organisms have experienced in the actual world, or some amount morally equivalent to that amount, is necessary for the natural evolution of conscious animals. I conclude that the first part of our defense is true for all we know: Every possible world that contains higher-level sentient creatures either contains patterns of suffering morally equivalent to those recorded by S, or else is massively irregular.

Let us now consider the second part of our defense: Some important intrinsic or extrinsic good depends on the existence of higher-level sentient creatures; this good is of sufficient magnitude that it outweighs the patterns of suffering recorded by S. It is not very hard to believe (is it?) that a world that was as the earth was just before the appearance of human beings would contain a much larger amount of intrinsic good, and would, in fact, contain a better balance of good over evil, than a world in which there were no organisms higher than worms. (Which is not to say that there could not be worlds lacking intelligent life that contained a still better balance of good over evil – say, worlds containing the same organisms, but significantly less suffering.) And then there is the question of extrinsic value. One consideration immediately suggests itself: intelligent life – creatures made in the image and likeness of God – could not evolve directly from worms or oysters; the immediate evolutionary predecessors of intelligent animals must possess higher-level sentience.

We now turn to the third part of our defense: Being massively irregular is a defect in a world, a defect at least as great as the defect of containing patterns of suffering morally equivalent to those recorded by S. We should recall that a defense is not a theodicy, and that we are not required to argue at this point that it is *plausible to suppose* that massive irregularity is a defect in a world, a defect so grave that creating a world containing animal suffering morally equivalent to the animal suffering of the actual world is a reasonable price to pay to avoid it. We are required to argue only that *for all we know* this judgment is correct.

The third part of our defense is objectionable only if we have some prima facie reason for believing that the actual sufferings of beasts are a graver defect in a world than massive irregularity would be. Have we any such reason? It seems to me that we do not. To begin with, it does seem that massive irregularity is a defect in a world. One minor point in favor of this thesis is the witness of deists and other thinkers who have deprecated the miraculous on the ground that *any* degree of irregularity in a world is a defect, a sort of unlovely jury-rigging of things that is altogether unworthy of the power and wisdom of God. Presumably such thinkers would regard *massive* irregularity as a very grave defect indeed. And perhaps there is something to this reaction. It does seem that there is something right about the idea that God would include no more irregularity than was necessary in His creation. A second point is that many, if not all, massively irregular worlds are not only massively irregular but massively *deceptive*. This is obviously true of a world which looks like the actual world but which began five minutes ago, or a world which looks like the actual world but in which beasts feel no pain. (And this is not surprising, for our beliefs about the world depend in large measure on our habit of drawing conclusions that are based on the assumption that the world is regular.) But it is plausible to suppose that deception, and, a fortiori, massive deception, is inconsistent with the nature of a perfect being. These points, however, are no more than suggestive, and, even if they amounted to proof, they would prove only that massive irregularity was a defect; they would not prove that it was a defect in any way comparable to the actual suffering of beasts. In any case, proof is not the present question: the question is whether there is a prima facie case for the thesis that the actual sufferings of beasts constitute a graver defect in a world than does massive irregularity.

What would such a case be based on? I would suppose that someone who maintained that there was such a case would have to rely on his moral intuitions, or, more generally, on his intuitions of value. He would have to say something like this: "I have held the two states of affairs – the actual sufferings of beasts and massive irregularity – before my mind and carefully compared them. My considered judgment is that the former is worse than the latter." This judgment presupposes that these two states of affairs are, in the sense that was explained above, comparable: one of them is worse than the other, or else they are of the same value

(or disvalue). It is not clear to me that there is any reason to suppose that this is so. If it is *not* so, then, as we have seen, it can plausibly be maintained that the two states of affairs are morally equivalent, and a Creator could not be faulted on moral grounds for choosing either over the other. But let us suppose that the two states of affairs are comparable. In that case, if the value-judgment we are considering is to be trusted, then human beings possess a faculty that enables them correctly to judge the relative values of states of affairs of literally cosmic magnitude, states of affairs, moreover, that are in no way (as some states of affairs of cosmic magnitude may be) connected with the practical concerns of human beings. Why should one suppose that one's inclinations to make judgments of value are reliable in this area? One's intuitions about value are either a gift from God or a product of evolution or socially inculcated or stem from some combination of these sources. Why should we suppose that any of these sources would provide us with the means to make correct value-judgments in matters that have nothing to do with the practical concerns of everyday life? (I do think we must be able to speak of *correct* value-judgments if the problem of evil is to be of any interest. An eminent philosopher of biology has said in one place that God, if He existed, would be indescribably wicked for having created a world like this one, and, in another place, that morality is an illusion, an illusion that we are subject to because of the evolutionary advantage it confers. These two theses do not seem to me to add up to a coherent position.) Earlier I advocated a form of modal skepticism: our modal intuitions, while they are no doubt to be trusted when they tell us that the table could have been placed on the other side of the room, are not to be trusted on such matters as whether there could be transparent iron or whether there could be a "regular" universe in which there were higher sentient creatures that did not suffer. And if this is true, it is not surprising. Assuming that there are "modal facts of the matter," why should we assume that God or evolution or social training has given us access to modal facts knowledge of which is of no interest to anyone but the metaphysician? God or evolution has provided us with a capacity for making judgments about size and distance which is very useful in hunting mammoths and driving cars, but which is no use at all in astronomy. It seems that an analogous restriction applies to our capacity for making modal judgments. How can we be sure that an analogous restriction does not also apply to our capacity for making *value*-judgments? My position is that we cannot be sure, and that for all we know our inclinations to make value-judgments are not veridical when they are applied to cosmic matters unrelated to the concerns of everyday life. (Not that our inclinations in this area are at all uniform. I myself experience no inclination to come down on one side or the other of the question whether massive irregularity or vast amounts of animal suffering is the graver defect in a world. I suspect that others do experience such inclinations. If they don't, of course, then I'm preaching to the converted.) But then there is no prima facie case for the thesis that the actual sufferings of beasts constitute a graver defect in a world than does massive irregularity. Or, at least, there is no case that is grounded in our intuitions about value. And in what else could such a case be grounded?

These considerations have to do with intrinsic value, with comparison of the intrinsic disvalue of two states of affairs. There is also the matter of extrinsic value. Who can say what the effects of creating a massively irregular world might be? What things of intrinsic value might be frustrated or rendered impossible in a massively irregular world? We cannot say. Christians have generally held that at a certain point God plans to hand over the government of the world to humanity. Would a massively irregular world be the sort of world that could be "handed over"? Perhaps a massively irregular world would immediately dissolve into chaos if an infinite being were not constantly making adjustments to it. We simply cannot say. If anyone insists that he has good reason to believe that nothing of any great value depends on the world's being regular, we must ask him why he thinks he is in a position to know things of that sort. We might remind him of the counsel of epistemic humility that was spoken to Job out of the whirlwind:

> Gird up now thy loins like a man; for I will
>   demand of thee, and answer thou me.
> Where wast thou when I laid the foundations of
>   the earth? Declare if thou hast understanding.
> Knowest thou it, because thou wast then born,
>   or because the number of thy days is great?
> Canst thou bind the sweet influences of Pleiades,
>   or loose the bands of Orion?
> Knowest thou the ordinances of heaven? Canst
>   thou set the dominion thereof in the earth?[16]

I have urged extreme modal and moral skepticism (or, one might say, humility) in matters unrelated to the concerns of everyday life. If such skepticism is accepted, then we have no reason to accept the evidentialist's premise that "an omniscient and omnipotent being will be able so to arrange matters that the world contains sentient beings among whom suffering, if it exists at all, is apportioned according to desert." More exactly, we have no reason to suppose that an omniscient and omnipotent being could do this without creating a massively irregular world; and, for all we know, the intrinsic or extrinsic disvalue of a massively irregular world is greater than the intrinsic disvalue of vast amounts of animal suffering (which, presumably, are not apportioned according to desert). If these consequences of modal and moral skepticism are accepted, then there is no reason to believe that the probability of S on HI is higher than the probability of S on theism, and the evidential argument from evil cannot get started. Even if we assume that the probability of S on HI is high (that the denial of S is very surprising on HI), this assumption gives us no reason to prefer HI to theism. If there were such a reason, it could be presented as an argument:

The probability of S on HI is high

We do not know what to say about the probability of S on theism

HI and theism are inconsistent

Therefore, for anyone in our epistemic situation, the truth of S constitutes a prima facie case for preferring HI to theism.

This argument is far from compelling. If there is any doubt about this, it can be dispelled by considering a parallel argument. Let L be the proposition that intelligent life exists, and let G be the proposition that God wants intelligent life to exist. We argue as follows:

The probability of L on G is high

We do not know what to say about the probability of L on atheism

G and atheism are inconsistent

Therefore, for anyone in our epistemic situation, the truth of L constitutes a prima facie case for preferring G to atheism.

The premises of this argument are true. (As to the second premise, there has been considerable debate in the scientific community as to whether the natural evolution of intelligent life is inevitable or extremely unlikely or something in between; let us suppose that "we" are a group of people who have tried to follow this debate and have been hopelessly confused by it.) But I should be very surprised to learn of someone who believed that the premises of the argument entailed its conclusion.

I will close this section by pointing out something that is not strictly relevant to the argument it contains, but is, in my view, of more than merely autobiographical interest. I have not accepted the extreme modal skepticism that figures so prominently in the argument of this section as a result of epistemic pressures exerted by the evidential argument from evil. I was an extreme modal skeptic before I was a theist, and I have, on the basis of this skepticism, argued (and would still argue) against both Swinburne's attempt to show that the concept of God is coherent and Plantinga's attempt to use the modal version of the ontological argument to show that theism is rational.[17]

III

Imagine an ancient Greek, an atomist who believes that the whole world is made of tiny, indestructible, immutable solids. Imagine that an opponent of atomism (call him Aristotle) presents our atomist with the following argument: "If fire were made of tiny solids, the same solids earth is made of, or ones that differ from them only in shape, then fire would not be Absolutely Light – it would not rise toward the heavens of its own nature. But that fire is not Absolutely Light is contrary to observation."[18] From our lofty twentieth-century vantage point, we might be inclined to regard Aristotle's argument as merely quaint. But this impression of quaintness rests on two features of the argument that can be removed without damage to what is, from one point of view anyway, its essential force. The two quaint features of Aristotle's argument, the idea that fire is a stuff and the idea of the Absolutely Light, can be removed from the argument by substituting air for fire and by substituting the behavior we nowadays associate with the gaseous state for the defining behavior of the Absolutely Light (that is, a natural tendency to move upward). The resulting argument would look something like this:

Suppose air were made of tiny solid bodies as you say. Then air would behave like fine dust: it would eventually settle to the ground and become a mere dusty coating on the surface of the earth. But this is contrary to observation.

Well, what is wrong with this argument? Why *don't* the O_2, N_2, CO_2, and other molecules that make up the atmosphere simply settle to the ground like dust particles? The answer is that air molecules, unlike dust particles, push on one another; they are kept at average distances that are large in comparison with their own sizes by repulsive forces (electromagnetic in nature), the strength of these forces in a given region being a function of the local temperature. At the temperatures one finds near the surface of the earth (temperatures maintained by solar radiation and the internal heat of the earth), the aggregate action of these intermolecular forces produces the kind of aggregate molecular behavior that, at the macroscopic level of description, we call the gaseous state.

We can see where the improved version of Aristotle's argument goes wrong. (We can also see that in one minor respect it's better than an ancient Greek could know: if it weren't for intermolecular forces, air molecules would not simply settle slowly to the ground; they would drop like rocks.) But what about our imaginary ancient atomist, who not only doesn't know all these things about intermolecular forces and temperature and so on, but who couldn't even conceive of them as epistemic possibilities? What shall he say in response to the improved version of Aristotle's argument?

In order to sharpen this question, let us imagine that a Greek philosopher called A-prime has actually presented our atomist with the air-and-dust argument, and let us imagine that A-prime has at his disposal the techniques of a late-twentieth-century analytical philosopher. Having presented the atomist with the simple argument that I have given above (the primitive or "whence, then, is air?" version of the argument from air), he presses his point by confronting the atomist with a much more sophisticated argument, the *evidential* argument from air. "Let HI, the Hypothesis of Independence, be the thesis that there are four independent and continuous elements, air among them, each of which has sui generis properties (you can find a list of them in any reputable physics text) that determine its characteristic behavior. Let S be a proposition that records the properties of air. The simple air-and-dust argument is sufficient to establish that S is not surprising given HI, but is very surprising given atomism. There are only three ways for you to respond to this prima facie case against atomism: you may argue that S is much more surprising, given HI, than one might suppose; or that S is much less surprising, given atomism, than one might suppose; or that there are reasons for preferring atomism to HI that outweigh the prima facie reason for preferring HI to atomism that is provided by the air-and-dust argument. The first I shall not discuss. The third is unpromising, unless you can come up with something better than the very abstract metaphysical arguments with which you have attempted to support atomism in the past, for they certainly do not outweigh the clear and concrete air-and-dust argument. The only course open to you is to construct an *atomodicy*. That is, you must find some auxiliary hypothesis *h* that explains how S could be true, given atomism. And you will have to show both that the probability of S is high (or at least not too low) on the conjunction of atomism and *h* and that the probability of *h* on atomism is high. While you may be able to find a hypothesis that satisfies the former condition, I think it very unlikely that you will be able to find one that satisfies the latter. In any case, unless you *can* find a hypothesis that satisfies both conditions, you cannot rationally continue to be an atomist."

Whatever else may be said about this argument, A-prime is certainly right about one thing: it is unlikely that the atomist will be able to produce a successful atomodicy. Even if he were told the modern story about air, he could not do it. At least, I don't think he could. What is the epistemic probability on atomism (relative to the epistemic situation of an ancient Greek) of our complicated modern story of intermolecular forces and the gaseous state? What probability should someone who knew nothing about the micro-structure of the material world except that it was composed of atoms (it is, of course, our "elementary particles" and not our "atoms" or our "molecules" that correspond to the atoms of the Greeks) assign to the modern story? As far as I am able to judge, the only rational thing such a person could do would be to decline to assign any probability to the modern story on atomism. (The answer of modern science to the air-and-dust argument does not take the form of a story that, relative to the epistemic situation of an ancient Greek, is highly probable on atomism.)

Fortunately for the atomist, A-prime's demand that he produce an atomodicy is unreasonable. The atomist need do nothing more in response to the evidential argument from air than find a defense – or, better, several independent defenses. A defense, of course, is a story that explains how there could be a stuff that has the properties of air (those known to an ancient Greek), given that the material world is made entirely of atoms. A defense need *not* be highly probable on atomism. It is required only that, given atomism, the defense be true for all anyone (sc. any ancient Greek) knows.

Here is one example of a defense: air atoms (unlike earth atoms) are spheres covered with a "fur" of long, thin, flexible spikes that are, unless flexed by contact with another atom, perpendicular to the surface of the atom's "nucleus" (i.e., its central sphere); the length of the spikes is large in comparison with the diameters of nuclei, and their presence thus tends to keep nuclei far apart. Since, for all anyone (anyone in the epistemic situation of an ancient Greek) knows, some atoms have such features – if there are atoms at all – the observed properties of air are not surprising on the assumption of atomism. Since there are defenses that are true for all anyone (anyone in the epistemic situation of an ancient Greek) knows, no ancient Greek was in a position to say anything about the probability on atomism of S, the proposition that sums up the properties of air that were known to him. A-prime, therefore, is left with no better argument than the following:

The probability of S on HI is high

We do not know what to say about the probability of S on atomism

HI and atomism are inconsistent

Therefore, for anyone in our epistemic situation, the truth of S constitutes a prima facie case for preferring HI to atomism.

And this argument is manifestly invalid.

IV

We know how it is that air can be composed of molecules and yet not drift to the ground like dust. This knowledge provides us with a certain rather Olympian perspective from which to view the "Problem of Air." I wish next to examine the epistemic situation of those of our contemporaries who believe that the Milky Way galaxy (ours) contains other intelligent species than humanity. (Since they are our contemporaries, we cannot view their situation from any such Olympian perspective.) Let us confront them with an argument analogous to the argument from evil and the argument from air. The essence of this argument is contained in a question of Enrico Fermi's, a question as pithy as "Whence, then, is evil?": Where are they?

If there are other intelligent species in the galaxy, the overwhelming probability is that at least one intelligent species existed at least a hundred million years ago. There has been life on the earth for at least thirty times that long, and there is nothing magical about the present time. The universe was just as suitable for intelligent life a hundred million years ago, and if the pace of evolution on the earth had been just three or four percent faster, there would have been intelligent life *here* a hundred million years ago. An intelligent and technologically able species will attempt to send messages to other species elsewhere in the galaxy (as we have begun to do). The most efficient way to do this is to send out self-reproducing robotic probes to other stars: when such a probe reaches another star, it makes two or more duplicates of itself out of local materials, and these duplicates proceed to further stars. Then it waits, perhaps for hundreds of millions of years, till it detects locally produced radio signals, at which point it reveals itself and delivers its message. (There are no fundamental technological barriers to this program. At our present rate of scientific progress, we shall be able to set such a process in motion within the next century.) It is not hard to show that the descendants of the original probes will reach every star in the galaxy within fifty million years. (We assume that the probes are capable of reaching one-tenth the speed of light.) But no such probe has revealed itself to us. Therefore, any nonhuman intelligence in the galaxy came into existence less than fifty million years ago. But it is statistically very unlikely that there are nonhuman intelligences *all* of which came into existence within the last fifty million years. (The reasoning is like this: if you know that such people as there are in the Sahara Desert are distributed randomly, and if you know that there are no people in the Sahara except, possibly, within a circular area one hundred miles in diameter that is hidden from you, you can conclude that there are probably no people at all in the Sahara.) Furthermore, it is not merely the absence of robotic probes that should disturb the

proponent of "extraterrestrial intelligence." There are also the absence of radio signals from thousands of nearby stars and several of the nearer galaxies[19] and the absence of manifestations of "hypertechnology" like the wide-angle infrared source that would signal the presence of a star that has been surrounded with a "Dyson sphere." We may refer collectively to all of these "absences" as *cosmic silence*, or simply *silence*. (If there are other intelligent species in the galaxy, or even in the nearby galaxies, they are *species absconditae*.) The obvious implication of these observations is that we are alone.[20]

Let us call the thesis that there is intelligent life elsewhere in the galaxy *noetism*. The above argument, the argument from cosmic silence, provides materials from which the antinoetist may construct an evidential argument against noetism analogous to the evidential argument from evil: "Let the Hypothesis of Isolation (HI) be the hypothesis that humanity is the only intelligent species that exists or has ever existed in the Milky Way galaxy or any of the nearby galaxies. Let S be a proposition that records all of the observations that constitute a failure to discover any manifestation whatever of life, and, a fortiori, of intelligent life, elsewhere in the universe. The argument from cosmic silence is sufficient to establish that the truth of S (which, of course, is not at all surprising given HI) is very surprising, given noetism. There are only three ways for you to respond to the argument from cosmic silence: you may argue that S is much more surprising, given HI, than one might suppose; or that S is much less surprising, given noetism, than one might suppose; or that there are reasons for preferring noetism to HI that outweigh the prima facie reason for preferring HI to noetism that is provided by the argument from cosmic silence. The first is no more than a formal possibility. The third is unpromising, unless you can come up with something better than those facile arguments for the prevalence of life in the cosmos that are so popular with astronomers and physicists and so exasperating to evolutionary biologists.[21] The only course open to you is to construct a *noödicy*. That is, you must find some auxiliary hypothesis *h* that explains how S could be true, given noetism. And you will have to show both that the probability of S is high (or at least not too low) on the conjunction of noetism and *h* and that the probability of *h* on noetism is high. While you may be able to find a hypothesis that satisfies the former condition, I think it very unlikely that you will be able to find one that satisfies the latter. In any case, unless you *can* find a hypothesis that satisfies both conditions, you cannot rationally continue to be a noetist."

The antinoetist is no doubt right in supposing that it is very unlikely that the noetist will be able to construct a successful noödicy. One example should suffice to make the point. Consider the elegantly simple, if rather depressing, Nuclear Destruction Scenario: intelligent species do not last long enough to make much of a mark on the cosmos; within at most a few decades of developing radio transmitters powerful enough to be detected across a distance of light-years (and long before they can make self-reproducing intersidereal robotic probes), they invariably destroy themselves in nuclear wars. It is clear that the Nuclear Destruction Scenario is a failure as a noödicy, for it is not highly probable on noetism. (That intelligent species invariably destroy themselves in nuclear wars is not highly probable on the hypothesis that intelligent species exist.) The proponents of extraterrestrial intelligence have provided a wide range of possible explanations of "cosmic silence" (intelligence does not necessarily imply technology; the desire to communicate with other intelligent species is a human idiosyncrasy; the most efficient means of intersidereal signaling, the one that all the extraterrestrials actually employ, is one we haven't yet thought of), but it is clear that none of these possible explanations should be regarded as *highly probable* on noetism. We simply do not know enough to make any such probability judgment. Shall the noetist therefore concede that we have shown his position to be irrational? No, for the antinoetist's demand that the noetist produce a noödicy is wholly unreasonable. The noetist need only produce one or more *defenses*, one or more explanations of the phenomenon of cosmic silence that entail noetism and are true for all we know. And this is just what the noetist has done. (I have already mentioned several of them.) Since there are defenses that for all anyone knows are true, no one knows what to say about the probability on noetism of S (the proposition that records all of our failed attempts to discover any manifestation of intelligent life elsewhere in the universe). The antinoetist has therefore failed to show that the truth of S constitutes a prima facie case in favor of preferring HI to noetism.

V

"This is all very well. But evil *is* a difficulty for the theist, and the gaseous state *was* a difficulty for the ancient atomist, and cosmic silence *is* a difficulty for the noetist. You seem to be saying that they can just ignore these difficulties."

Not at all. I have said that these difficulties (I accept the term "difficulty") do not render their beliefs irrational – not even if they are unable to find arguments that raise the probabilities of their hypotheses relative to the probabilities of competing hypotheses that do not face the same difficulties, and are also unable to devise auxiliary hypotheses that enable them to construct "-dicies." It doesn't follow that they should simply ignore the difficulties.

"Well, what *should* they do?"

To begin with, they can acknowledge the difficulties. They can admit that the difficulties exist and that they're not sure what to say about them. They might go on to offer some speculations about the causes of the phenomena that raise the difficulties: mechanisms that would account for the gaseous state, possible conditions that would interfere with communications across light-years, reasons God might have for allowing evil. Such speculations need not be (they almost certainly will not be) highly probable on the "-ism" in whose defense they are employed. And they need not be probable on anything that is known to be true, although they should not be improbable on anything that is known to be true. They are to be offered as explanations of the difficult phenomena that are, *for all anyone knows*, the correct ones. In sum, the way to deal with such difficulties is to construct defenses.

"But if a phenomenon is a 'difficulty' for a certain theory, does that not mean that it is evidence against that theory? Or if it is not evidence against that theory, in what sense can it raise a 'difficulty' for the theory? Are you not saying that it can be right to accept a theory to which there is counterevidence when there are competing theories to which there is no counterevidence?"

That sounds good, but it is really a recipe for rejecting just about any interesting theory. Just about any interesting theory is faced with phenomena that make the advocates of the theory a bit uncomfortable, this discomfort being signaled by the tendency to speculate about circumstances consistent with the theory that might produce the phenomena. For any theory that faces such a difficulty, there will always be available another "theory," or at least another hypothesis, that does not face that difficulty: its denial. (The denial of an interesting theory will rarely if ever itself be an interesting theory; it will be too general and non-specific.) Your suggestion would therefore appear to constrain us never to accept any interesting theory, but always either to accept its denial or else neither the theory nor its denial. The latter will be the more common result, since the denial of a theory can usually be partitioned into interesting theories that face individual difficulties. (For example, the denial of atomism can be partitioned into the following hypotheses: matter is continuous; matter is neither continuous nor atomically structured; matter does not exist. Each of these hypotheses faces difficulties.) This result might be avoided if you placed some sort of restriction on what counted as a "competing theory," but it is not clear what sort of restriction would be required. It will not do simply to rule out the denial of a theory as a competing theory, for contraries of the theory that were very general and nonspecific could produce equally counterintuitive results. If, moreover, you did produce a satisfactory solution to this problem, it is not clear what consequences your solution might have for the evidential argument from evil. Consider, for example, the Hypothesis of Indifference. This is not a very specific thesis: it tells us only that the nature and condition of sentient beings on earth do *not* have a certain (very narrowly delineated) cause. Perhaps it would not count as a proper "competitor" with the quite specific thesis we have called "theism." Perhaps it would be a consequence of your solution that only some proposition more specific than HI, some proposition that entailed but was not entailed by HI, could properly be in competition with theism. And this proposition might face difficulties of its own, difficulties not faced by HI.

But we may answer your question more directly and simply. A difficulty with a theory does not necessarily constitute evidence against it. To show that an acknowledged difficulty with a theory is not evidence against it, it suffices to construct a defense that accounts for the facts that raise the difficulty. (This thesis by no means provides an automatic "out" for a theory that is confronted with some recalcitrant observation, for a defense is not automatically available to the proponents of every theory that is confronted with a recalcitrant observation. A defense may not be improbable, either on the theory in whose cause it is employed or on anything we know to be true. In a particular case, it may be that no one can think of any hypothesis that satisfies these two conditions, and what was a mere difficulty for a theory will thereby attain to the status of evidence against the theory. It is perhaps worth pointing out that two or more difficulties may jointly constitute evidence against a theory, even if none of them taken individually counts as evidence against it. This could be the case if the defenses that individually "handle" the difficulties are inconsistent, or if – despite the fact that none of the defenses taken individually is improbable – their conjunction is improbable.)

The central thesis of this essay may be usefully summarized in the terminology that has been introduced in the present section: While the patterns of suffering we find in the actual world constitute a *difficulty* for theism and do not constitute a difficulty for the competing hypothesis HI, they do not – owing to the availability of the defense[22] I have outlined – attain to the status of *evidence* that favors HI over theism. It follows that the evidential argument from evil fails, for it is essential to the evidential argument that those patterns of suffering be evidence that favors HI over theism.[23]

Notes

1 My formulation of this argument owes a great deal to a recent article by Paul Draper ("Pain and Pleasure: An Evidential Problem for Theists," *Noûs* 23 (1989), 331–50). I do not, however, claim that the argument I shall present *is* Draper's intricate and subtle argument, or even a simplified version of it. (One important difference between the argument discussed in the present essay and Draper's argument is that the latter makes reference to the distribution of both pain and pleasure, while the former makes reference only to the distribution of pain.) Nevertheless, I hope that the version of the evidential argument from evil that I shall discuss is similar enough to Draper's that what I say about my version will at least suggest strategies that the theist can employ in dealing with Draper's argument. Draper (p. 332) credits Hume with being the first to ask the question whether there is "any serious hypothesis that is logically inconsistent with theism [and] explains some significant set of facts about evil . . . much better than theism does." (See *Dialogues Concerning Natural Religion*, Part XI.)

2 In Draper's argument, the role that corresponds to the role played by S in our argument is played by a proposition O that reports "both the observations one has made of humans and animals experiencing pain or pleasure and the testimony one has encountered concerning the observations others have made

of sentient beings experiencing pain or pleasure" (p. 332). I find that the argument goes more easily if it is stated in terms of the probability (on various hypotheses) of the pattern of suffering that it is reasonable to believe the actual world exhibits, rather than in terms of the probability (on those hypotheses) of the observations and testimony on which our reasonable belief in that pattern rests. I do not think that this modification of Draper's strategy leaves me with an argument that is easier to refute than the argument that would have resulted if I had retained this feature of his strategy.

3 Cf. Draper, "Pain and Pleasure," p. 331. Perhaps we should add that this being has not ceased to exist, and has never ceased to be omniscient, omnipotent, or morally perfect.

4 Cf. ibid., pp. 333 and 349 (note 2). Some difficulties with the notion of epistemic probability are discussed in note 7 below.

5 Cf. ibid., p. 332.

6 It is a currently popular view that one can have reasons for believing in God that are of a quite different kind from "arguments for the existence of God." For a sampling of versions of this view, see the essays by the editors and the essay by William P. Alston in *Faith and Rationality: Reason and Belief in God*, ed. Alvin Plantinga and Nicholas Wolterstorff (South Bend, Ind.: University of Notre Dame Press, 1983). My own position on this matter is that some version of this view is right, and that there are reasons for believing in God that are of the general kind described by Plantinga, Wolterstorff, and Alston. I believe, moreover, that these reasons not only can provide one with adequate justification for being a theist in the absence of a prima facie case against theism, but are strong enough to override any conceivable prima facie case against theism. (For a contrary view – which I believe rests on a misunderstanding – see Draper, "Pain and Pleasure," pp. 347–8.) But I shall not defend this thesis here, since the point of the present essay is that the patterns of suffering that exist in the actual world do not constitute even a prima facie case against theism.

7 I prefer to formulate the evidential argument from evil in terms of epistemic surprise, rather than in terms of high and low epistemic probability. (Draper's essay suggested this use of the concept of "surprise" to me. Although his "official" formulation of his argument is in terms of epistemic probability, he frequently employs the notion of "surprise" in his informal commentary on the argument. Indeed, at one place – see "Pain and Pleasure," p. 333 – he comes very close to explaining epistemic probability as I did in the text: by equating "has a lower epistemic probability" with "is more surprising.") Let me attempt to explain why I am uneasy about formulating the argument in terms of probabilities. If the argument is so formulated, it would appear to depend on the validity of the following inference-form: p; the probability of p on q is much higher than the probability of p on r; q and r are inconsistent; therefore, there exists a prima facie reason (viz., that p) for preferring q to r. The trouble with this inference-form is that the probability of p may be very low on q despite the fact that p is not at all *surprising* on q. For example, the probability of the hypothesis that the unobservable card that Alice is holding is the four of clubs is quite low on the hypothesis that she drew the card at random from a standard deck, but the former hypothesis is not at all surprising on the latter. Now let S be some true proposition that has a low probability on theism but is not at all surprising on theism. I should think that the proposition that states the exact number of dogs would do: in "most" possible worlds in which God exists, the number of dogs is not the actual number. It is clear that the following facts do not comprise a prima facie case for preferring "S and God does not exist" to "God exists": S; the probability of S on "S and God does not exist" is much higher than the probability of S on "God exists"; "S and God does not exist" and "God exists" are inconsistent.

These considerations show that the use of the language of high and low probabilities in formulating the evidential argument from evil is a source of possible confusion. Since, however, my criticisms of the argument have nothing to do with this point, I shall continue to employ this language. But I shall employ it only as a stylistic device: anything I say in this language could easily be restated in terms of epistemic surprise.

8 I can have *some* epistemically warranted expectations about how what I see displayed on the sheet of paper will look: it must in some sense "look like writing" – it can't be a detailed drawing of a cat or a series of a thousand identical marks. Similarly, I can have *some* epistemically warranted expectations about how suffering will be distributed if there is a God. I would suppose, for example, that it is highly improbable on theism that there be sentient creatures and that all of them be in excruciating pain at every moment of their existence.

9 Well, one might somehow know the probability of S on theism as a function of the probability of S on HI; one might know that the former probability was one-tenth the latter, and yet have no idea what either probability was. But that is not the present case. The evidentialist's argument essentially involves two independent probability-judgments: that the probability of S on HI is at least not too low and that the probability of S on theism is very low.

10 Indeed, in *one* sense of probability, the probability of a defense may be very low on theism. We have said that a defense may not be *surprising* on theism, but, as we saw in note 7, there is a perfectly good sense of probability in which a proposition that is not at all surprising on theism may nevertheless be very

improbable on theism. If the defender of theism had at his disposal a very large number of defenses, all of them inconsistent with the others and none of them epistemically preferable to any of the others, it is hard to see why he should not conclude that (relative to his epistemic situation) the probability of any given one of them was very low on theism.

11 "The Magnitude, Duration, and Distribution of Evil: A Theodicy," in *God, Knowledge, and Mystery* (Ithaca and London: Cornell University Press, 1995), pp. 66–95. Failure to appreciate this consideration is a weak point in many versions of the evidential argument from evil. Consider, for example, William L. Rowe's much-discussed article, "The Problem of Evil and Some Varieties of Atheism" (*American Philosophical Quarterly* 16 (1979), 335–41 [ch. 30, this volume]. In this article, Rowe employs the following premise:

> An omniscient, wholly good being would prevent the occurrence of any intense suffering it could, unless it could not do so without losing some greater good or permitting some evil equally bad or worse.

If there are alternative, morally equivalent amounts of (intense) suffering, then this premise is false. To make this point more concrete, let us consider Rowe's famous case of a fawn that dies in prolonged agony of burns that it suffers in a forest fire caused by lightning. God, I concede, could have miraculously prevented the fire, or miraculously saved the fawn, or miraculously caused its agony to be cut short by death. And, I will concede for the sake of argument, if He had done so, this would have thwarted no significant good and permitted no significant evil. But what of the hundreds of millions (at least) of similar incidents that have, no doubt, occurred during the long history of life? Well, I concede, He could have prevented any one of them, or any two of them, or any three of them . . . without thwarting any significant good or permitting any significant evil. But could he have prevented all of them? No – not without causing the world to be massively irregular. And, of course, there is no sharp cutoff point between a world that is massively irregular and a world that is not – just as there is no sharp cutoff point between a penalty that is an effective deterrent for armed assault and a penalty that is not. There is, therefore, no *minimum* number of cases of intense suffering that God could allow without forfeiting the good of a world that is not massively irregular – just as there is no shortest sentence that a legislature can establish as the penalty for armed assault without forfeiting the good of effective deterrence.

12 See "The Place of Chance in a World Sustained by God," in *God, Knowledge, and Mystery.*

13 "Ontological Arguments," in *God, Knowledge, and Mystery.* Review of *The Coherence of Theism* by

Richard Swinburne, *Philosophical Review 87* (1979), 668–72. See also George Seddon, "Logical Possibility," *Mind 81* (1972), 481–94.

14 These laws, being quantum mechanical, are indeterministic. God could not, therefore, have "fine-tuned" the initial state of a universe like ours so as to render an eventual universal hedonic utopia causally inevitable. It would seem to be almost certain that, owing to quantum mechanical indeterminacy, a universe that was a duplicate of ours when ours was, say, 10^{-45} seconds old could have evolved into a very different universe from our present universe. (There is also the point to be considered that there probably *was* no initial state of the universe.) Would it be possible for an omniscient and omnipotent being to create a universe that evolved deterministically out of a carefully selected initial state into a hedonic utopia? This question raises many further questions, questions that mostly cannot be answered. Nevertheless, the following facts would seem to be relevant to an attempt to answer it: life depends on chemistry, and chemistry depends on atoms, and atoms depend on quantum mechanics (classically speaking, an atom cannot exist: the electrons of a "classical" atom would spiral inward, shedding their potential energy in the form of electromagnetic radiation, till they collided with the nucleus), and quantum mechanics is essentially indeterministic.

15 This fact has been widely remarked on. See, e.g., John Leslie, "Modern Cosmology and the Creation of Life," in *Evolution and Creation*, ed. Ernan McMullin (South Bend, Ind.: University of Notre Dame Press, 1985), pp. 91–120.

16 This is not properly speaking a quotation; it is, rather, a selection of verses from chapter 38 of the book of Job. It comprises verses 3, 4, 21, 31, and 33.

17 See the essay and review cited in note 13.

18 Cf. *De Cælo IV*, especially 309ᵃ 18–310ᵃ 13.

19 This latter fact is very important in the debate about extraterrestrial intelligence. If someone in our galaxy aimed a powerful signal at, say, the Andromeda galaxy, then, two million years later, anyone in the Andromeda galaxy who aimed a sensitive receiver precisely at our galaxy would detect that signal. When we aim a sensitive receiver precisely at the Andromeda galaxy, however, we detect no signal. Therefore, no one on any planet circling any of the hundred billion or more stars in the Andromeda galaxy was aiming a signal at the Milky Way galaxy two million years ago. (This argument actually depends on the false assumption that all of the stars in the Andromeda galaxy are equally distant from us, but the essential point of the argument is sound.)

20 For an excellent popular article on the search for extraterrestrial intelligence, see Gregg Easterbrook, "Are We Alone?" *The Atlantic*, August 1988, pp. 25–38.

21 See, for example, Ernst Mayr, "The Probability of Extraterrestrial Intelligent Life," in *Philosophy of*

Biology, ed. Michael Ruse (New York: Macmillan, 1989), pp. 279–85.

22 Are there other defenses – other defenses that cover the same ground as the defense I have presented in Section II? I should like to think so, although I have not had any very interesting ideas about how additional defenses might be constructed. I should welcome suggestions.

23 This essay was read at Brandeis University. The author wishes to thank the members of the Brandeis Philosophy Department, and especially Eli Hirsch, for their helpful comments and criticisms.

33

Horrendous Evils and the Goodness of God

Marilyn McCord Adams

Introduction

Over the past thirty years, analytic philosophers of religion have defined "the problem of evil" in terms of the prima-facie difficulty in consistently maintaining

(1) God exists, and is omnipotent, omniscient, and perfectly good

and

(2) Evil exists.

In a crisp and classic article, "Evil and Omnipotence",[1] J. L. Mackie emphasized that the problem is not that (1) and (2) are logically inconsistent by themselves, but that they together with quasi-logical rules formulating attribute-analyses – such as

(P1) A perfectly good being would always eliminate evil so far as it could,

and

(P2) There are *no limits* to what an omnipotent being can do

Marilyn McCord Adams, "Horrendous Evils and the Goodness of God," reprinted by permission of Oxford University Press from Marilyn McCord Adams and Robert Merrihew Adams (eds.), *The Problem of Evil* (New York: Oxford University Press, 1990).

– constitute an inconsistent premiss-set. He added, of course, that the inconsistency might be removed by substituting alternative and perhaps more subtle analyses, but cautioned that such replacements of (P1) and (P2) would save "ordinary theism" from his charge of positive irrationality, only if true to its "essential requirements".[2]

In an earlier paper, "Problems of Evil: More Advice to Christian Philosophers",[3] I underscored Mackie's point and took it a step further. In debates about whether the argument from evil can establish the irrationality of religious belief, care must be taken, both by the atheologians who deploy it and by the believers who defend against it, to ensure that the operative attribute-analyses accurately reflect that religion's understanding of divine power and goodness. It does the atheologian no good to argue for the falsity of Christianity on the ground that the existence of an omnipotent, omniscient, pleasure-maximizer is incompossible with a world such as ours, because Christians never believed God was a pleasure-maximizer anyway. But equally, the truth of Christianity would be inadequately defended by the observation that an omnipotent, omniscient egoist could have created a world with suffering creatures, because Christians insist that God loves other (created) persons than Himself. The extension of "evil" in (2) is likewise important. Since Mackie and his successors are out to show that "the several parts of the *essential* theological doctrine are inconsistent with *one another*",[4] they can accomplish their aim only if they circumscribe the extension of "evil" as their religious opponents do. By the same token, it is not enough for Christian philosophers to explain how the power, knowledge, and goodness of God could coexist with some evils or other; a full account must exhibit the compossibility of divine perfection with evils in the amounts and of the kinds found in the actual world (and evaluated as such by Christian standards).

The moral of my earlier story might be summarized thus: where the internal coherence of a system of religious beliefs is at stake, successful arguments for its inconsistency must draw on premises (explicitly or implicitly) internal to that system or obviously acceptable to its adherents; likewise for successful rebuttals or explanations of consistency. The thrust of my argument is to push both sides of the debate towards more detailed attention to and subtle understanding of the religious system in question.

As a Christian philosopher, I want to focus in this paper on the problem for the truth of Christianity raised by what I shall call "horrendous" evils. Although our world is riddled with them, the biblical record punctuated by them, and one of them – namely, the passion of Christ; according to Christian belief, the judicial murder of God by the people of God – is memorialized by the Church on its most solemn holiday (Good Friday) and in its central sacrament (the Eucharist), the problem of horrendous evils is largely skirted by standard treatments for the good reason that they are intractable by them. After showing why, I will draw on other Christian materials to sketch ways of meeting this, the deepest of religious problems.

Defining the Category

For present purposes, I define "horrendous evils" as "evils the participation in (the doing or suffering of) which gives one reason prima facie to doubt whether one's life could (given their inclusion in it) be a great good to one on the whole".[5] Such reasonable doubt arises because it is so difficult humanly to conceive how such evils could be overcome. Borrowing Chisholm's contrast between *balancing off* (which occurs when the opposing values of *mutually exclusive* parts of a whole partially or totally cancel each other out) and *defeat* (which cannot occur by the mere addition to the whole of a new part of opposing value, but involves some "organic unity" among the values of parts and wholes, as when the positive aesthetic value of a whole painting defeats the ugliness of a small colour patch),[6] horrendous evils seem prima facie, not

only to balance off but to engulf the positive value of a participant's life. Nevertheless, that very horrendous proportion, by which they threaten to rob a person's life of positive meaning, cries out not only to be engulfed, but to be made meaningful through positive and decisive defeat.

I understand this criterion to be objective, but relative to individuals. The example of habitual complainers, who know how to make the worst of a good situation, shows individuals not to be incorrigible experts on what ills would defeat the positive value of their lives. Nevertheless, nature and experience endow people with different strengths; one bears easily what crushes another. And a major consideration in determining whether an individual's life is/has been a great good to him/her on the whole, is invariably and appropriately how it has seemed to him/her.[7]

I offer the following list of paradigmatic horrors: the rape of a woman and axing off of her arms, psychophysical torture whose ultimate goal is the disintegration of personality, betrayal of one's deepest loyalties, cannibalizing one's own offspring, child abuse of the sort described by Ivan Karamazov, child pornography, parental incest, slow death by starvation, participation in the Nazi death camps, the explosion of nuclear bombs over populated areas, having to choose which of one's children shall live and which be executed by terrorists, being the accidental and/or unwitting agent of the disfigurement or death of those one loves best. I regard these as *paradigmatic*, because I believe most people would find in the doing or suffering of them prima-facie reason to doubt the positive meaning of their lives.[8] Christian belief counts the crucifixion of Christ another: on the one hand, death by crucifixion seemed to defeat Jesus' Messianic vocation; for according to Jewish law, death by hanging from a tree made its victim ritually accursed, definitively excluded from the compass of God's people, *a fortiori* disqualified from being the Messiah. On the other hand, it represented the defeat of its perpetrators' leadership vocations, as those who were to prepare the people of God for the Messiah's coming, killed and ritually accursed the true Messiah, according to later theological understanding, God Himself.

The Impotence of Standard Solutions

For better and worse, the by now standard strategies for "solving" the problem of evil are powerless in the face of horrendous evils.

Seeking the reason-why

In his model article "Hume on Evil",[9] Pike takes up Mackie's challenge, arguing that (P1) fails to reflect ordinary moral intuitions (more to the point, I would add, Christian beliefs), and traces the abiding sense of trouble to the hunch that an omnipotent, omniscient being could have no reason compatible with perfect goodness for permitting (bringing about) evils, because all legitimate excuses arise from ignorance or weakness. Solutions to the problem of evil have thus been sought in the form of counter-examples to this latter claim, i.e. logically possible reasons-why that would excuse even an omnipotent, omniscient God! The putative logically possible reasons offered have tended to be *generic* and *global*: generic in so far as some *general* reason is sought to cover all sorts of evils; global in so far as they seize upon some feature of the world as a whole. For example, philosophers have alleged that the desire to make a world with one of the following properties – "the best of all possible worlds",[10] "a world a more perfect than which is impossible", "a world exhibiting a perfect balance of retributive justice",[11] "a world with as favorable a balance of (created) moral good over moral evil as God can weakly actualize"[12] – would constitute a reason compatible with perfect goodness for God's creating a world with evils in the amounts and of the kinds found in the actual world. Moreover, such general reasons are presented as so powerful as to do away with any need to catalogue types of evils one by one, and examine God's reason for permitting each in particular. Plantinga explicitly hopes that the problem of horrendous evils can thus be solved without being squarely confronted.[13]

The insufficiency of global defeat

A pair of distinctions is in order here: (i) between two dimensions of divine goodness in relation to creation – namely, "producer of global goods" and "goodness to" or "love of individual created persons"; and (ii) between the overbalance/defeat of evil by good on the global scale, and the overbalance/defeat of evil by good within the context of an individual person's life.[14] Correspondingly, we may separate two problems of evil parallel to the two sorts of goodness mentioned in (i).

In effect, generic and global approaches are directed to the first problem: they defend divine goodness along the first (global) dimension by suggesting logically possible strategies for the global defeat of evils. But establishing God's excellence as a producer of global goods does not automatically solve the second problem, especially in a world containing horrendous evils. For God cannot be said to be good or loving to any created persons the positive meaning of whose lives He allows to be engulfed in and/or defeated by evils – that is, individuals within whose lives horrendous evils remain undefeated. Yet, the only way unsupplemented global and generic approaches could have to explain the latter, would be by applying their general reasons-why to particular cases of horrendous suffering.

Unfortunately, such an exercise fails to give satisfaction. Suppose for the sake of argument that horrendous evil could be included in maximally perfect world orders; its being partially constitutive of such an order would assign it that generic and global positive meaning. But would knowledge of such a fact defeat for a mother the prima-facie reason provided by her cannibalism of her own infant to wish that she had never been born? Again, the aim of perfect retributive balance confers meaning on evils imposed. But would knowledge that the torturer was being tortured give the victim who broke down and turned traitor under pressure any more reason to think his/her life worth while? Would it not merely multiply reasons for the torturer to doubt that his/her life could turn out to be a good to him/her on the whole? Could the truck-driver who accidentally runs over his beloved child find consolation in the idea that this middle-known[15] but unintended side-effect was part of the price God accepted for a world with the best balance of moral good over moral evil he could get?

Not only does the application to horrors of such generic and global reasons for divine permission of evils fail to solve the second problem of evil; it makes it worse by adding *generic prima-facie* reasons to doubt whether human life would be a great good to individual human beings in possible worlds where such divine motives were operative. For, taken in isolation and made to bear the weight of the whole explanation, such reasons-why draw a picture of divine indifference or even hostility to the human plight. Would the fact that God permitted horrors because they were constitutive means to His end of global perfection, or that He tolerated them because He could obtain that global end anyway, make the participant's life more tolerable, more worth living for him/her? Given radical human vulnerability to horrendous evils, the ease with which humans participate in them, whether as victim or perpetrator, would not the thought that God visits horrors on anyone who caused them, simply because he/she deserves it, provide one more reason to expect human life to be a nightmare?

Those willing to split the two problems of evil apart might adopt a divide-and-conquer strategy, by simply denying divine goodness along the second dimension. For example, many Christians do not believe that God will ensure an overwhelmingly good life to each and every person He creates. Some say the decisive defeat of evil with good is promised only within the lives of the obedient, who enter by the narrow gate. Some speculate that the elect may be few. Many recognize that the sufferings of this present life are as nothing compared to the hell of eternal torment, designed to defeat goodness with horrors within the lives of the damned.

Such a road can be consistently travelled only at the heavy toll of admitting that human life in worlds such as ours is a bad bet. Imagine (adapting Rawls's device) persons in a pre-original position, considering possible worlds containing managers of differing power, wisdom, and character, and subjects of varying fates. The question they are to answer about each world is whether they would willingly enter it as a human being, from behind a veil of ignorance as to which position they would occupy. Reason would, I submit, dictate a negative verdict for worlds whose omniscient and omnipotent manager permits ante-mortem horrors that remain undefeated within the context of the human participant's life; *a fortiori*, for worlds in which some or most humans suffer eternal torment.

Inaccessible reasons

So far, I have argued that generic and global solutions are at best incomplete: however well their account of divine motivating reasons deals with the first problem of evil, the attempt to extend it to the second fails by making it worse. This verdict might seem prima facie tolerable to standard generic and global approaches and indicative of only a minor modification in their strategy: let the above-mentioned generic and global reasons cover divine permission of non-horrendous evils, and find other *reasons* compatible with perfect goodness *why* even an omnipotent, omniscient God would permit horrors.

In my judgement, such an approach is hopeless. As Plantinga[16] points out, where horrendous evils are concerned, not only do we not know God's *actual* reason for permitting them; we cannot even *conceive* of any plausible candidate sort of reason consistent with worthwhile lives for human participants in them.

The How of God's Victory

Up to now, my discussion has given the reader cause to wonder whose side I am on anyway. For I have insisted, with rebels like Ivan Karamazov and John Stuart Mill, on spotlighting the problem horrendous evils pose. Yet, I have signalled my preference for a version of Christianity that insists on both dimensions of divine goodness, and maintains not only (a) that God will be good enough to created persons to make human life a good bet, but also (b) that each created person will have a life that is a great good to him/her on the whole. My critique of standard approaches to the problem of evil thus seems to reinforce atheologian Mackie's verdict of "positive irrationality" for such a religious position.

Whys versus hows

The inaccessibility of reasons-why seems especially decisive. For surely an all-wise and all-powerful God, who loved each created person enough (a) to defeat any experienced horrors within the context of the participant's life, and (b) to give each created person a life that is a great good to him/her on the whole, would not permit such persons to suffer horrors for no reason.[17] Does not our inability even to conceive of plausible candidate reasons suffice to make belief in such a God positively irrational in a world containing horrors? In my judgement, it does not.

To be sure, motivating reasons come in several varieties relative to our conceptual grasp: There are (i) reasons of the sort we can readily understand when we are informed of them (e.g. the mother who permits her child to undergo painful heart surgery because it is the only humanly possible way to save its life). Moreover, there are (ii) reasons we would be cognitively, emotionally, and spiritually equipped to grasp if only we had a larger memory or wider attention span (analogy: I may be able to memorize small town street plans; memorizing the road networks of the entire country is a task requiring more of the same, in the way that proving Gödel's theorem is not). Some generic and global approaches insinuate that divine permission of evils has motivating reasons of this sort. Finally, there are (iii) reasons that we are cognitively, emotionally, and/or spiritually too immature to fathom (the way a two-year-old child is incapable of understanding its mother's reasons for permitting the surgery). I agree with Plantinga that our ignorance of divine reasons for permitting horrendous evils is not of types (i) or (ii), but of type (iii).

Nevertheless, if there are varieties of ignorance, there are also varieties of reassurance.[18] The two-year-old heart patient is convinced of its mother's love, not by her cognitively inaccessible reasons, but by her intimate care and presence through its painful experience. The story of Job suggests something similar is true with human participation in horrendous suffering: God does not give Job His reasons-why, and implies that Job isn't smart enough to grasp them; rather, Job is lectured on the extent of divine power, and sees God's goodness face to face! Likewise, I suggest, to exhibit the logical compossibility of both dimensions of divine goodness with horrendous suffering, it is not necessary to find logically possible reasons *why* God might permit them. It is enough to show *how* God can be good enough to created persons despite their participation in horrors – by defeating them within the context of the individual's life and by giving that individual a life that is a great good to him/her on the whole.

What sort of valuables?

In my opinion, the reasonableness of Christianity can be maintained in the face of horrendous evils only by drawing on resources of religious value theory. For one way for God to be *good to* created persons is by relating them appropriately to relevant and great goods. But philosophical and religious theories differ importantly on what valuables they admit into their ontology. Some maintain that "what you see is what you get", but nevertheless admit a wide range of valuables, from sensory pleasures, the beauty of nature and cultural artefacts, the joys of creativity, to loving personal intimacy. Others posit a transcendent good (e.g. the Form of the Good in Platonism, or God, the Supremely Valuable Object, in Christianity). In the spirit of Ivan Karamazov, I am convinced that the depth of horrific evil cannot be accurately estimated without recognizing it to be incommensurate with any package of merely non-transcendent goods and so unable to be balanced off, much less defeated, thereby.

Where the *internal* coherence of Christianity is the issue, however, it is fair to appeal to its own store of valuables. From a Christian point of view, God is a being a greater than which cannot be conceived, a good incommensurate with both created goods and temporal evils. Likewise, the good of beatific, face-to-face intimacy with God is simply incommensurate with any merely non-transcendent goods or ills a person might experience. Thus, the good of beatific face-to-face intimacy with God would *engulf* (in a sense analogous to Chisholmian balancing off) even the horrendous evils humans experience in this present life here below, and overcome any prima-facie reasons the individual had to doubt whether his/her life would or could be worth living.

Personal meaning, horrors defeated

Engulfing personal horrors within the context of the participant's life would vouchsafe to that individual a life that was a great good to him/her on the whole. I am still inclined to think it would guarantee that immeasurable divine goodness to any person thus benefited. But there is good theological reason for Christians to believe that God would go further, beyond engulfment to defeat. For it is the nature of persons to look for meaning, both in their lives and in the world. Divine respect for and commitment to created personhood would drive God to make all those sufferings which threaten to destroy the positive meaning of a person's life meaningful through positive defeat.[19]

How could God do it? So far as I can see, only by integrating participation in horrendous evils into a person's relationship with God. Possible dimensions of integration are charted by Christian soteriology. I pause here to sketch three.[20] (i) First, because God in Christ participated in horrendous evil through His passion and death, human experience of horrors can be a means of *identifying* with Christ, either through *sympathetic* identification (in which each person suffers his/her own pains, but their similarity enables each to know what it is like for the other) or through *mystical* identification (in which the created person is supposed literally to experience a share of Christ's pain[21]). (ii) Julian of Norwich's description of heavenly welcome suggests the possible defeat of horrendous evil through divine gratitude. According to Julian, before the elect have a chance to thank God for all He has done for them, God will say, "Thank you for all your suffering, the suffering of your youth." She says that the creature's experience of divine gratitude will bring such full and unending joy as could not be merited by the whole sea of human pain and suffering throughout the ages.[22] (iii) A third idea identifies temporal suffering itself with a vision into the inner life of God, and can be developed several ways. Perhaps, contrary to medieval theology, God is not impassible, but rather has matched capacities for joy and for suffering. Perhaps, as the Heidelberg catechism suggests, God responds to human sin and the sufferings of Christ with an agony beyond human conception.[23] Alternatively, the inner life of God may be, strictly speaking and in and of itself, beyond both joy and sorrow. But, just as (according to Rudolf Otto) humans experience divine presence now as *tremendum* (with deep dread and anxiety), now as *fascinans* (with ineffable attraction), so perhaps our deepest suffering as much as our highest joys may themselves be direct visions into the inner life of God, imperfect but somehow less obscure in proportion to their intensity. And if a face-to-face vision of God is a good for humans incommensurate with any non-transcendent goods or ills, so any vision of God (including horrendous suffering) would have a good aspect in so far as it is a vision of God (even if it has an evil aspect in so far as it is horrendous suffering). For the most part, horrors are not recognized as experiences of God (any more than the city slicker recognizes his visual image of a brown patch as a vision of Beulah the cow in the distance). But, Christian mysticism might claim, at least from the post-mortem perspective of the beatific vision, such sufferings will be seen for what they were, and retrospectively no one will wish away any intimate encounters with God from his/her life-history in this world. The created person's experience of the beatific vision, together with his/her knowledge that intimate divine presence stretched back over his/her antemortem life and reached down into the depths of his/her worst suffering, would provide retrospective comfort independent of comprehension of the reasons-why akin to the two-year-old's assurance of its mother's love. Taking this third approach, Christians would not need to commit themselves about what in any event we do not know: namely, whether we will (like the two-year-old) ever grow up enough to understand the reasons why God permits our participation in horrendous evils. For by contrast with the best of earthly mothers, such divine intimacy is an incommensurate good and would cancel out for the creature any need to know why.

Conclusion

The worst evils demand to be defeated by the best goods. Horrendous evils can be overcome only by the goodness of God. Relative to human nature, participation in horrendous evils and loving intimacy with God are alike disproportionate: for the former threatens to engulf the good in an individual human life with evil, while the latter guarantees the reverse engulfment of evil by good. Relative to one another, there is also disproportion, because the good that God *is*, and intimate relationship with Him, is incommensurate with created goods and evils alike. Because intimacy with God so outscales relations (good or bad) with any creatures, integration into the human person's relationship with God confers significant meaning and positive value even on horrendous suffering. This result coheres with basic Christian intuition: that the powers of darkness are stronger than humans, but they are no match for God!

Standard generic and global solutions have for the most part tried to operate within the territory common to believer and unbeliever, within the confines of religion-neutral value theory. Many discussions reflect the hope that substitute attribute-analyses, candidate reasons-why, and/or defeaters could issue out of values shared by believers and unbelievers alike. And some virtually make this a requirement on an adequate solution. Mackie knew better how to distinguish the many charges that may be levelled against religion. Just as philosophers may or may not find the existence of God plausible, so they may be variously attracted or repelled by Christian values of grace and redemptive sacrifice. But agreement on truth-value is not necessary to consensus on internal consistency. My contention has been that it is not only legitimate, but, given horrendous evils, necessary for Christians to dip into their richer store of valuables to exhibit the consistency of (1) and (2).[24] I would go one step further: assuming the pragmatic and/or moral (I would prefer to say, broadly speaking, religious) importance of believing that (one's own) human life is worth living, the ability of Christianity to exhibit how this could be so despite human vulnerability to horrendous evil constitutes a pragmatic/moral/religious consideration in its favour, relative to value schemes that do not.

To me, the most troublesome weakness in what I have said lies in the area of conceptual underdevelopment. The contention that God suffered in Christ or that one person can experience another's pain requires detailed analysis and articulation in metaphysics and philosophy of mind.

I have shouldered some of this burden elsewhere,[25] but its full discharge is well beyond the scope of this paper.

Notes

1   J. L. Mackie, "Evil and Omnipotence", *Mind*, 64 (1955); repr. in Nelson Pike (ed.), *God and Evil* (Englewood Cliffs, NJ: Prentice-Hall, 1964), pp. 46–60.

2   Ibid., p. 47.

3   Marilyn McCord Adams, "Problems of Evil: More Advice to Christian Philosophers", *Faith and Philosophy* (Apr. 1988), 121–43.

4   Mackie, "Evil and Omnipotence", pp. 46–7 (emphasis mine).

5   Stewart Sutherland (in his comment "Horrendous Evils and the Goodness of God – II", *Proceedings of the Aristotelian Society*, suppl. vol. 63 (1989), 311–23; esp. 311) takes my criterion to be somehow "first-person". This was not my intention. My definition may be made more explicit as follows: an evil e is horrendous if and only if participation in e by person p gives everyone prima-facie reason to doubt whether p's life can, given p's participation in e, be a great good to p on the whole.

6   Roderick Chisholm, "The Defeat of Good and Evil", in Marilyn McCord Adams and Robert Merrihew Adams (eds), *The Problem of Evil* (New York: Oxford University Press, 1990), ch. 3.

7   Cf. Malcolm's astonishment at Wittgenstein's dying exclamation that he had had a wonderful life, *Ludwig Wittgenstein: A Memoir* (London: Oxford University Press, 1962), p. 100.

8   Once again, more explicitly, most people would agree that a person p's doing or suffering of them constitutes prima-facie reason to doubt whether p's life can be, given such participation, a great good to p on the whole.

9   "Hume on Evil", *Philosophical Review*, 72 (1963), 180–97; reprinted in Pike (ed.), *God and Evil*, p. 88.

10 Following Leibniz, Pike draws on this feature as part of what I have called his Epistemic Defence ("Problems of Evil: More Advice to Christian Philosophers", pp. 124–5).

11 Augustine, *On Free Choice of Will*, iii. 93–102, implies that there is a maximum value for created worlds, and a plurality of worlds that meet it. All of these contain rational free creatures; evils are foreseen but unintended side-effects of their creation. No matter what they choose, however, God can order their choices into a maximally perfect universe by establishing an order of retributive justice.

12 Plantinga takes this line in numerous discussions, in the course of answering Mackie's objection to the Free Will Defence, that God should have made sinless free creatures. Plantinga insists that, given incompatibilist freedom in creatures, God cannot strongly actualize any world He wants. It is logically possible that a world with evils in the amounts and of the kinds found in this world is the best that He could do, Plantinga argues, given His aim of getting some moral goodness in the world.

13 Alvin Plantinga, "Self-Profile", in James E. Tomberlin and Peter van Inwagen (eds), *Profiles: Alvin Plantinga* (Dordrecht, Boston, Mass., and Lancaster, Pa.: Reidel, 1985), p. 38.

14 I owe the second of these distinctions to a remark by Keith De Rose in our Fall 1987 seminar on the problem of evil at UCLA.

15 Middle knowledge, or knowledge of what is "in between" the actual and the possible, is the sort of knowledge of what a free creature *would do* in every situation in which that creature could possibly find himself. Following Luis de Molina and Francisco Suarez, Alvin Plantinga ascribes such knowledge to God, prior in the order of explanation to God's decision about which free creatures to actualize (in *The Nature of Necessity* (Oxford: Clarendon Press, 1974), pp. 164–93). Robert Merrihew Adams challenges this idea in his article "Middle Knowledge and the Problem of Evil", *American Philosophical Quarterly*, 14 (1977); repr. in *The Virtue of Faith* (New York: Oxford University Press, 1987), pp. 77–93.

16 Alvin Plantinga, "Self-Profile", pp. 34–5.

17 This point was made by William Fitzpatrick in our Fall 1987 seminar on the problem of evil at UCLA.

18 Contrary to what Sutherland suggests ("Horrendous Evils", pp. 314–15), so far as the compossibility problem is concerned, I intend no illicit shift from reason to emotion. My point is that intimacy with a loving other is a good, participation in which can defeat evils, and so provide everyone with reason to think a person's life can be a great good to him/her on the whole, despite his/her participation in evils.

19 Note, once again, contrary to what Sutherland suggests ("Horrendous Evils", pp. 321–3) "horrendous evil e is defeated" entails *none* of the following propositions: "e was not horrendous", "e was not unjust", "e was not so bad after all". Nor does my suggestion that even horrendous evils can be defeated by a great enough (because incommensurate and uncreated) good, in any way impugn the reliability of our moral intuitions about injustice, cold-bloodedness, or horror. The judgement that participation in e constitutes prima-facie reason to believe that p's life is ruined, stands and remains a daunting measure of e's horror.

20 In my paper "Redemptive Suffering: A Christian Solution to the Problem of Evil", in Robert Audi and William J. Wainwright (eds), *Rationality, Religious Belief, and Moral Commitment: New Essays in Philosophy of Religion* (Cornell University Press, 1986), pp. 248–67, I sketch how horrendous suffering can be meaningful by being made a vehicle of divine redemption for victim, perpetrator, and onlooker, and thus an occasion of the victim's collaboration with God. In "Separation and Reversal in Luke–Acts", in Thomas Morris (ed.), *Philosophy and the Christian Faith* (Notre Dame, Ind.: Notre Dame University Press, 1988), pp. 92–117, I attempted to chart the redemptive plot-line whereby horrendous sufferings are made meaningful by being woven into the divine redemptive plot. My considered opinion is that such collaboration would be too strenuous for the human condition were it not to be supplemented by a more explicit and beatific divine intimacy.

21 For example, Julian of Norwich tells us that she prayed for and received the latter (*Revelations of Divine Love*, ch. 17). Mother Theresa of Calcutta seems to construe Matthew 25: 31–46 to mean that the poorest and the least *are* Christ, and that their sufferings *are* Christ's (Malcolm Muggeridge, *Something Beautiful for God* (New York: Harper & Row, 1960), pp. 72–5).

22 *Revelations of Divine Love*, ch. 14. I am grateful to Houston Smit for recognizing this scenario of Julian's as a case of Chisholmian defeat.

23 Cf. Plantinga, "Self-Profile", p. 36.

24 I develop this point at some length in "Problems of Evil: More Advice to Christian Philosophers", pp. 127–35.

25 For example in "The Metaphysics of the Incarnation in Some Fourteenth Century Franciscans", in William A. Frank and Girard J. Etzkorn (eds), *Essays Honoring Allan B. Wolter* (St Bonaventure, NY: The Franciscan Institute, 1985), pp. 21–57.

In the development of these ideas, I am indebted to the members of our Fall 1987 seminar on the problem of evil at UCLA – especially to Robert Merrihew Adams (its co-leader) and to Keith De Rose, William Fitzpatrick, and Houston Smit. I am also grateful to the Very Revd. Jon Hart Olson for many conversations in mystical theology.

34

Selves and Shadows

Mary Midgley

The Problem of Self-deception

We come back now to our original problem – the attempt to make wickedness understandable – absolved, if all has gone well, from various objections to the whole project, and equipped with some concepts which may help us. The problem, however, can still look an uncommonly awkward one. A cartoon of Edward Kliban's may suggest why.[1] It shows a cheerful mechanic, tools upraised in triumph, pointing to the open bonnet of a car and telling the owner with satisfaction, "Well, *there's* your problem." Inside the car there is nothing but a huge, prickly monster, crouched together in a sinister manner and baring its huge teeth in a knowing grin. The owner knows what's wrong now. But what is he going to do about it?

I have been suggesting that the wrong kind of approach to the problem of wickedness does make it look very much like this. Evil, considered as something positive, would indeed have to be an alien being, a demon which had taken possession. The only possible kind of treatment would then be to cast it out somehow from the possessed person. (That feat is indeed often expected, not only of witch-doctors and exorcists, but also of educators, of psychiatrists and of psycho-analysts.) This casting-out will not get far unless it is somehow replanned to take account of the fact that evil traits are not just something alien. In one sense they are

Mary Midgley, "Selves and Shadows," from *Wickedness: A Philosophical Essay* (London and Boston: Routledge and Kegan Paul, 1984), pp. 113–31.

simply qualities of the person who owns them, though in another they are indeed something extraneous which has attacked him. This duality is a most puzzling feature of our mental life, and a continual practical as well as theoretical problem. We try to avoid "owning" our bad motives, not just from vanity (though that is important) but because we feel that to own or acknowledge is to accept. We dread exposure to the hidden force whose power we sense. Our official idea of ourselves has no room for it. It therefore does not seem merely humiliating and depressing (as our known faults do), but alien, inhuman and menacing to an indefinite degree. When this sense of menace gets severe, it is almost certain to get projected on to the outside world, supplying fuel for those irrational fears and hatreds which play so central a part in human destructiveness.

In what may be called contentedly wicked people – and in all of us so far as we are contentedly wicked – this process is far gone, and may involve no more conflict in the inner life than in the front shown to the world. It is the fact that no conflict is visible that makes this kind of case so opaque. But this need not force us either to assume a special alternative morality at work, or to give up the attempt at understanding altogether. Instead, we can approach this kind of case by way of the much less opaque ones where conflict is still visibly raging. Hard though this is, it seems necessary to attempt it since self-deception, in spite of its chronic obscurity, is a topic which we badly need to understand. Bishop Butler, at the end of his discussion of it, cries out suddenly:

And, if people will be wicked, they had better of the two be so from the common vicious passions without such refinements, than from this deep and calm source of delusion, which undermines the whole principle of good, darkens that light, that *candle of the Lord within*, which is to direct our steps, and corrupts conscience, which is the guide of life.[2]

Does this mean that there are two quite separate alternatives, self-deception and vice? It seems not. Butler apparently takes "the common vicious passions" to be something conscious and acknowledged. But the more fully conscious they are, the nearer their owners come to what Aristotle called weakness, rather than vice.[3] They suffer spasms of (say) furious or covetous action alternating with fits of repentance. People who are weak in this sense are supposed still to keep so clear an intellectual grasp of the situation that they judge their own acts impartially, as they would other people's. This seems rather strange. The disadvantages of oscillating violently in this way are obvious, and in fact if we find people who seem to do it we tend to look for an explanation in some oscillation of their physical state. Without this extra factor, it is hard to see how the oscillator's clarity of vision can really be maintained. Some self-deception seems absolutely necessary, first so that he can have some kind of a story to tell himself during his vicious fits, but also, and more deeply, because the whole process of oscillation is going to need some justification of its own, and it will be uncommonly difficult to find an honest one. The question why one is behaving alternatively like two quite different people is one that cannot fail to arise. The answer "I just happen to be two people" has never been found to be very satisfactory. Butler's point, then, seems sound, but it is a matter of degree, not a complete dichotomy. The more chronic, continuous and well-established is the self-deception, the deeper and more pernicious the vice. But some self-deception is probably needed if actions are to be called vicious at all.

Inner Dialogue and Duality

I am suggesting that self-deception arises because we see motives which are in fact our own as alien to us and refuse to acknowledge them. This is not an isolated event, but is one possible outcome of a very common and pervasive inner dialogue, in which aspects of the personality appear to exchange views as if they were separate people. We are used to this interchange between alternating moods or viewpoints. (If we were not, we should probably find it much harder to disown some of them, because it would be harder to separate them from our official selves in the first place.) This inner dialogue is, I believe, the source of drama. Good plays and stories do not just show clashes between distinct individuals, externally related. They show ones which take place within us as well as outside. However black the villains, however strange the character-parts, we need to feel something within us respond to them. Drama helps inner conflict by crystallizing it. It can, of course, be used to help self-deception by externalizing villainy, but it can also help self-knowledge by showing up the participants clearly. Properly used, it always helps us to avoid that dangerous thing, an over-simple view of personal identity.

There is a great deal more to the problem of personal identity than meets the eye, or gets mentioned in current philosophical discussions. This connexion with inner conflict and the problem of evil, in particular, seems to have had very little academic attention of late. It is, however, very important, on account of the existence of shadows. In this century, academic philosophy, as much as psychology, has been reluctant to pay much attention to the shadow-side of human motivation. It has not occupied itself with the agonizing question "Can it really have been I who did that?" or with the genuine clash of reasons for answering yes or no to it. Nor has it dealt much with the still more startling division of the self into two or more embattled factions which marks the process of temptation. If we want to find a way into these problems, we had therefore better turn to those who have seriously and methodically considered them. Setting aside the religious traditions for a moment – because we are not sure how much of their conceptual equipment we shall want to accept – we are left, therefore, with works of imagination, and particularly of imaginative literature.

There is absolutely no shortage of shadows here. Resisting the urge to plunge in and round them all up, I shall deliberately start with a rather simple and schematic specimen, namely *The Strange Case of Dr Jekyll and Mr Hyde*. Critics have sometimes treated this story as a lightweight, but I think they are mistaken. Any crash course on evil must acknowledge a great debt to the Scots, and the debt to Stevenson here seems to be quite an important part of it. It is worth while, if one has not taken it very seriously, having another look.

What Stevenson brings out is the negativity of Hyde's character. Evil, in spite of its magnificent pretensions, turns out to be mostly a vacuum. That does not make it less frightening, but more so. Like darkness and cold, it destroys but it cannot replace. The thought is an old one, but we may have regarded it simply as a platitude. In the story, however, Hyde's first appearance shows it sharply:

Street after street and all the folks asleep. . . . All at once I saw two figures; one a little man who was stumping along eastwards at a good walk, and the other a girl of maybe eight or ten who was running as hard as she was able down a cross street. Well sir, the two ran into one another naturally enough at the corner; and then came the horrible part of the thing; for the man trampled calmly over the child's body and left her screaming on the ground. It sounds nothing to hear, but it was hellish to see.[4]

What makes it so is not deliberate cruelty, but callousness – the total absence of a normal human response. David Hume (a Scot of a different kind) asked, "Would any man, who is walking along, tread as willingly on another's gouty toes, whom he has no quarrel with, as on the hard flint and pavement?"[5] Well, here is that man, and his total blindness to any feeling but his own is central to his character. As Jekyll puts it, when he is eventually driven to attempt a choice between his two lives:

Hyde was indifferent to Jekyll, or but remembered him as the mountain bandit remembers the cavern in which he conceals himself from pursuit. Jekyll had more than a father's interest (because he shared Hyde's pleasures); Hyde had more than a son's indifference.[6]

This is why, although Hyde had

a soul boiling with causeless hatreds, and a body that seemed not strong enough to contain the raging energies of life, [Jekyll] . . . thought of Hyde, for all his energy of life, as of something not only hellish but inorganic. This was the shocking thing; that the slime of the pit seemed to utter cries and voices; that what was dead and had no shape, should usurp the offices of life.[7]

This fearful limitation is, of course, the reason why he cannot choose to settle for Hyde, but must continue the doomed effort to be Jekyll. He notes it again, as he draws his memoirs to a close:

Should the throes of change take me in the act of writing this, Hyde will tear it in pieces; but if some time shall have elapsed after I have laid it by, his wonderful selfishness and circumscription to the moment will probably save it again from the action of his ape-like spite.[8]

Hyde, appalling though he is, is no princely Lucifer; he is meanly sub-human. Mention of the "ape" here has its usual negative point. Symbolic animals stand merely for the absence of certain human powers and feelings, even though in real life animals may share these. Most animals in fact avoid trampling others underfoot, as has been noticed with annoyance when people have wanted to make horses or elephants do it. In the animal kingdom, Hyde is something special. But his specialness does not consist in a new, exciting, positive motivation. It is an emotional crippling, a partial death of his faculties.

Shadow-shedding

What has produced this crippling? It resulted in fact from a rather casual miscalculation on the part of Jekyll. (This casualness is, I think, what stops some people taking the story seriously. But the story is surely about the casualness, rather than being an expression of it.) Jekyll found, early in life, that his ambition was in conflict with his taste for dissipation, and decided to try and separate these two motives so that each could pursue its interests without hindrance from the other. He therefore accepted, and still defends to the end, the proposition that "man is not truly one, but truly two. I say two, because the state of my own knowledge does not pass beyond this point . . . [but perhaps] man will be ultimately known for a mere polity of multifarious, incongruous and independent denizens."[9] But of course he does not accept this idea seriously and literally as requiring a full separation, with an impartial distribution of chances to the multifarious denizens on a time-sharing basis. He sees it simply as providing a splendid disguise, which will allow the old Jekyll his fun while protecting his reputation and his complacency. (This is where the casualness comes in.)

"I do not think I ever met Mr Hyde?" asked Utterson. "Oh dear no sir. He never *dines* here," replied the butler.

"Indeed, we see very little of him on this side of the house; he mostly comes and goes by the laboratory."[10]

And again, as Jekyll puts it, "The moment I choose, I can be rid of Mr Hyde. I give you my hand upon that."[11] This was his whole plan for the relationship. His "discovery" of duality therefore means merely something which others have tried out before him, namely, the hypothesis that *it doesn't matter what you do with your shadow*. Peter Schlemihl sold his shadow to the devil, never supposing that he would need it.[12] He soon found out his mistake. Dorian Gray let his picture absorb the effects of his iniquities, supposing that he could ignore it, but it got him in the end. The dismissed shadow in Hans Andersen's story came back after many years, having grown a new body, though a thin one. It was embarrassingly obsequious at first, but rapidly grew more and more domineering, and reduced its former owner to the status of its shadow. When he tried to resist, it killed him. It is well known that you can't be too careful about these things. But the project of shadow-immunity which throws most light on our present subject is another Scottish one, James Hogg's novel, *The Confessions of a Justified Sinner.*[13]

This is an altogether deeper affair. The sinner, Robert Wringhim, has accepted with his whole heart the doctrine of justification by faith alone. He then becomes convinced of his own salvation, and thus believes himself to be henceforward incapable of sin. Going out to give thanks to God for this state of affairs, he is stopped by a mysterious stranger, his exact double. This person deflects him from his purpose by flattering words ("I am come to be a humble disciple of yours; to be initiated into the true way of true salvation by conversing with you, and perhaps of being assisted by your prayers").[14] Instead of joining Wringhim in thanking God, he points out to him that he is now a highly exceptional and privileged person, incapable of sin, and therefore free to commit every possible kind of action without blame. Are there not, therefore, remarkable acts to which he is called? Wringhim, who already believes most of those around him to be worthless enemies of the Lord, predestined to damnation, has no defence against the suggestion that it is his duty to kill many of them, including his own family. And this, in spite of his timidity

and some other natural objections, he is finally led on to do.

The ingenious use of Calvin's doctrine thus provides Wringhim's shadow-self with a quite exceptionally wide scope for exemption from responsibility. Dorian Gray's exemption covered only his appearance. Jekyll's, even in his most prosperous days, covered only the exploits of Hyde. His own life had still to be lived normally on its previous lines. But Wringhim (or the devil who counsels him) has so arranged things that his whole active life is to be immune from judgment and from serious consequences.

Two points emerge. One, that the price of this playground is high. Freed from consequences and from judgment, action altogether loses its meaning. Wringhim is very mad indeed. Two, that what he pays this price for is, again, something utterly squalid and negative. Certainly he is able to satisfy briefly his resentment against those who have not appreciated him, but this is hardly an aim proportioned to the tremendous metaphysical pretensions of the original scheme. His heroic acts are only a string of spiteful murders without any public or political point. The fate of all souls being in any case fixed, it is not even clear why cutting off the wicked in their prime should have the slightest value. It is a mean, unimpressive and disappointing enterprise, judged against the glittering hints dropped by the mysterious stranger, to whom Wringhim, in spite of his new-found importance and freedom, soon finds himself enslaved. Trying to get a hold on events, he asks the stranger for his name:

"I have no parents save one, whom I do not acknowledge", said he proudly. "Therefore pray drop that subject, for it is a disagreeable one. I am a being of a very peculiar temper, for, though I have servants and subjects more than I can number, yet, to gratify a certain whim, I have left them and retired to this city, and, for all the society which it contains, you see I have attached myself only to you. This is a secret . . . pray let it remain one, and say not another word about the matter."

It immediately struck me that this was no other than the Czar of Russia. . . . I had henceforward great and mighty hopes of high preferment as a defender and avenger of the oppressed Christian church, under the influence of this great potentate.[15]

Vanity is the key to Wringhim's enslavement. And it plays a central part also in that of Jekyll, who is throughout happy to sacrifice the whole integrity of his being for the sake of his spotless reputation. Vanity comes upon him at a fatal juncture, when he has for a time renounced Hyde, and been living as himself but has finally weakened and indulged, in his own person, in a night on the tiles. Next morning:

> [T]he Regent's Park was full of winter chirrupings and sweet with spring odours. I sat in the sun on a bench, the animal within me licking the chops of memory, the spiritual side a little drowsed, promising subsequent penitence, but not yet moved to begin. After all, I reflected, I was like my neighbours; and then I smiled, comparing myself with other men, comparing my active good-will with the lazy cruelty of their neglect. And at the very moment of that vainglorious thought, a qualm came over me, a horrid nausea and the most deadly shuddering. . . . I was once more Edward Hyde.[16]

The trouble is not, of course, that vanity is the worst of the vices. It is just that it is the one which makes admitting all the others unbearable, and so leads to the shadow-shedding project. And the reason why this project is doomed is because, as Jung sensibly points out, shadows have a function:

> Painful though it is, this [unwelcome self-knowledge] is in itself a gain – for what is inferior or even worthless belongs to me as my shadow and gives me substance and mass. How can I be substantial if I fail to cast a shadow? I must have a dark side also if I am to be whole; and inasmuch as I become conscious of my shadow I also remember that I am a human being like any other.[17]

The acknowledged shadow may be terrible enough. But it is the unacknowledged one which is the real killer.

Of course Stevenson's story is somewhat crude and schematic. But by being so it gets past our defences and makes us pay some attention to its topic. Jekyll was partly right: we *are* each not only one but also many. Might not this fact deserve a little more philosophic attention? Some of us have to hold a meeting every time we want to do something only slightly difficult, in order to find the self who is capable of undertaking it. We often fail, and

have to make do with an understudy who is plainly not up to the job. We spend a lot of time and ingenuity on developing ways of organizing the inner crowd, securing consent among it, and arranging for it to act as a whole. Literature shows that the condition is not rare. Others, of course, obviously do not feel like this at all, hear such descriptions with amazement, and are inclined to regard those who give them as dotty. There is not, however, the sort of difference between the conduct of those aware of constant internal debate and that of other people which would justify writing this awareness off as an aberration. When real difficulties arise, everybody becomes conscious of it, and has what is recognizably the same sort of trouble. There are then actually advantages in being used to it. Someone who has never felt gravely divided before is likely to be more bewildered than a habitual splitter. Most people, too, probably would recognize that serious troubles do give rise to such conflicts, that rather more of them go on than are sometimes noticed, and that, through the process of temptation, they do have an important bearing on wickedness. But just how does this connexion work? Can inner conflicts explain major crimes?

The Power of Projection

The difficulty for thought here is this. We feel that motives ought to be adequate for the actions they produce. In the case of good actions they often are so; indeed, it is common to find that the people who did something good were trying to do much more than they achieved. The frustration of really good schemes by outside difficulties is a commonplace. But in the case of evil actions this is much less clear. When we look for someone who conceived them we often cannot find him at all; when we can, we often find a number of culprits with no clear connexion with each other, none of whom was apparently trying to do what actually resulted. In such cases, we are inclined to retire baffled, give up the search for causes rooted in human motivation, and fall back on other sorts of explanation, such as the economic. But this is clearly not very satisfactory, since the human conduct in question – for instance, that of launching the First World War, and of carrying it on in the way that was in fact followed – is not a rational response to the economic factors. Although a few people profited from it, the damage which it did was so enormous, and the chance for any individual of immunity from that damage so small, that Hobbesian calculators of enlightened self-interest would not have been led to take such action. For instance, even the most selfish of politicians and generals did not want to lose their sons, nor to risk their careers in the chaos that follows defeat. The rational aims they were pursuing could have been followed up by methods which did not involve these dangers. And anyway most of those involved were not simply and clear-headed selfish; they thought they were doing their duty. We have therefore to look for diffused human motives, not clearly recognized, which blind people to their own interests as well as to other people's, and incline them to see as their duty actions which, if they viewed them impartially, they would consider wrong.

What makes these motives hard to see is the very same fact which gives them their force – namely, their immense diffusion. The habitual, half-conscious, apparently mild hostility of one people towards another is as little noticed, consciously, as the air they breathe. It also resembles that air in being a vital factor in their lives, and in the fact that a slight shift in its quality can make enormous changes. Yet it differs from it in being something for which they are, at root, responsible. To take the crudest case at once, it is what makes war possible. And a very interesting and significant point about the way in which it does so is its versatility – the ease with which it can be shifted from one opponent to another. Orwell's caricature in *1984*, where a political speaker in the middle of a speech changes fulminations directed against one enemy into ones directed against another, in response to a slip handed up to him showing that the High Command has changed its policy, contains a truth with which history has made us familiar, but whose oddness we need to notice. Alliances are changed far more easily than one might expect, and hostility is even more easily redirected. This is connected with another striking feature, the ease with which improbable charges are believed against anyone designated as an enemy, the invention of further charges when real data fail, and the general unreality with which enemy thought-processes are imagined. We need to notice again how contrary this habit of mind is to rational prudence. If one has enemies, it is surely of the first importance to discover their real intentions, to study them carefully, and assess realistically the dangers which they actually pose. No real enemy is unlimitedly hostile. All have particular aims, and between such aims compromise is nearly

always possible. Certainly some enemies are more threatening, some conflicts of interest harder to reconcile than others. But this only makes it all the more important to discover realistically which sort one is facing at the moment.

When we consider people's frequent failure to do this, and the extraordinary flourishing of violent hostility where no real threat is posed at all, we are (as far as I can see) forced to look for an explanation within. People who seriously believe that they are being attacked when they are not, and who attribute hostile planning groundlessly to their supposed attackers, have to be projecting their own unrecognized bad motives onto the world around them. For instance, the suspicion of witchcraft is a very common form for this projection, found in many cultures. The more convinced we are that witchcraft does not actually take place, the more necessary it surely is to account for this belief in terms of projection. In our own culture, the story of witch-hunting is a very remarkable one, since the early church actively discouraged it, and laid down rules which made the practice very difficult. In order to let loose the witch-hunting movement which was rife between the fifteenth and seventeenth centuries, it was necessary for those who saw witchcraft everywhere to break through established custom and reverse many ecclesiastical rulings.[18] This and many similar cases show how shallow it would be to attribute these beliefs merely to chance tradition and primitive ignorance of causes. Other obvious cases are anti-semitism and persecution of religious minorities. When we turn to disputes between nations things are, of course, often more complicated, since real conflicts of interests, and real threats, may be involved as well as irrational hostility. But when we look at these apparently more solid causes, complications appear. How rational is resentment? When one country has previously attacked another – for instance in the case of France and Germany after the war of 1870 – what follows? It is natural for the invaded party to fear that it will happen again, to want its provinces back, and in fact want revenge. But intense concentration of these aims is certainly not the best way to secure, in the end, harmonious relations with the neighbour. And those harmonious relations provide the only possible hope of arbitrating the conflict of interest effectively.

Even in the most reasonable kinds of dispute, uncontrolled, chronic hostility is a liability, not an asset, and this, again, gives us further grounds to suppose that it takes its rise in irrelevant, projected motives, not just in the specific, apparent causes of the outward dispute. Specific grievances wear out; the unchangingness of group hostilities marks them as fraudulent. They are not responses to real external dangers, but fantasies. We erect a glass at the border of our own group, and see our own anger reflected against the darkness behind it. Where we know a good deal about neighbouring groups, the darkness is not complete and the projection is imperfect. If we want to maintain it, we may then have to do quite a lot of arguing. But the more unfamiliar that group is, the deeper the darkness becomes. The illusion can then grow wholly convincing. This is the point at which even people who know perfectly well that the so-called *Protocols of the Elders of Zion* were deliberately forged by the Czarist police still find no difficulty in accepting them as evidence.[19] The dark vision is too vivid to be doubted; its force is its warrant. What we see out there is indeed real enough; it is our own viciousness, and it strikes us with quite appropriate terror. And by an unlucky chance, while it remains projected, there is no way to weaken or destroy it. Persecution and punishment of those to whom it is attributed do not soften it at all; indeed, to the persecutors' alarm, they often seem to intensify it. Hence the strange insatiability of persecution, the way in which suspicion seems to grow by being fed, and security never comes nearer.

Complicity Between Leaders and Led

This account of course raises many questions which we have still to deal with, notably about the origin of the projected feelings in the first place. But it has one great asset which, as it seems to me, makes some form of it a necessary move. This is that it resolves the difficulty about finding an adequate motive. The joint repressed aggression of a whole populace makes up a very powerful motive for communal crimes, such as pogroms, witch-hunts or gratuitous wars. It is a cause suitable to such effects. By invoking it, we can avoid a very odd and unconvincing feature of those explanations which ignore it, namely, that they divide populations sharply into a few guilty instigators and a majority of amazingly passive dupes or fools. Unless we think that a particular population is weak and foolish on all subjects, we must surely find it odd that they become so as soon as some particular feared or persecuted group comes in question. The picture of innocent passivity is not convincing because it

is too selective. We know very well that not every kind of political leader, and not every kind of cause, finds this kind of uncritical passive obedience. And if the picture of the passive herd is suspect, that of the wholly active, creative instigator, stamping his personality at will upon this wax, is still more so. Mass leaders must use the causes they can find. Konrad Heiden, in his life of Hitler, stresses the incoherence and vacillation of his policies, the random, opportunistic way in which he picked up his ideas, largely according to their saleability:

> Rather than a means of directing the mass mind, propaganda is a technique for riding with the masses. It is not a machine to make wind, but a sail to catch the wind. . . . The more passionately Hitler harps on the value of personality, the more clearly he reveals his nostalgia for something that is lacking. . . . Yes, he knows this mass world, he knows how to guide it by "compliance". . . . He did not have a plan and act accordingly; he acted, and out of his actions a plan arose.[20]

Influential psychopaths and related types, in fact, get their power not from originality, but from a perception of just what unacknowledged motives lie waiting to be exploited, and just what aspects of the world currently provide a suitable patch of darkness on to which they can be projected. In order to catch the wind, they must (if Heiden is right) be without any specific, positive motivation of their own which might distract them from taking up and using skilfully whatever has most popular appeal at the time. Many aspiring Caesars have come to grief here; they had too much individual character. They did not see the sharpness of the dilemma. To gain great popular power, you must either be a genuinely creative genius, able to communicate new ideas very widely, or you must manage to give a great multitude permission for things which it already wants, but for which nobody else is currently prepared to give that permission. In order to find these things, and to handle skilfully the process of permitting the unthinkable, absolute concentration on the main chance is required, and this seems only possible to those without serious, positive aims of their own. There is therefore a sense, and not a trivial one, in which such demagogues are themselves the tools of their supporters. This becomes disturbingly plain in causes where they eventually lose their influence and are cast aside to end their days in obscurity, like Titus Oates and Senator Joe

Mary Midgley

McCarthy. It then becomes a mystery, even to many of those who followed them, how they can ever have had such power. The only place where solutions to this mystery can be sought for seems to be the unconscious motivation of those who allowed themselves to be deceived.

All this does not, of course, mean that the difference between instigators and dupes is not a real one, only that it is a good deal less simple than we often suppose. Instigators are not wholly active nor dupes wholly passive. And many people, of course, fill both roles, adding a good deal on their own account to the suggestions they receive. The problem of understanding the instigators, however, still remains. And it may well seem to present particular difficulties for the notion which we have been considering, that evil is essentially negative. That notion is of course particularly easy to apply in the sort of cases we have looked at in this chapter – cases of conflict, resulting in weakness and self-deception. When we consider the strategies by which people who do not officially choose to be wicked still manage to do so while quieting their consciences and denying their shadows, a diagnosis which focuses on what they *fail* to do may seem plausible enough, or at least not surprising. And we have seen that it is possible for people in this situation to commit an immense proportion of the evil which is actually done in the world – a proportion which the impersonal complication of modern society may be continually raising. The harm that can be done by not thinking is literally immeasurable. All the same, there do still have to be some people to make the suggestions. No movement consists solely of followers. Might there still be a need for a different, entirely positive notion of evil there?

Summary

We come back to the problem of making wickedness understandable, after considering the objections that it (a) does not exist, and (b) has no real roots in us, being an external phenomenon induced by culture. This last view belongs to a group of ideas about evil, many of them quite old, which treat it as something quite foreign to us, external and therefore a positive force (demonic possession.) This approach necessarily obstructs the understanding which we need for dealing with it. But it springs from a real problem. Evil is in one sense part of ourselves; in another it is not. "Owning" bad motives can indeed lead to fatalism about them.

But disowning them can conceal their presence in us. We then tend to project them on to the outside world and attribute them to others.

Complete cases of this self-deception are rare and obscure, but partial ones, where conflict rages, are common and can be studied. The inner dialogue surrounding them finds natural expression in drama. Inner conflict is a normal, more or less constant feature of our personal identity. Our characters are constituted largely by the way we handle it. Transactions between people's official selves and their "shadows" – the aspects of their personalities which they try to reject – have not lately had much philosophic attention, but are often very shrewdly treated by imaginative writers. One example is *Dr Jekyll and Mr Hyde*. This story brings out, more subtly than is often noticed, the negative aspect of evil. Jekyll has not so much "become two people" as ceased to be anybody. He has become hollow, losing his centre, from refusing to acknowledge his shadow-side. Another example is *Confessions of a Justified Sinner*. Wringhim's ambitious vanity, taking him over, leaves him in the end no core to his personality – even no real motives except an obscure and quite impersonal terror. By denying and projecting his shadow, he has disintegrated altogether. ("Losing one's shadow" is how Peter Schlemihl puts it.)

These are stories about the loss of direction which results from denying one's shadow and its accompanying conflicts. If we find them convincing, they surely throw light on the familiar puzzle of finding adequate motives for bad actions – the puzzle which leads to calling them "mad". Communal projection of unacknowledged shadows is a possible cause – and seems the only plausible cause – for the strong element of fantasy in our hostility to outgroups (witchcraft, heresy-hunting, anti-semitism). Wild, paranoiac accusations seem hard to explain in any other way. The idea that a few wily leaders may have imposed this whole condition on an entirely passive mob of supporters is not plausible. The supporters must themselves be active. The leaders can only take them where they will go, and this particular direction is one which has succeeded too often to be a matter of chance. Leaders and led must surely be in collusion. Shared, half-conscious projected shadow-motivation supplies the steam.

If this (not very surprising) view is right, we can see the point of saying that evil in the supporters is negative. Their trouble lies in their *failure* to do something universally necessary. They have failed to acknowledge, and to deal with, powerful motives which are in origin their own, but which, through projection, are officially now no part of their personalities. What they do is, of course, positive action, but it proceeds, in a strange but familiar way, from a vacuum. By their own responsibility, they have let themselves become passive instruments of evil. Simply by not thinking, they can do immeasurable harm (Eichmann).

Notes

1 It appears on the cover of his collection of cartoons, appropriately called *Well, There's your Problem* (Penguin, Harmondsworth, 1980).

2 Bishop Butler, *Fifteen Sermons*, Sermon X "Upon Self-Deceit", section 16.

3 *Nicomachean Ethics* book VII, chs 1–10.

4 R. L. Stevenson, *The Strange Case of Dr Jekyll and Mr Hyde*, ch. 1 (Nelson, London, 1956), p. 6.

5 *Enquiry Concerning the Principles of Morals*, part ii, section V, 183.

6 Stevenson, *Dr Jekyll and Mr Hyde*, ch. 10, p. 86.

7 Ibid., pp. 94–5, 96–7.

8 Ibid., ch. 2, p. 25.

9 Ibid., p. 75.

10 Ibid., p. 21.

11 Ibid., p. 25.

12 These and other cases are well discussed by Ralph Timms in *Doubles in Literary Psychology* (Bowes & Bowes, Cambridge, 1949).

13 James Hogg, *The Confessions of a Justified Sinner* (1824; reprinted with an introduction by André Gide, Panther Books, London, 1970).

14 Ibid., p. 111.

15 Ibid., pp. 121–2.

16 Stevenson, *Dr Jekyll and Mr Hyde*, ch. 10, p. 90.

17 C. G. Jung, *Modern Man in Search of a Soul*, p. 40.

18 A remarkable story, well traced by Charles Williams in his *Witchcraft* (Faber, London, 1941).

19 For this extremely strange business, see Konrad Heiden, *Der Fuehrer: Hitler's Rise to Power* (trans. Ralph Mannheim; Gollancz, 1944), ch. 1.

20 Ibid., p. 118.

35

Buddhism and Evil

Martin Southwold

There is no concept of evil in Buddhism: so I concluded on the basis of my fieldwork among Sinhalese Buddhists in 1974–5.[1] But the literature implied that this must be wrong. Ling had published a book with the title *Buddhism and the Mythology of Evil* (1962), and Boyd another, covering similar ground, entitled *Satan and Māra: Christian and Buddhist Symbols of Evil* (1975). Obeyesekere's distinguished paper, "Theodicy, Sin and Salvation in a Sociology of Buddhism" (1968) mentions notions of evil among Sinhalese Buddhists, and can easily be read as discussing them at length. It was not to be supposed that such eminent scholars had enlarged on mere figments of their own imagination: more probable that my own fieldwork had been negligent.

Closer scrutiny revealed that the contradiction was more apparent than real. The key terms, "Buddhism" and "evil", are so ambiguous that it can be truly said both that there is and that there is not a concept of evil in Buddhism. Such ambiguity screens reality from view. When it is resolved, by clearly distinguishing the different senses of the terms, there comes into view a more nuanced and interesting scene. There are some concepts of evil in Buddhism; but there is no concept of evil in the strongest and most distinctive sense in which we use this term. Some Buddhists – and this is also significant – have notions that approach it more closely than do those of others.

Martin Southwold, "Buddhism and Evil," from David Parkin (ed.), *The Anthropology of Evil* (Oxford: Blackwell Publishers, 1985), pp. 128–41.

The term "Buddhism" itself suggests a more unitary phenomenon than actually exists. In this paper I consider only Buddhism of the Theravāda variety, and not Māhāyana. My first-hand evidence in fact is only of Sinhalese Buddhism, but I shall assume, as others have, that the Buddhisms of Burma and Thailand will differ only in minor ways (see particularly Spiro 1971: 16).

Within Theravāda Buddhism I distinguish two main interpretations, which do differ in some rather basic ways.[2] In what I have termed Meditation Buddhism, the goal is to attain Nirvana soon; this is to be done by withdrawing from the world and pursuing a life of austerity and intense meditation; it is assumed that this can hardly be done except by members of the Sangha, or clergy, and among these only by "forest monks" (see Carrithers 1983), living in monasteries or as hermits in the wilderness. In what I have termed Ministry Buddhism, Nirvana is an ultimate goal, not to be attained in ordinary time; the vocation of clergy is to serve the laity, especially by teaching, contributing thereby to their own spiritual progress as well as to that of those they serve.

It seems clear that Ministry Buddhism is now, and was in the past, the version preferred by most Buddhists, clergy as well as laity, and is thus the greater part of the ethnographic reality. This has too often been missed because most scholars have based their studies on the scriptures, in which Meditation Buddhism has a much larger place. The scholars also exaggerated the importance of the scriptures: partly because they had studied them; partly because they imagined that in them they found the words of the Buddha himself; partly because they overestimated the extent to which the scriptures are authoritative for Buddhists. In consequence, on matters where Meditation and Ministry Buddhism diverge, the accounts of scholars who have studied the scriptures differ from those of ethnographers who have studied people. On the present topic, this accounts for some differences of emphasis; more impressive, I think, is the fact that neither among the Meditation Buddhists of the scriptures nor among the Ministry Buddhists of real life is there to be found an entire concept of evil.

I have been helped by Kenneth Grayston's brief article on evil (1950) in Alan Richardson's *A Theological Word Book of the Bible*.[3] Strictly, Grayston discusses the meanings of the Hebrew and Greek words that are translated as "evil" in the Authorized Version of the Bible. The fact that they were so translated implies that "evil" had a similar range of meanings in the English of that period – and this can be readily confirmed from other sources.[4] Grayston distinguishes between the "descriptive" and the "moral" meaning of the terms. The latter is of course familiar – broadly, it refers to conduct that is morally wrong or bad. The former is less familiar, and is best explained in Grayston's own words:

> The Hebrew term *ra'* conveys the factual judgment that something is bad (e.g. figs, cattle), displeasing (e.g. a woman in the eyes of her husband), or harmful (e.g. wild beasts, poisonous herbs, disease). Quite generally it means anything that causes pain, unhappiness, or misery, including the discipline of punishment sent by God. (Grayston 1950: 73)

This descriptive meaning may have a moral connotation, i.e. the implication that the harm is due to someone's moral fault; or it may have no such connotation, in which case I would speak of the purely descriptive meaning. Grayston's account clearly implies that the purely descriptive meaning of *ra'* was the earliest, that at some period the word was normally used without any moral connotation (see Taylor 1985).

The descriptive meaning does survive in modern English: most familiarly as a noun, used to refer to such characteristic human afflictions as disease and death. It can still, just, be used adjectivally, as when an ugly face is termed an "evil countenance". But these are literary rather than colloquial usages, and

usually, I think, deliberately archaic.[5] In modern English the moral has become the primary, indeed unmarked,[6] meaning, and this makes it difficult to use the descriptive meaning without risk of misunderstanding. It is impossible now to use the purely descriptive meaning. Does one read "evil countenance" as merely "ugly" without understanding also "malevolent"? Could one read of an "evil wife" as merely unattractive to her husband, without supposing she is morally wicked?

There has been a shift in meaning of the word "evil" since Jacobean times; hence we tend to misinterpret passages in the Bible, or in Shakespeare, where it was used with the descriptive meaning. Anthropologists who write about the traditional religions of other peoples have a tendency to resort to biblical idiom, and this may produce misunderstanding. It is not always perfectly clear whether or not the word "evil" carries a moral connotation or meaning.

There is a further ambiguity, less widely recognized but more harmful than this: an ambiguity within the moral (or, as I would rather say, "ethical") meaning of "evil". When used with this meaning, "evil" is a term of ethical judgement or condemnation. It may be applied to an act of wrongdoing, to a course of such acts or a disposition or tendency thereto, or to the wrongdoer himself; especially as a noun, it tends to reify or personify a supposed principle or force of wrongness. There are differences of connotation between some of these applications. More basic, however, is a distinction between two major senses, which have notably different implications and consequences. I distinguish them as the "weak" and "strong" senses of the moral meaning.[7]

As an ethical term, "evil" sorts with a family of such terms, e.g. "immoral", morally "bad" or "wrong", "wicked", "sinful". In the weak sense, "evil" is no stronger in condemnation than these, is effectively synonymous and interchangeable with at least some of them. This sense is plain in the common expressions "good and evil", "good or evil", applied particularly to acts. Here the assumption is that, of acts to which moral judgement applies, and neglecting the band of the morally neutral, the universe divides between those that are good, to be approved, and those that are evil, to be disapproved. The term "evil" here has the same wide scope as "bad": whatever is not good (and not neutral).

In the strong sense, however, "evil" is far from synonymous with "bad", etc.: it expresses condemnation that is markedly more severe. If we order wrongdoings on a scale of gravity or heinousness, the range of application of "evil" tends toward the graver end. It is unacceptable to use it of a peccadillo, and uncomfortable to use it of a venial offence. At the other end of the scale, for a gross moral enormity "evil" is not only acceptable but almost required: perhaps only "wicked" will do as an alternative. If one were to describe and discuss what the Nazis did at Auschwitz and elsewhere in pursuit of their Final Solution, and conclude with the judgement that such conduct was "bad" or "wrong" or "immoral", one would outrage one's readers. Judgement in those terms would be perceived as quite inadequate, as close to condoning the conduct. Pocock's (1985: 42) observation that "evil" is cognate with "over" in the sense of "excessive" seems apt for this strong sense of the term. The bias towards the more severe end of the moral scale is still more marked when the reference is to the wrongdoer, not just wrongdoing: to term a person, or set of persons, "evil" is very severe – indeed, fighting talk.

There is plainly a notable difference between the weak and strong senses of "evil" as an ethical term. There is a simple test to distinguish between them: where we encounter the term "evil", can we, or can we not, substitute such other terms as "bad" or "immoral" without loss of meaning? In too many cases there is no certain answer; in others it becomes evident that an author slides, no doubt unawares, between one sense and the other. Sometimes he suggests, or leaves the reader to suppose, that the people he describes have a concept of evil in the strong sense, while the evidence presented warrants only the conclusion that they have a concept of evil in the weak sense.

We should understand other cultures, and indeed our own, better if we gave up using the misleading term "evil", or at least always qualified it. Instead of "evils" in the descriptive sense we might speak of "afflictions"; for "evil" in the weak ethical sense we should substitute the terms "immoral", morally "wrong" or "bad". I want to keep "evil" in the strong sense, the better to point to the problems that arise: I shall therefore specify this as "radical evil".

So far I have suggested that "radical evil" is like "bad" only more so – which does not make it obvious why it is important to distinguish. The important differences lie in the images and associations of the two concepts, and still more in the responses each tends to evoke. The notion of radical evil is notably associated with demonology, with the

imagery of hosts of malignant beings. But demonology need not entail this notion, which is more strictly associated with demonology of the Iranian (Zoroastrian) dualist kind. For obvious reasons, notions of hell may be, but need not be, indices of radical evil. More significant, I think, is the dogma that "there can be no compromise with evil". The other side of this is our feeling that to describe as "bad" what should properly be termed (radically) "evil" is to condone it. The radical evil is that which must not be condoned or admitted to compromise: and since we must oppose it, this is indeed fighting talk. My own very restricted explorations do indeed indicate a strong association of notions of radical evil with war. They seem to be favoured by the militarist and the bellicose, and the categorization of adversaries as evil is unmistakably a call to arms. This is probably the basis of their associations with demonology: evil demons or devils, in my view (and that of Buddhists[8]), are projections of the ill-will and pugnacity of those who suppose them.

The word "evil" is often used by anthropologists, as by others, with little or no attempt to distinguish its various senses. In consequence it is often impossible to be sure what concepts are being designated by it. Worse, it is all too easy to suppose that certain concepts (ours, usually) have been attributed to another people, when there is no sound evidence for it in the text. I am especially conscious of this because of the way that I, and some others, have misread Obeyesekere's (1968) paper. It is very easy to suppose that here we have an account of Sinhalese Buddhist concepts of evil broadly similar to our own. But it is not so. Obeyesekere does say something about Buddhist ideas of "evil", but this is always "evil" in the descriptive sense. He says more about ideas of moral wrongs among contemporary Sinhalese Buddhists, but he never uses the word "evil" in presenting them (mostly he terms these wrongs "sins").[9] There is no evidence here that Sinhalese verbally link afflictions and moral wrongs, as is done by our word "evil". Still less is there any evidence for a concept of "evil" in the strong ethical sense – indeed, I suspect that it is because there is no such concept that Obeyesekere avoided the word in describing moral views.

It would be consoling if Obeyesekere's paper were unusually obscure. On the contrary, it is remarkably clear once one thinks to look for the distinctions between various senses of "evil". My point is that we rarely do, and in consequence we fall all too readily into the trap of attributing our concept of evil to other cultures, without warrant.

What, then, are Sinhalese Buddhist notions about wrongdoing and about affliction, and do these form a complex sufficiently similar to our own to warrant our saying they have a concept of "evil"? I should say at once that I did not examine this question while I was doing fieldwork, and do not find much material in my notes or elsewhere that bears at all directly on it. I am moderately confident that what I say is sound, since there is much else that confirms it indirectly. But more research is needed.

Among the Sinhalese the word *naraka*, which means "bad" in a very wide sense, is applied to wrong acts and dispositions, and also sometimes to afflictions. But apart from this, it seems that one set of terms is used of wrong acts, etc., and another of afflictions and suffering. In my experience there is no word commonly used to link these two areas of reference as our word "evil" can. I do not think this is important, since the two are very strongly linked conceptually. According to the doctrine of *karma*, all one's afflictions are the consequences of one's own former misdeeds – which does not, in practice, exclude alternative etiologies. The commonest term for suffering and unhappiness is *duka*, or Pali *dukkha*, and in Buddhist analysis *dukkha* is caused entirely by one's own wrongness.

Affliction, physical "evil"[10] and wrongdoing, moral "evil", are then linked by the Sinhalese, and to that extent they have a concept like ours, if not a word of similar application. They are probably unremarkable in this, since it is likely that most peoples make some such link. Grayston writes, referring to the descriptive meaning of *ra'* among the early Hebrews, "the development of a moral connotation is very natural; a harmful action, as viewed by the injured party, is a wicked one" (1950: 74). Equally, in most ethical systems an act is identified as wrong because it is harmful, especially to others. It is likely, further, that the experience of punishment conditions people to think of affliction as a response to the victim's wrongdoing.

Examined more closely, the thinking of the Sinhalese may be significantly different from what I suggest is commonplace in human cultures. Grayston's remark assumes that the wrongdoer and the victim are different persons; and the harm that people anticipate from wrongdoing is mainly harm to others. But the theories of *karma* and *dukkha* that the Sinhalese use do not make that distinction: the stress is on the harm to oneself from one's own wrongdoing. For the same reason their theories are not, cognitively at least, extrapolations of the experi-

ence of punishment. Wrongdoing is not an offence against the command or authority or sacredness of some godlike being, for there is no such being. It is seen as a matter of natural law that suffering follows wrongdoing, much as smoke follows fire.

This is the basis of the fact that forbids us to attribute a concept of "evil" to Sinhalese Buddhists: the absence of any concept of radical evil. If one regularly blames others for one's misfortunes, it is easy (but not necessary) to come to see them as radically evil, meet to be destroyed. It is rather unlikely that one will see oneself in the same way – though some of the austerities of the more extreme Meditation Buddhists could be considered self-destructive.

It is, of course, always difficult to be certain of the absence of anything. I say that there is no concept of radical evil among Buddhists partly because all the words I have encountered, in fieldwork and in literature, that might be or might have been translated as "evil" quite clearly do not carry the strong sense, and partly because examination of the cultural contexts in which such a concept might more probably lurk fails to uncover it.

It is necessary to hold in mind the distinction between Meditation Buddhism and Ministry Buddhism, as I have termed them. I assume that this correlates strongly (but not perfectly) with the distinction between Buddhism as it appears to those who study scriptures, and Buddhism as it is found by those who study people. I further assume that, by his distinction between "monastic" and "lay" Buddhism, Ling had something similar in mind. I should further remark that, in studying the concepts of Buddhists, one ought to make the distinction they themselves make, between the Buddhist and the non-Buddhist parts of their culture; however, with regard to "evil" at least, the two are consistent.

In writings about Buddhism, the term "evil" is notably used in reference to the mythological figure of Māra. Māra is often called "the Evil One", and compared with Satan in the Christian tradition. If anywhere, it is here that we might expect to find a concept of radical evil among Buddhists.

Ling (1962: 43 and *passim*) remarks that the scriptures contain many references to Māra, who is thus an important figure within them. He is represented as the tempter, who tries to divert the Buddha and his followers from their quest. In particular, he sought to divert Gotama from attaining that Enlightenment by which he became a Buddha; then he sought to obstruct the teaching of that Enlightenment. He seeks every opportunity to destroy whatever insight has been gained by disciples of the Buddha, and especially opposes the practice of meditation (pp. 51–2). He is the upholder of false views arising from ignorance (or delusion) – *avijjā*; he seems like a symbolic image of ignorance (pp. 61–2).

What this evidence from the scriptures shows is that the figure of Māra was important for those Buddhists who produced the scriptures, whose views, I have suggested, were mainly those of Meditation Buddhism. He may be important today for those who take a similar view, and for those who read the scriptures much – which categories, in my experience, seem largely coincident. Ling also points out that Māra is unlikely to have been important in the popular instruction given to laymen. "Māra is almost entirely disregarded" in the non-canonical Jātaka stories, which laymen know much better than the canonical scriptures (Ling 1962: 73), while, according to the canonical scriptures, though ordinary villagers might be possessed by Māra, they would not perceive the fact (p. 75).

On the basis of my observation, I can say that the figure of Māra is more familiar to villagers than Ling's account suggests. He is mentioned in sermons, but is most familiar from imagery: notably in the statues and pictures in many temples which present Buddhist themes to the public in visual form. Pictures of him are also quite common on postcards, religious pictures and book illustrations. But it would be a gross error to infer from this that Māra the Evil One is a significant element in the religion of ordinary Buddhists. He is hardly ever spoken of, except by clergy in sermons and by people actually seeing his image in a temple. Nothing suggests to me that anyone imagines he might actually encounter Māra; on the contrary, Māra is simply a stock character in the scene of an event of long ago in the experience of that superhuman person, the Buddha. The scene is always the same: that in which Māra appeared with his three voluptuous daughters in a vain endeavour to tempt the Buddha-to-be from achieving enlightenment. I am rather sure that this scene is so often depicted because it gives the artists, and their clients, a religious pretext for relishing the depiction of voluptuous women. I would guess that, if any villager ever does imagine himself in such a scene, the emotion evoked is by no means fear. Māra, to be blunt, is a sort of pimp.

Ling's view of the matter (1962: 72–6), that Māra is a prominent symbol in monastic rather than in popular Buddhism, seems to be correct; though in my terms I would say that he sorts with Meditation rather than Ministry Buddhism. If, as we saw above, Māra is particularly opposed to meditation, this is understandable – I found that villagers were commonly indifferent to, if not disdainful of, meditation. Ling, apparently alluding to the scriptures, writes of "the frequently emphasized idea that only the Buddha sees Māra and recognizes him, and after him, those others who like the Buddha have become awakened, those who are devoted to the Dhamma and walk in the Buddha's holy path" (p. 75). The figure of the Evil One, it seems, occurs in the context of the quest for perfection.[11]

But is Māra properly termed "the Evil One"? Ling (1962) so frequently uses the expression that the identity is fixed in the reader's mind before there is any discussion of the indigenous term. On p. 47 he mentions, and on p. 56 begins briefly to discuss, the Pali term *pāpimā*, which has been translated as "evil". Though he asserts that it indicates "moral evil", his discussion strongly suggests that its sense is mainly descriptive, to designate "evil, an ill". Neither here nor elsewhere where the issue comes up is Ling clear. Similarly, though use of the word "evil" and the comparison with Satan would suggest to many readers that this is "evil" in the strong ethical sense, Ling fails to clarify the distinction, while presenting evidence that counts against this sense. As Ling points out, in all the scriptural passages, bar one, in which Māra confronts the Buddha, there is no real conflict. Simply "to recognise Māra is to deflate him", and the Buddha always immediately recognizes, deflates and then dismisses him (p. 50). Other Buddhists are counselled to do the same (pp. 63–5).

Boyd's discussion of the terminology is very much to be preferred. On the first page of that section of his book which deals with Māra he has a note:

> The rendering of the Pali and Buddhist Sanskrit term *pāpa* as "evil" is not done without hesitation, for though the English term "evil" is an accepted rendering . . . it runs the risk of retaining implicit Christian meanings which do not necessarily belong to the Buddhist understanding of *pāpa*. (Boyd 1975: 73 n. 1)

Boyd goes on to note that Rhys Davids related the term to Greek *pema*, which translates as "misery, calamity". Repeating this latter observation on p. 157, he continues: "The basic meaning of the term *pāpa*, therefore, most probably is: that which is essentially miserable, full of suffering, and inferior." He contrasts the meaning of *pāpa* with the connotations of the English term "evil", and suggests that the term "bad" may be a better rendering than "evil", as "The English word 'bad' in contemporary usage does not as readily carry the moralistic and strong malignant connotations as does the term 'evil'" (p. 158). Noting that there are contexts in which *pāpa* connotes moral wrong, as well as having (what I call) the descriptive sense, he writes, "Because the English term 'bad' embraces both connotative levels more readily than does the more forceful term 'evil', it appears to be a more appropriate general rendering of the Buddhist meaning of *pāpa*" (p. 159).

Finally, Boyd remarks another contrast between Christian and Buddhist concepts. For the Buddhist the source of *pāpa* as moral wrong is within the person, but for Christians the source of *ponēros* (evil) is external to man: "the early Christians understood the nature of *ponēros* to be ultimately an extrinsic power foreign and hostile to the rightful conditions of human existence." There is thus a "difference between the Christian affirmation and the Buddhist rejection of the externality of the source of 'evil' . . . " (Boyd 1975: 159–61).

In summary, then, Boyd considers that to render *pāpa* as "evil" is likely to be misleading, partly because the meaning is primarily descriptive rather than moral, partly because, to the extent that it is moral, it is without the strong sense; and he links this latter observation to the fact that the source of *pāpa* is within oneself, not external. This is so similar to my own analysis that I should point out that I had formulated mine before I read Boyd. On this point at least, analysis of modern ethnographic reality and analysis of the scriptures converge towards the same conclusion.

There is more evidence to be found in the Sinhalese notions concerning demons (*sing: yaksa*). For want of space I must refer the reader to Gombrich's account (1971: 160–3). In brief, there are at least three categories, of which only one might reasonably suggest a notion of radical evil: these are the named demons, such as Mahasōnā, which are "distinctly malevolent" and are, in the low country of Sri Lanka mainly, the objects of exorcism rites (p. 162).[12] The Sinhalese consider these to be no part of Buddhism, and in any case they are not radically evil: both because, as Kapferer (1983) makes clear, the rationale of the exorcisms rests on the assumption that the demons do not really have power to harm, and because, as Gombrich points out, *yaksas* and gods are not clearly distinguished (1971: 162). Sinhalese notions of *yaksas* are similar to those of *yakkhas,* as found in the Pali scriptures (pp. 160–2); but also, as Ling shows (1962: 44–6), the notions of Māra closely resemble these latter. Hence the lack of a concept of radical evil in both cases is unsurprising.

Again, if space permitted, Sinhalese notions of hell (or rather, hells – *apāya*) might be explored. My impression, among the villagers I knew, was that no one took these very seriously. People would sometimes say, of someone they considered unusually wicked, that he deserved or was likely to go to hell; it did not seem to me that anyone had ever supposed this might be his own fate. Carrithers points out that forest monks (in my terms, those most committed to Meditation Buddhism) often have an unusual fear of hell and fascination with hell-fire preaching (1983: 17–18, 78–9). This fits my suggestion that there is more that resembles our own notions of evil in Meditation than in Ministry Buddhism.

There is no concept of radical evil in Buddhism: does this matter? What does not exist is of no interest in itself, but only in a comparative context; and our discussion makes it uncertain what the comparative context is. People have talked and written confidently enough about notions of evil in Buddhism: more careful and critical scrutiny shows that the term is seriously misleading. The same may well be true of other cultures to which people have carelessly attributed concepts of evil. Is Buddhism unique, or unusual, in having no concept of evil in the full sense? Or is Buddhism normal in this regard, and our own culture of Christendom the odd stream out? One comparison at least I can make with some confidence, and it is that between Buddhendom and Christendom.

The widespread complacency of liberal intellectuals notwithstanding, the concept of radical evil is alive and festering among us – not least among the most educated and influential. The speech of President Reagan at Orlando, Florida, in which he described the Soviet Union as the "empire of evil" is a notorious instance. A more daunting example is in the first leader of *The Times* of 20 May 1982, pontificating on the imminent British invasion of the Falkland Islands; it is quoted, together with an analysis of its "tremulous repetition of 'evil'", in Barnett (1982: 98–100). A sadder instance occurs in *The Church and the Bomb* (Church of England 1982), the report of a working party of the Church of England. Much of the argument hinges on a crucial passage of ethical analysis on pp. 99–101: close attention will show that its plausibility rests on equivocation between the weak and strong senses of "evil".[13]

How could we account for the fact that some cultures (also some subcultures, some individuals) use the concept of evil in the strong sense, others only in the weak sense? I suggest that the practical difference between the two senses reflects less or more readiness to forgive. "There can be no compromise with [radical] evil"; to call the radical evil merely "bad" seems to condone it. What, then, might cause some to refuse to forgive what others would forgive? I have space to mention only a few factors in a very complex manifold. (1) To forgive is to re-admit the wrongdoer to community; to refuse is to exclude him. We might therefore expect indisposition to forgive, manifested in openness to a concept of radical evil, to be more marked among the more asocial. This clearly fits the difference between Ministry and Meditation Buddhists. (2) Forgiveness, I guess, is commonly in the spirit of "forgive that ye may be forgiven": hence those who are most aware of their own need for forgiveness, of their own proneness to sin, should be most forgiving. The stiff-necked and authoritarian would be unforgiving, and most ready to speak of radical evil. This fits many facts.

But, further (3) self-awareness of this kind might vary according to where the culture locates the source of wrongdoing. As Lienhardt pointed out in *Divinity and Experience* (1961), the Dinka tend to project on to supposed external occult agencies much that we attribute to the inward workings of mind (pp. 149–55). There is evidence that this is characteristic of "primitive" cultures;[14] whereas the tendency to reduce all occult agencies to inner psychic phenomena goes further among Buddhists than among ourselves. Buddhists are therefore taught to see the roots of wrongdoing within oneself. In other cultures these are blamed on external occult agencies, which can easily then be seen as alien in themselves, and as possessing the evildoers; which facilitates seeing the evildoer as an enemy to be destroyed.

This is why, as I have suggested, radical evil is associated with demonology, which itself is associated with theism. But the association is imperfect: the concept of radical evil seems to be more closely associated with monotheism.[15] Monotheism seems to me to be quite strongly associated, as both cause and effect, with intolerance. What is it that associates both of these with the Middle East, while both, with their bedfellow radical evil, are virtually absent from India?[16] Could it be that the much-maligned caste system, by producing a series of closed but interdependent communities, gives rise to polytheism and religious pluralism, hence the religious tolerance and the self-awareness that find no place for radical evil?

Notes

1 This fieldwork, lasting just over a year, was conducted in the Kurunegala District of Sri Lanka; I give more details in Southwold (1983).

2 I summarize here what I have set out at length in Southwold (1983: ch. 9).

3 The implication that I have not been helped by other books I have consulted is mostly true. I except works discussed in this paper; and also Doob (1978), an admirable discussion which is rich in empirical material.

4 E.g. Shakespeare's plays, of which some typical usages are summarized in Onions (1949: 73).

5 The *OED* also remarks that what little use the word has in colloquial English is due to literary influence (see Pocock 1985: 42). Is it possible that the concept of evil, especially radical evil (see below), has always flourished more in writing than in speech?

6 I.e. the meaning that is understood in the absence of any specification of the intended sense.

7 This is not the distinction that Macfarlane (1985) draws between a "strong" and a "weak" meaning; in his usage the latter is close to my "descriptive" meaning. Nor is it equivalent to the *OED*'s distinction between "positive" and "privative" senses.

8 Ortner (1978: 99); Southwold (1983: 52, 196).

9 There are four passages (pp. 23, 33, 34, n. 4) that seem to be exceptions; but in none of them does Obeyesekere unequivocally impute to living Sinhalese the use of a term translatable as "evil" in the ethical sense.

10 My distinction between the descriptive and ethical meanings is close to that in traditional moral theology between physical and moral evil; but as mine makes no space for metaphysical evil, the two schemas are not the same.

11 In the course of our discussions, Pocock suggested that the concept of (radical) evil seemed to be evoked by the desire for perfection.

12 On these rites, see especially Kapferer (1983).

13 I regret that I do not have the space to demonstrate this. Were space more ample, I should discuss at length the use of the term "evil" in this report.

Passages in which the term is frequent and the strong sense plain are markedly contrasted with those where the usage is infrequent and the sense "weak". They indicate very different theologies which are imperfectly harmonized in the report.

14　See, for example, Hallpike (1979: ch. 9). However bizarre in parts, Jaynes (1982) also contains much that points to the infrequency of notions of subjective consciousness like our own.

15　Professor Roy Wallis first pointed this out to me, in discussion, when I presented an earlier version of this paper in Belfast.

16　O'Flaherty notes that "Indologists have long maintained that there is no problem of evil in Indian thought", and quotes several writers (1976: 7, 4). She disagrees, choosing to translate the word *pāpa* (Boyd's discussion, of which I cited in the text) as "evil". There seems to be confusion here, O'Flaherty affirming the use of weak and descriptive senses, the Indologists denying the use of the strong sense. Ling refers to some of the same authors in support of his claim that India has a "mythology free from Iranian dualism" (1962: 25–6); evil in the strong sense seems to be closely linked with Iranian dualism.

References

Ahern, M. B. (1971). *The Problem of Evil*. London: Routledge and Kegan Paul.

Barnett, A. (1982). *Iron Britannia*. London: Allison and Busby.

Boyd, J. W. (1975). *Satan and Māra: Christian and Buddhist Symbols of Evil* (Studies in the History of Religions, xxvii). Leiden: E. J. Brill.

Carrithers, M. (1983). *The Forest Monks of Sri Lanka*. Delhi: Oxford University Press.

Church of England (Board for Social Responsibility) (1982). *The Church and the Bomb*. London: Hodder and Stoughton.

Doob, L. W. (1978). *Panorama of Evil: Insights from the Behavioral Sciences*. Westport and London: Greenwood Press.

Gombrich, R. F. (1971). *Precept and Practice: Traditional Buddhism in the Rural Highlands of Ceylon*. London: Oxford University Press.

Grayston, K. (1950). "Evil". In Alan Richardson (ed.), *A Theological Word Book of the Bible*. London: SCM Press.

Hallpike, C. R. (1979). *The Foundations of Primitive Thought*. Oxford: Oxford University Press.

Jaynes, J. (1982). *The Origin of Consciousness in the Breakdown of the Bicameral Mind* (first edition, 1976). Harmondsworth: Penguin.

Kapferer, B. (1983). *A Celebration of Demons*. Bloomington: Indiana University Press.

Lienhardt, G. (1961). *Divinity and Experience: The Religion of the Dinka*. London: Oxford University Press.

Ling, T. O. (1962). *Buddhism and the Mythology of Evil*. London: Allen and Unwin.

Macfarlane, A. (1985). "The Root of all Evil". In David Parkin (ed.), *The Anthropology of Evil*. Oxford: Blackwell Publishers.

Obeyesekere, G. (1968). "Theodicy, Sin and Salvation in a Sociology of Buddhism". In E. R. Leach (ed.), *Dialectic in Practical Religion* (Cambridge Papers in Social Anthropology, 5). Cambridge: Cambridge University Press.

O'Flaherty, W. D. (1976). *The Origins of Evil in Hindu Mythology*. Berkeley: University of California Press.

Onions, C. T. (1949). *A Shakespeare Glossary* (first edition, 1911). Oxford: Clarendon Press.

Ortner, S. B. (1978). *Sherpas Through their Rituals* (Cambridge Studies in Cultural Systems, 2). Cambridge: Cambridge University Press.

Plantinga, A. (1974). *God, Freedom and Evil*. London: Allen and Unwin.

Pocock, D. (1985). "Unruly Evil". In David Parkin (ed.), *The Anthropology of Evil*. Oxford: Blackwell Publishers.

Southwold, M. (1983). *Buddhism in Life*. Manchester: Manchester University Press.

Spiro, M. E. (1971). *Buddhism and Society: A Great Tradition and its Burmese Vicissitudes*. London: Allen and Unwin.

Taylor, D. (1985). "Theological Thoughts About Evil". In David Parkin (ed.), *The Anthropology of Evil*. Oxford: Blackwell Publishers.

36

Evil and Ethical Terror

Nel Noddings

People have always been fascinated by evil – by that which harms us or threatens to harm us. Primitive people sought to escape evil by magic, ritual, and appeasement. Philosophers have attempted to redeem evil by elaborate analyses designed to show that evil is somehow necessary, and theologians have produced a body of work on the "problem of evil." Women have until recently been relatively silent on evil, in part because they have been silent on most matters, but largely because they have themselves been closely identified with evil in the traditional view. Women who have attempted to speak on moral matters have often been effectively silenced by the accusation that speaking and thinking on such things automatically separates them from the feminine principle and thus from their only claim to goodness.

Today, of course, women have awakened to the injustice of this treatment, and feminist theologians are urging us to look with a new focus on what Mary Daly calls the "images and conceptualizations" of evil. Rosemary Radford Ruether says: "Feminism represents a fundamental shift in the valuations of good and evil. It makes a fundamental judgment upon some aspects of past descriptions of the nature and etiology of evil as themselves ratifications of evil."[1]

Nel Noddings, "Evil and Ethical Terror," from *Women and Evil* (Berkeley: University of California Press, 1989), pp. 5–34. Copyright © 1989 The Regents of the University of California, The University of California Press, Berkeley.

Further, the new look at evil will be phenomenological; it must look at evil from the viewpoint of experience. Ruether comments, however, "The uniqueness of feminist theology lies not in its use of the criterion of experience but rather in its use of *women's* experience, which has been almost entirely shut out of theological reflection in the past."[2] This is the task I will undertake [here], but before starting it, I must clarify the view that feminists are rejecting.

There has always been general agreement that evil involves pain, suffering, terror, and destruction. Feminists do not disagree on this appraisal. It has also been customary to separate natural evil from moral evil. Suffering that occurs without the deliberate or negligent agency of human beings is construed as natural evil; violent storms, drought, disease, earthquakes, and natural death are all examples of natural evil and part of the world we inhabit. Difficulties arise with attempts to justify natural evil. If, for example, we can find a justification for God's allowing us to suffer (or even for his inflicting pain on us), moral evil cannot be entirely identified with our infliction of pain on one another, for we too might be justified. If the God so justified is all good and all powerful, then clearly we are at his mercy, and we need to pay more attention to him than to one another. If he demands our obedience and we fail to give it, we have fallen into evil from which we cannot rescue ourselves. Moral evil, in this view, becomes sin.

The problem (or miscasting of it) begins with the attempt to rescue God from collaboration in evil. When men posited a God supposed to be all-powerful, all-knowing, and all-good, the "problem of evil" emerged. How can there be evil in a world created by such a God? "The problem of evil," says John Hick, "concerns the contradiction, or apparent contradiction, between the reality of evil on the one hand, and religious beliefs in the goodness and power of God or of the Ultimate on the other."[3] This concern gives rise to *theodicy*, the philosophical attempt to reconcile the goodness of God with the existence of evil. Theodicy is not the only philosophical approach to evil, of course, but it has been the most influential one, and it is associated with the problem of evil by definition.

We might try to redeem evil by arguing philosophically for its necessity without reference to God. At least one of these views will prove interesting, and it will be necessary to examine it from a feminist perspective. I will look closely at Nietzsche's notion that evil is necessary for good, that pain is necessary for pleasure, and suffering for joy. But the view I ultimately embrace will be closer to Sartre's in spirit. Speaking of evil and the need for people to retain a sense of evil as *evil*, he says:

We have been taught to take it seriously. It is neither our fault nor our merit if we lived in a time when torture was a daily fact. Châteaubriand, Oradour, the Rue des Saussaies, Tulle, Dachau, and Auschwitz have all demonstrated to us that Evil is not an appearance, that knowing its cause does not dispel it, that it is not opposed to Good as a confused idea is to a clear one, that (it) is not the effects of passions which might be cured, of a feat that might be overcome, of a passing aberration which might be excused, of an ignorance which might be enlightened, that it can in no way be diverted, brought back, reduced, and incorporated into idealistic humanism, like that shade of which Leibnitz has written that it is necessary for the glare of daylight.[4]

In this passage Sartre mentions all the prominent philosophical ploys to redeem evil; I will not discuss them individually except as they arise in connection with the standard treatment of evil or in the phenomenology of evil that I discuss later. He goes on to give experiential justification for dismissing all these arguments as failures:

Perhaps a day will come when a happy age, looking back at the past, will see in this suffer-

ing and shame one of the paths which led to peace. But we were not on the side of history already made. We were, as I have said, *situated* in such a way that every lived minute seemed to us like something irreducible. Therefore, in spite of ourselves, we came to the conclusion, which will seem shocking to lofty souls: Evil cannot be redeemed.[5]

Sartre's position, although admirable in its courageous rejection of the idea that evil can be redeemed, does not shed much light on the ways philosophical and theological views have actually contributed to evil. As we examine how scholars and ordinary people have dealt with evil, we will see that they have made significant choices. Plato's description of evil, for example, arises from a god's-eye view. From this perspective a thoroughly good person (one who understands what goodness really is) is safe from evil; what happens to the body is unimportant so long as the soul is incorrupt. Not only is this an other-worldly view that denigrates the body and the things of this world – thus denying the possibility of an ethic that grows out of, say, motherly love – but it also suggests that goodness and the happiness associated with it are within the control of the human agents who pursue them wisely. Aristotle's view is far more realistic and attractive to most of us. Here we find acceptance of our human interdependence, acknowledgment that goodness and happiness depend to some degree on luck and felicitous associations, and acceptance of tragedy in the lives of people of good character.[6] From the perspective of women, Aristotle's ethic is a vast improvement over Plato's detached and perfect soul.

A new difficulty arises, however, when Aristotle makes emotion depend on belief. To suggest, for example, that pity depends on our belief that the one suffering does not deserve to suffer opens the door to ethical cruelty; as we will see, Christian theodicy has used the notion to justify natural evil. Further, acceptance of a tragic view can lead in at least two directions. It can lead – but has not yet done so – to a rejection of divinities and great principles that ask us to accept and even to inflict suffering, or it can lead to a glorification of the tragic condition. That is, the insights of tragedy can be used to heighten our admiration for tragic heroes and distract us from the task of building a world in which a bit less will depend on luck. The main job of this chapter is to examine the possible choices we have in facing up to evil.

Early Views of Evil and the Possibility of an Evil God

The earliest views of evil are accessible to us only through the interpretation of artifacts and myths. Although it is not my purpose to provide a history of evil and our conceptions of it, we must explore the possibilities open to us. Which have led us astray and increased our pain? Which invite closer inspection? Because we depend on myth in this part of the investigation, it seems reasonable to begin with a discussion of myths and their role in increasing human understanding.

Paul Ricoeur tells us that the power of myths grows through a process of "demythologization"; that is, when a myth loses its early explanatory power, it takes on a new symbolic power. Deprived of its initial literal meaning, it opens up to manifold interpretations and thus contributes to knowledge of ourselves, the mythmakers. To label something a myth, then, does not destroy it – "only a myth" is an odd and contradictory juxtaposition of words – but rather enriches it by conferring on it the power of symbolism. In Ricoeur's terms, a myth grows more powerful as it loses its false logos.[7]

The earliest notions of evil described in myths were bound up with natural evil. Marie-Louise von Franz, a Jungian, comments: "The evil forces of nature . . . belong to the archetypal experience of evil: hunger, cold, fire, landslides and avalanches, snowstorms, drowning, storms at sea, being lost in the forest, the big enemy animals, the ice bear in the North, the lion or crocodile in Africa, etc."[8]

Jung and his followers construe the great natural evils as both concrete entities and archetypes – psychic realities that may present themselves symbolically and hence with a variety of meanings. The *sea*, for example, is a concrete cosmic entity; as archetype it represents not only a cosmic reality, but also a psychic reality with respect to which we are all somehow situated. Poetically it often stands as a sign of the feminine. Further, it can present itself in a variety of manifestations: in dreams of sailing, diving, drowning, walking on the shore, fishing, floating, being threatened by waves. Jungian analysis considers both archetypal and personal factors in interpretation. The presentation means something in itself (archetypally), but it also has special meaning arising from the particular personal unconscious. Similarly, a large enemy animal is a concrete reality and so a potential natural evil, but it may also be a monster in the psyche and poetically a metaphor for evil.

Views of evil almost always connect to the spiritual and often to the explicitly religious. A manifestation of evil strikes us with terror and a frantic desire to escape. In childhood it causes us to seek the security of a parent's loving arms; in its most elemental forms it continues to induce a similar urge. When the concrete parent is not present to protect us, we reach toward a spiritual parent or deity, and if this entity fails to aid us we often suppose that someone (we ourselves or some other) has done something to incur its righteous wrath. To avoid evil outcomes, then, we must avoid defilement – the contamination that is evil and leads to evil.

Here we see the beginnings of a great mistake that has followed us into the present century. Scholars have concentrated on the terror induced by disobeying a father, god, or authority and thereby incurring its wrath. They have paid relatively little attention to the desire for goodness that is aroused by loving relations with the mother. Freud, for example, almost ignores the pre-Oedipal child and locates the birth of the superego in the absolute terror of the Oedipal conflict.[9] This way of looking at things turns the protector into a source of new terror and constructs ethics on a foundation of fear.

Ricoeur describes a progression in the symbolism of evil from defilement to sin to guilt.[10] The symbolism of defilement springs from a primitive religious attitude, but the rituals connected to its removal are still embedded in contemporary religious practice. Even if Ricoeur is right in claiming that we can no longer coordinate ritual action with "any type of action for which we can construct a theory today," elaborate theorylike rationales are still created, promulgated, and believed. "What resists reflection," Ricoeur says, "is the idea of a quasi-material something that infects as a sort of filth, that harms by invisible properties, and that nevertheless works in the manner of a force in the field of our undividedly psychic and corporeal existence."[11] When he says that "we" can no longer understand such an orientation, he means, of course, that philosophy cannot make sense of such a position, not that there are no living persons who believe in forces of defilement. Later in this chapter we will see that belief in such forces is still active and is perhaps even growing. The history of the human psyche teems with devils, demons, and witches, and women have long been associated with evil in the form of defilement.

Women's bodies have been suspected of harboring evil, and menstrual taboos were established in congruence with this belief. The primitive notion that menstrual blood is a form of defilement has survived in contemporary Roman and Anglican church rituals that require the purification of women after childbirth.[12] Primitives considered not only menstrual blood but the menstruating woman herself to be a source of defilement. M. Esther Harding, a Jungian, comments:

> For it is believed that if a man "looks upon a menstruating woman his bones will soften, he will lose his manhood," will even die, while his weapons and implements will become useless, his nets will no longer catch fish, and his arrows will not kill deer. And, in addition, the power of the "war-bundle," which represents a warrior's commitment to the warlike undertaking and at the same time is a charm or amulet for its success, will be destroyed by such a contact, so fatal was the power of instinctive desire aroused by the woman's condition believed to be.[13]

Terror seems to be the basic affect of defilement. Ricoeur refers to "ethical terror," a fear of transgressing and thus calling forth harm, but surely pure uncritical terror historically and genetically precedes ethical terror. It will be necessary to explore the experiential roots of the turn from pure terror or dread to ethical terror. As I have noted, our childhood terrors are not first of this sort, and a loving parental embrace can banish them. Similarly, young children may comfort dolls or pets thought to be suffering terror. The young child in such situations may be showing the earliest signs of ethical concern – that is, concern to relieve the pain of an other. In our fear of defilement, however, we have passed from pure terror to an early stage of ethical terror. The turn to ethical terror rather than, say, ethical concern already posits a threatening parent or deity who may impose suffering for a mistake, transgression, or even a bit of misfortune. In contrast, ethical concern would be a move toward protecting loved others – a recognition that natural evil threatens all of us and that we should therefore band together lovingly to offer aid and comfort. A feminine phenomenology of evil will have to return to pure terror and see what next suggests itself to consciousness.

The move to ethical terror almost certainly represents an attempt to gain control through ritual

and taboo, but taboo may also signify a dangerous decision to locate evil in the other – to project the perceived evil of instinctive desire onto the object of desire, for example, onto menstruating women. Because the desire was apparently overwhelming, the remedies had to be powerful. Not only must women be periodically isolated and purified, but men must adhere to a strong code of honor. Men must not allow themselves to be diverted from their perceived duties by the allure of females. Over time this insistence on maintaining control over instinctive desire led to the justification of deeds construed as honorable by men and evil by women, although most explications of evil have been masculine. Jungians go so far as to say that men and women are mirror opposites in their spiritual assessments. Harding, for example, declares, "That which to man is spiritual, good, to be sought after, is to woman daemonic, powerful, and destructive, and vice versa."[14]

But Harding fails to resolve the apparent contradiction, and she does not explore the full moral potential in the feminine view. She seems to accept the male code of honor and blames the woman who distracts her man from it: "The typical story is that he must join his regiment. When he goes to say goodby to her she coaxes him to remain or is so alluring that he forgets his obligation, and the army entrains without him."[15]

When we look at evil from the standpoint of women's experience, we will question the whole tradition of honor that has grown up around war and violence. This will not be simple work, for it is not merely a matter of rejecting war and supposing that men enjoy killing one another; we cannot easily brush aside considerations of principles and fidelity to companions. Yet this way of thinking started somewhere in a way of life and mode of experience alien to women, and women have, in spite of their insights and sound intuitions, inexplicably agreed that they are somehow deeply wrong to tempt men toward what might be argued as *good*. Harding continues by evaluating the story of the regiment: "All true women blame the woman who acts in this way, rather than the man. They know that such an action takes an unfair advantage of the man's vulnerability."[16]

Jungians thus acknowledge a tremendous feminine power that is neither reasoned nor moral, but instinctive, unconscious, mysterious. Men striving for rationality would have to fear such a power and set up a countervailing force that could, by creating even greater terror, offset it. Hidden entirely in this account is the great protective love of the mother for her infant and the first stirrings of other-feeling in the young child who wants to please this loving parent and *give* love in return.[17]

Ethical terror, the fear of transgressing against gods, may have been in part a move to rescue men from both the moral and the biological power of women. If the deity so conceived was in their own image and all-good, so much the better, for it would become easier to draw the lines between good and evil. But primitive people did not draw that line so cleanly. Their gods were neither all-powerful nor all-good. Primitive gods were responsible for both creation and destruction, and primitive people made no attempt to justify destruction as ultimately good. Rather, they instituted elaborate rituals to turn away or mollify the destructive rage of the gods. The earliest gods seem to have been as capricious and whimsical as the forces of nature must have seemed to our predecessors.

Not only were good and evil mixed in individual deities, but, as differentiation occurred, good and evil deities competed for power. Hence even if the move to ethical terror were accepted as necessary, there are still alternatives fanning out from this unfortunate decision point. Why select and argue for an all-powerful god? Why posit one who is all-good? Ricoeur points out that the possibility of an evil god leads to a tragic sense of life; as we shall see next, there is something deeply rational and attractive in that view. Primitive views of evil often located good and evil in the same divinity, and the Greeks brought this view to its greatest sophistication in their tragedies. Ricoeur notes that the theme of divine wickedness is "expressed with surprising force and constancy" in Homer's *Iliad*; again and again the gods take possession of men and their acts. "This darkening, this leading astray, this seizure," says Ricoeur, "is not punishment for some fault; it is the fault itself, the origin of the fault."[18] He remarks, however, that although the theme is replayed in spectacle (drama), it resists expression in speculation (theory). We cannot, he says, conceptualize an evil god. Although Ricoeur's claim is questionable, most of us find the worship of an evil god (Satanism, for example) pathological. The great strength in a position that postulates an evil god in addition to a good one is that we need not try to justify evil as the work of the good god we worship. But, of course, we must give up the insistence on that god's omnipotence.

Resistance to the concept of an evil god can take several forms. The most dangerous may be exactly the one taken by the mainstream theologies that ordinary persons believe and use to guide their lives. They insist that the words and acts recorded of a god, say, Yahweh, would indeed be evil if spoken or performed by men, but that coming from the god they must somehow be justified. It is hard to deny the wickedness of Yahweh as he is portrayed in the Old Testament. In story after story Yahweh reveals himself as jealous, vengeful, and small-minded. The book of Numbers catalogs the destruction that Yahweh did directly and that the Israelites accomplished at his direction. In surveying that chapter Martin Gardner remarks, "Numbers 31 is not only the most infamous chapter of the Bible; it is hard to find its equal in any other sacred book." The biblical account of the destruction Yahweh ordered is consistent with an evil god: his killings of Nadab and Abihu for a mistake in the mixing of incense, the stoning of a young man for blasphemy, the swallowing up of rebels against Moses and Aaron, the plague that murdered 14,700 people because some complained about their god's cruelty, the fiery serpents sent to bite and kill when people objected to the taste of manna.[19]

From a feminist perspective, the killing of women and children is especially interesting, if deplorable. The Midianite women were almost certainly seen as a threat to the sovereignty of Yahweh, and the great campaigns of Joshua and Moses can be interpreted as violent moves to gain political and religious domination over an area in which the goddess was still worshiped. Merlin Stone, in her description of the cruelty of this campaign, comments on the irony of traditional interpretations: "At the risk of being repetitive, I cannot help thinking of Professor Albright's comment that the 'orgiastic nature worship' of Canaan 'was replaced by Israel with its pastoral simplicity and purity of life, its lofty monotheism and its severe code of ethics.' "[20]

Stone may or may not be right to interpret the slaughter of nonvirgin Midianite females as an attempt to stamp out female religion. Slaughters took place in those days – as in these – for a variety of reasons. In a feminine phenomenology of evil we will identify violence directly with evil through pain and terror, and we might well wonder why pain and violence came unstuck, as it were, from evil. We know in a sketchy way *how* it happened – through the move to ethical terror – but we still need to speculate on *why* it happened. From the perspective of persons whose experience centers on bearing and raising children, maintaining a secure and restful home, preparing food, making clothing, and nursing the ill, the separation of violence from evil seems inexplicable. One way of proceeding is, of course, the way suggested in the lines from Professor Albright: one simply brushes aside the actual violence, terror, and evil and concentrates on the progress of abstract thought. This way seems merely irrational – and perhaps blindly optimistic – but the way actually chosen, to justify violence and terror in the name of ultimate good, is far more frightening.

Even though we are clearly on the road to theodicy in our historical account, I must note that opportunities arise again and again for the notion of an evil or partly evil god to intrude itself. Indeed, a correlation between killing and godlike power has long held. As Marie-Louise von Franz notes, "The primitive idea that somebody who commits a murder or an outstanding crime is really not himself but performs something which only a God could do, expresses the situation very well."[21]

There is always the temptation, then, to equate the exercise of power with gods and with godlike behavior. Yet there remains a reluctance bordering on paranoic aversion to the association of the true God with evil. Indeed, historical accounts may be unable to catch the turning point, because they seem to involve notions of confession and repentance as far back as written records can take us. Confession and repentance, with which Ricoeur starts his discussion of evil, already contain the seeds of contradiction. Repentance makes it easy to recognize our own evil but to see it as temporary, inevitable, and redeemable; at the same time it tempts us to project true (unrepentant) evil outward onto others. Thus in our own time an American president called Russia "the Evil Empire," and many label the killing of children "terrorism" when done by other groups and "self-defense" when done by their own. Clearly the quest to establish a god who does all sorts of terrible things in the name of righteousness has a political as well as a spiritual basis. Von Franz notes that Christianity complicates the search for personal honesty in locating evil in ourselves, because at bottom only the unredeemed are permanently evil and therefore condemned. Further, we cannot find goodness by ourselves in Christianity but must be saved. Hence the things we do to one another are not nearly as important in our spiritual lives as our attitude and relation to God. Some argue, of course, that a right relation to God will inevitably bring forth a right relation to people, but this claim is one for which we cannot produce much empirical evidence.

Echoes of an evil god come down to us from the Greeks. Poets working in the Greek spirit have been bold enough to recognize the evil god:

Who shapes the soul, and makes her a barren wife
To the earthly body and grievous growth of clay;
Who turns the large limbs to a little flame,
And binds the great sea with a little sand;
Who makes desire, and slays desire with shame;
Who shakes the heaven as ashes in his hand;
Who, seeing the light and shadow for the same,
Bids day waste night as fire devours a brand,
Smites without sword, and scourges without rod—
The supreme evil, God.

In affirmation of this bold realization, Swinburne has the chorus continue:

That these things are not otherwise, but thus;
That each man in his heart sigheth, and saith,
That all men even as I,
All we are against thee, against thee,
O God most high.[22]

Swinburne's chorus sings a classic refrain on the evil god. No sooner are the recognition and bold renunciation announced than a retraction issues forth. It is agreed that silence is good, that reverence and fear make men whole, and that "silence is most noble till the end."[23] The injunction to be silent echoes in von Franz's comments on a story we will discuss later, that of Wassilissa and Baba-Yaga.[24] Human beings have always felt that it is unwise to point the finger at evil, especially at omnipotent evil, and so the fear of omnipotence has subdued the courage to construct a genuine ethicality. In the story of Job we also see fear overcome Job's sense of his own faultlessness. According to the story Job *is* faultless by his own assessment and even by God's, and so he appears to have a right to question God's goodness. But then he comes up flat against God's omnipotence. "Shall he that contendeth with the Almighty instruct *him*? he that reproveth God, let him answer it. Then Job answered the Lord, and said, Behold, I am vile; what shall I answer thee? I will lay mine hand upon my mouth" (Job 40: 2–4).

This is exactly Wassilissa's response to Baba-Yaga; it is best to be silent about evil in the presence of the evil one, particularly if there is a good side to which one might appeal. "This motif," says von Franz, "is widespread in folklore stories." It reveals the essence of the mixed god. "We can conclude from this story that the Baba-Yaga is not totally evil; she is ambiguous, she is light and dark, good and evil, though here the evil aspect is stressed."[25]

People have long recognized the possibility of divinities split between good and evil. Indeed, the recognition holds within itself the potential for coming to grips with the shadow side of ourselves. If the gods are part good and part evil but value their good side more, would it not be possible for us too to promote our good side while remaining warily alert for the appearance of our own evil? This is what Jung urges in his discussion of good and evil in the emerging biblical God. According to Jung, Job taught God an ethical lesson, and God responded by becoming man to redeem humankind from the evil into which he had led us.[26] Such thinking is, of course, anathema to many religious thinkers, and to others it leads merely to logical and epistemological problems. Gardner mentions his teacher, Charles Hartshorne, who held this sort of position on God. God was for Hartshorne "finite," located in time, struggling and learning much as we are.[27] Gardner objects to Hartshorne's arguments because they depend so heavily on the concept of time. For Gardner, time is a bigger mystery than God, and he prefers one great postulate to several. Hence Gardner, like so many other intelligent beings, turns – albeit reluctantly – down the road toward theodicy.

As we begin the examination of theodicy – which of necessity will be brief – it is important to keep in mind where we are headed. Three questions guide us: Is a religious view necessary to define and minimize evil? What harm have the dominant views on evil done to us? What are the alternatives? We will return again to the notion of an evil god as we examine views on the devil, on instinctive violence, and on destroying evil. More important, we will return to the notion of a god struggling toward goodness as we consider the possibility of spirituality in a feminist view of evil. In that discussion we will find that a notion of human love and compassionate living can guide the search for a god we can live with.[28]

Theodicy and Human Suffering

If we believe that God is all-good and all-powerful, and if at the same time we see that there really is evil in the world, we find it difficult to understand God as both giver of ethics and creator. "The clearer God becomes as legislator," Ricoeur says, "the more obscure he becomes as creator," and vice versa. We are inclined to blame God for a lack of ethicality. As we have seen, however, the blame is usually resisted. The idea of God as evil is close to unthinkable and, once thought, is hard to sustain. Only a minor god can be evil – surely not the one we worship. People long after a good god as children long after a good parent. As Ricoeur points out, "There begins the foolish business of trying to justify God: theodicy is born."[29]

The Augustinian tradition provided the main line of thinking on theodicy, but the Greek Epicureans had already posed the problem as a trilemma in response to Stoic attempts at theodicy: if God could have prevented evil and did not, he is malevolent; if God would have prevented evil but could not, he is impotent; if God could not and would not, why call him God?[30] The answer might be political. An all-good, all-powerful authority was thought to have considerably more clout than a loving, fallible parent-figure. Augustine followed the path of the Stoics. Since it is not my purpose to write an entire volume on theodicy, I will look at the central questions Saint Augustine and his followers raised and answered, and I will note missed alternatives as we move along. In the "lofty monotheism" of Augustine we have to deal with a deity who is all-knowing, all-powerful, and all-good. Further, all being emanating from his creative hand is also held to be good. Creation is itself, then, good.

How could evil enter into the all-good creation of an all-powerful God? Augustinians answer this question in two main ways, both of which lay the blame on human beings. First, human beings, as God's creation, must be perfect. But because we are endowed with free will, we may turn from the greatest good, God, toward a lesser good. This turning – perhaps inevitable for a creature born free and curious – is itself evil. It is not that we turn *toward* evil, for in Augustinian terms there is no evil-as-entity toward which to turn. The turning itself is the source of evil.

The Augustinian notion of hierarchically arranged goods begins the attempt to save God from complicity in evil by putting God at the top – the supreme good. (Recall Swinburne's chorus singing the alternative – God as supreme evil.) The angels risk evil when they look toward lower creations such as man, and man runs a similar risk when he looks with undue interest below him. Man runs a special risk when he looks toward the creature next below him in the hierarchy, woman. Thus in Augustine we find a reintroduction and interpretation of Plato's divided line: Man and things of the spirit are above the line – lower than God but on the "right" side of the line. Woman and material things are on the "wrong," or corporeal, side and hence represent a dreadful temptation that man must fear and avoid.

The attempt to rescue God from accusations of creating evil locates evil instead in the willful turning of men and angels from God to lower entities, even though these entities are themselves good – as is everything God created. But this account does not explain why God should allow creatures with this weakness for turning to exist. Here Augustine introduces an aesthetic argument, relying heavily on the principle of plenitude rooted in the work of Plotinus. John Hick explains:

> Plotinus saw the ultimate reality as so superabundantly full that it "gives off" being as the sun radiates light. The divine plenitude overflows, pouring itself outwards and downwards in a teeming cascade of ever-new forms of life until all the possibilities of existence have been actualized and the shores are reached of the unlimited ocean of nonbeing.[31]

God did not create the various forms as equal because there would then have been no reason to create such a multitude; indeed, there would have been a deprivation of being and, synonymously, of good. The resulting hierarchy of being actualizes the possibilities and maximizes *being*. Even the great philosopher Leibniz followed this line of thinking. He did not accept the Greek notion of *emanation* by which entities are created unconsciously – "as the sun radiates light" – but rather held that God in his omniscience considered all the logical possibilities for world building and from the vast array chose to actualize this best of all possible worlds.[32] Some theologians object to Leibniz's account on the grounds that it describes God as constrained by logic rather than as its master and thus threatens

his omnipotence. Such an objection illustrates the tangle of knots created by the insistence that God must be all-knowing, all-powerful, and all-good.

Having attributed to plenitude the creation of entities likely to fall or turn, both Augustine and Leibniz insist that human sin was not *caused*. God foresaw the fall but did not ordain it; things could have been otherwise. For both thinkers evil in the world results from contingent acts of human beings. The aesthetic argument continues by describing God's role in the suffering we associate with evil. Here Augustine introduces the principle of harmony. First, he denies that suffering from natural evil is evil at all. Only because we cannot see the larger picture as God sees it do we call such suffering "evil." In the long run – God's run – all things work together for good. Second, suffering is required to balance moral evil. Since God has allowed human choice and that choice has produced moral evil, God must exact retribution to maintain harmony or balance. For Augustine hell is a necessary part of a perfect universe, even if the vast majority of humankind has to be consigned to it to keep the balance. Leibniz too accepts the wisdom of God's decision to allow most human souls to suffer eternal damnation.[33]

John Hick observes that the notion of God's bringing good out of evil, that he "indeed brings an eternal and therefore infinite good out of a temporal and therefore finite evil, is a thought of great promise for Christian theodicy."[34] Hick assesses the Augustinian project as fatally flawed, however, because *eternal* damnation contradicts an eventual and infinite good. But if we hold that those so damned are of little or no consequence and that they have earned their own condemnation, their eternal suffering can be part of the picture of eternal happiness for those who have done right or who have been chosen. (We need not feel pity, as Aristotle said, for those who deserve to suffer.) Indeed, for Augustine the contrast between the comfort of the saved and the misery of sinners might augment the happiness of some souls in heaven. Hick is less cruel – and perhaps less astute on human nature – than Augustine.

When we look at evil from the perspective of women's experience – through the eyes of people who bear and raise children, try to maintain a comfortable and stable home, feed and nurture the hungry and developing – we find much more wrong with the Augustinian theodicy. First, it requires something like the Adamic myth, some account of the first sin, to hold it up. When the Adamic myth combines with Augustine's pronouncements on original sin, the burden on women becomes enormous, as we will see. But not only women have suffered. Ricoeur says: "The harm that has been done to souls, during the centuries of Christianity, first by literal interpretation of the story of Adam, and then by confusion of this myth, treated as history, with later speculations, principally Augustinian, about original sin, will never be adequately told."[35]

Second, it is not just eternal damnation that raises questions about the goodness of the God who decrees it. The problem of suffering is by no means adequately treated, and I will turn to that discussion shortly. Third, the explanation of suffering as retribution for sin sets the investigation of evil on the wrong track. This is a large part of the perversion Mary Daly, Rosemary Ruether, and other feminists condemn. The raw terror of natural evil is turned prematurely and arbitrarily into *ethical* terror, the fear of incurring the father-God's wrath. Our thinking, then, is distracted from the loving parent's attitude that would relieve and eliminate suffering to a long and perhaps hopeless quest to be justified in God's sight. In accepting this quest, we too often do harm to one another. It is odd that Freud, who looked on religion as something that should be outgrown, should suggest a mechanism – the Oedipal conflict – that leaves the basic evils of terror and righteous punishment intact.

Fourth, the image of God created in this long chain of arguments in theodicy has greatly favored his omnipotence and omniscience. Hence the religious tradition has blinded us ethically. Since God, who clearly has the knowledge and power to do otherwise, inflicts or allows the greatest of suffering, the infliction of pain cannot be a *primary* ethical abuse. Since God hides himself from us, the neglect of a loving personal relation cannot be a primary evil, and the responsibility for remaining in contact falls to the weak and dependent. Since God presents the world to us in impenetrable mystery, there is precedent for mystification, and the dependent and powerless must learn to trust authority. These will be the great themes of evil from the perspective of women's experience.

There are clearly many alternatives to the Augustinian God. Indeed, many theologians consider the Augustinian program to be intellectually weak and, in contemporary thought, almost a caricature of the Christian position. But this assessment, which sophisticated thinkers make so easily, is misleading. Not only do many laypersons still accept the elements of this tradition (a recent poll revealed that 53 percent of Americans still believe in hell, for example),[36] but the notion that the tradition is no longer worthy of our intellectual attention forecloses the possibility of a full discussion of the political programs that accompanied Augustinian theology. Mary Midgley is mistaken, then, when she supposes that we can ignore the Augustinian tradition in any thorough discussion of evil. I agree with her that simply getting rid of religion will not solve the problem either. She says of the idea of getting rid of religion, "Whatever may have been its plausibility in the eighteenth century, when it first took the centre of the stage, it is surely just a distraction today."[37] We cannot ignore either side of this long argument, because each accuses the other of a fundamental complicity in evil. Feminist theologians, as I noted, accuse the theological traditionalists of having "ratified" certain evils in their definition of evil; in contrast, fundamentalists see "secular humanism" as a radical evil. Reasonable thinkers like Midgley would understandably like to be rid of both extremes, but that banishment is not so easy. From a caring perspective, dialogue between these two groups is essential because, after all, both share some basic values that could be enhanced by their cooperation. Finally, the enormous influence of Augustinian theodicy on our political and social structures makes it imperative that all educated persons be familiar with its main points and effects.

Influential alternative theodicies exist, and although in my view none of these has been successful, I must consider at least one. The Irenaean type of theodicy (named for Irenaeus, ca. AD 120–202) views Adam not as a perfect creation who irrationally turns to evil but as a developing being – one who must seek knowledge and ethical understanding to achieve the capacity to communicate with God. From this perspective the Fall does not represent the loss of an original paradise but the beginning of a long quest for knowledge and goodness. Since the childlike weakness of Adam came to light in his Fall, the Fall itself turns out to be a blessing in disguise because it necessitates redemption. Adam's sin becomes a *necessarium peccatum* and a *felix culpa* – a necessary sin and a happy fault.

Although the Irenaean view is gentler in its assessment of human responsibility for evil and more generous in its emphasis on redemption, it too fails in its account of suffering. It leaves the problem not only in mystery (thus resigning its solution to faith), but in a state of contradiction as well. Accepting such a view, John Hick says:

> We thus have to say, on the basis of our present experience, that evil is really evil, really malevolent and deadly and also, on the basis of faith, that it will in the end be defeated and made to serve God's good purposes. From the point of view of that future completion it will not have been merely evil, for it will have been used in the creation of infinite good.[38]

This view does not deny evil as merely an appearance that we misinterpret. Evil is real but somehow useful. No longer the great aesthetician, God becomes the foremost Utilitarian. How strange that even Immanuel Kant seems to have accepted a version of this doctrine in his account of the Fall and its role in soul making.[39] In Kantian ethics principles are absolute, and morality lies in the acts and their connection to principle – not in the effective production of some valued non-moral good. The only way to avoid the awful contradiction of God's turning out to be a Utilitarian in a Kantian scheme is to fasten onto a grim and absolute conception of justice in which the infliction of suffering can be justified as obedience to a supreme law. This kind of thinking, transposed to the domain of human interaction, leads to the untold suffering of many people at the hands of righteous others.

The problem of suffering is central to theodicy and, as we have seen, the solutions often seem to ratify evil rather than to redeem it. Augustine tried to solve the problem through balance and harmony:

> If there were misery before there were sins, then it might be right to say that the order and government of the universe were at fault. Again, if there were sins and no consequent misery, that order is equally dishonored by lack of equity. But since there is happiness for those who do not sin, the universe is perfect; and it is no less perfect because there is misery for sinners.[40]

This solution is clearly unsatisfactory on several counts. First, even Augustine did not mean that all individual suffering was the direct penalty for individual sin; rather suffering is generally available in amounts to balance the sin that occurs. His is a long-run account; eventually the good will know happiness, and evildoers will reap misery. But all of us merit some suffering because we share in original sin. The doctrine of original sin – absent from older Hebraic versions of the Adamic myth – was invoked in part to explain the suffering of innocents. In this view there are no real innocents; all share in the guilt of original sin. In a later chapter [not included here] we will see how human beings have adapted this teaching to their own justification of killing innocents in warfare. When some questioned the bombing of German civilian populations in World War II, for example, part of the response included a description of German civilians – "innocents" by the usual rules of warfare – as *not* innocent by virtue of their Nazi contamination. This pernicious doctrine has penetrated our political and social life; it has not been confined to esoteric theologies.

Second, Augustine's harmony and balance cannot adequately explain suffering inflicted on the just, and we will see how weak his account is when we analyze the story of Job a bit later.

Third, his account does not in any way explain animal suffering. As Hick points out, Augustine seems to have been little moved by the pain of animals.[41] On the one hand, Augustine says that animal suffering helps human beings understand something called the "desire for bodily unity"; on the other, he finds something aesthetically pleasing in the transformation of one animal body into food for other animals. Nowhere does he consider prolonged agony, the starvation of young deprived of their mothers, or the terror of being constantly preyed on.[42] He does not ask what sort of god would deliberately create a world in which his creatures must eat one another to live.

The problem of animal pain provides another opportunity to consider a different, more fallible, sort of God or to adopt a tragic sense of life. Considering the problem of animal suffering, Schopenhauer says: "Brahma is said to have produced the world by a kind of fall or mistake; and in order to atone for his folly, he is bound to remain in it himself until he works out his redemption. As an account of the origin of things, that is admirable!"[43] Indeed, it is admirable, and it puts us into sympathy with both the erring god and our fallible human companions. There is a lofty arrogance in the strict monotheism that insists on the all-goodness of an all-powerful God who allows and uses such suffering for his own purposes, and this sort of thinking has maintained and promoted a social order in which disobedience or distrust of the patriarch (as church, state, or father) is the greatest sin. What could be greater in such a system? For God himself commits all the crimes we might, from a natural perspective, label evil.

Since the major project in this work is to redefine and describe evil from women's perspective, we must return to Augustine's account of human suffering. It is clear, however, that the existence of unjustified animal suffering is enough to discredit the notion of an all-good and all-powerful deity. Which characteristic should be sacrificed? When we discuss Satan we will see that it is tempting to give up God's alleged omnipotence; when we discuss Job it will be equally tempting to give up the claim of God's all-goodness.

The most prominent, but deeply flawed, solution to the problem of suffering lies in the concept of soul making. This idea, central to the Irenaean theodicy, echoes in Kant and in modern writers like C. S. Lewis. Ricoeur says of Kant that he understood "the fall, free and fated, of man as the painful road of all ethical life that is of an adult character and on an adult level."[44] This view helps explain why Kant felt that it was not our duty to contribute to another's moral perfection:

It is contradictory to say that I make another person's *perfection* my end and consider myself obliged to promote this. For the *perfection* of another man, as a person, consists precisely in *his own* power to adopt his end in accordance with his own concept of duty; and it is self-contradictory to demand that I do (make it my duty to do) what only the other person himself can do.[45]

In the coming analysis of evil I will contest this way of looking at perfection and, in general, at moral life and action. But here we see that Kant's ethical perspective is consistent with his religious (or metaphysical) perspective. God leaves us free to choose our moral course, and we in turn have no obligation to promote the moral perfection of our fellows. Life is a painful and lonely struggle designed to "make souls." In the Christian design faith may lighten the struggle, but the suffering is no less real. Instead of concentrating on the alleviation and possible elimination of suffering, Christians are urged to find meaning in it. C. S. Lewis, for example, said of his wife's relentless pain from cancer: "But is it credible that such extremities of torture should be necessary for us? Well, take your choice. The tortures occur. If they are unnecessary, then there is no God or a bad one. If there is

a good God, then these tortures are necessary. For no even moderately good Being could possibly inflict or permit them if they weren't."[46]

Completely immersed in a strict monotheism, Lewis fails to appreciate the possibilities in a fallible god – one who controls just so much and is perhaps still struggling toward an ethical vision. This sort of god – lovable and understandable to women – may be unattractive to many men because he cannot make absolute claims on us for worship, obedience, and authority, or if he makes such claims, we might be justified in challenging him and even charging the claim to his wicked or unfinished side. A fallible god shakes the entire hierarchy and endangers men in their relations to women, children, animals, and the whole living environment. Whether Lewis saw any of this is doubtful. He adhered to the Augustinian line, affirming with St. Paul "that the sufferings of this present time are not worthy to be compared with the glory that shall be revealed in us."[47] Justice will triumph.

In the story of Job we encounter another way to reconceptualize God. The doctrine of original sin was designed in part to explain why innocents must suffer. But why should the *just* suffer?

"There was a man in the land of Uz, whose name was Job; and that man was perfect and upright, and one that feared God, and eschewed evil" (Job 1: 1). In this biblical beginning we have something like a philosophical fiction – an ideal case to test. How might we explain the suffering of a *perfectly just* man? Despite Job's perfection, God allowed Satan to put him to terrible tests of his faithfulness. Previously rich and well blessed in family life, Job was undeservedly deprived of everything: his servants were killed, his herds stolen, his seven sons slain by the wind, and, at last, his body afflicted from head to foot with "sore boils." On top of all this physical and emotional pain he suffered the deepest of all pains, psychic or soul pain, as his friends suggested that he must have done something to deserve the evil that was visited on him and as he struggled to maintain a belief in the goodness of a God who willfully permitted him to suffer so. How could God be all-good and at the same time allow Satan to inflict deliberate pain on a just man? Why would an omniscient deity thunder on for seventy-one verses bragging about his omnipotence to a lowly servant long since convinced?[48]

Here again we might decide not simplistically and childishly that God is bad, but that God is fallible and himself subject to error and temptation. Jung, in his fascinating *Answer to Job*, asks us to consider a developing God (one Hartshorne mentioned and Gardner rejected, as I discussed earlier).[49] This God, says Jung, may have learned a moral lesson from Job, a mere man, and then was constrained to "answer Job" by becoming man himself, thus sharing the pain, ambiguity, and finiteness of the beings he had created.

This account reminds us of Schopenhauer's description of Brahma and his atonement for the mistakes of creation. But the story that follows in the New Testament is a strange mixture of loving redemption and savage destruction. In the final agonies of Revelation, the new God seems very like Yahweh, exacting terrible and irrevocable vengeance. Indeed, we human beings are sometimes exhorted to return good for evil not out of love for our erring fellows but in the full realization that by so doing we "heap coals of fire upon their heads." Further, the program of redemption involves two things that should be anathema to women: a disregard of human intimacy and a perpetuation of the ancient ritual of sacrificing the son.

Jung interprets this story as a signal that the growing God needs to be rejoined to Sophia, the feminine deity-companion, who will bring wisdom, compassion, and completion to divinity.[50] In this thinking Jung has made a bold choice. He accepts God as omnipotent and omniscient but not yet all-good. He sees God as striving to manage his omniscience, and the call for Sophia is a move to enhance this project. [. . .] [C]learly Jung's thinking has had little influence on patriarchal Christianity.

The foolishness of theodicy has led us to search for the meaning of suffering. We have supposed, as a result of this long search, that suffering may be justified for retributive, therapeutic, pedagogical, or redemptive reasons.[51] Because God visits suffering on us for these reasons, we have inferred that we may cause one another to suffer for the same reasons. I will call all this into question in the later phenomenological investigation of evil. But before turning to that project (in which we encounter suffering *as* suffering without justification), we must ask about alternatives not yet considered. Suppose God is all-good but not all-powerful? Suppose God is at war with an equally powerful evil force?

Devils

One way to explain evil in the world is to posit an evil entity of great power who acts directly to bring about evil. This is a view several Eastern religions put forward, and it is the Manichaean dualist solution. According to the Manichaeans two great powers, light and darkness, are locked in battle for control of the world. Augustine accepted this view for some time, but then he rejected it, recognizing that it entailed a god who was not all-powerful. Hick says of Augustine's critical rejection of Manichaeanism: "It pictured the God whom men worship as less than absolute, and as but one of two co-ordinate powers warring against each other."[52]

Such a view is, of course, incompatible with a strict monotheism. It saves God from complicity in evil but sacrifices his omnipotence. Further, a complex mythology grew up around the forces of good and evil, making the position both confusing and unpalatable to the growing scientific orientation. (Not only is there a hierarchy of angels as in Augustine, for example, but now there are devils, demons, and archons to arrange as well.) But this view reinforced and accentuated a tendency already present in the Christian church to devalue the body and associate it with materiality. Jeffrey Burton Russell comments: "The presence of such dualism at the edge of the tradition sharpened the tension between soul and body and enhanced the view of the Devil as lord of matter, using the human body as the vehicle for his temptations."[53]

Manichaean dualism sees the body as a prison – a situation in which the exiled soul must strive to find redemption. Describing this view, Russell says of Jesus' message:

> Jesus goes to Adam and tells him the truth: that his body is an evil imposture invented by demons, and that he must try to rescue his soul for the world of light. Thus the function of men and women in the world is to grasp the saving gnosis, the message of Jesus, and to work at freeing the soul from the body.[54]

In spite of the rejection of Manichaeanism, its denunciation of the body had tremendous influence on Christianity. [. . .] Although Augustine had to brand as heresy any view of the body as evil in itself, the weakness of bodies and the evils of "fleshiness" came to be major themes in Christianity.

The dualism of the Manichaeans is not entirely absent from contemporary Christianity. M. Scott Peck, a Christian psychiatrist, takes just such a view. Adopting what he frankly calls a "Christian model," he says: "According to this model, humanity (and perhaps the entire universe) is locked in a titanic struggle between the forces of good and evil, between God and the devil. The battleground of this struggle is the individual human soul. The only question of ultimate significance is whether the individual soul will be won to God or won to the devil." Peck then refers to a particular case in his practice:

> By establishing through his pact a relationship with the devil, George had placed his soul in the greatest jeopardy known to man. It was clearly the critical point of his life. And possibly even the fate of all humanity turned upon his decision. Choirs of angels and armies of demons were watching him, hanging on his every thought, praying continually for one outcome or the other. In the end, by renouncing his past and the relationship, George rescued himself from hell and to the glory of God and for the hope for mankind.[55]

Peck takes a "multifaceted" approach in his work that includes both a medical model and the Christian model described above, but he clearly accepts the notion of two warring powers. Another contemporary writer who believes in the reality of Satan, viewing Satan as "god of this world," is Hal Lindsey. He too believes in possession: "I believe that people are being given superhuman powers from Satan in order that they may promote his work on earth." And he believes in the host of demons and worker devils:

> How many believe they are making contact with a powerful, incredibly intelligent spiritual being who heads a vast, highly organized army of spiritual beings like himself? This host is dedicated to blinding men's minds to the gift of forgiveness and love which God offered through Jesus Christ and to destroying or neutralizing those who have already believed in Him.[56]

One possible advantage of dualistic systems (beyond their simple preservation of God's goodness) is their location of the source of evil in gods rather than human beings. From this perspective evil is not a mere privation or turning from the good; rather it is part chosen and part inherited. Ricoeur says "Evil does not begin because it is

always already there in some fashion; it is choice *and* heritage."[57]

Again the opportunity for a tragic sense of life arises, but Christianity rejects it. Although it acknowledges the power of evil forces, those not rescued from possession are damned. Further, those who *choose* to align themselves with evil are often held to be irredeemable. Satan and his host of devils and demons are therefore doomed forever. "Once having sinned," Russell says in explaining Augustine's position, "the Devil and the other fallen angels are bound forever to the shadows and can never more do good."[58] This view has done enormous mischief. Far from relieving human beings from complete blame for the introduction of evil, Augustine's view combines original sin and diabology. Just as the fallen angels cannot be saved, so some people cannot be saved. But how can we tell which persons fall into this category? The dilemma caused real problems not only in technical analyses of predestination but also in such practical matters as, for example, judging witches. Those who had sealed pacts with the devil had to be destroyed; others, who had merely flirted, so to speak, with evil, were punished less severely.

A tremendous body of lore has grown up around the devil, and the concept has been and remains important in Christianity. Russell goes so far as to say:

> To deny the existence and central importance of the Devil in Christianity is to run counter to apostolic teaching and to the historical development of Christian doctrine. Since defining Christianity in terms other than these is literally meaningless, it is intellectually incoherent to argue for a Christianity that excludes the Devil. If the Devil does not exist, then Christianity has been dead wrong on a central point right from the beginning.[59]

Christian thinkers can sharply dispute this point. In one sense, of course, Russell is right: the devil is there historically. In another he is clearly wrong, for Christianity is not a static body of lore and dogma. It can be redefined without the devil as a central character. The most important point, however, is similar to the one Elisabeth Schüssler Fiorenza made with respect to women and scripture.[60] She argues that scripture should not be discarded on feminist grounds; rather it should be read and critiqued as a way of remembering what our fore-mothers suffered. It is part of our heritage as women. Similarly, we must remember the devil if we are to develop a morality of evil. We must try to understand why our predecessors needed such an entity and why some people still need devils on which to project their own evil.

Russell contends that the devil finds a role in every viewpoint that can logically be taken with respect to religion and evil.[61] First, when evil is construed as privation or nonbeing, as in Augustine, the devil (a fallen angel, created good) becomes *princeps mundi*, prince of this world – ruling the earth not as a competing deity but with God's tolerance and for eventual purposes of good. The view persists even though there is something incoherent in insisting that the devil is real, evil, and irredeemable while at the same time defining evil as nonbeing. Second, if evil is defined as the purpose and reality of a deity warring with God, the devil has his most powerful role, and human beings then have a duty to help the good God establish his final rule. This position has long been branded a heresy, but, as we have seen, it continues to spring up in Christianity and other religions. Third – and this view was foreshadowed in the discussion of Jung and Job – the devil is sometimes seen as part of God himself.[62] I will return to this view in later chapters where I will show it as one religious view compatible with a feminine phenomenology of evil. Fourth and finally, the devil even plays a role in atheistic views of evil. The role is metaphorical, of course, but its continual recurrence testifies to the power and romance of the idea.

In the last view, the devil is an entity to be courted and then subdued by those who desire power. Both Goethe's *Faust* and Nietzsche's *Zarathustra* illustrate this theme. William Barrett remarks that "both attempt to elaborate in symbols the process by which the superior individual – whole, intact, and healthy – is to be formed; and both are identically 'immoral' in their content, if morality is measured in its usual conventional terms."[63]

Barrett points out that Gounod's *Faust* is a moralized (or Christianized) version of the story. Unlike Gounod's hero, Goethe's is not destroyed by Gretchen's tragic death but begins a process of self-development:

> The strong man survives such disasters and becomes harder. The Devil, with whom Faust has made a pact, becomes in a real sense his

servitor and subordinate, just as our devil, if joined to ourselves, may become a fruitful and positive force; like Blake before him Goethe knew full well the ambiguous power contained in the traditional symbol of the Devil.[64]

Nietzsche too advises us to incorporate our devils and become stronger. Nietzsche strongly attacked Christian debasement of the body; that which was evil in Christian terms became good in Nietzsche's. He chided Christianity for standing proper values "on their head." The spiritual men of Christianity, he said,

> smash the strong, contaminate great hopes, cast suspicion on joy in beauty, break down everything autocratic, manly, conquering, tyrannical, all the instincts proper to the highest and most successful of the type "man," into uncertainty, remorse of conscience, self-destruction, indeed reverse the whole love of the earthly and of dominion over the earth into hatred of the earth and the earthly.[65]

From a different perspective we would have to say that Nietzsche's great insights into the harm done by Christian abhorrence of the body and earthly life oddly intermixed with a profound misunderstanding of the church. When he referred to churchmen breaking down the "autocratic, manly, conquering, tyrannical," he spoke only of the church's gentle message – not of its actions or real intentions. Between the Christian moralist and the Nietzschean immoralist, we – both men and women – have little to choose if we seek a way of life free from domination, the deliberate infliction of suffering, and the unbridled power of a male hierarchy.

The notion of a Faustian science to combat evil is still popular. Ernest Becker in his analysis of evil claims that such a science must do three things:

> It will have to explain evil credibly, and offer a way to overcome it;
> It would have to define the True, the Good, and the Beautiful;
> And it would have to re-establish the unity of man and nature, the sense of intimacy with the cosmic process.

Becker sees all this as a necessary move from the old theodicies (which he, like other writers, wrongly claims are dead) to a new theodicy – one that he calls an "anthropodicy." This anthropodicy would "settle for a new *limited* explanation [of evil and] . . . cover only *those evils that allow for human remedy*."[66] As Becker admits, this was the project of the Enlightenment. (We recall here the error Midgley warns against.) We transfer our faith from God to science. Instead of asking how we can best live in the inevitably tragic situation presented to us at birth, Becker finds reasons for optimism in the social utopia of Marx and the "understanding of man" provided by Freud. But Freud, as we know, left the basic evil of ethical terror firmly in place.

There is much in Becker's work with which we might sympathize – his call for community, his attack on agonism (the ancient Greek notion of life as a contest).[67] But he moves in the traditional pattern to global and sweeping solutions. Is it really necessary (or even possible) to define "the True, the Good, and the Beautiful," or might this very project maintain some forms of evil? Do we require a sense "of intimacy with the cosmic process"? Or do we need to recognize that our recourse stands beside us in the form of other human beings through whom we really do live and define our being? Women are in a peculiarly advantaged position historically to analyze a way of life that has necessitated living with and loving powerful human beings, men, who might properly be described as part-god, part-devil.

Finally, Becker wants a way to overcome evil. In a later work he writes of an escape from evil and describes human beings as longing to overcome evil.[68] But this longing, activated by fear, translates into action that sustains and renews evil through ignorance. We project the devil onto enemies, and we slay our enemies in the hope of overcoming evil. We also intend to incorporate the strength of our slain enemies and achieve a temporary victory over death. Primitive man and Nietzsche have much in common. The urge is always toward power, control, autonomy, and standardization – an odd assortment of objectives.

Becker, for all his insights and valuable suggestions, forgets that theodicy was an attempt to *justify* God in the face of evil and that anthropodicy might well lead in a similar direction. The present work looks evil in the face as in a mirror and sees that the face hardens and softens, that it is capable of smiling – of turning away from evil with a firm "This I will not do" and of living patiently with the evil in ourselves and others.

Summary

The basic question of this chapter has been, Can evil be redeemed? At the outset I confessed some agreement with Sartre on the matter: evil cannot be redeemed. But I do not mean that persons who commit evil are irredeemable; and, of course, Sartre was not speaking the language of religion. He meant that no philosophical or theological attempt to justify evil or to show its nonexistence could succeed, and in this I agree with him.

In this brief look at views on evil we have seen the earliest recognized evil in the cosmos and tried to ward it off by rites and rituals. Human beings were afflicted and sometimes even directed into evil by gods; they were not thought to be the originators of evil through sin. The gods themselves were thought to incorporate both good and evil; one begged the good side for protection against the evil side. Although there is clearly something psychologically healthy in this early view, there is also a moral dullness in it. If one man killed another, for example, it was clear that evil had befallen the one killed, but the killer was not necessarily judged to have committed evil. Interestingly, this view persists in some cultures where Christianity and paganism have blended. A contemporary Masai, for example, answered a visitor's question whether it was "all right" to kill a man by saying. "It is not so bad to kill a man. If you do it and are successful, it is not so bad, because God allowed the man to die. God agreed, and so it happened."[69]

Properly developed, the early views might have led to a tragic view of life in which people banded together against cosmic evil [. . .]. Where a tragic view did develop, however, it more often emphasized the tragic necessity of *doing* evil and accepting evil rather than a sustained commitment to stand against it.

The idea of gods in whom good and evil are undifferentiated leads to the notion of an evil god. This idea has arisen again and again. Even in early Christian sects the notion of an evil deity in combat with the God of light was prominent. It is perhaps more logical – and certainly simpler – than the concept of an all-good, all-powerful god who must somehow be responsible for the evil that we see and suffer in the world. But we saw that the idea is not easy to sustain; the longing for goodness – particularly with respect to omnipotence – is too great. A few bold and imaginative thinkers have suggested alliances with the devil or devils in order to grow stronger and more powerful, but even these writers were not in search of something they truly believed to be *evil*. They were reacting against a notion of evil that robbed life of its passion and people of their autonomy and courage.

The idea of an evil being appears even in strictly monotheistic views. The devil might be regarded as a projection of evil. Evil, then, is the other, right from God on down the hierarchy: evil is not in God but in Satan, who is irredeemable; evil is in the archons or demons, not in the angels; evil is in those who do not believe what authority dictates, not in the select; and evil is far more congenial to women (whose bodies make them especially susceptible) than to men. Russell surmises that this projection – the devil (although he does not label the devil a projection) – will persist:

The concept of the Devil is very much alive today, in spite of opposition from many theologians as well as from those hostile to all metaphysics. Indeed, the idea is more alive now than it has been for many decades, because we are again aware of the ineradicable nature of perversity in our own behavior, a perversity that has perhaps been more evident in the twentieth century than ever before. . . . We have direct perception of evil, of deliberate malice and desire to hurt, constantly manifesting itself in

governments, in mobs, in criminals, and in our own petty vices. . . . This is the Devil.[70]

But unless we see these faults in our own governments and selves as well as in others, we are guilty of *projection*, an exteriorization of evil that leaves us blameless as we try to destroy it. An alternative, suggested in one form or another by Jung, Sontag, and James, is the integration of good and evil in both deity and humans. From this viewpoint God is still learning to control the evil within him and is good to the degree that he does so. So must we learn to recognize, control, and convert the evil within us. This is what Jung has in mind when he says that we need a morality of evil.[71]

The view that did perhaps the greatest harm in its definition of evil is the one described in the discussion of theodicy and suffering. Here we find human beings blamed for the introduction of evil into an originally good world, the identification of evil with the material and bodily world, a hierarchy of being that has been used to dominate women and exploit the animal world, and at bottom a thorough mystification of the problem of evil. This view justifies the infliction of suffering, and we lose the opportunity to investigate evil at its phenomenal roots. From the perspective that will guide the rest of this study, that long tradition has *ratified* evil in some of its most basic forms.

Notes

1 Rosemary Radford Ruether, *Sexism and God-Talk* (Boston: Beacon Press, 1983), p. 160.
2 Ibid., p. 13.
3 "The Problem of Evil," *Encyclopedia of Philosophy*, ed. Paul Edwards (London: Collier Macmillan; New York: Macmillan and Free Press, 1967), 3: 136.
4 Jean-Paul Sartre, *What Is Literature?* trans. Bernard Frechtman (New York: Philosophical Library, 1949), p. 217.
5 Ibid., p. 219.
6 See the extensive discussion in Martha C. Nussbaum, *The Fragility of Goodness* (Cambridge: Cambridge University Press, 1986).
7 Paul Ricoeur, *The Symbolism of Evil*, trans. Emerson Buchanan (Boston: Beacon Press, 1969), pp. 5, 161–74.
8 Marie-Louise von Franz, *Shadow and Evil in Fairy Tales* (Dallas: Spring, 1983), p. 146.
9 See Eli Sagan, *Freud, Women, and Morality* (New York: Basic Books, 1988).
10 Ricoeur, *Symbolism of Evil*, part 1.

11 Ibid., pp. 25–6.
12 See M. Esther Harding, *Woman's Mysteries* (New York: Harper Colophon Books, 1976), pp. 55–63.
13 Ibid., p. 58.
14 Ibid., p. 36.
15 Ibid., p. 81.
16 Ibid.
17 Sagan also makes the connection between love in early life and morality in *Freud, Women, and Morality*.
18 Ricoeur, *Symbolism of Evil*, p. 214.
19 Martin Gardner, *The Whys of a Philosophical Scrivener* (New York: Quill, 1983), p. 249. The list of horrors are among those Gardner selected.
20 Merlin Stone, *When God Was a Woman* (New York: Dial Press, 1976), p. 171.
21 Von Franz, *Shadow and Evil*, p. 37.
22 Algernon Charles Swinburne, "Atalanta in Calydon," in *Swinburne's Poems*, ed. Richard Henry Stoddard (New York: Thomas Crowell, 1884), pp. 24, 25.
23 Ibid., p. 25.
24 Von Franz, *Shadow and Evil*, pp. 163–7.
25 Ibid., pp. 167, 163.

26 See Carl G. Jung, *Answer to Job*, trans. R. F. C. Hull (Princeton: Princeton University Press, Bollingen Series, 1973).

27 Gardner, *Philosophical Scrivener*, p. 251.

28 See the essays in Paula M. Cooey, Sharon A. Farmer, and Mary Ellen Ross, eds., *Embodied Love* (San Francisco: Harper & Row, 1987).

29 Ricoeur, *Symbolism of Evil*, p. 315.

30 My thanks to Hazel Barnes for bringing this trilemma to my attention.

31 John Hick, *Evil and the God of Love* (London: Macmillan, 1966), p. 81.

32 G. W. Leibniz, *Theodicy*, trans. E. M. Huggard (New Haven: Yale University Press, 1952), para. 225.

33 See ibid., para. 237.

34 Hick, *Evil and the God of Love*, p. 95.

35 Ricoeur, *Symbolism of Evil*, p. 239.

36 Ronald Schiller, "How Religious Are We?" *Reader's Digest*, May 1986, pp. 102–4.

37 Mary Midgley, *Wickedness* (London: Routledge & Kegan Paul, 1984), p. 6.

38 Hick, *Evil and the God of Love*, p. 400.

39 See Immanuel Kant, *Religion Within the Limits of Pure Reason Alone*, trans. Theodore M. Greene and Hoyt H. Hudson (New York: Harper Torchbooks, 1960).

40 Augustine, *On Free Will*, in *Augustine: Earlier Writings*, ed. John H. S. Burleigh (London: S. C. M. Press; Philadelphia: Westminster Press, 1953), 3.9.26.

41 See Hick, *Evil and the God of Love*, pp. 91–3.

42 Augustine, *On Free Will* 3.23 and 3.15.42–3.

43 Arthur Schopenhauer, "On the Suffering of the World," in *Studies in Pessimism*, selected and trans. by T. Bailey Saunders (1893; London: Swan Sonnenschein, 1976), p. 22.

44 Ricoeur, *Symbolism of Evil*, p. 273.

45 Immanuel Kant, *The Metaphysics of Morals*, part 2, *The Doctrine of Virtue*, trans. Mary J. Gregor (New York: Harper & Row, 1964), pp. 44–5.

46 C. S. Lewis, *A Grief Observed* (Toronto: Bantam Books, 1976), p. 50.

47 C. S. Lewis, *The Problem of Pain* (New York: Macmillan, 1962), p. 144. Lewis quotes Romans 8: 18.

48 C. G. Jung raises this question in *Answer to Job*, p. 16.

49 See also Alfred North Whitehead, *Process and Reality* (Cambridge: Cambridge University Press, 1929); Charles Hartshorne, *The Logic of Perfection* (La Salle, Ill.: Open Court, 1962).

50 See Jung, *Answer to Job*.

51 These categories appear regularly in philosophical-religious writing. The last category, "redemptive," is sometimes called "vicarious." See David Little, "Human Suffering in a Comparative Perspective" (Paper presented at the conference Perspectives on Human Suffering, University of Colorado, Boulder, November 1985).

52 Hick, *Evil and the God of Love*, p. 45.

53 Jeffrey Burton Russell, *Satan: The Early Christian Tradition* (Ithaca and London: Cornell University Press, 1981), pp. 165–6.

54 Ibid., p. 165.

55 M. Scott Peck, *People of the Lie* (New York: Simon & Schuster, 1983), pp. 37–8.

56 Hal Lindsey, *Satan Is Alive and Well on Planet Earth* (Grand Rapids, Mich.: Zondervan, 1972), pp. 40, 42.

57 Ricoeur, *Symbolism of Evil*, p. 300.

58 Russell, *Satan*, p. 207.

59 Ibid., p. 25.

60 See Elisabeth Schussler Fiorenza, *In Memory of Her: A Feminist Theological Reconstruction of Christian Origins* (New York: Crossroad, 1983); see also Fiorenza, "Discipleship and Patriarchy: Early Christian Ethos and Christian Ethics in a Feminist Theological Perspective," in *Women's Consciousness, Women's Conscience*, ed. Barbara Hilkert Andolsen, Christine E. Gudorf, and Mary D. Pellauer (Minneapolis: Winston Press, 1985), pp. 143–60.

61 In a discussion of the Cathars, Russell lists four possible positions that might logically be taken on the problem of evil. See Jeffrey Burton Russell, *Lucifer: The Devil in the Middle Ages* (Ithaca and London: Cornell University Press, 1984), p. 187.

62 See, for example, Frederick Sontag, *The God of Evil* (New York: Harper & Row, 1970).

63 William Barrett, *Irrational Man* (Garden City, NY: Doubleday Anchor, 1962), pp. 189–90.

64 Ibid., p. 190.

65 Nietzsche, *Beyond Good and Evil*, trans. R. J. Hollingdale (Harmondsworth: Penguin Books, 1973), p. 70.

66 Ernest Becker, *The Structure of Evil* (New York: George Braziller, 1968), pp. 375, 17, 18.

67 See ibid., pp. 259–62.

68 Ernest Becker, *Escape from Evil* (New York: Free Press, 1975).

69 Lance Morrow, "Africa," *Time*, February 23, 1987.

70 Russell, *Satan*, p. 222.

71 Jung, *Answer to Job*, sections 696, 742 (pp. 434, 457).

PART VII

Religious Values

Introduction

Charles Taliaferro

Religious conceptions of the world seem to be saturated with values, whether these are distinctively religious (the value of prayer) or compatible with secular ethics (religious as well as secular, civic prohibitions against homicide).

We begin this section with a paper by Edward Langerak who seeks to define three important categories when addressing conflict: respect, tolerance, and cooperation. We believe that Langerak helps us to think more carefully about the different ways in which tolerance and intolerance may be practiced. Langerak's work has a bearing on both religious and secular conflict.

In what respects might religious beliefs form the foundation of moral judgments? Robert Merrihew Adams defends the thesis that the moral rightness and wrongness of acts may be accounted for by God's commanding or prohibiting such acts. Baruch Brody adopts a less sweeping position, but one with radical implications. He does not argue that moral rightness consists of God's commands, but he argues that if there is a God, we may well have obligations to obey God by virtue of the fact that God created us and conserves the cosmos in being. In George Mavrodes's contribution, the moral life of right and wrong, and all the things we value or disvalue, are set against two frameworks: theism and naturalism. If naturalism is assumed, do our moral duties wind up as "queer" or alien? Mavrodes argues that the allegiance to objective moral values invites a theistic framework.

In religious ethics we are often enjoined to love God and others. In "Pure Love," Adams considers the nature of love and self-interest. The essay raises general concerns which go beyond any specific religious tradition. Can there be "pure love"? Is truly self-less benevolence possible?

A key religious value (or set of values) in Christian tradition lies in the incarnation. Traditionally, Christians believe that God became incarnate as a human being. For Christians, this event sets in motion the occasion for the redemption of all people. Is belief in the incarnation coherent? Richard Swinburne contends that it is. In the next entry, John Hick takes up a competing position. Hick does not see religious traditions in exclusive terms, according to which if the Christian belief in the incarnation is correct then a Muslim's denial of it would be false. Hick sees world religions as converging on a reality (he refers to this as the Real) which transcends each religion. In this framework, different religions may be equally valuable in orienting us to what is deeply sacred. Anthony O'Hear assesses this pluralism and uses works of art to articulate the promise and difficulty of pluralism. "The real or the Real? Chardin or Rothko" is a good example of how philosophy of religion may interact with the world of art.

Religious values do not concern exclusively human or divine–human relations. Holmes Rolston considers the implications of religious convictions for how we think about the environment.

When, if ever, is religious faith a virtue? Blaise Pascal's famous wager argument points to the prudential value of religious faith. In the last entry Tim Chappell situates the good of religious faith in between two sorts of responsiveness: responsiveness to truth and to practical hope.

Further Reading

Historical Sources:

Kant, Immanuel: *Critique of Practical Reason*
Kant, Immanuel: *Critique of Pure Reason, Transcendental Doctrine of Method, Chapter 2*
Kant, Immanuel: *Religion Within the Limits of Reason Alone*

From The Blackwell Companion to Philosophy of Religion, *see the following entries:*

Childress, J. F., "Theism and Medical Ethics"
Comstock, G. L., "Theism and Environmental Ethics"
Idziak, J. M., "Divine Command Ethics"
Langerak, E., "Theism and Toleration"
Outka, G., "Agapeistic Ethics"
Porter, J., "Virtual Law Ethics"
Roberts, R. C., "Narrative Ethics"
Weithman, P. J., "Theism, Law, and Politics"

Other further reading:

Adams, R. M., "Moral Arguments for Theistic Belief," in C. F. Delaney (ed.), *Rationality and Religious Belief* (Notre Dame: University of Notre Dame Press, 1979).

Bertocci, P. A., *The Goodness of God* (Washington, DC: University Press of America, 1981). *Excellent.*

Hick, J. H., *God Has Many Names* (Philadelphia: Westminster Press; London: Macmillan, 1980). *Favors religious pluralism.*

Hick, J. H., *Problems of Religious Pluralism* (New York: St Martin's Press, 1985).

Jordan, J. (ed.), *Gambling on God: Essays on Pascal's Wager* (Lanham and London: Rowman and Littlefield, 1996). *On the probability of God's existence and the prudence of religious belief.*

Mackie, J. L., "Moral Arguments for the Existence of God," in *The Miracle of Theism: Arguments For and Against the Existence of God* (Oxford: Clarendon Press, 1982).

Morris, T. V., *The Logic of God Incarnate* (Ithaca: Cornell University Press, 1986).

Nielsen, K., *God and the Grounding of Morality* (Ottawa: University of Ottawa Press, 1991). *Critique of theism.*

Owen, H. P., *The Moral Argument for Christian Theism* (London: Allen and Unwin, 1965).

Phillips, D. Z. (ed.), *Religion and Morality* (New York: St Martin's Press, 1996). *A handsome collection of different positions.*

Phillips, D. Z., *Death and Immortality* (New York: St Martin's Press, 1970).

Rescher, N., *Pascal's Wager: A Study of Practical Reasoning in Philosophical Theology* (Notre Dame: University of Notre Dame Press, 1983). *Superb re-statement of Pascal's wager.*

Runzo, J. (ed.), *Ethics, Religion and the Good Society: New Directions in a Pluralistic World* (Louisville: Westminster/John Knox Press, 1992).

Zagzebski, L., "Does Ethics Need God?" *Faith and Philosophy* 4 (1987): 294–303. *A subtle, interesting case for linking God and values.*

37

Pluralism, Tolerance, and Disagreement

Edward Langerak

A dark side of tolerating diversity is that – as the Latin root *tolerare* connotes – it involves the enduring of something disagreeable, perhaps even abhorrent. If utopia involves agreement on everything that really matters, it has no place for tolerating anything. There is some debate about the extent to which the sort of disagreement relevant to toleration involves matters of morality. Some seem to claim that we cannot tolerate actions that we regard as morally wrong (Midgley 1991: 70), whereas others suggest that toleration applies only to matters of which we morally disapprove (Nicholson 1985; Raphael 1988: 139). Perhaps both sides are right, depending on the culture; it has been remarked that the genius of American politics is to treat matters of principle as if they were merely conflicts of interest, while the genius of French politics is to treat even conflicts of interests as if they were matters of principle (Wolff et al. 1969: 21). However, I agree with those who argue that we probably cannot draw a line between what we dislike and what we disapprove (Warnock 1987: 127) and that, in any case, the issue of toleration can arise whenever there is disagreement about any matters regarded as important, be they mores or morals. The point to notice is that everyone in this debate agrees that toleration is to be sharply distinguished from both indifference toward diversity as well as broadminded celebration of it.

Edward Langerak, "Pluralism, Tolerance, and Disagreement," *Rhetoric Society Quarterly* 24 (1994), pp. 95–106.

On the other hand, we sometimes think of tolerant persons as those who are very accepting of differences, and tolerant societies as those that encourage diversity. Here tolerance connotes the sort of affirming that renders the notion of begrudging endurance unnecessary, even offensive. In fact, a recent book suggests that liberalism's broadminded attitude is actually a threat to toleration (Fotion and Elfstrom 1992: 124). As the authors put it paradoxically: "the more tolerant we become the less tolerant . . . we become," that is, as liberalism cultivates a more open and approving attitude it pushes us beyond merely enduring diversity. They suggest we use "tolerance" to refer to an accepting attitude and "toleration" to refer to enduring the disagreeable. If we take this suggestion we might say that tolerance undermines toleration and that the genius of political liberalism is its ability to do precisely that. My thesis is that, although we do need a conceptual framework that allows us to respect many of the views we regard as wrong, it also must allow us to judge that these respectable views are disagreeable and even that sometimes actions based on them should not be tolerated.

I

First I want to note that ambivalence about the disagreement involved in toleration extends to the history of its justification. I take the following to be part of the consensus history of toleration in Europe: Even before the Reformation there were conflicts between religious outlooks – such as

Christianity and Islam – which, unlike the localized religious of Greece and Rome, believed in a revealed but universal doctrine of eternal salvation. In obedience to the only God and out of compassion for the unsaved, they sought to expand their control everywhere they could. Although commercial and even moral motivations sometimes elicited a practical *modus vivendi*, heresy was seldom tolerated whenever religious passions dominated. Obedience to God, concern for the general good, and even care for the heretic prevented a stable policy of peaceful coexistence. As long as this conflict was between different territories and races, societies could still flourish, at least away from borders and between crusades. But with the Reformation, one of these religions turned this sort of conflict in on itself. Hence the religious wars, with the atrocities on both sides that made life uncertain at best and, at worst, nasty, brutish, and short. Terror and exhaustion, if not prudence, motivated Europe to heed calls like Locke's *Letter Concerning Toleration*, which stressed the irrationality of coercing beliefs that must be voluntary (1983: 27), as well as the rationality of accommodating certain types of religious differences (ibid.: 44). Locke was not one to celebrate diversity; he merely argued the irrationality of not enduring it. Even then, he is notorious for not extending such begrudging toleration to "Papists" and atheists, on the grounds that they threatened harm to the state (the former because they pledged allegiance to a foreign prince and the latter because they were incapable of making any pledges at all (ibid.: 50–1)). Anglican and Puritan practices could be tolerated because, although one or the other of them was terribly wrong, they could be endured without undermining civil order.

So the early justifications for toleration allowed and, in fact, insisted on its disapproving dark side. Later justifications of toleration could also be comfortable with it, even when the justification appealed to moral or theological principle rather than to prudence or rationality. Respecting another's right to autonomy, whether motivated by moral commitment or by religious awe toward those created in the image of God,[1] is quite consistent with disliking, disapproving, and even abhorring the tolerated behavior. But with Mill's *On Liberty*, a new element was added. Of course, Mill did defend toleration of diversity on the prudential ground of its leading to truth (1978: 50) and on the moral ground of a utilitarian right to liberty (ibid.: 11). But, in addition, he supported measures that would nurture diversity and not merely endure it. Mill

himself may have had a personal taste for the eccentric (ibid.: 64), but he also argued that everyone should see human diversity as the means for human progress (ibid.: 54–71). Thus he listed public opinion, and not just legal coercion, as undesirable constraints on natural human growth (ibid.: 9). Indeed, he was fond of comparing the use of such traditional constraints to the Chinese practice of foot-binding (ibid.: 66). Not only did normal adults have the moral right to freedom, but encouraging them to pursue diverse visions of the good life was both necessary and sufficient for the ongoing improvement of society.[2] Therefore, as long as people were not allowed to harm each other, society should encourage and not merely allow diversity. It is clear that Mill's liberalism advocates a pluralism whose broadminded acceptance of diversity makes toleration (in the sense of enduring the disagreeable) as unnecessary as it is undesirable.

II

The above history of justification for toleration is, I hope, relatively uncontroversial (see, for example, Mendus 1989: 22–68; Rawls 1993: xxi–xxv; and Fotion and Elfstrom 1992: 75–80). It helps us understand some of what is behind the tension in political liberalism between tolerating differences and affirming them. It also reminds us that people would rather be celebrated than put-up-with, and that liberals find it nicer to accept something than endure it. What Bertrand Russell once said about friends also applies to strangers: "A sense of duty is useful in work, but offensive in personal relations. People wish to be liked, not to be endured with patient resignation" (1930: 157). However, this point reminds us why some worry that the "affirmation" side of liberalism flirts with relativism. The most stiff-necked dogmatist can tolerate disagreeable things, but can one accept (almost) everything and still have convictions of one's own, commitments that provide guidance, structure, and meaning for one's life?

The ambivalence in liberal attitudes toward toleration was underscored for me last year when I served on a "Cultural Diversity Task-force" for the local public schools. Our mandate was to develop a plan "to ensure that all students will have an appreciation for cultural diversity and global interdependence." A "strategic planning retreat," which had earlier written the mandate, provided us with ten basic beliefs, including the belief that "diversity enriches society." It became clear that much of the positive attitude toward diversity derived from the "inclusive education" approach that the State of Minnesota is pushing in all its school districts. Students should be affirmed rather than discounted because of differences in age, wellness, ability, social and economic class, sex, physical and psychological characteristics, color, race, religion, and so on. Although most of these sorts of differences can be found in even a homogeneous society (so they can hardly be construed as cultural diversity), many of them do involve differences that should be celebrated rather than endured, and not only because of political correctness. Thus those at the strategic retreat agreed on something like Mill's "diversity enriches society" thesis and it is not surprising that this attitude was generalized by some educators to almost all differences, including genuinely cultural differences. Indeed, the pedagogy that the teachers on our task force seemed most comfortable with stressed the importance of being non-judgmental when encountering customs that conflict with one's own.

Sometimes, "non-judgmental" simply translated into the wise policy of being very careful about making judgments and very selective about expressing them. Other times it seemed to reduce to the claim that we cannot really understand other cultures, a claim similar to the sort of "moral isolationism" that Midgley has argued is incoherent (1981: 160). Most often, those stressing a nonjudgmental attitude wanted students to avoid negative evaluations and felt that the best way to teach this was to nurture an open and affirming attitude toward cultural differences. (Thus they agreed that "non-judgmental" really means "positive-judgmental.") Of course, these teachers knew that some behavior must be judged wrong; however, they thought that such behavior is not about cultural differences but about the sort of mutual respect required for education, safety, and citizenship. Such teachers find support from Nick Fotion and Gerard Elfstrom in their very helpful book *Toleration* (1992). They emphasize "the repugnant nature of tolerating" (p. 129) and note that people "naturally wish for others to hold them in esteem rather than be objects of reined-in contempt." They believe that "substantive reasons exist for believing that liberal doctrine readily allows societies to be cleansed of toleration" (ibid.: 130).[3]

Such a cleansing might appeal to those interested in cross-cultural understanding. In terms of Robert Hanvey's "An Attainable Global Perspective" (copies of which the task-force received

and read), educators typically want students to go beyond the level I awareness of the exotic sort of differences noted by tourists and readers of *National Geographic*, and beyond the Level II awareness that relates these differences to the cultural traits noticed by those caught in cultural conflicts. They want students to acquire the Level III cognitive skills of understanding the outlooks of others in a way that makes them believable, and the Level IV empathy skills that enable one to see oneself in the others' situations. Having supervised an international college program in Asia, I certainly agree that these higher-level skills are important in a globally interdependent world. I also realize that one tempting pedagogy for nurturing them is to cultivate a reluctance to make disapproving judgments and to affirm whatever differences one finds.

But it should not be surprising that many parents oppose such a pedagogy. One does not have to be a fundamentalist to worry that this is a way to teach empathy by implying that one religion, morality, or practice is as good as any other. If students think that they have no grounds for believing that others are wrong, they will eventually infer that they also have no grounds for thinking anyone is right (Gardner 1992: 72, 76). When such relativism gets too closely associated with liberal tolerance and public school pedagogy, one can expect trouble.

One might try to cope with parental worries by asserting that "the child's right to an education must be seen as more fundamental than the parents' right to transmit their view of the world" (Kach and DeFaveri 1987: 135). Perhaps then the school board could patiently explain to the parents how "those cultural groups that see children merely as means of perpetuating their culture and not as ends in themselves must be seen as morally flawed" (ibid.: 175).[4] But, whatever one thinks of this hard-line Kantianism, its frank rejection of communitarian values in favor of individualism can hardly serve as an argument for being non-judgmental.

If one were somehow to cultivate the refusal to make negative cross-cultural evaluations, it could result in even more trouble. For one thing, it could provide rhetorical support for the violation of human rights by encouraging repressive regimes to classify toleration itself as little more than a Western hang-up. As 34 Arab and Asian governments argued in the "Bangkok Declaration" at the Vienna Conference on Human Rights (June 1993),[5] the notion of human rights can itself be seen as relative to the cultural, religious, and historical diversity of nations, and therefore it should not be used "as an instrument of political pressures." One cultural difference has to do with the metaphysics of individuals and groups. If individuals are not the basic unit in society – if they are primarily parts of a group – then role expectations may be a more important value than individual rights. Moreover, the locus of diversity would be between *groups* rather than *individuals* and, in order to maintain group diversity, there may have to be definite limits on freedoms available to individuals within the groups. Indonesia, for example, has long toyed with the idea of banning Hollywood movies in order to maintain a distinctive cultural identity. One can sympathize with its Foreign Minister, who proclaimed at the Vienna Conference that "no country or group of countries should arrogate unto itself the role of judge, jury, and executioner over other countries" on such "critical and sensitive" issues. However, Indonesia also contains groups which practice an especially mutilating form of female circumcision (Sherwin 1992: 61) and which cultivate female role responsibilities that, to Westerners, seem especially repressive. United States Secretary of State Warren Christopher, arguing at the conference for a new emphasis on women's rights, claimed that "We respect the religious, social and cultural characteristics that make each country unique, but we cannot let cultural relativism become the last refuge of repression." The question is how one can respect certain types of cultural diversity while, far from accepting them, be quite selective about tolerating them.

A related problem with a pedagogy that prefers tolerance as acceptance over toleration as endurance is that it has trouble with what has been called (Mendus 1989: 18; Raphael 1988: 149) the paradox of toleration: if I find that, in spite of my best efforts, I cannot approve of something, why should I tolerate it? If I am genuinely convinced that something is truly wrong, why shouldn't I try to persuade the majority to ban it? I believe the best answer is that sometimes my obligation to respect autonomy overrides my disapproval of another's behavior. But the pedagogical implication of this answer requires that we cultivate not the disposition to approve but the disposition (selectively) to endure what one disapproves. Then we can nurture strong convictions about right and wrong – even local loyalties and parochial solidarities – and still avoid dogmatic intolerance by teaching the appropriate role of tolerating (at least some of) the disagreeable. Therefore I conclude that we should teach toleration precisely because we should teach how to disagree.

III

So far I have suggested there is wisdom in keeping the disagreeable in the verb "tolerate" and the adjective "tolerant." Since these associate with both of the nouns "tolerance" and "toleration," I do not endorse the proposal (Fotion and Elfstrom 1992) that "tolerance" mean "acceptance" and "toleration" mean "enduring." Rather, I think confusion is best avoided if all of these terms retain the root meaning of enduring something disagreeable. Moreover, we should notice that generally it is behavior, rather than persons or beliefs, that are tolerated. Presumably the alternatives to enduring persons or (the mere holding of) beliefs are such drastic measures as death, banishment, or brainwashing, which generally are not realistic options in a pluralistic society. Hence I would like to see tolerance and toleration used interchangeably and defined as "I disagree with your position on this matter that I care about but I will not attempt to coerce your behavior." Intolerance,[6] of course, does try to coerce behavior – either directly, through personal interference or, indirectly, by trying to make the behavior illegal or proscribed in some way. It is important to notice that tolerance is quite compatible with trying to change the other person's mind by rational argument. Indeed, if one were to speak of tolerating beliefs (as opposed to the behavior of communicating them), presumably one would mean something like "not try to change the other person's opinion by any means other than rational argument" (Kordig 1982: 63).

Sometimes, especially in a pluralistic society, one can disagree with another's position and go beyond tolerance to cooperation. A cooperative stance says, "I may disagree with your decision but I will help you carry it out." Sometimes cooperation with what is disagreeable is motivated by timidity, moral cowardice, lack of integrity, or over-eagerness to please. But sometimes it can derive from principled compromise (Benjamin 1990) and from moral conviction, as when, for example, a physician respects a patient's autonomy enough to abide by the patient's decisions even when they do not seem medically indicated. Notice that an uncooperative stance is not yet intolerance. A nurse can refuse to assist during an abortion without trying to prevent others from carrying it out. Of course, there can be borderline cases, as when a public resignation is intended to create pressure to change a policy. But, in general, tolerance is not sufficient for cooperation. (Nor is tolerance necessary for cooperation, since we can cooperate on matters about which we agree or toward which we are indifferent.)

Tolerance is not the same as resigning oneself to the disagreeable out of a sense of helplessness. To be tolerant implies that one believes (perhaps falsely) that one could interfere in some way with the disagreeable behavior. Of course, one could decide that coercion would come at too high a price, which decision could elicit a begrudging tolerance.

Tolerance is very different from refusal to blame and from forgiveness toward the blameworthy. We can be intolerant of the behavior of parents who, on religious grounds, refuse necessary medical treatment for their children and, at the same time, either refuse to blame them or forgive them if we do. And we can blame and refuse to forgive pornographers while tolerating (within limits) their behavior. Similarly, sympathy and empathy cut across tolerance and intolerance.

IV

Having surveyed the conceptual geography of tolerance and having restricted it to disagreeable behavior that we endure, we need another notion to capture what is undeniably an important part of pluralism and of political liberalism, namely the willingness to admit that views we disagree with can still be entirely respectable. Although intelligent people may vary somewhat on their (largely implicit) standards for what makes positions respectable, there is likely to be a fair amount of overlap on such common-sense criteria as consistency, clarity, comprehensiveness, plausibility, and practicality. These criteria allow us to endorse a position's adequacy without endorsing its truth (Rescher 1978: 243). What makes a position respectable includes not just the propositional content of the belief but also the way in which the believer arrived at and defends the belief. The content of one's horoscope may be fairly intelligent, but most of us would regard as irrational believing it solely on the say-so of a fortune-teller (unless, of course, the latter has proved much more reliable than most soothsayers). Similarly, one might find implausible the content of another's religious belief about karma and reincarnation, but admit that the other's believing it is quite reasonable. So what I

call the attitude of respect applies more to believings than to beliefs or believers.[7] You can disrespect a particular position without disrespecting the person who holds it, though if you could not respect a fairly high percentage of a person's positions it probably would have implications for your attitude toward that person's character. Similarly, I could hold you in high regard and still think that you hold a few (perhaps charmingly) irrational views.

I suggest we characterize an attitude of respect as "I (may) disagree with your position but I believe that it is reasonable." As Rawls (1993: 48–54) has lately argued, "reasonable" has some moral as well as intellectual bite. Perhaps in some narrow sense a purely selfish decision could be *rational*, but a *reasonable* decision, while not necessarily altruistic, is sensitive to the interests of others; it has as much to do with Kant's practical reason as his theoretical reason. Rawls seems to build a commitment to equality right into the notion of reasonable (ibid.: 50), but I think that an intrinsic concern for others can be expressed in undemocratic ways. Hence some forms of theocracy or monarchy can be perfectly respectable positions. By the same token, respectable positions can evaluate each other as respectable but harmful to the public good. Thus, I claim that you can grant that a decision is respectable, and therefore reasonable, without accepting it, approving it, or even liking it. Indeed, you can be intolerant of it, as illustrated by the previous example of physicians who get a court order to override what they may regard as a respectable decision by parents who, on religious grounds, refuse to allow a life-saving medical treatment for their young child. Noticing that respect and intolerance can be combined is socially important in a pluralistic society where even friends sometimes have to let political force decide a dispute between themselves. On the other hand, you can tolerate and even cooperate with a position you do not respect, as when you work with knaves or fools to defeat a common opponent. Noticing that disrespect and tolerance and cooperation can be combined may also be important in a pluralistic society where even enemies sometimes have to join forces to win a political dispute.[8]

The attitude of respect requires one to be open-minded enough to understand and even appreciate the reasonableness of diverse and contradictory views. But it does not require Mill's broadminded delight in and affirmation of diversity. I submit that this latter feature of respect is a distinct advantage in a pluralistic society. We now know that our differences will remain deep and wide, that resolutions are more often the result of compromising than of convincing, and that sometimes sheer political power must be exercised. Instead of hoping for increasing consensus about the good, we are now trying to figure out how "incompatible yet reasonable comprehensive doctrines" (Rawls 1993: xvi) can coexist in one quarrelsome but non-violent political union. What reasonable citizens owe each other's views is not broadminded agreement, affirmation, approval, or admiration but open-minded[9] respect and, when appropriate, tolerance and co-operation. Even when tolerance seems inappropriate, as it does to some of the factions in the abortion conflict (who try to prevent violation of what each side regards as basic rights, by directly or indirectly interfering with each other's activities), opponents can grant that some of the opposing views are reasonable. Such recognition could at least raise the level of the debate, enhance civility, and perhaps even motivate the search for common ground.

Assuming that people should follow their conscience when it is reasonable, respect should be interpreted as what has been called "moral non-dogmatism" (Cohen 1967: 150). This is the view that if I believe your position is reasonable, then I should agree that you ought to try to do what you think is right. ("Try to" is necessary in the definition because, as noted earlier, I may also decide I ought not to tolerate your reasonable but wrong behavior.) Moral non-dogmatism has been rejected by some (ibid.: 159) because it seems to contradict the central moral criterion of universalizability. When we make a moral judgment, we universalize it because we agree that anyone who is in a relevantly similar situation is permitted or obliged to do what we think we are permitted or obliged to do. This is what distinguishes morality from mere matters of taste, one can plausibly argue. But if respect is interpreted as moral non-dogmatism, then when I respectfully disagree with your position I seem to say both that if I were in your position I would not do what you think is right and that you ought to try to do what you think is right. So if I respect your decision and I also universalize my moral judgment about what I should not do, I seem to say both that you should and that you should not try to do what you think is right.

I believe that the above argument is unsound for the same reason that universalizability does not entail specific universal obligations. People are often in relevantly different situations, so universalizability does not entail that they have the same specific obligations. And your having a different but reasonable position from mine will often put us in relevantly different situations. Of course, if having any sort of different beliefs would put us in relevantly different situations, universalizability would be trivialized. Saddam Hussein would have different obligations toward the Kurds just because he believes they do not have moral rights. But respect applies only to reasonable believings, so it implies only that different reasonable believings can put us in relevantly different moral situations. Therefore I think that the non-dogmatic interpretation of respect is consistent with universalizability and that using it can be socially important in a divided but non-violent pluralistic state. It can enable us to honor the consciences of those with whom we disagree, even when we feel obliged to oppose them.

Sometimes respect, like tolerance, is associated with uncertainty, skepticism, relativism, or even nihilism. However, it should be clear that one can respect or tolerate a position and simultaneously believe that one knows the objective truth that the position is wrong. Of course living in a pluralism of respectable yet conflicting doctrines is likely to elicit the humility of admitting that one might be wrong. And a powerful argument for tolerance is that it can be an instrument for correcting the human tendency to make mistakes (Popper 1987). But we can admit that we might be wrong and still believe that we are right. We can also admit we have a lot to learn from discussion with those who hold conflicting views and still believe that our own view is closest to the truth. We can even believe we do not have anything to learn from another position and still regard it as worthy of respectful discussion. I grant that those who reject the notions of objective truth or knowledge can give pragmatic justifications for respect and tolerance, but I think it is important in a pluralistic society to see that also those who believe they know right from wrong can respect and tolerate some positions and behaviors they believe are wrong.

V

I noted earlier that Fotion and Elfstrom say that in liberal doctrine there are good reasons for encouraging the replacement of tolerating diversity with the approval of it. I should also note that they recognize reasons for keeping "the prickly and uncomfortable concept of toleration in the liberal pantheon" (1992: 131). In particular, they say, there will always be groups like the Nazis, the Ku Klux Klan, and pornographers who are "genuinely despicable and worthless" (ibid.: 131) but who ought to be tolerated anyway. Moreover, precisely because of its dark side, tolerating them implies no compromise of one's convictions – one is enduring, not affirming, such groups.

However, I hope I have shown that it is a better idea to recognize the various combinations of respect, tolerance, and cooperation (and their opposites)[10] and to appreciate, if not celebrate, the disagreeable side of tolerance. This conceptual framework recognizes the important fact that in a pluralistic society there will be a diversity of respectable yet conflicting outlooks and that sometimes one must combine respect and intolerance. For example, even if the factions in the abortion dispute restrict themselves to "public reasons" (which liberals insist on as the way to keep church and state separate) when arguing their case, there will be respectable positions on opposite sides and, at some point, political power may have to decide

which activities will not be tolerated.[11] Meanwhile, keeping the social fabric in usable shape depends on the factions being able to take a political stand without pushing all of their opponents into the same boat with Nazis and the Ku Klux Klan. By keeping it clear that it is behaviors, not people, that are intolerable, and that even respectable positions can sometimes yield behavior that the majority has good reason not to tolerate, we can perhaps make sense of Warren Christopher's reply to Indonesia: we respect your religious and cultural traditions but we will not allow even a respectable tradition to become the refuge of repression.

The last point underscores how much remains unsettled, even if my conceptual framework is accepted. What are the legitimate reasons for intolerance? Can "harm to others" be explicated by "public reasons" or does it require a thicker theory of the good? Are the reasons different in different contexts, such as interpersonal, professional, community, national, and international contexts? Appreciating the disagreeable in tolerance is only the first step in answering such questions.[12]

Notes

1 I have defended such a theological grounding of respect for autonomy in *Christian Faith, Health, and Medical Practice* (1989: 57–66).

2 Mill thought that encouraging diversity was *necessary* for progress because only by exposure to diversity could one escape the confines of tradition (1978: 54). He thought it was *sufficient* because he believed in the perfectibility of humans – that they would, in the long run, choose the better options (ibid.: 60 and 61, 67). Some commentators (Edwards 1988: 94; Megone 1992: 140) note the tension in Mill between his celebration of diversity and his belief that, as society is challenged by diversity, it will move toward the truth and thereby toward conformity of belief (Mill 1978: 42). I suspect Mill thought that conformity on matters of truth was compatible with diversity in lifestyles and that the latter would always be necessary to nurture the best in human nature.

3 As I note later, they do recognize a remaining role for toleration.

4 As quoted by Dwight Boyd in *The Challenge of Pluralism*. F. Clark Power and Daniel Lapsley, eds., University of Notre Dame Press, 1992, pp. 155–6.

5 The information about and quotations from this conference come from a *Washington Post* report printed in the Minnesota *Star-Tribune*, 6/15/1993, p. 2A.

6 "Intoleration" is hardly ever used, which is another reason for using tolerance and toleration interchangeably.

7 Jackson (1992: 31) agrees that what reasonable people believe depends on social context so she defines "reasonable" in terms of a "credentials test" that applies to the believer rather than the belief. The believer must be well-informed, reflective, clear-headed, and of apparent good will (ibid.: 30). Since such a believer can still have unreasonable believings, I think it is better to apply "reasonable" to believings or positions. Rawls (1993: 48) defines "reasonable" primarily as a virtue of believers, though he also lists three elements of reasonable doctrines (ibid.: 59). Making the (counterfactual?) assumption that reasonable persons affirm only reasonable doctrines, he notes that a reasonable doctrine can be affirmed in an unreasonable way but it is still reasonable if it can be affirmed in a reasonable way (ibid.: 60n). I think it is clearer to apply "reasonable" to believings but all I note here is that my notion of respectable overlaps Rawls' notion of reasonable.

8 We can easily cooperate with a believing that was arrived at foolishly but has acceptable content, such as when we cooperate with those who believe the message in a fortune cookie. And we can give pragmatic or pedagogical reasons for sometimes cooperating with the foolish decisions of co-workers or

children, at least when the foolishness is not dangerous. But I think one can also give moral reasons for sometimes cooperating with, say, a foolish order from a superior. My students who are nurses have given me a number of examples in which cooperation involved little risk to third parties whereas uncooperation would have caused significant harm. Of course, when significant risk to patients is involved, the appropriate attitude is probably uncooperation or even intolerance.

9 By "open-minded" I do not mean Gardner's (1992: 69) notion of entertaining a belief without either believing or disbelieving it. One can be open-minded toward a position one regards as wrong by trying carefully to understand it as possibly respectable.

10 In my two publications listed in the References (both of which overlap some of my discussion here concerning respect, tolerance, and cooperation), I argue that six (rather than eight) combinations are possible and plausible. I rejected as incoherent any combination involving intolerance and cooperation. I have become convinced that my rejection depends on debatable views concerning the identity and description of events and actions. A few years ago, Minneapolis police chief Tony Bouza regularly had his officers arrest his wife, Erica, when she would join war protesters blocking the driveways of the Honeywell Corporation. He would also cooperatively give her a ride from home to the protest site. I've always interpreted his stance as a combination of respect, intolerance, and uncooperation, much like that of a judge who admires the view of a conscientious objector but, as a judge, sends her to prison anyway. (Erica Bouza spent several weeks in the county workhouse.) However, others have insisted to me that they can give a description of such activities which combines intolerance and cooperation in a coherent way. Incidentally, that marriages such as the Bouzas' can both survive and even thrive has always struck me as confirming the wisdom of sometimes combining respect and intolerance.

11 This point is underscored in *Life's Dominion* (1993), Ronald Dworkin's recent analysis of the abortion dispute.

12 I thank Steve Evans, Rick Fairbanks, and Charles Taliaferro for giving helpful comments on an earlier draft of this paper. A version of this paper, with the title "Disagreement: Appreciating the Dark Side of Tolerance," was read at a conference on *Intolerance and Toleration* at Mary Washington College, November 5–7, 1993. It is scheduled to be published in the forthcoming Proceedings of the conference.

References

Benjamin, Martin. 1990. *Splitting the Difference: Compromise and Integrity in Ethics and Politics.* Lawrence: University Press of Kansas.

Cohen, Brenda. 1967. "An Ethical Paradox." *Mind* LXXVI (April): 250–9.

Dworkin, Ronald. 1993. *Life's Dominion.* New York: Alfred A. Knopf.

Edwards, David. 1988. "Toleration and Mill's Liberty of Thought and Discussion." In *Justifying Toleration*, ed. Susan Mendus. Cambridge: Cambridge University Press.

Fotion, Nick, and Gerard Elfstrom. 1992. *Toleration.* Tuscaloosa: University of Alabama Press.

Gardner, Peter. 1992. "Propositional Attitudes and Multicultural Education, or Believing Others are Mistaken." In *Toleration: Philosophy and Practice*, ed. John Horton and Peter Nicholson. Aldershot: Avebury.

Jackson, Jennifer. 1992. "Intolerance on the Campus." In *Toleration: Philosophy and Practice*, ed. John Horton and Peter Nicholson. Aldershot: Avebury.

Kach, N., and I. DeFaveri. 1987. "What Every Teacher Should Know About Multiculturalism." In *Contemporary Educational Issues: The Canadian Mosaic*, ed. L. L. Stewin and S. J. H. McCann. Toronto: Copp Clark Pitman.

Kordig, Carl R. 1982. "Concepts of Toleration." *Journal of Value Inquiry* 16: 59–66.

Langerak, Edward. 1989. "Values Education and Learning to Disagree." In *Values in Teaching and Professional Ethics*, ed. Carlton T. Mitchell. Mercer University Press.

——. 1989. *Christian Faith, Health, and Medical Practice.* Co-authored with Hessel Bouma, Douglas Diekema, Theodore Rottman, and Allen Verhey. Grand Rapids: Eerdmans Publishing Co.

Locke, John. 1983. *A Letter Concerning Toleration.* (First published 1689.) Trans. William Popple. Hackett Publishing Co.

Megone, Christopher. 1992. "Truth, the Autonomous Individual, and Toleration." In *Toleration: Philosophy and Practice*, ed. John Horton and Peter Nicholson. Aldershot: Avebury.

Mendus, Susan. 1989. *Toleration and the Limits of Liberalism.* Atlantic Highlands: Humanities Press.

Midgley, Mary. 1991. *Can't We Make Moral Judgments?* New York: St. Martin's Press.

——. 1981. *Heart and Mind.* New York: St. Martin's Press.

Mill, John Stuart. 1978. *On Liberty.* Hackett Publishing Co. (First published 1859.)

Nicholson, Peter. 1985. "Toleration as a Moral Ideal." In *Aspects of Toleration*, ed. John Horton and Susan Mendus. London: Methuen.

Popper, Karl. 1987. "Toleration and Intellectual Responsibility." In *On Toleration*, ed. Susan Mendus and David Edwards. Oxford: Clarendon Press.

Raphael, D. D. 1988. "The Intolerable." In *Justifying Toleration*, ed. Susan Mendus. Cambridge: Cambridge University Press.

Rawls, John. 1993. *Political Liberalism*. New York: Columbia University Press.

Rescher, Nicholas. 1978. "Philosophical Disagreement." *Review of Metaphysics* 32: 217–51.

Russell, Bertrand. 1930. *The Conquest of Happiness*. Garden City: Garden City Publishing Co.

Sherwin, Susan. 1992. *No Longer Patient*. Philadelphia: Temple University Press.

Warnock, Mary. 1987. "The Limits of Toleration." In *On Toleration*, ed. Susan Mendus and David Edwards. Oxford: Clarendon Press.

Wolff, Robert Paul, Barrington Moore, Jr., and Herbert Marcuse. 1969. *A Critique of Pure Tolerance*. Boston: Beacon Press.

38

A Modified Divine Command Theory of Ethical Wrongness

Robert Merrihew Adams

I

It is widely held that all those theories are indefensible which attempt to explain in terms of the will or commands of God what it is for an act to be ethically right or wrong. In this paper I shall state such a theory, which I believe to be defensible; and I shall try to defend it against what seem to me to be the most important and interesting objections to it. I call my theory a *modified* divine command theory because in it I renounce certain claims that are commonly made in divine command analyses of ethical terms. (I should add that it is *my* theory only in that I shall state it, and that I believe it is defensible – not that I am sure it is correct.) I present it as a theory of ethical *wrongness* partly for convenience. It could also be presented as a theory of the nature of ethical obligatoriness or of ethical permittedness. Indeed, I will have occasion to make some remarks about the concept of ethical permittedness. But as we shall see (in Section IV) I am not prepared to claim that the theory can be extended to all ethical terms; and it is therefore important that it not be presented as a theory about ethical terms in general.

It will be helpful to begin with the statement of a simple, *un*modified divine command theory of ethical wrongness. This is the theory that ethical

Robert Merrihew Adams, "A Modified Divine Command Theory of Ethical Wrongness," from G. Outka and J. R. Reeder (eds.), *Religion and Morality* (Garden City: Anchor Press, 1975), pp. 318–47.

wrongness *consists in* being contrary to God's commands, or that the word "wrong" in ethical contexts *means* "contrary to God's commands." It implies that the following two statement forms are logically equivalent.

(1) It is wrong (for A) to do X.
(2) It is contrary to God's commands (for A) to do X.

Of course that is not all that the theory implies. It also implies that (2) is conceptually prior to (1), so that the meaning of (1) is to be explained in terms of (2), and not the other way round. It might prove fairly difficult to state or explain in what that conceptual priority consists, but I shall not go into that here. I do not wish ultimately to defend the theory in its unmodified form, and I think I have stated it fully enough for my present purposes.

I have stated it as a theory about the meaning of the word "wrong" in ethical contexts. The most obvious objection to the theory is that the word "wrong" is used in ethical contexts by many people who cannot mean by it what the theory says they must mean, since they do not believe that there exists a God. This objection seems to me sufficient to refute the theory if it is presented as an analysis of what *everybody* means by "wrong" in ethical contexts. The theory cannot reasonably be offered except as a theory about what the word "wrong" means as used by *some but not all* people in ethical contexts. Let us say that the theory offers an analysis of the meaning of "wrong" in Judeo-Christian religious ethical discourse. This restriction of scope will apply to my modified divine command theory too. This restriction obviously gives rise to a possible objection. Isn't it more plausible to suppose that Judeo-Christian believers use "wrong" with the same meaning as other people do? This problem will be discussed in Section VI.

In Section II, I will discuss what seems to me the most important objection to the unmodified divine command theory, and suggest how the theory can be modified to meet it. Section III will be devoted to a brief but fairly comprehensive account of the use of "wrong" in Judeo-Christian ethical discourse, from the point of view of the modified divine command theory. The theory will be further elaborated in dealing with objections in Sections IV to VI. In a seventh and final section, I will note some problems arising from unresolved issues in the general theory of analysis and meaning, and briefly discuss their bearing on the modified divine command theory.

II

The following seems to me to be the gravest objection to the divine command theory of ethical wrongness, in the form in which I have stated it. Suppose God should command me to make it my chief end in life to inflict suffering on other human beings, for no other reason than that He commanded it. (For convenience I shall abbreviate this hypothesis to "Suppose God should command cruelty for its own sake.") Will it seriously be claimed that in that case it would be wrong for me not to practice cruelty for its own sake? I see three possible answers to this question.

(1) It might be claimed that it is logically impossible for God to command cruelty for its own sake. In that case, of course, we need not worry about whether it would be wrong to disobey if He did command it. It is senseless to agonize about what one should do in a logically impossible situation. This solution to the problem seems unlikely to be available to the divine command theorist, however. For why would he hold that it is logically impossible for God to command cruelty for its own sake? Some theologians (for instance, Thomas Aquinas) have believed (a) that what is right and wrong is independent of God's will, *and* (b) that God always does right by the necessity of His nature. Such theologians, if they believe that it would be wrong for God to command cruelty for its own sake, have reason to believe that it is logically

impossible for Him to do so. But the divine command theorist, who does not agree that what is right and wrong is independent of God's will, does not seem to have such a reason to deny that it is logically possible for God to command cruelty for its own sake.

(2) Let us assume that it is logically possible for God to command cruelty for its own sake. In that case the divine command theory seems to imply that it would be wrong not to practice cruelty for its own sake. There have been at least a few adherents of divine command ethics who have been prepared to accept this consequence. William Ockham held that those acts which we call "theft," "adultery," and "hatred of God" would be meritorious if God had commanded them.[1] He would surely have said the same about what I have been calling the practice of "cruelty for its own sake."

This position is one which I suspect most of us are likely to find somewhat shocking, even repulsive. We should therefore be particularly careful not to misunderstand it. We need not imagine that Ockham disciplined himself to be ready to practice cruelty for its own sake if God should command it. It was doubtless an article of faith for him that God is unalterably opposed to any such practice. The mere logical possibility that theft, adultery, and cruelty might have been commanded by God (and therefore meritorious) doubtless did not represent in Ockham's view any real possibility.

(3) Nonetheless, the view that if God commanded cruelty for its own sake it would be wrong not to practice it seems unacceptable to me; and I think many, perhaps most, other Jewish and Christian believers would find it unacceptable too. I must make clear the sense in which I find it unsatisfactory. It is not that I find an internal inconsistency in it. And I would not deny that it may reflect, accurately enough, the way in which some believers use the word "wrong." I might as well frankly avow that I am looking for a divine command theory which at least might possibly be a correct account of how *I* use the word "wrong." I do not use the word "wrong" in such a way that I would say that it would be wrong not to practice cruelty if God commanded it, and I am sure that many other believers agree with me on this point.

But now have I not rejected the divine command theory? I have assumed that it would be logically possible for God to command cruelty for its own sake. And I have rejected the view that if God commanded cruelty for its own sake, it would be wrong not to obey. It seems to follow that I am

Robert Merrihew Adams

committed to the view that in certain logically possible circumstances it would not be wrong to disobey God. This position seems to be inconsistent with the theory that "wrong" means "contrary to God's commands."

I want to argue, however, that it is still open to me to accept a modified form of the divine command theory of ethical wrongness. According to the modified divine command theory, when I say, "It is wrong to do X," (at least part of) what I *mean* is that it is contrary to God's commands to do X. "It is wrong to do X" *implies* "It is contrary to God's commands to do X." But "It is contrary to God's commands to do X" implies "It is wrong to do X" only if certain conditions are assumed – namely, only if it is assumed that God has the character which I believe Him to have, of loving His human creatures. If God were really to command us to make cruelty our goal, then He would not have that character of loving us, and I would not say it would be wrong to disobey Him.

But do I say that it would be wrong to obey Him in such a case? This is the point at which I am in danger of abandoning the divine command theory completely. I do abandon it completely if I say both of the following things.

(A) It would be wrong to obey God if He commanded cruelty for its own sake.
(B) In (A), "wrong" is used in what is for me its normal ethical sense.

If I assert both (A) and (B), it is clear that I cannot consistently maintain that "wrong" in its normal ethical sense for me means or implies "contrary to God's commands."

But from the fact that I deny that it would be wrong to disobey God if He commanded cruelty for its own sake, it does not follow that I must accept (A) and (B). Of course someone might claim that obedience and disobedience would both be ethically permitted in such a case; but that is not the view that I am suggesting. If I adopt the modified divine command theory as an analysis of my present concept of ethical wrongness (and if I adopt a similar analysis of my concept of ethical permittedness), I will not hold either that it would be wrong to disobey, or that it would be ethically permitted to disobey, or that it would be wrong to obey, or that it would be ethically permitted to obey, if God commanded cruelty for its own sake. For I will say that my concept of ethical wrongness (and my concept of ethical permittedness) would

"break down" if I really believed that God commanded cruelty for its own sake. Or to put the matter somewhat more prosaically, I will say that my concepts of ethical wrongness and permittedness could not serve the functions they now serve, because using those concepts I could not call any action ethically wrong or ethically permitted, if I believed that God's will was so unloving. This position can be explained or developed in either of two ways, each of which has its advantages.

I could say that by "X is ethically wrong" I mean "X is contrary to the commands of a *loving* God" (i.e., "There is a *loving* God and X is contrary to His commands") and by "X is ethically permitted" I mean "X is in accord with the commands of a *loving* God" (i.e., "There is a *loving* God and X is not contrary to His commands"). On this analysis we can reason as follows. If there is only one God and He commands cruelty for its own sake, then presumably there is not a *loving* God. If there is not a loving God then neither "X is ethically wrong" nor "X is ethically permitted" is true of any X. Using my present concepts of ethical wrongness and permittedness, therefore, I could not (consistently) call any action ethically wrong or permitted if I believed that God commanded cruelty for its own sake. This way of developing the modified divine command theory is the simpler and neater of the two, and that might reasonably lead one to choose it for the construction of a theological ethical theory. On the other hand, I think it is also simpler and neater than ordinary religious ethical discourse, in which (for example) it may be felt that the statement that a certain act is wrong is *about* the will or commands of God in a way in which it is not about His love.

In this essay I shall prefer a second, rather similar, but somewhat untidier, understanding of the modified divine command theory, because I think it may lead us into some insights about the complexities of actual religious ethical discourse. According to this second version of the theory, the statement that something is ethically wrong (or permitted) says something about the will or commands of God, but not about His love. Every such statement, however, *presupposes* that certain conditions for the applicability of the believer's concepts of ethical right and wrong are satisfied. Among these conditions is that God does not command cruelty for its own sake – or, more generally, that God loves His human creatures. It need not be assumed that God's love is the only such condition.

The modified divine command theorist can say that the possibility of God commanding cruelty for its own sake is not provided for in the Judeo-Christian religious ethical system as he understands it. The possibility is not provided for, in the sense that the concepts of right and wrong have not been developed in such a way that actions could be correctly said to be right or wrong if God were believed to command cruelty for its own sake. The modified divine command theorist agrees that it is logically possible[2] that God should command cruelty for its own sake; but he holds that it is unthinkable that God should do so. To have *faith* in God is not just to believe that He exists, but also to trust in His love for mankind. The believer's concepts of ethical wrongness and permittedness are developed within the framework of his (or the religious community's) religious life, and therefore within the framework of the assumption that God loves us. The concept of the will or commands of God has a certain function in the believer's life, and the use of the words "right" (in the sense of "ethically permitted") and "wrong" is tied to that function of that concept. But one of the reasons why the concept of the will of God can function as it does is that the love which God is believed to have toward men arouses in the believer certain attitudes of love toward God and devotion to His will. If the believer thinks about the unthinkable but logically possible situation in which God commands cruelty for its own sake, he finds that in relation to that kind of command of God he cannot take up the same attitude, and that the concept of the will or commands of God could not then have the same function in his life. For this reason he will not say that it would be wrong to disobey God, or right to obey Him, in that situation. At the same time he will not say that it would be wrong to obey God in that situation, because he is accustomed to use the word "wrong" to say that something is contrary to the will of God, and it does not seem to him to be the right word to use to express his own personal revulsion toward an act against which there would be no divine authority. Similarly, he will not say that it would be "right," in the sense of "ethically permitted," to disobey God's command of cruelty; for that does not seem to him to be the right way to express his own personal attitude toward an act which would not be in accord with a divine authority. In this way the believer's concepts of ethical rightness and wrongness would break down in the situation in which he believed that God commanded cruelty for

its own sake – that is, they would not function as they now do, because he would not be prepared to use them to say that any action was right or wrong.

III

It is clear that according to this modified divine command theory, the meaning of the word "wrong" in Judeo-Christian ethical discourse must be understood in terms of a complex of relations which believers' use of the word has, not only to their beliefs about God's commands, but also to their attitudes toward certain types of action. I think it will help us to understand the theory better if we can give a brief but fairly comprehensive description of the most important features of the Judeo-Christian ethical use of "wrong," from the point of view of the modified divine command theory. That is what I shall try to do in this section.

(1) "Wrong" and "contrary to God's commands" at least contextually imply each other in Judeo-Christian ethical discourse. "It is wrong to do X" will be assented to by the sincere Jewish or Christian believer if and only if he assents to "It is contrary to God's commands to do X." This is a fact sufficiently well known that the known believer who says the one commits himself publicly to the other.

Indeed "wrong" and such expressions as "against the will of God" seem to be used interchangeably in religious ethical discourse. If a believer asks his pastor, "Do you think it's always against the will of God to use contraceptives?" and the pastor replies, "I don't see anything wrong with the use of contraceptives in many cases," the pastor has answered the same question the inquirer asked.

(2) In ethical contexts, the statement that a certain action is wrong normally expresses certain volitional and emotional attitudes toward that action. In particular it normally expresses an intention, or at least an inclination, not to perform the action, and/or dispositions to feel guilty if one has performed it, to discourage others from performing it, and to react with anger, sorrow, or diminished respect toward others if they have performed it. I think this is true of Judeo-Christian ethical discourse as well as of other ethical discourse.

The interchangeability of "wrong" and "against the will of God" applies in full force here. It seems to make no difference to the expressive function of an ethical statement in a Judeo-Christian context which of these expressions is used. So far as

I can see, the feelings and dispositions normally expressed by "It is wrong to commit suicide" in a Judeo-Christian context are exactly the same as those normally expressed by "It is against God's will to commit suicide," or by "Suicide is a violation of the commandments of God."

I am speaking of attitudes *normally* expressed by statements that it is wrong to do a certain thing, or that it would be against God's will or commands to do that thing. I am not claiming that such attitudes are *always* expressed by statements of those sorts. Neither am I now suggesting any analysis of the *meaning* of the statements in terms of the attitudes they normally express. The relation between the meaning of the statements and the attitudes expressed is a matter about which I shall have somewhat more to say, later in this section and in Section VI. At this point I am simply observing that in fact statements of the forms "It is wrong to do X," "It is against God's will to do X," "X is a violation of the commandments of God," normally do express certain attitudes, and that in Judeo-Christian ethical discourse they all typically express the same attitudes.

Of course these attitudes can be specified only within certain very wide limits of normality. The experience of guilt, for instance, or the feelings that one has about conduct of others of which one disapproves, vary greatly from one individual to another, and in the same individual from one occasion to another.

(3)   In a Judeo-Christian context, moreover, the attitudes expressed by a statement that something is wrong are normally quite strongly affected and colored by specifically religious feelings and interests. They are apt to be motivated in various degrees by, and mixed in various proportions with, love, devotion, and loyalty toward God, and/or fear of God. Ethical wrongdoing is seen and experienced as *sin*, as rupture of personal or communal relationship with God. The normal feelings and experience of guilt for Judeo-Christian believers surely cannot be separated from beliefs, and ritual and devotional practices, having to do with God's judgment and forgiveness.

In all sin there is offense against a person (God), even when there is no offense against any other human person – for instance, if I have a vice which harms me but does not importantly harm any other human being. Therefore in the Judeo-Christian tradition reactions which are appropriate when one has offended another person are felt to be appropriate reactions to any ethical fault, regardless of whether another human being has been offended. I think this affects rather importantly the emotional connections of the word "wrong" in Judeo-Christian discourse.

(4)   When a Judeo-Christian believer is trying to decide, in an ethical way, whether it would be wrong for him to do a certain thing, he typically thinks of himself as trying to determine whether it would be against God's will for him to do it. His deliberations may turn on the interpretation of certain religiously authoritative texts. They may be partly carried out in the form of prayer. It is quite possible, however, that his deliberations will take forms more familiar to the nonbeliever. Possibly his theology will encourage him to give some weight to his own intuitions and feelings about the matter, and those of other people. Such encouragement might be provided, for instance, by a doctrine of the leading of the Holy Spirit. Probably the believer will accept certain very general ethical principles as expressing commandments of God, and most of these may be principles which many nonbelievers would also accept (for instance, that it is always, or with very few exceptions, wrong to kill another human being). The believer's deliberation might consist entirely of reasoning from such general principles. But he would still regard it as an attempt to discover God's will on the matter.

(5)   Typically, the Judeo-Christian believer is a nonnaturalist objectivist about ethical wrongness. When he says that something is (ethically) wrong, he means to be stating what he believes to be a fact of a certain sort – what I shall call a "nonnatural objective fact." Such a fact is objective in the sense that whether it obtains or not does not depend on whether any human being thinks it does. It is harder to give a satisfactory explanation of what I mean by "nonnatural" here. Let us say that a nonnatural fact is one which does not consist simply in any fact or complex of facts which can be stated entirely in the languages of physics, chemistry, biology, and human psychology. That way of putting it obviously raises questions which it leaves unanswered, but I hope it may be clear enough for present purposes.

That ethical facts are objective and nonnatural has been believed by many people, including some famous philosophers – for instance, Plato and G. E. Moore. The term "nonnaturalism" is sometimes used rather narrowly, to refer to a position held by Moore, and positions closely resembling it. Clearly, I am using "nonnaturalist" in a broader sense here.

Given that the facts of wrongness asserted in Judeo-Christian ethics are nonnatural in the sense explained above, and that they accordingly do not consist entirely in facts of physics, chemistry, biology, and human psychology, the question arises, in what they do consist. According to the divine command theory (even the modified divine command theory), in so far as they are nonnatural and objective, they consist in facts about the will or commands of God. I think this is really the central point in a divine command theory of ethical wrongness. This is the point at which the divine command theory is distinguished from alternative theological theories of ethical wrongness, such as the theory that facts of ethical rightness and wrongness are objective, nonnatural facts about ideas or essences subsisting eternally in God's understanding, not subject to His will but guiding it.

The divine command account of the nonnatural fact-stating function of Judeo-Christian ethical discourse has at least one advantage over its competitors. It is clear, I think, that in stating that X is wrong a believer normally commits himself to the view that X is contrary to the will or commands of God. And the fact (if it is a fact) that X is contrary to the will or commands of God is surely a nonnatural objective fact. But it is not nearly so clear that in saying that X is wrong, the believer normally commits himself to belief in any *other* nonnatural objective fact. (The preceding sentence presupposes the rejection of the Moorean view that the fact that X is wrong[3] is an objective nonnatural fact which cannot and should not be analyzed in terms of other facts, natural or nonnatural.)

(6)   The modified divine command theorist cannot consistently claim that "wrong" and "contrary to God's commands" have exactly the same meaning for him. For he admits that there is a logically possible situation which he would describe by saying, "God commands cruelty for its own sake," but not by saying, "It would be wrong not to practice cruelty for its own sake." If there were not at least some little difference between the meanings with which he actually, normally uses the expressions "wrong" and "contrary to God's commands," there would be no reason for them to differ in their applicability or inapplicability to the far-out unthinkable case. We may now be in a position to improve somewhat our understanding of what the modified divine command theorist can suppose that difference in meaning to be, and of why he supposes that the believer is unwilling to say that disobedience to a divine command of cruelty for its own sake would be wrong.

We have seen that the expressions "It is wrong" and "It is contrary to God's commands" or "It is against the will of God" have virtually the same uses in religious ethical discourse, and the same functions in the religious ethical life. No doubt they differ slightly in the situations in which they are most likely to be used and the emotional overtones they are most apt to carry. But in all situations experienced or expected by the believer as a believer they at least contextually imply each other, and normally express the same or extremely similar emotional and volitional attitudes.

There is also a difference in meaning, however, a difference which is normally of no practical importance. All three of the following are aspects of the normal use of "it is wrong" in the life and conversation of believers. (a) It is used to state what are believed to be facts about the will or commands of God. (b) It is used in formulating decisions and arguments about what to do (i.e., not just in deciding what one *ought* to do, but in deciding *what to do*). (c) It expresses certain emotional and volitional attitudes toward the action under discussion. "It is wrong" is commonly used to do all three of those things at once.

The same is true of "It is contrary to God's commands" and "It is against the will of God." They are commonly used by believers to do the same three things, and to do them at once. But because of their grammatical form and their formal relationships with other straightforwardly descriptive expressions about God, they are taken to be, first and last, descriptive expressions about God and His relation to whatever actions are under discussion. They can therefore be used to state what are supposed to be facts about God, even when one's emotional and decision-making attitude toward those supposed facts is quite contrary to the attitudes normally expressed by the words "against the will of God."

In the case of "It is wrong," however, it is not clear that one of its functions, or one of the aspects of its normal use, is to be preferred in case of conflict with the others. I am not willing to say, "It would be wrong not to do X," when both my own attitude and the attitude of most other people toward the doing of X under the indicated circumstances is one of unqualified revulsion. On the other hand, neither am I willing to say, "It would be wrong to do X," when I would merely be expressing my own personal revulsion (and perhaps that of other people as well) but nothing that I could regard as clothed in the majesty of a divine authority. The believer's concept of ethical wrongness therefore breaks down if one tries to apply it to the unthinkable case in which God commands cruelty for its own sake.

None of this seems to me inconsistent with the claim that part of what the believer normally means in saying "X is wrong" is that X is contrary to God's will or commands.

IV

The modified divine command theory clearly conceives of believers as valuing some things independently of their relation to God's commands. If the believer will not say that it would be wrong not to practice cruelty for its own sake if God commanded it, that is because he values kindness, and has a revulsion for cruelty, in a way that is at least to some extent independent of his belief that God commands kindness and forbids cruelty. This point may be made the basis of both philosophical and theological objections to the modified divine command theory, but I think the objections can be answered.

The philosophical objection is, roughly, that if there are some things I value independently of their relation to God's commands, then my value concepts cannot rightly be analyzed in terms of God's commands. According to the modified divine command theory, the acceptability of divine command ethics depends in part on the believer's independent positive valuation of the sorts of things that God is believed to command. But then, the philosophical critic objects, the believer must have a prior, nontheological conception of ethical right and wrong, in terms of which he judges God's commandments to be acceptable – and to admit that the believer has a prior, nontheological conception of ethical right and wrong is to abandon the divine command theory.

The weakness of this philosophical objection is that it fails to note the distinctions that can be drawn among various value concepts. From the fact that the believer values some things independently of his beliefs about God's commands, the objector concludes, illegitimately, that the believer must have a conception of ethical right and wrong that is independent of his beliefs about God's commands. This inference is illegitimate because there can be valuations which do not imply or presuppose a judgment of ethical right or wrong. For instance, I may simply like something, or want something, or feel a revulsion at something.

What the modified divine command theorist will hold, then, is that the believer values some things independently of their relation to God's commands, but that these valuations are not judgments of ethical right and wrong and do not of themselves imply judgments of ethical right and wrong. He will maintain, on the other hand, that such independent valuations are involved in, or even necessary for, judgments of ethical right and wrong which also involve beliefs about God's will or commands. The adherent of a divine command ethics will normally be able to give reasons for his adherence. Such reasons might include: "Because I am grateful to God for His love"; "Because I find it the most satisfying form of ethical life"; "Because there's got to be an objective moral law if life isn't to fall to pieces, and I can't understand what it would be if not the will of God."[4] As we have already noted, the modified divine command theorist also has reasons why he would not accept a divine command ethics in certain logically possible situations which he believes not to be actual. All of these reasons seem to me to involve valuations that are independent of divine command ethics. The person who has such reasons wants certain things – happiness, certain satisfactions – for himself and others; he hates cruelty and loves kindness; he has perhaps a certain unique and "numinous" awe of God. And these are not attitudes which he has simply because of his beliefs about God's commands.[5] They are not attitudes, however, which presuppose judgments of moral right and wrong.

It is sometimes objected to divine command theories of moral obligation, or of ethical rightness and wrongness, that one must have some reason for obeying God's commands or for adopting a divine command ethics, and that therefore a nontheological concept of moral obligation or of ethical rightness and wrongness must be presupposed, in order that one may judge that one ought to obey God's commands.[6] This objection is groundless. For one can certainly have reasons for doing something which do not involve believing one morally ought to do it or believing it would be ethically wrong not to do it.

I grant that in giving reasons for his attitudes toward God's commands the believer will probably use or presuppose concepts which, in the context, it is reasonable to count as nontheological value concepts (e.g., concepts of satisfactoriness and repulsiveness). Perhaps some of them might count as moral concepts. But all that the defender of a divine command theory of ethical wrongness has to maintain is that the concept of ethical wrongness which occurs in the ethical thought and discourse of believers is not one of the concepts which are used or presupposed in this way. Divine command theorists, including the modified divine command theorist, need not maintain that *all* value concepts, or even all moral concepts, must be understood in terms of God's commands.

In fact some well-known philosophers have held forms of divine command theory which quite explicitly presuppose some nontheological value concepts. Locke, for instance, says in his *Essay*,

> Good and evil . . . are nothing but pleasure or pain, or that which occasions or procures pleasure or pain to us. *Morally good and evil*, then, is only the conformity or disagreement of our voluntary actions to some law, whereby good or evil is drawn on us from the will and power of the law-maker. (*Essay*, II.xxviii.5)[7]

Locke goes on to distinguish three laws, or types of law, by reference to which actions are commonly judged as to moral good and evil: "(1) The *divine* law. (2) The *civil* law. (3) The law of *opinion* or *reputation*, if I may so call it" (*Essay*, II.xxviii.7). Of these three, Locke says that the third is "the common *measure of virtue and vice*" (*Essay*, II.xxviii.11). In Locke's opinion the terms "virtue" and "vice" are particularly closely attached to the praise and blame of society. But the terms "duty" and "sin" are connected with the commandments of God. About the divine law Locke says,

> This is the only true touchstone of *moral rectitude*; and by comparing them to this law, it is that men judge of the most considerable *moral good* or *evil* of their actions: that is, whether, as *duties* or *sins*, they are like to procure them happiness or misery from the hands of the ALMIGHTY. (*Essay*, II.xxviii.8)

The structure of Locke's analysis is clear enough. By "good" and "evil" we *mean* (nontheologically enough) pleasurable and painful. By "morally good" and "morally evil" we *mean* that the actions so described agree or disagree with some law under which the agent stands to be rewarded or punished. By "duty" and "sin," which denote the most important sort of moral good and evil, we *mean* (theologically now) actions which are apt to cause the agent good or evil (in the nontheological sense) because they agree or disagree with the law of God. I take it that the divine command theory advocated by Peter

Geach,[8] and hinted at by Miss Anscombe,[9] is similar in structure, though not in all details, to Locke's.

The modified divine command theory that I have in mind does not rely as heavily as Locke's theory does on God's power to reward and punish, nor do I wish to assume Locke's analysis of "good" and "evil." The point I want to make by discussing Locke here is just that there are many different value concepts and it is clearly possible to give one or more of them a theological analysis while giving others a nontheological analysis. And I do assume that the modified divine command theorist will give a nontheological analysis of some value concepts although he gives a theological analysis of the concept of ethical wrongness. For instance, he may give a nontheological analysis, perhaps a naturalistic one or a noncognitivist one, of the meaning of "satisfactory" and "repulsive," as he uses them in some contexts. He may even regard as *moral* concepts some value concepts of which he gives a nontheological analysis.

For it is not essential to a divine command theory of ethical wrongness to maintain that all valuing, or all value concepts, or even all moral concepts, depend on beliefs about God's commands. What is essential to such a theory is to maintain that when a believer says something is (ethically) *wrong*, at least part of what he means is that the action in question is contrary to God's will or commands. Another way of putting the matter is this. What depends on beliefs about God and His will is: not all of the religious person's value concepts, nor in general his ability to value things, but only his ability to appraise actions (and possible actions) in terms of their relation to a superhuman, nonnaturally objective, law. Indeed, it is obvious that Judeo-Christian ethics presupposes concepts that have at least ethical overtones and that are not essentially theological but have their background in human social relations and political institutions – such as the concepts of promise, kindness, law, and command. What the specifically theological doctrines introduce into Judeo-Christian ethics, according to the divine command theory, is the belief in a law that is superior to all human laws.

This version of the divine command theory may seem *theologically* objectionable to some believers. One of the reasons, surely, why divine command theories of ethics have appealed to some theologians is that such theories seem especially congruous with the religious demand that God be the object of our highest allegiance. If our supreme commitment in life is to doing what is right just because it is right, and if what is right is right just because God wills or commands it, then surely our highest allegiance is to God. But the modified divine command theory seems not to have this advantage. For the modified divine command theorist is forced to admit, as we have seen, that he has reasons for his adherence to a divine command ethics, and that his having these reasons implies that there are some things which he values independently of his beliefs about God's commands. It is therefore not correct to say of him that he is committed to doing the will of God *just* because it is the will of God; he is committed to doing it partly because of other things which he values independently. Indeed it appears that there are certain logically possible situations in which his present attitudes would not commit him to obey God's commands (for instance, if God commanded cruelty for its own sake). This may even suggest that he values some things, not just independently of God's commands, but more than God's commands.

We have here a real problem in religious ethical motivation. The Judeo-Christian believer is supposed to make God the supreme focus of his loyalties; that is clear. One possible interpretation of this fact is the following. Obedience to whatever God may command is (or at least ought to be) the one thing that the believer values for its own sake and more than anything and everything else. Anything else that he values, he values (or ought to) only to a lesser degree and as a means to obedience to God. This conception of religious ethical motivation is obviously favorable to an *un*modified divine command theory of ethical wrongness.

But I think it is not a realistic conception. Loyalty to God, for instance, is very often explained, by believers themselves, as motivated by gratitude for benefits conferred. And I think it is clear in most cases that the gratitude presupposes that the benefits are valued, at least to some extent, independently of loyalty to God. Similarly, I do not think that most devout Judeo-Christian believers would say that it would be wrong to disobey God if He commanded cruelty for its own sake. And if I am right about that I think it shows that their positive valuation of (emotional/volitional pro-attitude toward) doing *whatever* God may command is not clearly greater than their independent negative valuation of cruelty.

In analyzing ethical motivation in general, as well as Judeo-Christian ethical motivation in particular, it is probably a mistake to suppose that there is (or can be expected to be) only one thing that is valued supremely and for its own sake, with nothing else being valued independently of it. The motivation for a person's ethical orientation in life is normally much more complex than that, and involves a plurality of emotional and volitional attitudes of different sorts which are at least partly independent of each other. At any rate, I think the modified divine command theorist is bound to say that that is true of his ethical motivation.

In what sense, then, can the modified divine command theorist maintain that God is the supreme focus of his loyalties? I suggest the following interpretation of the single-hearted loyalty to God which is demanded in Judeo-Christian religion. In this interpretation the crucial idea is *not* that some one thing is valued for its own sake and more than anything else, and nothing else valued independently of it. It is freely admitted that the religious person will have a plurality of motives for his ethical position, and that these will be at least partly independent of each other. It is admitted further that a desire to obey the commands of God (*whatever* they may be) may not be the strongest of these motives. What will be claimed is that certain beliefs about God enable the believer to integrate or focus his motives in a loyalty to God and His commands. Some of these beliefs are about what God commands or wills (contingently – that is, although He could logically have commanded or willed something else instead).

Some of the motives in question might be called egoistic; they include desires for satisfactions for oneself – which God is believed to have given or to be going to give. Other motives may be desires for satisfaction for other people; these may be called altruistic. Still other motives might not be desires for anyone's satisfaction, but might be valuations of certain kinds of action for their own sakes; these might be called idealistic. I do not think my argument depends heavily on this particular classification, but it seems plausible that all of these types, and perhaps others as well, might be distinguished among the motives for a religious person's ethical position. Obviously such motives might pull one in different directions, conflicting with one another. But in Judeo-Christian ethics beliefs about what God does in fact will (although He could have willed otherwise) are supposed to enable one to *fuse* these motives, so to speak, into one's devotion to God and His will, so that they all pull together. Doubtless the believer will still have some motives which conflict with his loyalty to God. But the religious ideal is that these should all be merely momentary desires and impulses, and kept under control. They ought not to be allowed to influence voluntary action. The deeper, more stable, and controlling desires, intentions, and psychic energies are supposed to be fused in devotion to God. As I interpret it, however, it need not be inconsistent with the Judeo-Christian ethical and religious ideal that this fusion of motives, this integration of moral energies, depends on belief in certain propositions which are taken to be contingent truths about God.

Lest it be thought that I am proposing unprecedented theological positions, or simply altering Judeo-Christian religious beliefs to suit my theories, I will call to my aid on this point a theologian known for his insistence on the sovereignty of God. Karl Barth seems to me to hold a divine command theory of ethics. But when he raises the question of why we should obey God, he rejects with scorn the suggestion that God's *power* provides the basis for His claim on us. "By deciding for God [man] has definitely decided not to be obedient to power as power."[10] God's claim on us is based rather on His grace. "God calls us and orders us and claims us by being gracious to us in Jesus Christ."[11] I do not mean to suggest that Barth would agree with everything I have said about motivation, or that he offers a lucid account of a divine command theory. But he does agree with the position I have proposed on this point, that the believer's loyalty is not to be construed as a loyalty to God *as* allpowerful, nor to God *whatever* He might conceivably have willed. It is a loyalty to God *as* having a certain attitude toward us, a certain will for us, which God was free not to have, but to which, in Barth's view, He has committed Himself irrevocably in Jesus Christ. The believer's devotion is not to merely possible commands of God as such, but to God's actual (and gracious) will.

V

The ascription of moral qualities to God is commonly thought to cause problems for divine command theories of ethics. It is doubted that God, as an agent, can properly be called "good" in the moral sense if He is not subject to a moral law that is not of His own making. For if He is morally good, mustn't He do what is right *because* it is right? And how can He do that, if what's right is right because He wills it? Or it may be charged that divine command theories trivialize the claim that God is good. If "X is (morally) good" means roughly "X does what God wills," then "God is (morally) good"

means only that God does what He wills – which is surely much less than people are normally taken to mean when they say that God is (morally) good. In this section I will suggest an answer to these objections.

Surely no analysis of Judeo-Christian ethical discourse can be regarded as adequate which does not provide for a sense in which the believer can seriously assert that God is good. Indeed an adequate analysis should provide a plausible account of what believers do in fact mean when they say, "God is good." I believe that a divine command theory of ethical (rightness and) wrongness can include such an account. I will try to indicate its chief features.

(1) In saying "God is good" one is normally expressing a favorable emotional attitude toward God. I shall not try to determine whether or not this is part of the meaning of "God is good"; but it is normally, perhaps almost always, at least one of the things one is doing if one says that God is good. If we were to try to be more precise about the type of favorable emotional attitude normally expressed by "God is good," I suspect we would find that the attitude expressed is most commonly one of *gratitude*.

(2) This leads to a second point, which is that when God is called "good" it is very often meant that He is *good to us*, or *good to* the speaker. "Good" is sometimes virtually a synonym for "kind." And for the modified divine command theorist it is not a trivial truth that God is kind. In saying that God is good in the sense of "kind," one presupposes, of course, that there are some things which the beneficiaries of God's goodness value. We need not discuss here whether the beneficiaries must value them independently of their beliefs about God's will. For the modified divine command theorist does admit that there are some things which believers value independently of their beliefs about God's commands. Nothing that the modified divine command theorist says about the meaning of ("right" and) "wrong" implies that it is a trivial truth that God bestows on His creatures things that they value.

(3) I would not suggest that the descriptive force of "good" as applied to God is exhausted by the notion of kindness. "God is good" must be taken in many contexts as ascribing to God, rather generally, qualities of character which the believing speaker regards as virtues in human beings. Among such qualities might be faithfulness, ethical consistency, a forgiving disposition, and, in general, various aspects of love, as well as kindness. Not that

there is some definite list of qualities, the ascription of which to God is clearly implied by the claim that God is good. But saying that God is good normally commits one to the position that God has some important set of qualities which one regards as virtues in human beings.

(4) It will not be thought that God has *all* the qualities which are virtues in human beings. Some such qualities are logically inapplicable to a being such as God is supposed to be. For example, aside from certain complications arising from the doctrine of the incarnation, it would be logically inappropriate to speak of God as controlling His sexual desires. (He doesn't have any.) And given some widely held conceptions of God and His relation to the world, it would hardly make sense to speak of Him as *courageous*. For if He is impassible and has predetermined absolutely everything that happens, He has no risks to face and cannot endure (because He cannot suffer) pain or displeasure.[12]

Believers in God's goodness also typically think He lacks some human virtues which would *not* be logically inapplicable to a being like Him. A virtuous man, for instance, does not intentionally cause the death of other human beings, except under exceptional circumstances. But God has intentionally brought it about that all men die. There are agonizing forms of the problem of evil; but I think that for most Judeo-Christian believers (especially those who believe in life after death), this is not one of them. They believe that God's making men mortal and His commanding them not to kill each other, fit together in a larger pattern of harmonious purposes. How then can one distinguish between human virtues which God must have if He is good and human virtues which God may lack and still be good? This is an interesting and important question, but I will not attempt here to formulate a precise or adequate criterion for making the distinction. I fear it would require a lengthy digression from the issues with which we are principally concerned.

(5) If we accept a divine command theory of ethical rightness and wrongness, I think we shall have to say that *dutifulness* is a human virtue which, like sexual chastity, is logically inapplicable to God. God cannot either do or fail to do His duty, since He does not have a duty – at least not in the most important sense in which human beings have a duty. For He is not subject to a moral law not of His own making. Dutifulness is one virtuous disposition which men can have that God cannot have. But there are other virtuous dispositions which God

can have as well as men. Love, for instance. It hardly makes sense to say that God does what He does *because* it is right. But it does not follow that God cannot have any reason for doing what He does. It does not even follow that He cannot have reasons of a type on which it would be morally virtuous for a man to act. For example, He might do something because He knew it would make His creatures happier.

(6) The modified divine command theorist must deny that in calling God "good" one presupposes a standard of moral rightness and wrongness superior to the will of God, by reference to which it is determined whether God's character is virtuous or not. And I think he can consistently deny that. He can say that morally virtuous and vicious qualities of character are those which agree and conflict, respectively, with God's commands, and that it is their agreement or disagreement with God's commands that makes them virtuous or vicious. But the believer normally thinks he has at least a general idea of what qualities of character are in fact virtuous and vicious (approved and disapproved by God). Having such an idea, he can apply the word "good" descriptively to God, meaning that (with some exceptions, as I have noted) God has the qualities which the believer regards as virtues, such as faithfulness and kindness.

I will sum up by contrasting what the believer can mean when he says, "Moses is good," with what he can mean when he says, "God is good," according to the modified divine command theory. When the believer says, "Moses is good," (a) he normally is expressing a favorable emotional attitude toward Moses – normally, though perhaps not always. (Sometimes a person's moral goodness displeases us.) (b) He normally implies that Moses possesses a large proportion of those qualities of character which are recognized in the religious-ethical community as virtues, and few if any of those which are regarded as vices. (c) He normally implies that the qualities of Moses' character on the basis of which he describes Moses as good are qualities approved by God.

When the believer says, "God is good," (a) he normally is expressing a favorable emotional attitude toward God – and I think exceptions on this point would be rarer than in the case of statements that a man is good. (b) He normally is ascribing to God certain qualities of character. He may mean primarily that God is kind or benevolent, that He is *good* to human beings or certain ones of them. Or he may mean that God possesses (with some exceptions) those qualities of character which are regarded as virtues in the religious-ethical community. (c) Whereas in saying, "Moses is good," the believer was stating or implying that the qualities of character which he was ascribing to Moses conform to a standard of ethical rightness which is independent of the will of Moses, he is not stating or implying that the qualities of character which he ascribes to God conform to a standard of ethical rightness which is independent of the will of God.

VI

As I noted at the outset, the divine command theory of ethical wrongness, even in its modified form, has the consequence that believers and nonbelievers use the word "wrong" with different meanings in ethical contexts, since it will hardly be thought that nonbelievers mean by "wrong" what the theory says believers mean by it. This consequence gives rise to an objection. For the phenomena of common moral discourse between believers and nonbelievers suggest that they mean the same thing by "wrong" in ethical contexts. In the present section I shall try to explain how the modified divine command theorist can account for the facts of common ethical discourse.

I will first indicate what I think the troublesome facts are. Judeo-Christian believers enter into ethical discussions with people whose religious or antireligious beliefs they do not know. It seems to be possible to conduct quite a lot of ethical discourse, with apparent understanding, without knowing one's partner's views on religious issues. Believers also discuss ethical questions with persons who are known to them to be nonbelievers. They agree with such persons, disagree with them, and try to persuade them, about what acts are morally wrong. (Or at least it is normally *said*, by the participants and others, that they agree and disagree about such issues.) Believers ascribe, to people who are known not to believe in God, beliefs that certain acts are morally wrong. Yet surely believers do not suppose that nonbelievers, in calling acts wrong, mean that they are contrary to the will or commandments of God. Under these circumstances how can the believer really mean "contrary to the will or commandments of God" when he says "wrong"? If he agrees and disagrees with nonbelievers about what is wrong, if he ascribes to them beliefs that certain acts are wrong, must he not be using "wrong" in a nontheological sense?

What I shall argue is that in some ordinary (and I fear imprecise) sense of "mean," what believers and nonbelievers mean by "wrong" in ethical contexts may well be partly the same and partly different. There are agreements between believers and nonbelievers which make common moral discourse between them possible. But these agreements do not show that the two groups mean exactly the same thing by "wrong." They do not show that "contrary to God's will or commands" is not part of what believers mean by "wrong."

Let us consider first the agreements which make possible common moral discourse between believers and nonbelievers.

(1) One important agreement, which is so obvious as to be easily overlooked, is that they use many of the same ethical terms – "wrong," "right," "ought," "duty," and others. And they may utter many of the same ethical sentences, such as "Racial discrimination is morally wrong." In determining what people believe we rely very heavily on what they say (when they seem to be speaking sincerely) – and that means in large part, on the words that they use and the sentences they utter. If I know that somebody says, with apparent sincerity, "Racial discrimination is morally wrong," I will normally ascribe to him the belief that racial discrimination is morally wrong, even if I also know that he does not mean *exactly* the same thing as I do by "racial discrimination" or "morally wrong." Of course if I know he means something *completely* different, I would not ascribe the belief to him without explicit qualification.

I would not claim that believers and nonbelievers use *all* the same ethical terms. "Sin," "law of God," and "Christian," for instance, occur as ethical terms in the discourse of many believers, but would be much less likely to occur in the same way in nonbelievers' discourse.

(2) The shared ethical terms have the same basic grammatical status for believers as for nonbelievers, and at least many of the same logical connections with other expressions. Everyone agrees, for instance, in treating "wrong" as an adjective and "Racial discrimination is morally wrong" as a declarative sentence. "(All) racial discrimination is morally wrong" would be treated by all parties as expressing an A-type (universal affirmative) proposition, from which consequences can be drawn by syllogistic reasoning or the predicate calculus. All agree that if X is morally wrong, then it isn't morally right and refraining from X is morally obligatory. Such grammatical and

formal agreements are important to common moral discourse.

(3) There is a great deal of agreement, among believers and nonbelievers, as to what types of action they call "wrong" in an ethical sense and I think that that agreement is one of the things that make common moral discourse possible.[13] It is certainly not complete agreement. Obviously there is a lot of ethical disagreement in the world. Much of it cuts right across religious lines, but not all of it does. There are things which are typically called "wrong" by members of some religious groups, and not by others. Nonetheless there are types of action which everyone or almost everyone would call morally wrong – such as torturing someone to death because he accidentally broke a small window in your house. Moreover any two people (including any one believer and one nonbeliever) are likely to find some actions they both call wrong that not everyone does. I imagine that most ethical discussion takes place among people whose area of agreement in what they call wrong is relatively large.

There is probably much less agreement about the most basic issues in moral theory than there is about many ethical issues of less generality. There is much more unanimity in what people (sincerely) say in answer to such questions as "Was what Hitler did to the Jews wrong?" or "Is it normally wrong to disobey the laws of one's country?" than in what they (sincerely) say in answer to such questions as "Is it always right to do the act which will have the best results?" or "Is pleasure the only thing that is good for its own sake?" The issue between adherents and nonadherents of divine command ethics is typical of basic issues in ethical and metaethical theory in this respect.

(4) The emotional and volitional attitudes normally expressed by the statement that something is "wrong" are similar in believers and nonbelievers. They are not exactly the same; the attitudes typically expressed by the believer's statement that something is "wrong" are importantly related to his religious practice and beliefs about God, and this doubtless makes them different in some ways from the attitudes expressed by nonbelievers uttering the same sentence. But the attitudes are certainly similar, and that is important for the possibility of common moral discourse.

(5) Perhaps even more important is the related fact that the social functions of a statement that something is (morally) "wrong" are similar for be-lievers and nonbelievers. To say that something someone else is known to have done is "wrong" is commonly to attack him. If you say that something you are known to have done is "wrong," you aban-don certain types of defense. To say that a public policy is "wrong" is normally to register oneself as opposed to it, and is sometimes a signal that one is willing to be supportive of common action to change it. These social functions of moral discourse are extremely important. It is perhaps not surprising that we are inclined to say that two people agree with each other when they both utter the same sentence and thereby indicate their readiness to take the same side in a conflict.

Let us sum up these observations about the conditions which make common moral discourse between believers and nonbelievers possible. (1) They use many of the same ethical terms, such as "wrong." (2) They treat those terms as having the same basic grammatical and logical status, and many of the same logical connections with other expressions. (3) They agree to a large extent about what types of action are to be called "wrong." To call an action "wrong" is, among other things, to classify it with certain other actions, and there is consider-able agreement between believers and nonbelievers as to what actions those are. (4) The emotional and volitional attitudes which believers and non-believers normally express in saying that some-thing is "wrong" are similar, and (5) saying that something is "wrong" has much the same social functions for believers and nonbelievers.

So far as I can see, none of this is inconsistent with the modified divine command theory of ethical wrongness. According to that theory there are several things which are true of the believer's use of "wrong" which cannot plausibly be supposed to be true of the nonbeliever's. In saying, "X is wrong," the believer commits himself (subjectively, at least, and publicly if he is known to be a believer) to the claim that X is contrary to God's will or commandments. The believer will not say that anything would be wrong, under any possible circumstances, if it were not contrary to God's will or commandments. In many contexts he uses the term "wrong" interchangeably with "against the will of God" or "against the commandments of God." The heart of the modified divine command theory, I have suggested, is the claim that when the believer says, "X is wrong," one thing he means to be doing is stating a nonnatural objective fact about X, and the nonnatural objective fact he means to be stating is that X is contrary to the will or commandments of God. This claim may be true even though the uses of "wrong" by believers and nonbelievers are similar in all five of the ways pointed out above.

Suppose these contentions of the modified divine command theory are correct. (I think they are very plausible as claims about the ethical discourse of at least some religious believers.) In that case believers and nonbelievers surely do not mean exactly the same thing by "X is wrong" in ethical contexts. But neither is it plausible to suppose that they mean entirely different things, given the phenomena of common moral discourse. We must suppose, then, that their meaning is partly the same and partly different. "Contrary to God's will or commands" must be taken as expressing only part of the meaning with which the believer uses "wrong." Some of the similarities between believers' and nonbelievers' use of "wrong" must also be taken as expressing parts of the meaning with which the believer uses "wrong." This view of the matter agrees with the account of the modified divine command theory in Section III above, where I pointed out that the modified divine command theorist cannot mean exactly the same thing by "wrong" that he means by "contrary to God's commands."

We have here a situation which commonly arises when some people hold, and others do not hold, a given theory about the nature of something which everyone talks about. The chemist, who believes that water is a compound of hydrogen and oxygen, and the man who knows nothing of chemistry, surely do not use the word "water" in entirely different senses; but neither is it very plausible to suppose that they use it with exactly the same meaning. I am inclined to say that in some fairly ordinary sense of "mean," a phenomenalist, and a philosopher who holds some conflicting theory about what it is for a physical object to exist, do not mean exactly the same thing by "There is a bottle of milk in the refrigerator." But they certainly do not mean entirely different things, and they can agree that there is a bottle of milk in the refrigerator.

VII

These remarks bring us face to face with some important issues in the general theory of analysis and meaning. What are the criteria for determining whether two utterers of the same expression mean exactly the same thing by it, or something partly different, or something entirely different? What is the relation between philosophical analyses, and philosophical theories about the natures of things, on the one hand, and the meanings of terms in ordinary discourse on the other hand? I have permitted myself the liberty of speaking as if these issues did not exist. But their existence is notorious, and I certainly cannot resolve them in this essay. Indeed, I do not have resolutions to offer.

In view of these uncertainties in the theory of meaning, it is worth noting that much of what the modified divine command theorist wants to say can be said without making claims about the *meaning* of ethical terms. He wants to say, for instance, that believers' claims that certain acts are wrong normally express certain attitudes toward those acts, whether or not that is part of their meaning; that an act is wrong if and only if it is contrary to God's will or commands (assuming God loves us); that nonetheless, if God commanded cruelty for its own sake, neither obedience nor disobedience would be ethically wrong or ethically permitted; that if an act is contrary to God's will or commands that is a nonnatural objective fact about it; and that that is the only nonnatural objective fact which obtains if and only if the act is wrong. These are among the most important claims of the modified divine command theory – perhaps they include the very most important. But in the form in which I have just stated them, they are not claims about the *meaning* of ethical terms.

I do not mean to reject the claims about the meanings of terms in religious ethical discourse which I have included in the modified divine command theory. In the absence of general solutions to general problems in the theory of meaning, we may perhaps say what seems to us intuitively plausible in particular cases. That is presumably what the modified divine command theorist is doing when he claims that "contrary to the will or commands of God" is part of the meaning of "(ethically) wrong" for many Judeo-Christian believers. And I think it is fair to say that if we have found unresolved problems about meaning in the modified divine command theory, they are problems much more about what we mean in general by "meaning" than about what Judeo-Christian believers mean by "wrong."[14]

Notes

1 Guillelmus de Occam, *Super 4 libros sententiarum*, bk. II, qu. 19, O, in vol. IV of his *Opera plurima* (Lyon, 1494–6; réimpression en facsimilé, Farnborough, Hants., England: Gregg Press, 1962). I am not claiming that Ockham held a divine command theory of exactly the same sort that I have been discussing.

2 Perhaps he will even think it is causally possible, but I do not regard any view on that issue as an integral part of the theory. The question whether it is causally possible for God to act "out of character" is a difficult one which we need not go into here.

3 Moore took goodness and badness as primitive, rather than rightness and wrongness; but that need not concern us here.

4 The mention of moral law in the last of these reasons may presuppose the ability to *mention* concepts of moral right and wrong, which may or may not be theological and which may or may not be concepts one uses oneself to make judgments of right and wrong. So far as I can see, it does not *presuppose* the *use* of such concepts to make judgments of right and wrong, or one's adoption of them for such use, which is the crucial point here.

5 The independence ascribed to these attitudes is not a *genetic* independence. It may be that the person would not have come to have some of them had it not been for his religious beliefs. The point is that he has come to hold them in such a way that his holding them does not now depend entirely on his beliefs about God's commands.

6 I take A. C. Ewing to be offering an objection of this type on p. 112 of his book *Ethics* (London: English Univs. Press, 1953).

7 I quote from John Yolton's edition of *An Essay Concerning Human Understanding*, 2 vols. (London and New York: Everyman's Library, 1967).

8 In *God and the Soul* (London: Routledge, 1969), ch. 9.

9 G. E. M. Anscombe, "Modern Moral Philosophy," *Philosophy*, XXXIII (1958), pp. 1–19.

10 Karl Barth, *Church Dogmatics*, vol. II, pt. 2, trans. G. W. Bromiley and others (Edinburgh: T. & T. Clark, 1957), p. 553.

11 Ibid., p. 560.

12 The argument here is similar to one which is used for another purpose by Ninian Smart in "Omnipotence, Evil, and Superman," *Philosophy*, XXXVI (1961), reprinted in Nelson Pike, ed., *God and Evil* (Englewood Cliffs, NJ: Prentice-Hall, 1964), pp. 103–12.

I do not mean to endorse the doctrines of divine impassibility and theological determinism.

13 Cf. Ludwig Wittgenstein, *Philosophical Investigations*, 2nd edn. (Oxford: Blackwell, 1958), pt. I, sec. 242: "If language is to be a means of communication there must be agreement not only in definitions but also (queer as this may sound) in judgments." In contemporary society I think it may well be the case that because there is not agreement in ethical definitions, common ethical discourse requires a measure of agreement in ethical judgments. (I do not mean to comment here more broadly on the truth or falsity of Wittgenstein's statement as a statement about the conditions of linguistic communication in general.)

14 I am indebted to many who have read, or heard, and discussed versions of this essay, and particularly to Richard Brandt, William Frankena, John Reeder, and Stephen Stich, for helpful criticisms.

39

Morality and Religion Reconsidered

Baruch A. Brody

There are many people who believe that, in one way or another, morality needs a religious backing. One of the many things that might be meant by this vague and ambiguous claim[1] is the following: there are certain moral truths that are true only because of the truth of certain religious truths. In particular, the truth of certain claims about the rightness (wrongness) of a given action is dependent upon the truth of certain religious claims to the effect that God wants us to do (refrain from doing) that action. This belief, in effect, bases certain parts of morality upon the will of God.

Philosophers have not commonly agreed with such claims. And there is an argument, whose ancestor is an argument in the *Euthyphro*,[2] that is supposed to show that such claims are false. It runs as follows: the proponents of the claim in question have reversed the order of things. Doing a given action *A* is not right (wrong) because God wants us to do (refrain from doing) *A*; rather, God wants us to do (refrain from doing) *A* because of some other reason which is the real reason why *A* is right (wrong) for us to do. For, if the situation were the way it is depicted by the proponents of the claim in question, we would have moral truths based upon the arbitrary desires of God

as to what we should do (refrain from doing), and this is objectionable.

I would like to reexamine this issue and to show that the situation is far more complicated than philosophers normally imagine it to be. I should like to show (a) that the general argument suggested by the *Euthyphro* is not as persuasive as it is ordinarily thought to be, and (b) that it is even less persuasive when we see the religious claim applied to specific moral issues, and that this is so because the claims about the will of God can be supplemented by additional theological claims.

I

Let us begin by looking at the argument more carefully. We shall formulate it as follows:

(1) Let us suppose that it is the case that there is some action *A* that is right (wrong) only because God wants us to do (refrain from doing) it.

(2) There must be some reason for God's wanting us to do (refrain from doing) *A*, some reason that does not involve God's wanting us to do (refrain from doing) it.

(3) Therefore, that reason must also be a reason why *A* is right (wrong).

(4) So we have a contradiction, (1) is false, and either there are no actions that are right (wrong) because God wants us to do (refrain from doing) them or, if there are such actions, that is not the only reason why those actions are right (wrong).

What can be said by way of defense on (2)? The basic idea behind it seems to be the following: if God wanted us to do (refrain from doing) A, but he had no reason for that want that was independent of his act of wanting, then his act of wanting would be an arbitrary act, one that entails some imperfection in him. But God is a perfect being. Therefore, he must have some reason for wanting us to do (refrain from doing) A, some reason that is, of course, independent of that want of his. Now it is not entirely clear that this argument is sound, for it is not clear that the performance by an agent of an arbitrary act (even an arbitrary act of willing) entails some imperfection in the agent.[3] But we shall let that issue pass for now and focus, for the moment, on the crucial step (3).

It is clear that step (3) must rest upon some principle like the following:[4]

(Trans.) If p because of q and q because of r, then p because of r.

There are two things that should be noted about this principle. The first is that if we are to use it in our context we will have to take it as ranging over different types of cases in which we say "because." After all, there are significant differences between cases in which we make claims of the form "A is right (wrong) because God wants us to do (refrain from doing) A" and cases in which we make claims of the form "God wants us to do (refrain from doing) A because r," for it is only in the latter type of case that we have the reason-for-wanting, "because." The second point is that there are real problems with this principle. While Joe may go home because his wife wants him to do so, and she may want him to do so because she wants to have it out with him, it may well not be the case that he goes home because she wants to have it out with him. So the principle is going to need some modifying, and it is not clear how one is to do this while still preserving the inference from (1) and (2) to (3).

Still, let us suppose that this can be done. Our argument faces the following further objection: God's wanting us to do (refrain from doing) A is not the whole of the reason why the action is right (wrong); the additional part of the reason is that he is our creator to whom we owe obedience. And when we take into account the full reason, the argument collapses. After all, the *Euthyphro* argument would then run as follows:

(1') Let us suppose that there is some action A that is right (wrong) only because God wants us to do (refrain from doing) A and he is our creator to whom we owe obedience.

(2') There must be some reason for God's wanting us to do (refrain from doing) A, some reason that does not involve God's wanting us to do (refrain from doing) A.

(3') Therefore, that reason must also be a reason why A is right (wrong).

(4') So we have a contradiction, (1') is false, and either there are no actions that are right (wrong) because God, who is our creator and to whom we owe obedience, wants us to do (refrain from doing) them, or, if there are such actions, that is not the only reason why those actions are right (wrong).

And, even supposing that (Trans.) is true, (3') would not follow from (1') and (2').

It is clear that the proponents of the *Euthyphro* argument have got to block this move. How might they do so? The most straightforward move is to deny the moral relevance of the fact that God is our creator, to claim that even if he is, we have no obligation to obey his wishes and that, therefore, the reason advanced in (1') cannot be a reason why A is right (wrong).

Is this move acceptable? Consider, for a moment, our special obligation to obey the wishes of our parents.[5] Why do we have that obligation? Isn't it because they created us? And since this is so, we seem to have an obligation, in at least some cases, to follow their wishes. So, x's being our creator can be part of a reason for doing (refraining from doing) an action A if the other part is that that is x's wish. And if this is so in the case of our parents, why shouldn't it also be so in the case of God? How then can the defendents of the *Euthyphro* argument say that the fact that God created us cannot, together with some facts about his wishes, be a reason for doing (refraining from doing) some action A?

The proponents of the *Euthyphro* argument have a variety of ways, of differing plausibilities, of objecting to this defense of (1'). They might claim: (a) that we have no special obligations at all to our parents; (b) that it is no part of the special obligations that we have to our parents to do (refrain from doing) what they want us to do (refrain from doing); (c) that our special obligations to our parents are due to something that they do other than merely creating us, something that God does not do, so the whole question of our special obligations to our parents has nothing to do with the truth of (1').[6]

But there is another move open to the proponents of the *Euthyphro* argument. Rather than attempting to object to (1'), they might construct the following alternative argument against it, one that has the additional merit of not depending upon (Trans.):

(1') Let us suppose that there is some action A that is right (wrong) only because God wants us to do (refrain from doing) A and he is our creator to whom we owe obedience.

(2'*) There must be some reason for God's wanting us to do (refrain from doing) A, some reason that does not involve God's wanting us to do (refrain from doing) A, and some reason that is, by itself, a reason why A is right (wrong).

(4') So we have a contradiction, (1') is false, and either there are no actions that are right (wrong) because God, who is our creator and to whom we owe obedience, wants us to do (refrain from doing) them, or, if there are such actions, that is not the only reason why those actions are right (wrong).

The trouble with this move, of course, is that it rests upon the extremely strong assumption (2'*), and even if, to avoid the problem with arbitrary acts of willing, we are prepared to grant (2'), there seems to be little reason to grant this stronger (2'*) with its extra assumption about what are the types of reasons that God has for his acts of willing.

In short, then, the traditional argument that the rightness or wrongness of an action cannot depend upon the will of God rests upon some dubious premises, and things get worse when we add the idea that we have an obligation to follow God's wishes because he is our creator. There is, however, more to say about this issue, for there are reasons to suppose that some particular moral truths may depend in a special way upon the idea that God is the creator. We turn, therefore, to a consideration of these special cases.

II

Let us begin by considering a set of issues surrounding the idea of property rights. What is involved in one's owning a piece of property, in one's having a right to it? It seems to mean, in part, that while one may not use that property so as to infringe upon the rights of others, one may, if one wants, use it in such a way as to benefit while others lose. No doubt this distinction is unclear for there are cases in which it is difficult to say whether someone's rights have been infringed upon or whether he has simply lost out.[7] But the distinction is clear enough for our purposes.

How does one come to own a piece of property? One intuitively attractive picture runs as follows: if there is a physical object that belongs to no one, and if some person comes along and does something with it (mixes his labor with it), then the object in question belongs to that person.[8] He may then, in one way or another, transfer that property to someone else, who then has property rights in that object. Indeed, transference is now the most prevalent way of acquiring property. But all property rights are ultimately based, in this picture, upon these initial acts of acquisition through the mixing of one's labor with unowned objects. This picture certainly faces some familiar objections.[9] To begin with, what right does a person have to appropriate the ownerless piece of property for himself, thereby depriving all of us of the right to use it? And secondly, does the act of mixing his labor with it give him ownership rights over the initial, ownerless object or simply over the products (if any) of his interaction with it? But we shall leave aside these worries for now and suppose that something like this account is correct, for the question that we want to consider is whether or not it would have to be modified in light of any theological truths.

This picture clearly presupposes that, if there is such a thing as property owned by human beings, then there was, at least at one point in human history, such a thing as ownerless property, property that one could acquire if one mixed one's labor with it. But suppose that the universe was created by a personal God. Then, it might well be argued, he owns the whole universe, and there is not, and never has been, such a thing as ownerless property. Now suppose further that this creator allows men to use for their purposes the property that they mix their labor with, but he does so with the restriction that they must not use it in such a way as to cause a great loss to other people (even though the rights of these people are not infringed upon). That is to say, suppose that this creator allows people to take his property only if they follow certain of his wishes. Then, don't they have an obligation to do so, or, at least, an obligation to either return the property or to do so?[10] So, in short, if God, the creator, does wish us not to use the things of the world in certain ways, this will entail certain moral restrictions on property rights that might not be present otherwise.

Let us, at this point, introduce the idea of stewardship over property. We shall say that someone has stewardship over a piece of property just in case they own that piece of property subject to certain restrictions as to how they may use it and/or subject to certain requirements as to how they must use it, restrictions and/or requirements that were laid down by some previous owner of that piece of property. Now, what I have been arguing for is the idea that, if certain theological beliefs (that God created the universe but allows man to appropriate the property in it subject to certain restrictions and requirements that he lays down) are true, then men will have rights of stewardship, and not property rights, over the property that they possess. And if this is so, then there will be moral truths (about restrictions and requirements that property-possessors must follow)[11] that might not be true if these theological beliefs were false. So we have here a set of moral claims whose truth or falsehood might depend upon the truth or falsehood of certain theological claims.

The question that we must now consider is whether or not the *Euthyphro* argument, even if sound in general, could be used against the claim we are now considering. How would it run in this context? Presumably, it would run as follows:

(1″) Let us suppose that there are certain restrictions on property rights and that they exist only because God, from whom we get our stewardship over the earth, has imposed them.
(2″) There must be some reason why God has imposed these restrictions, a reason that does not involve his wanting us to follow them.
(3″) Therefore, that reason must also be a reason why we should follow those restrictions.
(4″) So we have a contradiction, (1″) is false, and either there are no such restrictions or there is some additional reason as to why they exist.

As we saw in the last section, when we considered (1′)–(4′), even if we grant (2″) and (Trans.), (3″) doesn't follow from (1″) and (2″). Now even if we grant what we are reluctant to grant in the last section, viz., that (1′) is objectionable because the mere fact that someone created us gives us no moral reason for following his wishes, we would still have

no reason for independently objecting to (1″). For if we have mere stewardship over the property we possess, then surely we do have an obligation to follow the wishes of him from whom we got our stewardship, and if God did create the world, then it certainly looks as though our property possession is a property stewardship gotten ultimately from God.

This point can also be put as follows. Neither (3′) nor (3″) follows from the previous steps in their respective arguments, even if we grant the truth of (Trans.), because the reasons they provide for the moral claims in question involve some other theological facts besides God's willing certain things. Now the defenders of the *Euthyphro* argument may try to attack (1″) on independent grounds, but it is difficult to see the grounds that they would have. So it looks then as though certain theological claims are relevant to certain moral truths having to do with the existence and extent of rights over property.

To be sure, the defenders of the *Euthyphro* argument might, in desperation, trot out the following argument:

(1″) Let us suppose that there are certain restrictions on property rights and that they exist only because God, from whom we get our stewardship over the earth, has imposed them.
(2″*) There must be some reason why God has imposed these restrictions, a reason that does not involve his wanting us to follow them, and one that is, by itself, a reason why we should follow these restrictions.
(4″) So we have a contradiction, (1″) is false, and either there are no such restrictions or there is some additional reason as to why they exist.

But like step (2′*) of the previous section, step (2″*) has little to recommend it. Even if a perfect God has to have reasons for wanting us to behave in certain ways, and, a fortiori, for imposing restrictions on our behavior, it is unclear why they must meet the very strong final requirement laid down by (2″*).

III

In the previous section, we have discussed the implications of the theological idea that God, the creator, owns the universe for the issue of property rights. It is sometimes felt that this idea also has implications for the moral issue of the permissibility of suicide.[12] We will, in this section, explore that possibility.

The liberal argument for the permissibility of suicide is stated very clearly early on in the *Phaedo*:

> . . . sometimes and for some people death is better than life. And it probably seems strange to you that it should not be right for those to whom death would be an advantage to benefit themselves, but that they should have to await the services of someone else. [62A]

It will do no good, of course, to object that the person might have some extremely important obligations that he would leave unfulfilled if he committed suicide, and this is why it is wrong for him to do so, because we could easily confine the discussions to cases in which he has no such obligations or to cases in which he could arrange for the executors of his estate to fulfill them. And moreover, such an argument would really only show that one should not be remiss in fulfilling one's obligations, it would not really show that there was something particularly wrong with the way the person who committed suicide did that.

Plato himself does not accept this argument for suicide (although he does think one can accede in being condemned to death), and he is opposed to suicide on the grounds that we are the possessions of the gods. His argument runs as follows:

> If one of your possessions were to destroy itself without intimation from you that you wanted it to die, wouldn't you be angry with it and punish it, if you had any means of doing so . . . so if you look at it this way, I suppose it is not unreasonable to say that we must not put an end to ourselves until God sends more compulsions like the one we are facing now. [62C]

Leaving aside the peculiarity of the idea that one ought, if one can, to punish those who succeed in destroying themselves – as opposed to the more reasonable idea that one ought to punish those who merely try – the idea that Plato is advancing is that the gods' property rights extend to us, and that we therefore have no right to destroy ourselves unless they give their permission.[13]

There are cases in which many religious people want to allow that suicide is permissible. One such case[14] is that of the person who commits suicide rather than face being compelled to do some very evil act. Thus, in a great many religious traditions, it would even be thought to be a meritorious act to commit suicide rather than face being tortured into committing acts of apostasy. Another such case is that of the person who commits suicide rather than reveal under torture secrets that would lead to the destruction of many innocent people. Can these exceptions be reconciled with the argument against suicide that we have been considering? It seems to me that they can. After all, the crucial objection to our destroying ourselves is that we have no right to do so without the permission of our owner, God, and the religious person might well add the additional claim that God has (perhaps in a revelation) already given his permission in these cases.

Obviously, the *Euthyphro* argument cannot be raised against the claim that we are considering. After all, the crucial first premise[15] would be the claim that

(1‴) Let us suppose that we cannot take our own lives only because we are the property of God, who created us, and he does not want us to destroy this piece of his property.

Then even if we add

(2‴) There must be some reason why he doesn't want us to do so, some reason that does not involve this want of his.

we will not, even assuming (Trans.), get the crucial

(3‴) Therefore, that reason must also be a reason why we should not take our own lives.

We can, no doubt, consider using

(2‴*) There must be some reason why he doesn't want us to do so, some reason that does not involve this want of his, and which is, by itself, a reason why we should not take our own lives.

instead of (2‴), but it is no more plausible than (2'*) and (2″*). Nor can we easily object to (1‴) in the way that we did to (1'). Even if we have no obligation to listen to the wishes of him who has created us, just because he has created us, we do have an obligation not to destroy someone else's property, and, if God created us, then perhaps we are God's property.

Having said this, we can now see that more is at stake here than a mere prohibition of suicide. For if we are the property of God, then perhaps we just have an obligation to do whatever he says, and then perhaps we can return to our initial general claims about morality and consider the possible claim that

(1'#) actions are right (wrong) for us to do just in case and only because God, who has created us and owns us and whom we therefore have an obligation to follow, wants us to do (refrain from doing) them.

So a great deal hinges on this point.

Despite all that we have seen, it is unclear that this argument against suicide (and, a fortiori, the more general claim just considered) will do. In the case of property rights, the crucial idea was that God, who created the world, owns all property, and this claim seemed a coherent one. But here, in (1'''), the crucial idea is that God, because he created us, owns us. And perhaps one can object directly to (1''') that it is incoherent. Does it make sense, after all, to talk of an all-just being owning or possessing a human being? Isn't doing that an unjust act, one that cannot meaningfully be ascribed to an all-just being?

It is difficult to assess this objection. There is no doubt that the objection to the institution of slavery is exactly that we think it unjust for one human being to own another human being, to have another human being as his possession. But is it unjust for God, who is vastly superior to us and is our creator, to possess human beings? To put this question another way, is slavery unjust because it is wrong for one human being to possess another (in which case, both the argument against suicide and the general claim, with their supposition that we are the possessions of God, can stand) or because it is wrong that a human being be a possession, a piece of property (in which case, both collapse on the grounds of incoherence)? Religious people have, very often, opted for the former alternative,[16] and as it is difficult to see an argument to disprove their contentions; we have, probably, to conclude that theological claims might make a difference to the truth or falsity of moral claims concerning suicide, and perhaps to a great many other issues as well.

IV

There is still one final issue about which it is often claimed that theological beliefs about the will of a God who created the world are relevant to the truth of moral beliefs about that issue. This is the moral issue raised by vegetarians. At least some vegetarians argue as follows: we normally suppose that it is wrong, except in certain very special cases, to take the life of an innocent human being. But we normally have no objections to taking the life of members of many other species to obtain from their bodies food, clothing, etc. Let us call these normal moral views the conventional consciousness. Now, argues the vegetarian, it is difficult to defend the conventional consciousness. What characteristics are possessed by all human beings, but by no members of any other species, and are such as to justify such a sharp moral distinction as the one drawn by the conventional consciousness?

I think that no one would deny that there is a gradation of development between different species, and most would concede that this gives rise to a gradation of rights. While few would object to killing a mosquito if it is being a minor nuisance, many would object to killing a dog on the same grounds. The interesting point, says the vegetarian, is that when we get to the case of human beings, the conventional consciousness accords to them many rights (including the strong right to life) even though there is not a sufficiently dramatic biological difference between these species to justify such a sharp moral difference. Therefore, concludes the vegetarian, we should reject the conventional consciousness and accord more of these rights (especially the right to life) to members of more species of animals.

This vegetarian argument draws further support from the fact that the intuitions embedded in the conventional consciousness are about species. After all, there are a variety of extreme cases (newly born infants, severely retarded individuals, people who are near death) in which many of the subtler features of human beings are not present but in which the conventional consciousness accords to the people in question far more rights than those normally accorded to animals. This makes it far more difficult to believe that there are some characteristics (a) possessed by all human beings, (b) not possessed by all animals, and (c) which justify the moral distinctions drawn by the conventional consciousness. So, the vegetarian concludes, we must reject the conventional consciousness.

There is a religious response to this vegetarian argument which runs as follows: when God created the world, he intended that man should use certain other species for food, clothing, etc. God did not, of course, give man complete freedom to do what he wants with these creatures. They are not, for example, to be treated cruelly. But, because that was God's intention, man can, and should use these creatures to provide him with food, clothing, etc. This view is embodied in the following Talmudic story:[17]

> A calf was being taken to the slaughter, when it broke away, hid his head under Rabbi's skirts, and lowed in terror. *Go, said he, for this wast thou created.* [B. Metzia, 85a]

It is pretty clear, once more, that the *Euthyphro* argument will not do against the claim we are considering. It is

(1''''') Man can take the lives of animals so that he can obtain from their bodies food, clothing, etc., only because God, who created the world and owns everything in it, intended that he do so.

and even if we grant

(2''''') There is some reason why he intended things that way, some reason that does not involve that intention.

and (Trans.), we do not get the crucial

(3''''') This must also be a reason why it is permissible for us to take the lives of animals for the sake of obtaining food, clothing, etc.

The crucial objection to this claim has to do with the coherency of (1'''''). Let us suppose that we are not troubled by the religious claims discussed in the previous section; let us suppose that we find nothing objectionable with the idea that God owns us. Then, presumably, even if we are impressed with the vegetarian argument, we will still find nothing objectionable with the idea that God owns animals as well. But we may still find (1''''') objectionable. For it, in effect, supposes that God's property rights extend so far as to allow the life of the piece of property in question to be taken by others, indeed, to so order things that this is done. And is this compatible with the idea of an all-just being? After all, even enlightened systems of slavery did not allow the slave-owner to take (or to have taken) the life of his slave. Does God's majesty really mean then that he can do even this?

We are straining here with the limits of the idea that everything is God's property because he is the creator of everything. When we applied the idea to inanimate objects, we saw that it could have important implications for the question of property rights. If we didn't object to applying it to human beings, we saw that it could (at least) have important applications for the question of the permissibility of suicide. If we are now prepared to take it to further extremes, it could serve as a response to the vegetarian's argument about animals and their right to life.

V

In a way, this essay can be seen as a gloss on the Psalmist's remarks that "the earth and all that fill it belong to God." We have tried to show that this idea may have important moral implications, and that it would therefore be wrong to suppose that there are no moral claims whose truth or falsehood may depend upon the truth or falsehood of theological claims. But it is, of course, clear that this is not the only theological belief that may have moral consequences.

Notes

I should like to thank David Rosenthal for his many insightful comments on an earlier version of this paper.

1 Other things that might be meant are: (a) we know that certain moral truths are true because we know the truth of certain religious truths (perhaps, that God has revealed to us that the action is right), and (b) we have a reason to do what is right because of the truth of certain religious truths (perhaps, that God will reward us if we do). We will not discuss these claims in this paper.

2 We leave aside, for this paper, the question as to exactly what was the argument in the *Euthyphro*. On that issue, see R. Sharvy's "Euthyphro 9d–11b", *Nous* (1972) which influenced the way I constructed the argument to be considered below.

3   This is a claim that would certainly be denied by writers in the Calvinist tradition. Thus, Jonathan Edwards writes as follows in connection with the question of salvation and damnation:

> It is meet that God should order all these things according to his own pleasure. By reason of his greatness and glory, by which he is infinitely above all, he is worthy to be sovereign, and that his pleasure should in all things take place. [*Jonathan Edwards* (Hill and Wang: 1935), p. 119]

4   It could, of course, rest upon the weaker principle, that only held in cases where *q* was some agent's wanting something. But all of the points we will make are equally applicable to this weaker principle.

5   This analogy between our obeying the will of God and the will of our parents is based upon the Talmudic discussion (in *Tractate Kedushin*, 30^b) of the obligation to honor one's parents.

6   Of the three moves, the third seems most plausible. But religious people might well respond to it as follows: let us grant that our special obligations to our parents are due to additional facts about the parent–child relationship (e.g., the way parents raise and sustain their children, etc.). God has those additional relations to all of his creations, and they therefore still have to him the special obligation of obedience.

7   Here is just one: let us suppose that I build a high wall at the back of my property, thereby depriving your yard of sunlight. There is no doubt that you have suffered a loss, but have I deprived you of any of your rights?

8   See, for example, chapter 5 of Locke's *Second Treatise of Civil Government*.

9   See, for example, chapter 3 of the First Memoir of Proudhon's *What is Property?*

10 If the individual was aware of what these wishes are before he takes the property, then it would seem that he has the obligation to follow them. But if he was not, and if they turn out to be strange and/or arbitrary, then perhaps he only has the weaker obligation, and then only from that time at which he becomes aware of what the wishes are.

11 It goes without saying that what exactly these restrictions are will vary from one theological system to another. The cases that are of the most interest for current discussions of property rights have to do, of course, with those systems in which the restrictions require one, in effect, at least to take into account the interests of other people and not merely their rights.

12 R. F. Holland, in "Suicide" in Rachels's *Moral Problems* (Harper and Row: 1971), discusses other ways in which the moral issues surrounding suicide are intertwined with theological questions.

13 Plato here is assuming the overly strong thesis that we never have a right to destroy someone else's property without their permission. Whether and how he could get a weaker thesis that would still leave the argument intact is something that cannot be considered here.

14 For a discussion of such cases, see the opinion of Rabenu Tam mentioned in the Tosafot glosses to *Talmud, Tractate Avodat Zarah*, 18a.

15 Notice that the obligation to listen to the wishes of the property owner is stronger here than in the previous case. Even if his wishes are strange and/or arbitrary, that does not give us a right to disregard them and destroy the property.

16 This is evidenced in the Talmudic idea (*Kedushin*, 22^b) that it is wrong for man to sell himself into slavery because God would object on the grounds that "they are my slaves, and not the slaves of slaves."

17 To be sure, Rabbi is punished for his answer, but only, as the text makes clear, because he fails to show compassion, not because his answer is unacceptable.

40

Religion and the Queerness of Morality

George I. Mavrodes

Many arguments for the existence of God may be construed as claiming that there is some feature of the world that would somehow make no sense unless there was something else that had a stronger version of that feature or some analogue of it. So, for example, the cosmological line of argument may be thought of as centering upon the claim that the way in which the world exists (called "contingent" existence) would be incomprehensible unless there were something else – that is, God – that had a stronger grip upon existence (that is, "necessary" existence).

Now, a number of thinkers have held a view something like this with respect to morality. They have claimed that in some important way morality is dependent upon religion – dependent, that is, in such a way that if religion were to fail, morality would fail also. And they have held that the dependence was more than psychological, that is, if religion were to fail, it would somehow be *proper* (perhaps logically or perhaps in some other way) for morality to fail also. One way of expressing this theme is by Dostoevsky's "If there is no God, then everything is permitted," a sentiment that in this century has been prominently echoed by Sartre. But perhaps the most substantial philosophical thinker of the modern period to espouse this view, though in a rather idiosyncratic way, was Immanuel Kant, who held that the existence of God was a

necessary postulate of "practical" (that is, moral) reason.[1]

On the other hand, it has recently been popular for moral philosophers to deny this theme and to maintain that the dependence of morality on religion is, at best, merely psychological. Were religion to fail, so they apparently hold, this would grant no sanction for the failure of morality. For morality stands on its own feet, whatever those feet may turn out to be.

Now, the suggestion that morality somehow depends on religion is rather attractive to me. It is this suggestion that I wish to explore in this paper, even though it seems unusually difficult to formulate clearly the features of this suggestion that make it attractive. I will begin by mentioning briefly some aspects that I will not discuss.

First, beyond this paragraph I will not discuss the claim that morality cannot survive psychologically without the support of religious belief. At least in the short run, this proposal seems to me false. For there certainly seem to be people who reject religious belief, at least in the ordinary sense, but who apparently have a concern with morality and who try to live a moral life. Whether the proposal may have more force if it is understood in a broader way, as applying to whole cultures, epochs, and so forth, I do not know.

Second, I will not discuss the attempt to define some or all moral terms by the use of religious terms, or vice versa. But this should not be taken as implying any judgment about this project.

Third, beyond this paragraph I shall not discuss the suggestion that moral statements may be entailed by religious statements and so may be "justified" by religious doctrines or beliefs. It is popular now to hold that no such alleged entailment can be valid. But the reason usually cited for this view is the more general doctrine that moral statements cannot be validly deduced from nonmoral statements, a doctrine usually traced to Hume. Now, to my mind the most important problem raised by this general doctrine is that of finding some interpretation of it that is both significant and not plainly false. If it is taken to mean merely that there is *some* set of statements that entails no moral statement, then it strikes me as probably true, but trivial. At any rate, we should then need another reason to suppose that religious statements fall in this category. If, on the other hand, it is taken to mean that one can divide the domain of statements into two classes, the moral and the nonmoral, and that none of the latter entail any of the former, then it is false. I, at any rate, do not know a version of this doctrine that seems relevant to the religious case and that has any reasonable likelihood of being true. But I am not concerned on this occasion with the possibly useful project of deducing morality from religion, and so I will not pursue it further. My interest is closer to a move in the other direction, that of deducing religion from morality. (I am not quite satisfied with this way of putting it and will try to explain this dissatisfaction later on.)

For the remainder of this discussion, then, my project is as follows. I will outline one rather common nonreligious view of the world, calling attention to what I take to be its most relevant features. Then I shall try to portray some sense of the odd status that morality would have in a world of that sort. I shall be hoping, of course, that you will notice that this odd status is not the one that you recognize morality to have in the actual world. But it will perhaps be obvious that the "world-view" amendments required would move substantially toward a religious position.

First, then, the nonreligious view. I take a short and powerful statement of it from a 1903 essay by Bertrand Russell, "A Free Man's Worship."

That man is the product of causes which had no prevision of the end they were achieving; that his origin, his growth, his hopes and fears, his loves and his beliefs are but the outcome of accidental collocations of atoms; that no fire, no heroism, no intensity of thought and feeling, can preserve an individual life beyond the grave; that all the labors of the ages, all the devotion, all the inspiration, all the noonday brightness of human genius, are destined to extinction in the vast death of the solar system, and that the whole temple of man's achievement must inevitably be buried beneath the debris of a universe in ruins – all these things, if not quite beyond dispute, are yet so nearly certain that no philosophy which rejects them can hope to stand. Only within the scaffolding of these truths, only on the firm foundation of unyielding despair, can the soul's habitation henceforth be safely built.[2]

For convenience, I will call a world that satisfies the description given here a "Russellian world." But we are primarily interested in what the status of morality would be in the actual world if that world should turn out to be Russellian. I shall therefore sometimes augment the description of a Russellian world with obvious features of the actual world.

What are the most relevant features of a Russellian world? The following strike me as especially important: (1) Such phenomena as minds, mental activities, consciousness, and so forth are the products of entities and causes that give no indication of being mental themselves. In Russell's words, the causes are "accidental collocations of atoms" with "no prevision of the end they were achieving." Though not stated explicitly by Russell, we might add the doctrine, a commonplace in modern science, that mental phenomena – and indeed life itself – are comparative latecomers in the long history of the earth. (2) Human life is bounded by physical death and each individual comes to a permanent end at his physical death. We might add to this the observation that the span of human life is comparatively short, enough so that in some cases we can, with fair confidence, predict the major consequences of certain actions insofar as they will affect a given individual throughout his whole remaining life. (3) Not only each individual but also the human race as a species is doomed to extinction "beneath the debris of a universe in ruins."

So much, then, for the main features of a Russellian world. Because the notion of benefits and goods plays an important part in the remainder of my discussion, I want to introduce one further technical expression – "Russellian benefit." A Russellian benefit is one that could accrue to a person in a Russellian world. A contented old age would be, I suppose, a Russellian benefit, as would a thrill of sexual pleasure or a good reputation. Going to heaven when one dies, though a benefit, is not a Russellian benefit. Russellian benefits are only the benefits possible in a Russellian world. But one can have Russellian benefits even if the world is not Russellian. In such a case there might, however, also be other benefits, such as going to heaven.

Could the actual world be Russellian? Well, I take it to be an important feature of the actual world that human beings exist in it and that in it their actions fall, at least sometimes, within the sphere of morality – that is, they have moral obligations to act (or to refrain from acting) in certain ways. And if they do not act in those ways, then they are properly subject to a special and peculiar sort of adverse judgment (unless it happens that there are special circumstances that serve to excuse their failure to fulfill the obligations). People who do not fulfill their obligations are not merely stupid or weak or unlucky; they are morally reprehensible.

Now, I do not have much to say in an illuminating manner about the notion of moral obligation, but I could perhaps make a few preliminary observations about how I understand this notion. First, I take it that morality includes, or results in, judgments of the form "N ought to do (or to avoid doing)____" or "It is N's duty to do (or to avoid doing)____." That is, morality ascribes to particular people an obligation to do a certain thing on a certain occasion. No doubt morality includes other things as well – general moral rules, for example. I shall, however, focus on judgments of the sort just mentioned, and when I speak without further qualification of someone's having an obligation I intend it to be understood in terms of such a judgment.

Second, many authors distinguish prima facie obligations from obligations "all things considered." Probably this is a useful distinction. For the most part, however, I intend to ignore prima facie obligations and to focus upon our obligations all things considered, what we might call our "final obligations." These are the obligations that a particular person has in some concrete circumstance at a particular place and time, when all the aspects of the situation have been taken into account. It identifies the action that, if not done, will properly subject the person to the special adverse judgment.

Finally, it is, I think, a striking feature of moral obligations that a person's being unwilling to fulfill the obligation is irrelevant to having the obligation and is also irrelevant to the adverse judgment in case the obligation is not fulfilled. Perhaps even more important is the fact that, at least for some obligations, it is also irrelevant in both these ways

for one to point out that he does not see how fulfilling the obligations can do him any good. In fact, unless we are greatly mistaken about our obligations, it seems clear that in a Russellian world there are an appreciable number of cases in which fulfilling an obligation would result in a loss of good to ourselves. On the most prosaic level, this must be true of some cases of repaying a debt, keeping a promise, refraining from stealing, and so on. And it must also be true of those rarer but more striking cases of obligation to risk death or serious injury in the performance of a duty. People have, of course, differed as to what is good for humans. But so far as I can see, the point I have been making will hold for any candidate that is plausible in a Russellian world. Pleasure, happiness, esteem, contentment, self-realization, knowledge – all of these can suffer from the fulfillment of a moral obligation.

It is not, however, a *necessary* truth that some of our obligations are such that their fulfillment will yield no net benefit, within Russellian limits, to their fulfiller. It is not contradictory to maintain that, for every obligation that I have, a corresponding benefit awaits me within the confines of this world and this life. While such a contention would not be contradictory, however, it would nevertheless be false. I discuss below one version of this contention. At present it must suffice to say that a person who accepts this claim will probably find the remainder of what I have to say correspondingly less plausible.

Well, where are we now? I claim that in the actual world we have some obligations that, when we fulfill them, will confer on us no net Russellian benefit – in fact, they will result in a Russellian loss. If the world is Russellian, then Russellian benefits and losses are the only benefits and losses, and also then we have moral obligations whose fulfillment will result in a net loss of good to the one who fulfills them. I suggest, however, that it would be very strange to have such obligations – strange not simply in the sense of being unexpected or surprising but in some deeper way. I do not suggest that it is strange in the sense of having a straightforward logical defect, of being self-contradictory to claim that we have such obligations. Perhaps the best thing to say is that were it a fact that we had such obligations, then the world that included such a fact would be absurd – we would be living in a crazy world.

Now, whatever success I may have in this paper will in large part be a function of my success (or lack thereof) in getting across a sense of that absurdity, that queerness. On some accounts of morality, in a Russellian world there would not be the strangeness that I allege. Perhaps, then, I can convey some of that strangeness by mentioning those views of morality that would eliminate it. In fact, I believe that a good bit of their appeal is just the fact that they do get rid of this queerness.

First, I suspect that morality will not be queer in the way I suggest, even in a Russellian world, if judgments about obligations are properly to be analyzed in terms of the speaker rather than in terms of the subject of the judgment. And I more than suspect that this will be the case if such judgments are analyzed in terms of the speaker's attitude or feeling toward some action, and/or his attempt or inclination to incite a similar attitude in someone else. It may be, of course, that there is something odd about the supposition that human beings, consciousness, and so forth, could arise at all in a Russellian world. A person who was impressed by that oddity might be attracted toward some "teleological" line of reasoning in the direction of a more religious view. But I think that this oddity is not the one I am touching on here. Once given the existence of human beings with capacities for feelings and attitudes, there does not seem to be anything further that is queer in the supposition that a speaker might have an attitude toward some action, might express that attitude, and might attempt (or succeed) in inciting someone else to have a similar attitude. Anyone, therefore, who can be satisfied with such an analysis will probably not be troubled by the queerness that I allege.

Second, for similar reasons, this queerness will also be dissipated by any account that understands judgments about obligations purely in terms of the feelings, attitudes, and so forth of the subject of the judgment. For, given again that there are human beings with consciousness, it does not seem to be any additional oddity that the subject of a moral judgment might have feelings or attitudes about an actual or prospective action of his own. The assumption that morality is to be understood in this way takes many forms. In a closely related area, for example, it appears as the assumption – so common now that it can pass almost unnoticed – that guilt could not be anything other than guilt *feelings*, and that the "problem" of guilt is just the problem generated by such feelings.

In connection with our topic here, however, we might look at the way in which this sort of analysis

enters into one plausible-sounding explanation of morality in a Russellian world, an explanation that has a scientific flavor. The existence of morality in a Russellian world, it may be said, is not at all absurd because its existence there can be given a perfectly straightforward explanation: morality has a survival value for a species such as ours because it makes possible continued cooperation and things of that sort. So it is no more absurd that people have moral obligations than it is absurd that they have opposable thumbs.

I think that this line of explanation will work only if one analyzes obligations into feelings, or beliefs. I think it is plausible (though I am not sure it is correct) to suppose that everyone's having feelings of moral obligation might have a survival value for a species such as Man, given of course that these feelings were attached to patterns of action that contributed to such survival. And if that is so, then it is not implausible to suppose that there may be a survival value for the species even in a moral feeling that leads to the death of the individual who has it. So far so good. But this observation, even if true, is not relevant to the queerness with which I am here concerned. For I have not suggested that the existence of moral feelings would be absurd in a Russellian world; it is rather the existence of moral *obligations* that is absurd, and I think it important to make the distinction. It is quite possible, it seems to me, for one to feel (or to believe) that he has a certain obligation without actually having it, and also vice versa. Now, beliefs and feelings will presumably have some effect upon actions, and this effect may possibly contribute to the survival of the species. But, so far as I can see, the addition of actual moral obligations to these moral beliefs and feelings will make no further contribution to action nor will the actual obligations have an effect upon action in the absence of the corresponding feelings and beliefs. So it seems that neither with nor without the appropriate feelings will moral obligations contribute to the survival of the species. Consequently, an "evolutionary" approach such as this cannot serve to explain the existence of moral obligations, unless one rejects my distinction and equates the obligations with the feelings.

And finally, I think that morality will not be queer in the way I allege, or at least it will not be as queer as I think, if it should be the case that every obligation yields a Russellian benefit to the one who fulfills it. Given the caveat expressed earlier, one can perhaps make some sense out of the notion of a Russellian good or benefit for a sentient organism in a Russellian world. And one could, I suppose, without further queerness imagine that such an organism might aim toward achieving such goods. And we could further suppose that there were certain actions – those that were "obligations" – that would, in contrast with other actions, actually yield such benefits to the organism that performed them. And finally, it might not be too implausible to claim that an organism that failed to perform such an action was defective in some way and that some adverse judgment was appropriate.

Morality, however, seems to require us to hold that certain organisms (namely, human beings) have in addition to their ordinary properties and relations another special relation to certain actions. This relation is that of being "obligated" to perform those actions. And some of those actions are pretty clearly such that they will yield only Russellian losses to the one who performs them. Nevertheless, we are supposed to hold that a person who does not perform an action to which he is thus related is defective in some serious and important way and an adverse judgment is appropriate against him. And that certainly does seem odd.

The recognition of this oddity – or perhaps better, this absurdity – is not simply a resolution to concern ourselves only with what "pays." Here the position of Kant is especially suggestive. He held that a truly moral action is undertaken purely out of respect for the moral law and with no concern at all for reward. There seems to be no room at all here for any worry about what will "pay." But he also held that the moral enterprise needs, in a deep and radical way, the postulate of a God who can, and will, make happiness correspond to virtue. This postulate is "necessary" for practical reason. Perhaps we could put this Kantian demand in the language I have been using here, saying that the moral enterprise would make no sense in a world in which that correspondence ultimately failed.

I suspect that what we have in Kant is the recognition that there cannot be, in any "reasonable" way, a moral demand upon me, unless reality itself is committed to morality in some deep way. It makes sense only if there is a moral demand on the world too and only if reality will in the end satisfy that demand. This theme of the deep grounding of morality is one to which I return briefly near the end of this paper.

The oddity we have been considering is, I suspect, the most important root of the celebrated and somewhat confused question, "Why should I be moral?" Characteristically, I think, the person who asks that question is asking to have the queerness of that situation illuminated. From time to time there are philosophers who make an attempt to argue – perhaps only a halfhearted attempt – that being moral really is in one's interest after all. Kurt Baier, it seems to me, proposes a reply of this sort. He says:

> Moralities are systems of principles whose acceptance by everyone as overruling the dictates of self-interest is in the interest of everyone alike though following the rules of a morality is not of course identical with following self-interest. . . .
>
> The answer to our question "Why should we be moral?" is therefore as follows. We should be moral because being moral is following rules designed to overrule self-interest whenever it is in the interest of everyone alike that everyone should set aside his interest.[3]

As I say, this seems to be an argument to the effect that it really is in everyone's interest to be moral. I suppose that Baier is here probably talking about Russellian interests. At least, we must interpret him in that way if his argument is to be applicable in this context, and I will proceed on that assumption. But how exactly is the argument to be made out?

It appears here to begin with a premise something like

(A) It is in everyone's best interest (including mine, presumably) for everyone (including me) to be moral.

This premise itself appears to be supported earlier by reference to Hobbes. As I understand it, the idea is that without morality people will live in a "state of nature," and life will be nasty, brutish, and short. Well, perhaps so. At any rate, let us accept (A) for the moment. From (A) we can derive

(B) It is in my best interest for everyone (including me) to be moral.

And from (B) perhaps one derives

(C) It is in my best interest for me to be moral.

And (C) may be taken to answer the question, "Why should I be moral?" Furthermore, if (C) is true, then moral obligation will at least not have the sort of queerness that I have been alleging.

Unfortunately, however, the argument outlined above is invalid. The derivation of (B) from (A) *may* be all right, but the derivation of (C) from (B) is invalid. What does follow from (B) is

(C') It is in my best interest for me to be moral *if everyone else is moral.*

The argument thus serves to show that it is in a given person's interest to be moral only on the assumption that everyone else in the world is moral. It might, of course, be difficult to find someone ready to make that assumption.

There is, however, something more of interest in this argument. I said that the derivation of (B) from (A) may be all right. But in fact is it? If it is not all right, then this argument would fail even if everyone else in the world were moral. Now (A) can be interpreted as referring to "everyone's best interest" ("the interest of everyone alike," in Baier's own words) either collectively or distributively; that is, it may be taken as referring to the best interest of the whole group considered as a single unit, or as referring to the best interest of each individual in the group. But if (A) is interpreted in the collective sense, then (B) does not follow from it. It may not be in *my* best interest for everyone to act morally, even if it is in the best interest of the group as a whole, for the interest of the group as a whole may be advanced by the sacrificing of my interest. On this interpretation of (A), then, the argument will not answer the question "Why should I be moral?" even on the supposition that everyone else is moral.

If (A) is interpreted in the distributive sense, on the other hand, then (B) does follow from it, and the foregoing objection is not applicable. But another objection arises. Though (A) in the collective sense has some plausibility, it is hard to imagine that it is true in the distributive sense. Hobbes may have been right in supposing that life in the state of nature would be short, etc. But some lives are short anyway. In fact, some lives are short just because the demands of morality are observed. Such a life is not bound to have been shorter in the state of nature. Nor is it bound to have been less happy, less pleasurable, and so forth. In fact, does it not seem obvious that *my* best Russellian interest will be further advanced in a situation in which everyone else acts morally but I act immorally (in

selected cases) than it will be in case everyone, including me, acts morally? It certainly seems so. It can, of course, be observed that if I act immorally then so will other people, perhaps reducing my benefits. In the present state of the world that is certainly true. But in the present state of the world it is also true, as I observed earlier, that many other people will act immorally *anyway*, regardless of what I do.

A more realistic approach is taken by Richard Brandt.[4] He asks, "Is it *reasonable* for me to do my duty if it conflicts seriously with my personal welfare?" After distinguishing several possible senses of this question, he chooses a single one to discuss further, presumably a sense that he thinks important. As reformulated, the question is now: "Given that doing x is my duty and that doing some conflicting act y will maximize my personal welfare, will the performance of x instead of y satisfy my reflective preferences better?" And the conclusion to which he comes is that "the correct answer may vary from one person to another. It depends on what kind of person one is, what one cares about." And within Russellian limits Brandt must surely be right in this. But he goes on to say, "It is, of course, no defense of one's failure to do one's duty, before others or society, to say that doing so is not 'reasonable' for one in this sense." And this is just to bring the queer element back in. It is to suppose that besides "the kind of person" I am and my particular pattern of "cares" and interests there is something else, my duty, which may go against these and in any case properly overrides them. And one feels that there must be some sense of "reasonable" in which one can ask whether a world in which that is true is a reasonable world, whether such a world makes any sense.

This completes my survey of some ethical or metaethical views that would eliminate or minimize this sort of queerness of morality. I turn now to another sort of view, stronger I think than any of these others, which accepts that queerness but goes no further. And one who holds this view will also hold, I think, that the question "Why should I be moral?" must be rejected in one way or another. A person who holds this view will say that it is simply a fact that we have the moral obligations that we do have, and that is all there is to it. If they sometimes result in a loss of good, then that too is just a fact. These may be puzzling or surprising facts, but there are lots of puzzling and surprising things about the world. In a Russellian world, morality will be, I suppose, an "emergent" phenomenon; it will be a feature of certain effects though it is not a feature of their causes. But the wetness of water is an emergent feature, too. It is not a property of either hydrogen or oxygen. And there is really nothing more to be said; somewhere we must come to an end of reasons and explanations. We have our duties. We can fulfill them and be moral, or we can ignore them and be immoral. If all that is crazy and absurd – well, so be it. Who are we to say that the world is not crazy and absurd?

Such a view was once suggested by William Alston in a criticism of Hasting Rashdall's moral argument for God's existence.[5] Alston attributed to Rashdall the view that "God is required as a locus for the moral law." But Alston then went on to ask, "Why could it not just be an ultimate fact about the universe that kindness is good and cruelty bad? This seems to have been Plato's view." And if we rephrase Alston's query slightly to refer to obligations, we might be tempted to say, "Why not indeed?"

I say that this is perhaps the strongest reply against me. Since it involves no argument, there is no argument to be refuted. And I have already said that, so far as I can see, its central contention is not self-contradictory. Nor do I think of any other useful argument to the effect that the world is not absurd and crazy in this way. The reference to Plato, however, might be worth following for a moment. Perhaps Plato did think that goodness, or some such thing related to morality, was an ultimate fact about the world. But a Platonic world is not very close to a Russellian world. Plato was not a Christian, of course, but his world view has very often been taken to be congenial (especially congenial compared to some other philosophical views) to a religious understanding of the world. He would not have been satisfied, I think, with Russell's "accidental collocations of atoms," nor would he have taken the force of the grave to be "so nearly certain." The idea of the Good seems to play a metaphysical role in his thought. It is somehow fundamental to what *is* as well as to what ought to be, much more fundamental to reality than are the atoms. A Platonic man, therefore, who sets himself to live in accordance with the Good aligns himself with what is deepest and most basic in existence. Or to put it another way, we might say that whatever values a Platonic world imposes on a man are values to which the Platonic world itself is committed, through and through.

Not so, of course, for a Russellian world. Values and obligations cannot be deep in such a world. They have a grip only upon surface phenomena, probably only upon man. What is deep in a Russellian world must be such things as matter and energy, or perhaps natural law, chance, or chaos. If it really were a fact that one had obligations in a Russellian world, then something would be laid upon man that might cost a man everything but that went no further than man. And that difference from a Platonic world seems to make all the difference.

This discussion suggests, I think, that there are two related ways in which morality is queer in a Russellian world. Or maybe they are better construed as two aspects of the queerness we have been exploring. In most of the preceding discussion I have been focusing on the strangeness of an overriding demand that does not seem to conduce to the *good* of the person on whom it is laid. (In fact, it does not even promise his good.) Here, however, we focus on the fact that this demand – radical enough in the human life on which it is laid – is *superficial* in a Russellian world. Something that reaches close to the heart of my own life, perhaps even demanding the sacrifice of that life, is not deep at all in the world in which (on a Russellian view) that life is lived. And that, too, seems absurd.

This brings to an end the major part of my discussion. If I have been successful at all you will have shared with me to some extent in the sense of the queerness of morality, its absurdity in a Russellian world. If you also share the conviction that it cannot in the end be absurd in that way, then perhaps you will also be attracted to some religious view of the world. Perhaps you also will say that morality must have some deeper grip upon the world than a Russellian view allows. And, consequently, things like mind and purpose must also be deeper in the real world than they would be in a Russellian world. They must be more original, more controlling. The accidental collocation of atoms cannot be either primeval or final, nor can the grave be an end. But of course that would be only a beginning, a sketch waiting to be filled in.

We cannot here do much to fill it in further. But I should like to close with a final, and rather tentative suggestion, as to a direction in which one might move in thinking about the place of morality in the world. It is suggested to me by certain elements in my own religion, Christianity.

I come more and more to think that morality, while a fact, is a twisted and distorted fact. Or perhaps better, that it is a barely recognizable version of another fact, a version adapted to a twisted and distorted world. It is something like, I suppose, the way in which the pine that grows at timberline, wind blasted and twisted low against the rock, is a version of the tall and symmetrical tree that grows lower on the slopes. I think it may be that the related notions of sacrifice and gift represent (or come close to representing) the fact, that is, the pattern of life, whose distorted version we know here as morality. Imagine a situation, an "economy" if you will, in which no one ever buys or trades for or seizes any good thing. But whatever good he enjoys it is either one which he himself has created or else one which he receives as a free and unconditional gift. And as soon as he has tasted it and seen that it is good he stands ready to give it away in his turn as soon as the opportunity arises. In such a place, if one were to speak either of his rights or his duties, his remark might be met with puzzled laughter as his hearers struggled to recall an ancient world in which those terms referred to something important.

We have, of course, even now some occasions that tend in this direction. Within some families perhaps, or even in a regiment in desperate battle, people may for a time pass largely beyond morality and live lives of gift and sacrifice. On those occasions nothing would be lost if the moral concepts and the moral language were to disappear. But it is probably not possible that such situations and occasions should be more than rare exceptions in the daily life of the present world. Christianity, however, which tells us that the present world is "fallen" and hence leads us to expect a distortion in its important features, also tells us that one day the redemption of the world will be complete and that then all things shall be made new. And it seems to me to suggest an "economy" more akin to that of gift and sacrifice than to that of rights and duties. If something like that should be true, then perhaps morality, like the Marxist state, is destined to wither away (unless perchance it should happen to survive in hell).

Christianity, then, I think is related to the queerness of morality in one way and perhaps in two. In the first instance, it provides a view of the world in which morality is not an absurdity. It gives morality a deeper place in the world than does a Russellian view and thus permits it to "make sense." But in the second instance, it perhaps suggests that morality is not the deepest thing, that it is provisional and transitory, that it is due to serve its use and then to pass away in favor of something richer and deeper. Perhaps we can say that it begins by inverting the quotation with which I began and by telling us that, since God exists, not everything is permitted; but it may also go on to tell us that, since God exists, in the end there shall be no occasion for any prohibition.

Notes

1 Perhaps, however, Kant was not entirely clear on this point, for in some places he talks as though it is only the *possibility* of God's existence that is a necessary postulate of morality. For a discussion of this point see M. Jamie Ferreira, "Kant's Postulate: The Possibility or the Existence of God?" *Kant-Studien* 17, no. 1 (1983): 75–80.

2 In Bertrand Russell, *Mysticism and Logic* (New York: Barnes & Noble, 1917), pp. 47–8.

3 Kurt Baier, *The Moral Point of View* (Ithaca: Cornell University Press, 1958), p. 314.

4 Richard Brandt, *Ethical Theory* (Englewood Cliffs, NJ: Prentice-Hall, 1959), pp. 375–8.

5 William P. Alston, ed., *Religious Belief and Philosophical Thought* (New York: Harcourt, Brace & World, 1963), p. 25.

41

Pure Love

Robert Merrihew Adams

In a standard handbook of teachings of the Roman Catholic Church we find the statement,

> There is a habitual state of love for God, which is pure charity without admixture of the motive of self-interest. Neither fear of punishments nor desire of rewards have any more part in it. God is no longer loved for the sake of the merit, nor for the sake of the perfection, nor for the sake of the happiness to be found in loving Him. (Denzinger, 1911: par. 1327)

This is not a surprising proposition to find in a compendium of Christian beliefs. The surprising thing is that it is not there to be endorsed, but to be condemned as "rash, scandalous, bad sounding, offensive to pious ears, pernicious in practice," or "even . . . erroneous." It is a fairly accurate quotation from Fénelon's *Explanation of the Maxims of the Saints Concerning the Interior Life*,[1] and is the first of the propositions from that book that were condemned by Pope Innocent XII in 1699 in the denouement of the famous dispute between Fénelon and Bossuet.

It is not my purpose here to tell the story, or sift through all the rights and wrongs, of that aftershock of the Quietist controversy. Fénelon attracts my attention because he articulated an extreme form of an ideal of disinterested love which has been

Robert Merrihew Adams, "Pure Love," from *Journal of Religious Ethics* 8 (1980), pp. 88–99. Copyright © *Journal of Religious Ethics*, Inc., published by Blackwell Publishers, Oxford.

attractive to Christians in many times and places. Ideals, like metals, reveal some of their properties most clearly when stretched or pressed; and I believe that reflection on Fénelon's views will shed light on the relations between love and various sorts of self-concern.

Holy Indifference

Fénelon distinguishes three basic types of love for God.

1 Love "for the gifts of God distinguished from him, and not for himself, may be called, *merely servile love*." Fénelon has little to say about it because, as he remarks, it is not love of God at all, strictly speaking (Fénelon, 1697: 13f, lf, my italics).

2 *Concupiscential love* is "that love wherewith God is loved only as the only means and instrument of happiness," as "the only object, the sight of which can render us happy" (ibid.: 14, 2f). It is the lover himself, rather than God, who is the "ultimate end" of this sort of love. But in concupiscential love it is at least by the vision of God himself that one seeks to be happy, whereas in merely servile love one seeks satisfaction in gifts much more separate from God.

3 *Charity* is love of God for himself. Its "formal object . . . is the goodness or beauty of God taken simply and absolutely in itself, without any idea that is relative to us" (ibid.: 42). Many passages in Fénelon's works suggest that charity consists

in desiring that God's will be done, desiring it for its own sake, as an ultimate end.

Fénelon distinguished two intermediate states in which concupiscential love for God is mingled with charity. His conception of these states is complex and subtle, and changed significantly during the two-year period of intense controversy with Bossuet. We shall not be concerned with them, however, but only with the contrast between concupiscential love and the *pure* state of charity, unmingled with other motives, which Fénelon, following St Francis de Sales, calls *holy indifference*.

In calling this state "indifference" he does not mean that it is "a stupid insensibility, an inward inactivity, a non-willing . . . [or] a perpetual equilibrium of the soul." On the contrary, "as [that] indifference is love itself, it is a very real and very positive principle. It is a positive and formal will which makes us really will or desire every volition of God that is known to us" (ibid.: 51). Fénelon quotes with approval St Francis de Sales as saying,

> Indifference . . . loves nothing except for the sake of the will of God. . . . The indifferent heart is like a ball of wax between the hands of its God, to receive in like manner all the impressions of the eternal good pleasure. It is a heart without choice, equally disposed to everything, without any other object of its will but the will of its God. It does not set its love on the things that God wills, but on the will of God that wills them. (ibid.: 55f; quoted pretty accurately, from Sales, 1969: 770, Book IX, ch. 4)

The state of pure love is one of indifference because in that state the soul is indifferent to all created things, and specifically to her own good, except insofar as she believes that God's will is concerned. "The indifferent soul no longer wills anything for herself by the motive of her own self-interest" (Fénelon, 1697: 49).

The most dramatic feature that characterizes the state of holy indifference is the sacrifice of eternal happiness. For one's eternal happiness is not excluded from the thesis that in this highest state of Christian perfection one wills *nothing* as an end in itself except that God's will be done. The logical consequence of the thesis had already been rigorously drawn by St Francis de Sales (1969: 770; Book IX, ch. 4; partly quoted by Fénelon, 1697: 56):

In sum, the good pleasure of God is the supreme object of the indifferent soul. Wherever she sees it she runs "to the fragrance of" its "perfumes," and always seeks the place where there is more of it, without consideration of any other thing. . . . [The indifferent person] would rather have hell with the will of God than Paradise without the will of God – yes indeed, he would prefer hell to Paradise if he knew that there were a little more of the divine good pleasure in the former than in the latter; so that if (to imagine something impossible) he knew that his damnation were a little more agreeable to God than his salvation, he would leave his salvation, and run to his damnation.

Fénelon (1697: 87) emphasizes the conditional aspect of this sacrifice. "It is certain that all the sacrifices which the most disinterested souls make ordinarily concerning their eternal happiness are conditional. One says, my God, if by an impossibility you willed to condemn me to the eternal pains of Hell without losing your love, I would not love you less for it. But this sacrifice cannot be absolute in the ordinary state."

Fénelon (ibid.: 90, 87) does speak of an "absolute [i.e., unconditional] sacrifice of her own self-interest for eternity," which a soul in the state of holy indifference can make if persuaded "that she is justly reprobated by God." This absolute sacrifice was much more controversial than the conditional sacrifice, and Fénelon's exposition of it is tangled and tormented, and changed (I suspect) during the period of the controversy. It involves a very questionable claim about contrary beliefs being held in different "parts" of the soul. Fortunately our arguments need not depend on the doctrine of the absolute sacrifice; the conditional sacrifice of eternal happiness will provide us with plenty of food for thought.

The reason why the sacrifice of salvation cannot normally be unconditional is that Christians should believe that God does will their salvation. They should therefore will it too, not out of self-interest, but because God wills it. Hence Fénelon (ibid.: 73) can speak of "the disinterested love that we owe to ourselves as to our neighbor for the love of God." Precisely here another important consequence of Fénelon's conception of holy indifference comes into view. On his account the disinterested desire for one's own salvation clearly is just a special case of the desire one ought to have for the salvation of all human beings, as willed by God. More generally, indeed, if all one wills as an end in itself is that God's will be done, one will regard oneself, volitionally, as just another person. One will not be special in one's own volitional eyes, except as the only agent that one can directly control.

> Souls attracted to pure love may be as disinterested with respect to themselves as to their neighbor, because they do not see or desire in themselves, any more than in the most unknown neighbor, anything but the glory of God, his good pleasure, and the fulfillment of his promises. In this sense these souls are like strangers to themselves. (ibid.: 106)

This neutralizing of the specialness of one's own self may be attractive to many moralists. It is a characteristic that Fénelon's theory shares with more than one ethical secular theory, including the most stringent form of utilitarianism. But my principal aim in this paper is to show that it does not belong in a theory of Christian Love.

Some Objections

One of the first objections to Fénelon's views that is likely to occur to us is that the state of holy indifference, as he describes it, is psychologically impossible. Could we really have no desire for anything, for its own sake, except that God's will be done? Perhaps not; but we should realize that Fénelon's exclusion of self-interested desires from the state of pure love was not as sweeping as might appear from the statements quoted thus far. For having said that "the indifferent soul . . . has no longer any interested desire," he adds, "'Tis true, that there remain in her still some involuntary inclinations and aversions, which she submits [to the will of God]; but she has no longer any voluntary and deliberate desires for her own interest, except on those occasions wherein she does not cooperate faithfully with all her grace" (Fénelon, 1697: 49f). There is an emphasis here on the voluntary as the only morally significant functions of the soul, which is congenial to the tradition within which Fénelon is working. The "voluntary and deliberate" desires, I take it, are conditional and unconditional choices, intentions, and resolutions. These can be in the indifferent soul, according to Fénelon, only to the extent that they are derived from a decision that in every possible (or even impossible) situation, she would choose whatever

would best fulfil the will of God. The "involuntary inclinations and aversions," on the other hand – the desires that we know we have, not because we decide on them but because we feel them – are seen as assailing the commandpost of the soul from outside, so to speak, and may be self-interested even in a perfectly indifferent soul, provided they are controlled and not allowed to influence choice. The indifferent soul will normally have, for example, both a natural, self-interested, involuntary aversion to physical illness, and a deliberate intention to do, ordinarily, what is necessary to avoid or cure physical illness. But the intention will be based on the belief that God commands us to care for our health, and will not be influenced in the least by the aversion. This extreme separation between impulse and will strikes me as both unrealistic and undesirable, but I will not bear down on that point here. When I ascribe to Fénelon views about desires, they should be understood to be about *voluntary* desires, unless otherwise indicated.

I shall be more concerned here with a series of objections in which Fénelon's opponents claimed that his views would exclude from the Christian ideal some of the most important Christian virtues – particularly hope, penitence, gratitude, and even the desire to love God. Some of the fiercest controversy raged about the theological virtue of *hope*. Because he held that even salvation, or eternal happiness, is not desired with a self-interested desire in the state of pure love, Fénelon was accused of leaving no room for this virtue in the highest state of the Christian life in this world; and he was at pains to defend himself against the charge. The indifferent or fully disinterested soul, he insists, will still hope for her own salvation. In hoping, she will will to be saved. But this is not "a falling away from the perfection of her disinterest," nor "a return to the motive of self-interest." For "the purest love never prevents us from willing, and even causes us to will positively, everything that God wills that we should will" (Fénelon, 1697: 44). "Whoever loves from pure love without any mixture of self-interest . . . wills happiness for himself only because he knows that God wills it, and that he wills that each of us should will it for his glory" (ibid.: 26f). "Then I will that which really is, and is known by me to be, the greatest of all my interests, without any interested motive determining me to it" (ibid.: 46). As the controversy progressed, Fénelon (1698: 12) added that in holy indifference we would desire our own salvation "precisely for the reason that it is our good, since it is for this reason that God wills it, and for which he commands us also to will it. Therefore . . . precisely the reason that it is our good, really moves and excites the will of man" in hoping for the intuitive vision of God. But if, on this account, the indifferent soul desires her salvation because it is her own good, she desires her own good only because God desires it – she desires it only in order that his desires may be satisfied.

The indifferent soul can will, conditionally, that she be saved *if* God wills it. And believing that God does will it, she can detach the consequent and will that she be saved, *since* God wills it. But it is hard to see how she can will that God will her salvation. For she could hardly want God to will her salvation solely in order that his will might be done. I have not found any place where Fénelon explicitly draws this conclusion. It would probably have seemed damaging, since the desire it would exclude seems to be central to much of Christian piety and prayer. But despite the strangeness of this consequence of Fénelon's position, I do not think this is the most promising point at which to try to show that he excludes something that is important for Christian ethics to maintain.

Self-Concern, Self-Interest, and the Desire to Love God

Fénelon's opponents charged that he would not have even charity itself to be sought for as a virtue (Noailles et al., 1698: 224). They dwelt much less on this objection than on that about hope, but they struck here a much more sensitive spot in Fénelon's position – one at which I believe that he himself was driven into inconsistency. Fénelon inherited from St Francis de Sales a strong suspicion against desires in which one aims ultimately at one's own virtue or perfection or even one's own love for God. St Francis de Sales (1969: 785, Book IX, ch. 9; cf. p. 1549 (first draft)) had spoken of the danger of coming to love one's love for God instead of loving God. And Fénelon (1697: 10f) declared that in pure charity God is no longer loved "for the sake of the merit, nor for the sake of the perfection . . . to be found in loving him." Yet they certainly also thought that we ought to want to be virtuous, and that the chief point of virtue we ought to desire is to love God with charity.

The only way of reconciling these concerns that is consistent with the general thesis that the only thing that is desired for its own sake in pure love is

that God's will be done, is to say that in pure love the soul does indeed want to love God, but only because (as she believes) he wills that we love him. Yet Fénelon was not in fact prepared to accept every consequence of this view, as can be seen in his treatment of (a) the desire that God's will be done, and (b) the desire that I love and obey God. We might suppose that these desires could never be opposed to each other. But such a conflict seems at least thinkable. Fénelon accepts a distinction between God's *signified will*, revealed to us primarily in his commandments and counsels, which is often violated, and his *good pleasure*, contrary to which nothing happens. It is not just God's signified will, but his good pleasure, that the indifferent soul wants to be done. Suppose it were God's good pleasure that my heart be hardened so that I would hate him and disobey his signified will. In that case it would seem that my hatred and disobedience are what God would really want, rather than the love and obedience that he commands. So if my heart is in holy indifference, shouldn't I desire, conditionally, that I should hate and disobey God if it were his good pleasure?

Fénelon's first response will be that the supposition of God's actively willing my sin is impossible. Sins that happen, though not contrary to God's good pleasure, are not willed but only permitted by God, according to Fénelon's theology; and God's "permissive will" is not proposed as a rule for even the indifferent soul (Fénelon, 1697: article XVIII, True). Nonetheless, Fénelon does demand of the indifferent soul a conditional desire regarding another impossible supposition – the supposition, namely, that God would torment her forever in hell though she loved him purely. I cannot see any good (or indeed any morally tolerable) reason for thinking that that supposition is any less impossible than the supposition of God's wanting me to hate and disobey him. So if we are to have conditional preferences regarding impossible suppositions, it would seem that the indifferent soul ought to will that she should hate and disobey God if that were his good pleasure.

But Fénelon vehemently rejects any such desire. This is most explicit in his treatment of "the ultimate trials" in which an indifferent soul makes an absolute or unconditional sacrifice of her own self-interest for eternity. Even in that case, he says,

She loves God more purely than ever. Far from consenting positively to hate him, she does not consent even indirectly to cease for a single instant from loving him, nor to diminish in the least her love, nor to put ever to the increase of that love any voluntary bounds, nor to commit any fault, not even a venial fault. (ibid.: 91)

It would be blasphemous to say that a soul in trials "may consent to hate God, because God will have her hate him; or that she may consent never more to love God, because he will no more be beloved by her; or that she may voluntarily confine her love, because God will have her to limit it; or that she may violate his law, because God will have her to transgress it" (ibid.: 93f).

Even a conditional desire to hate God if he should will it seems to be ruled out by saying that the indifferent soul "does not consent even indirectly" to cease, diminish, or limit her love for God. And, in the course of his controversy with Bossuet, Fénelon stated explicitly that the conditional sacrifice envisaged by St Francis de Sales is a sacrifice of one's supernatural happiness (which consists in the eternal rapture of an intuitive vision of God, accompanied by all the gifts of body and soul), but is not a sacrifice of "the love that we necessarily owe to God in every state" (Fénelon, 1838a: 89, Letter V, §3; cf. 1838b: 134, Letter III, §5).

There is thus an important difference between Fénelon's treatment of (b), the desire that I love and obey God, and his treatment of (c), the desire that I be happy rather than miserable eternally, if I have charity. It is impossible that God should will the opposite of either (b) or (c), according to Fénelon. Yet he holds that if my love were pure, I should desire conditionally to be miserable eternally, without ceasing to have charity, if God willed it; but he denies that I should desire conditionally to hate or disobey God, or even to lessen my love for him, if God willed it. This difference in the conditional desires of the soul in pure love can be accounted for only on the supposition that the soul has desire (b) independently of (a), the desire that God's will be done. For if I desired to love and obey God only in order that his will might be done, it would seem that I should want to cease loving and obeying him if he willed it. If I ought not to have that conditional desire, then presumably my loving and obeying God is something that I would desire at least partly for its own sake if I were a perfect Christian.

One might try to avoid this conclusion by supposing that desire (b) ought to be derived from (d) the desire that as many people as possible love and obey God. On this account I ought not to desire my own loving God for its own sake, but only as a means to the satisfaction of (d). But this view is not suggested by Fénelon, and would require him to say that I ought to have a conditional desire to hate God if that would result in more other people coming to love and obey him. But he would surely refuse to say that, and so is still left with the conclusion that my loving and obeying God is something I ought to want at least partly for its own sake.

But if part of what I am to desire for its own sake is not only that God's will be done, but also that *I* love and obey God, then it seems that my love for him is not to be completely disinterested; there is to be an element of self-concern in it. Thus Fénelon seems forced to admit an element of self-concern even in perfect love for God.

Of course the fact that even Fénelon did not manage consistently to exclude all self-concerned attitudes from the state of holy indifference does not prove that there is a rightful place for self-concern in pure or perfect love; but I think in fact there is. Not to care, literally not to care at all, whether I will be one who loves or hates God, so long as God's will will be done, would not be an attitude of love toward God on my part, but of something much more impersonal.[2]

Perhaps Fénelon would not have been too troubled by this. What he meant to insist on most of all was the ideal of a love for God completely free of *self-interest*. To desire, for its own sake, to be related in any way to another person is self-concerned, in the sense that it is aiming ultimately at a state of affairs that essentially involves oneself. I suspect Fénelon would say that while the desire to be one who loves and obeys God is self-concerned in this broad sense, it is not self-interested in the sense that concerns him.

This response has some plausibility. In wanting to love or serve God, or someone else, one is not necessarily aiming at one's own advantage. It may be part of one's desire that one wants to give up something, or make some sacrifice of one's own advantage, for the beloved. Fénelon is particularly interested in a desire to love and obey God even if one were eternally miserable. Such desires are concerned in part with the desirer, but it would seem strange, in many cases, to call them "self-interested." This suggests that not all self-concerned desires are self-interested; self-interest is a species of self-concern.

Which species, is not easy to say, however. There is perhaps a broad sense in which it is self-interested to desire anything *for one's own sake*. But "for one's own sake" is a very vague expression, and no account of it, or of a broad sense of "self-interested," that has occurred to me seems really satisfactory. I prefer therefore to use "self-interested" in a narrower sense. Historically, to speak of a person's "interest" is to speak of his good-on-the-whole; a state of affairs is "in his interest" if and only if it is good for him, on the whole, that it should obtain. I think this agrees well enough with Fénelon's use of "interest" (*intérêt*). We may say, then, that a desire is *self-interested*, in the strict or narrower sense, if and only if it is a desire in which one aims ultimately at one's own good-on-the-whole. Butler (1970: 101, 104, sermon XI) adopts a sense very much like this for "interested." (When I speak of a desire in which one *aims ultimately* at an end or state of affairs X, I mean a desire for X for its own sake, or at least partly for its own sake; or a desire for something else for the sake of X, where one does desire X at least partly for its own sake.) Even this narrower conception of self-interestedness is not without its problems, for it is doubtful whether anyone has a satisfactory conception of a person's good. But let us ignore that problem for present purposes. We do speak with some confidence of states of affairs being good (or bad) for a person on the whole – whether we are entitled to that confidence or not.

Fénelon's position can be modified, in terms of this distinction between self-concern and self-interest, to make it consistent. He could say that Christian love ought to be completely free of self-interested desire, though not completely free of self-concern. This certainly would be a modification of his views, as it involves abandoning the thesis that one who has perfect charity wants nothing for its own sake except that God's will be done. But I think the weaker claim is much more plausible than the stronger, and is sufficient to account for much of what Fénelon wanted to say.

In particular, the Salesian and Fénelonian suspicion against love for one's own love of God can be interpreted as something less than a complete rejection of self-concerned desires to love God. This may be done in at least three ways.

(1) Most obviously, Fénelon may still consistently object to desires in which love for God is desired not for its own sake but as a means to one's own good. Similarly, St Francis de Sales was particularly worried that one might begin to prize one's love for God for the sake of the pleasure that one

found in it. Wanting pleasure for oneself is not necessarily a self-interested motive, in the narrower sense defined above; for one can pursue one's own pleasure without pursuing one's own good-on-the-whole, as in smoking a cigarette, or eating a hot fudge sundae, that one thinks will be enjoyable but bad for one. But it seems to be consistent to maintain that in perfect charity one's love for God would be desired for its own sake, but one's own pleasure, as well as one's own good, would not.

I do not mean to suggest that St Francis de Sales does maintain this explicitly. When he speaks of the danger of loving one's love of God, "not for the good pleasure and satisfaction of God, but for the pleasure and satisfaction that we ourselves derive from it" (Sales, 1969: 785f, Book IX, ch. 9), he considers only the possibilities that the love is desired for the lover's pleasure and that it is desired for God's pleasure. He is correct in pointing out that love for God could be desired primarily as a pleasant experience of one's own, and that that would be a perversion. I agree with him about this, though I do not think there is necessarily anything wrong with wanting, for its own sake, to *enjoy* loving God, so long as one's interest in the subjective pleasure is subsidiary to one's desire for the objective relationship. But it is just this desire for the objective relationship that St Francis de Sales fails to mention. Desiring charity as pleasing to God is not the only alternative to desiring it for one's own pleasure. Love for God can also be desired for its own sake as a relation to God; and I think some aspects of the Salesian position imply that it ought to be desired in that way.

(2) Another characterization of the perversion that St Francis de Sales fears is that "instead of loving this holy love because it tends toward God who is the beloved, we love it because it proceeds from us who are the lovers" (Sales, 1969: 785, Book IX, ch. 9). More vividly, as he wrote in an earlier draft of his *Treatise*,

Who does not see that [in this perversion] it is no longer God that I regard, but from God I have returned to myself, and that I love this love because it is mine, not because it is for God. (Sales, 1969: 1550)

The point of these statements is not obvious, but we may conjecture that it has to do, not with what is *desired* in love, but with what is *admired*. Our interest in loving God is perverted when the focus of our admiration shifts from God's perfection, from his worthiness to be loved, to our own possible perfection. This seems to be correct, and is consistent with the view that our own righteousness and love for God are among the ends that we ought to desire at least partly for their own sake.

(3) A sense of proportion provides a final, and reasonable, ground of suspicion against one's interest in one's own love for God, and more broadly in one's own virtue. Even if self-concerned desires to love and obey God, and to be morally and religiously perfect, have a rightful or indeed a necessary place in the best Christian piety, it is clear that they all too easily assume too large a place. It is sinfully self-centered to care too much about one's own perfection in proportion to one's concern for the good of other people and the glorification of God in his whole creation. If one aims ultimately *only* at one's own perfection, one's attitude is not one of love for God. In this way it would indeed be possible to love one's (supposed) love for God instead of loving God.

Penitence and Gratitude

The suggestion that Christian love ought to be completely free of self-interested desire, but not completely free of self-concern, can be tested against other Christian virtues, to see if it is consistent with a satisfactory account of them. It works out very well in the case of *penitence*. It was charged that Fénelon overthrew "the proper and intrinsical motive of repentance" by holding that redeemed souls ought to engage in penitential behavior, "not for their own purification and deliverance, but as a thing that God wills" (Noailles et al., 1698: 226). Insofar as the accent falls here on "deliverance," implying that in penitence one should have a self-interested motive, fearing some loss or diminution of one's own good, this criticism shows an ignoble misunderstanding of the nature of penitence. In this respect Fénelon's sharp retort seems fully justified: "You annihilate the acts of perfect contrition, where one makes oneself suffer for one's sin, not for the sake of the happiness that one desires, but for the sake of the righteousness that one loves in itself" (Fénelon, 1838a: 87, Letter IV, §20; cf. 1838b: 143, Letter III, §12). The value of penitence is not enhanced by self-interest.

But penitence is certainly self-concerned. For it involves remorse, and remorse is not just regret that something bad has happened; it is being particularly sorry that one has done something bad *oneself.* The best sort of penitence involves wanting, for its own sake, not to be a wrongdoer. In penitence one cannot regard oneself as "just another person." Insofar as the accent, in the charge against Fénelon, falls on "purification," implying that in penitence one's own moral or religious improvement should be sought as an end in itself, the objectors seem to have a correct view of penitence. It is a view that Fénelon himself appears to share, in proposing "the righteousness that one loves in itself" as the right motive of penitence. And it requires the admission of self-concern, though not necessarily of self-interest, to the Christian ideal.

Thus far we have not found any Christian virtue that requires self-interest. But we have yet to consider *gratitude*. Fénelon's opponents charged that he omits mention of gratitude as a motive of love toward God (Noailles et al., 1698: 252). He responded that gratitude is useful in the earlier stages of the spiritual life, by helping us to see and attend to the perfections of God, and by diminishing concupiscence and increasing grace; "finally, in the most perfect state, the acts of . . . thankfulness become more and more frequent, but that is because they are commanded by charity" (Fénelon, 1838b: 132, Letter III, §2). This answer fails to come to grips with the problem. Where acts of thankfulness have to be commanded by charity – a charity not motivated by benefits received (ibid.) – there cannot be much real gratitude.

The first question to ask here is whether the occasion of gratitude must be something that is good for the grateful person and that he desires *ultimately because* it is good for him. Certainly one cannot appropriately be said to be *grateful* to just anyone for just any good deed that he does. Suppose a stranger risks his life to save the life of a child who is equally a stranger to you. No matter how much you admire the hero, or how much you feel for the child, it would be odd to say that you are *grateful* to the hero. You are not sufficiently involved. But you need not be *benefited* by the act for which you are grateful. You may be grateful to a second person for doing something for a third person at your request, even though it is not you but the third person who is benefited. Your request involves you enough to render both the fact and the concept of gratitude appropriate in such a case.

But would God's answers to our prayers for others provide adequate occasion for Christian gratitude to God? I think not. The Christian is supposed to be conscious of God's goodness *to him*, and grateful for that. And this is not an arbitrary demand. It is rooted in the needs of love. You might be very grateful to me for my making a contribution in your name to your favorite charity. But such a gift does not fully take the place of giving you something for your own benefit or pleasure. The good and happiness of the beloved are central ends in themselves for love. The full expression of love requires some actions that aim ultimately at those ends; and one ought to respond to such acts with gratitude.

Christians are supposed to be grateful to God for acting to promote their good. In the best sort of gratitude one must like something about what the benefactor did or meant to accomplish. And in gratitude to God it won't do to like only "the thought behind" the deed, as if he were a cousin who had knitted you a sweater of the wrong size. God makes no such mistakes. So it seems in the best sort of gratitude to God one must like one's own good; one must prefer that it have been promoted rather than not. And I think one must prefer it for one's own sake; that is, the preference must be self-interested. Suppose one were glad to have had one's own good promoted, but only as a means, saying to oneself, "This will help me glorify God," or "This will enable me to do a lot of good for other people." Such an inability to accept a gift *for oneself*, when one's own good was the chief goal of the giver, is *ungrateful*.

This argument does not show that the grateful Christian ought to pursue his own good as an end in itself, but only that he ought to like its having been promoted when it has been promoted by God. It is a self-interest already satisfied, rather than a striving self-interest that is required here. But it is a sort of self-interest, favoring one's own good for its (and one's) own sake.

Our review of the motivational requirements of several Christian virtues suggests that certain sorts of self-concern hold an important place in the Christian life; and that self-interest does indeed hold a place there, but a much less important place than some other sorts of self-concern. The right approach to Christian self-denial is not by an attempt at complete exclusion of self-interest or self-concern, but by a subtler study of their right and wrong relation to other motives.

Eros in Agape

Our discussion thus far has been about love for God, but it can also be applied to love for fellow human beings. The purest and ethically most interesting sort of love for another person is often identified with *benevolence* – that is, with desire for the other person's good. The natural extension of this view to the case of love for God is to identify perfect love for God with the desire that God's will be done.

Similarly, the contrast between *Agape* and *Eros* is popularly seen as a special case of the contrast between altruism and self-interest. *Agape*, Christian love, is identified with benevolence, and *Eros* is identified with self-interested desire for relationship with another person.[3] Benevolence is a motive that can hardly be praised too highly, and the contrast between altruistic and self-interested desires is legitimate and useful. But it has too often been treated as a dichotomy. That is, it is too often assumed, particularly where personal relations are in question, that what is desired is desired either for one's own good or for another person's good. The conception of love, and particularly of *Eros*, has suffered much from being forced into this dichotomy.

For *Eros* need not be either self-interested or altruistic. This is not a claim about what Plato (for example) meant, but about the character of the attitudes that we would normally recognize as concrete paradigms of *Eros*. The central case of *Eros* is passionate desire for a personal relationship. And such desire for a personal relationship need not be based on the belief that it would be good for anyone. This is most obvious in the case of a tragic or destructive *Eros*. There are doubtless instances in which a close personal relationship is strongly desired by both of the parties to it although neither of them believes it will be good for either of them. Perhaps if they truly love each other they will prefer on balance to break off the relationship; but that does not change the fact that they have a desire for the relationship – a desire which is neither self-interested nor altruistic in the present sense.

It is happily more usual in human relations that the lover believes that the relationship he desires would be good both for him and for the beloved. But it is *not* usual for the lover to desire the relationship only because he believes it would be good for one or both of them. Indeed if he desires the relationship in such a way that he would have no interest in it at all if he did not think it would be beneficial, we may doubt that he really loves. *Eros* is not based on calculations or judgments of utility or benefit, and must therefore at least partly escape classification as self-interested or altruistic. The mistake, in trying to force love into a dichotomy of self-interest and altruism, is a failure to recognize a desire for a relationship for its own sake as a third type of desire that is not just a combination or consequence of desire for one's own good and desire for another person's good. It is indeed this third type of desire – which is self-concerned but not self-interested in the sense explained above – that is most characteristic of *Eros*.

Thus the identification of *Eros* with self-interested desire for personal relationships is in error; and so is the identification of *Agape* with benevolence. The ideal of Christian love includes not only benevolence but also desire for certain kinds of personal relationship, for their own sakes. Were that not so, it would be strange to call it "love." It is an abuse of the word "love" to say that one *loves* a person, or any other object, if one does not care, except instrumentally, about one's relation to that object. Even St Francis de Sales (1969: 843, Book X, ch. 10) said that "if . . . there were an infinite goodness . . . with which we could not have any union or communication, we would certainly esteem it more highly than ourselves . . . and . . . we could have mere wishes to be able to love it; but strictly speaking we would not love it, because love has to do with union."

In saying that love involves caring about one's relationship with its object in a way that benevolence does not, I have in mind a wide variety of relationships, and not just those intimate social relationships that we think of first in connection with love. To take an example that is closely related to Fénelon's ideas: the lover will commonly want to *serve* the beloved – to satisfy his desires or promote his well-being. It may be thought that the benevolent person also wants to serve, by promoting the happiness of the object of his benevolence. But that is not quite right. The benevolent person need not care who promotes the well-being of the one whom he wishes well, so long as it is promoted. But to the lover it is not indifferent who promotes the good of his beloved. He wants to be the one who serves his beloved – or at least one of those who do.

Similarly the lover not only desires that misfortune and annoyances should not befall his beloved; he is particularly concerned that *he* not cause harm or displeasure to his beloved. And in general it is normally a part of love to want one's own actions and their consequences to express one's love. That this is true of love for God as well as love for fellow human beings seems to be one of the factors that led Fénelon into inconsistency.

The claim that Christian love – New Testament *Agape* – is not solely benevolence can be supported by at least two arguments from the Bible.

(1)   Whatever else *Agape* may be in the New Testament, it is first of all God's love for us. And God's love for us is surely seen as involving a desire for certain relationships between God and us, for their own sakes and not merely as good for us. The jealous husband of Israel (Jeremiah 2: 1–3: 5; Hosea 2), he made the whole human race so that they might seek and find him (Acts 17: 26–7). He desires our worship and devotion. Why did Christ give himself up for the Church? Because he loved her and wanted to present her to himself in splendor as a bride (Ephesians 5: 25–7). No doubt it would be possible to interpret all of this on the hypothesis that God desires to be related to us only because it will be good for us. But I think that is implausible. The Bible depicts a God who seems at least as interested in divine-human relationships as in human happiness *per se*. Even Anders Nygren, who is most emphatic about the unselfishness of *Agape*, presents it as one of the distinctive characteristics of *Agape* that it creates *fellowship* between God and human beings. But if such fellowship is desired for its own sake by God, God's desire is self-concerned inasmuch as the object of the desire involves him as essentially as it involves us. And would we have it otherwise? Let him who would rather be the object of benevolence than of love cast the first stone.

(2)   The New Testament sets a very high value on reconciliation and friendly relations between people. Loving enemies and strangers seems to be first of all a matter of desiring good for them, but also of greeting them (Matthew 5: 43–7). Christians are to "greet one another with a kiss of love [*Agape*]" (I Peter 5: 14). The incentive of love is to lead them to be in harmony with each other (Philippians 2: 1–2). One might try to explain this on the hypothesis that reconciliation, harmony, and friendship are to be pursued solely out of benevolence, as being good for the other persons involved. But that seems a strained interpretation. There is no reason to think that reconciliation and friendly relations are always a benefit to people, except insofar as they are worth pursuing for their own sake. Perhaps a good fight would sometimes be better for people. The Christian interest in harmonious

relations, as a goal of love, seems to go beyond any merely instrumental value they may have. And I believe that moral intuition, as well as Scriptural authority, favors regarding the desire for friendly relations, for their own sake, as a good motive.

Conceived as I have argued they ought to be, *Eros* and *Agape* are not opposites. *Eros* is generally present as a strand in love. It is the lover's desire for relationship with the beloved. It may be self-interested, but it need not be. It manifests itself most fully in a desire for the relationship for its own sake, and not just for the good of either party. Benevolence, the desire for the good of the beloved, is also present as a strand in love. I have argued that *Agape* is not to be identified with this strand. It includes both strands. Specifically, *Agape* includes a sort of *Eros* – not every sort of *Eros*, for there are certainly selfish, sick, and destructive forms of *Eros* that have no place in the Christian ethical ideal. One of the distinguishing characteristics of *Agape* is the kind of *Eros* that it includes – the kind of relationship that is desired in *Agape*.

It is a striking fact that while benevolence (the desire for another person's well-being) and *Eros*, as a desire for relationship with another person, seem to be quite distinct desires, we use a single name, "love" or "*Agape*," for an attitude that includes both of them, at least in typical cases. Why do we do this? I find it a tempting hypothesis that the central element in *Agape*, the element that holds the concept together, is the agapic type of *Eros*. In an exemplary case of *Agape* the lover wants a certain type of relationship with the beloved. That relationship includes mutual benevolence. Thus benevolence is desired in agapic *Eros*. Desiring benevolence is not the same as having it, but there is at any rate a natural affinity between benevolence and agapic *Eros*, which springs from the nature of agapic *Eros*.

To say that the agapic type of *Eros* is the *central* element in *Agape*, in this sense, is not to deny that benevolence is *ethically* the most *important* element in *Agape*. Benevolence is not only the most important, but also the most *essential* element in *Agape*. There cannot be *Agape* at all without benevolence; but when it is demanded of me that I have *Agape* toward the starving millions of Bangladesh, or even toward a multitude of strangers in my own city, perhaps no more of *Eros* is demanded of me than that I should want *not* to have *unfriendly* relations with them – which is hardly enough to count as *Eros*. Ethically important (indeed necessary) as it is, however, I think that *Agape* with so little *Eros* in it should be seen by Christians as only an incomplete and fragmentary participation in the fullness of God's *Agape*.[4]

Notes

1 Fénelon, 1697. I quote always from this first edition. The critical edition (Fénelon, 1911) presents a revised text made but not published by Fénelon, though the first edition can be reconstructed from Cherel's apparatus. The first edition seems to me the more important document. I have allowed my translations to be influenced in a number of cases by the language of a rather good contemporary English translation, which exists in at least two significantly different (and differently paginated) editions (*The Maxims of the Saints Explained, concerning the Interior Life*. London: H. Rhodes, 1698, and London: G. Thompson, R. Dampier, W. Manson, and J. Bland, no date).

2 This argument is an objection to the ideal of holy indifference as caring about nothing for its own sake except that God's will be done. It is not so clearly an objection to what Fénelon called "holy resignation," in which one prefers the accomplishment of God's will above all other ends although one does desire some other ends for their own sakes. The conditional sacrifices follow from holy resignation as well as from holy indifference, and I am not offering an opinion here as to what Fénelon ought to have said about the conditional sacrifices.

3 There is much in Nygren (1969) to encourage this interpretation of the distinction, though it is not fully explicit in Nygren and does not fit everything he says about *Agape*. It fits his conception of *Eros* better. Nygren's discussion, however, is less focused on the ends of diverse loves than on their causes and conditions.

4 An earlier version of this paper was read at the annual meeting of the American Society of Christian Ethics in January 1979. The ideas in it have been discussed with a number of individuals and groups, and provided approximately half of the substance of the thirty-second annual Willson Lectures at Southwestern University in March 1979. I am particularly indebted to Rogers Albritton, David Blumenfeld, John Giuliano, and Warren Quinn for their comments. I also particularly prize Giles Milhaven's comments, but have not altered the paper in the light of them, since it appears with his response.

References

Butler, Joseph. 1970. *Fifteen Sermons Preached at the Rolls Chapel*. Edited, with Butler's *Dissertation on the Nature of Virtue*, by T. A. Roberts. London: SPCK.

Denzinger, Heinrich. 1911. *Enchiridion symbolorum, definitionum, et declarationum de rebus fidei et morum*. Editio undecima quam paravit Clemens Bannwart. Freiburg im Breisgau: Herder.

Fénelon, François de Salignac de la Mothe. 1697. *Explication des maximes des saints sur la vie intérieure*. Paris: Pierre Aubouin, Pierre Emery, and Charles Clousier.

—— 1698. *Instruction pastorale de Messire Franc. de Salignac de la Mothe Fénelon . . . touchant son livre des maximes des saints*. Edition nouvelle, corrigée & augmentée. Amsterdam: Henri Wetstein.

—— 1838a. *Lettres à Mgr. l'évêque de Meaux, en réponse aux divers écrits ou mémoires sur le livre intitulé* Explication des maximes des saints. In 1838c.

—— 1838b. *Lettres en réponse à celle de Mgr. l'évêque de Meaux*. In 1838c.

—— 1838c. *Oeuvres de Fénelon, Archévêque de Cambrai*, précédées d'études sur sa vie, par M. Aimé-Martin. Tome II. Paris: Firmin Didot Frères.

—— 1911. *Explication des maximes des saints sur la vie intérieure*. Édition critique publiée d'après des documents inédits par Albert Cherel. Paris: Bloud.

Noailles, Louis Antoine de, Jacque-Bénigne Bossuet, and Paul Godet Desmarais. 1698. *Declaratio . . . circa librum cui titulus est*: Explication des maximes des saints sur la vie intérieure, etc. Text dated Paris, August 6, 1697. Republished, with facing French translation, among the "additions" to a "new edition" of Fénelon, 1697. Amsterdam: Henri Wetstein.

Nygren, Anders. 1969. *Agape and Eros*. Translated by Philip S. Watson. New York and Evanston: Harper & Row.

Sales, St François de. 1969. *Traité de l'amour de Dieu*. In *Oeuvres*, edited by André Ravier. Paris: Gallimard (Bibliothèque de la Pléiade).

42

The Possibility of Incarnation

Richard Swinburne

The Coherence of Chalcedon

The central doctrine of Christianity is that God intervened in human history in the person of Jesus Christ in a unique way; and that quickly became understood as the doctrine that in Jesus Christ the second person of the Trinity became man, that is, human. In AD 451 the Council of Chalcedon formulated that doctrine in a precise way utilizing the then current philosophical terminology, which provided a standard for the orthodoxy of subsequent thought on this issue. It affirmed its belief in "our Lord Jesus Christ . . . truly divine ($\theta\epsilon\delta s$) and truly human ($\ddot{a}\nu\theta\rho\omega\pi os$) . . . in two natures . . . the distinction of natures being in no way annulled by the union, but rather the characteristics of each nature being preserved and coming together to form one person".[1] One individual ($\dot{v}\pi\delta\sigma\tau a\sigma\iota s$), one thing that is; and being a rational individual, one person. An individual's nature are those general properties that make it the sort of individual it is. The nature of my desk is to be a solid material object of a certain shape; the nature of the oak tree in the wood is to take in water and light, and to grow into a characteristic shape with characteristic leaves and give off oxygen. Chalcedon affirmed that the one individual Jesus Christ had a divine nature, was a divine individual that is; and it assumed that the

divine nature was an essential nature. That is, any individual who is divine cannot cease to be divine and become something else instead, and could not ever have been anything else instead. If you lose your essential nature you cease to be [. . .]. The desk's nature, as described above, is an essential property of the desk. If you chop the desk up for firewood or vaporize it, so that there is no longer the material object of a certain shape, then there is no longer the desk. Chalcedon assumed that human nature is not (or not invariably) an essential nature. That is, just occasionally, an individual could become human or cease to be human while remaining the same individual. It then affirmed that the one individual, the second person of the Trinity, who was eternally divine, became also (at a certain moment of human history, about AD 1) human (i.e. man). He acquired the characteristics of man in addition to those of divinity.

Let us call this claim of the Council of Chalcedon the Chalcedonian definition. My object in this chapter is to investigate first whether the Chalcedonian definition is internally consistent (i.e. coherent), and secondly whether it is consistent with the picture of Christ in the New Testament, utilized in theories of the Atonement, and summarized in another affirmation of the Council of Chalcedon that Christ was "like us, in all respects, apart from sin". Is the Chalcedonian definition, that is, consistent with a wider spectrum of Christian teaching? [. . .]

My analysis of what it is to be divine shares with Chalcedon the view that divine nature is an essential nature. The Word of God, the second person of the Trinity, could not cease to be divine. [. . .]

I [suggest] that we have a rather vague understanding of what it is to be human (and my reading does not suggest to me that the Fathers of Chalcedon had any more precise understanding). A human being has as its essential core a human soul, normally connected to a human body. A soul is clearly a human soul if it is capable of having sensations, thoughts (including logical sequences thereof), and purposes (freely chosen); a structure of beliefs and desires (including moral beliefs); all of this caused by an underlying essence, with the right ancestry, with a limitation imposed by the human's body on the extent of his powers and knowledge. But our rather vague ordinary-language understanding of "human" allows an individual still to count as human even if not all these conditions are satisfied. You get wider and wider understandings of humanity as you drop more and more conditions; and clearly if many of the conditions are not satisfied, it becomes unreasonable to call an individual human.

Given that the soul is the principle of identity of the individual human, nothing can become a human being (while remaining what it is) unless it has, as its principle of identity, the soul which is subsequently the human soul. Becoming a human would involve that soul acquiring the features essential to humanity. In the case of ordinary humans such as ourselves, that individual soul [. . .] was an individual essence, a restriction on a universal such as "animate being". But if I am right in what I have suggested [elsewhere], that a divine individual, though by analogy a "personal" being in having like us a mental life, does not have thisness, what individuates it is the divine essence with certain individuating relational properties. In virtue of it being the subject of mental life, such an individual is, on my [. . .] definition, a soul. On which understanding of what are the features essential to humanity, could the soul which is divine, the divine being who is the second person of the Trinity, become also human?

A divine individual could certainly acquire a human body in the sense of a body through which he acts on the world and acquires beliefs about it. Many of the effects he produces through the body will be ones he could (but need not) bring about in other ways. The beliefs which the divine individual would acquire through his body are ones he would have anyway – but now he would acquire them through a new route. He would also, through his sense-organs, acquire some inclinations to hold false beliefs caused by illusion or misinformation striking the ears of his human body. But these inclinations would be overborne by his strongly held true beliefs, which were his through his divine omniscience. A divine individual could also acquire sensations through a human body; and, more generally, a mental life with all the features of a human mental life. For in acting he would have purposes; and being conscious of his beliefs he would have thoughts. And, with two apparent crucial qualifications, he could even have desires. A desire is an inclination to perform an action of some kind, an inclination which causally influences the agent. It does not necessarily determine him to act, but, if there is no countervailing stronger desire, he needs to "fight against" its influence in order not to act upon it. The first qualification is that, in order to maintain his perfect freedom (that no thing from without causally influences how he acts), a divine individual would himself have continually to cause in himself his desires. And secondly, it would seem that a divine individual can only allow himself to be subject to desires, non-rational inclinations, which, as it were, top up his rational inclinations. A normal agent need not desire to do actions in proportion to his beliefs about the worth of doing them. He may, for example, have no strong desire to do what he believes that he ought to do. For a divine individual, however, desires would have to be aligned with believed worth, and given that in virtue of his omniscience such an individual will have true beliefs about the worth of actions, that means actual worth. A divine individual could desire to do every good action, but he could only have a strongest desire to do what is best to do. Any other desire would be a non-rational influence limiting his perfect freedom of choice. It would do this even if it were to incline him to act in ways compatible with his perfect goodness – for instance, inclining him to do a certain one among a number of equal best actions or a certain one among the infinite number of good actions, each less good than some other good but incompatible action. Above all, a divine individual could not have what we normal humans so often have – a strong desire, not outweighed by a contrary desire, to do an action less good than the best available, let alone a wrong action (i.e. one obligatory not to do). For if the divine individual had such a desire, he might yield to the influence of the desire; and so he could not be necessarily perfectly good.

A divine individual clearly has the four further characteristics [. . .] of logical thought, moral awareness, free will, and a structured soul, possessed by humans and not animals. What of the three additional conditions suggested there? Could his body and mental life be caused by the same underlying essence as ours? Yes, an embryo which developed into the divine individual's body could have our genes, and (connected with it) whatever else was necessary to produce human mental life. The natural mechanism which gives rise to souls cannot dictate which soul will arise, for in general souls do not exist before birth, and so there can be no law dictating that a particular bodily process will give rise to this soul as opposed to that one. All the mechanism can do is to ensure that it gives rise to *a* soul, which will then have a certain mental life. That soul, a divine individual could ensure, without violating that mechanism, was his own soul.

Clearly a divine individual would not fulfil the limitation condition. If there is a maximum to abilities (including the ability to acquire true beliefs) if they are to be human abilities, the divine individual would have abilities which exceeded it. On the other hand a divine individual could fulfil the historical condition in that the physical causes which gave rise to his body could be genes derived from the human gene pool.[2] [. . .] We might reasonably deem the historical condition to be fulfilled sufficiently by genes being derived from one parent rather than two.

I conclude that the only qualifications on the possibility of a divine individual becoming human concern a limit to the kind of desires he can have, and that he cannot satisfy any limitation condition. Clearly the Council of Chalcedon understood "human" in such a way that it did not involve a limitation condition. For a divine individual could not become human, if to be human an individual has to have limited powers; and this is so obvious that the Fathers of Chalcedon could not have failed to notice it. [. . .] We can readily suppose Councils or individuals to make claims that are internally inconsistent, but only if the inconsistency is not too obvious. If Chalcedon had understood "human" in such a way that being human involved a limitation condition, the inconsistency in supposing that a divine individual became human (while remaining divine) would have been too obvious to escape notice, and the definition would not have been adopted in its original form.

So if we do not draw the limit of the human too strictly, certainly a divine individual can become human. He would do this by acquiring a human body (joining his soul to an unowned human body), acting, acquiring beliefs, sensations, and desires through it. Remaining divine, he would have become human by acquiring an extension to his normal modes of operation. A divine individual who became incarnate in Christ in this way would, I suggest, have satisfied the Chalcedonian definition of being one individual with both a divine and a human nature, on a not unreasonable interpretation of the latter. Chalcedon also declared that Christ had a "reasonable soul" ($\psi v \chi \acute{\eta} \ \lambda o \gamma \iota \kappa \acute{\eta}$) and by this it seems to have meant an acquired "human soul". But the Council could not have meant by this that there were in Christ both a divine and a human soul in my sense of "soul". For that would have been to say that Christ was two individuals, a doctrine to which Chalcedon was greatly opposed. Rather in the affirmation that Christ had a "reasonable soul", "soul" is to be understood in an Aristotelian sense; and so the affirmation is to be understood as saying that Christ had a human way of thinking and acting, as well as his divine way.

Although both divine and human properties belonged to the same individual, Christ, it was customary to say that some of them were his *qua* (as) divine, and others were his *qua* human – "Christ as God was omnipotent", "Christ as man suffered". What was being said by saying that various actions and properties were his, *qua* human, was that they were his in virtue of his having taken on a human body and a human way of thinking; and what was meant by saying that various actions and properties were his, *qua* divine, was that they were his apart from his having taken on any limitations.

Suffering for example, the Fathers and Church Councils wished to insist, was Christ's only *qua* man. Christ did indeed feel pain, hunger, thirst, and weariness. But *qua* divine, Christ was impassible, unable to suffer. There seems to be one clear correct point here. Suffering is something, pain, happening to you. A divine individual as the cause of all does not have things happen to him, unless he allows them to happen to him. So only if he puts himself in a special position, e.g. by taking on a human nature, can he suffer. But the denial that Christ, *qua* God, suffered cannot be read as a denial that God suffered. For a very clearly advocated patristic doctrine – and one to my mind clearly implied by the Chalcedonian definition – was the doctrine later called *communicatio idiomatum* ($\dot{\alpha} v \tau \acute{\iota} \delta o \sigma \iota s \ \acute{\iota} \delta \iota \omega \mu \acute{\alpha} \tau \omega v$), the doctrine that the human and divine attributes are predicable of the same individual, Christ. In virtue of that, it may be said that God was born of Mary, and so Mary may be called $\theta \epsilon \acute{o} \tau o \kappa o s$, the Mother of God – as proclaimed by the Council of Ephesus in AD 431. If God can have a mother, he can certainly suffer – although of course he only has either of these properties *qua* man. The Second Council of Constantinople recognized this when it declared it an article of faith that "one of the Trinity was crucified".[3]

The controversy resolved by the Council of Chalcedon's declaration that there were two natures in the individual who was Christ, revived two centuries later in an attenuated form in the monothelite controversy – did Christ have only one will (θέλησις or θέλημα) and one source of action (ἐνέργεια) or two? The third Council of Constantinople in AD 681 resolved the controversy by declaring that there were in Christ two natural wills, and two natural sources of action, the human will being "subject" to the divine.[4]

I do not think that this declaration added very much significant to the Chalcedonian definition. But to see that, we need to understand clearly what it was saying. Both the dyothelites ("two wills") and the monothelites ("one will") firmly held that there was only one individual who willed and acted; and, θέλησις and ἐνέργεια not previously having been given sharp technical senses, the Council could have expressed this point by saying that there was only one will and one source of action. It would thus have construed θέλησις and ἐνέργεια in such a way that their principle of individuation (e.g. what makes a θέλησις the unique one it is) was the individual who had them – for instance, a θέλησις being individuated by whose it is. But in fact the Council chose so to understand these terms that they were individuated by the kind of willing and acting they designated. There was a human kind of willing and acting and a divine kind, and Christ had both, since he acted and willed in both divine and human ways.

The sayings of Christ that, above all, were the source of the two wills doctrine, were the sayings in which Christ contrasts his will with that of the Father to which he submits – for example, the saying in Gethsemane, "not my will but thine be done" (Luke 22: 42). Now given that the three persons of the Trinity, apart from any incarnation, would have no tendency for their wills to conflict, such sayings must be read, as Gregory of Nyssa urged, as "Not what I as man will, but what thou and so I as God will."[5]

By a human kind of willing, I mean a willing of the kind of actions available to humans subject to the kind of desires to which humans are normally subject. By a divine kind of willing I mean a willing to do actions of the kind available to God subject only to desires of the limited kind described earlier. The "subjection" of the human will to the divine is then naturally interpreted as any human desires always being kept in place by stronger divine desires, so that Christ, although subject to human desires, is subject to no balance of human desires which in any way impedes his perfect freedom. Christ could be subject to a desire to avoid pain, but when it was not good to avoid pain, he would also have a stronger desire not to avoid pain. Christ would not, on this account, even be subject on balance to any desire to do just one of two or more equal best actions – for that would impair his perfect freedom to choose between them. He could not be subject on balance to a desire to befriend one disciple more than the others, unless there were a good reason so to do – for that desire would impair his perfect freedom to choose which disciple to befriend most. (Of course it would often be that the mere fact of his incarnation would make certain acts best acts or even obligatory for him when they would not otherwise be so – e.g. to show more love to Mary than to all other humans, because she was his mother.) All of this is a perfectly internally coherent further explication of Chalcedon.

The Limitedness of Christ

As so far expounded, the Chalcedonian definition simply says that God the Son acquired an additional nature to the divine nature; and, as he walked on earth, he continued to have all the divine properties, such as necessary omnipotence, omniscience, perfect freedom, and perfect goodness. In consequence it seems to fit badly with certain things said about Christ in the New Testament, and also to make it so easy for Christ to live a good human life that his doing so would not be the costly sacrifice needed to achieve our salvation.

It seems to fit badly with certain things said about Christ in the New Testament in respect of his ignorance, his weakness, and the extent to which he was open to temptation. St Luke's Gospel asserts that the boy Jesus "advanced in wisdom" (Luke 2: 52), that is, grew in knowledge, which seems to imply that he was not omniscient all the time. So too does the passage in St Mark's Gospel, to which I referred earlier, in which Jesus is reported as claiming that he, "the Son", does not know something which the Father does know – "the hour" at which "Heaven and Earth shall pass away" (Mark 13: 31f). And Christ's cry of dereliction from the

Cross, "My God, my God, why hast thou forsaken me?" (Mark 15: 34) might seem to suggest that Christ at that moment ceased to believe that God was sustaining him. There is a passage in St Mark that casts similar doubt on Christ's omnipotence. It is reported that in a visit to his own country, Jesus "could do there no mighty work" (Mark 6: 5). The Epistle to the Hebrews claims of our "High Priest", namely, Jesus, that he is not one who "cannot be touched with the feeling of our infirmities", and that suggests (though does not entail) that Jesus is weak, and so again not omnipotent. And, finally, although perhaps not formally incompatible with any obvious biblical passage, the view that Christ's being tempted was simply a matter of his being subject to a desire to which he could never yield, does not seem the natural picture suggested by the agony of Gethsemane, nor by two remarks in the Epistle to the Hebrews. Christ is said to have "learned obedience by the things which he suffered", and to have been "made perfect" (i.e. over time) (Heb. 5: 8f); this might suggest that he was not immune to temptation to begin with, but by not yielding to it became immune. And if Christ was "in *all* points tempted like as we are" (Heb. 4: 15), more openness to temptation would seem to be suggested.

Some of these passages are susceptible of other interpretations which have some plausibility and I have urged elsewhere that biblical passages should be interpreted in the light of Christian doctrines.[6] Nevertheless the general feeling which many readers of the New Testament surely get is that it pictures a Jesus rather more like ourselves than the Christ of the Chalcedonian definition. Other Christian doctrines also suggest that the traditional exposition of Chalcedon needs improvement. The Chalcedonian definition itself rephrases the Epistle to the Hebrews to assert that Christ was "like us in all respects, apart from sin". All Christian theories of the Atonement have claimed that it was effected by Christ doing good when men did ill, although he was no better equipped than they for doing good; if he was as knowledgeable and predetermined to do the best as the traditional exposition affirms, that claim would be hard to justify.[7] As St Gregory Nazianzen famously remarked, "What Christ has not assumed, he has not healed; but what has been united with God is saved."[8] The traditional exposition of Chalcedon might not seem adequately to affirm that he has taken on board all of us.

Many of the Fathers, especially the earlier ones and especially those of the Antiochene tradition,

held that Christ was more like ourselves in the respects described than the traditional interpretation of Chalcedon later allowed.[9] Can we interpret the Chalcedonian definition in a way that respects their viewpoint? I think that we can with the aid of a modern idea, the divided mind. It was Freud above all who helped us to see how an agent can have two systems of belief to some extent independent of each other. In performing some actions, the agent is acting on one system of belief and not guided by beliefs of the other system; and conversely. Although all his beliefs are accessible – they would not be his beliefs unless he had privileged access to them – he refuses to admit to his consciousness beliefs relevant to his action, on which he is not acting. Thus, to take a well-worn example, a mother may refuse to acknowledge to herself a belief that her son is dead or to allow some of her actions to be guided by it. When asked if she believes that he is dead, she says "No", and this is an honest reply, for it is guided by those beliefs of which she is conscious. Yet other actions of hers may be guided by the belief that he is dead – for instance, she may throw away some of his possessions – even though she does not admit that belief to consciousness. The refusal to admit a belief to consciousness is of course itself also something that the agent in this example refuses to admit to herself to be happening.

The Freudian account of the divided mind was of course derived from analysis of cases of human self-deception, when the beliefs of one belief system and the belief that the systems have been separated are not consciously acknowledged, and where the self-deception is a pathetic state from which the individual needs to be rescued. But such cases and the Freudian account of them helps us to see the logical possibility of an individual for good reason with conscious intention keeping a lesser belief system separate from his main belief system, and simultaneously doing different actions guided by different sets of beliefs of which he is consciously aware. Indeed even those of us who do not suffer from bad cases of a Freudian divided mind can sometimes perform at once two quite separate tasks – for example, having a conversation with someone and writing a letter to someone else – in directing which quite distinct beliefs are involved, which we can recognize as "on the way to" a divided mind in which the beliefs of both parts are consciously acknowledged.

Now a divine individual could not give up his knowledge, and so his beliefs; but he could, in becoming incarnate in Christ and acquiring a human belief-acquisition system, through his choice, keep the inclinations to belief resulting therefrom to some extent separate from his divine knowledge-system. Different actions would be done in the light of different systems. The actions done through the human body, the thoughts consciously entertained connected with the human brain, the interpretation of perceptual data acquired through the human eyes, would all be done in the light of the human belief-system. So, too, would any public statement made through his human mouth. However, his divine knowledge-system will inevitably include the knowledge that his human system contains the beliefs that it does; and it will include those among the latter which are true. The separation of the belief-systems would be a voluntary act, knowledge of which was part of the divine knowledge-system but not of the human knowledge-system. We thus get a picture of a divine consciousness and a human consciousness of God Incarnate, the former including the latter, but not conversely.[10]

The beliefs in the two parts of a divided mind may sometimes be explicitly contradictory (e.g. a belief that the son is alive and a belief that the son is dead). In such a case, it is misleading to call both beliefs "beliefs" without qualification, since at least one does not form part of a general view of the world but merely guides the subject's actions in certain circumstances. The overall constant and ever-present view of the world of a God who became incarnate in the way described would be his divine view; and so the "beliefs" belonging to that view could be described as "beliefs", whereas the "beliefs" belonging to the human perspective would be mere inclinations to belief or propositions guiding a limited set of actions. But it would be those inclinations belonging to the human perspective which guided Christ's honest public statements (honest, because guided by those beliefs of which he is conscious in his human acting).

Christ's human acts are the public acts done through his human body and the private mental acts correlated with the brain-states of that body; and if it is to be a human body its capacities must not be radically different from those of our bodies. So there is a limit to Christ's power *qua* man. If the human actions of God the Son are done only in the light of his human belief-inclinations, then he will feel the limitations that we have. God, in becoming incarnate, will not have limited his powers, but he will have taken on a way of operating which is limited and feels limited. So using the notion of

divided mind we can coherently suppose a divine individual to become incarnate while remaining divine, and yet act and feel much like ourselves.

But could he become like us in our liability to yield to temptation? For if he could, his failure to yield would seem so much more the victory over evil which the New Testament and later theories of the Atonement picture it.

Let us take a few steps backwards in order to sort out what is at stake here. [. . .] Wrong is of two kinds – objective and subjective. Objective wrong is failing in your obligations (or duties) to someone whether you realize it or not: for example, taking money that is not yours, whether or not you reasonably believe it to be yours. Subjective wrong is seeking to do what you believe to be failing in your obligations. In both cases, a wrong is, I suggest, a wrong to someone. If you take what is not yours, you wrong the person from whom you take it. If you take, believing that you are taking what is not yours, that is, stealing, you wrong the person from whom you believe that you are stealing. God has, I suspect, relatively few duties to humans – for example, plausibly, he could kill a human without wronging him, for, as the source of his being, he may keep him in being as long or as short a time as he chooses. But, with majority Christian tradition, I suggest that a divine individual does have some duties to human beings – for instance, to keep promises. God Incarnate must keep his promises to humans. If he failed in any of the duties he has to humans, he would wrong them. He would wrong a human objectively if he failed to fulfil some duty to him, for instance, failed to keep a promise to him, whether or not he realized that he was failing to fulfil the duty. He would wrong a human subjectively if he did (or merely tried to do) what he believed was failing in his duty to him.

The narrow range of duties to which a divine individual is subject does, however, give him vast scope for supererogatory good actions (i.e. good actions beyond the call of duty) benefitting humans. We humans have a limited number of duties to our fellows, and endless scope for good action beyond the call of duty. Exactly where the line is to be drawn is disputed, but there is a line. For example, the act of saving the life of a comrade at the expense of one's own is hardly a duty owed to him, but it is evidently a good action. Doing a supererogatory act is praiseworthy, but failing to do one is not blameworthy.[11] For by so failing you wrong no one. Plausibly, as Christian thinkers have normally maintained, no divine individual had any obligation to create a world (for if he failed to do so, there would not ever have been any creatures who had been wronged), let alone become incarnate. If he did so, it was an act of supererogatory goodness.

[. . .] An agent will do intentionally what he sees reason for doing, that is, what he believes to be good to do, in so far as he is rational. Hence he will only fail to pursue what he believes to be good if he is subject to desires inclining him to act contrary to reason, and in that case if he is to do the believed good, he has to struggle against the temptation which those desires provide. And if he is to do intentionally what is in fact good, he needs true beliefs about what is good.

Now it would, I suggest, have been wrong of a divine individual to allow himself to become incarnate in such a way as to open the possibility of his doing objective or subjective wrong. Hence it is incompatible with his perfect goodness that he should do so. For it is wrong of anyone to put themselves in a position where they are liable to wrong another – intentionally allow themselves to forget their duties, or to take drugs which would lead to their being strongly tempted (without having a stronger contrary desire) to do some wrong. A divine individual in becoming incarnate must ensure that in his human actions he has access to such beliefs as will allow him to be aware of his duties, and must ensure that he is not subject to a balance of desire to do believed wrong. Even though he cannot do wrong, he may however, through not allowing himself to be aware of his divine beliefs, be inclined to believe that he may succumb to temptation to do wrong and thus, in the situation of temptation, he may *feel* as we do.[12]

Now, while it is wrong to put oneself in a position where one is liable to do wrong, there is nothing wrong in putting oneself in a position where one is liable not to do the best action (or best kind of action), if there is such. Indeed, an action which had the foreseen consequence of putting oneself in that position might itself occasionally be the best thing to do. A generous man might well give away so much in order to do some supererogatory good that thereby he greatly endangered the possibility of his doing even more supererogatory good in future. Compatibly with his perfect goodness, a divine individual could choose to allow himself to act on a limited set of beliefs which included inadequate beliefs about what is most worth doing; and he could allow himself to be subject to a balance of desires to do lesser goods, to a weakness of will, so

long as it did not include any proneness to wrong anyone. He would then need to discover what was most worth doing; and he would need to fight against the balance of desire to do the lesser good and it would be possible that he should yield to the temptation to do a lesser good. He might choose to put himself in this position in order to share our lot as fully as possible. God the Son, in his divine consciousness, in perfect freedom would continually will (as part of the good of his incarnation) that he would do whatever (other than the wrong) he chooses to do under the influence of desire and limited belief. The former (second-order) will or choice would not be influenced by desire; only its execution would be so influenced, but it is good that it should be. Desire would have influenced God, but only to the extent to which God, uninfluenced by desire, allowed it to do so.

If in his human consciousness Christ were on occasion subject to a balance of desire not to do the best action, then his overcoming this balance would be a free act for which he would be praiseworthy. Almost all the actions by which he is supposed to have made available atonement for the sins of the world – his sacrificial service, culminating in allowing himself to be crucified – were not obligatory but supererogatory.[13] No divine individual had any obligation to allow himself to be crucified, and Christ must have been subject to desires of considerable force not to go through with the Crucifixion, and highly plausibly a balance of desire not to go through with it. In that latter case he was crucified as a result of a free choice contrary to temptation. It was a supererogatory act, and one which surely he believed to be supererogatory; and hence highly praiseworthy. In doing that supreme act and other supererogatory acts during his life freely and contrary to desire, he would have used well the freedom which we ordinary humans have abused by our sins. If he had failed to perform those acts, he would have done us no wrong; but doing them he did us great benefit. Yet if such heroic acts were inevitable, he would have had an advantage that we sinners did not have, and his redeeming acts would have been taking on and rightly directing a human nature crucially unlike ours in the respect in which we had gone wrong. That he performed supererogatory good actions, while we ordinary humans did wrong, although both he and we were equally well positioned to do good or ill, is, I repeat, crucial for theories of the Atonement.

So, yes, God the Son could subject himself to temptation, but only to do a lesser good, not to do wrong. He must protect himself from the prone-ness to do wrong which is original sinfulness. Ori-ginal sin includes minimally this original sinfulness, this proneness to do wrong. It has, however, been thought of by many as including some responsib-ility for the sin of others, including our ancestors ("Adam"). Yet any "solidarity" with them in sin can arise only as a result of their being responsible in very small part for our existence, which would not arise in the case of Christ, who, being God, does not owe his existence to them at all. So, since such solidarity has no application to an incarnate God, if God protects himself – as he must – from original sinfulness, then in becoming incarnate, he does so, as many creeds vigorously affirmed, without inheriting original sin at all.[14]

One important form of wrongdoing which the divine Word must ensure that the incarnate Christ does not do is deceive his hearers and thus the Church with respect to the content of revelation. He must not tell us that God wished the Church to celebrate the eucharist regularly or to incorporate new members by baptism, if that was not what he really wished it to do; or that the pure in heart and peacemakers are blessed, if they are not. For that would be deceiving people with respect to the way to salvation.[15]

If it can be good that Christ allow himself to act subject to a balance of desire to do an action less than the best, *a fortiori* it can be good for Christ to allow himself to be subject to desire to do some one among equal best actions (or one of an infinite number of good acts, each less good than some other of the number) – for example, to be subject to particular desires to benefit particular people more than others (when reason does not dictate such a choice). His perfect freedom would not be impaired, so long as he continually chooses (in his divine consciousness) as a best act that he act under the influence of some good (but not necessarily best) particular desire.

So then God the Son, being divine, must remain omniscient, but he can allow his human actions to be guided only by his humanly acquired inclina-tions to belief. He must remain omnipotent, but there is a limit to what he can do in a human way and, when he does act in a human way, he need not be fully aware of having more power than that. Being divine, he must remain perfectly good and perfectly free, but he can in perfect freedom, and because of the perfect goodness of doing so, allow himself to make a choice under the influence of desire to do a lesser good and allow himself to be subject to particular desires to benefit particular individuals. But an incarnate God could not do wrong. The Chalcedonian definition is not merely self-consistent but consistent with the New Testa-ment picture of Christ as acting in ignorance and weakness, and subject to temptation. A divine indi-vidual could become human in a rather fuller sense than its traditional interpretation allowed.

What in effect the "divided mind" view is claim-ing is that the divine and human natures are to some extent separated, and that allows the human nature of Christ to be not a nature as perfect as a human nature could be (e.g. in Heaven), but a nature more like our human nature on Earth, subject to ignorance and disordered desire, yet one connected enough with the divine nature so that Christ does no wrong. In particular the two wills are kept to some extent separate, so that when Christ wills under human conditions, he wills under the conditions, not of perfect humanity, but under conditions more like those of our humanity, i.e. conditions of ignorance of some of the remote consequences of his actions, limited awareness of power, and open to the influence of desire. The "subjection" of the human will to the divine must then be read only as a subjection which ensured no wrongdoing, but not in the more full-blooded way that always Christ had to will as he would will if he knew all the possibilities open to him and was not subject to influence by desire.

The monothelites saw that having two natures and only one will (in the relevant sense) would ensure that the human aspect of Jesus was purely passive; whereas the dyothelites and especially Maximus the Confessor and his disciple Anastasius saw that a genuine humanity needed a certain active independence.[16] I have suggested that the divided mind can give content to that requirement.

Total Interpenetration

The monothelites had objected to Maximus – does not dyothelitism have the consequence that "the Logos and man would be related to each other as strangers"?[17] In answer, Maximus adumbrated a doctrine, which was fully developed by St John Damascene in the eighth century, which ruled out the "divided mind" account and, I believe, lay behind the unsatisfactory way in which Chalcedon was expounded by the scholastics. This was the doctrine of $\pi\epsilon\rho\iota\chi\acute{\omega}\rho\eta\sigma\iota\varsigma$ $\phi\upsilon\sigma\acute{\epsilon}\omega\nu$, the "interpen-etration" of the two natures of Christ.[18] It is "each nature giving in exchange to the other its own properties";[19] or more correctly, as St John corrects himself a little later, it is the permeation of the human nature by the divine – the divine nature "imparts to the flesh its own peculiar glories, while abiding itself impassible and without participation in the affections of the flesh".[20] What this means is that the human properties of Christ are as divinized as they can be, that is, made as like those of a divine individual as the properties of a creature can be.

Hence as a man Christ was omniscient, not necessarily omniscient, or with a divine way of knowing – but he knows as man all a human could conceivably know.[21] So, John denies that Christ really advanced in wisdom and knowledge. Like Augustine before him, John Damascene held that Christ had always before his mind things that God alone can know, such as "the hour" at which "Heaven and Earth shall pass away"; the apparent denial by Christ that he knew this hour was, said Augustine, to be read simply as a claim that he was not prepared to announce the hour.[22] Likewise, although Christ's human nature was "not by nature omnipotent. But yet it was omnipotent because it truly and by nature had its origin in the God-Word."[23]

Likewise, given total permeation, the perfect goodness of the divine nature so permeated the human nature that Christ's strongest desires were always for the perfectly good; any sensory desires for food, drink, etc., in a situation where it was not overall a best act that he should eat or drink (as in the temptation in the wilderness – see e.g. Matt. 4: 2ff) were automatically overruled by stronger desires, so that there was not the slightest possibility that he would yield to any inclination to do a lesser good. Thus Damascene wrote: "The soul of the Lord . . . willed . . . those things which his divine will willed it to will. It was not in inclination but in natural power that the two wills differed from each other."[24]

John Damascene is an author quoted very frequently by Aquinas – after the Bible, Aristotle, Augustine, and Pseudo-Dionysius, probably the author most quoted – and we find in Aquinas, as in Damascene, "interpenetration of the natures", but not, I think, quite as total an interpenetration as in Damascene. Thus the human Christ knows everything actual (e.g. about past and future) but not all the possible actions that God could do and does not do.[25] And the human Christ was not, claimed Aquinas, omnipotent. And although there was not the slightest possibility that Christ would do wrong, Aquinas did not always sharply distinguish between

doing wrong, and failing to do supererogatory good; however, he does in one place say that "difficulty in doing good"[26] was among the disabilities Christ did not acquire. In these matters Duns Scotus followed Aquinas.[27]

Christological controversy flared up again in a mild way at the Reformation – between Lutherans on the one side and the "Reformed" tradition in a more technical sense, i.e. Calvinists (together with some Catholics), on the other side.[28] What was at stake here was explicitly the doctrine of total interpenetration advocated by Lutherans who used John Damascene as an explicit source. The Lutheran *Formula of Concord* recognized three "genera" of communication of properties, divine and human, in Christ. The first genus was simply the *communicatio idiomatum* – that the human and divine properties were predicable of the same individual, Jesus Christ who was the Son of God. This was accepted by all disputants; but the other genera involved the interpretation of the *communicatio* so as to involve total interpenetration. The second genus of communication was that by which "the perfections that are truly divine, together with the authority and power resulting from them, the honour and supreme glory, are communicated to the human nature of Christ."[29] Hence, Christ was omnipotent in virtue of his human nature. The third genus involved Christ's actions, which pertained to his office: "The union of the two natures in Christ occurred so that the work of redemption, atonement, and salvation might be accomplished in, with and through both natures of Christ."[30] So both the divine essential properties and the actions of redemption belonged to Christ in virtue of belonging both to his human nature and to his divine nature. In this controversy the Calvinists stressed Chalcedon's affirmation that the union of the natures was "without confusion" (ἀσυγχύτως), while the Lutherans stressed Chalcedon's affirmation that the union was "without division, without separation" (ἀδιαιρέτως, ἀχωρίστως).[31] I suggest that we support the Calvinists in this controversy. Calvin was right to comment that the Lutherans "deprive [Christ] of his flesh".[32] Total interpenetration rules out the divided mind view which alone does justice to the New Testament and makes for a viable theory of the Atonement. Total interpenetration is not a necessary development of Chalcedon. St John Damascene's reason for advocating the doctrine was clearly to affirm the divinity of Christ in an unattenuated form, but I have argued that it is not needed for that purpose. Even Aquinas resisted total interpenetration; and, I have argued, we need significantly less interpenetration than he allowed.

Hypostatizing the Natures

The final development of the Chalcedonian definition on which I need to comment was a simple piece of philosophical muddle by the scholastics.

Christ was divine and human and so he had a divine and human nature. But human nature as Aristotle and, I suspect, almost everyone else up to the fifth century AD understood it, is a universal. What made a human the particular human he was, [. . .] according to Aristotle, was the matter of which he was made. I saw reason [elsewhere] to consider this last view unsatisfactory, and argued that a human is the human he is in virtue of the individual soul (in my sense) which is joined to matter (whether physical matter, or soul-stuff, or perhaps no stuff at all). The resulting individual is human if the soul and body have [certain] universal characteristics. [. . .] In the case of normal humans the individual soul is an individual essence which is a restriction of a wider form, for example, animate being; in the case of Christ, I have suggested, it is a divine nature individuated by its relational properties. So in the Incarnation the divine soul of Christ, in acquiring a human nature, acquires those additional properties that are necessary for the humanity of any other individual, and also, no doubt, acquires some properties that are peculiar to the human which was Christ but which could in principle be possessed by many other humans. He also acquired a particular body, but that is not what individuated him.

Now what makes an individual the individual he is cannot be possessed by anything else. If ordinary human beings could not be other than human, [. . .] each human soul would be an individual human nature (instead of being an individual animate nature). But such a nature would be the essential core of the individual – what made him who he is – and could not be possessed temporarily or accidentally by anyone else. Christ therefore could not have an individual human nature. His human nature must be universal, in no way peculiar to Christ – it is just a set of properties which he acquires. I have also claimed that, since humans can become animate beings of other kinds, the same applies to ordinary humans too.

Many of the Fathers saw that the human nature of Christ is a universal, in no way necessarily peculiar to Christ. There was no such thing as an ἀνυπόστατος φύσις, a nature which exists without existing in an individual or hypostasis, claimed the sixth-century Leontius of Byzantium; the human nature of Christ, not being a hypostasis, exists only ἐνυπόστατος, that is, in virtue of the hypostasis in which it exists;[33] or what Leontius was, I believe, getting at – to speak of an individual human nature is merely to speak (misleadingly) of the universal human nature as joined to a hypostasis. Christ's human nature is impersonal (in my view just as also ours is) – but that makes him no less of an individual human being when that nature is united to the soul (in my sense) that is the Second Person of the Trinity.

That clear philosophical point began to get forgotten, and theologians began to think of the Incarnation as the Second Person of the Trinity adopting an individual human nature. This mistake was already adumbrated by earlier talk of Christ's divine nature or human nature being able to do or suffer this or that. But natures do not do things (unless they are themselves individuals); individuals do things, and their nature or natures give them the power to do or suffer this or that. Thus the Prologue to the definition of the Council of Chalcedon denied that the divine nature of Christ was παθητής (passible, able to suffer);[34] what it should have said was that Christ was not παθητής in virtue of his divine nature, only in virtue of his human nature. By a similar mistake the "rational soul" of Christ began to take on a life of its own – not being a human way of thinking that belonged to Christ, but more a soul in the sense in which I have used the term.

Aquinas too had adopted such a way of talking which was bound to lead to trouble. For all humans other than Christ Aquinas held (and in this he was followed by Scotus and Ockham),[35] the human person is the same thing as his or her individual human nature; a human nature is a substance composed of a body and a rational soul. (The necessity of a body is something against which I have argued, but that is not where Aquinas goes wrong in this matter.) What, according to Aquinas, distinguishes Christ from other humans is that while Christ is a person who is a human being, he is not a human person – I suppose that what this means is that Christ is not essentially human, while the rest of us are. I have suggested that the rest of us are not essentially human either. But if the only contrast to be made is between the human and divine (and the possibility of us becoming angels or crocodiles is ignored), then Aquinas's point may be allowed. Since Christ is not a human person, what makes him human is not something essential to his being the person he is. So far so good. But now, Aquinas assumed that since it is for ordinary humans, so also for Christ, a human nature is an individual substance and it is this which is joined to Christ in the Incarnation and makes him human. The union of human soul and body constitutes us ordinary humans as the individuals we are; but in Christ that union that forms a nature is joined to God the Son; "The composite comes to an already existing person or hypostasis."[36] But the question then arises as to why this human nature has to be joined to Christ; could it not be joined to someone else, temporarily or permanently? Aquinas seems to claim that this nature depends on the divine individual to which it is joined for its very existence.[37] But the question remains – why should it be thus? Why cannot a composite of soul and body exist on its own?

Scotus and Ockham took this way of talking to its logical conclusion and said that these things were possible; the human nature which Christ assumed was only contingently assumed by him. Christ need not have assumed it, in which case it would be a complete human person on its own; or

he could temporarily have taken the human nature of Socrates for two weeks, in which case Socrates would not exist for two weeks although his nature would. But then how can Socrates be the same thing as his nature if these things are possible?[38]

This whole mess has been produced by forgetting that human nature, and certainly Christ's human nature, is a universal; what individuates him is something else. Even if what individuates other humans is an individual human soul, in the sense of a restriction in the form of humanity, a divine individual cannot acquire such a soul. For such a soul would already be the individuating principle of a human. He can only take on a human soul in the sense of a human way of thinking and acting; and a soul in this sense (even with a body) is not enough to individuate a human.

My conclusion to this chapter is that the Chalcedonian definition is an internally coherent account of the Incarnation; and, spelled out in a certain way, coherent with things said in the New Testament about Christ and with doctrines of the Atonement. John Damascene's doctrine of the total interpenetration of the two natures is not however consistent with my favoured explication of Chalcedon and should be rejected, as should the hypostatization of the human nature of Christ.

Notes

1 Henricus Denzinger and Adolf Schönmetzer (eds), *Enchiridion Symbolorum*, § 302.
2 The Fathers did not regard satisfaction of the historical condition as necessary for humanity. "God could have taken upon himself to be man . . . from some other source, and not from the race of that Adam who bound the human race by his sin." Augustine, *De Trinitate*, 13. 18.
3 Denzinger, 432. It follows that if the Father took on, for a split second or permanently, another nature, he could also suffer. But it does not follow from that that the Father did suffer when Christ was crucified.
4 Denzinger, 556.
5 *Antirheticus*, 32.
6 See my *Revelation* (Clarendon Press, 1992), *passim*, esp. ch. 10.
7 For such theories, and the role of Christ's supererogatory acts, according to my favoured theory of the Atonement, the Sacrifice Theory, see *Responsibility and Atonement* (Clarendon Press, 1989), esp. ch. 10.
8 *Epistola* 101. 7 (PG 37: 181).
9 On the ignorance of Christ, see e.g. J. Tixeront, *History of Dogmas*, 2nd edn. (B. Herder Book Co., 1926), ii. 287f.

10 Models of Christ's knowledge on these lines are developed in David Brown, *The Divine Trinity* (Duckworth, 1985), 260–7; and in Thomas V. Morris, *The Logic of God Incarnate* (Cornell University Press, 1986), 102–7. The Freudian model of the divided mind has been applied to Christology quite a bit in this century, beginning with W. Sanday, *Christologies Ancient and Modern* (Oxford University Press, 1910).
11 For fuller discussion of this claim see my *Responsibility and Atonement*, especially ch. 2.
12 Morris, *Logic of God Incarnate*, 147, urges that "it is the *epistemic* possibility of sinning rather than a broadly logical, or metaphysical, or even physical possibility that is conceptually linked to temptation". Our concern in this context is with doing wrong rather than with sinning in the sense of doing wrong against God. But, if we take that into account, Morris's point would seem to be that you are tempted if and only if you believe that you have open to you a choice of what is wrong to which you may yield. That seems doubtful to me; if you do not really have such a choice, then you have the mere illusion of temptation. However, as I concede in the text,

someone falsely believing that he can choose what is wrong is indeed in an unfortunate situation which is like our situation of temptation in its psychological aspect. Morris's useful point is spoiled by his examples that concern agents who correctly believe that they can try to do some wrong action which it is physically impossible that they succeed in doing. But subjective wrongdoing is trying to do a believed wrong, and although objective wrongdoing is not possible for those agents, subjective wrongdoing is. Hence the felt inclination to do subjective wrong is a temptation. The "metaphysical or physical" possibility of subjective wrongdoing remains open to agents in Morris's examples, which do not therefore illustrate his point.

13 The supererogatory character of Christ's work consists in his living a holy life and allowing himself to be killed rather than deny his vocation as Messiah (see Mark 14: 61f for his affirmation of his Messiahship before Caiaphas, and the parallel passages in the other Gospels in which he refuses to deny his Messianic role which he has affirmed before his disciples); and in intending that supererogatory work to be the means of our salvation. On my account of the Atonement (see *Responsibility and Atonement*, ch. 10) it is the means of our salvation by being something which we can offer to God in place of the lives which we ought to have lived. In order to be supererogatory in the latter respect, the life must have been lived and laid down with the intention that it should be so available. That is, in his human consciousness Christ must have intended that his life and death be in some way the means of our salvation. It is hard to interpret Christ's words of institution at the Last Supper, "This is my body", and "This is my blood" (e.g. Mark 14: 22–4) in any other way than as expressing an intention that they commemorate the sacrifice of his life, which benefits those who partake of the Supper.

14 As I have argued elsewhere, such "solidarity" in sin which we have with our ancestors is not guilt for their sin – see *Responsibility and Atonement*, ch. 9.

15 I distinguish between the content of Christ's teaching and the assumptions of his culture in terms of which it may have been expressed. On how this distinction is to be made see my *Revelation*, ch. 2. I also distinguish between the content of Christ's solemn teaching on matters of religious doctrine, his revealed teaching given with authority (often, it seems, introduced by the phrase, "Verily I say unto you") and any other bits of information which he might have sought to convey (e.g. about the dates of the kings of Judah). I cannot see that God the Word needs to ensure that the incarnate Christ does not convey any false pieces of information (that he is inclined to believe in his human consciousness) which are such that no great harm will come to anyone who believes them; any more than any of us have any obligation not to overtire ourselves lest we honestly mislead someone on trivial matters.

16 On these arguments of dyothelites and monothelites, see J. A. Dorner, *History of the Development of the Doctrine of the Person of Christ*, div. 2, vol. i (Edinburgh, 1861), 186–90.

17 Ibid. 190.

18 περιχώρησις φυσέων, the interpenetration of the natures of Christ, is not to be confused with the περιχώρησις ὑποστάτων – the interpenetration of the persons of the Trinity, i.e. the mutual knowledge and support of each of the persons by the others, taught by Gregory Nazianzen and other Cappadocian theologians who sought thereby to explain in what consisted the unity of the persons of the Trinity and thus defend themselves against the charge of tritheism.

19 St John Damascene, *De fide orthodoxa*, 3. 4.

20 Ibid. 3. 7.

21 "His human nature does not in essence possess the knowledge of the future, but the soul [i.e. the human or rational soul] through its union with God the Word himself and its identity in subsistence was enriched . . . with the knowledge of the future, as well as with the other miraculous powers", ibid. 3. 21.

22 St Augustine, *De Trinitate*, 1. 23.

23 St John Damascene, *De fide orthodoxa*, 3. 18.

24 Ibid.

25 *Summa theologiae*, 3. 10. 2.

26 Ibid. 3. 14. 4.

27 See e.g. on the human Christ not being omnipotent, Duns Scotus, *Commentary on the Sentences*, 3. 14.

28 On this controversy, see (e.g.) J. Pelikan, *The Christian Tradition*, vol. iv. *Reformation of Church and Dogma* (University of Chicago Press, 1984), 352–9.

29 J. W. Baier, *Compendium of Positive Theology*, cited in Pelikan, ibid. 357.

30 Pelikan, *The Christian Tradition*, 358.

31 Denzinger, 302.

32 J. Calvin, *Institutes of the Christian Religion*, 4. 17. 32. The Lutheran/Calvinist controversy about the relation of the two natures of Christ came to prominence in connection with the alternative doctrines of the eucharist to which they led; and this quotation from Calvin comes from his discussion of the eucharist.

33 The "nature" (φύσις) of Christ "has its being in another" (ἐν ἑτέρῳ ἔχειτὸ εἶναι), wrote Leontius (PG 86: 1277D), just as a shape has its being in the body of which it is the shape. (See also Leontius, PG 86: 1944.)

34 Denzinger, 300.

35 For the subsequent analysis of the difference between the Christologies of Aquinas on the one hand

and those of Scotus and Ockham on the other, I am much indebted to Alfred J. Freddoso, "Human Nature, Potency, and the Incarnation", *Faith and Philosophy*, 3 (1986), 27–53.

36 *Summa theologiae*, 3. 2. 5. ad 1.

37 See Freddoso, "Human Nature", app., for an exegesis of Aquinas's views on this.

38 For detailed references to Scotus and Ockham, and demonstration of the contradictions to which their account leads, see Freddoso, "Human Nature".

43

Religious Pluralism

John Hick

Until recently the philosophy of religion, as practiced in the West, has meant the philosophy of the Christian religion and has concentrated primarily on the Christian (or the Judeo-Christian) concept of God. However, it is clear that in principle the philosophy of religion has no confessional boundaries and is concerned with religion throughout the world and in its wide variety of forms. Also, during the last decade or so Western philosophers of religion have increasingly felt obliged to take note of the fact that Christianity is only one of the great world faiths and that monotheism is only one of the major types of religion, so that it is now common for new texts on the subject to include a chapter on the problems of religious pluralism. These problems, or areas for research, are of several kinds.

Analysis of Religious Concepts

There is the philosophical analysis of non-Christian, including non-monotheistic, religious concepts. Some work has been done on Eastern descriptions of unitive mysticism; on Hindu and Buddhist notions of reincarnation, centering on the question of personal identity from life to life; on such Buddhist ideas as *anatta* ("no self"), *sunyata* ("emptiness"); and on a number of other important

John Hick, "Religious Pluralism," from Philip L. Quinn and Charles Taliaferro (eds.), *A Companion to Philosophy of Religion* (Oxford: Blackwell Publishers, 1997), pp. 607–14.

concepts. But much remains to be done and many other major concepts await attention, both individually and comparatively. Indeed this area of philosophical inquiry has almost unlimited scope for development as Western philosophers of religion take a wider view of their subject and extend their interests to include the Eastern religions.

The Epistemology of Religion and Conflicting Truth-Claims

A recent major development in the epistemology of religion has highlighted the problem of the conflicting truth-claims of the different religions. With the widespread consensus that the traditional theistic arguments fail to prove, and that the idea of probability has no useful purchase here – although there are prominent thinkers who resist these conclusions – a different approach to the rationality or otherwise of theistic belief has emerged. This centers upon religious experience as a putative cognition of God. Religious people report a wide range of forms of distinctively religious experience, including mystical experiences of direct awareness of, and even union with, God; a sense of divine presence in moments of worship or of contemplation; an indirect consciousness of God in the feeling of absolute dependence upon a creator, or of a divine presence and activity mediated through the beauties and sublimities of nature, the claims of conscience, the profound significance of human love, the crises of birth and death, and many kinds of personal and historical events. Can such modes of experience count as good grounds for belief in the reality of God?

The older kind of apologetic used religious experience as a phenomenon that points to God as its cause. This is open to the objection that such experiences may have a purely natural origin in the powers of the human imagination. The universe, including human religious experience, thus remains objectively ambiguous. But the new type of apologetic starts at this point. It involves a shift from an external, or third person, use of religious experience to an internal, or first person, use. Instead of asking whether it is rational to infer God from the reported religious experiences of others, it asks whether it is rational for religious experiencers themselves to believe in the reality of God on the basis of their own experience. To take a paradigm case, was it rational for Jesus, continuously conscious of God's presence, so that the heavenly Father was as real to him as his human neighbors, to believe in God's reality? Would it not indeed have been irrational, a kind of cognitive suicide on his part, not so to believe?

At this point the "principle of credulity," or better, the principle of rational credulity, is invoked, according to which it is rational to trust our experience as cognitive of reality except in so far as we have reason to distrust it. We apply this principle in our ordinary experience of our physical environment: we do not need a reason to trust sense experience in general but rather a reason to distrust it on particular occasions. And it is claimed that the same principle should apply, impartially, to religious experience as a form of apparently cognitive experience. Prima facie it is an awareness of a non-physical divine reality; and the critical task is to examine and assess possible overriding considerations.

This approach has been most massively and systematically presented by William Alston (1991). Given the basic principle that religious experience has parity with sense experience as a prima facie ground of rational belief, discussion centers upon reasons to trust one whilst distrusting the other. Such reasons are: first, whereas sense experience is universal and compulsory, religious experience is optional and confined to a limited number of people, so that whilst sensory reports can in principle be confirmed by anyone, religious experience reports cannot; and second, whereas sense experience produces a universally agreed description of the physical world, religious experience within the different traditions produces different and often incompatible descriptions of the divine.

The first objection has met with the reply that whereas our basic freedom as persons is not undermined by a compulsory awareness of the natural world, it would be undermined by a compulsory awareness of an unlimitedly valuable reality whose very existence lays a total claim upon us. Thus the difference on which the objection is based is matched by a corresponding difference between the putative objects of sensory and religious experience respectively. Hence it is appropriate for consciousness of God not to be forced upon us, as is our consciousness of the physical world; and it is accordingly possible for many people, as a result of upbringing or of a conscious or unconscious choice, to shut it out.

The second objection, however, is more formidable. Alston claims (as do many other philosophers who adopt the same kind of apologetic) that because it is rational to base beliefs on religious experience, Christian religious experience entitles those who participate in it to hold distinctively Christian beliefs. But it is obvious that by the same principle Islamic religious experience entitles Muslims to hold distinctively Islamic beliefs, Buddhist religious experience entitles Buddhists to hold distinctively Buddhist beliefs, and so on. Alston acknowledges that and regards it as "the most difficult problem for my position" (Alston 1991, p. 255). It is an equally difficult problem for other related positions, such as the claim that the core Christian beliefs require no justification because they are "properly basic."

Alston's response is based upon the traditional assumption that there can be, at most, only one true religion, in the sense of a religion that teaches the truth. This is David Hume's principle that in matters of religion, whatever is different is contrary. From a religious point of view the question now becomes: which is the true religion? Alston argues that since the beliefs of each major world faith are equally well based in religious experience, and there are no neutral grounds on which to choose between them, I must simply rely on my own form of religious experience and presume that the other forms are (wholly or partly) delusory. On analogy with rival ways of construing the world, "the only rational course for me is to sit tight with the [epistemic] practice of which I am master and which serves me so well in guiding my activity in the world. Hence, by parity of reasoning, the rational thing for a practitioner of CP [Christian epistemic practice] to do is to continue to form Christian M-beliefs [beliefs about divine manifestations], and, more generally, to continue to accept, and operate in accordance with, the system of Christian belief" (Alston 1991, p. 274).

The problem raised by this defense does not lie in the advice to "sit tight" in the situation as Alston defines it, but in the way in which he defines the situation. For the Humean assumption that only one of the competing sets of religious beliefs can be true conflicts with Alston's basic principle that religious experience, like sense experience, gives rise (specific "defeaters" apart) to true beliefs. Indeed it reverses this basic principle by making religious experience within one's own tradition the sole exception to the general rule that religious experience gives rise to *false* beliefs! For the only-one-true-religion premise, together with the fact that the experientially based beliefs of the different religions are often incompatible, entails that religious experience can be a valid basis for belief in the case of only one religion at most. In all other cases beliefs based upon religious experience are false in so far as they conflict with the privileged exception of one's own religion. Thus the fact of religious diversity undermines the entire argument that religious experience has prima facie parity with sense experience in producing true beliefs.

The Relation Between Religions

I place this area of discussion third because any solution to the problem just noted must be derived from it.

From a naturalistic point of view, according to which religion in all its forms is a delusory projection upon the universe of our human hopes, fears, and ideals, the truth-claims of the different religions are all false, and the fact that they conflict with one another does not present any problem. However, from a religious point of view, according to which religious experience is not purely human projection but, whilst obviously involving imaginative projection, is at the same time a cognitive response to a transcendent reality, the problem is acute.

A variety of religious, as distinguished from naturalistic, interpretations of religion have been offered, each of which would solve the conflicting truth-claims problem in its own way.

Truth-Claims Exclusivism

The most widely, if usually implicitly, held view is that there can only be one true religion, and that this is one's own. The others are false, at least in so far as their beliefs are incompatible with those taught by one's own. This is what most of the adherents of each religion, including some but not all of its reflective thinkers, have generally assumed.

However, a "hermeneutic of suspicion" is provoked by the evident fact that in perhaps 99 percent of cases the religion to which one adheres (or against which one reacts) is selected by the accident of birth. Someone born to devout Muslim parents in Iran or Indonesia is very likely to be a Muslim; someone born to devout Buddhist parents in Thailand or Sri Lanka is very likely to be a Buddhist; someone born to devout Christian parents in Italy or Mexico is very likely to be a Catholic Christian; and so on. Thus there is a certain non-rational arbitrariness in the claim that the particular tradition within which one happens to have been born is the one and only true religion. And if the conviction is added that salvation and eternal life depend upon accepting the truths of one's own religion, it may well seem unfair that this saving truth is known only to one group, into which only a minority of the human race have had the good fortune to be born.

This thought has been countered by some Christian philosophers by an appeal to middle knowledge – God's knowledge of what everyone *would* do in all possible circumstances – proposing that God knows of every individual who, because of the circumstances of his or her birth, has not had an opportunity to respond to the Christian gospel, that they *would* have freely rejected it if they had heard it. This suggestion, which could of course be deployed from within each religion, involves an idea that is theologically objectionable to many, namely that God has created vast numbers of people whom God knows will forfeit salvation. There is, however, among contemporary Christian thinkers a strong inclusivist trend which separates knowing the truth from receiving salvation, and holds that some (or all) of those who do not in this life come to know the truth may nevertheless, by divine grace, either be counted now as "anonymous Christians" or may receive Christian salvation in or beyond death. The question here is whether there is not still an arbitrary privileging of one's own religion as the sole channel of salvation.

There are, however, other religious interpretations of religion which do not presuppose that there can only be one religion that knows the truth and is a locus of salvation. These are broadly described as pluralistic.

John Hick

The Transcendent Unity of Religions

Proponents of the "perennial philosophy" such as Frithjof Schuon (1975), Rene Guenon, Ananda Coomaraswamy, Seyyed Hossein Nasr, and Huston Smith distinguish between the esoteric religion of the mystics and the exoteric religions of the mass of believers. The former is, in its innermost core, identical across the different religions, whereas the latter, consisting of culturally conditioned concepts, doctrines, imagery, lifestyle, and spiritual practices, differ and are indeed at many points mutually incompatible. Each exoteric tradition (historical Christianity, Islam, Hinduism, Buddhism, etc.) should accordingly maintain its own unique individuality, because each is a valid expression of the ultimate reality that is directly known by the mystics in an experience that constitutes the transcendent unity of religion. Mysticism is here seen as the core of religion. A question for this approach is whether it can avoid, as some of its proponents wish to do, a relativizing of the different religious belief-systems and ways of life.

Considerable discussion has centered upon the question whether unitive mysticism constitutes (as is claimed for it) a direct and unmediated awareness of the ultimate divine reality, or whether even this experience is conditioned by the thought-forms of the mystic's tradition (see Katz 1978). For whilst some unitive mystics report union with a divine Person, others report union with a non-personal reality. Are these differences to be attributed to varying theological interpretations of a common ineffable experience, or are the reports to be accepted as accounts of genuinely different experiences? Or should we hold that a preconscious interpretative activity enters into the formation of the conscious experience, so that it may be true both that mystics of different traditions are encountering the same reality and yet also that their actual conscious experiences are characteristically different? This latter possibility is developed in the theory next to be discussed.

The Kantian-type "Pluralistic Hypothesis"

This (Hick 1989, and elsewhere) is based upon a Kantian-type distinction between the Real (or the Divine or the Ultimate) in itself and the Real as variously humanly conceived and experienced. The modern consensus that the perceiver always contributes to the form in which the environment is perceived was most influentially introduced into philosophy by Immanuel Kant, but has been reinforced by work in cognitive psychology, in the sociology of knowledge, and also in quantum physics. It is now a commonplace that we do not perceive the physical world as it is in itself, unobserved, but always and necessarily as it appears to beings with our particular sensory equipment and conceptual resources.

Kant sought to identify the concepts in terms of which we order and give meaning to our experience in the activity of bringing it to consciousness. We can apply the same method to religious experience. The pluralistic hypothesis is that the Real (to select this term from several equally available ones) in itself is present to us, or impinges upon us, all the time and that when this impingement comes to consciousness it takes the form of what we call religious experience. Such experience is, however, very diverse, depending upon the set of religious concepts in terms of which it is constructed. The two basic concepts are deity, or the Real as personal, and the absolute, or the Real as non-personal, the former issuing in the theistic and the latter in the non-theistic forms of religion. We are not, however, aware of deity in general or of the absolute in general. These concepts are (in Kantian language) schematized or made more concrete, not, however, as in Kant's system, in terms of abstract time but in terms of the filled time of history and culture. Thus human beings are specifically aware of the Yahweh who chose and specially treasures the children of Israel; or of the Vishnu or the Siva worshiped within the Hindu traditions; or of the Holy Trinity of Christian devotion; or of the God whose angel revealed to the prophet Muhammad the words of the Qur'an; and so on. These, and the many other God figures, are *personae* of the Real, each jointly formed by its universal presence to humanity and by the particular conceptualities and spiritual practices of the different religious traditions. Again, the non-personal Brahman, Dao, Dharmakaya, Nirvana, Sunyata, are *impersonae* of the Real, formed similarly but by means of very different concepts. A Thomistic principle states that things known are in the knower according to the mode of the knower, and in the case of religion the mode of the knower differs from tradition to tradition.

On this hypothesis the nature of the Real in itself is beyond the range of our (other than purely formal) human concepts. It is in Western terms ineffable, or in Eastern terms formless. In Kantian language, the noumenal Real is humanly experienced as a range of divine phenomena.

The criterion by which religions are judged to be authentic or inauthentic, for this hypothesis, arises within a circular argument which is entered through the acceptance of the religious experience of one's own tradition as not purely imaginative projection but at the same time a cognitive response to a transcendent reality; and through the extension of this principle to other religions whose moral and spiritual fruits seem to be more or less on a par with those of one's own. These fruits thus provide a common criterion by which to recognize the salvific transformation of human existence from natural self-centeredness to a new orientation centered in the Real, a transformation which takes different concrete forms within different religious cultures.

This Kantian-type hypothesis addresses the problem of the conflicting truth-claims of the different religions by the proposal that they do not in fact conflict because they are claims about different manifestations of the Real to different human faith communities, each operating with its own conceptuality, spiritual practices, form of life, treasury of myths and stories, and historical memories. One of the main critical questions about this hypothesis is whether, in reducing the distinctive belief-systems of the different religions from absolute truths to reports of one human perception amongst others of the divine reality, it does not contradict the cherished self-understanding of each. Is it not inherently revisionary rather than purely descriptive?

Other Pluralistic Theories

Ninian Smart (in Kellenberger 1993, and elsewhere) and Keith Ward (1994, and elsewhere) stress the idea of the complementarity of the world religions.

Ward, rejecting the Kantian-type distinction between the Ultimate in itself and the Ultimate as humanly thought and experienced, speaks of "a Supreme Reality which wills all to be consciously related to it" (1994, p. 340), complementary aspects of this Reality being revealed within the different world religions. Thus, for example, "the Semitic and Indian traditions are complementary, emphasizing the active and unchanging poles respectively of the Supreme Spiritual Reality to which they both seek to relate" (p. 331). And through their friendly interactions, each seeking to learn from the others, a "convergent spirituality" may emerge in ways which cannot be known in advance. The question here is whether in the end the conflicting-truth-claims problem has been addressed.

To some (e.g. John Cobb, in Kellenberger 1993 and elsewhere) it seems more realistic to recognize a plurality of ultimates, including at least the personal God affirmed by monotheistic religion and the ever-changing interdependent process of the universe (*pratitya-samutpada*) affirmed by Buddhism. Here the critical questions concern the relationship between the different ultimates.

There is already a considerable literature discussing these and the other theories currently in the field (offered, e.g., by such philosophers as David Basinger, William Craig, Paul Griffiths, James Kellenberger, David Krieger, Robert McKim, Sarvepalli Radhakrishnan, Joseph Runzo, etc.; and also by a large number of Christian theologians, most of whom seek to defend in various ways the unique centrality of their own tradition). Each theory brings with it its own problems, and the entire subject is ripe for new approaches and new proposals.

The whole subject of the relation between the religions is so obviously a major problem within the philosophy of religion, and presents so obvious a challenge to a dominant contemporary form of confessional religious apologetic, that it seems inevitable that it will be increasingly widely discussed in the coming decades.

References

Alston, W. 1991. *Perceiving God* (Ithaca and London: Cornell University Press).

Christian, W. 1987. *Doctrines of Religious Communities: A Philosophical Study* (New Haven and London: Yale University Press).

Hick, J. 1989. *An Interpretation of Religion* (London: Macmillan; New Haven: Yale University Press).

Katz, S. (ed.) 1978. *Mysticism and Philosophical Analysis* (New York: Oxford University Press; London: Sheldon Press).

John Hick

Kellenberger, J. (ed.) 1993. *Inter-Religious Models and Criteria* (London: Macmillan; New York: St Martin's Press). (Contains a variety of viewpoints.)

Schuon, F. 1975. *The Transcendent Unity of Religions* (Paris, 1948) (New York and London: Harper & Row).

Smith, W. C. 1991. *The Meaning and End of Religion* (New York, 1962) (Minneapolis: Fortress Press).

(Deconstructs the modern Western concept of "a religion.")

Vroom, H. (ed.) 1989. *Religions and the Truth: Philosophical Reflections and Perspectives* (Amsterdam: Rodopi; Grand Rapids: Eerdmans).

Ward, K. 1994. *Religion and Revelation* (Oxford: Clarendon Press).

44

The real or the Real? Chardin or Rothko?

Anthony O'Hear

I

I will begin by considering some themes from Proust's wonderful essay on Chardin, *Chardin and Rembrandt* (Proust, 1988). Proust speaks of the young man "of modest means and artistic taste", his imagination filled with the splendour of museums, of cathedrals, of mountains, of the sea, sitting at table at the end of lunch, nauseated at the "traditional mundanity" of the unaesthetic spectacle before him: the last knife left lying on the half turned-back table cloth, next to the remains of an underdone and tasteless cutlet. He cannot wait to get up and leave, and if he cannot take a train to Holland or Italy, he will at least go to the Louvre to have sight of the palaces of Veronese, the princes of van Dyck and the harbours of Claude. Doing this will, of course, make his return to his home and its familiar surroundings seem yet more drab and exasperating.

> If I knew this young man I would not deter him from going to the Louvre, but rather accompany him there . . . I would make him stop . . . in front of the Chardins. And once he had been dazzled by this opulent depiction of what he had called mediocrity . . . I should say to him: Are you happy? Yet what have you seen but

. . . dining or kitchen utensils, not the pretty ones, like Saxe chocolate-jars, but those you find most ugly, a shiny lid, pots of every shape and material (the salt-cellar, the strainer), the sights that repel you, dead fish lying on the table, and the sights that nauseate you, half-emptied glasses and too many full glasses. (1988, p. 123)

Proust then goes on to note that if one finds all this beautiful to look at, it is because Chardin found it beautiful to paint; and the underlying reason he and you find it all beautiful is because you have already unconsciously experienced the pleasure afforded by still life and modest lives, a pleasure Chardin had the power to summon to explicit recognition with his "brilliant and imperative language".

In sum:

> from Chardin we had learnt that a pear is as alive as a woman, that common crockery is as beautiful as a precious stone. The painter had proclaimed the divine equality of all things before the mind that contemplates them, before the light that beautifies them. (1988, p. 129)

He thus brings us out from a false ideal of conventional beauty, to a wider reality, in which, in accordance with what Proust says, we are enabled to find beauty everywhere. Perhaps Proust is wrong about this: perhaps there are areas in which there is no beauty to be found, in a dying child's bootless agony, for example. But the underlying drift of what Proust says, and the substance of Chardin's

Anthony O'Hear

aesthetic, is surely right: that there is a real beauty in the midst of everyday domesticity, a beauty that may well be overlooked by aesthetic young men and other visionaries, who have a false ideal of beauty, one constrained by grandiosity and sublimity. Proust does not say this either, but one aspect of the false ideal of beauty is doubtless the tendency – so prevalent in the contemporary world – to treat the mundane as disposable; to fail to cherish it, to let it grow old and so become touched with humanity through use and familiarity; to fail to design it with care for its conformability to our sensibility, but to crush all that with a brash and ultimately impersonal dehumanizing aesthetic of function.

Another aspect of Chardin, to which I shall return, is the way in which in his still lives – in contrast to those of some of his brilliant Dutch predecessors, such as Kalf or Coorte – the objects emerge shyly, from a soft and often indeterminate background, against which they quiver in the light almost on the edge of visibility. Their being seen, and us seeing them, is then represented by Chardin as what it is, a human achievement: the objects are summoned, as Proust puts it, "out from the everlasting darkness in which they had been interred". We may well be reminded by all this of Cézanne's words "le paysage se reflète, s'humanise, se pense en moi". These words, indeed, encapsulate what I want to emphasize in this article, particularly if they are considered alongside Cézanne's own mature *oeuvre*, which consists not of dead versions of life, so to speak, but of canvasses in which the appearances of things are vividly reconstituted for us out of the equally visible pigments of the paint (which is one reason why photographic reproductions are particularly faithless to the reality in the case of Cézanne).

In his essay, Proust goes on to contrast the reality Chardin evokes for us with what he calls the transcendence of reality in Rembrandt; in some of Rembrandt's works, objects become no more than the vehicles by which something else, another light, another meaning, is reflected. Whatever we might say about Rembrandt himself, it is possible to discern in western painting an oscillation of emphasis and interest between the everyday and the transcendent. Early Italian painters such as Duccio and Fra Angelico made little attempt to be fully realistic, being more concerned to give expression to the religious truths underlying the myths they painted. It was not that in their painting there was a complete inability to represent the appearances of things; they do and they can, but that is not the focus

of their interest. In Raphael we find, to sublime effect, a balance of the physical and the religious, a balance which has been quite lost – though to stunning effect – in the opulent sensuality of Titian and Veronese. It is not for nothing that Titian has been seen as ushering in the materialism of the modern age, though to see him simply in such terms is to discount the pantheistic overtones and allegorical subject matter of paintings such as *The Flaying of Marsyas* and *The Death of Actaeon*. Given that painting is about the appearances of things, and that it is thus intimately related to our experience of seeing, it is even arguable that no painting can be regarded as materialistic in a reductionist sense; thus Monet – who is often taken to be the epitome of modernistic materialism in painting – in many paintings certainly emphasizes sensation at the expense of anything deeper or more inward, but his work also testifies to the intrinsic interest and value of our perspective on the world, and would thus resist analysis of that perspective as "mere" epiphenomenon.

If Monet was not interested in his art in anything specifically religious, there were other painters in the nineteenth century who were, and who, for a time, managed to combine a stylistic naturalism with an overtly religious content. We can think here of the Nazarenes in Germany and the Pre-Raphaelites in England. But this affected naivety could not last. As Peter Fuller graphically described in *Theoria* (1988) under the assault of Darwinism, the hope expressed in *The Light of the World* quickly turned to the desolation of Holman Hunt's *Scapegoat* and Dyce's *Pegwell Bay*. In the former, a visit to the Holy Land failed to elicit anything more uplifting than a mangy animal and a waterless, wasted landscape. In the latter, women and children hunt for fossils on an empty beach beneath a sickly sky across which Donati's comet is passing. The symbolism would in both cases have had a direct impact on the intended audience, even if it needs conscious retrieval on our part. Moreover, if the natural world could no longer be seen as directly revelatory of the divine hand, what point was there in its literal depiction, particularly when the camera could do that painlessly? At least some of the Pre-Raphaelite Brotherhood retreated into highly-charged medieval fantasy (and not *just*, I surmise, because Rossetti was no natural draughtsman).

Other religiously motivated artists worked in more oblique ways than the Pre-Raphaelites. Caspar David Friedrich's romantic landscapes turn out to be carefully crafted allegories of the Christian's journey through the world, but in them there is little enough sense either of the divine nature of the world – which is all too often a hostile environment redeemed only by the distant presence of a cross or of a vision of a cathedral – or of the concrete detail of the Christian myth.

Another approach is that of van Gogh: to transform the natural in a visionary manner: to see stars, olive trees, cypresses and the like, not as they appear in everyday life but as transfigured symbols of a deeper more vibrant life pulsating beneath the empirical surface, and visible to the man of faith. Van Gogh and Friedrich, whatever their differences in approach and in painterly quality, concur in their desire to preserve what they would see as the essence of the Christian message and in their refusal in the main either to represent that message literally or to see the natural world as it is to the normal eye as a straightforward manifestation of the divine. And in all these respects, they have been followed by many artists in this century.

With the decline of natural theology and the collapse of credal religion, the problem for a religiously motivated artist is to devise a way of presenting the essence of religion without illegitimate recourse to either creed or nature. It is hardly surprising that some artists should have sought abstraction as a way forward, nor indeed that some critics and commentators have seen Barnett Newman and Mark Rothko as among the supreme religious painters of our time. Newman indeed told us that we should take him in this way, providing elaborate references to Kabbalistic themes in his titles and commentaries. I must confess to some difficulty in accepting Newman on his own terms. His huge rectangular expanses of flat colour punctuated by vertical stripes are not easily experienced as pointers to the numinous, although the canvasses can, like those of Rothko, engulf the perceiver by their sheer size, and one can be amazed for a time at Newman's sheer effrontery.

By comparison with Newman, Rothko's major canvasses are not so big (a mere 2 metres wide in many cases), but they all produce an experience of engulfing the perceiver, as much by their working from a ragged, indeterminate edge to quasi-rectangular expanses of deep colour, as by their size. They are, in a way, perfect expressions of the world as a stage on which everything is about to happen, or has already happened. In Rothko's work, there is no trace of the concrete, nothing appears; we are overwhelmed by hazy, empty sublimity. And

before long, I find them deeply unsatisfying, longing to turn to the modesty and concreteness of a Chardin. Is engulfment, the wiping away of all determinations and horizons, what life – and art – is all about? If it is, then human effort and perception and perspective are, in the final analysis, mocked. There is, in fact, more than a grain of truth in Patrick Heron's barbed comment: "that having painted 800 such canvasses, Rothko was led nowhere, but to the dealers and suicide!" (1989, p. 39).

II

My excursion into the history of painting is not simple self-indulgence. I have engaged in it in order to illustrate as vividly as I can the reason why I am unable to rest content with approaches to existence and experience which would undervalue human perception and human experience.

Either there is some cosmic point to human existence, or there is not. In either case, the value of human experience remains irreducible, despite temptations on both accounts to discount it.

Let us suppose, first, that human beings are simply products of a mindless, purposeless cosmos, thrown up by the random or mechanistic activities of more basic particles. Then it will be true that our perspective on the world (including our perceptions, our feelings and our meaning) is itself a by-product of more fundamental processes and reflective of no deeper reality or purpose. It may even be that knowledge of these fundamental processes and the laws which govern them would enable us to predict human perceptions and actions. Relative to the more fundamental processes which underlie our perceptions, the modalities of our perceptions (colour, taste, smell, touch, sound) will be regarded as consisting of secondary qualities, qualities which arise only as a result of the interaction of colourless, tasteless, odourless, textureless and silent particles with our sense organs. But even if this were true, our perceptions, and artistic works devoted to the exploration and development of human perspectives would not lose any value they have for us. The value of a Monet landscape lies not in its genesis, but in the satisfactions and delights and insights it affords us, satisfactions and delights and insights which would not be corroded completely even were we to adopt the scientific view from nowhere, that which displaces the human subject from the centre of things, and sees

525

human life and perception as part of more inclusive causal processes. But even accepting a story of this sort at an intellectual level, we still feel and experience things as we do, and it is in our lives and experiences as lived and experienced that value lies.

Indeed, even seeing our *Lebenswelt* as the product of primary material processes does not make what is revealed in our world *false*. It is open to us, even while accepting the scientific view as causally fundamental, to regard what is revealed in our experience as a legitimate disclosure of the world, one which is available only to us. Just because the world of so-called secondary qualities arises only in the interaction of particles with our sense organs, does not mean that that world is unreal or in some derogatory sense subjective, any more than the pictures a television set emits are unreal or subjective just because a television receiver has to transform invisible radio waves into visible images.

The idea that there is in human perception a singular and irreducible revelation of the real world becomes even more plausible if we see human existence as cosmically intended in some way. For what, from the cosmic point of view, could be the point of human existence, other than that the cosmos should be experienced and understood in a human way? It is worth noting here that not even God, being a-temporal, a-spatial and immaterial, could know what it is like to be a human being; however much God might have foreknowledge of our thoughts, experiences and actions, this foreknowledge would necessarily be schematic, abstract and theoretical.

It has for long seemed to me, as it did to Oliver Soskice in "Painting and the Absence of Grace", that if we are here for a purpose, and if human life has something unique to contribute to the cosmos, it is this:

Sind wir vielleicht *hier*, um zu sagen: Haus,
Brücke, Brunnen, Tor, Krug, Obstbaum,
      Fenster —
höchstens: Säule, Turm . . . aber zu *sagen*,
      verstehs,
oh zu sagen *so*, wie selber die Dinge niemals
innig meinten zu sein.

"Are we perhaps here to say: House,
Bridge, Well, Gate, Jug, Fruit Tree, Window
— at most, Pillar, Tower . . . but to say – oh!
to say in this way, as the things themselves
never so intently meant to be."
(R. M. Rilke, *Ninth Duino Elegy*, lines 32–6)

That is, we are here to experience and articulate something about things, something which things themselves can neither articulate nor experience, but which also (as Rilke goes on to say) is beyond the power of angels to know and experience.

We can, of course, see value in doing what Rilke says we are here to do, even if we are not put here to do anything, and that valuing need not be impugned by scientific explanations or views from nowhere. It is, perhaps, strange then that religion, which does see us as being on earth for a reason, all too often downgrades our Rilkean task, for doing what Rilke says we are here to do is the one thing we alone can do; and is the reason I place a higher value on the aesthetic experiencing of the world than many theological writers. I see the contemplation of what arises in human practice as the singular contribution we as humans can make to the cosmos. That is to say, through our practices and the associated sensory apparatus, we divide the world up in various ways, but because we are self-conscious we can reflect on enjoying these perceptions and evaluate the significance of what is revealed in our practices and perceptions. Because of our status as sensory *and* intellectual, we alone are in a position to enjoy particular perceptions of the world, and to evaluate the fruits of those perceptions. A merely sensory consciousness could not reflect on what it perceives, while a purely intellectual being (an angel) would perceive or experience nothing.

Religion, though, would take us all too quickly from the human to something we cannot envisage or articulate at all. In so doing, it all too easily downgrades and wipes away the human. Soskice refers in his article to Hölderlin's *Griechenland*:

. . . where the longing for eternity knows no
      bounds
Divine things are overcome with sleep.
There is no trust in God, no proportion . . .

I find more than a trace of this lack of proportion in John Hick's *An Interpretation of Religion* (1989). I am now going to turn to this book as it is, I believe, a brave and radical attempt to salvage something of religious value from the downfall of dogmatic religion; or, more precisely, from the dilemma which arises for any would-be religious believer from the existence of a plurality of religious faiths, all of which seem to have some good claim to be regarded as offering genuine insights into the divine.

Hick is also faced with the problem that straight-forward dogmatic religion is hardly credible in the late twentieth century. For him, there is to be no return to a Pre-Raphaelitic naivety. Moreover, he is well aware that Christianity is not the only credal contender. Right at the start of his book he speaks of the transcendent being perceived through different and distinctive cultural lenses (1989, p. 8).

Nevertheless, he is convinced that there is a Real behind the different religious traditions: that is to say, that the God of Abraham, Isaac and Jacob, the Holy Trinity, Allah, Vishnu, Brahman, the Dharmakāya/Nirvāṇa/Śūnyatā, Zen and the Tao, all represent ways of affirming the same ultimate.

I presume that Zeus, Jupiter, Wotan, and the other limited, personal deities are not included in Hick's list because they are limited; they are them-selves subject to fate and to contract and are not transcendent. Be that as it may, and leaving aside the point that Jahweh, Jesus and Allah are all con-ceived in personal – and hence determinate and limited – terms, I want now to consider the implica-tions for us of conceiving what he calls the real as Hick does, as a metaphysical or noumenal ground underlying all religious objects, whether personal (as often in Western tradition) or impersonal (as characteristically in eastern traditions): that is, some-thing divine and real behind the various humanly mediated revelations or intimations of divinity.

There is, indeed, as Hick points out, a drive in human thought to seek the utterly transcendent or the self-subsistent ground of our beliefs and valuations. We are not just conscious, we are also self-conscious. We have beliefs and values, and we are aware of having them. I am aware that any belief or judgment I make is mine, and that my perspective is just that – *my* perspective on a world which has an existence independent of me, and in which there are other agents also making judg-ments of value. I thus become aware that my belief or judgment is not the only possible belief or way of according value. I become aware of my route through the world as only one of many possible routes, and thereby open to question.

My self-consciousness may well be sparked into reflective activity by the realization that there are people other than me and cultures other than mine. But once activated, we begin to realize the limited nature of any actual sets of beliefs or values we have. We thus formulate for ourselves the concep-tion of an absolute truth, an absolute good. But in formulating such notions, we realize that no merely human sets of beliefs or values can be guaranteed to be absolute: all will be more or less limited by the particular perspective we adopt.

Hick sees a great upsurge of self-conscious dissatisfaction with local and particular beliefs and customs around the fifth century BC, the time of Confucius, Lao Tzu, the Buddha, Mahavira, Zoroaster, the Hebrew prophets – and Socrates. As he puts it, following Karl Jaspers, at what is dubbed, the "axial" age,

> [I]ndividuals were emerging into self-consciousness out of the closely-knit communal mentality of their society.... Religious value no longer resided in total identification with the group but began to take the form of personal openness to transcendence. And since the new religious messages of the axial age were ad-dressed to individuals as such, rather than as cells in a social organism, these messages were in principle universal in their scope. (1989, p. 30)

This "post-axial" quest for individuality and uni-versality is in fact based in our very nature as self-conscious beings, as I have been arguing, and is not just a product of specific historical circumstances, however much some circumstances might encour-age its development. The drive to individualism and the search for universal, unlimited truth and value are inherent in human nature, and cannot be totally suppressed. Nevertheless, we should realize that both these tendencies carried with them two, probably connected problems. First, they destroy culture and secondly they encourage a religion of unknowing, whose effect may well be to under-mine the human.

In saying that individualistic and universalistic attitudes destroy culture, what I have in mind is the complaint raised by Aristophanes (in *The Frogs*) and by Nietzsche (in *The Birth of Tragedy*) against Socrates. In their view, the greatness of ancient Athens stemmed in part from the fact that its cit-izens were united in reverence for a myth or set of myths which bound them together (and which also, doubtless, enabled them to make culturally crucial distinctions between the best and the rest of soci-ety, between themselves as Athenians and other Hellenes, and between Hellenes and barbarians). But Socrates and, to an extent, Euripides, taught ordinary men to question the myths and to cease to respect their superiors or to regard Greeks as Greeks first and as men second.

527

In *The Decline of the West* (1926), Spengler characterized the transition from what he called Culture to Civilization in the following terms, which certainly have a bearing on Hick's characterization of axiality:

> In place of a type-true people, born of and grown on the soil, there is a new sort of nomad, cohering unstably in fluid masses, the parasitical city-dweller, traditionless, utterly matter-of-fact, religionless, clever, unfruitful, deeply contemptuous of the countryman, and especially that highest form of countryman, the country gentleman. (1926, p. 32)

And Spengler goes on to speak of the "uncomprehending hostility" of the new city-dweller to "all the traditions representative of the Culture (nobility, church, privileges, dynasties, conventions in art and limits of knowledge in science)", of his "keen and cold intelligence that confounds the wisdom of the peasant" and of his apparently new-fashioned but actually quite primitive and instinctual naturalism in all matters of sex and society.

While there will in city-dwelling civilizations tend to be a decline of local and particular ways of doing things, in favour of the universal, the reproducible, the purely functional and the disposable, intellectually the decline of (Spenglerian) culture presages an attempt to discern a unity underlying apparently disparate forms of similar activity. This, of course, is what Hick attempts in the case of religion, and whose aesthetic analogue is the *œuvre* of Rothko. I say this in the case of Rothko because I take it that what he is presenting is not just colour as an end in itself, but colour as a symbol of the ineffable.[1]

The attempt to fuse what, on the face of it, is unfusable (e.g. Islam, Christianity, Hinduism and Buddhism) together with the religious drive to find an underlying ultimate reality conspire to produce a religion which is, practically speaking, without content. Drawing, indeed, on ancient religious texts and traditions, Hick speaks of God, Brahman, the Dharmakāya as unlimited, "not to be equated without remainder with anything that can be humanly experienced and defined" (1989, p. 236); the Real in itself cannot be said to be "one or many, person or thing, substance or process, good or evil, purposive or non-purposive" (1989, p. 246); "we postulate the real *an sich* as the ultimate ground of the intentional objects of the different forms of religious thought-and-experience" (1989, p. 350). Even if it is said that there is *something* (the Real) which underlies all the phenomenal divinities, the fact is that we can say nothing about this real. It is hard to see the difference between faith in a non-describable Real and agnosticism.

I hope that by now the point of my earlier reference to the work of Mark Rothko is now clear. Instead of anything specific we are, in both cases, being offered a void, an emptiness, which is said to be pregnant with noumenal meaning and to underlie the merely phenomenal. Hick does urge us to respect and to maintain the disparate phenomenal manifestations of the Real (i.e. the actual world-religions). But given the superior viewpoint he is urging us to adopt, whereby each of these religions is seen as a radically incomplete version of something utterly ungraspable, of which we are told there are other equally valid (though I would add) mutually inconsistent manifestations, it is hard to see how one could in all good conscience continue to worship in, say, a Christian church or a Muslim mosque.

Even if the exclusivist and particular claims of the actual world-religions could somehow be mutually reconciled against the background of a noumenal we know not what, I am extremely dubious about the moral and human effects of worshipping and directing our efforts to a Being as indeterminate for us as Hick's unknowable Real. If this Real can be said to be neither person nor thing, good or evil, purposive or non-purposive, loving or hating, as Hick avers (1989, p. 350), what ultimate reason is there for us to love, to be good, to respect others or to engage in purposive activity at all? Hick does indeed struggle manfully with the Buddhist śūnyatā (emptiness, transcendence of all perspective (cf. 1989, pp. 288–92)); śūnyatā seems to be the natural end of life if the Real is as Hick conceives it. At any rate, it is hard to value human activity or to see how our way of perceiving things could be a worthwhile revelation of a Reality which is essentially unknowable.

Hick doubtless would say that there is a reason for us to cultivate loving and truthful attitudes, given that we are aiming to eradicate our ignorance and delusion with respect to the Real, and also that such attitudes are propagated by all the great world-religions. But I have to say that from Hick's perspective of radical agnosticism, even loving and truthful attitudes on our part will get us no closer to the Real: we will still have nothing to say about it, and nothing to grasp, except possibly by some incommunicable, and hence dumb, religious experience. I can, indeed, see nothing in Hick's account to rule out a Real whose ultimate nature was not, say, closer to a Nietzschean will-to-power than to a Catholic Sacred Heart; nor indeed am I convinced that compassion for suffering humanity is always to the forefront of the world-religions, as opposed to a chronic carelessness about individual life and suffering in face of cosmic dramas of global, rather than individual redemption or transformation. What is there in the notion of the unknowable, transcendent Real to rule but the possibility that our idea of a compassionate divinity is simply the ultimate fantasy of a deluded humanity whose final fate is to be broken on the wheel of existence? And I do not think it can be denied that some religious seekers after an ultimate divine reality have found

not bliss but an emptiness, even a cruelty, too terrible to contemplate.[2]

Against such a background the emptiness – at its worst, the rhetoric – of Rothko would be vindicated against the painstaking and human modesty of Chardin, and what Chardin presents to us as an all-too-fragile achievement will be swallowed up in the abyss of the divine. At the same time, it is doubtless true that we come to see Chardin's achievement as the achievement it is just when we begin to understand that we are standing above an abyss, cosmically speaking, and that human domesticity and human perception rest on no secure foundation. In terms of my illustrative analogy, then, Rothko's Real might be seen to serve as the background from which Chardin's reality – and ours – emerges and is perceived.

Notes

I intend, in this place, to develop further some of the argument of Oliver Soskice in his article "Painting and the Absence of Grace", *Modern Painters*, vol. 4, no. 1 (Spring 1991, pp. 63–5). I thank Michael McGhee for percipient comments on an earlier draft.

1 This might raise the question as to what I would say about a work – an Ellsworth Kelly, say – in which the aim might well be taken to be just the presentation of an experience of colour, as it is in itself and for itself, in which a painting "stands", as a large and public sense-datum. Leaving aside the gigantism such works are typically prone to, I would have to say that this is a further area in which I would distance myself from a Proustian equality of all things; that there is more meaning, more humanity, in a wineglass or a firedog than in a patch of yellow, however large or small – and that the effort of a painter to render the one is potentially more worthwhile from a human point of view than the effort to represent the

other. We value Vermeer's little patch of yellow but we do not value it just because it is what it is in itself. We value it because it is part of an extraordinarily gentle and precarious humanization of the world.

2 In the light of that dark night of the soul which is a recurring theme throughout the history of religious practice, I have to say that I find the efforts made by Hick in his book (1989, pp. 304–6) to link religious practice to "politico-economic liberation" (i.e. anticapitalism) sentimental and misguided religiously as well as economically. His endorsement of the "basic intent" of Marx, Lenin, Trotsky and Mao, as a "dispositional response of the modern sociologically conditioned consciousness to the real" (p. 306), serves, I think, to underline the extent to which religious thinkers, of all ages, get embroiled in the delusions of their time. Invoking a Real underlying the delusion will be of little consolation to those whose lives, domesticity and all, are ruined by projects of politico-economic liberation.

References

Fuller, P. 1988. *Theoria* (London: Chatto and Windus).
Heron, P. 1989. "Can Mark Rothko's Work Survive?", *Modern Painters*, vol. 2, no. 2 (Summer), pp. 36–9.
Hick, J. 1989. *An Interpretation of Religion* (London: Macmillan).

Proust, M. 1988. *Against Sainte-Beuve and Other Essays*, trans. J. Sturrock (Harmondsworth: Penguin Books).
Spengler, O. 1926. *The Decline of the West*, trans. C. F. Atkinson (New York: Barnes & Noble).

45

Does Nature Need to be Redeemed?

Holmes Rolston III

Bible and Biology

Biologists believe in genesis, but if a biologist begins reading Genesis, the opening story seems incredible. The trouble is not so much the six days of creation in chapters 1 and 2, though most of the controversy is usually thought to lie there, as in chapter 3, where, spoiling the Garden Earth, the first couple fall and Earth becomes cursed. A biologist realizes that prescientific peoples expressed themselves in parables and stories. The Earth arising from a formless void, inspired by a command to bring forth swarms of creatures, generated in the seas, filling the land, multiplying and filling the Earth, eventuating in the appearance of humans, made of dust and yet remarkably special – all of this is rather congenial with the evolutionary genesis. The real problem is with the Fall, when a once-paradisiacal nature becomes recalcitrant as a punishment for human sin.

That does not fit into the biological paradigm at all. Suffering in a harsh world did not enter chronologically after sin and on account of it. There was struggle for long epochs before the human arrival, however problematic the arrival of sinful humans may also be. This has been Darwin's century, and biology has been painting an ambivalent picture of nature. Nature is prolific and fertile

enough, creative, and the panorama of life across the epochs of natural history is a good thing, a mysterious thing. This calls for a respect for life, perhaps even a reverence for life. But nature is also where the fittest survive, "red in tooth and claw," fierce and indifferent, a scene of hunger, disease, death. And nature is what it is regardless of human moral failings, indeed regardless of humans at all.

Darwin, a biologist who started his career considering studying theology, ends with two contrary moods. He closes the *Origin of Species* resolute about how the Creator began with a few forms and produced many by natural selection:

> Thus, from the war of nature, from famine and death, the most exalted object which we are capable of conceiving, namely, the production of the higher animals, directly follows. There is grandeur in this view of life, with its several powers, having been originally breathed into a few forms or into one; and that, whilst this planet has gone cycling on according to the fixed law of gravity, from so simple a beginning endless forms most beautiful and most wonderful have been, and are being, evolved. (Darwin [1859] 1968: 459–60)

Darwin also exclaims that the process is "clumsy, wasteful, blundering, low, and horribly cruel" (Darwin, quoted in de Beer 1962: 43).

Biologists, disturbed by the first pages of the Bible, will likely not get to later chapters. But if so, there will be more ambivalence. Often the Bible extols the beauties of creation. "O Lord, how manifold are thy works! In wisdom hast thou made them all; the earth is full of thy creatures" (Psalm 104: 24). Nature is a wonderland, perhaps not a paradise, but a realm to be encountered in awe. Beside these passages, the biologist will find laments over creation. Nature, sighs the Preacher, is "vanity of vanities" (Ecclesiastes 1: 2). "The whole creation," asserts Paul, "has been groaning in travail until now." "The creation was subjected to futility" (Romans 8: 19–22).

Should the biologist read on to the closing chapters, the Bible abandons this ambivalence and portrays a new heaven and a new earth, one fulfilling the prophetic vision of the day when "the wolf shall dwell with the lamb, and the leopard shall lie down with the kid" (Isaiah 11: 6). Paul promises, "The creation itself will be set free from its bondage to decay and obtain the glorious liberty of the children of God" (Romans 8: 21). The Bible closes with Eden restored, a Garden City.

What can all of this mean, wonders the biologist, either fallen nature or its idyllic redemption? Has it any relevance for understanding biology? Can a theologian who takes these passages seriously even understand biology? Does nature need to be saved? Thus the biologist carries to the Bible a problematic concept of nature, having no doubt that there has been genesis of some sort, but ambivalent about nature's prolific fecundity, the struggle for life, the goodness of creation. The biologist is also sure that whatever nature is, its fundamental character has nothing to do with human sinfulness. Human sin did not throw nature out of joint; nature does not need to be redeemed on that account.

Biologists have no wish to talk theologians out of genesis. They do not mind being religious. Ernst Mayr, one of the most eminent living biologists, concludes, "Virtually all biologists are religious, in the deeper sense of the word, even though it may be a religion without revelation. . . . The unknown and maybe unknowable instills in us a sense of humility and awe" (Mayr 1982: 81). Biologists find nature spectacular, startling by any criteria. They also find nature stark and full of suffering, sometimes dreadful. They are almost all conservation biologists; they want to save nature. But do they think nature needs to be saved? Do theologians think nature needs to be saved?

One line of answer dissolves the questions. The Bible does not have anything to say about biology at all, nor does biology have anything to say about the Bible – a two-languages view. The Creation and Fall story is a piece of poetry, as is the lion eating straw like the ox (Isaiah 11: 7), or the crystal city in the new creation. These are peace pictures imaging the hoped-for end of violence in culture. And we may hope for the end of violence in culture, but this goal has nothing to do with natural selection in nature, where lions must eat meat, and predation must continue. The wolf lying down with the lamb does not make any biological sense, since ecological harmony includes the violence of eating and being eaten, a conflict and resolution essential to biological creativity at the higher trophic levels. The wolf with the lamb makes sense only poetically, expressing human hopes for redemption within culture. Such passages do not have any biological application. Shalom in nature and shalom in culture are different categories.

But perhaps the two languages of Bible and biology are not wholly unrelated, for they do each offer a concept of nature, a worldview. The biblical language may sometimes be poetry, but not always. *Genesis* sounds like a biological word, showing up, for instance, in genes and regeneration. Both biology and Bible do seek to characterize nature and, even if one does so scientifically and one poetically, the two descriptions need to be congenial. Even if Genesis is taken to be not so much about origins as about the present dependence of nature on God, is ecology in present-day nature conceptually any different in its operation from evolution in historical nature? There is emergence in nature, the present is more than the past. Still, in nature the process and the product, the origins and the continuing character are hardly separable. Ecology is a time-slice out of evolution.

Even prophets and poets have to come back to Earth at times; they too need to tell it like it is. Both biology and theology, then, have two views in dialectic: nature as prolific; nature as problematic. The two languages have to be spoken by one person, whether biologist or theologian. Are they commensurable?

Theologians themselves speak two languages. If we consult Luther, after human sin, nature stands under the left hand of God. "The earth is indeed innocent and would gladly produce the best products, but it is prevented by the curse which was placed on man because of sin." "And what of thorns, thistles, water, fire, caterpillars, flies, fleas, and bedbugs? Collectively and individually, are not all of them messengers who preach to us concerning sin and God's wrath, since they did not exist before sin or at least were not harmful and troublesome?"

(Luther 1958: 205, 208). Likewise Calvin: "Adam ... ruined his posterity by his defection, which has perverted the whole order of nature in heaven and earth. ... Undoubtedly ... they [the creatures] sustain part of the punishment due to the demerits of man" (Calvin 1936, II, I, V, vol. 1: 270).

Augustine insists that nature is not cursed; the whole creation groaning in travail does not apply to the nonhuman creation. The creatures are mutable, but they are not fallen (Clarke 1956). Only humans are fallen and subject to vanity. Aquinas agrees: "Man's sin did not so change the nature of animals, that those whose nature it is now to eat other animals, like lions and hawks, would then have lived on a vegetable diet" (Aquinas 1964: 1.96.1, vol. 13: 125). Perhaps theologians need to figure out what they believe before they talk to biologists; perhaps theologians will not be able to figure out what they believe until they have studied biology.

The Promised Earth

Let us come to the Bible story from a different perspective. The Creation stories are poetry, and sometimes also the prophecies, but overall the Bible is a historical book. We doubt the six days, we doubt the Fall; we doubt the lion lying down with the lamb. But we do not doubt that there was Israel in Palestine, with a claim of covenant and promised land. That land is to be inhabited justly and charitably, and the twin commandments of biblical faith are to love God and to love neighbor. Israel is to be a holy people, a righteous nation, and the principal focus of biblical faith is not nature in the land, but the culture established there. At the same time, the Bible is full of constant reminders of the natural givens that undergird all cultural achievements.

Justice is to run down like waters, and the land flows with milk and honey. "The land which you are going over to possess is a land of hills and valleys, which drinks water by the rain from heaven, a land which the Lord your God cares for; the eyes of the Lord your God are always upon it, from the beginning of the year to the end of the year" (Deuteronomy 11: 11–12). The Hebrew covenant of Redemption is prefaced by the covenant of Creation. The creatures of the landscape are again and again included in that covenant.

Jesus said, "My kingdom is not of this world." Teaching as he did in the Imperial Roman world,

his reference in "this" is to the fallen world of the culture he came to redeem, to false trust in politics and economics, in armies and kings. God loves "the world," and in the landscape surrounding him Jesus found ample evidence of the presence of God. He taught that the power organically manifest in the growing grain and the flowers of the field is continuous with the power spiritually manifest in the kingdom he announces. There is an ontological bond between nature and spirit.

In contrast with the surrounding faiths from which biblical faith emerged, the natural world is disenchanted; it is neither God, nor is it full of gods, but it remains sacred, a sacrament of God. Although nature is an incomplete revelation of God's presence, it remains a mysterious sign of divine power. The birds of the air neither sow nor reap yet are fed by the heavenly Father, who notices the sparrows that fall. Not even Solomon is arrayed with the glory of the lilies, though the grass of the field, today alive, perishes tomorrow (Matthew 6). There is in every seed and root a promise. Sowers sow, the seed grows secretly, and sowers return to reap their harvests. God sends rain on the just and unjust. "A generation goes, and a generation comes, but the earth remains forever" (Ecclesiastes 1: 4). "Thou crownest the year with thy bounty; the tracks of thy chariot drip with fatness. The pastures of the wilderness drip, the hills gird themselves with joy, the meadows clothe themselves with flocks, the valleys deck themselves with grain, they shout and sing together for joy" (Psalm 65: 11–13).

This records an experience in Palestine, but it characterizes nature as a whole. The Hebrews are moving from the particular, in Canaan, to the global Earth. This does not sound like a nature cursed and needing to be redeemed; it rather praises a promised land experienced in Israel and universal on this promised Earth.

Wildness

Biblical writers are principally concerned with the culture Israel established on this promised land, but they regularly appreciate the wild nature that surrounds them on their landscape. A wildland is a wonderland, a miracle. "Praise the Lord from the earth, you sea monsters and all deeps, fire and hail, snow and frost, stormy wind fulfilling his command! Mountains and all hills, fruit trees and all cedars! Beasts and all cattle, creeping things and flying birds!" (Psalm 148: 7–9). "Who has cleft a channel for the torrents of rain, and a way for the thunderbolt, to bring rain on a land where no man is, on the desert in which there is no man; to satisfy the waste and desolate land, and to make the ground put forth grass?" (Job 38: 25–7). God not only sends rain on the just and the unjust; God sends rain to satisfy wildlands. God not only blesses humans; God blesses the desolate wastes. These fierce landscapes, sometimes supposed to be ungodly places, are godly after all.

That the fair land of Palestine, with its cities and fields, should again become desert and wilderness is a frequent prophetic threat. The collapse of cultural life in the Promised Land is indeed a tragedy, and in that sense a relapse to the wild is sometimes used in the Bible as a symbol for judgment on an aborted, promised culture. Jackals roam the land, destroyed in punishment for sin. Such wildness is a tragedy only in foil to failed culture, but taken for what it is in itself, prior to using it to symbolize human hopes and disappointments, wildness in the Bible is never a bad thing.

"Who has let the wild ass go free? Who has loosed the bonds of the swift ass, to whom I have given the steppe for his home, and the salt land for his dwelling place? He scorns the tumult of the city; he hears not the shouts of the driver. He ranges the mountain as his pasture, and he searches after every green thing" (Job 39: 5–8). God is not "for us" humans alone. God is "for" these wild creatures too. God loves wildness as well as God loves culture, and in this love God both blesses and satisfies wildness and also leaves it to its own spontaneous autonomy. To be self-actualizing under God is a good thing for humans, and it is a good thing, *mutatis mutandis*, for coyotes and columbines. That is the blessing of divinity in them.

"Is it by your wisdom that the hawk soars, and spreads his wings toward the south? Is it at your command that the eagle mounts up and makes his nest on high? On the rock he dwells and makes his home in the fastness of the rocky crag. Thence he spies out the prey; his eyes behold it afar off. His young ones suck up blood; and where the slain are, there is he. . . . Shall a faultfinder contend with the Almighty? He who argues with God, let him answer it" (Job 39: 26–40: 2). "The high mountains are for the wild goats; the rocks are a refuge for the badgers. . . . The young lions roar for their prey, seeking their food from God" (Psalm 104: 18–21). None of this suggests that nature is fallen and needs to be redeemed. Is there more to be said?

Perpetual Perishing

If redemption means being saved from the guilt of sin, then fauna, flora, rocks, and rivers have no guilt and cannot be redeemed. If redemption means being saved from the consequences of sin, then nature can be redeemed only so far as it has been ruined by human sin that infects the natural course. That hardly seems credible before humans arrive on Earth, and it hardly seems credible where nature continues to run its spontaneous course unaffected by human vices or virtues. We may want to keep the word *redemption* in that kind of a soteriological context; certainly that is where the biblical writers are usually focused. We might be making a category mistake to try to stretch it over to nonhuman domains of experience.

If redemption can also mean being rescued from harm (Latin: *redimo* to release, to buy back), then our inquiry is still open. If redemption can mean that value in one life is rescued and restored, or that value in one life survives to contribute to lives beyond one's own, then our inquiry is promising. If redemption can mean that there is a transformation by which destruction of the old, lower life is not really destruction but renovation, the creation of newer, higher levels of life, then our inquiry is promising indeed.

Redemption is not a word that biologists are likely to use, but consider the word *regeneration*. It can serve as a crossover between biology and theology. *Reproduction* is more likely to be the word that shows up in the index of a biology text; nevertheless *regeneration* is omnipresent in biology. Every species has to reproduce itself from generation to generation; it absolutely must regenerate or else go extinct. Every organism, even when not reproducing, has constantly to regenerate itself, day by day, hour by hour, moment by moment. Your body has regenerated millions of cells during the time you have been reading this article. Life is lived in the midst of an ever-threatening relapse into chaos.

What does nature need to be redeemed from? What does nature need to be redeemed to? That does not quite phrase the question correctly for a biologist – not initially at least. But if we ask, Does nature need regenerating from day to day, from generation to generation? the biologist at once answers, Yes, without doubt. The organism ever stands in close proximity to failure, a failure (death) that will sooner or later overtake every individual life. These individual failures are kept from being final only by regeneration from life to life. Life is an uphill climb against the downhill tug of entropy. Without regeneration, life collapses into a sand heap. Does nature need to be redeemed? If this asks whether life must be perpetually redeemed in the midst of its perishing,[1] then nature needs to be redeemed as much as humanity. In the Psalmist's metaphors, life is lived in green pastures and in the valley of the shadow of death, nourished by eating at a table prepared in the midst of its enemies.

The biblical writers, lacking paleontological museums, had no access to the distant origins of life in evolutionary time, any more than, lacking microscopes, they had access to biochemistry and cellular biology. But they did encounter nature directly; indeed, they lived nearer to raw nature than do we. They were inspired to see into its inner character, a dialectical character, which, if not all of the truth, is part of the truth about nature. At this point, perhaps the poetry of nature as garden and as groaning in travail can be demythologized, or remythologized, for our scientific era. Also, since good and evil, about which biblical writers thought a lot, are not words that biologists handle with ease, perhaps they can teach biologists something, at least when those biologists are in a philosophical mood. Is there good and evil in nature?

Natural Evils

Though there is no sin in amoral nature, there is quite a list of candidate evils from which nature might need to be redeemed: predation, parasitism, selfishness, randomness, blindness, disaster, indifference, waste, struggle, suffering, death. There are natural evils, incontestably so – at least at a first level of analysis – and this element in nature has suggested to some that nature is fallen. Biblical writers, though they rejoice in nature, can also speak of nature laboring in travail. *Travail*, in fact, is a key to understanding these evils. The root idea is that of *birthing*, of a woman in labor as she delivers her child. Now we find regeneration coupled with suffering. *Birthing*, which is really also the root for the word *nature* (Greek: *natans*, "giving birth"), is a transformative experience where suffering is the prelude to creation, indeed struggle is the principle of creation. Struggle is always going on, and it is this struggle in which life is regenerated. Nature is always giving birth, regenerating, always in travail.

Nature is random, contingent, blind, disastrous, wasteful, indifferent, selfish, cruel, clumsy, ugly, struggling, full of suffering, and, ultimately, death? Yes, but this sees only the shadows, and there has to be light to cast shadows. Nature is orderly, prolific, efficient, selecting for adapted fit, exuberant, complex, diverse, regenerating life generation after generation. There are disvalues in nature as surely as there are values, and the disvalues systemically drive the value achievements (Rolston 1992). Translated into theological terms, the evils are redeemed in the ongoing story.

Look, for instance, at predation. Certainly from the perspective of any particular animal as prey, being eaten is a bad thing. But then again the disvalue to the prey is a value to the predator, and, further, with a systemic turn, perspectives change. There is not value loss so much as value capture; there is appropriation of nutrient materials and energy from one life stream to another, with selective pressures to be efficient about the transfer. The pains of the prey are redeemed, we might say, by the pleasures of the predator. There are many biological achievements in muscle, power, sentience, and intelligence that could only have evolved, at least in life as we know it on Earth, with predation.

Could, should God have created a world with only flora, no fauna? Possibly. Possibly not, since in a world in which things are assembled something has to disassemble them for recycling. In any case, we do not think that a mere floral world would be of more value than a world with fauna also. In a mere floral world, there would be no one to think. Heterotrophs must be built on autotrophs, and no autotrophs are sentient or cerebral. Could we have had only plant-eating fauna, only grazers, no predators? Possibly, though probably we never did, since predation preceded photosynthesis. Even grazers are predators of a kind, though what they eat does not suffer. Again, an Earth with only herbivores and no omnivores or carnivores would be impoverished – the animal skills demanded would be only a fraction of those that have resulted in actual zoology – no horns, no fleet-footed predators or prey, no fine-tuned eyesight and hearing, no quick neural capacity, no advanced brains. We humans stand in this tradition, as our ancestors were hunters. We really cannot envision a world, on any Earth more or less like our own, which can give birth to the myriad forms of life that have been generated here, without some things eating other things.

Life preys on life; all advanced life requires food pyramids, eating and being eaten. Humans are degenerate in the sense that we cannot synthesize all that we need, compared with, say, the flora, which are autotrophs. But in such degeneracy lies the possibility of advancement. If the higher forms had to synthesize all the life materials from abiotic materials (also degrading their wastes), they could never have advanced very far, not even as organisms, much less as humans in culture. The upper levels are freed for more advanced synthesis because they depend on syntheses (and decompositions) carried out by lesser organisms below. From a systemic point of view, we see the conversion of a resource from one life stream to another – the anastomosing of life threads that characterizes an ecosystem. Plants become insects, which become chicks, which become foxes, which die to fertilize plants.

Or take bad luck. Again, it is certainly true that the creatures can be unlucky and by accident find themselves in peril. Does anything redeem the bad luck? Often not so for particular individuals. And yet, when we place local bad luck into the larger system, we realize that in a world without chance there can be no creatures with integrity, no adventures, surprises, taking risks, and the skills of life would be very different. The organism by its genetic programming, instincts, perceptions, and conditioned learning modifies its exposure to luck and thus acts as a preference sieve through a world with luck in it, partially but not wholly accumulating the lucky upstrokes and discarding the unlucky downstrokes. The organism is redeemed in the midst of its perpetual perishing as it catches its opportunities and dodges its threats.

Bad luck is sometimes catastrophic. Violent forces in nature with random probability strike animals, plants, and people; disaster often results. There is no question but that such forces can and do destroy individuals. Is there any redemption from them? Possibly these violent forces are bad, but there are good ones that overcome them. Possibly the catastrophic, negative forces are integrated with the uniformitarian, positive forces. Floods, windstorms, lightning storms, volcanic eruptions, and all such violences would become more or less like wildfire in natural ecosystems, a bad thing to individuals burned and in short range, but not really all that bad a thing systemically and in long range, given nature's restless creativity.

In March 1872, John Muir was in Yosemite Valley when it was struck by the great Inyo earthquake. He records: "I ran out of my cabin, near the Sentinel Rock, both glad and frightened, shouting, 'A noble earthquake!' . . . a terribly sublime and beautiful spectacle" (Muir 1954: 166–7). "It is delightful to be trotted and dumpled on our

Mother's mountain knee" (Muir 1980: 125). It was "as if God had touched the mountains with a muscled hand" (Muir, in Cohen 1984: 134). Later, Muir concludes that the earthquake was "wild beauty-making business." "On the whole, by what at first sight seemed pure confusion and ruin, the landscapes were enriched; for gradually every talus, however big the boulders composing it, was covered with groves and gardens, and made a finely proportioned and ornamental base for the sheer cliffs." "Storms of every sort, torrents, earthquakes, cataclysms, 'convulsions of nature,' etc., however mysterious and lawless at first sight they may seem, are only harmonious notes in the song of creation, varied expressions of God's love" (Muir 1954: 169). Muir certainly has an intensive faith in natural systems, but such faith is not without some impressive evidence. The great destructive forces are followed by – indeed they are part of – nature's creativity. That amounts to saying that nature is redeemed from catastrophic tragedy.

The list of candidate evils in nature is a long one, and we cannot examine all of them here. The very fact that there is such a list and that it has to be examined indicates that the inquiry is not just, Is there evil in nature? It is, What more is there to be said? The inquiry is whether there is any redemption from these evils, and often as not there indeed is. Here again, biologist and theologian need not quarrel that nature is perpetually renewed in the midst of its perishing. That is a fact of the matter. Indeed, biologist and theologian may agree that the logic of creation requires destruction as well as construction, on scales both large and small, both before humans arrived and after as well.

Struggling Through to Something Higher

The question of whether nature needs to be redeemed is essentially an appraisal of the role of struggle in the genesis of life. Suffering is not a feature of mere causal relations; there is no suffering in astronomy or geology. It appears in bioscience, where we meet not only a functional capacity unprecedented in physical science, but something still more novel. Irritability is universally present in life; suffering in some sense seems copresent with neural structures. Matter can be meaningless, as when so much cosmic material seems tossed forth in waste; but it cannot suffer. Sentient life can suffer, most obviously with the higher forms in their subjectivity. Causality deepens into sentience.

In chemistry, physics, astronomy, geomorphology, meteorology, nothing suffers; in botany life is stressed. In some weakened sense, even nonsentient forms struggle bodily, objectively to avoid death. They have needs and endure stress. But only in zoology does pain emerge. Each seeming advance – from plants to animals, from instinct to learning, from ganglia to brains, from sentience to self-awareness, from herbivores to carnivores – steps up the pain. We are not much troubled by seeds that fail, but it is difficult to avoid pity for nestling birds fallen to the ground.

Though biology introduces suffering, understanding it is not a scientific problem. All the descriptions of science only present the facts, including any feelings (for which it has minimal descriptive power); science has no resources with which to evaluate them. The question metamorphoses into one of the meaning of problematic experiences. So much of Earth's life seems tossed forth in waste, only now the process seems cruel, at least at its advancing levels. This observation torments the possibility of divine design and can seem to reduce natural history to a desolate, evil scene. But "tragic" is not a scientific word. The question of suffering in natural history escapes the competences of science. Yet it is one of the central issues we face.

Emptiness and vastness in an oversized universe is the challenge to interpret in modern physics. The time span of ceaseless struggle is the challenge to interpret in biology. Something stirs in the cold mathematical beauty of physics, in the heated energies supplied by matter, and there is first an assembling of living information centers, and still later suffering subjects. Energy turns into pain. Is this now ugliness emergent for the first time? Or is it a more sophisticated form of beauty? Is it the emerging of life that can and must be redeemed? Bioscience as such can only amorally and nonaesthetically describe what has happened, and to assess whether this is good or bad requires valuational judgment.

An organism can have needs, which is not possible in inert physical nature. A planet moves through an environment, but only an organism can need its world, a feature simultaneously of its prolife program and of the requirement that it overtake materials and energy. But if the environment can be a good to it, that brings also the possibility of deprivation as a harm. To be alive is to have problems. Things can go wrong just because they can

also go right. In an open, developmental, ecological system, no other way is possible. All this first takes place at insentient levels, where there is bodily duress, as when a plant needs water.

Sentience brings the capacity to move about deliberately in the world, and also the possibility of being hurt by it. We might have sense organs – sight or hearing – without any capacity to be pained by them. But sentience does more than permit observation of the world. It rather evolves to awaken some concern for it. Sentience coevolves with a capacity to separate the helps from the hurts in the world. Even in animal life, sentience with its counterpart, suffering, is an incipient form of love and freedom. A neural animal can love something in its world and is free to seek this, a capacity greatly advanced over anything known in immobile, insentient plants. It has the power to move through and experientially to evaluate the environment. The appearance of sentience is the appearance of caring, when the organism is united with or torn from its loves – the step up that brings more drama brings suffering.

When we deal with nature in physics and astronomy, we meet a *causal* puzzle, one of *creatio ex nihilo*. That remains true in biology, when life appears, not out of nothing, but out of matter in which there was no-life before. How could life appear where absolutely none was before? But biology adds, in the higher if not also the lower species, a *meaning* puzzle, one of *creatio per passionem*. Life arises in passionate endurance. Struggle is the dark side of creation. This existential fact, discovered by sensitive souls, is a truth written into life's creation, though it was obscured by the facile Newtonian notion of a Divine Designer fabricating his world machine.

Organic life requires an entirely different model, one of suffering through toward something higher. Only later on, in humans, can this goal be consciously entertained. Prior to that, there is only an instinctive biological drive to survive at the cost of ordeal, present at every biostructural level. If irritability seems at first an unwelcome, adventitious intruder into the life project, by this switch of gestalts it becomes part of the biologic and logic of meanings. All advances come in contexts of problem solving, with a central problem in sentient life being the prospect of hurt. We do not really have available to us any coherent alternative models by which, in a painless world, there might have come to pass anything like these dramas of nature that have happened, events that in their central thrusts we greatly treasure. There are sorts of creation that cannot occur without death, and these include the highest created goods. Death can be meaningfully put into the biological processes as a necessary counterpart to the advancing of life.

The logic here is not so much formal or universal as it is dialectical and narrative. In natural history, whatever might be true in other imaginable worlds, the pathway to psychosomatic consciousness, the only kind of experience we know, is through flesh that can feel its way through that world. There is some sentience without much capacity to be pained by it; we do not much suffer through our eyes or ears. But neither would we have those eyes and ears had they not evolved for the protection of the kinesthetic core of an experiential life that can suffer, whether by lack of food for which eyes may search or by predators whom ears may hear.

In general, the element of suffering and tragedy is always there; it does indeed seem that subjectively to evolve is invariably to suffer. Yet the suffering is both corollary and cause in the larger currents of life. We want to ask not whether Earth is a well-designed paradise for all its inhabitants, nor whether it was a former paradise from which humans were anciently expelled. The question is not whether the world is, or ever was, a happy place. Rather, the question is whether it is a place of significant suffering through to something higher.

We can recognize here a principle both of redemptive and of vicarious suffering, one whereby success is achieved by sacrifice. This principle does not operate in its pronounced and existential forms until evolution advances to the level of mind, reaching there layers of meaning untouched in nonhuman nature. But we can see that the biological process anticipates what later becomes paramount, and this forces us to ask about the meaning of suffering, although that question is one which biological science is incompetent to answer.

Cruciform Creation

Whatever is in travail needs redemption, whether or not there is any sin to be dealt with. If we take the moral component out of redemption (or, better, if we restrict the moral component to the redemption of humans, who are moral and immoral) and ask whether the biodiverse amoral values present in nature need to be saved, then the answer is most certainly that they do. "Conserved" is the biological word; life is the unrelenting conservation of

biological identity above all else, an identity that is threatened every moment, every hour, every generation. But that threatened life has prevailed for several billion years. If we make the correct translation into theology, we will not say that nature does not need to be redeemed, nor that it has never been redeemed; to the contrary, it is ever redeemed.

The Earth is a divine creation and scene of providence. The whole natural history is somehow contained in God, God's doing, and that includes even suffering, which, if it is difficult to say simply that it is immediately from God, is not ultimately outside of God's plan and redemptive control. God absorbs suffering and transforms it into goodness. There is ample preparation for this conviction in Judaism, but it reaches its apex in the crucifixion and resurrection of a suffering Messiah, who produces life out of death in his followers. But we must be careful here. It is not simply the experience of divine design, of architectural perfection, that has generated the Christian hypothesis of God. Experiences of the power of survival, of new life rising out of the old, of the transformative character of suffering, of good resurrected out of evil, are even more forcefully those for which the theory of God has come to provide the most plausible hypothesis.

Christianity seeks to draw the harshness of nature into the concept of God, as it seeks by a doctrine of providence to draw all affliction into the divine will. This requires penetrating backward from a climaxing cross and resurrection to see how this is so. Nature is intelligible. Life forms are logical systems. But nature is also *cruciform*. The world is not a paradise of hedonistic ease, but a theater where life is learned and earned by labor, a drama where even the evils drive us to make sense of things. Life is advanced not only by thought and action, but by suffering, not only by logic but by pathos.

The Greek word is *pathos*, "suffering," and there are pathologies in nature, such as the diseases of parasitism. But pathology is only part of the disvalue; even in health there is suffering. Life is indisputably prolific; it is just as indisputably pathetic, almost as if its logic were pathos, as if the whole of sentient nature were pathological. "Horribly cruel!" exclaimed Darwin. This pathetic element in nature is seen in faith to be at the deepest logical level the pathos in God. God is not in a simple way the Benevolent Architect, but is rather the Suffering Redeemer. The whole of the earthen metabolism needs to be understood as having this character. The God met in physics as the divine wellspring from which matter-energy bubbles up, as the upslope epistemic force, is in biology the suffering and resurrecting power that redeems life out of chaos. The point is not to paint the world as better or worse than it actually is in the interests of a religious doctrine but to see into the depths of what is taking place, what is inspiring the course of natural history, and to demand for this an adequate explanation.

The secret of life is seen now to lie not so much in the heredity molecules, not so much in natural selection and the survival of the fittest, not so much in life's informational, cybernetic learning. The secret of life is that it is a passion play. Things perish in tragedy. The religions knew that full well, before biology arose to reconfirm it. But things perish with a passing over in which the sacrificed individual also flows in the river of life. Each of the suffering creatures is delivered over as an innocent sacrificed to preserve a line, a blood sacrifice perishing that others may live. We have a kind of "slaughter of the innocents," a nonmoral, naturalistic harbinger of the slaughter of the innocents at the birth of the Christ, all perhaps vignettes hinting of the innocent lamb slain from the foundation of the world. They share the labor of the divinity. In their lives, beautiful, tragic, and perpetually incomplete, they speak for God; they prophesy as they participate in the divine pathos. All have "borne our griefs and carried our sorrows."

The abundant life that Jesus exemplifies and offers to his disciples is that of a sacrificial suffering through to something higher. There is something divine about the power to suffer through to something higher. The Spirit of God is the genius that makes alive, that redeems life from its evils. The cruciform creation is, in the end, deiform, godly, just because of this element of struggle, not in spite of it. There is a great divine yes hidden behind and within every no of crushing nature. God, who is the lure toward rationality and sentience in the upcurrents of the biological pyramid, is also the compassionate lure in, with, and under all purchasing of life at the cost of sacrifice. God rescues from suffering, but the Judeo–Christian faith never teaches that God eschews suffering in the achievement of the divine purposes. To the contrary, seen in the paradigm of the cross, God too suffers, not less than God's creatures, in order to gain for the creatures a more abundant life.

In the natural course there is creaturely suffering, autonomously owned, necessitated by the natural drives, though unselected by those caught in the drama. Yet this drive too may be construed, in the panentheistic whole, as God suffering with and for the Creation, diffused divine omnipresence, since each creature both subsists in the divine ground and is lured on by it. The Son of God is an innocent led to slaughter, and his production of new life for the many climaxes a *via dolorosa*, in which the struggling survivors stand under the divine watching over.

In the biblical model in either testament, to be chosen by God is not to be protected from suffering. It is a call to suffer and to be delivered as one passes through it. The election is for *struggling* with and for God, seen in the very etymology of the name Israel, "a limping people." The divine son takes up and is broken on a cross, "a man of sorrows and acquainted with grief." Redemptive suffering is a model that makes sense of nature and history. Far from making the world absurd, suffering is a key to the whole, not intrinsically, not as an end in itself, but as a transformative principle, transvalued into its opposite. The capacity to suffer through to joy is a supreme emergent and an essence of Christianity. Yet the whole evolutionary upslope is a lesser calling of this kind, in which renewed life comes by blasting the old. Life is gathered up in the midst of its throes, a blessed tragedy, lived in grace through a besetting storm.

The enigmatic symbol of this is the cross, a symbol Christians adopt for God, and for an extrahistorical miracle in the atonement of Christ, but one which, more than they have known, is a parable of all natural and cultural history. The Garden Earth, we now understand, is a symbol for a flowering Earth, and there can be little doubt that life has flourished on Earth. The Bible writers experienced that exuberance of life, and biology since has confirmed and reconfirmed it. But we cannot take this Garden Earth as paradise in which there was neither labor nor pain; even in the Garden Earth, life has to be redeemed in the midst of its perpetual perishing. The Garden Earth forebodes the Garden of Gethsemane. Creation is cruciform.

The Human Fall into Sin

The Genesis story concerns, superficially, a couple who live in paradise and are cast out of it as a result of sin. Traditionally, this has been called the Fall. Moral evil in history amplifies the spontaneous evils of nature and deeply compounds the story. By logic alone, the possibility of morality contains the possibility of immorality; and by the logistics of life, we cannot help each other in a world where we cannot hurt each other. We cannot have responsibilities in a world without caring. This education and evolution of moral caring inevitably introduces guilt into our storied awareness. This leads on to themes of forgiveness and reconciliation, likewise gathered into the symbol of the cross. Here, supremely, one suffers through to joy.

Humans have a superiority of opportunity, capacities unattained in animal life. Alas, however, the human capacity is forever unattained, brokenly attained. Much of the history that humans have made is sordid enough. The typical biblical verdict is condemnation of these adventures. The beast made to image God has fallen into sin. Religion has tried to face full on, cognitively, existentially, and redemptively, the stark reality of suffering and tragedy in historical life. All the classical religions find the human condition to be deeply flawed; humans are in trouble, needing salvation. Christian monotheism has insisted that there is something "original" about sin, something in our origins that produces sin perennially, something in our biology, our flesh, that makes it all but inevitable for humans to lapse into sin. At this point theology and at least some kinds of biology, sociobiology for example, are well within dialogue; indeed they can seem to be saying almost the same thing. When biology finds within humans an innate "selfishness," this concurs with what the classical religions have been teaching for millennia.

In this genesis of spirit, humans do have to break out of their animal natures. When animals act "like beasts," as nonmoral beings, nothing is amiss, evil, or ungodly. To the contrary, spectacular values have been achieved, coded, used for coping over the millennia of evolutionary time. But if humans go no further, something is amiss; indeed, in theological terms, something is ungodly. They "fall back" into evil, rather than rise up to their destiny. Stagnating in animal nature, "the natural man [who] does not receive the gifts of the Spirit of God" (I Corinthians 2: 14) is not so much "fallen" as nonrisen, failing rather than falling, failing to rise to the destiny of a child of God, languishing in animal nature.

There is no greater drama in Earth's history than this long struggle (late in the evolutionary story) of the climb to humanity, with perennial failing back to the animal levels. That is the story-parable of Genesis 1–3, a story that is both once upon a time, and once upon all times, aboriginal and perennial. This story discloses our human situation, the situation into which we are now born; but it also discloses the ancient past, the story of how we humans fell into that situation. The Genesis plot is the creation of life, culminating with the creation of human life, coupled with its tragic perennial falling into a real that is less than the ideal. That is the prologue, sketched mythically there, and profoundly orienting the whole story of salvation to follow. What was and is in the animals a good thing becomes ("falls into") a bad thing when it is the only thing in human life. This arrests advancement to the next, the human, humane stage.

The New Testament speaks of the struggle of "spirit" (Greek: *pneuma*) against "flesh" (*sarx*), sometimes of "mind" (*nous*) or "soul" (*psyche*) versus "body" (*soma*). The command to love one's neighbor summarizes the human-divine law; by contrast the animal law is eat or be eaten. That is not a bad law for animals; for humans to live by that law is tragic, since they fail to reach their humanity. The flesh (*sarx*) is too weak for this humane, divine achievement. The "natural man," left to biological inheritance alone, finds that this does not sufficiently empower humans for what they ought to do socially, morally, spiritually. The "natural man" – and woman – need to become the spiritual man and woman; they need their broken spirits inspired by the divine spirit (*pneuma*, "wind," in-spiring), divine inspiriting elevating the mere biology. That does not despise the flesh, which is valuable enough in its place, good creation. But it knows that humans have to rise to spirit to become what they are destined to be. Only that can "save" the natural man or woman from lapsing into beastliness. This genesis of spirit, recompounded from nature, requires the second birth superposed on the first, transcending natural possibilities.

In this sense, religion, carried by cultural inheritance, requires experiences beyond the previous attainment and power of biology. Those experiences come creatively, with struggle, with an arduous passage through a twilight zone of spirit in exodus from nature. This does not mean that nature is bad; nature is pronounced to be very good – not perfect, because culture is yet to come – but intrinsically good. Humans are made godward, to turn toward God, but they shrink back and act like beasts. Genesis is the story, not of the Fall from perfection, but of the "Fall" of the aboriginal couple from innocence into sin. There is awakening. After the sin, "the eyes of both were opened, and they knew that they were naked" (Genesis 3: 7).

Life under natural selection is perpetually perishing, but the process systemically is prolific. When humans emerge in culture, we emerge into, and at the same time fall into a process that contains the seeds of its own destruction, which was not true before. We rise to, and fall into, a moral process. We rise to a vision of the good that has evil as its shadow side. We rise to the possibility of being sons and daughters of God, in love, justice, and freedom at the same time that we fall into being demonic, into arrogance, into lust, into bondage to sin.

Self-actualizing is a good thing for humans as well as animals. The organism does well what it has the capacity to do, a vital, productive capacity, resulting in the earthen genesis, with its swarms of creatures embedded in ecology and community. The amoral fauna and flora are checked in their possessive impulses by the limitations of their eco-systems – which provide a satisfactory place, a niche, for each specific form of life, but limit each species to its appropriate sector, where it has adapted fit. The human species is not so checked, but tempted by the fearful power of hand and mind to possess the whole. The human species has no natural niche, no limits by natural selection, which is relaxed progressively as the human species rises to culture as its niche, superposed on nature. There, too, our possessive power is tempted to concupiscence. This power can only be checked by duty or by tragedy, and not by duty alone but by duty empowered by a vision of the whole, by duty empowered by spirit. We have moved out of biology into ethics, but further, out of ethics into spirituality.

Religion warns that, when humans arrive, they are warped by ambiguity, by the evil that besets their loftiest aspirations toward the good. Both morality and rationality, unredeemed from self-love, will prove dysfunctional and tragic. This is the value crisis again, taken to a new level. Symbolically put, those who want themselves to be God fail tragically; those who wish to image God can become children of God, though made of the dust of Earth. Now selfishness in the moral sense does appear, when the organism-become-person fails to emerge and acts like a beast in culture. The dusty beast reaches to be god; that is biology gone amuck, the original sin. Culture has, in that sense, to constrain the biology, or better, to constrain what the biology becomes if extrapolated into culture without any narrative development. Better still, culture has to elevate the biology, to humanize us by lifting us higher than "nothing but" biology, to

make exodus into a promised land, where humans can live as the people of God. This they do as "Israelites," those who struggle with the question and the presence of God.

There is a great story told in the transposition from nature to culture, one not without its tragic epochs. With humans, the fourth movement of this symphony accentuates the minor key already introduced in the third movement, with animals, and even in the second movement, with plants, though it could not be detected in the first movement, with matter. The music becomes more beautiful for its conflict and resolution, for the struggling through to something higher. We will expect that the values achieved in history are checkered with disvalues, checked with lapses and falls. No one can deny that the evolutionary epic, when it comes to the human chapter at least, is the story of good and evil.

When humans arrive, and go wrong, the pain is intensified, as sin produces suffering at new levels. To sin is to betray oneself and others. Sin introduces affliction. The need for redemption becomes more urgent. It is this human problem that the Bible principally addresses. There is an obvious sense in which redemption is for people and for people alone. All the vocabulary of redemption – sin, forgiveness, repentance, faith, hope, love, righteousness – is addressed to humans; animals are incapable of these vices and virtues.

But when moral responsibility does come, this does not change the sign of natural history. It rather intensifies a theme already crucially there, enriching this motif because it adds moral self-awareness. After this, history begins to turn on concepts of right and wrong, justice and guilt, obligation and retribution. But the way of history too, like that of nature, only more so, is a *via dolorosa*. In that sense, the aura of the cross is cast backward across the whole global story, and it forever outlines the future.

The Human Threat to Creation

Look to the future we must, for we face peril and promise. Nature today is in crisis, a crisis generated by human culture. The two great marvels of our planet are life and mind, so far unknown elsewhere. Life is a product of evolutionary natural history, the toil and achievement of three and one-half billion years. For perhaps two hundred thousand years, the human brain and hand have produced cultures superposed on natural systems – cultures broken and failed enough in the midst of their glories. Meanwhile, diverse combinations of nature and culture worked well enough for nature to continue over many millennia, but no more. In the last century, our modern cultures threaten the stability, beauty, and integrity of Earth and thereby of the cultures superposed on Earth. Behind the vision of one world is the shadow of none.

The late-coming moral species, *Homo sapiens*, has still more lately gained startling powers for the rebuilding and modification, including the degradation, of nature. Human desires for maximum development drive population increases, escalate exploitation of the environment, and fuel the forces of war. Those who are not at peace with one another find it difficult to be at peace with nature, and vice versa. We are sowing the seeds of our destruction. We worried throughout most of this century, the first century of great world wars, that humans would destroy themselves in interhuman conflict. Fortunately, that fear has subsided. Unfortunately, it is rapidly being replaced by a new one. The worry for the next century is that humans may destroy their planet and themselves with it.

We are turning a millennium. The challenge of the last millennium was to pass from the medieval to the modern world, building modern cultures and nations. In the ancient world, in millennia before that, the challenge was to build civilization in Greece and Rome and to baptize it with the religion of the Hebrews. Or so we thought in the West, at least. The Western conquest of nature is the story of such civilization, increasing its power with the coming of modern science and the Enlightenment. The Hebrews put humans over nature, under God, and urged them to subdue and conquer their Earth. This vision blended with and transformed the Greek rationalistic bent, sustained the medieval centuries, and produced the modern era.

In the secularizing of the modern age, though the monotheism lapsed, the axioms about human dominion persisted. We rejoiced in our exodus from nature. We admired the pilgrim, the settler, the explorer, the scientist, the engineer for their prowess against the recalcitrance of nature. We tamed continents, cleared forests, built roads, bridged rivers, and, often in the name of religion, urged the conquest of nature and redeeming of the fallen world. And yet we have discovered that our most modern civilizations, whatever their genius, remain infected with the original sin of concupiscence, of desiring to be God. Technology becomes god; consumption becomes god. The spirit of conquest becomes an Earth-eating mentality. The planet is plundered, poisoned. The wildlife are decimated. Species are endangered and lost. On our present heading, much of the integrity of the natural world will be destroyed within the next century. It is five hundred years since Columbus discovered the New World, but the spirit of the conquistadors cannot continue. The next five hundred years cannot be like the last five hundred years.

The biologist is sure that whatever nature is in itself, today and for millennia past, its fundamental character has nothing to do with human sinfulness. Yet the biologist, in consensus with the theologian, now does fear that human sin can henceforth throw nature out of joint. Both can agree that nature does now need to be redeemed on that account. Sin pollutes the world. An ancient insight is breaking over us anew. We had almost thought that geology, biology, and anthropology had drained the truth out of the Genesis stories. They enshrined, we conceded at length, only theological truth, not biological truth, and we were increasingly less sure of that.

But then we discover that these stories contain a profound myth of aboriginal community and the human fall from it. We are made for fellowship at multiple levels: with God, with persons, with the Earth. When that sense of community breaks, the world begins to fall apart. Now we see anew the difference so subtly put in those stories between being God and being like God. Those who image God will use the Earth with justice and charity, but those who want to be God will use the Earth any way they please, any way they find the power to dominate it. They think they are God; they play God. They make of the world something to boss around.

The root sin is pride – the theologians say. It is concupiscence, covetous lust. It is ingratitude. Animals are incapable of such vices; but humans, simultaneously with their rise into humanity, fall into a perennial struggle with moral evil, from which we do need to be redeemed. Such sin destroys human relationships; sin alienates from God. And sin is also ecological. Dissatisfied with their ecological niche, the man and the woman reach to be gods. The crown of creation humans are, and it is proper for us to be stewards over Earth, our home. But creature among creatures we humans would not be. We reached to decide our own goods and evils. Imaging God on Earth was not enough; we did not know when to say, Enough! Nor have we yet, over the millennia since, learned when and how to say, Enough! We have fallen into a consumption mentality. Earth is our resource, nothing more; and treated with such lust, it frustrates us.

Now, if we ask the question whether nature needs to be redeemed, we must answer: Yes, urgently, more urgently today than ever before! Humans, as a result of their failings, degrade the natural world, and nature is at peril owing to human cultures on Earth. There is something perverse about an ethic, held by the dominant class of *Homo sapiens*, that regards the welfare of only one of several million species as an object and beneficiary of duty. We lust. We are proud. We are selfish. These escalating human desires, coupled in this century with more power than ever before to transform the earth, have put nature in travail. In this sense, the fall of nature, far from being archaic, is among the most imminent threats; nature is at more peril today than at any time in the last two and one-half billion years. We may face the end of nature, unless human cultures can be redeemed.

Several billion years worth of creative toil, several million species of teeming life, have been handed over to the care of this late-coming species in which mind has flowered and morals have emerged. Yet this sole moral species has not yet been able to do anything less self-interested than count all the products of an evolutionary ecosystem as resources for our consumption. That does not sound like trusteeship; that sounds like corruption, a fall from human nobility. Insatiable overconsumption is cancerous, if not psychotic. Worse still, it is depraved.

The New Creation

What are we to make of the biblical vision of a new creation? Perhaps there is some eschatological sense in which there will, in the further future, come an ultimate redemption of both heaven and earth, of culture and of nature. I am not sure that I know what that means. Looking past, this Earth is very old; looking forward, if we can redeem it now, Earth might last a very long time. But I do not believe that this Earth will last forever. One day it will perish. Can God find a way to redeem Earth in that ultimate perishing? Who knows? It is hard enough to look back several billion years; it is impossible to look forward several billion more. Perhaps some transfigured Earth lies ahead. Perhaps God saves more than souls. Like the human body,

which Saint Paul considers a kind of seed planted here that will flourish in a life beyond the grave, the fauna and flora will perish here to be regenerated in an age beyond our own. The end of the Earth story will not be dust and ashes; it will end by being lifted up into God.

The book of Revelation portrays every creature in heaven and on earth and under the earth and in the sea joining the saints who surround the throne of God to sing God's praises (Revelation 5: 9–14). If such redemption comes, it will be God's doing. In a world where what lies behind us has actually managed to happen, almost anything can happen. Paul's image of planting a seed can seem naive; when we plant grass seed we do get more grass, but we get just more grass, nothing transformed. But if we place Paul's image on an evolutionary scale, you can plant a protozoan and get, a billion years later, a person. If we plant persons, and wait a million years, what might we get?

The same God that lured protozoans into persons may be still at work on scales that we cannot imagine scientifically but can only hope for mythically. The miracle of a new heaven and a new earth would be a lesser miracle than the fact that this past and present heaven and earth are and have been here in the first place. The story of the last several billion years has not been so much the loss of value as of its transformation into new levels of attainment and power. Perhaps that will be the story of the next several billion years. Perhaps God is able to save all that is of value in the story, not just human spirits.

Meanwhile, this we do know. Nature has been redeemed across the last several billion years, but the current threat is the greatest that nature has yet faced. Unless we can in the next millennium, indeed in the next century, regulate and control the escalating human devastation of our planet, there will be little or nothing to worry about after that. To recall the Pauline lament, the Creation is being subjected to futility, and it cannot be set free from this degradation until the human race rises to its glory, imaging God and governing in suffering love. Does nature need to be redeemed? It can, it must, and let us work and pray that such redemption is at hand.

Pride is the original sin. It was feared by some that the space flights, reaching for the stars, were acts of human arrogance, hubris in extreme, more of the conquest and dominion by *Homo sapiens* that had already ravaged the planet. But people responded unexpectedly. The haughty, the high, and the mighty of spirit failed to materialize with the flight into space. Rather humility, from *humus*, meaning "earthy," also the root of "human," was the dominant experience. The value and beauty of the home planet and our destiny in caring for it has been the repeated reaction. One reason that we have so seldom gone back to space is the conviction that our more urgent responsibilities are earthbound: they lie in constructing a human future on Earth in harmony with conserving nature. Perhaps that is a truth in the beatitude: "Blessed are the meek, for they shall inherit the Earth." For Earth is indeed a planet with promise, a promised planet, and we humans have both the right to share in and the responsibility to help to keep that promise.

Note

1 This idea, even the phrase, goes back through Whitehead to Locke and eventually Heraclitus, where it is not necessarily restricted to living organisms (Whitehead [1927–28] 1978, 29, 60, 146–7, and others).

References

Aquinas, Thomas. 1964. *Summa Theologiae*, Latin text and English translation. New York: McGraw-Hill.

Calvin, John. 1936. *Institutes of the Christian Religion*. Philadelphia: Presbyterian Board of Christian Education.

Clarke, Thomas E. 1956. *The Eschatological Transformation of the Material World According to Saint Augustine*. Woodstock, Md.: Woodstock College Press.

Cohen, Michael P. 1984. *The Pathless Way: John Muir and American Wilderness*. Madison: Univ. of Wisconsin Press.

Darwin, Charles. [1859] 1968. *Origin of Species*. Baltimore: Penguin Books.

de Beer, Gavin. 1962. *Reflections of a Darwinian*. London: Thomas Nelson.

Luther, Martin. 1958. Lectures on Genesis, chaps. 1–5. Vol. 1 of *Luther's Works*, ed. Jaroslav Pelikan. St Louis, Mo.: Concordia Publishing House.

Mayr, Ernst. 1982. *The Growth of Biological Thought*. Cambridge: Harvard Univ. Press.

Muir, John. 1954. *The Wilderness World of John Muir*, ed. Edwin Way Teale. Boston: Houghton Mifflin.

—— 1980. *To Yosemite and Beyond: Writings from the Years 1863–1875*, ed. Robert Engberg and Donald Wesling. Madison: Univ. of Wisconsin Press.

Rolston, Holmes. 1992. "Disvalues in Nature." *The Monist* 75: 250–78.

Whitehead, Alfred North. [1927–8] 1978. *Process and Reality*, corrected edition. New York: Free Press.

46

Pascal's Wager

Blaise Pascal

Let us now speak according to natural lights.

If there is a God, He is infinitely incomprehensible, since, having neither parts nor limits, He has no affinity to us. We are then incapable of knowing either what He is or if He is. This being so, who will dare to undertake the decision of the question? Not we, who have no affinity to Him.

Who then will blame Christians for not being able to give a reason for their belief, since they profess a religion for which they cannot give a reason? They declare, in expounding it to the world, that it is a foolishness, *stultitiam*; and then you complain that they do not prove it! If they proved it, they would not keep their word; it is in lacking proofs that they are not lacking in sense. "Yes, but although this excuses those who offer it as such, and takes away from them the blame of putting it forward without reason, it does not excuse those who receive it." Let us then examine this point, and say, "God is, or He is not." But to which side shall we incline? Reason can decide nothing here. There is an infinite chaos which separated us. A game is being played at the extremity of this infinite distance where heads or tails will turn up. What will you wager? According to reason, you can do neither the one thing nor the other; according to reason, you can defend neither of the propositions.

Do not then reprove for error those who have made a choice; for you know nothing about it. "No, but I blame them for having made, not this choice, but a choice; for again both he who chooses heads and he who chooses tails are equally at fault, they are both in the wrong. The true course is not to wager at all."

Yes; but you must wager. It is not optional. You are embarked. Which will you choose then? Let us see. Since you must choose, let us see which interests you least. You have two things to lose, the true and the good; and two things to stake, your reason and your will, your knowledge and your happiness; and your nature has two things to shun, error and misery. Your reason is no more shocked in choosing one rather than the other, since you must of necessity choose. This is one point settled. But your happiness? Let us weigh the gain and the loss in wagering that God is. Let us estimate these two chances. If you gain, you gain all; if you lose, you lose nothing. Wager, then, without hesitation that He is. – "That is very fine. Yes, I must wager; but I may perhaps wager too much." – Let us see. Since there is an equal risk of gain and of loss, if you had only to gain two lives, instead of one, you might still wager. But if there were three lives to gain, you would have to play (since you are under the necessity of playing), and you would be imprudent, when you are forced to play, not to chance your life to gain three at a game where there is an equal risk of loss and gain. But there is an eternity of life and happiness. And this being so, if there were an infinity of chances, of which one only would be for you, you would still be right in wagering one to win two, and you would act stupidly, being obliged to play, by refusing to stake one life against three at a game in which out of an infinity of chances there is one for you, if there were an infinity of an infinitely happy life to gain. But there is here an infinity of an infinitely happy life to gain, a chance of gain against a finite number of chances of loss, and what you stake is finite. It is all divided; wherever the infinite is and there is not an infinity of chances of loss against that of gain, there is no time to hesitate, you must give all. And thus, when one is forced to play, he must renounce reason to preserve his life, rather than risk it for infinite gain, as likely to happen as the loss of nothingness.

For it is no use to say it is uncertain if we will gain, and it is certain that we risk, and that the infinite distance between the *certainty* of what is staked and the *uncertainty* of what will be gained, equals the finite good which is certainly staked against the uncertain infinite. It is not so, as every player stakes a certainty to gain an uncertainty, and yet he stakes a finite certainty to gain a finite uncertainty, without transgressing against reason. There is not an infinite distance between the certainty staked and the uncertainty of the gain; that is untrue. In truth, there is an infinity between the certainty of gain and the certainty of loss. But the uncertainty of the gain is proportioned to the certainty of the stake according to the proportion of the chances of gain and loss. Hence it comes that, if there are as many risks on one side as on the other, the course is to play even; and then the certainty of the stake is equal to the uncertainty of the gain, so far is it from fact that there is an infinite distance between them. And so our proposition is of infinite force, when there is the finite to stake in a game where there are equal risks of gain and of loss, and the infinite to gain. This is demonstrable; and if men are capable of any truths, this is one.

"I confess it, I admit it. But, still, is there no means of seeing the faces of the cards?" – Yes, Scripture and the rest, etc. "Yes, but I have my hands tied and my mouth closed; I am forced to wager, and am not free. I am not released, and am so made that I cannot believe. What, then, would you have me do?"

True. But at least learn your inability to believe, since reason brings you to this, and yet you cannot believe. Endeavour then to convince yourself, not by increase of proofs of God, but by the abatement of your passions. You would like to attain faith, and do not know the way; you would like to cure yourself of unbelief, and ask the remedy for it. Learn of those who have been bound like you, and who now stake all their possessions. These are people who know the way which you would follow, and who are cured of an ill of which you would be cured. Follow the way by which they began; by acting as if they believed, taking the holy water, having masses said, etc. Even this will naturally make you believe, and deaden your acuteness. – "But this is what I am afraid of." – And why? What have you to lose?

But to show you that this leads you there, it is this which will lessen the passions, which are your stumbling-blocks.

The end of this discourse. – Now, what harm will befall you in taking this side? You will be faithful, honest, humble, grateful, generous, a sincere friend, truthful. Certainly you will not have those poisonous pleasures, glory and luxury; but will you not have others? I will tell you that you will thereby gain in this life, and that, at each step you take on this road, you will see so great certainty of gain, so much nothingness in what you risk, that you will at last recognize that you have wagered for something certain and infinite, for which you have given nothing.

"Ah! This discourse transports me, charms me," etc.

If this discourse pleases you and seems impressive, know that it is made by a man who has knelt, both before and after it, in prayer to that Being, infinite and without parts, before whom he lays all he has, for you also to lay before Him all you have for your own good and for His glory, that so strength may be given to lowliness.

47

Why is Faith a Virtue?

Tim Chappell

1. The Meaning of "Faith"

By faith I mostly mean *religious* faith, i.e. that (whatever it is) which distinguishes the religious believer, as such, from the unbeliever, as such. Although an important qualification to this remark will appear in due course (see section 8), I am not primarily concerned with faith as in "Have you no faith in me?", or "I doubted his good faith". I am concerned with faith as in "I wish I had your faith", or "I'm afraid I've lost my faith", or "other faiths". Talking of which, I am also thinking primarily within the confines of the Christian religion.

2. The Importance of Not Failing to Notice the Importance of the Word "Virtue"

Kantians and consequentialists are likely to think, though not of course bound to think, that "virtue" just means "good thing about a person". (Perhaps not even necessarily about a person; spades and plans of attack may have virtues too, may they not?[1]) These sorts of moralist will (usually) say that talk about virtues should be, and unproblematically can be, ironed out into more straightforward theoretical talk about states of affairs or acts of

Tim Chappell, "Why is Faith a Virtue?" reprinted by permission of Cambridge University Press from *Religious Studies* 32 (1996), pp. 27–36. Copyright © 1996 Cambridge University Press.

the will. So much the worse for Kantians and consequentialists. And so much the better for Aristotelians, who will rather focus directly on the notion of a virtue, will have a rich and non-reducible account of what a virtue is, and will consequently meet, or so we hope, with much fairer success in their thinking about ethics.

If then we take the Aristotelian route, as I do here, our next question is bound to be:

3. What is a Virtue?

Some Aristotelians[2] say that a virtue is a disposition of character which we humans need to have to have a flourishing human life. Others (such as myself) would say it is a disposition of character which instantiates or promotes responsiveness to one or more basic good. These two sorts of definition are not, of course, necessarily in conflict. The reason why we need the virtues to have "a flourishing human life" can be because the virtues instantiate or promote responsiveness to one or more basic goods, and because a flourishing human life essentially involves responsiveness to basic goods. If so, our question "Why is faith a virtue?" can be paraphrased as "Why is faith needed for a flourishing human life?", and that question in turn can be paraphrased as "To what basic good(s) is faith a responsiveness, or source of responsiveness?". I think the third paraphrase is the most revealing, and the most useful. It does however prompt a further question, which I must spend some time answering:

4. What is a Basic Good?

A basic good, as some[3] say, is "an *intrinsic* good, i.e. [one] that is considered good for its own sake and not merely as something sought under some such description as 'what will enable me to impress my audience' or 'what will confirm my instinctive beliefs' or 'what will contribute to my survival' . . . to say that [something] is a [basic] value is simply to say that reference to the pursuit of [it] makes intelligible (though not necessarily reasonable-all-things-considered) any particular instance of the human activity and commitment involved in such a pursuit".

As others say, a basic good is a good, generally recognized as such by humans, of a sort which can appropriately provide an end to chains of subsumptive explanation (CSEs). What then is a CSE? Compare these two dialogues:

1A. I am running for the train because I want to get to Oxford on time.
1B. Why do you want to get to Oxford on time?
1C. Well, because . . .

2A. I am going to the National Gallery because I think it will be fun.
2B. Why do you want fun?
2C. ?!?!?

1B is a question which calls for a further explanation of a kind which, in general, we can see how to supply. (Perhaps I am going to Oxford to meet my beloved, or for a job interview, or for a party, or . . .)

By contrast, if someone asks 2B as if *this* were another question of the same sort as the question before it, then they display a misunderstanding – or they have read too much modern moral philosophy. In normal circumstances, the most natural response to 2B is a puzzled stare. Why so? Because 2B refers us immediately to a recognized basic good or goods (to fun, which by the way is not the same thing as pleasure); whereas 1B does not.

Quite generally, asking the question "Why do you want X?", about anyone's voluntary pursuit of any X, can meet with only two kinds of legitimate response: (i) those responses which refer us immediately to some basic good which our respondent sees as instantiated or promoted by the pursuit of X; and (ii) those responses which refer us ultimately to some basic good which our respondent

sees as instantiated or promoted by the pursuit of X, i.e. those responses which prompt further questions, which prompt further responses, which (eventually) will refer us immediately to some basic good which our respondent sees as instantiated or promoted by the pursuit of X.

In other words, any complete CSE must, sooner or later, terminate. A CSE that went on for ever, or indefinitely, would not yield any intelligible justification. Moreover, any such complete CSE must terminate in a reference to a basic good. If a CSE does not, or cannot, refer back at some stage to some basic good, then it is not a chain of explanation – not an intelligible account of the action's motivation – at all. Why is (e.g.) the thought that "I must get there on time", in certain circumstances, a motivating thought? This question is to be answered by referring the inquirer to some good which "getting there on time" is seen by the agent as a way of achieving in those circumstances. There can be no question of the same sort about the good to which the inquirer is, ultimately or immediately, so referred. This latter kind of good – the basic good – is foundational to practical rationality of the subsumptive kind I am talking about. If there are no basic goods of this sort there will be no subsumptive practical reasoning, because there will not be anything for it to aim at.

Such basic goods, then, are foundational to, the first principles of, subsumptive practical rationality. This in two senses: (a) subsumptive practical rationality could have no point or terminus without these basic goods, and (b) subsumptive rationality shows us what sort of things the basic goods are when we identify its termini. However, we need a different kind of practical rationality, not subsumptive, but narrative, for an account of why the basic goods are the particular goods they are. Their nature and number is to be established by reflection on what kind of ingredients we would need for a good life; on what kind of story would be a good story to be the subject of, what elements it would contain, how combined, and why.

Another point about basic goods is (c) that they are either evident or self-evident goods, or both. By "an evident good" I mean "a good such that no one would normally dream of denying its goodness"; by "a self-evident good" I mean "a good such that it is self-defeating to deny its goodness". Pleasure, for example, is an evident good, so much so that the utilitarians base a whole moral system on its goodness. No one except a philosopher could deny that the prospect of pleasure is, in the absence of special circumstances, something that gives us a *prima facie* reason to act.[4] By contrast rationality – the ability to reason, to do logic, to see a contradiction, to frame an argument – is a self-evident good (and no doubt an evident good as well). For consider any argument that shows that rationality is not a good, not worth having. Any such argument, whether successful or not, is itself guaranteed to be not worth having. For its success would show that no argument is worth having (and so neither is this one); but its failure would show that this argument is not worth having.

Note also (d) that basic goods are mutually irreducible. Nothing is a basic good if it is not or cannot intelligibly be sought in itself, for its own sake. Now there is more than one basic good. Therefore more than one thing is sought for its own sake, and those who say, as Aristotle apparently did[5] and as many utilitarians certainly have,[6] that everything we do is for the sake of one end only – whatever end that may be – are simply wrong. Even if their position is not in itself unsustainably contorted or incoherent, the best they can hope to do with the phenomenology of our actual experience of choice is distort it.

5. Faith as a Virtue

With this much in place, I can now suggest that faith is a virtue because it instantiates a responsiveness to two basic goods: truth, and what I shall call "practical hope". Not just truth, and not just practical hope, but both. So first I need to show that truth and practical hope are basic goods, and then I need to show that faith is a responsiveness to them.

If truth and practical hope are basic goods, then they will be (a) the kinds of goods that give subsumptive practical reasoning its point, (b) considerations typically, or at least often, found at the termini of CSEs, (c) either evident or self-evident goods, and (d) mutually irreducible goods. (d) The irreducibility of truth and practical hope is shown by the possibility that they could be in tension with each other. To put it crudely, the truth could be such as to make it irrational to have practical hope. What of (a)–(c)?

6. Truth as a Basic Good

Truth is a basic good of the same sort as rationality, as just discussed, because (a) it is an intelligibly

complete explanation of what John is doing, to say that he is seeking the truth; and (b) one will typically need no further explanation, than that seeking the truth is what John is doing, to understand what John is doing; (c) truth is, like rationality, a self-evident good, and presumably an evident good as well. For consider the claim that truth is not a good, not worth having. Any such claim is itself guaranteed to be not worth having. For if it is true, then *no* true claim is worth having (and so neither is this one). But if it is false, then this claim is not worth having.

7. Practical Hope as a Basic Good

What is "practical hope"? The condition of practical hope is the condition of believing that I am not, either continually or typically, confronted with situations in which my endeavours, both practical and intellectual, are either doomed to disaster from the start, or else can make no possible difference. It is the attitude that practical choice and action, or theoretical inquiry, is not inevitably going to be vain or fruitless in the situation(s) with which I am confronted. Something like this may be what Aristotle has in mind when he writes that

> There is no deliberate choice of impossibilities . . . We deliberate about what comes about through us and not always in the same way. (*Nicomachean Ethics* 1111b21, 1112b3–4)

and again when he remarks that, if logical fatalism were true, then "there would be no point in deliberating or taking pains" (*de Interpretatione* 18b30). One good reason for thinking that logical fatalism is not true is that we do find, or seem to find, it worthwhile to deliberate and take trouble over our projects.

"There can be no deliberate choice of impossibilities"; the belief that one is confronted (a) by possibilities, (b) by more than one of them, and (c) by some possibilities to bring about which will be a good and worthwhile outcome – these beliefs are a necessary precondition of deliberate choice. Deliberate choice is about our projects; so that to have these beliefs and not their opposites, and to act and inquire accordingly, is a precondition of any intellectual or practical project's even getting started. The possibility of holding the beliefs in question is what I mean by the basic good of practical hope. The connections of this good with the goods realized in practical activity in general, and with the rather special good of free will, may already be plain. Practical hope, I suspect, is going to be a good in rather the same way that free will is.

But have I yet shown that practical hope is any more than an instrumental good? I have said something about how practical hope might be an irreducible form of good, and an evident, maybe even a self-evident, good. But it may be that instrumental goods too can be evident goods. Moreover, on my own principles, practical hope cannot be seen as an irreducibly basic form of good unless we already have other reasons for thinking that it is more than a merely instrumental good. And in any case, what I have said so far is not enough to show that practical hope is a basic good unless it is also the kind of good that can give subsumptive practical reasoning its point, and the kind of consideration typically or often found at the termini of CSEs. So: is practical reasoning ever about achieving no other objective than practical hope? To put it another way: is practical hope ever itself the terminus of a CSE?

I think the answer to this is Yes, although, of course, that doesn't mean that any non-philosopher would ever put it quite as I have just put it. People do act in ways designed to make it true that they are confronted (a) by possibilities, (b) by more than one of them, and (c) by some possibilities to bring about which will be a good and worthwhile outcome. We do seek to be in positions where we have a variety of options, and where as many of those options as possible are good options. For example we seek political freedom; we seek breadth of choice; we seek so to be habituated that we will not be the slaves of habit or addiction or laziness. We seek these goods for ourselves, and also for others (e.g. our children); and, this being the crucial point, we seek them for their own sake. Likewise we do prize the fact that it is possible to be in such situations, and to act so as to put ourselves in such situations, in and of itself. I can take delight in my health, in (say) a feeling of physical well-being and energy, as well as, and quite apart from, prizing what I can do with that energy and well-being, like sprinting or wrestling or climbing mountains. Similarly I can take delight in the very fact that I am confronted by different possibilities for good (or evil), as well as in any of the good possibilities themselves; just as I can take delight not only in particular truths but in the possibility of any truth; not only in particular pieces of logical argument, but in the possibility of any logic at all; not only in particular experiences but in the possibility of any experience; not only in the kind of life I actually have here and now, but in being alive itself.

I am arguing then that practical hope is a possible objective of action, a basic good lying at the end of possible CSEs, in and of itself. But recall that acting to attain any basic good (in fact any good at all) is itself an exercise of practical hope. So then is this one: acting to attain the basic good of practical hope is itself an exercise of practical hope. Contrariwise: acting in any way which directly denies or rejects the basic good of practical hope is itself going to be an exercise of practical hope, albeit an exercise in which practical hope is strangely at odds with itself. From here we can perhaps see our way to the claim that practical hope is, in fact, not merely an evident good, but a self-evident good: a good such that it is self-defeating to act so as to reject or deny it. In this respect, I suggest, practical hope is like free will, truth, reason, knowledge, experience, perception, health, and life itself; to act so as to reject or deny any of these forms of good is to act, in one way or another, self-defeatingly. For self-refutation, global scepticism in the sense of a denial of the possibility of knowledge or truth, determinism, solipsism, suicide are all, in different but related ways, cases of the sort of self-defeatingness I mean.

8. Truth, Practical Hope, and Faith

If all this is right, then I seem to have established my case for thinking that practical hope is indeed a form of basic good, in a sense surprisingly close to the sense in which truth is a form of basic good. A critic might now ask, indeed probably several critics are already asking: "What has all this got to do with (religious) faith, which is supposed to be a responsiveness to truth and to practical hope? Religious faith just doesn't seem to be in the picture yet. For, apparently, someone could be fully responsive to truth and to practical hope, and thereby (according to you) have the virtue of faith, without their having any positive religious beliefs at all!".

Indeed so. *If* someone could be fully responsive to truth and to practical hope without having any positive religious beliefs at all, then – we may provisionally suggest – they *would* have the virtue of faith. For faith (as I would define it) is the virtue about religious truth, and if religion (all religion) is false, then the person who has the virtue about religious truth is the atheist, the person who does not in any positive sense go in for religion at all. Faith *would* have little or nothing to do with religion if religion were false. Here then is my first shot at an answer to the question of my title: "Faith is a virtue because it is a proper responsiveness to the basic goods of practical hope and truth; but religious faith, i.e. faith in the usual sense of the word as outlined in section 1, is only a virtue if religion is true".

But this, I think, is not quite right, because there is more to the virtue of faith than proper responsivenesses to the basic goods of practical hope and truth. If religious beliefs were all false, it might be that our responsivenesses to these goods were widely separate, i.e. that there was no single disposition of character which instantiated and/or promoted *both* sorts of responsiveness at once. The atheist, then, if he is right, will have a proper responsiveness to truth, and a proper responsiveness to practical hope. But he will not have them together in the same disposition of character; and no such disposition of character will be a virtue. In short, if God does not exist, there will be no one disposition which is the virtue of faith.

More than this: if God does not exist, then there will come a point at which proper responsivenesses to truth and practical hope will be not only separate, but in tension. For my being properly responsive to practical hope means my believing that I am confronted (a) by possibilities, (b) by more than one of them, and (c) by some possibilities to bring about which will be a good and worthwhile outcome. But if (the Christian's) God does not exist, and if accordingly there is, e.g., no eternal life, there will be situations where these beliefs are no longer true; and not just accidentally or possibly temporarily no longer true, but inevitably and irrevocably no longer true. Such a situation – for example, the situation of an atheist on his death bed – will be one where to be responsive to practical hope is to believe what responsiveness to truth forbids me to believe. The atheist on his death bed (and, perhaps more importantly, the atheist who is thinking ahead to his death) must, in short, either surrender responsiveness to truth, or else responsiveness to practical hope; he cannot keep both.

Of course, it is still true of the dying atheist that he can choose good or bad ways of dying, and also that he can make good or bad arrangements, e.g. in a will, for the world which will still be there after his death. So even at the moment of his death, and beyond it, he can still be confronted by some possibilities – albeit ones of a sort which must be peripheral to the living of life. But not by any that the theist is not also confronted by; whereas the

theist sees, however dimly and uncertainly, a great and central possibility that the atheist does not.

If, then, (Christian) religious belief is right, our interdependent responsivenesses to practical hope and to truth need never be in finally irresoluble tension with one another. My responsiveness to practical hope will be expressed in my belief in the doctrine of providence: in my belief that, if there is a God, then he will never put me in a situation where it is irrevocably or inevitably false that I am confronted by possibilities, by more than one of them, and by some possibilities to bring about which will be good and worthwhile. My responsiveness to truth will be expressed by a corresponding belief that there *is* such a God. Now without the belief that there is such a God, the attitude of practical hope will be, ultimately, simply wrong. But without the belief that the God who truly exists is a good and providential God, a God who makes practical hope an appropriate and justified attitude, the responsiveness to truth which is expressed by my belief that God exists will be, ultimately, futile. Thus in faith responsiveness to truth and to practical hope will be intimately linked – provided God exists; and if God does exist, then the answer to the question of my title will be that faith is a virtue, a responsiveness to basic goods which we need to have if we are to live well, because, in the words of Hebrews 11: 6, God both is, and is a rewarder of them that diligently seek him.

9. Some Other Positions Reviewed

I have presented no argument, nor anything like an argument, that God exists. But I have pointed out how intimately the very possibility of there being a virtue of faith at all is related to the question whether God exists or not. What kinds of people we ought to be does depend, in a crucial way, on whether there is a God. If God does not exist, then we have no reason to try to have the disposition of character of (religious) faith: that is, faith is not a virtue. Moral reasons and factual reasons are very closely interrelated here, and there is (I am arguing) no question of separating them, of arguing (say) what Pascal argues in the *Pensées*, that we have compelling reason to want to have the disposition of faith whether or not God exists.

On the other hand, I have argued that we do have *some* reason, though not compelling reason, to want to have the disposition of religious faith. For Kant was quite right to hold that the ultimate reconcilability of various sorts of basic good which (as a matter of empirical fact) people do seek depends upon whether religious faith is justified, i.e. upon whether God exists. However, this premiss cannot possibly license the Kantian "moral argument", i.e. transcendental practical argument, for God's existence, that

> the postulate of the possibility of a highest derivative good (the best world) is at the same time the postulate of the reality of a highest original good, namely, the postulate of the existence of God. Now it was our duty to promote the highest good; and it is not merely our privilege but a necessity connected with duty as a requisite to presuppose the possibility of this highest good. This presupposition is made only under the condition of the existence of God, and this condition inseparably connects this supposition with duty. Therefore, it is morally necessary to assume the existence of God.[7]

Kant – to put it crudely – is saying that "Morality would be undermined if God did not exist; therefore God exists". But if my argument here has been correct, then any such attitude as that expressed here by Kant is mistaken; for it embodies an offence against the basic good of truth in the name of the basic good of practical hope.

In any case, Kant's argument, at least in my crude paraphrase, is a *non sequitur*: the "therefore" is simply unwarranted. Nonetheless, it is a *non sequitur* with a true antecedent. Morality, or in my non-Kantian terms the unity or reconcilability of the virtues, is indeed imperilled if God does not exist. It would be an immense disaster for humanity if he did not exist; for then the kinds of goods we seek would be irreconcilable. Recognizing the threat of this disaster does not entitle us to infer that God does exist. But it may help us to see more clearly why the question whether he exists is of crucial importance, and why a negative answer to that question is something we have reason to want to be false.

10. Faith and Knowledge

In conclusion, a few words on the question which may seem to some to be the most obvious question about faith of all, namely how faith is to be contrasted with knowledge. I have been emphasizing the way in which, if someone's faith is to be a virtue in them, it must be a proper responsiveness both to practical hope and to truth. Now faith is (Hebrews 11: 1) "the substance (*hypostasis*) of things hoped for, the evidence (*elenchos*) of things not seen"; and in this life (2 Cor. 5: 7) "we walk by faith and not by sight". It is evident, when we consider the difficulties of this world, that my responsivenesses to practical hope and to truth are often going to be, to some extent, in tension or at least only precariously in balance.

How, to take an obvious example, is one to deal with the problem of suffering without either falling into a self-deceiving optimism which flouts the good of truth, or into a clear-eyed pessimism which flouts the good of practical hope? Another example: the adoption of faith is partly a matter of responsiveness to evidence taken to be true, and partly a matter of a decision that "this is the way to live", which often means "the most practically-hopeful way to live". But adopting the Christian faith could not be merely accepting the facts at issue. Firstly, the facts *are* at issue, they have not been simply accepted by all parties; anyway, secondly, one could (and many do) accept all the facts at issue without being in any sense a Christian. ("The devils too believe in God, and tremble": James 2: 19.) Yet neither could adopting the Christian faith be merely an assertion of practical hope. If that is all there is to faith, one might as well believe in fairy-land. Faith would then simply be a matter of deliberate self-deception: moreover, faith adopted on this sort of grounds would still be self-deception even if the claims of faith are true. But I have taken it as obvious that the self-deceived way is not a good way to live.

Faith, then, for us imperfect and in-process creatures, is a matter of finding a balance between responsiveness to these two goods of practical hope and truth; a balance which rejects neither good and does honour to both. (Notice incidentally that if this sort of balancing is typically only going to be possible if God exists, then the very attempt to perform this balancing, in the exercise of faith, may well involve the presupposition that success in such attempts is possible, i.e. that God exists.) I do not here propose to attempt the difficult and detailed and situation-specific question of exactly how that balance is to be found by each or any one of us. I only want to say that this is the right question to pose, and that seeing faith as *this* sort of balancing act between responsiveness to truth and responsiveness to practical hope – a balance attained perhaps in what Iris Murdoch has called "loving, truthful attention"[8] to what is around us – is seeing faith in the right way.

Tim Chappell

Notes

1   In any non-metaphorical sense of "virtue", no, they may not.
2   Such as Rosalind Hursthouse, "Virtue Theory and Abortion", *Philosophy and Public Affairs* 20 (1991), p. 224.
3   J. M. Finnis, *Natural Law and Natural Rights* (Oxford: Clarendon Press, 1980), pp. 62ff.
4   Cf. Aristotle, *Nicomachean Ethics* 1153b27.
5   In the opening lines of *Nicomachean Ethics*; but the evidence is ambiguous.
6   Bentham and James Mill are obvious examples; J. S. Mill's distinction between "higher" and "lower" pleasures, in chapter 2 of his *Utilitarianism* (ed. Warnock; London: Fontana, 1962), begins to complicate the picture.
7   Kant, *Critique of Practical Reason* (trans. Lewis White Beck: Oxford, Maxwell Macmillan, 3rd edn. 1993), p. 132: Part 1, Bk. 2, Ch. 2, S. V, "The existence of God as a postulate of pure practical reason".
8   Iris Murdoch, "On 'God' and 'Good'", pp. 59ff, in her *The Sovereignty of Good* (reprinted by Routledge Kegan Paul, 1991).

PART VIII

Personal Identity and Death

Introduction

Paul J. Griffiths

The questions of what persons are and of what happens to them when they die are intimately linked and are both of great importance to the world's religious traditions. These are also among the questions on which religious traditions diverge most. Christians and Muslims, for instance, tend to think that persons are substances of some sort (spiritual, physical, or both), and that when they die they enter upon an everlasting condition from which thereafter there will be no change. Buddhists, by contrast, tend to think that persons endure through time only as continua of causally connected events, continua that may come to an end but which ordinarily continue through many human lives in a world like the one we inhabit. There are, of course, other possible positions as well.

Roger Trigg identifies the question about persons (in the first of the essays in this section) in the following way: "What is the 'I' that appears to be the subject of all 'my' thoughts and imaginings, my experiences and desires?" His answer is that our ways of talking and forming social relations imply that we both have and need some idea of ourselves as enduring through time in such a way that we can be bound to and by our own futures (we can make promises, for example); and that such an idea sits well with, even if it does not require, some metaphysical concept of self as other than its world, its language, and even its body – some idea, that is, of what is usually called dualism. Views such as Trigg's sit well with, though do not require, specifically Christian and (some) Islamic and Hindu views; they are much less easily combined with Buddhist or Jewish views about what happens at death. We include Hume's famous argument about miracles here because of its upshot, which is that while it is not incoherent to suppose that there might be miracles (including that of a human being coming back from the dead), we always have more reason to doubt our evidence for such miracles than to suppose them to have happened.

Grace Jantzen's "Do We Need Immortality?" and Charles Taliaferro's "Why We Need Immortality" take opposing views on the centrality of the hope for immortality to Christian thought and practice. Jantzen raises questions about the coherence of the idea of personal immortality, the propriety of a love of God motivated by hope for the reward of immortality, and about the connection between God's love for us and our immortality. Need it be the case, she asks, that God will give us immortality because he loves us? Taliaferro argues in response that it is not obviously incoherent to think that there might be goods whose value is neither lost nor diminished by being extended infinitely in time; and that if this is a possibility, immortality might be such a good, and it might be reasonable to suppose that God gives it to us. There are other particular disagreements between Taliaferro and Jantzen about the effects that a belief in and hope for immortality might have upon our beliefs and attitudes (to death and other things) prior to our death, and about the logical coherence of the idea of personal immortality. But the deep disagreement between them has to do with whether Christianity may properly be construed in such a way as to dispense altogether with a hope for immortality.

The last essay in this section (and in the book) is Arindam Chakrabarti's essay on whether liberation is pleasant. The problem here is that many Indian schools which postulate a final liberation from rebirth and redeath (from *saṃsāra*) are faced with what looks like a dilemma: if such a final liberation is not said to be pleasant, then there might seem little reason to seek it. If, on the other hand, it is described as pleasant (even blissful or ecstatic), then it will be hard to distinguish desire for it from desire for the ordinary joys of *saṃsāra*, and therefore also difficult to distinguish its character from that of *saṃsāra*. Chakrabarti treats this question by distinguishing the question of what ought to motivate seeking release from *saṃsāra* from the question of what such liberation is like. He argues that it would be better not to seek liberation for its supposed delights, but to remain agnostic about whether in fact it has any.

Further Reading

From **The Blackwell Companion to the Philosophy of Religion,** *see the following entry: Hick, J., "Religious pluralism"*

Other further reading:

Adams, R. M. (ed.), *The Virtue of Faith and Other Essays in Philosophical Theology* (New York: Oxford University Press, 1987).

Badham, P. and Badham, L., *Immortality or Extinction?* (New York: Barnes and Noble, 1981). *A good resource.*

Braine, D., *The Human Person: Animal and Spirit* (London: Duckworth, 1993).

Cooper, J. W., *Body, Soul, and Life Everlasting: Biblical Anthropology and the Monist–Dualism Debate* (Grand Rapids: Eerdmans, 1989). *A rigorous dualist treatment of the Bible.*

Davis, S. T. (ed.), *Encountering Evil: Live Options in Theodicy* (Atlanta: John Knox Press, 1981; 2nd edn, 2001).

Davis, Stephen (ed.), *Death and Afterlife* (New York: St Martin's Press, 1989). *A variety of good-quality papers on a range of views.*

Evans, C. S., "Separable Souls: A Defense of 'Minimal Dualism'," *The Southern Journal of Philosophy* 19 (1981): 313–31.

Evans, C. Stephen, *The Historical Christ and the Jesus of Faith* (Oxford: Oxford University Press, 1996). *A trenchant, balanced treatment of revelation claims.*

Feenstra, R. J. and Plantinga, C. (eds.), *Trinity, Incarnation, and Atonement: Philosophical and Theological Essays* (Notre Dame: University of Notre Dame Press, 1990).

Hick, J. H., *Death and Eternal Life* (London: Collins; New York: Harper and Row, 1976). *Classic, of great interest for a cross-cultural perspective.*

Holland, R. F., "The Miraculous," *American Philosophical Quarterly* 2 (1965): 43–51.

Kvanvig, J. L., *The Problem of Hell* (Oxford: Oxford University Press, 1993).

Lewis, H. D., *Persons and the Life after Death* (New York: Barnes and Noble, 1978).

Lucas, J. R., *Freedom and Grace* (London: SPCK Press; Grand Rapids: Eerdmans, 1976).

Penelhum, T., *Survival and Disembodied Existence* (New York: Humanities Press, 1970). *Meticulous, critical approach to an individual after-life.*

Shoemaker, S. and Swinburne, R., *Personal Identity* (Oxford: Basil Blackwell, 1984). *Shoemaker is a materialist, Swinburne a dualist.*

Swinburne, R., *The Evolution of the Soul* (Oxford: Clarendon Press, 1986).

Taliaferro, C., *Consciousness and the Mind of God* (Cambridge: Cambridge University Press, 1994). *A defense of the coherence of God and persons in non-materialist terms.*

Van Inwagen, P., "The Possibility of Resurrection," *International Journal for Philosophy of Religion* 9 (1978): 114–21.

Walls, J. L., *The Logic of Damnation* (Notre Dame: University of Notre Dame Press, 1992).

Williams, B., "The Makropulos Case: Reflections on the Tedium of Immortality," in *Problems of the Self, Philosophical Papers 1956–1972* (Cambridge: Cambridge University Press, 1973).

48

The Metaphysical Self

Roger Trigg

1. Subject and Object

What is the self? What is the "I" that appears to be the subject of all "my" thoughts and imaginings, my experiences and desires? This is not simply about problems of identification. How I pick you out or you recognize me are questions related to the problem of what it is to be me or you, but they are not the same issue. If our "true selves" are inaccessible to public scrutiny, how we are identified and re-identified publicly will be different from who "we" are. The problem of the self is a genuinely metaphysical question which cannot be reduced to the epistemological one of how we know each other, without further argument.

Antony Flew argues that we use bodily criteria to establish bodily continuity and that is a "large part, if not the whole of what is meant by personal identity". He continues: "It would be, wouldn't it, if persons just are, as I maintain that we all know that we are, a very special sort of creatures of flesh and blood."[1] This makes it clear that whatever the merits of bodily continuity as a measure of personal identity, the major issue is a metaphysical one. Are we *just* creatures of flesh and blood?

This is a venerable problem in philosophy, and in modern times the terms of the discussion have been set by Descartes. He recognized that even though he could think everything false, nevertheless there was still a subject of that thought. He

Roger Trigg, "The Metaphysical Self," reprinted by permission of Cambridge University Press from *Religious Studies* 24 (1988), pp. 277–89.

himself was thinking. This is the context of his "*cogito, ergo sum*". He declared that he was a substance, the whole nature of which was to think, with no need of any location, and independent of any material thing. His conclusion was: "This 'me', that is to say the soul by which I am what I am, is entirely distinct from the body, and is even more easy to know than is the latter: and even if body were not, the soul would not cease to be what it is."[2]

The notion of an unanalysable subject, the substratum of all thought, conceivable apart from the body, was thus given a powerful impetus. It is a notion that fits well with the structure of our language, dividing everything into subject and predicate. This may mean that we have been misled and have reified ideas that have a merely grammatical status. Certainly our language should reflect our metaphysics and not the other way round. Nevertheless the distinction between subject and object runs deep and the problem is how far the subject, particularly the subject of thought, can be devalued without affecting the position of the object. When I kick a stone, the presumption is that there is a relationship between two physical objects, but if I know a truth the position is not so clear. Is it possible to deny that "I" refers to some thing (or substance) without thereby casting doubt on the separate status of what is known? Nearly every view of truth must distinguish what is the case from the beliefs of any individual. What I believe and whether it is true are totally different issues. Many would hold that what is true is objective, independent of the conceptions of individuals or groups. In contrast, beliefs are subjective, so that whether I believe something is a matter about me. Just because I am wrong in my beliefs does not mean that I do not hold them. The world is full of people who have beliefs and are mistaken. What makes beliefs true is what the beliefs are about.

These remarks may seem obvious but they utilize a strong contrast between the possessor of beliefs and the objects of that cognitive state. As a believing, and even a knowing, subject, I gain much of my status by contrast with the world I try to grasp. The real world does not become moulded to my will, but is what it is, whatever I think. It includes me and my so-called "mental states", and it is not brought into existence by me. I discover truth and do not create it. Even an idealist, making a general connection between mind, or language, and reality, would differentiate between my beliefs and what is the case, or between what *I* think and what is generally thought. An identity could only result in solipsism, according to which my beliefs and my world are co-extensive. Solipsism, however, itself trades on the tacit distinction between self and reality, but merely refuses to detach the concept of reality from that of self. I create the world, while *I* still exist in splendid and impregnable isolation. It could be argued that this is the inevitable outcome of Cartesian dualism. The more sure I am of myself and my thought, the less sure I may be of anything lying beyond. At this point, though, dualism has been superseded by monism. Mind (and my mind at that) has become the only reality. Everything I believe has to be true, since I cannot be wrong about the world I myself create. The only complication that can arise is if my beliefs are internally inconsistent, although presumably this must mean that my world itself has inconsistent features, as dream-worlds often have.

The opposite danger is that of the physicalist who is so sure of the reality of the physical world that the place of *me* and *my* thoughts becomes of secondary importance. I am a physical object, and knowledge becomes a matter of the relation of one physical object to another. The difficulty is how to differentiate one mode of causal interaction from another. Assuming, as a physicalist will, that all beliefs have a physical foundation and are physically caused, there is no way left of saying which causes link our beliefs to the world and which do not. We can identify deviant beliefs, but that is all they are. The normal beliefs of the majority can set the standard for truth. Given our beliefs, we then have a standard to enable us to decide which are

correct. A premium has to be placed on coherence and consensus, and it may be claimed that we cannot hope for more. We cannot step outside all our beliefs in order to confront reality. Yet the result is that the world then ceases to be independent of our systems of beliefs. It has to be a construction out of them.

The paradox is that the more that belief is thought the product of the physical world and itself an aspect of it, the more the physical world loses its status as something against which beliefs can be measured. We cannot start wondering which beliefs are justified and which are not, since we cannot discriminate between different causal chains. To do so would be to admit that we have a prior view of what is true and already know the proper paths to it. Without independent access to truth, we can only build up a picture of the world from the beliefs we already have. We cannot assume that these must mirror a world that exists apart from our conceptions of it. If beliefs are part of the physical world, identified perhaps with states of the brain, all that can be said is that we are physical organisms disposed to act in particular ways.

Evolution through natural selection has presumably ensured that these ways are likely to be advantageous to us. Some would imagine that this shows there is likely to be a "fit" between our beliefs and the world. Creatures that misjudge their environment, it may be said, are unlikely to survive. Beliefs, however, do not have to be true to be advantageous. Sociobiologists are prone to argue that moral beliefs are advantageous even if illusory. The notion of a moral claim or obligation being "objective" and demanding our allegiance is said to be beneficial, even though such a belief has been programmed in us to discourage anti-social behaviour, and need not correspond with the way things are. Reality may be morally neutral. It is the belief that is advantageous and it does not matter whether it is true, as long as we hold it. Questions of biological advantage are different from questions of truth. The monism of a physicalist similarly changes the subject from questions of what is true to those concerning the fact of belief. That people believe something becomes of greater significance than the content of their beliefs, since we have no independent means of adjudicating the latter.

Both forms of monism, whether mental or physical, can lead to positions which make us powerless to distinguish between truth and falsehood. The solipsist can never be wrong. Even if he changes his mind, there is no guarantee that his second thoughts are better than his first. The physicalist has to take our collective beliefs on trust, and may indeed conceive it a virtue that we cannot be radically mistaken. For both idealist and physicalist, truth must depend on consensus, since one can appeal to nothing beyond people's conceptions of reality, however they are understood.

Is the desirable position to have two items which have to be fitted together? Idealism and physicalism typically deny this by accepting the dualist framework but then emphasizing one of the sides of the potential equation. Monists deny either the separate existence of "mind" or "the world". Yet a critic might say that in so doing they are accepting and arguing within a distinction that should never be made. The distinction between subject and object lies at the root of the argument, and it may be suggested that this should be discarded. This would block the worry that we are all *only* subjects or *only* objects.

There is a powerful current in modern philosophy that tries to sweep aside the dichotomy. The metaphysical subject is as much anathema as the world existing in itself apart from human conceptions of it. Much of this approach can be exemplified in the writings of Nietzsche. He boldly asserted:

There exists neither spirit, nor reason, nor thinking, nor consciousness, nor soul, nor will, nor truth; all are fictions that are of no use. There is no question of "subject and object".[3]

He maintained that the concept of substance is a consequence of our concept of the subject, and denounced the "fiction" that beneath our various states there lies a substratum. Following Heraclitus, he believed that everything is in flux, so that we find in "things" what we bring to them. Everything is linked to everything else. Nothing is determinate, and all is a question of interpretation and perspective. He says: "Truth is the kind of error without which a certain species of life could not live." It is difficult for anyone challenging the metaphysics which shines through our language to do so without apparently using language in contradictory ways. The question must not be whether one can transcend the categories to language without doing violence to language, but whether such a programme is rationally defensible.

Talk of reality as indeterminate or chaotic, and reference to "becoming" instead of "being" may be to attack a particular kind of metaphysics, but it is hard to make much sense of it except as a way of telling us something of the character of reality. When Nietzsche says "facts are precisely what there is not, only interpretations",[4] he is not saying anything at all unless he is talking about what there really is. He senses a difficulty when he asks whether an interpretation implies an interpreter. He maintains that even this is "invention" but, again, the notion of invention only gains its power by contrast with what is not invented. Our whole metaphysics can be questioned, but there has to come a point at which denial stops. If everything is fiction, and nothing is real, we so lose our grip on the concepts of fact and fiction, truth and falsity, and reality and unreality, that the argument cannot even be stated. There comes a point at which an attack on the presuppositions of *our* language becomes an attack on those of *any* language.

The world may be indeterminate, and Nietzsche alleges there is no limit to the ways in which it can be interpreted, but if any interpretation is as good as any other, nothing can ever be ruled out. Nietzsche's own objections to Platonic and Christian metaphysics fall to the ground. The problem is that if they are mistaken in claiming objective truth, Nietzsche apparently wants them to be "objectively" mistaken. Their views, in that case, do not match the character of the world. In fact, the dichotomy between the world and what is said about it can never be finally transcended. Anything can be said with impunity, without some distinction between what is and is not the case, and that can only mean that language is reduced to meaningless sound. It is not coincidence that Heraclitus was much admired by Nietzsche and that his followers were confronted with this very difficulty by Plato.[5] The less check that is put by reality on what can be said, the less in the end can be said.

What is the connection between the possibility of metaphysics and the notion of the self? Since my beliefs about the world are seen to be *about* something, we have to take the possibility of mistake seriously. That means that we must differentiate between the stance I take to the world and "the world". The basic distinction between subject and object makes language possible. The distinction between what is the case and what is thought to be the case runs very deep. Part of what enables me to differentiate myself from the world is the knowledge that my conception of the world is not co-existent with the world. *My* world is not necessarily *the* world, not just because of my limitations but also because of my proneness to error.

2.   The Idea of the Self

The distinction between what is taken to be true and what is true provides one of the bases for conceiving of the self. Yet impressions of the world can be distinguished from it, without invoking any notion of a principle of unity underlying them. Why should one talk of *the* self, as if there is one thing underlying reactions to the world? It might perhaps be sufficient for perceptions, beliefs and so on to be associated in some way with a particular body. The question remains why the nature of *the* self needs a metaphysical rather than a physical basis. It is even alleged that the idea of an incorporeal substance somehow subsisting within the human personality is dangerous. It inevitably invites a contrast between the self and the body, so that the body can be thought of as weighing down, impeding and limiting the true self. The latter yearns, it may be imagined, for its freedom, not wishing to be restricted by place and time. Further, the notion, it is claimed, is excessively individualist. The self is envisaged as totally apart from other beings. The "solitary ego" is, it seems, independent of the influences of biology or society. Just as it is distinct from the body, it is detached from its social background, in which, it is claimed by some, human beings find their identity.

A doctrine of the metaphysical self envisages it as something more than the product of biological and social influences. The uniqueness of each individual is stressed in a way that transcends the context, whether physical or social, in which the self is placed. Without such an idea, our notion of the human person becomes exceedingly problematic. It is always tempting to wield Ockham's razor, and the intrinsic difficulty of discovering the self in the midst of myriad experiences (as Hume found) can make it tempting to dispense with the notion. We do not need to give up a distinction between the subject and object of belief to reinforce the idea of some substance or substratum. There perhaps need not be one thing making me what I am, and "I" may be produced in a different way. Certainly our genetic inheritance and our social environment are powerful influences and interact in a complex manner. Yet the subtraction of the metaphysical self means that our dispositions, beliefs and desires are merely the effects of particular causal chains. We are then (whoever "we" are) merely responding to a combination of biological and environmental pressures, and the individuality that seems

so precious is merely the result of different causal influences. Some would even go so far as to claim that not only is the "self" created in the main by social pressures, but that the idea of the individual self that we have is itself social in origin. It is not something we each naturally have, and may not, indeed, be present in the same way in each society.

This raises the possibility that people could live in an ordered way in society without distinguishing themselves from other people. Yet notions of such arrangements are difficult to grasp. If there is a "self" it must be the starting point for my interaction with the world. One can imagine communities in which there are different ideas of who or what may belong to me. Human society does not inevitably have to rely on ideas of property or the nuclear family. My responsibilities can easily vary. How, though, could a society function in which I do not understand that there is any difference between myself and others? Biological organisms may have evolved so as to interact with each other, without understanding what they are doing, but it is hard to believe that a human society could work like that. Indeed a strong sense of one's own identity could prove to be biologically advantageous. I am better placed to pursue my own advantage when I can appreciate who "I" am. This notion of a self, however, involves not much more than a grasp of oneself as a physical organism in a world of other such organisms. It seems that more has to be added before any idea of a metaphysical self is arrived at.

Yet the concept of a physical organism is not as metaphysically empty as might first appear. Any such conception necessarily involved the thought that I am the *same* organism persisting through time. There would be no point in the conscious pursuit even of biological advantage if I did not have the concept of myself as a continuing entity. Even if a desire for children has biological origins, I have to have the idea that they would be *my* children and that presupposes that *I* persist through their conception, birth and growth. Similarly, there must be a presumption that they persist *themselves* through the various stages of their growth. It may well be that the fact of consciousness, and even of self-consciousness, has helped to give humanity a major evolutionary advantage.

The idea of the self would seem also to be more a precondition of society than a consequence of it. Our moral views are based firmly on questions of personal responsibility and thus on the idea of a person. Without a strong conception of the self, I could not hold myself responsible or other people either. I must be able to hold that the same person can persist through time, to be able to feel remorse or pride myself or to praise or blame others. I cannot feel guilty if someone else did something wrong. I should not punish anyone for something they did not do. Perhaps this reflects a particular view of morality, so that notions of personal responsibility could change if we no longer believed in the persistence of persons. It is difficult, however, to envisage a society whose members could not be re-identified. There would be a succession of different persons, so that the society would exist in a flux of constant change.

A remark made by Nietzsche draws attention to the problem of a society whose members do not continue through time. In a slightly different context he asks:

> To breed an animal with the right to make promises – is not this the paradoxical task that nature has set itself in the case of man? Is it not the real problem regarding man?[6]

Yet to make a promise, I must be able to recognize myself as persisting into the future. To enter into an obligation with others implies that I will try to fulfil it. This obviously entails that "I" will still be "me". I cannot now promise to act in the future in a particular way without assuming that I will still exist at the future time. However much I may change, I must still be bound by the promise. Part therefore of what should be meant by what gives the "right to make promises" is the fact of the continuance of the self. Indeed without some notion of persons persisting, it is difficult to see how many of the central notions of morality can be retained. Some forms of utilitarianism encouraging pleasant experiences and discouraging unpleasant ones, might be possible, even if the experiences had no persisting owners. Whether, however, this could provide a sufficient basis for a stable society is dubious. Certainly there could be no moral responsibility for the conduct of such a policy. No one could be wrong in failing to maximize pleasure and minimize pain, since "they", whoever "they" are supposed to be, would not exist long enough to be blamed for what they were or were not doing. No society can exist without some conception of the human subject, responsible for his or her actions, and ready and willing to accept that responsibility.

It may be objected that the notion of a responsible agent does not of itself add up to the concept of self, particularly a metaphysical one. There is,

however, something of great importance common to the two ideas, and that is the fact of persistence through change. The concept of substance has had a chequered philosophical history, but it began by picking out that which persists through alteration. A substance is at least the subject of change, and without such a conception there can only be a confusing flux of characteristics and properties. That is a desperate enough position for would-be physical objects, but in the area of human experience, it means that nothing can bind together different feelings, thoughts, memories and experiences. Without a common subject, even the idea that experiences can come in bundles is suspect. What criteria are there for gathering them up into this bundle rather than that?

The problem is not just that we need some principle of unity which can relate the pain in my leg to the thoughts I am at present having. They may not be causally related, but they have in common the fact that they are all *mine*. We also need to be able to relate past experiences, and present memories, present actions with future memories. My whole life is an on-going unity in which each part is related to every other by virtue of the simple but crucial fact that it concerns me. It is not enough to introduce questions of causation and argue that my present memory is caused by my past experience. This already assumes a grasp of who or what is to count as me. We will still have to distinguish which causal chains begin and end with me and which involve other people. Even some causal links between my previous experience and my memory of it can be deviant, in that they rely on other people's accounts of what happened to me. It is only a short step from this to my apparently remembering as an event in my life something which in fact happened to someone else. Memory is not so much a source of a sense of personal identity as a consequence of it. I cannot remember what I once felt without some preconception of myself as a persisting person. Otherwise all I can be confronted with is a flux of ownerless impressions and feelings.

It is a common human experience to be aware of oneself as continuing through time and space. One can be convinced that one is the same person as when one was a child, even though one may have changed in many ways, both obvious and subtle. This may indeed be one of the main foundations for a belief in the metaphysical self, transcending the various stages of bodily growth and decay. Yet as a philosophical argument, it is not perhaps very convincing to those who vehemently deny having any such experience and who claim their life (whoever "they" may be) has no overall unity. Maybe they conceive of it as a series of overlapping experiences, each causally related to one another, but in no way united by any common principle. Yet it is very difficult to conceive of one's life in this way. Indeed, conceiving "it" as a whole, to be divided into stages, would already be self-contradictory, just as thinking of "my" life would be.

Without any overall unity for a life, notions of meaning and purpose become very elusive. I cannot discover any overall purpose for my life if the very notion of what it is for a life to be "mine" dissolves into the mists of uncertainty. It is perhaps not a coincidence that the most vociferous atheists, such as Nietzsche, tend also to be the major opponents of any notion of a metaphysical self. It might be just an aversion to all metaphysics, so that all metaphysical entities are fair game, but there may be more to it than that. The idea of a continuing self, as the subject of consciousness, and as a moral agent, giving unity to the personality, stems from a picture of the world in which stability rather than flux, purpose rather than chance, and meaning rather than nihilism all play important parts. This then inevitably raises the question as to the source of such stability and purpose. Who or what has endowed the world with meaning? Merely to raise such a question begins to point the way to a theistic answer. The alternative view, which Nietzsche exemplifies at its extreme, has to make individual humans the source of meaning. Life is what the "will to power" makes it. "Stability" is what we put into the world and not what we find there. Because there are no substances, no continuing entities, there are no selves and no God, and even the idea of an individual seems hard to sustain.

There is certainly a general connection between the notion of the metaphysical self and belief in God. What point is there in looking beyond this world to a loving Creator, who loves *me*, if my life has no unity and hence no meaning? Any God would certainly have no interest in *me*, because in a real sense, I, as a continuing person, do not exist. Similarly an attack on the notion of God can in the end undermine belief in my own importance and my own value. This can lead to doubts about my own substantiality, in the sense of continued existence. Whilst it might be pointed out that a strong sense of one's own importance is not an unmixed blessing, what is at issue is the value of anyone. If "I" am not important, because no sense can be given to the notion of "I", it follows that no one

else is either. Yet that is a conclusion with tremendous ethical consequences. Although Nietzsche thought that religion "has debased the concept man, by extolling the paltry and weak, and belittling the strong and great",[7] what he meant was that Christianity had preached the value of each individual. He complained that "through Christianity, the individual was made so important, so absolute, that he could no longer be sacrificed".[8] A universal love for man is in practice, he says, the preference for the suffering, under-privileged and degenerate. Christian altruism is, he holds, "the mass egoism of the weak". We should not hesitate to sacrifice the weak for the strong in the interests of eventually producing a "higher kind of man", as superman. It may be unfair to hold Nietzsche in any way responsible for the Third Reich, but it is notable that nothing in his outlook could have acted as a moral restraint on an Adolf Hitler.

Nietzsche portrayed in graphic terms the consequences for human life of overturning Christian metaphysics. In some ways, he was more honest than those who would abandon the metaphysics but wish to retain the morality depending on it. He believed that "the soul is only a word for something about the body" and emphasized the role of basic instinctual drives, an emphasis which to some extent echoed Darwin, and which was certainly to influence Freud. Nietzsche's views nearly made it impossible for him to talk consistently about "the world" or "bodies" in the first place, but his statement is very close to Wittgenstein's that "the human body is the best picture of the human soul". The metaphysical self thus becomes the physical self and everything, it might seem, can go on virtually unchanged. Some may wish to introduce the notion of humans as "psycho-somatic unities", and this is certainly a nod in the direction of recognizing that we are not *just* bodies. Once, however, the idea of self that can be distinguished in any way from a body is denied, there is a problem. Experiences which are causally related to a body do not add up to being *me*. We still need a principle of unity. It is hard not to conclude that if we are identified in some way with our bodies, then our individual distinctiveness and indeed our very existence as persons is put at risk.

3. The Self and Language

The Cartesian idea of the solitary ego may seem to open up an intolerable gap between mind and body, but closing the gap can bring about a diminution of the ego to the point of extinction. The later Wittgenstein was opposed to any form of dualism, and his celebrated argument against the possibility of a private language symbolizes his deep suspicion of the self-conscious ego as a source of knowledge. His belief that language has to be public and social was all the more significant when coupled with his reluctance to give credence to any notion of the pre-linguistic. Thoughts were not firmly enough anchored for him until they were expressed in language. Language, in fact, was to be a formative influence on thought, with linguistic categories determining how we saw the world.

The picture of an isolated self trying to come to grips with the real world was then rejected as radically ill conceived. Instead, the social world is thought to have logical priority over the private world of the individual. We are all participants in forms of life of varying complexity, and membership of a linguistic community becomes of greater importance than who we individually are. One recent commentator on Wittgenstein can interpret him as saying:

> I discover myself not in some pre-linguistic inner space of self-presence, but in the network of multifarious social and historical relationships in which I am willy-nilly involved.[9]

I become, it seems, what I am, not because of some metaphysical fact, but through the social practices in which I grew up, and the language I learn. Language, indeed, apparently grants us the power of self-consciousness, and the self has been created by society. The public has become the precondition of the private, and the community is logically prior to the individual. Perhaps most significant of all is the way in which language is no longer viewed as being about an independently existing reality. The later Wittgenstein emphasized that the meaning of a word lay not in its relation to what it referred to, but in the way it was used in a particular community. The very same position which removes the autonomous self from the philosophic stage also lays waste any notion of extra-linguistic reality. Indeed, since the extra-linguistic self is part of that reality, it is hardly surprising that it is treated in the same way.

Kerr associates the notion of a self and that of extra-linguistic reality when he remarks: "Perhaps it is only if we are already strongly tempted to treat the self as a solitary intellect locked within a space that is inaccessible to anyone else that language looks instinctively like a system of referring to things."[10]

According to Kerr, Wittgenstein was right to insist that we do things with words, rather than simply associate them with objects. He considers that as a consequence the locus of meaning has been moved "from the ego's mental enclosure to the social world". Instead of a relationship between three independent items, a private self, a public language, and an objective world, we have only one left.[11] For Wittgenstein language creates the self and moulds the world. There is an intimate connection between his repudiation of the metaphysical self and his apparent rejection of an objective world. If we each had the power to abstract ourselves from language and recognize the world independently of its categories, the objectivity of reality would not seem so problematic. If we were able to recognize parts of reality *before* we learnt language, and only afterwards learnt the relevant words, our own independence from language would be as assured as the independence of reality. Many have held, and would still hold, that this is precisely what makes language learning, not to mention translation between languages, possible in the first place. Wittgenstein's understanding of our social immersion makes it impossible to explain how we ever learnt language, since if we cannot identify *things* independently, we cannot learn to use language in the appropriate contexts. We must, indeed, be able to recognize a context as appropriate before we can learn how to use the word properly.

There is no such thing as language in the abstract, because there are only particular languages. It follows that being given one's identity and one's world by the concepts of the language one learns reduces the fundamental concepts of metaphysics to the quirks of a particular language. It may be alleged that the alternative vision is to erect the parochial standards of one's own linguistic community into eternal ones binding on all times and places. This is to reiterate the point that the subject–predicate form which makes talk of selves and substances seem so natural is merely a feature of a particular set of languages. Nevertheless, the result is to remove the possibility of all metaphysics. The more explicitly relativism is embraced, the easier it is to slip into the kind of nihilism which confronted Nietzsche. Once one has lost grip on the notion that certain things *are* the case, and becomes content with the idea that this is merely what is agreed in one form of life, it is not long before one is confronted with the question why one should go on accepting even that. There can be no satisfactory answer to that, and the denial of metaphysical underpinning becomes a prescription for total despair.

The concepts of reality and of myself as a continuing person set in that reality, but also in a sense separated from it, are indissolubly linked. Denying one must lead us into difficulties with the other. In this sense, any proper theory of the self must be dualistic. It must recognize that I cannot be wholly identified with "the world". The subject and object of belief cannot be absorbed into each other, as long as we take the possibility of error seriously. *The world is not necessarily *my* world*, since my judgements often do not coincide with the way things really are. I am not a passive recipient of would-be knowledge, but also an active agent, having to make my way in a world of objects and other people. I have to decide how to behave, and there are moral, as well as epistemological, claims on the self. How I treat others depends very largely on the kind of person I am.

This distinction between the self and the world, between subject and object, separates human agents from the rest of the world in a manner that may seem anathema to many. There are clear connections between such a view of the self, and religious conceptions of the soul. Those who search for a monistic vision of a unified self and world will vehemently oppose any sharp distinction between mind and matter of the kind practised by Cartesian dualism. This is, of course, one of the most important and long-lasting controversies in Western philosophy, stemming from the pre-Socratics and Plato. However, if anyone persists in the wholesale repu-

diation of metaphysics, there are obvious dangers, not least that of self-refutation. The most ardent physicalist will find it difficult not to view himself and his beliefs as somehow claiming truth, and distinct from the rest of the world. Yet the concept of the self is one of the central notions of metaphysics. Any notion of the self has to be metaphysical and is linked very firmly to other metaphysical conceptions, such as that of objective reality. Those who begin by attacking the one will inevitably find themselves also attacking the other.

If thought and language are to be possible (and presumably writing this sentence shows that they are) questions of truth and of the nature of those beings who can accept or reject truth can never be set aside. The genuine nihilist has no alternative but to be silent. This of itself does not prove that any particular religious claims about the soul and its eternal destiny are correct. It merely leaves room for them to be made. To these metaphysical conclusions about the necessary pre-conditions of language must be added the importance of the moral responsibility of the persisting self for the existence of society. So far from being the creation of language or society, the existence of the self is the absolute pre-condition for both. Some form of dualism seems inescapable in our view of reality. Indeed, the very notion of such a view already encapsulates a dualistic approach. How far we are thereby led towards theism is another question. Many theists would themselves repudiate any dualistic vision. There is, though, no doubt that many philosophers have followed Nietzsche in his repudiation of the distinction between subject and object, precisely because they feared a connection.

Notes

1 "The Presuppositions of Survival", *Philosophy*, LXII (1987): 28.
2 *Philosophical Works of Descartes*, trans. E. Haldane and G. R. T. Ross (Cambridge, 1931), p. 101.
3 *Will to Power* (no. 480), ed. W. Kaufmann (New York, 1967).
4 Ibid., no. 493.
5 E.g. *Theaetetus* 182D.
6 *Genealogy of Morals*, ed. W. Kaufmann (New York, 1969), p. 57.
7 *Will to Power*, no. 136.
8 Ibid., no. 240.
9 F. Kerr, *Theology after Wittgenstein* (Oxford, 1986), p. 69.
10 Ibid., p. 57.
11 See my "Thought and Language", *Proceedings of the Aristotelian Society*, LXXIX (1978–9).

49

Of Miracles

David Hume

Part I

There is, in Dr Tillotson's writings, an argument against the *real presence*,[1] which is as concise, and elegant, and strong as any argument can possibly be supposed against a doctrine so little worthy of a serious refutation. It is acknowledged on all hands, says that learned prelate, that the authority, either of the scripture or of tradition, is founded merely in the testimony of the apostles, who were eye-witnesses to those miracles of our Saviour by which he proved his divine mission. Our evidence, then, for the truth of the *Christian* religion is less than the evidence for the truth of our senses; because, even in the first authors of our religion, it was no greater; and it is evident it must diminish in passing from them to their disciples; nor can any one rest such confidence in their testimony, as in the immediate object of his senses. But a weaker evidence can never destroy a stronger; and there-fore, were the doctrine of the real presence ever so clearly revealed in scripture, it were directly contrary to the rules of just reasoning to give our assent to it. It contradicts sense, though both the scripture and tradition on which it is supposed to be built carry not such evidence with them as sense, when they are considered merely as external

David Hume, "Of Miracles," reprinted by permission of Hackett Publishing Company Inc. from David Hume, *An Enquiry Concerning Human Understanding*, 2nd edn, edited by Eric Steinberg (Indianapolis: Hackett, 1977), pp. 72–90. All rights reserved.

evidences, and are not brought home to every one's breast by the immediate operation of the Holy Spirit.

Nothing is so convenient as a decisive argument of this kind, which must at least *silence* the most arrogant bigotry and superstition, and free us from their impertinent solicitations. I flatter myself that I have discovered an argument of a like nature, which, if just, will, with the wise and learned, be an everlasting check to all kinds of superstitious delusion, and consequently will be useful as long as the world endures. For so long, I presume, will the accounts of miracles and prodigies be found in all history, sacred and profane.

Though experience be our only guide in reason-ing concerning matters of fact, it must be acknow-ledged that this guide is not altogether infallible, but in some cases is apt to lead us into errors. One who in our climate should expect better weather in any week of June than in one of December, would reason justly, and conformably to experience; but it is certain that he may happen, in the event, to find himself mistaken. However, we may observe that, in such a case, he would have no cause to complain of experience, because it commonly in-forms us beforehand of the uncertainty, by that contrariety of events, which we may learn from a diligent observation. All effects follow not with like certainty from their supposed causes. Some events are found, in all countries and all ages, to have been constantly conjoined together. Other are found to have been more variable, and sometimes to dis-appoint our expectations; so that, in our reasonings concerning matter of fact, there are all imaginable degrees of assurance, from the highest certainty to the lowest species of moral evidence.

A wise man, therefore, proportions his belief to the evidence. In such conclusions as are founded on an infallible experience, he expects the event with the last degree of assurance, and regards his past experience as a full *proof* of the future existence of that event. In other cases, he proceeds with more caution: He weighs the opposite experiments; he considers which side is supported by the greater number of experiments; to that side he inclines, with doubt and hesitation; and when at last he fixes his judgement, the evidence exceeds not what we properly call *probability*. All probability, then, supposes an opposition of experiments and observations, where the one side is found to overbalance the other, and to produce a degree of evidence, proportioned to the superiority. A hundred instances or experiments on one side, and fifty on another, afford a doubtful expectation of any event; though a hundred uniform experiments, with only one that is contradictory, reasonably beget a pretty strong degree of assurance. In all cases, we must balance the opposite experiments, where they are opposite, and deduct the smaller number from the greater, in order to know the exact force of the superior evidence.

To apply these principles to a particular instance; we may observe, that there is no species of reasoning more common, more useful, and even necessary to human life than that which is derived from the testimony of men, and the reports of eye-witnesses and spectators. This species of reasoning, perhaps, one may deny to be founded on the relation of cause and effect. I shall not dispute about a word. It will be sufficient to observe that our assurance in any argument of this kind is derived from no other principle than our observation of the veracity of human testimony, and of the usual conformity of facts to the reports of witnesses. It being a general maxim that no objects have any discoverable connexion together, and that all the inferences which we can draw from one to another are founded merely on our experience of their constant and regular conjunction; it is evident, that we ought not to make an exception to this maxim in favour of human testimony, whose connexion with any event seems, in itself, as little necessary as any other. Were not the memory tenacious to a certain degree; had not men commonly an inclination to truth and a principle of probity; were they not sensible to shame, when detected in a falsehood: were not these, I say, discovered by *experience* to be qualities, inherent in human nature, we should never repose the least confidence in human testimony. A man delirious, or noted for falsehood and villainy, has no manner of authority with us.

And as the evidence derived from witnesses and human testimony is founded on past experience, so it varies with the experience, and is regarded either as a *proof* or a *probability*, according as the conjunction between any particular kind of report and any kind of object has been found to be constant or variable. There are a number of circumstances to be taken into consideration in all judgements of this kind; and the ultimate standard, by which we determine all disputes that may arise concerning them, is always derived from experience and observation. Where this experience is not entirely uniform on any side, it is attended with an unavoidable contrariety in our judgements, and with the same opposition and mutual destruction of argument as in every other kind of evidence. We frequently hesitate concerning the reports of others. We balance the opposite circumstances, which cause any doubt or uncertainty; and when we discover a superiority on any side, we incline to it, but still with a diminution of assurance, in proportion to the force of its antagonist.

This contrariety of evidence, in the present case, may be derived from several different causes; from the opposition of contrary testimony, from the character or number of the witnesses, from the manner of their delivering their testimony, or from the union of all these circumstances. We entertain a suspicion concerning any matter of fact, when the witnesses contradict each other; when they are but few, or of a doubtful character; when they have an interest in what they affirm; when they deliver their testimony with hesitation, or on the contrary, with too violent asseverations. There are many other particulars of the same kind, which may diminish or destroy the force of any argument derived from human testimony.

Suppose, for instance, that the fact, which the testimony endeavours to establish, partakes of the extraordinary and the marvellous; in that case, the evidence resulting from the testimony admits of a diminution, greater or less, in proportion as the fact is more or less unusual. The reason why we place any credit in witnesses and historians is not derived from any *connexion*, which we perceive a priori, between testimony and reality, but because we are accustomed to find a conformity between them. But when the fact attested is such a one as has seldom fallen under our observation, here is a contest of two opposite experiences; of which the one destroys the other, as far as its force goes, and the superior can only operate on the mind by the force which remains. The very same principle of experience, which gives us a certain degree of assurance in the testimony of witnesses, gives us also, in this case, another degree of assurance against the fact which they endeavour to establish, from which contradiction there necessarily arises a counterpoise, and mutual destruction of belief and authority.

I should not believe such a story were it told me by Cato was a proverbial saying in Rome, even during the lifetime of that philosophical patriot.[2] The incredibility of a fact, it was allowed, might invalidate so great an authority.

The Indian prince who refused to believe the first relations concerning the effects of frost, reasoned justly; and it naturally required very strong testimony to engage his assent to facts that arose from a state of nature with which he was unacquainted, and which bore so little analogy to those events of which he had had constant and uniform experience. Though they were not contrary to his experience, they were not conformable to it.

But in order to increase the probability against the testimony of witnesses, let us suppose that the fact which they affirm, instead of being only marvellous, is really miraculous; and suppose also that the testimony, considered apart and in itself, amounts to an entire proof; in that case, there is proof against proof, of which the strongest must prevail, but still with a diminution of its force in proportion to that of its antagonist.

A miracle is a violation of the laws of nature; and as a firm and unalterable experience has established these laws, the proof against a miracle, from the very nature of the fact, is as entire as any argument from experience can possibly be imagined. Why is it more than probable that all men must die; that lead cannot, of itself, remain suspended in the air; that fire consumes wood, and is extinguished by water; unless it be that these events are found agreeable to the laws of nature, and there is required a violation of these laws, or in other words a miracle to prevent them? Nothing is esteemed a miracle if it ever happen in the common course of nature. It is no miracle that a man, seemingly in good health, should die on a sudden: because such a kind of death, though more unusual than any other, has yet been frequently observed to happen. But it is a miracle that a dead man should come to life, because that has never been observed, in any age or country. There must, therefore, be a uniform experience against every miraculous event, otherwise the event would not merit that appellation. And as an uniform experience amounts to a proof, there is here a direct and full *proof*, from the nature of the fact, against the existence of any miracle; nor can such a proof be destroyed, or the miracle rendered credible, but by an opposite proof, which is superior.

The plain consequence is (and it is a general maxim worthy of our attention), "That no testimony is sufficient to establish a miracle, unless the testimony be of such a kind that its falsehood would be more miraculous than the fact which it endeavours to establish: and even in that case there is a mutual destruction of arguments, and the superior only gives us an assurance suitable to that degree of force, which remains, after deducting the inferior." When any one tells me that he saw a dead man restored to life, I immediately consider with myself, whether it be more probable that this person should either deceive or be deceived, or that the fact which he relates should really have happened. I weigh the one miracle against the other; and according to the superiority which I discover, I pronounce my decision, and always reject the greater miracle. If the falsehood of his testimony would be more miraculous than the event which he relates; then, and not till then, can he pretend to command my belief or opinion.

Part II

In the foregoing reasoning we have supposed that the testimony, upon which a miracle is founded, may possibly amount to an entire proof, and that the falsehood of that testimony would be a real prodigy: But it is easy to show, that we have been a great deal too liberal in our concession, and that there never was a miraculous event established on so full an evidence.

For *first*, there is not to be found, in all history, any miracle attested by a sufficient number of men, of such unquestioned good-sense, education, and learning as to secure us against all delusion in themselves; of such undoubted integrity as to place them beyond all suspicion of any design to deceive others; of such credit and reputation in the eyes of mankind as to have a great deal to lose in case of their being detected in any falsehood; and at the same time attesting facts, performed in such a public manner and in so celebrated a part of the world, as to render the detection unavoidable: All which circumstances are requisite to give us a full assurance in the testimony of men.

Secondly. We may observe in human nature a principle, which, if strictly examined, will be found to diminish extremely the assurance which we might, from human testimony, have in any kind of prodigy. The maxim, by which we commonly conduct ourselves in our reasonings, is that the objects of which we have no experience resemble those of which we have; that what we have found to be most usual is always most probable; and that where there is an opposition of arguments, we ought to give the preference to such as are founded on the greatest number of past observations. But though, in proceeding by this rule, we readily reject any fact which is unusual and incredible in an ordinary degree; yet in advancing farther, the mind observes not always the same rule; but when anything is affirmed utterly absurd and miraculous, it rather the more readily admits of such a fact, upon account of that very circumstance which ought to destroy all its authority. The passion of *surprise* and *wonder* arising from miracles, being an agreeable emotion, gives a sensible tendency towards the belief of those events from which it is derived. And this goes so far that even those who cannot enjoy this pleasure immediately, nor can believe those miraculous events of which they are informed, yet love to partake of the satisfaction at second-hand or by rebound, and place a pride and delight in exciting the admiration of others.

With what greediness are the miraculous accounts of travellers received, their descriptions of sea and land monsters, their relations of wonderful adventures, strange men, and uncouth manners? But if the spirit of religion join itself to the love of wonder, there is an end of common sense; and human testimony, in these circumstances, loses all pretensions to authority. A religionist may be an enthusiast, and imagine he sees what has no reality. He may know his narrative to be false, and yet persevere in it, with the best intentions in the world, for the sake of promoting so holy a cause. Or even where this delusion has not place, vanity, excited by so strong a temptation, operates on him more powerfully than on the rest of mankind in any other circumstances; and self-interest with equal force. His auditors may not have, and commonly have not, sufficient judgement to canvass his evidence: what judgement they have, they renounce by principle, in these sublime and mysterious subjects: or if they were ever so willing to employ it, passion

and a heated imagination disturb the regularity of its operations. Their credulity increases his impudence: and his impudence overpowers their credulity.

Eloquence, when at its highest pitch, leaves little room for reason or reflection; but addressing itself entirely to the fancy or the affections, captivates the willing hearers, and subdues their understanding. Happily, this pitch it seldom attains. But what a Tully or a Demosthenes could scarcely effect over a Roman or Athenian audience, every *Capuchin*, every itinerant or stationary teacher can perform over the generality of mankind, and in a higher degree, by touching such gross and vulgar passions.

The many instances of forged miracles, and prophecies, and supernatural events, which in all ages have either been detected by contrary evidence, or which detect themselves by their absurdity, prove sufficiently the strong propensity of mankind to the extraordinary and the marvellous, and ought reasonably to beget a suspicion against all relations of this kind. This is our natural way of thinking, even with regard to the most common and most credible events. For instance: There is no kind of report which rises so easily, and spreads so quickly, especially in country places and provincial towns, as those concerning marriages; insomuch that two young persons of equal condition never see each other twice, but the whole neighbourhood immediately join them together. The pleasure of telling a piece of news so interesting, of propagating it, and of being the first reporters of it, spreads the intelligence. And this is so well known that no man of sense gives attention to these reports till he find them confirmed by some greater evidence. Do not the same passions, and others still stronger, incline the generality of mankind to believe and report, with the greatest vehemence and assurance, all religious miracles?

Thirdly. It forms a strong presumption against all supernatural and miraculous relations, that they are observed chiefly to abound among ignorant and barbarous nations; or if a civilized people has ever given admission to any of them, that people will be found to have received them from ignorant and barbarous ancestors, who transmitted them with that inviolable sanction and authority, which always attend received opinions. When we peruse the first histories of all nations, we are apt to imagine ourselves transported into some new world, where the whole frame of nature is disjointed, and every element performs its operations in a different manner from what it does at present. Battles, revolutions, pestilence, famine, and death are never the effect of those natural causes which we experience. Prodigies, omens, oracles, judgments quite obscure the few natural events that are intermingled with them. But as the former grow thinner every page, in proportion as we advance nearer the enlightened ages, we soon learn that there is nothing mysterious or supernatural in the case, but that all proceeds from the usual propensity of mankind towards the marvellous, and that, though this inclination may at intervals receive a check from sense and learning, it can never be thoroughly extirpated from human nature.

It is strange, a judicious reader is apt to say, upon the perusal of these wonderful historians, *that such prodigious events never happen in our days.* But it is nothing strange, I hope, that men should lie in all ages. You must surely have seen instances enough of that frailty. You have yourself heard many such marvellous relations started, which, being treated with scorn by all the wise and judicious, have at last been abandoned even by the vulgar. Be assured that those renowned lies, which have spread and flourished to such a monstrous height, arose from like beginnings; but being sown in a more proper soil, shot up at last into prodigies almost equal to those which they relate.

It was a wise policy in that false prophet, Alexander, who, though now forgotten, was once so famous, to lay the first scene of his impostures in Paphlagonia, where, as Lucian tells us,[3] the people were extremely ignorant and stupid, and ready to swallow even the grossest delusion. People at a distance, who are weak enough to think the matter at all worth enquiry, have no opportunity of receiving better information. The stories come magnified to them by a hundred circumstances. Fools are industrious in propagating the imposture; while the wise and learned are contented, in general, to deride its absurdity, without informing themselves of the particular facts by which it may be distinctly refuted. And thus the impostor-above-mentioned was enabled to proceed, from his ignorant Paphlagonians, to the enlisting of votaries, even among the Grecian philosophers and men of the most eminent rank and distinction in Rome. Nay, could engage the attention of that sage emperor Marcus Aurelius; so far as to make him trust the success of a military expedition to his delusive prophecies.

The advantages are so great of starting an imposture among an ignorant people that, even though the delusion should be too gross to impose on the generality of them (which, though seldom, is sometimes the case), it has a much better chance for succeeding in remote countries than if the first scene had been laid in a city renowned for arts and knowledge. The most ignorant and barbarous of these barbarians carry the report abroad. None of their countrymen have a large correspondence, or sufficient credit and authority to contradict and beat down the delusion. Men's inclination to the marvellous has full opportunity to display itself. And thus a story which is universally exploded in the place where it was first started, shall pass for certain at a thousand miles distance. But had Alexander fixed his residence at Athens, the philosophers of that renowned mart of learning had immediately spread, throughout the whole Roman empire their sense of the matter; which, being supported by so great authority, and displayed by all the force of reason and eloquence, had entirely opened the eyes of mankind. It is true; Lucian, passing by chance through Paphlagonia, had an opportunity of performing this good office. But, though much to be wished, it does not always happen that every Alexander meets with a Lucian, ready to expose and detect his impostures.

I may add as a *fourth* reason which diminishes the authority of prodigies, that there is no testimony for any, even those which have not been expressly detected, that is not opposed by an infinite number of witnesses; so that not only the miracle destroys the credit of testimony, but the testimony destroys itself. To make this the better understood, let us consider that, in matters of religion, whatever is different is contrary; and that it is impossible the religions of ancient Rome, of Turkey, of Siam, and of China should, all of them, be established on any solid foundation. Every miracle, therefore, pretended to have been wrought in any of these religions (and all of them abound in miracles), as its direct scope is to establish the particular system to which it is attributed, so has it the same force, though more indirectly, to overthrow every other system. In destroying a rival system, it likewise destroys the credit of those miracles on which that system was established; so that all the prodigies of different religions are to be regarded as contrary facts, and the evidences of these prodigies, whether weak or strong, as opposite to each other. According to this method of reasoning, when we believe any miracle of Mahomet or his successors, we have for our warrant the testimony of a few barbarous Arabians: And on the other hand, we are to regard the authority of Titus Livius, Plutarch, Tacitus, and, in short, of all the authors and witnesses, Grecian, Chinese, and Roman Catholic, who have related any miracle in their particular religion; I say, we are to regard their testimony in the same light as if they had mentioned that Mahometan miracle, and had in express terms contradicted it with the same certainty as they have for the miracle they relate. This argument may appear over subtile and refined; but is not in reality different from the reasoning of a judge, who supposes that the credit of two witnesses, maintaining a crime against any one, is destroyed by the testimony of two others, who affirm him to have been two hundred leagues distant at the same instant when the crime is said to have been committed.

One of the best attested miracles in all profane history is that which Tacitus reports of Vespasian, who cured a blind man in Alexandria by means of his spittle, and a lame man by the mere touch of his foot, in obedience to a vision of the god Serapis, who had enjoined them to have recourse to the Emperor for these miraculous cures. The story may be seen in that fine historian;[4] where every circumstance seems to add weight to the testimony, and might be displayed at large with all the force of argument and eloquence, if any one were now concerned to enforce the evidence of that exploded and idolatrous superstition. The gravity, solidity, age, and probity of so great an emperor who through the whole course of his life conversed in a familiar manner with his friends and courtiers, and never affected those extraordinary airs of divinity assumed by Alexander and Demetrius. The historian, a contemporary writer, noted for candour and veracity, and withal the greatest and most penetrating genius, perhaps, of all antiquity; and so free from any tendency to credulity that he even lies under the contrary imputation of atheism and profaneness: the persons, from whose authority he related the miracle, of established character for judgement and veracity, as we may well presume, eye-witnesses of the fact, and confirming their testimony after the Flavian family was despoiled of the empire and could no longer give any reward as the price of a lie. *Utrumque, qui interfuere, nunc quoque memorant, postquam nullum mendacio pretium.*[5] To which if we add the public nature of the facts as related, it will appear that no evidence can well be supposed stronger for so gross and so palpable a falsehood.

There is also a memorable story related by Cardinal de Retz,[6] which may well deserve our consideration. When that intriguing politician fled into Spain to avoid the persecution of his enemies,

he passed through Saragossa, the capital of Arragon, where he was shown, in the cathedral, a man who had served seven years as a door-keeper, and was well known to every body in town, that had ever paid his devotions at that church. He had been seen, for so long a time, wanting a leg, but recovered that limb by the rubbing of holy oil upon the stump; and the cardinal assures us that he saw him with two legs. This miracle was vouched by all the canons of the church; and the whole company in town were appealed to for a confirmation of the fact; whom the cardinal found by their zealous devotion to be thorough believers of the miracle. Here the relater was also contemporary to the supposed prodigy, of an incredulous and libertine character, as well as of great genius; the miracle of so *singular* a nature as could scarcely admit of a counterfeit, and the witnesses very numerous and all of them, in a manner, spectators of the fact to which they gave their testimony. And what adds mightily to the force of the evidence, and may double our surprise on this occasion, is that the cardinal himself, who relates the story, seems not to give any credit to it, and consequently cannot be suspected of any concurrence in the holy fraud. He considered justly that it was not requisite, in order to reject a fact of this nature, to be able accurately to disprove the testimony, and to trace its falsehood through all the circumstances of knavery and credulity which produced it. He knew that, as this was commonly altogether impossible at any small distance of time and place, so was it extremely difficult, even where one was immediately present, by reason of the bigotry, ignorance, cunning, and roguery of a great part of mankind. He therefore concluded, like a just reasoner, that such an evidence carried falsehood upon the very face of it, and that a miracle, supported by any human testimony, was more properly a subject of derision than of argument.

There surely never was a greater number of miracles ascribed to one person, than those which were lately said to have been wrought in France upon the tomb of Abbé Paris, the famous Jansenist, with whose sanctity the people were so long deluded. The curing of the sick, giving hearing to the deaf, and sight to the blind, were every where talked of as the usual effects of that holy sepulchre. But what is more extraordinary; many of the miracles were immediately proved upon the spot, before judges of unquestioned integrity, attested by witnesses of credit and distinction, in a learned age, and on the most eminent theatre that is now in the world. Nor is this all: a relation of them was published and dispersed every where; nor were the *Jesuits*, though a learned body, supported by the civil magistrate and determined enemies to those opinions, in whose favour the miracles were said to have been wrought, ever able distinctly to refute or detect them. Where shall we find such a number of circumstances agreeing to the corroboration of one fact? And what have we to oppose to such a cloud of witnesses, but the absolute impossibility or miraculous nature of the events which they relate? And this surely, in the eyes of all reasonable people, will alone be regarded as a sufficient refutation.

Is the consequence just, because some human testimony has the utmost force and authority in some cases, when it relates the battle of Philippi or Pharsalia for instance; that therefore all kinds of testimony must in all cases have equal force and authority? Suppose that the Caesarean and Pompeian factions had, each of them, claimed the victory in these battles, and that the historians of each party had uniformly ascribed the advantage to their own side; how could mankind, at this distance, have been able to determine between them? The contrariety is equally strong between the miracles related by Herodotus or Plutarch, and those delivered by Mariana, Bede, or any monkish historian.

The wise lend a very academic faith to every report which favours the passion of the reporter; whether it magnifies his country, his family, or himself, or in any other way strikes in with his natural inclinations and propensities. But what greater temptation than to appear a missionary, a prophet, an ambassador from heaven? Who would not encounter many dangers and difficulties in order to attain so sublime a character? Or if, by the help of vanity and a heated imagination, a man has first made a convert of himself, and entered seriously into the delusion; who ever scruples to make use of pious frauds in support of so holy and meritorious a cause?

The smallest spark may here kindle into the greatest flame; because the materials are always prepared for it. The *avidum genus auricularum*,[7] the gazing populace, receive greedily, without examination, whatever soothes superstition and promotes wonder.

How many stories of this nature have, in all ages, been detected and exploded in their infancy? How many more have been celebrated for a time, and have afterwards sunk into neglect and oblivion? Where such reports, therefore, fly about, the solution of the phenomenon is obvious; and we judge in conformity to regular experience and observation when we account for it by the known and natural principles of credulity and delusion. And shall we, rather than have a recourse to so natural a solution, allow of a miraculous violation of the most established laws of nature?

I need not mention the difficulty of detecting a falsehood in any private or even public history, at the place where it is said to happen; much more when the scene is removed to ever so small a distance. Even a court of judicature, with all the authority, accuracy, and judgement which they can employ, find themselves often at a loss to distinguish between truth and falsehood in the most recent actions. But the matter never comes to any issue if trusted to the common method of altercation and debate and flying rumours, especially when men's passions have taken part on either side.

In the infancy of new religions, the wise and learned commonly esteem the matter too inconsiderable to deserve their attention or regard. And when afterwards they would willingly detect the cheat, in order to undeceive the deluded multitude, the season is now past, and the records and witnesses which might clear up the matter have perished beyond recovery.

No means of detection remain but those which must be drawn from the very testimony itself of the reporters: and these, though always sufficient with the judicious and knowing, are commonly too fine to fall under the comprehension of the vulgar.

Upon the whole, then, it appears that no testimony for any kind of miracle has ever amounted to a probability, much less to a proof; and that, even supposing it amounted to a proof, it would be opposed by another proof, derived from the very nature of the fact which it would endeavour to establish. It is experience only which gives authority to human testimony; and it is the same experience which assures us of the laws of nature. When, therefore, these two kinds of experience are contrary, we have nothing to do but subtract the one from the other, and embrace an opinion, either on one side or the other, with that assurance which arises from the reminder. But according to the principle here explained, this substraction, with regard to all popular religions, amounts to an entire annihilation; and therefore we may establish it as a maxim that no human testimony can have such force as to prove a miracle, and make it a just foundation for any such system of religion.

I beg the limitations here made may be remarked, when I say that a miracle can never be proved, so as to be the foundation of a system of religion. For

I own that otherwise there may possibly be miracles, or violations of the usual course of nature, of such a kind as to admit of proof from human testimony; though perhaps it will be impossible to find any such in all the records of history. Thus, suppose, all authors, in all languages agree that from the first of January 1600 there was a total darkness over the whole earth for eight days: Suppose that the tradition of this extraordinary event is still strong and lively among the people: That all travellers, who return from foreign countries, bring us accounts of the same tradition, without the least variation or contradiction. It is evident that our present philosophers, instead of doubting the fact, ought to receive it as certain, and ought to search for the causes whence it might be derived. The decay, corruption, and dissolution of nature, is an event rendered probable by so many analogies, that any phenomenon which seems to have a tendency towards that catastrophe comes within the reach of human testimony, if that testimony be very extensive and uniform.

But suppose that all the historians who treat of England should agree that, on the first of January 1600, Queen Elizabeth died; that both before and after her death she was seen by her physicians and the whole court, as is usual with persons of her rank; that her successor was acknowledged and proclaimed by the parliament; and that, after being interred a month, she again appeared, resumed the throne, and governed England for three years. I must confess that I should be surprised at the concurrence of so many odd circumstances, but should not have the least inclination to believe so miraculous an event. I should not doubt of her pretended death, and of those other public circumstances that followed it: I should only assert it to have been pretended, and that it neither was, nor possibly could be real. You would in vain object to me the difficulty, and almost impossibility of deceiving the world in an affair of such consequence; the wisdom and solid judgement of that renowned queen; with the little or no advantage which she could reap from so poor an artifice: all this might astonish me; but I would still reply that the knavery and folly of men are such common phenomena, that I should rather believe the most extraordinary events to arise from their concurrence, than admit of so signal a violation of the laws of nature.

But should this miracle be ascribed to any new system of religion; men in all ages have been so much imposed on by ridiculous stories of that kind, that this very circumstance would be a full proof of a cheat, and sufficient, with all men of sense, not only to make them reject the fact, but even reject it without farther examination. Though the Being to whom the miracle is ascribed be, in this case, Almighty, it does not upon that account become a whit more probable; since it is impossible for us to know the attributes or actions of such a Being, otherwise than from the experience which we have of his productions in the usual course of nature. This still reduces us to past observation, and obliges us to compare the instances of the violation of truth in the testimony of men, with those of the violation of the laws of nature by miracles, in order to judge which of them is most likely and probable. As the violations of truth are more common in the testimony concerning religious miracles than in that concerning any other matter of fact, this must diminish very much the authority of the former testimony, and make us form a general resolution never to lend any attention to it, with whatever specious pretence it may be covered.

Lord Bacon seems to have embraced the same principles of reasoning. "We ought," says he, "to make a collection or particular history of all monsters and prodigious births or productions, and in a word of every thing new, rare, and extraordinary in nature. But this must be done with the most severe scrutiny, lest we depart from truth. Above all, every relation must be considered as suspicious which depends in any degree upon religion, as the prodigies of Livy: And no less so, every thing that is to be found in the writers of natural magic or alchimy, or such authors who seem, all of them, to have an unconquerable appetite for falsehood and fable."[8]

I am the better pleased with the method of reasoning here delivered, as I think it may serve to confound those dangerous friends or disguised enemies to the *Christian Religion*, who have undertaken to defend it by the principles of human reason. Our most holy religion is founded on *Faith*, not on reason; and it is a sure method of exposing it to put it to such a trial as it is by no means fitted to endure. To make this more evident, let us examine those miracles related in scripture; and not to lose ourselves in too wide a field, let us confine ourselves to such as we find in the *Pentateuch*, which we shall examine according to the principles of these pretended Christians, not as the word or testimony of God himself, but as the production of a mere human writer and historian. Here then we are first to consider a book, presented to us by a barbarous and ignorant people, written in an age when they were still more barbarous, and in all probability long after the facts which it relates, corroborated by no concurring testimony, and resembling those fabulous accounts which every nation gives of its origin. Upon reading this book, we find it full of prodigies and miracles. It gives an account of a state of the world and of human nature entirely different from the present: of our fall from that state: of the age of man, extended to near a thousand years: of the destruction of the world by a deluge: of the arbitrary choice of one people, as the favourites of heaven, and that people the countrymen of the author: of their deliverance from bondage by prodigies the most astonishing imaginable. I desire any one to lay his hand upon his heart, and after a serious consideration declare whether he thinks that the falsehood of such a book, supported by such a testimony, would be more extraordinary and miraculous than all the miracles it relates; which is, however, necessary to make it be received, according to the measures of probability above established.

What we have said of miracles may be applied, without any variation, to prophecies; and indeed all prophecies are real miracles, and as such only can be admitted as proofs of any revelation. If it did not exceed the capacity of human nature to foretell future events, it would be absurd to employ any prophecy as an argument for a divine mission or authority from heaven. So that, upon the whole, we may conclude, that the *Christian Religion* not only was at first attended with miracles, but even at this day cannot be believed by any reasonable person without one. Mere reason is insufficient to convince us of its veracity: and whoever is moved by *Faith* to assent to it is conscious of a continued miracle in his own person, which subverts all the principles of his understanding, and gives him a determination to believe what is most contrary to custom and experience.

Notes

1 The presence of the body and blood of Christ in the bread and wine of the Eucharist.
2 Plutarch, in vita Catonis Min. 19 (*Life of Cato* (the Younger)).
3 In *Alexander, the False Prophet*, the Greek author Lucian (born *c.* 120) relates how Alexander of Abonoteichos was hailed as an oracle because of a hoax perpetrated on the people of Paphlagonia, whereby he made it appear that the god Asclepius was being born in the form of a serpent from a goose's egg.
4 Hist. Bk. IV, chap 81 Suetonius gives nearly the same account *in vita* Vesp.
5 Of each event, those who were present, even now keep speaking, though they get no reward for lying.
6 Cardinal de Retz (1613–79), a French political leader. His *Mémoires* (1717) provide insight into the court life of his time.
7 Literally, "a gossip-hungry race"; this is an adaptation or misquotation of *Humanum genus est avidum nimus auricularum*: "the human race is too gossip-hungry" (Lucretius, *De Rerum Natura*, iv. 594).
8 Nov. Org. lib, ii. aph. 29.

50

Do We Need Immortality?

Grace M. Jantzen

The doctrine of life after death is often taken to be an essential ingredient in Christian theology. Baron Friedrich Von Hügel, when he said that "Religion, in its fullest development, essentially requires, not only this our little span of earthly years, but a life beyond,"[1] was only echoing the words of St Paul: "If in this life only we have hope in Christ, we are of all men most miserable."[2] And more recently, others, among them John Hick, have devoted much energy to a consideration of life after death. Hick writes that "Any religious understanding of human existence – not merely one's own existence but the life of humanity as a whole – positively requires some kind of immortality belief and would be radically incoherent without it."[3]

In this article I propose to look behind the arguments for and against the possibility of life after death, to investigate the various motives for wanting it, ranging from the frivolously irreligious to the profound. I shall argue that the belief in immortality is not so central to Christian thought and practice as is often believed, and indeed that a rich Christian faith does not require a doctrine of life after death in order to be profound and meaningful.

Self-Regarding Motives

To begin with the obvious, our desire for immortality is not a desire for just any sort of continued

Grace M. Jantzen, "Do We Need Immortality?" from *Modern Theology* 1:1 (1984), pp. 33–44. Copyright © Blackwell Publishers Ltd., Oxford.

existence: the less musical among us might prefer extinction to an eternity of playing harps and singing hymns, and given a choice, we would all prefer extinction to hell. H. H. Price has offered a picture of a life after death which is entirely the product of our desires – but which might turn out to be a highly undesirable state. In his description, the post-mortem world is a world in which our wishes would immediately fulfil themselves, a world whose laws "would be more like the laws of Freudian psychology than the laws of physics".[4] As Price points out, this might be much less pleasant than we might have thought; because our desires, when we include all those we have repressed, are not in mutual harmony. They incorporate, for instance, desires for punishment and suffering for the wrongs we have done. He offers the following grim comments: "Each man's purgatory, would be just the automatic consequence of his own desires; if you like, he would punish himself by having just those images which his own good feelings demand. But, if there is any consolation in it, he would have those unpleasant experiences because he wanted to have them; exceedingly unpleasant as they might be, there would still be something in him which was satisfied by them."[5] Price's point is that if all our repressed desires suddenly came true, this would be horrifying, and we would have to set about the difficult process of altering our characters so that when we get what we want, we want what we get.

The popular desire for immortality is very little like this. Life after death is often pictured, rather, as the fulfilment of longings for pleasure: it will be a paradise where there will be no more suffering and pain, where we will be happily reunited with those we love in perpetual feasting and gladness. It must be admitted that some religious pictures of heaven reinforce this frankly hedonistic conception. In the Koran we find that heaven is a beautiful garden filled with fruits and flowers. "There the Muslims drink the wine they have been denied on earth, wine that has no after-effects. It is brought to them by handsome youths, and dark-eyed houris wait on their every pleasure."[6] Similar descriptions of a hedonistic paradise of feasting and delight can be found in Christian writings, except that the dark-eyed houris are conspicuously absent, probably because of Christianity's long-standing suspicion of the sorts of delights the presence of these creatures would signal.

One of the appeals of such a description of paradise is that in this eternal delight there is no more separation from those we love; we are all eternally reunited. This, however, might prove a mixed blessing. Apart from the fact that with some of those we love, the relationship improves if there are periods of space between our togetherness, there is also the consideration that heaven would not be a private party – everyone is invited. Now, what might it be like to find oneself at the heavenly feast seated next to a Neanderthal man? Surely conversation would lag, and it is doubtful whether the silences could be filled by enjoyment of the same food. Christianity has sometimes avoided this social embarrassment by consigning the vast majority of mankind to hell, but that is not a possibility with which many of us could acquiesce and still enjoy the feast.

The point behind these frivolous comments is that it is not quite so easy to give a picture of unending delight as might be thought; it is against scenarios of this sort that Bernard Williams' comments on the tedium of immortality have some point.[7] A paradise of sensuous delights would become boring; it would in the long run be pointless and utterly unfulfilling. We can perhaps imagine ways of making a very long feast meaningful; we do, after all, cope with lengthy terrestrial social occasions by choosing interesting conversational partners, and making the dinner occasions not merely for food and drink but also for stimulating discussion and for giving and receiving friendship the value of which extends beyond the termination of the dinner. But if the feasting literally never came to an end, if there were no progress possible from the sensuous enjoyment of paradise to anything more meaningful, then we might well wish, like Elina Macropolis, to terminate the whole business

and destroy the elixir of youth. It is important to notice, however, that on this view survival is tedious simply because there is no progress, no point to the continued existence except the satisfaction of hedonistic desires. But this picture is much too simple-minded. Christians (and Muslims too, of course) have long recognized this, and have taken the hedonistic descriptions of the Scriptures as symbolic of something more meaningful than eternal self-indulgence, as we shall see.

Death is sometimes seen as evil because it means the curtailment of projects; immortality would be required to give significance to life because it would allow those projects to be meaningfully continued. Of course, most of our projects would not require all eternity to complete. But even in this life, one enterprise leads to another, and provided endless progress were possible, we might pursue an endless series of challenging and absorbing tasks, each one developing into another, without any risk of boredom. This might also give more point to some of our earthly projects: the painstaking acquisition of languages and techniques would be worthwhile beyond the few years we have to employ them here. This way of thinking about survival is probably more attractive to an intellectual whose current projects could easily be extended into the future, than, say, to a labourer who considers the prospect of endless projects as enough to make him feel tired already. Still, given the opportunity, perhaps he too would develop interests which he would genuinely like to pursue.

The notion that life after death would provide an opportunity for the fulfilment of projects is not, of course, presented as an argument for the likelihood of survival but as an argument for its desirability. But does it succeed? There is considerable pull toward saying that it does, especially for those who have far more interests than they can possibly develop even assuming an average life-span. An after-life in which we could all pursue what we are really interested in without worrying about earning daily bread or having the notion that the project itself is fulfilling – so that a fulfilled person is one who completes fulfilling projects – but then we have gone round in a circle. Personal fulfilment involves something like actualizing our potential, completing projects which "do ourselves justice". But this then is problematical again: what is meant by "our potential"? If it means the whole variety of things that many of us would enjoy doing and could do well with suitable training, then this life is much too short for fulfilment, and immortality appears attractive.

Grace M. Jantzen

But while this shows that immortality may be desirable (for some people, in some forms) it is possible to give an alternative account of fulfilment which does not require survival. If death is seen as the limit of life, then "death gains what significance it has, not by serving as a state characterizing things, but as a function which orders members of the limited series".[8] Thus if we take seriously the fact that our existence will terminate, this will affect our choice about life: if we will not live forever, then we must do while we can those things which are really important to do. On this view, a fulfilled person would be a person who picked such projects for his life that were genuinely worthwhile and suitable for his abilities and aptitudes, and was able to bring them to completion: Einstein, who lived to an old age and had accomplished significant projects, would be described as fulfilled, but a person who never had any projects at all, and lived in continuous aimless frustration, "In the evening saying 'Would it were morning' and in the morning saying 'Would it were evening'" would not be so describable. Neither would be the person who had projects but died before he could accomplish them. We do distinguish fulfilled and unfulfilled people in these ways, without reference to immortality. This does not of course mean that immortality is not desirable, especially for those who through no fault of their own are not able to complete their projects in their life-times. But it does mean that we do not have to postulate an after-life to make sense of the very concept of fulfilled and meaningful human life.

Also, if death is a limit, this gives a significance and urgency to our choices which they would not otherwise have. If we could go on pursuing an endless series of projects, it might not matter very much which ones we chose first: we could always do others later. Nor would it matter how vigorously we pursued them – for there would always be more time – nor how challenging they were or how well they developed us and brought out the best in us – for there would always be other opportunities. But if fulfilment is something which must be reached in this life if it is to be reached at all, we will be far less cavalier about the choices we make affecting our own fulfilment, and also, very importantly, in our relationships with others for whose fulfilment we are partly responsible. A great many of our projects, and arguably the most significant of them, have to do not merely with ourselves but with others: our fulfilment is not simply a matter of, say, satisfying our individual intellectual curiosities, but is bound up with the fulfilment of family, friends, students.

If we really have only this life, then enjoyment and fulfilment cannot be postponed to another, either for ourselves or for those we care about.

Moral Motives

It is sometimes argued that immortality is required on moral grounds. Such an argument can take the Kantian form: immortality is necessary as a postulate of practical reason. Since the Summum Bonum involves happiness as well as virtue, and since in this life we often find a disparity between the two, it is necessary to postulate a life after death where the imbalance will be redressed. Otherwise the universe is ultimately unjust, out of joint.

I do not wish to linger long over this, but simply make three points, none of them original. First, maybe we should just admit that the universe is out of joint; it hardly seems obvious, even (or especially) from the point of view of Christian theology, that it is not. Second, even if it is, that does not rob morality – even on a Kantian system – of its point. An act of intrinsic worth is still worthwhile even if it will never receive any happiness in reward; furthermore, morality retains its meaning even if we are all going to perish. (It is not pointless for the dying to show kindness to one another.) Those who say that if there is no life after death then nothing – including morality – in this life is meaningful are implicitly admitting that there is nothing in this life which is worthwhile for its own sake, independent of eternal consequences; that everything, even love, is only a means to an end, and an end which this life cannot give. Kant himself could not have accepted such a view. Third, the Kantian view of reward has a peculiarity. What sort of happiness is it which is to be the reward of virtue? Suppose we think of it as some variant of the hedonistic paradise described earlier: then for reasons already given, the more moral one was – the more one valued that which was intrinsically good – the less happiness one would find in such ultimately pointless eternal self-indulgence. On the other hand, if Kant was speaking of the satisfactions of fulfilment rather than of a hedonistic utopia, then for the one who truly pursues virtue, becoming virtuous will itself be the fulfilment; virtue will be its own reward.

A more interesting argument for the requirement of immortality arises, not from the idea that virtue needs to be rewarded, but from the fact that none of us is sufficiently virtuous. If part of the point of life is moral development, and none of us develops fully in this life, would it not be desirable for this process to continue beyond the grave? There is considerable connection between this argument and the previous ones; except that here there is no request for happiness as a compensation for virtue, but rather for fulfilment of the very virtue that one has sought, albeit with only moderate success. There are at least two aspects of this, which I shall consider separately.

The first is encapsulated by Dostoyevsky in *The Brothers Karamazov*. "Surely I haven't suffered simply that I, my crimes and my sufferings, may manure the soil of the future harmony for somebody else. I want to see with my own eyes the hind lie down with the lion and the victim rise up and embrace his murderer. I want to be there when everyone suddenly understands what it has all been for."[9] This is not a desire for happiness in any hedonistic sense, but a desire to see the point, the fruition of all one's efforts. It is a natural enough human desire, of course; yet I do not think that it can be used as an argument that morality requires immortality, for the assumption here surely is that all the toil and suffering does have a point, whether we are "there" to understand it in the end or not. Even if we are not present at the final denouement, this does not make working toward it less worthwhile, for once again, the value of doing that cannot depend on what we individually get out of it. Although Dostoyevsky here touches, as he so often does, a very deep nerve of desire, he surely cannot be interpreted to mean that if that desire remains forever unfulfilled, there was no meaning to the suffering in the first place.

The second aspect of the longing for immortality is the longing for perfection in virtue. This is part of what prompted the more positive conceptions of purgatory, where that was seen not as a place of retributive punishment until one had suffered proportionately to the sins one had committed on earth, but rather as a place of moral purification and advance, "Where human spirits purge themselves, and train / To leap up into joy celestial."[10] This, clearly, is not an unworthy motive for desiring life after death (though in more cynical moments one might wonder how universally it is shared – how many people desire immortality because they truly want to become better). Yet it too has some problems.

In the first place, it is not obvious that simple extension of life would result in moral improvement: more time can be opportunity for deterioration as well as for advance; the person who says, "I would

be better, if only I had a little longer" is justifiably suspect. Still, although time does not automatically produce growth, it may be true that it is necessary for growth. But once again it is worth thinking about the concept of death as a limit. If immortality is denied, and if moral growth is valued, there is an urgency to moral improvement, both for oneself and for others, which might easily be ignored if it were thought that there was endless time available. And as we have already seen, it will not do to say that such moral improvement, with its struggle and frequent failure, would be worthless if all ends at death, for this would hold true only if moral improvement were a means to an end, rather than intrinsically valuable.

Religious Motives

Those who say that immortality will be the scene of moral progress do not, of course, usually have in mind nothing but temporal extension to bring this about: as Fichte once said, "By the mere getting oneself buried, one cannot arrive at blessedness."[11] Rather, they believe that in the life after death there will be some strong inducements to improvement. In Price's non-theistic purgatory the unpleasantness of getting what we want may lead us to revise our desires and characters, while according to some theistic conceptions of purgatory, the punishments for our sins will purge us – sometimes in Clockwork Orange fashion – of our innate sinfulness. The most interesting theory of inducement to moral perfection, and one that forms a bridge to specifically religious arguments for the need for immortality, is the idea that the lure of divine love, more obvious in the next life than in this one, will progressively wean us from our self-centeredness and purify us so that at last our response will be perfect love reciprocated. John Hick, in his discussion of universal salvation, argues that given the assumption that man has been created by God and is "basically oriented towards him, there is no final opposition between God's saving will and our human nature acting in freedom".[12] Thus God, extending his love ever again towards us, will not take "no" for an answer but will ultimately woo successfully, not by overriding our freedom, but by winning us over so that eventually we freely choose him and his perfection. Hick says, "if there is continued life after death, and if God is ceaselessly at work for the salvation of his children, it follows that he will continue to be at work until the work is done; and I have been arguing that it is logically possible for him eventually to fulfil his saving purpose without at any point overriding our human freedom."[13]

But even granting Hick's basic assumptions of humanity's created bias toward God, God in loving pursuit of men and women, and endless time for "the unhurried chase", there are still problems with his conclusion. It is not clear that genuine freedom could be preserved while still guaranteeing the ultimate result: surely if there is freedom there is always the possibility of refusal. Hick's response, presumably, would be to agree that refusal is possible but that, given his assumptions, it becomes less and less likely as time goes on. Yet significantly to the extent that theists, Hick among them, wish to use the fact of human freedom as a (partial) resolution of the problem of evil, one aspect of their defence is that, though persons were created with a bias toward God, their freedom made it possible for them to choose rebellion, thus bringing moral evil in its train: evil is the price of freedom gone wrong. I do not see how one can have it both ways: if evil choices were made in the past even when there seemed no particular reason for them, how can Hick be confident that they will not be repeated endlessly in the future, especially since in the latter case they are made by characters already considerably warped by previous evil choices? The only way that I can see out of this for Hick is by increasing the emphasis on the divine pressure, but that runs the risk of undermining the very freedom which must here be preserved.

It is important to see the implications of human freedom for a Christian doctrine of redemption. One aspect of choice not sufficiently considered is its finality. Of course decisions can sometimes be reversed; we can often change our minds. And when we do so, when there is genuine repentance and conversion, Christianity teaches that God "makes all things new", brings creativity out of chaos, Easter out of Calvary. But the fact that we can sometimes freely change our minds is not the same as saying that in the end it makes no difference what our intermediate choices are because ultimately we will all (freely) be brought to the same goal. If it is true that whether I choose p or not-p, in the end I will get p, the idea of choice has been robbed of all significance – and that is so even if I can be persuaded that in the end it will really be p that I do want. So if I perpetually choose selfishness and distrust and dishonesty, and my character is formed by these choices, it seems perverse to say

that eventually these choices will be reversed and I will attain the same moral perfection as I would have if I had all along chosen integrity and compassion. Part of what it means to be free is that our choices have consequences; it is playing much too lightly with the responsibility of freedom to suggest that these consequences, at least in their effects upon ourselves, are always reversible, even if only in the endless life to come. For that matter, if everyone is perfected, then even the consequences of our choices upon others will finally be overridden: all, in the end, will be as though no one had ever chosen evil at all. Morally revolting as is the thought of God committing people to eternal flames, one of the reasons why traditional theology has so long retained a doctrine of hell is surely to guard this aspect of freedom: there is no such thing as automatic salvation.

In spite of the strong reinforcement which the belief in immortality receives from Scripture and Christian tradition, a surprising amount can also be found which calls into question the idea that immortality is a religious requirement. In the first place, it is sometimes held that, of all the evils and sufferings in this world, death is the worst. On a traditional theistic view, evil must eventually be overcome, and all the wrongs made good; and this requires that death, "the last enemy", may not be proud. Death, too, shall die, when all who have ever lived will live again. This assumes, of course, that death is an evil; and if what I have said about death as a limit is correct, then that cannot be retained without some qualifications. Still, although death is not the worst evil, and not an unqualified evil, this does not amount to saying that it is not an evil at all; consequently in a world where evil was eradicated, death, too, would have no place.

But can this be used as an argument for a religious requirement of life after death? I am not sure that it can. If the perfect world dawns, death will perhaps not be found in it; but does this mean that death in this very imperfect world is followed by immortality? One might argue that only if it is, is God just: the sufferings of this present world can only be justified by the compensation of eternal life. But this, in the first place, is shocking theodicy: it is like saying that I may beat my dog at will provided that I later give him a dish of his favourite liver chowder. What happens after death – no matter how welcome – does not make present evil good.[14] But if life after death cannot be thought of as a compensation for otherwise unjustified present evils, surely death itself – permanent extinction

– must be an evil from which a Christian may hope to escape? Well, on what grounds? We do not escape other evils and sufferings which a perfect world would not contain; why should we expect to escape this one? A Christian surely must recognize that there are many aspects of the problem of evil which he cannot explain; maybe he should just accept that death is another one. But would not death make the problem of evil not just more mysterious than it already is, but actually in principle unsolvable? Wouldn't we have to conclude that God is unjust? I don't know. If we can retain a belief in divine justice amid present evil and suffering, horrific as it is, I am not sure that relinquishing the prospect of life after death would necessarily alter the case. Of course it might tip the balance psychologically, making us "of all men, most miserable", but that is another matter. If the present evils can be relegated to the mysterious purposes of God, it seems presumptuous to assume that these purposes could not include our extinction.

A very persuasive argument for the requirement for immortality for Christian theology gathers up strands from several of these lines of thought, but places special emphasis on the personal love of God. If, as Christians maintain, God loves and values each of us individually, then we can trust him not to allow us to perish forever. We are worth more to him than that. Thus Helen Oppenheimer, in her discussion of problems of life after death, recognizes the great philosophical complexities regarding personal identity, resurrection, and the rest, but finally says that if we believe in God at all, we must also believe that if we keep on looking we will find the solution to these problems, because it is as unthinkable that a loving God would permit a relationship with one he loves to be severed by extinction of that loved one as it is to think that we would willingly allow our dearest friends to perish if it were in our power to provide them with a full and rich life.[15]

This approach has the merit, first of not pretending that the puzzles of identity and/or resurrection are easily solvable, second, of treating death seriously, and third, of placing the doctrine of immortality within the context of a doctrine of personal relationship with God. Death is not seen as a mild nuisance which can be quickly left behind never to be repeated; immortality is not automatic, and could not be expected at all were it not for the intervention of an omnipotent God. It is only because Christianity stakes itself on the unfailing love of God, following the man who dared to call

God "Father" rather than "Judge", that life after death can even be considered.

But even though this seems to me a sounder starting place, given basic assumptions of Christian theology, than the belief that human beings are endowed with naturally immortal souls, I still have problems with it. It is comforting to be told that the love of God will not allow the termination of a relationship with him; it is also much more religiously satisfying to see this relationship as of central importance, and all the descriptions of the delights of paradise as mere symbolic gropings after the enjoyment of this divine fellowship. Nevertheless, Christian theology does hold that there are other things which are precious to God and which, in spite of that, perish forever. Christian theologians increasingly recognize that it is not the case that the whole earth, every primrose, every songbird, all the galaxies of all the heavens, exist for the benefit of humanity alone. Yet if it is true that God brought about the existence of all these things and takes delight in them, then it is also true that some of the things he delights in perish forever: a popular book of natural history estimates that 99 per cent of all species of animals which have lived on earth are now extinct.[16]

We cannot have it both ways. "Are not three sparrows sold for a farthing?" Jesus asked. "Yet not one of them falls to the ground without your heavenly Father's knowledge."[17] These words of Jesus have often (and rightly) been taken as his teaching of the tender concern of the Father for all his creatures; what has not been noticed so often is that Jesus never denies that sparrows do fall. If the analogy which Jesus is drawing to God's care for persons (who, he says, "are of more value than many sparrows") is taken to its logical conclusion, the implication, surely, is not that we will not die but that our death will not go unnoticed. If a Christian admits that God allows some things which he values to perish, it will need further argument to show why this should not also be true of human beings: the primroses, presumably, are not loved less simply because they are temporary.

But perhaps they are temporary because they are loved less? Because they are not of such enduring worth to God (as human beings are) they are allowed to perish? This still leaves me uneasy. It is one thing to believe that we are individually valued by God, and valued perhaps in a way that other things are not; it is quite another to say that this value must result in our immortality. How can we be so sure? The analogy with persons we love whom we would not willingly allow to perish assumes that our relationship with God is in this respect just like our relationship with them. But even if we accept this analogy as the best we have for our relationship with God, we must still admit that there must be considerable disanalogies as well: how do we know that the case of endless preservation is not one of them? We may believe that God looks upon us with love and compassion, but that does not seem to me to be any guarantee that he wills our everlasting existence – that is a further (very large) step. We are taught, to be sure, that God wishes to bring us to eternal life; but it is a glaring confusion to equate eternal life with endless survival. As the notion of eternal life is used in the Johannine writings, for instance, it is spoken of as a present possession, a quality of life, not a limitless quantity; nor is it something that happens after death but in this present lifetime.

Furthermore, if there were no life after death, this in itself would not mean that religion would be pointless. Just as that which is morally valuable is valuable for its own sake and not for the reward it can bring, so also trust in God, if it is worthwhile at all, is worthwhile even if it cannot go on forever. A relationship with another human being does not become pointless just because at some time it will end with the death of one of the partners; why should it be thought that a relationship with God would be pointless if one day it too should end? Shneur Zalman, the Jewish founder of the Chabad, once exclaimed, "Master of the Universe! I desire neither Paradise nor Thy bliss in the world to come. I desire Thee and Thee alone."[18] And the hymn of Fenelon has become the common property of Christendom:

My God I love Thee: not because I hope for
heaven thereby,
Nor yet because who love Thee not are lost
eternally . . .

Not for the sake of winning heaven, nor of
escaping hell;
Not from the hope of gaining aught, not
seeking a reward;
But as thyself hast loved me, O ever loving
Lord . . .
Solely because thou art my God and my most
loving King.[19]

It is true, of course, that these words (and many more examples could be given) were written by men who did believe in immortality; the point, however, is that according to them, the value of the relationship with God, the vision of God, cannot be measured by measuring its temporal duration.

But perhaps it will still be objected that if God will one day allow me to perish, this shows that all the teaching about his love for me is a vast fraud – if he really loved me, he would preserve my life. I can only reply that for reasons already given, this does not seem obvious to me. I cannot forget the primroses. They perish. Must we conclude that they are not precious to God?

I am not arguing that there is no life beyond the grave or that it is irrational to hope for it or for Christians to commit their future to God in trust. But if what I have said is correct, then it would be presumptuous to be confident that life after death is a matter of course, guaranteed, whatever the problems, by the requirements of morality and religion. We should not neglect the significant change of verb in the Nicene Creed: from affirmations "I believe in God", "I believe in Jesus Christ", and so on, we come to the rather more tentative "And I look for the resurrection of the dead and the life of the world to come." Christian faith and Christian commitment bases itself not first and foremost on a hope of survival of death, but on the intrinsic value of a relationship with God, without any reservations about what the future holds – here or hereafter.

Notes

1 Baron F. Von Hügel, *Eternal Life*, 2nd edition (Edinburgh: T. & T. Clark, 1913), p. 396.
2 I Cor. 15: 19.
3 John Hick, *Death and Eternal Life* (London: Fontana, 1976), p. 11.
4 H. H. Price, "Survival and the Idea of 'Another World'", in J. Donnelly (ed.), *Language, Metaphysics and Death* (New York: Fordham University Press, 1978), p. 193.
5 Ibid., p. 192.
6 Alfred Guillaume, *Islam*, 2nd edition (Harmondsworth, Middlesex: Penguin, 1954), p. 198.
7 Bernard Williams, "The Macropolis Case: Reflections of the Tedium of Immortality", in his *Problems of the Self* (Cambridge: Cambridge University Press, 1973).
8 James Van Evra, "On Death as a Limit", in Donnelly, *Language, Metaphysics and Death*, p. 25.

9   F. Dostoyevsky, *The Brothers Karamazov*, II. V. 4.

10 Dante, *The Divine Comedy: Purgatory*, I. 5 & 6.

11 Fichte, *Sämmtliche Werke Vol. 5* (1845–6), p. 403, quoted in Von Hügel, *Eternal Life*, p. 176.

12 Hick, *Death and Eternal Life*, p. 254.

13 Ibid., p. 258. "Salvation" as Hick uses the term involves moral perfection.

14 And of course it may put a different complexion on things that were perceived as evil in our imperfect state of knowledge, so that we see that it was a necessary condition for good; but that is not at issue here.

15 Helen Oppenheimer in a University Sermon preached in St Mary's, Oxford, in 1979.

16 Richard E. Leakey, *The Making of Mankind* (London: Book Club Associates, 1981), p. 20.

17 Matt. 10: 29.

18 Quoted in Isidore Epstein, *Judaism* (Harmondsworth, Middlesex: Penguin, 1959), p. 279.

19 Quoted from *Hymns Ancient and Modern*, 106.

51

Why We Need Immortality

Charles Taliaferro

There is no such thing as a natural death: nothing that happens to a man is ever natural, since his presence calls the world into question. All men must die: but for every man his death is an accident and, even if he knows it and consents to it, an unjustifiable violation.

Simone de Beauvoir[1]

In an early volume of *Modern Theology* Grace Jantzen raises doubts about whether we should give an affirmative answer to the question in her article title "Do We Need Immortality?"[2] She does not argue that there is no life after death, nor that it is irrational for anyone to hope for immortality. But she does contend that certain portraits of the afterlife are religiously and morally suspect, that the existence of an afterlife does not substantially alter the theistic problem of evil, and that our survival of death cannot be inferred from the fact that God is loving. I am in agreement with Ms Jantzen's characteristically stimulating and astute paper at many points, especially with her stance that "Christian faith and Christian commitment bases itself not first and foremost on a hope of survival of death, but on the intrinsic value of a relationship with God" (p. 43 [580]). Nonetheless, I believe she does not sufficiently appreciate the nature and desirability of life after death as it is envisioned in classical Christianity.

Charles Taliaferro, "Why We Need Immortality," from *Modern Theology* 6:4 (1990), pp. 367–77. Copyright © Blackwell Publishers Ltd., Oxford.

The Value of Life After Death

Ms Jantzen correctly points out that bare survival of death may not be at all desirable, but could be horrifying. Moreover, few would argue with her that certain forms of the afterlife may also be undesirable owing to their boring or tedious character. Ms Jantzen underscores some of the drawbacks of dining with neanderthals (p. 34 [575]) and the rich but limited value to endless feasting.

> A paradise of sensuous delights would become boring, it would in the long run be pointless and utterly unfulfilling. We can perhaps imagine ways of making a very long feast meaningful; we do, after all, cope with lengthy terrestrial social occasions by choosing interesting conversational partners, and making the dinner occasions not merely for food and drink but also for stimulating discussion and for giving and receiving friendship the value of which extends beyond the termination of the dinner. But if the feasting literally never came to an end, if there were no progress possible from the sensuous enjoyment of paradise to anything more meaningful, then we might well wish, like Elina Macropolis, to terminate the whole business and destroy the elixir of youth. (pp. 34–5 [575])

Even an eternal life of intellectually stimulating projects would become wearisome. She paints the outcome of pursuing everlasting projects in terms which may please the procrastinator.

If we could go on pursuing an endless series of projects, it might not matter very much which ones we chose first: we could always do others later. Nor would it matter how vigorously we pursued them – for there would always be more time – nor how challenging they were or how well they developed us and brought out the best in us – for there would always be other opportunities. But if fulfillment is something which must be reached in this life if it is to be reached at all, we will be far less cavalier about the choices we make affecting our own fulfillment, and also, very importantly, in our relationships with others for whose fulfillment we are partly responsible. (p. 36 [576])

If there is no life after death, the projects of this life as well as the feasts, friendships, and sensuous delights assume a great importance and value. If there is an afterlife we face the problem of being cavalier with this one.

In assessing Ms Jantzen's position, let us distinguish two general sorts of goods, what we may call time-enclosed goods and non-time-enclosed goods. A time-enclosed good is any good project, thing, event, state or process which is good but its good value is not preserved if it is temporally unlimited in extent. Thus, your eating a tasty meal is good, but a time-enclosed good, for surely your meal would lose its good value if it were to continue uninterrupted for a year or a thousand years or be everlasting in temporal extent. It is not necessarily bad or evil for a time-enclosed good to cease to be. A non-time-enclosed good is any good project, event, state or process which is good and its good value is not lost if it is temporally unlimited in extent.

If everlasting life after death for you and me is something good and, thus, something to be desired, this continued life must be imagined to consist in more than pursual of a singular time-enclosed good. Perhaps there could be one exception to this which I mention only to set to one side. Imagine you endlessly pursue some singular time-enclosed good, but owing, say, to a continuous lapse of memory you fail to realize your ongoing activity. The meal before you is the same you have had for several millennia but, not being aware of your endless dining, the meal surprises you and seems as fresh and unusual as ever. This strategy could also be deployed against the problem of being cavalier noted above. Perhaps we would only treat some projects in a cavalier fashion if we *knew* there would be endless opportunity to pursue them. The problem

could be avoided if we posit a world in which there are endless opportunities for us to act upon but we do not realize it. Imagine we will live forever but we think our lives could end at any point. Such a defense of the afterlife is too desperate. The resulting portrait of God's hampering our memory and forever keeping secret our immortality so that we may not be bored with life after death seems pitiful at best. Let us also put to one side what may be called biological skepticism. A critic may allow that there could, in principle, be a non-time-enclosed good for you and me, but, owing to our biological makeup, our need for sleep and so on, it is not possible for us to partake in it. If the God who preserves us in existence after death is omnipotent, presumably none of these biological obstacles need keep us from partaking in the good. I know of no reason why you and I might not enjoy a life after death in a profoundly different embodiment.[3]

In my view, Ms Jantzen fails to give sufficient attention to the possibility of there being some singular non-time-enclosed good. In this life we may not be able to appreciably grasp the character of this great good, but then it might be odd if we could conceptually grasp it now. Orthodox and Catholic theology has identified this non-time-bound good as the beatific vision in which our beatitude is achieved in an experience of God's glory. It would be useful to explore the historical development of this understanding of final grace from philosophical, and religious sources (scriptural references Matt. 5: 8 and I John 3: 2 have figured prominently in its early theological development). However, as even the proponents of this understanding of "last things" insist on our present inability to imaginatively grasp this great good, appeal to a beatific vision will carry little weight with the skeptic, and I shall therefore pursue an alternative stance in what follows.

I do not think Ms Jantzen gives sufficient weight to the possibility of an afterlife with a great, perhaps indefinite variety or alteration of time-enclosed goods. Many ethicists have recognized the good of variety, *bonum variationis*.[4] We may well imagine an afterlife replete with an ever-altering mixture of goods including the sensuous, aesthetic, moral, intellectual, and religious. Such a portrait of the afterlife makes no appeal to experiences altogether dissimilar to those we are capable of having now, albeit in a piecemeal sometimes marred form. I believe that being a person is itself a non-time-enclosed good precisely because it is possible for a person to engage in a rich, perhaps endless variety of time-enclosed goods. In other words, it is good and desirable for you to forever partake of goods in an ever-altering pattern despite the fact that only partaking of a single one of these goods without interruption would become undesirable. Some time-enclosed goods may involve enterprises which lose their value after being performed only once. But it is difficult to believe all our time-enclosed goods have this character. Of course, there may come a point when an individual person, Miriam, loses the desire to live and whose life becomes so engulfed in pain that we think her death would be merciful. But if we are to make any sense out of the sorrow we feel over her death, surely we must see her death as the ending of something valuable. I submit that Miriam's good or value cannot be exhausted or fulfilled in any absolute final sense in this life. She is dying, and death under current physical conditions may be the least worst alternative, but surely (if we love her) her continued life under healthier, perhaps we should say glorious, conditions is what we should prefer, if such an alternative were available. I argue later that if we have reason to believe God loves her fully and deeply, we have reason to believe God will preserve the life of Miriam who, as a person, possesses a good or value which is not exhausted over time.

Ms Jantzen makes no suggestion that God is bored with either Godself or the world. If Ms Jantzen is correct in her view of the limited goods of an endless life, why should not God desire "to terminate the whole business"? Perhaps God has no desire to do so because God is a non-time-enclosed good or because of the endless created order of ever-changing time-enclosed goods God delights in. If God has reason not to be bored or weary of a deathless life, why could not you and I find everlasting life of value in virtue of even a minute participation in the goods that God delights in?[5]

If there are goods worthy of pursuit and interest, the problem of procrastination and being cavalier about one's projects seems to be a case of the problem of evil.

The Problem of Evil and Immortality

Ms Jantzen holds that the existence of an afterlife does not substantially alter the problem of evil facing the theist. She puts her point succinctly:

One might argue that only if it [the afterlife] is, is God just: the sufferings of this present world

can only be justified by the compensation of eternal life. But this, in the first place, is shocking theodicy: it is like saying that I may beat my dog at will provided that I later give him a dish of his favourite liver chowder. What happens after death – no matter how welcome – does not make present evil good. (p. 40 [578])

I agree that what occurs after death does not make what evil that occurs in this life good. But there are two important points that are overlooked.

First, whether or not there is an afterlife and what its character consists in has a bearing upon the extent of evil that exists in this life. Erik murdered Miriam out of deep malice. Imagine there is no afterlife. He is responsible for annihilating a person. Miriam has ceased to exist as a result of Erik's hateful act. Imagine there is an afterlife. Erik is still profoundly guilty for endeavoring to annihilate Miriam. Miriam has lost a great good, her present life and relations; perhaps the murder itself involved profound suffering. But Erik did not extinguish her life altogether. Belief in an afterlife need in no way reduce our moral convictions about the moral outrage and obscenity of murder. Still, if there is no afterlife, I judge the murder to have resulted in a far greater evil (Miriam's perishing altogether) than if there is an afterlife (Miriam still exists and some companionship and exchange with her is possible after death). I believe this to be the case with respect to the world's great evils as well. Consider the holocaust under two conditions: one in which millions were annihilated in an absolute sense, the other one in which the millions died but are not annihilated. Under either condition, Nazism remains a moral outrage and horror, but the evil perpetrated by the Nazis is worse if their victims ceased to be altogether and God allowed the millions who suffered to perish everlastingly.

Second, there are respects in which an evil may give rise to some good. Thus, many ethicists have argued that sorrowing over some past evil one has committed constitutes a good. It would be better if the evil Erik performed had never occurred. Given that it has occurred, his taking pleasure in his deed tends to enhance or aggravate the evil. In a converse fashion, there is a respect in which a sorrowful regret for a past act can be good.[6] You have grown to have a right relation to values, values you yourself imperiled. Giving a dog a nice meal after beating him does not make your having beaten him good. But just as the act could give rise to an additional evil (your later relishing the act and pleasure in the memory) it could also give rise to a good (perhaps you will embrace your dog with Franciscan tenderness). And if there is some afterlife for Erik and Miriam, perhaps too there is the opportunity for forgiveness and an altered profoundly good relationship. A world in which there is no such afterlife is one in which this greater good is unrealizable after death. Does it not seem that a loving Creator would want to provide occasion for this greater good?

What about the problem of the procrastinator who is given an opportunity to pursue the great goods of an afterlife and elects to reject them? Arguably, the mere fact that someone is confronted with something of great value and he is apprised of its goodness does not entail that he will love it. Grace Jantzen herself raises doubts about the depiction of an afterlife in works by John Hick in which all creatures come to embrace the love of God. On her view, Mr Hick's portrait of the afterlife involves an inadequate appreciation of the value of free will.

> Part of what it means to be free is that our choices have consequences. It is playing too lightly with the responsibility of freedom to suggest that these consequences, at least in their effects upon ourselves, are always reversible, even if only in the endless life to come. (p. 40 [578])

While I hope that the lives of all created persons here are followed by renewed opportunities for turning to God and overturning some of the evils we perpetrate in this life (through sorrowing over past evils and achieving some reconciliation with those we harm and have harmed us), I share Ms Jantzen's insistence upon the value of freedom. I therefore believe that the afterlife will not be forced on persons who continuously and relentlessly freely elect to perish everlastingly. But voluntary choices like this are only fully voluntary when made under certain conditions. Ignorance and connative impairment tend to vitiate freedom. For the choice of extinction to be fully voluntary, I think it needs to be made under conditions different from the ones that now prevail, conditions which can profoundly distort our exercise of free will. If someone elects to voluntarily perish then I think the person voluntarily wills an evil end, the destruction of a person. But if possession of freedom is good and it is good that persons have this power to elect a Godward life or Godless death, then this perishing must

be seen as a real possibility. The good of an afterlife and the good of this life is in no way lessened by supposing that a person may lose her life absolutely only under condition of fully voluntarily choosing to do so.[7]

The Love of God

I believe one of the most weighty motives for thinking there is an afterlife rests in the conviction that God is loving.[8] Ms Jantzen questions whether the appeal to Divine love provides a foundation for belief in an individual's survival of death.

> Christian theology does hold that there are other things which are precious to God and which, in spite of that, perish forever. Christian theologians increasingly recognize that it is not the case that the whole earth, every primrose, every songbird, all the galaxies of all the heavens, exist for the benefit of humanity alone. Yet it is true that God brought about the existence of all these things and delights in them, then it is also true that some of the things he delights in perish forever. (pp. 41–2 [579])

She goes on to point out that the limited, temporally finite character of many of our valued relationships is not to be valued less for its limitation.

> Just as that which is morally valuable is valuable for its own sake and not for the reward it can bring, so also trust in God, if it is worthwhile at all, is worthwhile even if it cannot go on forever. A relationship with another human being does not become pointless just because at some point it will end with the death of one of the partners; why should it be thought that a relationship with God would be pointless if one day it too should end. (pp. 42–3 [580])

I do not think this is altogether wrong. The commonplace dictum "A friendship that ends is no friendship" may not hold in all cases.

My reservations about Ms Jantzen's stance here rest upon her neglecting an important correlation between love and preferring the existence of the beloved to her non-existence. There may be different forms of love; some theologians distinguish love in terms of *philia*, *eros*, *amor*, *agape*, and *caritas*. Whatever its form, I believe there is what may be termed a vivifying feature of love. Consider Thomas

Charles Taliaferro

Carson's characterization of love in *The Status of Morality*:

> Whether someone loves or hates something on the whole is ultimately a function of how he is disposed to act. A person who loves something will choose or prefer its existence or occurrence to its non-existence or non-occurrence, all other things being equal, a person who hates something will choose or prefer its non-existence or non-occurrence to its existence or occurrence, all other things being equal.[9]

In his lively masterpiece, *On Love*, Ortega y Gasset expresses an analogous position in more poetic terms.

> Love itself is, by nature, a transitive act in which we exert ourselves on behalf of what we love. Although we are quiescent, when we are a hundred leagues from the object and not even thinking about it, if we love the object an indefinable flow of a warm and affirmative nature will emanate from us. This is clearly observable if we compare love with hate. To hate something or someone is not "being" passive, like being sad, but, in some way, it is a terribly negative action, ideally destructive of the hated object.[10]

While hatred aims at crippling the one hated and is often expressed in a pleasure in an enemy's misfortune, love delights in the fulfillment of the beloved and is expressed in a desire that the beloved find such fulfillment.

The Ortega–Carson account seems to me to be fundamentally correct, though I do not think their characterization of love succeeds as an *analysis* of what it is to love and hate. It is instead plausible to think that loving and the requisite preferring are two distinct acts or undergoings rather than a single state or thing. If the Ortega–Carson account were an analysis, love would be understood as not simply leading to the requisite preferences; love would be the preference designated. But as an analysis this faces the problem of accounting for the fact that I may prefer your existence to non-existence *because* I love you. My loving you may be the reason for my preference and thus my loving you does not consist solely in the preference itself. (Consider an analogy, Erik's being an unmarried male is not what explains his being a bachelor.

Being a bachelor simply is being an unmarried male. Loving you and preferring your existence seem different from this case, however, as the former can be employed to explain the latter.)

While Ortega's and Carson's depiction of love does not count as an analysis of what love is in itself, they are on the right track in their insistence upon the correlation of love and preference. Cases that appear to belie their thesis can be accounted for by specifying the many respects in which we love and hate others. Erik may claim to hate his parents and yet prefer their existence to their non-existence. But what precisely does Erik hate about his parents? He may hate their smugness, pretension, and abusiveness. According to our understanding of love and hatred, Erik's hatred of his parents' faults involves his preferring the non-existence of these faults rather than their existence. This is consistent with his preferring, all things considered, that his parents exist rather than not exist.[11]

Fundamental to Christianity is the belief that the cosmos is the result of God's creative loving activity. Insofar as God loves something, God prefers its existence to its non-existence. Insofar as God loves you and me, and loves us absolutely, God prefers our existence to non-existence and we may have confidence that God will uphold us in existence to the degree that we are confident that God loves us.

Let us return to Ms Jantzen's objections to this form of argument. Is it not true that God loves many things including many animals who pass out of existence? I am not sure how many things pass out of existence, nor am I sure whether (or how many) non-human animals enjoy some afterlife. However, I suggest that our theological reflection in this area be guided by our consideration of what constitutes the fulfillment or good of the thing loved. Earlier I contended that persons are themselves non-time-enclosed goods. That is, the complete fulfillment of a person is not exhausted by the fulfillment of some singular time-enclosed personal good activity (feasting). There is a transcendental character to persons such that our good or value is greater than the good or value of such undertakings. As such, to love a person deeply and profoundly is to prefer her rich and endless fulfillment rather than her non-existence or her existence under dire, unfulfilled conditions. Consider Ms Jantzen's case of a friendship between persons which is valuable despite the fact that it "cannot go on forever". Her stance seems plausible when the friends are both human and it is not within the power of either friend to preserve the other from annihilation. But I would seriously doubt the "love" of a partner who had it within her power to sustain me in existence, an existence in which I can flourish, and yet she either actively brought about my extinction or passively allowed me to perish irretrievably.

Perhaps God loves many things which do perish. My own conviction is that insofar as any creature has the kind of non-time-enclosed good which characterizes being a person, God will preserve it in being. If the case for treating dolphins and chimpanzees as persons is plausible, the case for their having an afterlife is plausible.

I defend this view further in the course of considering three objections:

1 Belief in an afterlife for persons introduces an undesirable dichotomy between persons and non-persons, humans and nature. Even if we believe that not all non-human animals will perish, our attitude to much of the "lower" animals is bound to be cavalier.

I do not think this follows at all. To love a person must be distinguishable from loving a non-person because persons have features non-persons do not. But the natural world of songbirds, plants, rocks and planets may still be loved and cherished as real, *bona fide* goods. That there is a natural world is good, and we must be careful to respect our kinship to fellow creatures who do not possess the transcendental powers of personhood.[12] I do not think my doubting that there is an afterlife for elephants compromises my concern for their preservation nor my convictions about the evils over our present cruel treatment of those and other non-human animals. As some proponents of animal rights have argued, the fact (if it is a fact) that non-human animals will not enjoy an afterlife may constitute an important case for vegetarianism and legal sanctions against killing non-human animals on the grounds that we should ensure that their lives are no shorter than they would be naturally.[13]

2 Belief in an afterlife is belief in something logically or metaphysically impossible. Created persons simply cannot survive death.

If this objection holds, then to desire to survive death is to desire something unrealizable.

Insofar as love is rational and it is irrational to desire or prefer something impossible, then the argument from Divine love falters indeed. But it is by no means obvious that an afterlife for humans is impossible. I have argued for its conceivability elsewhere and note that many philosophers who do not think we will survive death concede that such survival is at least possible.[14]

3 Isn't there something pretentious or presumptuous for us to believe in an afterlife? Such belief seems to be more of an expression of vain self-regard than disinterested love.

A true belief can be held for morally suspect reasons and undoubtedly some persons believe in an afterlife out of some colossal self-inflation. But surely it need not be vain or pompous of me to desire and hope for your survival of death out of my love for you. If our critic finds this impossible, I suspect he would "discover" egotism and pretentiousness behind all acts of love and compassion whatever.

I believe Ms Jantzen has ably brought to light the fact that Christians should not think "life after death is a matter of course" and "guaranteed", though our reasons for thinking this diverge somewhat. I think we should not do so because God's love of us and the created order has the character of a gracious, free gift and is not itself a matter of course. That God should have lovingly created us to begin with was not guaranteed. Thus, I do not think persons as such have a moral right to an afterlife. But I do think that if we have reason to believe God loves us deeply, we have reason to expect an afterlife and even to feel that our perishing absolutely would be a violation (to use Simone de Beauvoir's strong language). It would be a violation because it would violate a fundamental feature of love.[15]

In the course of my arguments I have not shown Ms Jantzen to be incorrect that "*a* rich Christian faith does not require a doctrine of life after death in order to be profound and meaningful" (p. 33 [574]; emphasis mine). There can be a variety of forms of Christianity and various levels of profundity and meaning. But I do hope to have drawn fuller attention to the motives behind why classical Christianity has found belief in the afterlife to have its peculiar centrality, meaning and profundity.

Notes

1 Simone de Beauvoir, *A Very Easy Death*, translated by Patrick O'Brien (New York: G. P. Putnam's Sons, 1966), p. 106.

2 Grace M. Jantzen, "Do We Need Immortality", *Modern Theology*, vol. 1, no. 1 (October 1984). All references to Jantzen's paper are noted in the text. [See also ch. 50, this volume; page numbers given in square brackets.]

3 I have defended the coherence of Divine omnipotence in "The Magnitude of Omnipotence", *International Journal for Philosophy of Religion*, vol. 14 (1983), pp. 99–106, and discussed ways in which God might enhance our powers in "Nagel's Vista or Taking Subjectivity Seriously", *The Southern Journal of Philosophy*, vol. XXVI, no. 3 (1988), pp. 395–6. See references in note 14 below.

4 The good of variety itself is underscored by various ethicists, including F. Brentano, G. E. Moore, and George Kratkov. See R. M. Chisholm's *Brentano and Intrinsic Value* (Cambridge: Cambridge University Press, 1986) for a defense of the *bonum variationis* as a distinctive category of values.

5 Thomas Morris makes a related point in his criticism of the process theological treatment of life after death, "God and the World", *Process Theology*, edited by Ronald Nash (Grand Rapids: Baker Book House, 1987).

6 See Chisholm, *Brentano and Intrinsic Value*. This has also been argued vigorously by Robert Nozick in *Philosophical Explanations* (Cambridge: Harvard University Press, 1981).

7 I address this issue in "Does God Violate Your Right to Privacy?", *Theology*, vol. XCII (May 1989).

8 Traditional Christian apologetics has emphasized the evidence of the historical resurrection of Jesus Christ as a principal reason for believing in life after death. In this paper I lay stress on an argument from the love of God as the early Christian portrayal of Christ's resurrection is itself supposed to be evidence of God's special loving activity.

9 Thomas Carson, *The Status of Morality* (Boston: Reidel, 1984), p. 3.

10 Ortega y Gasset, *On Love* (New York: Meridian, 1957), p. 47.

11 For an illuminating account of love and attendant notions of preferring the existence to the non-existence of the beloved, see William Hasker, "On Regretting the Evils of this World", *Southern Journal of Philosophy*, vol. XIX, no. 4 (1981), pp. 425–37.

12 The existence of a rock may be good, even a non-time-enclosed good, and worthy of our taking pleasure in. But the language of love in which we desire not just the existence but the fulfillment of the beloved makes little sense when used of a rock. There is a large difference between being a fulfilled person and an unfulfilled person, but I have no idea of what it would mean for there to be an unfulfilled rock. I follow Joel Feinberg's view of rocks, plants and non-human animals in "The Rights of Animals and Unborn Generations", *Rights, Justice and the Bounds of Liberty* (Princeton: Princeton University Press, 1980).

13 See Tom Regan's *The Case for Animal Rights* (Berkeley: University of California Press, 1983).

14 See "Pollock's Body Switching", *The Philosophical Quarterly*, vol. 36, no. 4 (October 1985), pp. 57–61; "Dualism and the Problem of Individuation", *Religious Studies*, 22 (1986), pp. 263–76; "A Modal Argument for Dualism", *Southern Journal of Philosophy*, vol. XXIV, no. 1 (Spring 1986), pp. 95–108. In the last article I critically assess works by John Pollock, D. M. Armstrong, Richard Boyd, and David Lewis, all of whom think a kind of bodiless, post-mortem personal life is possible but will not occur. My own work has aimed at establishing the coherence of an afterlife on the basis of a plausible dualist understanding of persons. Ms Jantzen's own philosophical anthropology and theistic world-view is non-dualist in character. See her fascinating *God's World, God's Body* (Philadelphia: The Westminster Press, 1984) and our debate about Divine incorporeality in *Modern Theology*, vol. 3, no. 2 (January 1987). Even if a dualist understanding of created persons is rejected, I believe that a plausible alternative physicalist account of individual afterlife can be constructed. See Bruce Reichenbach's *Is Man the Phoenix? A Study* of *Immortality* (Grand Rapids: Wm. B. Eerdmans, 1978).

15 It would be obviously fallacious to argue that there is an afterlife simply on the grounds that we would find it desirable. A more sophisticated argument from desire can be developed and I refer the reader to Robert Holyer's "The Argument from Desire", *Faith and Philosophy*, vol. 5, no. 1 (January 1988), pp. 61–71.

52

Is Liberation (*mokṣa*) Pleasant?

A. Chakrabarti

I thus perceived that I was in a state of great peril, and I compelled myself to seek with all my strength for a remedy, *however uncertain it might be*; as a sick man struggling with a deadly disease . . . is compelled to seek such a remedy with all his strength, inasmuch as his whole hope lies therein.

Spinoza

I

Rabindranath Tagore, the prophetic poet of India, remarked that most of us worldly ordinary people are slaves. We are enslaved to our petty belongings, our small individual prides, and even to our subordinates. For a being so profoundly in love with bondage the message of freedom is quite without appeal, if not positively fearsome. It is not that we are quite insensitive to the sorry sides of human life. But, for all those long stretches of worried waiting and bitter aftertaste, deadly boredom, and the terrible chill of loneliness – we are still not ready to forgo the often brief but intense pleasures that this worldly existence undoubtedly allows us to enjoy. "Isn't it foolish," the hedonist Cārvāka argues, "to give up eating rice simply because the grains come enfolded with husk?" Since we love our little terrestrial joys so acutely that for their

sake we are even prepared to "fall upon the thorns of life and bleed," now and then we find the notion of a liberated state of the soul – with all its promised painlessness – an out-and-out negative one. This attitude of the man in the street towards *mokṣa* or complete liberation is counted as one among many of his "false cognitions."

In his commentary on Gautama's *Nyāya Sūtras* (1.1.2), Vātsyāyana gives this very faithful account of our mundane reasons for recoiling from the philosophically glorified prospect of getting rid of the sorrowful cycle of birth and death that is generally called *saṃsāra* in Indian philosophy.

About liberation (the idea), that it is indeed gruesome, consisting of a cessation of all activity. With such a liberation which divorces us from everything, so many good things of life would be finished. How, therefore, can any intelligent person find that sort of liberation characterized by absence of all the pleasures and even of consciousness at all palatable?[1]

Since all the Darśanas (except Cārvāka) of India make some kind of liberation from *saṃsāra* their explicit goal, it falls on their part to demonstrate that such a liberation *is*, after all, worth seeking. It is not sheer human weakness of the will or unthinking involvement with the world that stands in the way. There are also prima facie theoretical positions challenging the desirability of *mokṣa* or *apavarga* or *nirvāṇa*. There can be interesting discussions questioning the objective validity of the general premise that life as it is (that is, *saṃsāra*) is made of, or is full of, suffering. What about those who do not feel it to be so? And these admittedly outnumber those who do. Since, unlike "is red" or "is solid," "is painful" is *not* primarily an objectively testable predicate, one cannot issue rectificatory judgments of the form: "Well, *saṃsāra* is painful, though you do not feel it to be so." Yet, this is precisely what the liberation-obsessed philosopher says to the happy-go-lucky ordinary man! Compared to other considerations like, "the present inevitable mixture of pain offers the best combination with pleasure we can aspire after" or "the pleasures of life are compensating," the major argument of the *mokṣa*-averse – "I *find saṃsāra* enjoyable, hence it is so" – stands out with a characteristic appeal of incorrigibility concerning beliefs about our own hedonic states. It has been suggested that *duḥkha* or suffering be taken no longer as a descriptive hedonic term, but as an evaluative term which claims the same objectivity and mistakability that "good" or "beautiful" (and according to some) "true" does.

In his prologue to the *Nyāya Vārtika*, Uddyotakara says things which confirm the suspicion that *duḥkha* (sorrow) was taken at least more objectively than a mere subjective feeling. He incidentally gives a list of twenty-one types of *duḥkhas* among which *sukha* (pleasure) is one. In explanation, we get the cryptic remark: "Pleasure is so (i.e., of the nature of pain) because it is inextricably intermingled with pain."[2]

Elsewhere, he explains the term "intermingling" (*anuṣaṅga*) rather too elaborately as meaning either

(a) causing (*nimittārtho 'nuṣaṅgaḥ*);
(b) being instrumental to (*sādhanārtho 'nuṣaṅgaḥ*); or
(c) being never found without (*avinābhāvo 'nuṣaṅgaḥ*)[3]

and says that the third is the relation that prevails between pleasure and pain. Since pain is defined as *whatever* is thus intermingled with the feeling of suffering or torture (or any kind of deprivation),[4] we cannot raise the plausible-looking question, why not the other way around? Why not *call* pain "pleasure" because it is never found without the latter? And it is not an arbitrary decision to define "sorrow" more pervasively than "happiness," but, for the empirically slanted Naiyāyika, it is an empirically supported finding that the *avinābhāvo* (non-without-staying) relation of pain and pleasure is not reversible. We find an explicit statement of this in Udayana's *Ātmatattvaviveka*:

But there are some [who would not mind going through patches of sorrow to enjoy the accompanying pleasures] who need no more. No, the symmetry does not exist. It is suffering which is [more] abundant. Not all sufferings are intermingled with pleasures, although all pleasures are, as a rule, intermingled with pains.[5]

It becomes clearer that the Naiyāyika does not mean the statement "life is painful" to be taken as an a priori metaphysical truth but as a plain empirical factual assertion, as Udayana goes on to support the onesided equation of pleasures with "pain" (in the wider sense), by such poetic remarks as the following:

Thus, indeed, even when we try to enjoy commodities earned by fair and just means, how little joy like the flickers of a fire-fly – we actually feel, compared to the great amount [of worries and tensions] we suffer regarding their procurement and protection. The [calamities] that attend [our enjoyment of] unrighteously earned objects are beyond my powers of imagination![6]

Whether we agree with his generalization or not, we can see clearly what he means when he says that reflective and spiritually ambitious souls *can* and *do* (notice: not an empty, formal *ought to*) run after the goal of absolute freedom from suffering together with all its roots and accessories – knowing full well that such a freedom would also be necessarily devoid of the "sweet sparks of joy." Taking the mocked-at rice-and-the-husk argument to an extremity, he gives the illustration of a delicious poison (rice soaked with honey and poison). The point of the new illustration is that the threat of the poison is strong enough to win away our temptation towards the delicacy. But, practically, is it simply the threat of the poison or is it some assurance of a sweeter nectar as a prize for our sacrifice of the worldly enjoyments that motivates, or is adequate to motivate, the *mumukṣu* (aspirant after liberation)? The search for *mokṣa* is indeed a protracted and arduous one. Is the negative motive of "avoidance of worldly sufferings" enough to keep up the spirits all through that long and thorny path? Isn't the Naiyāyikas' description of *mokṣa* – as a state of the soul when it sheds off not only its relation with mortal bodies but also all its cognitive and affective faculties, retaining only formal properties like its oneness, separation from other souls, and so forth – too bleak? The "ultimate good" (*niḥśreyasa*) seems to demand more as its conceptual content than just "complete and permanent cessation of suffering." It is to answer this question that the bulk of this essay will be devoted. We shall use as text mainly Vātsyāyana's commentary on *Nyāya Sūtras* 1.1.22, looking off and on into Vācaspati's *Tātparyaṭīkā* on that and the relevant sections of *Ātmatattvaviveka*. Some reference to Maṇḍana Miśra's *Brahmasiddhi* will be made in connexion with the rival view that liberation is a state of *positive* unending happiness (bliss, to be more accurate) and not a mere *lack* of suffering. We shall also try towards the end to arrive at a solution of the problem in the light of what I think is the Kantian position about a connected but distinct problem.

II

The question *Need liberation be a state of positive happiness?* – as it has been discussed in the literature – can be broken up into two distinct questions, the first *speculative*, the second *practical*.

1 Does an individual, when he is released from the bondage of *saṃsāra*, really enjoy some kind of eternal unmixed positive pleasure?
2 Should an individual, while aiming at liberation, wish to attain positive pleasure?

Logically, there are four alternative positions possible regarding their answers: We may answer "Yes" to both, "No" to both, "Yes" to the first and "No" to the second, and "No" to the first but "Yes" to the second. Accordingly we get the following four positions:

(1) The position adopted as standard by the Advaita Vedāntin (and, I presume, by other devotional schools of theological thought is well) is that the soul really feels an intense, unrelieved, perpetual bliss in being liberated because that joy is the very essence of his being which was hitherto engulfed with the veil of ignorance or because he starts to enjoy the bliss-breathing company of his truly beloved Lord (a personal God of some sort). Practically, also, it is quite appropriate (any *other* motive being inappropriate) for the aspirant to be motivated by a hankering for that ethereal joy. The Vaiṣṇavas go farther to assert that the only price by which the ultimate goal (for them, a pure consciousness which is imbued with love for the Lord) can be purchased is "greed" (an intense uncompromising craving for nothing short of the Love of God). Tagore seemed to have a lifelong sympathy with this *positive* picture of the spiritual *summum bonum* and says, in an exquisite poem,

> [the lucky one that receives Your grace] is the greediest of all
> because he removes all his greeds to make place for You.[7]

We shall refer to this view as the Positive Joy (PJ) view.

(2) The standard Naiyāyika view is the opposite. It maintains that, in reality, the liberated soul does *not* enjoy any special happiness on top of an absolute absence of pain. Although Vātsyāyana gives a sublime description of the state as one of "fearlessness, freedom from death and decay," and even echoes the Upaniṣads by comparing it to the pure benignness of Brahman, he makes it very clear that there is no additional happiness to it. Happiness is caused by virtuous acts as a result of their moral merit; and the soul, when it casts off its captivating ties with birth and death also casts off all merit and demerit, virtue and vice. Hence there is no room left for any emotional state whatsoever – however favourable it might be. And there is no need for it either. Because the aspirant never wanted it. It is dangerous and counterproductive according to the orthodox Naiyāyika to allow the seeker of liberation to be guided by a desire for permanent happiness in *mokṣa*. For, as Udayana observes, the idea that *mokṣa* guarantees us a permanent state of happiness is not only irrelevant to our attainment of that state, but is also an obstacle to it (*na kevalam iyaṃ nityasukhadṛṣṭir mokṣānupayoginī pratyuta virodhinītyevaha*).[8] The desire for happiness of any sort is a hindrance to the attainment of *mokṣa* as much as any other desire is. This austere view will be referred to as the No Joy (NJ) view.

(3) We can also hold that the liberated soul does really get more than just cessation of pain, but ought not to seek after it. It is simply because one develops a genuine disinterest for the worldly life and wants to put an end to the sufferings of earthly existence that one should pursue the goal of liberation. But in fact when one becomes free in this spiritual sense one does enjoy a bliss – of a kind that one did not wish for – because one could not do more than imagine its magnitude and intensity! Something similar, I presume, was Kant's view

about virtue and happiness. Man becomes truly virtuous when he totally gives up the inclination for happiness and pursues the moral principles for their own sake. (In this respect Kant's moral aspirant is worse off than our religious seeker because he does not have even the negatively spurring motive of avoidance of pain upon which to base his actions.) But Kant also holds, and quite strongly (as a piece of practical knowledge about the realm of ontic necessity which surpasses the phenomenal world), that the virtuous man really is rewarded by the maximum of well-being. Happiness thus comes to us only as an unwished-for object. To quote Tagore again: "it is something that we get only if we don't want it, it comes near only when we have given it up." We shall discuss this view as the Kantian view, towards the end of the paper, although, as we shall also see, it has obvious un-Kantian implications.

(4) The fourth view, which we shall leave out as not serious, is nevertheless a popular stance taken by religious teachers to attract the disciples (for their own good, of course) by a sort of bait. This is the position that although in reality liberation brings no happiness over and above complete absence of suffering, the seekers can (at least at a primary level) look for some promised prospect of greater pleasures to win over their yearnings for the worldly ones. Apart from the popular story of Buddha's unruly brother, who had to be told that *nirvāṇa* would bring all sorts of voluptuous pleasures before he could really start an ascetic life with very much unascetic intentions, eventually, of course, getting quiet satisfaction out of a pure *end* of suffering, there is also another beautiful illustrative story in the *avadāna* literature about such pious lies. A mother whose newborn baby has died comes to Buddha praying for the life of her child. Buddha promises to reenliven the dead child if the mother can fetch a handful of grains from a household where no *sorrow* has ever entered. The mother fails to find such a household, realizes the noble truth, and returns to the Master wiser in spirit, although the child never comes back to life. The practical efficacy of such a pedagogic device apart, this does not represent a genuine theoretical position. So we shall ignore it.

The positive joy view, attested as it is by a number of scriptural descriptions, was upheld not only by the Vedāntin; a section of slightly recalcitrant Kashmīrī Naiyāyikas believed in it as well – consciously going against Vātsyāyana the commentator. Thus

Bhāsarvajña in his *Nyāya-Sāra* mentions the orthodox Nyāya (No Joy) view and refutes it. The *Bṛhadāraṇyaka Upaniṣad* (3.9.28) says that the bliss which constitutes the true nature of the Absolute – who is said to be identical with (or characterized by, as you wish) pure consciousness and pure joy – manifests itself (in the individual soul) at liberation ("*Ānandaṃ Brahmaṇo rūpaṃ tac ca mokṣe 'bhivyajyate*"). Spinoza's *Ethics* (Prop. 33 to Prop. 42) describes the state of freedom (through the intellectual love of God – which, in its turn, is a necessary consequence of our perfect knowledge of God through *scientia intuitiva*) as one of eternal, maximum happiness, a blessedness of which God is recognized to be the source. Even the *Gītā* gives ample support to such a (PJ) view of the state of freedom:

> After the yogin's *rajas* (restlessness) has subsided, all sins have been purged away, and he becomes mentally quietened, being one with (or similar to) the Brahman, and the Highest Happiness descends on him. (VI. 27)

This happiness, of course, is different in kind from the happiness that the fettered souls felt at the contact of their desired (perishable) objects. It is not only a pure and intense but also an intellectual (as against sensual) supra-sensible happiness: the *Gītā* describes it as something the attainment of which dwarfs all other attainments.

All this evidence, together with the testimony of the alleged *jīvanmuktas* (people who stay alive after *mukti*), provides a very strong case for at least an affirmative answer to the first, that is, the speculative, question.

The exponent of the NJ theory which gives negative answers to both the questions refutes the above view in the following manner: we cannot assert that there is a feeling of eternal happiness in liberation because (a) it is theoretically indefensible that such a state would comprise such a feeling, and (b) if we assert it, then the seeker of liberation (the *mumukṣu*) will hanker for it, and once "by way of the assurance of a permanent state of Pleasure, this seed of desire is nurtured in our hearts, the wicked witch of lust getting a little scope will tempt the person back to the material objects of desire – thus throwing him far away from the prospect of liberation."[9]

Let us call (a) the speculative argument and (b) the practical argument. It is plain that the practical argument takes for granted a negative answer to the second, that is, the practical, question. Its force lies in demonstrating that if *mokṣa* consists of permanent pleasure it would be *known* to do so by the *mumukṣu* who would then be actuated by a sort of allurement for a – however pure or beatific – *pleasure*, and allurement will bind him again in *saṃsāra*, because it is its nature to bind. Hence if *mokṣa* is pleasant then it cannot be ever attained by the seeker who knows it to be so. And this is supposed to be enough to show that *mokṣa* is *not* pleasant.

The speculative argument meets the first part of the PJ view more directly. It, however, has two distinct parts.

(1) It is said that in *mokṣa* the already existent eternal happiness of the soul becomes manifested (*abhivyakta*). But is this manifestation (or *feeling*) of eternal happiness itself eternal or not? If the manifestation (like the essential property of joyousness which it makes felt) itself is eternal, that is, beginningless, too, then we must say that the soul eternally – hence even before the *mukti*-state – feels happy. Then the fettered and the free alike would feel the blessedness that is claimed to be a prerogative of the free alone. This being absurd, the manifestation cannot be said to be eternal or uncaused.

If on the other hand the manifestation has a beginning, marked by the moment of being liberated, we must be able to account for its emergence at that particular point of time by some causal explanation. Here there are two sorts of explanations forthcoming: Vātsyāyana considers a view according to which it is a special kind of co-ordination between the self and the inner sense (the instrument of inner perception, for example of *sukha* (happiness), and so forth) – helped by the special merit of value – resulting from a Yogic state of *samādhi* – which causes the feeling of the eternal happiness of liberation. But *mokṣa* is by definition a state where the soul gives up all its previous equipment of merits and demerits, virtues and vices, and does not accumulate any new results of action. The positive *dharma* which is caused by *yogasamādhi* will therefore exhaust itself, thus causing the feeling of joy also to cease. If the feeling ceases, the existence of the joy would be impossible to ascertain because one could not be sure whether it is the joy which has vanished or only the feeling of it. We cannot say that this special *samādhi* and the merit it produces never gets exhausted, because all positive entities which are caused or have the property of being brought into existence necessarily have

to have an end too. Thus a non-eternal feeling which has a beginning would not be permanent, as the happiness of liberation is alleged to be, and unfelt happiness is as good as no happiness at all.

Bhāsarvajña[10] plays ingenious scholastic tricks at this point to preserve the position that the feeling of bliss of the liberated soul has no reason to cease to be felt, although it starts to be (is caused), because nothing can lead to the destruction of the relation between the essentially eternal happiness and an awareness of it once that relation has been established by removing all intervening obstacles. As Vātsyāyana argues:

> Whatever is produced comes to an end.
> The manifestation or feeling (of the joy of *mukti*) is produced
> ∴ It comes to an end.[11]

The argument is said to be fallacious because the *vyāpti* that it is based upon (the major premise) does not hold universally (in other words, the *hetu* is *anaikāntika*, non-pervasive). A counterexample to the major premise would be: the absence of an object after the destruction. Such a posterior absence has a beginning, is produced by the act of destruction but never comes to an end because the same thing cannot come back to existence.

But to preclude such a counterexample, the *vyāpti* may be re-cast with a reservation clause: Whatever is produced, *and is a positive entity* (*vastu*) must have an end. But Bhāsarvajña argues[12] that there is no evidence that the feeling of happiness which consists in the "relation between a cognition and the object, viz. happiness" is a positive entity of a sort which has to be perishable if it is producible. For one thing, it is not included explicitly in any of the six categories of *positive* entities (substance, quality, action, particularity, universal, and inherence). If we try to include it somewhere in the list we are at a loss to say which category will subsume such a relation of intentionality *viṣayaviṣayisambandha* under itself. The above list of Vaiśeṣika categories is said to be so arranged that nothing which belongs in the category of an earlier item can reside in any of the later ones. Thus if we are to make room for the cognitive relation we must make it after universals – so that the possibility of such a relation taking universals (and all other four categories of things) as its relata is left open. But in that case, too, we have to say that such a relation can never exist between a cognition and the relation of inherence itself, or not even between a cognition and an *absence*. But we do admit (the Vaiśeṣika himself does) the knowability of inherence and of absence – the latter being said to be directly perceptible. Then, there seems to be no way of categorizing the cognitive relational tie itself as a positive item. If someone puts forward the further argument that all cognitive ties are due to some result of previous action or merit due to virtue, and so forth, and since such merits are perishable (as in the case of merit due to *yogisamādhi*) the cognitive tie too must be perishable. That argument is easily invalidated: for, if all cognitive ties have to be established through an unseen destiny (*adṛṣṭa*), then God, who has no such destiny, would have to be deprived of any such tie with any object and would be far from omniscient. He would not have a chance to know a single object.

If the above evasion of the perishability of a produced feeling does not sound persuasive, one might resort to construing the production of feeling not by a positive factor but by removal of some obstacle. It is often urged that just as the existent jar is not seen by the eyes until the intervening obstruction (of a wall, or curtain) is removed, the essential blissfulness of the self cannot be felt (by those in bondage) because of obstructing factors like our sins, ignorance, physical involvements. But Vātsyāyana asks:[13] What, precisely, are these obstructions? If it is held that it is our embodiment in a mortal body that stands in the way, that hardly sounds persuasive. Is it not the main purpose of the body to enable us to enjoy and suffer pleasures and pain? How can the instrument and medium of enjoyment of happiness itself be a hurdle to such enjoyment? Here, too, Vātsyāyana seems obstinately to ignore the alleged distinction of kind between the pleasures of ordinary worldly life and the supra-sensible "*atīndriya*"-pleasures of the emancipated soul! When he issues such generalizations as: "There is no evidence that a bodiless soul has any enjoyment" (*na cāsty anumānaṃ aśarīrasya ātmano bhogaḥ kaścid astīti*),[14] he obviously overlooks the emphasized disparity between the enjoyment of sensible objects and the enjoyment of eternal Bliss – the latter being of a sort where even the distinction between subject and object is said (sometimes) to disappear. Is it not plausible that for such an ethereal bliss to be felt, our body *is* an obstacle rather than an instrument?

Uddyotakara tries to strengthen the above argument of the commentator by adding another reason for rejecting the alleged explanation of the body being an obstacle. "Like the happiness which (though unfelt) is imagined to reside in the self eternally we can also imagine the body to be eternal in some sense." It is not clear what he is implying by this hypothesis. The subsequent chain of polemics brings out that it is considered just *as* indefensible to hold that the happiness of the soul is ever-present *as* to hold that the soul's body is so.

We can give some sense to the line of attack above by pointing out that the Vedāntin sometimes admits that it is possible to be liberated while alive. Others who talk about *mukti* being a blissful state talk of some type of purified transformed body. So it seems that the *body as such* can coexist with the state of liberation – according to these philosophers. So they at least cannot argue that the eternal bliss cannot be eternally *felt* because of the presence of the body. Both Uddyotakara and Vācaspati were aware of the alleged distinctiveness of the joy of *mukti*. They anticipated arguments like the following: "Since, unlike ordinary pleasures which are inextricably associated with pain, the pleasure felt by the *mukta* is free from any possible contamination by pain – there is no question of wanting to avoid this latter sort of lofty unadulterated pleasure for fear of any attendant pains." Udayana, in his *Ātmatattvaviveka*, takes up the debate from this point and tries to show that the claimed self-illuminating, uncaused, untainted nature of such a positive joy would make it also unseekable, unachievable, unknowable, and unobtainable. "Since it is said to be eternal it cannot be sought. One does not search for what one already possesses. If one compares it to a *forgotten* piece of possession – like the golden chain which is all the time round our neck while we are frantically searching for it – it becomes incoherent with its alleged self-manifesting nature."[15]

Finally, Udayana answers Bhāsarvajña's technical trick by pointing out that the category of positive entity and that of absence exclude any middle which is neither (*bhāvābhāvayoḥ prakārāntarābhāvāt*). Since the relation between a cognition and its object (here, the feeling and the eternal happiness) is not of the nature of an absence (for, if it is, *whose* absence can it be called?), then it must be a positive entity – and hence be perishable if producible – because there is no other exception to that rule except a certain kind of absence.

If, on the other hand, that much-glorified "attainment" is identified with the destruction of nescience or *avidyā* (which destruction could surely generate a state which has a beginning but has no end), then the Naiyāyika has no quarrel with that negative description of the state of liberation and its means. Since our nescience is so invincibly hard to eliminate the mere eradication of it looks like a great positive achievement. Even the enjoyment of the highest heavenly pleasures – insofar as they are unevenly distributed – have a tint of pain by way of envy, dissatisfaction, fear of falling, and so forth. The mixture is so essential that we cannot hope to separate the two like rice and husk. But just as we heave a sigh of great relief after we have merely taken out a thorn from our foot or have quenched our thirst, although these are just *removals* of certain pains, we feel exalted just by being able to dispel the ageless shroud of "original illusion" although we do not thereby *gain* anything new.

(2) The second part of the speculative argument repeats the point already touched that liberation cannot consist of pleasure of any sort because pleasures are so uniformly co-present with pains that it is not possible to isolate the one and avoid only the pain-bit and retain the pleasure. We have already seen the reasons for the Naiyāyika's charting of *sukha* as a kind of *duḥkha*, and from that it follows, by definition, that if *mokṣa* is a state of absolute release from all the twenty-one sets of *duḥkhas* it is, *eo ipso*, a "release" from *sukha* as well. It is needless to rehearse the possible retort to this from the PJ camp. Instead, let us pass on to the positive arguments adduced by the PJ proponents.

As Vātsyāyana represents them, the positive-joy view may contend that it is found that people hanker after liberation, and scriptures prescribe ways to bring it about. Unless liberation was a positive state of happiness, how can this hankering and this instruction be accounted for? Men cannot direct their volition toward a mere "absence." The inference when properly arranged (by Vācaspati) looks like this: "*Mokṣa* must be a state of happiness, because it is *aimed at* (*iṣṭa*) and nothing but a state of happiness can be aimed at."[16] But the generalization "nothing but a state of happiness can be desirable" can be rebutted. It was rebutted by all of Mill's critics. In this particular case, the Naiyāyika would say, we cannot aim at what is apparently desirable because it is so inseparably blended with what is counterbalancingly undesirable. The guiding motive, thus, becomes avoidance of the undesirable, as already shown by the example of the poisonous delicacy. That this has to be the case was admitted by Mill himself, who was otherwise eager to vindicate the happiness principle.

Since utility includes not solely the pursuit of happiness but the prevention or mitigation of unhappiness, and if the *former aim be chimerical*, there will be all the greater scope and *more important* need for the latter.[17]

The Naiyāyika seriously believes that from an ultimate point of view the possibility of combining happiness with complete absence of suffering is indeed chimerical; hence the counterbalancing importance and urgency of getting rid of suffering even at the cost of foregoing all pleasure. But this practical argument against the speculative thesis begins, as it were, with confusing the two different questions. For the solution of the speculative problem, namely, whether, in reality, liberation brings a feeling of eternal happiness with it, it takes as a clue an answer to the ethical problem, namely, whether the seeker should desire happiness, and so forth. If, it proceeds, the seeker desires happiness (of however refined or pure a sort), this desire (*rāga*) will bind him, eventually blocking his way to liberation, because it is in the very nature of desire to bind. Once we give in to the desire for happiness, there is every chance that, being tired of the hard struggle which our seeking involves, we might choose the easier means to get happiness and thus lose ourselves in *saṃsāra* again. This worry goes back to the traditional charge against hedonism that it is impracticable to make distinctions of (nobler and baser) quality while confining oneself within the happiness principle. Mill, who wanted to establish Utilitarianism as the sole principle of moral worth by adding to the other dimensions of variation of happiness the new dimension of *higher/ lower* or *more/less valuable kinds*, admitted that: "Men, often from infirmity of character make their election for the *nearer good*, though they know it to be less valuable"[18] and thus: "Many who begin with youthful enthusiasm for everything noble, as they advance in years sink into indolence and selfishness."[19] Udayana, in the *Ātmattattvaviveka* gives the following rather obnoxious illustration of this sound principle:

That [hankering for happiness] dies hard. Since [by past associations] the idea of happiness is accompanied by the traces of [ordinarily enjoyed] happiness, if we pursue that idea those mental traces are going to reawaken in us the memory of [hence the desire for] worldly pleasures; the man who desires [the allegedly] special kind of happiness is likely to be propelled toward

A. Chakrabarti

ordinary earthly pleasures, too – in this way.
An example:

It is found that being unable to get a glam-
orously beautiful lady one sometimes perversely
loves some subhuman animal.[20]

The basic psychological truth behind this is that
when an ideal is pursued, not out of sheer regard
for the ideal but for the sake of the pleasure that
it brings, a little frustration leads us to inferior
pleasures: despairing of the lofty, we often desperately bury our heads in the low. The impure
motive of desire for happiness (sukharāga), therefore, is a precarious ground for our endeavour
after liberation.

It is this apprehension that prevents the
Naiyāyika from taking terms like "happiness"
(sukha) or "joy" (ānanda), which the scriptures
use when describing the state of liberation in their
primary, that is, literal, positive significance. They
are hence taken in their secondary import of
"absence or destruction of suffering" (duḥkhābāva
or dhvaṃsa). The support from usage of such
secondary meaning of sukha has been already
cited. Do we not call the relief from the agony of
a bruise or the removal of a painful thorn "a great
happiness"?

Against this psychological argument, one can
counterargue that absence of pain cannot by itself
or always (necessarily) be equated with pleasure.
Maṇḍana[21] gives the simple instance of a man
scorched by summer heat dipping into cool lake
water and remaining half-plunged in it. Can this
man be said to be "happy" because his pain due to
heat (over half his body) has been removed? But
this niggling counter-example can easily be got
around by qualifying "absence of pain" by "complete, absolute, in all parts," and so forth. The big
objection, however, remains that the interpretation
of all those frequent references in the texts (and
testimonies of self-fulfilled mukta souls) to an immense unending joy – as simply signifying a mere
absence of suffering – seems quite unconvincing.
As to the argument that the so-called blessedness
of mukti descends only upon the untrammelled calm
mind, whereas the mind which is stirred by the
yearning for happiness is not calm – we can retort
in this way:

If desire for sukha is a seed of saṃsāra – is not
aversion to duhka equally so? Are not love and
hate equally hindering obstacles for the seeker?

Yet, the seeker, after the Nyāya model, is
a man who constantly hates his worldly life
because of its sorrowful nature. How can such
a soul, actuated as it is by the motive of aversion toward certain objects, ever hope to get
liberated?

To this Uddyotakara replies that "No, the motive
of warding off sorrow is not counter-productive."[22]

Vācaspati explains this reply as follows: true,
a piece of anger, spitefulness, or aversion is an
element of bondage. But that is the aversion which
is of the type of a blazing fire (jvalanātmaka), and
this is not how the seeker should feel toward worldly
sufferings. His characteristic mood is that of a non-
attached person for whom the earthly life is of no
taste whatsoever. (The Sanskrit word "Vairāgya"
here seems almost untranslatable.) We can have a
sense of not wanting something (alaṃpratyaya) without feeling aggressively scornful about it. This quiet
cognition of dispensability (upekṣābuddhi) is what
we think the seeker ought to feel towards the plights
of human bondage.

But, here, the supporter of the PJ view may join
the issue: just as not every "willingness to avoid" is
"aversion," not every "wish to attain" is "desire."
The pure, unblemished eagerness for an enlightened tranquility of mind and the supreme joy
thereof is not to be identified with the tiny desires
for corporeal objects. The latter captivates us to
saṃsāra, but why should the former do so? It is as
improper to describe the seeker's attraction towards
the sublime happiness of mokṣa as a case of "desire
for pleasure" as it is to describe his flight from
suffering as an "aversion to pain."

Maṇḍana strengthens his positive answer to the
ethical question (namely, that the seeker should
run after a great, positive, eternal happiness) by
citing the general psychological principle that a great
desire devours smaller ones for its own fulfilment.
Even if the wish to be eternally and absolutely
happy is a strong desire, it precludes the possibility
of our surrendering to any smaller temptation while
we are prompted by such a great motivating force.
Just as a man who wants to be a great political
leader or an emperor (for the sake of power and
pride) easily forgoes hundreds of tiny pleasures
and courts hardships, we can easily forget immediate pleasures and pains, profits and losses while we
are searching for that great attainment of a permanent and boundless ocean of joy, which is mukti.
The fear, unless the desire for eternal happiness be

self-baffling, is therefore groundless. It is such a not-easily-quenched thirst for nothing short of supreme Beatitude, that is the proper motive-force for liberation.

III

We have discussed, up to this point, the two following views:

(PJ): The liberated soul does get positive happiness, and the seeker for liberation ought to look for such an ecstatic joy, and so forth.
(NJ): The liberated soul does not get any happiness beyond simple cessation of sufferings, and the seeker *should not* look for such happiness.

It is clear that neither of the above-mentioned views maintains a clear distinction between the two initial questions, namely, the ontological and the psycho-ethical. The PJ thinks that we can quite safely look for supreme endless joy while seeking release from *saṃsāra* because we ultimately are guaranteed to get it, along with such a release. The NJ thinks that that state *really* cannot be said to consist of such positive happiness because if it is so, then people seeking it would have the risky motive of desire for such a happiness which in its turn might captivate them forever in *saṃsāra*. A consistent view seems to emerge out of combining the elements which are convincingly cogent in both the accounts. We can, as indicated above, maintain that the seeker ought to model himself after the Naiyāyika fashion with a stoic negative attitude towards all worldly objects – apparently pleasurable and painful alike. As reflected in the passage quoted from Spinoza at the head of this article, his attitude should be like that of "a man with his head on fire – running madly towards water" – without ever imagining to get anything more than merely a putting out of the fire of sorrows. But as Kant thought that the truly virtuous man is, in the intelligible world (where everything happens as it ought to), rewarded by supreme happiness, although he never, by definition, *qua* a *virtuous* moral agent acted *for the sake* of such happiness, we might imagine that the true seeker of liberation attains eternal happiness even if he did not look for it.

The analogy with Kant's position is, of course, in one important sense quite misleading. The moral actor, in Kant's view, not only gives up all inclinations for happiness but does not even act out of any tendency to put an end to sufferings. Popular representations of Kantian morality make the ethically perfect person rather prone to pains, whereas the chief motive of the seeker for liberation is, according to our position, the motive of putting an end to sufferings of all kinds and forever. Thus while Kant's moral actor is supposed to have no end other than doing his duty out of a respect for the moral law (which, according to some interpreters, does supply some positive psychological ground for his motivation), the Naiyāyikas' *mumukṣu* yearns for liberation out of his utter disillusionment with this mortal life. But this disanalogy does not make the comparison absolutely pointless. If we replace virtue by liberation (= *end of duḥkha*) we can get the very Kantian-looking view that liberation ought to be sought for its own sake, although when attained it incidentally (out of a necessity which is not available to discursive reasoning or theoretical knowledge or proof) brings with it an eternal happiness – which is incomparably superior to all mundane happiness. In short, we make a sharp distinction between the two questions, answering the speculative with a tentative (optimistic) affirmative and the ethical with a negative: *Man cannot be advised to wish for eternal happiness in liberation but he actually gets it if he is liberated.* But there was a certain point in "confusing" the two questions. As the Naiyāyika would argue (and I suppose a critic of Kant's moral theology would also, in parallel, argue): When you describe the state of liberation as a pleasant one, you thereby motivate the seeker with an improper impetus, thus rendering it impossible for him to attain it. Kant solved this paradox by maintaining that we do not and cannot *know* that virtue brings happiness, although it is *true* that it does (and we have a "hope" or "practical certainty" to that effect). If we really know, that is, theoretically be certain, that *mukti* would give us endless joy, how can we resist hankering after *mukti* without looking for the joy it involves? If, on the other hand, we do not have any means to prove that we here are not actuated by any such premise of eternal pleasure, it nevertheless seems possible, and psychologically feasible, to seek liberation for its own sake, provided some basic emotional and intellectual conditions are fulfilled.

Emotionally, it requires an intense feeling of worthlessness and disvalue for the mortal existence. As the *Gītā* describes the mood in the classic way: "Unperturbed by pains and disinterested in pleasures" – or, as *Aśvaghoṣa* describes the ascetic indifference of the young prince Siddhartha, surrounded by the luxuries of the royal palace: "Musing anxiously over the mortality of things he neither rejoiced nor winced."

The urgency of getting rid of this shackled life must reach a maximum point before one can really want to attain a *freedom* from this predominantly sorry life even at the cost of foregoing all its flickering bits of pleasure. We must be so tired of repeated births and deaths as to feel earnestly anxious just to get away from it – without the slightest speculation as to how rewarding liberation might be.

Just as out of excessive longing we go for an object ignoring its defects, we do also turn away from an object ignoring its (apparent) good sides if we are genuinely disgusted with it.[23]

The *intellectual* condition is the requirement that one should be discriminating enough to see through the genesis of the worldly sufferings. The step-by-step process by which Gautama says an individual can attain the *summum bonum* of liberation has "destruction of false apprehension" as its penultimate stage. It is because we reconcile ourselves to the idea that we have to suffer certain plights in order to enjoy our shares of happiness that we don't mind them and are careless about trying to get rid of them absolutely. So many people are consciously struck by the "*Duhkhakhayābhighāta*" (blow of the threefold sorrow) but only a handful have "*jijñāsā tadavaghātake hetau*" (inquiry into the conditions for its eradication).[24] This is because the intellectual condition of being philosophically aware is so rarely fulfilled. Thus, to cross over the biggest hurdle, namely, one's craving for pleasure, one has just to contemplate the very essence of worldly pleasures which makes it impossible to enjoy them without a counterbalancingly greater amount of pain before and after.

These emotional and intellectual requirements being met, it might be possible for someone to strive for a pure freedom from all sorts of pain without the faintest desire for any additional feeling of happiness. And that seems the most appropriate and secure psychological ground for a seeker after liberation.

As to the answer to the ontological question – whether the fire-extinguishing water of the river of *mokṣa* is also positively soothing – our stance must remain to some extent open. The scriptural descriptions or the testimonies of liberated souls can only give us a secondary and sketchy idea of what it is really like to be liberated. One cannot really convey the exact taste of an experience without making the audience taste it for themselves. Thus, it is possible

(a) that *mokṣa* feels like a sheer absence of any feeling of pain of any sort; *or*
(b) that *mokṣa* feels like a great positive state of boundless ecstatic joy; *or*
(c) that the sheer absolute absence of suffering feels like the greatest joy possible.

And we cannot and need not decide between the alternatives. Interestingly enough, such a position is already hinted at by Vātsyāyana himself at the end of his commentary on 1.1.22 (N.S.B.):

If, in like manner, the liberated soul does have an eternal happiness or does not have it – neither of these alternative situations make any difference to the attainment of *mokṣa* [for one who has given up all *desire* for eternal happiness][25]

Our final position therefore is definite about the practical question: the seeker should not make desire for happiness his basis for seeking liberation; but our attitude towards the speculative question is rather indifferent: the question must remain open. All our answers to such a speculative question must be conjectural. As the Buddha said, it is idle to ask what the real nature of this or that state of things is. Our problem is a practical one: how to put an end to all these agonies of existence. As to whether we shall get anything more than cessation of suffering when we attain the final release, we are free to take the scripture's descriptions of that state as "joyous" either literally or as a figurative way of describing a complete relief from unhappiness. As Udayana remarks in the *Kiraṇāvalī*: "Being petty dealers in ginger, why should we bother about information concerning large cargo-ships?" To us poor mortals whose highest conceivable model of pleasure is still tarnished by some pain (a phenomenon we euphemistically call the beauty of contrast) it is not given to know how an absolute absence of pain feels.

Notes

1 *Nyāyadarśana of Gautama*, with Bhāṣya, Vārtika, Ṭīkā and Pariśuddhis, edited by A. Thakur (Mittula Institute, 1967), vol. 1, p. 150.

2 Ibid., p. 6.

3 Ibid., p. 450.

4 Ibid.

5 *Ātmatattvaviveka of Udayana*, edited by Ḍhuṇḍhirāja Śāstrī (Benares: Chowkhamba Sanskrit Series, 1940), p. 440.

6 Ibid., pp. 440–1.

7 *Gītāñjali*, poem no. 66.

8 *Nyāyadarśana*, p. 459.

9 Ibid.

10 *Nyāyasāra of Bhāsarvajña*, edited by Abhyankara E. Devadhara (Poona, 1922), pp. 96–7.

11 *Nyāyadarśana*, p. 454.

12 *Nyāyasāra*, pp. 96–7.

13 *Nyāyadarśana*, p. 454.

14 Ibid.

15 *Ātmatattvaviveka*, p. 442.

16 *Nyāyadarśana*, p. 459.

17 J. S. Mill, *Utilitarianism*, chap. 2.

18 Ibid.

19 Ibid.

20 *Ātmatattvaviveka*, p. 445.

21 *Brahmasiddhi of Maṇḍana* (Madras, 1937), pp. 1–2.

22 *Nyāyadarśana*, p. 457.

23 *Ātmatattvaviveka*, pp. 439–40.

24 *Sāṃkhyakārika*, no. 1.

25 *Nyāyadarśana*, p. 455.

Index